continued on back inside cover

E-commerce

business. technology. society.

FIFTH EDITION

Kenneth C. Laudon
New York University

Carol Guercio Traver
Azimuth Interactive, Inc.

PEARSON
Prentice
Hall

Prentice Hall, Upper Saddle River, New Jersey 07458

Library of Congress Cataloging-in-Publication Information is Available

Executive Editor: Bob Horan
Editorial Director: Sally Yagan
Editor in Chief: Eric Svendsen
Product Development Manager: Ashley Santora
Assistant Editor: Kelly Loftus
Marketing Manager: Anne Fahlgren
Marketing Assistant: Susan Osterlitz
Permissions Project Manager: Charles Morris
Senior Managing Editor: Judy Leale
Associate Managing Editor: Suzanne DeWorken
Senior Operations Specialist: Arnold Vila
Operations Specialist: Carol O'Rourke
Senior Art Director: Janet Slowik
Art Director: Steve Frim
Cover Designer: Steve Frim
Composition: Azimuth Interactive, Inc.
Full Service Project Management: Azimuth
    Interactive, Inc.
Printer/Binder: Edwards Brothers, Inc.
Typeface: ITC Veljovic Std. Book, 9.5pt

Pearson Education Ltd, London
Pearson Education Singapore, Pte. Ltd
Pearson Education, Canada, Ltd
Pearson Education—Japan
Pearson Education Australia PTY, Limited

Pearson Education North Asia Ltd.
Pearson Educación de Mexico, S.A. de C.V.
Pearson Education Malaysia, Pte. Ltd.
Pearson Education Upper Saddle River, New Jersey

10 9 8 7 6 5 4 3 2 1
ISBN-13: 978-0-13-600711-1
ISBN-10: 0-13-600711-2

PREFACE

WELCOME TO THE NEW E-COMMERCE

In the 13 years since it began in 1995, electronic commerce has grown in the United States from a standing start to a $258 billion retail business and a $3.6 trillion business-to-business juggernaut, bringing about enormous change in business firms, markets, and consumer behavior. Economies and business firms around the globe, in Europe, Asia, and Latin America, are being similarly affected. In the next five years, e-commerce in all of its forms is projected to continue growing at double-digit rates, becoming the fastest-growing form of commerce in the world. Just as automobiles, airplanes, and electronics defined the twentieth century, so will e-commerce of all kinds define business and society in the twenty-first century. The rapid movement toward an e-commerce economy and society is being led by both established business firms such as Wal-Mart, JCPenney, and General Electric, and new entrepreneurial firms such as Google, Amazon, E*Trade, MySpace, Facebook, Photobucket, and YouTube. Students of business and information technology need a thorough grounding in electronic commerce in order to be effective and successful managers in the next decade. This book is written for tomorrow's managers.

The focus of the 5th edition is on the new breed of e-commerce services that have emerged since the last edition. These new online services provide social networking, video and photo-sharing, and communication services, as well as a forum for online advertising that firms of all kinds are anxious to exploit. Sometimes called Web 2.0, new sites such as Facebook, MySpace, Photobucket, Del.icio.us, YouTube, and Blinkx, have grown explosively in the last two years.

The traditional forms of retail e-commerce and services also remain vital and continue to show double-digit growth. The experience of these firms over the last decade is also a focus of this book. The defining characteristic of these firms is that they are profitable, sustainable, efficient, and innovative firms with powerful brand names. Many of these now-experienced retail and service firms, such as eBay, Amazon, E*Trade, Priceline, and Expedia, are survivors of the first era of e-commerce, from 1995 to spring 2000. These surviving firms have evolved their business models, integrated their online and offline operations, and changed their revenue models to become profitable. Students must understand how to build these kinds of e-commerce businesses in order to help the business firms they manage to succeed in the e-commerce era.

It would be foolish to ignore the lessons learned in the early period of e-commerce. Like so many technology revolutions in the past—automobiles, electricity, telephones, television, and biotechnology—there was an explosion of entrepreneurial efforts, followed by consolidation. By 2005, the survivors of the early period were moving to establish profitable businesses while maintaining rapid growth in revenues. In 2008–2009, e-commerce is entering a new period of explosive entreprenurial activity, quite similar to the early years of e-commerce. E-commerce is alive, well, once again vibrant and exciting, and growing very fast at more than 15% a year (as traditional retail stores show little if any growth in 2008), bringing about extraordinary changes to markets, industries, individual businesses, and society as a whole. E-commerce is generating thousands of new jobs for young managers in all fields from marketing to management, entrepreneurial studies, and information systems. Today, e-commerce has moved into the mainstream life of established businesses that have the market brands and financial muscle required for the long-term deployment of e-commerce technologies and methods. If you are working in an established business, chances are the firm's e-commerce capabilities and Web presence are important factors for its success. If you want to start a new business, chances are very good that the knowledge you learn in this book will be very helpful.

BUSINESS. TECHNOLOGY. SOCIETY.

We believe that in order for business and technology students to really understand e-commerce, they must understand the relationships among e-commerce business concerns, Internet technology, and the social and legal context of e-commerce. These three themes permeate all aspects of e-commerce, and therefore in each chapter we present material that explores the business, technological, and social aspects of that chapter's main topic.

Given the continued growth and diffusion of e-commerce, all students—regardless of their major discipline—must also understand the basic economic and business forces driving e-commerce. E-commerce is creating new electronic markets where prices are more transparent, markets are global, and trading is highly efficient, though not perfect. E-commerce is having a direct impact on the firm's relationship with suppliers, customers, competitors, and partners, as well as how firms market products, advertise, and use brands. Whether you are interested in marketing and sales, design, production, finance, information systems, or logistics, you will need to know how e-commerce technologies can be used to reduce supply chain costs, increase production efficiency, and tighten the relationship with customers. This text is written to help you understand the fundamental business issues in e-commerce.

We spend a considerable amount of effort analyzing the business models and strategies of "pure-play" online companies and established businesses now forging "bricks-and-clicks" business models. We explore why many early e-commerce firms failed and the strategic, financial, marketing, and organizational challenges they faced. We also describe how contemporary e-commerce firms learned from the mistakes of early firms, and how established firms are using e-commerce to succeed. Above all, we attempt to bring a strong sense of business realism and sensitivity to the often exaggerated descriptions of e-commerce. As founders of a dot.com company and participants in the e-commerce revolution, we have learned that the "E" in e-commerce does not stand for "easy."

The Web and e-commerce is causing a major revolution in marketing and advertising in the United States. We spend two chapters discussing how marketing and advertising dollars are moving away from traditional media, and towards online media, causing significant growth in search engine marketing, targeted display advertising, and online rich media/video ads.

E-commerce is driven by Internet technology. Internet technology, and information technology in general, is perhaps the star of the show. Without the Internet, e-commerce would be virtually nonexistent. Accordingly, we provide three specific chapters on the Internet and e-commerce technology, and in every chapter we provide continuing coverage by illustrating how the topic of the chapter is being shaped by new information technologies. For instance, Internet technology drives developments in security and payment systems, marketing strategies and advertising, financial applications, business-to-business trade, and retail e-commerce. We describe new wireless and mobile commerce technology, new telecommunications technologies that lower business costs, new software applications such as widgets and gadgets and new software languages such as XML that enable Web 2.0, and new types of Internet-based information systems that support electronic business-to-business markets.

E-commerce is not only about business and technology, however. The third part of the equation for understanding e-commerce is society. E-commerce and Internet technologies have important social consequences that business leaders can ignore only at their peril. E-commerce has challenged our concepts of privacy, intellectual property, and even our ideas about national sovereignty and governance. Google, Amazon, and assorted advertising networks maintain profiles on millions of U.S. and foreign online shoppers. The proliferation of illegally copied music and videos on the Internet, and the growth of social networking sites often based on displaying copyrighted materials without permission, are challenging the intellectual property rights of record labels, studios, and artists. And many countries—including the United States—are demanding to control the content of Web sites displayed within their borders for political and social reasons. Tax authorities in the United States and Europe are demanding that e-commerce sites pay sales taxes. As a result of these challenges to existing institutions, e-commerce and the Internet are the subject of increasing investigation, litigation, and legislation. Business leaders need to understand these societal developments, and they cannot afford to assume any longer that the Internet is borderless, beyond social control and regulation, or a place where market efficiency is the only consideration. In addition to an entire chapter devoted to the social and legal implications of e-commerce, each chapter contains material highlighting the social implications of e-commerce.

FEATURES AND COVERAGE

Strong Conceptual Foundation We analyze e-commerce, digital markets, and e-business firms just as we would ordinary businesses and markets using concepts from economics, marketing, finance, philosophy, and information systems. We try to avoid ad hoc theorizing of the sort that sprang breathlessly from the pages of many journals in the early years of e-commerce.

Some of the important concepts from economics and marketing that we use to explore e-commerce are transaction cost, network externalities, perfect digital markets, segmentation, price dispersion, targeting, and positioning. Important concepts from the study of information systems and technologies play an important role in the book, including public key encryption, multi-tier server systems, Internet standards and protocols, wireless technologies, and client/server computing. From the literature on ethics and society, we use important concepts such as intellectual property, privacy, information rights and rights management, governance, public health, and welfare.

From the literature on business, we use concepts such as business process design, return on investment, strategic advantage, industry competitive environment, oligopoly, and monopoly. One of the witticisms that emerged from the early years of e-commerce and that still seems apt is the notion that e-commerce changes everything except the rules of business. Businesses still need to make a profit in order to survive in the long term.

Real-World Business Firm Focus From Akamai Technologies, to Google, Microsoft, Apple, and Amazon, to Liquidation.com, this book contains well over 100 real-company examples that place coverage in the context of actual dot.com businesses. You'll find these examples in each chapter, as well as in special features such as chapter-opening and chapter-closing cases, and "Insight on" boxes.

E-commerce in Action Cases Part IV of the book analyzes the business strategies and financial operating results of five public e-commerce companies in retail, services, B2B, auctions, and digital media content. The companies we analyze in-depth are some of the leaders of their respective industries: Amazon, Expedia, Yahoo, CNET Networks, and Ariba. For each company, we identify the vision of the company, analyze its financial performance, review its current strategy, and assess the near-term future prospects for the firm. These cases are ideal real-world instructional guides for students interested in understanding the financial foundation of e-commerce firms, their strategic visions and customer value propositions, and their changing strategic objectives. They can also be used as projects where students update the case materials using the most current financial and business news, or provide additional analysis.

In-depth Coverage of B2B E-commerce We devote an entire chapter to an examination of B2B e-commerce. In writing this chapter, we developed a unique and easily understood classification schema to help students understand this complex arena of e-commerce. This chapter covers four types of Net marketplaces (e-distributors, e-procurement companies, exchanges, and industry consortia) as well as the development of private industrial networks and collaborative commerce.

Current and Future Technology Coverage Internet and related information technologies continue to change rapidly. The most important changes for e-commerce include dramatic price reductions in e-commerce infrastructure (making it much less expensive to develop sophisticated Web sites), the explosive growth in the mobile digital platform such as iPhones, and expansion in the development of social technologies. What was once a shortage of telecommunications capacity has now turned into a surplus, PC prices have continued to fall, new client-side devices have emerged, Internet high-speed broadband connections are now typical and are continuing to show double-digit growth, and wireless technologies such as Wi-Fi and cellular broadband are playing a larger role in mobile Internet access. While we thoroughly discuss the current Internet environment, we devote considerable attention to describing Web 2.0 and Internet II technologies and applications such as the advanced network infrastructure, fiber optics, wireless Web and 3G technologies, Wi-Fi, IP multicasting, and future guaranteed service levels.

Up-to-Date Coverage of the Research Literature This text is well grounded in the e-commerce research literature. We have sought to include, where appropriate, references and analysis of the latest e-commerce research findings, as well as many classic articles, in all of our chapters. We have drawn especially on the disciplines of economics, marketing, and information systems and technologies, as well as law journals and broader social science research journals including sociology and psychology.

Special Attention to the Social and Legal Aspects of E-commerce We have paid special attention throughout the book to the social and legal context of e-commerce. Chapter 8 is devoted to a thorough exploration of four ethical dimensions of e-commerce: information privacy, intellectual property, governance, and protecting public welfare on the Internet. We have included an analysis of the latest Federal Trade Commission and other regulatory and nonprofit research reports, and their likely impact on the e-commerce environment.

OVERVIEW OF THE BOOK

The book is organized into four parts.

Part 1, "Introduction to E-commerce," provides an introduction to the major themes of the book. Chapter 1 defines e-commerce, distinguishes between e-commerce and e-business, and defines the different types of e-commerce. Chapter 2 introduces and defines the concepts of business model and revenue model, describes the major e-commerce business and revenue models for both B2C and B2B firms, and introduces the basic business concepts required throughout the text for understanding e-commerce firms including industry structure, value chains, and firm strategy.

Part 2, "Technology Infrastructure for E-commerce," focuses on the technology infrastructure that forms the foundation for all e-commerce. Chapter 3 traces the historical development of Internet I—the first Internet—and thoroughly describes how today's Internet works. A major focus of this chapter is the new Web 2.0

applications, and the emerging Internet II that is now under development and will shape the future of e-commerce. Chapter 4 builds on the Internet chapter by focusing on the steps managers need to follow in order to build a commercial Web site. This e-commerce infrastructure chapter covers the systems analysis and design process that should be followed in building an e-commerce Web site; the major decisions surrounding the decision to outsource site development and/or hosting; and how to choose software, hardware, and other tools that can improve Web site performance. Chapter 5 focuses on Internet security and payments, building on the e-commerce infrastructure discussion of the previous chapter by describing the ways security can be provided over the Internet. This chapter defines digital information security, describes the major threats to security, and then discusses both the technology and policy solutions available to business managers seeking to secure their firm's sites. This chapter concludes with a section on Internet payment systems. We identify the stakeholders in payment systems, the dimensions to consider in creating payment systems, and the various types of online payment systems (credit cards, stored value payment systems such as PayPal, digital wallets such as Google Checkout and others).

Part 3, "Business Concepts and Social Issues," focuses directly on the business concepts and social-legal issues that surround the development of e-commerce. Chapter 6 focuses on e-commerce consumer behavior, the Internet audience, and introduces the student to the basics of online marketing and branding, including online marketing technologies and marketing strategies. Chapter 7 is devoted to online marketing communications, such as online advertising, e-mail marketing, and search-engine marketing. Chapter 8 provides a thorough introduction to the social and legal environment of e-commerce. Here, you will find a description of the ethical and legal dimensions of e-commerce, including a thorough discussion of the latest developments in personal information privacy, intellectual property, Internet governance, jurisdiction, and public health and welfare issues such as pornography, gambling, and health information.

Part 4, "E-commerce in Action," focuses on real-world e-commerce experiences in retail and services, online media, auctions, portals, and social networks, and business-to-business e-commerce. These chapters take a sector approach rather than a conceptual approach as used in the earlier chapters. E-commerce is different in each of these sectors. Chapter 9 takes a close look at the experience of firms in the retail marketplace for both goods and services, including both "pure-play" online firms such as Amazon and Expedia, and also mixed strategy "bricks-and-clicks" firms such as Wal-Mart and JCPenney. Chapter 10 explores the world of online content and digital media, and examines the enormous changes in online publishing and entertainment industries that have occurred over the last two years. Chapter 11 explores the online world of auctions, portals, and social networks. We describe a number of successful ventures here, including eBay and Yahoo, and communities such as Facebook, MySpace, and iVillage. Chapter 12 explores the world of B2B e-commerce, describing both electronic Net market-places and the less-heralded, but very large arena of private industrial networks and the movement toward collaborative commerce.

CHAPTER OUTLINE

Each chapter contains a number of elements designed to make learning easy as well as interesting.

Learning Objectives A list of learning objectives that highlights the key concepts in the chapter guides student study.

Chapter-Opening Cases Each chapter opens with a story about a leading e-commerce company that relates the key objectives of the chapter to a real-life e-commerce business venture.

Online Groceries:
Up from the Embers

When Webvan flamed out in July 2001 after having spent almost $1 billion trying to build the Web's largest online grocery store based on huge distribution warehouses in seven U.S. cities, most pundits and investors thought the entire online grocery business model was either a failure or a fraud. Facing the costs of building an entirely new distribution system of warehouses and truck fleets to compete with existing grocery businesses, not to mention the expense of marketing, Webvan compounded its problems by offering below-market prices and free delivery of even small orders at just about any time of the day or night in urban areas often clogged with traffic. But the pundits did not count on Manhattan's FreshDirect—or the ability of traditional grocery chains to move into the ashes of the online grocery business to create solid, profitable businesses. Jupiter Research estimates that online grocery sales will garner sales of $7.5 billion in 2008, and by 2012, sales are expected to grow to $13.5 billion, a compound annual growth rate of about 17%. FreshDirect and other traditional firms are learning how to exploit this potential market with profitable business models.

Today, traditional firms such as California's huge Safeway Stores and Royal Ahold (Dutch owner of the U.S. Stop & Shop and Giant food stores, among others, and the Internet firm Peapod, which handles Internet shopping for Stop & Shop and Giant) are following the lead of the successful British grocer Tesco. Tesco is the largest chain of supermarkets in Britain and opened an online division in 1990. It differed from Webvan's effort because Tesco uses its current warehouse infrastructure and existing stores to put together the baskets of food for consumers. Customers can either pick up their baskets or have them delivered within a chosen time window for a fee that recoups most of the delivery costs. Tesco dominates the online grocery shopping market in the United Kingdom, with over 5.4 million unique visitors during the period March-May 2008, more than three times as many as its nearest competitor Tesco takes over 30,000 online orders per day. In the United States, Safeway's wholly-owned subsidiary GroceryWorks.com provides online shopping and delivery services for Safeway stores in

63

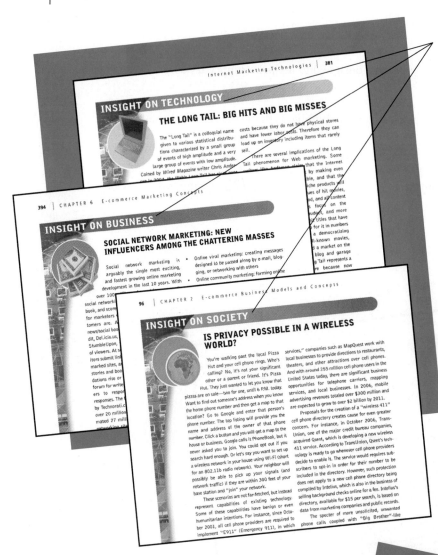

"Insight on" Cases Each chapter contains three real-world short cases illustrating the themes of technology, business, and society. These cases create an integrated framework and coverage throughout the book for describing and analyzing the full breadth of the field of e-commerce. The cases probe such issues as the ability of governments to regulate Internet content, how to design Web sites for accessibility, the challenges faced by luxury marketers in online marketing, and the potential anti-competitiveness of Net marketplaces.

Margin Glossary Throughout the text, key terms and their definitions appear in the text margin where they are first-introduced.

Real-Company Examples Drawn from actual e-commerce ventures, well over 100 pertinent examples are used throughout the text to illustrate concepts.

Chapter-Closing Case Studies Each chapter concludes with a robust case study based on a real-world organization. These cases help students synthesize chapter concepts and apply this knowledge to concrete problems and scenarios such as evaluating the ethics and legality of advertising spyware, the marketing plans of Liquidation.com, and the business model behind Siemens' Click2procure B2B marketplace.

Chapter-Ending Pedagogy Each chapter contains end-of-chapter materials designed to reinforce the learning objectives of the chapter.

Key Concepts Keyed to the learning objectives, Key Concepts present the key points of the chapter to aid student study.

Review Questions Thought-provoking questions prompt students to demonstrate their comprehension and apply chapter concepts to management problem solving.

Projects At the end of each chapter are a number of projects that encourage students to apply chapter concepts and to use higher level evaluation skills. Many make use of the Internet and require students to present their findings in an oral presentation or written report. For instance, students are asked to evaluate publicly available information about a company's financials at the SEC Web site, assess payment system options for companies across international boundaries, or search for the top ten cookies on their own computer and the sites they are from.

Web Resources A section at the end of the chapter directs students to Web resources on the Companion Web site at www.prenhall.com/laudon that can extend their knowledge of each chapter with projects and exercises and additional content. The Web site contains the following content provided by the authors:

- Additional projects, exercises, and tutorials.
- Material on how to build a business plan and revenue models.
- Reports on the recent activities of venture capitalists in the e-commerce space.
- Essays on careers in e-commerce, including marketing, technology, web design, and web metrics.

SUPPORT PACKAGE

The following supplementary materials are available to qualified instructors through the Companion Web site. Contact your Prentice Hall sales representative for information about how to access them.

- **Instructor's Manual with solutions** This comprehensive manual pulls together a wide variety of teaching tools so that instructors can use the text easily and effectively. Each chapter contains an overview of key topics, a recap of the key learning objectives, lecture tips, discussion of the chapter-ending case, and answers to the Case Study Questions, Review Questions, and Student Projects.
- **Test Bank** For quick test preparation, the author-created Test Bank contains multiple-choice, true/false, and short-essay questions that focus both on content and the development of critical/creative thinking about the issues evoked by the chapter. The Test Bank is available in Microsoft Word and TestGen format. The TestGen is also available in WebCT and BlackBoard-ready format. TestGen allows instructors to view, edit, and add questions.
- **PowerPoint lecture presentation slides** These slides illustrate key points, tables, and figures from the text in lecture-note format. The slides can be easily converted to transparencies or viewed electronically in the classroom.

ACKNOWLEDGMENTS

Pearson Education sought the advice of many excellent reviewers, all of whom strongly influenced the organization and substance of this book. The following individuals provided extremely useful evaluations of this and previous editions of the text:

Carrie Andersen, Madison Area Technical College

Dr. Shirley A. Becker, Northern Arizona University

Prasad Bingi, Indiana-Purdue University, Fort Wayne

Christine Barnes, Lakeland Community College

Cliff Butler, North Seattle Community College

Joanna Broder, University of Arizona

James Buchan, College of the Ozarks

Ashley Bush, Florida State University

Andrew Ciganek, Jacksonville State University

Daniel Connolly, University of Denver

Tom Critzer, Miami University

Dursan Delen, Oklahoma State University

Abhijit Deshmukh, University of Massachusetts

Brian L. Dos Santos, University of Louisville

Robert Drevs, University of Notre Dame

Akram El-Tannir, Hariri Canadian University, Lebanon

Kimberly Furumo, University of Hawaii at Hilo

John H. Gerdes, University of California, Riverside

Philip Gordon, University of California at Berkeley

Allan Greenberg, Brooklyn College

Peter Haried, University of Wisconsin-Milwaukee

Sherri Harms, University of Nebraska at Kearney

Sharon Heckel, St. Charles Community College

David Hite, Virgina Intermont College

Ellen Kraft, Georgian Court University

Gilliean Lee, Lander University

Zoonky Lee, University of Nebraska, Lincoln

Andre Lemaylleux, Boston University, Brussels

Haim Levkowitz, University of Massachusetts, Lowell

Yair Levy, Nova Southeastern University

Richard Lucic, Duke University

John Mendonca, Purdue University

Dr. Abdulrahman Mirza, DePaul University

Kent Palmer, MacMurray College

Karen Palumbo, University of St. Francis

Wayne Pauli, Dakota State University

Jamie Pinchot, Theil College

Barry Quinn, University of Ulster, Northern Ireland

Jay Rhee, San Jose State University

Jorge Romero, Towson University

John Sagi, Anne Arundel Community College

Patricia Sendall, Merrimack College

Dr. Carlos Serrao, ISCTE/DCTI, Portugal

Neerja Sethi, Nanyang Business School, Singapore

Amber Settle, DePaul CTI

Vivek Shah, Texas State University-San Marcos

Seung Jae Shin, Mississippi State University

Sumit Sircar, University of Texas at Arlington

Hongjun Song, University of Memphis

Pamela Specht, University of Nebraska at Omaha

Esther Swilley, Kansas State University

Tony Townsend, Iowa State University

Bill Troy, University of New Hampshire

Susan VandeVen, Southern Polytechnic State University

Hiep Van Dong, Madison Area Technical College

Mary Vitrano, Palm Beach Community College

Andrea Wachter, Point Park University

Catherine Wallace, Massey University, New Zealand

Biao Wang, Boston University

Harry Washington, Lincoln University

Rolf Wigand, University of Arkansas at Little Rock

Erin Wilkinson, Johnson & Wales University

Alice Wilson, Cedar Crest College

Dezhi Wu, Southern Utah University

Gene Yelle, SUNY Institute of Technology

David Zolzer, Northwestern State University

We would like to thank eMarketer, Inc. and David Iankelevich for their permission to include data and figures from their research reports in our text. eMarketer is one of the leading independent sources for statistics, trend data, and original analysis covering many topics related to the Internet, e-business, and emerging technologies. eMarketer aggregates e-business data from multiple sources worldwide.

In addition, we would like to thank all those at Prentice Hall who have worked so hard to make sure that this book is the very best that it can be. We want to thank Bob Horan, Executive Editor of the Prentice Hall MIS list and Kelly Loftus, Assistant Editor for their editorial support; Suzanne DeWorken and Karalyn Holland for overseeing production of this project; and Steve Frim for the outstanding cover design. Very special thanks to Megan Miller and Will Anderson at Azimuth Interactive, Inc., and Ann Cohen, for all their hard work on the production of, and supplements for, this book.

A special thanks also Susan Hartman Sullivan, Executive Editor for the first and second editions and to Frank Ruggirello, Publisher at Addison-Wesley when we began this project, and now Publisher at Benjamin-Cummings.

Finally, last but not least, we would like to thank our family and friends, without whose support this book would not have been possible.

Kenneth C. Laudon
Carol Guercio Traver

Brief Contents

PART 4 E-commerce in Action

Contents

---

2   E-COMMERCE BUSINESS MODELS AND CONCEPTS   62

PART 2 Technology Infrastructure for E-commerce

PART 3 Business Concepts and Social Issues

6   E-COMMERCE MARKETING CONCEPTS   336

PART 4   E-commerce in Action

---

11   SOCIAL NETWORKS, AUCTIONS, AND PORTALS   708

| 12 | B2B E-COMMERCE: SUPPLY CHAIN MANAGEMENT AND COLLABORATIVE COMMERCE | 766 |

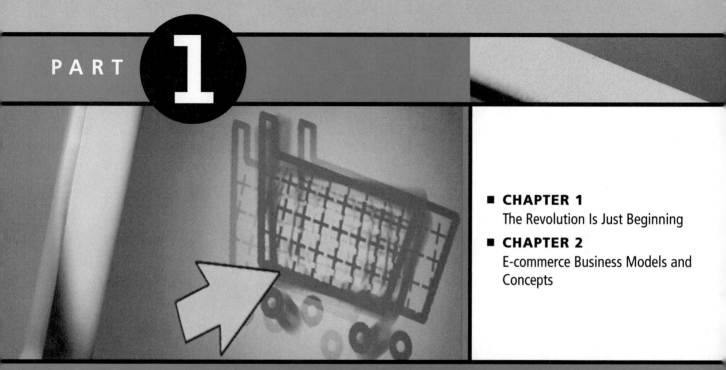

Introduction to E-commerce

The Revolution Is Just Beginning

After reading this chapter, you will be able to:

- Define e-commerce and describe how it differs from e-business.
- Identify and describe the unique features of e-commerce technology and discuss their business significance.
- Recognize and describe Web 2.0 applications.
- Describe the major types of e-commerce.
- Discuss the origins and growth of e-commerce.
- Understand the evolution of e-commerce from its early years to today.
- Identify the factors that will define the future of e-commerce.
- Describe the major themes underlying the study of e-commerce.
- Identify the major academic disciplines contributing to e-commerce.

Myspace and Facebook:
It's All About You

How many people watched the final episode of one of the most popular American television shows in history, The Sopranos? Answer: about 12 million (out of a total television audience size of 111 million).

Now, how many people in the United States do you think visit MySpace and Facebook, the two most popular social networking sites, each month? Answer: during the summer of 2008, MySpace had about 72 million unique U.S. visitors a month, while Facebook had around 40 million. That makes the television audience for The Sopranos

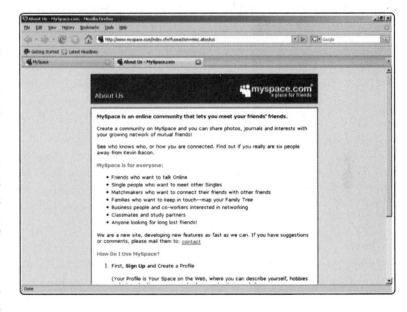

seem puny in comparison. Worldwide, Facebook and MySpace attract an even bigger audience: over 130 million unique visitors a month for Facebook and about 115 million for MySpace. Both sites also each have over 100 million personal profiles.

MySpace and Facebook, along with other "social" sites such as YouTube, Photobucket, and Second Life, exemplify the new face of e-commerce in the 21st century. When we think of e-commerce we tend to think of selling things online, a retail model based on selling physical products. While this iconic vision of e-commerce is still very powerful, and online retail is the fastest growing form of retail in the United States, growing up alongside is a whole new value stream based on selling services—not just goods. It's the service model of e-commerce.

What are these services and how much are they worth? How can you make money selling online services and how much can you make? Here, a little background will help.

The founders of MySpace, Tom Anderson and Chris DeWolfe, wanted to create a Web site that would make it possible for people to talk about the things they loved, and do it in a personal way—a sort of bulletin board combined with the capability of building your own Web pages with ease. Their vision was that people would like to talk about themselves, even promote themselves, and find others online to talk with. Anderson and DeWolfe started the business in January 2004, experienced an immediate unparalleled growth spurt, and today MySpace is among the top five most visited sites on the Internet, and on some days, in the top spot, rivaling and surpassing Google, Amazon, and eBay! Only Yahoo consistently draws more visitors.

MySpace is supported by advertising. That's where audience size is critical: a very large number of firms are willing to pay premium prices to contact 100 million people. For instance, in June 2008, the luxury jewelry company Cartier launched product pages for its "Love by Cartier" product line with new music by 12 different artists. Procter & Gamble has used MySpace to launch new products by linking their product pages to the MySpace pages of musicians whose visitors have the right demographics. Toyota has used MySpace to set up a profile of its Yaris car, and users can become "friends" of Yaris.

In July 2005, Rupert Murdoch's News Corporation bought MySpace for what then was thought to be an outrageous price of $580 million. Even more unusual was the buyer. Here was a traditional newspaper and television company buying an Internet venture that at the time was not profitable. In retrospect, many believe the real value of MySpace was in the billions of dollars. In August 2006, MySpace struck a deal with Google for $900 million, allowing Google to display short text ads next to search results generated by MySpace. In one year, Murdoch had made back his investment and then some. Analysts believe that MySpace had about $685 million in total revenue for its fiscal year ending in June 2008 and will have over $1 billion by 2010, primarily on the basis of Google search revenue and other advertising deals. For instance, in June 2008, MySpace, together with other Web sites operated by its parent company News Corp's Fox Interactive Media, took over the lead in the U.S. market for online display advertising from Yahoo for the first time. Fox served 52.3 billion ad (of which MySpace accounted for 51 billion) compared to Yahoo's 34.7 billion. However, Yahoo's ad rates are 5 times higher than MySpace's. News Corporation does not report independent financial results for MySpace, so no one really knows if MySpace is profitable, although the division that includes MySpace reported a $42 million profit for the 2008 fiscal year compared to a loss of $193 million a year earlier.

MySpace was not a new vision—other sites such as Friendster preceded it. But MySpace learned from Friendster's limitations. MySpace allowed bands and artists to promote themselves on the site, while Friendster banned self-promoting bands and artists. At MySpace, users could find the bands they liked and share that with their friends, starting a word-of-mouth buzz that promoted the bands, but also promoted MySpace as the place to find great music. However, because it allows users to post just about anything they want, it has been banned from many business firms, as well as schools. Nevertheless, more than half of the MySpace audience is older than 34 years.

MySpace has rivals. In fact, it has spawned hundreds of more focused, niche social networks. There are investor, teen, business, career, family, fishing, music and travel networks, just to name a few. But its largest rival is Facebook. Founded as thefacebook.com at Harvard by student Mark Zuckerberg as a hobby, the idea behind Facebook was to create an online digital version of the traditional student class picture or "facebook." It quickly became popular at Harvard, expanded to Yale and

Stanford, and then to the nation's 3,000 plus college campuses, creating a "social networking phenomenon" on campus. About 90% of college students in the United States have a Facebook profile, along with lists of favorites, activities, and accomplishments. Like MySpace, Facebook quickly developed into a general-purpose platform for conducting social life.

Originally restricted to college students, and relying on fixed templates rather than user-designed Web pages, Facebook initially was easily eclipsed by MySpace in terms of sheer numbers of subscribers. In 2006, in an effort to expand its subscriber base, Facebook made itself available to anyone, not just college students, and opened up its Web pages to thousands of widgets—small software programs that users can find on the Web that make posting of photos, music, and video easy. Facebook even allows users to post ads and make money from their own advertising campaigns. MySpace does not allow posting of user advertising, and does not allow outside vendors to develop software applications to run on its site. Facebook, in contrast, supplies other firms with its source code and is encouraging outside firms to build applications that run on the Facebook site. As a result, Facebook is attracting MySpace users looking for a more structured, defined, and refined environment. Facebook is growing at twice the rate of MySpace in 2008. As with MySpace, no one knows if Facebook is profitable, and the owners of this private company are not saying. In May 2008, eMarketer estimated that Facebook would have around $300 million in revenue for 2008.

For Zuckerberg, still the CEO of Facebook, the goal is to become "the social operating system of the Internet," at the center of users' online lives. This is right up there with the ambitions of Google ("to organize the world's information") and Amazon (becoming the "Earth's Biggest Selection"). But they will have to go through MySpace first.

SOURCES: "MySpace Tops in Display Ads", by Kenneth Corbin, August 27, 2008; Internetnews.com; "Facebook's 100 Million Users: How Much are They Worth?" by Stan Schroeder, Mashable.com, August 26, 2008; "Monetizing MySpace Traffic," by Debra Aho Williamson, eMarketer, August 11, 2008a; "Cartier Pretties up MySpace with Ad Campaign," by Caroline McCarthy, Cnet News, June 26, 2008; "comScore: Facebook is Beating MySpace Worldwide," by Caroline McCarthy, Cnet News, June 20, 2008; "Facebook Privacy Flap Should Spark Concern for Business," by Jim Carr, SCMagazineUS.com, March 26, 2008; "Facebook CEO Seeks Help as Site Grows Up," by Vauhini Vara, *Wall Street Journal*, March 5, 2008; "Social Networks Find Ways to Monetize User Data," by Thomas Claburn, InformationWeek, November 10, 2007; "In Facebook, Investing In a Theory," by Brad Stone, *New York Times*, October 4, 2007 "MySpace Outperforms All Other Social Networking Sites," News Corporation, July 12, 2007; "The Guys Behind MySpace.com," by Matt Krantz, *USA Today*, June 27, 2007; "Facebook Gets Help From Its Friends," *Wall Street Journal*, June 22, 2007; "'Sopranos' Whacks Most Rivals," by *Associated Press*, June 13, 2007; "Social Networking's Next Phase," by Brad Stone, *New York Times*, March 3, 2007; "Turning an Online Community Into a Business," by David Enrich, *Wall Street Journal*, February 27, 2007.

MySpace and Facebook, and hundreds of other niche-oriented social networking sites, are emblematic of the new e-commerce. These sites and others, such as YouTube, Photobucket, and Second Life, are defining a new and vibrant model of e-commerce growing up alongside the more traditional e-commerce retail sales model exemplified by Amazon and eBay. In this new model, services—not retail goods—are provided both to subscribers as well as to business firms advertising to entirely new audiences. Second, the movement of eyeballs towards social networking and user-generated content sites means fewer viewers of television and Hollywood movies, and fewer readers of newspapers and magazines. Never before in the history of media have such large audiences been aggregated and made accessible. Social networks are a technology that is highly disruptive of traditional media firms. Social networks are becoming the place where new products can be introduced and where new sales can be achieved to highly targeted and segmented audiences with a precision heretofore impossible. Welcome to the new service-based e-commerce!

This is not the first time e-commerce has reinvented itself. In the past 10 years, e-commerce has gone through two transitions. The early years of e-commerce, during the late 1990s, were a period of business vision, inspiration, and experimentation, followed by the realization that establishing a successful business model based on those visions would not be easy, which then ushered in a period of retrenchment and reevaluation. The retrenchment led to the stock market crash of March 2000 to April 2001, when the stock market value of e-commerce, telecommunications, and other technology stocks plummeted in the space of a year by more than 90%. After the bubble burst, many people were quick to write off e-commerce and predicted that e-commerce growth would stagnate, and the Internet audience itself would plateau. But they were wrong. In this first transition, the surviving firms refined and honed their business models, ultimately leading to models that actually produced profits, resulting in e-commerce retail growth rates of over 25% per year.

The second transition is toward services such as creating and publishing photos, software applications, blogs and videos, and developing new communities and professional ties through network sites, even as the e-commerce retail goods trade continues to expand at 14% a year. And it's probably safe to predict that this will not be the last transition for e-commerce.

1.1   E-COMMERCE: THE REVOLUTION IS JUST BEGINNING

In fact, the e-commerce revolution is just beginning. For instance, in 2008:

- Online consumer sales (retail, travel and online content) expanded around 14% to an estimated $255 billion (eMarketer, Inc., 2008b; Internet Retailer, 2008).
- The major source of online retail growth is now increased spending by existing online buyers rather than new buyers as trust and consumer confidence build. Shoppers are buying expensive, "high-touch" goods online such as consumer electronics, home furnishings, and apparel.

- The number of individuals online in the United States increased to 173 million, up from 170 million in 2007, and 150 million in 2006. (The total population of the United States is about 300 million). (eMarketer, Inc., 2008c)

- Of the total 120 million households in the United States, the number online increased to 84 million or about 70% of all households (eMarketer, Inc., 2008c).

- On an average day, 112 million people go online. Around 97 million send e-mail, 33 million share music on peer-to-peer networks, and 35 million research a product. About 62 million have used Wikipedia, 28 million have created a social network profile, 21 million have created a blog, and 55 million have used the Internet to rate a person, product, or service (Pew Internet and American Life Project, 2008).

- The number of people who have purchased something online expanded to about 117 million, with an additional 21 million just shopping (gathering information but not purchasing) (eMarketer, Inc., 2008b).

- The demographic profile of new online adult shoppers broadened to become more like ordinary American shoppers while at the same time significant generational differences in purchase patterns have emerged (eMarketer, Inc., 2008b).

- B2B e-commerce—use of the Internet for business-to-business commerce—expanded about 13% to more than $3.8 trillion (U.S. Census Bureau, 2008; authors' estimates).

- The Internet technology base gained greater depth and power, as more than 72 million households have broadband cable or DSL access to the Internet—about 62% of all U.S. households (eMarketer, Inc., 2008c).

These developments signal many of the themes in the new edition of this book (see **Table 1.1**). More and more people and businesses will be using the Internet to conduct commerce; smaller, local firms are learning how to take advantage of the Web; the e-commerce channel will deepen as more products and services come online; more industries will be transformed by e-commerce, including all forms of traditional media (from movies, television, music, and news), software, education, and finance; Internet technology will continue to drive these changes as broadband telecommunications comes to more households; pure e-commerce business models will be refined further to achieve higher levels of profitability; and traditional retail brands such as Sears, JCPenney, and Wal-Mart will further extend their multi-channel, bricks-and-clicks strategies and retain their dominant retail positions by strengthening their Internet operations. At the societal level, other trends are apparent. The Internet has created a platform for millions of people to create and share content, establish new social bonds and strengthen existing ones through social networking sites, blogging, and video posting sites such as YouTube. The major digital copyright owners have increased their pursuit of online file-swapping services with mixed success. States have successfully moved toward taxation of Internet sales, while Internet gaming sites have been severely curtailed through criminal prosecutions in the United States. Sovereign nations have expanded their surveillance of, and control over, Internet communications and content as a part of their anti-terrorist activities and their traditional interest in snooping on citizens. Privacy seems to have lost much of its meaning in an age when millions create public online personal profiles.

In 1994, e-commerce as we now know it did not exist. In 2008, just 14 years later, around 117 million American consumers are expected to spend about $255 billion purchasing online retail products and services on the Internet's World Wide Web (eMarketer, Inc., 2008d). Although the terms Internet and World Wide Web are often used interchangeably, they are actually two very different things. The *Internet* is a worldwide network of computer networks, and the *World Wide Web* is one of the Internet's most popular services, providing access to over 40 billion Web pages. We describe both more fully later in this chapter and in Chapter 3. In 2008, businesses are expected to spend over $3.8 trillion purchasing goods and services from other businesses on the Web (U.S. Census Bureau, 2008). From a standing start in 1995, this type of commerce, called *electronic commerce* or *e-commerce*, has experienced growth rates of well over 100% a year, although the rate has slowed and is now growing at about 14% a year. These developments have created the first widespread digital electronic marketplaces. Even more impressive than its spectacular initial growth is its future predicted growth. By 2012, analysts estimate that consumers will be spending over $400 billion and businesses about $6.3 trillion in online transactions (eMarketer, Inc., 2008d; U.S. Census Bureau, 2008).

TABLE 1.1	MAJOR TRENDS IN E-COMMERCE 2008–2009

BUSINESS

- New business models emerge based on social technologies and consumer-generated content from videos and photos, to blogs and reviews.
- Search engine marketing challenges traditional marketing and advertising media as consumers switch their eyes to the Web.
- Retail consumer e-commerce continues to grow at double-digit rates.
- Online population growth slows, but average purchase expands.
- The online demographics of shoppers continues to broaden with the fastest growth among teens and tweens, and older adults.
- Online sites continue to strengthen profitability by refining their business models and leveraging the capabilities of the Internet.
- The first wave of e-commerce transformed the business world of books, music, brokerage, and air travel. Today industries facing a similar transformation include marketing/advertising, telecommunications, entertainment, print media, real estate, hotels, bill payments, and software.

TABLE 1.1	MAJOR TRENDS IN E-COMMERCE 2008–2009 (CONTINUED)

- The breadth of e-commerce offerings grows, especially in travel, entertainment, retail apparel, appliances, and home furnishings.
- Small businesses and entrepreneurs continue to flood into the e-commerce marketplace, often riding on the infrastructures created by industry giants such as Amazon, eBay, and Google.
- Brand extension through the Internet grows as large firms such as Sears, JCPenney, L.L.Bean, and Wal-Mart pursue integrated, multi-channel bricks-and-clicks strategies.
- B2B supply chain transactions and collaborative commerce continue to strengthen and grow beyond the $3.8 trillion mark.

TECHNOLOGY

- Wireless Internet connections (Wi-Fi, WiMax, and 3G telephone) grow rapidly.
- A new mobile computing and communications platform emerges based on smart iPhones and Blackberries to rival the PC platform.
- Podcasting takes off as a new media format for distribution of video, radio, and user-generated content. iTunes becomes an operating system within Windows for the play of music and video.
- The Internet broadband foundation becomes stronger in households and businesses. Bandwidth prices fall as telecommunications companies re-capitalize their debts.
- Computing and networking component prices continue to fall dramatically.
- New Internet-based models of computing such as .NET and Web services expand B2B opportunities.

SOCIETY

- Consumer and user-generated content, and syndication in the form of blogs, wikis, virtual lives, and social networks, grow to form an entirely new self-publishing forum that engages millions of consumers.
- Virtual life sites such as Second Life emerge as a new form of Internet-based entertainment that causes millions to reduce television viewing.
- Traditional media such as newspapers, television broadcasters, and magazine publishers continue to lose subscribers, and adopt online, interactive models.
- Conflicts over copyright management and control grow in significance.
- Explosive growth in online viewing of video and television programs
- Over 76 million adults join a social network on the Internet, with the majority over 35 years of age.
- Taxation of Internet sales becomes more widespread and accepted by large online merchants.
- Controversy over content regulation and controls increases.
- Surveillance of Internet communications grows as a part of the "war on terror."
- Concerns over commercial and governmental privacy invasion grow as firms provide access to government agencies of private personal information.
- Internet fraud, abuse, and identity theft occurrences increase.
- Spam grows despite new laws and promised technology fixes.
- Invasion of personal privacy on the Web expands as marketers expand their capabilities to track users.
- China and India Internet populations continue to grow at over 20% annually.

THE FIRST THIRTY SECONDS

It is important to realize that the rapid growth and change that has occurred in the first 14 years of e-commerce represents just the beginning—what could be called the first 30 seconds of the e-commerce revolution. The same technologies that drove the first decade of e-commerce (described in Chapter 3) continue to evolve at exponential rates. This underlying ferment in the technological groundwork of the Internet and Web presents entrepreneurs with new opportunities to both create new businesses and new business models in traditional industries, and also to destroy old businesses. Business change becomes disruptive, rapid, and even destructive, while offering entrepreneurs new opportunities and resources for investment.

Changes in underlying information technologies and continuing entrepreneurial innovation in business and marketing promise as much change in the next decade as seen in the last decade. The twenty-first century will be the age of a digitally enabled social and commercial life, the outlines of which we can barely perceive at this time. It appears likely that e-commerce will eventually impact nearly all commerce, and that most commerce will be e-commerce by the year 2050.

Is there a terminal velocity, or a terminal point, towards which e-commerce is hurtling? Can e-commerce continue to grow at its current rate indefinitely? It's possible that at some point, e-commerce growth may slow just because people have no more time to watch yet another Internet television show, or open more and more e-mail. However, currently, there is no foreseeable limit to the continued exponential development of the technology, or limits on the inventiveness of entrepreneurs to develop new uses for the technology. Therefore, for now at least, the disruptive process will continue.

Business fortunes are made—and lost—in periods of extraordinary change such as this. The next five years hold out extraordinary opportunities—as well as risks—for new and traditional businesses to exploit digital technology for market advantage. For society as a whole, the next few decades offer the possibility of extraordinary gains in social wealth as the digital revolution works its way through larger and larger segments of the world's economy, offering the possibility of high rates of productivity and income growth in an inflation-free environment.

As a business or technology student, this book will help you perceive and understand the opportunities and risks that lie ahead. By the time you finish, you will be able to identify the technological, business, and social forces that have shaped the growth of e-commerce and extend that understanding into the years ahead.

WHAT IS E-COMMERCE?

e-commerce
the use of the Internet and the Web to transact business. More formally, digitally enabled commercial transactions between and among organizations and individuals

Our focus in this book is **e-commerce**—the use of the Internet and the Web to transact business. More formally, we focus on digitally enabled commercial transactions between and among organizations and individuals. Each of these components of our working definition of e-commerce is important. *Digitally enabled transactions* include all transactions mediated by digital technology. For the most part, this means transactions that occur over the Internet and the Web. *Commercial transactions* involve the exchange of value (e.g., money) across organizational or individual boundaries in return for products and services. Exchange of value is important for understanding the limits of e-commerce. Without an exchange of value, no commerce occurs.

THE DIFFERENCE BETWEEN E-COMMERCE AND E-BUSINESS

There is a debate among consultants and academics about the meaning and limitations of both e-commerce and e-business. Some argue that e-commerce encompasses the entire world of electronically based organizational activities that support a firm's market exchanges—including a firm's entire information system's infrastructure (Rayport and Jaworski, 2003). Others argue, on the other hand, that e-business encompasses the entire world of internal and external electronically based activities, including e-commerce (Kalakota and Robinson, 2003).

We think that it is important to make a working distinction between e-commerce and e-business because we believe they refer to different phenomena. E-commerce is not "anything digital" that a firm does. For purposes of this text, we will use the term **e-business** to refer primarily to the digital enabling of transactions and processes *within* a firm, involving information systems under the control of the firm. For the most part, in our view, e-business does not include commercial transactions involving an exchange of value across organizational boundaries. For example, a company's online inventory control mechanisms are a component of e-business, but such internal processes do not directly generate revenue for the firm from outside businesses or consumers, as e-commerce, by definition, does. It is true, however, that a firm's e-business infrastructure provides support for online e-commerce exchanges; the same infrastructure and skill sets are involved in both e-business and e-commerce. E-commerce and e-business systems blur together at the business firm boundary, at the point where internal business systems link up with suppliers or customers, for instance (see **Figure 1.1**). E-business applications turn into e-commerce precisely when an exchange of value occurs (see Mesenbourg, U.S. Department of Commerce, 2001, for a similar view). We will examine this intersection further in Chapter 12.

e-business

the digital enabling of transactions and processes within a firm, involving information systems under the control of the firm

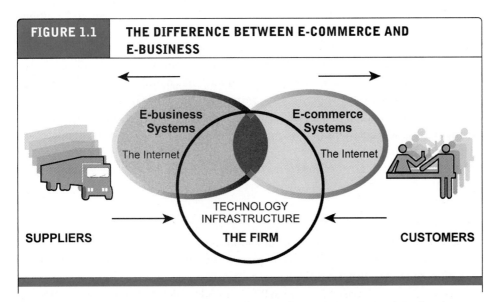

| FIGURE 1.1 | THE DIFFERENCE BETWEEN E-COMMERCE AND E-BUSINESS |

E-commerce primarily involves transactions that cross firm boundaries. E-business primarily involves the application of digital technologies to business processes within the firm.

WHY STUDY E-COMMERCE?

Why are there college courses and textbooks on e-commerce when there are no courses or textbooks on "TV Commerce," "Radio Commerce," "Direct Mail Commerce," "Railroad Commerce," or "Highway Commerce," even though these technologies had profound impacts on commerce in the twentieth century and account for far more commerce than e-commerce? Many colleges, including Massachusetts Institute of Technology (MIT), University of Michigan, Cornell University, University of California at Berkeley, and NSEAD Business School (France), are also developing courses on social interaction technologies and techniques, online social networks, online community development, and consumer-generated media. At least one college offers a YouTube 101 course called "Learning from YouTube."

The reason for the interest specifically in e-commerce is that e-commerce technology (discussed in detail in Chapters 3 and 4) is different and more powerful than any of the other technologies we have seen in the past century. E-commerce technologies—and the digital markets that result—promise to bring about some fundamental, unprecedented shifts in commerce. While these other technologies transformed economic life in the twentieth century, the evolving Internet and other information technologies will shape the twenty-first century.

Prior to the development of e-commerce, the marketing and sale of goods was a mass-marketing and sales force-driven process. Marketers viewed consumers as passive targets of advertising "campaigns" and branding blitzes intended to influence their long-term product perceptions and immediate purchasing behavior. Companies sold their products via well-insulated "channels." Consumers were trapped by geographical and social boundaries, unable to search widely for the best price and quality. Information about prices, costs, and fees could be hidden from the consumer, creating profitable "information asymmetries" for the selling firm. **Information asymmetry** refers to any disparity in relevant market information among parties in a transaction. It was so expensive to change national or regional prices in traditional retailing (what are called *menu costs*) that "one national price" was the norm, and dynamic pricing to the marketplace—changing prices in real time—was unheard of. In this environment, manufacturers prospered by relying on huge production runs of products that could not be customized or personalized. One of the shifts that e-commerce appears to be bringing about is a large reduction in information asymmetry among all market participants (consumers and merchants). Preventing consumers from learning about costs, price discrimination strategies, and profits from sales becomes more difficult with e-commerce, and the entire marketplace potentially becomes highly price competitive.

information asymmetry
any disparity in relevant market information among parties in a transaction

EIGHT UNIQUE FEATURES OF E-COMMERCE TECHNOLOGY

Table 1.2 lists eight unique features of e-commerce technology that both challenge traditional business thinking and explain why we have so much interest in e-commerce. These unique dimensions of e-commerce technologies suggest many new possibilities for marketing and selling—a powerful set of interactive, personalized, and rich messages are available for delivery to segmented, targeted audiences.

TABLE 1.2	EIGHT UNIQUE FEATURES OF E-COMMERCE TECHNOLOGY
E-COMMERCE TECHNOLOGY DIMENSION	**BUSINESS SIGNIFICANCE**
Ubiquity—Internet/Web technology is available everywhere: at work, at home, and elsewhere via mobile devices, anytime.	The marketplace is extended beyond traditional boundaries and is removed from a temporal and geographic location. "Marketspace" is created; shopping can take place anywhere. Customer convenience is enhanced, and shopping costs are reduced.
Global reach—The technology reaches across national boundaries, around the Earth.	Commerce is enabled across cultural and national boundaries seamlessly and without modification. "Marketspace" includes potentially billions of consumers and millions of businesses worldwide.
Universal standards—There is one set of technology standards, namely Internet standards.	There is a common, inexpensive, global, technology foundation for businesses to use.
Richness—Video, audio, and text messages are possible.	Video, audio, and text marketing messages are integrated into a single marketing message and consuming experience.
Interactivity—The technology works through interaction with the user.	Consumers are engaged in a dialog that dynamically adjusts the experience to the individual, and makes the consumer a co-participant in the process of delivering goods to the market.
Information density—The technology reduces information costs and raises quality.	Information processing, storage, and communication costs drop dramatically, while currency, accuracy, and timeliness improve greatly. Information becomes plentiful, cheap, and accurate.
Personalization/Customization—The technology allows personalized messages to be delivered to individuals as well as groups.	Personalization of marketing messages and customization of products and services are based on individual characteristics.
Social technology—User content generation and social networking.	New Internet social and business models enable user content creation and distribution, and support social networks.

E-commerce technologies make it possible for merchants to know much more about consumers and to be able to use this information more effectively than was ever true in the past. Potentially, online merchants can use this new information to develop new information asymmetries, enhance their ability to brand products, charge premium prices for high-quality service, and segment the market into an endless number of subgroups, each receiving a different price. To complicate matters further, these same technologies make it possible for merchants to know more about other merchants than was ever true in the past. This presents the possibility that merchants might collude on prices rather than compete and drive overall average prices up. This strategy works especially well when there are just a few suppliers (Varian, 2000b). We examine these different visions of e-commerce further in Section 1.2 and throughout the book.

Each of the dimensions of e-commerce technology and their business significance listed in Table 1.2 deserves a brief exploration, as well as a comparison to both traditional commerce and other forms of technology-enabled commerce.

Ubiquity

marketplace

physical space you visit in order to transact

ubiquity

available just about everywhere, at all times

marketspace

marketplace extended beyond traditional boundaries and removed from a temporal and geographic location

In traditional commerce, a **marketplace** is a physical place you visit in order to transact. For example, television and radio typically motivate the consumer to go some place to make a purchase. E-commerce, in contrast, is characterized by its **ubiquity**: it is available just about everywhere, at all times. It liberates the market from being restricted to a physical space and makes it possible to shop from your desktop, at home, at work, or even from your car, using mobile commerce. The result is called a **marketspace**—a marketplace extended beyond traditional boundaries and removed from a temporal and geographic location. From a consumer point of view, ubiquity reduces *transaction costs*—the costs of participating in a market. To transact, it is no longer necessary that you spend time and money traveling to a market. At a broader level, the ubiquity of e-commerce lowers the cognitive energy required to transact in a marketspace. *Cognitive energy* refers to the mental effort required to complete a task. Humans generally seek to reduce cognitive energy outlays. When given a choice, humans will choose the path requiring the least effort—the most convenient path (Shapiro and Varian, 1999; Tversky and Kahneman, 1981).

Global Reach

reach

the total number of users or customers an e-commerce business can obtain

E-commerce technology permits commercial transactions to cross cultural and national boundaries far more conveniently and cost-effectively than is true in traditional commerce. As a result, the potential market size for e-commerce merchants is roughly equal to the size of the world's online population (over 1.4 billion in 2008, and growing rapidly, according to industry sources) (Internet Worldstats, 2008). The total number of users or customers an e-commerce business can obtain is a measure of its **reach** (Evans and Wurster, 1997).

In contrast, most traditional commerce is local or regional—it involves local merchants or national merchants with local outlets. Television and radio stations, and newspapers, for instance, are primarily local and regional institutions with limited but powerful national networks that can attract a national audience. In contrast to e-commerce technology, these older commerce technologies do not easily cross national boundaries to a global audience.

Universal Standards

universal standards

standards that are shared by all nations around the world

One strikingly unusual feature of e-commerce technologies is that the technical standards of the Internet, and therefore the technical standards for conducting e-commerce, are **universal standards**—they are shared by all nations around the world. In contrast, most traditional commerce technologies differ from one nation to the next. For instance, television and radio standards differ around the world, as does cell telephone technology. The universal technical standards of the Internet and e-commerce greatly lower *market entry costs*—the cost merchants must pay just to bring their goods to market. At the same time, for consumers, universal standards reduce *search costs*—the effort required to find suitable products. And by creating a single, one-world marketspace, where prices and product descriptions can be inexpensively displayed for all to see, *price discovery* becomes simpler, faster, and more accurate (Banerjee, et. al., 2005; Bakos, 1997; Kambil, 1997). And users of the Internet, both businesses and individuals, experience *network externalities*—benefits that arise because everyone uses the same technology. With e-commerce technologies, it is possible for the first time in history to easily find many of the suppliers, prices, and delivery terms of a specific product anywhere in the world, and to view them in a coherent, comparative environment. Although this is not necessarily realistic today for all or many products, it is a potential that will be exploited in the future.

Richness

Information **richness** refers to the complexity and content of a message (Evans and Wurster, 1999). Traditional markets, national sales forces, and small retail stores have great richness: they are able to provide personal, face-to-face service using aural and visual cues when making a sale. The richness of traditional markets makes them a powerful selling or commercial environment. Prior to the development of the Web, there was a trade-off between richness and reach: the larger the audience reached, the less rich the message (see **Figure 1.2**). The Internet has the potential for offering considerably more information richness than traditional media such as printing presses, radio, and television because it is interactive and can adjust the message to individual users. Chatting with an online sales person, for instance, comes very close to the customer experience in a small retail shop. The richness of the Web allows retail and service merchants to market and sell "complex" goods and services that heretofore really did require a face-to-face presentation by a sales force. Complex goods have multiple attributes, are typically expensive, and cannot be compared easily, such as used cars, non-standard financial instruments, and even diamond rings (Fink, et. al., 2004).

richness
the complexity and content of a message

Interactivity

Unlike any of the commercial technologies of the twentieth century, with the possible exception of the telephone, e-commerce technologies allow for interactivity, meaning they enable two-way communication between merchant and consumer. Traditional television, for instance, cannot ask viewers any questions or enter into conversations with them, and it cannot request that customer information be entered into a form. In contrast, all of these activities are possible on an e-commerce Web site. **Interactivity** allows an online merchant to

interactivity
technology that allows for two-way communication between merchant and consumer

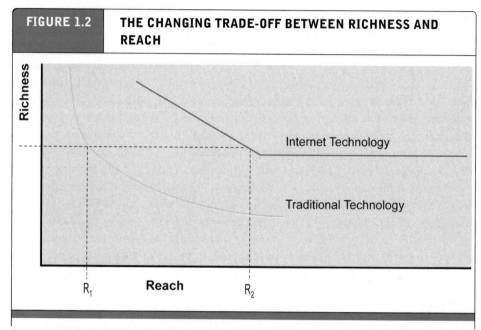

FIGURE 1.2   THE CHANGING TRADE-OFF BETWEEN RICHNESS AND REACH

E-commerce technologies have changed the traditional trade-off between richness and reach. The Internet and Web can deliver, to an audience of millions, "rich" marketing messages with text, video, and audio, in a way not possible with traditional commerce technologies such as radio, television, or magazines.
SOURCE: Evans and Wurster, 2000.

engage a consumer in ways similar to a face-to-face experience, but on a much more massive, global scale.

Information Density

information density
the total amount and quality of information available to all market participants

The Internet and the Web vastly increase **information density**—the total amount and quality of information available to all market participants, consumers, and merchants alike. E-commerce technologies reduce information collection, storage, processing, and communication costs. At the same time, these technologies increase greatly the currency, accuracy, and timeliness of information—making information more useful and important than ever. As a result, information becomes more plentiful, less expensive and of higher quality.

A number of business consequences result from the growth in information density. In e-commerce markets, prices and costs become more transparent. *Price transparency* refers to the ease with which consumers can find out the variety of prices in a market; *cost transparency* refers to the ability of consumers to discover the actual costs merchants pay for products (Sinha, 2000). But there are advantages for merchants as well. Online merchants can discover much more about consumers; this allows merchants to segment the market into groups willing to pay different prices and permits them to engage in *price discrimination*—selling the same goods, or nearly the same goods, to different targeted groups at different prices. For instance, an online merchant can discover a consumer's avid interest in expensive exotic vacations, and then pitch expensive exotic vacation plans to that consumer at a premium price, knowing this person is willing to pay extra for such a vacation. At the same time, the online merchant can pitch the same vacation plan at a lower price to more price-sensitive consumers. Merchants also have enhanced abilities to differentiate their products in terms of cost, brand, and quality.

Personalization/Customization

E-commerce technologies permit **personalization**: merchants can target their marketing messages to specific individuals by adjusting the message to a person's name, interests, and past purchases. The technology also permits **customization**—changing the delivered product or service based on a user's preferences or prior behavior. Given the interactive nature of e-commerce technology, much information about the consumer can be gathered in the marketplace at the moment of purchase. With the increase in information density, a great deal of information about the consumer's past purchases and behavior can be stored and used by online merchants. The result is a level of personalization and customization unthinkable with existing commerce technologies. For instance, you may be able to shape what you see on television by selecting a channel, but you cannot change the contents of the channel you have chosen. In contrast, the online version of *The Wall Street Journal* allows you to select the type of news stories you want to see first, and gives you the opportunity to be alerted when certain events happen. Personalization and customization allow firms to precisely identify market segments and adjust their messages accordingly.

personalization
the targeting of marketing messages to specific individuals by adjusting the message to a person's name, interests, and past purchases

customization
changing the delivered product or service based on a user's preferences or prior behavior

Social Technology: User Content Generation and Social Networking

In a way quite different from all previous technologies, the Internet and e-commerce technologies have evolved to be much more social by allowing users to create and share content in the form of text, videos, music, or photos with a worldwide community. Using these forms of communication, users are able to create new social networks and strengthen existing ones. All previous mass media in modern history, including the printing press, use a broadcast model (one-to-many) where content is created in a central location by experts (professional writers, editors, directors, actors, and producers) and audiences are concentrated in huge aggregates to consume a standardized product. The telephone would appear to be an exception but it is not a "mass communication" technology. Instead the telephone is a one-to-one technology. The new Internet and e-commerce technologies have the potential to invert this standard media model by giving users the power to create and distribute content on a large scale, and permit users to program their own content consumption. The Internet provides a many-to-many model of mass communications that is unique.

WEB 2.0: PLAY MY VERSION

Many of the unique features of e-commerce and the Internet come together in a set of applications and social technologies referred to as Web 2.0. The Internet started out as a simple network to support e-mail and file transfers among remote computers. Communication among experts was the purpose. The World Wide Web (the Web) started out as a way to use the Internet to display simple pages and allow the user to navigate among the pages by linking them together electronically. You can think of this as Web 1.0—the first Web. By 2007 something else was happening. The Internet and the Web have evolved to the point where users can now create, edit, and distribute content to millions of others; share with one another their preferences, bookmarks, and online personas; participate in virtual lives; and build online communities. This "new" Web is called by many "**Web 2.0**," and while it draws heavily on the "old" Web 1.0, it is nevertheless a clear evolution from the past.

Let's look at some examples of Web 2.0 applications and sites:

Web 2.0

a set of applications and technologies that allows users to create, edit, and distribute content; share preferences, bookmarks, and online personas; participate in virtual lives; and build online communities

- Photobucket zooms from 4 million to 50 million users and 5 billion consumer-generated images and videos to become the most popular Web photo posting site, offering users an easy way to post and send photos and video, and provides a convenient link to YouTube, MySpace, and blog pages (Photobucket.com, 2008).

- YouTube, owned by Google after a $1.65 billion purchase, grows to the largest online consumer-generated video posting site and still searches for a profitable business model. Over 65,000 videos are uploaded each day and 3 billion video streams are launched each month to more than 70 million monthly visitors. This one site accounts for over 60% of all videos watched online (Nielsen, 2008).

- MySpace ("A place for friends") and Facebook rocket to the lead of online networking sites, each with over 100 million Web socialites (Facebook, 2008; News Corporation, 2007). Adult professional sites such as LinkedIn attract additional millions of adults looking for online connections.

- Joost.com becomes the first Internet Television channel with financing of $50 million and agreements with networks to deliver TV programs to any Internet-connected device such as an iPod, MP3 player, cell phone, TV set top box, or any wirelessly connected PC or device. In 2008, Joost offers 28,000 TV shows and 250 channels. Suddenly TV is unleashed from cables, wires and national television networks or even local stations. Programming becomes user programming (Joost.com, 2008).

- Google attracts the largest Internet audience with 140 million unique monthly U.S. users, and over 575 million international users, with a continual stream of innovations such as Google Apps, Google Maps, GoogleView (a photo database of U.S. neighborhoods from the street level), video and photo posting and sharing, Gmail, and Google Scholar. Over 25% of Google search results on the world's top 20 brands provide links to consumer-generated content such as reviews, blogs, and photos. Google Apps is a group of Web-based services offering free office productivity tools such as Google Docs, calendar, spreadsheet, and collarobrative tools.

- Second Life is a 3-D virtual world built and owned by its residents who have established lives by building over almost 15 million avatars in "The World," spending Linden dollars, owning real estate, and building and sharing "creations," which include clothing, interior designs, or writing, among other items. Second Life had over 27 million unique visitors each month in 2008. Residents spend over $2 million real dollars each day to buy things on the site for their virtual lives, and convert the real dollars to Lindens (Secondlife.com, 2008).

- Wikipedia allows contributors around the world to share their knowledge and in the process has become the most successful online encyclopedia, far surpassing early "professional" encyclopedias such as Encarta or even Britannica. Wikipedia is one of the largest collaboratively edited reference projects in the world. As of August 2008, there were over 2.5 million articles in English, and over 75,000 active contributors working on more than 10 million articles in 250 languages. Garnering over 20% of the online reference market, Wikipedia relies on volunteers, makes no money, and accepts no advertising. The Wikimedia Foundation, Inc., a not-for-profit organization that relies on fund-raising and donations to survive, owns Wikipedia. Wikipedia is one of the top 10 most visited sites on the Web with about 62 million users Wikipedia.org, 2008; Pew Internet and American Life Project, 2008).

What do all these applications and new sites have in common? First, they rely on user- and consumer-generated content. These are all "applications" created by people, especially people in the 18–34 year-old demographic, and heavily in the 7–17 age group as well. "Regular" people (not just experts or professionals) are creating, sharing, modifying, and broadcasting content to huge audiences. Second, easy search capability is a key to their success. Third, they are inherently highly interactive, creating new opportunities for people to socially connect to others. They are "social" sites because they support interactions among users. Fourth, they rely on broadband connectivity to the Web. Fifth, with the exception of Google, they are currently marginally profitable, and their business models unproven despite considerable investment. Sixth, they attract extremely large audiences when compared to traditional Web 1.0 applications, exceeding in many cases the audience size of national broadcast and cable television programs. These audience relationships are intensive and long-lasting interactions with millions of people. In short, they attract eyeballs in very large numbers. Hence, they present marketers with extraordinary opportunities for targeted marketing and advertising. They also present consumers with the opportunity to rate and review products, and entrepreneurs with ideas for future business ventures. Last, these sites act as application development platforms where users can contribute and use software applications for free. Briefly, it's a whole new world from what has gone before. You'll learn more about Web 2.0 in later chapters.

---

[1]Business-to-Government (B2G) e-commerce can be considered yet another type of e-commerce. For the purposes of this text, we subsume B2G e-commerce within B2B e-commerce, viewing the government as simply a form of business when it acts as a procurer of goods and/or services.

TABLE 1.3	MAJOR TYPES OF E-COMMERCE
TYPE OF E-COMMERCE	EXAMPLE
B2C—Business-to-Consumer	Amazon is a general merchandiser that sells consumer products to retail consumers.
B2B—Business-to-Business	Foodtrader is an independent third-party commodity exchange, auctions provider, and market information source that serves the food and agricultural industry.
C2C—Consumer-to-Consumer	On a large number of Web auction sites such as eBay, and listing sites such as Craigslist, consumers can auction or sell goods directly to other consumers.
P2P—Peer-to-Peer	BitTorrent is a software application that permits consumers to share videos and other high-bandwidth content with one another directly, without the intervention of a market maker as in C2C e-commerce.
M-commerce—Mobile commerce	Wireless mobile devices such as PDAs (personal digital assistants) and cell phones can be used to conduct commercial transactions.

TYPES OF E-COMMERCE

There are a variety of different types of e-commerce and many different ways to characterize these types. **Table 1.3** lists the five major types of e-commerce discussed in this book.[1]

For the most part, we distinguish different types of e-commerce by the nature of the market relationship—who is selling to whom. The exceptions are P2P and m-commerce, which are technology-based distinctions.

Business-to-Consumer (B2C) E-commerce

Business-to-Consumer (B2C) e-commerce
online businesses selling to individual consumers

The most commonly discussed type of e-commerce is **Business-to-Consumer (B2C) e-commerce**, in which online businesses attempt to reach individual consumers. Even though B2C is comparatively small (about $255 billion in 2008), it has grown exponentially since 1995, and is the type of e-commerce that most consumers are likely to encounter. Within the B2C category, there are many different types of business models. Chapter 2 has a detailed discussion of seven different B2C business models: portals, online retailers, content providers, transaction brokers, service providers, and community providers.

Business-to-Business (B2B) E-commerce

Business-to-Business (B2B) e-commerce
online businesses selling to other businesses

Business-to-Business (B2B) e-commerce, in which businesses focus on selling to other businesses, is the largest form of e-commerce, with about $3.8 trillion in transactions in the United States in 2008. There was an estimated $12 trillion in business-to-business exchanges of all kinds, online and offline, suggesting that B2B e-commerce has significant growth potential. The ultimate size of B2B e-commerce could be huge. There are two primary business models used within the B2B arena: Net marketplaces, which include e-distributors, e-procurement companies, exchanges and industry consortia, and private industrial networks, which include single firm networks and industry-wide networks.

Consumer-to-Consumer (C2C) E-commerce

Consumer-to-Consumer (C2C) e-commerce provides a way for consumers to sell to each other, with the help of an online market maker such as the auction site eBay or the classified site Craigslist. Given that in 2008, eBay generated more than $60 billion in gross merchandise volume around the world, it is probably safe to estimate that the size of the global C2C market in 2008 is over $70 billion (eBay, 2008). In C2C e-commerce, the consumer prepares the product for market, places the product for auction or sale, and relies on the market maker to provide catalog, search engine, and transaction-clearing capabilities so that products can be easily displayed, discovered, and paid for.

Consumer-to-Consumer (C2C) e-commerce
consumers selling to other consumers

Peer-to-Peer (P2P) E-commerce

Peer-to-peer technology enables Internet users to share files and computer resources directly without having to go through a central Web server. In peer-to-peer's purest form, no intermediary is required, although in fact, most P2P networks make use of intermediary "super servers" to speed operations. Since 1999, entrepreneurs and venture capitalists have attempted to adapt various aspects of peer-to-peer technology into **Peer-to-Peer (P2P) e-commerce**. To date, the most widely used P2P networks are BitTorrent (which is used for downloading large video files, and accounts for nearly 25% of all Internet traffic) and eDonkey (used mostly for music files). Together these two P2P network programs account for 50%–70% of all Internet traffic worldwide—a startling figure. Some of this downloading and sharing is legal, but most is not. Legal commercial applications of P2P networking are beginning to emerge as Hollywood film studios move towards a digital distribution platform. The business models that support P2P commerce are unusual, in many cases illegal, and under constant attack by authorities.

Peer-to-Peer (P2P) e-commerce
use of peer-to-peer technology, which enables Internet users to share files and computer resources directly without having to go through a central Web server, in e-commerce

Napster, which was established to aid Internet users in finding and sharing online music files, was the most well-known example of P2P e-commerce until it was put out of business in 2001 by a series of negative court decisions. However, other file-sharing networks, such as Kazaa and Grokster, quickly emerged to take Napster's place. These networks were also put out of business by a variety of court opinions. The Supreme Court issued a decision in the case against the file-sharing networks in June 2005. Read the case study at the end of the chapter for a further look at how the music industry has been transformed both by file-sharing networks and legal sites such as Apple's iTunes and Real Networks' Rhapsody.

mobile commerce (m-commerce)
use of wireless digital devices to enable transactions on the Web

Mobile Commerce (M-commerce)

Mobile commerce, or **m-commerce**, refers to the use of wireless digital devices to enable transactions on the Web. Described more fully in Chapter 3, m-commerce involves the use of wireless networks to connect cell phones, handheld devices such as iPhones, Android G1s, and BlackBerries, and personal computers to the Web. Once connected, mobile consumers can conduct transactions, including stock trades, in-store price comparisons, banking, travel reservations, and more. Thus far, m-commerce is used most widely in Japan and Europe (especially in Scandinavia), where cell phones are more prevalent than in the United States. However, as discussed in the next section, m-commerce is expected to grow rapidly in the United States over the next five years because of the growth of "smart phones" and broadband cellular networks..

GROWTH OF THE INTERNET AND THE WEB

Internet
worldwide network of computer networks built on common standards

The technology juggernauts behind e-commerce are the Internet and the World Wide Web. Without both of these technologies, e-commerce as we know it would be impossible. We describe the Internet and the Web in some detail in Chapter 3. The **Internet** is a worldwide network of computer networks built on common standards. Created in the late 1960s to connect a small number of mainframe computers and their users, the Internet has since grown into the world's largest network, connecting over 1.2 billion computers worldwide. The Internet links businesses, educational institutions, government agencies, and individuals together, and provides users with services such as e-mail, document transfer, newsgroups, shopping, research, instant messaging, music, videos, and news.

Figure 1.3 illustrates one way to measure the growth of the Internet, by looking at the number of Internet hosts with domain names. (An *Internet host* is defined by the Internet Software Consortium, which conducts this survey, as any IP address that returns a domain name in the in-addr.arpa domain, which is a special part of the DNS namespace that resolves IP addresses into domain names.) In January 2008, there were over 540 million Internet hosts in over 245 countries, up from a mere 70 million in 2000. The number of Internet hosts has been growing at a rate of around 35% a year since 2000 (Internet Systems Consortium, Inc., 2008).

The Internet has shown extraordinary growth patterns when compared to other electronic technologies of the past. It took radio 38 years to achieve a 30% share of U.S. households. It took television 17 years to achieve a 30% share. Since the invention of a graphical user interface for the World Wide Web in 1993, it took only 10 years for the Internet/Web to achieve a 53% share of U.S. households.

World Wide Web (the Web)
the most popular service that runs on the Internet; provides easy access to Web pages

The **World Wide Web (the Web)** is the most popular service that runs on the Internet infrastructure. The Web is the "killer application" that made the Internet commercially interesting and extraordinarily popular. The Web was developed in the early 1990s and hence is of much more recent vintage than the Internet. We describe the Web in some detail in Chapter 3. The Web provides easy access to over 50 billion Web pages indexed by Google and other search engines. These pages are created in a language called *HTML (HyperText Markup Language)*. HTML pages

| FIGURE 1.3 | THE GROWTH OF THE INTERNET, MEASURED BY THE NUMBER OF INTERNET HOSTS WITH DOMAIN NAMES |

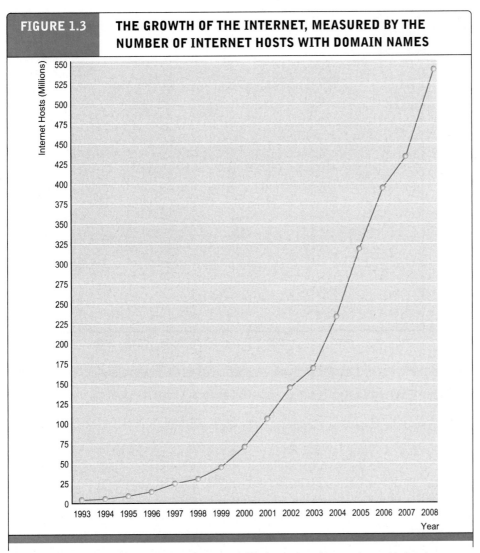

Growth in the size of the Internet 1993–2008 as measured by the number of Internet hosts with domain names.
SOURCE: Based on data from Internet Systems Consortium, Inc., 2008.

contain information—including text, graphics, animations, and other objects—made available for public use. You can find an exceptionally wide range of information on Web pages, ranging from the entire catalog of Sears Roebuck, to the entire collection of public records from the Securities and Exchange Commission, to the card catalog of your local library, to millions of music tracks (some of them legal) and videos. The Internet prior to the Web was primarily used for text communications, file transfers, and remote computing. The Web introduced far more powerful and commercially interesting, colorful multimedia capabilities of direct relevance to commerce. In essence, the Web added color, voice, and video to the Internet, creating a communications infrastructure and information storage system that rivals television, radio, magazines, and even libraries.

| FIGURE 1.4 | THE GROWTH OF WEB CONTENT, AS MEASURED BY WEB PAGES INDEXED BY GOOGLE |

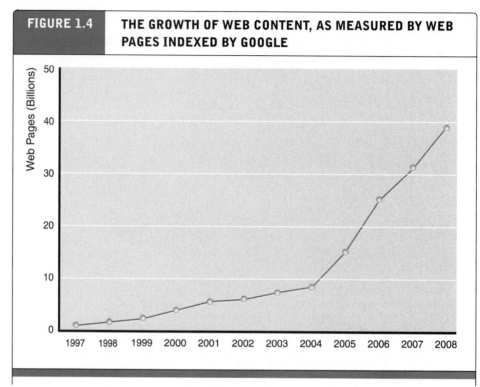

The number of Web pages indexed by Google has grown from about 1 billion in 1998 to nearly 40 billion in 2008.

SOURCE: Based on data from Google Inc.,2008, and authors' estimates.

There is no precise measurement of the number of Web pages in existence, in part because today's search engines index only a portion of the known universe of Web pages, and also because the size of the Web universe is unknown. It is estimated that Google, the Web's most popular and perhaps most comprehensive Web search engine, currently indexes nearly 40 billion pages. There are also an estimated 900 billion Web pages in the so-called "deep Web" that are not indexed by ordinary search engines such as Google. Nevertheless, it would be accurate to say that Web content has grown exponentially since 1993. **Figure 1.4** describes the growth of Web content as measured by the number of pages indexed by Google.

Read *Insight on Technology: Spider Webs, Bow Ties, Scale-Free Networks, and the Deep Web* on pages 26–27 for the latest view of researchers on the structure of the Web.

ORIGINS AND GROWTH OF E-COMMERCE

It is difficult to pinpoint just when e-commerce began. There were several precursors to e-commerce. In the late 1970s, a pharmaceutical firm named Baxter Healthcare initiated a primitive form of B2B e-commerce by using a telephone-based modem that permitted hospitals to reorder supplies from Baxter. This system was later expanded during the 1980s into a PC-based remote order entry system and was widely copied throughout the United States long before the

FIGURE 1.5	THE GROWTH OF B2C E-COMMERCE

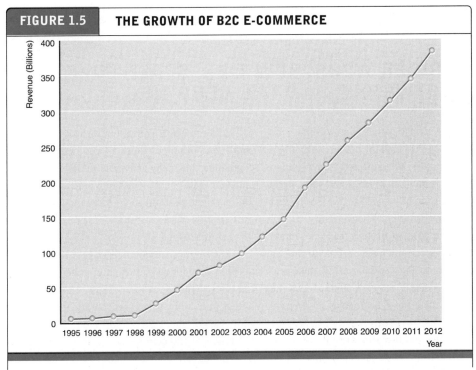

In the early years, B2C e-commerce was doubling or tripling each year. Today, B2C e-commerce is growing at about 10%-15% per yea. (Note: Revenue shown includes retail sales and travel services revenues.)

SOURCES: Based on data from eMarketer, Inc., 2008d; U.S. Census Bureau, 2008; authors' estimates.

Internet became a commercial environment. The 1980s saw the development of Electronic Data Interchange (EDI) standards that permitted firms to exchange commercial documents and conduct digital commercial transactions across private networks.

In the B2C arena, the first truly large-scale digitally enabled transaction system was deployed in France in 1981. The French Minitel was a videotext system that combined a telephone with an 8-inch screen. By the mid-1980s, more than 3 million Minitels were deployed, and over 13,000 different services were available, including ticket agencies, travel services, retail products, and online banking. The Minitel service continued in existence until December 31, 2006, when it was finally discontinued by its owner, France Telecom.

However, none of these precursor systems had the functionality of the Internet. Generally, when we think of e-commerce today, it is inextricably linked to the Internet. For our purposes, we will say e-commerce begins in 1995, following the appearance of the first banner advertisements placed by ATT, Volvo, Sprint, and others on Hotwired in late October 1994, and the first sales of banner ad space by Netscape and Infoseek in early 1995. Since then, e-commerce has been the fastest growing form of commerce in the United States. **Figure 1.5** and **Figure 1.6** (on page 28) chart the development of B2C e-commerce and B2B e-commerce,

INSIGHT ON TECHNOLOGY

SPIDER WEBS, BOW TIES, SCALE-FREE NETWORKS, AND THE DEEP WEB

The World Wide Web conjures up images of a giant spider web where everything is connected to everything else in a random pattern and you can go from one edge of the web to another by just following the right links. Theoretically, that's what makes the Web different from a typical index system: You can follow hyperlinks from one page to another. In the "small world" theory of the Web, every Web page is thought to be separated from any other Web page by an average of about 19 clicks. In 1968, sociologist Stanley Milgram invented small-world theory for social networks by noting that every human was separated from any other human by only six degrees of separation. On the Web, the small world theory was supported by early research on a small sampling of Web sites. But research conducted jointly by scientists at IBM, Compaq, and AltaVista found something entirely different. These scientists used a Web crawler to identify 200 million Web pages and follow 1.5 billion links on these pages.

The researchers discovered that the Web was not like a spider web at all, but rather like a bow tie (see figure below). The bow-tie Web had a "strongly connected component" (SCC) composed of about 56 million Web pages. On the right side of the bow tie was a set of 44 million OUT pages that you could get to from the center, but could not return to the center from. OUT pages tended to be corporate intranet and

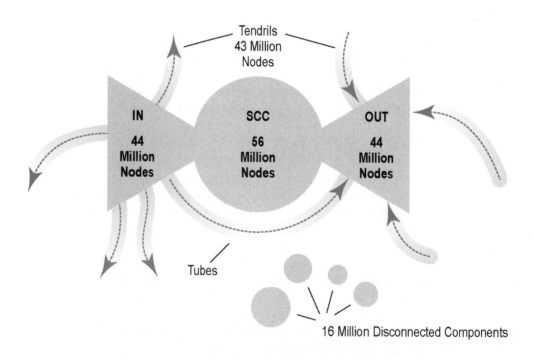

Tendrils
43 Million
Nodes

IN
44
Million
Nodes

SCC
56
Million
Nodes

OUT
44
Million
Nodes

Tubes

16 Million Disconnected Components

(continued)

other Web site pages that are designed to trap you at the site when you land. On the left side of the bow tie was a set of 44 million IN pages from which you could get to the center, but that you could not travel to from the center. These were recently created pages that had not yet been linked to by many center pages. In addition, 43 million pages were classified as "tendrils," pages that did not link to the center and could not be linked to from the center. However, the tendril pages were sometimes linked to IN and/or OUT pages. Occasionally, tendrils linked to one another without passing through the center (these are called "tubes"). Finally, there were 16 million pages totally disconnected from everything.

Further evidence for the non-random and structured nature of the Web is provided in research performed by Albert-Lazlo Barabasi at the University of Notre Dame. Barabasi's team found that far from being a random, exponentially exploding network of 50 billion Web pages, activity on the Web was actually highly concentrated in "very-connected super nodes" that provided the connectivity to less well-connected nodes. Barabasi dubbed this type of network a "scale-free" network and found parallels in the growth of cancers, disease transmission, and computer viruses. As its turns out, scale-free networks are highly vulnerable to destruction: Destroy their super nodes and transmission of messages breaks down rapidly. On the upside, if you are a marketer trying to "spread the message" about your products, place your products on one of the super nodes and watch the news spread. Or build super nodes and attract a huge audience.

Thus, the picture of the Web that emerges from this research is quite different from earlier reports. The notion that most pairs of Web pages are separated by a handful of links, almost always under 20, and that the number of connections would grow exponentially with the size of the Web, is not supported. In fact, there is a 75% chance that there is no path from one randomly chosen page to another. With this knowledge, it now becomes clear why the most advanced Web search engines only index a very small percentage of all Web pages, and only about 2% of the overall population of Internet hosts (about 550 million). Search engines cannot find most Web sites because their pages are not well-connected or linked to the central core of the Web. Another important finding is the identification of a "deep Web" composed of over 900 billion Web pages that are not indexed at all. The pages are not easily accessible to Web crawlers that most search engine companies use. Instead, these pages are either proprietary (not available to crawlers and non-subscribers) like the pages of *The Wall Street Journal*) or are not easily available from home pages. In the last few years newer search engines (such as the medical search engine Mammahealth) and older ones such as Yahoo have been revised to search the deep Web. Because e-commerce revenues in part depend on customers being able to find a Web site using search engines, Web site managers need to take steps to ensure their Web pages are part of the connected central core, or "super nodes" of the Web. One way to do this is to make sure the site has as many links as possible to and from other relevant sites, especially to other sites within the SCC.

▬ **SOURCES:** "Invisible or Deep Web: What it is, Why it exists, How to find it, and Its inherent ambiguity," http://www.lib.berkeley.edu, accessed August, 2008; "Accessing the Deep Web," by Bin He, Mitesh Patel, Zhen Zhang, and Kevin Chen-Chuan Chang; *Communications of the ACM (CACM)* 50 (2): 94-101, May 2007; "Deep Web Research 2007," Marcus P. Zillman, llrx.com, December 17, 2006; "Yahoo Mines the "Deep Web," by Tim Gray, InternetNews.com, June 17, 2005; *Linked: The New Science of Networks,* by Albert-Lazlo Barabasi. Cambridge, MA: Perseus Publishing (2002); "The Bowtie Theory Explains Link Popularity," by John Heard, Searchengineposition.com, June 1, 2000. "Graph Structure in the Web," by A. Broder, R. Kumar, F. Maghoul, P. Raghaven, S. Rajagopalan, R. Stata, A. Tomkins, and J. Wiener, Proceedings of the 9th International World Wide Web Conference, Amsterdam, The Netherlands, pages 309-320. Elsevier Science, May 2000.

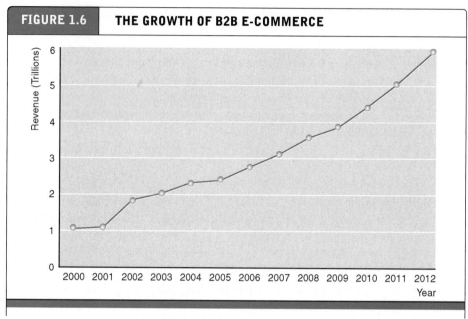

| FIGURE 1.6 | THE GROWTH OF B2B E-COMMERCE |

B2B e-commerce is about ten times the size of B2C e-commerce. In 2012, B2B e-commerce is projected to be about $6.3 trillion. (Note: Does not include EDI transactions.)

SOURCES: Based on data from U.S. Census Bureau, 2008; authors' estimates.

respectively, with projections for the next several years. Both graphs show a strong projected growth rate, but the dollar amounts of B2B e-commerce dwarf those of B2C.

TECHNOLOGY AND E-COMMERCE IN PERSPECTIVE

Although in many respects, e-commerce is new and different, it is also important to keep e-commerce in perspective. First, the Internet and the Web are just two of a long list of technologies that have greatly changed commerce in the United States and around the world. Each of these other technologies spawned business models and strategies designed to leverage the technology into commercial advantage and profit. They were also accompanied by explosive early growth, which was characterized by the emergence of thousands of entrepreneurial start-up companies, followed by painful retrenchment, and then a long-term successful exploitation of the technology by larger established firms. In the case of automobiles, for instance, in 1915, there were over 250 automobile manufacturers in the United States. By 1940, there were five. In the case of radio, in 1925, there were over 2,000 radio stations across the United States, with most broadcasting to local neighborhoods and run by amateurs. By 1990, there were fewer than 500 independent stations. There is every reason to believe e-commerce will follow the same pattern—with notable differences discussed throughout the text.

Second, although e-commerce has grown explosively, there is no guarantee it will continue to grow forever at these rates and much reason to believe e-commerce growth will cap as it confronts its own fundamental limitations. For instance, B2C e-commerce is still a small part (about 6%) of the overall retail market of $4 trillion. Under current projections, in 2012, all of B2C commerce will roughly equal the projected revenue of Wal-Mart in 2012 (about $400 billion). Wal-Mart is the world's largest and most successful retailer.. On the other hand, with only 6% of all retail sales revenue now being generated online, there is tremendous upside potential.

POTENTIAL LIMITATIONS ON THE GROWTH OF B2C E-COMMERCE

A recent headline in *The New York Times* read "Online Sales Lose Steam," reporting on a Forrester Research report in 2007 (Richtel and Tedeschi, 2007). Forrester believes online sales will slow down from 25% annual growth to 9% by 2010. Unfortunately, the research confuses online retail sales of goods with all of e-commerce revenues, forgetting that online sales of services are exploding even faster than 25% and are likely to continue at this pace for some time. Our data suggests that B2C e-commerce will continue to grow by about 15% annually, slower than in earlier years, but much faster than traditional retail sales (about 4%). Nevertheless, there are several reasons to believe that e-commerce revenues from goods and services together will not expand forever at these very high rates. As online sales become a larger percentage of all sales, which grow in the 5%–6% range annually, online sales growth will approach the growth in all of retail and service sales. This point still appears to be a long way off. Online service sales, everything from music, to video, medical information, games and entertainment, have an even longer period to grow before they hit any ceiling effects.

There are other limitations on B2C e-commerce that have the potential to cap its growth rate and ultimate size. **Table 1.4** describes some of these limitations.

TABLE 1.4	**LIMITATIONS ON THE GROWTH OF B2C E-COMMERCE**
LIMITING FACTOR	COMMENT
Expensive technology	Using the Internet requires a $400 PC (minimal) and a connect charge ranging from about $10 to $100 depending on the speed of service.
Sophisticated skill set	The skills required to make effective use of the Internet and e-commerce capabilities are far more sophisticated than, say, for television or newspapers.
Persistent cultural attraction of physical markets and traditional shopping experiences	For many, shopping is a cultural and social event where people meet directly with merchants and other consumers. This social experience has not yet been fully duplicated in digital form (although social shopping is a major new development).
Persistent global inequality limiting access to telephones and personal computers	Much of the world's population does not have telephone service, PCs, or cell phones.
Saturation and ceiling effects	Growth in the Internet population slows as its approaches the size of the at risk population.

Some of these limitations may be eradicated in the next decade. For instance, it is likely that the price of entry-level PCs will fall to $200 by the year 2010. Other Internet-client gadgets as well as cell phones are within this price range now. This, coupled with enhancements in capabilities such as integration with television, access to entertainment film libraries on a pay-per-view basis, and other software enhancements, will likely raise U.S. Internet household penetration rates to the level of cable television penetration (about 80%) by 2010. The PC operating system will also likely evolve from the current Windows platform to far simpler choice panels similar to the interface found on iPhones, iPods and Palm OS handheld devices.

The most significant technology that can reduce barriers to Internet access is wireless Web technology (described in more detail in Chapter 3). Today, consumers can access the Internet via a variety of different mobile devices, such as mobile computers, cell phones, BlackBerries, and personal digital assistants (PDAs). In 2008, approximately half of the 173 million Internet users in the United States had a laptop with a wireless Wi-Fi capability, or a cell phone that can access the Internet. There are about 255 million cellular phone subscribers in the United States in 2008 and increasingly these phones are Web-enabled (CTIA, 2008). **Figure 1.7** illustrates the rapid growth projected for both broadband home connections and wireless Web devices in the United States.

On balance, the current technological limits on e-commerce growth, while real, are likely to recede in importance over the next decade. The social and cultural limitations of e-commerce are less likely to change as quickly, but the Web is fast developing virtual social shopping experiences and virtual realities that millions find as entertaining as shopping or seeing their friends face-to-face.

1.2 E-COMMERCE: A BRIEF HISTORY

Although e-commerce is a very recent phenomenon of the late 1990s, it already has a brief, tumultuous history. The history of e-commerce can be usefully divided into three periods. The early years of e-commerce were a period of explosive growth and extraordinary innovation, beginning in 1995 with the first widespread use of the Web to advertise products. This period of explosive growth was capped in March 2000 when stock market valuations for dot-com companies reached their peak and thereafter began to collapse. A sobering period of reassessment occurred, followed by strong double-digit growth through the current period. In 2006, e-commerce entered a period of re-definition with the appearance of social networking and user-generated content sharing Web sites that have attracted huge audiences.

E-COMMERCE 1995–2000: INNOVATION

The early years of e-commerce were one of the most euphoric of times in American commercial history. It was also a time when key e-commerce concepts were developed and explored. Thousands of dot-com companies were formed, backed by over $125 billion in financial capital—one of the largest outpourings of venture capital in United States history (PricewaterhouseCoopers, National Venture Capital

FIGURE 1.7	GROWTH PROJECTIONS FOR BROADBAND HOME CONNECTIONS AND WIRELESS WEB DEVICES IN THE UNITED STATES

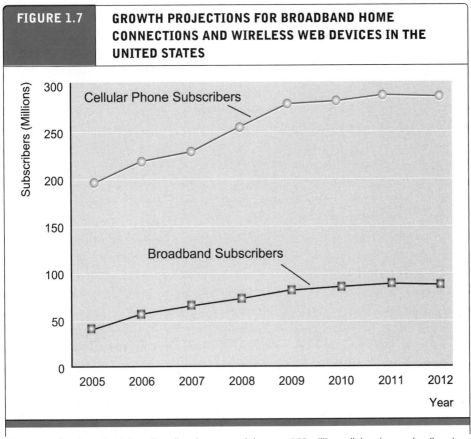

About 72 million households have broadband access and there are 255 million cellular phone subscribers in the United States who are increasingly connected to the Internet. Both of these developments provide a significant stimulus to mobile e-commerce.

SOURCES: Based on data from eMarketer, Inc. 2008c; Telecommunications Industry Association, 2008; authors' estimates.

Association MoneyTree Report, Data: Thomson Financial 2008). **Figure 1.8** (on page 32) depicts the amounts invested by venture capital firms in Internet-related businesses in the period 1995–2007. While venture investment has trended markedly lower since 2000, it is still significantly larger than pre-1996 levels, and investing in dot-com and Internet businesses continues at a strong pace through the second quarter of 2008. By 2004, dot-com IPOs were again being successfully floated on Wall Street, encouraged by Google's successful IPO in 2004, which raised more than $1.67 billion, and the fact that Google shares have since shot up from its offering price of $85 to almost $700 in 2008.

For computer scientists and information technologists, the early success of e-commerce was a powerful vindication of a set of information technologies that had developed over a period of forty years—extending from the development of the early Internet to the PC, to local area networks. The vision was of a universal communications and computing environment that everyone on Earth could access with cheap, inexpensive computers—a worldwide universe of knowledge stored on HTML pages created by hundreds of millions of individuals and thousands of

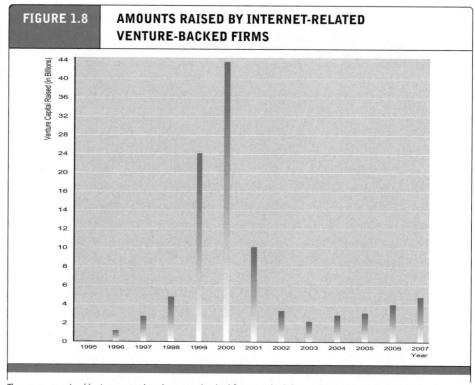

FIGURE 1.8 | **AMOUNTS RAISED BY INTERNET-RELATED VENTURE-BACKED FIRMS**

The amounts raised by Internet-related venture-backed firms peaked during the 1999–2001 period, but the amount raised in the 2002–2007 period is still much higher than that raised in the periods prior to 1999.

SOURCES: Based on data from PricewaterhouseCoopers/National Venture Capital Association MoneyTree Report, Data: Thomson Financial, 2008.

libraries, governments, and scientific institutes. Technologists celebrated the fact that the Internet was not controlled by anyone or any nation, but was free to all. They believed the Internet—and the e-commerce that rose on this infrastructure—should remain a self-governed, self-regulated environment.

For economists, the early years of e-commerce raised the realistic prospect of a nearly perfect competitive market: where price, cost, and quality information is equally distributed, a nearly infinite set of suppliers compete against one another, and customers have access to all relevant market information worldwide. The Internet would spawn digital markets where information would be nearly perfect—something that is rarely true in other real-world markets. Merchants in turn would have equal direct access to hundreds of millions of customers. In this near-perfect information marketspace, transaction costs would plummet because search costs—the cost of searching for prices, product descriptions, payment settlement, and order fulfillment—would all fall drastically (Bakos, 1997). New shopping bot programs would automatically search the entire Web for the best prices and delivery times. For merchants, the cost of searching for customers would also fall, reducing the need for wasteful advertising. At the same time, advertisements could be personalized to the needs of every customer. Prices and even costs would be increasingly transparent to the consumer, who could now know exactly and instantly the worldwide best price, quality, and availability of most products. Information asymmetry would be greatly reduced. Given the instant nature of Internet communications, the availability of powerful sales information systems, and the low cost involved in changing prices on a Web site (low menu costs), producers could dynamically price their products to reflect actual demand, ending the idea of one national price, or one suggested manufacturer's list price. In turn, market middlemen—the distributors, wholesalers, and other factors in the marketplace who are intermediates between producers and consumers, each demanding a payment and raising costs while adding little value—would disappear (**disintermediation**). Manufacturers and content originators would develop direct market relationships with their customers. The resulting intense competition, the decline of intermediaries, and the lower transaction costs would eliminate product brands, and along with it, the possibility of *monopoly profits* based on brands, geography, or special access to factors of production. Prices for products and services would fall to the point where prices covered costs of production plus a fair, "market rate" of return on capital, plus additional small payments for entrepreneurial effort (that would not last long). Unfair competitive advantages (which occur when one competitor has an advantage others cannot purchase) would be eliminated, as would extraordinary returns on invested capital. This vision was called **friction-free commerce** (Smith et al., 2000).

For real-world entrepreneurs, their financial backers, and marketing professionals, the idea of friction-free commerce was far from their own visions. For these players, e-commerce represented an extraordinary opportunity to earn far above normal returns on investment, far above the cost of borrowing capital. The e-commerce marketspace represented access to millions of consumers worldwide who used the Internet and a set of marketing communications technologies (e-mail and Web pages) that was universal, inexpensive, and powerful. These new technologies would permit marketers to practice what they always had done—segmenting the market into groups with different needs and price sensitivity, targeting the segments with branding and promotional messages, and positioning the product and pricing for each group—but with even more precision. In this new marketspace, extraordinary profits would go to **first movers**—those firms who were first to market in a particular area and who moved quickly to gather market share. In a "winner take all" market, first movers could establish a large customer base quickly, build brand name recognition early, create an entirely new distribution channel, and then inhibit competitors (new entrants) by building in *switching costs* for their customers through proprietary interface designs and features available only at one site. The idea for entrepreneurs was to create near monopolies online based on size, convenience, selection, and brand. Online businesses using the new technology could create informative, community-like features unavailable to traditional merchants. These "communities of consumption" also would add value and be difficult for traditional merchants to imitate. The thinking was that once customers became accustomed to using a company's unique Web interface and feature set, they could not easily be switched to competitors. In the best case, the entrepreneurial firm would invent proprietary technologies and techniques that almost everyone adopted, creating a **network effect**. A network effect occurs where all participants receive value from the fact that everyone else uses

disintermediation
displacement of market middlemen who traditionally are intermediaries between producers and consumers by a new direct relationship between manufacturers and content originators with their customers

friction-free commerce
a vision of commerce in which information is equally distributed, transaction costs are low, prices can be dynamically adjusted to reflect actual demand, intermediaries decline, and unfair competitive advantages are eliminated

first mover
a firm that is first to market in a particular area and that moves quickly to gather market share

network effect
occurs where users receive value from the fact that everyone else uses the same tool or product

the same tool or product (for example, a common operating system, telephone system, or software application such as a proprietary instant messaging standard or an operating system such as Windows), all of which increase in value as more people adopt them.[2] Successful first movers would become the new intermediaries of e-commerce, displacing traditional retail merchants and suppliers of content, and becoming profitable by charging fees of one sort or another for the value customers perceived in their services and products.

To initiate this process, entrepreneurs argued that prices would have to be very low to attract customers and fend off potential competitors. E-commerce was, after all, a totally new way of shopping that would have to offer some immediate cost benefits to consumers. However, because doing business on the Web was supposedly so much more efficient when compared to traditional "bricks-and-mortar" businesses (even when compared to the direct mail catalog business) and because the costs of customer acquisition and retention would supposedly be so much lower, profits would inevitably materialize out of these efficiencies. Given these dynamics, market share, the number of visitors to a site ("eyeballs"), and gross revenue became far more important in the earlier stages of an online firm than earnings or profits. Entrepreneurs and their financial backers in the early years of e-commerce expected that extraordinary profitability would come, but only after several years of losses.

Thus, the early years of e-commerce were driven largely by visions of profiting from new technology, with the emphasis on quickly achieving very high market visibility. The source of financing was venture capital funds. The ideology of the period emphasized the ungoverned "Wild West" character of the Web and the feeling that governments and courts could not possibly limit or regulate the Internet; there was a general belief that traditional corporations were too slow and bureaucratic, too stuck in the old ways of doing business, to "get it"—to be competitive in e-commerce. Young entrepreneurs were therefore the driving force behind e-commerce, backed by huge amounts of money invested by venture capitalists. The emphasis was on *deconstructing* (destroying) traditional distribution channels and disintermediating existing channels, using new pure online companies who aimed to achieve impregnable first mover advantages. Overall, this period of e-commerce was characterized by experimentation, capitalization, and hypercompetition (Varian, 2000a). Read *Insight on Business: Dot-com Déjà Vu* on pages 35–36 for a further look at the financing of e-commerce ventures.

The crash in stock market values for e-commerce throughout 2000 is a convenient marker for ending the early period in the development of e-commerce. Looking back at the first years of e-commerce, it is apparent that e-commerce has been, for the most part, a stunning technological success as the Internet and the Web ramped up from a few thousand to billions of e-commerce transactions per year, generating $255 billion in B2C revenues and around $3.8 trillion in B2B revenues in 2008, with around 117 million online buyers in the United States, and another 140 million worldwide. With enhancements and strengthening, described in later chapters, it is clear the e-commerce's digital infrastructure is solid enough to sustain significant growth in

[2]The network effect is quantified by Metcalfe's Law, which argues that the value of a network grows by the square of the number of participants.

INSIGHT ON BUSINESS

DOT-COM DÉJÀ VU

E-commerce was built on Internet technology, but what makes it run is money—big money. Between 1998 and 2000, venture capitalists poured an estimated $120 billion into approximately 12,450 dot-com start-up ventures. Investment bankers then took 1,262 of these companies public in what is called an initial public offering (IPO) of stock. To prepare for an IPO, investment bankers analyze a company's finances and business plans and attempt to arrive at an estimate of how much the company is "worth"—how much the investing public might be willing to pay for the shares and how many shares might be purchased by the public and other institutions. The bankers then underwrite the stock offering and sell the stock on a public stock exchange, making enormous fees for underwriting in the process. The basic process has not changed over time, but the style and fashions have changed since the good old "bad days" of e-commerce.

In the early years of e-commerce, from 1998 to 2000, dot-com IPO shares often skyrocketed within minutes of hitting the trading floor. Some shares tripled and quadrupled in the first day, and a 50% "pump" (or increase in value) was considered just a reasonable showing. IPO shares for dot-com companies were often targeted to open at around $15 per share, and it was not uncommon for them to be trading at $45 a share or even much more later the same day. Therefore, getting in on the ground floor of an IPO—which meant arranging to purchase a fixed number of shares prior to actual trading on the first day—was a privilege reserved for other large institutions, friends of the investment bankers, or other investment bankers. In what was called "stock spinning," the underwriter would sell IPO shares to entrepreneurs it hoped to obtain business from

in the future. The Securities and Exchange Commission made this practice illegal in 1999.

What has happened to the dot-com IPOs of this period? According to a financial services research firm, Thomson Financial, 12% of the companies that went public between 1998 and 2000 were trading at $1 or less a share in April 2001, a fairly shocking development when one considers that just a relatively short time previously, those companies' shares were trading at upwards of 10 to 100 times that price. Among the companies that fell below $1 in share price were Autoweb, iVillage, and Drugstore.com. In mid-2005, Autoweb merged with Autobytel and the combined company sells for about $4 a share; iVillage sold to NBC Universal in 2006 and remains the most popular Web destination for women—but not as an independent company. Drugstore.com sells in the $2–$4 range. Each of these companies is showing strong growth (10% a year or more). In 2007, seven years after the peak of the dot-com frenzy, at least 5,000 Internet companies have either been acquired or shut down. On a more positive note, recent research shows that the attrition rate of these early firms was about 20% a year, on par with what occurred in other industries during their early boom years. More than half the early dot-coms are still in business in 2007.

Nevertheless, after the big bust of March 2000, venture capitalists turned away from the "Get Big Fast" and "First Mover Advantage" religion, and instead focused on companies that demonstrated a profitable prior history. In this second period of IPOs, the VCs invested over $200 billion for the purchase of over 4,000 Web companies. In this period, the hot properties included Internet shopping sites (such as Shopping.com, purchased for $620 million by eBay and Shopzilla, purchased for $525 million

(continued)

by The E.W. Scripps Company), Internet advertising firms (such as DoubleClick, purchased for $1.1 billion by buyout firm Hellman & Friedman), search engine properties (such as Ask Jeeves (now Ask.com), purchased by IAC/InterActive Corp for $1.85 billion), and community sites (such as About.com, purchased by The New York Times for $410 million, and Intermix, owner of the social networking site MySpace, purchased by News Corp.'s Fox Interactive Media division for $580 million). This period of solid investing based on fundamentals (such as profit) culminated with Google's IPO in late 2004. Google had been profitable for three years before going public.

But then something strange happened on the way to the bank, and the period of capital discipline was history. As Google's shares soared from the $85 offering price to almost $750 in November 2007, VCs and investors returned to their bad old ways—investing in ideas, Get Big Fast companies, and revenue growth (not profits). About 62% of tech firms going public since 2006 were not profitable companies (still short of the all-time 85% unprofitable in 2000). King of the Get Big Fast mentality is YouTube, an unprofitable company with an estimated $200 million in revenue in 2008, for which Google paid $1.65 billion. Facebook, which has not yet been acquired, is currently being valued by investors at up to $15 billion, estimated to be 32 times its current revenue.

▬ **SOURCES:** "Microsoft Swoops In on Yahoo" by Catherine Holahan, BusinessWeek, February 1, 2008; "Google Closes In on DoubleClick Deal," by Catherine Holahan, BusinessWeek, December 20, 2007; "Silicon Valley Start-Ups Awash in Dollars, Again," by Brad Stone and Matt Richtel, *New York Times*, October 17, 2007; "Tech Companies Bleeding Red Ink Pursue IPO Gold," by Pui-Wing Tam, *Wall Street Journal*, March 13, 2007; "The Dot Com Bubble is Reconsidered—and Maybe Relived," by Lee Gomes, *Wall Street Journal*, November 8, 2006; "Was There Too Little Entry During the Dot Com Era?" by Brent Goldfarb, David Kirsch, and David Miller, Robert H. Smith School Research Paper No. RHS 06-029, April 24, 2006.

e-commerce during the next decade. The Internet scales well. The "e" in e-commerce has been an overwhelming success.

From a business perspective, though, the early years of e-commerce were a mixed success, and offered many surprises. Only about 10% of dot-coms formed since 1995 have survived as independent companies in 2008. Only a very tiny percentage of these survivors are profitable. Yet online B2C sales of goods and services are still growing in 2008 at around 15% per year. Consumers have learned to use the Web as a powerful source of information about products they actually purchase through other channels, such as at a traditional "bricks-and-mortar" store. This is especially true of expensive consumer durables such as appliances, automobiles, and electronics. For instance, over 70% of new car buyers research on the Web first, then purchase from a dealer (Pew Internet and American Life Project, 2008; Tedeschi, 2007). This "Internet-influenced" commerce is very difficult to estimate, but is believed to be somewhere between $400 billion and $1.4 trillion (Forrester Research, Inc., 2007; eMarketer, Inc., 2008d). Altogether then, B2C e-commerce (both actual purchases and purchases influenced by Web shopping but actually buying in a store) amounts to over $600 billion in 2008, or about 17% of total retail sales. The "commerce" in e-commerce is basically very sound, at least in the sense of attracting a growing number of customers and generating revenues.

E-COMMERCE 2001–2006: CONSOLIDATION

E-commerce entered a period of consolidation beginning in 2001 and lasting until 2006. Emphasis shifted to a more "business driven" approach rather than technology driven; large traditional firms learned how to use the Web to strengthen their market positions; brand extension and strengthening became more important than creating new brands; financing shrunk as capital markets shunned start-up firms; and traditional bank financing based on profitability returned.

E-COMMERCE 2006—PRESENT: REINVENTION

E-commerce entered a third period in 2006 that extends through the present day and into the uncertain future. Google has been one of the driving forces, but so have other large media firms who have quickly bought out very fast-moving entrepreneurial firms, such as MySpace and YouTube. It is a period of reinvention involving the extension of Internet technologies, the discovery of new business models based on consumer-generated content, social networking, and virtual online lives. This period is as much a sociological phenomenon, as it is a technological or business phenomenon. Few of the new models have been able to monetize their huge audiences into profitable operations yet, but many eventually will.

Table 1.5 on page 38 summarizes e-commerce in each of these three periods.

ASSESSING E-COMMERCE: SUCCESSES, SURPRISES, AND FAILURES

Although e-commerce has continued to grow at an extremely rapid pace in customers and revenues throughout its history, it is clear that many of the visions, predictions, and assertions about e-commerce developed in the early years have not have been fulfilled. For instance, economists' visions of "friction-free" commerce have not been entirely realized. Prices are sometimes lower on the Web, but the low prices are sometimes a function of entrepreneurs selling products below their costs. Consumers are less price sensitive than expected; surprisingly, the Web sites with the highest revenue often have the highest prices. There remains considerable persistent and even increasing price dispersion on the Web: the difference between the lowest price and the average price for a basket of goods increased from 8% of the average price in 2000 to 10% in 2008 (Nash-equilibrium.com, 2008). In other words, the standard deviation in Web prices is about 10% of the average price for the same product on the Web. Shop around! The concept of one world, one market, one price has not occurred in reality as entrepreneurs discover new ways to differentiate their products and services. While for the most part Internet prices save consumers about 20% on average when compared to in-store prices, sometimes prices on the Web are higher than for similar products purchased offline, especially if shipping costs are considered. For instance, prices on books and CDs vary by as much as 50%, prices for airline tickets as much as 20% (Baye, 2004; Baye, et al., 2004; Bailey, 1998a, b; Brynjolfsson and Smith, 2001). Merchants have adjusted to the competitive Internet environment by engaging in "hit-and-run pricing" or changing prices every day or hour so competitors never know what they are charging (neither do customers); by making their prices hard to discover and sowing confusion among consumers by "baiting and switching" customers from low-margin products to high-margin products with supposedly "higher quality." Finally, brands remain very important in e-commerce—consumers trust some firms more than others to deliver a high-quality product on time (Slatalla, 2005).

The 'perfect competition' model of extreme market efficiency has not entirely come to pass. Merchants and marketers are continually introducing information asymmetries. Search costs have fallen overall, but the overall transaction cost of actually completing a transaction in e-commerce remains high because users have a bewildering number of new questions to consider: Will the merchant actually deliver? What is the time frame of delivery? Does the merchant really stock this item? How do I fill out this form? Nearly 60% of potential e-commerce purchases are terminated in the shopping cart stage because of these consumer uncertainties. In many product areas, it is easier to call a trusted catalog merchant on the telephone than order on a

TABLE 1.5	EVOLUTION OF E-COMMERCE		
1995–2000 **INNOVATION**	**2001–2006** **CONSOLIDATION**	**2006–FUTURE** **RE-INVENTION**
Technology-driven	Business-driven	Audience, customer, and community driven
Revenue growth emphasis	Earnings and profits emphasis	Audience and social network growth emphasis
Venture capital financing	Traditional financing	Smaller VC investments; early small firm buyouts by large online players
Ungoverned	Stronger regulation and governance	Extensive government surveillance
Entrepreneurial	Large traditional firms	Large pure Web-based firms
Disintermediation	Strengthening intermediaries	Proliferation of small online intermediaries renting business processes of larger firms
Perfect markets	Imperfect markets, brands, and network effects	Continuation of online market imperfections; commodity competition in select markets
Pure online strategies	Mixed "bricks and clicks" strategies	Return of pure online strategies in new markets; extension of bricks and clicks in traditional retail markets
First-mover advantages	Strategic follower strength; complimentary assets	First-mover advantages return in new markets as traditional Web players catch up
Low complexity retail products	High complexity retail products	Services

Web site. Finally, intermediaries have not disappeared as predicted, and few manufacturers or producers have actually developed a one-to-one sales relationship with their ultimate consumers. Most manufacturers, for instance, have not adopted the Dell model of online sales, and Dell itself in 2008 has moved towards a mixed model heavily reliant on in-store sales where customers can kick the tires, or try the keyboard. Apple Stores are very successful physical retail locations, and marketing devices. People still like to shop in a physical store.

If anything, e-commerce has created many new opportunities for middlemen to aggregate content, products, and services into portals and search engines and thereby introduce themselves as the "new" intermediaries. Yahoo, MSN, Google, and Amazon, along with third-party travel sites such as Orbitz and Expedia, are all examples of this kind of new intermediary. As illustrated in **Figure 1.9**, e-commerce did not drive existing retail chains and catalog merchants out of business although it has created opportunities for new entrepreneurial Web-only firms to succeed. In fact, existing retail chains with physical stores as well as Web sites earned the largest portion of online sales in 2007.

The visions of many entrepreneurs and venture capitalists for e-commerce have not materialized exactly as predicted. First-mover advantage appears to have succeeded only for a very small group of sites. Historically, first movers have been long-term losers, with the early-to-market innovators usually being displaced by established "fast-follower" firms with the financial, marketing, legal, and production complimentary assets needed to develop mature markets, and this has proved true for e-commerce as well. A number of e-commerce first movers, such as eToys, FogDog (sporting goods), WebVan (groceries), and Eve.com (beauty products) are out of business. Customer acquisition and retention costs during the early years of e-commerce were extraordinarily high, with some firms, such as E*Trade and other financial service firms, paying up to $400 to acquire a new customer. In 2004, certain law firms engaged in asbestos and tobacco liability suits were paying $90 each time

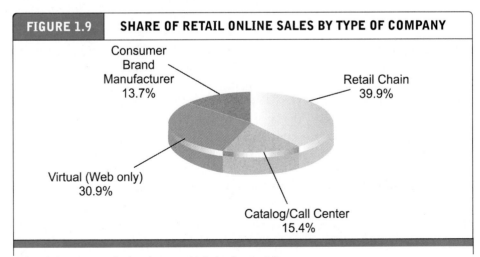

| FIGURE 1.9 | SHARE OF RETAIL ONLINE SALES BY TYPE OF COMPANY |

Consumer Brand Manufacturer 13.7%

Retail Chain 39.9%

Virtual (Web only) 30.9%

Catalog/Call Center 15.4%

Web-only firms account for less than one-third of online retail firm revenues.
SOURCE: eMarketer, Inc., 2008e.

someone clicked on their Google ad (Bialik, 2004). The overall costs of doing business on the Web—including the costs of technology, site design and maintenance, and warehouses for fulfillment—are no lower than the costs faced by the most efficient bricks-and-mortar stores. A large warehouse costs tens of millions of dollars regardless of a firm's Web presence. The knowledge of how to run the warehouse is priceless, and not easily moved. The start-up costs can be staggering. Attempting to achieve profitability by raising prices has often led to large customer defections. From the e-commerce merchant's perspective, the "e" in e-commerce does not stand for "easy."

PREDICTIONS FOR THE FUTURE: MORE SURPRISES

Given that e-commerce has changed greatly in the last two years, its future cannot be predicted except to say watch for more surprises. There are five main factors that will help define the future of e-commerce. First, there is little doubt that the technology of e-commerce—the Internet, the Web, and the growing number of wireless Internet devices that make up the emerging "mobile digital platform," including cellular devices such as the iPhone, Android G1, and BlackBerry, continue to propagate through all commercial activity. The overall revenues from e-commerce (goods and services) will continue to rise on a steep growth path, most likely in the range of 12%–18% per year through 2012. The number of products and services sold on the Web and the size of the average purchase order are both growing at double-digit rates. The number of online shoppers in the United States will continue to grow at a modest rate of less than 5% per year. There has also been a significant broadening of the online product mix compared to the early years when books, computer software, and hardware dominated e-commerce (see **Table 1.6**). This trend will continue as trust in e-commerce transactions grows. The fastest-growing major non-travel e-commerce categories include home products, office supplies, sporting goods, and apparel/accessories. (See Chapter 9 for changes in retail products and services.)

Second, e-commerce prices will rise to cover the real costs of doing business on the Web, and to pay investors a reasonable rate of return on their capital. Third, e-commerce *margins* (the difference between the revenues from sales and the cost of goods) and profits will rise to levels more typical of all retailers. Fourth, the cast of players will change radically. Traditional well-endowed, experienced Fortune 500 companies will play a growing and dominant role in e-commerce while at the same time new start-up ventures will quickly gain large online audiences for new products and services not dominated by the large players. There will also be a continuation of audience consolidation on the Internet in general, with the top 25 sites garnering over 90% of the audience share, and nearly one-third of all online sales. **Table 1.7** on page 42 lists the top 25 online retailers, as ranked by 2007 online sales. The table shows an unmistakable trend toward the appearance in the top 25 sites of some very well-known, traditional brands from strong traditional businesses, with Staples, Office Depot, Hewlett-Packard, OfficeMax, Sears, Sony, Best Buy, JCPenney, and Wal-Mart all in the top 15.

Fifth, the number of successful pure online companies will remain smaller than integrated online/offline stores that combine traditional sales channels such

TABLE 1.6	ONLINE RETAIL SALES BY CATEGORY, 2007		
CATEGORY	ANNUAL SALES (IN BILLIONS)	ANNUAL SALES (IN BILLIONS)	COMPOUND ANNUAL GROWTH RATE (CAGR)
	2007	**2012**	**2007–2012**
Mass merchant/department store	$29.3	$33.1	12.9%
Computers/electronics	$23.3	$26.7	14.7%
Office supplies	$13.9	$16.1	16.0%
Apparel/accessories	$12.3	$14.2	15.8%
Books/CDs/DVDs	$4.1	$4.7	14.5%
Housewares/Home furnishings	$3.8	$4.4	16.3%
Specialty/non-apparel	$3.4	$3.8	12.0%
Health/beauty	$2.4	$2.9	21.6%
Food/drug	$2.3	$2.6	15.0%
Sporting goods	$1.5	$1.7	16.0%
Flower/gifts	$1.3	$1.5	13.0%
Hardware/home improvement	$1.3	$1.5	16.3%
Toys/hobbies	$1.1	$1.2	9.8%
Jewelry	$1.0	$1.1	13.5%

SOURCES: Based on data from eMarketer, 2008f; Internet Retailer, 2008; authors' estimates.

as physical stores and printed catalogs with online efforts. For instance, traditional catalog sales firms such as L.L.Bean have transformed themselves into integrated online and direct mail firms with more than half of their sales coming from the online channel. Procter & Gamble will continue to develop informative Web sites such as Tide.com; and the major automotive companies will continue to improve the content and value of their Web sites even if they do not enter into direct sales relationships with consumers, but instead use the Web to assist sales through dealers (thereby strengthening traditional intermediaries and channels).

The future of e-commerce will include the growth of regulatory activity both in the United States and worldwide. Governments around the world are challenging the early vision of computer scientists and information technologists that the Internet remain a self-regulating and self-governing phenomenon. The Internet and e-commerce have been so successful and powerful, so all-pervasive, that they directly involve the social, cultural, and political life of entire nations and cultures. Throughout history, whenever technologies have risen to this level of social importance, power, and visibility, they become the target of efforts to regulate and control the technology to ensure that positive social benefits result from their use and to guarantee the public's health and welfare. Radio, television, automobiles,

TABLE 1.7	TOP 25 ONLINE RETAILERS RANKED BY ONLINE SALES
ONLINE RETAILER	ONLINE SALES (2007) (IN BILLIONS)
Amazon	$14.8
Staples	$ 5.6
Office Depot	$ 4.9
Dell.com	$ 4.2
HP Home and Office	$ 3.3
Office Max	$ 3.1
Apple Computer	$ 2.7
Sears Holdings Corporation	$ 2.5
CDW Corp	$ 2.4
Newegg.com	$ 1.9
QVC Corp	$ 1.8
SonyStyle.com	$ 1.7
Best Buy Co.	$ 1.7
JC Penney	$ 1.5
Wal-Mart Stores	$ 1.5
Circuit City Stores	$ 1.4
Netflix.com	$ 1.2
Costco Wholesale Corp.	$ 1.2
Victoria's Secret Direct	$ 1.1
Target Corp.	$ 1.1
Williams Sonoma Inc.	$ 1.1
L.L. Bean	$ 0.9
Systemax Inc.	$ 0.9
GAP	$ 0.9
HSN	$ 0.9

SOURCES: Based on data from Internet Retailer, 2008; Company Reports on Form 10-K filed with the Securities and Exchange Commission.

electricity, and railroads are all the subject of regulation and legislation. Likewise, with e-commerce. In the U.S. Congress, there have already been hundreds of bills proposed to control various facets of the Internet and e-commerce, from consumer privacy to pornography, child abuse, gambling, and encryption. We can expect these efforts at regulation in the United States and around the world to increase as e-commerce extends its reach and importance.

A relatively new factor that will influence the growth of e-commerce is the cost of energy, in particular gasoline and diesel. As fuel costs rise, shopping at suburban physical malls can be a very expensive form of shopping. Buying online can save customers time, and energy costs. There is growing evidence that shoppers are changing their shopping habits and locales because of fuel costs, and pushing the sales of online retailers to higher levels

In summary, the future of e-commerce will be a fascinating mixture of traditional retail, service and media firms extending their brands to online markets, early period e-commerce firms such as Amazon and eBay strengthening their financial results and dominant positions, and a bevy of entirely new entrepreneurial firms with the potential to rocket into prominence by developing huge new audiences in months. Firms that fit this pattern include MySpace, Facebook, Twitter, and PhotoBucket.

1.3 UNDERSTANDING E-COMMERCE: ORGANIZING THEMES

Understanding e-commerce in its totality is a difficult task for students and instructors because there are so many facets to the phenomenon. No single academic discipline is prepared to encompass all of e-commerce. After teaching the e-commerce course for several years and preparing this book, we have come to realize just how difficult it is to "understand" e-commerce. We have found it useful to think about e-commerce as involving three broad interrelated themes: technology, business, and society. We do not mean to imply any ordering of importance here because this book and our thinking freely range over these themes as appropriate to the problem we are trying to understand and describe. Nevertheless, as in previous technologically driven commercial revolutions, there is an historic progression. Technologies develop first, and then those developments are exploited commercially. Once commercial exploitation of the technology becomes widespread, a host of social, cultural, and political issues arise.

TECHNOLOGY: INFRASTRUCTURE

The development and mastery of digital computing and communications technology is at the heart of the newly emerging global digital economy we call e-commerce. To understand the likely future of e-commerce, you need a basic understanding of the information technologies upon which it is built. E-commerce is above all else a technologically driven phenomenon that relies on a host of information technologies as well as fundamental concepts from computer science developed over a 50-year period. At the core of e-commerce are the Internet and the World Wide Web, which we describe in detail in Chapter 3. Underlying these technologies are a host of complementary technologies: personal computers, hand-held cell phone/computers such as the iPhone, local area networks, relational databases, client/server computing, and fiber-optic switches, to name just a few. These technologies lie at the heart of sophisticated business computing applications such as enterprise-wide computing systems, supply chain management systems, manufacturing resource planning systems, and customer relationship management systems. E-commerce

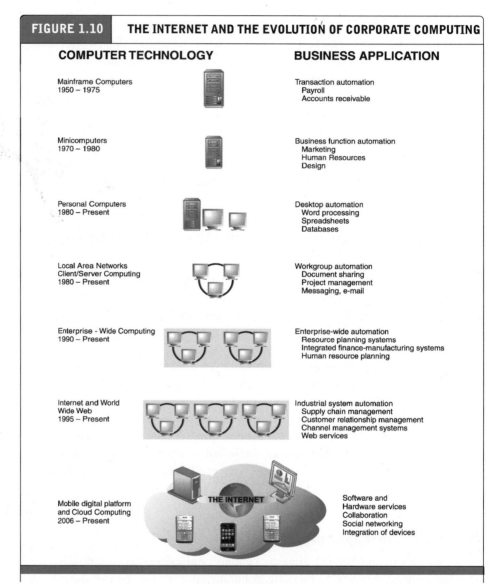

FIGURE 1.10   THE INTERNET AND THE EVOLUTION OF CORPORATE COMPUTING

The Internet and World Wide Web , and the emergence of a mobile digital platform held together by the Internet Cloud, are the latest in a chain of evolving technologies and related business applications, each of which builds on its predecessors.

relies on all these basic technologies—not just the Internet. The Internet—while representing a sharp break from prior corporate computing and communications technologies—is nevertheless just the latest development in the evolution of corporate computing and part of the continuing chain of computer-based innovations in business.

Figure 1.10 illustrates the major stages in the development of corporate computing and indicates how the Internet and the Web fit into this development trajectory.

To truly understand e-commerce, then, you will need to know something about client/server computing, packet-switched communications, protocols such as TCP/IP, Web servers, HTML, mobile digital platforms, and the Internet Cloud computing platform.. All of these topics are described fully in Part 2 of the book (Chapters 3–5).

BUSINESS: BASIC CONCEPTS

While the technology provides the infrastructure, it is the business applications—the potential for extraordinary returns on investment—that create the interest and excitement in e-commerce. New technologies present businesses and entrepreneurs with new ways of organizing production and transacting business. New technologies change the strategies and plans of existing firms: old strategies are made obsolete and new ones need to be invented. New technologies are the birthing grounds where thousands of new companies spring up with new products and services. New technologies are the graveyard of many traditional firms, like record stores. To truly understand e-commerce, you will need to be familiar with some key business concepts, such as the nature of digital electronic markets, digital goods, business models, firm and industry value chains, value webs, industry structure, and consumer behavior in digital markets. We'll examine each of these concepts further in Chapter 2 and throughout the book.

SOCIETY: TAMING THE JUGGERNAUT

With around 175-200 million adult Americans now using the Internet, many for e-commerce purposes, and over 1 billion users worldwide, the impact of the Internet and e-commerce on society is significant and global. Increasingly, e-commerce is subject to the laws of nations and global entities. You will need to understand the pressures that global e-commerce places on contemporary society in order to conduct a successful e-commerce business or understand the e-commerce phenomenon. The primary societal issues we discuss in this book are intellectual property, individual privacy, and public welfare policy (such as the protection of children from Internet pornography). Because the cost of distributing digital copies of copyrighted intellectual property—tangible works of the mind such as music, books, and videos—is nearly zero on the Internet, e-commerce poses special challenges to the various methods societies have used in the past to protect intellectual property rights.

Since the Internet and the Web are exceptionally adept at tracking the identity and behavior of individuals online, e-commerce raises difficulties for preserving privacy—the ability of individuals to place limits on the type and amount of information collected about them, and to control the uses of their personal information. Read *Insight on Society: Holding On To Your Privacy Online* to get a view of some of the ways e-commerce sites use personal information.

The global nature of e-commerce also poses public policy issues of equity, equal access, content regulation, and taxation. For instance, in the United States, public telephone utilities are required under public utility and public accommodation laws to make basic service available at affordable rates so everyone can

INSIGHT ON SOCIETY

HOLDING ON TO YOUR PRIVACY ONLINE

Ever have the feeling you've lost control over your personal information on the Internet? Feel people are following you around online? Do you ever have the feeling that you no longer control your computer screen, or your e-mail inbox? Join the crowd: most Internet users often feel that way too. Today, upwards of 75% of all e-mail is unsolicited junk mail called spam. In a year, thousands of "display" ads (banners) will appear on your screen that you never asked for and are often irrelevant to you. Yet one of the virtues, or vices (depending on your perspective), of e-commerce technology is that it permits online merchants to send you advertising that supposedly reflects personal information the merchant has gathered about you. This is called "one-to-one" marketing or "personalization." This personal information might include what products you have previously purchased from the merchant, what kind of content you have viewed at its site, how you arrived at the site (where you were previously), as well as all of your clicking behavior at the site or all other sites on the Web. This clickstream becomes the basis for constructing a digital profile of you. Your clickstream and resulting profile is a marketer's and merchant's gold mine: if you know what people like and what they have recently purchased, you stand a good chance of being able to sell them something else. How does a Web-based company find out about your clickstream?

Let's start with Google—the site that 80 million people in the United States use everyday to find what they're looking for. So what does Google know about your clicks? Here's a sampler:

- Google Search: Search terms
- Google Desktop: Index of users' computer files, e-mail, music, photos, and chat and Web browser history

- Google Talk: instant message chats
- Google Maps: addresses, including user home address
- Google Mail: user e-mail history
- Google Calendar: users' schedules
- Google YouTube: video viewing history
- Google Checkout: credit card, payment information

Google keeps this information for 18–24 months, and uses it to pitch ads to you. Google claims it does not really know who you are, only your computer's IP address and browser information. But critics point out that nearly 90% of Americans can be identified by name with just three pieces of information: birth date, gender, and ZIP code.

Actually just about any four pieces of information stored by Google from the list above would identify the vast majority of users by name.

There are no legal or technical restrictions on how Google uses this personally identifiable information. If you've ever wondered how much this information is worth, consider Google's stock price has been as high as $750 a share, and its market capitalization over $200 billion. This value derives from "monetizing" the consumer information Google owns, i.e. selling it to the highest bidder.

Under pressure from privacy groups, Google has announced it would "anonymize" its search logs in 18-24 months. Privacy groups were not impressed: why keep the logs that long? Why not 12 months or six months? Part of the answer is unexpected: many countries and states require record retention for purposes of official investigations into personal behavior. For instance, in a $1 billion lawsuit against Google's YouTube, a federal judge ordered YouTube to turn over all its records of which users watched which videos. The

(continued)

judge reasoned it was the only way Viacom could prove most of the videos streamed on YouTube are copyright protected. Meanwhile, Apple has added to its latest version of iTunes the ability to monitor every song you listen to on your computer (as well as all the songs you listen to on the iTunes Web site).

Social networking sites are ideal places to collect personal information. Facebook proposed its Beacon program in 2007 which broadcast user activities on other sites to their friends. Consumer backlash forced Facebook to allow this sharing only with user consent.

Another way your clickstream gets privatized by Web marketers is through advertising networks such as DoubleClick, ValueClick Media, and 24/7 Real Media. These advertising networks insert themselves between you and the merchant, and track your movements through their networks. They do this so well that Google bought DoubleClick in April 2007 for $3.1 billion; Yahoo bought RightMedia in the same month for $580 million; and Microsoft, fast on their heels, bought aQuantive for $6 billion in May 2007. There's money to be made invading people's privacy.

When you visit any of thousands of Web sites in these ad networks, the network firms log your access to the site, and then follow your movements through the site (as does the merchant). Your clickstream behavior is merged with that of thousands of other consumers, and then these firms pop banner ads on your browser when visiting the other network sites.

Merchant sites also keep a complete contact log of every click you make and every object you choose to see on their Web sites. This is a built-in capability of Web server software. This data is stored and can be mined to create a profile of your behavior on the site. All Web sites use cookies and many use Web bugs. A cookie is a small text file downloaded onto your hard drive by a Web site. The cookie file contains whatever identifying information the merchant chooses to put in it. They can

be read by other Web sites you visit and used to track your movement among sites. A Web bug is a tiny graphic, typically one pixel wide and one pixel deep, embedded within a Web page or e-mail. It usually is transparent or blends into the background color. A Web bug in a Web page can report information such as a visitor's IP address, cookie information, and referring URL back to the sending server or to the server of a third party, such as a Web advertising company. Hidden inside e-mail messages, a Web bug can tell the merchant whether you opened the e-mail, and even more alarming to privacy advocates, can match the e-mail address with a previously set cookie, thereby allowing the merchant to coordinate a specific individual with their actions on the Web. The merchant then has a great deal of both clickstream behavior and personal information about you generated at the merchant's site, including all the information entered into shopping carts and payment information. So when you return to Amazon, Amazon knows your purchase history and can recommend new titles.

Now let's go over the top: spyware, sometimes also known as adware. People often make a distinction between adware and spyware: adware is designed to serve you ads, and spyware is designed to record information from your computer (such as your credit card number or any other personal information) and send it to a remote server. Both operate on the same principle: these are small software programs that secretly install themselves on your computer by piggybacking on larger applications, or by downloading potentially any file from the Web. The most common source of adware and spyware are music-sharing P2P network programs such as eDonkey and BitTorrent and online contests where you need to download a program in order to participate. Once installed, adware calls out to other sites to send banner ads and other obnoxious unsolicited material to your screen. Spyware also can report your movements on the

(continued)

Internet to other computers. If, for instance, you ask your browser to go to Llbean.com, adware can divert you to a competitor, or pop a banner ad on your screen offering a 10% discount if you visit the competitor's site. Spyware really lives up to its name when it is used to transmit user keystrokes to remote servers. In this application, anything you enter on your keyboard—including passwords, personal names, your address or financial information—can all be sent to remote servers without you knowing about it.

All of this tracking behavior of large advertising, media and retail firms makes Web users nervous and distrustful. Over 50% of Internet users are more concerned about security and privacy this year than last year. More than 36% of Internet users never buy online for fear of privacy and security issues. Many people feel that efforts to market products and services based on their online behavior is an invasion of their privacy. They believe that while it may increase sales in the short term, violating personal privacy on the Web is bad business. In its annual Digital Future Report, the USC Annenberg School found 87% of Internet users reported some level of concern about the lack of online privacy, and 46% were "very or extremely concerned" about privacy while shopping online. eMarketer and Forrester Research report that 52% of Internet users think Web sites ask for too much information when registering, 45% believe their privacy has eroded since going online, and 56% oppose Web sites collecting non-personally identifiable information even if it results in more relevant advertising. On the other hand, millions of online consumers willingly give up their private information in return for a benefit such as premium information content (reports and white papers), or simply the chance to win a contest. Other millions give up their names, pictures, friends, and contact information on social networking sites.

Can you protect your privacy in the Internet age (and still use the Web for convenient shopping)? There are several kinds of solutions: merchant privacy policy, advertising network privacy policy, technology, and enforcement of existing laws, passage of new laws, and consumer market resistance.. Some new technologies that can help are called anonymizers. Companies such as Anonymizer.com have developed software packages and their own Web servers that you can use to hide your identity online. Software programs such as SpySweeper and Ad-aware can help remove spyware programs.

Laws and aggressive prosecutors help also. In August 2006, Washington State attorney general Rob McKenna a filed a lawsuit under the state's Computer Spyware Act against Movieland.com and its associates alleging that this movie sharing site used malware tactics to bombard millions of visitors with aggressive pop-up ads that demanded payment for its download service. The pop-ups demanding payment took up users' screens and prevented further work on the computer until they agreed to pay $19.95 to Movieland.

Do customers in an open marketplace have a "right" to privacy, or a legitimate expectation of privacy? As we describe in later chapters (especially Chapter 8), efforts to regulate online privacy and create new laws to protect online commercial privacy have not been widely successful, although self-regulation by advertising networks has produced some progress.

Most Web merchants are learning that it pays to be sensitive to customers' concerns about privacy. Trust is critical to successful e-commerce. Almost all sites have "opt-out" check boxes that allow visitors the option to not receive e-mail and other marketing information

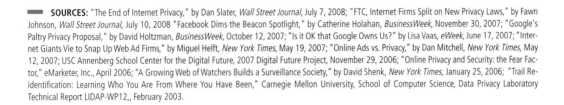

from the site. Many sites have "opt-in" poli-cies that require customers to check a box if they want to receive additional marketing mes-sages. All of the Web's top 25 e-merchants, as well as many others, have privacy policies posted on their sites. The question remains: Do these Web site privacy policies achieve what consumers want?

SOURCES: "The End of Internet Privacy," by Dan Slater, *Wall Street Journal*, July 7, 2008; "FTC, Internet Firms Split on New Privacy Laws," by Fawn Johnson, *Wall Street Journal*, July 10, 2008 "Facebook Dims the Beacon Spotlight," by Catherine Holahan, *BusinessWeek*, November 30, 2007; "Google's Paltry Privacy Proposal," by David Holtzman, *BusinessWeek*, October 12, 2007; "Is it OK that Google Owns Us?" by Lisa Vaas, *eWeek*, June 17, 2007; "Inter-net Giants Vie to Snap Up Web Ad Firms," by Miguel Helft, *New York Times*, May 19, 2007; "Online Ads vs. Privacy," by Dan Mitchell, *New York Times,* May 12, 2007; USC Annenberg School Center for the Digital Future, 2007 Digital Future Project, November 29, 2006; "Online Privacy and Security: the Fear Fac-tor," eMarketer, Inc., April 2006; "A Growing Web of Watchers Builds a Surveillance Society," by David Shenk, *New York Times*, January 25, 2006; "Trail Re-identification: Learning Who You Are From Where You Have Been," Carnegie Mellon University, School of Computer Science, Data Privacy Laboratory Technical Report LIDAP-WP12,, February 2003.

have telephone service. Should these laws be extended to the Internet and the Web? If goods are purchased by a New York state resident from a Web site in California, shipped from a center in Illinois, and delivered to New York, what state has the right to collect a sales tax? Should some heavy Internet users who consume extraordinary amounts of bandwidth be charged extra for service or should the Internet be neutral with respect to usage? If some societies choose to ban selected images, selected commercial activity (such as gambling), or political messages from their public media, then how can that society exercise content and activity control over a global e-commerce site? What rights do nation-states and their citizens have with respect to the Internet, the Web, and e-commerce?

ACADEMIC DISCIPLINES CONCERNED WITH E-COMMERCE

The phenomenon of e-commerce is so broad that a multidisciplinary perspective is required (see **Figure 1.11**). There are two primary approaches to e-commerce: technical and behavioral.

Technical Approaches

Computer scientists are interested in e-commerce as an exemplary application of Internet technology. They are concerned with the development of computer hardware, software, and telecommunications systems, as well as standards, encryp-tion, and database design and operation. Management scientists are primarily interested in building mathematical models of business processes and optimizing these processes. They are interested in e-commerce as an opportunity to study how business firms can exploit the Internet to achieve more efficient business operations.

Behavioral Approaches

In the behavioral area, information systems researchers are primarily interested in e-commerce because of its implications for firm and industry value chains, industry

---

| FIGURE 1.11 | DISCIPLINES CONCERNED WITH E-COMMERCE |

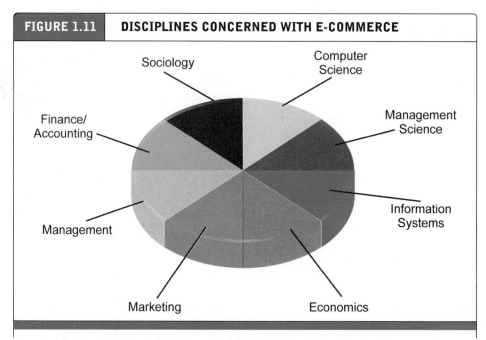

Many disciplines are directly involved in the study and understanding of e-commerce.

structure, and corporate strategy. The information systems discipline spans the technical and behavioral approaches. For instance, technical groups within the information systems specialty also focus on data mining, search engine design, and artificial intelligence. Economists have focused on consumer behavior at Web sites, pricing of digital goods, and on the unique features of digital electronic markets. The marketing profession is interested in marketing, brand development and extension, consumer behavior on Web sites, and the ability of Internet technologies to segment and target consumer groups, and differentiate products. Economists share an interest with marketing scholars who have focused on e-commerce consumer response to marketing and advertising campaigns, and the ability of firms to brand, segment markets, target audiences, and position products to achieve above-normal returns on investment.

Management scholars have focused on entrepreneurial behavior and the challenges faced by young firms who are required to develop organizational structures in short time spans. Finance and accounting scholars have focused on e-commerce firm valuation and accounting practices. Sociologists—and to a lesser extent psychologists—have focused on general population studies of Internet usage, the role of social inequality in skewing Internet benefits, and the use of the Web as a social networking and group communications tool. Legal scholars are interested in issues such as preserving intellectual property, privacy, and content regulation.

No one perspective dominates research about e-commerce. The challenge is to learn enough about a variety of academic disciplines so that you can grasp the significance of e-commerce in its entirety.

CASE STUDY

P2P NETWORKS ROCK,
Music Industry Rolls.

In 2005, after several years of heated court battles, the case of *Metro Goldwyn Mayer Studios v. Grokster, et al.* finally reached the U.S. Supreme Court. In June 2005, the Court handed down its unanimous decision: Internet file-sharing services such as Grokster, StreamCast, BitTorrent, and Kazaa can be held liable for copyright infringement because they intentionally sought to induce, enable, and encourage users to share music that was owned by the record labels. Indeed, it was their business model: steal the music, gather a huge audience, and monetize the audience by advertising. Since the court ruling, Kazaa, Morpheus, Grokster, BearShare, iMesh, and many others have either gone out of business or settled with the music label firms and converted themselves into legal file-sharing sites by entering into relationships with the labels.

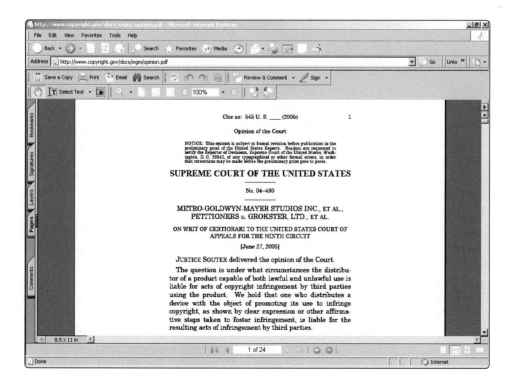

But, this legal victory has not proven to be the magic bullet that miraculously solves all the problems facing the music industry. In addition to the issue of illegal downloads, legitimate digital music sales have so far failed to make up for the falling CD sales revenues. These two problems are interrelated: if customers can get the music for free, why should they buy a digital copy or a CD?

CD sales have continued to slide, leading to a disastrous financial performance not just at the music label firms but also among their music distributors—the large retail outlets that sell CDs such as Tower Records, Sam Goody, Wal-Mart, and Best Buy. The big three record labels (EMI, Warner Music, and Sony Music) make nearly all their money selling CDs—collections of 12 or more songs in a physical bundle. Sales of CDs started falling in 2004 as the Internet ramped up its broadband connectivity. In 2007, sales of CDs plunged 20% in one year and will drop another 11% per year in 2008 and 2009; 800 music retail stores closed in 2006 and 400 followed suit in 2007; Wal-Mart cut back its shelfspace devoted to CDs and now carries only the top titles. And yet while physical unit album sales are down, overall purchases of music (including legal digital downloads) are up 15%.

Downloading music—legal or illegal—is a major American pastime. About 70 million people downloaded music in 2008. Approximately 35 million of these use illegal P2P networks, and the rest download from legal sites that charge for music. Those who use the illegal free sites are predominantly young, tech-savvy males in the 14–21 year age group. People older than 21 tend to use legitimate downloading sites such as iTunes. The presence of so many young people on illegal P2P sites makes selling advertising on these sites very lucrative. Every month, about 1 billion songs are shared on illegal file-sharing P2P networks. In contrast, it took Apple iTunes about two years to achieve that many downloads! Illegal downloads are about 90% of the music download traffic. How can this be if the Supreme Court declared these networks illegal?

At the same time, legal sales of music at iTunes, Rhapsody, and eMusic have been growing at about 50% per year since 2006. While a hopeful sign, these revenues are typically generated by sales of individual songs at 99 cents each, not entire albums at $15–$20 retail. Digital music sales have just not been strong enough to compensate for the plunging CD sales. Why not?

Let's take these questions one at a time. Why has illegal file sharing continued if these sites are illegal and can be prosecuted? To answer this question you need to know a bit about P2P networks.

Peer-to-peer computer networks rely on the computing power of participants in the network rather than on a single central server or group of servers. A software program coordinates the communications among the participant computers who "donate" their storage, communication, and processing power. As more people join the network, the more power it has, and the faster you can find and exchange files.

P2P networks followed in the footsteps of Napster—the first world champion of free music downloads. Founded in 1999, Napster had over 80 million users worldwide by 2001, but it was put out of business by a U.S. federal court decision in 2001 that required Napster to shut down its central servers that indexed music titles stored on users' computers. By maintaining a central index of available music located on network members' computers, Napster was directly enabling the sharing of music and the violation of copyright protections, i.e., users were not paying the owners of the music for listening.

Later P2P networks operate differently and do not require a central index of titles. Kazaa relies on a software program called FastTrack, which was invented in 1997 by two engineers: Niklas Zennstrom (Swedish) and Janus Friis (Dutch). Here's how it works: Users download the FastTrack software free from any of several sources on the Internet. The software helps users create a local shared directory where they can store music tracks they are willing to share and download tracks from others on the network. When users want to search the Web for new tracks, they launch FastTrack and the software searches first for FastTrack "super nodes" on the Internet— high-speed servers volunteered by other users—that contain pointers to other users who have the desired music tracks. From there, the requesting and sharing computers use their local client Fast Track software to establish a direct peer-to-peer link, and the file swap occurs. The super nodes speed up file transfer by identifying several sources of the same music track and establishing multiple download links. The software automatically identifies which computers on the network are capable of acting as super nodes without direction from outside.

A much more powerful P2P network, BitTorrent, was created by Bram Cohen in 2001, and is distributed by BitTorrent Inc. Ideally suited for sharing movies online, BitTorrent is a protocol (and a client program) in which very large files are distributed in chunks over a large number of Internet client computers. When you request a file (such as a movie), the BitTorrent program finds machines in your vicinity which are storing parts of the movie, and requests their download to your client computer. The downloading process is much faster than downloading from a single server.

How do P2P networks make money? In the early years, downloading FastTrack brought with it many other programs and occasional viruses. In order to make money, Kazaa loaded FastTrack with so-called spyware and adware programs (discussed in the *Insight on Society* story in this chapter, and in later chapters), which in turn go out on the Internet and request pop-up advertisements and unsolicited e-mail from vendors who pay for this service. In that sense, FastTrack was an "advertising network" that made its money not from selling music but from selling to advertisers access to millions of users.

The music available on Kazaa functioned as a draw to a huge Internet audience. Most other file-sharing services operate under the same principles, with few variations on the central theme of using copyrighted music to create an audience that downloads software, which in turn displays ads on users' computers. After settling their lawsuits with the record labels in 2006, sites such as Kazaa have cleaned up their software and no longer force users to accept spyware or adware. Instead they make money from music sales, advertising directly on their sites (they are popular among millions of people) and through their distributed software.

After the major U.S. P2P networks were shut down or changed their business models to become legitimate music vendors, the software itself has propagated throughout the Web, and many new open source P2P programs have also propagated (such as eDonkey, the most popular). Anyone can download the programs and protocols for P2P file sharing. The result is that thousands of smaller P2P networks have sprung up around the world, many in foreign countries such as Sweden and Russia where they cannot be held liable for illegal sharing of music. Sites in these countries claim to be operating within the copyright laws of their countries. An estimated 95% of online music in Russia is pirated, a figure which is true throughout much of the world including Europe. The Russian authorities shut down the leading Russian site, AllofMP3.com, during President Putin's visit to the United States in July 2007.

Enter "free music" into a search engine and you will receive over 3 million entries, many of which are illegal file-sharing sites. Caution: It's user beware when it comes to downloading these files and programs. Some of them have been corrupted by the record labels, and others may contain viruses, adware, or spyware. About 10 million people are logged onto to P2P music-sharing sites during a typical day in the United States.

So P2P networks are likely to propagate and pirated music is likely to be with us and the music industry for a very long time. Independent bands ("Indie music"), and even some well-known stars are starting to distribute their music on their own Web sites without a company label backing them. This spells more trouble for the traditional record label business and requires a new digital business model for the industry.

Why haven't sales of digital music made up for the loss of CD sales? At 99 cents a song, about the same price as a typical blank CD, one would think the record labels are making as much on songs as before. The difference is they are not selling 12–15 songs on a CD, but single songs, one at a time. The loss of the bundle concept—the CD—has reduced sales drastically. Because consumers can buy one song at a time on the Internet, the whole concept of "an album" is lost on the consumer. The culture of music has changed for consumers. Also, the legal sites use fairly complex digital rights management software to prevent users from freely playing the songs on a variety of devices, or moving them among client computers, such as from a laptop to a desktop PC. When you buy a CD you own it. When you purchase a song online at iTunes, you license the song for limited use, and you can't play it on other players or move it from one machine to another without a lot work. EMI, along with other labels, as well as Apple are considering the elimination of digital rights management protections and moving to a "pay once" concept with unlimited playback. But Apple's entire business model is based on its proprietary audio format ACC. Apple is not considering making its audio compression software and file standards available to other device manufacturers. So the question of how to play your iTunes tunes on a Zune or other player is still hard to answer for the average consumer.

Other changes the industry is making includes developing "teaser" tracks of video and audio and distributing these on BitTorrent and other P2P networks, in essence, using the P2P networks to advertise their products; and selling MP3s directly online without any copyright protection or allowing others such as Yahoo to sell their MP3s.

SOURCES: "U.S. Album Sales Fell 9.5% in 2007," by the Associated Press, *New York Times*, January 4, 2008; "Amazon to Sell Music Without Copy Protection," by Brad Stone and Jeff Leeds, *New York Times*, May 17, 2007; "The Album, a Commodity in Disfavor," by Jeff Leeds, *New York Times*, March 26, 2007; "Sales of Music, Long in Decline, Plunge Sharply," by Ethan Smith, *Wall Street Journal*, March 21, 2007; "EMI Mulls Lifting Online-Music Restrictions," by Ethan Smith and, *Wall Street Journal*, February 9, 2007; "Digital Music Up 80% but Shy of Lost Revenue," by Eric Pfanner, *New York Times*, January 18, 2007; "Record Labels Turn Piracy Into a Marketing Opportunity," *Wall Street Journal*, October 18, 2006.

Until the labels and device makers can agree on how to sell music on the Internet at a fair price and with few limitations on playback, the greatest music box on Earth—the Internet—will remain a threat to the very industry that makes the music.

Case Study Questions

1. How can P2P file-sharing networks make money if they do not sell music?

2. Into which category or categories of e-commerce do P2P file-sharing networks fall?

3. What social issues are raised by P2P file-sharing protocols and programs such as BitTorrent? Is the record industry justified in attempting to shut them down? Why or why not?

4. Will the Supreme Court's decision inhibit the development of P2P technology or the Internet itself, as proponents of P2P services have claimed?

5. Why do people older than 21 tend to use legitimate downloading sites whereas younger people tend to use illegal sites?

6. What difference would it make if the existing music labels disappeared for lack of revenue? What legitimate function do the music labels perform in the creation and distribution of original music?

1.5 REVIEW

KEY CONCEPTS

■ Define e-commerce and describe how it differs from e-business.

- E-commerce involves digitally enabled commercial transactions between and among organizations and individuals. Digitally enabled transactions include all those mediated by digital technology, meaning, for the most part, transactions that occur over the Internet and the Web. Commercial transactions involve the exchange of value (e.g., money) across organizational or individual boundaries in return for products or services.

- E-business refers primarily to the digital enabling of transactions and processes within a firm, involving information systems under the control of the firm. For the most part, e-business does not involve commercial transactions across organizational boundaries where value is exchanged.

■ Identify and describe the unique features of e-commerce technology and discuss their business significance.

There are eight features of e-commerce technology that are unique to this medium:

- *Ubiquity*—available just about everywhere, at all times, making it possible to shop from your desktop, at home, at work, or even from your car.
- *Global reach*—permits commercial transactions to cross cultural and national boundaries far more conveniently and cost-effectively than is true in traditional commerce.
- *Universal standards*—shared by all nations around the world. In contrast, most traditional commerce technologies differ from one nation to the next.
- *Richness*—refers to the complexity and content of a message. It enables an online merchant to deliver marketing messages with text, video, and audio to an audience of millions, in a way not possible with traditional commerce technologies such as radio, television, or magazines.
- *Interactivity*—allows for two-way communication between merchant and consumer and enabling the merchant to engage a consumer in ways similar to a face-to-face experience, but on a much more massive, global scale.
- *Information density*—is the total amount and quality of information available to all market participants. The Internet reduces information collection, storage, processing, and communication costs while increasing the currency, accuracy, and timeliness of information.
- *Personalization* and *customization*—merchants can target their marketing messages to specific individuals by adjusting the message to a person's name, interests, and past purchases. Because of the increase in information density, a great deal of information about the consumer's past purchases and behavior can be stored and used by online merchants. The result is a level of personalization and customization unthinkable with existing commerce technologies.
- *Social technology*—provides a many-to-many model of mass communications. Millions of users are able to generate content consumed by millions of other users. The result is the formation of social networks on a wide scale and the aggregation of large audiences on social network platforms.

■ Describe and identify Web 2.0 applications

- A new set of applications has emerged on the Internet, loosely referred to as Web 2.0. These applications attract huge audiences and represent significant new opportunities for e-commerce revenues. Web 2.0 applications such as social networks, photo-and video-sharing sites, Wikipedia, and virtual life sites support very high levels of interactivity compared to other traditional media.

■ Describe the major types of e-commerce.

There are five major types of e-commerce:
- B2C involves businesses selling to consumers and is the type of e-commerce that most consumers are likely to encounter. In 2008, consumers spent about $255 billion in B2C transactions.
- B2B e-commerce involves businesses selling to other businesses and is the largest form of e-commerce, with an estimated $3.8 trillion in transactions occurring in 2008.
- C2C is a means for consumers to sell to each other. In C2C e-commerce, the consumer prepares the product for market, places the product for auction or sale, and relies on the market maker to provide catalog, search engine, and transaction clearing capabilities so that products can be easily displayed, discovered, and paid for.

- P2P technology enables Internet users to share files and computer resources directly without having to go through a central Web server. Music and file-sharing services, such as BitTorrent, Kazaa, and eDonkey, are prime examples of this type of e-commerce, because consumers can transfer files directly to other consumers without a central server involved.
- M-commerce involves the use of wireless digital devices to enable transactions on the Web.

■ **Understand the evolution of e-commerce from its early years to today.**

E-commerce has gone through three stages: innovation, consolidation, and reinvention. The early years of e-commerce were a period of explosive growth, beginning in 1995 with the first widespread use of the Web to advertise products and ending in 2000 with the collapse in stock market valuations for dot-com ventures.

- The early years of e-commerce were a technological success, with the digital infrastructure created during the period solid enough to sustain significant growth in e-commerce during the next decade, and a mixed business success, with significant revenue growth and customer usage, but low profit margins.
- E-commerce during its early years did not fulfill economists' visions of the perfect Bertrand market and friction-free commerce, or fulfill the visions of entrepreneurs and venture capitalists for first-mover advantages, low customer acquisition and retention costs, and low costs of doing business.
- E-commerce entered a period of consolidation beginning in March 2000 and extending through 2005.
- E-commerce entered a period of reinvention in 2006 with the emergence of social networking and Web 2.0 applications that attracted huge audiences in a very short time span.

■ **Identify the factors that will define the future of e-commerce.**

Factors that will define the future of e-commerce include the following:
- E-commerce technology will continue to propagate through all commercial activity, with overall revenues from e-commerce, the number of products and services sold over the Web, and the amount of Web traffic all rising.
- E-commerce prices will rise to cover the real costs of doing business on the Web.
- E-commerce margins and profits will rise to levels more typical of all retailers.
- Traditional well-endowed and experienced Fortune 500 companies will play a growing and more dominant role.
- Entrepreneurs will continue to play an important role in pioneering new social applications.
- The number of successful pure online companies will continue to decline and most successful e-commerce firms will adopt an integrated, multi-channel bricks-and-clicks strategy.
- Regulation of e-commerce and the Web by government will grow both in the United States and worldwide.

■ **Describe the major themes underlying the study of e-commerce.**

E-commerce involves three broad interrelated themes:
- *Technology*—To understand e-commerce, you need a basic understanding of the information technologies upon which it is built, including the Internet and the

World Wide Web, and a host of complimentary technologies—personal computers, local area networks, client/server computing, packet-switched communications, protocols such as TCP/IP, Web servers, HTML, and relational databases, among others.

- *Business*—While technology provides the infrastructure, it is the business applications—the potential for extraordinary returns on investment—that create the interest and excitement in e-commerce. New technologies present businesses and entrepreneurs with new ways of organizing production and transacting business. Therefore, you also need to understand some key business concepts such as electronic markets, information goods, business models, firm and industry value chains, industry structure, and consumer behavior in electronic markets.

- *Society*—Understanding the pressures that global e-commerce places on contemporary society is critical to being successful in the e-commerce marketplace. The primary societal issues are intellectual property, individual privacy, and public policy.

■ **Identify the major academic disciplines contributing to e-commerce.**

There are two primary approaches to e-commerce: technical and behavioral. Each of these approaches is represented by several academic disciplines. On the technical side:

- Computer scientists are interested in e-commerce as an application of Internet technology.
- Management scientists are primarily interested in building mathematical models of business processes and optimizing them to learn how businesses can exploit the Internet to improve their business operations.
- Information systems professionals are interested in e-commerce because of its implications for firm and industry value chains, industry structure, and corporate strategy.
- Economists have focused on consumer behavior at Web sites, and on the features of digital electronic markets.

On the behavioral side:

- Sociologists have focused on studies of Internet usage, the role of social inequality in skewing Internet benefits, and the use of the Web as a personal and group communications tool.
- Finance and accounting scholars have focused on e-commerce firm valuation and accounting practices.
- Management scholars have focused on entrepreneurial behavior and the challenges faced by young firms who are required to develop organizational structures in short time spans.
- Marketing scholars have focused on consumer response to online marketing and advertising campaigns, and the ability of firms to brand, segment markets, target audiences, and position products to achieve higher returns on investment.

QUESTIONS

1. What is e-commerce? How does it differ from e-business? Where does it intersect with e-business?
2. What is information asymmetry?
3. What are some of the unique features of e-commerce technology?
4. What is a marketspace?
5. What are three benefits of universal standards?
6. Compare online and traditional transactions in terms of richness.
7. Name three of the business consequences that can result from growth in information density.
8. What is Web 2.0? Give examples of Web 2.0 sites and explain why you included them in your list.
9. Give examples of B2C, B2B, C2C, and P2P Web sites besides those listed in the chapter materials.
10. How are the Internet and the Web similar to or different from other technologies that have changed commerce in the past?
11. Describe the three different stages in the evolution of e-commerce.
12. What are the major limitations on the growth of e-commerce? Which is potentially the toughest to overcome?
13. What are three of the factors that will contribute to greater Internet penetration in U.S. households?
14. Define disintermediation and explain the benefits to Internet users of such a phenomenon. How does disintermediation impact friction-free commerce?
15. What are some of the major advantages and disadvantages of being a first mover?
16. Discuss the ways in which the early years of e-commerce can be considered both a success and a failure.
17. What are five of the major differences between the early years of e-commerce and today's e-commerce?
18. What factors will help define the future of e-commerce over the next five years?
19. Why is a multidisciplinary approach necessary if one hopes to understand e-commerce?

PROJECTS

1. Search the Web for an example of each of the five major types of e-commerce described in Section 1.1. Create a PowerPoint slide presentation or written report describing each Web site (take a screenshot of each, if possible), and explain why it fits into one of the five types of e-commerce.

2. Choose an e-commerce Web site and assess it in terms of the eight unique features of e-commerce technology described in Table 1.2. Which of the features does the site implement well, and which features poorly, in your opinion? Prepare a short memo to the president of the company you have chosen detailing your findings and any suggestions for improvement you may have.

3. Given the development and history of e-commerce in the years from 1995–2008, what do you predict we will see during the next five years of e-commerce? Describe some of the technological, business, and societal shifts that may occur as the Internet continues to grow and expand. Prepare a brief PowerPoint slide presentation or written report to explain your vision of what e-commerce looks like today.

4. Follow up on events at Facebook and MySpace subsequent to September 2008 (when the opening case was prepared). Has Facebook continued to challenge the dominance of MySpace (the world's largest social networking site)? What are its current prospects for success or failure? Prepare a short report on your findings.

WEB SITE RESOURCES www.prenhall.com/laudon

- ■ Additional projects, exercises, and tutorials
- ■ Careers: Explore career opportunities in e-commerce
- ■ Raising capital and business plans

E-commerce Business Models and Concepts

After reading this chapter, you will be able to:

- Identify the key components of e-commerce business models.
- Describe the major B2C business models.
- Describe the major B2B business models.
- Recognize business models in other emerging areas of e-commerce.
- Understand key business concepts and strategies applicable to e-commerce.

Online Groceries:
Up from the Embers

When Webvan flamed out in July 2001 after having spent almost $1 billion trying to build the Web's largest online grocery store based on huge distribution warehouses in seven U.S. cities, most pundits and investors thought the entire online grocery business model was either a failure or a fraud. Facing the costs of building an entirely new distribution system of warehouses and truck fleets to compete with existing grocery businesses, not to mention the expense of marketing, Webvan compounded its problems by offering below-market prices and free delivery of even small orders at just about any time of the day or night in urban areas often clogged with traffic. But the pundits did not count on Manhattan's FreshDirect—or the ability of traditional grocery chains to move into the ashes of the online grocery business to create solid, profitable businesses. Jupiter Research estimates that online grocery sales will garner sales of $7.5 billion in 2008, and by 2012, sales are expected to grow to $13.5 billion, a compound annual growth rate of about 17%. FreshDirect and other traditional firms are learning how to exploit this potential market with profitable business models.

Today, traditional firms such as California's huge Safeway Stores and Royal Ahold (Dutch owner of the U.S. Stop & Shop and Giant food stores, among others, and the Internet firm Peapod, which handles Internet shopping for Stop & Shop and Giant) are following the lead of the successful British grocer Tesco. Tesco is the largest chain of supermarkets in Britain and opened an online division in 1990. It differed from Webvan's effort because Tesco uses its current warehouse infrastructure and existing stores to put together the baskets of food for consumers. Customers can either pick up their baskets or have them delivered within a chosen time window for a fee that recoups most of the delivery costs. Tesco dominates the online grocery shopping market in the United Kingdom, with over 5.4 million unique visitors during the period March-May 2008, more than three times as many as its nearest competitor Tesco takes over 30,000 online orders per day. In the United States, Safeway's wholly-owned subsidiary GroceryWorks.com provides online shopping and delivery services for Safeway stores in

California, Oregon, Washington, Arizona, Maryland, Virginia, and the District of Columbia; and for Vons stores in Southern California and Las Vegas, Nevada. Customers register online, entering their personal information, including their frequent shopper cards. They are shown lists of recently purchased items to speed selection. The prices of goods are the same as those in the stores. Safeway has so-called "pickers" roam the aisles of nearby stores using a computerized picklist that directs them through the store in an efficient pattern, and even specifies the order of packing goods into bags. The orders are put into a van and delivered to the customer within a two-hour window for a fee of $10. At Peapod.com, which serves Stop & Shop and Giant Food store customers in 18 regional markets, shoppers can view both their online ordering history and their off-line purchases at nearby stores during the previous four months. The Web site also features a shopping list that displays items in the order they can be found at the customer's local store. Customers have the option of ordering online or printing the shopping list and taking it to the store. For these traditional supermarket chains, the value being offered to customers is convenience and time savings at prices only marginally higher than self-shopping.

FreshDirect has a more revolutionary but also successful approach. In July 2002, Joe Fedele and Jason Ackerman founded FreshDirect as a new kind of high-quality and high-tech food preparation and delivery service in Manhattan, and raised $120 million in venture funding. Operating out of a 300,000-square-foot plant in Queens—just across the river from Manhattan—FreshDirect trucks deliver groceries to densely populated Manhattan, Brooklyn, and Queens at prices 25% below what most New York grocers charge. It charges a $5.49–$6.79 delivery fee, depending on location and size of order, and requires a minimum order of $30. The value proposition to consumers is convenience and time savings, but also higher quality at lower prices.

How can FreshDirect succeed at these prices? One answer is that FreshDirect concentrates on very fresh perishable foods and stays away from low-margin dry goods. For instance, the FreshDirect Web site features around 3,000 perishables and 3,000 packaged goods compared to the typical 25,000 packaged goods and 2,200 perishable items that a typical grocery store offers. To do so, FreshDirect created the most modern automated perishable food processing plant in the United States. While most of the factory is kept at 36 degrees to ensure freshness and quality control, dedicated areas vary from a low of minus 25 degrees for frozen foods to a high of 62 degrees in one of its specially designed fruit and vegetable rooms. At the factory, FreshDirect butchers meat from whole carcasses, makes its own sausage, cuts up its own fish, grinds coffee, bakes bread and pastries, and cooks entire prepared meals. FreshDirect co-founder Jason Ackerman likens FreshDirect to Dell Inc. in this regard: FreshDirect employs the same "make-to-order," manufacturer-direct philosophy as does Dell. Cleanliness is an obsession—the factory was built to exceed U.S. Department of Agriculture standards. The firm uses SAP software (an enterprise resource planning system) to track inventory, compile financial reports, tag products to fulfill customers' orders, and precisely control production down to the level of telling bakers how many bagels to cook each day and what temperature to use. It uses automated carousels and conveyors to bring orders to food-prep workers and packers. The FreshDirect Web site is powered by BEA Systems'

Weblogic platform, which can track customer preferences, such as the level of fruit ripeness desired, or the preferred weight of a cut of meat. FreshDirect also uses NetTracker, Web site traffic and online behavior analysis software, to help it better understand and market to its online customers. At peak times, the Web site has handled up to 18,000 simultaneous shopping sessions. The final piece in the formula for profit is a supply chain that includes dealing directly with manufacturers and growers, thus cutting out the costs of middle-level distributors and the huge chains themselves. FreshDirect does not accept slotting fees—payments made by manufacturers for shelf space. Instead, it asks suppliers to help it direct market to consumers and to lower prices. To further encourage lower prices from suppliers, FreshDirect pays them in four business days after delivery, down from the industry pattern of 35 days.

As of July 2008, FreshDirect delivers to around 160 zip codes in the New York City metropolitan area and adjacent suburbs. It has fulfilled more than 6 million orders since opening for business, had annual revenue in 2007 of around $240 million, and is reportedly profitable. Typical order size has grown from $79 to over $145 dollars; the number of orders per week averages around 40,000; and the company has about 250,000 active customers. But despite all this success, FreshDirect has remained conservative. According to Jason Ackerman, what FreshDirect learned from Webvan's demise was that: "This is a very complex business, and the customer demands perfection every time we fill an order. Webvan's rapid expansion was unmanageable... no matter how good the executive team." Although in January 2007, FreshDirect reaffirmed that it had no plans to take its business model nationwide any time soon, by January 2008, the company had begun to change its tune, with FreshDirect's chief marketing officer Steve Druckman stating, "We won't just stay regional. It's a matter of time."

FreshDirect also says its not concerned about the prospect of competing with Amazon, which entered the online grocery marketspace in June 2006. Initially, Amazon offered only nonperishable foods, such as pasta, cereal, and canned goods. But in August 2007, Amazon, taking a page from the FreshDirect playbook, launched a micro site, Fresh.Amazon.com, which offers locally grown fresh meat, fruit, and vegetables. The site was initially available only to invited customers who lived on Mercer Island, a suburb located near Amazon's Seattle distribution center, but has since expanded to serve 24 zip codes in the Seattle metropolitan area. According to business analyst John Hauptman, "What they are doing with this pilot looks a lot like the business model FreshDirect successfully implemented in New York."

Should FreshDirect start to worry?

SOURCES: "FreshDirect-Help-FAQs," FreshDirect.com, July 3, 2008; Peapod LLC Corporate Fact Sheet," Peapod.com, July 3, 2008; "SimonDelivers More," by Gene Rebeck, *Twin Cities Business*, March 2008; "Safeway.com Grows by Nearly 33% in 2007," *Internet Retailer*, February 27, 2008; "FreshDirect Sees Broader Market Horizons Ahead," *Internet Retailer*, January 16, 2008; "Grocery-Works.com, LLC," Google Finance, August 22, 2007; "Amazon Gets Fresh with an Expanded Grocery Service," *Internet Retailer*, August 3, 2007; "FreshDirect Celebrates Five Year Anniversary," PRNewswire, July 9, 2007; "FreshDirect Staying Close to Home," *Internet Retailer*, January 24, 2007; "Online Grocer Peapod Goes Multi-Channel with Stop & Shop and Giant Food," *Internet Retailer*, January 31, 2007; "Tesco Dominates Internet Shopping," ZDNet.co.uk, August 24, 2006; "A Fresh Approach to Technology," by Darrell Dunn, *Information Week*, January 24, 2005; "Web Grocer Hits Refresh," by Jennifer Harsany, *PC Magazine*, May 18, 2004; "FreshDirect: Ready to Deliver," by Larry Dignan, *Baseline*, February 17, 2004; "What FreshDirect Learned from Dell," by Tim Laseter, Barrie Berg, and Martha Turner, *Stategy+ Business*, Spring 2003.

The story of FreshDirect illustrates the difficulties of turning a good business idea into a good business model. FreshDirect and the other "new" online groceries work as business models because their managers have very carefully thought out the operational details of their ideas, and they have executed these ideas with efficiency and precision.

In the early days of e-commerce, thousands of firms discovered they could spend other people's invested capital much faster than they could get customers to pay for their products or services. In most instances of failure, the business model of the firm was faulty from the very beginning. In contrast, successful e-commerce firms have business models that are able to leverage the unique qualities of the Web, provide customers real value, develop highly effective and efficient operations, avoid legal and social entanglements that can harm the firm, and produce profitable business results. In addition, successful business models must scale. The business must be able to achieve efficiencies as it grows in volume. But what is a business model, and how can you tell if a firm's business model is going to produce a profit?

In this chapter, we focus on business models and basic business concepts that you must be familiar with in order to understand e-commerce.

2.1 E-COMMERCE BUSINESS MODELS

INTRODUCTION

business model
a set of planned activities designed to result in a profit in a marketplace

business plan
a document that describes a firm's business model

e-commerce business model
a business model that aims to use and leverage the unique qualities of the Internet and the World Wide Web

A **business model** is a set of planned activities (sometimes referred to as *business processes*) designed to result in a profit in a marketplace. A business model is not always the same as a business strategy although in some cases they are very close insofar as the business model explicitly takes into account the competitive environment (Magretta, 2002). The business model is at the center of the business plan. A **business plan** is a document that describes a firm's business model. A business plan always takes into account the competitive environment. An **e-commerce business model** aims to use and leverage the unique qualities of the Internet and the World Wide Web (Timmers, 1998).

EIGHT KEY ELEMENTS OF A BUSINESS MODEL

If you hope to develop a successful business model in any arena, not just e-commerce, you must make sure that the model effectively addresses the eight elements listed in **Table 2.1**. These elements are: value proposition, revenue model, market opportunity, competitive environment, competitive advantage, market strategy, organizational development, and management team (Ghosh, 1998). Many writers focus on a firm's value proposition and revenue model. While these may be the most important and most easily identifiable aspects of a company's business model, the other elements are equally important when evaluating business models and plans, or when attempting to understand why a particular company has succeeded or failed (Kim and Mauborgne, 2000). In the following section, we describe each of the key business model elements more fully.

TABLE 2.1	KEY ELEMENTS OF A BUSINESS MODEL
COMPONENTS	KEY QUESTIONS
Value proposition	Why should the customer buy from you?
Revenue model	How will you earn money?
Market opportunity	What marketspace do you intend to serve, and what is its size?
Competitive environment	Who else occupies your intended marketspace?
Competitive advantage	What special advantages does your firm bring to the marketspace?
Market strategy	How do you plan to promote your products or services to attract your target audience?
Organizational development	What types of organizational structures within the firm are necessary to carry out the business plan?
Management team	What kinds of experiences and background are important for the company's leaders to have?

Value Proposition

A company's value proposition is at the very heart of its business model. A **value proposition** defines how a company's product or service fulfills the needs of customers (Kambil, Ginsberg, and Bloch, 1998). To develop and/or analyze a firm's value proposition, you need to understand why customers will choose to do business with the firm instead of another company and what the firm provides that other firms do not and cannot. From the consumer point of view, successful e-commerce value propositions include: personalization and customization of product offerings, reduction of product search costs, reduction of price discovery costs, and facilitation of transactions by managing product delivery (Kambil, 1997; Bakos, 1998).

FreshDirect, for instance, primarily is offering customers the freshest perishable food in New York, direct from the growers and manufacturers, at the lowest prices, delivered to their homes at night. Although local supermarkets can offer fresh food also, customers need to spend an hour or two shopping at those stores every week. Convenience and saved time are very important elements in FreshDirect's value proposition to customers.

Before Amazon existed, most customers personally traveled to book retailers to place an order. In some cases, the desired book might not be available and the customer would have to wait several days or weeks, and then return to the bookstore to pick it up. Amazon makes it possible for book lovers to shop for virtually any book in print from the comfort of their home or office, 24 hours a day, and to know immediately whether a book is in stock. Amazon's primary value propositions are unparalleled selection and convenience.

value proposition
defines how a company's product or service fulfills the needs of customers

In many cases, companies develop their value proposition based on current market conditions or trends. Consumers' increasing emphasis on fresh perishable foods—as opposed to frozen or canned goods—is a trend FreshDirect's founders took note of, just as Starbucks' founders saw the growing interest in and demand for coffee bars nationwide. Both companies watched the market and then developed their value proposition to meet what they perceived to be consumers' demand for certain products and services.

Revenue Model

revenue model

describes how the firm will earn revenue, produce profits, and produce a superior return on invested capital

A firm's **revenue model** describes how the firm will earn revenue, generate profits, and produce a superior return on invested capital. We use the terms *revenue model* and *financial model* interchangeably. The function of business organizations is both to generate profits and to produce returns on invested capital that exceed alternative investments. Profits alone are not sufficient to make a company "successful" (Porter, 1985). In order to be considered successful, a firm must produce returns greater than alternative investments. Firms that fail this test go out of existence.

Retailers, for example, sell a product, such as a personal computer, to a customer who pays for the computer using cash or a credit card. This produces revenue. The merchant typically charges more for the computer than it pays out in operating expenses, producing a profit. But in order to go into business, the computer merchant had to invest capital—either by borrowing or by dipping into personal savings. The profits from the business constitute the return on invested capital, and these returns must be greater than the merchant could obtain elsewhere, say, by investing in real estate or just putting the money into a savings account.

Although there are many different e-commerce revenue models that have been developed, most companies rely on one, or some combination, of the following major revenue models: the advertising model, the subscription model, the transaction fee model, the sales model, and the affiliate model.

advertising revenue model

a company provides a forum for advertisements and receives fees from advertisers

In the **advertising revenue model**, a Web site that offers its users content, services, and/or products also provides a forum for advertisements and receives fees from advertisers. Those Web sites that are able to attract the greatest viewership or that have a highly specialized, differentiated viewership and are able to retain user attention ("stickiness") are able to charge higher advertising rates. Yahoo, for instance, derives a significant amount of revenue from search engine and other forms of online advertising.

subscription revenue model

a company offers its users content or services and charges a subscription fee for access to some or all of its offerings

In the **subscription revenue model**, a Web site that offers its users content or services charges a subscription fee for access to some or all of its offerings. For instance, the online version of *Consumer Reports* provides access to premium content, such as detailed ratings, reviews and recommendations, only to subscribers, who have a choice of paying a $5.95 monthly subscription fee or a $26.00 annual fee. Experience with the subscription revenue model indicates that to successfully overcome the disinclination of users to pay for content on the Web, the content offered must be perceived as a high-value-added, premium offering that is not read-

| FIGURE 2.1 | ANCESTRY.COM SUBSCRIPTION SERVICES |

Ancestry.com offers a variety of different membership options for different subscription fees.
SOURCE: Ancestry.com, 2008

ily available elsewhere nor easily replicated. Companies successfully offering content or services online on a subscription basis include Match.com and eHarmony (dating services), Ancestry.com (see **Figure 2.1**) and Genealogy.com (genealogy research), Microsoft's Xboxlive.com (video games), Rhapsody Online (music), among others.

In the **transaction fee revenue model**, a company receives a fee for enabling or executing a transaction. For example, eBay provides an online auction marketplace and receives a small transaction fee from a seller if the seller is successful in selling the item. E*Trade, an online stockbroker, receives transaction fees each time it executes a stock transaction on behalf of a customer.

In the **sales revenue model**, companies derive revenue by selling goods, information, or services to customers. Companies such as Amazon (which sells books, music, and other products), LLBean.com, and Gap.com, all have sales revenue models.

In the **affiliate revenue model**, sites that steer business to an "affiliate" receive a referral fee or percentage of the revenue from any resulting sales. For example, MyPoints makes money by connecting companies with potential customers by offering special deals to its members. When they take advantage of an offer and make a purchase, members earn "points" they can redeem for

transaction fee revenue model
a company receives a fee for enabling or executing a transaction

sales revenue model
a company derives revenue by selling goods, information, or services

affiliate revenue model
a company steers business to an affiliate and receives a referral fee or percentage of the revenue from any resulting sales

TABLE 2.2	FIVE PRIMARY REVENUE MODELS	
REVENUE MODEL	EXAMPLES	REVENUE SOURCE
Advertising	Yahoo	Fees from advertisers in exchange for advertisements
Subscription	WSJ.com Consumerreports.org	Fees from subscribers in exchange for access to content or services
Transaction Fee	eBay E-Trade	Fees (commissions) for enabling or executing a transaction
Sales	Amazon LLBean Gap JCPenny.com	Sales of goods, information, or services
Affiliate	MyPoints	Fees for business referrals

freebies, and MyPoints receives a fee. Community feedback sites such as Epinions receive much of their revenue from steering potential customers to Web sites where they make a purchase.

Table 2.2 summarizes these major revenue models.

Market Opportunity

market opportunity
refers to the company's intended marketspace and the overall potential financial opportunities available to the firm in that marketspace

marketspace
the area of actual or potential commercial value in which a company intends to operate

The term **market opportunity** refers to the company's intended **marketspace** (i.e., an area of actual or potential commercial value) and the overall potential financial opportunities available to the firm in that marketspace. The market opportunity is usually divided into smaller market niches. The realistic market opportunity is defined by the revenue potential in each of the market niches where you hope to compete.

For instance, let's assume you are analyzing a software training company that creates software-learning systems for sale to corporations over the Internet. The overall size of the software training market for all market segments is approximately $70 billion. The overall market can be broken down, however, into two major market segments: instructor-led training products, which comprise about 70% of the market ($49 billion in revenue), and computer-based training, which accounts for 30% ($21 billion). There are further market niches within each of those major market segments, such as the Fortune 500 computer-based training market and the small business computer-based training market. Because the firm is a startup firm, it cannot compete effectively in the large business, computer-based training market (about $15 billion). Large brand-name training firms dominate this niche. The startup firm's real market opportunity is to sell to the thousands of small business firms who spend about $6 billion on computer-based software training and who desperately need a cost-effective training solution. This is the size of the firm's realistic market opportunity (see **Figure 2.2**).

FIGURE 2.2	MARKETSPACE AND MARKET OPPORTUNITY IN THE SOFTWARE TRAINING MARKET

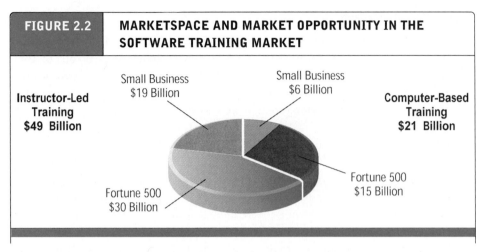

Marketspaces are composed of many market segments. Your realistic market opportunity will typically focus on one or a few market segments.

Competitive Environment

A firm's **competitive environment** refers to the other companies selling similar products and operating in the same marketspace. It also refers to the presence of substitute products and potential new entrants to the market, as well as the power of customers and suppliers over your business. We discuss the firm's environment later in the chapter. The competitive environment for a company is influenced by several factors: how many competitors are active, how large their operations are, what the market share of each competitor is, how profitable these firms are, and how they price their products.

Firms typically have both direct and indirect competitors. Direct competitors are those companies that sell products and services that are very similar and into the same market segment. For example, Priceline and Travelocity, both of whom sell discount airline tickets online, are direct competitors because both companies sell identical products—cheap tickets. Indirect competitors are companies that may be in different industries but still compete indirectly because their products can substitute for one another. For instance, automobile manufacturers and airline companies operate in different industries, but they still compete indirectly because they offer consumers alternative means of transportation. CNN.com, a news outlet, is an indirect competitor of ESPN.com not because they sell identical products, but because they both compete for consumers' time online.

The existence of a large number of competitors in any one segment may be a sign that the market is saturated and that it may be difficult to become profitable. On the other hand, a lack of competitors could either signal an untapped market niche ripe for the picking or a market that has already been tried without success because there is no money to be made. Analysis of the competitive environment can help you decide which it is.

competitive environment
refers to the other companies operating in the same marketspace selling similar products

Competitive Advantage

competitive advantage
achieved by a firm when it can produce a superior product and/or bring the product to market at a lower price than most, or all, of its competitors

Firms achieve a **competitive advantage** when they can produce a superior product and/or bring the product to market at a lower price than most, or all, of their competitors (Porter, 1985). Firms also compete on scope. Some firms can develop global markets, while other firms can only develop a national or regional market. Firms that can provide superior products at lowest cost on a global basis are truly advantaged.

Firms achieve competitive advantages because they have somehow been able to obtain differential access to the factors of production that are denied to their competitors—at least in the short term (Barney, 1991). Perhaps the firm has been able to obtain very favorable terms from suppliers, shippers, or sources of labor. Or perhaps the firm has more experienced, knowledgeable, and loyal employees than any competitors. Maybe the firm has a patent on a product that others cannot imitate, or access to investment capital through a network of former business colleagues or a brand name and popular image that other firms cannot duplicate. An **asymmetry** exists whenever one participant in a market has more resources—financial backing, knowledge, information, and/or power—than other participants. Asymmetries lead to some firms having an edge over others, permitting them to come to market with better products, faster than competitors, and sometimes at lower cost.

asymmetry
exists whenever one participant in a market has more resources than other participants

For instance, when Steven Jobs, CEO and founder of Apple Computer, announced iTunes, a new service offering legal, downloadable individual song tracks for 99 cents a tune that would be playable on Apple iPods or Apple desktops, the company was given better than average odds of success simply because of Apple's prior success with innovative hardware designs, and the large stable of music labels which Apple had meticulously lined up to support its online music catalog. Few competitors could match the combination of cheap, legal songs and powerful hardware to play them on.

first-mover advantage
a competitive market advantage for a firm that results from being the first into a marketplace with a serviceable product or service

One rather unique competitive advantage derives from being first mover. A **first-mover advantage** is a competitive market advantage for a firm that results from being the first into a marketplace with a serviceable product or service. If first movers develop a loyal following or a unique interface that is difficult to imitate, they can sustain their first-mover advantage for long periods (Arthur, 1996). Amazon provides a good example. However, in the history of technology-driven business innovation, most first movers lack the **complimentary resources** needed to sustain their advantages, and often follower firms reap the largest rewards (Rigdon, 2000; Teece, 1986). Indeed, many of the success stories we discuss in this book are those of companies that were slow followers—businesses that gained knowledge from failure of pioneering firms and entered into the market late.

complimentary resources
resources and assets not directly involved in the production of the product but required for success, such as marketing, management, financial assets, and reputation

unfair competitive advantage
occurs when one firm develops an advantage based on a factor that other firms cannot purchase

Some competitive advantages are called "unfair." An **unfair competitive advantage** occurs when one firm develops an advantage based on a factor that other firms cannot purchase (Barney, 1991). For instance, a brand name cannot be purchased and is in that sense an "unfair" advantage. As we will discuss in Chapter 6, brands are built upon loyalty, trust, reliability, and quality. Once obtained, they are difficult to copy or imitate, and they permit firms to charge premium prices for their products.

In **perfect markets**, there are no competitive advantages or asymmetries because all firms have access to all the factors of production (including information and knowledge) equally. However, real markets are imperfect, and asymmetries leading to competitive advantages do exist, at least in the short term. Most competitive advantages are short term, although some—such as the competitive advantage enjoyed by Coca-Cola because of the Coke brand name—can be sustained for very long periods. But not forever: Coke is increasingly being challenged by fruit, health, and unique flavor drinks.

Companies are said to **leverage** their competitive assets when they use their competitive advantages to achieve more advantage in surrounding markets. For instance, Amazon's move into the online grocery business leverages the company's huge customer database and years of e-commerce experience.

perfect market
a market in which there are no competitive advantages or asymmetries because all firms have equal access to all the factors of production

leverage
when a company uses its competitive advantages to achieve more advantage in surrounding markets

Market Strategy

No matter how tremendous a firm's qualities, its marketing strategy and execution are often just as important. The best business concept, or idea, will fail if it is not properly marketed to potential customers.

Everything you do to promote your company's products and services to potential customers is known as marketing. **Market strategy** is the plan you put together that details exactly how you intend to enter a new market and attract new customers.

Part of FreshDirect's strategy, for instance, is to develop close supply chain partnerships with growers and manufacturers so it purchases goods at lower prices directly from the source. This helps FreshDirect lower its prices for consumers. By partnering with suppliers that could benefit from FreshDirect's access to consumers, FreshDirect is attempting to extend its competitive advantages.

YouTube and PhotoBucket have a social network marketing strategy which encourages users to post their content on the sites for free, build personal profile pages, contact their friends, and build a community. In these cases, the customer is the marketing staff!

market strategy
the plan you put together that details exactly how you intend to enter a new market and attract new customers

Organizational Development

Although many entrepreneurial ventures are started by one visionary individual, it is rare that one person alone can grow an idea into a multi-million dollar company. In most cases, fast-growth companies—especially e-commerce businesses—need employees and a set of business procedures. In short, all firms—new ones in particular—need an organization to efficiently implement their business plans and strategies. Many e-commerce firms and many traditional firms who attempt an e-commerce strategy have failed because they lacked the organizational structures and supportive cultural values required to support new forms of commerce (Kanter, 2001).

Companies that hope to grow and thrive need to have a plan for **organizational development** that describes how the company will organize the work that needs to be accomplished. Typically, work is divided into functional departments, such as production, shipping, marketing, customer support, and finance. Jobs within these functional areas are defined, and then recruitment begins for specific job titles and

organizational development
plan describes how the company will organize the work that needs to be accomplished

responsibilities. Typically, in the beginning, generalists who can perform multiple tasks are hired. As the company grows, recruiting becomes more specialized. For instance, at the outset, a business may have one marketing manager. But after two or three years of steady growth, that one marketing position may be broken down into seven separate jobs done by seven individuals.

For instance, eBay founder Pierre Omidyar started an online auction site, according to some sources, to help his girlfriend trade PEZ dispensers with other collectors, but within a few months the volume of business had far exceeded what he alone could handle. So he began hiring people with more business experience to help out. Soon the company had many employees, departments, and managers who were responsible for overseeing the various aspects of the organization.

Management Team

management team

employees of the company responsible for making the business model work

Arguably, the single most important element of a business model is the **management team** responsible for making the model work. A strong management team gives a model instant credibility to outside investors, immediate market-specific knowledge, and experience in implementing business plans. A strong management team may not be able to salvage a weak business model, but the team should be able to change the model and redefine the business as it becomes necessary.

Eventually, most companies get to the point of having several senior executives or managers. How skilled managers are, however, can be a source of competitive advantage or disadvantage. The challenge is to find people who have both the experience and the ability to apply that experience to new situations.

To be able to identify good managers for a business startup, first consider the kinds of experiences that would be helpful to a manager joining your company. What kind of technical background is desirable? What kind of supervisory experience is necessary? How many years in a particular function should be required? What job functions should be fulfilled first: marketing, production, finance, or operations? Especially in situations where financing will be needed to get a company off the ground, do prospective senior managers have experience and contacts for raising financing from outside investors?

CATEGORIZING E-COMMERCE BUSINESS MODELS: SOME DIFFICULTIES

There are many e-commerce business models, and more are being invented every day. The number of such models is limited only by the human imagination, and our list of different business models is certainly not exhaustive. However, despite the abundance of potential models, it is possible to identify the major generic types (and subtle variations) of business models that have been developed for the e-commerce arena and describe their key features. It is important to realize, however, that there is no one correct way to categorize these business models.

Our approach is to categorize business models according to the different e-commerce sectors—B2C, B2B, C2C, etc.—in which they are utilized. You will note, however, that fundamentally similar business models may appear in more than one sector. For example, the business models of online retailers (often called e-tailers) and e-distributors are quite similar. However, they are distinguished by the market focus of the sector in which they are used. In the case of e-tailers in the B2C sector, the business model focuses on sales to the individual consumer, while in the case of the e-distributor, the business model focuses on sales to another business.

The type of e-commerce technology involved can also affect the classification of a business model. M-commerce, for instance, refers to e-commerce conducted over wireless networks. The e-tail business model, for instance, can also be used in m-commerce, and while the basic business model may remain fundamentally the same as that used in the B2C sector, it will nonetheless have to be adapted to the special challenges posed by the m-commerce environment.

Finally, you will also note that some companies use multiple business models. For instance, eBay can be considered as a B2C market maker. At the same time, eBay can also be considered as having a C2C business model. If eBay adopts wireless mobile computing, allowing customers to bid on auctions from their cell phone or wireless Web devices, then eBay may also be described as having a B2C m-commerce business model. We can expect many companies will have closely related B2C, B2B, and m-commerce variations on their basic business model. The purpose will be to leverage investments and assets developed with one business model into a new business model.

2.2   MAJOR BUSINESS-TO-CONSUMER (B2C) BUSINESS MODELS

Business-to-consumer (B2C) e-commerce, in which online businesses seek to reach individual consumers, is the most well-known and familiar type of e-commerce. **Table 2.3** illustrates the major business models utilized in the B2C arena.

PORTAL

Portals such as Yahoo, MSN/Windows Live, and AOL offer users powerful Web search tools as well as an integrated package of content and services, such as news, e-mail, instant messaging, calendars, shopping, music downloads, video streaming, and more, all in one place. Initially, portals sought to be viewed as "gateways" to the Internet. Today, however, the portal business model is to be a destination site. They are marketed as places where consumers will want to start their Web searching and hopefully stay a long time to read news, find entertainment, and meet other people (think of destination resorts). Portals do not sell anything directly—or so it seems—and in that sense they can present themselves as unbiased. The market opportunity is very large: In 2008, about 173 million people in the United States had access to the Internet at work or home (eMarketer, Inc., 2008a). Portals generate revenue primarily by charging advertisers for ad placement, collecting referral fees for steering customers to other sites, and charging for premium services. AOL, MSN (in conjunction with Verizon), and Yahoo (in conjunction with AT&T)—which in addition to being portals are also Internet Service Providers (ISPs) that provide access to the Internet and the Web—add an additional revenue stream: monthly subscription fees for access.

Although there are numerous portal/search engine sites, the top five sites (Google, Yahoo, MSN/Windows Live, AOL, and Ask.com) gather more than 95% of the search engine traffic because of their superior brand recognition (Nielsen Online,

portal
offers users powerful Web search tools as well as an integrated package of content and services all in one place

TABLE 2.3	B2C BUSINESS MODELS			
BUSINESS MODEL	VARIATIONS	EXAMPLES	DESCRIPTION	REVENUE MODEL
Portal	Horizontal/General	Yahoo AOL MSN	Offers an integrated package of content and content-search, services news, e-mail, chat, music downloads, video streaming, calendars, etc. Seeks to be a user's home base	Advertising, subscription fees, transaction fees
	Vertical/Specialized (Vortal)	Sailnet	Offers services and products to specialized marketplace	Same
	Search	Google Ask.com	Focuses primarily on offering search services	Advertising, affiliate referral
	Virtual Merchant	Amazon	Online version of retail store, where customers can shop at any hour of the day or night without leaving their home or office	Sales of goods
	Bricks-and-clicks	Walmart.com Sears.com	Online distribution channel for a company that also has physical stores	Same
	Catalog Merchant	LLBean.com LillianVernon.com	Online version of direct mail catalog	Same
	Manufacturer-direct	Dell.com Mattel.com Sony.com	Manufacturer uses online channel to sell direct to customer	Same
Content Provider		WSJ.com Sportline.com CNN.com ESPN.com RealRhapsody	Information and entertainment providers such as newspapers, sports sites, and other online sources that offer customers up-to-date news and special interest how-to guidance and tips and/or information sales	Advertising, subscription fees, affiliate referral fees
Transaction Broker		E-Trade Expedia Monster Travelocity Hotels.com Orbitz	Processors of online sales transactions, such as stockbrokers and travel agents, that increase customers' productivity by helping them get things done faster and more cheaply	Transaction fees
Market Creator		eBay Priceline	Web-based businesses that use Internet technology to create markets that bring buyers and sellers together	Transaction fees
Service Provider		VisaNow.com xDrive.com Linklaters BlueFlag	Companies that make money by selling users a service, rather than a product	Sales of services
Community Provider		iVillage Friendster MySpace Facebook About.com	Sites where individuals with particular interests, hobbies, common experiences, or social networks can come together and "meet" online	Advertising, subscription, affiliate referral fees

2008). Many of the top sites were among the first to appear on the Web and therefore had first-mover advantages. Being first confers advantage because customers come to trust a reliable provider and experience switching costs if they change to late arrivals in the market. By garnering a large chunk of the marketplace, first-movers—just like a single telephone network—can offer customers access to commonly shared ideas, standards, and experiences (something called *network externalities* that we describe in later chapters).

Yahoo, AOL, MSN/Windows Live, and others like them are considered to be horizontal portals because they define their marketspace to include all users of the Internet. Vertical portals (sometimes called vortals) attempt to provide similar services as horizontal portals, but are focused around a particular subject matter or market segment. For instance, Sailnet specializes in the consumer sailboat market that contains about 8 million Americans who own or rent sailboats. Although the total number of vortal users may be much lower than the number of portal users, if the market segment is attractive enough, advertisers are willing to pay a premium in order to reach a targeted audience. Also, visitors to specialized niche vortals spend more money than the average Yahoo visitor. Google and Ask.com can also be considered portals of a sort, but currently focus primarily on offering search services. They generate revenues primarily from search engine advertising sales and also from affiliate referral fees. For more information, see *Insight on Technology: Search, Ads, and Apps: the Future for Google (and Microsoft)*.

E-TAILER

Online retail stores, often called **e-tailers**, come in all sizes, from giant Amazon to tiny local stores that have Web sites. E-tailers are similar to the typical bricks-and-mortar storefront, except that customers only have to connect to the Internet to check their inventory and place an order. Some e-tailers, which are referred to as "bricks-and-clicks," are subsidiaries or divisions of existing physical stores and carry the same products. JCPenney, Barnes & Noble, Wal-Mart, and Staples are four examples of companies with complementary online stores. Others, however, operate only in the virtual world, without any ties to physical locations. Amazon, BlueNile.com, and Drugstore.com are examples of this type of e-tailer. Several other variations of e-tailers—such as online versions of direct mail catalogs, online malls, and manufacturer-direct online sales—also exist (Gulati and Garino, 2000).

e-tailer
online retail store

Given that the overall retail market in the United States in 2008 is estimated to be around $4 trillion, the market opportunity for e-tailers is very large (U.S. Census Bureau, Economic and Statistics Administration, 2008). Every Internet user is a potential customer. Customers who feel time-starved are even better prospects, since they want shopping solutions that will eliminate the need to drive to the mall or store (Bellman, Lohse, and Johnson, 1999). The e-tail revenue model is product-based, with customers paying for the purchase of a particular item.

This sector is extremely competitive, however. Since **barriers to entry** (the total cost of entering a new marketplace) into the Web e-tail market are low, tens of thousands of small e-tail shops have sprung up on the Web. Becoming profitable and surviving is very difficult, however, for e-tailers with no prior brand name or experi-

barriers to entry
the total cost of entering a new marketplace

INSIGHT ON TECHNOLOGY

SEARCH, ADS, AND APPS: THE FUTURE FOR GOOGLE (AND MICROSOFT)

When the Web was first invented, no one envisaged that by 2008 online search would grow to a more than $10 billion dollar business. In fact, early pundits thought that online search would be a commodity business, at best a small niche player in e-commerce. But in 2008, with paid search spending comprising more than 40% of the U.S. online advertising market, and paid search ad spending growing at around 20% a year over the past several years, the search engine market is booming, along with the larger Internet advertising marketplace now estimated at about $26 billion. About 85% of Internet users in the United States use a search engine at least once during a month. The top ten search engines in May 2008 conducted an estimated 7.8 billion searches, an average of about 250 million a day. No one knows the ultimate demand for search on the Web, but as the cost (both in terms of money and time) of searching declines, and the power of search engines increases, it is now apparent that search will be a major Web-based industry driven in large part by advances in technology. What is less apparent is who exactly will dominate this marketspace and what role technology (as opposed to marketing muscle or economics) will play in the ultimate outcome. Where's the money in search? A related question is how many search engines will remain when the competition is over.

Today, five Web sites account for over 95% of all Web searches: Google (59.3%), Yahoo (16.9%), MSN/Windows Live Search (13.3%), AOL (4.1%), and Ask.com (2.1%). The real powerhouses of search are Google and Yahoo, which provide over 75% of all searches. Microsoft unveiled its own proprietary search technology in February 2005, and has made some progress at the expense of Yahoo and Ask.com.

AOL does not have an independent search capability but instead purchases all of its search results and online ads from Google.

Of these firms, Google stands out as the only "pure" search engine for which search is the major line of business, whereas the other firms are either content portals (Yahoo and AOL) or, in the case of Microsoft, the provider of 95% of the world's desktop computer operating systems. In 2004, Google became a public company, greatly expanding its capital foundation to support further growth. Google's securities filings with the Securities and Exchange Commission show just how profitable the search business has become. In 2007, Google reported revenue of $16.6 billion, 99% of which it derived from various forms of search-based advertising. Google's net income (profit) was $4.2 billion. While Google started out as a search company with unique technology as the basis of its business model, search and search engine advertising growth have started to slow somewhat (from 100% annual increases, to 20% in 2007, and an estimated 15% in 2011). In response, Google is turning into a three-play company: search, advertising, and apps (applications).

Leadership in the search engine industry has changed hands several times. In the first round of the search engine wars, the original keyword search engines such as Alta Vista were replaced by Google, which claimed to possess superior technology, and Yahoo, which offered content, not just search. In the second round, an upstart firm named GoTo.com exploded onto the scene and created the marketplace for paid placement on search engines. Rather than be at the mercy of obscure search engine ranking rules, pay-for-placement allowed firms to pay for

(continued)

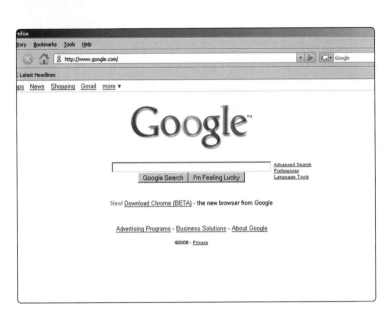

most important criteria for ranking pages, as well as the page content. The more other Web pages link to a particular page, the higher it jumps in Google's ranking structure called Page-Rank. This is called "link analysis" and is run independently of the query being made. Once all the Web's indexed pages are ranked, Google also factors in other information, such as the text content of a page, its link structure, proximity of search words to one another on the page, fonts, heading, and text of nearby pages. The company uses a number of software algorithms to carry out each search, drawing on the power of an undisclosed number of servers (rumored to be anywhere from 100,000 to 450,000) located in server "farms" throughout the world. Some people believe Google has the largest computing system in the world.

It is unclear if Google can maintain its technological edge in search given the investments being made by both Yahoo and Microsoft, as well as the proliferation of several other smaller but popular search engines such as AOL (4% of searches) and Ask.com (2% of searches). The original PageRank patent is owned by Stanford University, where it was created, and expires in 2017. Larry Page and Sergey Brin have an exclusive license until 2011, after which time their license is not exclusive. The validity of that patent has not been tested and there are ways to design around it. The concept of analyzing a social network, and ranking the "influence of participants" in terms of who receives and sends the most

a top ranking, and then pay only when they received a click. GoTo.com grew to become Overture.com and in a few years equaled the size of Google. Overture was purchased by Yahoo in 2003.

Google achieved its early and powerful lead in the search business through superior software technology, a highly efficient computer hardware architecture, and excellent Web site design. Google was started in 1998 by two enterprising Stanford grad students, Sergey Brin and Larry Page, who were studying data mining and the process of analyzing data for patterns. That research later became the basis of their business, Google, which can search millions of Web pages in less than a second. Early search engines like Alta Vista (which once had 90% of the search market) merely counted how many times a search term appeared on a given Web page to determine where to rank a particular page. If you searched on "iPhone," Alta Vista would show you pages ranked in terms of the number of times the Web site's home page, and other pages, contained the word "iPhone." Google's search, on the other hand, uses the popularity of Web pages as the

(continued)

communications (links) is hardly original to Google, but instead was a basic insight of sociologists in the 1950s who studied communities as social networks. In the competition among search engines, it is clear that search alone is not the key ingredient, just the foundation for the winning hand. It's a necessary but not sufficient condition for success.

Google's strategy has been to extend its advantages in search into two areas and try to "out-invent" the competition. These new areas are advertising and applications: in the words of CEO Eric Schmidt, Google is all about "search, ads, and apps." It has extended search to include images, books, scholars, content, finance, and news. It has extended its advertising services through its AdWords and AdSense programs. AdWords is an auction program that allows advertisers to bid for placement on Google pages. AdSense allows Google to place ads on publisher Web sites (basically any Web site is a "publisher" Web site) based on the content of that site's Web pages. Other services include Google Geo (maps, Earth, and local content), and Google Checkout (an online wallet).

Google is also starting to push into Microsoft's territory in the applications market. Google's applications include Gmail, Docs and Spreadsheets, Calendar, Groups, Orkut (a social networking environment), and Blogger. In case you've missed the last two decades, most of these are "Office" applications where Microsoft currently has a near monopoly. Where to put Google's $1.65 billion purchase of YouTube? Wall Street analysts have had a tough time with this question too. YouTube is all three: it's an online application for storing and sharing videos; it's a search system for videos; and it's an advertiser's dream come true: according to comScore, nearly 80 million users watched more than 3 billion user posted videos in January 2008.

While Google's software applications may be popular, they have not yet turned into big money makers, and Microsoft still "owns" 95% of the world's PC office environment. Almost all (99%) of Google's revenue still comes from search and advertising (including AdWords and AdSense). And while Microsoft has invested billions developing its own search engine, so far it has gained only at the expense of AOL and Ask.com, and seems stuck at about 13%-14% of the market (an improvement over previous years when it was below 10%). Google has increased its share of search a bit to 53% from 51%.

In a "life imitates art" moment, both companies purchased advertising networks to help target banner ads within a month of one another. Google bought DoubleClick for $3.1 billion in April 2007, and Microsoft protested the purchase to the Department of Justice as "anti-competitive." A month later, Microsoft bought aQuantive for $6 billion, the largest purchase in Microsoft history. Earlier in 2006, it bought in-game advertising pioneer Massive Inc. There's just no shame among monopolists and oligopolists!

The future portends an expensive battle among the world's largest Internet technology titans for control of search, advertising, and applications on your PC. Stay tuned.

■ **SOURCES**: "Nielsen Online Announces May U.S. Search Share Rankings," Nielsen Online, June 19, 2008; eMarketer, Inc., "US Online Advertising: Resilient in a Rough Economy," by David Hallerman, March 2008; Google Inc. Form 10-K for the year ended December 31, 2007 filed with the Securities and Exchange Commission, February 15, 2008; "YouTube Looks for the Money Clip," by Yi-Wyn Yen, *Fortune*, March 25, 2008; "Google Keeps Tweaking Its Search Engine," by Saul Hansell, *New York Times*, June 3,2007; "Out of Chaos, Order. Or So Google Says," by Miguel Helft, *New York Times*, May 11, 2007; "Is Google Too Powerful," by Rob Hof, *BusinessWeek*, April 9, 2007; "Google Looks To Boost Ads with YouTube," by Kevin Delaney, *New York Times*, October 10, 2006.

ence. The e-tailer's challenge is differentiating its business from existing stores and Web sites.

Companies that try to reach every online consumer are likely to deplete their resources quickly. Those that develop a niche strategy, clearly identifying their target market and its needs, are best prepared to make a profit. Keeping expenses low, selection broad, and inventory controlled are keys to success in e-tailing, with inventory being the most difficult to gauge. Online retail is covered in more depth in Chapter 9.

CONTENT PROVIDER

Although there are many different ways the Internet can be useful, "information content," which can be defined broadly to include all forms of intellectual property, is one of the largest types of Internet usage. **Intellectual property** refers to all forms of human expression that can be put into a tangible medium such as text, CDs, or the Web (Fisher, 1999). **Content providers** distribute information content, such as digital video, music, photos, text, and artwork, over the Web. According to the Online Publishers Association, in 2005, U.S. consumers spent $2 billion for online content (Online Publishers Association, 2006). Since then, digital music, movies, and television have become an increasingly important part of the market, and are expected to generate over $3.6 billion in revenues alone during 2008 (eMarketer, Inc. 2007b; 2007c; author estimates).

Content providers make money by charging a subscription fee. For instance, in the case of Real.com's Rhapsody Unlimited service, a monthly subscription fee provides users with access to thousands of song tracks. Other content providers, such as WSJ.com (*The Wall Street Journal's* online newspaper), *Harvard Business Review*, and many others, charge customers for content downloads in addition to or in place of a subscription fee. Micropayment systems technology provides content providers with a cost-effective method for processing high volumes of very small monetary transactions (anywhere from $.25 to $5.00 per transaction). Micropayment systems have greatly enhanced the revenue model prospects of content providers who wish to charge by the download.

Of course, not all online content providers charge for their information: just look at Sportsline.com, CIO.com, CNN.com, and the online versions of many newspapers and magazines. Users can access news and information at these sites without paying a cent. These popular sites make money in other ways, such as through advertising and partner promotions on the site. Increasingly, however, "free content" is limited to headlines and text, whereas premium content—in-depth articles or video delivery—is sold for a fee.

Generally, the key to becoming a successful content provider is owning the content. Traditional owners of copyrighted content—publishers of books and newspapers, broadcasters of radio and television content, music publishers, and movie studios—have powerful advantages over newcomers to the Web who simply offer distribution channels and must pay for content, often at oligopolistic prices.

Some content providers, however, do not own content, but syndicate (aggregate) and then distribute content produced by others. *Syndication* is a major variation of the

intellectual property
refers to all forms of human expression that can be put into a tangible medium such as text, CDs, or the Web

content provider
distributes information content, such as digital news, music, photos, video, and artwork, over the Web

standard content provider model. Another variation here is Web aggregators, who collect information from a wide variety of sources and then add value to that information through post-aggregation services. For instance, Shopping.com collects information on the prices of thousands of goods online, analyzes the information, and presents users with tables showing the range of prices and Web locations. Shopping.com adds value to content it aggregates, and re-sells this value to advertisers who advertise on its site (Madnick and Siegel, 2001).

Any e-commerce startup that intends to make money by providing content is likely to face difficulties unless it has a unique information source that others cannot access. For the most part, this business category is dominated by traditional content providers.

Online content is discussed in further depth in Chapter 10.

TRANSACTION BROKER

transaction broker
site that processes transactions for consumers that are normally handled in person, by phone, or by mail

Sites that process transactions for consumers normally handled in person, by phone, or by mail are **transaction brokers**. The largest industries using this model are financial services, travel services, and job placement services. The online transaction broker's primary value propositions are savings of money and time. In addition, most transaction brokers provide timely information and opinions. Sites such as Monster.com offer job searchers a national marketplace for their talents and employers a national resource for that talent. Both employers and job seekers are attracted by the convenience and currency of information. Online stock brokers charge commissions that are considerably less than traditional brokers, with many offering substantial deals, such as cash and a certain number of free trades, to lure new customers (Bakos, Lucas, et al., 2000).

Given rising consumer interest in financial planning and the stock market, the market opportunity for online transaction brokers appears to be large. However, while millions of customers have shifted to online brokers, many have been wary about switching from their traditional broker who provides personal advice and a brand name. Fears of privacy invasion and the loss of control over personal financial information also contribute to market resistance. Consequently, the challenge for online brokers is to overcome consumer fears by emphasizing the security and privacy measures in place, and, like physical banks and brokerage firms, providing a broad range of financial services and not just stock trading. This industry is covered in greater depth in Chapter 9.

Transaction brokers make money each time a transaction occurs. Each stock trade, for example, nets the company a fee, based either on a flat rate or a sliding scale related to the size of the transaction. Attracting new customers and encouraging them to trade frequently are the keys to generating more revenue for these companies. Job sites generate listing fees from employers up front, rather than charging a fee when a position is filled.

Competition among brokers has become more fierce in the past few years, due to new entrants offering ever more appealing offers to consumers to sign on. Those who prospered initially were the first movers such as E*Trade, Ameritrade, Datek, and Schwab. During the early days of e-commerce, many of these firms engaged in expensive marketing campaigns and were willing to pay up to $400 to acquire a single customer. However, online brokerages are now in direct competition with traditional brokerage firms who have joined the online marketspace. Significant consolidation is occurring in this industry. The number of job sites has also multiplied, but the largest sites (those with the largest number of job listings) are pulling ahead of smaller niche companies. In both industries, only a few, very large firms are likely to survive in the long term.

MARKET CREATOR

Market creators build a digital environment in which buyers and sellers can meet, display products, search for products, and establish prices. Prior to the Internet and the Web, market creators relied on physical places to establish a market. Beginning with the medieval marketplace and extending to today's New York Stock Exchange, a market has meant a physical space for transacting. There were few private digital network marketplaces prior to the Web. The Web changed this by making it possible to separate markets from physical space. A prime example is Priceline, which allows consumers to set the price they are willing to pay for various travel accommodations and other products (sometimes referred to as a reverse auction) and eBay, the online auction site utilized by both businesses and consumers.

For example, eBay's auction business model is to create a digital electronic environment for buyers and sellers to meet, agree on a price, and transact. This is different from transaction brokers who actually carry out the transaction for their customers, acting as agents in larger markets. At eBay, the buyers and sellers are their own agents. Each sale on eBay nets the company a commission based on the percentage of the item's sales price, in addition to a listing fee. eBay is one of the few Web sites that has been profitable virtually from the beginning. Why? One answer is that eBay has no inventory or production costs. It is simply a middleman.

The market opportunity for market creators is potentially vast, but only if the firm has the financial resources and marketing plan to attract sufficient sellers and buyers to the marketplace. At the end of June 2008, eBay had about 84.5 million active users, and this makes for an efficient market (eBay, 2008). There are many sellers and buyers for each type of product, sometimes for the same product, for example, laptop computer models. New firms wishing to create a market require an aggressive branding and awareness program to attract a sufficient critical mass of customers. Some very large Web-based firms such as Amazon have leveraged their large customer base and started auctions. Many other digital auctions have sprung up in smaller, more specialized vertical market segments such as jewelry and automobiles.

In addition to marketing and branding, a company's management team and organization can make a difference in creating new markets, especially if some managers have had experience in similar businesses. Speed is often the key in such situations. The ability to become operational quickly can make the difference between success and failure.

market creator
builds a digital environment where buyers and sellers can meet, display products, search for products, and establish a price for products

SERVICE PROVIDER

While e-tailers sell products online, **service providers** offer services online. There's been an explosion in online services that is often unrecognized. Web 2.0 applications such as photo sharing, video sharing, and user-generated content (in blogs and social networking sites) are all services provided to customers. Google has led the way in developing online applications such as Google Maps, Google Docs and Spreadsheets, and Gmail. ThinkFree and Buzzword are online alternatives to Microsoft Word provided as services (rather than boxed software—a product). More personal services such as online medical bill management, financial and pension planning, and travel recommender sites are showing strong growth.

Service providers use a variety of revenue models. Some charge a fee, or monthly subscriptions, while others generate revenue from other sources, such as through advertising and by collecting personal information that is useful in direct marketing. Some services are free but are not complete. For instance, Google Apps' basic edition is free, but a "Premier" model with virtual conference rooms and advanced tools costs $50 per employee a year. Much like retailers who trade products for cash, service providers trade knowledge, expertise, and capabilities, for revenue.

Obviously, some services cannot be provided online. For example, dentistry, medical services, plumbing, and car repair cannot be completed via the Internet. However, online arrangements can be made for these services. Online service providers may offer computer services, such as information storage, provide legal services, such as at Linklaters BlueFlag, or offer advice and services to high-net worth individuals, such as at MyCFO.com. Grocery shopping sites such as FreshDirect and Peapod are also providing services.[1] To complicate matters a bit, most financial transaction brokers (described previously) provide services such as college tuition and pension planning. Travel brokers also provide vacation-planning services, not just transactions with airlines and hotels. Indeed, mixing services with your products is a powerful business strategy pursued by many hard-goods companies (for example, warranties are services).

The basic value proposition of service providers is that they offer consumers valuable, convenient, time-saving, and low-cost alternatives to traditional service providers or—in the case of search engines and most Web 2.0 applications—they provide services that are truly unique to the Web. Where else can you search 50 billion Web pages, or share photos with as many other people instantly? Research has found, for instance, that a major factor in predicting online buying behavior is *time starvation*. Time-starved people tend to be busy professionals who work long hours and simply do not have the time to pick up packages, buy groceries, send photos, or visit with financial planners (Bellman, Lohse, and Johnson, 1999). The market opportunity for service providers is as large as the variety of services that can be provided and potentially is much larger than the market opportunity for physical goods. We live in a service-based economy and society; witness the growth of fast food restaurants, package delivery services, and wireless cellular phone services. Consumers'

---

[1]FreshDirect and other e-commerce businesses can also be classified as online retailers insofar as they warehouse commonly purchased items and make a profit based on the spread between their buy and sell prices.

increasing demand for convenience products and services bodes well for current and future online service providers.

Marketing of service providers must allay consumer fears about hiring a vendor online, as well as build confidence and familiarity among current and potential customers. Building confidence and trust is critical for service providers just as it is for retail product merchants. Kodak, for instance, has a powerful brand name over a century old, and has translated that brand into a trusted online provider of photo services. In the process, Kodak is transforming itself from a products-only company (cameras and paper) into a more contemporary digital services company.

COMMUNITY PROVIDER

Although community providers are not a new entity, the Internet has made such sites for like-minded individuals to meet and converse much easier, without the limitations of geography and time to hinder participation. **Community providers** are sites that create a digital online environment where people with similar interests can transact (buy and sell goods); share interests, photos, videos; communicate with like-minded people; receive interest-related information; and even play out fantasies by adopting online personalities called avatars. The social networking sites MySpace, Facebook, Friendster, and hundreds of other smaller, niche sites such as Doostang, Twitter, and Sportsvite, all offer users community building tools and services.

The basic value proposition of community providers is to create a fast, convenient, one-stop site where users can focus on their most important concerns and interests, share the experience with friends, and learn more about their own interests. Community providers typically rely on a hybrid revenue model that includes subscription fees, sales revenues, transaction fees, affiliate fees, and advertising fees from other firms that are attracted by a tightly focused audience.

Community sites such as iVillage make money through affiliate relationships with retailers and from advertising. For instance, a parent might visit Babystyle for tips on diapering a baby and be presented with a link to Huggies.com; if the parent clicks the link and then makes a purchase from Huggies.com, Babystyle gets a commission. Likewise, banner ads also generate revenue. At About.com, visitors can share tips and buy recommended books from Amazon, giving About.com a commission on every purchase. Some of the oldest communities on the Web are Well.com, which provides a forum for technology and Internet-related discussions, and The Motley Fool (Fool.com), which provides financial advice, news, and opinions. The Well offers various membership plans ranging from $10 to $15 a month. Motley Fool supports itself through ads and selling products that start out "free" but turn into annual subscriptions.

Consumers' interest in communities is mushrooming. Community is, arguably, the fastest growing online activity. While many community sites have had a difficult time becoming profitable, over time many have succeeded. Newer community sites such as Facebook and MySpace may not be profitable at this time, but they are quickly developing advertising revenues as their main avenue of revenue. Both the very large social networking sites (MySpace and Facebook each have over 100 million profiles) as

community provider
sites that create a digital online environment where people with similar interests can transact (buy and sell goods); share interests, photos, and videos; communicate with like-minded people; and receive interest-related information

TABLE 2.4

BUSINESS
(1) NET M
E-distributor
E-procuremen
Exchange
Industry Cons
(2) PRIVA
Single firm
Industry-wide

E-PROCUREM
Just as e-distrib
and sell access
created softwar
mini-digital ma
(where supplie
Ariba helps ve
creation, shippi
to generically a
B2B servi
number of worl
ing firms a soph
firms to reduce
sometimes also

scale economies
efficiencies that arise from increasing the size of a business

firms much lower costs of software by achieving scale economies. **Scale economies** are efficiencies that result from increasing the size of a business, for instance, when large, fixed-cost production systems (such as factories or software systems) can be operated at full capacity with no idle time. In the case of software, the marginal cost of a digital copy of a software program is nearly zero, and finding additional buyers for an expensive software program is exceptionally profitable. This is much more efficient than having every firm build its own supply chain management system, and it permits firms such as Ariba to specialize and offer their software to firms at a cost far less than the cost of developing it.

EXCHANGES

exchange
an independent digital electronic marketplace where suppliers and commercial purchasers can conduct transactions

Exchanges have garnered most of the B2B attention and early funding because of their potential market size even though today they are a small part of the overall B2B picture. An **exchange** is an independent digital electronic marketplace where hundreds of suppliers meet a smaller number of very large commercial purchasers (Kaplan and Sawhney, 2000). Exchanges are owned by independent, usually entrepreneurial startup firms whose business is making a market, and they generate revenue by charging a commission or fee based on the size of the transactions conducted among trading parties. They usually serve a single vertical industry such as steel, polymers or aluminum, and focus on the exchange of direct inputs to production and short-term contracts or spot purchasing. For buyers, B2B exchanges make it possible to gather information, check out suppliers, collect prices, and keep up to date on the latest happenings all in one place. Sellers, on the other hand, benefit from expanded access to buyers. The greater the number of sellers and buyers, the lower the sales cost and the higher the chances of making a sale. The ease, speed, and volume of transactions are summarily referred to as *market liquidity*.

In theory, exchanges make it significantly less expensive and time-consuming to identify potential suppliers, customers and partners, and to do business with each other. As a result, they can lower transaction costs—the cost of making a sale or purchase. Exchanges can also lower product costs and inventory-carrying costs—the cost of keeping a product on hand in a warehouse. In reality, as discussed in Chapter 12, B2B exchanges have had a difficult time convincing thousands of suppliers to move into singular digital markets where they face powerful price competition, and an equally difficult time convincing businesses to change their purchasing behavior away from trusted long-term trading partners. As a result, the number of exchanges has fallen to less than 200, down from over 1,500 in 2002, although the surviving firms have experienced some success (Ulfelder, 2004; Day, Fein, Ruppersberger, 2003). Read *Insight on Business: Onvia Evolves* for a look at how a former B2B high flyer has evolved its business model in order to survive.

e-distributor
a company that products and s directly to indiv businesses

INDUSTRY CONSORTIA

industry consortia
industry-owned vertical marketplaces that serve specific industries

Industry consortia are industry-owned *vertical marketplaces* that serve specific industries, such as the automobile, aerospace, chemical, floral, or logging industries. In contrast, *horizontal marketplaces* sell specific products and services to a wide range of companies. Vertical marketplaces supply a smaller number of companies with products and services of specific interest to their industry, while horizontal marketplaces supply companies in different industries with a particular type of

INSIGHT ON BUSINESS

ONVIA EVOLVES

Few e-commerce start-ups reflect the nimble behavior of entrepreneurial firms better than Onvia. Founded in 1996 by Vancouver entrepreneur Glenn Ballman, Onvia started out as a market hub or exchange aimed at helping the 15 million small businesses in America shop for the best deals on products and services. Starting out at home, Ballman created a Web site where small businesses could buy and sell products, access small business information, and purchase business software. Originally called Megadepot.com, in 1998 Ballman moved to Seattle in part to attract venture capital funding, and renamed the company Onvia.com (in Latin, "on the road"). After several rounds of venture capital investment that accumulated to more than $71 million in 1999, Onvia went public in March 2000, at the offering price of $21, raising an addition $240 million.

By 2000, Onvia had over a million small business users, and thousands of suppliers, and also had built strategic relationships with Visa and AOL to build co-branded Web sites for the small business market. But the company remained unprofitable because, like so many other exchanges, it could not attract enough suppliers willing to compete against one another in an open

marketplace. This reduced the goods and services available in the marketplace and reduced trading volume. Because Onvia made money only when goods were exchanged, Onvia revenues never achieved a profitable level. By December 2000, Onvia had laid off over 200 employees, and its stock sank to $1, the delisting price for stocks on NASDAQ.

Not one to give up easily, founder Ballman initiated a recovery plan. He sold off Onvia's online purchasing of software, hardware, and business products to a competitor, Firstsource Corporation, retaining only the Onvia procurement network that matches buyers and sellers. Then the company completely switched markets from the small business service market to the government procurement and service market. In this new marketspace, Onvia planned to provide procurement services to local, state, and federal government agencies and feed sales leads to small businesses wanting to serve that market.

(continued)

In March 2001, Onvia purchased DemandStar Inc., a leading provider of buyer-side business-to-government platforms that had over 270 government agency subscribers. In June 2001, Onvia purchased ProjectGuides, the nation's largest online bid gathering and distribution service. This acquisition permitted the company to greatly increase the flow of bids from agencies into the marketplace. It also began compiling a proprietary database, called Onvia Dominion, that now contains 5 million procurement records, 275,000 vendor profiles, and coverage of more than 78,000 government purchasing offices nationwide. In 2005, the company introduced Onvia Business Builder, a business intelligence tool that allows companies to mine the Onvia Dominion database for information relevant to their business, and in 2006, added Onvia Navigator, an enhanced search tool for the database. In February 2008, Onvia launched yet another new product, Onvia Planning and Construction, which expands its solutions for the commercial and residential development market. Onvia makes money by charging clients a subscription fee for access to its products and services, by licensing its content to third parties who then resell the data, and by selling custom market information reports.

The changes in its business model have enabled Onvia to regain stability, although it is not yet profitable. During the period from 2002 to 2007, revenue almost tripled, from $7 million to over $20 million, and in 2007, Onvia recorded its first annual net profit.. As of June 2008, Onvia had approximately 8,100 clients with an annual contract value of approximately $18.2 million. According to Mike Pickett, Onvia's Chairman and Chief Executive Office, Onvia is very pleased with its progress. In 2008. Onvia jumped from 120th to 26th in the Seattle Times 2008 rankings of Northwest businesses. It appears that Onvia has finally discovered a viable business model. Onvia's stock currently sells in the $4–$6 range.

SOURCES: "About Onvia," Onvia.com, July 7, 2008; Onvia.com Inc. Form 10-Q for the quarter ended June 30, 2008, filed with the Securities and Exchange Commission on August 13, 2008; "Onvia's Quarterly Revenue Grows 10% Over Q1 2007," Onvia, Inc., April 29, 2008; Onvia.com Inc. Form 10-K for the fiscal year ended December 31, 2007, filed with the Securities and Exchange Commission on March 31, 2008.

product and service, such as marketing-related, financial, or computing services For example, Exostar is an online trading exchange for the aerospace and defense industry, founded by BAE Systems, Boeing, Lockheed Martin, Raytheon, and Rolls-Royce in 2000. Exostar connects with over 300 procurement systems in 20 different countries and has registered more than 40,000 trading partners worldwide.

Industry consortia have tended to be more successful than independent exchanges in part because they are sponsored by powerful, deep-pocketed industry players, and also because they strengthen traditional purchasing behavior rather than seek to transform it.

PRIVATE INDUSTRIAL NETWORKS

Private industrial networks (sometimes referred to as *private trading exchanges* or *PTXs*) constitute about 75% of all B2B expenditures by large firms and far exceed the expenditures for all forms of Net marketplaces. Private industrial networks are digital networks (often but not always Internet-based networks) designed to coordinate the flow of communications among firms engaged in business together. For instance, Wal-Mart operates one of the largest private industrial networks in the world for its suppliers, who on a daily basis use Wal-Mart's network to monitor the sales of their goods, the status of shipments, and the actual inventory level of their goods. B2B e-commerce relies overwhelmingly on a technology called electronic data interchange (EDI) (U.S. Census Bureau, 2008). EDI is useful for one-to-one relationships between a single supplier and a single purchaser, and originally was designed for proprietary networks, although it is migrating rapidly to the Internet. Many firms have begun to supplement their EDI systems, however, with more powerful Web technologies that can enable many-to-one, and many-to-many market relationships where there are many suppliers selling to a single or small group of very large purchasers, or, in the case of independent exchanges, there may be many sellers and many buyers simultaneously in the marketplace. EDI is not designed for these types of relationships. There are two types of private industrial networks: single-firm networks and industry-wide networks.

Single-firm private industrial networks are the most common form of private industrial network. These single-firm networks are owned by a single large purchasing firm, such as Wal-Mart or Procter & Gamble. Participation is by invitation only to trusted long-term suppliers of direct inputs. Single-firm networks typically evolve out of a firm's own enterprise resource planning system (ERP), and they are an effort to include key suppliers in the firm's own business decision making (eMarketer, Inc., 2004).

Industry-wide private industrial networks often evolve out of industry associations. These networks are usually owned by a consortium of the large firms in an industry and have the following goals: providing a neutral set of standards for commercial communication over the Internet; having shared and open technology platforms for solving industry problems; and in some cases, providing operating networks that allow members of an entire industry to closely collaborate. To some extent, these industry-wide networks are a response to the success of single-firm private industrial networks. For instance, Wal-Mart has refused to open its very successful network to other members of the retail industry, in effect to become an industry standard, for fear it will be sharing technology secrets with other retailers like Sears.

In response, Sears and other retailers around the world have created their own set of organizations and networks that are open to all in the industry. For instance, Agentrics is an industry-wide private industrial network for retailers and suppliers designed to facilitate and simplify trading among retailers, suppliers, partners, and distributors. Agentrics' members currently include more than half of the world's top 25 retailers and over 200 suppliers from Africa, Asia, Europe, North America, and South America, with combined sales of approximately $1.2 trillion. Agentrics provides collaborative design tools; planning and management; negotiations and auctions; order execution; demand

private industrial networks
digital network designed to coordinate the flow of communications among firms engaged in business together

aggregation; worldwide item management; worldwide logistics; and a global catalog in English, French, German, and Spanish containing trading relationship data for member-sponsored suppliers totaling more than 30,000 items (Agentrics LLC, 2008). From this list of services and capabilities, it is clear that industry-wide private industrial networks offer much more functionality than industry consortia, although the two models appear to be moving closer together (Gebauer and Zagler, 2000). We discuss these developments and other nuances of B2B commerce in Chapter 12.

2.4 BUSINESS MODELS IN EMERGING E-COMMERCE AREAS

When we think about a business, we typically think of a business firm that produces a product or good, and then sells it to a customer. But the Web has forced us to recognize new forms of business, such as consumer-to-consumer e-commerce, peer-to-peer e-commerce, and m-commerce. **Table 2.5** lists some of the business models that can be found in these emerging markets.

CONSUMER-TO-CONSUMER (C2C) BUSINESS MODELS

Consumer-to-consumer (C2C) ventures provide a way for consumers to sell to each other, with the help of an online business. The first and best example of this type of business is eBay, utilizing a market creator business model.

Before eBay, individual consumers used garage sales, flea markets, and thrift shops to both dispose of and acquire used merchandise. With the introduction of online auctions, consumers no longer had to venture out of their homes or offices in order to bid on items of interest, and sellers could relinquish expensive retail space that was no longer needed in order to reach buyers. In return for linking like-minded buyers and sellers, eBay takes a small commission. The more auctions, the more

TABLE 2.5	BUSINESS MODELS IN EMERGING E-COMMERCE AREAS		
BUSINESS	EXAMPLES	DESCRIPTION	REVENUE MODEL
Consumer-to-consumer	eBay Half.com	Helps consumers connect with other consumers to conduct business	Transaction fees
Peer-to-peer	Kazaa Cloudmark	Technology enabling consumers to share files and services via the Web, without a common server	Subscription fees, advertising, transaction fees
M-commerce	eBay Mobile PayPal Mobile Checkout AOL Moviefone	Extending business applications using wireless technology	Sales of goods and services

money eBay makes. In fact, it is one of the few Web companies that has been profitable from day one—and has stayed so for several years.

Consumers who don't like auctions but still want to find used merchandise can visit Half.com (also owned by eBay), which enables consumers to sell unwanted books, movies, music, and games to other consumers at a fixed price. In return for facilitating the transaction, Half.com takes a commission on the sale, ranging from 5%–15%, depending on the sale price, plus a fraction of the shipping fee it charges.

PEER-TO-PEER (P2P) BUSINESS MODELS

Like the C2C models, P2P business models link users, enabling them to share files and computer resources without a common server. The focus in P2P companies is on helping individuals make information available for anyone's use by connecting users on the Web. Historically, peer-to-peer software technology has been used to allow the sharing of copyrighted music files in violation of digital copyright law. The challenge for P2P ventures is to develop viable, legal business models that will enable them to make money. In Chapter 1, we discussed the difficulties faced by Kazaa, one of the most prominent examples of a P2P business model in action. To date, there are few if any examples of successful P2P e-commerce business models outside of the music and content file-swapping sites. However, one company that has successfully used this model outside those two arenas is Cloudmark, which offers a P2P anti-spam solution called Cloudmark Desktop. Cloudmark currently protects over 180 million e-mailboxes in 163 countries.

M-COMMERCE BUSINESS MODELS

M-commerce, short for *mobile-commerce*, takes traditional e-commerce models and leverages emerging new wireless technologies—described more fully in Chapter 3— to permit mobile access to the Web. Wireless Web technology will be used to enable the extension of existing Web business models to service the mobile work force and consumer of the future. Wireless networks utilize newly available bandwidth and communication protocols to connect mobile users to the Internet. These technologies have already taken off in Asia and Europe, and will expand greatly in the United States in a few years. The major advantage of m-commerce is that it provides Internet access to anyone, anytime, and anywhere, using wireless devices. The key technologies here are cell phone-based 3G (third-generation wireless), Wi-Fi (wireless local area networks), and Bluetooth (short-range radio frequency Web devices).

There are many more cell phone subscribers (an estimated 3 billion worldwide in 2008) than there are Internet users (TIA, 2008). Cell phone usage is still considerably higher in Asia and Europe than it is in the United States. However, in the United States, the introduction of the iPhone in June 2007 and the 3G version in July 2008 has brought about a resurgence of interest in 3G technologies and their potential role in e-commerce. The standards implementing Wi-Fi were first introduced in 1997, and since then it has exploded in the United States and elsewhere. Analysts estimate that there are around 225,000 wireless hot spots (locations that enable a Wi-Fi–enabled device to connect to a nearby wireless LAN and access the Internet) worldwide in 2008 (JiWire.com, 2008). Likewise, the number of Bluetooth-enabled cell phones is also expanding exponentially. For instance, 70% of all the cell phones sold the fourth quarter of 2007 in the United States supported Bluetooth. Two new wireless technologies that may have an impact are Ultrawideband (wireless USB technology), which will be able to transfer large files such as movies over short distances, and Zigbee, which, like Bluetooth, will connect devices to each other but at a longer range and with lower power requirements.

Despite all of the technological advancements in the last several years, mobile commerce in the United States has been a disappointment to date. According to a 2007 report, only 2% of the retail brands in the top 1,000 U.S. brands in 2007 operated a mobile Web site, and in many instances, they were used purely as a marketing and branding vehicle (Siwicki, 2007). However, with the introduction of the iPhone and other phones with similar capabilities, this has begun to change (**Figure 2.3**) and a September 2008 Internet Retailer survey found that almost 7% of Web retailers now have an m-commerce site (Brohan, 2008). The server-side hardware and software platform is in place, and the basic bandwidth is ready. As with all areas of e-commerce, the challenge for businesses will be finding ways to use m-commerce to make money while serving customer needs. Currently, demand is highest for digital content such as customized ringtones, games, and wallpaper. With the introduction of the iPhone, mobile search applications are likely to become more popular. Consumer applications are also beginning to appear in high-volume personal transaction areas,

| FIGURE 2.3 | APPLE iPHONE: INTERNET IN YOUR POCKET |

The Apple iPhone combines both cellular voice and Internet, as well as Wi-Fi local area network access to the Web. Over 3 million 3G iPhones were sold in the first month following its introduction in July 2008, and over 7 million regular iPhones have been sold in the United States since it was first introduced in June 2007.
SOURCE: Apple, Inc., 2008.

such as AOL's Moviefone reservation system, eBay's Mobile system, and mobile pay-ment platforms such as PayPal's Mobile Checkout.

M-commerce business models that hope to rely on push advertising, as described in *Insight on Society: Is Privacy Possible in a Wireless World?* also may face an uphill battle.

E-COMMERCE ENABLERS: THE GOLD RUSH MODEL

Of the nearly 500,000 miners who descended on California in the Gold Rush of 1849, less than 1% ever achieved significant wealth. However, the banking firms, shipping companies, hardware companies, real estate speculators, and clothing companies such as Levi Strauss built long-lasting fortunes. Likewise in e-commerce. No discus-sion of e-commerce business models would be complete without mention of a group of companies whose business model is focused on providing the infrastructure necessary for e-commerce companies to exist, grow, and prosper. These are the e-commerce enablers: the Internet infrastructure companies. They provide the hardware, operating system software, networks and communications technology, applications software, Web designs, consulting services, and other tools that make e-commerce over the Web possible (see **Table 2.6**). While these firms may not be conducting e-commerce per se (although in many instances, e-commerce in its traditional sense is in fact one of their sales channels), they as a group have perhaps profited the most from the development of e-commerce. We will discuss many of these players in the following chapters.

TABLE 2.6	E-COMMERCE ENABLERS
INFRASTRUCTURE	**PLAYERS**
Hardware: Web Servers	IBM, HP, Dell, Sun
Software: Operating Systems and Server Software	Microsoft, RedHat Linux, Sun, Apache Software Foundation
Networking: Routers	Cisco, JDS Uniphase, Lucent
Security: Encryption Software	VeriSign, Check Point, Entrust, RSA
E-commerce Software Systems (B2C, B2B)	IBM, Microsoft, Ariba, BroadVision, BEA Systems
Streaming and Rich Media Solutions	Real Networks, Microsoft, Apple, Audible
Customer Relationship Management Software	Oracle, SAP, E.piphany
Payment Systems	VeriSign, PayPal, Cybersource
Performance Enhancement	Akamai, Kontiki
Databases	Oracle, Microsoft, Sybase, IBM
Hosting Services	Interland, IBM, WebIntellects, Quest

INSIGHT ON SOCIETY

IS PRIVACY POSSIBLE IN A WIRELESS WORLD?

You're walking past the local Pizza Hut and your cell phone rings. Who's calling? No, it's not your significant other or a parent or friend. It's Pizza Hut. They just wanted to let you know that pizzas are on sale—two for one, until 6 P.M. today. Want to find out someone's address when you know the home phone number and then get a map to that location? Go to Google and enter that person's phone number. The top listing will provide you the name and address of the owner of that phone number. Click a button and you will get a map to the house or business. Google calls it PhoneBook, but it never asked you to join. You could opt out if you search hard enough. Or let's say you want to set up a wireless network in your house using Wi-Fi (short for an 802.11b radio network). Your neighbor will possibly be able to pick up your signals (and network traffic) if they are within 300 feet of your base station and "join" your network.

These scenarios are not far-fetched, but instead represent capabilities of existing technology. Some of these capabilities have benign or even humanitarian intentions. For instance, since October 2001, all cell phone providers are required to implement "E911" (Emergency 911), in which your cell phone's embedded GPS chips (global positioning system chips) can be tracked by emergency responders or law enforcement even if the phone is not turned on, and to automatically track the location of phones that are turned on. In true emergencies, these capabilities are helpful. If you are in an emergency and use your cell phone to call for help, authorities can find your location nearly instantly.

But while the primary goal of these wireless tracking capabilities is enhanced public safety, companies are already developing business models centered on applications that will allow them to exploit the technology. Called "location-based services," companies such as MapQuest work with local businesses to provide directions to restaurants, theaters, and other attractions over cell phones. And with around 255 million cell phone users in the United States today, there are significant business opportunities for telephone carriers, mapping services, and local businesses. In 2006, mobile advertising revenues totaled over $300 million and are expected to grow to over $2 billion by 2011.

Proposals for the creation of a "wireless 411" cell phone directory creates cause for even greater concern. For instance, in October 2006, TransUnion, one of the major credit bureau companies, acquired Qsent, which is developing a new wireless 411 service. According to TransUnion, Qsent's technology is ready to go whenever cell phone providers decide to enable it. The service would requires subscribers to opt-in in order for their number to be included in the directory. However, such protection does not apply to a new cell phone directory being compiled by Intelius, which is also in the business of selling background checks online for a fee. Intelius's directory, available for $15 per search, is based on data from marketing companies and public records.

The specter of more unsolicited, unwanted phone calls coupled with "Big Brother"-like location tracking has privacy advocates raising the alarm. "Developing wireless technology shows many indications of repeating two privacy disasters of the wired Internet—spam and nonconsensual tracking," said one privacy expert.

The wireless industry, mindful of the privacy issues raised in the online e-commerce context, has issued calls for stringent self-regulation in an attempt to avoid government-imposed regulation. For instance, the Mobile Marketing Association (MMA) has a Code of Conduct for wireless marketing campaigns, developed by an MMA board-appointed Privacy Advisory Committee

(continued)

whose members included Cingular Wireless, Procter & Gamble, and VeriSign, among others. The MMA has also established a wireless anti-spam committee. TRUSTe, a not-for-profit organization that operates an Internet privacy seal program, has Wireless Privacy Principles and Implementation Guidelines, drafted by a Wireless Advisory Committee that included TRUSTe, AT&T Wireless, Microsoft, HP, the MMA, the Wireless Location Industry Association, and various consumer advocacy groups such as the Center for Democracy and Technology. The guidelines cover such topics as notice, third-party sharing of personally identifiable information, and the use of location-based information. Under the guidelines, wireless service providers are encouraged to provide a full privacy statement to the consumer prior to or during the collection of personally identifiable information, or upon first use of a service. They should only disclose that information to a third party for uses unrelated to the provision of services if the consumer has provided "opt-in" consent prior to such use. Finally, the guidelines state that wireless service providers should only use location information for services other than those related to placing or receiving voice calls if consumers opt-in. According to Verizon Wireless spokesperson Jeffrey Nelson, "We are more concerned with maintaining the relationship with our customers than with someone who wants to use their location information."

And what about government regulation? The 2003 CAN-SPAM Act requires the Federal Communications Commission to issue rules to protect wireless subscribers from unwanted mobile service commercial messages, and provides that consumers can list their cell phone numbers in the National Do Not Call Registry. In August 2004, in accordance with the CAN-SPAM Act, the FCC proposed regulations, most of which went into effect in October 2004. The FCC prohibits sending wireless commercial e-mail messages unless the individual addressee has given the sender express prior authorization. The FCC also created a publicly available FCC wireless domain names list with the domain names used for mobile service messaging so that senders of commercial mail could more easily determine which addresses are directed at mobile services.

To date, wireless location-based services remain largely unregulated. The Wireless Communications and Public Safety Act (often called the "911 Act") added the term "location" to the definition of customer proprietary network information (CPNI) held by telecommunication carriers, to make it eligible for certain privacy protections offered by the Communications Act of 1934. The 911 Act also required that the FCC establish rules regarding how telecommunications carriers treat CPNI. The FCC did so in July 2002, adopting an approach that requires an individual's affirmative consent (opt-in) for some circumstances and assuming consent is granted unless an individual indicates otherwise (opt-out) in others. The Wireless Location Industry Association has also developed draft wireless policy standards for its members that combines an opt-in and out-out approach. Congress continues to debate how to protect wireless subscribers further, but thus far none have passed since CAN-SPAM in 2003. Will consumers be so enthralled with the idea of services tailored to their specific location that they won't mind being tracked? Privacy watchdogs don't think so and predict that any company whose business model is predicated on that assumption is underestimating the increasing sensitivity of the American public to privacy concerns.

■■■ **SOURCES**: "Cellphone Directory Grabs Your Number," by Tricia Duryee, *Seattle Times*, August 13, 2007; "US Mobile Advertising and Search Markets, " Frost & Sullivan, July 24, 2007; "World Telecommunication Indicators Database," International Telecommunication Union, June 2007; "Wireless Location Tracking Draws Privacy Questions," Anne Broache, C/Net News.com, May 17, 2006; "Wireless Privacy and Spam: Issues for Congress," by Marcia S. Smith, CRS Report for Congress, December 22, 2004; "FCC Seeks Comment on Rules to Eliminate Spam from Mobile Phones," Federal Communications Commission Press Release, FCC.gov, March 11, 2004; "TRUSTe Announces First Wireless Privacy Standards to Protect Mobile Users," TRUSTe Press Release, Truste.org,; "Mobile Marketing Association Releases Code of Conduct for Wireless Campaigns, " Mobile Marketing Association Press Release, Mmaglobal.com, December 2, 2003.

2.5 HOW THE INTERNET AND THE WEB CHANGE BUSINESS: STRATEGY, STRUCTURE, AND PROCESS

Now that you have a clear grasp of the variety of business models used by e-commerce firms, you also need to understand how the Internet and the Web have changed the business environment in the last decade, including industry structures, business strategies, and industry and firm operations (business processes and value chains). We will return to these concepts throughout the book as we explore the e-commerce phenomenon. In general, the Internet is an open standards system available to all players, and this fact inherently makes it easy for new competitors to enter the marketplace and offer substitute products or channels of delivery. The Internet tends to intensify competition. Because information becomes available to everyone, the Internet inherently shifts power to buyers who can quickly discover the lowest-cost provider on the Web. On the other hand, the Internet presents many new opportunities for creating value, for branding products and charging premium prices, and for enlarging an already powerful offline physical business such as Wal-Mart or Sears.

Recall Table 1.1 in Chapter 1 that describes the truly unique features of e-commerce technology. **Table 2.7** suggests some of the implications of each unique feature for the overall business environment—industry structure, business strategies, and operations.

INDUSTRY STRUCTURE

industry structue
refers to the nature of the players in an industry and their relative bargaining power

E-commerce changes industry structure, in some industries more than others. **Industry structure** refers to the nature of the players in an industry and their relative bargaining power. An industry's structure is characterized by five forces: *rivalry among existing competitors*, the *threat of substitute products, barriers to entry into the industry*, the *bargaining power of suppliers*, and the *bargaining power of buyers* (Porter, 1985). When you describe an industry's structure, you are describing the general business environment in an industry and the overall profitability of doing business in that environment. E-commerce has the potential to change the relative strength of these competitive forces (see **Figure 2.4** on page 100).

industry structural analysis
an effort to understand and describe the nature of competition in an industry, the nature of substitute products, the barriers to entry, and the relative strength of consumers and suppliers

When you consider a business model and its potential long-term profitability, you should always perform an industry structural analysis. An **industry structural analysis** is an effort to understand and describe the nature of competition in an industry, the nature of substitute products, the barriers to entry, and the relative strength of consumers and suppliers.

E-commerce can affect the structure and dynamics of industries in very different ways. Consider the recorded music industry, an industry that has experienced significant change because of the Internet and e-commerce. Historically, the major record label firms owned the exclusive rights to the recorded music of various artists. With the entrance into the marketplace of substitute providers such as Kazaa, millions of consumers began to use the Internet to bypass traditional music labels and their distributors entirely. In the travel industry, entirely new

TABLE 2.7	EIGHT UNIQUE FEATURES OF E-COMMERCE TECHNOLOGY
FEATURE	SELECTED IMPACTS ON BUSINESS ENVIRONMENT
Ubiquity	Alters industry structure by creating new marketing channels and expanding size of overall market. Creates new efficiencies in industry operations and lowers costs of firms' sales operations. Enables new differentiation strategies.
Global reach	Changes industry structure by lowering barriers to entry, but greatly expands market at same time. Lowers cost of industry and firm operations through production and sales efficiencies. Enables competition on global scope.
Universal standards	Changes industry structure by lowering barriers to entry and intensifying competition within an industry. Lowers costs of industry and firm operations by lowering computing and communications costs. Enables broad scope strategies.
Richness	Alters industry structure by reducing strength of powerful distribution channels. Changes industry and firm operations cost by reducing reliance on sales forces. Enhances post-sales support strategies.
Interactivity	Alters industry structure by reducing threat of substitutes through enhanced customization. Reduces industry and firm costs by reducing reliance on sales forces. Enables Web-based differentiation strategies.
Personalization/ customization	Alters industry structure by reducing threats of substitutes, raising barriers to entry. Reduces value chain costs in industry and firms by lessening reliance on sales forces. Enables personalized marketing strategies.
Information density	Changes industry structure by weakening powerful sales channels, shifting bargaining power to consumers. Reduces industry and firm operations costs by lowering costs of obtaining, processing, and distributing information about suppliers and consumers.
Social networking technologies	Changes industry structure by shifting programming and editorial decisions to consumers; creates substitute entertainment products; energizes a large group of new suppliers.

middlemen such as Travelocity have entered the market to compete with traditional travel agents. After Travelocity, Expedia, CheapTickets, and other travel services demonstrated the power of e-commerce marketing for airline tickets, the actual owners of the airline seats—the major airlines—banded together to form their own Internet outlet for tickets, Orbitz, for direct sales to consumers, potentially eliminating the middlemen entirely. Clearly, e-commerce and the Internet create *new industry dynamics* that can best be described as the give and take of the marketplace, the changing fortunes of competitors.

Yet in other industries, the Internet and e-commerce have strengthened existing players. In the chemical and automobile industries, e-commerce is being used effectively by manufacturers to strengthen their traditional distributors. In these industries, e-commerce technology has not fundamentally altered the competitive forces—bargaining power of suppliers, barriers to entry, bargaining power of buyers,

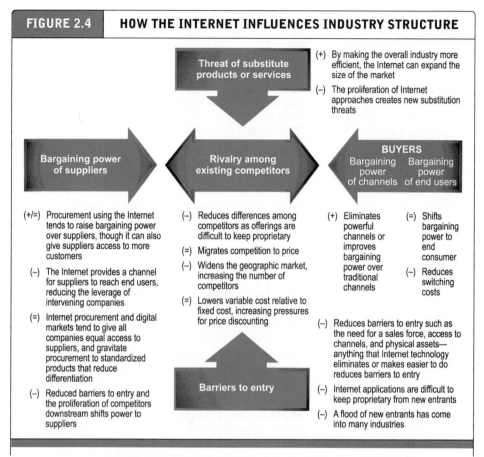

FIGURE 2.4 **HOW THE INTERNET INFLUENCES INDUSTRY STRUCTURE**

The Internet and e-commerce have many impacts on industry structure and competitive conditions. From the perspective of a single firm, these changes can have negative or positive implications. In this figure, "+" indicates a positive development for the firm, "−" a negative development, and "=" that neither positive nor negative impacts can be predicted. Each industry will be affected differently and must be analyzed separately. SOURCE: Porter, 2001.

threat of substitutes, or rivalry among competitors—within the industry. Hence, each industry is different and you need to examine each one carefully to understand the impacts of e-commerce on competition and strategy.

New forms of distribution created by new market entrants can completely change the competitive forces in an industry. For instance, if a software firm such as Microsoft discovers that consumers will gladly substitute a $50 or even free encyclopedia on a CD-ROM (a digital information product) for a $2,500 set of Britannica encyclopedias (a physical information product), then the competitive forces in the encyclopedia industry are radically changed. Even if the substitute is an inferior product, consumers are able to satisfy their anxieties about their children's education at a much lower cost (Gerace, 1999).

Inter-firm rivalry (competition) is one area of the business environment where e-commerce technologies have had an impact on most industries. In general, the

Internet has increased price competition in nearly all markets. It has been relatively easy for existing firms to adopt e-commerce technology and attempt to use it to achieve competitive advantage vis-à-vis rivals. For instance, the Internet inherently changes the scope of competition from local and regional to national and global. Because consumers have access to global price information, the Internet produces pressures on firms to compete by lowering prices (and lowering profits). On the other hand, the Internet has made it possible for some firms to differentiate their product or services from others. Amazon has patented one-click purchasing for instance, while eBay has created a unique, easy-to-use interface and a differentiating brand name. REI, Inc.—a specialty mountain climbing-oriented sporting goods company— has been able to use its Web site to maintain its strong niche focus on outdoor gear. Therefore, although the Internet has increased emphasis on price competition, it has also enabled businesses to create new strategies for differentiation and branding so that they can retain higher prices.

It is impossible to determine if e-commerce technologies have had an overall positive or negative impact on firm profitability in general. Each industry is unique, so it is necessary to perform a separate analysis for each one. Clearly, in some industries, in particular, information product industries such as the music, newspaper, book, and software industries, as well as other information-intense industries such as financial services, e-commerce has shaken the foundations of the industry. In these industries, the power of consumers has grown relative to providers, prices have fallen, and overall profitability has been challenged. In other industries, especially manufacturing, the Internet has not greatly changed relationships with buyers, but has changed relationships with suppliers. Increasingly, manufacturing firms in entire industries have banded together to aggregate purchases, create industry digital exchanges or marketplaces, and outsource industrial processes in order to obtain better prices from suppliers. Throughout this book, we will document these changes in industry structure and market dynamics introduced by e-commerce and the Internet.

INDUSTRY VALUE CHAINS

While an industry structural analysis helps us understand the impact of e-commerce technology on the overall business environment in an industry, a more detailed industry value chain analysis can help identify more precisely just how e-commerce may change business operations at the industry level (Benjamin and Wigand, 1995). One of the basic tools for understanding the impact of information technology on industry and firm operations is the value chain. The concept is quite simple. A **value chain** is the set of activities performed in an industry or in a firm that transforms raw inputs into final products and services. Each of these activities adds economic value to the final product; hence, the term *value chain* as an interconnected set of value-adding activities. **Figure 2.5** illustrates the six generic players in an industry value chain: suppliers, manufacturers, transporters, distributors, retailers, and customers.

By reducing the cost of information, the Internet offers each of the key players in an industry value chain new opportunities to maximize their positions by

value chain
the set of activities performed in an industry or in a firm that transforms raw inputs into final products and services

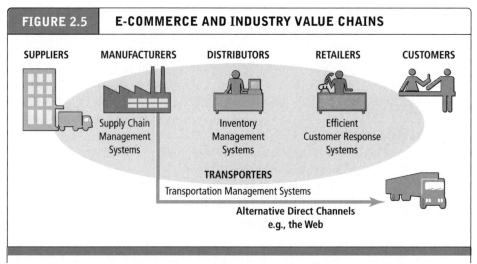

FIGURE 2.5   **E-COMMERCE AND INDUSTRY VALUE CHAINS**

Every industry can be characterized by a set of value-adding activities performed by a variety of actors. E-commerce potentially affects the capabilities of each player as well as the overall operational efficiency of the industry.

lowering costs and/or raising prices. For instance, manufacturers can reduce the costs they pay for goods by developing Web-based B2B exchanges with their suppliers. Manufacturers can develop direct relationships with their customers through their own Web sites, bypassing the costs of distributors and retailers. Distributors can develop highly efficient inventory management systems to reduce their costs, and retailers can develop highly efficient customer relationship management systems to strengthen their service to customers. Customers in turn can use the Web to search for the best quality, fastest delivery, and lowest prices, thereby lowering their transaction costs and reducing prices they pay for final goods. Finally, the operational efficiency of the entire industry can increase, lowering prices and adding value to consumers, and helping the industry to compete with alternative industries. Dell Inc., for instance, employs a number of these stratagems, most notably a sales model for personal computers that bypasses traditional retail distribution channels by selling directly to consumers over the Web. Dell also has developed a highly efficient supply chain management system to reduce its costs, and an equally efficient customer relationship management system to support customers and add to the value of its products.

FIRM VALUE CHAINS

firm value chain
the set of activities a firm engages in to create final products from raw inputs

The concept of value chain can be used to analyze a single firm's operational efficiency as well. The question here is: How does e-commerce technology potentially affect the value chains of firms within an industry? A **firm value chain** is the set of activities a firm engages in to create final products from raw inputs. Each step in the process of production adds value to the final product. In addition, firms develop support activities that coordinate the production process and

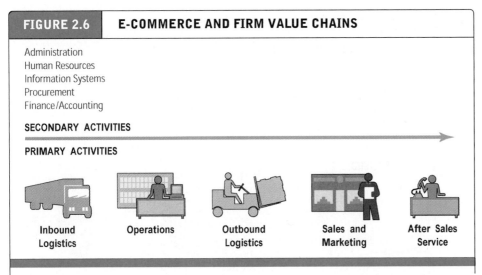

| **FIGURE 2.6** | **E-COMMERCE AND FIRM VALUE CHAINS** |

Administration
Human Resources
Information Systems
Procurement
Finance/Accounting

SECONDARY ACTIVITIES

PRIMARY ACTIVITIES

Inbound Logistics   Operations   Outbound Logistics   Sales and Marketing   After Sales Service

Every firm can be characterized by a set of value-adding primary and secondary activities performed by a variety of actors in the firm. A simple firm value chain performs five primary value-adding steps: inbound logistics, operations, outbound logistics, sales and marketing, and after sales service.
SOURCE: Laudon, 2006.

contribute to overall operational efficiency. **Figure 2.6** illustrates the key steps and support activities in a firm's value chain.

The Internet offers firms many opportunities to increase their operational efficiency and differentiate their products. For instance, firms can use the Internet's communications efficiency to outsource some primary and secondary activities to specialized, more efficient providers without such outsourcing being visible to the consumer. In addition, firms can use the Internet to more precisely coordinate the steps in the value chains and reduce their costs. Finally, firms can use the Internet to provide users with more differentiated and high-value products. For instance, Amazon uses the Internet to provide consumers with a much larger inventory of books to choose from, at a lower cost, than traditional book stores. It also provides many services—such as instantly available professional and consumer reviews, and information on buying patterns of other consumers—that traditional bookstores cannot.

FIRM VALUE WEBS

While firms produce value through their value chains, they also rely on the value chains of their partners—their suppliers, distributors, and delivery firms. The Internet creates new opportunities for firms to cooperate and create a value web. A **value web** is a networked business ecosystem that uses Internet technology to coordinate the value chains of business partners within an industry, or at the first level, to coordinate the value chains of a group of firms. **Figure 2.7** illustrates a value web.

value web
networked trans-business system that coordinates the value chains of several firms

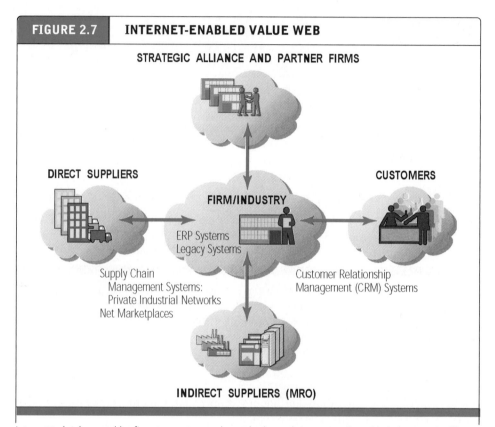

Internet technology enables firms to create an enhanced value web in cooperation with their strategic alliance and partner firms, customers, and direct and indirect suppliers.

A value web coordinates a firm's suppliers with its own production needs using an Internet-based supply chain management system. We discuss these B2B systems in Chapter 12. Firms also use the Internet to develop close relationships with their logistics partners. For instance, Amazon relies on UPS tracking systems to provide its customers with online package tracking, and it relies on the U.S. Postal Service systems to insert packages directly into the mail stream. Amazon has partnership relations with hundreds of firms to generate customers and to manage relationships with customers. (Online customer relationship management systems are discussed in Chapter 6.) In fact, when you examine Amazon closely, you realize that the value it delivers to customers is in large part the result of coordination with other firms and not simply the result of activities internal to Amazon. The value of Amazon is, in large part, the value delivered by its value web partners. This is difficult for other firms to imitate in the short run.

business strategy

a set of plans for achieving superior long-term returns on the capital invested in a business firm

profit

the difference between the price a firm is able to charge for its products and the cost of producing and distributing goods

BUSINESS STRATEGY

A **business strategy** is a set of plans for achieving superior long-term returns on the capital invested in a business firm. A business strategy is therefore a plan for making profits in a competitive environment over the long term. **Profit** is simply the difference between the price a firm is able to charge for its products and the cost of producing and distributing goods. Profit represents economic value. Economic value is created anytime customers are willing to pay more for a product than it costs to produce. Why would anyone pay more for a product than it costs to produce? There are multiple answers. The product may be unique (there are no other suppliers), it may be the least costly product of its type available, consumers may be able to purchase the product anywhere in the world, or it may satisfy some unique needs that other products do not. Each of these sources of economic value defines a firm's strategy for positioning its products in the marketplace. There are four generic strategies for achieving a profitable business: differentiation, cost, scope, and focus. We describe each of these below. The specific strategies that a firm follows will depend on the product, the industry, and the marketplace where competition is encountered.

Although the Internet is a unique marketplace, the same principles of strategy and business apply. As we will see throughout the book, successful e-commerce strategies involve using the Internet to leverage and strengthen existing business (rather than destroy your business), and to use the Internet to provide products and services your competitors cannot copy (in the short term anyway) and that means developing unique products, proprietary content, distinguishing processes (like Amazon's one-click shopping), and personalized or customized services and products (Porter, 2001). Let's examine these ideas more closely.

Differentiation refers to all the ways producers can make their products unique and distinguish them from those of competitors. The opposite of differentiation is **commoditization**—a situation where there are no differences among products or services, and the only basis of choosing a product is price. As economists tell us, when price alone becomes the basis of competition and there are many suppliers and many customers, eventually the price of the good falls to the cost to produce it (marginal revenues from the nth unit equal marginal costs). And then profits are zero! This is an unacceptable situation for any business person. The solution is to differentiate your product and to create a monopoly-like situation where you are the only supplier.

There are many ways businesses differentiate their products. A business may start with a core generic product, but then create expectations among users about the "experience" of consuming the product—"Nothing refreshes like a Coke!" or "Nothing equals the experience of driving a BMW." Businesses may also augment products by adding features to make them different from those of competitors. And businesses can differentiate their products further by enhancing the products' abilities to solve related consumer problems. For instance, tax programs such as TurboTax can import data from spreadsheet programs, as well as be used to electronically file tax returns. These capabilities are enhancements to the product that solve a customer's problems. The purpose of marketing is to create these differentiation features and to make the consumer aware of the unique qualities of products, creating in the process a "brand" that stands for these features. We discuss marketing and branding in Chapter 6.

differentiation
refers to all the ways producers can make their products unique and different to distinguish them from those of competitors

commoditization
a situation where there are no differences among products or services, and the only basis of choosing products is price

In their totality, the differentiation features of a product constitute the customer value proposition we described in earlier sections of this chapter. The Internet and the Web offer some unique ways to differentiate products. The ability of the Web to personalize the shopping experience and to customize the product or service to the particular demands of each consumer are perhaps the most significant ways in which the Web can be used to differentiate products. E-commerce businesses can also differentiate products by leveraging the ubiquitous nature of the Web (by making it possible to purchase the product from home, work, or on the road); the global reach of the Web (by making it possible to purchase the product anywhere in the world); richness and interactivity (by creating Web-based experiences for people who use the product, such as unique interactive content, videos, stories about users, and reviews by users); and information density (by storing and processing information for consumers of the product, such as warranty information on all products purchased through a site or income tax information online).

Adopting a *strategy of cost competition* means a business has discovered some unique set of business processes or resources that other firms cannot obtain in the marketplace. Business processes are the atomic units of the value chain. For instance, the set of value-creating activities called Inbound Logistics in Figure 2.6 is in reality composed of many different collections of activities performed by people on the loading docks and in the warehouses. These different collections of activities are called business processes—the set of steps or procedures required to perform the various elements of the value chain.

When a firm discovers a new, more efficient set of business processes, it can obtain a cost advantage over competitors. Then it can attract customers by charging a lower price, while still making a handsome profit. Eventually, its competitors go out of business as the market decisively tilts toward the lowest-cost provider. Or, when a business discovers a unique resource, or lower-cost supplier, it can also compete effectively on cost. For instance, switching production to low-wage-cost areas of the world is one way to lower costs.

Competing on cost can be a short-lived affair and very tricky. Competitors can also discover the same or different efficiencies in production. And competitors can also move production to low-cost areas of the world. Also, competitors may decide to lose money for a period as they compete on cost.

The Internet offers some new ways to compete on cost, at least in the short term. Firms can leverage the Internet's ubiquity by lowering the costs of order entry (the customer fills out all the forms, so there is no order entry department); leverage global reach and universal standards by having a single order entry system worldwide; and leverage richness, interactivity, and personalization by creating customer profiles online and treating each individual consumer differently—without the use of an expensive sales force that performed these functions in the past. Finally, firms can leverage the information intensity of the Web by providing consumers with detailed information on products, without maintaining either expensive catalogs or a sales force.

While the Internet offers powerful capabilities for intensifying cost competition, making cost competition appear to be a viable strategy, the danger is that competitors have access to the same technology. The *factor market*s—where producers buy their supplies—are open to all. Assuming they have the skills and organizational will to use the technology, competitors can buy many of the same cost-reducing techniques in the marketplace. Even a skilled labor force can be purchased, ultimately. However, self-knowledge, proprietary tacit knowledge (knowledge that is not published or codified), and a loyal, skilled workforce are in the short term difficult to purchase in factor markets. Therefore, cost competition remains a viable strategy.

Two other generic business strategies are scope and focus. A *scope strategy* is a strategy to compete in all markets around the globe, rather than merely in local, regional, or national markets. The Internet's global reach, universal standards, and ubiquity can certainly be leveraged to assist businesses in becoming global competitors. Yahoo, for instance, along with all of the other top 20 e-commerce sites, has readily attained a global presence using the Internet. A *focus strategy* is a strategy to compete within a narrow market segment or product segment. This is a specialization strategy with the goal of becoming the premier provider in a narrow market. For instance, L.L.Bean uses the Web to continue its historic focus on outdoor sports apparel; and W.W.Grainger—the Web's most frequently visited B2B site—focuses on a narrow market segment called MRO: maintenance, repair, and operations of commercial buildings. The Internet offers some obvious capabilities that enable a focus strategy. Firms can leverage the Web's rich interactive features to create highly focused messages to different market segments; the information intensity of the Web makes it possible to focus e-mail and other marketing campaigns on small market segments; personalization—and related customization—means the same product can be customized and personalized to fulfill the very focused needs of specific market segments and consumers.

Industry structure, industry and firm value chains, value webs, and business strategy are central business concepts used throughout this book to analyze the viability of and prospects for e-commerce sites. In particular, the signature case studies found at the end of each chapter are followed with questions that may ask you to identify the competitive forces in the case, or analyze how the case illustrates changes in industry structure, industry and firm value chains, and business strategy. *E-commerce in Action* cases (found in Chapters 9–12) also use these concepts when analyzing specific firms.

Priceline.com

and the Search for a Business Model that Works

Priceline is one of the Web's most well-known companies. Its "Name Your Own Price" reverse-auction pricing system is a unique business model that uses the information sharing and communications power of the Internet to create a new way of pricing products and services. At Priceline, consumers can enter a bid for travel, hotels, rental cars, and even home financing. Priceline queries its vendors (airline, hotel, and financial service firms) to see if anyone will accept the bid. Priceline offers a compelling value proposition to customers, allowing them to save money by trading off flexibility about brands, product features, and/or sellers in return for lower prices. Vendors also can gain additional revenue by selling products they might not otherwise be able to sell by accepting below-retail price offers, without disrupting their existing distribution channels or retail pricing structure. Priceline is an example of using the Web to achieve efficient price discrimination: charging some consumers much more than others for the same product. In 2007, Priceline sold about 2.9 million airline tickets, 27.7 million hotel room nights, and 8.6 million rental car days.

The original vision of Priceline's founder Jay Walker was called "demand collection." Walker poured millions into the concept of a one-stop shopping center for goods and services from trucks, to toothpaste, to vacation travel. But for much of its early history, Priceline was not profitable. In 1999, it lost over $1 billion. It pared losses to $15 million by 2001, but then, as travel declined after the September 11, 2001, World Trade Center tragedy, regressed in 2002, posting a $23 million dollar loss. Key executives resigned. Headlines such as "Priceline on the Ropes" and "Curtain Call for Priceline.com" predominated.

However, in 2003, Priceline recorded its first ever annual profit, recording $10.4 million in net income. The good news has continued since. In 2004, Priceline recorded operating income (income before tax adjustments) of $30 million; in 2005, $35 million; in 2006, $61 million; and in 2007, 155.5 million. (During the period between June 2003 and December 2006, Priceline's stock held relatively steady in the mid-$20–$30 range, but has since steadily increased, reaching a high of $144 in May 2008 before dropping back down into the $95-$100 range in the months following). In 2008, Priceline continued to exceed analyst expectations, with operating income for the second quarter of 2008 totaling $54.1 million compared to $34.6 million for the same period in 2007. Suddenly, Priceline was the darling of Wall Street with its stock price doubling in the course of a year, and far outstripping rivals like Orbitz and Travelocity, both of whom were have earnings declines. Priceline's rise occurred when worldwide travel was declining due to rising oil prices.

How has Priceline engineered this seeming turnaround? Has it finally found a business model that works? What went wrong with its original business, which initially seemed so promising?

Priceline commenced operations on April 6, 1998, with the sale of airline tickets. To purchase a Name Your Own Price ticket, a customer logs onto Priceline's Web site, specifies the origin and destination of the trip, the dates he or she wishes to depart, the price the customer is willing to pay, and a valid credit card to guarantee the offer. The customer must agree to fly on any major airline, leave at any time of day between 6 A.M. and 10 P.M., accept at least one stop or connection, receive no frequent flier miles or upgrades, and accept tickets that cannot be refunded or changed. Upon receiving the offer, Priceline checks the available fares, rules, and inventory provided by its participating airlines and determines whether it will fulfill the order at the requested price. If so, it notifies the customer within an hour that his or her offer has been accepted. On the consumer side, a central premise of Priceline's Name Your Own Price business model is that in many product and service categories, there are a significant number of consumers for whom brands, product features, and sellers are interchangeable, particularly if agreeing to a substitution among brands or sellers will result in saving money. On the vendor side, the Priceline Name Your Own Price business model is predicated on the assumption that sellers almost invariably have excess inventory or capacity that they would sell at lower prices, if they could do so without either lowering their prices to retail customers or advertising that lower prices are available. Priceline believed that its business model was ideally suited to industries characterized by expiring or rapidly aging inventory (for example, airline seats not sold by the time a flight takes off or hotel rooms not rented), although it did not think that it would be limited to such industries.

Priceline extended its system to hotel reservations in October 1998, and in January 1999, introduced home financing services. It went public in March 1999, and later that year, it added rental cars and even new cars to the mix. To promote its products and the Priceline brand, Priceline embarked on an extensive (and expensive) advertising campaign, hiring William Shatner to become the voice of Priceline, and it quickly became one of the most recognizable brands on the Web.

At the beginning of 2000, Priceline licensed the Name Your Own Price business model to several affiliates, including Priceline Webhouse Club, which attempted to extend the model to groceries and gasoline, and Perfect Yardsale, which used the model to sell used goods online, and added long distance calling and travel insurance. Priceline also had ambitious plans to expand internationally, and in 2000, licensed its business model to companies planning to set up similar operations in Asia and Australia.

However, by fall 2000, the picture no longer looked so rosy. In October 2000, after only 10 months of operation, Priceline's affiliate Priceline Webhouse Club, unable to raise additional financing, shut down its business, after running through $363 million. The financial climate at the time, with its renewed emphasis on profitability, made it impossible for Jay Walker, Priceline's founder, to raise the additional hundreds of millions that would be required before Webhouse might become profitable. Walker did not see the closure as a failure of the Priceline business model, however. Instead, he characterized it as the result of the "fickle sentiments" of investors. Many analysts did not accept Walker's characterization. Instead, they pointed to other factors. First, many of the major manufacturers of food and dried goods chose not to participate in Priceline Webhouse. So, to generate consumer interest, Priceline Webhouse subsidized discounts on most products itself. Although some major manufacturers, such as Kellogg's and Hershey's, did eventually sign up, many, such as Kraft, Procter & Gamble, and Lever Brothers, did not. The second miscalculation was that bidding on groceries and gasoline did not exactly provide a "hassle-free" way to shop. Customers were required to bid on and pay for groceries online, then use a special identification card to pick them up at a participating supermarket. If the particular items purchased were not available at the store, the customer would either have to go to another store or return at another time. To many, the demise of Priceline Webhouse highlighted potential cracks in the Priceline business model and raised strong concerns about its ultimate extensibility. Priceline's founder Jay Walker resigned in December 2000.

New management sharply curtailed Priceline's expansion and laid off over 1,000 employees. Priceline Chairman Richard Braddock said, "Priceline will entertain selective expansion... with stringent financial controls. We're going to make money on this and move forward." In 2002, Priceline focused on its core business of travel reservations, shedding its auto sales and long distance telephone units. Its only non-travel business today is its 49% interest in Priceline Mortgage. And in 2003–2004, it tweaked its business model once again, adding new discount "retail" airline ticket and rental car services to complement its hallmark Name Your Own Price offerings, in order to compete more effectively with firms such as Expedia, Travelocity, Hotwire, and Orbitz for the business of the consumer who prefers to book a specific airline or rental car. Although these services are not as lucrative as the Name Your Own Price model (it takes 1.5 to 2.5 retail plane tickets to bring in the same gross profit as a single Name Your Own Price ticket), and to a certain extent "cannibalize" its Name Your Own Price tickets, Priceline has made up at least some of the difference in increased volume. To further support this strategy, Priceline acquired a majority interest in TravelWeb, a consortium of five large hotel chains that provides Priceline with access to discount hotel rooms, purchased Active Hotels and Bookings B.V., a European hotel reservation service, and in 2005 extended its retail strategy to the hotel market. In 2006 and 2007, Priceline focused on adding to its full-service travel offerings in the United States, and recognizing that the growth of the domestic online market for travel services had slowed, on building its brand in Europe and Asia. Its international business represented approximately 56% of its gross bookings during 2007, and was a substantial contributor to its operating income during that period. Prior to the fourth quarter of 2004, substantially all of its revenues were generated in the United States. Priceline expects that the international segment of its business will represent a growing percentage of its business in the years to come. In 2008 Priceline eliminated the $5 to $11 booking fee which nearly all travel sites charge for airline bookings. Other sites have not stopped charging this fee. As a result, Priceline has become the undisputed low cost air reservation site.

As noted above, these strategic moves by Priceline have succeeded in generating annual profits since 2004. However, although Priceline is currently "in the black," a rosy future is by no means assured. Priceline faces industry-wide shrinkage in all forms of travel caused by the fear of terrorism, war, high fuel prices and economic recession. In addition, Priceline faces extraordinary competition, not just from other online middlemen such as Expedia, Travelocity, Hotels.com, Hotwire, and CheapTickets, but also from the direct discount sales by airlines. Priceline's competitors could easily drop their airline booking fees. Its business model today (discount travel services) is a mere shadow compared to Jay Walker's expansive vision. So even though right now it looks as if Priceline will survive, the question remains: for how long and on what terms?

SOURCES: Priceline.com Incorporated Form 10-Q Quarterly Report for quarterly period ended June 30, 2008, filed with the Securities and Exchange Commission on August 8, 2008; "Hot Growth Companies:Priceline Is Really Going Places," by Aaron Pressman, BusinessWeek Online, May 29, 2008; "Priceline Outshines Its Rivals," by Rick Munarriz, The Motley Fool, May 12, 2008; Priceline.com Incorporated Report on Form 10-K for the fiscal year ended December 31, 2007, filed with the Securities and Exchange Commission on March 1, 2008; "Priceline.com Reports Financial Results for 4th Quarter and Full-Year 2007", Priceline.com Press Release, February 14, 2008; "Beam Me Up, Priceline" by Rick Munarriz, The Motley Fool, August 8, 2007.

Case Study Questions

1. What are the core components of Priceline's business model?

2. Do you think Priceline will ultimately succeed or fail? Why?

3. How has Priceline (and similar online services) impacted the travel services industry?

4. Follow up on developments at Priceline since September 2008 when this case study was prepared. Has its business model and/or strategy changed at all, and if so, how? Who are its strongest competitors? Is it profitable or operating at a loss?

2.7 REVIEW

KEY CONCEPTS

■ **Identify the key components of e-commerce business models.**

A successful business model effectively addresses eight key elements:

- *Value proposition*—how a company's product or service fulfills the needs of customers. Typical e-commerce value propositions include personalization, customization, convenience, and reduction of product search and price delivery costs.
- *Revenue model*—how the company plans to make money from its operations. Major e-commerce revenue models include the advertising model, subscription model, transaction fee model, sales model, and affiliate model.
- *Market opportunity*—the revenue potential within a company's intended marketspace.
- *Competitive environment*—the direct and indirect competitors doing business in the same marketspace, including how many there are and how profitable they are.
- *Competitive advantage*—the factors that differentiate the business from its competition, enabling it to provide a superior product at a lower cost.
- *Market strategy*—the plan a company develops that outlines how it will enter a market and attract customers.
- *Organizational development*—the process of defining all the functions within a business and the skills necessary to perform each job, as well as the process of recruiting and hiring strong employees.
- *Management team*—the group of individuals retained to guide the company's growth and expansion.

■ **Describe the major B2C business models.**

There are a number of different business models being used in the B2C e-commerce arena. The major models include the following:

- *Portal*—offers powerful search tools plus an integrated package of content and services; typically utilizes a combined subscription/advertising revenue/transaction fee model; may be general or specialized (vortal).
- *E-tailer*—online version of traditional retailer; includes virtual merchants (online retail store only), bricks-and-clicks e-tailers (online distribution channel for a company that also has physical stores), catalog merchants (online version of direct mail catalog), and manufacturers selling directly over the Web.

- *Content provider*—information and entertainment companies that provide digital content over the Web; typically utilizes an advertising, subscription, or affiliate referral fee revenue model.
- *Transaction broker*—processes online sales transactions; typically utilizes a transaction fee revenue model.
- *Market creator*—uses Internet technology to create markets that bring buyers and sellers together; typically utilizes a transaction fee revenue model.
- *Service provider*—offers services online.
- *Community provider*—provides an online community of like-minded individuals for networking and information sharing; revenue is generated by advertising, referral fees, and subscriptions.

■ **Describe the major B2B business models.**

The major business models used to date in the B2B arena include:
- *E-distributor*—supplies products directly to individual businesses.
- *E-procurement*—single firms create digital markets for thousands of sellers and buyers.
- *Exchange*—independently owned digital marketplace for direct inputs, usually for a vertical industry group.
- *Industry consortium*—industry-owned vertical digital market.
- *Private industrial network*—industry-owned private industrial network that coordinates supply chains with a limited set of partners.

■ **Recognize business models in other emerging areas of e-commerce.**

A variety of business models can be found in the consumer-to-consumer e-commerce, peer-to-peer e-commerce, and m-commerce areas:
- *C2C business models*—connect consumers with other consumers. The most successful has been the market creator business model used by eBay.
- *P2P business models*—enable consumers to share files and services via the Web without common servers. A challenge has been finding a revenue model that works.
- *M-commerce business models*—take traditional e-commerce models and leverage emerging wireless technologies to permit mobile access to the Web.
- *E-commerce enablers*—focus on providing the infrastructure necessary for e-commerce companies to exist, grow, and prosper.

■ **Understand key business concepts and strategies applicable to e-commerce.**

The Internet and the Web have had a major impact on the business environment in the last decade, and have affected:
- *Industry structure*—the nature of players in an industry and their relative bargaining power by changing the basis of competition among rivals, the barriers to entry, the threat of new substitute products, the strength of suppliers, and the bargaining power of buyers.
- *Industry value chains*—the set of activities performed in an industry by suppliers, manufacturers, transporters, distributors, and retailers that transforms raw inputs into final products and services by reducing the cost of information and other transaction costs.

- *Firm value chains*—the set of activities performed within an individual firm to create final products from raw inputs by increasing operational efficiency.
- *Business strategy*—a set of plans for achieving superior long-term returns on the capital invested in a firm by offering unique ways to differentiate products, obtain cost advantages, compete globally, or compete in a narrow market or product segment.

QUESTIONS

1. What is a business model? How does it differ from a business plan?
2. What are the eight key components of an effective business model?
3. What are Amazon's primary customer value propositions?
4. Describe the five primary revenue models used by e-commerce firms.
5. Why is targeting a market niche generally smarter for a community provider than targeting a large market segment?
6. Besides music, what other forms of information could be shared through peer-to-peer sites? Are there legitimate commercial uses for P2P commerce?
7. Would you say that Amazon and eBay are direct or indirect competitors? (You may have to visit the Web sites to answer.)
8. What are some of the specific ways that a company can obtain a competitive advantage?
9. Besides advertising and product sampling, what are some other market strategies a company might pursue?
10. What elements of FreshDirect's business model may be faulty? Does this business scale up to a regional or national size?
11. Why is it difficult to categorize e-commerce business models?
12. Besides the examples given in the chapter, what are some other examples of vertical and horizontal portals in existence today?
13. What are the major differences between virtual storefronts, such as Drugstore.com, and bricks-and-clicks operations, such as Walmart.com? What are the advantages and disadvantages of each?
14. Besides news and articles, what other forms of information or content do content providers offer?
15. What is a reverse auction? What company is an example of this type of business?
16. What are the key success factors for exchanges? How are they different from portals?
17. What is an application service provider?
18. What are some business models seen in the C2C and P2P e-commerce areas?
19. How have the unique features of e-commerce technology changed industry structure in the travel business?
20. Who are the major players in an industry value chain and how are they impacted by e-commerce technology?
21. What are four generic business strategies for achieving a profitable business?

PROJECTS

1. Select an e-commerce company. Visit its Web site and describe its business model based on the information you find there. Identify its customer value proposition, its revenue model, the marketspace it operates in, who its main competitors are, any comparative advantages you believe the company possesses, and what its market strategy appears to be. Also try to locate information about the company's management team and organizational structure. (Check for a page labeled "the Company," "About Us," or something similar.)

2. Examine the experience of shopping on the Web versus shopping in a traditional environment. Imagine that you have decided to purchase a digital camera (or any other item of your choosing). First, shop for the camera in a traditional manner. Describe how you would do so (for example, how you would gather the necessary information you would need to choose a particular item, what stores you would visit, how long it would take, prices, etc.). Next, shop for the item on the Web. Compare and contrast your experiences. What were the advantages and disadvantages of each? Which did you prefer and why?

3. Visit eBay and look at the many types of auctions available. If you were considering establishing a rival specialized online auction business, what are the top three market opportunities you would pursue, based on the goods and auction community in evidence at eBay? Prepare a report or slide presentation to support your analysis and approach.

4. During the early days of e-commerce, first-mover advantage was touted as one way to success. On the other hand, some suggest that being a market follower can yield rewards as well. Which approach has proven to be more successful— first mover or follower? Choose two e-commerce companies that prove your point, and prepare a brief presentation to explain your analysis and position.

5. Prepare a research report (3 to 5 pages) on the current and potential future impacts of e-commerce technology on the book publishing industry.

WEB SITE RESOURCES www.prenhall.com/laudon

- Additional projects, exercises and tutorials
- Careers: Explore career opportunities in e-commerce
- Raising capital and business plans

Technology Infrastructure for E-commerce

CHAPTER 3

The Internet and World Wide Web: E-commerce Infrastructure

LEARNING OBJECTIVES

After reading this chapter, you will be able to:

- Discuss the origins of the Internet.
- Identify the key technology concepts behind the Internet.
- Describe the role of Internet protocols and utility programs.
- Explain the current structure of the Internet.
- Understand the limitations of today's Internet.
- Describe the potential capabilities of Internet II.
- Understand how the World Wide Web works.
- Describe how Internet and Web features and services support e-commerce.

All Mashed Up

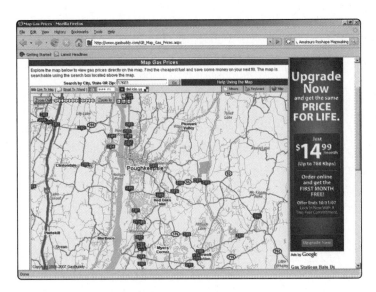

Mashups were initially developed by the music industry. Disk jockeys—at first in England and later in the United States and other countries—developed a new style of remix, known as mashups, in which two or more songs are melded together. Often, the resulting track features the melody of one song and the vocals of another. The idea is to take different sources and produce a new work that is "greater" than the sum of its parts. Generally, the more the sources differ from one another, the more fun they are to listen to, and the more humorous the process of discovering the source soundtracks.

On the Web, the term mashup has taken on a whole new meaning. Part of a movement called Web 2.0, and in the spirit of musical mashups, Web mashups combine the capabilities of two or more online applications to create a hybrid that provides more customer value than the original sources alone. So far, the area of greatest innovation involves the mashup of mapping and satellite image software with local content. For instance, the City of Portland, Oregon, created a site called PortlandMaps.com which integrates Google Earth's satellite imagery with city data on land use, zoning, street construction, household income, crime rates, and other data locked in City computers. GasBuddy.com provides searchable maps showing current gasoline prices. And thousands of real estate agents have integrated Google Earth or Microsoft Maps into their Web sites so customers can see online what a house and neighborhood really looks like.

In May 2007, Google introduced a toolkit called Google Gears that allows programmers and just ordinary folks to integrate eight Google applications such as Web search, chat, maps, calendars, scheduling, and advertising into their own Web sites. Its MyMaps service makes it easy for users to create customized maps. Yahoo and Microsoft are providing similar tools. You can think of mashups as a kind of software Legos.

While building communication links among software applications using Web-based tools is not new (these are called Web services), online mashup applications are driving a whole new set of recombinant applications. The Web services movement is being driven by the increased use of the programming language XML—eXtensible Markup Language—and a new set of computer communication standards that make it possible for computer programs to "talk" with one another without special programming.

For Calin Uioreanu, creator of a site called Simplest-shop.com, Web services means that he can offer his customers the same functionality as Amazon—because it is Amazon's system he is using. Uioreanu rents a server that communicates with Amazon servers throughout the day and night to obtain continual updates on prices, availability, products, and shipping information. On some items, customers have a choice of buying from Amazon or from Simplest-Shop.com. Uioreanu makes a 15% referral fee on Amazon sales, and a full markup on products he sells. Uioreanu won't discuss profits or revenue, but claims he has about 2 million monthly hits.

What's different about the mashup programs of today is that the major vendors have greatly simplified the process of building mashups, which can involve as little work as inserting four lines of JavaScript into a program. With publicly available Application Programming Interfaces (APIs), programmers are able to get the tools needed to pull data from many different Web sites and to combine it with other information to make an entirely new Web service. The result is that instead of the Web being merely a collection of pages, it is becoming a collection of capabilities, a platform that enables programmers to create new services quickly and inexpensively.

Probably the fastest growing type of mashups are geomashups which combine maps with specialized niche information and knowledge. Between April 2007, when Google released MyMaps, through July 2008, users created over 8 million customized maps. Examples include HealthMap.org, a site that provides a global mapping of current infectious diseases and Chicagocrime.org, which uses Google Maps to display where crimes occur in Chicago. Other non-map-based mashups include Plaxo.com, a site that provides the integration of your contact information including built-in calendar and schedules; Bookburro.com, which allows users to compare book prices based on Amazon's API and other screen-scrapping tools that scour the Web for other book sites' prices; and Indeed.com, which pulls job listings from many different Web job sites and organizes them by city. The YouTube Plugin allows you to search YouTube, select a video from the results and add it to your post. Even the browser developers are getting into the action. An add-on to the Firefox browser called Greasemonkey allows users to install scripts on their computer that customize the way a Web site works on a specific computer.

Mashups are also being taken seriously by business. IBM developed the IBM Mashup Center in February 2008. It allows their customers and employees to create applications, or mashups, by remixing information from anywhere to gain business insight and do their jobs more efficiently. Even non-technical users will be able to exploit standards and Web-based technology to gain access to myriad sources of information, such as Web sites and feeds, spreadsheets, databases, applications, unstructured text from an e-mail, video, audio and other information on the Web, and make sense of it, all in minutes.

So how do mashups effect e-commerce? Mashups represent one of the key technologies that is driving down the costs of building Web sites and applications. This, in turn, drives down the cost of Web entrepreneurship, the cost of initial financing, and increases the number of new Web applications that can be built. Mashups make it possible for thousands of Web entrepreneurs to create sites using free or very low cost applications built by much larger firms. For large Web players, such as Google, Microsoft, Yahoo, and others who create plug-in program modules, mashups enable them to distribute their brand names across the Web at no cost. Frequently, advertising opportunities will result: you can place Google's AdSense advertising on your Web site to display Web ads with just a few lines of code. Mashups are also likely to cause an eruption of e-commerce tied to local destinations—an area today where the Web is somewhat weak. The advertising industry is looking for ways to contact consumers when they are seeking local addresses: contextual advertising tied to specific locations. With a Google or Microsoft map mashup, you can easily direct customers to local restaurants, museums, and sites. Potentially, there are billions of dollars of e-commerce revenues waiting to be developed by local advertising that occurs just at the right moment for consumers.

SOURCES: "IBM Empowers Business People With Customized Web 2.0 Software," ibm.com, June 5, 2008; Google, Inc. Form 10K for the fiscal year ending December 31, 2007, March 31, 2008; "Social Media Will Change Your Business," by Stephen Baker and Heather Green, *BusinessWeek*, February 20, 2008; 'With Tools on Web, Amateurs Reshape Mapmaking," *New York Times*, July 27, 2007; "Businesses Embrace 'Mashups,'" by Lee Gomes, *Wall Street Journal*, July 3, 2007; "Moving Web-Based Software Offline," by Miguel Helft, *New York Times*, May 31, 2007; "City Sites," by Kevin Delaney, *Wall Street Journal*, March 26, 2007.

his chapter examines the Internet and World Wide Web of today and tomorrow, how it evolved, how it works, and how the present and future infrastructure of the Internet and the Web enables new business opportunities.

The opening case about mashups and Web services illustrates how important it is for business people to understand how the Internet and related technologies work, and to be aware of what's new on the Internet. It could change your business drastically, and open up new opportunities as well. Operating a successful small business on the Web such as Simplest-Shop.com, or implementing key Web business strategies such as personalization, customization, market segmentation, and price discrimination, all require that business people understand Web technology and keep track of Web developments.

The Internet and its underlying computer technology is not a static phenomenon in history, but instead is changing very rapidly. The Internet happened, but it is also happening. Computers are merging with cell phone services; broadband access in the home and broadband wireless access to the Internet via wireless devices are expanding rapidly; self-publishing on the Web via blogging, social networking, and podcasting now engages millions of Internet users; and new software technologies such as Web services, grid computing, and peer-to-peer applications are being deployed. Looking forward a few years to the emerging Internet II of 2012, the business strategies of the future will require a firm understanding of these new technologies to deliver products and services to consumers.

3.1 THE INTERNET: TECHNOLOGY BACKGROUND

What is the Internet? Where did it come from, and how did it support the growth of the World Wide Web? What are the Internet's most important operating principles? How much do you really need to know about the technology of the Internet?

Let's take the last question first. The answer is: it depends on your career interests. If you are on a marketing career path, or general managerial business path, then you need to know the basics about Internet technology, which you'll learn in this and the following chapter. If you are on a technical career path and hope to become a Web designer, or pursue a technical career in Web infrastructure for businesses, you'll need to start with those basics and then build from there. You'll also need to know about the business side of e-commerce, which you will learn about throughout this book.

Internet

an interconnected network of thousands of networks and millions of computers linking businesses, educational institutions, government agencies, and individuals

As noted in Chapter 1, the **Internet** is an interconnected network of thousands of networks and millions of computers (sometimes called *host computers* or just *hosts*) linking businesses, educational institutions, government agencies, and individuals. The Internet provides approximately 1.2 billion people around the world (including about 175-200 million people in the United States) with services such as e-mail, newsgroups, shopping, research, instant messaging, music, videos, and news (Internetworldstats.com, 2008). No single organization controls the Internet or how it functions, nor is it owned by anybody, yet it has provided the infrastructure for a transformation in commerce, scientific research, and culture. The word Internet is derived from the word *internetwork*, or the connecting together of two or more computer networks. The **World Wide Web**, or **Web** for short, is one of the Internet's most popular services, providing access to over 50 billion Web pages, which are documents created in a programming language called HTML that can contain text, graphics, audio, video, and other objects, as well as "hyperlinks" that permit users to jump easily from one page to another.

THE EVOLUTION OF THE INTERNET: 1961—THE PRESENT

Today's Internet has evolved over the last forty or so years. In this sense, the Internet is not "new;" it did not happen yesterday. Although journalists talk glibly about "Internet" time—suggesting a fast-paced, nearly instant, worldwide global change mechanism, in fact, it has taken over forty years of hard work to arrive at today's Internet.

The history of the Internet can be segmented into three phases (see **Figure 3.1**). In the first phase, the *Innovation Phase,* from 1961 to 1974, the fundamental building blocks of the Internet were conceptualized and then realized in actual hardware and software. The basic building blocks are: packet-switching hardware, client/server computing, and a communications protocol called TCP/IP (all described more fully later in this section). The original purpose of the Internet, when it was conceived in the 1960s, was to link large mainframe computers on different college campuses. This kind of one-to-one communication between campuses was previously only possible through the telephone system or postal mail.

In the second phase, the *Institutionalization Phase*, from 1975 to 1994, large institutions such as the Department of Defense and the National Science Foundation

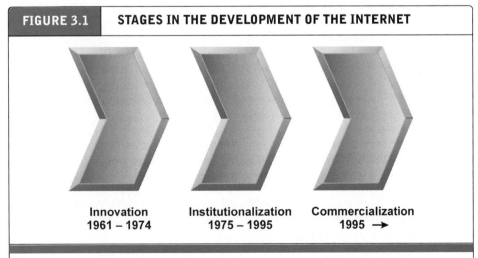

| FIGURE 3.1 | STAGES IN THE DEVELOPMENT OF THE INTERNET |

Innovation
1961 – 1974

Institutionalization
1975 – 1995

Commercialization
1995 →

The Internet developed in three stages over a 40-year period from 1961 to the present. In the Innovation stage, basic ideas and technologies were developed; in the Institutionalization stage, these ideas were brought to life; in the Commercialization stage, once the ideas and technologies had been proven, private companies brought the Internet to millions of people worldwide.

(NSF) provided funding and legitimization for the fledging invention called the Internet. Once the concepts behind the Internet had been proven in several government-supported demonstration projects, the Department of Defense contributed $1 million to further develop them into a robust military communications system that could withstand nuclear war. This effort created what was then called ARPANET (Advanced Research Projects Agency Network). In 1986, the NSF assumed responsibility for the development of a civilian Internet (then called NSFNET) and began a ten-year-long $200 million expansion program.

In the third phase, the *Commercialization Phase*, from 1995 to the present, government agencies encouraged private corporations to take over and expand both the Internet backbone and local service to ordinary citizens—families and individuals across America and the world who were not students on campuses. By 2000, the Internet's use had expanded well beyond military installations and research universities. See **Table 3.1** for a closer look at the development of the Internet from 1961 on.

THE INTERNET: KEY TECHNOLOGY CONCEPTS

In 1995, the Federal Networking Council (FNC) took the step of passing a resolution formally defining the term *Internet* (see **Figure 3.2**).

Based on that definition, the Internet means a network that uses the IP addressing scheme, supports the Transmission Control Protocol (TCP), and makes services available to users much like a telephone system makes voice and data services available to the public.

FIGURE 3.2	**RESOLUTION OF THE FEDERAL NETWORKING COUNCIL**

"The Federal Networking Council (FNC) agrees that the following language reflects our definition of the term 'Internet.'

'Internet' refers to the global information system that—

(i) is logically linked together by a globally unique address space based on the Internet Protocol (IP) or its subsequent extensions/follow-ons;

(ii) is able to support communications using the Transmission Control Protocol/Internet Protocol (TCP/IP) suite or its subsequent extensions/follow-ons, and/or other IP-compatible protocols; and

(iii) provides, uses or makes accessible, either publicly or privately, high level services layered on the communications and related infrastructure described herein."

Last modified on October 30, 1995.

SOURCE: Federal Networking Council, 1995.

TABLE 3.1	DEVELOPMENT OF THE INTERNET TIMELINE

YEAR EVENT	SIGNIFICANCE

INNOVATION PHASE 1961–1974

1961 Leonard Kleinrock (MIT) publishes a paper on "packet switching" networks.	The concept of packet switching is born.
1972 E-mail is invented by Ray Tomlinson of BBN. Larry Roberts writes the first e-mail utility program permitting listing, forwarding, and responding to e-mails.	The first "killer app" of the Internet is born.
1973 Bob Metcalfe (XeroxPark Labs) invents Ethernet and local area networks.	**Client/server computing is invented.** Ethernet permitted the development of local area networks and client/server computing in which thousands of fully functional desktop computers could be connected into a short-distance (<1,000 meters) network to share files, run applications, and send messages. Although the Apple and IBM personal computers had not yet been invented, at XeroxPark Labs, the first powerful desktop computers connected into a local network were created in the late 1960s.
1974 "Open architecture" networking and TCP/IP concepts are presented in a paper by Vint Cerf (Stanford) and Bob Kahn (BBN).	**TCP/IP invented.** The conceptual foundation for a single common communications protocol that could potentially connect any of thousands of disparate local area networks and computers, and a common addressing scheme for all computers connected to the network, are born.
	These developments made possible "peer-to-peer" "open" networking. Prior to this, computers could only communicate if they shared a common proprietary network architecture, e.g., IBM's System Network Architecture. With TCP/IP, computers and networks could work together regardless of their local operating systems or network protocols.

INSTITUTIONAL PHASE 1975–1995

1980 TCP/IP is officially adopted as the DoD standard communications protocol.	The single largest computing organization in the world adopts TCP/IP and packet-switched network technology.
1980 Personal computers are invented.	Altair, Apple, and IBM personal desktop computers are invented. These computers become the foundation for today's Internet, affording millions of people access to the Internet and the Web.
1984 Apple Computer releases the HyperCard program as part of its graphical user interface operating system called Macintosh.	The concept of "hyperlinked" documents and records that permit the user to jump from one page or record to another is commercially introduced.
1984 Domain Name System (DNS) introduced.	DNS provides a user-friendly system for translating IP addresses into words that people can easily understand.

(continued)

TABLE 3.1	DEVELOPMENT OF THE INTERNET TIMELINE (CONTINUED)

YEAR EVENT	SIGNIFICANCE
1989 Tim Berners-Lee of the physics lab CERN in Switzerland proposes a worldwide network of hyperlinked documents based on a common markup language called HTML—HyperText Markup Language.	**The concept of an Internet-supported service called the World Wide Web based on HTML pages is born.** The Web would be constructed from "pages" created in a common markup language, with "hyperlinks" that permitted easy access among the pages. The idea does not catch on rapidly and most Internet users rely on cumbersome FTP and Gopher protocols to find documents.
1990 NSF plans and assumes responsibility for a civilian Internet backbone and creates NSFNET.[1] ARPANET is decommissioned.	The concept of a "civilian" Internet open to all is realized through non-military funding by NSF.
1993 The first graphical Web browser called Mosaic is invented by Mark Andreesen and others at the National Center for Supercomputing at the University of Illinois.	Mosaic makes it very easy for ordinary users to connect to HTML documents anywhere on the Web. The browser-enabled Web takes off.
1994 Andreesen and Jim Clark form Netscape Corporation.	The first commercial Web browser—Netscape—becomes available.
1994 The first banner advertisements appear on Hotwired.com in October 1994.	**The beginning of e-commerce.**

COMMERCIALIZATION PHASE 1995–PRESENT	
1995 NSF privatizes the backbone, and commercial carriers take over backbone operation.	The fully commercial civilian Internet is born. Major long-haul networks such as AT&T, Sprint, GTE, UUNet, and MCI take over operation of the backbone. Network Solutions (a private firm) is given a monopoly to assign Internet addresses.
1995 Jeff Bezos founds Amazon; Pierre Omidyar forms AuctionWeb (eBay).	E-commerce begins in earnest with pure online retail stores and auctions.
1998 The U.S. federal government encourages the founding of Internet Corporation for Assigning Numbers and Names (ICANN).	Governance over domain names and addresses passes to a private nonprofit international organization.
1999 The first full-service Internet-only bank, First Internet Bank of Indiana, opens for business.	Business on the Web extends into traditional services.
2003 The Internet2 Abilene high-speed network is upgraded to 10 Gbps. Internet2 now has over 200 university, 60 corporate, and 40 affiliate members.	A major milestone toward the development of ultra-high-speed transcontinental networks several times faster than the existing backbone is achieved.
2005 NSF proposes the Global Environment for Networking Investigations (GENI) Initiative to develop new core functionality for the Internet, including new naming, addressing, and identity architectures; enhanced capabilities, including additional security architecture and a design that supports high availability; and new Internet services and applications.	Recognition that future Internet security and functionality needs may require the thorough rethinking of existing Internet technology.

[1] "Backbone" refers to the U.S. domestic trunk lines that carry the heavy traffic across the nation, from one metropolitan area to another. Universities are given responsibility for developing their own campus networks that must be connected to the national backbone.

(continued)

TABLE 3.1	DEVELOPMENT OF THE INTERNET TIMELINE (CONTINUED)

YEAR EVENT	SIGNIFICANCE
2006 The U.S. Senate Committee on Commerce, Science, and Transportation holds hearings on "Network Neutrality."	The debate grows over differential pricing based on utilization that pits the backbone utility owners against the online content and service providers, and device makers.
2007 BBN Technologies selected by the NSF to plan and design the next generation Internet (GENI).	Work begins on the new Internet which can provide differential service levels, guaranteed service levels, and differential pricing.
2008 The Internet Society (ISOC) identifies Trust and Indentity as a primary design element for every layer of the Internet, and launches an initiative in 2008-2010 to address these issues.	The leading Internet policy group recognizes the current Internet is threatened by breaches of security and trust that are build into the existing network.
2008 National Lambdarail develops the first 40 gigabit per second network, and the first transcontinental Ethernet network.	Using Cisco optical routers, this leading consortium of universities and businesses provides a nationwide platform for experimentation in very high speed Internet platforms.
2008 The Federal Communications Commission (F.C.C.) finds Comcast illegally inhibited users of its Internet service from using popular file-sharing software like BitTorrent.	Puts the F.C.C. on record as supporting "net neutrality" and opposed to congestion pricing plans advocated by Internet service providers.
2008 Internet "cloud computing" becomes a billion dollar industry.	Internet capacity is sufficient to support on-demand computing resources (processing and storage), as well as software applications, for large corporations and individuals.

SOURCES: Based on Leiner, et al., 2000; Zakon, 2005; Gross, 2005; Geni.net, 2007; nlr.org, 2008; ISOC.org, 2008.

Behind this formal definition are three extremely important concepts that are the basis for understanding the Internet: packet switching, the TCP/IP communications protocol, and client/server computing. Although the Internet has evolved and changed dramatically in the last 30 years, these three concepts are at the core of the way the Internet functions today and are the foundation for Internet II.

Packet Switching

Packet switching is a method of slicing digital messages into discrete units called **packets**, sending the packets along different communication paths as they become available, and then reassembling the packets once they arrive at their destination (see **Figure 3.3**). Prior to the development of packet switching, early computer networks used leased, dedicated telephone circuits to communicate with terminals and other computers. In circuit-switched networks such as the telephone system, a complete point-to-point circuit is put together, and then communication can proceed. However, these "dedicated" circuit-switching techniques were expensive and wasted available communications capacity—the circuit would be maintained regardless of whether any data was being sent. For nearly 70% of the time, a dedicated voice circuit is not being fully used because of pauses between words and delays in assembling the circuit segments, both of which increase the length of time required to find and connect circuits. A better technology was needed.

packet switching
a method of slicing digital messages into packets, sending the packets along different communication paths as they become available, and then reassembling the packets once they arrive at their destination

packet
the discrete units into which digital messages are sliced for transmission over the Internet

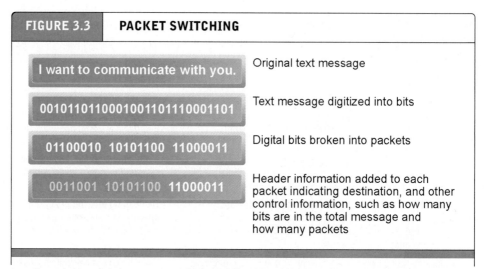

| FIGURE 3.3 | **PACKET SWITCHING** |

I want to communicate with you.
Original text message

0010110110001001101110001101
Text message digitized into bits

01100010 10101100 11000011
Digital bits broken into packets

0011001 10101100 11000011
Header information added to each packet indicating destination, and other control information, such as how many bits are in the total message and how many packets

In packet switching, digital messages are divided into fixed-length packets of bits (generally about 1,500 bytes). Header information indicates both the origin and the ultimate destination address of the packet, the size of the message, and the number of packets the receiving node should expect. Because the receipt of each packet is acknowledged by the receiving computer, for a considerable amount of time, the network is not passing information, only acknowledgments, producing a delay called latency.

The first book on packet switching was written by Leonard Kleinrock in 1964 (Kleinrock, 1964), and the technique was further developed by others in the defense research labs of both the United States and England. With packet switching, the communications capacity of a network can be increased by a factor of 100 or more. The communications capacity of a digital network is measured in terms of bits per second.[1] Imagine if the gas mileage of your car went from 15 miles per gallon to 1,500 miles per gallon—all without changing too much of the car!

In packet-switched networks, messages are first broken down into packets. Appended to each packet are digital codes that indicate a source address (the origination point) and a destination address, as well as sequencing information and error-control information for the packet. Rather than being sent directly to the destination address, in a packet network, the packets travel from computer to computer until they reach their destination. These computers are called routers. A **router** is a special-purpose computer that interconnects the different computer networks that make up the Internet and routes packets along to their ultimate destination as they travel. To ensure that packets take the best available path toward their destination, routers use a computer program called a **routing algorithm**.

Packet switching does not require a dedicated circuit, but can make use of any spare capacity that is available on any of several hundred circuits. Packet switching makes nearly full use of almost all available communication lines and capacity. Moreover, if some lines are disabled or too busy, the packets can be sent on any available line that eventually leads to the destination point.

router
special-purpose computer that interconnects the computer networks that make up the Internet and routes packets to their ultimate destination as they travel the Internet

routing algorithm
computer program that ensures that packets take the best available path toward their destination

[1]A bit is a binary digit, 0 or 1. A string of eight bits constitutes a byte. A home telephone dial-up modem connects to the Internet usually at 56 Kbps (56,000 bits per second). Mbps refers to millions of bits per second, whereas Gbps refers to billions of bits per second.

Transmission Control Protocol/Internet Protocol (TCP/IP)

While packet switching was an enormous advance in communications capacity, there was no universally agreed upon method for breaking up digital messages into packets, routing them to the proper address, and then reassembling them into a coherent message. This was like having a system for producing stamps but no postal system (a series of post offices and a set of addresses). The answer was to develop a **protocol** (a set of rules and standards for data transfer) to govern the formatting, ordering, compressing, and error-checking of messages, as well as specify the speed of transmission and means by which devices on the network will indicate they have stopped sending and/or receiving messages.

In 1974, Vint Cerf and Bob Kahn laid the conceptual foundation for **Transmission Control Protocol/Internet Protocol (TCP/IP)**, which has become the core communications protocol for the Internet (Cerf and Kahn, 1974). **TCP** establishes the connections among sending and receiving Web computers, and makes sure that packets sent by one computer are received in the same sequence by the other, without any packets missing. **IP** provides the Internet's addressing scheme and is responsible for the actual delivery of the packets.

TCP/IP is divided into four separate layers, with each layer handling a different aspect of the communication problem (see **Figure 3.4**). The **Network Interface Layer** is responsible for placing packets on and receiving them from the network medium, which could be a LAN (Ethernet) or Token Ring network, or other network technology. TCP/IP is independent from any local network technology and can adapt to changes at the local level. The **Internet Layer** is responsible for addressing, packaging, and routing messages on the Internet. The **Transport Layer** is responsible for providing communication with the application by acknowledging and sequencing the packets to and from the application. The **Application Layer** provides a wide variety of applications with the ability to access the services of the lower layers. Some of the best known applications are HyperText Transfer Protocol (HTTP), File Transfer Protocol (FTP), and Simple Message Transfer Protocol (SMTP), all of which we will discuss later in this chapter.

IP Addresses

The IP addressing scheme answers the question "How can 500 million computers attached to the Internet communicate with one another?" The answer is that every computer connected to the Internet must be assigned an address—otherwise it cannot send or receive TCP packets. For instance, when you sign onto the Internet using a dial-up, DSL, or cable modem, your computer is assigned a temporary address by your Internet Service Provider. Most corporate and university computers attached to a local area network have a permanent IP address.

There are two versions of IP currently in use. IPv4 (Version 4) is still the most frequently used version. An IPv4 **Internet address** is a 32-bit number that appears as a series of four separate numbers marked off by periods, such as 64.49.254.91. Each of the four numbers can range from 0–255. This "dotted quad" addressing scheme contains up to 4 billion addresses (2 to the 32nd power). In a typical Class C network, the first three sets of numbers identify the network (in the preceding

protocol
a set of rules and standards for data transfer

Transmission Control Protocol/Internet Protocol (TCP/IP)
the core communications protocol for the Internet

TCP
protocol that establishes the connections among sending and receiving Web computers and handles the assembly of packets at the point of transmission, and their re-assembly at the receiving end

IP
protocol that provides the Internet's addressing scheme and is responsible for the actual delivery of the packets

Network Interface Layer
responsible for placing packets on and receiving them from the network medium

Internet Layer
responsible for addressing, packaging, and routing messages on the Internet

Transport Layer
responsible for providing communication with the application by acknowledging and sequencing the packets to and from the application

Application Layer
provides a wide variety of applications with the ability to access the services of the lower layers

Internet address
Internet address expressed as a 32-bit number that appears as a series of four separate numbers marked off by periods, such as 64.49.254.91

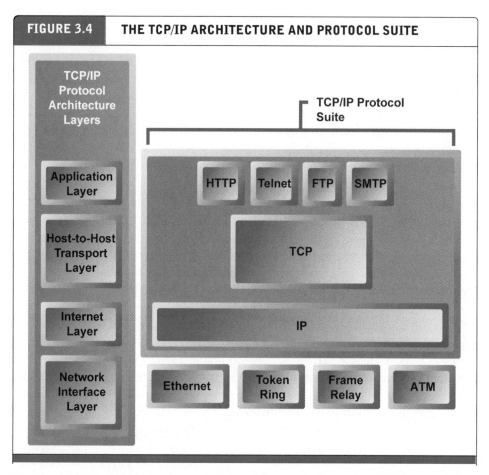

FIGURE 3.4 | **THE TCP/IP ARCHITECTURE AND PROTOCOL SUITE**

TCP/IP is an industry-standard suite of protocols for large internetworks. The purpose of TCP/IP is to provide high-speed communication network links.

example, 64.49.254 is the local area network identification) and the last number (91) identifies a specific computer.

Because many large corporate and government domains have been given millions of IP addresses each (to accommodate their current and future work forces), and with all the new networks and new Internet-enabled devices requiring unique IP addresses being attached to the Internet, a newer version of the IP protocol, called IPv6, has been developed. IPv6 provides for 128-bit addresses, or about 1 quadrillion (10 to the 15th power) (National Research Council, 2000).

Figure 3.5 illustrates how TCP/IP and packet switching work together to send data over the Internet.

---

[3]You can check the IP address of any domain name on the Internet. In Windows, bring up the DOS program or use Start/Run/cmd to open the DOS prompt. Type "ping < Domain Name >". You will receive the IP address in return.

FIGURE 3.5	ROUTING INTERNET MESSAGES: TCP/IP AND PACKET SWITCHING

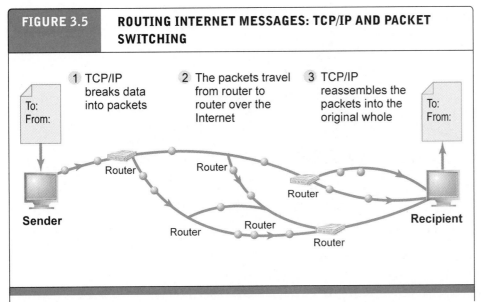

The Internet uses packet-switched networks and the TCP/IP communications protocol to send, route, and assemble messages. Messages are broken into packets, and packets from the same message can travel along different routes.

Domain Names, DNS, and URLs

Most people cannot remember 32-bit numbers. An IP address can be represented by a natural language convention called a **domain name**. The **Domain Name System (DNS)** allows expressions such as Cnet.com to stand for a numeric IP address (cnet.com's numeric IP is 216.239.115.148).[3] A **Uniform Resource Locator (URL)**, which is the address used by a Web browser to identify the location of content on the Web, also uses a domain name as part of the URL. A typical URL contains the protocol to be used when accessing the address, followed by its location. For instance, the URL http://www.azimuth-interactive.com/flash_test refers to the IP address 208.148.84.1 with the domain name "azimuth-interactive.com" and the protocol being used to access the address, HTTP. A resource called "flash_test" is located on the server directory path /flash_test. A URL can have from two to four parts; for example, name1.name2.name3.org. We discuss domain names and URLs further in Section 3.4. **Figure 3.6** illustrates the Domain Name System and **Table 3.2** summarizes the important components of the Internet addressing scheme

Client/Server Computing

While packet switching exploded the available communications capacity and TCP/IP provided the communications rules and regulations, it took a revolution in computing to bring about today's Internet and the Web. That revolution is called client/server computing and without it, the Web—in all its richness—would not exist. **Client/server computing** is a model of computing in which powerful personal computers called

domain name
IP address expressed in natural language

Domain Name System (DNS)
system for expressing numeric IP addresses in natural language

Uniform Resource Locator (URL)
the address used by a Web browser to identify the location of content on the Web

client/server computing
a model of computing in which powerful personal computers are connected in a network together with one or more servers

---

FIGURE 3.6 | **THE HIERARCHICAL DOMAIN NAME SYSTEM**

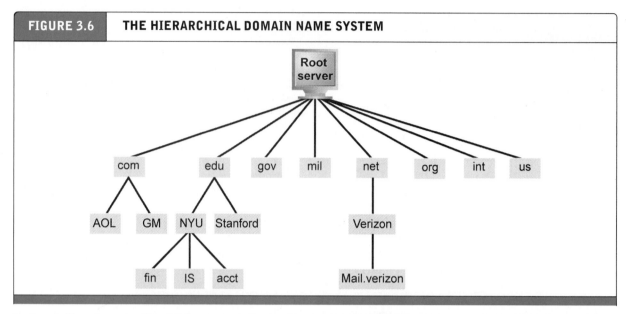

The Domain Name System is a hierarchical namespace with a root server at the top. Top-level domains appear next and identify the organization type (such as .com, .gov, .org, etc.) or geographic location (such as .uk (Great Britain) or .ca (Canada)). Second-level servers for each top-level domain assign and register second-level domain names for organizations and individuals such as IBM.com, Microsoft.com, and Stanford.edu. Finally, third-level domains identify a particular computer or group of computers within an organization, e.g., www.finance.nyu.edu.

client

a powerful personal computer that is part of a network

server

networked computer dedicated to common functions that the client computers on the network need

clients are connected in a network to one or more server computers. These clients are sufficiently powerful to accomplish complex tasks such as displaying rich graphics, storing large files, and processing graphics and sound files, all on a local desktop or handheld device. **Servers** are networked computers dedicated to common functions that the client computers on the network need, such as file storage, software

TABLE 3.2	PIECES OF THE INTERNET PUZZLE: NAMES AND ADDRESSES
IP addresses	Every computer connected to the Internet must have a unique address number called an Internet Protocol address. Even computers using a modem are assigned a temporary IP address.
Domain names	The Domain Name System allows expressions such as Prenhall.com (Prentice Hall's Web site) to stand for numeric IP locations.
DNS servers	DNS servers are databases that keep track of IP addresses and domain names on the Internet.
Root servers	Root servers are central directories that list all domain names currently in use for specific domains; for example, the .com root server. DNS servers consult root servers to look up unfamiliar domain names when routing traffic.

FIGURE 3.7   **THE CLIENT/SERVER COMPUTING MODEL**

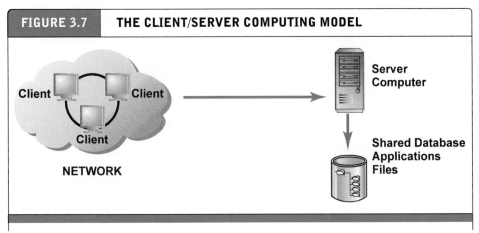

In the client/server model of computing, client computers are connected in a network together with one or more servers.

---

applications, utility programs such as Web connections, and printers (see **Figure 3.7**). The Internet is a giant example of client/server computing in which millions of Web servers located around the world can be easily accessed by millions of client computers, also located throughout the world.

To appreciate what client/server computing makes possible, you must understand what preceded it. In the mainframe computing environment of the 1960s and 1970s, computing power was very expensive and limited. For instance, the largest commercial mainframes of the late 1960s had 128k of RAM and 10 megabyte disk drives, and occupied hundreds of square feet. There was insufficient computing capacity to support graphics or color in text documents, let alone sound files or hyperlinked documents and databases.

With the development of personal computers and local area networks during the late 1970s and early 1980s, client/server computing became possible. Client/server computing has many advantages over centralized mainframe computing. For instance, it is easy to expand capacity by adding servers and clients. Also, client/server networks are less vulnerable than centralized computing architectures. If one server goes down, backup or mirror servers can pick up the slack; if a client computer is inoperable, the rest of the network continues operating. Moreover, processing load is balanced over many powerful smaller computers rather than being concentrated in a single huge computer that performs processing for everyone. Both software and hardware in client/server environments can be built more simply and economically.

Today there are over 1 billion personal computers in existence worldwide (Gartner, 2008). Personal computing capabilities are also moving to handheld devices such as BlackBerries, Palms, HP iPAQ Pocket PCs, and cell phones such as Apple's iPhone and T-Mobile's Android G1(much "thinner clients"). In the process, more computer processing will be performed by central servers (reminiscent of mainframe computers of the past). Read *Insight on Business: Peer-to Peer-Networks Rescue Hollywood and*

INSIGHT ON BUSINESS

PEER TO PEER NETWORKS RESCUE HOLLYWOOD AND TV STUDIOS

In June 2005, the Supreme Court ruled that peer-to-peer (P2P) file sharing networks such as Grokster, StreamCast, and Kazaa could be held liable for copyright infringement. However, the Court did not rule P2P networks themselves illegal, and the ruling does not impair the future development of this technology for legitimate purposes. Whether or not the Court's ruling has an impact on illegal music file sharing, there are many legitimate uses of this technology which are bound to expand in the next five years.

Take video and Hollywood movies for example. The bane of Hollywood and the nightmare of television production and broadcasting is the existing open source peer-to-peer networks which make thousands of pirated movies, videos and television shows, or snippets of them, available on the Web for free. Yet these same owners of content know that the future of the Internet for them involves users pointing a mouse, clicking and watching movies and television.

While this sounds simple, achieving this objective is anything but. A greatly compressed movie can be downloaded in an hour (compared to seconds for a single song) and the result is jerky small video. A television quality movie takes three hours to download with a high-bandwidth connection. Hardly point, click, and watch. High definition DVD quality can take overnight to download. The same is true for television shows. Hold the popcorn till morning, folks, or just rent a DVD.

One solution is to stream video content. Instead of downloading the entire movie file and saving it to your hard drive, the file can be sent in chunks over the Internet and stored in cache memory on your computer, and then played almost instantly. The movie can only be played once, and is not stored on your hard drive. You don't own it, and you can't replay it.

Both streaming and downloading face the same problem: scale. When video files are streamed from a single server, or downloaded from a single server, that server and the routers along the way can load up very quickly. The result is a slowdown in transmission, overwhelming other traffic on the Web. Multiplying the number of servers helps up to a point, but at some point the Internet itself is the choke point. If 10 million Americans suddenly wanted to see *American Idol* over the Internet some evening, the Internet would come to its knees using a client/server model.

Oddly, the favorite tool of movie and music pirates is also the solution to copyright owners' problems. Hollywood studios, television companies, and video distributors are embracing P2P networks as the only way to achieve the goal of point, click, and watch. The most commonly used P2P network software today is BitTorrent. A P2P network uses the computing power and bandwidth of participants rather than the power of central file and application servers in a typical client/server network. In peer-to-peer computing, two things happen. First, client computers can establish file sharing and sharing workspaces with one another without the intervention of a central server. Second, idle computers on the network can be used to share hard drives, processing power, and bandwidth for collective complex tasks. When a client computer seeks a movie file, a P2P network will fetch parts of the file distributed across hundreds of other nearby client machines logged into the network, and then reassemble them on your computer. The larger the network, the more people logged on, the more computing power connected, the faster the network becomes. Scale problem solved.

Netflix—the Web's largest online DVD store—is changing its business model to include online streaming of movies using BitTorrent protocols. ReelTime, Joost, Limelight, Bright-cove, and FEARNet (a horror movie site), along with the Hollywood-owned CinemaNow have developed P2P network streaming and download-ing sites, or work with the BitTorrent network. Now, instead of waiting 30 minutes or even overnight for a download or a stream to start, a BitTorrent stream can be started in a few seconds. A complete high-quality download takes half the time, and you can play the movie for 24 hours with no restrictions. After that, the downloaded movies are not playable. You also have options to buy or pay later when you view the movie. In addi-tion to speed, there's the marketing potential of P2P networks. Viacom's Spike Cable channel is promoting its new television series through P2P networks.

Currently, the largest legitimate source of television programs and movies on the Web is Apple's iTunes store, but this situation could change rapidly. The BitTorrent Network does not allow downloading to portable devices such as an iPod, and the digital rights management used by BitTorrent is not compatible with Apple's DRM software. Apple uses its own servers to download video and TV shows, and buys sufficient bandwidth to move this content to end users. It is unclear if this method can scale up to a truly large national audience. If network ISPs get their way in Washington, they will charge firms such as Apple a premium for consuming so much network bandwidth. At some point, Apple will need to use a P2P network technology such as BitTorrent, or strike a deal with BitTorrent.

While promoters of illegal file sharing claimed that the Supreme Court's 2005 decision would prevent P2P technology from flourishing, this is most likely not the case. P2P networking promises to greatly enhance the ability to collaborate and share information, while also increasing the efficiency of existing bandwidth. Point, click, and watch.

▬ **SOURCES**: "Promoting New TV Through P2P," *Los Angeles Times*, June 10, 2008; "Off New York Streets, Film Piracy is Online," by Eric Taub, *New York Times*, April 14, 2008; "Nothing to Watch on TV? Streaming Video Appeals to Niche Audiences," by Michel Marriottt, *New York Times*, August 6, 2007; "Soft-ware Tool of Pirates Gets Work in Hollywood," by Brad Stone, *New York Times*, February 26, 2007.

TV Studios for a discussion of a new form of computing that does not directly involve central servers.

THE INTERNET "CLOUD COMPUTING" MODEL: SOFTWARE AND HARDWARE AS A SERVICE

The growing bandwidth power of the Internet has pushed the client/server model one step further, towards what is called the "cloud computing model."

Cloud computing refers to a model of computing in which firms and individu-als obtain computing power and software applications over the Internet, rather than purchasing the hardware and software, and installing it on their own computers. Cur-rently, cloud computing is the fastest growing form of computing, with an estimated

Cloud computing
model of computing in which firms and individuals obtain computing power and software over the Internet

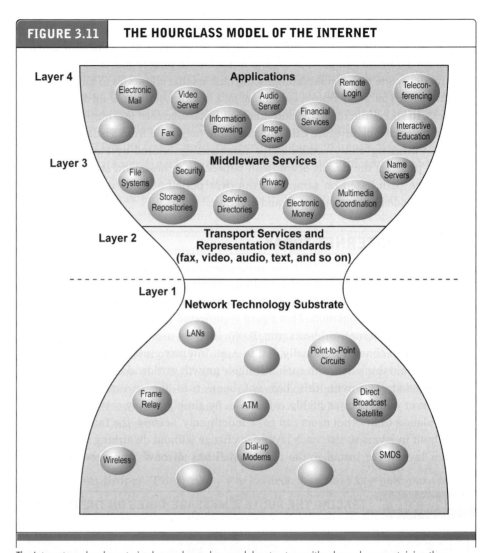

| FIGURE 3.11 | THE HOURGLASS MODEL OF THE INTERNET |

The Internet can be characterized as an hour-glass modular structure with a lower layer containing the bit-carrying infrastructure (including cables and switches) and an upper layer containing user applications such as e-mail and the Web. In the narrow waist are transportation protocols such as TCP/IP.

SOURCE: Adapted from Computer Science and Telecommunications Board (CSTB), 2000.

Network Technology Substrate layer
layer of Internet technology that is composed of telecommunications networks and protocols

Transport Services and Representation Standards layer
layer of Internet architecture that houses the TCP/IP protocol

Applications layer
layer of Internet architecture that contains client applications

Internet can go through radical changes to make service faster without being disruptive to your desktop applications running on the Internet.

Figure 3.11 illustrates the "hourglass" and layered architecture of the Internet. The Internet can be viewed conceptually as having four layers: the Network Technology Substrate, Transport Services and Representation Standards, Middleware Services, and Applications.[4] The **Network Technology Substrate layer** is composed of telecommunications networks and protocols. The **Transport Services and Representation Standards layer** houses the TCP/IP protocol. The **Applications layer** contains client applications such as the World Wide Web, e-mail, and audio or

[4]Recall that the TCP/IP communications protocol also has layers, not to be confused with the Internet architecture layers.

video playback. The **Middleware Services layer** is the glue that ties the applications to the communications networks, and includes such services as security, authentication, addresses, and storage repositories. Users work with applications (such as e-mail) and rarely become aware of middleware that operates in the background. Because all layers use TCP/IP and other common standards linking all four layers, it is possible for there to be significant changes in the network layer without forcing changes in the applications layer. The Network Technology Substrate layer is further described below.

THE INTERNET BACKBONE

Figure 3.12 illustrates some of the main physical elements of today's Internet. Originally, the Internet had a single backbone, but today's Internet has several backbones that are physically connected with each other and which transfer information from one private network to another. These private networks are referred to as **Network Service Providers (NSPs)**, which own and control the major backbone networks (see **Table 3.3**). For the sake of clarity we will refer to these networks of backbones as a single "backbone." The **backbone** has been likened to a giant pipeline that transports data around the world in milliseconds. In the United States, the backbone is composed entirely of fiber-optic cable with bandwidths ranging

Middleware Services layer
the "glue" that ties the applications to the communications networks, and includes such services as security, authentication, addresses, and storage repositories

Network Service Provider (NSP)
owns and controls one of the major networks comprising the Internet's backbone

backbone
high-bandwidth fiber-optic cable that transports data across the Internet

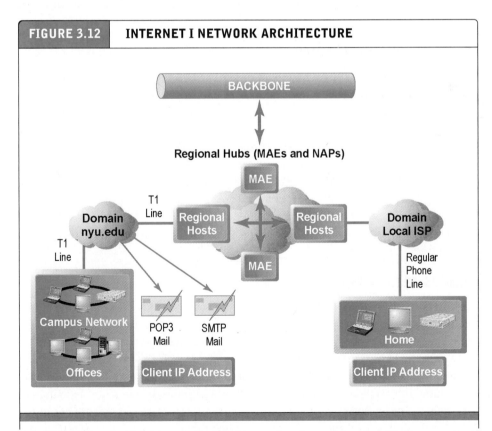

| FIGURE 3.12 | INTERNET I NETWORK ARCHITECTURE |

Today's Internet has a multi-tiered open network architecture featuring multiple national backbones, regional hubs, campus area networks, and local client computers.

TABLE 3.3	MAJOR U.S INTERNET BACKBONE OWNERS
AT&T	NTT/Verio
AOL Transit Data Network (ATDN)	Qwest
Cable & Wireless	Sprint
Global Crossing	Verizon
Level 3	

bandwidth

measures how much data can be transferred over a communications medium within a fixed period of time; is usually expressed in bits per second (bps), kilobits per second (Kbps), megabits per second (Mbps),or gigabits per second (Gbps)

redundancy

multiple duplicate devices and paths in a network

from 155 Mbps to 2.5 Gbps. **Bandwidth** measures how much data can be transferred over a communications medium within a fixed period of time, and is usually expressed in bits per second (bps), kilobits (thousands of bits) per second (Kbps), megabits (millions of bits) per second (Mbps), or gigabits (billions of bits) per second (Gbps).

Connections to other continents are made via a combination of undersea fiber-optic cable and satellite links. The backbones in foreign countries typically are operated by a mixture of private and public owners. The U.S. backbone is one of the most developed because the Internet's infrastructure was developed here. The backbone has built-in redundancy so that if one part breaks down, data can be rerouted to another part of the backbone. **Redundancy** refers to multiple duplicate devices and paths in a network.

INTERNET EXCHANGE POINTS

Internet Exchange Point (IXP)

hub where the backbone intersects with local and regional networks and where backbone owners connect with one another

In the United States, there are a number of hubs where the backbone intersects with regional and local networks, and where the backbone owners connect with one another (see **Figure 3.13**). These hubs were originally called Network Access Points (NAPs) or Metropolitan Area Exchanges (MAEs), but now are more commonly referred to as **Internet Exchange Points (IXPs)**. IXPs use high-speed switching computers to connect the backbone to regional and local networks, and exchange messages with one another. The regional and local networks are owned by local Bell operating companies (RBOCs—pronounced "ree-bocks"), and private telecommunications firms; they generally are fiber-optic networks operating at over 100 Mbps. The regional networks lease access to ISPs, private companies, and government institutions.

CAMPUS AREA NETWORKS

campus area network (CAN)

generally, a local area network operating within a single organization that leases access to the Web directly from regional and national carriers

Campus area networks (CANs) are generally local area networks operating within a single organization—such as New York University or Microsoft Corporation. In fact, most large organizations have hundreds of such local area networks. These organizations are sufficiently large that they lease access to the Web directly from regional and national carriers. These local area networks generally are running Ethernet (a local area network protocol) and have network operating systems such as Windows 2000/2003, Novell NetWare, or Linux that permit desktop clients to connect to the Internet through a local Internet server attached to their campus networks. Connection speeds in campus area networks are in the range of 10–100 Mbps to the desktop.

FIGURE 3.13	SOME MAJOR U.S. INTERNET EXCHANGE POINTS (IXPs)

Region	Name	Location	Operator
EAST	MAE East	Virginia and Miami	MCI
	New York International Internet Exchange (NYIIX)	New York	Telehouse
	Peering and Internet Exchange (PAIX)	New York, Philadelphia and Northern Virginia	Switch and Data
	NAP of the Americas	Miami	Terramark
CENTRAL	MAE Chicago	Chicago	MCI
	Chicago NAP	Chicago	SBC
	MAE Central	Dallas and Atlanta	MCI
	Peering and Internet Exchange (PAIX)	Atlanta	Switch and Data
WEST	MAE West	San Jose and Los Angeles	MCI
	Peering and Internet Exchange (PAIX)	Palo Alto, San Jose, and Seattle	Switch and Data
	Los Angeles International Internet Exchange (LAIIX)	Los Angeles	Telehouse

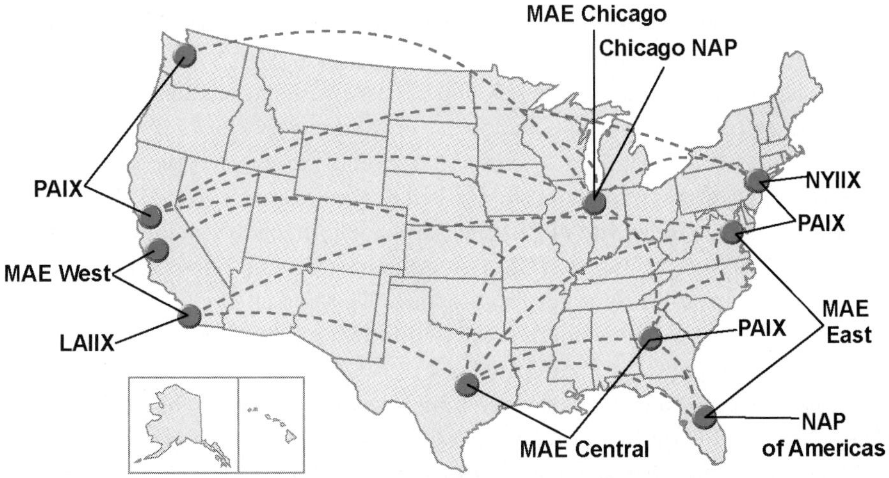

INTERNET SERVICE PROVIDERS

Internet Service Provider (ISP)

firm that provides the lowest level of service in the multi-tiered Internet architecture by leasing Internet access to home owners, small businesses, and some large institutions

The firms that provide the lowest level of service in the multi-tiered Internet architecture by leasing Internet access to home owners, small businesses, and some large institutions are called **Internet Service Providers (ISPs)**. ISPs are retail providers—they deal with "the last mile of service" to the curb—homes and business offices. About 84 million U.S. households connect to the Internet through either a local or national ISP (eMarketer, Inc., 2008a). ISPs typically connect to IXPs with high-speed telephone or cable lines (45 Mbps and higher).

There are a number of major ISPs, such as AOL, Earthlink, MSN Network, AT&T WorldNet, Comcast (Optimum Online), Verizon, Sprint, and about 3,500 local ISPs in the United States, ranging from local telephone companies offering dial-up and DSL telephone access to cable companies offering cable modem service, to small "mom-and-pop" Internet shops that service a small town, city, or even county with mostly dial-up phone access. If you have home or small business Internet access, an ISP likely provides the service to you. Satellite firms also offer Internet access, especially in remote areas where broadband service is not available, but satellite firms have had a difficult time penetrating the ISP market because they can offer high-speed download service but they require a telephone service for uplink.

narrowband

the traditional telephone modem connection, now operating at 56.6 Kbps

broadband

refers to any communication technology that permits clients to play streaming audio and video files at acceptable speeds—generally anything above 100 Kbps

Table 3.4 summarizes the variety of services, speeds, and costs of ISP Internet connections. There are two types of ISP service: narrowband and broadband. **Narrowband** service is the traditional telephone modem connection now operating at 56.6 Kbps (although the actual throughput hovers around 30 Kbps due to line noise that causes extensive resending of packets). This used to be the most common form of connection worldwide but is quickly being replaced by broadband connections in the United States, Europe, and Asia. Broadband service is based on DSL, cable modem, telephone (T1 and T3 lines), and satellite technologies. **Broadband**—in the context of Internet service—refers to any communication technology that permits clients to play streaming audio and video files at acceptable speeds—generally anything above 100 Kbps. In the United States, broadband users surpassed dial-up users in 2004, and in 2008 there were 75 million broadband households and only 9 million dial-up households (eMarketer, Inc., 2008a).

The actual throughput of data will depend on a variety of factors including noise in the line and the number of subscribers requesting service. T1 lines are publicly regulated utility lines that offer a guaranteed level of service, but the actual throughput of the other forms of Internet service is not guaranteed.

Digital Subscriber Line (DSL)

a telephone technology for delivering high-speed access through ordinary telephone lines found in homes or businesses

Digital Subscriber Line (DSL) service is a telephone technology for delivering high-speed access to the Internet through ordinary telephone lines found in a home or business. Service levels range from about 768 Kbps all the way up to 3 Mbps. DSL service requires that customers live within two miles (about 4,000 meters) of a neighborhood telephone switching center.

cable modem

a cable television technology that piggybacks digital access to the Internet on top of the analog video cable providing television signals to a home

Cable modem refers to a cable television technology that piggybacks digital access to the Internet using the same analog or digital video cable providing television signals to a home. Cable Internet is a major broadband alternative to DSL service, generally providing faster speeds and a "triple play" subscription: telephone, television, and Internet

TABLE 3.4	ISP SERVICE LEVELS AND BANDWIDTH CHOICES	
SERVICE	COST/MONTH	SPEED TO DESKTOP (KBPS)
Telephone modem	$10–$25	30–56 Kbps
DSL	$15–$50	1 Mbps–3 Mbps
Cable modem	$20–$50	1 Mbps–15 Mbps
Satellite	$20–$50	250 Kbps–1 Mbps
T1	$1,000–$2,000	1.54 Mbps
T3	$10,000–$30,000	45 Mbps

for a single monthly payment. Cable modem services range from 1 Mbps up to 15 Mbps. Comcast, Time Warner Road Runner, and Cox are the largest cable Internet providers.

T1 and T3 are international telephone standards for digital communication. **T1** lines offer guaranteed delivery at 1.54 Mbps, while T3 lines offer delivery at a whopping 45 Mbps. T1 lines cost about $1,000–$2,000 per month, and **T3** lines between $10,000 and $30,000 per month. These are leased, dedicated, guaranteed lines suitable for corporations, government agencies, and businesses such as ISPs requiring high-speed guaranteed service levels.

Some satellite companies offer broadband high-speed digital downloading of Internet content to homes and offices that deploy 18″ satellite antennas. Service is available beginning at 256 Kbps up to 1 Mbps. In general, satellite connections are not viable for homes and small businesses because they are only one-way—you can download from the Internet at high speed, but cannot upload to the Internet at all. Instead, users need a phone or cable connection to upload.

Prices are falling drastically to as low as $14.95 per month for DSL service. Cable broadband accounts for nearly 60% of all broadband users and nearly all large business firms and government agencies have broadband connections to the Internet. Demand for broadband service has grown so rapidly simply because it greatly speeds up the process of downloading Web pages and increasingly large video and audio files located on Web pages (see **Table 3.5**). As the quality of Internet service offerings expands to include Hollywood movies, music, games, and other rich media-streaming content, the demand for broadband access will continue to swell. In order to compete with cable companies, telephone companies have introduced an advanced form of DSL called FiOS (fiber optic service) that provides up to 50 Mbps speeds for households, much faster than cable systems.

INTRANETS AND EXTRANETS

The very same Internet technologies that make it possible to operate a worldwide public network can also be used by private and government organizations as internal networks. An **intranet** is a TCP/IP network located within a single organization for purposes of communications and information processing. Internet technologies are generally far less expensive than proprietary networks, and there is a global source of new applications that can run on intranets. In fact, all the applications

T1
an international telephone standard for digital communication that offers guaranteed delivery at 1.54 Mbps

T3
an international telephone standard for digital communication that offers guaranteed delivery at 45 Mbps

intranet
a TCP/IP network located within a single organization for purposes of communications and information processing

TABLE 3.5	TIME TO DOWNLOAD A 10-MEGABYTE FILE BY TYPE OF INTERNET SERVICE
TYPE OF INTERNET SERVICE	TIME TO DOWNLOAD
NARROWBAND SERVICES	
Telephone modem	25 minutes
BROADBAND SERVICES	
DSL @ 1 Mbps	1.33 minutes
Cable modem @ 10 Mbps	8 seconds
T1	52 seconds
T3	2 seconds

available on the public Internet can be used in private intranets. The largest providers of local area network software are Microsoft's Windows 2000/2003 server software, followed by open source Linux, both of which use TCP/IP networking protocols.

extranet

formed when firms permit outsiders to access their internal TCP/IP networks

Extranets are formed when firms permit outsiders to access their internal TCP/IP networks. For instance, General Motors permits parts suppliers to gain access to GM's intranet that contains GM's production schedules. In this way, parts suppliers know exactly when GM needs parts, and where and when to deliver them.

Intranets and extranets generally do not involve commercial transactions in a marketplace, and they are mostly beyond the scope of this text. Extranets will receive some attention as a technology that supports certain types of B2B exchanges (described in Chapter 12).

WHO GOVERNS THE INTERNET?

Aficionados and promoters of the Internet often claim that the Internet is governed by no one, and indeed cannot be governed, and that it is inherently above and beyond the law. What these people forget is that the Internet runs over private and public telecommunications facilities which are themselves governed by laws, and subject to the same pressures as all telecommunications carriers. In fact, the Internet is tied into a complex web of governing bodies, national legislatures, and international professional societies. There is no one governing organization that controls activity on the Internet. Instead, there are several organizations that influence the system and monitor its operations. Among the governing bodies of the Internet are:

- The *Internet Architecture Board (IAB)*, which helps define the overall structure of the Internet.
- The *Internet Corporation for Assigned Names and Numbers (ICANN)*, which assigns IP addresses, and the *Internet Network Information Center (InterNIC)*, which assigns

domain names. ICANN was created in 1998 by the U.S. Department of Commerce to eventually take over the domain name system and the 13 root servers that are at the heart of the Internet addressing scheme.

- The *Internet Engineering Steering Group (IESG)*, which oversees standard setting with respect to the Internet.

- The *Internet Engineering Task Force (IETF)*, a private-sector group which forecasts the next step in the growth of the Internet, keeping watch over its evolution and operation.

- The *Internet Society (ISOC)*, which is a consortium of corporations, government agencies, and nonprofit organizations that monitors Internet policies and practices.

- The *World Wide Web Consortium (W3C)*, a largely academic group that sets HTML and other programming standards for the Web.

- The *International Telecommunication Union (ITU)*, which helps set technical standards.

While none of these organizations has actual control over the Internet and how it functions, they can and do influence government agencies, major network owners, ISPs, corporations, and software developers with the goal of keeping the Internet operating as efficiently as possible.

In addition to these professional bodies, the Internet must also conform to the laws of the sovereign nation-states in which it operates, as well as the technical infrastructures that exist within the nation-state. Although in the early years of the Internet and the Web there was very little legislative or executive interference, this situation is changing as the Internet plays a growing role in the distribution of information and knowledge, including content that some find objectionable.

While, as noted previously, the U.S. Department of Commerce originally created ICANN with the intent that it take over control of the Domain Name System, this is no longer the case. The United States changed its policy in June 2005, when the Department of Commerce announced it would retain oversight over the 13 root servers which serve as master directories for Web browsers and e-mail programs throughout the world. Observers give several reasons for this move, including the use of the Internet for basic communications services by terrorist groups, and the uncertainty that might be caused should an international body take over. Countries who refuse to accept U.S. control over the Internet could set up their own separate domain name systems, fracturing today's single Web into many different, potentially incompatible networks. A United Nations panel set up to devise a global plan for the Internet has failed to come to an agreement. The Working Group on Internet Governance (WGIG) decided instead to set up a permanent forum to carry on the debate and issued a report in July 2005, calling for international governance of the Internet. There have been no further meetings of WGIG.

Read *Insight on Society: Government Regulation of the Internet* for a further look at the issue of censorship of Internet content and substance.

INSIGHT ON SOCIETY

GOVERNMENT REGULATION OF THE INTERNET

The Internet is often hailed as a unique media that empowers average citizens to make their voices heard. Some people believe they are anonymous on the Internet. After all, who could possibly be reading the billions of e-mail messages that are sent daily in the United States alone? Many people assume that because the Internet is so widely dispersed, it must be difficult to control or monitor.

But, in reality, controlling the Internet and its content turns out to be pretty easy. In fact, just about all governments assert some kind of control over how the Web operates within their countries. For instance, in 2007 an Egyptian court sentenced a blogger to four years in jail for outraging religious authorities. A Turkish judge ordered YouTube blocked because of videos mocking the country's founder, Attaturk. Thailand's military government also blocked YouTube because of videos offending the country's king. In India, the government temporarily banned sixteen Web sites because they insulted local customs. Russia has passed a law requiring that 50% of all radio news be "positive," and routinely applies this standard to Web sites which are not "positive" or which damage state interests, closing them down.

In China, citizens who use the Internet to make their voices heard run the risk of losing their freedom, and sometimes their lives. Internet traffic in all countries runs through huge fiber-optic trunk lines. In China, there are three such lines, and China requires the companies that own these lines to configure their routers for both internal and external service requests. When a request originates in China for a Web page in Chicago, the Chinese routers examine the request to see if the site is on a blacklist, and then examine words in the requested Web page to see if they contain blacklisted terms. The most famous blacklisted terms are "falun" (a suppressed religious group in China) and "Tiananmen Square massacre" (or any symbols that might lead to such results such as "198964" which signifies June 4, 1989, the date of the massacre). The system is often referred to as "The Great Firewall of China," and is implemented with the assistance of Cisco Systems—the U.S. firm that is the largest manufacturer of routers in the world.

In August 2008, China was host of the Olympics. Despite earlier promises to the International Olympic Committee, the Chinese government at the last minute decided to restrict the international press from accessing certain Web sites both in China and outside China that were objectionable to the government. There went Wikipedia and BBC News. So much for the Olympic spirit of cooperation among nations!

In addition to the Great Firewall of China, the Chinese government relies on a much more effective tactic called "self censorship" (or intimidation). In 2002, the Chinese government summarily shut off access to Google's servers from inside China. Even before this action, Google's results were often slowed by the Great Firewall. After this incident, Google decided to locate its servers on Chinese soil (Google.cn), where they became directly subject to China's censorship regime, which bans from the Internet anything that "damages the honor or interests of the state," "disturbs the public order," or "infringes upon national customs and habits." Why does Google, an American company whose mottos are "Don't be evil," and "Organize the world's information," collaborate with a repressive regime?

Even more questions were raised by Yahoo's behavior in China. Beginning in 2002, Yahoo's Chinese operations in Hong Kong identified to the Chinese government the names of human rights activists who had submitted articles critical of the government to an anonymous Yahoo Group bulletin board. As a result, four of these Web bloggers and a journalist were arrested and imprisoned for up to ten years in Chinese prisons. In 2007, Yahoo was sued in the United States by a journalist and his wife under the Alien Tort Claims Act and the Torture Victims Protection Act. Yahoo continues to cooperate with the Chinese government's pursuit of bloggers and journalists as a condition of its continuing business in China. Other American-based firms identified by human rights groups as complicit with Chinese censorship and repression are Microsoft (for complying with a request to delete the blogging of a Chinese journalist from its U.S.-based servers, and to delete the search term "freedom" from its search service), and MySpace (for self-censoring any content that might upset the Chinese government). If you think MySpace is a wild outpost that its owners just can't control, you should visit the Chinese MySpace. Owner Rupert Murdoch's News Corp. and its local partners have implemented filtering software to prohibit users from discussing the usual banned topics or displaying photos or videos of teens that reveal too much flesh. Even better, MySpace China encourages users to click a button if they spot any "misconduct" by other users. This "misconduct" includes actions such as "endangering national security, leaking state secrets, subverting the government, undermining national unity, spreading rumors, or disturbing the social order." There are probably a lot of parents in the United States who would appreciate the approach taken by MySpace China!

In February 2006, members of the House of Representatives held hearings on the behavior of U.S. Internet firms in China which led to widespread denunciations of these firms, and an effort to define in legislation how these firms should behave in the future. However, such legislation has not yet been passed.

In their defense, all these firms say they are simply abiding by the laws of the countries where they do business. Google claims it is not identifying specific individuals to Chinese authorities because it operates no e-mail or bulletin board services in China, just search services, which it censors to avoid trouble with the Chinese government. Cisco says it does not cooperate with governments for such uses, though it notes the hardware "can be used for many different purposes." In a joint statement to the caucus, Yahoo and Microsoft said they were exploring the voluntary approach and have also spoken to the Bush administration about raising the issue of Internet service directly with Beijing. "Our leverage and ability to influence government policies in various countries is severely limited," the companies said. They are looking for U.S. government help to avoid having to comply with foreign government requests for surveillance and censorship.

Not to be outdone, both Europe and the United States have at various times taken steps to control Internet and Web content and communications, although not to the extent of China. European and American countries generally ban the sale, distribution, or even possession of online child pornography. Both France and Germany bar online Nazi memorabilia. The United States has passed laws attempting to restrict ordinary pornographic content, but most of these have been struck down by courts. The United States does ban Internet gambling, and has arrested several European entrepreneurs on U.S. soil for promoting or engaging in Internet gambling sites. In response to terrorism threats, European countries are preparing legislation to retain Internet identity and usage data for up to two years. In the United States, the most recent changes to the Foreign Intelligence Surveillance Act (FISA) permit law enforcement agencies to wiretap domestic phone conversations with foreign parties without a warrant from a court.

And there are many groups who would like to ban entire topics or Web sites (such as those related to sex, drugs, tax-free cigarettes, Internet pharmacies, and gambling).

As the Internet becomes a vital tool for communication, self-expression, and for user-generated content of all kinds, efforts to control and regulate the Internet have grown. What at first appeared to be a liberating tool is, in some cases, becoming a tool for surveillance, and even repression. Different cultures and states around the world impose their own values on the Internet rather than changing to accommodate the Internet culture in the United States and Europe.

There is the distinct possibility that the single World Wide Web will become a collection of loosely connected country Web sites, each with its own form of censorship. The irony here is that the Internet was developed as a means of fostering global communication. Yet it is now very clear that many countries will put stricter limits on freedom of expression than is true in the United States.

SOURCES: "IOC Agrees to Internet Blocking at the Games", by Andrew Jacobs, *International Herald Tribune*, July 30, 2008; "Senate Approves Bill to Broaden Wiretap Powers", Eric Lichtblau, *New York Times*, July 10, 2008; "Bush Signs Law to Widen Reach for Wiretapping," by James Risen, *New York Times*, August 6, 2007; "Thailand Bans YouTube," by Thomas Fuller, *New York Times*, April 5, 2007; "Europe's Plan to Track Phone and Net Use," by Victoria Shannon, *New York Times*, February 20, 2007; "U.S. Firms in China Face Ethical Issues," by Representative Chris Smith, Letter to the Editor, *New York Times*, February 10, 2007; "Google's China Problem (and China's Google Problem)," by Clive Thompson, *New York Times*, April 23, 2006.

3.3 INTERNET II: THE FUTURE INFRASTRUCTURE

The Internet is changing as new technologies appear and new applications are developed. We refer to the future infrastructure as Internet II. The second era of the Internet is being built today by private corporations, universities, and government agencies. To appreciate the benefits of Internet II, you must first understand the limitations of the Internet's current infrastructure.

LIMITATIONS OF THE CURRENT INTERNET

Much of the Internet's current infrastructure is several decades old (equivalent to a century in Internet time). It suffers from a number of limitations, including:

- *Bandwidth limitations*. There is insufficient capacity throughout the backbone, the metropolitan switching centers, and most importantly, the "last mile" to the house and small businesses. The result is slow peak-hour service (congestion) and a limited ability to handle high volumes of video and voice traffic.

- *Quality of service limitations*. Today's information packets take a circuitous route to get to their final destinations. This creates the phenomenon of **latency**—delays in messages caused by the uneven flow of information packets through the network. In the case of e-mail, latency is not noticeable. However, with streaming video and synchronous communication, such as a telephone call, latency is noticeable to the user and perceived as "jerkiness" in movies or delays in voice communication. Today's Internet uses "best-effort" quality of service (QOS), which makes no guarantees about when or whether data will be delivered, and provides each packet with the same level of service, no matter who the user is or what type of data is

latency
delays in messages caused by the uneven flow of information packets through the network

contained in the packet. A higher level of service quality is required if the Internet is to keep expanding into new services, such as video on demand and telephony.

- *Network architecture limitations.* Today, a thousand requests for a single music track from a central server will result in a thousand efforts by the server to download the music to each requesting client. This slows down network performance as the same music track is sent out a thousand times to clients that might be located in the same metropolitan area. This is very different from television, where the program is broadcast once to millions of homes.

- *Language development limitations.* HTML, the language of Web pages, is fine for text and simple graphics, but poor at defining and communicating "rich documents," such as databases, business documents, or graphics. The tags used to define an HTML page are fixed and generic.

- *Wired Internet.* The Internet is based on cables—fiber-optic and coaxial copper cables. Copper cables use a centuries-old technology, and fiber-optic cable is expensive to place underground. The wired nature of the Internet restricts mobility of users although it is changing rapidly as Wi-Fi hotspots proliferate, and cellular phone technology advances.

Now imagine an Internet at least 100 times as powerful as today's Internet, one that is not subjected to the limitations of bandwidth, protocols, architecture, physical connections, and language detailed previously. Welcome to the world of Internet II, and the next generation of e-commerce services and products!

THE INTERNET2® PROJECT

Internet2® is a consortium of more than 200 universities working in partnership with government agencies and private businesses in an effort to make the Internet more efficient.[5] Their work together is a continuation of the kind of cooperation among government, private, and educational organizations that created the original Internet.

Internet2®
a consortium of more than 200 universities, government agencies, and private businesses that are collaborating to find ways to make the Internet more efficient

The idea behind Internet2 is to create a "giant test bed" where new technologies can be tested without impacting the existing Internet. The three primary goals of Internet2 are to:

- Create a leading-edge very high-speed network capability for the national research community

- Enable revolutionary Internet applications

- Ensure the rapid transfer of new network services and applications to the broader Internet community

Some of the areas Internet2 participants are focusing on in this pursuit are advanced network infrastructure, new networking capabilities, middleware, and advanced applications. The advanced networks created and in use by Internet2 members provide the environment in which new technologies can be tested and enhanced. Several new networks have been established, including Abilene and vBNS.

[5]The Internet2® project is just one aspect of the larger second generation Internet we call Internet II.

Abilene and vBNS (short for *very high performance Backbone Network Service*) are high-performance backbone networks with bandwidths ranging from 2.5 Gbps to 10 Gbps that interconnect the GigaPoPs used by Internet2 members to access the network. A **GigaPoP** is a regional Gigabit Point of Presence, or point of access to the Internet2 network that supports data transfers at the rate of 1 Gbps or higher (see **Figure 3.14**). In February 2004, Internet2 upgraded all segments of the Abilene network to 10 Gbps. In 2007, Internet2 deployed a 100 Gbps East-West link. At these speeds, the ability of the network to process data begins to exceed the speed at which client computers can pull data off their hard drives. With a 100 Gbps Internet, a high-quality version of the movie "The Matrix" could be sent in a few seconds rather than half a minute over the current Internet2 and two days over a typical home broadband line.

THE LARGER INTERNET II TECHNOLOGY ENVIRONMENT: THE FIRST MILE AND THE LAST MILE

The Internet2 project is just the tip of the iceberg when it comes to near-term future enhancements to the Internet. In 2007, the NSF began work on the Global Environment for Networking Innovations (GENI) Initiative to develop new core functionality for the Internet, including new naming, addressing and identity architectures; enhanced capabilities, including additional security architecture and a design that supports high availability; and new Internet services and applications (Geni.net, 2008). The most significant privately initiated (but often government-

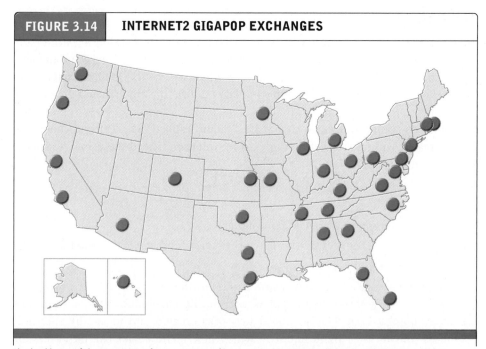

| FIGURE 3.14 | **INTERNET2 GIGAPOP EXCHANGES** |

The backbone of the Internet2 infrastructure is a fiber-optic cable OC-192 network connecting regional GigaPoP servers (represented by the blue circles) that operate at billions of bits per second.
SOURCE: Internet2.edu, 2008.

influenced) changes are coming in two areas: fiber-optic trunk line bandwidth and wireless Internet services. Fiber optics is concerned with the first mile or backbone Internet services that carry bulk traffic long distances. Wireless Internet is concerned with the last mile—from the larger Internet to the user's cell phone or laptop.

Fiber Optics and the Bandwidth Explosion in the First Mile

Fiber-optic cable consists of up to hundreds of strands of glass that use light to transmit data. It is frequently replacing existing coaxial and twisted pair cabling because it can transmit much more data at faster speeds, with less interference and better data security. Fiber-optic cable is also thinner and lighter, taking up less space during installation. The hope is to use fiber optics to expand network bandwidth capacity in order to prepare for the expected increases in Web traffic once Internet II services are widely adopted.

The enormous increase in long-haul backbone capacity from 1998 to 2001, coupled with a decline in demand, caused over 60 telecommunications companies including WorldCom and Global Crossing Ltd. to declare bankruptcy and others to struggle with large deficits, leading to painful losses in shareholder value. The cost of a 1.5 Mbps dedicated line between Los Angeles and New York has fallen from $1.8 million in early 2000 down to $100,000 in 2008. Thousands of miles of fiber-optic cable in the United States are "dark" or "unlit". The decline in the cost of fiber-optic cable is due in part to the continued technical improvement in switching equipment which allows firms to achieve exponentially higher throughput from the existing fiber-optic cables by improvements in processors and technique. For this reason, the installation of long-haul fiber-optic cable is likely to remain relatively flat for years to come, and the prices companies can charge for long-haul digital transmission will also likely remain flat through 2010.

However, there is a silver lining in this cloudy picture. The fiber-optic cable will not disappear or degrade over time, and it represents a vast digital highway that is currently being exploited by YouTube (Google), MySpace, and other high-bandwidth applications; telecommunications companies are re-capitalizing and building new business models based on market prices for digital traffic. The net result is that society will ultimately benefit from extraordinarily low-cost, long-haul, very high-bandwidth communication facilities that are already paid for.

Demand for fiber-optic cable is likely to strengthen as consumers demand integrated telephone, broadband access, and video from a single source. Interactive online television, online Hollywood movies, inexpensive Voice over Internet Protocol (VoIP) telephone, and Internet access all from the same company that provides a single cable into the home is the vision driving Verizon, other local Bells, and cable firms. Verizon began in 2004 to run fiber into 3 million homes. The technology, called FiOS (for fiber-optic service), costs consumers from $40 to $200 a month. FiOS provides download speeds of up to 50 Mbps and upload speeds of up to 10 Mbps. Verizon will spend $23 billion by 2010 wiring 18 million homes (about half its customer base) (Mehta, 2007). This so-called FTTP (Fiber to the Premises) will be the fastest growing form of broadband connection in the next decade.

fiber-optic cable
consists of up to hundreds of strands of glass or plastic that use light to transmit data

TABLE 3.6	MAJOR PHOTONICS OPPORTUNITIES AND PLAYERS	
TECHNOLOGY	OPPORTUNITY	PLAYERS
Dense Wavelength Division Multiplexing	Transform single strand of fiber-optic cable into multiple virtual fibers	Cisco, Cogent Communications
Optical switches and transmission equipment	Expand capacity, drop costs, speed service	Broadwing
Gigabit Ethernet over fiber switches	Increased access to metro regional equipment networks	World Wide Packets, Zuma Networks
Optical service accounting platforms	Packet size metering and billing; bytes to bucks	Ellacoya Networks
Optical switching	Building blocks for all optical systems conponents	ADC Telecommunications, JDS Uniphase, Bookham
Optical integrated circuits	Powerful optical chips with mirrors and lasers	Bookham, Avanex
Passive Optical Networks (PON)	Low-cost, high-performance networks	Zhone, Broadlight
Fiber-optic cable	The highway material	Corning, AT&T

photonics

the study of communicating with light waves

Table 3.6 describes some of the **photonic** technologies that are being used to expand the capacity of the installed long-haul fiber lines. Together these improvements will allow the Internet to move from narrowband to broadband digital services, and from stationary Web access to mobile Web access.

Figure 3.15 gives a comparative look at bandwidth demand for various applications.

The Last Mile: Mobile Wireless Internet Access

Fiber-optic networks carry the long-haul bulk traffic of the Internet—and in the future will play an important role in bringing BigBand to the household and small business. But along with fiber optics and photonics, arguably the most significant development for the Internet and Web in the last five years has been the emergence of mobile wireless Internet access.

Wireless Internet is concerned with the last mile of Internet access to the user's home, office, car, or cell phone anywhere. Up until 2000, the last-mile access to the Internet—with the exception of a small satellite Internet connect population—was bound up in land lines of some sort: copper coaxial TV cables or telephone lines or, in some cases, fiber-optic lines to the office. Internet II will increasingly rely on wireless technology to connect users' handheld telephones/computers, personal organizers, and laptop and desktop computers to the Web and LANs and to one another (such as a digital connection between your cell phone and your laptop computer or TV).

In 2008, about 75 million personal computers were sold in the United States, about half of which were mobile laptop computers, most with wireless networking built in. By 2010, nearly 60% of all personal computers will be mobile laptops (IDC, 2008). In 2008, there were around 77,000 wireless hotspots in the United States, which

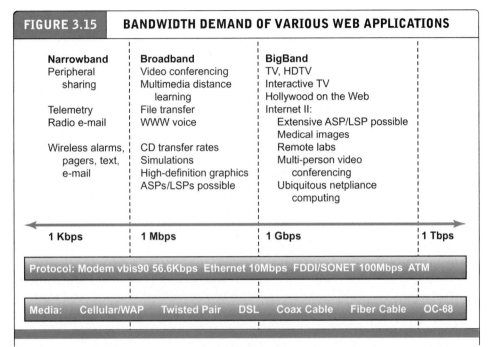

FIGURE 3.15 | **BANDWIDTH DEMAND OF VARIOUS WEB APPLICATIONS**

Narrowband	**Broadband**	**BigBand**
Peripheral sharing	Video conferencing	TV, HDTV
	Multimedia distance learning	Interactive TV
		Hollywood on the Web
Telemetry	File transfer	Internet II:
Radio e-mail	WWW voice	Extensive ASP/LSP possible
		Medical images
Wireless alarms, pagers, text, e-mail	CD transfer rates	Remote labs
	Simulations	Multi-person video conferencing
	High-definition graphics	Ubiquitous netpliance computing
	ASPs/LSPs possible	

| 1 Kbps | 1 Mbps | 1 Gbps | 1 Tbps |

Protocol: Modem vbis90 56.6Kbps Ethernet 10Mbps FDDI/SONET 100Mbps ATM

Media: Cellular/WAP Twisted Pair DSL Coax Cable Fiber Cable OC-68

The really exciting e-commerce applications such as high definition television (HDTV) and interactive TV and movies require much higher levels of bandwidth to the home than are currently available. than are widely available in the United States. Verizon's FiOS fiber optic network operating at 15 Mbps is a suitable option.

around 20 million mobile laptops are capable of using to connect to the Internet (eMarketer, Inc., 2008a; TIA, 2008). As cell phones add Wi-Fi capabilities, such as Apple's iPhone or T-Mobile's Android G1, millions of cell phone users will gain Internet access. Clearly, a large part of the future Internet will be mobile, access anywhere, broadband service for the delivery of video, music, and Web search.

Telephone-Based versus Computer Network-Based Wireless Internet Access There are two different basic types of wireless Internet connectivity: telephone-based and computer network-based systems. Within each of these basic types there are many variations (and a veritable jungle of acronyms).

Telephone-based wireless Internet access connects the user to a global telephone system (land, satellite, and microwave) that has a long history of dealing with thousands of users simultaneously and already has in place a large-scale transaction billing system and related infrastructure. Cellular telephones and the telephone industry are currently the largest providers of wireless access to the Internet today if only because the telephone is the single most widely adopted electronic device in human history. In 2008, there were about 1.2 billion cell phones sold in the world worth $650 billion (eMarketer, Inc., 2008b).

The challenge for telephone-based wireless systems is to move from the historically slow and inefficient circuit-switched phone networks of the past to higher speed, cellular, digital packet-switched networks. The whole point of the cell phone future is to deliver entertainment (music and video) along with traditional voice service.

second generation (2G) cellular networks
relatively slow circuit-switched digital network that can transmit data at about 10 Kbps

2.5G network
interim cellular network that provides speeds of 60–144 Kbps using General Packet Radio Services (GPRS)

GPRS (General Packet Radio Services)
next generation technology carries data in packets, just like the Internet, but over radio frequencies that make wireless communication possible

Third generation (3G) cellular network
new generation of cellular phone standards that can connect users to the Web at 2.4 Mbps

GSM (Global System for Mobile Communications)
mobile communications system widely used in Europe and Asia that uses narrowband Time Division Multiple Access (TDMA)

CDMA (Code Division Multiple Access)
mobile communications system widely used in the United States that uses the full spectrum of radio frequencies and digitally encrypts each call

The first generation of cellular networks were analog-based. **Second generation (2G) cellular networks** are relatively slow circuit-switched digital networks that can transmit data at about 10 Kbps—one-fifth the speed of a home modem. In the United States, cell phone companies developed what they called 2.5G as an interim step. A **2.5G network** provides speeds of 60 to 144 Kbps using **GPRS (General Packet Radio Services)**, a packet-switched technology that is much more efficient (and hence faster) than dedicated circuit-switched networks. An enhanced version of GPRS called EDGE can carry data at up to 384 Kbps. **Third generation (3G) cellular networks** have speeds ranging from 384 Kbps to up to around 2 Mbps.

The cellular telephone story is further complicated by the existence of two different competing standards: GSM and CDMA. In over 100 countries (including all of Europe), the standard is **GSM**, short for **Global System for Mobile Communications**, in which a specific frequency is shared by up to eight different phone users and the space or bandwidth is divided among users using TDMA (Time Division Multiple Access) in which each user is allocated a portion of time on the frequency.

In the United States, a different standard called **CDMA (Code Division Multiple Access)**, developed by the military in World War II, transmits over several frequencies, occupies the entire spectrum, and randomly assigns users to a range of frequencies over time. The basic patents for CDMA chipsets are owned by a U.S. firm called Qualcomm (San Diego). In general, CDMA is cheaper to implement, is more efficient in use of spectrum, and provides higher quality throughput of voice and data. However, three out of four of the world's estimated 2.3 billion cell phones are GSM, including most of those in China, the world's largest cell phone market. Because of its inherent efficiency, a standard called W-CDMA (wide-band CDMA) is the long-term objective of existing GSM systems in the future. But in the interim, GSM providers have developed so-called 2.5G networks using GSM/GPRS technologies operating in the 60–144 Kbps range. In the United States, in the meantime, a different 3G version of CDMA known as CDMA2000 has been developed. For instance, Sprint and Verizon are currently offering 3G services on CDMA2000/1xRTT and CDMA2000/EV-DO networks with a real-world data transfer rates of about 1 Mbps.

We apologize for all these confusing terms and acronyms. It's a part of digital life we cannot seem to escape. **Table 3.7** summarizes the various telephone technologies used for wireless Internet access.

Regardless of which standard is involved, the advent of higher speed cellular networks has created an entire new class of Web appliances that utilize a new kind of telecommunications service called "hybrid PCS," or just PCS for personal communication devices. Also known as 'smart phones', these devices combine the functionality of a PDA with that of a cell phone, such as an Apple iPhone, T-Mobile G1, or RIM BlackBerry, and that of a mobile laptop computer with Wi-fi capability. This makes it possible to combine in one device music, video, Web access, and telephone service. When these same cellular devices also can provide Wi-Fi connections to the Web, and switch seamlessly from one network to the other, they are referred to as fully converged devices. **Table 3.8** on page 158 illustrates the some of the types of handheld products available as of July 2008.

Once a connection is established with a user's PDA/cell phone, there are a number of different ways to deliver Web pages. The Apple iPhone has a such a high resolution and large screen that Web pages are delivered as ordinary HTML pages and the user can scroll around the page to navigate. Likewise with BlackBerry 8820s. Older devices with less-capable screens either use Wireless Application Protocol (WAP) or iMode, a proprietary standard owned by the Japanese company NTT DoCoMo.

Wireless local area network (WLAN)-based Internet access derives from a completely different background from telephone-based wireless Internet access. Popularly known as Wi-Fi, WLANs are based on computer local area networks where the task is to connect client computers (generally stationary) to server computers within local areas of, say, a few hundred meters. WLANs function by sending radio signals that are broadcast over the airwaves using certain radio frequency ranges (2.4 GHz to 5.875 GHz, depending on the type of standard involved). The major technologies here are the various versions of the Wi-Fi standard and Bluetooth. Emerging WLAN technologies include WiMAX, Ultra-Wideband (UWB), and ZigBee (see **Table 3.9** on page 159).

TABLE 3.7	WIRELESS INTERNET ACCESS TELEPHONE TECHNOLOGIES		
TECHNOLOGY	**SPEED**	**DESCRIPTION**	**PLAYERS**
2G			
GSM (Global System for Mobile Communications)	10 Kbps	European and some American companies' basic cell phone service; text messaging; uses TDMA.	Vodafone (Europe), Cingular, T-Mobile
TDMA (Time Division Multiple Access)	10 Kbps	An early standard for cell phone service. Used by GSM networks worldwide.	GSM networks in Europe and Japan
CDMA	10 Kbps	American standard for basic cell phone service; text messaging. Developed by Qualcomm.	Verizon, Sprint
2.5G			
GPRS (General Packet Radio Services) EDGE	30–170 Kbps	Enhanced GSM service. Interim step toward 3G in the United States. Fast enough for Web access.	Cingular, T-Mobile, Apple iPhone, Vodafone
3G (THIRD GENERATION)			
CDMA2000 1xRTT CDMA2000 EV-DO W-CDMA	144 Kbps–2 Mbps	High-speed, mobile, always on for e-mail, browsing, instant messaging. Implementing technologies include versions of CDMA2000 (used by CDMA providers) and W-CDMA (used by GSM providers). Truly a broadband cellular service as fast as Wi-Fi.	Apple iPhone 3G; TMobile G1; All cellular network providers

TABLE 3.8	EXAMPLE HYBRID CELLULAR WIRELESS DEVICES		
PRODUCT	FUNCTIONALITY	PROVIDER/ NETWORK	SPEED
Apple iPhone; Apple iPhone 3G; TMobile G1	Phone, Web, e-mail, organizer. Fully converged Wi-Fi/ cellular device	AT&T	60–284 Kbps EVDO network/ 11 Mbps Wi-Fi/ 1 Mbps 3G
Palm T|X Handheld; Palm Treo	Wi-Fi Web, e-mail, video, photos, organizer	Wi-Fi hotspots	11 Mbps
Samsung SCH-A950	Phone, Web (EV-DO), e-mail, V-cast video, and Verizon music store; camera	Verizon 3G network	144–2 Mbps
Motorola Razr V3	Phone, e-mail, Web GSM, Bluetooth, camera, organizer	Cingular GSM network; CDMA2000 EV-DO network	60–170 Kbps
BlackBerry Curve BlackBerry Bold BlackBerry Pearl	Phone, Web (EDGE), music, e-mail, organizer ; 8820 is a fully converged phone with Wi-Fi and EDGE access	BlackBerry network; Verizon GSM/GPRS network; EDGE network	60–170 Kbps

Wi-Fi (Wireless Fidelity)

also referred to as 802.11b, 802.11a (Wi-Fi5), and 802.16 (WiMAX). Wireless standard for Ethernet networks with greater speed and range than Bluetooth

IEEE 802.11b (also referred to as **Wi-Fi**) was the first commercially viable standard for wireless local networks in the 2.4 GHz frequency range set aside by the U.S. government for unregulated use. Subsequent versions offered greater speed. Version 802.11n became the standard in 2008.

In a Wi-Fi network, a *wireless access point* (also known as a "hot spot") connects to the Internet directly via a broadband connection (cable, DSL telephone, or T1 line) and then transmits a radio signal to a transmitter/receiver installed in a laptop computer or PDA, either as a PCMCIA card or built-in at manufacture (such as Intel's Centrino processor, which provides built-in support for Wi-Fi in portable devices). **Figure 3.16** on page 160 illustrates how a Wi-Fi network works.

Wi-Fi offers extremely high bandwidth capacity of from 11 Mbps to 70 Mbps—far greater than any 3G service even planned—but has a limited range of 300 meters, with the exception of WiMax discussed below. Wi-Fi is also exceptionally inexpensive. The cost of creating a corporate Wi-Fi network in a single fourteen-story building with an access point for each floor is less than $100 an access point. It would cost well over $500,000 to wire the same building with Ethernet cable. Admittedly, the Ethernet cable would be operating at a theoretical 100 Mbps—ten times as fast as Wi-Fi. However, in some cases, this capacity is not needed and Wi-Fi is an acceptable alternative.

While initially a grass roots, "hippies and hackers" public access technology, billions of dollars have subsequently been poured into private ventures seeking to create for-profit Wi-Fi networks. The most prominent network has been created by

TABLE 3.9	WIRELESS INTERNET ACCESS NETWORK TECHNOLOGY		
TECHNOLOGY	**RANGE/SPEED**	**DESCRIPTION**	**PLAYERS**
Wi-Fi (IEEE 802.11a –802.11n)	300 feet/11–70 Mbps	Evolving high-speed, fixed broadband wireless local area network for commercial and residential use	Linksys, Cisco, and other Wi-Fi router manufacturers; entrepreneurial network developers
WiMAX (IEEE 802.16)	30 miles/50–70 Mbps	High-speed, medium-range, broadband wireless metropolitan area network	Fujitsu, Intel, Alcatel, Proxim/Terabeam
Bluetooth (wireless personal area network)	1–30 meters/ 1–3 Mbps	Modest speed, low power, short range connection of digital devices	Ericson, Nokia, Apple, HP, and other device makers
Ultra-Wideband (UWB) (wireless personal area networks)	30 feet/5–10 Mbps	Low-power, short-range, high bandwidth network technology useful as cabling replacement in home and office networks	Ultrawideband Forum, Intel, Freescale
ZigBee (wireless personal area network)	30 feet/250 Kbps	Short-range, very low-power, wireless network technology useful for remotely controlling industrial, medical, and home automation devices	Zigbee Alliance, Chipcon, Freescale, Mitsubishi, Motorola, Maxstream, San Juan Software

Boingo Wireless with over 100,000 hot spots around the globe (Boingo Wireless, Inc., 2008). Wayport has created another large network that provides Wi-Fi service at hotels, airports, McDonalds, IHOPs, and Hertz airport rental offices, with over 12,000 hot spots worldwide (Wayport, Inc., 2008). Even phone companies are establishing networks: T-Mobile and Sprint both have established nationwide Wi-Fi services at 2,000 Starbuck's coffee shops, and thousands of other public locations. Apple, in turn, has made Wi-Fi automatically available to iPhone handsets as an alternative to the more expensive and much slower 2.5G cellular systems it also uses.

Will WLAN compete directly against far more expensive telephone 3G services? The answer is "eventually but not right now." Wi-Fi was originally a local area network technology of limited range, for stationary client computers, but with high capacity suitable for most Web surfing and some corporate uses with modest bandwidth demands. Cellular phone systems are wide area networks of nearly unlimited range, for mobile client computers and handhelds, and with modest but rapidly increasing capacity suitable for e-mail, photos, and some Web browsing (on very small screens). However, the rock bottom price of Wi-Fi coupled with ambitious plans for a 30-mile-

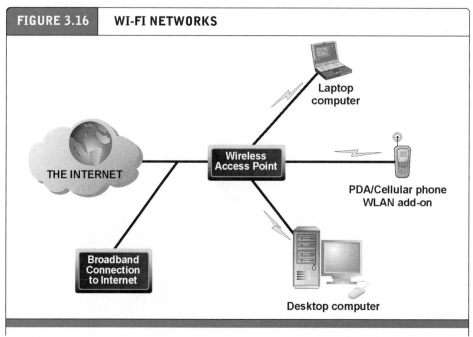

| FIGURE 3.16 | WI-FI NETWORKS |

In a Wi-Fi network, wireless access points connect to the Internet using a land-based broadband connection. Clients, which could be laptops, desktops, cell phones, or suitably equipped PDAs, connect to the access point using radio signals.

range WiMAX (802.16) service suggests that Wi-Fi could drain significant business from far more capital-intensive cellular systems.

A second WLAN technology for connecting to the Internet, and for connecting Internet devices to one another, is called Bluetooth. Bluetooth is an industry standard that emanated from Scandinavian telecommunications firms such as Ericsson, Nokia, and Siemens in the 1990s. **Bluetooth** is a personal connectivity technology that enables links between mobile computers, mobile phones, PDAs, and connectivity to the Internet (Bluetooth SIG, 2005). Bluetooth is the universal cable cutter, promising to get rid of the tangled mess of wires, cradles, and special attachments that plague the current world of personal computing. With Bluetooth, users wear a cell phone wireless earbud, share files in a hallway or conference room, synchronize their PDA with their laptop without a cradle, send a document to a printer, and even pay a restaurant bill from the table to a Bluetooth-equipped cash register. Bluetooth also is an unregulated media operating in the 2.4 GHz spectrum but with very limited range of 30 feet or less. It uses a frequency hopping signal with up to 1,600 hops per second over 79 frequencies, giving it good protection from interference. Bluetooth-equipped devices—which could be cell phones, PDAs, or laptops—constantly scan their environments looking for connections to compatible devices. Today, almost all cell phones and PDAs are Bluetooth-enabled.

A more recent arrival on the wireless connectivity front is ZigBee. **ZigBee** is a less-expensive, low-power, and simpler form of radio network operating in the 2.4 GHz frequency range that allows small appliances and sensors to communicate

Bluetooth
new technology standard for short-range wireless communication under 10 meters

ZigBee
a less-expensive, low-power, and simpler form of radio network operating in the 2.4 GHz band and other bands that allows small appliances and sensors to talk with one another

with one another. The current focus of ZigBee is developing simple networks for industrial controls, medical devices, smoke and intruder alarms, building automation, and home automation. These networks use very small amounts of power, so individual devices might run for a year or two with a single alkaline battery (ZigBee Alliance, 2008).

Table 3.10 summarizes some of the e-commerce services that can be supported by wireless Internet access. Some of these services are *push services*—the transmission of data at a predetermined time, or under determined conditions. This could include unsolicited information such as news delivery or stock market values. Other services are *pull services*—transmission of data resulting from user requests. Geographical information services—advertising for local pizza shops, restaurants, and museums—are a major growth area for cell phone services in part due to the Wireless Communications and Public Safety Act of 1999, which required all cell phone carriers in the United States to feature E911 technology by 2006. E911 (Enhanced 911) service allows a person's cell phone to be located at a physical address when that person calls the 911 emergency number used throughout the United States. This requires all cell phones to be equipped with GPS receivers (Global Positioning System), which provide

TABLE 3.10	POTENTIAL WIRELESS INTERNET E-COMMERCE SERVICES
SERVICE	DESCRIPTION
Horizontal Market Services	**Services that apply across industries and firms**
Personalized information	Stock values, news, quotes based on user profiles and needs
Geographical-based local content	Local maps, hotel finders, movie locations and times, and restaurant locations and reviews
Media services	Video, photos, news, and music
Banking services	Balance checking, money transfer, bill payment, and overdraft alerts
Financial services	Trading, stock alerts, and interest rates based on user account information
Vertical Market Services	**Services that apply within a firm or industry**
Sales support	Stock and production information, remote orders, calendars, and planning information
Reservation systems	Airline, train, hotel, and event reservations coordinated with inventory
Dispatching	Communication of job details, parts information, and repair routines
Fleet management	Control of fleet delivery or service staff; monitoring locations and work schedules
Parcel delivery	Tracking of packages, queries, and performance monitoring
Home automation	Coordinating alarm and other digital services and devices in a home
Industrial automation	Coordinating machine controllers in a factory

a fairly precise latitude and longitude location. In fact, all cell phone carriers can identify the GPS location of a cell phone regardless of what number is called. This enhanced geographic locating capability can easily be used to send locally based advertising to cell phone users either over the Web or using the cellular network itself.

BENEFITS OF INTERNET II TECHNOLOGIES

The increased bandwidth and expanded wireless network connectivity of the Internet II era will result in benefits beyond faster access and richer communications. First-mile enhancements created by fiber-optic networks will enhance reliability and quality of Internet transmissions and create new business models and opportunities. Some of the major benefits of these technological advancements include IP multicasting, latency solutions, guaranteed service levels, lower error rates, and declining costs. Widespread wireless access to the Internet will also essentially double or even triple the size of the online shopping marketspace because consumers will be able to shop and make purchases just about anywhere. This is equivalent to doubling the physical floor space of all shopping malls in America. We describe some of these benefits in more detail in the following sections.

IP Multicasting

The future of the Internet is clearly to become the entertainment center of American life, replacing radio, television, and movie theaters. This means Hollywood movies, television shows, and all the music ever digitized will have to routinely move across the Internet from coast to coast on demand from 175-200 million users. Today, this would cause a near collapse of the Internet. Internet II will potentially solve this problem. One capability of Internet II is IP multicasting.

IP multicasting
a set of technologies that enables efficient delivery of data to many locations on a network

IP multicasting is a set of technologies that enables efficient delivery of very large files to many locations on a network. Rather than making multiple copies of a message intended to be distributed to multiple recipients at the point of origin of a message, multicasting initially sends just one message and does not copy it to the individual recipients until it reaches the closest common point on the network, thereby minimizing the bandwidth consumed (see **Figure 3.17**). At that point, routers make copies as needed to serve requesting clients, and the sender sends only a single copy over the Internet. Network performance is significantly improved because it isn't bogged down with the processing and transmission of several large data files; each receiving computer doesn't have to query the transmitting server for the file. Multicasting technologies are already making their way into today's Internet through the use of Mbone (a special-purpose backbone for delivering video data). Used in combination with protocols like BitTorrent, IP multicasting has the potential to scale up to serve an entire nation of Internet users.

Latency Solutions

One of the challenges of packet switching, where data is divided into chunks and then sent separately to meet again at the destination, is that the Internet does not

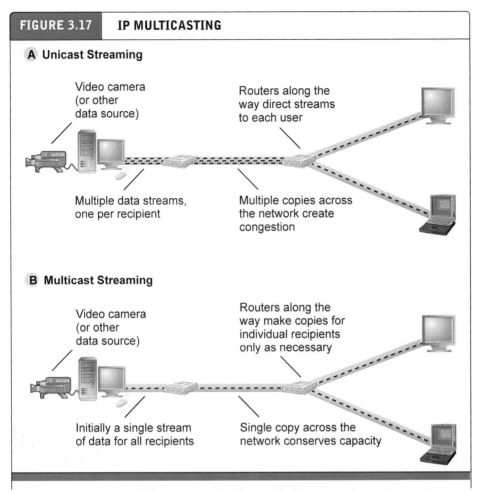

| FIGURE 3.17 | IP MULTICASTING |

A Unicast Streaming

Video camera
(or other
data source)

Routers along the
way direct streams
to each user

Multiple data streams,
one per recipient

Multiple copies across
the network create
congestion

B Multicast Streaming

Video camera
(or other
data source)

Routers along the
way make copies for
individual recipients
only as necessary

Initially a single stream
of data for all recipients

Single copy across the
network conserves capacity

IP multicasting is a method for efficiently sending high-bandwidth video files to clients without causing Internet congestion and delay for other traffic.

SOURCES: Adapted from Cisco Systems, 2007; Internet2.edu, 2000.

differentiate between high-priority packets, such as video clips, and those of lower priority, such as self-contained e-mail messages. Because the packets cannot yet be simultaneously reassembled, the result is distorted audio and video streams.

Internet II holds the promise of **diffserv**, or differentiated quality of service—a new technology that assigns levels of priority to packets based on the type of data being transmitted. Video conference packets, for example, which need to reach their destination almost instantaneously, would receive much higher priority than e-mail messages. In the end, the quality of video and audio will skyrocket without undue stress on the network. Live and on-demand television and movies will be possible once Internet II is completed. But differential service is very controversial because it means some users will get more bandwidth than others, and potentially they may have to pay a higher price for more bandwidth.

diffserv (differentiated quality of service)
a new technology that assigns levels of priority to packets based on the type of data being transmitted

Guaranteed Service Levels and Lower Error Rates

In today's Internet, there is no service-level guarantee and no way to purchase the right to move data through the Internet at a fixed pace. Today's Internet promises only "best effort." The Internet is democratic—it speeds or slows everyone's traffic alike. With Internet II, it will be possible to purchase the right to move data through the network at a guaranteed speed in return for higher fees.

Improved capacity and packet switching will also inevitably impact quality of data transmissions, reducing error rates and boosting customer satisfaction.

Declining Costs

As the Internet pipeline is upgraded, the availability of broadband service will expand beyond major metropolitan areas, significantly reducing the costs of access. More users means lower cost, as products and technology catch on in the mass market. Higher volume usage enables providers to lower the cost of both access devices, or clients, and the service required to use such products. Both broadband and wireless service fees are expected to decline as geographic service areas increase, in part due to competition for that business.

3.4   THE WORLD WIDE WEB

Without the World Wide Web, there would be no e-commerce. The invention of the Web brought an extraordinary expansion of digital services to millions of amateur computer users, including color text and pages, formatted text, pictures, animations, video, and sound. In short, the Web makes nearly all the rich elements of human expression needed to establish a commercial marketplace available to nontechnical computer users worldwide.

While the Internet was born in the 1960s, the Web was not invented until 1989–1991 by Dr. Tim Berners-Lee of the European Particle Physics Laboratory, better known as CERN (Berners-Lee et al., 1994). Several earlier authors—such as Vannevar Bush (in 1945) and Ted Nelson (in the 1960s)—had suggested the possibility of organizing knowledge as a set of interconnected pages that users could freely browse (Bush, 1945; Ziff Davis Publishing, 1998). Berners-Lee and his associates at CERN built on these ideas and developed the initial versions of HTML, HTTP, a Web server, and a browser, the four essential components of the Web.

First, Berners-Lee wrote a computer program that allowed formatted pages within his own computer to be linked using keywords (hyperlinks). Clicking on a keyword in a document would immediately move him to another document. Berners-Lee created the pages using a modified version of a powerful text markup language called SGML (Standard Generalized Markup Language).

Berners-Lee called this language HyperText Markup Language, or HTML. He then came up with the idea of storing his HTML pages on the Internet. Remote client computers could access these pages by using HTTP (introduced earlier in Section 3.2 and described more fully in the next section). But these early Web pages still appeared as black and white text pages with hyperlinks expressed inside brackets.

The early Web was based on text only; the original Web browser only provided a line interface.

Information being shared on the Web remained text-based until 1993, when Marc Andreesen and others at the NCSA (National Center for Supercomputing Applications) at the University of Illinois created a Web browser with a graphical user interface (GUI) called **Mosaic** that made it possible to view documents on the Web graphically—using colored backgrounds, images, and even primitive animations. Mosaic was a software program that could run on any graphically based interface such as Macintosh, Windows, or Unix. The Mosaic browser software read the HTML text on a Web page and displayed it as a graphical interface document within a graphical user interface operating system such as Windows or Macintosh. Liberated from simple black and white text pages, HTML pages could now be viewed by anyone in the world who could operate a mouse and use a Macintosh or PC.

Mosaic
Web browser with a graphical user interface (GUI) that made it possible to view documents on the Web graphically

Aside from making the content of Web pages colorful and available to the world's population, the graphical Web browser created the possibility of **universal computing**, the sharing of files, information, graphics, sound, video, and other objects across all computer platforms in the world, regardless of operating system. A browser could be made for each of the major operating systems, and the Web pages created for one system, say, Windows, would also be displayed exactly the same, or nearly the same, on computers running the Macintosh or Unix operating systems. As long as each operating system had a Mosaic browser, the same Web pages could be used on all the different types of computers and operating systems. This meant that no matter what kind of computer you used, anywhere in the world, you would see the same Web pages. The browser and the Web have introduced us to a whole new world of computing and information management that was unthinkable prior to 1993.

universal computing
the sharing of files, information, graphics, sound, video, and other objects across all computer platforms in the world, regardless of operating system

In 1994, Andreesen and Jim Clark founded Netscape, which created the first commercial browser, **Netscape Navigator**. Although Mosaic had been distributed free of charge, Netscape initially charged for its software. In August 1995, Microsoft Corporation released its own version of a browser, called **Internet Explorer**. In the ensuing years, Netscape has faltered, falling from a 100% market share to less than .5% in 2008. The fate of Netscape illustrates an important e-commerce business lesson. Innovators usually are not long-term winners, whereas smart followers often have the assets needed for long-term survival.

Netscape Navigator
the first commercial Web browser

Internet Explorer
Microsoft's Web browser

HYPERTEXT

Web pages can be accessed through the Internet because the Web browser software on your PC can request Web pages stored on an Internet host server using the HTTP protocol. **Hypertext** is a way of formatting pages with embedded links that connect documents to one another, and that also link pages to other objects such as sound, video, or animation files. When you click on a graphic and a video clip plays, you have clicked on a hyperlink. For example, when you type a Web address in your browser such as http://www.sec.gov, your browser sends an HTTP request to the sec.gov server requesting the home page of sec.gov.

Hypertext
a way of formatting pages with embedded links that connect documents to one another, and that also link pages to other objects such as sound, video, or animation files

HTTP is the first set of letters at the start of every Web address, followed by the domain name. The domain name specifies the organization's server computer that is housing the document. Most companies have a domain name that is the same as or closely related to their official corporate name. The directory path and document name are two more pieces of information within the Web address that help the browser track down the requested page. Together, the address is called a Uniform Resource Locator, or URL. When typed into a browser, a URL tells it exactly where to look for the information. For example, in the following URL:

http://www.megacorp.com/content/features/082602.html

http = the protocol used to display Web pages

www.megacorp.com = domain name

content/features = the directory path that identifies where on the domain Web server the page is stored

082602.html = the document name and its format (an html page)

The most common domain extensions (known as general top-level domains, or gTLDs) currently available and officially sanctioned by ICANN are shown in **Table 3.11**. Countries also have domain names, such as .uk, .au, and .fr (United Kingdom, Australia, and France, respectively). These are sometimes referred to as country-code top-level domains, or ccTLDs. In June 2008, ICANN approved an expansion of domain names, based on communities, such as .nyc, .berlin, .writers, and so on, but this has not yet been implemented.

MARKUP LANGUAGES

Although the most common Web page formatting language is HTML, the concept behind document formatting actually had its roots in the 1960s with the development of Generalized Markup Language (GML).

Standard Generalized Markup Language (SGML)

In 1986, the International Standards Organization adopted a variation of GML called Standard Generalized Markup Language, or SGML. The purpose of SGML was to help very large organizations format and categorize large collections of documents. The advantage of SGML is that it can run independent of any software program but, unfortunately, it is extremely complicated and difficult to learn. Probably for this reason, it has not been widely adopted.

HyperText Markup Language (HTML)
one of the next generation of GMLs that is relatively easy to use in Web page design. HTML provides Web page designers with a fixed set of markup "tags" that are used to format a Web page

HyperText Markup Language (HTML)

HyperText Markup Language (HTML) is a GML that is relatively easy to use. HTML provides Web page designers with a fixed set of markup "tags" that are used to format a Web page (see **Figure 3.18**). When these tags are inserted into a Web page, they are read by the browser and interpreted into a page display. You can see the source HTML code for any Web page by simply clicking on the "Page Source" command found in all browsers. In Figure 3.18, the HTML code in the first screen produces the display in the second screen.

TABLE 3.11	TOP-LEVEL DOMAINS		
GENERAL TOP-LEVEL DOMAIN (gTLD)	YEAR(S) INTRODUCED	PURPOSE	SPONSOR/ OPERATOR
.com	1980s	Unrestricted (but intended for commercial registrants)	VeriSign
.edu	1980s	U.S. educational institutions	Educause
.gov	1980s	U.S. government	U.S. General Services Administration
.mil	1980s	U.S. military	U.S. Department of Defense Network Information Center
.net	1980s	Unrestricted (but originally intended for network providers, etc.)	VeriSign
.org	1980s	Unrestricted (but intended for organizations that do not fit elsewhere)	Public Interest Registry (was operated by VeriSign until December 31, 2002)
.int	1998	Organizations established by international treaties between governments	Internet Assigned Numbers Authority (IANA)
.aero	2001	Air-transport industry	Societe Internationale de Telecommunications Aeronautiques SC (SITA)
.biz	2001	Businesses	NeuLevel
.coop	2001	Cooperatives	DotCooperation LLC
.info	2001	Unrestricted use	Afilias LLC
.museum	2001	Museums	Museum Domain Name Association (MuseDoma)
.name	2001	For registration by individuals	Global Name Registry Ltd.
.pro	2002	Accountants, lawyers, physicians, and other professionals	RegistryPro Ltd
.jobs	2005	Job search	Employ Media LLC
.travel	2005	Travel search	Triallance Corporation
.mobi	2005	Web sites specifically designed for mobile phones	mTLD Top Level Domain, Ltd.
.cat	2005	Individuals, organizations, and companies that promote the Catalan language and culture	Fundació puntCAT
.asia	2006	Regional domain for companies, organizations, and individuals based in Asia	DotAsia Organization
.tel	2006	Telephone numbers and other contact information	Telnic, Ltd.

SOURCES: Based on data from ICANN, 2008.

| FIGURE 3.18 | EXAMPLE HTML CODE (A) AND WEB PAGE (B) |

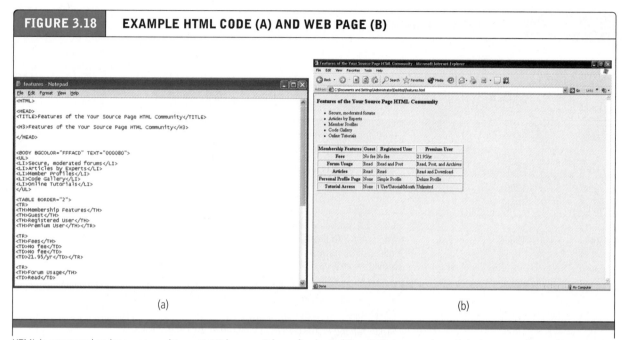

(a)   (b)

HTML is a text markup language used to create Web pages. It has a fixed set of "tags" that are used to tell the browser software how to present the content on screen. The HTML shown in Figure 3.17 (a) creates the Web page seen in Figure 3.17 (b).

HTML defines the structure and style of a document, including the headings, graphic positioning, tables, and text formatting. Since its introduction, the major browsers have continuously added features to HTML to enable programmers to further refine their page layouts. Unfortunately, some browser enhancements may work only in one company's browser. Whenever you build an e-commerce site, you should take care that the pages can be viewed by the major browsers, even outdated versions of browsers. HTML Web pages can be created with any text editor, such as Notepad or WordPad, using Microsoft Word (simply save the Word document as a Web page) or any one of several Web page development tools such as such as FrontPage or Dreamweaver.[6]

eXtensible Markup Language (XML)

eXtensible Markup Language (XML)

a markup language specification developed by the W3C (World Wide Web Consortium) that is designed to describe data and information

eXtensible Markup Language (XML) takes Web document formatting a giant leap forward. XML is a markup language specification developed by the W3C (World Wide Web Consortium) that is similar to HTML, but has a very different purpose. Whereas the purpose of HTML is to control the "look and feel" and display of data on the Web page, XML is designed to describe data and information. For example, consider the sample XML document in **Figure 3.19**. The first line in the sample document is the XML declaration, which is always included; it defines the XML version of the document. In this case, the document conforms to the 1.0 specification of XML. The next line defines the first element of the document (the root element): < note >. The next four lines define four child elements of the root (to, from, heading, and

[6]A detailed discussion of how to use HTML is beyond the scope of this text.

FIGURE 3.19   **A SIMPLE XML DOCUMENT**

```
<?xml version="1.0"?>
<note>
<to>George</to>
<from>Carol</from>
<heading>Just a Reminder</heading>
<body>Don't forget to order the groceries from FreshDirect!</body>
</note>
```

The tags in this simple XML document, such as <note>, <to>, and <from> are used to describe data and information, rather than the look and feel of the document.

body). The last line defines the end of the root element. Notice that XML says nothing about how to display the data, or how the text should look on the screen. HTML is used for information display in combination with XML, which is used for data description.

Figure 3.20 shows how XML can be used to define a database of company names in a company directory. Tags such as < Company >, < Name >, and < Specialty > can be defined for a single firm, or an entire industry. On an elementary level, XML is extraordinarily easy to learn and is very similar to HTML except that you can make up your own tags. At a deeper level, XML has a rich syntax and an enormous set of

---

FIGURE 3.20   **SAMPLE XML CODE FOR A COMPANY DIRECTORY**

```
<?xml version="1.0"?>
<Companies>
    <Company>
          <Name>Azimuth Interactive Inc.</Name>
       <Specialties>
                <Specialty>HTML development</Specialty>
                  <Specialty>technical documentation</Specialty>
               <Specialty>ROBO Help</Specialty>
               <Country>United States</Country>
       </Specialties>
       <Location>
                <Country>United States</Country>
             <State />
              <City>Chicago</City>
       </Location>
            <Telephone>301-555-1212</Telephone>
    </Company>
    <Company>
       ...
    </Company>
   ...
</Companies>
```

This XML document uses tags to define a database of company names.

software tools, which make XML ideal for storing and communicating many types of data on the Web.

XML is "extensible," which means the tags used to describe and display data are defined by the user, whereas in HTML the tags are limited and predefined. XML can also transform information into new formats, such as by importing information from a database and displaying it as a table. With XML, information can be analyzed and displayed selectively, making it a more powerful alternative to HTML. This means that business firms, or entire industries, can describe all of their invoices, accounts payable, payroll records, and financial information using a Web-compatible markup language. Once described, these business documents can be stored on intranet Web servers and shared throughout the corporation.

XML is not yet a replacement for HTML; however, most contemporary browsers support XML. Currently, XML and HTML work side by side on the same Web pages.

WEB SERVERS AND CLIENTS

We have already described client/server computing and the revolution in computing architecture brought about by client/server computing. You already know that a server is a computer attached to a network that stores files, controls peripheral devices, interfaces with the outside world—including the Internet—and does some processing for other computers on the network.

Web server software

software that enables a computer to deliver Web pages written in HTML to client computers on a network that request this service by sending an HTTP request

But what is a Web server? **Web server software** refers to the software that enables a computer to deliver Web pages written in HTML to client computers on a network that request this service by sending an HTTP request. The two leading brands of Web server software are Apache, which is free Web server shareware that accounts for about 50% of the market, and Microsoft's Internet Information Services (IIS), which accounts for about 35% of the market (Netcraft.com, 2008).

Aside from responding to requests for Web pages, all Web servers provide some additional basic capabilities such as the following:

- *Security services*—These consist mainly of authentication services that verify that the person trying to access the site is authorized to do so. For Web sites that process payment transactions, the Web server also supports SSL, the Internet protocol for transmitting and receiving information securely over the Internet. When private information such as names, phone numbers, addresses, and credit card data needs to be provided to a Web site, the Web server uses SSL to ensure that the data passing back and forth from the browser to the server is not compromised.

- *FTP*—This protocol allows users to transfer files to and from the server. Some sites limit file uploads to the Web server, while others restrict downloads, depending on the user's identity.

- *Search engine*—Just as search engine sites enable users to search the entire Web for particular documents, search engine modules within the basic Web server software package enable indexing of the site's Web pages and content, and permit easy keyword searching of the site's content. When conducting a search, a search engine makes use of an index, which is a list of all the documents on the server. The search term is compared to the index to identify likely matches.

- *Data capture*—Web servers are also helpful at monitoring site traffic, capturing information on who has visited a site, how long the user stayed there, the date and time of each visit, and which specific pages on the server were accessed. This information is compiled and saved in a log file, which can then be analyzed. By analyzing a log file, a site manager can find out the total number of visitors, average length of each visit, and the most popular destinations, or Web pages.

The term *Web server* is also used to refer to the physical computer that runs Web server software. Leading manufacturers of Web server computers include IBM, Dell, and Hewlett-Packard. Although any personal computer can run Web server software, it is best to use a computer that has been optimized for this purpose. To be a Web server, a computer must have the Web server software described installed and be connected to the Internet. Every public Web server computer has an IP address. For example, if you type http://www.prenhall.com/laudon in your browser, the browser software sends a request for HTTP service to the Web server whose domain name is prenhall.com. The server then locates the page named "laudon" on its hard drive, sends the page back to your browser, and displays it on your screen. Of course, firms also can use Web servers for strictly internal local area networking in intranets.

Aside from the generic Web server software packages, there are actually many types of specialized servers on the Web, from **database servers** that access specific information within a database, to **ad servers** that deliver targeted banner ads, to **mail servers** that provide e-mail messages, and **video servers** that provide video clips. At a small e-commerce site, all of these software packages might be running on a single computer, with a single processor. At a large corporate site, there may be hundreds or thousands of discrete server computers, many with multiple processors, running specialized Web server functions. We discuss the architecture of e-commerce sites in greater detail in Chapter 4.

A **Web client**, on the other hand, is any computing device attached to the Internet that is capable of making HTTP requests and displaying HTML pages. The most common client is a Windows or Macintosh computer, with various flavors of Unix/Linux computers a distant third. However, the fastest-growing category of Web clients are not computers at all, but cell phones and handheld PDAs outfitted with wireless Web access software. In general, Web clients can be any device—including a refrigerator, stove, home lighting system, or automobile instrument panel—capable of sending and receiving information from Web servers.

WEB BROWSERS

Web browsers are software programs whose primary purpose is to display Web pages. Browsers also have added features, such as e-mail and newsgroups (an online discussion group or forum). The leading Web browsers are Internet Explorer, with about 73% of the market as of June 2008. Firefox (Mozilla) is currently the second most popular Web browser, with about 19% of the U.S. Web browser market

database server
server designed to access specific information with a database

ad server
server designed to deliver targeted banner ads

mail server
server that provides e-mail messages

video server
server that serves video clips

Web client
any computing device attached to the Internet that is capable of making HTTP requests and displaying HTML pages, most commonly a Windows PC or Macintosh

(Net Applications, 2008). First released in 2004, Firefox is a free, open source Web browser for the Windows, Linux and Macintosh operating systems, based on Mozilla open source code (which originally provided the code for Netscape). It is small and fast and offers many new features such as pop-up blocking and tabbed browsing. Other browsers include Apple's Safari, Opera, and Netscape Navigator, which collectively make up 5% of the market.

In September 2008, Google released a beta version of its entry into the Web browser competition, a small, yet technologically advanced open-source browser called Chrome. With the development of Chrome, Google hopes to create a browser that improves upon other browsers' speed, security, and stability, while also serving as a streamlined platform for even the most complex web pages as well as a wide variety of applications. In the process, the company hopes to make inroads against the market share of Firefox and, more importantly, Internet Explorer.

3.5 THE INTERNET AND THE WEB: FEATURES

The Internet and the Web have spawned a number of powerful new software applications upon which the foundations of e-commerce are built. You can think of these all as Web services, and it is interesting as you read along to compare these services to other traditional media such as television or print media. If you do, you will quickly realize how rich is the Internet environment.

E-MAIL

electronic mail (e-mail)

the most-used application of the Internet. Uses a series of protocols to enable messages containing text, images, sound, and video clips to be transferred from one Internet user to another

Since its earliest days, **electronic mail**, or **e-mail**, has been the most-used application of the Internet. In the United States about 97 million people send e-mail every day, and worldwide over 600 million send e-mail daily. The total number of e-mail messages (including commercial, personal, and spam) sent daily in the United States in 2008 is estimated to be around 80 billion (EmailStatcenter.com, 2008; Evert, 2007). Estimates vary on the amount of spam, ranging from 40% to 90%. E-mail marketing and spam are examined in more depth in Chapter 7.

attachment

a file inserted within an e-mail message

E-mail uses a series of protocols to enable messages containing text, images, sound, and video clips to be transferred from one Internet user to another. Because of its flexibility and speed, it is now the most popular form of business communication—more popular than the phone, fax, or snail mail (the U.S. Postal Service). In addition to text typed within the message, e-mail also allows **attachments**, which are files inserted within the e-mail message. The files can be documents, images, sounds, or video clips.

INSTANT MESSAGING

instant messaging (IM)

displays words typed on a computer almost instantaneously. Recipients can then respond immediately to the sender the same way, making the communication more like a live conversation than is possible through e-mail

One of the fastest growing forms of online human communication is **instant messaging (IM)**. An instant messenger is a client software program that signs onto an instant messaging server. IM sends text messages in real time, one line at a time, unlike e-mail. E-mail messages have a time lag of several seconds to minutes between when messages are sent and received. IM displays lines of text entered on a computer almost instantaneously. Recipients can then respond immediately to the sender the same way, making the communication more like a live conversation than is possible through e-mail. To use IM, users identify a buddy list they want to communicate with, and then enter short text messages that their buddies will receive instantly (if they are online at the time). And although text remains the primary communication mechanism in IM, users can insert audio clips or photos into their instant messages, and even participate in video conferencing.

The major IM systems are AOL (which first introduced IM as a proprietary consumer service in 1997), with around 40 million unique users; Microsoft's Windows Live Messenger, with about 18 million; Yahoo Messenger, with about 27 million; and Google Talk with 2 million. IM systems were initially developed as proprietary systems, with competing firms offering versions that did not work with one another. However, in 2006, Yahoo and MSN joined together to provide a level of interoperability between their respective systems, and in June 2008, Google has announced talks with Yahoo to do the same.

SEARCH ENGINES

No one knows for sure how many Web pages there really are. The surface Web is that part of the Web which search engines visit and record information about. For instance, Google currently searches about 40 billion Web pages and stores information about those pages in its massive computer network located throughout the United States. Microsoft and Yahoo presumably index a similar number of pages, AskJeeves is estimated to index 10 billion pages. But there is also a "deep Web" that contains an estimated 900 billion additional Web pages, many of them proprietary (such as the pages of the online version of *The Wall Street Journal*, which cannot be visited without an access code) or behind corporate firewalls (Zillman, 2005). Cuil (pronounced "cool"), a new search company, announced in July 2008 that it had indexed 120 billion Web pages (Cuil, Inc., 2008)

But obviously with so many Web pages, finding Web specific pages that can help you or your business, nearly instantly, is an important problem. The question is: how can you find the one or two Web pages you really want and need out of the 50 billion indexed Web pages?

Search engines solve the problem of finding useful information on the Web nearly instantly, and, arguably, they are the "killer app" of the Internet era. About 71 million Americans use search engines each day, generating about 7.5 to 10 billion queries a month (Pew Internet & American Life Project, 2008, Nielsen Online, 2008). There are hundreds of different search engines in the world, but the vast majority of the search results are supplied by the top five providers (see **Figure 3.21**).

Web search engines started out in the early 1990s shortly after Netscape released the first commercial Web browser. Early browsers were relatively simple software programs that roamed the nascent Web, visiting pages, and gathering information about the content of each Web page. These early programs were called variously crawlers, spiders, and wanderers; the first full-text crawler that indexed the contents of an entire Web page was called WebCrawler, released in 1994. AltaVista (1995), one

search engine
identifies Web pages that appear to match keywords, also called queries, typed by the user and provides a list of the best matches

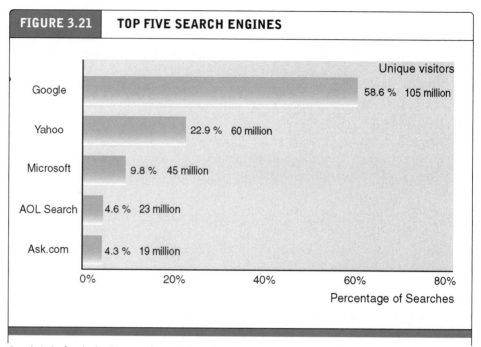

| FIGURE 3.21 | TOP FIVE SEARCH ENGINES |

Google is, by far, the leading search engine based on its percentage share of the number of searches. In terms of unique visitors, however, the top three sites are much more tightly bunched.

SOURCE: Based on data from eMarketer, Inc., 2008e; and Nielsen Online, 2008.

of the first widely used search engines, was the first to allow "natural language" queries such as "history of Web search engines" rather than "history + Web search + search engine".

The Google search engine is continuously crawling the Web, indexing the content of each page, calculating its popularity, and caching the pages so that it can respond quickly to your request to see a page. The entire process takes about one-half of a second.

The first search engines employed simple keyword indexes of all the Web pages visited. They would count the number of times a word appeared on the Web page, and store this information in an index. These search engines could be easily fooled by Web designers who simply repeated words on their home pages. The real innovations in search engine development occurred through a program funded by the Department of Defense called the Digital Library Initiative, designed to help the Pentagon find research papers in large databases. Stanford, Berkeley, and three other universities became hotbeds of Web search innovations in the mid-1990s. At Stanford in 1994, two computer science students, David Filo and Jerry Yang, created a hand-selected list of their favorite Web pages and called it "Yet Another Hierarchical Officious Oracle" or Yahoo!. Yahoo initially was not a real search engine, but rather an edited selection of Web sites organized by categories the editors found useful. Yahoo has since developed "true" search engine capabilities.

In 1998, Larry Page and Sergey Brin, two Stanford computer science students, released their first version of Google. This search engine was different: not only did it index each Web page's words, but Page had discovered that the AltaVista search engine not only collected keywords from sites but also calculated what other sites linked to each page. By looking at the URLs on each Web page, they could calculate an index of popularity. AltaVista did nothing with this information. Page took this idea and made it a central factor in ranking a Web page's appropriateness to a search query. He patented the idea of a Web page ranking system (PageRank System), which essentially measures the popularity of the Web page. Brin contributed a unique Web crawler program that indexed not just keywords on a Web page, but combinations of words (such as authors and their article titles). These two ideas became the foundation for the Google search engine (Brandt, 2004). **Figure 3.22** illustrates how Google works.

Search engine Web sites have became so popular and easy to use that they also serve as major portals for the Internet (see Chapter 11). The search marketplace has become very competitive despite the dominance of Google. Both Microsoft and Yahoo have invested over a billion dollars each to match Google's search engine.

Initially, few understood how to make money out of search engines. That changed in 2000 when Goto.com (later Overture) allowed advertisers to bid for placement on their search engine results, and Google followed suit in 2003 with its AdWords program which allowed advertisers to bid for placement of short text ads on Google search results. The spectacular increase in Internet advertising revenues (which have been growing over the last few years at around 20%–25% annually), has helped search engines transform themselves into major shopping tools and created an entire new industry called "search engine marketing." Search engine marketing has been the fastest-growing form of advertising in the United States,

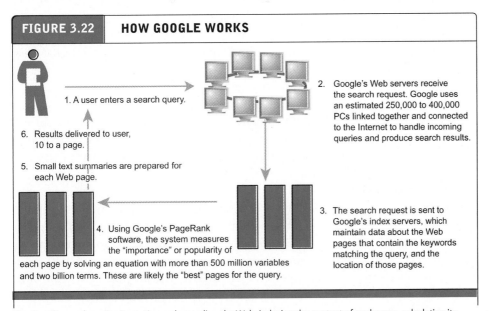

FIGURE 3.22   **HOW GOOGLE WORKS**

1. A user enters a search query.

2. Google's Web servers receive the search request. Google uses an estimated 250,000 to 400,000 PCs linked together and connected to the Internet to handle incoming queries and produce search results.

3. The search request is sent to Google's index servers, which maintain data about the Web pages that contain the keywords matching the query, and the location of those pages.

4. Using Google's PageRank software, the system measures the "importance" or popularity of each page by solving an equation with more than 500 million variables and two billion terms. These are likely the "best" pages for the query.

5. Small text summaries are prepared for each Web page.

6. Results delivered to user, 10 to a page.

The Google search engine is continuously crawling the Web, indexing the content of each page, calculating its popularity, and caching the pages so that it can respond quickly to your request to see a page. The entire process takes about one-half of a second.

reaching about $11 billion in 2008. When users enter a search term at Google, MSN Search, Yahoo, or any of the other Web sites serviced by these search engines, they receive two types of listings: sponsored links, for which advertisers have paid to be listed (usually at the top of the search results page) and unsponsored "organic" search results. In addition, advertisers can purchase small text ads on the right side of the search results page. Although the major search engines are used for locating general information of interest to users, search engines have also become a crucial tool within e-commerce sites. Customers can more easily search for the product information they want with the help of an internal search program; the difference is that within Web sites, the search engine is limited to finding matches from that one site. In addition, search engines are extending their services to include maps, satellite images, computer images, e-mail, group calendars, group meeting tools, and indexes of scholarly papers. Outside of e-mail, search engines are the most common online daily activity and produce the largest online audiences.

INTELLIGENT AGENTS (BOTS)

intelligent agent

software program that gathers and/or filters information on a specific topic and then provides a list of results for the user

An **intelligent agent** (also known as a software robot, or bot, for short) is a software program that gathers and/or filters information on a specific topic, and then provides a list of results for the user ranked in a number of ways, such as from lowest price to availability or to delivery terms. Intelligent agents were originally invented by computer scientists interested in the development of artificial intelligence (a family of related technologies that attempt to imbue computers with human-like intelligence). However, with the advent of e-commerce on the Web, interest quickly turned to exploiting intelligent agent technology for commercial purposes. Today, there are a number of different types of bots used in e-commerce on the Web, and more are being developed every day (see **Table 3.12**).

For instance, as previously noted, many search engines employ Web crawlers or spiders that crawl from server to server, compiling lists of URLs that form the database for the search engine. These Web crawlers and spiders are actually bots, automated programs that search the Web for a variety of reasons.

The shopping bot is another common type of bot. Shopping bots search online retail sites all over the Web and then report back on the availability and pricing of a range of products. For instance, you can use MySimon's shopping bot to search for a Sony digital camera. The bot provides a list of online retailers that carry a particular camera model, as well as report about whether it is in inventory and the price and shipping charges. Orbitz provides bots that find the lowest prices for airfares, hotels, and rental cars. Shopzilla.com is the leading comparison shopping Web site with an estimated 25 million unique monthly visitors in 2008, followed by Yahoo Shopping with an estimated 22 million, and Shopping.com with an estimated 18 million. About 60% of consumers have used a comparison shopping Web site. The number of shoppers visiting such sites is also growing rapidly at about 15% annually overall, with some sites like Yahoo Shopping growing over 50% in 2008 (Internet Retailer, 2008).

Another type of bot, called a Web monitoring bot, allows you to monitor for updated materials on the Web, and will e-mail you when a selected site has new or

TABLE 3.12	TYPES OF WEB BOTS
TYPE	**EXAMPLES**
Search bot	Searchbot.com Altavista.com Webcrawler.com
Shopping Bot	Shopzilla.com Shopping.com MySimon.com Orbitz.com
Web Monitoring Bot	WebSite Watcher TimelyWeb.com
News Bot	WebClipping.com SportSpider.net
Chatter Bot	Anna (Ikea) Ask Vic (Qantas) Virtual Advisor (Ultralase)

changed information. News bots will create custom newspapers or clip articles for you in newspapers around the world. RSS (Really Simple Syndication), discussed later in this chapter, is also a kind of automated program that sends updates and news to subscribers, and is quickly becoming the most common type of Web content monitoring tool.

Read *Insight on Technology: Chatterbots Meet Avatars*, to see how a bot with academic roots has morphed into an e-commerce customer-support tool.

ONLINE FORUMS AND CHAT

An **online forum** (also referred to as a message board, bulletin board, discussion board, discussion group, or simply a board or forum) is a Web application that enables Internet users to communicate with each other, although not in real time. A forum provides a container for various discussions (or "threads") started (or "posted") by members of the forum, and depending on the permissions granted to forum members by the forum's administrator, enables a person to start a thread and reply to other people's threads. Most forum software allows more than one forum to be created. The forum administrator typically can edit, delete, move, or otherwise modify any thread on the forum. Unlike an electronic mailing list (such as a listserv), which automatically sends new messages to a subscriber, an online forum typically requires that the member visit the forum to check for new posts. Some forums offer an "e-mail notification" feature that notifies users that a new post of interest to them has been made.

Online chat differs from an online forum in that, like IM, chat enables users to communicate via computer in real time, that is, simultaneously. However, unlike IM, which works only between two people, chat can occur among several users. Typically, users log in to a "chat room" where they can text message others. Some chat rooms offer virtual chat, which enable users to incorporate 2-D and 3-D graphics along with

online forum
a Web application that allows Internet users to communicate with each other, although not in real time

online chat
enables users to communicate via computer in real time, that is, simultaneously. Unlike IM, chat can occur among several users

INSIGHT ON TECHNOLOGY

CHATTERBOTS MEET AVATARS

In the early 1960s, Joseph Weizenbaum, a professor of computer science at the Massachusetts Institute of Technology, created a software program known as Eliza. Eliza was one of the first software programs to allow a computer to "converse" with a human in natural language. Weizenbaum programmed Eliza so that it was able to recognize certain key words in a statement or question. Eliza would then respond based on a set of preprogrammed rules. Sometimes Eliza was able to carry on a passable conversation—for a short period of time. More often than not, though, the conversation quickly degenerated into something no person would mistake for a human interaction. The trick behind Eliza was to answer a human's statements and questions with reasonable-sounding but ultimately meaningless questions drawn from Rogerian psychotherapy that were intended to encourage the patient to talk more about themselves.

From this rudimentary beginning in computer science departments sprang chatterbots: commercial-quality intelligent agents (computer programs) that could converse with a customer over the telephone or the Web either in text or voice modes. Sometimes called "virtual reps" or "remote agents," later chatterbots were programmed to both recognize human speech and to respond with meaningful suggestions or questions. Chatterbots are viewed as one possible answer to the customer service difficulties plaguing many e-commerce sites, problems that will cost e-tailers billions of dollars in 2007. For instance, one study found that the response times of Fortune 100 companies to simple e-mail queries left much to be desired, with only 13% responding within 24 hours; 37% of Fortune 500 companies did not respond to general inquiries submitted to their Web sites at all. Another study found that over 65% of those who start to fill up a shopping cart abandon it before going through the check-out process, for a variety of reasons, including poor Web site design, a confusing check-out process, or questions that were unanswered.

If you call a large bank, credit card provider, or your cell service provider, chances are good you will be encouraged to talk with a chatterbot. They are on duty 24/7, cost very little to operate, and can answer many questions of consumers using natural language interfaces and synthesized voices. No one knows for sure, but millions of transactions in the United States and Europe are handled by chatterbots every day. One of the largest commercial providers of virtual reps is the U.K firm Creativevirtual.com. They supply virtual online sales reps to BP, Lloyds, Sky.com, and Schering-Plough. Ikea's "Anna" is available on Ikea's Web sites worldwide in several different languages and acts as a guide to customers who land on the Ikea home page and don't have a clue about where to go next.

The problem with chatterbots is that they are not human, just computer programs with funny voices. Avatars may be an alternative. Increasingly, chatterbots are taking on the characteristics of 3-D Second Life avatars, or let's say the two are merging, or is it marrying?

An avatar is a computer-based representations of a person, usually as an animated graphic. They are created using a variety of different programs, and once created, they can be used in computer games, on instant messaging services, blogs, or in virtual communities such as Second Life, an "online 3-D digital world" that is

(continued)

"home" to 8 million Internet users. Avatars, unlike chatterbots, use the mind of their creators when interacting with other avatars as opposed to a computer program, and they express themselves using text, or online voice using VoIP. Avatars can be recorded on video, and the video played back.

Firms are beginning to experiment with virtual business centers on Second Life. A virtual business center is a location on Second Life where a firm can construct a building or office space, and where it can display its products and services to other avatars who come visit. For instance, IBM has set up a virtual business center staffed by IBM sales representatives from around the world. Clients who want buy or shop for hardware, software, or services can get help from IBM avatars who, in reality, are live IBM sales reps. The avatars can handle all aspects of customer requests up to the actual money transaction, sharing of credit information, or signing legal documents. Those aspects of the sales transaction are transferred to real people. The IBM sales reps' avatars are available in English, Portuguese, German, Spanish, Dutch, Italian, and French.

Reebok, Adidas, American Apparel, and 1-800-Flowers are also setting up shop on Second Life using avatars to present their products. At Reebok, users can create and buy tennis shoes for their avatars, and go to Reebok.com and purchase real-world tennis shoes for themselves. 1-800-Flowers sells both virtual bouquets and directs users to the real-world site for people bouquets.

So why should a business invest in avatars? Some possibilities include using avatars to place and time shift, for instance, by creating a presence at a trade show without actually traveling there, or by creating sales demonstrations of products, recording them, and playing them back to visiting avatars. Kohl's, Sears, and American Apparel are using avatars to display and sell clothes to children.

At this point, the commercial uses of avatars are just being explored. But as thousands of businesses join digital environments such as Second Life, avatars will play a growing role in remote sales and service. The problem with avatars is that there's an expensive human behind the pretty graphics. One solution might be to add a little artificial intelligence to the avatar's front end. Whether or not humans will be fooled by this artifice is not known.

■■■ **SOURCES**: "Retailers 'Sell' to Young Virtually, Children Clothe Their Avatars Online," by Cheryl Lu-Lien, *Wall Street Journal*, August 19, 2008; "Advertising Coke Promotes Iself in a New Virtual World," by Louise Story, *The New York Times*, December 7, 2007; "'That Looks Great on You': Online Sales People Get Pushy," *Wall Street Journal*, January 3, 2007; "In 3-D Virtual World, Business Never Sleeps," by Dwight Adams, *Indianapolis Star*, June 25, 2007;" Awaiting Real Sales From Virtual Shoppers," by Bob Tedeschi, *New York Times*, June 11, 2007; "IBM Opens Sales Center in Second Life," by Jon Brodkin, *Networkworld*, May 15, 2007; "Chatterbots," by Jill Ruchala, *New York Press*, August 17, 2005.

avatars (an icon or representation of the user) into their chat, or offer the ability to communicate via audio and/or video. Chat systems include Internet Relay Chat (IRC), Jabber, and a number of proprietary systems based on the Microsoft Windows or Java platform. E-commerce firms typically use online forums and online chat to help develop community and as customer service tools. We will discuss the use of online forums as a community-building tool further in Chapter 11.

STREAMING MEDIA

Streaming media enables live Web video, music, video, and other large bandwidth files to be sent to users in a variety of ways that enable the user to play back the files. In some situations, such as live Web video, the files are broken into chunks and served

streaming media
enables music, video, and other large files to be sent to users in chunks so that when received and played, the file comes through uninterrupted

by specialized video servers to users in chunks. Client software puts the chunks together and plays the video. In other situations, such as YouTube, a single large file is downloaded from a standard Web server to users who can begin playing the video before the entire file is downloaded. Streamed files must be viewed "live": they cannot be stored on client hard drives without special software. Streamed files are "played" by a software program such as Microsoft's Media Player, Apple QuickTime, Flash, and RealMedia Player. There are a number of tools used to create streaming files but one of the most common is Adobe's Flash program. The Flash player has the advantage of being built into most client browsers; no plug-in is required to play Flash files.

Sites such as YouTube, MetaCafe, and GoogleVideo have popularized user-generated video streaming. Web advertisers increasingly use video to attract viewers. Streaming audio and video segments used in Web ads and news stories are perhaps the most frequently used streaming services. As the capacity of the Internet grows, streaming media will play an even larger role in e-commerce.

COOKIES

cookie

a tool used by Web sites to store information about a user. When a visitor enters a Web site, the site sends a small text file (the cookie) to the user's computer so that information from the site can be loaded more quickly on future visits. The cookie can contain any information desired by the site designers

A **cookie** is a tool used by a Web site to store information about a user. When a visitor enters a Web site, the site sends a small text file (the cookie) to the user's computer so that information from the site can be loaded more quickly on future visits. The cookie can contain any information desired by the Web site designers, including customer number, pages visited, products examined, and other detailed information about the behavior of the consumer at the site. Cookies are useful to consumers because the Web site will recognize returning patrons and not ask them to register again. Cookies are also used by advertisers to ensure visitors do not receive the same advertisements repeatedly. Cookies can also help personalize a Web site by allowing the site to recognize returning customers and make special offers to them based on their past behavior at the site. Cookies allow Web marketers to customize products and segment markets—the ability to change the product or the price based on prior consumer information (described more fully in later chapters). As we will discuss throughout the book, cookies also can pose a threat to consumer privacy, and at times they are bothersome. Many people clear their cookies at the end of every day. Some disable them entirely using tools built into most browsers.

WEB 2.0 FEATURES AND SERVICES

Today's broadband Internet infrastructure has greatly expanded the services available to users. These new capabilities have formed the basis for new business models. Digital content and digital communications are the two areas where innovation is most rapid.

Blogs

weblog (blog)

personal Web page that is created by an individual or corporation to communicate with readers

There are so many "killer apps" on the Web that it's hard to pick one super app. But blogs arguably are a super app. A **blog**, or **weblog**, is a personal Web page that typically contains a series of chronological entries (newest to oldest) by its author, and links to related Web pages. The blog may include a blogroll (a collection of links to other blogs) and TrackBacks (a list of entries in other blogs that refer to a post on the first blog). Most blogs allow readers to post comments on the blog entries as well. The act of creating a blog is often referred to as "blogging." Blogs are either hosted by a third-party site such as Blogger.com (owned by Google), LiveJournal, Typepad, Xanga, Wordpress, or Microsoft's Windows LiveSpaces, or prospective bloggers can download software such as Moveable Type and bBlog to create a blog that is hosted by the user's ISP. Blog pages are usually variations on templates provided by the blogging service or software and hence require no knowledge of HTML. Therefore, millions of people without HTML skills of any kind can post their own Web pages, and share content with friends and relatives. The totality of blog-related Web sites is often referred to as the blogoshpere.

The content of blogs range from individual musings to corporate communications. Blogs have had a significant impact on political affairs, and have gained increasing notice for their role in breaking and shaping the news. Blogs have become hugely popular. While estimates on the number of blogs vary, Technorati, a weblog research firm, claims there were over 112 million blogs as of 2008, with 175,000 created each day, and 1.6 million postings (Technorati, 2008). No one knows how many of these blogs are kept up to date or just yesterday's news. And no one knows how many of these blogs have a readership greater than one (the blog author). Other, perhaps more reliable surveys find about 21 million people have created a blog, and 67 million read blogs regularly in the United States (Pew Internet & American Life Report, 2008). In fact, there are so many blogs you need a blog search engine just to find them (such as Google's search engine), or you can just go to a list of the most popular 100 blogs and dig in. We discuss blogs further in Chapter 6 as a marketing mechanism, and in Chapter 10 as one part of the significant growth in user-generated content enabled by the Internet.

Really Simple Syndication (RSS)

The rise of blogs is correlated with a new distribution mechanism for news and information from Web sites that regularly update their content. **Really Simple Syndication (RSS)** is an XML format that allows users to have digital content, including text, articles, blogs and podcast audio files, automatically sent to their computers over the Internet. An RSS aggregator software application that you install on your computer gathers material from the Web sites and blogs that you tell it to scan and it brings new information from those sites to you. Sometimes this is referred to as "syndicated" content because it is distributed by news organizations and other syndicators (or distributors). Users download RSS aggregators and then "subscribe" to the RSS "feeds." When you go to your RSS aggregator's page, it will display the most recent updates for each channel to which you have subscribed.

RSS has rocketed from a "techie" pastime to a broad-based movement. No one knows how many people have downloaded RSS client programs, but at *The New York Times,* the subscriber base for RSS feeds (which include headlines, summaries, and links to full articles) went from 500,000 when first introduced in 2003 to more than 8 million today. In fact, so many users are requesting RSS feeds that online publishers are developing ways to present advertising along with the content. Microsoft has

Really Simple Syndication (RSS)
program that allows users to have digital content, including text, articles, blogs and podcast audio files, automatically sent to their computers over the Internet

included an integrated RSS reader in Vista, the current version of its Windows operating system, and Google and Yahoo are selling advertising options for RSS.

Podcasting

podcast

an audio presentation—such as a radio show, audio from a movie, or simply personal audio presentations—stored as an audio file and posted to the Web

A **podcast** is an audio presentation—such as a radio show, audio from a movie, or simply personal audio presentations—stored as an audio file and posted to the Web. Listeners download the files from the Web and play them on their players or computers. While commonly associated with Apple's iPod portable music player, you can listen to podcast MP3 files with any MP3 player. Podcasting has transitioned from an amateur independent producer media in the "pirate radio" tradition, to a professional news and talk content distribution channel. More than one third of American adults own an iPod or an MP3 player and about 20% of all Internet users report that they have downloaded a podcast (Pew Internet & American Life Project, 2008).

Celebrities such as Paris Hilton and Fortune 500 firms now vie with thousands of independent producers by posting podcasts to get their messages out. Major advertisers are looking at podcasts as a new advertising channel. Microsoft has included podcast creation tools in Vista. No one knows for sure how many podcasts exist, but Apple's iTunes Web site provides a directory to over 300,000 podcasts. Podcasting is discussed further in Chapter 10 as one aspect of the growth in user-generated digital content.

Wikis

wiki

Web application that allows a user to easily add and edit content on a Web page

A **wiki** is a Web application that allows a user to easily add and edit content on a Web page. (The term wiki derives from the "wiki wiki" (quick or fast) shuttle buses at Honolulu Airport.) Wiki software enables documents to be written collectively and collaboratively. Most wiki systems are open source, server-side systems that store content in a relational database. The software typically provides a template that defines layout and elements common to all pages, displays user-editable source code (usually plain text), and then renders the content into an HTML-based page for display in a Web browser. Some wiki software allows only basic text formatting, whereas others allow the use of tables, images, or even interactive elements, such as polls and games. Since wikis by their very nature are very open in allowing anyone to make changes to a page, most wikis provide a means to verify the validity of changes via a "Recent Changes" page, which enables members of the wiki community to monitor and review the work of other users, correct mistakes, and hopefully deter "vandalism."

Wikis are another Web 2.0 killer app. The most well-known wiki is Wikipedia, an online encyclopedia that contains over 2.5 million English-language articles on a variety of topics. The Wikimedia Foundation, which operates Wikipedia, also operates a variety of related projects, including Wikibooks, a collection of collaboratively written free textbooks and manuals; Wikinews, a free content news source; and Wiktionary, a collaborative project to produce a free multilingual dictionary in every language, with definitions, etymologies, pronunciations, quotations, and synonyms. Wikimedia's sites had over 50 million unique visitors in July 2008 and are routinely among the top ten visited sites on the Web (comScore, 2008). Wikis are also discussed further in Chapter 10.

Internet and the Web:Features** | **183**

New Music and Video Services

With the low bandwidth connections of the early Internet, audio and video files were difficult to download and share, but with the huge growth in broadband connections, these files are not only commonplace but at major universities and other places where those under 25 years of age log on, they are the majority of Web traffic. Spurred on by the worldwide sales of more than 150 million iPods through March 2008, and an additional 33 million other MP3 players, the Internet has become a virtual digital river of music files. In 2005, Apple introduced video files to its iTunes service, offering music videos licensed from the major record labels, Pixar short films, and hit TV shows. In 2008, 138 million Americans are expected to watch some online video at least once a month (Comscore Media Metrix, 2008). The iTunes Store has a catalog with over 8 million tracks, 20,000 television episodes and over 2,000 movies, and has sold over 5 billion songs, rented 50,000 television episodes every day, and typically rents over 50,000 movies a day, making it the world's most popular online music, TV, and movie store (Apple, 2008).

Video clips, Flash animations, and photo images are now routinely displayed either as part of Web sites or sent as attached files. Companies that want to demonstrate use of their products have found video clips to be extremely effective. And audio reports and discussions have also become commonplace, either as marketing materials or customer reports.

Digital video on demand is considered by many to be the "killer app" for the future Internet. Future digital video networks will be able to deliver better-than-broadcast-quality video over the Internet to computers and other devices in homes and on the road. High-quality interactive video and audio makes sales presentations and demonstrations more effective and lifelike and enable companies to develop new forms of customer support. New video, audio, and presentation approaches are also dramatically changing the nature of the media and news business. One can easily foresee the Internet as a major new distribution channel for Hollywood movies (see Chapter 10).

Internet Telephony

If the telephone system were to be built from scratch today, it would be an Internet-based packet-switched network using TCP/IP because it would be less expensive and more efficient than the alternative existing system, which involves a mix of circuit-switched legs with a digital backbone. Likewise, if cable television systems were built from scratch today, they most likely would use Internet technologies for the same reasons.

Already, nearly all pre-paid long distance phone cards use the Internet for the long-distance portion of calls. About 30% of the international calls from or to the United States use the Internet. Internet telephony is not entirely new. **IP telephony** is a general term for the technologies that use **Voice over Internet Protocol (VoIP)** and the Internet's packet-switched network to transmit voice, fax, and other forms of audio communication over the Internet. VoIP avoids the long distance charges imposed by traditional phone companies.

IP telephony
a general term for the technologies that use VoIP and the Internet's packet-switched network to transmit voice and other forms of audio communication over the Internet

Voice over Internet Protocol (VoIP)
protocol that allows for transmission of voice and other forms of audio communication over the Internet

Figure 3.23 illustrates the growth in Internet telephony in terms of the number of access lines through 2011.

There will be about 25 million VoIP subscribers in the North America in 2009, and this number is expanding rapidly as cable systems provide telephone service as part of their "triple play": voice, Internet, and TV as a single package. VoIP's share of international traffic has grown even faster, rising from 0.2% in 1998 to over 20% of the 344 billion minutes of voice traffic worldwide in 2007. Skype, the most popular VoIP service in the United States, accounts for 4% of all international calling (eMarketer, 2008a).

VoIP is a disruptive technology. In the past, voice and fax were the exclusive provenance of the regulated telephone networks. With the convergence of the Internet and telephony, however, this dominance is already starting to change, with local and long distance telephone providers and cable companies becoming ISPs, and ISPs getting into the phone market (see **Table 3.13**). Independent service providers such as VoIP pioneers Vonage and Skype accounted for over 60% of VoIP service in the United States in 2004, but this percentage dropped significantly by 2008 as traditional players such as Comcast, Time Warner, Verizon, AT&T, Cox, and other telephone and cable companies moved aggressively into the market. ISPs are also joining the fray: AOL developed its own Internet phone service; Yahoo bought

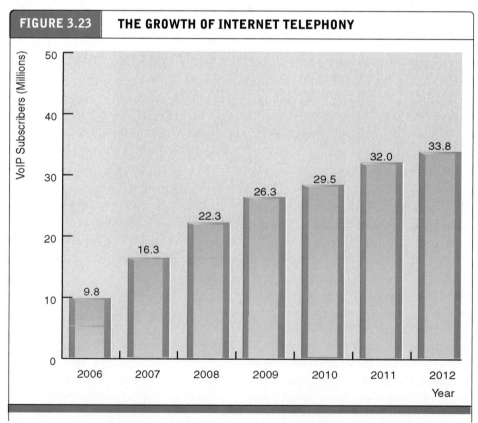

FIGURE 3.23 — THE GROWTH OF INTERNET TELEPHONY

The number of VoIP subscribers is expected to grow at around 20% a year for the next several years.
SOURCES: Telecommunications Industry Association, 2007; eMarketer, Inc., 2007g; International Data Corporation, 2006.

Dialpad Communications, a VoIP service provider; and Microsoft moved to build its presence in the market with the purchase of Internet phone company Teleo Inc. In September 2005, eBay purchased Skype for $2.6 billion. Although it was forced to write down the value of its investment in Skype by $900 million in 2007, eBay still sees big potential for Skype's voice services.

Internet Television

IThere are three ways in which people watch television over the Internet: as a streaming Flash-based video (such as YouTube videos), as download video podcasts from a variety of sites such as Apple's iTunes store, or as very high definition streaming files which use the IPTV protocol. By far the most common type of Internet video is provided by YouTube, with more than 4 billion video streams a month, some of them short clips taken from television networks. Television and movie producers use video podcasts as a marketing tool, and sites such as Apple's iTunes and independent sites like videopodcasts.tv distribute millions of television downloads a month. There is very little data on the amount of television content per se (syndicated television shows vs. movies or home-made videos) that is being download. Clearly, the largest source of legal, paid television content is the iTunes store where you can purchase entire seasons of TV shows.

IPTV, the third method of watching television on the Internet, uses high-bandwidth Internet connection to deliver television programming to the home. Standard quality television requires about 3 Mbps Internet connectivity using MPEG2 compression, but high definition TV requires about 19 Mbps. MPEG4 compression requires about half as much bandwidth, but still a substantial connection.

The definition of IPTV is still fluid and many different protocols are used such as IP multicasting to move compressed digital television streams over the Internet. Quality is an issue and typical broadband connection speeds can support standard quality television streams, but high definition television (HDTV) requires much more bandwidth. Commercial IPTV is not yet widely available in the United States, and is grow-

IPTV
uses high-bandwidth Internet connections to deliver television programming to the home

TABLE 3.13	KEY IP TELEPHONY PLAYERS
SPECIALTY	COMPANY
Independent Facilities-based Service Providers	Vonage Time Warner Digital Comcast Digital Voice Cablevision/Optimum Voice Cox Digital Phone Verizon AT&T SBC
Client-based Service Providers	Skype (eBay) Net2Phone MSN Yahoo Messenger GoogleTalk AOL Phoneline

ing slowly in Europe. France has the largest commercial IPTV audience, currently about 5 million viewers.

Video Conferencing

Although video conferencing has been available for years, few have used it due to the cost of video equipment and telephone line rental fees. However, in recent years, Internet-based video conferencing has begun to overtake traditional telephone-based systems. Internet video conferencing is accessible to anyone with a broadband Internet connection and a Web camera (Webcam). The most widely used Web conferencing suite of tools is WebEx (now owned by Cisco). VoIP companies such as Skype also provide more limited Web conferencing capabilities.

As Internet II develops, it will continue to significantly reduce the cost of video conferencing, making it even more affordable to share information that involves either an image or audio component. Meetings of geographically dispersed workers or colleagues will be easy to arrange, using VoIP technology, and the quality of image and audio transmission will be much higher.

Online Software and Web Services: Web Apps, Widgets, and Gadgets

We are all used to installing software on our PCs. But as the Web and e-commerce moves towards a service model, applications increasingly will be running off Web servers. Instead of buying a "product" in a box, you will be paying for a Web service instead. There are many kinds of Web services now available, many free, all the way from full-function applications, to much smaller chunks of code called "widgets" and "gadgets" that you can drag to your blog, or MySpace pages. Widgets can put some bling in your blog!

Widgets pull content and functionality from one place on the Web to a place where you need it, such as on your Web page, blog, or Facebook page. You can see these new Web widget services most clearly in the photo sites such as Picnic.com, which offers a free photo editing application that is powerful and simple to use. Or drag a copy of one of the fastest growing widgets, iLike, to your Facebook page and share your favorite musicians, songs, movies, and concert plans with your friends. In its first six months on Facebook, iLike signed up 1 million users. Wal-Mart, eBay, and Amazon, along with many other retailers, are creating shopping widgets that users can drag to their networking pages or blogs so visitors can shop at a full function online store without leaving your blog or Facebook page. Yahoo, Google, MSN, and Apple all have useful collections of hundreds of widgets available on their Web sites, and companies are expected to spend over $40 million on widgets in 2008 as marketing tools (eMarketer, 2008c).

Gadgets are closely related to widgets. They are small chunks of code that usually supply a single limited function such as a clock, calendar, or diary. You can see a collection of gadgets at http://desktop.google.com/plugins.

As bandwidth capabilities of the Internet have increased, major software firms have begun to move away from the boxed model and towards Web distribution of software as a service. The clear leader here is Google, which has online versions of word processing, spreadsheet, and presentation programs, all of which are becoming competitive with Microsoft's Office suite. Microsoft is planning for a future where Microsoft Office is a Web application, but the revenue implications are uncertain.

In the business world, digital libraries of software applications have begun that permit companies and individuals to rent software (or purchase software services) rather than buy it. For instance, SalesForce.com sells customer and sales force management software services to companies over the Internet for a subscription fee instead of a purchase price. Accessing a Web server enables a user to download the desired software. Most enterprise software firms such as SAP and Oracle are moving towards a Web services model for small businesses. This service is especially useful for expensive software packages, such as graphic design or software development tools, that few individuals or small businesses can afford.

Application Service Providers can assist both in processing data and in storing it, dispersing it to multiple servers rather than having it reside on just one. Backing up online has many advantages. You do not need to buy extra hard drives, and your information is backed up entirely offline in a secure environment run by a professional staff. Both iBackup.com and Xdrive.com offer backup and data distribution services such as FTP servers for sharing large media and other files.

M-commerce Applications: The Next Big Thing

In many places around the world, mobile commerce is a viable part of e-commerce. Combining voice, data, images, audio, and video on a handheld wireless device in a high-bandwidth network is common in Japan and parts of southeast Asia. In Japan, NTT DoCoMo, Japan's largest wireless and landline phone company, offers cell phones with embedded credit cards. These permit mobile consumers to make payments easily from their cell phones, unleashing a torrent of potential "mobile commerce" applications. Already in Korea and Europe, mobile payments systems of various types are becoming firmly established. In addition, mobile computers in the form of laptops are now estimated to be 25% of the world's population of personal computers, growing at a rate of 16% annually.

In the United States, prior to 2007, mobile commerce was not yet a success in part because the mobile cellular networks had not developed enough bandwidth to display Web pages conveniently, and in part because the cell phone devices had poor display properties. All that changed in 2008, and the path towards mobile e-commerce is open. Apple's iPhone, T-Mobile's Android G1, and BlackBerry's Curve, along with competitor phones, now offer Web browsing at acceptable speeds and resolutions. Google has also entered the fray by developing its own prototype cell phones to support its mobile search and ad placement applications, and by urging the Federal Communications Commission to support "open" cellular networks which would allow all devices to run on high speed networks, not just the devices approved by the carriers such as ATT and Verizon.

As mobile devices grow in power, their use in e-commerce is inevitable. Currently, m-commerce in the United States is tiny, less than 1% of all B2C e-commerce. But the list of services available on cell phones—from both the Internet and cell networks—is growing and includes downloads of ringtones, music, video content, television, news, listings, reviews, and notices. The wireless carriers and Internet giants such as Google are on a collision course over the potential future mobile content and advertising markets. We will examine m-commerce applications in further depth in later chapters.

3.6   CASE STUDY

Akamai Technologies:
The Web's Jukebox

Most people love the Web, but hate the wait. Studies have shown that most won't stay on a Web site if the Web page and its contents take more than a few seconds to load. Other studies show that if a video ad or sports video takes too long to buffer, shows jerky frames, or poor visual quality, over half the customers will seek out a competitor's Web site. For online publishers and marketers, online video is rapidly becoming a serious component of their business strategies. In order for these initiatives to pay off, the viewing experience needs to be nearly flawless. For marketers who increasingly are using video to establish a more intimate relationship with the consumer and the brand, the quality of the Internet video experience is critical.

In today's broadband cable and DSL environment, the threshold of patience is probably much lower than a few seconds. Increased video and audio customer expectations are bad news for anyone seeking to use the Web for delivery of high-quality multimedia content such as CD quality music and high definition video. YouTube and MySpace have unleashed a torrent of video downloads, causing total Internet traffic to expand yearly at somewhere between 50% and 100%. BitTorrent files used to share

videos now account for half of U.S. Internet traffic, and on college campuses more than 80% of campus Internet use. If you are SIRIUS/XM Radio and you want to stream online music to a several million users a day, you will definitely need some help. If you are MTV and want to stream music video to your 6 million customers online, or Apple iTunes and want to download music or video files to your 10 million online customers, you will also need some help. Akamai is one of the Web's major helpers, and each of the preceding companies, along with the Web's top 20,000 domains, use Akamai's services to speed the delivery of content.

Slow-loading Web pages and Web content—from music to video—sometimes results from poor design, but more often than not, the problem stems from the underlying infrastructure of the Internet. As you have learned in this chapter, the Internet was originally developed to carry text-based e-mail messages among a relatively small group of researchers, not bandwidth-hogging graphics, sound, and video files to tens of millions of people all at once. The Internet is a collection of networks that has to pass information from one network to another. Sometimes the handoff is not smooth. Every 1,500-byte packet of information sent over the Internet must be verified by the receiving server and an acknowledgment sent to the sender. This slows down not only the distribution of content such as music, but also slows down interactive requests, such as purchases, that require the client computer to interact with an online shopping cart. Moreover, each packet may go through many different servers on its way to its final destination, multiplying by several orders of magnitude the number of acknowledgments required to move a packet from New York to San Francisco. The Internet today spends much of its time and capacity verifying packets, contributing to a problem called "latency" or delay.

Today's Internet traffic has also changed drastically. Instead of handling text messages, today's Internet must devote 33% of its total capacity to moving BitTorrent and other P2P network music! Music lovers dominate the Web's traffic. On average, there are over 500,000 visitors per minute to U.S. music sites. Another 10% of capacity is devoted to video sites that spew out everything from full-length movies and trailers to short marketing videos. Video traffic will increase to more than 30% of Internet capacity by 2010. The explosion in user-generated content sites, streaming news sites, music, movies, games, and Big-Band applications like high definition television and video, all point to a potential crisis for the Internet, leading to delays and breakdowns. Akamai, and other firms in the CDN (content distribution networks) industry are one of the reasons why the Web has not disintegrated under the load.

There are many other causes of Internet delay or failure, including bandwidth constraints at the end-user site, Internet traffic exceeding the capacity of routers at local ISPs, malfunctioning peering points at the hand-off of data between ISPs, and traffic bottlenecks at corporate data centers. The result is that, realistically, and without special efforts, the average throughput on a busy day from San Francisco to New York is about 30 Kbps—enough for text e-mail but not enough for CNN news videos or music downloads. The solution Akamai came up with is EdgeNetwork: it places copies of content close to the user so the content only has to move across country once and can be delivered to users from local servers.

Akamai (which means intelligent, clever, or "cool" in Hawaiian) Technologies was founded by Tom Leighton, an MIT professor of applied mathematics, and Daniel Lewin, an MIT grad student, with the idea of expediting Internet traffic to overcome these limitations. When Timothy Berners-Lee, founder of the World Wide Web, realized that congestion on the Internet was becoming an enormous problem, he issued a challenge to Leighton's research group to invent a better way to deliver Internet content. The result was a set of breakthrough algorithms that became the basis for Akamai. Lewin received his masters degree in electrical engineering and computer science in 1998. His master's thesis was the theoretical starting point for the company. It described storing copies of Web content such as pictures or video clips at many different locations around the Internet so that one could always retrieve a nearby copy, making Web pages load faster.

Officially launched in August 1998, Akamai's main product is EdgeSuite, a suite of services that allows corporations to maximize their Web performance and minimize costs while distributing their content on the Internet. EdgeSuite allows customers to move their Web content closer to end users so a user in New York City, for instance, will be served L.L.Bean pages from the New York Metro area Akamai servers, while users of the L.L.Bean site in San Francisco will be served pages from Akamai servers in San Francisco. Presto! Faster Internet. Akamai has a wide range of large corporate and government clients, from SIRIUS/XM Radio, Apple iTunes, and Yahoo to NAS-DAQ, General Motors, the National Basketball Association, and FedEx. Today, Akamai has over 20,000 corporate and government customers and operates over 20,000 servers worldwide, which makes it possible for customers' Web pages and other content to load and run quickly. In 2009, Akamai accounts for over 20% of all Internet content distribution in the United States. Other competitors in this space are Blue-Coat, LimeLight, SAVVIS, and Mirror Image Internet. At this moment, on average in 2008, there are about 900,000 live streams being delivered by Akamai.

Accomplishing this seemingly simple task—what Akamai calls "edge computing"—requires that Akamai monitor the entire Internet, locating potential sluggish areas and devising faster routes for information to travel. Frequently used portions of a client's Web site, or large video or audio files that would be difficult to send to users quickly, are stored on Akamai's 20,000 servers on 1,100 networks located in 70 countries around the world. When a user requests a song or a video file, his or her request is redirected to an Akamai server nearby and the content served from this local server. Akamai's servers are placed in Tier 1 backbone supplier networks, large ISPs, universities, and other networks. Akamai's software determines which server is optimum for the user and then transmits the "Akamaized" content locally. Web sites that are "Akamaized" can be delivered anywhere from four to ten times as fast as non-Akamaized content.

Akamai has developed a number of other business services based on its Internet savvy, including content targeting of advertising based on user location and zip code, content security, business intelligence, disaster recovery, on-demand bandwidth, and computing capacity during spikes in Internet traffic in partnership with IBM, storage, global traffic management, and streaming services.

For marketing and advertising firms, Akamai offers a product called EdgeScape. EdgeScape provides enterprises with intelligence generated by the Internet's most accurate and comprehensive knowledge base of Internet network activity. Akamai's massive server deployment and relationships with networks throughout the world enable optimal collection of geography and bandwidth-sensing information. As a result of these unparalleled data-gathering techniques, Akamai provides a highly accurate knowledge base with worldwide coverage. Customers integrate a simple program into their Web server or application server. This program communicates with the Akamai database to retrieve the very latest information. The Akamai global network of servers is constantly mapping the Internet, and at the same time, each enterprise's EdgeScape software is in continual communication with the Akamai network. The result: data is always current. Advertisers can deliver ads based on country, region, city, market area, area code, county, zip code, connection type, and speed. You can see several interesting visualizations of the Internet which log basic real-time Web activity by visiting the Akamai Web site and clicking on "View Visualizations."

While Akamai is one of the leaders in its field, the burst of the Internet bubble in 2001 and 2002 deeply impacted its corporate and stock performance. When Akamai went public in 1999, its stock soared to $345 a share. In August 2008, its stock trades in the $20 range despite a huge growth of nearly 50% in revenues and 100% in earnings on a revenue base of $636 million. Akamai's Chief Financial Officer told Wall Street analysts in July 2008 that "media growth has moderated from the pace we saw for several years during the period of rapid broadband adoption." In a tough economic environment, consumers aren't exactly rushing to upgrade their computing systems, so for the time being, Akamai may have run into a bottleneck. Some analysts feel Akamai's technology is challenged by new upstart companies using less expensive technology such as P2P video delivery networks. But many still remain positive about Akamai's prospects, and feel that that the company's infrastructure, "best of breed" status, and Fortune 500 client base will help it stave off competition.

SOURCES: "F.C.C. Chief Would Bar Comcast From Imposing Web Restrictions," By Saul Hansell, *The New York Times*, July 12, 2008; "State of the Internet," by Akamai, Inc., June, 2008; Akamai Technologies Inc. Form 10-K for the fiscal year ended December 31, 2007, filed with the Securities and Exchange Commission on March 30, 2008; "Video Surge Divides Web Watchers," by Kevin Delaney and Bobby White, *Wall Street Journal*, August 14, 2007; "Akamai, Exxon Slide, While Apple Shines," by Thomas Gryta, *Wall Street Journal*, July 27, 2007.

Case Study Questions

1. Why does Akamai need to geographically disperse its servers to deliver its customers' Web content?

2. If you wanted to deliver software content over the Internet, would you sign up for Akamai's service? Why or why not?

3. What advantages does an advertiser derive from using Akamai's EdgeScape service? What kinds of products might benefit from this kind of service?

4. With the demand for high-bandwidth music and video exploding, why isn't Akamai's stock performing better? If you were an investor, what factors would encourage you to invest in Akamai? What factors would discourage you?

3.7 REVIEW

KEY CONCEPTS

- **Discuss the origins of the Internet.**

The Internet has evolved from a collection of mainframe computers located on a few U.S. college campuses to an interconnected network of thousands of networks and millions of computers worldwide. The history of the Internet can be divided into three phases:

- During the *Innovation Phase* (1961–1974), the Internet's purpose was to link researchers nationwide via computer.
- During the *Institutionalization Phase* (1975–1994), the Department of Defense and National Science Foundation provided funding to expand the fundamental building blocks of the Internet into a complex military communications system and then into a civilian system.
- During the *Commercialization Phase* (1995 to the present), government agencies encouraged corporations to assume responsibility for further expansion of the network, and private business began to exploit the Internet for commercial purposes.

- **Identify the key technology concepts behind the Internet.**

The Internet's three key technology components are:

- *Packet switching*, which slices digital messages into packets, routes the packets along different communication paths as they become available, and then reassembles the packets once they arrive at their destination.
- *TCP/IP*, which is the core communications protocol for the Internet. TCP establishes the connections among sending and receiving Web computers and makes sure that packets sent by one computer are received in the sequence by the other, without any packets missing. IP provides the addressing scheme and is responsible for the actual delivery of the packets.
- *Client/server technology*, which makes it possible for large amounts of information to be stored on Web servers and shared with individual users on their client computers.

- **Describe the role of Internet protocols and utility programs.**

Internet protocols and utility programs make the following Internet services possible:

- *HTTP* delivers requested Web pages, allowing users to view them.
- *SMTP* and *POP* enable e-mail to be routed to a mail server and then picked up by the recipient's server, while *IMAP* enables e-mail to be sorted before being downloaded by the recipient.
- *SSL* ensures that information transmissions are encrypted.
- *FTP* is used to transfer files from servers to clients and vice versa.
- *Telnet* is a utility program that enables work to be done remotely.
- *Ping* is a utility program that allows users to verify a connection between client and server.

- *Tracert* lets you track the route a message takes from a client to a remote computer.
- *Pathping* combines the functionality offered by Ping and Tracert.

■ Explain the structure of the Internet today.

The main structural elements of the Internet are:
- The *backbone*, which is composed primarily of high-bandwidth fiber-optic cable operated by a variety of providers.
- *IXPs*, which are hubs that use high-speed switching computers to connect the backbone with regional and local networks.
- *CANs*, which are local area networks operating within a single organization that connect directly to regional networks.
- *ISPs*, which deal with the "last mile" of service to homes and offices. ISPs offer a variety of types of service, ranging from dial-up service to broadband DSL, cable modem, T1 and T3 lines, and satellite link service.
- *Governing bodies*, such as IAB, ICANN, IESG, IETF, ISOC, W3C, and ITU, which although they do not control the Internet, have influence over it and monitor its operations.

■ Understand the limitations of today's Internet.

To envision what the Internet of tomorrow—Internet II—will look like, we must first look at the limitations of today's Internet.
- *Bandwidth limitations*. Today's Internet is slow and incapable of effectively sharing and displaying large files, such as video and voice files.
- *Quality of service limitations*. Data packets don't all arrive in the correct order, at the same moment, causing latency; latency creates jerkiness in video files and voice messages.
- *Network architecture limitations*. Servers can't keep up with demand. Future improvements to Internet infrastructure will improve the way servers process requests for information, thus improving overall speed.
- *Language development limitations*. The nature of HTML restricts the quality of "rich" information that can be shared online. Future languages will enable improved display and viewing of video and graphics.
- *Limitations arising from the "wired" nature of the Internet*. The Internet is based primarily on physical cables, which restricts the mobility of users.

■ Describe the potential capabilities of Internet II.

Internet2 is a consortium working together to develop and test new technologies for potential use on the Internet. Internet2 participants are working in a number of areas, including advanced network infrastructure, new networking capabilities, middleware, and advanced applications that incorporate audio and video to create new services.

In addition to the Internet2 project, other groups are working to expand Internet bandwidth via improvements to fiber-optic and photonics. Wireless LAN and 3G telephone technologies will provide users of cellular phones and PDAs with increased access to the Internet and its various services.

The increased bandwidth and expanded connections of the Internet II era will result in a number of benefits, including IP multicasting, which will enable more efficient delivery of data; latency solutions; guaranteed service levels; lower error rates; and declining costs

■ Understand how the World Wide Web works.

The Web was developed during 1989-1991 by Dr. Tim Berners-Lee, who created a computer program that allowed formatted pages stored on the Internet to be linked using keywords (hyperlinks). In 1993, Marc Andreesen created the first graphical Web browser, which made it possible to view documents on the Web graphically and created the possibility of universal computing. The key concepts you need to be familiar with in order to understand how the Web works are the following:

- *Hypertext*, which is a way of formatting pages with embedded links that connect documents to one another and that also link pages to other objects.
- *HTTP*, which is the protocol used to transmit Web pages over the Internet.
- *URLs*, which are the addresses at which Web pages can be found.
- *HTML*, which is the programming language used to create most Web pages and which provides designers with a fixed set of tags that are used to format a Web page.
- *XML*, which is a newer markup language that allows designers to describe data and information.
- *Web server software*, which is software that enables a computer to deliver Web pages written in HTML to client computers that request this service by sending an HTTP request. Web server software also provides security services, FTP, search engine, and data capture services. The term Web server also is used to refer to the physical computer that runs the Web server software.
- *Web clients*, which are computing devices attached to the Internet that are capable of making HTTP requests and displaying HTML pages.
- *Web browsers*, which display Web pages and also have added features such as e-mail and newsgroups.

■ Describe how Internet and Web features and services support e-commerce.

Together, the Internet and the Web make e-commerce possible by allowing computer users to access product and service information and to complete purchases online. Some of the specific features that support e-commerce include:

- *E-mail*, which uses a series of protocols to enable messages containing text, images, sound, and video clips to be transferred from one Internet user to another. E-mail is used in e-commerce as a marketing and customer support tool.
- *Instant messaging*, which allows messages to be sent between two users almost instantly, allowing parties to engage in a two-way conversation. In e-commerce, companies are using instant messaging as a customer support tool.
- *Search engines*, which identify Web pages that match a query submitted by a user. Search engines assist users in locating Web pages related to items they may want to buy.
- *Intelligent agents (bots)*, which are software programs that gather and/or filter information on a specific topic and then provide a list of results for the users.
- *Online forums* (message boards), which enable users to communicate with each other, although not in real time, and online chat, which allows users to communicate in real time (simultaneously), are being used in e-commerce as community-building tools.

- *Streaming media*, which enables music, video, and other large files to be sent to users in chunks so that when received and played, the file comes through uninterrupted. Like standard digital files, streaming media may be sold as digital content and used as a marketing tool.

- *Cookies*, which are small text files that allow a Web site to store information about a user, are used by e-commerce as a marketing tool. Cookies allow Web sites to personalize the site to the user and also permit customization and market segmentation.

The Internet II infrastructure will permit the rapid deployment of new services and greatly expand e-commerce opportunities. Emerging services include:

- *Blogs*, which are personal Web pages that typically contain a series of chronologyical entries (newest to oldest) by the author and links to related Web pages.

- *RSS*, which is an XML format that allows users to have digital content, including text, articles, blogs and podcast audio files, automatically sent to their computers over the Internet.

- *Podcasts*, which are audio presentations—such as a radio show, audio from a movie, or simply personal audio presentations—stored as an audio file and posted to the Web.

- *Wikis*, which are Web applications that allow a user to easily add and edit content on a Web page.

- *New music and video services*, such as iTunes and digital video on demand.

- *Internet telephony*, which uses VoIP to transmit audio communication over the Internet, and *Internet television (IPTV)*.

- *Online software and services*, such as Web apps, widgets, gadgets, and distribution of software applications and distributed storage offered by ASPs.

- *M-commerce applications*, which permit mobile consumers to make payments easily from their cell phones.

QUESTIONS

1. What are the three basic building blocks of the Internet?
2. What is latency, and how does it interfere with Internet functioning?
3. Explain how packet switching works.
4. How is the TCP/IP protocol related to information transfer on the Internet?
5. What technological innovation made client/server computing possible? What impact has client/server computing had on the Internet?
6. Despite the number of PCs connected to the Internet, rich information sharing is still limited. Why?
7. Why isn't the Internet overloaded? Will it ever be at capacity?
8. What types of companies form the Internet backbone today?
9. What function do the IXPs serve?
10. What is a campus area network, and who uses them?
11. Compare and contrast intranets, extranets, and the Internet as a whole.
12. What are the four major limitations of today's Internet?
13. What are some of the challenges of policing the Internet? Who has the final say when it comes to content?
14. Compare and contrast the capabilities of Wi-Fi and 3G wireless networks.
15. What are some of the new wireless standards, and how are they relevant to Internet II?

16. What are the major technological advancements that are anticipated will accompany Internet II? Define and discuss the importance of each.
17. Why was the development of the browser so significant for the growth of the Web?
18. Name the different Web markup languages and explain the differences among them.
19. Name and describe five services currently available through the Web.
20. What are at least three new services that will be available through the next generation of the Internet?

PROJECTS

1. Visit the MySimon.com Web site and investigate the following types of purchases: an iPod, a copy of the book *The Tales of Beetle the Bard*, and a dozen red roses. What did you find as you searched for these items? Describe the process, the search results, and any limitations you encountered. What are the major advantages and disadvantages of such intelligent agents?

2. Locate where cookies are stored on your computer. (They are probably in a folder entitled "cookies" within your browser program.) List the top 10 cookies you find and write a brief report describing the kinds of sites that placed the cookies. What purpose do you think the cookies serve? Also, what do you believe are the major advantages and disadvantages of cookies? In your opinion, do the advantages outweigh the disadvantages, or vice versa?

3. Call a local ISP, cable provider, and DSL provider to request information on their services. Prepare a brief report summarizing the features, benefits, and costs of each. Which is the fastest? What, if any, are the downsides of selecting any of the three for Internet service (such as additional equipment purchases)?

4. Select two countries (excluding the United States) and prepare a short report describing their basic Internet infrastructure. Are they public or commercial? How and where do they connect to backbones within the United States?

5. We have mentioned several high-speed gigabit networks throughout this chapter. Investigate the topic of high-speed networks on the Web and try to find the fastest recorded network (usually used for research purposes). Then try to find the fastest commercial network handling routine Internet traffic.

WEB SITE RESOURCES www.prenhall.com/laudon

- Additional projects, exercises, and tutorials
- Careers: Explore career opportunities in e-commerce
- Raising capital and business plans

CHAPTER 4

Building an E-commerce Web Site

After reading this chapter, you will be able to:

- Explain the process that should be followed in building an e-commerce Web site.
- Describe the major issues surrounding the decision to outsource site development and/or hosting.
- Identify and understand the major considerations involved in choosing Web server and e-commerce merchant server software.
- Understand the issues involved in choosing the most appropriate hardware for an e-commerce site.
- Identify additional tools that can improve Web site performance.

Right-Sizing a Web Site

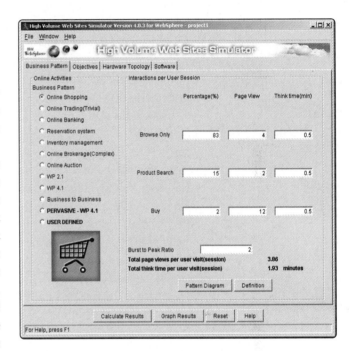

Let's say you've decided to create a Web site for your successful garden equipment company. You've been in business for five years, have established a regional brand for high-quality gardening tools, and have about 12,000 retail customers and 21 wholesale dealers who purchase from you. Based on a marketing report you commissioned, you expect that in the first year your Web site will have about 1,400 visitors a day. The average visitor will look at eight pages, producing about 4 million page views a year. About 10% will purchase something, and the rest will browse to explore prices and products. However, in peak times (during the months of April, May, June, and December), you expect peak loads of 3,000 customers a day, con-centrated during the hours of 9 A.M. to 5 P.M., producing about 375 visitors per hour or 6 per second. During this time, your Web site will have to serve up about 40 screens per second, with most of the content being read from a database of product and price information. Pages must be served up within 2 seconds of a customer click during peak times or customers may lose patience and go elsewhere.

Before you can proceed, there are some questions you will need answered. How many Web servers will your site require? How many CPUs should each server have? How powerful does the site's database server need to be? What kind of connection speed do you need to the Internet? Until recently, finding the answers to questions such as these was often done on a trial-and-error basis. However, hardware and software vendors such as IBM, Microsoft, and Hewlett-Packard have developed a number of simulation tools that can help you find the right answers.

IBM's simulator is called the On Demand Performance Advisor (OPERA) (formerly known as the High Volume Web Sites Simulator). OPERA enables users to estimate the performance and capacity of a Web server based on workload patterns, performance objectives, and specific hardware and software. OPERA has a very easy-to-use interface that includes pre-built workload patterns for various e-commerce applications, such as shopping, banking, brokerage, auction, portal, B2B, and reservation systems, that can be modified as necessary based on the user's own data or assumptions. It can provide what-if analyses for various performance parameters such as throughput, response time, resource utilization, number of concurrent users, and page view rate. It also provides special algorithms to address increases in Web traffic during peak usage periods. The simulator includes built-in performance characteristics for various types of hardware (such IBM, Sun, and HP servers), software, and infrastructure models. OPERA uses an analytic model to generate reports that allow users to assess the adequacy of proposed hardware and software configurations, forecast performance, and graphically identify bottlenecks that might develop. IBM also offers Sonoma, a Web service based on OPERA, that can be used to estimate the performance and capacity of service-oriented architecture (SOA) workloads.

Users of the simulator have included Charles Schwab, Aetna, Fidelity, Visa, Bank of America, Walmart.com, and eBay, among others. eBay first turned to the simulator when it was attempting to cope with dramatic increases in customer demand. In its early years, eBay needed to serve up only about 1 million pages per hour, but as its customer base grew, and the number of page views per hour significantly increased, its original Web site hardware and software became insufficient, creating customer resistance. After running a simulation of its current and likely future workload, eBay decided to rebuild its auction system around IBM's WebSphere application that integrates a variety of software tools into an integrated Web site design. Later, eBay returned to OPERA to examine the performance of its Sell Your Item application on its new three-tier Web server architecture. The simulation enabled eBay to determine both the number of servers (36) and the optimal CPU (the IBM x335, which provided a 30% performance increase due to a higher-speed CPU, increased amount of RAM, and faster bus speed) required to meet current workloads and future growth targets.

But let's say you're not eBay or Fidelity, and are just creating the proverbial "one-person-in-a-garage-just-getting-started" kind of Web site. For instance, Dave Novak created Steamshowers4Less.com using a MacBook Pro computer in a spare bedroom. He now sells over $1 million a year in bath fixtures. For really small sites, micro-businesses with just a few people, there are many less costly alternatives to sizing issues. One solution is to build a Web site using pre-built templates offered by Yahoo Merchant Solutions, Amazon, eBay, Design.NetworkSolutions.com, or hundreds of other online sites. Fees range from a few hundred dollars to several thousand. These firms host your Web site and they worry about capacity and scale issues as your firm grows. For instance, Yahoo Merchant Solutions offers three different packages—Starter, Standard, and Professional. As the business grows, you can move up to a more comprehensive package. Another solution is to hire a local professional designer (for about $1,000–$5,000) and have them build you an e-commerce installation that runs off a single computer and broadband connection. If you need more computing power, buy a newer PC with more speed and storage. Get a faster Web connection. Still another solution is to do everything yourself (design the Web site, procure and build the Web servers, and connect to the Internet) at first until you start attracting customers. However, in both of these do-it-yourself solutions, you will have to worry about how to keep up with growth.

SOURCES: "Online Tools Give Home-Based Firms Office-Style Services," by Gwendolyn Bounds, *Wall Street Journal*, September 11, 2007; "Keeping Costs Low For Online Business," by Kelly Spors, *New York Times*, April 24, 2007; "Guide to E-commerce Technology, 2007-2008 Edition," *Internet Retailer*, 2007; "Sonoma: Web Service for Estimating Capacity and Performance of Service-Oriented Architecture (SOA) Workloads", by Eugene Hung, Qi He, Jinzy Zhu, IBM Working Paper, October 9, 2006; "HiPODs Model: An eBay Case Study," by Noshir C. Wadia, Jayashree Subrahmonia, and Umesh Talwalkar, IBM Conference on Performance Engineering and Best Practices, June 21, 2004; "More about High Volume Web Sites," by High-Volume Web Sites Team, IBM Redbook, March 8, 2004; "HVWS Simulator: An eBay Case Study," High Performance On Demand Solutions Team and eBay, February 27, 2004.

In Chapter 3, you learned about the infrastructure of the Internet and the Web, e-commerce's technological foundation. Now it's time to focus on the next step: building an e-commerce site. In this chapter, you will examine the important factors that a manager needs to consider when building an e-commerce site. The focus will be on the managerial and business decisions you must make before you begin to build Web pages and Web sites, and which you will continually need to make during the life of your Web site. While building a sophisticated e-commerce site isn't easy, today the tools for building Web sites are much less expensive and far more powerful than they were during the early days of e-commerce. You do not have to be Amazon or eBay to create a successful Web site. In this chapter, we focus on both small and medium-sized businesses that want to build a Web site, and much larger corporate entities that serve thousands of customers a day, or even an hour. As you will see, although the scale may be very different, the principles and considerations are basically the same.

4.1 BUILDING AN E-COMMERCE WEB SITE: A SYSTEMATIC APPROACH

Building a successful e-commerce site requires a keen understanding of business, technology, and social issues, as well as a systematic approach. E-commerce is just too important to be left totally to technologists and programmers.

The two most important management challenges in building a successful e-commerce site are (1) developing a clear understanding of your business objectives and (2) knowing how to choose the right technology to achieve those objectives. The first challenge requires you to build a plan for developing your firm's site. The second challenge requires you to understand some of the basic elements of e-commerce infrastructure. Let the business drive the technology.

Even if you decide to outsource the entire e-commerce site development and operation to a service provider, you will still need to have a site development plan and some understanding of the basic e-commerce infrastructure issues such as cost, capability, and constraints. Without a plan and a knowledge base, you will not be able to make sound management decisions about e-commerce within your firm (Laudon and Laudon, 2009).

PIECES OF THE SITE-BUILDING PUZZLE

Let's assume you are a manager for a medium-sized, industrial parts firm of around 10,000 employees worldwide, operating in 10 countries in Europe, Asia, and North America. Senior management has given you a budget of $1 million to build an e-commerce site within one year. The purpose of this site will be to sell and service the firm's 20,000 customers, who are mostly small machine and metal fabricating shops around the world. Where do you start?

First, you must be aware of the main areas where you will need to make decisions (see **Figure 4.1**). On the organizational and human resources fronts, you will have to bring together a team of individuals who possess the skill sets needed to build and manage a successful e-commerce site. This team will make the key decisions about technology, site design, and the social and information policies that will be applied at your site. The entire site development effort must be closely managed if you hope to avoid the disasters that have occurred at some firms.

You will also need to make decisions about your site's hardware, software, and telecommunications infrastructure. While you will have technical advisors help you make these decisions, ultimately the operation of the site is your responsibility. The demands of your customers should drive your choices of technology. Your customers will want technology that enables them to find what they want easily, view the product, purchase the product, and then receive the product from your warehouses quickly. You will also have to carefully consider your site's design. Once you have identified the key decision areas, you will need to think about a plan for the project.

PLANNING: THE SYSTEMS DEVELOPMENT LIFE CYCLE

Your second step in building an e-commerce site will be creating a plan document. In order to tackle a complex problem such as building an e-commerce site, you will have to proceed systematically through a series of steps. One methodology for developing an e-commerce site plan is the systems development life cycle (see **Figure 4.2**).

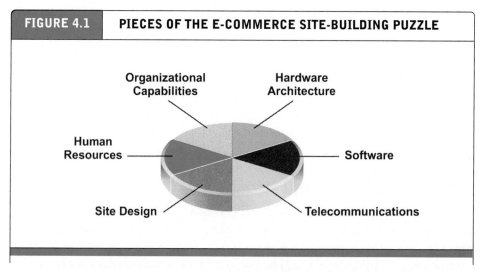

| FIGURE 4.1 | PIECES OF THE E-COMMERCE SITE-BUILDING PUZZLE |

Building an e-commerce Web site requires that you systematically consider the many factors that go into the process.

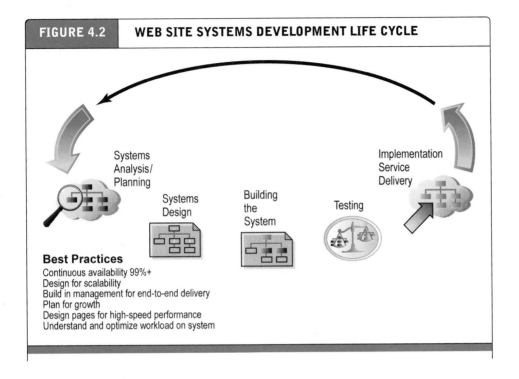

FIGURE 4.2 **WEB SITE SYSTEMS DEVELOPMENT LIFE CYCLE**

The systems development life cycle (SDLC) is a methodology for understanding the business objectives of any system and designing an appropriate solution. Adopting a life cycle methodology does not guarantee success, but it is far better than having no plan at all. The SDLC method also helps in creating documents that communicate to senior management the objectives of the site, important milestones, and the uses of resources. The five major steps involved in the systems development life cycle for an e-commerce site are:

- Systems Analysis/Planning
- Systems Design
- Building the System
- Testing
- Implementation

systems development life cycle (SDLC)
a methodology for understanding the business objectives of any system and designing an appropriate solution

SYSTEMS ANALYSIS/PLANNING: IDENTIFY BUSINESS OBJECTIVES, SYSTEM FUNCTIONALITY, AND INFORMATION REQUIREMENTS

The systems analysis/planning step of the SDLC tries to answer the question, "What do we want the e-commerce site to do for our business?" The key lesson to be learned here is to let the business decisions drive the technology, not the reverse. This will ensure that your technology platform is aligned with your business. We will assume here that you have identified a business strategy and chosen a business model to achieve your strategic objectives (see Chapter 2). But how do you translate your strategies, business models, and ideas into a working e-commerce site?

business objectives
a list of capabilities you want your site to have

system functionalities
a list of the types of information systems capabilities you will need to achieve your business objectives

information requirements
the information elements that the system must produce in order to achieve the business objectives

One way to start is to identify the specific business objectives for your site, and then develop a list of system functionalities and information requirements. **Business objectives** are simply a list of capabilities you want your site to have.

System functionalities are a list of the types of information systems capabilities you will need to achieve your business objectives. The **information requirements** for a system are the information elements that the system must produce in order to achieve the business objectives. You will need to provide these lists to system developers and programmers so they know what you as the manager expect them to do.

Table 4.1 describes some basic business objectives, system functionalities, and information requirements for a typical e-commerce site. As shown in the table, there are nine basic business objectives that an e-commerce site must deliver. These objectives must be translated into a description of system functionalities and ultimately into a set of precise information requirements. The specific information requirements for a system typically are defined in much greater detail than Table 4.1 indicates. To a large extent, the business objectives of an e-commerce site are not that different from those of an ordinary retail store. The real difference lies in the system functionalities and information requirements. In an e-commerce site,

TABLE 4.1	SYSTEM ANALYSIS: BUSINESS OBJECTIVES, SYSTEM FUNCTIONALITY, AND INFORMATION REQUIREMENTS FOR A TYPICAL E-COMMERCE SITE	
BUSINESS OBJECTIVE	**SYSTEM FUNCTIONALITY**	**INFORMATION REQUIREMENTS**
Display goods	Digital catalog	Dynamic text and graphics catalog
Provide product information (content)	Product database	Product description, stocking numbers, inventory levels
Personalize/customize product	Customer on-site tracking	Site log for every customer visit; data mining capability to identify common customer paths and appropriate responses
Execute a transaction payment	Shopping cart/payment system	Secure credit card clearing; multiple options
Accumulate customer information	Customer database	Name, address, phone, and e-mail for all customers; online customer registration
Provide after-sale customer support	Sales database	Customer ID, product, date, payment, shipment date
Coordinate marketing/advertising	Ad server, e-mail server, e-mail, campaign manager, ad banner manager	Site behavior log of prospects and customers linked to e-mail and banner ad campaigns
Understand marketing effectiveness	Site tracking and reporting system	Number of unique visitors, pages visited, products purchased, identified by marketing campaign
Provide production and supplier links	Inventory management system	Product and inventory levels, supplier ID and contact, order quantity data by product

the business objectives must be provided entirely in digital form without buildings or salespeople, twenty-four hours a day, seven days a week.

SYSTEM DESIGN: HARDWARE AND SOFTWARE PLATFORMS

Once you have identified the business objectives and system functionalities, and have developed a list of precise information requirements, you can begin to consider just how all this functionality will be delivered. You must come up with a **system design specification**—a description of the main components in the system and their relationship to one another. The system design itself can be broken down into two components: a logical design and a physical design. A **logical design** includes a data flow diagram that describes the flow of information at your e-commerce site, the processing functions that must be performed, and the databases that will be used. The logical design also includes a description of the security and emergency backup procedures that will be instituted, and the controls that will be used in the system.

A **physical design** translates the logical design into physical components. For instance, the physical design details the specific model of server to be purchased, the software to be used, the size of the telecommunications link that will be required, the way the system will be backed up and protected from outsiders, and so on.

Figure 4.3(a) presents a data flow diagram for a simple high-level logical design for a very basic Web site that delivers catalog pages in HTML in response to HTTP requests from the client's browser, while **Figure 4.3(b)** shows the corresponding physical design. Each of the main processes can be broken down into lower-level designs that are much more precise in identifying exactly how the information flows and what equipment is involved.

BUILDING THE SYSTEM: IN-HOUSE VERSUS OUTSOURCING

Now that you have a clear idea of both the logical and physical design for your site, you can begin considering how to actually build the site. There are many choices here and much depends on how much money you are willing to spend. Choices range from outsourcing everything (including the actual systems analysis and design) to building everything yourself (in-house). **Outsourcing** means that you will hire an outside vendor to provide the services involved in building the site that you cannot perform with in-house personnel. You also have a second decision to make: Will you host (operate) the site on your firm's own servers or will you outsource the hosting to a Web host provider? These decisions are independent of each other, but they are usually considered at the same time. There are some vendors who will design, build, and host your site, while others will either build or host (but not both). **Figure 4.4** on page 207 illustrates the alternatives.

Build Your Own versus Outsourcing

Let's take the building decision first. If you elect to build your own site, there are a range of options. Unless you are fairly skilled, you should use a pre-built template to create the Web site. For example, Yahoo Merchant Solutions, Amazon Stores, and eBay

system design specification
description of the main components in a system and their relationship to one another

logical design
describes the flow of information at your e-commerce site, the processing functions that must be performed, the databases that will be used, the security and emergency backup procedures that will be instituted, and the controls that will be used in the system

physical design
translates the logical design into physical components

outsourcing
hiring an outside vendor to provide the services you cannot perform with in-house personnel

FIGURE 4.3	A LOGICAL AND PHYSICAL DESIGN FOR A SIMPLE WEB SITE

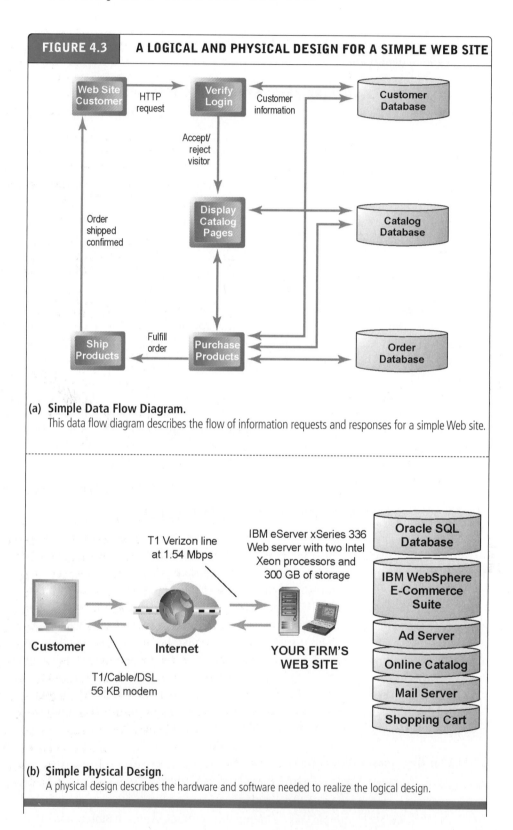

(a) Simple Data Flow Diagram.
This data flow diagram describes the flow of information requests and responses for a simple Web site.

(b) Simple Physical Design.
A physical design describes the hardware and software needed to realize the logical design.

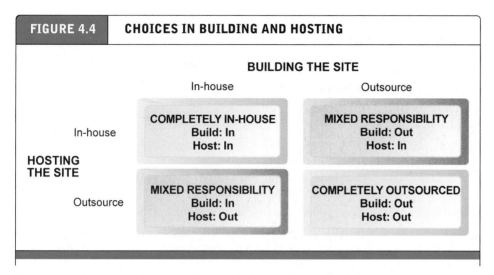

FIGURE 4.4   **CHOICES IN BUILDING AND HOSTING**

You have a number of alternatives to consider when building and hosting an e-commerce site.

all provide templates that merely require you to input text, graphics, and other data, as well as the infrastructure to run the Web site once it has been created. This is the least costly and simplest solution but you will be limited to the "look and feel" and functionality provided by the template and infrastructure.

If you have some experience with computers, you might decide to build the site yourself "from scratch." There is a broad variety of tools, ranging from those that help you build everything truly "from scratch," such as Adobe Dreamweaver and Microsoft Expression, to top-of-the-line prepackaged site-building tools that can create sophisticated sites customized to your needs. **Figure 4.5** illustrates the spectrum of tools available. We will look more closely at the variety of e-commerce software available in Section 4.2.

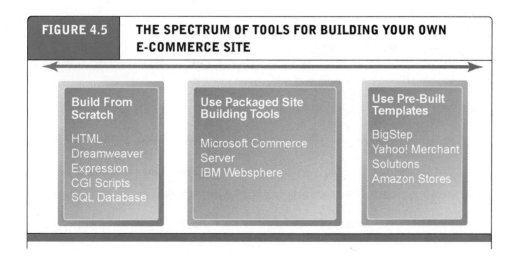

FIGURE 4.5   **THE SPECTRUM OF TOOLS FOR BUILDING YOUR OWN E-COMMERCE SITE**

The decision to build a Web site on your own has a number of risks. Given the complexity of features such as shopping carts, credit card authentication and processing, inventory management, and order processing, the costs involved are high, as are the risks of doing a poor job. You will be reinventing what other specialized firms have already built, and your staff may face a long, difficult learning curve, delaying your entry to market. Your efforts could fail. On the positive side, you may be better able to build a site that does exactly what you want, and more important, develop the in-house knowledge to allow you to change the site rapidly if necessary due to a changing business environment.

If you choose more expensive site-building packages, you will be purchasing state-of-the art software that is well tested. You could get to market sooner. However, to make a sound decision, you will have to evaluate many different packages and this can take a long time. You may have to modify the packages to fit your business needs and perhaps hire additional outside vendors to do the modifications. Costs rise rapidly as modifications mount. A $4,000 package can easily become a $40,000 to $60,000 development project (see **Figure 4.6**). If you choose the template route, you will be limited to the functionality already built into the templates, and you will not be able to add to the functionality or change it.

In the past, bricks-and-mortar retailers in need of an e-commerce site typically designed the site themselves (because they already had the skilled staff in place and had extensive investments in information technology capital such as databases and telecommunications). However, as Web applications have become more sophisticated, larger retailers today rely heavily on vendors to provide sophisticated Web site capabilities, while also maintaining a substantial internal staff. Small startups may build their own sites from scratch using in-house technical personnel in an effort to

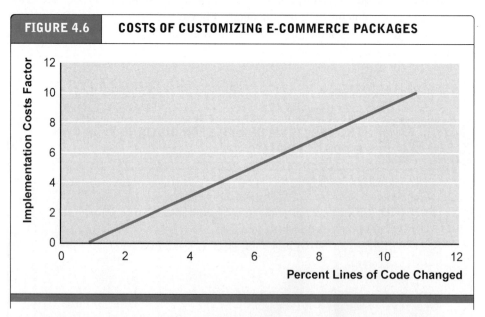

FIGURE 4.6 | **COSTS OF CUSTOMIZING E-COMMERCE PACKAGES**

While sophisticated site development packages appear to reduce costs and increase speed to market, as the modifications required to fit the package to your business needs rise, costs also rise exponentially.

keep costs low. Medium-size startups will often purchase a sophisticated package and then modify it to suit their needs. Very small mom-and-pop firms seeking simple storefronts will use templates. For e-commerce sites, the costs of building has dropped dramatically in the last five years, resulting in lower capital requirements for all players (see *Insight on Business: Curly Hair and Tattoos: Getting Started on the Cheap*).

Host Your Own versus Outsourcing

Now let's look at the hosting decision. Most businesses choose to outsource hosting and pay a company to host their Web site, which means that the hosting company is responsible for ensuring the site is "live," or accessible, twenty-four hours a day. By agreeing to a monthly fee, the business need not concern itself with many of the technical aspects of setting up a Web server and maintaining it, telecommunications links, nor with staffing needs.

You can also choose to *co-locate*. With a **co-location** agreement, your firm purchases or leases a Web server (and has total control over its operation) but locates the server in a vendor's physical facility. The vendor maintains the facility, communications lines, and the machinery. Co-location has expanded with the spread of virtualization where one server has multiple processors (4–16) and can operate multiple Web sites at once with multiple operating systems. In this case, you do not buy the server but rent its capabilities on a monthly basis, usually at one-quarter of the cost of owning the server itself. See **Table 4.2** for a list of some of the major hosting/co-location providers. There is an extraordinary range of prices for co-hosting, ranging from $4.95 a month, to several hundred thousands of dollars per month depending on the size of the Web site, bandwidth, storage, and support requirements.

Hosting and co-location have become a commodity and a utility: costs are driven by very large providers (such as IBM and Qwest) who can achieve large economies of scale by establishing huge "server farms" located strategically around the country and the globe. What this means is that the cost of pure hosting has fallen as fast as the fall in server prices, dropping about 50% every year! Telecommunications costs have also fallen. As a result, most hosting services seek to differentiate themselves from the commodity hosting business by offering extensive site design, marketing, optimization and other services. Small, local ISPs also can be used as hosts, but service reliability is an issue. Will the small ISP be able to provide uninterrupted service, 24x7x365? Will they have service staff available when you need it?

co-location
when a firm purchases or leases a Web server (and has total control over its operation) but locates the server in a vendor's physical facility. The vendor maintains the facility, communications lines, and the machinery

TABLE 4.2	KEY PLAYERS: HOSTING/CO-LOCATION SERVICES
GoDaddy.com	Qwest Communications
Oneandone.com	NTT/Verio
IBM Global Services	Rackspace
MOSSO	ServerBeach

INSIGHT ON BUSINESS

CURLY HAIR AND TATTOOS: GETTING STARTED ON THE CHEAP

With so many big companies with national brand names dominating the e-commerce scene, and with the top 100 retail firms collecting over 90% of the revenues, you may wonder if there's a chance for the little guy anymore, the complete amateurs. The answer is yes: there's still at least about $20 billion left in potential online retail sales to go for, with additional money to be made from advertising revenues. As it turns out, being big does not make you nimble.

NaturallyCurly.com is a good example of a low entry cost, niche-oriented portal site. Two reporters, Gretchen Heber and Michelle Breyer, started the site with $500 in 1998. Both had naturally curly hair. "We had long diatribes complaining about our curly hair on very muggy days," says Heber. Or they'd talk about how good it looked on other days. Based on a hunch that other people also needed help coping with curly hair issues, they launched NaturallyCurly.com. They spent $200 on the domain name, and bought some curly hair products to review on the site. The site was built with a simple Web server and the help of a 14-year-old Web page designer. The idea was to act as a content site with community feedback. They added a bulletin board for users to send in their comments.

There were no competitors at first, and even without advertising on Google, they started showing up in Google searches for "curly hair" near or at the top of the search results list.

(continued)

In 2000, after a year of operation, they got an e-mail from Procter & Gamble, the world's largest personal care products company, asking if they would accept advertising for $2,000 a month for two years. From there, the site grew by adding additional advertising from leading hair care products companies such as Aveda, Paul Mitchell, and Redken, among others. Today the site has close to 200,000 monthly visitors and revenue in excess of $1 million from advertising and sales of products on curlmart.com, its online boutique for curly hair products.. In May 2007, the firm received an investment of $600,000 from a venture capital firm that will be used to hire a marketing person and support staff, improve its Web technology, and expand its shipping and handling operations. Ms. Breyer said the company is still not profitable because they have poured money back into the firm, but it's good enough that both quit their jobs in 2004.

Internet incubators—firms that provide technology, money, and space to small ventures in return for a part of the company—are another source of small, niche-oriented e-commerce sites that are largely advertising-supported. In a development reminiscent of the early years of e-commerce, when incubators such as IdeaLab and CMGI provided backing for dozens of retail-oriented e-commerce sites, a company called RIVR Media Interactive will produce 15 online-only video Web sites. RIVR produces television programming for cable channels such as A&E and Nickelodeon. Leveraging this video background, RIVR launched its first advertising-supported site, Needled.com. The site offers video clips, photos, multimedia histories, artists, and contact information to the needled crowd—those who have tattoos. As it turns out, 67 million Americans have some kind of tattoo, and 34% of 18-to-34-year-olds have tattoos. The site runs video ads for all things young—motorcycles, video games, beverages, and cars. Needled.com was started as a blog by Marisa DeMattia, and purchased by RIVR for an undisclosed sum. Other RIVR sites include Widgetgames.com, aimed at the casual gamer and SyncLive.com, which allows users to broadcast live concerts from venues across the country and the world.

The lesson here is that building startup Web sites is much less expensive and much easier these days than in the past.

SOURCES: "About Us", NaturallyCurly.com, 2008; " Curl Tamers," *Jewish Woman*, Summer 2008; "RIVR Media Interactive Creating Syndicated Internet Network Geared toward Male Demographic", PR Newswire, June 25, 2008; "Turning Curls into Dollar Signs," Business Opportunities Weblog, March 2008; "Bad Hair Days Lead Pair to Web Incubator and Venture Capital," by Bob Tedeschi, *New York Times*, May 21, 2007; "Naturally Curly Raises $600,000 in Funding," by Kristen Nicole, Mashable.com, May 20, 2007; "The Perils of Spending Hard-Raised Money," by Maureen Farrell, Forbes.com, May 3, 2007.

There are several disadvantages to outsourcing hosting. If you choose a vendor, make sure the vendor has the capability to grow with you. You need to know what kinds of security provisions are in place for backup copies of your site, internal monitoring of activity, and security track record. Is there a public record of a security breach at the vendor? Most Fortune 500 firms do their own hosting so they can control the Web environment. On the other hand, there are risks to hosting your own site if you are a small business. Your costs will be higher than if you had used a large outsourcing firm because you don't have the market power to obtain low-cost hardware and telecommunications. You will have to purchase hardware and software, have a physical facility, lease communications lines, hire a staff, and build security and backup capabilities yourself.

TESTING THE SYSTEM

Once the system has been built and programmed, you will have to engage in a testing process. Depending on the size of the system, this could be fairly difficult and lengthy. Testing is required whether the system is outsourced or built in-house. A complex e-commerce site can have thousands of pathways through the site, each of which must be documented and then tested. **Unit testing** involves testing the site's program modules one at a time. **System testing** involves testing the site as a whole, in the same way a typical user would when using the site. Because there is no truly "typical" user, system testing requires that every conceivable path be tested. Final **acceptance testing** requires that the firm's key personnel and managers in marketing, production, sales, and general management actually use the system as installed on a test Internet or intranet server. This acceptance test verifies that the business objectives of the system as originally conceived are in fact working. It is important to note that testing is generally under-budgeted. As much as 50% of the software effort can be consumed by testing and rebuilding (usually depending on the quality of initial design).

IMPLEMENTATION AND MAINTENANCE

Most people unfamiliar with systems erroneously think that once an information system is installed, the process is over. In fact, while the beginning of the process is over, the operational life of a system is just beginning. Systems break down for a variety of reasons—most of them unpredictable. Therefore, they need continual checking, testing, and repair. Systems maintenance is vital, but sometimes not budgeted for. In general, the annual system maintenance cost will roughly parallel the development cost. A $40,000 e-commerce site will likely require a $40,000 annual expenditure to maintain. Very large e-commerce sites experience some economies of scale, so that, for example, a $1 million site will likely require a maintenance budget of $500,000 to $700,000.

Why does it cost so much to maintain an e-commerce site? Unlike payroll systems, for example, e-commerce sites are always in a process of change, improvement, and correction. Studies of traditional systems maintenance have found 20% of the time is devoted to debugging code and responding to emergency situations (a new server was installed by your ISP, and all your hypertext links were lost and CGI scripts disabled—the site is down!) (Lientz and Swanson, 1980; Banker and Kemerer, 1989). Another 20% of the time is concerned with changes in reports, data files, and links to backend databases. The remaining 60% of maintenance time is devoted to general administration (making product and price changes in the catalog) and making changes and enhancements to the system. E-commerce sites are never finished: they are always in the process of being built and rebuilt. They are dynamic—much more so than payroll systems.

The long-term success of an e-commerce site will depend on a dedicated team of employees (the Web team) whose sole job is to monitor and adapt the site to changing market conditions. The Web team must be multi-skilled; it will typically include programmers, designers, and business managers drawn from marketing, production, and sales support. One of the first tasks of the Web team is to listen to customers' feedback on the site and respond to that feedback as necessary. A second task is to develop a systematic monitoring and testing plan to be followed weekly to ensure all the links are operating, prices are correct, and pages are updated. A large business may have thousands of Web pages, many of them linked, that require systematic monitoring. Other important tasks of the Web team include **benchmarking** (a process in which the site is compared with those of competitors in terms of response speed, quality of layout, and design) and keeping the site current on pricing and promotions. The Web is a competitive environment where you can very rapidly frustrate and lose customers with a dysfunctional site.

benchmarking

a process in which the site is compared with those of competitors in terms of response speed, quality of layout, and design

FACTORS IN OPTIMIZING WEB SITE PERFORMANCE

The purpose of a Web site is to deliver content to customers and to complete transactions. The faster and more reliably these two objectives are met, the more effective the Web site is from a commerce perspective. If you are a manager or marketing executive, you will want the Web site operating in a way that fulfills customers' expectations. You'll have to make sure the Web site is optimized to achieve this business objective. The optimization of Web site performance is more complicated than it seems and involves at least three factors: page content, page generation, and page delivery (see **Figure 4.7**). In this chapter, we describe the software and hardware choices you will need to make in building an e-commerce site; these are also important factors in Web site optimization.

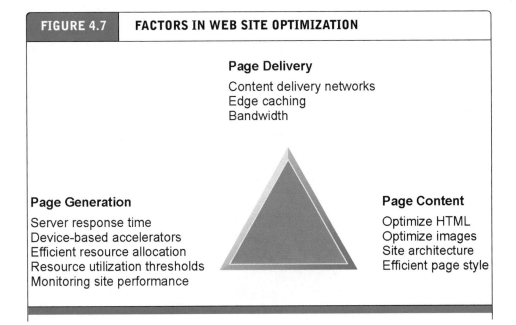

FIGURE 4.7	FACTORS IN WEB SITE OPTIMIZATION

Page Delivery
Content delivery networks
Edge caching
Bandwidth

Page Generation
Server response time
Device-based accelerators
Efficient resource allocation
Resource utilization thresholds
Monitoring site performance

Page Content
Optimize HTML
Optimize images
Site architecture
Efficient page style

Web site optimization requires that you consider three factors: page content, page generation, and page delivery.

Using efficient styles and techniques for *page design* and *content* can reduce response times by two to five seconds. Simple steps include reducing unnecessary HTML comments and white space, using more efficient graphics, and avoiding unnecessary links to other pages in the site. *Page generation* speed can be enhanced by segregating computer servers to perform dedicated functions (such as static page generation, application logic, media servers, and database servers), and using various devices from vendors to speed up these servers. Using a single server or multiple servers to perform multiple tasks reduces throughput by over 50%. *Page delivery* can be speeded up by using edge-caching services such as Akamai, or specialized content delivery networks such as RealNetworks, or by increasing local bandwidth. We will discuss some of these factors throughout the chapter, but a full discussion of Web site optimization is beyond the scope of this text.

WEB SITE BUDGETS

How much you spend on a Web site depends on what you want it to do. Simple Web sites can be built and hosted with a first-year cost of $5,000 or less. The Web sites of large firms that offer high levels of interactivity and linkage to corporate systems can cost several hundred thousand to millions of dollars a year to create and operate. For instance, in September 2006, Bluefly, which sells women's and men's designer clothes online, embarked on the process of developing an improved version of its Web site based on software from Art Technology Group (ATG). It hopes to launch the new site by early 2009. To date, it has capitalized over $3.6 million in connection with the redevelopment of the Web site. (Bluefly, Inc., 2008).

While how much you spend to build a Web site depends on how much you can afford, and, of course, the size of the opportunity, **Figure 4.8** provides some idea of the relative size of various Web site costs. In general, the cost of hardware, software and telecommunications for building and operating a Web site has fallen

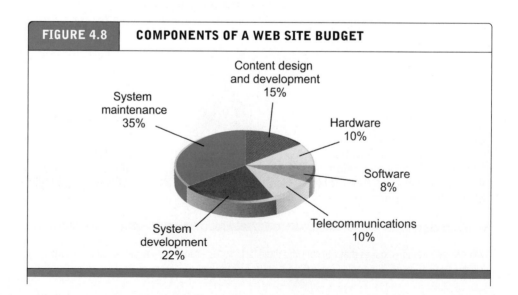

FIGURE 4.8 **COMPONENTS OF A WEB SITE BUDGET**

dramatically (by over 50%) since 2000, making it possible for very small entrepreneurs to build fairly sophisticated sites. At the same time, while technology has lowered the costs of system development, the costs of system maintenance and content creation have risen to make up more than half of typical Web site budgets. Providing content and smooth 24x7 operations are both labor intensive.

4.2   CHOOSING SOFTWARE

Much of what you are able to do at an e-commerce site is a function of the software. As a business manager in charge of building the site, you will need to know some basic information about e-commerce software. The more sophisticated the software and the more ways you can sell goods and services, the more effective your business will be. This section describes the software needed to operate a contemporary e-commerce site. Section 4.3 discusses the hardware you will need to handle the demands of the software.

SIMPLE VERSUS MULTI-TIERED WEB SITE ARCHITECTURE

Prior to the development of e-commerce, Web sites simply delivered Web pages to users who were making requests through their browsers for HTML pages with content of various sorts. Web site software was appropriately quite simple—it consisted of a server computer running basic Web server software. We might call this arrangement a single-tier system architecture. **System architecture** refers to the arrangement of software, machinery, and tasks in an information system needed to achieve a specific functionality (much like a home's architecture refers to the arrangement of building materials to achieve a particular functionality). The SteamShowers4Less and NaturallyCurly sites both started this way—there were no monetary transactions. Tens of thousands of dot-com sites still perform this way. Orders can always be called in by telephone and not taken online.

system architecture
the arrangement of software, machinery, and tasks in an information system needed to achieve a specific functionality

However, the development of e-commerce required a great deal more interactive functionality, such as the ability to respond to user input (name and address forms), take customer orders for goods and services, clear credit card transactions on the fly, consult price and product databases, and even adjust advertising on the screen based on user characteristics. This kind of extended functionality required the development of Web application servers and a multi-tiered system architecture to handle the processing loads. *Web application servers*, described more fully later in this section, are specialized software programs that perform a wide variety of transaction processing required by e-commerce.

In addition to having specialized application servers, e-commerce sites must be able to pull information from and add information to pre-existing corporate databases. These older databases that predate the e-commerce era are called *backend* or *legacy* databases. Corporations have made massive investments in these systems to store their information on customers, products, employees, and vendors. These backend systems constitute an additional layer in a multi-tiered site.

two-tier architecture

e-commerce system architecture in which a Web server responds to requests for Web pages and a database server provides backend data storage

multi-tier architecture

e-commerce system architecture in which the Web server is linked to a middle-tier layer that typically includes a series of application servers that perform specific tasks as well as to a backend layer of existing corporate systems

Figure 4.9 illustrates a simple two-tier and more complex multi-tier e-commerce system architecture. In **two-tier architecture**, a Web server responds to requests for Web pages and a database server provides backend data storage. In a **multi-tier architecture**, in contrast, the Web server is linked to a middle-tier layer that typically includes a series of application servers that perform specific tasks, as well as to a backend layer of existing corporate systems containing product, customer, and pricing information. A multi-tiered site typically employs several or more physical computers, each running some of the software applications and sharing the workload across many physical computers.

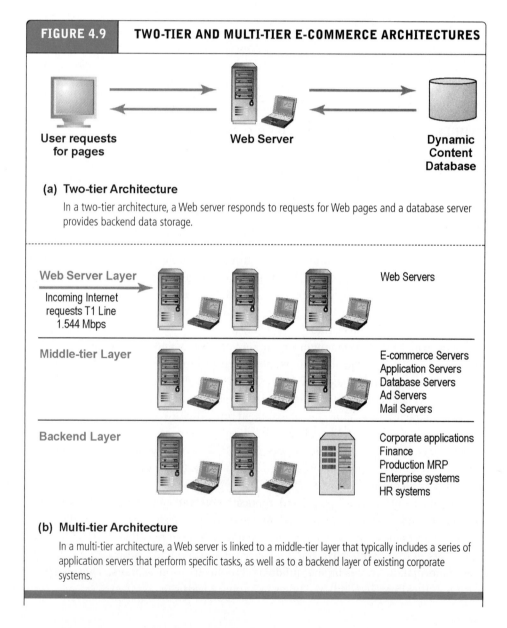

FIGURE 4.9   TWO-TIER AND MULTI-TIER E-COMMERCE ARCHITECTURES

(a) Two-tier Architecture

In a two-tier architecture, a Web server responds to requests for Web pages and a database server provides backend data storage.

(b) Multi-tier Architecture

In a multi-tier architecture, a Web server is linked to a middle-tier layer that typically includes a series of application servers that perform specific tasks, as well as to a backend layer of existing corporate systems.

The remainder of this section describes basic Web server software functionality and the various types of Web application servers.

WEB SERVER SOFTWARE

All e-commerce sites require basic Web server software to answer requests from customers for HTML and XML pages. The leading Web server software choices are shown in **Figure 4.10**.

When you choose Web server software, you will also be choosing an operating system for your site's computers. Looking at all servers on the Web, the leading Web server software, with 50% of the market, is Apache, which works with Linux and Unix operating systems. Unix is the original programming language of the Internet and Web, and Linux is a derivative of Unix designed for the personal computer. Apache was developed by a worldwide community of Internet innovators. Apache is free and can be downloaded from many sites on the Web; it also comes installed on most IBM Web servers. Literally thousands of programmers have worked on Apache over the years; thus, it is extremely stable. There are thousands of utility software programs written for Apache that can provide all the functionality required for a contemporary e-commerce site. In order to use Apache, you will need staff that is knowledgeable in Unix or Linux.

Microsoft Internet Information Services (IIS) is the second major Web server software available, with about 35% of the market. IIS is based on the Windows operating system and is compatible with a wide selection of Microsoft utility and support programs. These numbers are different among the Fortune 1000 firms (55% of which use Microsoft IIS), and different again if you include blogs which are served up by Microsoft and Google at their own proprietary sites.

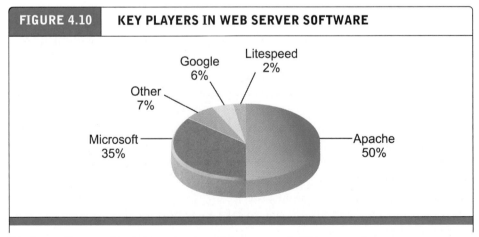

| FIGURE 4.10 | **KEY PLAYERS IN WEB SERVER SOFTWARE** |

This diagram illustrates the relative market share of the most popular Web server software.
SOURCE: Based on data from E-Soft, Inc, 2008.

TABLE 4.3	BASIC FUNCTIONALITY PROVIDED BY WEB SERVERS
FUNCTIONALITY	DESCRIPTION
Processing of HTTP requests	Receive and respond to client requests for HTML pages
Security services (Secure Sockets Layer)	Verify username and password; process certificates and private/public key information required for credit card processing and other secure information
File Transfer Protocol	Permits transfer of very large files from server to server
Search engine	Indexing of site content; keyword search capability
Data capture	Log file of all visits, time, duration, and referral source
E-mail	Ability to send, receive, and store e-mail messages
Site management tools	Calculate and display key site statistics, such as unique visitors, page requests, and origin of requests; check links on pages

There are also at least 100 other smaller providers of Web server software, most of them based on the Unix or Sun Solaris operating systems. Note that the choice of Web server has little effect on users of your system. The pages they see will look the same regardless of the development environment. There are many advantages to the Microsoft suite of development tools—they are integrated, powerful, and easy to use. The Unix operating system, on the other hand, is exceptionally reliable and stable, and there is a worldwide open software community that develops and tests Unix-based Web server software.

Table 4.3 shows the basic functionality provided by all Web servers.

Site Management Tools

In Chapter 3, we described most of the basic functionality of the Web servers listed in Table 4.3. Another functionality not described previously is site management tools. **Site management tools** are essential if you want to keep your site working, and if you want to understand how well it is working. Site management tools verify that links on pages are still valid and also identify orphan files, or files on the site that are not linked to any pages. By surveying the links on a Web site, a site management tool can quickly report on potential problems and errors that users may encounter. Your customers will not be impressed if they encounter a "404 Error: Page Does Not Exist" on your Web site. Links to URLs that have moved or been deleted are called dead links; these can cause error messages for users trying to access that link. Regularly checking that all links on a site are operational helps prevent irritation and frustration in users who may decide to take their business elsewhere to a better functioning site.

Even more importantly, site management tools can help you understand consumer behavior on your Web site. Site management software and services, such as

site management tools
verify that links on pages are still valid and also identify orphan files

those provided by WebTrends, can be purchased in order to more effectively monitor customer purchases and marketing campaign effectiveness, as well as keep track of standard hit counts and page visit information. **Figure 4.11** contains several screenshots that illustrate the different types of functionality provided by WebTrends software.

Dynamic Page Generation Tools

One of the most important innovations in Web site operation has been the development of dynamic page generation tools. Prior to the development of e-commerce, Web sites primarily delivered unchanging static content in the form of HTML pages. While this capability might be sufficient to display pictures of products, consider all the elements of a typical e-commerce site today by reviewing Table 4.1, or visit what you believe is an excellent e-commerce site. The content of successful e-commerce sites is always changing, often day by day. There are new products and promotions, changing prices, news events, and stories of successful users. E-commerce sites must intensively interact with users who not only request pages but also request product, price, availability, and inventory information. One of the most dynamic sites is eBay—the auction site. There, the content is changing minute by minute. E-commerce sites are just like real markets—they are dynamic. News sites, where stories change constantly, are also dynamic.

The dynamic and complex nature of e-commerce sites requires a number of specialized software applications in addition to static HTML pages. Perhaps one of the most important is dynamic page generation software. With **dynamic page generation**, the contents of a Web page are stored as objects in a database, rather than being hard-coded in HTML. When the user requests a Web page, the contents for that page are then fetched from the database. The objects are retrieved from the database using CGI (Common Gateway Interface), ASP (Active Server Pages), JSP (Java Server Pages), or other server-side programs. CGI, ASP, and JSP are described in the last section of this chapter. This technique is much more efficient than working directly in HTML code. It is much easier to change the contents of a database than it is to change the coding of an HTML page. A standard data access method called *Open Database Connectivity (ODBC)* makes it possible to access any data from any application regardless of what database is used. ODBC is supported by most of the large database suppliers such as Oracle, Sybase, and IBM. ODBC makes it possible for HTML pages to be linked to backend corporate databases regardless of who manufactured the database. Web sites must be able to pull information from, and add information to, these databases. For example, when a customer clicks on a picture of a pair of boots, the site can access the product catalog database stored in a DB2 database, and access the inventory database stored in an Oracle database to confirm that the boots are still in stock and to report the current price.

Dynamic page generation gives e-commerce several significant capabilities that generate cost and profitability advantages over traditional commerce. Dynamic page generation lowers *menu* costs (the costs incurred by merchants for changing product descriptions and prices). Dynamic page generation also permits easy online *market segmentation*—the ability to sell the same product to different

dynamic page generation
the contents of a Web page are stored as objects in a database, rather than being hard-coded in HTML. When the user requests a Web page, the contents for that page are then fetched from the database

---

FIGURE 4.11 | **WEBTRENDS MARKETING LAB2**

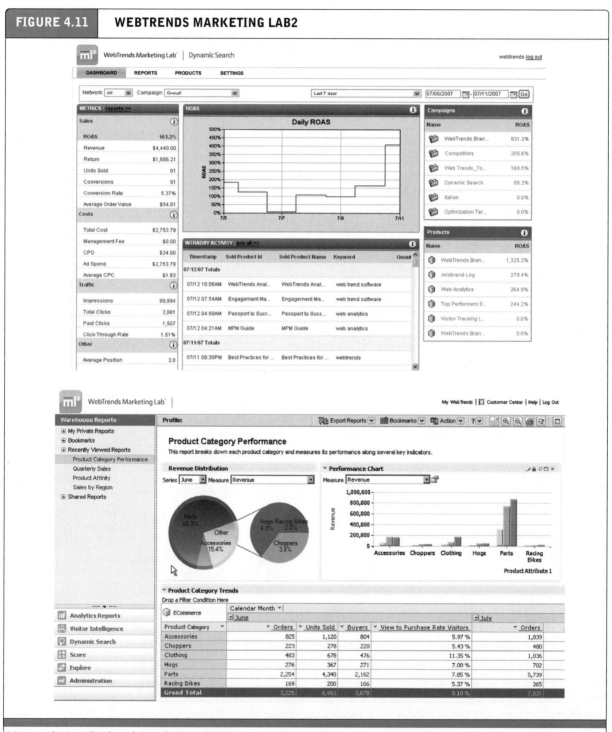

Using a sophisticated Web analytics solution such as WebTrends Marketing Lab2, managers can quickly understand the return on investment of their online marketing efforts and determine how to improve conversion by drilling down into abandoment paths, product preferences, and successful campaign elements for different types of customers.

SOURCE: WebTrends, Inc., 2007.

markets. For instance, you might want variations on the same banner ad depending on how many times the customer has seen the ad. In the first exposure to a car ad, you might want to emphasize brand identification and unique features. On the second viewing you might want to emphasize superlatives like "most family friendly" to encourage comparison to other brands (Story, 2007). The same capability makes possible nearly cost-free *price discrimination*—the ability to sell the same product to different customers at different prices. For instance, you might want to sell the same product to corporations and government agencies but use different marketing themes. Based on a cookie you place on client files, or in response to a question on your site that asks visitors if they are from a government agency or a corporation, you would be able to use different marketing and promotional materials for corporate clients and government clients. You might want to reward loyal customers with lower prices, say on DVDs or musical tracks, and charge full price to first-time buyers. Dynamic page generation allows you to approach different customers with different messages and prices.

Dynamic page generation also enables the use of Web content management systems. As its name implies, a **Web content management system (WCMS or WebCMS)** is used to create and manage Web content. A WCMS separates the design and presentation of content (such as HTML documents, images, video, audio) from the content creation process. The content is maintained in a database and dynamically linked to the Web site. A WCMS usually includes templates that can be automatically applied to new and existing content, WYSIWIG editing tools that make it easy to edit and describe (tag) content, and collaboration, workflow and document management tools. Typically, an experienced programmer is needed to install the system, but thereafter, content can be easily created and managed by non-technical staff. There are a wide range of commercial WCMSs available, from top-end enterprise systems offered by Interwoven, Vignette, Documentum, RedDot, IBM, and Oracle, to mid-market systems by Ingenuix, PaperThin, Ektron and Hot Banana, as well as hosted SAAS (software as a service) versions by Clickability, Marqui, and CrownPeak Technologies. There are also several open source content management systems available, such as Joomla, Drupal, OpenCMS, and others (CMSWatch.com, 2008).

Web content management system (WCMS, WebCMS)
used to create and manage Web content

APPLICATION SERVERS

Web application servers are software programs that provide the specific business functionality required of a Web site. The basic idea of application servers is to isolate the business applications from the details of displaying Web pages to users on the front end and the details of connecting to databases on the back end. Application servers are a kind of middleware software that provides the glue connecting traditional corporate systems to the customer as well as all the functionality needed to conduct e-commerce. In the early years, a number of software firms developed specific separate programs for each function, but increasingly, these specific programs are being replaced by integrated software tools that combine all the needed functionality for an e-commerce site into a single development environment, a packaged software approach.

web application server
software programs that provide specific business functionality required of a Web site

TABLE 4.4	APPLICATION SERVERS AND THEIR FUNCTION
APPLICATION SERVER	FUNCTIONALITY
Catalog display	Provides a database for product descriptions and prices
Transaction processing (shopping cart)	Accepts orders and clears payments
List server	Creates and serves mailing lists and manages e-mail marketing campaigns
Proxy server	Monitors and controls access to main Web server; implements firewall protection
Mail server	Manages Internet e-mail
Audio/video server	Stores and delivers streaming media content
Chat server	Creates an environment for online real-time text and audio interactions with customers
News server	Provides connectivity and displays Internet news feeds
Fax server	Provides fax reception and sending using a Web server
Groupware server	Creates workgroup environments for online collaboration
Database server	Stores customer, product, and price information
Ad server	Maintains Web-enabled database of advertising banners that permits customized and personalized display of advertisements based on consumer behavior and characteristics
Auction server	Provides a transaction environment for conducting online auctions
B2B server	Implements buy, sell, and link marketplaces for commercial transactions

Table 4.4 illustrates the wide variety of application servers available in the marketplace. The table focuses on "sell side" servers that are designed to enable selling products on the Web. So-called "buy side" and "link" servers focus on the needs of businesses to connect with partners in their supply chains or find suppliers for specific parts and assemblies. These buy side and link servers are described more fully in Chapter 12, *B2B E-commerce, Supply Chain Management, and Collaborative Commerce*. There are several thousand software vendors that provide application server software. For Linux and Unix environments, many of these capabilities are available free on the Internet from various sites. Most businesses—faced with this bewildering array of choices—choose to use integrated software tools called merchant server software.

e-commerce merchant server software

software that provides the basic functionality needed for online sales, including an online catalog, order taking via an online shopping cart, and online credit card processing

E-COMMERCE MERCHANT SERVER SOFTWARE FUNCTIONALITY

E-commerce merchant server software provides the basic functionality needed for online sales, including an online catalog, order taking via an online shopping cart, and online credit card processing.

Online Catalog

A company that wants to sell products on the Web must have a list, or **online catalog**, of its products, available on its Web site. Merchant server software typically includes a database capability that will allow for construction of a customized online catalog. The complexity and sophistication of the catalog will vary depending on the size of the company and its product lines. Small companies, or companies with small product lines, may post a simple list with text descriptions and perhaps color photos. A larger site might decide to add sound, animations, or videos (useful for product demonstrations) to the catalog, or interactivity, such as customer service representatives available via instant messaging to answer questions. Today, larger firms make extensive use of streaming video.

online catalog
list of products available on a Web site

Shopping Cart

Online **shopping carts** are much like their real-world equivalent; both allow shoppers to set aside desired purchases in preparation for checkout. The difference is that the online variety is part of a merchant server software program residing on the Web server, and allows consumers to select merchandise, review what they have selected, edit their selections as necessary, and then actually make the purchase by clicking a button. The merchant server software automatically stores shopping cart data.

shopping cart
allows shoppers to set aside desired purchases in preparation for checkout, review what they have selected, edit their selections as necessary, and then actually make the purchase by clicking a button

Credit Card Processing

A site's shopping cart typically works in conjunction with credit card processing software, which verifies the shopper's credit card and then puts through the debit to the card and the credit to the company's account at checkout. Integrated e-commerce software suites typically supply the software for this function. Otherwise, you will have to make arrangements with a variety of credit card processing banks and intermediaries.

MERCHANT SERVER SOFTWARE PACKAGES (E-COMMERCE SUITES)

Rather than build your site from a collection of disparate software applications, it is easier, faster, and generally more cost-effective to purchase a **merchant server software package** (also called an **e-commerce server suite**). Merchant server software/e-commerce suites offer an integrated environment that promises to provide most or all of the functionality and capabilities you will need to develop a sophisticated, customer-centric site. E-commerce suites come in three general ranges of price and functionality.

merchant server software package (e-commerce server suite)
offers an integrated environment that provides most or all of the functionality and capabilities needed to develop a sophisticated, customer-centric site

Basic packages for elementary e-commerce business applications are provided by Bizland, Hypermart, and Yahoo! Merchant Solutions. Freewebs.com also offers free Web building tools and hosting services. PayPal can be used as a payment system on simple Web sites, and widgets can add interesting capabilities.

Midrange suites include IBM's WebSphere Commerce Express Edition and Microsoft's Commerce Server 2007. High-end enterprise solutions for large global firms are provided by IBM WebSphere's Commerce Professional and Enterprise Editions, Broadvision Commerce, and others. There are several hundred software firms

TABLE 4.5	WIDELY USED MIDRANGE AND HIGH-END E-COMMERCE SUITES
PRODUCT	APPROXIMATE PRICE
Microsoft Commerce Server	Standard Edition, $6,999 per processor Enterprise Edition, $19,999 per processor
IBM WebSphere Commerce	Express Edition, single user license, $3,610; Processor Value Unit (PVU) license, $20,000
	Professional edition, PVULlicense, $100,000
	Enterprise Edition, PVU license, $159,000
Broadvision Commerce	$60,000 per processor
IntershopEnfinity Suite 6 Consumer Channel	$125,000–$250,000
ATG (Art Technology Group)	$380,000 for a four-CPU license

that provide e-commerce suites, which raises the costs of making sensible decisions on this matter. Many firms simply choose vendors with the best overall reputation. Quite often this turns out to be expensive but ultimately a workable solution. **Table 4.5** lists some of the most widely adopted midrange and high-end e-commerce suites.

Choosing an E-commerce Suite

With all of these vendors, how do you choose the right one? Evaluating these tools and making a choice is one of the most important and uncertain decisions you will make in building an e-commerce site. The real costs are hidden—they involve training your staff to use the tools and integrating the tools into your business processes and organizational culture. The following are some of the key factors to consider:

- Functionality
- Support for different business models
- Business process modeling tools
- Visual site management tools and reporting
- Performance and scalability

- Connectivity to existing business systems
- Compliance with standards
- Global and multicultural capability
- Local sales tax and shipping rules

For instance, although e-commerce suites promise to do everything, your business may require special functionality—such as streaming audio and video. You will need a list of business functionality requirements. Your business may involve several different business models—such as a retail side and a business-to-business side; you may run auctions for stock excess as well as fixed-price selling. Be sure the package can support all of your business models. You may wish to change your business processes, such as order taking and order fulfillment. Does the suite contain tools for modeling business process and work flows? Understanding how your site works will require visual reporting tools that make its operation transparent to many different people in your business. A poorly designed software package will drop off significantly in performance as visitors and transactions expand into the thousands per hour, or minute. Check for performance and scalability by stress testing a pilot edition or obtaining data from the vendor about performance under load. You will have to connect the e-commerce suite to your traditional business systems. How will this connection to existing systems be made, and is your staff skilled in making the connection? Because of the changing technical environment—in particular, changes in mobile commerce platforms—it is important to document exactly what standards the suite supports now, and what the migration path will be toward the future. Finally, your e-commerce site may have to work both globally and locally. You may need a foreign language edition using foreign currency denominations. And you will have to collect sales taxes across many local, regional, and national tax systems. Does the e-commerce suite support this level of globalization and localization?

BUILDING YOUR OWN E-COMMERCE SITE: WEB SERVICES AND OPEN SOURCE OPTIONS

While existing firms often have the financial capital to invest in commercial merchant server software suites, many small firms and startup firms do not. They have to build their own Web sites, at least initially. There are really two options here, the key factor being how much programming experience and time you have. One option is to utilize the e-commerce merchant services provided by hosting sites such as Yahoo's Merchant Solutions. For a $50 setup fee, and a starter plan of $39.95, the service will walk you through setting up your Web site and provide Web hosting, a shopping cart, technical help by phone, and payment processing. Other less well-known hosting services include Freemerchant.com, which offers a free turnkey (complete) solution that enables you to build a fair sophisticated online store. Bigstep.com takes users step by step through the process of building an online store. Entrabase.com and Tripod provide easy-to-use site-building tools and e-commerce templates for e-commerce sites. An e-commerce template is a pre-designed Web site that allows users to customize the look and feel of the site to fit their business needs and provides a standard set of functionality. Most templates today contain ready-to-go site designs with built-in e-commerce suite functionality like shopping carts, payment clearance, and site management tools.

If you have considerable, or at least some, programming background, then you can consider open source merchant server software. Open source software, as described in Chapter 3, is software developed by a community of programmers and designers, and is free to use and modify. **Table 4.6** provides a description of some open source options.

The advantage of using open source Web building tools is that you get exactly what you want, a truly customized unique Web site. The disadvantage is that it will take several months for a single programmer to develop the site and get all the tools

TABLE 4.6	OPEN SOURCE SOFTWARE OPTIONS
MERCHANT SERVER FUNCTIONALITY	**OPEN SOURCE SOFTWARE**
Web server, online catalog	Apache (the leading Web server for small and medium businesses)
Shopping cart	Many providers: ZenCart.com; AgoraCart.com; X-Cart.com; OSCommerce.com
Credit card processing	Many providers: Echo Internet Gateway; ASPDotNetStorefront. Credit card acceptance is typically provided in shopping cart software but you may need a merchant account from a bank as well.
Database	MySQL (the leading open source SQL database for businesses)
Programming/scripting language	PHP (a scripting language embedded in HTML documents but executed by the server providing server-side execution with the simplicity of HTML editing). PERL is an alternative language. JavaScript programs are client side programs that provide user interface components.
Analytics	Analytics keep track of your site's customer activities and the success of your Web advertising campaign. You can also use Google Analytics if you advertise on Google, which provides good tracking tools; most hosting services will provide these services as well.

to work together seamlessly. How many months do you want to wait before you get to market with your ideas?

One alternative to building a Web site first is to create a blog first, and develop your business ideas and a following of potential customers on your blog. Once you have tested your ideas with a blog, and attract a Web audience, you can then move on to developing a simple Web site.

4.3   CHOOSING THE HARDWARE FOR AN E-COMMERCE SITE

As the manager in charge of building an e-commerce site, you will be held accountable for its performance. Whether you host your own site or outsource the hosting and operation of your site, you will need to understand certain aspects of the computing hardware platform. The **hardware platform** refers to all the underlying computing equipment that the system uses to achieve its e-commerce functionality. Your objective is to have enough platform capacity to meet peak demand (avoiding an overload condition), but not so much platform that you are wasting money. Failing to meet peak demand can mean your site is slow, or actually crashes. Remember, the

hardware platform

refers to all the underlying computing equipment that the system uses to achieve its e-commerce functionality

TABLE 4.7	FACTORS IN RIGHT-SIZING AN E-COMMERCE PLATFORM				
SITE TYPE	PUBLISH/ SUBSCRIBE	SHOPPING	CUSTOMER SELF-SERVICE	TRADING	WEB SERVICES/B2B
Examples	WSJ.com	Amazon	Travelocity	E*Trade	Ariba e-procurement exchanges
Content	Dynamic Multiple authors High volume Not user specific	Catalog Dynamic items User profiles with data mining	Data in legacy applications Multiple data sources	Time sensitive High volatility Multiple suppliers and consumers Complex transactions	Data in legacy applications Multiple data sources Complex transactions
Security	Low	Privacy Non-repudiation Integrity Authentication Regulations	Privacy Non-repudiation Integrity Authentication Regulations	Privacy Non-repudiation Integrity Authentication Regulations	Privacy Non-repudiation Integrity Authentication Regulations
Percent secure pages	Low	Medium	Medium	High	Medium
Cross session information	No	High	High	High	High
Searches	Dynamic Low volume	Dynamic High volume	Non dynamic Low volume	Non dynamic Low volume	Non dynamic Moderate volume
Unique items (SKUs)	High	Medium to high	Medium	High	Medium to high
Transaction volume	Moderate	Moderate to high	Moderate	High to extremely high	Moderate
Legacy integration complexity	Low	Medium	High	High	High
Page views (hits)	High to very high	Moderate to high	Moderate to low	Moderate to high	Moderate

Web site may be your only or principal source of cash flow. How much computing and telecommunications capacity is enough to meet peak demand? How many hits per day can your site sustain?

To answer these questions, you will need to understand the various factors that affect the speed, capacity, and scalability of an e-commerce site.

RIGHT-SIZING YOUR HARDWARE PLATFORM: THE DEMAND SIDE

The most important factor affecting the speed of your site is the demand that customers put on the site. **Table 4.7** lists the most important factors to consider when estimating the demand on a site.

Demand on a Web site is fairly complex and depends primarily on the type of site you are operating. The number of simultaneous users in peak periods, the nature of customer requests, the type of content, the required security, the number of items in inventory, the number of page requests, and the speed of legacy applications that may be needed to supply data to the Web pages are all important factors in overall demand on a Web site system.

Certainly, one important factor to consider is the number of simultaneous users who will likely visit your site. In general, the load created by an individual customer on a server is typically quite limited and short-lived. A Web session initiated by the typical user is **stateless**, meaning that the server does not have to maintain an ongoing, dedicated interaction with the client. A Web session typically begins with a page request, then a server replies, and the session is ended. The sessions may last from tenths of a second per user, to a minute. Nevertheless, system performance does degrade as more and more simultaneous users request service. Fortunately, degradation (measured as "transactions per second" and "latency" or delay in response) is fairly graceful over a wide range, up until a peak load is reached and service quality becomes unacceptable (see **Figure 4.12**).

Serving up static Web pages is **I/O intensive**, which means it requires input/output (I/O) operations rather than heavy-duty processing power. As a result, Web site performance is constrained primarily by the server's I/O limitations and the telecommunications connection, rather than speed of the processor.

There are some steps you can take to make sure that you stay within an acceptable service quality. One step is to simply purchase a server with faster CPU processors, multiple CPU processors, or larger hard disk drives. However, the improvement that results is not linear and at some point becomes cost-ineffective. **Figure 4.13** on page 230 shows the theoretical performance of a Web server as processors are added from a single processor up to eight processors. By increasing processors by a factor of eight, you get only three times more load capacity.

A second factor to consider on the demand side is the **user profile**, which refers to the nature of customer requests and customer behavior on your site (how many pages customers request and the kind of service they want). Web servers can be very efficient at serving static Web pages. However, as customers request more advanced services, such as site searches, registration, order taking via shopping carts, or downloads of large audio and video files, all of which require more processing power, performance can deteriorate rapidly.

The nature of the content your site offers is a third factor to consider. If your site uses dynamic page generation, then the load on the processor rises rapidly and performance will degrade. Dynamic page generation and business logic (such as a shopping cart) are **CPU-intensive** operations—they require a great deal of processing power. For instance, a site with only dynamic page content can expect performance of a single processor server to fall to one-tenth the levels described in Figure 4.13. Instead of effectively serving 8,000 users, you can only service 1,000 concurrent users. Any interaction with the user requiring access to a database—filling out forms, adding to carts, purchasing, and completing questionnaires—puts a heavy processing load on the server.

A final factor to consider is the telecommunications link that your site has to the Web, and also the changing nature of the client connection to the Web. **Figure 4.14** on page 231 shows that the number of hits per second your site can handle depends

stateless
refers to the fact that the server does not have to maintain an ongoing, dedicated interaction with the client

I/O intensive
requires input/output operations rather than heavy-duty processing power

user profile
refers to the nature of customer requests and customer behavior at a site

CPU-intensive
operations that require a great deal of processing power

FIGURE 4.12	DEGRADATION IN PERFORMANCE AS NUMBER OF USERS INCREASES

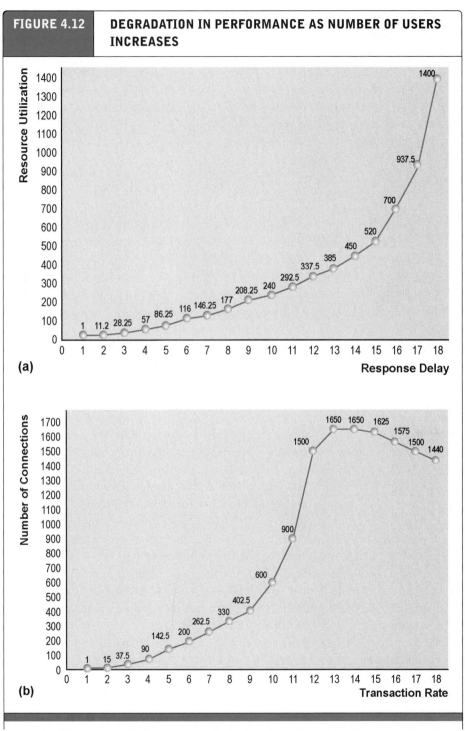

Degradation in Web server performance occurs as the number of users (connections) increases, and as the systems resources (processors, disk drives) become more utilized. In (a), user-experienced delay rises gracefully until an inflection point is reached, and then delay rises exponentially to an unacceptable level. In (b), the transaction rate rises gracefully until the number of users rapidly escalates the transaction rate, and at a certain inflection point, the transaction rate starts declining as the system slows down or crashes.

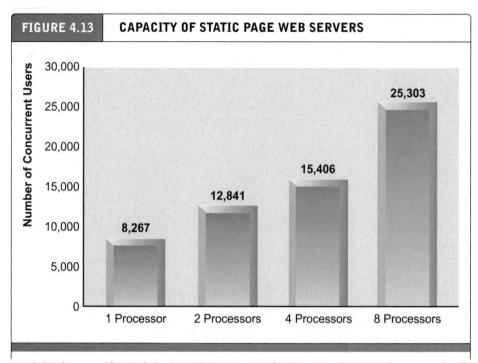

FIGURE 4.13 — **CAPACITY OF STATIC PAGE WEB SERVERS**

A typical Web server with a single Pentium 4.2 GHz processor that is serving only static Web pages can handle about 8,000 concurrent users. With eight processors, the same computer could handle about 25,000 concurrent users.

on the bandwidth connection between your server and the Web. The larger the bandwidth available, the more customers can simultaneously hit your site. For example, if your connection to the Web is a 1.5 Mbps DSL line, the maximum number of visitors per second for 1 kilobyte files is probably about 100. Most businesses host their sites at an ISP or other provider that contractually is (or should be) obligated to provide enough bandwidth for your site to meet peak demands. However, there are no guarantees and ISPs can blame Web congestion for their own bandwidth limitations. Check your ISP's bandwidth and your site performance daily.

While server bandwidth connections are less a constraint today with the widespread deployment of fiber-optic cable, the connection to the client is improving and this will have implications for your customers' expectations. In 2008, there are approximately 72 million broadband households in the United States, and this number is expected to increase to around 87 million by 2012 (eMarketer, Inc., 2008; Telecommunications Association of America, 2008). This means your customers will be able to make far more frequent requests and demand far richer content like videos, games, podcasts, and simulations. This demand will translate quickly into dynamic content and the need for additional capacity.

scalability
refers to the ability of a site to increase in size as demand warrants

RIGHT-SIZING YOUR HARDWARE PLATFORM: THE SUPPLY SIDE

Once you estimate the likely demand on your site, you will need to consider how to scale up your site to meet demand. **Scalability** refers to the ability of a site to

FIGURE 4.14	THE RELATIONSHIP OF BANDWIDTH TO HITS

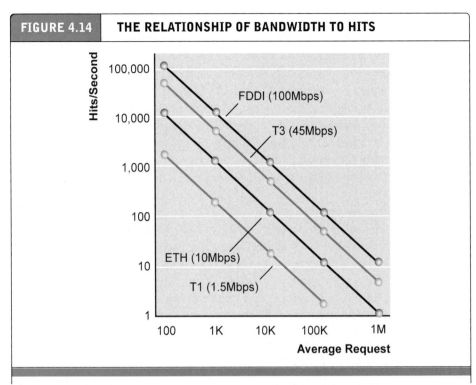

The greater the bandwidth available, the more customers can simultaneously access a Web site without any perceived degradation in performance.

SOURCE: IBM, 2003

increase in size as demand warrants. There are three steps you can take to meet the demands for service at your site: scale hardware vertically, scale hardware horizontally, and/or improve the processing architecture of the site (see **Table 4.8**).

TABLE 4.8	VERTICAL AND HORIZONTAL SCALING TECHNIQUES

TECHNIQUE	APPLICATION
Use a faster computer	Applies to edge servers, presentation servers, data servers, etc.
Create a cluster of computers	Use computers in parallel to balance loads
Use appliance servers	Special-purpose computers optimized for their task
Segment workload	Segment incoming work to specialized computers
Batch requests	Combine related requests for data into groups, process as a group
Manage connections	Reduce connections between processes and computers to a minimum
Aggregate user data	Aggregate user data from legacy applications in single data pools
Cache	Store frequently used data in cache rather than on the disk

horizontal scaling
employing multiple computers to share the workload

vertical scaling
increasing the processing power of individual components

Vertical scaling refers to increasing the processing power of individual components. **Horizontal scaling** refers to employing multiple computers to share the workload and increase the "footprint" of the installation (IBM, 2002).

You can scale your site vertically by upgrading the servers from a single processor to multiple processors (see **Figure 4.15**). You can keep adding processors to a computer depending on the operating system and upgrade to faster chip speeds as well.

There are two drawbacks to vertical scaling. First, it can become expensive to purchase new computers with every growth cycle, and second, your entire site becomes dependent on a small number of very powerful computers. If you have two such computers and one goes down, half of your site, or perhaps your entire site, may become unavailable.

Horizontal scaling involves adding multiple single-processor servers to your site and balancing the load among the servers. You can also then partition the load so that some servers handle only requests for HTML or ASP pages, while others are dedicated to handling database applications. You will need special load-balancing software (provided by a variety of vendors such as Cisco, Microsoft, and IBM) to direct incoming requests to various servers (see **Figure 4.16**).

There are many advantages to horizontal scaling. It is inexpensive and often can be accomplished using older PCs that otherwise would be disposed of. Horizontal scaling also introduces redundancy—if one computer fails, chances are that another computer can pick up the load dynamically. However, when your site grows from a single computer to perhaps 10 to 20 computers, the size of the physical facility required (the "footprint") increases and there is added management complexity.

A third alternative—improving the processing architecture—is a combination of vertical and horizontal scaling, combined with artful design decisions. **Table 4.9** on page 232 lists some of the more common steps you can take to greatly improve performance of your site. Most of these steps involve splitting the workload into I/O-intensive activities (such as serving Web pages) and CPU-intensive activities (such

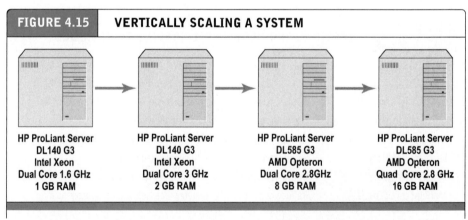

| FIGURE 4.15 | VERTICALLY SCALING A SYSTEM |

HP ProLiant Server
DL140 G3
Intel Xeon
Dual Core 1.6 GHz
1 GB RAM

HP ProLiant Server
DL140 G3
Intel Xeon
Dual Core 3 GHz
2 GB RAM

HP ProLiant Server
DL585 G3
AMD Opteron
Dual Core 2.8GHz
8 GB RAM

HP ProLiant Server
DL585 G3
AMD Opteron
Quad Core 2.8 GHz
16 GB RAM

You can scale a site vertically by both improving the processors and adding additional CPUs into a single physical server.

FIGURE 4.16	HORIZONTALLY SCALING A SYSTEM

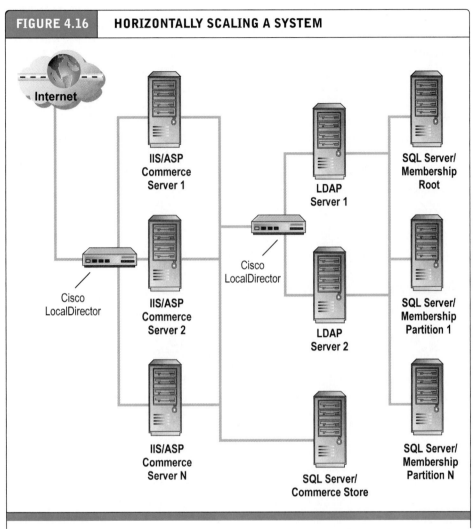

You can horizontally scale a system to meet demands by adding inexpensive single-processor servers to the site and using load-balancing software to allocate incoming customer requests to the correct server, shown in the diagram as a Cisco LocalDirector.

as taking orders). Once you have this work separated, you can fine-tune the servers for each type of load. One of the least expensive fine-tuning steps is to simply add RAM to a few servers and store all your HTML pages in RAM. This reduces load on your hard drives and increases speed dramatically. RAM is thousands of times faster than hard disks, and RAM is inexpensive. The next most important step is to move your CPU-intensive activities, such as order taking, onto a high-end, multiple processor server that is totally dedicated to handling orders and accessing the necessary databases. Taking these steps can permit you to reduce the number of servers required to service 10,000 concurrent users from 100 down to 20, according to one estimate.

TABLE 4.9	IMPROVING THE PROCESSING ARCHITECTURE OF YOUR SITE
ARCHITECTURE IMPROVEMENT	DESCRIPTION
Separate static content from dynamic content	Use specialized servers for each type of workload.
Cache static content	Increase RAM to the gigabyte range and store static content in RAM.
Cache database lookup tables	Cache tables used to look up database records.
Consolidate business logic on dedicated servers	Put shopping cart, credit card processing, and other CPU-intensive activity on dedicated servers.
Optimize ASP code	Examine your code to ensure it is operating efficiently.
Optimize the database schema	Examine your database search times and take steps to reduce access times.

4.4 OTHER E-COMMERCE SITE TOOLS

Now that you understand the key factors that affect the speed, capacity, and scalability of your site, we can consider some other important requirements for your Web site. You will need a coherent Web site design effort that makes business sense—not necessarily a site to wow visitors or excite them, but to sell them something. You will also need to know how to build active content and interactivity into your site—not just display static HTML pages. You will definitely want to be able to track customers who come, leave, and return to your site in order to be able to greet return visitors ("Hi Sarah, welcome back!"). You will also want to track customers throughout your site so you can personalize and customize their experience. Finally, you will need to establish a set of information policies for your site—privacy, accessibility, and access to information policies.

In order to achieve these business capabilities, you will need to be aware of some design guidelines and additional software tools that can cost-effectively achieve the required business functionality.

WEB SITE DESIGN: BASIC BUSINESS CONSIDERATIONS

This is not a text about how to design Web sites. (In Chapter 7, we discuss Web site design issues from a marketing perspective.) Nevertheless, from a business manager's perspective, there are certain design objectives you must communicate to your Web site designers to let them know how you will evaluate their work. At a minimum, your customers will need to find what they need at your site, make a purchase, and leave. A Web site that annoys customers runs the risk of losing the customer forever. For instance, a survey by Hostway found that about 75% of respondents said they were extremely or somewhat likely to not visit an offending site again and to unsubscribe from the offending company's promotional messages when they encounter one of their "pet peeves," and around 71% said they might refuse to purchase from the Web site and would view the company in a negative way. About 55% said they would complain about the Web site to friends and associates, and 45% said they might even refuse to make purchases in the company's offline stores (Hostway, 2007). See **Figure 4.17** for a list of the most common consumer complaints about Web sites.

Some critics believe poor design is more common than good design. It appears easier to describe what irritates people about Web sites than to describe how to design a good Web site. The worst e-commerce sites make it difficult to find information about their products and make it complicated to purchase goods; they have missing pages and broken links, a confusing navigation structure, and annoying graphics or sounds that you cannot turn off. **Table 4.10** on page 236 restates these negative experiences as positive goals for Web site design.

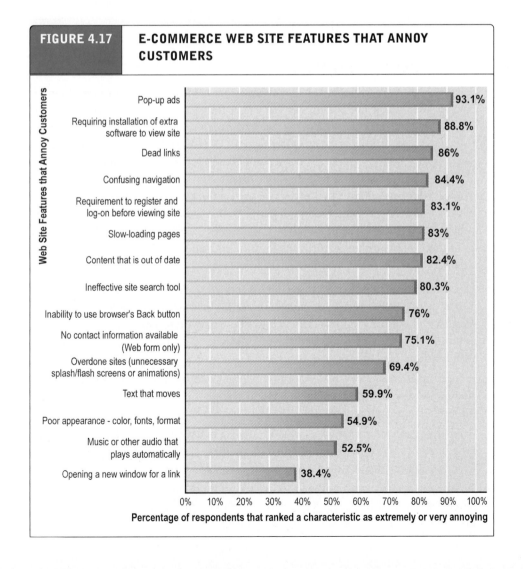

| FIGURE 4.17 | E-COMMERCE WEB SITE FEATURES THAT ANNOY CUSTOMERS |

Web Site Features that Annoy Customers

Feature	Percentage
Pop-up ads	93.1%
Requiring installation of extra software to view site	88.8%
Dead links	86%
Confusing navigation	84.4%
Requirement to register and log-on before viewing site	83.1%
Slow-loading pages	83%
Content that is out of date	82.4%
Ineffective site search tool	80.3%
Inability to use browser's Back button	76%
No contact information available (Web form only)	75.1%
Overdone sites (unnecessary splash/flash screens or animations)	69.4%
Text that moves	59.9%
Poor appearance - color, fonts, format	54.9%
Music or other audio that plays automatically	52.5%
Opening a new window for a link	38.4%

Percentage of respondents that ranked a characteristic as extremely or very annoying

TABLE 4.10	THE EIGHT MOST IMPORTANT FACTORS IN SUCCESSFUL E-COMMERCE SITE DESIGN
FACTOR	DESCRIPTION
Functionality	Pages that work, load quickly, and point the customer toward your product offerings
Informational	Links that customers can easily find to discover more about you and your products
Ease of use	Simple fool-proof navigation
Redundant navigation	Alternative navigation to the same content
Ease of purchase	One or two clicks to purchase
Multi-browser functionality	Site works with the most popular browsers
Simple graphics	Avoids distracting, obnoxious graphics and sounds that the user cannot control
Legible text	Avoids backgrounds that distort text or make it illegible

TOOLS FOR WEB SITE OPTIMIZATION

A Web site is only as valuable from a business perspective as the number of people who visit. Web site optimization (as we use it here) means how to attract lots of people to your site. One answer, of course, is through search engines such as Google, Yahoo, MSN, Ask, and several hundred others. The first stop for most customers looking for a product or service is to start with a search engine, and follow the listings on the page, usually starting with the top three to five listings, then glancing to the sponsored ads to the right. The higher you are on the search engine pages, the more traffic you will receive. Page 1 is much better than Page 2. So how do you get to Page 1 in the natural (unpaid) search listings? While every search engine is different, and none of them publish their algorithms for ranking pages, there are some basic ideas that work well.

- Keywords and page titles: Search engines "crawl" your site and identify keywords as well as title pages and then index them for use in search arguments. Pepper your pages with keywords that accurately describe what you sell or do. Experiment: use different keywords to see which work. "Vintage cars" may attract more visitors than "antique cars," or "restored cars."

- Identify market niches: instead of marketing "jewelry," be more specific, such as "Victorian jewelry," or "1950s jewelry" to attract small, specific groups who are intensely interested in period jewelry.

- Offer expertise: White papers, industry analyses, FAQ pages, guides, and histories are excellent ways to build confidence on the part of users and to encourage them to see your Web site as the place to go for help and guidance.

- Get linked up: Encourage other sites to link to your site; build a blog that attracts people and who will share your URL with others and post links in the process. List your site with Yahoo Directory for $300 a year.

- Buy ads: Complement your natural search optimization efforts with paid ads on search engines. Choose your keywords and purchase direct exposure on Web pages. You can set your budget and put a ceiling on it to prevent large losses. See what works, and observe the number of visits to your site produced by each keyword string.

- Local e-commerce: Developing a national market can take a long time. If your Web site is particularly attractive to local people, or involves products sold locally, then use keywords that connote your location so people can find you nearby. Town and city names in your keywords, or regions can be helpful, such as "Vermont cheese" or "San Francisco blues music."

TOOLS FOR INTERACTIVITY AND ACTIVE CONTENT

As a manager responsible for building a Web site, you will want to ensure that users can interact with your Web site quickly and easily. As we describe in later chapters, the more interactive a Web site is, the more effective it will be in generating sales and encouraging return visitors.

Although functionality and ease of use are the supreme objectives in site design, you will also want to interact with users and present them with a lively "active" experience. You will want to personalize the experience for customers by addressing their individual needs, and customize the content of your offerings based on their behavior or expressed desires. For example, you may want to offer customers free mortgage calculations or free pension advice, based on their interaction with programs available at your site. In order to achieve these business objectives, you will need to consider carefully the tools necessary to build these capabilities. Simple interactions such as a customer submitting a name, along with more complex interactions involving credit cards, user preferences, and user responses to prompts, all require special programs. Here is a brief description of some commonly used software tools for achieving high levels of site interactivity.

Bling for Your Blog: Web 2.0 Design Elements

One easy way to pump up the energy on your Web site is to include some appropriate widgets (sometimes called gadgets, plug-ins, or snippets). **Widgets** are small chunks of code that execute automatically in your HTML Web page. They are pre-built and many are free. Millions of social network and blog pages use widgets to present users with content drawn from around the Web (news headlines from specific news sources, announcements, press releases and other routine content), calendars, clocks, weather, live TV, games and other functionality. You can copy the code to an HTML Web page. A good place to start is Google Gadgets and Yahoo Widgets.

Mashups are a little more complicated, and as explained in Chapter 3, involve pulling functionality and data from one program and including it another. The most common mashup involves using Google Maps data and software and combining it with other data. For instance, if you have a local real estate Web site, you can download Google Maps and satellite images applications to your site so visitors can

widget

a small, pre-built chunk of code that executes automatically in your HTML Web page; capable of performing a wide variety of tasks get a sense of the neighborhood. There are thousands of Google Map mashups, from maps of Myanmar political protests, to maps of the Fortune 500 companies, all with associated news stories and other content. Other mashups involve sports, photos, video, shopping and news.

The point of these Web 2.0 applications is to enhance user interest and involvement in your site, and to easily include sophisticated functionality and unique data in your Web site.

Common Gateway Interface (CGI)

CGI (Common Gateway Interface)

a set of standards for communication between a browser and a program running on a server that allows for interaction between the user and the server

Common Gateway Interface (CGI) is a set of standards for communication between a browser and a program running on a server that allows for interaction between the user and the server. CGI permits an executable program to access all the information within incoming requests from clients. The program can then generate all the output required to make up the return page (the HTML, script code, text, etc.), and send it back to the client via the Web server. For instance, if a user clicks the Display the Contents of My Shopping Cart button, the server receives this request and executes a CGI program. The CGI program retrieves the contents of the shopping cart from the database and returns it to the server. The server sends an HTML page that displays the contents of the shopping cart on the user's screen. Notice all the computing takes place on the server side (this is why CGI programs and others like it are referred to as "server-side" programs).

CGI programs can be written in nearly any programming language as long as they conform to CGI standards. Currently, Perl is the most popular language for CGI scripting. Generally, CGI programs are used with Unix servers. CGI's primary disadvantage is that it is not highly scalable because a new process must be created for each request, thereby limiting the number of concurrent requests that can be handled. CGI scripts are best used for small to medium-sized applications that do not involve a high volume of user traffic. There are also Web server extensions available, such as FastCGI, that improve CGI's scalability (Doyle and Lopes, 2005).

Active Server Pages (ASP)

Active Server Pages (ASP)

a proprietary software development tool that enables programmers using Microsoft's IIS package to build dynamic pages

Active Server Pages (ASP) is Microsoft's version of server-side programming for Windows. Invented by Microsoft in late 1996, ASP has grown rapidly to become the major technique for server-side Web programming in the Windows environment. ASP enables developers to easily create and open records from a database and execute programs within an HTML page, as well as handle all the various forms of interactivity found on e-commerce sites. Like CGI, ASP permits an interaction to take place between the browser and the server. ASP uses the same standards as CGI for communication with the browser. ASP programs are restricted to use on Windows 2003/2000/NT Web servers running Microsoft's IIS Web server software.

Java, Java Server Pages (JSP), and JavaScript

Java is a programming language that allows programmers to create interactivity and active content on the client computer, thereby saving considerable load on the server.

Java was invented by Sun Microsystems in 1990 as a platform-independent programming language for consumer electronics. The idea was to create a language whose programs (so-called Write Once Run Anywhere [WORA] programs) could operate on any computer regardless of operating system. This would be possible if every operating system (Macintosh, Windows, Unix, DOS, and mainframe MVS systems) had a Java Virtual Machine (VM) installed that would interpret the Java programs for that environment.

By 1995, it had become clear, however, that Java was more applicable to the Web than to consumer electronics. Java programs (known as Java applets) could be downloaded to the client over the Web and executed entirely on the client's computer. Applet tags could be included in an HTML page. To enable this, each browser would have to include a Java VM. Today, the leading browsers do include a VM to play Java programs. When the browser accesses a page with an applet, a request is sent to the server to download and execute the program and allocate page space to display the results of the program. Java can be used to display interesting graphics, create interactive environments (such as a mortgage calculator), and directly access the Web server.

Different vendors, including Microsoft, IBM, HP, and others, have produced several versions of the Java language, and even different VMs. Java applets built using Microsoft Java can play well only on Microsoft's Internet Explorer browser. Therefore, the objective of having Java applets play the same on all Web clients has not succeeded. Many corporations will not allow Java applets through their firewalls for security reasons. Despite the fact that Java applets do not have access to local client system resources (they operate in a "sandbox" for security reasons), information system security managers are extremely reluctant to allow applets served from remote servers to come through the firewall. Many Java applets crash or do not perform well, wasting system resources, and when they do perform, the functions are often trivial (such as flashing logos).

Java Server Pages (JSP), like CGI and ASP, is a Web page coding standard that allows developers to use a combination of HTML, JSP scripts, and Java to dynamically generate Web pages in response to user requests. JSP uses Java "servlets," small Java programs that are specified in the Web page and run on the Web server to modify the Web page before it is sent to the user who requested it. JSP is supported by most of the popular application servers on the market today.

JavaScript is a programming language invented by Netscape that is used to control the objects on an HTML page and handle interactions with the browser. It is most commonly used to handle verification and validation of user input, as well as to implement business logic. For instance, JavaScript can be used on customer registration forms to confirm that a valid phone number, zip code, or even e-mail address has been given. Before a user finishes completing a form, the e-mail address given can be tested for validity. JavaScript appears to be much more acceptable to corporations and other environments in large part because it is more stable and also it is restricted to the operation of requested HTML pages. *Insight on Technology: Pumping Up the Customer Experience Using AJAX and Flash* further describes the use of JavaScript and other tools to create highly interactive Web sites.

Java
a programming language that allows programmers to create interactivity and active content on the client computer, thereby saving considerable load on the server

Java Server Pages (JSP)
like CGI and ASP, a Web page coding standard that allows developers to dynamically generate Web pages in response to user requests

JavaScript
a programming language invented by Netscape that is used to control the objects on an HTML page and handle interactions with the browser

INSIGHT ON TECHNOLOGY

PUMPING UP THE CUSTOMER EXPERIENCE USING AJAX AND FLASH

The truth is, despite the success of e-commerce retail and services, many people still prefer to shop in real stores so they can feel, touch, and see the goods. The online shopping experience has until recently been limited to online catalogs with pretty pictures and a cumbersome check-out procedure euphemistically called a "shopping cart." There's very little meaningful interactivity in most online retail shopping. Less than 20% of the people who visit even the best Web sites buy something, while most Web sites find less than 5% buy anything. Arpund 60% of shopping carts are abandoned before purchase. Over 50% of those who visit but do not buy say they cannot see or touch the product as the main reason.

If ordinary physical retail stores performed this badly they would not call the United States a "consumer economy" and Macy's and Wal-Mart would go broke. Looked at another way: if shopping cart abandonment went to zero and everyone who visited a Web site bought something, it is likely that retail e-commerce would double to over $300 billion a year. That's the upside.

The days of static HTML pages are hopefully coming to an end, and the shopping experience made more virtual, highly interactive and enjoyable through the use of a set of techniques called AJAX. You can see these new techniques most clearly in mapping services such as Google Maps, MapQuest, and Yahoo Maps. Once the map is drawn on the screen, you can grab the map to move it in any direction without causing the entire HTML page to reload. On the retail products side, you can see AJAX at work in product configurators that allow you to grab the product with your mouse, and rotate it so you can see the product from different angles, all without re-loading the HTML Web page. For instance, at Timberland.com, you can build a custom boot with colors, initials, embroidery, and designs all in real-time, without interruption. Many automobile Web sites use these same techniques.

Most Web sites today still work on the standard Web model: a client computer asks for a Web page, and a Web server delivers the page. This occurs every time you press a Continue or Search button. Today's highly graphical Web pages often contain several hundred kilobytes of data. But even if you have entered only a few lines of information containing a few hundred bytes of data in the traditional Web client/server model, all the processing is done on a remote server computer, and the client is not much more than a keyboard, screen, and interface. With this traditional model, entire Web pages of information are transferred across the Web, creating delays for the user and hogging bandwidth on the Web.

But there is a different way to create Web pages. Using "AJAX" (for Asynchronous JavaScript and XML, also sometimes just called "rich Internet applications" or RIA), the client and server work in the background to transfer information immediately as the user enters it, and the server responds immediately, all without the user being aware of the transfer. The result is a smooth, seamless, seemingly continuous user experience. How does RIA work? There are several ways of building rich Internet applications, but they all involve downloading a small program to the client. AJAX and RIA use existing tools to improve the user experience. One method is to download a small JavaScript program to a client computer that has a Java-enabled browser. JavaScript was one of the first client-side

(continued)

languages and technologies with the ability to run a computer program delivered over the Web. This small program carries on a background conversation with the server, retrieving only the information the user needs at whatever interval the application program requires. This method requires that the JavaScript program be capable of running on all target client computers, which may be using any one of several different browsers, and which may or may not be Java-enabled.

A different method is supported by Adobe's Flash plug-in, which nearly 98% of U.S. client computers are currently using. In this method, a Flash program is downloaded to the client. This program runs within the Flash Player installed in most browsers. Flash provides a nearly universal client-side solution.

Whatever method is chosen, the results at consumer Web sites are encouraging. Tests at TJMaxx.com and HomeGoods.com showed that about 50% more customers completed a one-page, AJAX-enabled shopping cart (which combined checkout, billing, and shipping pages) compared to a multiple-page shopping cart used earlier. TravelClicks, an iHotelier unit that sells hotel reservation systems to other hotels, licenses a reservation program built using Adobe's Flex program (a program specifically designed by Adobe to create RIAs). On the roughly 2,000 hotel sites using iHotelier, customers now can see instantly the impact of changing rooms, or changing dates, without loading new pages.

As AJAX applications spread, the original vision of the Web as a highly interactive medium—as opposed to a slow page-turner—will become a reality. And hopefully, shopping carts will not become places where transactions go to die, but instead the last stop for a pleasing customer shopping journey.

SOURCES: "The Business Benefits of Developing Applications in AJAX," by Andre Charland, UIresourcecenter.com, 2008; "Shopping Cart Abandonment Rises," eMarketer, Inc., May 29, 2008; "Making Web 2.0 Usable: Ajax Case Study," Molecular Inc. 2007; ; "Ajax Builds a Better Way to Find Ocean Carrier Timetables," by Heather Havenstein, *Computerworld*, March 9, 2007; "E-commerce: AJAX, Flash Make Websites More Engaging," by Meredith Levinson, *CIO Magazine*, March 1, 2006.

ActiveX and VBScript

Microsoft—not to be outdone by Sun Microsystems and Netscape—invented the **ActiveX** programming language to compete with Java and **VBScript** to compete with JavaScript. When a browser receives an HTML page with an ActiveX control (comparable to a Java applet), the browser simply executes the program. Unlike Java, however, ActiveX has full access to all the client's resources—printers, networks, and hard drives. VBScript performs in the same way as JavaScript. Of course, ActiveX and VBScript work only if you are using Internet Explorer. Otherwise, that part of the screen is blank.

In general, given the conflicting standards for Java, ActiveX, and VBScript and the diversity of user client computers, many e-commerce sites choose to steer clear of these tools. CGI scripts, JSP, and JavaScript are the leading tools for providing active, dynamic content.

ActiveX
a programming language created by Microsoft to compete with Java

VBScript
a programming language invented by Microsoft to compete with JavaScript

ColdFusion

ColdFusion is an integrated server-side environment for developing interactive Web applications. Originally developed by Macromedia and now offered by Adobe, ColdFusion combines an intuitive tag-based scripting language and a tag-based server scripting language (CFML) that lowers the cost of creating interactive features.

ColdFusion
an integrated server-side environment for developing interactive Web applications

ColdFusion offers a powerful set of visual design, programming, debugging, and deployment tools.

PERSONALIZATION TOOLS

You will definitely want to know how to treat each customer on an individual basis and emulate a traditional face-to-face marketplace. *Personalization* (the ability to treat people based on their personal qualities and prior history with your site) and *customization* (the ability to change the product to better fit the needs of the customer) are two key elements of e-commerce that potentially can make it nearly as powerful as a traditional marketplace, and perhaps even more powerful than direct mail or shopping at an anonymous suburban shopping mall. Speaking directly to the customer on a one-to-one basis, and even adjusting the product to the customer is quite difficult in the usual type of mass marketing, one-size-fits-all commercial transaction that characterizes much of contemporary commerce.

There are a number of methods for achieving personalization and customization. For instance, you could personalize Web content if you knew the personal background of the visitor. You could also analyze the pattern of clicks and sites visited for every customer who enters your site. We discuss these methods in later chapters on marketing. The primary method for achieving personalization and customization is through the placement of cookie files on the user's client computer. As we discussed in Chapter 3, a cookie is a small text file placed on the user's client computer that can contain any kind of information about the customer, such as customer ID, campaign ID, or purchases at the site. And then, when the user returns to the site, or indeed goes further into your site, the customer's prior history can be accessed from a database. Information gathered on prior visits can then be used to personalize the visit and customize the product.

For instance, when a user returns to a site, you can read the cookie to find a customer ID, look the ID up in a database of names, and greet the customer ("Hello Mary! Glad to have you return!"). You could also have stored a record of prior purchases, and then recommend a related product ("How about the wrench tool box now that you have purchased the wrenches?"). And you could think about customizing the product ("You've shown an interest in the elementary training programs for Word. We have a special "How to Study" program for beginners in Office software. Would you like to see a sample copy online?").

We further describe the use of cookies and their effectiveness in achieving a one-to-one relationship with the customer in Chapter 8.

THE INFORMATION POLICY SET

privacy policy
a set of public statements declaring to your customers how you treat their personal information that you gather on the site

accessibility rules
a set of design objectives that ensure disabled users can effectively access your site

In developing an e-commerce site, you will also need to focus on the set of information policies that will govern the site. You will need to develop a **privacy policy**—a set of public statements declaring to your customers how you treat their personal information that you gather on the site. You also will need to establish **accessibility rules**—a set of design objectives that ensure disabled users can effectively access your site. There are more than 50 million Americans who are disabled and require special access routes to buildings as well as computer systems (see *Insight on Society: Designing Accessibility in Web 2.0*). E-commerce information policies are described in greater depth in Chapter 8.

INSIGHT ON SOCIETY

DESIGNING FOR ACCESSIBLITY WITH WEB 2.0

In 1998, Congress amended the Rehabilitation Act to require U.S. agencies, government contractors, and others receiving federal money to make electronic and information technology services accessible to people with disabilities. Known as Section 508, this legislation requires Web sites of federally funded organizations to be accessible to users who are blind, deaf, blind and deaf, or unable to use a mouse. However, the legislation applies only to U.S. agencies, government contractors, and others receiving federal money, not to the broader e-commerce environment.

In one of the first law suits seeking to enforce Section 508 for Internet services, Access Now Inc., an advocacy group for the disabled, sued Southwest Airlines in 2001 on behalf of more than 50 million disabled Americans for operating a Web site that was inaccessible to the disabled, on the grounds that this violated of the 1990 Americans with Disability Act (ADA). In November 2002, a Federal District Court in Florida, in one of the first court decisions on the applicability of the ADA to Web sites, ruled that ADA applies only to physical spaces, not virtual spaces. However, the judge noted in a footnote that she was surprised that a customer-oriented firm like Southwest Airlines did not "employ all available technologies to expand accessibility to its Web site for visually impaired customers who would be an added source of revenue."

Since this early decision however, both the interpretation of the law and public sentiment have resulted in many well-known Web sites conforming to the spirit of Section 508, sometimes voluntarily and sometimes under threat from advocacy groups. For instance, RadioShack, Amazon, Ramada, and Priceline have entered into agreements with the American Council for the Blind, and the American Foundation for the Blind. Meanwhile, the National Federation of the Blind brought a class-action suit against Target for failing to make its site accessible for the blind. They claimed that blind people could not use Target's shopping cart because it required use of a mouse, used inaccessible image maps and graphics, and lacked compliant alt-text, an invisible code embedded beneath graphics that allows screen reading software to vocalize a description of the image. Target claimed the ADA did not apply to Web sites.

In September 2006, a federal district court ruled that ADA did indeed apply to Web sites. The court held "the 'ordinary meaning' of the ADA's prohibition against discrimination in the enjoyment of goods, services, facilities, or privileges is that whatever goods or services the place provides, it cannot discriminate on the basis of disability in providing enjoyment of those goods and services." The court thus rejected Target's argument that only its physical store locations were covered by the civil rights laws, ruling instead that all services provided by Target, including its Web site, must be accessible to persons with disabilities. In October 2007, the court granted class-action status to the lawsuit.

In August 2008, Target and the NFB settled the suit. Target made no admission or concession that its Web site violated the ADA, but agreed to bring it into compliance with certain online assistive technology guidelines by February 28, 2009, and to have the NFB certify that it is compliant with those guidelines. In addition, Target agree to pay damages of $6 million. Many accessibility advocates expressed disappointment that the res-

(continued)

olution of the case via a settlement failed to provide any clear legal precedent.

So how does a blind person access the Web and how should designers build in accessibility for blind persons? Most blind persons use the same PCs as everyone else. But a blind person's PC uses screen access software that translates information on the screen into synthesized speech or Braille. The program used to surf the Web will most likely be Internet Explorer, although other browsers are also available, such as Lynx (a text-only browser written originally to run under Unix) and IBM's Home Page Reader, which generate their own speech.

A blind person enters a Web page by checking out the hypertext links that are on the page. This is usually accomplished by jumping from link to link with the Tab key; the screen access software automatically reads the highlighted text as the focus moves from link to link. If the highlighted text is something like "How to Contact Us" or "Visit Your Shopping Cart," the blind user will be able to make some sense out of the link. If, however, the highlighted text is "Click Here," or "Here," it will be difficult if not impossible for the blind user to interpret the meaning of the link without using a different navigation strategy. With the more recent screen access software/browser combinations, it is possible for a blind Web surfer to explore the page one line at a time, thus alleviating this problem. However, being forced to examine every detail of a Web page just to learn the meaning of a hypertext link is a time-consuming process that, ideally, should be avoided. The important point to keep in mind is that the screen access software is looking for ASCII text, which it can convert to speech or Braille.

Once the desired hypertext link has been located, the blind person presses the Enter key (clicks on the link) to go where the link points. If there is a form to fill out on the page, the blind person will usually tab to the appropriate input field and type the information in the usual way. Other controls such as checkboxes, combo boxes, radio buttons, and the like can all be used if the screen access software can detect them.

There are several simple strategies Web designers can use to improve accessibility. Embedding text descriptions behind images is one example that allows screen readers to announce those descriptions. So instead of saying "Image," when a screen reader passes over an image, the visually impaired user can hear "Photo of a cruise ship sitting in a harbor." Allowing users to set the color and font schemes can also make a difference for the visually impaired. Adding screen magnification tools and sound labels where hyperlinks appear are two additional ways to increase accessibility.

These are examples of "equivalent alternatives" to visual content that disability advocates suggest should be required, both for visual and auditory content, to ensure individuals with disabilities have equal access information that appears on-screen. Guidelines for creating accessible Web pages include ensuring that text and graphics are understandable when viewed without color, using features that enable activation of page elements via a variety of input devices (such as keyboard, head wand, or Braille reader), and providing clear navigation mechanisms (such as navigation bars or a site map) to aid users.

Business firms pay a cost for making their sites accessible to the blind. Today, only about 10% of all Web sites in the United States are accessible and conform to the international Web Accessibility Initiative of the World Wide Web Consortium. But, as graphical elements such as video come to play an ever more important role in Web content and navigation, it becomes even more important for these elements to be accessible to the blind. There are about 10 million visually impaired persons in the United States alone who represent a formidable economic force.

SOURCES: "Target Settles Lawsuit with Advocates for Blind," by Andrea K. Walker, Baltimore Sun, August 28, 2008; "Develop a Web Site Accessible by Visually Impaired Users and Comply with the Law," by Joe Gross, Tech Republic, February 21, 2008; "Lawsuit Seeks to Improve Web Access for the Blind," by Carolyn Said, Sfgate.com, October 3, 2007; "Point, Click, and Sue," by Sherry Karabin, *Corporate Counsel*, September, 2007; "Web Accessibility: Making Your Site Accessible to the Blind," by Curtiss Chong, National Federation of the Blind, September 2007; "Legal Precedent Set for Web Accessibility," Press Release, National Federation for the Blind, September 7, 2006; "Do the Rights of the Disabled Extend to the Blind on the Web?," by Bob Tedeschi, *New York Times*, November 6, 2006.

REI Climbs the Web Mountain

Washington-based Recreational Equipment, Inc. (REI) is the world's largest online retailer of outdoor gear. REI is a somewhat unusual company. Lloyd and Mary Anderson, mountain climbers from Seattle, Washington, founded REI in 1938. The Andersons imported a special ice axe from Austria for themselves and decided to set up a cooperative to help their friends and other fellow outdoor enthusiasts acquire high-quality climbing and camping gear at reasonable prices. Today, REI is the largest consumer cooperative in the United States, with nearly 3.4 million members who have paid a one-time membership fee of $20 that entitles them to an annual dividend equal to about 10% of their annual purchases. And the business has grown. Today, REI operates 96 retail stores in 28 states, two online stores, an international mail order operation, and REI Adventures, a travel agency. Kiosks in every store allow customers to access products at either of REI's Web sites: REI.com and REI-Outlet.com. REI employs over 9,500 people, and in 2007, generated over $1.3 billion in gross revenues, about $225 million of which comes from its online stores.

REI first started exploring the Internet in the summer of 1995. Netscape had just gone public, and e-commerce was just getting started. As with many business success stories, REI's online venture began with senior executives who recognized the potentially transformative power of the Web, and the mixture of opportunity and possible threat that it represented.

Many traditional bricks-and-mortar retailers at that time feared cannibalization of their retail and/or catalog sales if they introduced an online sales outlet. Their nightmare was that starting an online store would merely "steal" their own customers from their regular sales channels. But REI wasn't deterred. As Dennis Madsen, REI's former president and chief executive officer, said, "We knew that if we could not serve our customers who were looking to shop with us online, they would turn to someone else online. It was never a question for us. Being online meant better serving the customer. Our experience has proven that cannibalization is largely a myth and that our multi-channel customers are our best customers. For instance, dual-channel customers who shopped both online and at stores spent 114% more than single-channel customers. And customers who shop three channels—retail stores, Web, and kiosks—spent 48% more than dual-channel customers."

REI charged Matt Hyde, who had previously helped start REI Adventures, the company's travel service (and who now serves as the company's senior vice president of marketing and merchandising), with the mission of launching REI's first Web site on a budget of approximately $500,000. At the time, Netscape was the only company offering a complete e-commerce suite, so REI chose Netscape's Merchant

Server software installed on an IBM RS/6000 server. And although Hyde recognized that REI was a retailer by trade, not a programming shop, he chose to keep design of the site in-house, using off-the-shelf Web authoring tools rather than outsource creation of the Web site. The rationale: "When [we] took the leap of faith that we could launch this compelling value proposition, and that it could be big, [we] realized we needed to make this a core competency. It couldn't be outsourced." The decision was not without its costs, however: managing REI.com's growth internally, with no outsourcing, strained REI's human resources. REI soon discovered that finding people with the requisite skills could be difficult, and even if they could be found, they were a lot more expensive than salespeople. In September 1996, at a time when few traditional retailers were even looking at online sales, REI.com launched, promoted primarily through direct mail and in-store notices. The first order arrived 20 minutes later. By February 1997, Hyde and his team knew they were on the right track. Traffic was up by 50% in the two months following Christmas. But that in itself posed a problem. As Hyde remembers, "We chose Netscape early on, and they were clearly the leader [at that time]. But not long after getting the system up, we realized that it was too limited. When you go from a few thousand people checking out your site to a million every month, you need a lot of infrastructure."

He also noted, "On the surface, e-commerce sounds relatively easy. It's not until you have experience trying to integrate a high-volume, high-functionality Web site into existing business processes and applications that you realize that it's a lot harder than it seems. It's like an iceberg—the view from the browser is only 10% of what it takes to build a successful and profitable Web site."

REI had originally hoped to upgrade with Netscape, but, as Hyde said, "that wasn't working out." This time they had more of a choice, and looked at offerings from all the major vendors, including Microsoft, IBM, Broadvision, and OpenMarket. "When you change commerce packages, there's a huge learning curve. I was going to make this change once, but I wasn't going to do it again, so I wanted to pick the right package ... for the next several years." In early 1998, REI decided on IBM's Net.Commerce server software. An important factor in the decision was IBM's ability to preserve all the custom coding REI had done over the past two years to connect its online store to its legacy system. "I had hundreds of thousands, if not millions of dollars tied up in this [system], and we didn't want to throw it away. And since Net.Commerce [would also lessen] the need to do custom coding in the future, it's a two-fold benefit."

In August 1998, REI launched a second Web site, REI-Outlet.com, using Net.Commerce server software. Once REI-Outlet.com was successfully launched, REI then turned to migrating REI.com to the new system, completing the move in October 1998.

In 2002, REI began a third re-building of its Web site by standardizing on a single platform, IBM's WebSphere, an integrated set of e-commerce site development and operational tools. Prior to this point, REI's e-commerce infrastructure was a mixture of software applications written both in-house and by a variety of different technology vendors. In the period since REI's second re-build in 1998, IBM had developed a suite of tools and functionalities built on standards such as Java and Unix that included

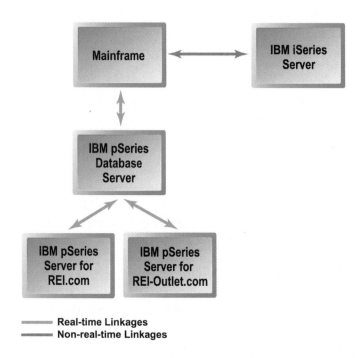

than 40% of all orders generated on REI.com's Web site are delivered to stores for pickup, and one-third of the customers who pick up orders purchase an additional $90 in merchandise during the visit. REI's multi-channel gift registry is another example. The registry can be set up, monitored, and updated through an in-store kiosk, over the phone, or at REI.com. All modifications to the list or purchases are updated to the list in real time. According to REI, gift registries created online bring customers into its retail stores, many of whom are first-time customers.

With the ascendancy of Google and search engine marketing, it has also become critical that REI's online catalog pages appear in the first page of search engine queries. REI worked with a Web firm called Netconcepts to redesign its Web pages, end the practice of using dynamic URLs for pages, and in general make the catalog Web pages more friendly to search engine Web crawlers so its pages could be properly read. The result was a 200% gain in "natural search" sales produced without making payments to search engines. In 2006, REI began using a software service, Mercent Retail, to help it better manage referrals from comparison shopping portals such as Shopping.com, and manufacturer Web sites. The service, which is integrated with REI's back-end retail management software systems, helps REI maintain brand and merchandising consistency between its own Web sites and the various third-party sites, and optimizes the product links sent to each of its channel partners. In 2007, REI switched from its proprietary search engine to one from Mercado Software, enabling customers to quickly search for items by brand, price, or best sellers.

As a result of its efforts, REI has been rewarded with steadily increasing online sales, which have grown from $111 million in 2004 to $226 million in 2007, and according to Internet Retailer's Top 500 Guide, ranked second in the online Sport-

WebSphere Application Server, WebSphere Commerce, MQ Series Integrator, and IBM VisualAge for Java, all running on IBM pSeries Unix-based computer servers, which can be configured with multiple processors in order to scale with a business. By that time, REI had come to the realization that it was less costly in the long run to rely on a single vendor such as IBM to provide an integrated set of e-commerce applications, rather than building the applications in-house.

Today, REI offers around 16,000 unique products online—more than in any of its physical stores—at prices that are the same as in the retail stores; thousands of pages of in-depth product information; an interactive community system; and a complete adventure travel service. The outlet store, REI-Outlet.com, sells merchandise that the company buys specifically for the outlet.

REI's technology platform continues to rely on IBM pSeries and iSeries servers that link the Web sites and stores to backend legacy databases that are used to store product and customer information (see figure). The WebSphere applications provide end-to-end business to consumer commerce from shopping and checkout to fulfillment. Orders from the Web site are processed as seamlessly as those from retail stores or mail-order sales.

The system appears to be working well. REI has won a "Best in E-commerce Innovation" Retail Systems Achievement award and been named by Forrester Research as one of the best multi-channel companies in Forrester's U.S. multi-channel retail evaluation, which measures the top 30 things a retailer must do to deliver a great multi-channel experience. REI scored highest for "customer experience" and "technical integration."

With its focus on an integrated platform from a single vendor, REI has implemented extensive customer features utilizing the platform's capabilities in personalized service and information, as well as more convenience for both online and in-store shoppers. For instance, REI has the ability to refer new Web customers to nearby stores that are having sales. It can e-mail coupons for bike helmets redeemable at local stores or online to customers who purchased a bicycle. WebSphere can drop an image of hiking boots featured at REI onto the screen of a customer reading an REI "Learn and Share" article on backpacking.

REI's clicks-and-bricks strategy has paid off handsomely. In addition to improving relationships with existing customers, the online stores have helped create new customers. About 36% of the online customers are not members of the REI cooperative, meaning they are likely new customers, compared to 15% of REI's retail customers. And despite management's early fears, the online stores haven't cannibalized traditional store sales. In fact, the opposite has occurred: The Web site has attracted new customers and strengthened the relationship with existing customers. Two services enabled by the WebSphere Commerce platform, REI Store Pickup service, and REI's gift registry, are a case in point. REI Store Pickup service provides in-store pickup as a free shipping option for online orders. To implement the service, REI combined its Web and store fulfillment systems, shipping customer merchandise to the stores on the same trucks that deliver the store's bi-weekly stock orders. The service has proved to be a tremendous success. In its first 12 months, in-store pickups from online sales accounted for $40 million in revenue, and they now account for about a third of online sales. Today, more ing Goods market and 62st overall. But REI isn't satisfied with just 20% annual growth. According to Brad Brown, REI's vice president of e-commerce and web strategy, "We want to grow more aggressively." To do so, it is implementing more rich media, videocasts, and other Web 2.0 tools. For example, shoppers can watch a video on how to change a flat bicycle tire. Links for related products appear on the same page. Rich media applications from Heck Yes Productions enable shoppers to see products in 3D and from different angles. RSS is another new tool that REI is using. As you learned in Chapter 3, RSS is a data feed that delivers updated information from selected Web sites directly to a subscriber's desktop. REI uses RSS to drive traffic to REI-Outlet.com's "deal of the day." They have added customer reviews of its products, an option which has proved quite popular. And during 2008, it is putting the finishing touches on three-year-long, multi-million dollar project to create a new data warehouse that will combine information collected in stores, on the Web, from call centers, and all other customer contacts into a single database. The data warehouse will allow REI to deliver highly targeted marketing messages and customer service. Staying atop the Web mountain requires both continuing innovation and investment.

But REI is not without competitors. In 2007, Cabela's, another leading sporting goods retailer, leapfrogged past REI to the top online spot according to Internet Retailer, with $459 million in online sales, and a 30% share of the online market, compared to REI's $226 million and 15% share. Cabela's is using many of the same techniques as REI, such as online order/store pick-up, interactive kiosks, advanced search functions, enlarged product views, product ratings, etc., but apparently with more success. During the 2007 holiday season, MegaView Online Retail listed Cabela's as one of the top 10 "power converters," with a 16.8% conversion rate. Cabela's was also cited by Keynote Systems for having the industry's best reliability over the holiday season, as well as the best site responsiveness, as measured by how quickly pages loaded and how many customer transactions were completed. In February 2008, Cabela's implemented RightNow Technologies' on demand customer relationship management solution, which enables Cabela's customer representatives to chat with customers online, and as a result the company has significantly reduced the number of abandoned shopping carts. Cabela's has also built a searchable, online knowledge database that ensures consumers can easily find the information they need on the company's Web site, and also provides an information resource for Cabela employees. The system also automatically routes customer e-mails to the appropriate staff member, based on customer needs. Cabela's can now reply to most customer e-mails within 2.5 hours, and the volume of phone calls to Cabela's contact center has dropped. In September 2008, Cabela's added MicroStrategy as its provider of business intelligence software, which will allow Cabela's employees to review every item purchased online and better understand the items that customers typically purchase together, which should enable Cabela's to be able to better present complementary product offerings to its online customers.

With competition such as Cabela's now in front, and other's such as Bass Pro Outdoor Online nipping at its heels, REI cannot afford to rest on its laurels if it hopes to reclaim its top spot atop the Web sporting goods mountain.

SOURCES: "About Us," REI.com, October 2008; "Cabela's Chooses MicroStrategy as Enterprise Reporting Standard," Internet Retailer, September 30, 2008; "REI Combines 20 Sources of Customer Information into One Data Warehouse," Internet Retailer, March 18, 2008; "Driving Sales," Internet Retailer, March 2008; "RightNow Helps Cabela's Deliver Exceptional Customer Experiences and Support Renowned Service-Centric Brand," Internet Retailer, February 12, 2008; "Holiday Web Performance at 26 Leading Online Retailers Improved," Internet Retailer, February 1, 2008; "In December, 10 Retailers Were Power Converters," Internet Retailer, January 29, 2008; "REI's Online Performance Climbs with Mercent Retail," March 20, 2007; "Top 500 Guide, 2008 Edition," *Internet Retailer*, 2008; Case Study: REI", Netconcepts.com, July 28, 2006; "REI.com Expands Its Store Pickup Program," *Internet Retailer*, March 15, 2006; "REI Optimizes Sales with Cross-channel Commerce Solution," IBM Case Study, August 2004; "How REI Scaled the E-commerce Mountain, " by Megan Santosus, *CIO*, May 19, 2004; "REI Personalizes Online Shopping with WebSphere Commerce Suite," IBM Global Industries: Retail Case Studies, IBM Case Study, April 2003.

Case Study Questions

1. Create a simple logical design and physical design for REI.com using information provided in the case study, supplemented as necessary by your own research.

2. After reading the case study, identify the key reasons for REI.com's success thus far.

3. Visit REI.com and rate its performance on the eight factors listed in Table 4.10 on a scale of 1 to 10 (with 1 being the lowest and 10 the highest). Provide reasons for your ratings.

4. Prepare a short industry analysis of the online outdoor sporting goods and apparel industry. Who are REI's primary competitors? How well have they developed multi-channel retailing?

4.6 REVIEW

KEY CONCEPTS

■ **Explain the process that should be followed in building an e-commerce Web site.**

Factors you must consider when building an e-commerce site include:
- hardware architecture
- software
- telecommunications capacity
- site design
- human resources
- organizational capabilities

The systems development life cycle (a methodology for understanding the business objectives of a system and designing an appropriate solution) for building an e-commerce Web site involves five major steps:
- Identify the specific business objectives for the site and then develop a list of system functionalities and information requirements.
- Develop a system design specification (both logical design and physical design).
- Build the site, either by in-house personnel or by outsourcing all or part of the responsibility to outside contractors.
- Test the system (unit testing, system testing, and acceptance testing).
- Implement and maintain the site.

The nine basic business and system functionalities an e-commerce site should contain include:

- *Digital catalog*—allows a site to display goods using text and graphics.
- *Product database*—provides product information, such as a description, stocking number, and inventory level.
- *Customer on-site tracking*—enables a site to create a site log for each customer visit, aiding in personalizing the shopping experience and identifying common customer paths and destinations.
- *Shopping cart/payment system*—provides an ordering system, secure credit-card clearing, and other payment options.
- *Customer database*—includes customer information such as the name, address, phone number, and e-mail address.
- *Sales database*—contains information regarding the customer ID, product purchased, date, payment, and shipment to be able to provide after-sale customer support.
- *Ad server*—tracks the site behavior of prospects and customers that come through e-mail or banner ad campaigns.
- *Site tracking and reporting system*—monitors the number of unique visitors, pages visited, and products purchased.
- *Inventory management system*—provides a link to production and suppliers in order to facilitate order replenishment.

■ **Describe the major issues surrounding the decision to outsource site development and/or hosting.**

Advantages of building a site in-house include:
- the ability to change and adapt the site quickly as the market demands
- the ability to build a site that does exactly what the company needs

Disadvantages of building a site in-house include:
- the costs may be higher
- the risks of failure may be greater, given the complexity of issues such as security, privacy, and inventory management
- the process may be more time-consuming than if you had hired an outside specialist firm to manage the effort
- staff may experience a longer learning curve that delays your entry into the market

Using design templates cuts development time, but pre-set templates can also limit functionality.

A similar decision is also necessary regarding outsourcing the hosting of the site versus keeping it in-house. Relying on an outside vendor to ensure that the site is live twenty-four hours a day places the burden of reliability on someone else, in return for a monthly hosting fee. The downside is that if the site requires fast upgrades due to heavy traffic, the chosen hosting company may or may not be capable of keeping up. Reliability versus scalability are the issues in this instance.

■ **Identify and understand the major considerations involved in choosing Web server and e-commerce merchant server software.**

Early Web sites used single-tier system architecture and consisted of a single-server computer that delivered static Web pages to users making requests through their browsers. The extended functionality of today's Web sites required the development of a multi-tiered systems architecture, which utilizes a variety of specialized Web servers, as well as links to pre-existing "backend" or "legacy" corporate databases.

All e-commerce sites require basic Web server software to answer requests from customers for HTML and XML pages. When choosing Web server software, companies are also choosing what operating system the site will run on; Apache, which runs on the Unix system, is the market leader.

Web servers provide a host of services, including:

- Processing user HTML requests
- Security services
- File transfer protocol
- Search engine
- Data capture
- E-mail
- Site management tools

Dynamic server software allows sites to deliver dynamic content, rather than static, unchanging information. Web application server programs enable a wide range of e-commerce functionality, including creating a customer database, creating an e-mail promotional program, and accepting and processing orders, as well as many other services.

E-commerce merchant server software is another important software package that provides catalog displays, information storage and customer tracking, order taking (shopping cart), and credit card purchase processing. E-commerce suites can save time and money, but customization can significantly drive up costs. Factors to consider when choosing an e-commerce suite include its functionality, support for different business models, visual site management tools and reporting systems, performance and scalability, connectivity to existing business systems, compliance with standards, and global and multicultural capability.

- ■ **Understand the issues involved in choosing the most appropriate hardware for an e-commerce site.**

Speed, capacity, and scalability are three of the most important considerations when selecting an operating system, and therefore the hardware that it runs on.

To evaluate how fast the site needs to be, companies need to assess the number of simultaneous users the site expects to see, the nature of their requests, the type of information requested, and the bandwidth available to the site. The answers to these questions will provide guidance regarding the processors necessary to meet customer demand. In some cases, adding additional processing power can add capacity, thereby improving system speed.

Scalability is also an important issue. Increasing processing supply by scaling up to meet demand can be done through:

- *Vertical scaling*—improving the processing power of the hardware, but maintaining the same number of servers
- *Horizontal scaling*—adding more of the same processing hardware

- *Improving processing architecture*—identifying operations with similar workloads and using dedicated tuned servers for each type of load

■ Identify additional tools that can improve Web site performance.

In addition to providing a speedy Web site, companies must also strive to have a well-designed site that encourages visitors to buy. Building in interactivity improves site effectiveness, as does personalization techniques that provide the ability to track customers while they are visiting the site. Commonly used software tools for achieving high levels of Web site interactivity and customer personalization include:

- *Common Gateway Interface (CGI) scripts*—a set of standards for communication between a browser and a program on a server that allows for interaction between the user and the server
- *Active Server Pages (ASP)*—a Microsoft tool that also permits interaction between the browser and the server
- *Java applets*—programs written in the Java programming language that also provide interactivity
- *JavaScript*—used to validate user input, such as an e-mail address
- *ActiveX and VBScript*—Microsoft's version of Java and JavaScript, respectively
- *Cookies*—text files stored on the user's hard drive that provide information regarding the user and his or her past experience at a Web site

QUESTIONS

1. Name the six main pieces of the e-commerce site puzzle.
2. Define the systems development life cycle and discuss the various steps involved in creating an e-commerce site.
3. Discuss the differences between a simple logical and simple physical Web site design.
4. Why is system testing important? Name the three types of testing and their relation to each other.
5. Compare the costs for system development and system maintenance. Which is more expensive, and why?
6. Why is a Web site so costly to maintain? Discuss the main factors that impact cost.
7. What are the main differences between single-tier and multi-tier site architecture?
8. Name five basic functionalities a Web server should provide.
9. What are the three main factors to consider when choosing the best hardware platform for your Web site?
10. Why is Web server bandwidth an important issue for e-commerce sites?
11. Compare and contrast the various scaling methods. Explain why scalability is a key business issue for Web sites.
12. What are the eight most important factors impacting Web site design, and how do they affect a site's operation?
13. What are Java and JavaScript? What role do they play in Web site design?
14. Name and describe three methods used to treat customers individually. Why are they significant to e-commerce?

15. What are some of the policies e-commerce businesses must develop before launching a site, and why must they be developed?

PROJECTS

1. Go to Freewebs.com or NetworkSolutions.com. Both sites allow you to create a simple e-tailer Web site for a free trial period. The site should feature at least four pages, including a home page, product page, shopping cart, and contact page. Extra credit will be given for additional complexity and creativity. Come to class prepared to present your e-tailer concept and Web site.

2. Visit several e-commerce sites, not including those mentioned in this chapter, and evaluate the effectiveness of the sites according to the eight basic criteria/functionalities listed in Table 4.10. Choose one site you feel does an excellent job on all the aspects of an effective site and create a presentation, including screen shots, to support your choice.

3. Imagine that you are the head of information technology for a fast-growth e-commerce startup. You are in charge of development of the company's Web site. Consider your options for building the site in-house with existing staff, or outsourcing the entire operation. Decide which strategy you believe is in your company's best interest and create a brief presentation outlining your position. Why choose that approach? And what are the estimated associated costs, compared with the alternative? (You'll need to make some educated guesses here—don't worry about being exact.)

4. Choose two of the e-commerce suite software packages listed in Table 4.5 and prepare an evaluation chart that rates the packages on the key factors discussed in the section "Choosing an E-commerce Suite." Which package would you choose if you were developing a Web site of the type described in this chapter, and why?

5. Choose one of the open source Web content management systems such as Joomla or Drupal or another of your own choosing and prepare an evaluation chart similar to that required by Project 4. Which system would you choose and why?

WEB SITE RESOURCES www.prenhall.com/laudon

- Additional projects, exercises, and tutorials
- Careers: Explore career opportunities in e-commerce
- Raising capital and business plans

CHAPTER 5

Online Security and Payment Systems

After reading this chapter, you will be able to:

- Understand the scope of e-commerce crime and security problems.
- Describe the key dimensions of e-commerce security.
- Understand the tension between security and other values.
- Identify the key security threats in the e-commerce environment.
- Describe how technology helps protect the security of messages sent over the Internet.
- Identify the tools used to establish secure Internet communications channels, and protect networks, servers, and clients.
- Appreciate the importance of policies, procedures, and laws in creating security.
- Describe the features of traditional payment systems.
- Understand the major e-commerce payment mechanisms.
- Describe the features and functionality of electronic billing presentment and payment systems.

Cyberwar Becomes a Reality

Estonia is a very small country with a little more than 1 million citizens in northeastern Europe, bounded by Russia to the east, the Gulf of Finland to the north, and the Baltic Sea and Sweden to the west. Despite its small size, it was the location of a momentous Internet security event on April 26, 2007—perhaps the most significant Internet security event in history, in terms of size, scale, and sheer chutzpah. It all started in early April 2007, when the Estonian government began dismantling a bronze statue of a World War II-era Soviet soldier, and began moving the statue from its previous location in a park to a suburban cemetery. Ethnic Russians took

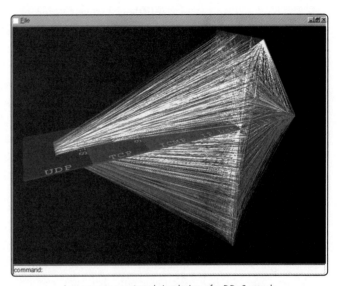

A computer-generated simulation of a DDoS attack.

to the streets in protest, but by April 29, the streets of capital city Tallinn were calm. Estonia's Internet infrastructure, however, was under attack.

Beginning on April 26, the Internet addresses of the Estonian government and some Estonian banks began to receive the first trickle of requests for service from an unusual number of foreign Internet addresses, some identified as Russian government sites located inside the Kremlin, and a part of Russian premier Vladimir Putin's administration. Within hours, on April 27, the trickle became a flood of highly distributed requests from millions of computers worldwide. It was the beginning of a massive, unparalleled Distributed Denial of Service (DDoS) attack launched by a global network of so-called zombie computers linked together in a botnet.

Attackers began with a trickle of requests to identify Estonian servers, and then sent a huge burst of data to measure the capacity of the network. Once the throughput capacity of the network was estimated, the attackers contracted with botnet operators worldwide, and used botnets under their own control, to initiate a sustained multi-week attack on the Estonian servers. In ten large assaults, over 1 million computers worldwide slammed the Estonia servers with junk messages and requests, producing streams of 90 megabits of data a second for ten hours, far beyond the capacity of Estonia's routers, switches, and Web servers.

259

In Estonia, the Web is a little more important than it is in the United States or Europe. In Estonia, people use the Web to pay for groceries, pay for newspapers using mobile digital wallets, and file their taxes, as well as pay traffic fines. In Estonia, the Web and Internet are a basic utility and infrastructure for the economy. While the Estonian government's software engineers were able to survive the attacks, the Bank of Estonia was forced to shut down and also cut off access to banks outside the country for a period of time. E-mail, purchases, and payments all slowed to a crawl. Government agencies temporarily slowed and closed in some cases.

A little over a year later, as the world tuned in to the opening of the 2008 Summer Olympic Games on August 8, 2008, many were shocked to learn that Russia had invaded the former Soviet Republic of Georgia in support of a separatist group within Georgia. What most did not know was that like in Estonia, this attack, had been preceded in the previous two weeks by DDOS attacks aimed at Georgian government, media, banking and transportation web sites. Hackers shut down the Web site of the Georgian president for 24 hours and defaced the Georgian parliament Web site. Although the Georgian government blamed Russia, the Russia government denied that it was involved. As in Estonia, Georgia's attackers used botnets.

While cyberwar has been written about in novels, and has been demonstrated on a small scale, the Georgian and Estonian situations, malicious strikes against Web sites of specific companies (often as part of a blackmail plot), and a major attack against VeriSign illustrate that cyberwar is now a reality on a much scarier scale. In the VeriSign case, several botnets involving several hundred thousand computers around the globe attempted to overwhelm all of the 13 root server systems—the top level domains such as .com, .org, .net, and others. The attack failed but severely stressed the United States Internet infrastructure, slowing down the Internet and demonstrating how fragile the entire system is to such attacks.

Imagine: about 10% of the world's billion computers connected to the Internet worldwide are captured by stealth malware programs that users unintentionally install by opening e-mail attachments or clicking malicious links that download files, or as a result of using pirated "free" software. RustockB is one common stealth program that adds unwitting users to botnets. These programs then take over the computer without the user knowing and are controlled remotely by a Command and Control server. Once under control, the botnet is used to send spam. Botnets are responsible for over 80% of the spam sent throughout the world. This is the most profitable use of botnets. They are also used to collect credit card information, personal IDs, and bank information, feeding the underground economy with identity theft candidates. The botnets can be "rented" to run DDoS attacks against any site on the Internet. It could be your company, or your bank. ShadowServer, an organization of volunteer computer security experts, tracks 400,000 known infected computers (a small fraction of the total) and about 1,500 active controllers.

Defense authorities, government agencies, and businesses are unlikely to be able to fend off these attacks forever without some re-design of the Internet itself because the scale of the botnets is growing faster than the scale of the defensive moves.

SOURCES: "U.S. at Risk of Cyberattacks, Experts Say," by Brandon Griggs, cnn.com, August 18, 2008; "Georgia Takes a Beating in the Cyberwar with Russia," by John Markoff, *New York Times*, August 11, 2008; Net Attack," by Aaron Mannes and James Hendler, *Wall Street Journal*, June 5, 2007; "War Fears Turn Digital After Data Siege in Estonia," by Mark Lander and John Markoff, *New York Times*, May 29, 2007; "VeriSign Moves to Address an Internet Security Problem," by John Markoff, *New York Times*, February 8, 2007; "Attack of the Zombie Computers Is Growing Threat," by John Markoff, *New York Times*, January 7, 2007.

As *Cyberwar Becomes a Reality* illustrates, the Internet and Web are increasingly vulnerable to large-scale attacks and potentially large-scale failure. Increasingly, these attacks are led by organized gangs of criminals operating globally—an unintended consequence of globalization. However, there are steps you can take to protect your Web sites and your personal information when using online e-commerce sites.

In this chapter, we will examine e-commerce security and payment issues. First, we will identify the major security risks and their costs, and describe the variety of solutions currently available. Then, we will look at the major payment methods and consider how to achieve a secure payment environment.

5.1 THE E-COMMERCE SECURITY ENVIRONMENT

For most law-abiding citizens, the Internet holds the promise of a huge, convenient, global marketplace, providing access to people, goods, services and businesses worldwide, all at a bargain price. For criminals, the Internet has created entirely new—and lucrative—ways to steal from the more than 1 billion consumers in the world on the Internet. From products and services to cash to information, it's all there for the taking on the Internet.

It's also less risky to steal online. Rather than rob a bank in person, the Internet makes it possible to rob people remotely and almost anonymously. Rather than steal a CD at a local record store, on the Internet you can download the same music for free and almost without risk. The potential for anonymity on the Internet cloaks many criminals in legitimate-looking identities, allowing them to place fraudulent orders with online merchants, steal information by intercepting e-mail, or simply shut down e-commerce sites by using software viruses and swarm attacks. The Internet was never designed to be a global marketplace with a billion users, and lacks many basic security features found in older networks such as the telephone system or broadcast television networks. Who ever heard of the telephone system being hacked and "brought down" by programmers in Eastern Europe? By comparison, the Internet is an open, vulnerable-design network. The actions of cybercriminals are costly for both businesses and consumers, who are then subjected to higher prices and additional security measures. However, the overall security environment is strengthening as business managers and government officials make significant investments in security equipment and business procedures.

THE SCOPE OF THE PROBLEM

Cybercrime is becoming a more significant problem for both organizations and consumers. Bot networks, DoS, and DDoS attacks (all described in the opening case), Trojans, phishing (fraudulently obtaining financial information from a victim, typically via e-mail), data theft, identity theft, credit card fraud, and spyware are just some of the threats that are making daily headlines. But despite the increasing attention being paid to cybercrime, it is difficult to accurately estimate the actual amount of such crime, in part because some companies may be hesitant to report crime due to fear of losing the trust of its customers, and because even if crime is reported, it may be difficult to quantify the actual dollar amount of the loss.

One source of information is the Internet Crime Complaint Center ("IC3"), a partnership between the National White Collar Crime Center and the Federal Bureau of Investigation. The IC3 data is useful for gauging the types of e-commerce crimes most likely to be reported by consumers and the typical amount of loss experienced. In 2007, the IC3 processed more than 200,000 Internet crime complaints and referred more than 90,000 of them to federal, state, and local law enforcement agencies. The total dollar loss from all referred cases was nearly $240 million, a 21% increase over 2006; and the average dollar loss was about $2,650. **Figure 5.1** provides a summary of the top 5 categories of reported complaints, and **Figure 5.2** shows the average dollar loss for various categories. Auction fraud was the most frequently reported complaint, while the highest dollar loss per incident arose from Nigerian letter fraud (a form of phishing) (National White Collar Crime Center and the Federal Bureau of Investigation, 2008).

The Computer Security Institute's annual *Computer Crime and Security Survey* is another source of information. In 2007, the survey was based on the responses of almost 500 security practitioners in U.S. corporations, government agencies, financial institutions, medical institutions, and universities. The survey reported that 46% of

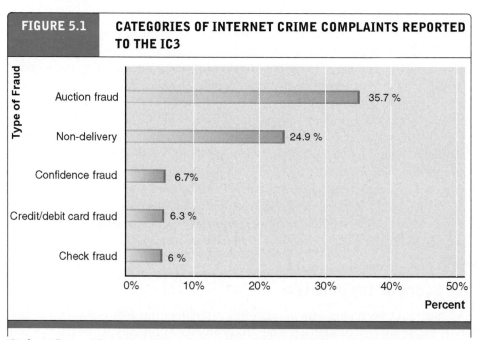

| FIGURE 5.1 | CATEGORIES OF INTERNET CRIME COMPLAINTS REPORTED TO THE IC3 |

This figure illustrates the top 5 categories of reported complaints to the FBI's Internet Crime Complaint Center. The most common complaint involves auction fraud, accounting for about 36% of reported complaints, followed by non-delivery of merchandise or payment.

SOURCE: Based on data from National White Collar Crime Center and the Federal Bureau of Investigation, 2008.

| FIGURE 5.2 | AVERAGE REPORTED LOSSES FOR VARIOUS TYPES OF INTERNET COMPLAINTS |

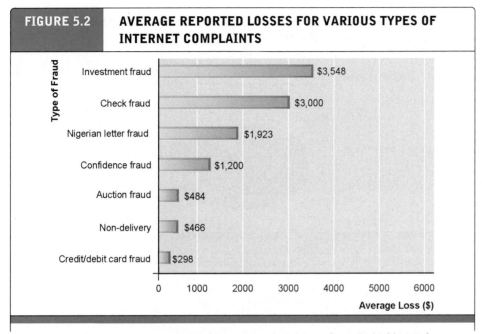

The average loss for the top seven categories of Internet complaints ranges from a high of $3,500 for investment fraud to around $300 for credit/debit card fraud.

SOURCE: Based on data from National White Collar Crime Center and the Federal Bureau of Investigation, 2008.

responding organizations experienced a computer security incident within the past year. **Figure 5.3** illustrates the various types of attacks against computer systems reported. Not all of these necessarily involve e-commerce, although many of them do. The total loss reported was $67 million, and the average annual loss was approximately $350,000. The most costly categories of attacks were financial fraud ($21 million), viruses ($8 million), and system penetration by an outsider ($6.8 million) (Computer Security Institute, 2007).

Reports issued by security product providers, such as Symantec, are another source of data. Symantec, for instance, issues a semi-annual *Internet Security Threat Report*, based on 40,000 sensors monitoring Internet activity in over 180 countries, and malicious code reports from over 120 million systems that utilize Symantec's anti-virus products. In the second half of 2007, almost 500,000 new malicious code threats were reported to Symantec, a 700% increase over the second half of 2006. It observed an average of about 61,940 active bot-infected computers per day and there were 87,963 phishing hosts, up 559% from the prior year (Symantec, 2008). However, Symantec does not attempt to quantify any actual crimes and/or losses related to these threats.

Online credit card fraud and phishing attacks are perhaps the most high-profile form of e-commerce crimes. Although the average amount of credit card fraud loss experienced by any one individual is typically relatively small (for instance, about $430 for those credit card/debit card fraud complaints reported in 2006 to the Internet Crime Complaint Center), the overall amount is substantial. The research firm

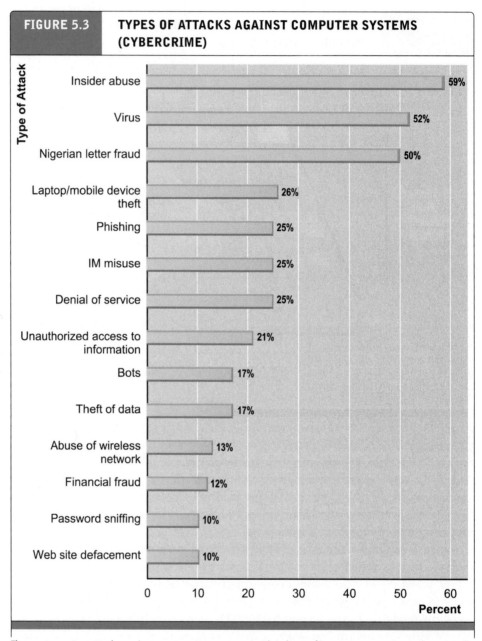

FIGURE 5.3   **TYPES OF ATTACKS AGAINST COMPUTER SYSTEMS (CYBERCRIME)**

The most common attacks against computer systems are insider abuse of Internet access, viruses, laptop and mobile device theft, phishing, IM misuse, and denial of service. Some of these are specifically related to e-commerce, while others are not.

SOURCE: Based on data from Computer Security Institute, 2007.

CyberSource estimates online credit card fraud in the United States amounted to about $3.6 billion in 2007 (CyberSource, 2008). The overall rate of online credit card fraud is estimated to be about 1.6%–1.8% of all online card transactions, roughly twice the rate of offline credit card fraud. As a percentage of all e-commerce revenues, credit card fraud is declining as merchants and credit companies expand security systems to prevent the most common types of low-level fraud. But the nature of credit card fraud has changed greatly from the theft of a single credit card number and efforts to purchase goods at a few sites, to the simultaneous theft of millions of credit card numbers and their distributions to thousands of criminals operating as gangs of thieves. The emergence of "identify theft," described further later in this chapter, as a major online/offline type of fraud, may well increase markedly the incidence and amount of credit card fraud, since identity theft often includes the use of stolen credit card information and the creation of phony credit card accounts.. According to a 2007 Gartner study, around 15 million Americans experienced identity theft in 2006 and lost an average of $3,257 (eMarketer, Inc., 2007). However, some analysts think online identity theft concerns are overblown. For instance, the 2008 Identity Fraud Survey by Javelin Strategy & Research found that in 2007, identity theft incidents were on the decline, with 3.6% of adults in the United States victims, compared to 4.25% in 2006. According to Javelin, the total loss was $51 billion (compared to $54 billion in 2006), while the average cost per consumer was $691, up from $554 in 2006 (eMarketer, 2008b, 2008c).

The Underground Economy Marketplace: The Value of Stolen Information

Criminals who steal information on the Internet do not always use this information themselves, but instead derive value by selling the information to others on so-called "underground economy servers." There are several thousand known underground economy servers around the world that sell stolen information (about half of these are in the United States). **Table 5.1** lists some recently observed prices.

Finding these servers is difficult for the average user (and for law enforcement agencies), and you need to be vetted by other criminals before gaining access. This vetting process takes place through e-mail exchanges of information, money and reputation. Criminals have fairly good, personalized security!

Note that not every cybercriminal is necessarily after money. In some cases, such criminals aim to just deface, vandalize and/or disrupt a Web site, rather than actually steal goods or services. The cost of such an attack includes not only the time

TABLE 5.1	THE UNDERGROUND ECONOMY MARKETPLACE
U.S. credit card	$.40–$20
A full identity (U.S. bank account, credit card, date of birth, social security, etc.)	$1–$10
Bank account	$10–$100
A single compromised computer	$6–$20
Social security number	$5–$7
Phishing Web site hosting	$3–$5
E-mail passwords	$4-$30

SOURCE: Based on data from Symantec, 2008, 2007a, 2007b.

and effort to make repairs to the site but also damage done to the site's reputation and image as well as revenues lost as a result of the attack.

So, what can we can conclude about the overall size of cybercrime? Cybercrime against e-commerce sites is dynamic and changing all the time, with new risks appearing often. The amount of losses to businesses appears to be significant but stable, and may represent a declining percentage of overall sales, because firms have invested in security measures to protect against the simplest crimes. Individuals face new risks of fraud, many of which (unlike credit cards where federal law limits the loss to $50 for individuals) involve substantial uninsured losses involving debit cards and bank accounts. The managers of e-commerce sites must prepare for an ever-changing variety of criminal assaults, and keep current in the latest security techniques.

WHAT IS GOOD E-COMMERCE SECURITY?

What is a secure commercial transaction? Any time you go into a marketplace, you take risks, including the loss of privacy (information about what you purchased). Your prime risk as a consumer is that you do not get what you paid for. In fact, you might pay and get nothing! Worse, someone steals your money while you are at the market! As a merchant in the market, your risk is that you don't get paid for what you sell. Thieves take merchandise and then either walk off without paying anything, or pay you with a fraudulent instrument, stolen credit card, or forged currency.

E-commerce merchants and consumers face many of the same risks as participants in traditional commerce, albeit in a new digital environment. Theft is theft, regardless of whether it is digital theft or traditional theft. Burglary, breaking and entering, embezzlement, trespass, malicious destruction, vandalism—all crimes in a traditional commercial environment—are also present in e-commerce. However, reducing risks in e-commerce is a complex process that involves new technologies, organizational policies and procedures, and new laws and industry standards that empower law enforcement officials to investigate and prosecute offenders. **Figure 5.4** illustrates the multi-layered nature of e-commerce security.

To achieve the highest degree of security possible, new technologies are available and should be used. But these technologies by themselves do not solve the problem. Organizational policies and procedures are required to ensure the technologies are not subverted. Finally, industry standards and government laws are required to enforce payment mechanisms, as well as investigate and prosecute violators of laws designed to protect the transfer of property in commercial transactions.

The history of security in commercial transactions teaches that any security system can be broken if enough resources are put against it. Security is not absolute. In addition, perfect security forever is not needed, especially in the information age. There is a time value to information—just as there is to money. Sometimes it is sufficient to protect a message for a few hours, days, or years. Also, because security is costly, we always have to weigh the cost against the potential loss. Finally, we have also learned that security is a chain that breaks most often at the weakest link. Our locks are often much stronger than our management of the keys.

FIGURE 5.4	THE E-COMMERCE SECURITY ENVIRONMENT

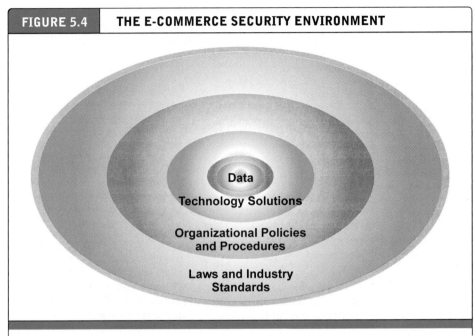

E-commerce security is multi-layered, and must take into account new technology, policies and procedures, and laws and industry standards.

We can conclude then that good e-commerce security requires a set of laws, procedures, policies, and technologies that, to the extent feasible, protect individuals and organizations from unexpected behavior in the e-commerce marketplace.

DIMENSIONS OF E-COMMERCE SECURITY

There are six key dimensions to e-commerce security: integrity, nonrepudiation, authenticity, confidentiality, privacy, and availability (see **Table 5.2**).

Integrity refers to the ability to ensure that information being displayed on a Web site, or transmitted or received over the Internet, has not been altered in any way by an unauthorized party. For example, if an unauthorized person intercepts and changes the contents of an online communication, such as by redirecting a bank wire transfer into a different account, the integrity of the message has been compromised because the communication no longer represents what the original sender intended.

Nonrepudiation refers to the ability to ensure that e-commerce participants do not deny (i.e., repudiate) their online actions. For instance, the availability of free e-mail accounts with alias names makes it easy for a person to post comments or send a message and perhaps later deny doing so. Even when a customer uses a real name and e-mail address, it is easy for that customer to order merchandise online and then later deny doing so. In most cases, because merchants typically do not obtain a physical copy of a signature, the credit card issuer will side with the customer because the merchant has no legally valid proof that the customer ordered the merchandise.

integrity

the ability to ensure that information being displayed on a Web site or transmitted or received over the Internet has not been altered in any way by an unauthorized party

nonrepudiation

the ability to ensure that e-commerce participants do not deny (i.e., repudiate) their online actions

TABLE 5.2	CUSTOMER AND MERCHANT PERSPECTIVES ON THE DIFFERENT DIMENSIONS OF E-COMMERCE SECURITY	
DIMENSIONS	CUSTOMER'S PERSPECTIVE	MERCHANT'S PERSPECTIVE
Integrity	Has information I transmit or receive been altered?	Has data on the site been altered without authorization? Is data being received from customers valid?
Nonrepudiation	Can a party to an action with me later deny taking the action?	Can a customer deny ordering products?
Authenticity	Who am I dealing with? How can I be assured that the person or entity is who they claim to be?	What is the real identity of the customer?
Confidentiality	Can someone other than the intended recipient read my messages?	Are messages or confidential data accessible to anyone other than those authorized to view them?
Privacy	Can I control the use of information about myself transmitted to an e-commerce merchant?	What use, if any, can be made of personal data collected as part of an e-commerce transaction? Is the personal information of customers being used in an unauthorized manner?
Availability	Can I get access to the site?	Is the site operational?

authenticity
the ability to identify the identity of a person or entity with whom you are dealing on the Internet

confidentiality
the ability to ensure that messages and data are available only to those who are authorized to view them

privacy
the ability to control the use of information about oneself

availability
the ability to ensure that an e-commerce site continues to function as intended

Authenticity refers to the ability to identify the identity of a person or entity with whom you are dealing on the Internet. How does the customer know that the Web site operator is who it claims to be? How can the merchant be assured that the customer is really who she says she is? Someone who claims to be someone he is not is "spoofing" or misrepresenting himself.

Confidentiality refers to the ability to ensure that messages and data are available only to those who are authorized to view them. Confidentiality is sometimes confused with **privacy**, which refers to the ability to control the use of information a customer provides about himself or herself to an e-commerce merchant.

E-commerce merchants have two concerns related to privacy. They must establish internal policies that govern their own use of customer information, and they must protect that information from illegitimate or unauthorized use. For example, if hackers break into an e-commerce site and gain access to credit card or other information, this not only violates the confidentiality of the data, but also the privacy of the individuals who supplied the information.

Availability refers to the ability to ensure that an e-commerce site continues to function as intended.

E-commerce security is designed to protect these six dimensions. When any one of them is compromised, it is a security issue.

THE TENSION BETWEEN SECURITY AND OTHER VALUES

Can there be too much security? The answer is yes. Contrary to what some may believe, security is not an unmitigated good. Computer security adds overhead and expense to business operations, and also gives criminals new opportunities to hide their intentions and their crimes.

Ease of Use

There are inevitable tensions between security and ease of use. When traditional merchants are so fearful of robbers that they do business in shops locked behind security gates, ordinary customers are discouraged from walking in. The same can be true on the Web. In general, the more security measures added to an e-commerce site, the more difficult it is to use and the slower the site becomes. As you will discover reading this chapter, digital security is purchased at the price of slowing down processors and adding significantly to data storage demands on storage devices. Security is a technological and business overhead that can detract from doing business. Too much security can harm profitability, while not enough security can potentially put you out of business.

Public Safety and the Criminal Uses of the Internet

There is also an inevitable tension between the desires of individuals to act anonymously (to hide their identity) and the needs of public officials to maintain public safety that can be threatened by criminals or terrorists. This is not a new problem, or even new to the electronic era. The U.S. government began informal tapping of telegraph wires during the Civil War in the mid-1860s in order to trap conspirators and terrorists, and the first police wiretaps of local telephone systems were in place by the 1890s—twenty years after the invention of the phone (Schwartz, 2001). No nation-state has ever permitted a technological haven to exist where criminals can plan crimes or threaten the nation-state without fear of official surveillance or investigation. In this sense, the Internet is no different from any other communication system. Drug cartels make extensive use of voice, fax, and data encryption devices; a number of large international organized criminal groups steal information from commercial Web sites and resell it to other criminals who use it for financial fraud. Over the years, the U.S. government has successfully pursued various "carding forums" (Web sites that facilitate the stale of stolen credit card and debit card numbers), such as Shadowcrew.com and Carderplanet.com, resulting in the arrest and prosecution of a number of their members and the shutting down of the sites. However, other criminal organizations have emerged to take their place, including Cardersmarket.com, which reportedly has thousands of members worldwide, and CCpowerForums.com.

Terrorists are also fond users of the Internet and have been for many years. Encrypted files sent via e-mail were used by Ramsey Yousef—a member of the terrorist group responsible for bombing the World Trade Center in 1993—to hide plans for bombing 11 U.S. airliners. The Internet was also used to plan and coordinate the subsequent attacks on the World Trade Center on September 11, 2001. In addition, the

Aum Shinrikyo religious cult in Japan that spread poison gas in the Tokyo subway in March 1995 (killing 12 and hospitalizing 6,000 people) stored their records detailing plans for attacks on other countries on computers using a powerful form of encryption called RSA, described later. Fortunately, authorities were lucky to find the encryption key stored on a floppy disk (Denning and Baugh, 1999).

More recently, Al Qaeda and its offshoots "have understood that both time and space have in many ways been conquered by the Internet," said John Arquilla, a professor at the Naval Postgraduate School who coined the term "netwar" more than a decade ago. Al Qaeda, according to security experts in the United States and Britain, use the Web as a dynamic library of training materials on poison mixing and explosive construction, tactical coordination of imminent attacks, and building a larger terrorist community of like-minded people. The Internet is both anonymous and pervasive, an ideal communication tool for criminal and terrorist groups (Peretti, 2008).

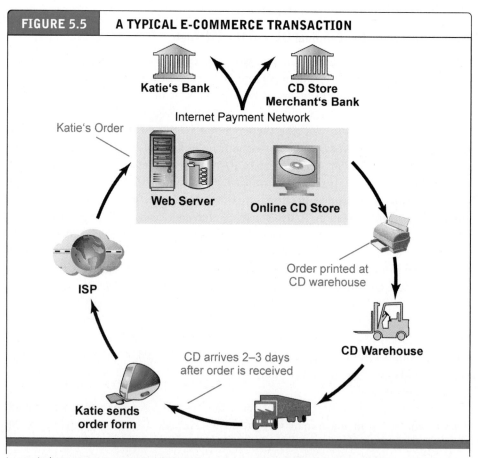

FIGURE 5.5 | **A TYPICAL E-COMMERCE TRANSACTION**

In a typical e-commerce transaction, the customer uses a credit card and the existing credit payment system. The transaction has many vulnerable points.
SOURCE: Boncella, 2000.

FIGURE 5.6	**VULNERABLE POINTS IN AN E-COMMERCE TRANSACTION**

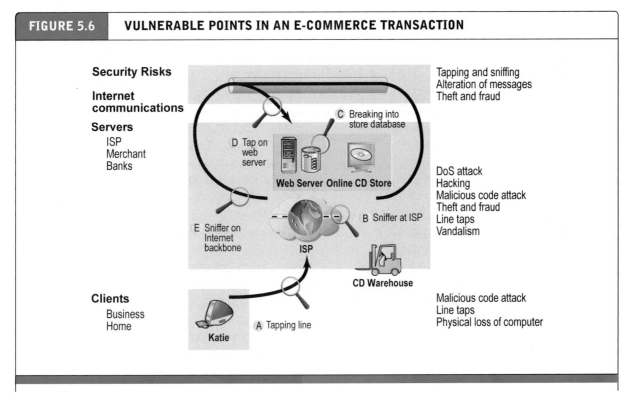

There are three vulnerable points in e-commerce transactions: Internet communications, servers, and clients.
SOURCE: Boncella, 2000.

5.2 SECURITY THREATS IN THE E-COMMERCE ENVIRONMENT

From a technology perspective, there are three key points of vulnerability when dealing with e-commerce: the client, the server, and the communications pipeline. **Figure 5.5** illustrates a typical e-commerce transaction with a consumer using a credit card to purchase a product. **Figure 5.6** illustrates some of the things that can go wrong at each major vulnerability point in the transaction—over Internet communications channels, at the server level, and at the client level.

In this section, we describe a number of the most common and most damaging forms of security threats to e-commerce consumers and site operators: malicious code, unwanted programs, phishing and identity theft, hacking and cybervandalism, credit card fraud/theft, spoofing (pharming) and spam (junk) Web sites, Denial of Service (DoS) and Distributed Denial of service (DDoS) attacks, sniffing, insider attacks, and finally, poorly designed server and client software.

MALICIOUS CODE

malicious code (malware)

includes a variety of threats such as viruses, worms, Trojan horses, and bots

Malicious code (sometimes referred to as "malware") includes a variety of threats such as viruses, worms, Trojan horses, and bots. In 2008, Microsoft reported that its Malicious Software Removal Tool had removed malware from an estimated 25 million distinct computers during 2007 (Microsoft, 2008). Malicious code in the past often was intended simply to impair computers, and was often authored by a lone hacker, but increasingly the intent is to steal e-mail addresses, logon credentials, personal data and financial information. Increasingly, malicious code is used to develop integrated malware networks that organize the theft of information and money.

virus

a computer program that has the ability to replicate or make copies of itself, and spread to other files

A **virus** is a computer program that has the ability to replicate or make copies of itself, and spread to other files. In addition to the ability to replicate, most computer viruses deliver a "payload." The payload may be relatively benign, such as the display of a message or image, or it may be highly destructive—destroying files, reformatting the computer's hard drive, or causing programs to run improperly.

One of the latest innovations in virus distribution is to embed them in the online advertising chain, including at Google and other ad networks. For instance, in May 2007, Google users who clicked on Tomshardware.com were re-directed to a server that downloaded viruses and destroyed computers. Approximately 100,000 computers were affected. A recent survey of search engine text ads found that 7% led to suspicious sites (Steel, 2007). In August 2008, Flash-based ads infected with malicious script were discovered to be inserting URLS for sites offering phony security software onto the clipboards of both PCs and Macs running Windows (Keizer, 2008). Viruses embedded in PDF files have also been discovered. Virus authors are also increasingly using links embedded within e-mail instead of the more traditional file attachments to infect computers. The links lead directly to a malicious code download or Web sites that include malicious JavaScript code (Keizer, 2007). Equally important, there has been a major shift in the writers of malware from amateur hackers and adventurers to organized criminal efforts to defraud companies and individuals. In other words, it's now more about the money than ever before.

Computer viruses fall into several major categories as follows:

- *Macro viruses* are application-specific, meaning that the virus affects only the application for which it was written, such as Microsoft Word, Excel, or PowerPoint. When a user opens an infected document in the appropriate application, the virus copies itself to the templates in the application, so that when new documents are created, they are infected with the macro virus as well. Macro viruses can easily be spread when sent in an e-mail attachment.

- *File-infecting viruses* usually infect executable files, such as *.com, *.exe, *.drv, and * .dll files. They may activate every time the infected file is executed by copying themselves into other executable files. File-infecting viruses are also easily spread through e-mails and any file transfer system.

- *Script viruses* are written in script programming languages such as VBScript (Visual Basic Script) and JavaScript. The viruses are activated simply by double-clicking an infected *.vbs or *.js file. The ILOVEYOU virus (also known as the Love Bug), which overwrites *.jpg and *.mp3 files, is one of the most famous examples of a script virus.

Viruses are often combined with a worm. Indeed, most researchers agree that classic viruses—the original malicious programs—have become much less common, while the far more dangerous worm has grown exponentially. Some of the reason is simple: viruses infect a single computer, and may destroy but produce very little cash. As the nature of the criminal changes from amateur hacker to professional criminal interested in cash, it is much more lucrative to create a worm that can propagate from one computer to another, perhaps to millions.

Instead of just spreading from file to file, a **worm** is designed to spread from computer to computer. A worm does not necessarily need to be activated by a user or program in order for it to replicate itself. For example, the Slammer worm, which targeted a known vulnerability in Microsoft's SQL Server database software, infected more than 90% of vulnerable computers worldwide within 10 minutes of its release on the Internet; crashed Bank of America cash machines, especially in the southwestern part of the United States; affected cash registers at supermarkets such as the Publix chain in Atlanta, where staff could not dispense cash to frustrated buyers; and took down most Internet connections in South Korea, causing a dip in the stock market there. Other well-known worms include the MyDoom worm, the Sasser worm, the Zotob worm, and the Nymex worm (Symantec, 2007; United States Government Accountability Office, 2005).

A **Trojan horse** appears to be benign, but then does something other than expected. The Trojan horse is not itself a virus because it does not replicate, but is often a way for viruses or other malicious code such as bots or *rootkits* (a program whose aim is to subvert control of the computer's operating system) to be introduced into a computer system. The term *Trojan horse* refers to the huge wooden horse in Homer's *Iliad* that the Greeks gave their opponents, the Trojans—a gift that actually contained hundreds of Greek soldiers. Once the people of Troy let the massive horse within their gates, the soldiers revealed themselves and captured the city. In today's world, a Trojan horse may masquerade as a game, but actually hide a program to steal your passwords and e-mail them to another person. According to Symantec, of the top 10 new malicious code families detected in the last six months of 2007, four were Trojans; during the second half of 2007, Trojans made up 71% of the volume of the top 50 malicious code reports, an increase over the 54% reported in the first half of 2007 (Symantec, 2008). In August 2007, Monster.com suffered a highly publicized attack from a Trojan horse called Infostealer.Monstres that stole more than 1.6 million records, such as names, e-mail addresses, home addresses, and phone numbers of job seekers who had filed resumes with Monster (Kreizer, 2007b).

Bots (short for robots) are a type of malicious code that can be covertly installed on your computer when attached to the Internet. Once installed, the bot responds to external commands sent by the attacker, and your computer becomes a "zombie," and is able to be controlled by an external third party (the "bot-herder"). **Botnets** are collections of captured computers used for malicious activities such as sending spam, participating in a Distributed Denial of Service attack (described later), stealing information from computers, and storing network traffic for later analysis. In the last six months of 2007, Symantec identified an average of 61,940 active bot-infected computers per day and observed over 5 million distinct bot-infected computers. Arguably, bots and bot networks are the single most important threat to the Internet

worm
malware that is designed to spread from computer to computer

Trojan horse
appears to be benign, but then does something other than expected. Often a way for viruses or other malicious code to be introduced into a computer system

bot
type of malicious code that can be covertly installed on a computer when attached to the Internet. Once installed, the bot responds to external commands sent by the attacker

botnet
collection of captured bot computers

and e-commerce in 2007 because they can be used to launch very large-scale attacks using many different techniques. In 2007, the authors of the Storm worm (which can also be described as a Trojan horse) assembled a massive botnet to propagate the worm. It is estimated that 5,000 to 6,000 computers are dedicated to spreading the worm through the use of e-mail with infected attachments, with over 1.2 billion virus messages sent by the botnet since January 2007 (Gaudin, 2007).

Malicious code is a threat at both the client and the server level, although servers generally engage in much more thorough anti-virus activities than do consumers. At the server level, malicious code can bring down an entire Web site, preventing millions of people from using the site. Such incidents are infrequent. Much more frequent malicious code attacks occur at the client level, and the damage can quickly spread to millions of other computers connected to the Internet. **Table 5.3** lists some well-known examples of malicious code.

While the number of viruses and worms is increasing, so too has prosecution of those who create viruses. Increasingly, European and Asian authorities are coordinating arrests with American authorities. In the United States, the FBI's Operation BotRoast has resulted in a number of arrests (FBI, 2007). In 2006, a Moroccan teenager was sent to jail for two years for releasing the Zotob worm virus that ravaged U.S. computer networks. In July 2005, the 18-year-old creator of the Sasser worm was convicted in Germany on charges including computer sabotage.

UNWANTED PROGRAMS

In addition to malicious code, the e-commerce security environment is further challenged by unwanted programs such as adware, browser parasites, spyware, and other applications that install themselves on a computer, typically without the user's informed consent. Such programs are increasingly being found on social networking and user-generated content sites where users are fooled into downloading them (Symantec, 2007). Once installed, these applications are usually exceedingly difficult to remove from the computer.

Adware (described further in Chapter 7) is typically used to call for pop-up ads to display when the user visits certain sites. While annoying, adware is not typically used for criminal activities. ZangoSearch and PurityScan are examples of adware programs that open the Web pages or display pop-up ads of partner sites when certain keywords are used in Internet searches. A **browser parasite** is a program that can monitor and change the settings of a user's browser, for instance, changing the browser's home page, or sending information about the sites visited to a remote computer. Browser parasites are often a component of adware. For example, Websearch is an adware component that modifies Internet Explorer's default home page and search settings.

browser parasite
a program that can monitor and change the settings of a user's browser

spyware
a program used to obtain information such as user's keystrokes, e-mail, instant messages, and so on

Spyware, on the other hand, can be used to obtain information such as a user's keystrokes, copies of e-mail and instant messages, and even take screenshots (and thereby capture passwords or other confidential data). One example of spyware is SpySheriff, which claims to be a spyware removal program but is actually a malicious spyware application. Spyware (along with phishing, described in the next section) is often used for identity theft.

TABLE 5.3	\multicolumn{2}{l}{**NOTABLE EXAMPLES OF MALICIOUS CODE**}
NAME	TYPE	DESCRIPTION
Silentbanker	Trojan horse	First appeared in December 2007. Steals online banking information, diverts legitimate transactions and steals money from accounts. Records keystrokes, captures screen images, steals confidential financial information and sends it to remote attacker.
Netsky.P	Worm/Trojan horse	First appeared in early 2003; still one of the most common computer worms. It spreads by gathering target e-mail addresses from the computers it infects, and sending e-mail to all recipients from the infected computer. It is commonly used by bot networks to launch spam and Denial of Service attacks.
Storm (Peacomm, NuWar)	Worm/Trojan horse	First appeared in January 2007. It spreads in a manner similar to the Netsky.P worm. May also download and run other Trojan programs and worms.
Nymex	Worm	First discovered in January 2006. Spreads by mass mailing; activates on the 3rd of every month, and attempts to destroy files of certain types.
Zotob	Worm	First appeared in August 2005. Well-known worm that infected a number of U.S. media companies.
Sasser	Worm	First appeared in 2004. Exploited a vulnerability in LSASS, causing network problems.
Mydoom	Worm	First appeared in January 2004. One of the fastest-spreading mass-mailer worms.
Slammer	Worm	Launched in January 2003. Caused widespread problems.
Klez	Worm	Most prolific virus of 2002. Was distributed via an e-mail with a random subject line and message body. Once launched, the worm sent itself to all addresses in the Windows Address Book, the database of instant-messaging program ICQ, and local files.
CodeRed	Worm	Appeared in 2001. It achieved an infection rate of over 20,000 systems within 10 minutes of release and ultimately spread to hundreds of thousands of systems.
Melissa	Macro virus/worm	First spotted in March 1999. At the time, Melissa was the fastest-spreading infectious program ever discovered. It attacked Microsoft Word's Normal.dot global template, ensuring infection of all newly created documents. It also mailed an infected Word file to the first 50 entries in each user's Microsoft Outlook Address Book.
Chernobyl	File-infecting virus	First appeared in 1998. It wipes out the first megabyte of data on a hard disk (making the rest useless) every April 26, the anniversary of the nuclear disaster at Chernobyl.

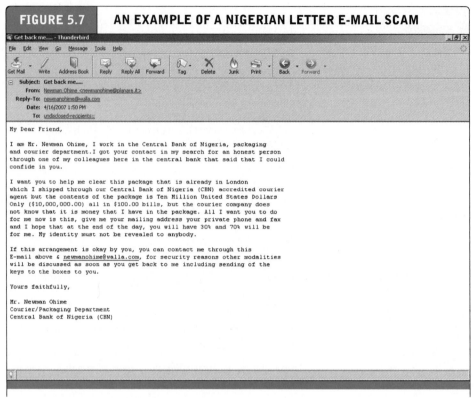

This is an example of a typical Nigerian letter e-mail scam.

PHISHING AND IDENTITY THEFT

phishing

any deceptive, online attempt by a third party to obtain confidential information for financial gain

Phishing is any deceptive, online attempt by a third party to obtain confidential information for financial gain. Phishing attacks do not involve malicious code but instead rely on straightforward misrepresentation and fraud, so-called "social engineering" techniques. The most popular phishing attack is the e-mail scam letter. The scam begins with an e-mail: a rich former oil minister of Nigeria is seeking a bank account to stash millions of dollars for a short period of time, and requests your bank account number where the money can be deposited. In return, you will receive a million dollars. This type of e-mail scam is popularly known as a "Nigerian letter" scam (see **Figure 5.7**).

Thousands of other phishing attacks use other scams, some pretending to be eBay, PayPal, or Citibank writing to you for "account verification." Click on a link in the e-mail and you will be taken to a Web site controlled by the scammer, and prompted to enter confidential information about your accounts, such as your account number and PIN codes (see **Figure 5.8**). On any given day, millions of these phishing attack e-mails are sent, and, unfortunately, some people are fooled and disclose their personal account information.

Phishers rely on traditional "con man" tactics, but use e-mail to trick recipients into voluntarily giving up financial access codes, bank account numbers, credit card

| FIGURE 5.8 | AN EXAMPLE OF A PHISHING ATTACK |

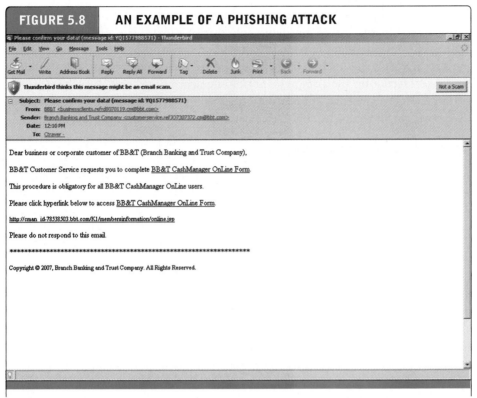

This is an example of a typical phishing e-mail that seeks to obtain personal information from an unwary respondent.

numbers, and other personal information. Often, phishers create ("spoof") a Web site that purports to be a legitimate financial institution and con users into entering financial information. Phishers use the information they gather to commit fraudulent acts such as charging items to your credit cards or withdrawing funds from your bank account, or in other ways "steal your identity" (identity theft). Phishing attacks are one of the fastest-growing forms of e-commerce crime. During the last six months of 2007, Symantec detected 207,547 unique new phishing e-mail messages, an increase of 20% compared to the second half of 2006 (Symantec, 2008). In October 2007, OpenDNS published the PhishTank Annual Report, based on over 300,000 phishing scams it examined. The report found that the top two spoofed brands were eBay and PayPal, with a variety of banks, the IRS, and several large retailers (Amazon and Wal-Mart) rounding out the top 10. It also found that just over 30% of phishing Web sites were hosted on U.S.-based networks, but that the three IP addresses with the most attacks—responsible for a total of 18% of all verified phishing Web sites—were located in Korea, Turkey, and Chile (OpenDNS, 2007).

Many of the security vulnerabilities described throughout this section use what are called "social engineering" techniques to propagate. These techniques involve fraud or misrepresentation, or in other words, pretending to be something that it is not. For instance, the Netsky.P worm uses an e-mail message that takes the form of an e-mail delivery notification to trick recipients into thinking that the e-mail is from a valid source, encouraging them to open an attached file that, in reality, is an executable program that contains a virus or worm. Once the attachment is opened, the worm begins to execute on the computer. Social engineering not only aids the worm in getting the target recipient to open the infected e-mail, it also allows the worm to evade content filters or scanners, often by masquerading as a compressed zip file.

HACKING AND CYBERVANDALISM

A **hacker** is an individual who intends to gain unauthorized access to a computer system. Within the hacking community, the term **cracker** is typically used to denote a hacker with criminal intent, although in the public press, the terms hacker and cracker tend to be used interchangeably. Hackers and crackers gain unauthorized access by finding weaknesses in the security procedures of Web sites and computer systems, often taking advantage of various features of the Internet that make it an open system that is easy to use. Hackers and crackers typically are computer aficionados excited by the challenge of breaking into corporate and government Web sites. Sometimes they are satisfied merely by breaking into the files of an e-commerce site. Others have more malicious intentions and commit **cybervandalism**, intentionally disrupting, defacing, or even destroying the site.

For instance, Robert Lyttle of San Francisco and Benjamin Stark of St. Petersburg, Florida, were convicted of breaking into and "hacking" a computer at NASA's Ames Research Center in Moffett Field, California. They stole information about members of the agency's Astrobiology Institute and used that information to deface the home page of the NASA Astrobiology Institute. Calling themselves "The Deceptive Duo," Lyttle and Stark stated that their attacks were intended to demonstrate vulnerabilities in the government's computer security systems. The pair also hacked into the Defense Department's Defense Logistics Information Service Web site and the agency's Office of Health Affairs. Lyttle pleaded guilty to the attacks, and the U.S. District Court in Oakland, California, sentenced him to four months in prison, restitution payment of $71,181, and three years probation. Stark, who also pleaded guilty, was sentenced to two years probation and to pay $29,006 in restitution (Butterfield, 2005).

The hacker phenomenon has diversified over time. In general, benign hacking and defacement hacking has receded as law enforcement and private agencies learn how to detect perpetrators. Hacker activities have broadened beyond mere system intrusion to include theft of goods and information, as well as vandalism and system damage. Financial hacking is on the rise, especially from foreign countries. For instance, hackers invaded the Web sites of the Miami Dolphins in January 2007, and the World Cup Web site, in order to install key-logging software on visitors' computers.

Groups of hackers called *tiger teams* are sometimes used by corporate security departments to test their own security measures. By hiring hackers to break into the system from outside, the company can identify weaknesses in the computer system's armor. These "good hackers" became known as **white hats** because of their role in

hacker

an individual who intends to gain unauthorized access to a computer system

cracker

within the hacking community, a term typically used to denote a hacker with criminal intent

cybervandalism

intentionally disrupting, defacing, or even destroying a site

white hats

"good" hackers who help organizations locate and fix security flaws helping organizations locate and fix security flaws. White hats do their work under contract, with agreement from clients that they will not be prosecuted for their efforts to break in.

In contrast, **black hats** are hackers who engage in the same kinds of activities but without pay or any buy-in from the targeted organization, and with the intention of causing harm. They break into Web sites and reveal the confidential or proprietary information they find. These hackers believe strongly that information should be free, so sharing previously secret information is part of their mission.

Somewhere in the middle are the **grey hats**, hackers who believe they are pursuing some greater good by breaking in and revealing system flaws. Grey hats discover weaknesses in a system's security, and then publish the weakness without disrupting the site or attempting to profit from their finds. Their only reward is the prestige of discovering the weakness. Grey hat actions are suspect, however, especially when the hackers reveal security flaws that make it easier for other criminals to gain access to a system.

black hats
hackers who act with the intention of causing harm

grey hats
hackers who believe they are pursuing some greater good by breaking in and revealing system flaws

CREDIT CARD FRAUD/THEFT

Theft of credit card data is one of the most feared occurrences on the Internet. Fear that credit card information will be stolen frequently prevents users from making online purchases. Interestingly, this fear appears to be largely unfounded. Incidences of stolen credit card information are much lower than users think, around 1.6%–1.8% of all online card transactions (CyberSource, 2008).

In traditional commerce, there is substantial credit card fraud, but the consumer is largely insured against losses by federal law. In the past, the most common cause of credit card fraud was a lost or stolen card that is used by someone else, followed by employee theft of customer numbers and stolen identities (criminals applying for credit cards using false identities). Federal law limits the liability of individuals to $50 for a stolen credit card. For amounts over $50, the credit card company generally pays the amount, although in some cases, the merchant may be held liable if it failed to verify the account or consult published lists of invalid cards. Banks recoup the cost of credit card fraud by charging higher interest rates on unpaid balances, and by merchants who raise prices to cover the losses.

But today the most frequent cause of stolen cards and card information is the systematic hacking and looting of a corporate server where the information on millions of credit card purchases are stored. The largest and most damaging mass credit card theft to date occurred at TJX Companies, owner of 2,500 retail stores. Information from 47.5 million credit and debit cards was stolen by hackers who gained access to TJX's customer information database via a poorly protected wireless local area network in 2003. The theft was not discovered until 2006, and was not reported until 2007. The information was sold on underground economy sites to criminals who subsequently made hundreds of thousands of purchases, both offline and online (Dash, 2007; Vijayan, 2007).

International orders have been particularly prone to repudiation. If an international customer places an order and then later disputes it, online merchants often have no way to verify that the package was actually delivered and that the credit card holder is the person who placed the order.

The solution for many Web sites is to institute new identity verification mechanisms that are currently in development; these will be discussed in the next section. Until a customer's identity can be guaranteed, online companies are at a much higher risk of loss than traditional offline companies. The federal government has attempted to address this issue through the Electronic Signatures in Global and National Commerce Act (the "E-Sign" law), which gives digital signatures the same authority as hand written signatures in commerce. This law also intended to make digital signatures more commonplace, and easier to use. Except for large businesses conducting transactions over the Internet, the law has had little impact on B2C commerce, but that may be changing.

SPOOFING (PHARMING) AND SPAM (JUNK) WEB SITES

spoof

to misrepresent oneself by using fake e-mail addresses or masquerading as someone else

Hackers attempting to hide their true identity often **spoof**, or misrepresent themselves by using fake e-mail addresses or masquerading as someone else. Spoofing a Web site is also called "pharming," which involves redirecting a Web link to an address different from the intended one, with the site masquerading as the intended destination. Links that are designed to lead to one site can be reset to send users to a totally unrelated site—one that benefits the hacker. Spam Web sites are a little different. These are sites that promise to offer some product or service, but in fact are a collection of advertisements for other sites, some of which contain malicious code. For instance, you may search for "[name of town] weather," and then click on a link that promises your local weather, but then discover that all the site does is display ads for weather-related products or other Web sites.

Although spoofing does not directly damage files or network servers, it threatens the integrity of a site. For example, if hackers redirect customers to a fake Web site that looks almost exactly like the true site, they can then collect and process orders, effectively stealing business from the true site. Or, if the intent is to disrupt rather than steal, hackers can alter orders—inflating them or changing products ordered—and then send them on to the true site for processing and delivery. Customers become dissatisfied with the improper order shipment and the company may have huge inventory fluctuations that impact its operations.

In addition to threatening integrity, spoofing also threatens authenticity by making it difficult to discern the true sender of a message. Clever hackers can make it almost impossible to distinguish between a true and a fake identity or Web address.

Junk or spam Web sites typically appear on search results, and do not involve e-mail. These sites cloak their identities by using domain names similar to legitimate firm names, post their names on open Web forums, and redirect traffic to known spammer-redirection domains such as vip-online-search.info, searchadv.com, and webresourses.info. Recent research on junk Web sites found more than 30% of the results on keywords "drugs" and "ringtones" led to fake Web pages supported by major advertisers. One study found that 11% of the pages returned for 1,000 keywords were fake (Wang, et al., 2007).

DENIAL OF SERVICE (DOS) AND DISTRIBUTED DENIAL OF SERVICE (DDOS) ATTACKS

In a **Denial of Service (DoS)** attack, hackers flood a Web site with useless page requests that inundate and overwhelm the site's Web servers. Increasingly, DoS attacks involve the use of bot networks and so-called "distributed attacks" built from thousands of compromised client computers. According to Symantec, during the second half of 2007, the United States was subject to the most DoS attacks, accounting for 56% of the worldwide total (Symantec, 2008). DoS attacks typically cause a Web site to shut down, making it impossible for users to access the site. For busy e-commerce sites, these attacks are costly; while the site is shut down, customers cannot make purchases. And the longer a site is shut down, the more damage is done to a site's reputation. Although such attacks do not destroy information or access restricted areas of the server, they can destroy a firm's online business. Often, DoS attacks are accompanied by attempts at blackmailing site owners to pay tens or hundreds of thousands of dollars to the hackers in return for removing the DoS attack.

A **Distributed Denial of Service (DDoS)** attack uses numerous computers to attack the target network from numerous launch points. DoS and DDoS attacks are threats to a system's operation because they can shut it down indefinitely. Major Web sites such as Yahoo and Microsoft have experienced such attacks, making the companies aware of their vulnerability and the need to introduce new measures to prevent future attacks. The largest DDoS attack to date occurred in February 2007, when a botnet composed of several thousand computers attempted to bring down the part of the Internet domain name system operated by VeriSign. The attack affected all of the thirteen domain name servers operated by VeriSign, including the .com and .org domains (Markoff, 2007). The attack impeded but did not bring down any of the servers. Had it succeeded, the Internet itself would have failed for a period of time.

SNIFFING

A **sniffer** is a type of eavesdropping program that monitors information traveling over a network. When used legitimately, sniffers can help identify potential network trouble-spots, but when used for criminal purposes, they can be damaging and very difficult to detect. Sniffers enable hackers to steal proprietary information from anywhere on a network, including e-mail messages, company files, and confidential reports. The threat of sniffing is that confidential or personal information will be made public. For both companies and individuals, such an occurrence can be disruptive.

E-mail wiretaps are a variation on the sniffing threat. An e-mail wiretap is hidden code in an e-mail message that allows someone to monitor all succeeding messages forwarded with the original message. E-mail wiretaps can be installed on servers and client computers. For instance, the USA PATRIOT Act permits the FBI to compel ISPs to install a black box on their mail servers that can impound the e-mail of a single person or group of persons for later analysis. In the case of American citizens communicating with other citizens, an FBI agent or government lawyer need only certify to a judge on the secret 11-member U.S. Foreign Intelligence Surveillance Court (FISC) that the

Denial of Service (DoS) attack
flooding a Web site with useless traffic to inundate and overwhelm the network

Distributed Denial of Service (DDoS) attack
using numerous computers to attack the target network from numerous launch points

sniffer
a type of eavesdropping program that monitors information traveling over a network

information sought is "relevant to an ongoing criminal investigation" to get permission to install the program. Judges have no discretion. They must approve wiretaps based on government agents' unsubstantiated assertions (Associated Press, 2005). Congress adopted a new amendment to the 1978 Foreign Intelligence Surveillance Act, known as FISA, that provides new powers to the National Security Agency to monitor international e-mail and telephone communications where one person is in the United States, and where the purpose of such interception is to collect foreign intelligence (Foreign Intelligence Surveillance Act of 1978; Protect America Act of 2007).

INSIDER ATTACKS

We tend to think of security threats to a business as originating outside the organization. In fact, the largest financial threats to business institutions come not from robberies but from embezzlement by insiders. Bank employees steal far more money than bank robbers. The same is true for e-commerce sites. Some of the largest disruptions to service, destruction to sites, and diversion of customer credit data and personal information have come from insiders— once trusted employees. Employees have access to privileged information, and in the presence of sloppy internal security procedures, they are often able to roam throughout an organization's systems without leaving a trace. The 2007 CSI survey reports that insider abuse of systems was the second most frequent type of attack during the preceding 12 months, and that 64% of survey respondents believed that insiders contributed to some portion of the firm's financial losses during the previous year (Computer Security Institute, 2007). A Michigan State University study found that as much as 70% of all identity theft, including credit card theft, is the work of "insiders" (Borden, 2007). In some instances, the insider might not have criminal intent, but inadvertently expose data that can then be exploited by others. For instance, in September 2007, Citigroup confirmed that it was investigating a data breach that involved the names, social security numbers, and credit card information of over 5,000 customers by an employee of its ABN Amro Mortgage Group unit onto the LimeWire P2P file-sharing network (Vass, 2007).

POORLY DESIGNED SERVER AND CLIENT SOFTWARE

Many security threats prey on poorly designed server and client software, sometimes in the operating system and sometimes in the application software, including browsers. The increase in complexity and size of software programs, coupled with demands for timely delivery to markets, has contributed to an increase in software flaws or vulnerabilities that hackers can exploit. Each year security firms identify about 5,000 software vulnerabilities in Internet and PC software. For instance, in the second half of 2007, Symantec identified 18 vulnerabilities in Internet Explorer, 88 in Mozilla browsers, 22 in Apple Safari, and 12 in Opera. Some of these vulnerabilities were critical (Symantec, 2008). All the top 10 Internet attacks launched in 2008 were attacks against the Microsoft Windows server and client software, exploiting weaknesses in Microsoft's Win32 application programming interface (API). The very design of the personal computer includes many open communication ports that can be used, and indeed are designed to be used, by external computers to send and receive messages. The port typically attacked is TCP port 445. However, given their complexity and design objectives, all operating systems and application software, including Linux and Macintosh, have vulnerabilities. There are also a growing number of "zero-day" vulnerabilities, where the vulnerability is unknown to security experts and is actively exploited before there is a patch available, requiring firms to scurry to develop patches. In the single week of September 1, 2008, the U.S. Computer Emergency Readiness Team (US-CERT; Department of Homeland Security) reported on 112 newly discovered vulnerabilities in server and application software, 54 of them rated "high severity" (US-CERT, 2007).

5.3 TECHNOLOGY SOLUTIONS

At first glance it might seem like there is not much that can be done about the onslaught of security breaches on the Internet. Reviewing the security threats in the previous section, it is clear that the threats to e-commerce are very real, potentially devastating, and likely to be increasing in intensity along with the growth in e-commerce. But in fact a great deal of progress has been made by private security firms, corporate and home users, network administrators, technology firms, and government agencies. There are two lines of defense: technology solutions and policy solutions. In this section, we consider some technology solutions, and in the following section, we look at some policy solutions that work.

The first line of defense against the wide variety of security threats to an e-commerce site is a set of tools that can make it difficult for outsiders to invade or destroy a site. **Figure 5.9** illustrates the major tools available to achieve site security. In the next section, we describe these tools in greater detail.

PROTECTING INTERNET COMMUNICATIONS

Because e-commerce transactions must flow over the public Internet, and therefore involve thousands of routers and servers through which the transaction packets flow, security experts believe the greatest security threats occur at the level of Internet communications. This is very different from a private network where a dedicated communication line is established between two parties. A number of tools are available to protect the security of Internet communications, the most basic of which is message encryption.

ENCRYPTION

Encryption is the process of transforming plain text or data into **cipher text** that cannot be read by anyone other than the sender and the receiver. The purpose of encryption is (a) to secure stored information and (b) to secure information transmission. Encryption can provide four of the six key dimensions of e-commerce security referred to in Table 5.2:

encryption
the process of transforming plain text or data into cipher text that cannot be read by anyone other than the sender and the receiver. The purpose of encryption is (a) to secure stored information and (b) to secure information transmission

cipher text
text that has been encrypted and thus cannot be read by anyone other than the sender and the receiver

FIGURE 5.9	TOOLS AVAILABLE TO ACHIEVE SITE SECURITY

There are a number of tools available to achieve site security.

- *Message integrity*—provides assurance that the message has not been altered.
- *Nonrepudiation*—prevents the user from denying he or she sent the message.
- *Authentication*—provides verification of the identity of the person (or computer) sending the message.
- *Confidentiality*—gives assurance that the message was not read by others.

key (cipher)
any method for transforming plain text to cipher text

This transformation of plain text to cipher text is accomplished by using a key or cipher. A **key** (or **cipher**) is any method for transforming plain text to cipher text.

Encryption has been practiced since the earliest forms of writing and commercial transactions. Ancient Egyptian and Phoenician commercial records were encrypted using substitution and transposition ciphers. In a **substitution cipher**, every occurrence of a given letter is replaced systematically by another letter. For instance, if we used the cipher "letter plus two"—meaning replace every letter in a word with a new letter two places forward—then the word "Hello" in plain text would be transformed into the following cipher text: "JGNNQ." In a **transposition cipher**, the ordering of the letters in each word is changed in some systematic way. Leonardo Da Vinci recorded his shop notes in reverse order, making them readable only with a mirror. The word "Hello" can be written backwards as "OLLEH." A more complicated cipher would (a) break all words into two words and (b) spell the first word with every other letter beginning with the first letter, and then spell the second word with all the remaining letters. In this cipher, "HELLO" would be written as "HLO EL."

substitution cipher
every occurrence of a given letter is replaced systematically by another letter

transposition cipher
the ordering of the letters in each word is changed in some systematic way

Symmetric Key Encryption

In order to decipher these messages, the receiver would have to know the secret cipher that was used to encrypt the plain text. This is called **symmetric key encryption** or **secret key encryption**. In symmetric key encryption, both the sender and the receiver use the same key to encrypt and decrypt the message. How do the sender and the receiver have the same key? They have to send it over some communication media or exchange the key in person. Symmetric key encryption was used extensively throughout World War II and is still a part of Internet encryption.

The possibilities for simple substitution and transposition ciphers are endless, but they all suffer from common flaws. First, in the digital age, computers are so powerful and fast that these ancient means of encryption can be broken quickly. Second, symmetric key encryption requires that both parties share the same key. In order to share the same key, they must send the key over a presumably *insecure* medium where it could be stolen and used to decipher messages. If the secret key is lost or stolen, the entire encryption system fails. Third, in commercial use, where we are not all part of the same team, you would need a secret key for each of the parties with whom you transacted, that is, one key for the bank, another for the department store, and another for the government. In a large population of users, this could result in as many as n(n–1) keys. In a population of millions of Internet users, thousands of millions of keys would be needed to accommodate all e-commerce customers (estimated at about 120 million in the United States). Potentially, 120 million[2] different keys would be needed. Clearly this situation would be too unwieldy to work in practice.

Modern encryption systems are digital. The ciphers or keys used to transform plain text into cipher text are digital strings. Computers store text or other data as binary strings composed of 0s and 1s. For instance, the binary representation of the capital letter "A" in ASCII computer code is accomplished with eight binary digits (bits): 01000001. One way in which digital strings can be transformed into cipher text is by multiplying each letter by another binary number, say, an eight-bit key number 0101 0101. If we multiplied every digital character in our text messages by this eight-bit key, sent the encrypted message to a friend along with the secret eight-bit key, the friend could decode the message easily.

The strength of modern security protection is measured in terms of the length of the binary key used to encrypt the data. In the preceding example, the eight-bit key is easily deciphered because there are only 2^8 or 256 possibilities. If the intruder knows you are using an eight-bit key, then he or she could decode the message in a few seconds using a modern desktop PC just by using the brute force method of checking each of the 256 possible keys. For this reason, modern digital encryption systems use keys with 56, 128, 256, or 512 binary digits. With encryption keys of 512 digits, there are 2,512 possibilities to check out. It is estimated that all the computers in the world would need to work for 10 years before stumbling upon the answer.

The **Data Encryption Standard (DES)** was developed by the National Security Agency (NSA) and IBM in the 1950s. DES uses a 56-bit encryption key. To cope with

[1]For instance: DESX and RDES with 168-bit keys; the RC Series: RC2, RC4, and RC5 with keys up to 2,048 bits; and the IDEA algorithm, the basis of PGP, e-mail public key encryption software described later in this chapter, which uses 128-bit keys.

symmetric key encryption (secret key encryption)
both the sender and the receiver use the same key to encrypt and decrypt the message

Data Encryption Standard (DES)
developed by the National Security Agency (NSA) and IBM. Uses a 56-bit encryption key

much faster computers, it has been improved by *Triple DES*—essentially encrypting the message three times each with a separate key. Today, the most widely used symmetric key encryption algorithm is **Advanced Encryption Standard (AES)**, which offers key sizes of 128, 192, and 256 bits. There are also many other symmetric key systems with keys up to 2,048 bits.[1]

Public Key Encryption

In 1976, a new way of encrypting messages called **public key cryptography** was invented by Whitfield Diffie and Martin Hellman. Public key cryptography solves the problem of exchanging keys. In this method, two mathematically related digital keys are used: a public key and a private key. The private key is kept secret by the owner, and the public key is widely disseminated. Both keys can be used to encrypt and decrypt a message. However, once the keys are used to encrypt a message, that same key cannot be used to unencrypt the message. The mathematical algorithms used to produce the keys are *one-way functions*. A one-way irreversible mathematical function is one in which, once the algorithm is applied, the input cannot be subsequently derived from the output. Most food recipes are like this. For instance, it is easy to make scrambled eggs, but impossible to retrieve whole eggs from the scrambled eggs. Public key cryptography is based on the idea of irreversible mathematical functions. The keys are sufficiently long (128-, 256-, and 512-bit keys) that it would take enormous computing power to derive one key from the other using the largest and fastest computers available. **Figure 5.10** illustrates a simple use of public key cryptography and takes you through the important steps in using public and private keys.

Public Key Encryption Using Digital Signatures and Hash Digests

In public key encryption, some elements of security are missing. Although we can be quite sure the message was not understood or read by a third party (message confidentiality), there is no guarantee the sender really is the sender; that is, there is no authentication of the sender. This means the sender could deny ever sending the message (repudiation). And there is no assurance the message was not altered somehow in transit. For example, the message "Buy Cisco @ $25" could have been accidentally or intentionally altered to read "Sell Cisco @ $25." This suggests a potential lack of integrity in the system.

A more sophisticated use of public key cryptography can achieve authentication, nonrepudiation, and integrity. **Figure 5.11** on page 288 illustrates this more powerful approach.

To check the confidentiality of a message and ensure it has not been altered in transit, a hash function is used first to create a digest of the message. A **hash function** is an algorithm that produces a fixed-length number called a *hash* or *message digest*. A hash function can be simple, and count the number of digital 1s in a message, or it can be more complex, and produce a 128-bit number that reflects the number of 0s and 1s, the number of 00s, 11s, and so on. Standard hash functions are available (MD4 and MD5 produce 128- and 160-bit hashes) (Stein, 1998). These more complex hash functions produce hashes or hash results that are unique to every message. The results of applying the hash function are sent by the sender to the recipient.

Advanced Encryption Standard (AES)
The most widely used symmetric key encryption algorithm. Offers 128-, 192-, and 256-bit keys.

public key cryptography
two mathematically related digital keys are used: a public key and a private key. The private key is kept secret by the owner, and the public key is widely disseminated. Both keys can be used to encrypt and decrypt a message. However, once the keys are used to encrypt a message, that same key cannot be used to unencrypt the message

hash function
an algorithm that produces a fixed-length number called a hash or message digest

FIGURE 5.10 PUBLIC KEY CRYPTOGRAPHY—A SIMPLE CASE

STEP	DESCRIPTION
1. The sender creates a digital message.	The message could be a document, spreadsheet, or any digital object.
2. The sender obtains the recipient's public key from a public directory and applies it to the message.	Public keys are distributed widely and can be obtained from recipients directly.
3. Application of the recipient's key produces an encrypted ciphertext message.	Once encrypted using the public key, the message cannot be reverse-engineered or unencrypted using the same public key. The process is irreversible.
4. The encrypted message is sent over the Internet.	The encrypted message is broken into packets and sent through several different pathways, making interception of the entire message difficult (but not impossible).
5. The recipient uses his/her private key to decrypt the message.	The only person who can decrypt the message is the person who has possession of the recipient's private key. Hopefully, this is the legitimate recipient.

In the simplest use of public key cryptography, the sender encrypts a message using the recipient's public key, and then sends it over the Internet. The only person who can decrypt this message is the recipient, using his or her private key. However, this simple case does not ensure confidentiality or an authentic message.

Upon receipt, the recipient applies the hash function to the received message and checks to verify the same result is produced. If so, the message has not been altered. The sender then encrypts both the hash result and the original message using the recipient's public key (as in Figure 5.10), producing a single block of cipher text.

FIGURE 5.11	PUBLIC KEY CRYPTOGRAPHY WITH DIGITAL SIGNATURES

STEP	DESCRIPTION
1. The sender creates an original message.	The message could be any digital file.
2. The sender applies a hash function, producing a 128-bit hash result.	Hash functions create a unique digest of the message based on the message contents.
3. The sender encrypts the message and hash result using recipient's public key.	This irreversible process creates a cipher text that can be read only by the recipient using his or her private key.
4. The sender encrypts the result, again using his or her private key.	The sender's private key is a digital signature. There is only one person who could create this digital mark.
5. The result of this double encryption is sent over the Internet.	The message traverses the Internet as a series of independent packets.
6. The receiver uses the sender's public key to authenticate the message.	Only one person could send this message, namely, the sender.
7. The receiver uses his or her private key to decrypt the hash function and the original message. The receiver checks to ensure the original message and the hash function results conform to one another.	The hash function is used here to check the original message. This ensures the message was not changed in transit.

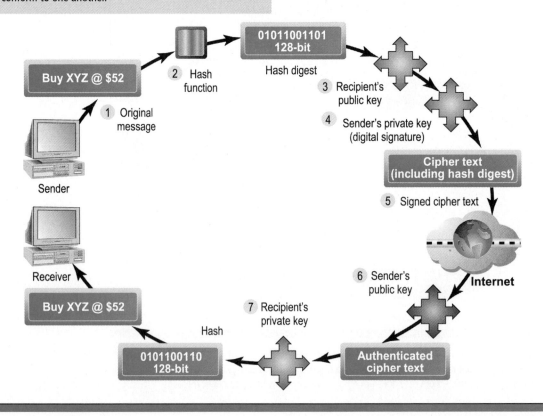

A more realistic use of public key cryptography uses hash functions and digital signatures to both ensure the confidentiality of the message and authenticate the sender. The only person who could have sent the above message is the owner or the sender using his/her private key. This authenticates the message. The hash function ensures the message was not altered in transit. As before, the only person who can decipher the message is the recipient, using his/her private key.

One more step is required. To ensure the authenticity of the message and to ensure nonrepudiation, the sender encrypts the entire block of cipher text one more time using the sender's private key. This produces a **digital signature** (also called an *e-signature*) or "signed" cipher text that can be sent over the Internet.

A digital signature is a close parallel to a handwritten signature. Like a handwritten signature, a digital signature is unique—only one person presumably possesses the private key. When used with a hash function, the digital signature is even more unique than a handwritten signature. In addition to being exclusive to a particular individual, when used to sign a hashed document, the digital signature is also unique to the document, and changes for every document.

The recipient of this signed cipher text first uses the sender's public key to authenticate the message. Once authenticated, the recipient uses his or her private key to obtain the hash result and original message. As a final step, the recipient applies the same hash function to the original text, and compares the result with the result sent by the sender. If the results are the same, the recipient now knows the message has not been changed during transmission. The message has integrity.

Early digital signature programs required the user to have a digital certificate, and were far too difficult for an individual to use. Newer programs from several small companies are Internet-based and do not require users to install software, or understand digital certificate technology. DocuSign, EchoSign, and Sertifi are companies offering online digital signatures. Fidelity National Financial and other insurance, finance, and surety companies are beginning to permit customers to electronically sign documents (although not mortgage documents yet) (Buckman, 2007).

digital signature (e-signature)
"signed" cipher text that can be sent over the Internet

Digital Envelopes

Public key encryption is computationally slow. If one used 128- or 256-bit keys to encode large documents—such as this chapter or the entire book—significant declines in transmission speeds and increases in processing time would occur. Symmetric key encryption is computationally faster, but as we pointed out previously, it has a weakness—namely, the symmetric key must be sent to the recipient over insecure transmission lines. One solution is to use the more efficient symmetric encryption and decryption for large documents, but public key encryption to encrypt and send the symmetric key. This technique is called using a **digital envelope**. See **Figure 5.12** for an illustration of how a digital envelope works.

In Figure 5.12, a diplomatic document is encrypted using a symmetric key. The symmetric key—which the recipient will require to decrypt the document—is itself encrypted, using the recipient's public key. So we have a "key within a key" (a *digital envelope*). The encrypted report and the digital envelope are sent across the Web. The recipient first uses his/her private key to decrypt the symmetric key, and then the recipient uses the symmetric key to decrypt the report. This method saves time because both encryption and decryption are faster with symmetric keys.

digital envelope
a technique that uses symmetric encryption for large documents, but public key encryption to encrypt and send the symmetric key

Digital Certificates and Public Key Infrastructure (PKI)

There are still some deficiencies in the message security regime described previously. How do we know that people and institutions are who they claim to be?

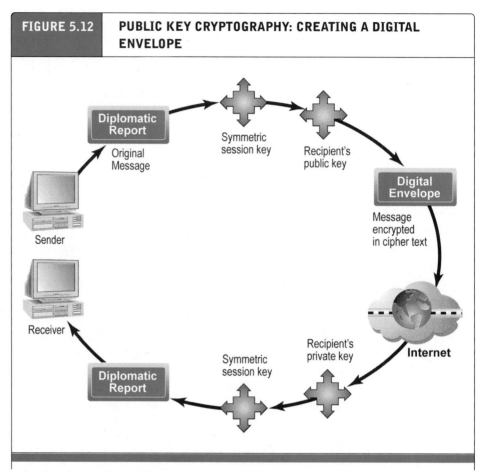

| FIGURE 5.12 | PUBLIC KEY CRYPTOGRAPHY: CREATING A DIGITAL ENVELOPE |

A digital envelope can be created to transmit a symmetric key that will permit the recipient to decrypt the message and be assured the message was not intercepted in transit.

digital certificate

a digital document issued by a certification authority that contains the name of the subject or company, the subject's public key, a digital certificate serial number, an expiration date, an issuance date, the digital signature of the certification authority, and other identifying information

certification authority (CA)

a trusted third party that issues digital certificates

Anyone can make up a private and public key combination and claim to be someone they are not. Before you place an order with an online merchant such as Amazon, you want to be sure it really is Amazon.com you have on the screen and not a spoofer masquerading as Amazon. In the physical world, if someone asks who you are and you show a social security number, they may well ask to see a picture ID or a second form of certifiable or acceptable identification. If they really doubt who you are, they may ask for references to other authorities and actually interview these other authorities. Similarly, in the digital world, we need a way to know who people and institutions really are.

Digital certificates, and the supporting public key infrastructure, are an attempt to solve this problem of digital identity. A **digital certificate** is a digital document issued by a trusted third-party institution known as a **certification authority (CA)** that contains the name of the subject or company, the subject's public key, a digital certificate serial number, an expiration date, an issuance date, the digital signature of

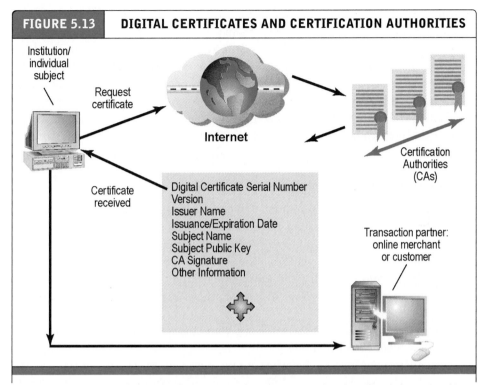

| FIGURE 5.13 | DIGITAL CERTIFICATES AND CERTIFICATION AUTHORITIES |

The PKI includes certification authorities that issue, verify, and guarantee digital certificates that are used in e-commerce to assure the identity of transaction partners.

the certification authority (the name of the CA encrypted using the CA's private key), and other identifying information (see **Figure 5.13**).

In the United States, private corporations such as VeriSign and government agencies such as the U.S. Postal Service act as CAs. In fact, a hierarchy of CAs is emerging with less well-known CAs being certified by larger and better-known CAs, creating a community of mutually verifying institutions. **Public key infrastructure (PKI)** refers to the CAs and digital certificate procedures that are accepted by all parties.

To create a digital certificate, the user generates a public/private key pair and sends a request for certification to a CA along with the user's public key. The CA verifies the information (how this is accomplished differs from CA to CA). The CA issues a certificate containing the user's public key and other related information. Finally, the CA creates a message digest from the certificate itself (just like a hash digest) and signs it with the CA's private key. This signed digest is called the *signed certificate*. We end up with a totally unique cipher text document—there can be only one signed certificate like this in the world.

There are several ways the certificates are used in commerce. Before initiating a transaction, the customer can request the signed digital certificate of the merchant and decrypt it using the merchant's public key to obtain both the message digest and the certificate as issued. If the message digest matches the certificate, then the merchant and the public key are authenticated. The merchant may in return request certification of the user, in which case the user would send the merchant his or her

public key infrastructure (PKI)
CAs and digital certificate procedures that are accepted by all parties

individual certificate. There are many types of certificates: personal, institutional, Web server, software publisher, and CAs themselves.

Pretty Good Privacy (PGP)

a widely used e-mail public key encryption software program

You can easily obtain a public and private key for personal, noncommercial use at the International PGP Home Page Web site, Pgpi.org. **Pretty Good Privacy (PGP)** was invented in 1991 by Phil Zimmerman, and has become one of the most widely used e-mail public key encryption software tools in the world. Using PGP software installed on your computer, you can compress and encrypt your messages as well as authenticate both yourself and the recipient. The *Insight on Society* story, *In Pursuit of E-mail Security*, describes additional efforts to ensure e-mail security.

Limitations to Encryption Solutions

PKI is a powerful technological solution to security issues, but it has many limitations. PKI applies mainly to protecting messages in transit on the Internet and is not effective against insiders—employees—who have legitimate access to corporate systems including customer information. Most e-commerce sites do not store customer information in encrypted form. Other limitations are apparent. For one, how is your private key to be protected? Most private keys will be stored on insecure desktop or laptop computers.

There is no guarantee the person using your computer—and your private key— is really you. Under many digital signature laws (such as those in Utah and Washington), you are responsible for whatever your private key does even if you were not the person using the key. This is very different from mail-order or telephone order credit card rules, where you have a right to dispute the credit card charge. Second, there is no guarantee the verifying computer of the merchant is secure. Third, CAs are self-selected organizations seeking to gain access to the business of authorization. They may not be authorities on the corporations or individuals they certify. For instance, how can a CA know about all the corporations within an industry to determine who is or is not legitimate? A related question concerns the method used by the CA to identify the certificate holder. Was this an e-mail transaction verified only by claims of applicants who filled out an online form? For instance, VeriSign acknowledged in one case that it had mistakenly issued two digital certificates to someone fraudulently claiming to represent Microsoft. Digital certificates have been hijacked by hackers, tricking consumers into giving up personal information. Last, what are the policies for revoking or renewing certificates? The expected life of a digital certificate or private key is a function of the frequency of use and the vulnerability of systems that use the certificate. Yet most CAs have no policy or just an annual policy for re-issuing certificates (Ellison and Schneier, 2000).

SECURING CHANNELS OF COMMUNICATION

The concepts of public key encryption are used routinely for securing channels of communication.

Secure Sockets Layer (SSL)

The most common form of securing channels is through the *Secure Sockets Layer (SSL)* of TCP/IP (described briefly in Chapter 3). When you receive a message from a server

INSIGHT ON SOCIETY

IN PURSUIT OF E-MAIL SECURITY

You just sent a poisonous e-mail to a friend about a colleague at work with whom you compete for position and recognition. Now you wish you could expunge that e-mail because you now remember that the two share several common friends and you are afraid the e-mail will make the rounds of friends of friends. You just wish you could say "kablooey" and away it would go.

You are in New York and you would like to use e-mail to negotiate a deal with another company in London but are afraid they will forward your offer to competitors seeking the same deal and seek a higher price than you are willing to start with. You are looking for a private deal, not a public conversation.

You sent an e-mail to a distributor telling them to stop shipment of a train-car load of parts to a retail dealer that just went bankrupt. If the goods are shipped and received by the retailer, they will be tied up in bankruptcy proceedings as that company's assets. You need undeniable evidence your distributor received the message. If the distributor shipped, then it is liable, not you. What you need is a registered, certified, and return receipt capability like regular postal mail. Good luck!

About 80 billion e-mail messages are generated every business day in the United States, up from 10 billion e-mail messages daily just five years ago. Most e-mail programs offer little if any help in terms of controlling who sees your e-mail, how long it remains live, and who if anyone received it. E-mail is easily denied or altered. In fact, your e-mail theoretically can be seen by anybody, forever, or by no one if they so choose. Therefore, you need to think carefully about what you say, how you say it, and in the end you might want to avoid e-mail altogether. But help is on the way.

There are now a number of free services that allow users to send self-destructing emails, which expire/disappear automatically after a specified time interval. One example is BigString, which recalls or retracts a message after it has been sent, basing on the number of times the message is read, and/or the age of the e-mail message. It also blocks the recipient from copying, forwarding or printing the message. There is also a plug-in being developed to allow those using the services to do so through any e-mail client. Others include Self-destructing-email.com, which works with Web-based e-mail clients and Willselfdestruct.com, which allows the user to create a one-time secure page for the recipient. The message is accessed through a specific url, and then it is deleted. Kicknotes.com's messages self-destruct based on times read and age; Stealthmessage.com stores encrypted messages anonymously (the user can set the self-destruct options, and there is no forwarding of messages); Sdmessage.com (Self Destruct Message) is web-based, and messages self-destruct 60 seconds after they are viewed.

If you've ever wondered why e-mail can't be "registered" like postal mail, a solution is now provided by RPost.com as an add-on to Microsoft Outlook. For 59 cents per e-mail message, RPost alerts the sender that an e-mail was received and opened. It can also verify that the content of the e-mail was not altered.

According to Microsoft's William Kennedy, general manager of Office communications services, Microsoft will be adding many of these features to its Outlook 2007 application over time, such as electronic postmarks (the mail was processed and delivered), non-forwarding mail, and non-printing mail.

But the ability to eliminate, delete, destroy, or alter e-mail runs flat up against the drift of

(continued)

modern corporate law. E-mail is increasingly playing a role similar to postal mail and contracts in courts. It is used as evidence of action, intention, and consequence. Corporate e-mail messages have achieved the same status as other commonly used business documents. A number of new laws, such as the Sarbanes-Oxley Act of 2002 (also known as SOX, or the Public Company Accounting Reform and Investor Protection Act of 2002), requires all public firms to develop a reasonable policy of business record retention, including e-mail and instant messages. The retention period must be "reasonable" and clearly set in the policy. A good retention policy cannot be selective—all documents need to be saved. As a result, most public firms are storing all e-mail and IMs in perpetuity. Under SOX, if you are convicted of changing, altering, or deleting business e-mail that is needed for a judicial process, you can be sentenced for up to 20 years in jail. In the current environment, therefore, you will need to be careful to balance user control over e-mail with corporate responsibilities for record retention.

■■■ SOURCES: "Unintentional Employee Misuse Top Driver for Enterprise Email Risk," Messagegate.com, July 9, 2008; "Office Space: Career Couch. The Risk Is All Yours in Office E-Mail," by Matt Villano, *New York Times*, August 31, 2007; "Key Issues for Electronic Discovery," by Whit Andrews, EMC White Paper, August 20, 2007; "Don't Let Your E-Evidence Get Trashed," by Jerold S. Solovy and Robert L. Byman, *National Law Journal*, June 11, 2007; "10 Free Services to Send Self-destructing Emails which Expire/Disappear Automatically after a Specified Time Interval, " Tech.blog.com July 25, 2007; "Sarbanes-Oxley Has Major Impact on Electronic Evidence," by Michele Lange, *National Law Journal*, January 2, 2007.

secure negotiated session

a client-server session in which the URL of the requested document, along with the contents, contents of forms, and the cookies exchanged, are encrypted

session key

a unique symmetric encryption key chosen for a single secure session

on the Web with which you will be communicating through a secure channel, this means you will be using SSL to establish a secure negotiated session. (Notice that the URL changes from HTTP to HTTPS.) A **secure negotiated session** is a client-server session in which the URL of the requested document, along with the contents, contents of forms, and the cookies exchanged, are encrypted (see **Figure 5.14**). For instance, your credit card number that you entered into a form would be encrypted. Through a series of handshakes and communications, the browser and the server establish one another's identity by exchanging digital certificates, decide on the strongest shared form of encryption, and then proceed to communicate using an agreed-upon session key. A **session key** is a unique symmetric encryption key chosen just for this single secure session. Once used, it is gone forever. Figure 5.14 shows how this works.

In practice, most private individuals do not have a digital certificate. In this case, the merchant server will not request a certificate, but the client browser will request the merchant certificate once a secure session is called for by the server.

The SSL protocol provides data encryption, server authentication, optional client authentication, and message integrity for TCP/IP connections. SSL is available in 40-bit and 128-bit levels, depending on what version of browser you are using. The strongest shared encryption is always chosen.

SSL was designed to address the threat of authenticity by allowing users to verify another user's identity or the identity of a server. It also protects the integrity of the messages exchanged. However, once the merchant receives the encrypted credit and order information, that information is typically stored in unencrypted format on the merchant's servers.

While the SSL protocol provides secure transactions between merchant and consumer, it only guarantees server-side authentication. Client authentication is optional.

FIGURE 5.14 | SECURE NEGOTIATED SESSIONS USING SSL

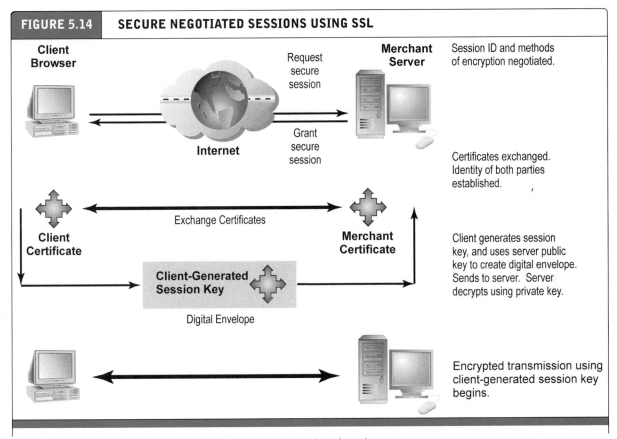

Client Browser

Request secure session

Grant secure session

Internet

Merchant Server

Session ID and methods of encryption negotiated.

Certificates exchanged. Identity of both parties established.

Exchange Certificates

Client Certificate

Merchant Certificate

Client-Generated Session Key

Digital Envelope

Client generates session key, and uses server public key to create digital envelope. Sends to server. Server decrypts using private key.

Encrypted transmission using client-generated session key begins.

Certificates play a key role in using SSL to establish a secure communications channel.

In addition, SSL cannot provide irrefutability—consumers can order goods or download information products, and then claim the transaction never occurred. Other protocols for protecting financial transactions such as *SET (Secure Electronic Transaction Protocol)* have emerged that require all parties to a transaction to use digital certificates.

Secure Hypertext Transfer Protocol (S-HTTP)

A competing method is called **Secure Hypertext Transfer Protocol (S-HTTP)**. S-HTTP is a secure message-oriented communications protocol designed for use in conjunction with HTTP. It is designed to coexist with HTTP and to be easily integrated with HTTP applications. Whereas SSL is designed to establish a secure connection between two computers, S-HTTP is designed to send individual messages securely. Not all browsers and not all Web sites support S-HTTP. You know you are dealing with a supporting site when the URL starts with "SHTTP." The use of this as part of an anchor tag indicates that the target server is S-HTTP capable. Using S-HTTP, any message may be signed, authenticated, encrypted, or any combination of these. Basically, S-HTTP attempts to make HTTP more secure.

Secure Hypertext Transfer Protocol (S-HTTP)

a secure message-oriented communications protocol designed for use in conjunction with HTTP. Cannot be used to secure non-HTTP messages

Virtual Private Networks (VPNs)

virtual private network (VPN)

allows remote users to securely access internal networks via the Internet, using the Point-to-Point Tunneling Protocol (PPTP)

A **virtual private network (VPN)** allows remote users to securely access internal networks via the Internet, using the **Point-to-Point Tunneling Protocol (PPTP)**. PPTP is an encoding mechanism that allows one local network to connect to another using the Internet as the conduit. A remote user can dial into a local ISP, and PPTP makes the connection from the ISP to the corporate network as if the user had dialed into the corporate network directly. The process of connecting one protocol (PPTP) through another (IP) is called *tunneling,* because PPTP creates a private connection by adding an invisible wrapper around a message to hide its content. As the message travels through the Internet between the ISP and the corporate network, it is shielded from prying eyes by PPTP's encrypted wrapper.

Point-to-Point Tunneling Protocol (PPTP)

an encoding mechanism that allows one local network to connect to another using the Internet as the conduit

A VPN is "virtual" in the sense that it appears to users as a dedicated secure line when in fact it is a temporary secure line. The primary use of VPNs is to establish secure communications among business partners—larger suppliers or customers. A dedicated connection to a business partner can be very expensive. Using the Internet and PPTP as the connection method significantly reduces the cost of secure communications.

PROTECTING NETWORKS

Once you have protected communications as well as possible, the next set of tools to consider are those that can protect your networks, as well as the servers and clients on those networks.

Firewalls

Firewalls and proxy servers are intended to build a wall around your network and the attached servers and clients, just like physical-world firewalls protect you from fires for a limited period of time. Firewalls and proxy servers share some similar functions, but they are quite different.

firewall

refers to either hardware or software that filters communication packets and prevents some packets from entering the network based on a security policy

A **firewall** refers to either hardware or software that filters communication packets and prevents some packets from entering the network based on a security policy. The firewall controls traffic to and from servers and clients, forbidding communications from untrustworthy sources, and allowing other communications from trusted sources to proceed. Every message that is to be sent or received from the network is processed by the firewall, which determines if the message meets security guidelines established by the business. If it does, it is permitted to be distributed, and if it doesn't, the message is blocked. Firewalls can filter traffic based on packet attributes such as source IP address, destination port or IP address, type of service (such as WWW or HTTP), the domain name of the source, and many other dimensions. Most hardware firewalls that protect local area networks connected to the Internet have default settings that require little if any administrator intervention and accomplish simple but effective rules that deny incoming packets from a connection that does not originate from an internal request—the firewall only allows connections from servers that you requested service from. A common default setting on hardware firewalls (DSL and cable modem routers) simply ignores efforts to communicate with TCP port 445, the most commonly attacked port. The increasing use of firewalls by home and business Internet users has greatly reduced the effectiveness of attacks, and forced hackers to focus more on e-mail attachments to distribute worms and viruses.

There are two major methods firewalls use to validate traffic: packet filters and application gateways. *Packet filters* examine data packets to determine whether they are destined for a prohibited port or originate from a prohibited IP address (as specified by the security administrator). The filter specifically looks at the source and destination information, as well as the port and packet type, when determining whether the information may be transmitted. One downside of the packet filtering method is that it is susceptible to spoofing, since authentication is not one of its roles.

Application gateways are a type of firewall that filters communications based on the application being requested, rather than the source or destination of the message. Such firewalls also process requests at the application level, farther away from the client computer than packet filters. By providing a central filtering point, application gateways provide greater security than packet filters, but can compromise system performance.

Proxy servers (proxies) are software servers (usually located on a dedicated computer) that handle all communications originating from or being sent to the Internet, acting as a spokesperson or bodyguard for the organization. Proxies act primarily to limit access of internal clients to external Internet servers, although some proxy servers act as firewalls as well. Proxy servers are sometimes called *dual home systems* because they have two network interfaces. To internal computers, a proxy server is known as the *gateway*, while to external computers it is known as a *mail server* or *numeric address*.

> **proxy server (proxy)**
> software server that handles all communications originating from or being sent to the Internet, acting as a spokesperson or bodyguard for the organization

When a user on an internal network requests a Web page, the request is routed first to the proxy server. The proxy server validates the user and the nature of the request, and then sends the request onto the Internet. A Web page sent by an external Internet server first passes to the proxy server. If acceptable, the Web page passes onto the internal network Web server and then to the client desktop. By prohibiting users from communicating directly with the Internet, companies can restrict access to certain types of sites, such as pornographic, auction, or stock-trading sites. Proxy servers also improve Web performance by storing frequently requested Web pages locally, reducing upload times, and hiding the internal network's address, thus making it more difficult for hackers to monitor. **Figure 5.15** illustrates how firewalls and proxy servers protect a local area network from Internet intruders and prevent internal clients from reaching prohibited Web servers.

PROTECTING SERVERS AND CLIENTS

Operating system features and anti-virus software can help further protect servers and clients from certain types of attacks.

Operating System Security Enhancements

The most obvious way to protect servers and clients is to take advantage of Microsoft's and Apple's automatic computer security upgrades. Windows Server 2003 and the Windows XP and Windows Vista client operating systems are continuously being upgraded by Microsoft to patch vulnerabilities discovered by hackers. These patches are autonomic; that is, when using Windows XP or Vista on the Internet, you are

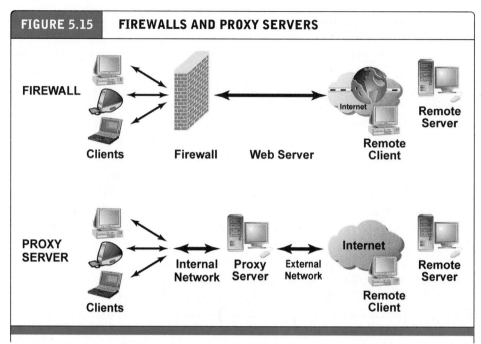

| FIGURE 5.15 | **FIREWALLS AND PROXY SERVERS** |

The primary function of a firewall is to deny access by remote client computers to local computers. The primary purpose of a proxy server is to provide controlled access from local computers to remote computers.

prompted and informed that operating system enhancements are available. Users can easily download these security patches for free. The most common known worms and viruses can be prevented by simply keeping your server and client operating systems and applications up to date. Application vulnerabilities are also fixed in the same manner. For instance, both the Mozilla browser and Internet Explorer are updated automatically with little user intervention.

Anti-Virus Software

The easiest and least expensive way to prevent threats to system integrity is to install anti-virus software. Programs by McAfee, Symantec (Norton AntiVirus), and many others provide inexpensive tools to identify and eradicate the most common types of malicious code as they enter a computer, as well as destroy those already lurking on a hard drive. Anti-virus programs can be set up so that e-mail attachments are inspected prior to you clicking on them, and the attachments are eliminated if they contain a known virus or worm. It is not enough, however, to simply install the software once. Since new viruses are developed and released every day, daily routine updates are needed in order to prevent new threats from being loaded. Some premium-level anti-virus software is updated hourly.

Anti-virus suite packages and stand-alone programs are available to eliminate intruders such as bot programs, adware, and other security risks. Such programs work much like anti-virus software in that they look for recognized hacker tools or signature actions of known intruders. Designed to trigger an alarm when such an action is noted, these systems must be monitored by staff members or intrusion detection services in order to work properly.

5.4 MANAGEMENT POLICIES, BUSINESS PROCEDURES, AND PUBLIC LAWS

U.S. business firms and government agencies spend about 10% of their information technology budgets on security hardware, software, and services. That will add up to about $100 billion in 2008. This expenditure explains why attacks against organizational computer systems at business firms and government agencies are, in general, modestly down, and dollar losses are also down since 2000. The exception is attacks against Web sites, and the financial losses caused by unauthorized access to information and theft of proprietary information, which increased in 2007 over previous years. Attacks against Web sites and cyberattacks against individual clients, and individual financial records and identities that are Web-based, are much higher, and the cost of these attacks has grown.

Most CEOs and CIOs of existing e-commerce operations believe that technology is not the sole answer to managing the risk of e-commerce. The technology provides a foundation, but in the absence of intelligent management policies, even the best technology can be easily defeated. Public laws and active enforcement of cybercrime statutes are also required to both raise the costs of illegal behavior on the Internet and guard against corporate abuse of information. Let's consider briefly the development of management policy.

A SECURITY PLAN: MANAGEMENT POLICIES

In order to minimize security threats, e-commerce firms must develop a coherent corporate policy that takes into account the nature of the risks, the information assets that need protecting, and the procedures and technologies required to address the risk, as well as implementation and auditing mechanisms. **Figure 5.16** illustrates the key steps in developing a solid security plan.

A security plan begins with **risk assessment**—an assessment of the risks and points of vulnerability. The first step is to inventory the information and knowledge assets of the e-commerce site and company. What information is at risk? Is it customer information, proprietary designs, business activities, secret processes, or other internal information, such as price schedules, executive compensation, or payroll? For each type of information asset, try to estimate the dollar value to the firm if this information were compromised, and then multiply that amount by the probability of the loss occurring. Once you have done so, rank order the results. You now have a list of information assets prioritized by their value to the firm.

Based on your quantified list of risks, you can start to develop a **security policy**—a set of statements prioritizing the information risks, identifying

risk assessment
an assessment of the risks and points of vulnerability

security policy
a set of statements prioritizing the information risks, identifying acceptable risk targets, and identifying the mechanisms for achieving these targets

| FIGURE 5.16 | DEVELOPING AN E-COMMERCE SECURITY PLAN |

There are five steps involved in building an e-commerce security plan.

acceptable risk targets, and identifying the mechanisms for achieving these targets. You will obviously want to start with the information assets that you determined to be the highest priority in your risk assessment. Who generates and controls this information in the firm? What existing security policies are in place to protect the information? What enhancements can you recommend to improve security of these most valuable assets? What level of risk are you willing to accept for each of these assets? Are you willing, for instance, to lose customer credit data once every 10 years? Or will you pursue a 100-year hurricane strategy by building a security edifice for credit card data that can withstand the once-in-100-year disaster? You will need to estimate how much it will cost to achieve this level of acceptable risk. Remember, total and complete security may require extraordinary financial resources. By answering these questions, you will have the beginnings of a security policy.

implementation plan
the action steps you will take to achieve the security plan goals

Next consider an **implementation plan**—the steps you will take to achieve the security plan goals. Specifically, you must determine how you will translate the levels of acceptable risk into a set of tools, technologies, policies, and procedures. What new technologies will you deploy to achieve the goals, and what new employee procedures will be needed?

To implement your plan, you will need an organizational unit in charge of security, and a security officer—someone who is in charge of security on a daily basis. For a small e-commerce site, the security officer will likely be the person in charge of Internet services or the site manager, whereas for larger firms, there typically is a dedicated team with a supporting budget. The **security organization** educates and trains users, keeps management aware of security threats and breakdowns, and maintains the tools chosen to implement security.

The security organization typically administers access controls, authentication procedures, and authorization policies. **Access controls** determine which outsiders and insiders can gain legitimate access to your networks. Outsider access controls include firewalls and proxy servers, while insider access controls typically consist of login procedures (usernames, passwords, and access codes).

Authentication procedures include the use of digital signatures, certificates of authority, and PKI. Now that e-signatures have been given the same legal weight as an original pen-and-ink version, companies are in the process of devising ways to test and confirm a signer's identity. Companies frequently have signers type their full name and click on a button indicating their understanding that they have just signed a contract or document.

Biometric devices are used along with digital signatures to verify physical attributes associated with an individual, such as a fingerprint or retina (eye) scan or speech recognition system. (**Biometrics** is the study of measurable biological, or physical, characteristics.) A company could require, for example, that an individual undergo a fingerprint scan before being allowed access to a Web site, or before being allowed to pay for merchandise with a credit card. Biometric devices make it even more difficult for hackers to break into sites or facilities, significantly reducing the opportunity for spoofing.

Authorization policies determine differing levels of access to information assets for differing levels of users. **Authorization management systems** establish where and when a user is permitted to access certain parts of a Web site. Their primary function is to restrict access to private information within a company's Internet infrastructure. Although there are several authorization management products currently available, most operate in the same way: the system encrypts a user session to function like a passkey that follows the user from page to page, allowing access only to those areas that the user is permitted to enter, based on information set at the system database. By establishing entry rules up front for each user, the authorization management system knows who is permitted to go where at all times.

The last step in developing an e-commerce security plan is performing a security audit. A **security audit** involves the routine review of access logs (identifying how outsiders are using the site as well as how insiders are accessing the site's assets). A monthly report should be produced that establishes the routine and non-routine accesses to the systems and identifies unusual patterns of activities. As previously noted, tiger teams are often used by large corporate sites to evaluate the strength of existing security procedures. Many small firms have sprung up in the last five years to provide these services to large corporate sites.

The *Insight on Technology* story, *Securing Your Information: Cleversafe Hippie Storage*, discusses a new method for securing information using the Internet.

security organization
educates and trains users, keeps management aware of security threats and breakdowns, and maintains the tools chosen to implement security

access controls
determine who can gain legitimate access to a network

authentication procedures
include the use of digital signatures, certificates of authority, and public key infrastructure

biometrics
the study of measurable biological or physical characteristics

authorization policies
determine differing levels of access to information assets for differing levels of users

authorization management system
establishes where and when a user is permitted to access certain parts of a Web site

security audit
involves the routine review of access logs (identifying how outsiders are using the site as well as how insiders are accessing the site's assets)

INSIGHT ON TECHNOLOGY

SECURING YOUR INFORMATION: CLEVERSAFE HIPPIE STORAGE

Normally when you think of keeping your computer data secure you think about making multiple copies of the information and putting them on separate storage devices, such as backing up your desktop files to a central server, and/or or copying them to a USB jump drive and taking it home at night. Three copies are generally considered the corporate norm for securing data in a distributed file system method known as LOCKSS: lots of copies keeps stuff safe. This is the method offered by Microsoft and most data security companies to e-commerce firms. But there are just a few problems with this brute force method.

LOCKSS increases the number of servers and storage devices by at least 200% just to store files. This makes hard disk and server manufacturers happy but ends up being very costly to firms. In a world that's swimming in digital information, this does not seem like an intelligent choice. For instance, Google stores so much information that it was forced to create one of the world's largest data storage facilities (68,000 square feet of disk drives and PCs) in Dalles, Oregon, on the banks of the Columbia River—one of America's largest—so it could take advantage of cheap Columbia River hydroelectric power and the cooling waters of the river to keep its PCs humming. With the amount of digital information now exceeding 5 exabytes (roughly 37,000 Libraries of Congress) and doubling every three years, it is conceivable that at some point there won't be enough electricity on earth to make three copies of our really important files.

Also, traditional methods are not very secure: if one storage system is hacked, or if one laptop containing a copy is misplaced, you lose all security. Ask TJMaxx, which lost control of

over 47 million customer credit card records because one storage system was hacked. Their files were all backed up with multiple copies, some buried inside mountains, but one server was compromised. Moreover, communicating the data to remote storage locations increases the risk of interception.

Cleversafe, an open source company located at the Illinois Institute of Technology, is developing a different system. Whereas Google aims to organize all the world's information, Cleversafe wants to store all the world's information. In this method—variously called hippie storage or grid storage—an algorithm known as an information dispersal algorithm is used to slice the information into pieces, encrypt the pieces, and distribute them to different servers across the Internet. The algorithm adds redundancy, error checking, and encryption as it moves through the data file. The idea is similar to the SETI@Home project, a shared computing system that allows individual PC users to contribute their idle computer time to create a distributed computer project that looks for meaning in signals from space.

Based on a paper by computer scientist Adi Shamir ("How to Share a Secret"), the original data can be reconstructed from a majority of the slices. In most examples of this method, the data is distributed to 11 interconnected servers on the Internet, and can be reconstructed from any four of these servers. Depending on your needs and risks, you can determine how many dispersed servers to use and how many are needed to reconstruct your data. This is referred to as a computing grid: an interconnected set of computers that share the processing load across all computers on the grid. Losing anywhere from one to six of the servers to fire, flood, hacking or

(continued)

another problem, and your data is still available from the four remaining servers. If hackers break into one or two servers, or three or four, not a problem: they would need to crack into more to reconstruct your data. The overhead cost is a fraction of the LOCKSS brute force strategy. The largest cost reduction comes from eliminating separate copies for backups, archives, or disaster recovery. Compared with ratios of 5-to-1 or 6-to-1 of "extra" versus original data in copy-based storage environments, Cleversafe requires ratios of 1.3-to-1 or less.

In March 2008, Cleversafe launched its first commercial dispersed storage product. The product divides digital content into slices using information dispersal algorithms and disperses the slices to multiple storage nodes on a dispersed storage network. A typical configuration of equipment that includes 24 terabytes of raw storage capacity costs $127,000. In August 2008, Cleversafe announced a partnership with 5 key partners, a U.S-based consortium of ISPs, hosting companies and telecommunications providers, to deploy the product.

With more than 1 billion PCs connected to the Web, and grid computing becoming more common, it is likely in the near future that confidential data generated in e-commerce will be stored and shared across thousands of Internet computers, in plain site. It's an economical and "green" way of sharing secrets to protect them.

▬ **SOURCES:** "Cleversafe Launches First 'Dispersed' Storage Network," by Chris Preimesberger, Eweek.com, August 21, 2008; "First Steps into the Cloud," by George Crump, Information Week, July 11, 2008; "Cleversafe Announces Availability of First Commercial Products to Create Dispersed Storage Networks," Reuters, February 19, 2008; "Cleversafe's Dispersed Storage," by Robert Scheier, *Computerworld*, August 20, 2007; "Cleversafe Presents Alternative to Google's Triple Storage Philosophy at Linux World," by Alexander Ljungberg, *Linux/Unix/Open Source*, August 10, 2007; "A Move to Secure Data by Scattering the Pieces," by John Markoff, *New York Times*, August 21, 2006; "How to Share a Secret," by Adi Shamir, *Communications of the ACM*, November, 1979.

THE ROLE OF LAWS AND PUBLIC POLICY

The public policy environment today is very different from the early days of e-commerce. The net result is that the Internet is no longer an ungoverned, unsupervised, self-controlled technology juggernaut. Just as with financial markets in the last 70 years, there is a growing awareness that e-commerce markets work only when a powerful institutional set of laws and enforcement mechanisms are in place. These laws help ensure orderly, rational, and fair markets. This growing public policy environment is becoming just as global as e-commerce itself. Despite some spectacular internationally based attacks on U.S. e-commerce sites, the sources and persons involved in major harmful attacks have almost always been uncovered and, where possible, prosecuted.

Voluntary and private efforts have played a very large role in identifying criminal hackers and assisting law enforcement. Since 1995, as e-commerce has grown in significance, national and local law enforcement activities have expanded greatly. New laws have been passed that grant local and national authorities new tools and mechanisms for identifying, tracing, and prosecuting cybercriminals. **Table 5.4** lists the most significant federal e-commerce security legislation.

Following passage of the National Information Infrastructure Protection Act of 1996, which makes DoS attacks and virus distribution federal crimes, the FBI and the Department of Justice established the National Infrastructure Protection Center (NIPC). Now subsumed within the National Cyber Security Division of the Depart-

TABLE 5.4	E-COMMERCE SECURITY LEGISLATION
LEGISLATION	**SIGNIFICANCE**
Computer Fraud and Abuse Act (1986)	Primary federal statute used to combat computer crime
Electronic Communications Privacy Act (1986)	Imposes fines and imprisonment for individuals who access, intercept, or disclose the private e-mail communications of others
National Information Infrastructure Protection Act (1996)	Makes DOS attacks illegal; creates NIPC in the FBI
Cyberspace Electronic Security Act (2000)	Reduces export restrictions
Computer Security Enhancement Act (2000)	Protects federal government systems from hacking
Electronic Signatures in Global and National Commerce Act (the "E-Sign Law") (2000)	Authorizes the use of electronic signatures in legal documents
USA PATRIOT Act (2001)	Authorizes use of computer-based surveillance of suspected terrorists
Homeland Security Act (2002)	Authorized establishment of the Department of Homeland Security, which is assigned responsibility for developing a comprehensive national plan for security the key resources and critical infrastructures of the United States; DHS becomes the central coordinator for all cyberspace security efforts
CAN-SPAM Act (2003)	Although primarily a mechanism for civil and regulatory lawsuits against spammers, the CAN-SPAM Act also creates several new criminal offenses intended to address situations in which the perpetrator has taken steps to hide his or her identity or the source of the spam from recipients, ISPs, or law enforcement agencies. Also contains criminal sanctions for sending sexually explicit e-mail without designating it as such.
U.S. SAFE WEB Act (2006)	Enhances FTC's ability to obtain monetary redress for consumers in cases involving spyware, spam, Internet fraud and deception: also improves FTC's abiltty to gather information and coordinate investigations with foreign counterparts

ment of Homeland Security, this organization's sole mission is to identify and combat threats against the United States' technology and telecommunications infrastructure.

By increasing the punishment for cybercrimes, the U.S. government is attempting to create a deterrent to further hacker actions. And by making such actions federal crimes, the government is able to extradite international hackers and prosecute them within the United States.

After September 11, 2001, Congress passed the USA PATRIOT Act, which broadly expanded law enforcement's investigative and surveillance powers. The act has provisions for monitoring e-mail and Internet use. Currently, this is a temporary act, but there are efforts to make it permanent and to further expand law enforcement's monitoring powers. The Homeland Security Act of 2002 also attempts to fight cyberterrorism and increases the government's ability to compel information disclosure by computer and ISP sources.

Private and Private-Public Cooperation Efforts

The good news is that e-commerce sites are not alone in their battle to achieve security on the Internet. Several organizations—some public and some private— are devoted to tracking down criminal organizations and individuals engaged in attacks against Internet and e-commerce sites. One of the better-known private organizations is the **CERT Coordination Center** (formerly known as the Computer Emergency Response Team) at Carnegie Mellon University. CERT monitors and tracks online criminal activity reported to it by private corporations and government agencies that seek out its help. CERT is composed of full-time and part-time computer experts who can trace the origins of attacks against sites despite the complexity of the Internet. Its staff members also assist organizations in identifying security problems, developing solutions, and communicating with the public about widespread hacker threats. The CERT Coordination Center also provides product assessments, reports, and training in order to improve the public's knowledge and understanding of security threats and solutions. The U.S. Department of Homeland Security (DHS) operates the **United States Computer Emergency Readiness Team (US-CERT)**, which coordinates cyber incident warnings and responses across both the government and private sectors.

CERT Coordination Center monitors and tracks online criminal activity reported to it by private corporations and government agencies that seek out its help

US-CERT division of the U.S. Department of Homeland Security that coordinates cyber incident warnings and responses across government and private sectors

Government Policies and Controls on Encryption Software

As noted in the beginning of this chapter, governments have sought to restrict availability and export of encryption systems as a means of detecting and preventing crime and terrorism. In the United States, both Congress and the executive branch have sought to regulate the uses of encryption. At the international level, four organizations have influenced the international traffic in encryption software: OECD (Organization for Economic Cooperation and Development), G-7/G-8 (the heads of state of the top eight industrialized countries in the world), the Council of Europe, and the Wassnaar Arrangement (law enforcement personnel from the top 33 industrialized counties in the world) (EPIC, 2000). Various governments have proposed schemes for controlling encryption software or at least preventing criminals from obtaining strong encryption tools (see **Table 5.5**).

OECD Guidelines

In July 2002, the OECD formally released its *Guidelines for the Security of Information Systems and Networks*. The Guidelines consist of nine principles that aim to increase public awareness, promote education, share information, and provide training that can lead to a better understanding of online security and the adoption of best practices. "A Culture of Security" represents a new way of thinking—one in which everyone using computers and networks like the Internet has a role to play. The

TABLE 5.5	GOVERNMENT EFFORTS TO REGULATE AND CONTROL ENCRYPTION
REGULATORY EFFORT	**IMPACT**
Restrict export of strong security systems	Supported primarily by the United States. Widespread distribution of encryption schemes weakens this policy. The policy is changing to permit exports except to pariah countries.
Key escrow/key recovery schemes	France, the United Kingdom, and the United States supported this effort in the late 1990s, but now have largely abandoned it. There are few trusted third parties.
Lawful access and forced disclosure	Growing support in recent U.S. legislation and in OECD countries.
Official hacking	All countries are rapidly expanding budgets and training for law enforcement "technical centers" aimed at monitoring and cracking computer-based, encryption activities of suspected criminals.

Guidelines represent the consensus views of all 30 OECD member countries and support the OECD's larger goal of promoting economic growth, trade, and development.

5.5 PAYMENT SYSTEMS

TYPES OF PAYMENT SYSTEMS

In order to understand e-commerce payment systems, you first need to be familiar with the various types of generic payment systems. Then you will be able to clarify the different requirements that e-commerce payments systems must meet and identify the opportunities provided by e-commerce technology for developing new types of payment systems. There are five main types of payment systems: cash, checking transfer, credit cards, stored value, and accumulating balance.

Cash

cash
legal tender defined by a national authority to represent value

Cash, which is legal tender defined by a national authority to represent value, is the most common form of payment in terms of number of transactions. The key feature of cash is that it is instantly convertible into other forms of value without the intermediation of any other institution. For instance, free airline miles are not cash because they are not instantly convertible into other forms of value—they require intermediation by a third party (the airline) in order to be exchanged for value (an airline ticket). Private organizations sometimes create a form of private cash called *scrip* that can be instantly redeemed by participating organizations for goods or cash. Examples include trading stamps, "point" programs, and other forms of consumer loyalty currency.

Why is cash still so popular today? Cash is portable, requires no authentication, and provides instant purchasing power for those who possess it. Cash allows for micropayments (payments of small amounts). The use of cash is "free" in that neither merchants nor consumers pay a transaction fee for using it. Using cash does not require any complementary assets, such as special hardware or the existence of an account, and it puts very low cognitive demands on the user. Cash is anonymous and difficult to trace, and in that sense it is "private." Other forms of payment require significant use of third parties and leave an extensive digital or paper trail.

On the other hand, cash is limited to smaller transactions (you can't easily buy a car or house with cash), it is easily stolen, and it does not provide any "**float**" (the period of time between a purchase and actual payment for the purchase); when it is spent, it is gone. With cash, purchases tend to be final and irreversible (i.e., they are irrefutable) unless otherwise agreed by the seller.

Checking Transfer

A **checking transfer**, which represents funds transferred directly via a signed draft or check from a consumer's checking account to a merchant or other individual, is the second most common form of payment in the United States in terms of number of transactions, and the most common in terms of total amount spent.

Checks can be used for both small and large transactions, although typically they are not used for micropayments (less than $1). Checks have some float (it can take up to 10 days for out-of-state checks to clear), and the unspent balances can earn interest. Checks are not anonymous and require third-party institutions to work. Checks also introduce security risks for merchants: They can be forged more easily than cash, so authentication is required. For merchants, checks also present some additional risk compared to cash because they can be canceled before they clear the account or they may bounce if there is not enough money in the account.

Credit Card

A **credit card** represents an account that extends credit to consumers, permits consumers to purchase items while deferring payment, and allows consumers to make payments to multiple vendors at one time. **Credit card associations** such as Visa and MasterCard are nonprofit associations that set standards for the **issuing banks**—such as Citibank—that actually issue the credit cards and process transactions. Other third parties (called **processing centers** or **clearinghouses**) usually handle verification of accounts and balances. Credit card issuing banks act as financial intermediaries, minimizing the risk to transacting parties.

Credit cards offer consumers a line of credit and the ability to make small and large purchases instantly. They are widely accepted as a form of payment, reduce the risk of theft associated with carrying cash, and increase consumer convenience. Credit cards also offer consumers considerable float. With a credit card, for instance, a consumer typically need not actually pay for goods purchased until receiving a credit card bill 30 days later. Merchants benefit from increased consumer spending resulting from credit card use, but they pay a hefty transaction fee of 3% to 5% of the purchase price to the issuing banks. In addition, federal Regulation Z places the risks of the transaction (such as credit card fraud, repudiation of the transaction, or nonpayment) largely on the merchant and credit card issuing bank. Regulation Z

float
the period of time between a purchase and actual payment for the purchase

checking transfer
funds transferred directly via a signed draft or check from a consumer's checking account to a merchant or other individual

credit card
represents an account that extends credit to consumers, permits consumers to purchase items while deferring payment, and allows consumers to make payments to multiple vendors at one time

credit card association
nonprofit association that sets standards for issuing banks

issuing bank
bank that actually issues credit cards and processes transactions

processing center (clearinghouse)
institution that handles verification of accounts and balances

limits cardholder liability to $50 for unauthorized transactions that occur before the card issuer is notified. Once a card is reported stolen, consumers are not liable for any subsequent charges.

Credit cards have less finality than other payment systems because consumers can refute or repudiate purchases under certain circumstances, and they limit risk for consumers while raising risk for merchants and bankers.

Stored Value

stored-value payment system

account created by depositing funds into an account and from which funds are paid out or withdrawn as needed

debit card

immediately debits a checking or other demand-deposit account

Accounts created by depositing funds into an account and from which funds are paid out or withdrawn as needed are **stored-value payment systems**. Stored-value payment systems are similar in some respects to checking transfers—which also store funds—but do not involve writing a check. Examples include debit cards, gift certificates, prepaid cards, and smart cards (described in greater detail later in the chapter). **Debit cards** immediately debit a checking or other demand-deposit account. For many consumers, the use of a debit card eliminates the need to write a paper check. Today, there are nearly 300 million debit cards in use nationwide. However, because debit cards are dependent on funds being available in a consumer's bank account, larger purchases are still typically paid for by credit card, and their use in the United States still lags behind that of other developed nations, in part because they do not have the protections provided by Regulation Z and they do not provide any float.

P2P payment systems such as PayPal (discussed further in Section 5.6) are variations on the stored value concept. P2P payment systems do not insist on prepayment, but do require an account with a stored value, either a checking account with funds available or a credit card with an available credit balance. PayPal is often referred to as a P2P payment system because it allows small merchants and individuals to accept payments without using a merchant bank or processor to clear the transaction.

Accumulating Balance

accumulating balance payment system

account that accumulates expenditures and to which consumers makes periodic payments

Accounts that accumulate expenditures and to which consumers make periodic payments are **accumulating balance payment systems**. Traditional examples include utility, phone, and American Express accounts, all of which accumulate balances, usually over a specified period (typically a month), and then are paid in full at the end of the period.

Table 5.6 summarizes how payment systems differ on a variety of dimensions and highlights a number of points about payment systems. First, evaluating payment systems is a complex process; there are many dimensions that must be considered. Table 5.6 suggests how difficult it is for entrepreneurs to devise new payment mechanisms to displace current payment systems (cash, checks, and credit cards). As we will discuss below, consumers in the United States have not, as a general matter, accepted alternative online payment systems and rely primarily on credit cards for online payments.

Table 5.6 also suggests that the various parties that have an interest in payment systems (stakeholders) may have different preferences with respect to the different dimensions. The main stakeholders in payment systems are consumers, merchants, financial intermediaries, and government regulators.

Consumers are interested primarily in low-risk, low-cost, refutable (able to be repudiated or denied), convenient, and reliable payment mechanisms. Consumers have demonstrated they will not use new payment mechanisms unless they are equally or more beneficial to them than existing systems. In general, most consumers use cash, checks, and/or credit cards. The specific payment system chosen will change depending on the transaction situation. For instance, cash may be preferred to keep certain transactions private and anonymous, but the same consumer may want a record of transaction for the purchase of a car.

Merchants are interested primarily in low-risk, low-cost, irrefutable (i.e., final), secure, and reliable payment mechanisms. Merchants currently carry much of the risk of checking and credit card fraud, refutability of charges, and much of the hardware cost of verifying payments. Merchants typically prefer payments made by cash, check, and to a lesser extent credit cards, which usually carry high fees and allow transactions to be repudiated after the fact by consumers.

TABLE 5.6	DIMENSIONS OF PAYMENT SYSTEMS				
DIMENSION	CASH	PERSONAL CHECK	CREDIT CARD	STORED VALUE (DEBIT CARD)	ACCUMULATING BALANCE
Instantly convertible without intermediation	yes	no	no	no	no
Low transaction cost for small transactions	yes	no	no	no	yes
Low transaction cost for large transactions	no	yes	yes	yes	yes
Low fixed costs for merchant	yes	yes	no	no	no
Refutable (able to be repudiated)	no	yes	yes	no (usually)	yes
Financial risk for consumer	yes	no	up to $50	limited	no
Financial risk for merchant	no	yes	yes	no	yes
Anonymous for consumer	yes	no	no	no	no
Anonymous for merchant	yes	no	no	no	no
Immediately respendable	yes	no	no	no	no
Security against unauthorized use	no	some	some	some	some
Tamper-resistant	yes	no	yes	yes	yes
Requires authentication	no	yes	yes	yes	yes
Special hardware required	no	no	yes—by merchant	yes—by merchant	yes—by merchant
Buyer keeps float	no	yes	yes	no	yes
Account required	no	yes	yes	yes	yes
Has immediate monetary value	yes	no	no	yes	no

SOURCE: Adapted from MacKie-Mason and White, 1996.

Financial intermediaries, such as banks and credit card networks, are primarily interested in secure payment systems that transfer risks and costs to consumers and merchants, while maximizing transaction fees payable to themselves. The preferred payment mechanisms for financial intermediaries are checking transfers, debit cards, and credit cards.

Government regulators are interested in maintaining trust in the financial system. Regulators seek to protect against fraud and abuse in the use of payment systems; ensure that the interests of consumers and merchants are balanced against the interests of the financial intermediaries whom they regulate; and enforce information reporting laws. The most important regulations of payment systems in the United States are Regulation Z, Regulation E, and the Electronic Funds Transfer Act (EFTA) of 1978, regulating ATM machines. Regulation Z limits the risk to consumers when using credit cards. In contrast, EFTA and Regulation E place more risk on consumers when using debit or ATM cards. For instance, if you lose an ATM card or debit card, you are potentially liable for any losses to the account. However, in reality, Visa and MasterCard have issued policies that limit consumer risk for loss of debit cards to the same $50 that applies to credit cards.

5.6 E-COMMERCE PAYMENT SYSTEMS

The emergence of e-commerce has created new financial needs that in some cases cannot be effectively fulfilled by traditional payment systems. For instance, new types of purchasing relationships—such as auctions between individuals online—have resulted in the need for peer-to-peer payment methods that allow individuals to e-mail payments to other individuals. New types of online information products such as iTunes, video purchases and rentals, newspaper and magazine articles, and other information services require micropayments of less than $5. Yet, for the most part, existing payment mechanisms used in most societies have been able to adapt to the new online environment. E-commerce technology offers a number of possibilities for creating new payment systems that substitute for existing systems, as well as for creating enhancements to existing systems. In this section, we provide an overview of e-commerce payment systems in use today.

In the United States, the primary form of online payment is the existing credit card system. In 2008, credit cards are estimated to account for around 60% of online transactions in the United States, although the use of debit cards has been increasing. **Figure 5.17** illustrates the approximate usage of various payment types. PayPal is the most popular alternative to usage of credit and debit cards online. (see the "Online Stored Value Payment Systems" section for more information on PayPal).

In other parts of the world, e-commerce payments can be very different depending on traditions and infrastructure. Credit cards are not nearly as dominant a form of online payment as in the United States. If you plan on operating a Web site in Europe, Asia, or Latin America, you will need to develop different payment systems for each region. Consumers in Europe rely for the most part on bank debit cards (especially in Germany) and some credit cards. Online purchases in China are typically paid for by check or cash when the consumer picks up the goods at a local store.

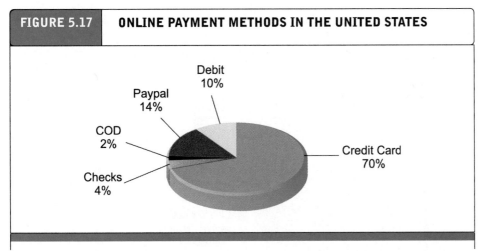

ONLINE PAYMENT METHODS IN THE UNITED STATES

Traditional credit cards are the dominant method of payment for online purchases, although PayPal is gaining ground.

SOURCE: Based on data from eMarketer, Inc., 2008; Javelin Strategy & Research, 2008;; U.S. Census Bureau, 2007; authors' estimates.

In Japan, consumers use postal and bank transfers and CODs, using local convenience stores (konbini) as the pickup and payment point. Japanese consumers also use accumulated balance accounts with the telephone company for Internet purchases made from their home computers.

ONLINE CREDIT CARD TRANSACTIONS

Because credit cards are the dominant form of online payment, it is important to understand how they work and to recognize the strengths and weaknesses of this payment system. Online credit card transactions are processed in much the same way that in-store purchases are, with the major differences being that online merchants never see the actual card being used, no card impression is taken, and no signature is available. Online credit card transactions most closely resemble *MOTO* (Mail Order-Telephone Order) transactions. These types of purchases are also called CNP (Cardholder Not Present) transactions and are the major reason that charges can be disputed later by consumers. Since the merchant never sees the credit card, nor receives a hand-signed agreement to pay from the customer, when disputes arise, the merchant faces the risk that the transaction may be disallowed and reversed, even though he has already shipped the goods or the user has downloaded a digital product.

Figure 5.18 illustrates the online credit card purchasing cycle. There are five parties involved in an online credit card purchase: consumer, merchant, clearinghouse, merchant bank (sometimes called the "acquiring bank"), and the consumer's card issuing bank. In order to accept payments by credit card, online merchants must have a merchant account established with a bank or financial institution. A **merchant account** is simply a bank account that allows companies to process credit card payments and receive funds from those transactions.

merchant account
a bank account that allows companies to process credit card payments and receive funds from those transactions

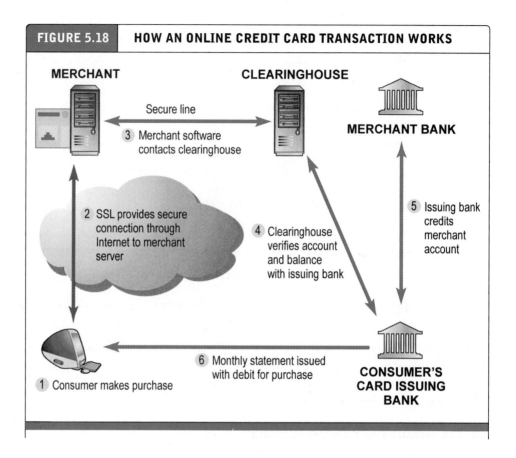

FIGURE 5.18 **HOW AN ONLINE CREDIT CARD TRANSACTION WORKS**

As shown in Figure 5.18, an online credit card transaction begins with a purchase (1). When a consumer wants to make a purchase, he or she adds the item to the merchant's shopping cart. When the consumer wants to pay for the items in the shopping cart, a secure tunnel through the Internet is created using SSL. Using encryption, SSL secures the session during which credit card information will be sent to the merchant and protects the information from interlopers on the Internet (2). SSL does not authenticate either the merchant or the consumer. The transacting parties have to trust one another.

Once the consumer credit card information is received by the merchant, the merchant software contacts a clearinghouse (3). As previously noted, a clearinghouse is a financial intermediary that authenticates credit cards and verifies account balances. The clearinghouse contacts the issuing bank to verify the account information (4). Once verified, the issuing bank credits the account of the merchant at the merchant's bank (usually this occurs at night in a batch process) (5). The debit to the consumer account is transmitted to the consumer in a monthly statement (6).

Credit Card E-commerce Enablers

Companies that have a merchant account still need to buy or build a means of handling the online transaction; securing the merchant account is only step one in a two-part process. Today, Internet payment service providers can provide both a merchant account and the software tools needed to process credit card purchases online.

For instance, Authorize.net is an Internet payment service provider. Authorize.net helps a merchant secure an account with one of its merchant account provider partners and then provides payment processing software for installation on the merchant's server. The software collects the transaction information from the merchant's site and then routes it via the Authorize.net "payment gateway" to the appropriate bank, ensuring that customers are authorized to make their purchases. The funds for the transaction are then transferred to the merchant's merchant account.

Limitations of Online Credit Card Payment Systems

There are a number of limitations to the existing credit card payment system. The most important limitations involve security, merchant risk, cost, and social equity.

The existing system offers poor security. Neither the merchant nor the consumer can be fully authenticated. The merchant could be a criminal organization designed to collect credit card numbers, and the consumer could be a thief using stolen or fraudulent cards. The risk facing merchants is high: consumers can repudiate charges even though the goods have been shipped or the product downloaded. The banking industry attempted to develop a secure electronic transaction protocol (SET) in 2000, but this effort failed because it was too complex for consumers and merchants alike.

Credit costs for merchants are also significant—roughly 3.5% of the purchase plus a transaction fee of 20–30 cents per transaction, plus other setup fees. Stored value systems such as PayPal that rely on the credit card system are even more costly: in addition to paying the credit card fee of 3.5%, PayPal tacks on a variable fee of from 1.5%–3% depending on the size of the transaction. The high costs make it undesirable to sell goods that cost less than $10 on the Web. The sale of individual articles, music tracks, or other small items is not particularly feasible with credit cards. One way around this problem is to aggregate a consumer's purchases over a period of time before actually charging the credit card. This is the tack taken by Apple's iTunes Music Store, which charges 99 cents per song. Instead of charging your credit card for each individual song, Apple aggregates any purchases you make within a 24-hour period so that they're posted to your credit card account as a total for the period, not as individual song purchases. iTunes barely breaks even on a 99 cent sale, but can start making money if you purchase several songs. In general, credit companies are opposed to "aggregating" because it reduces their profits.

Credit cards are not very democratic, even though they seem ubiquitous. Millions of young adults do not have credit cards, along with almost 100 million other adult Americans who cannot afford cards or who are considered poor risks because of low incomes.

DIGITAL WALLETS

Aside from credit cards, there are also a number of new forms of payment that have been attempted, with mixed success. These include digital wallets, digital cash, online stored value payment systems, digital accumulating balance systems, and digital checking systems

digital wallet

emulates the functionality of a regular wallet by authenticating the consumer, storing and transferring value, and securing the payment process from consumer to merchant

A **digital wallet** seeks to emulate the functionality of a regular wallet that you carry on your person. The most important functions of a digital wallet are to (a) authenticate the consumer through the use of digital certificates or other encryption methods, (b) store and transfer value, and (c) secure the payment process from the consumer to the merchant. Early efforts by many companies failed to popularize the idea of a digital wallet. Even Microsoft, which offered a proprietary server-side digital wallet with first Passport and then MSN Wallet, ultimately abandoned the effort in February 2005. The latest effort to develop something like a digital wallet is Google's Checkout, which is a payment processing system designed to make online shopping more convenient and easier. It does not store value like PayPal, but communicates a shopper's credit card and personal information necessary for a transaction to the merchant. The merchant receives some additional transaction guarantees that the user has been authenticated by Google. It is not clear at this time how successful this system will be. As of September 2008, despite aggressively promoting Checkout to its search advertisers, Google has yet to match PayPal's strength or popularity, in part due to eBay's refusal to allow merchants to use Checkout.

DIGITAL CASH

digital cash

an alternative payment system developed for e-commerce in which unique, authenticated tokens representing cash value are tramsmitted from consumers to merchants

Digital cash (sometimes called *e-cash*) was one of the first forms of alternative payment systems developed for e-commerce. The basic idea behind all digital cash systems is payment over the Internet by transmitting unique, authenticated tokens representing cash value from consumer to merchants. In these schemes, users would deposit money in a bank or provide a credit card. Banks would issue digital tokens (unique encrypted numbers) for various denominations of cash, and consumers could "spend" these at merchants' sites. Merchants would in turn deposit these electronic tokens in its bank. DigiCash, First Virtual, and Millicent, all early pioneers in digital cash, no longer offer services in the form originally envisioned. In general, the protocols and practices required to make digital cash a reality were far too complex. However, there are still several firms that are continuing to pursue the idea of digital cash. Some firms, such as E-gold and GoldMoney, have focused on electronic currency backed by gold bullion.

ONLINE STORED VALUE PAYMENT SYSTEMS

online stored value payment system

permits consumers to make instant, online payments to merchants and other individuals based on value stored in an online account

Online stored value payment systems permit consumers to make instant, online payments to merchants and other individuals based on value stored in an online account.

PayPal (purchased by eBay in 2002) enables individuals and businesses with e-mail accounts to make and receive payments up to a specified limit. PayPal transferred about $30 billion in payments among individuals and businesses during the first six months of 2008, a 34% increase over the same period in 2007. PayPal is now available in 190 countries and at June 30, 2008 had about 165 million account holders, of which about 62.6 million are considered to be active accounts. PayPal builds on the existing financial infrastructure of the countries in which it operates. You establish a PayPal account by specifying a credit, debit, or checking account you wish to have charged or paid when conducting online transactions. When you make a payment using PayPal, you e-mail the payment to the merchant's PayPal account. PayPal transfers the amount from your credit or checking account to the merchant's bank account. The beauty of PayPal is that no personal credit information has to be shared among the users, and the service can be used by individuals to pay one another even in small amounts. Issues with PayPal include its high cost, and lack of consumer protections when a fraud occurs or a charge is repudiated. PayPal is discussed in further depth in the case study at the end of the chapter.

There are also several different categories of online stored value systems in addition to PayPal. Some, such as Valista, are merchant platforms. Others, such as QPass, are primarily aimed at the micropayments market for wireless carriers and publishers selling individual articles.

Smart cards are another kind of stored value system based on credit-card-sized plastic cards with embedded chips that store personal information that can be used to support mobile wireless e-commerce payments. They are not used from home PCs to purchase goods, but can be used to pay for generally small ticket items by waving the card at a reader, or passing it through a reader. Whereas credit cards store a single charge account number in the magnetic strip on the back, smart cards can hold 100 times more data, including multiple credit card numbers and information regarding health insurance, transportation, personal identification, bank accounts, and loyalty programs, such as frequent flyer accounts. This capacity makes them an attractive alternative to carrying a dozen or so credit and ID cards in a physical wallet. Smart cards can also require a password, unlike credit cards, adding another layer of security.

There are actually two types of smart cards—*contact and contactless*—depending on the technology embedded. In order for contact cards to be read, they must be physically placed into a card reader, while contactless cards have an antenna built in that enables transmission of data without direct contact using RFID technology. **Radio frequency identification (RFID)** is a method of automatic identification that uses short range radio signals to identify objects and users. A stored-value smart card, such as a retail gift card purchased in a certain dollar value, is an example of a contact card because it must be swiped through a smart card reader in order for payment to be processed. A highway toll payment system such as EZPass is an example of a contactless smart card because the EZPass device in the card is read by a remote sensor, with the appropriate toll automatically deducted from the card at the end of the trip.

Smart cards as payment vehicles are more common in Europe and Asia. The Mondex card is one of the original smart cards, invented in 1990 by NatWest Bank in England. The card allows users to download cash from a bank account to the card via a Mondex-compatible telephone or a card reader attached to a PC, and spend large or small amounts. It can carry five different currencies simultaneously and can be accepted by merchants who have readers installed. Mondex is part of MasterCard's worldwide suite of smart card products.

The Octopus card is a rechargeable contactless stored value smart card used in Hong Kong. The card debuted in 1997 as a fare collection system for Hong Kong's mass transit system. Today, it has become the world's most successful stored value

smart card
a credit-card sized plastic cards with an embedded chip that stores personal information; can be used to support mobie wireless e-commerce payments

radio frequency identification (RFID)
a method of automatic identification that uses short range radio signals to identify objects and users

smart card. It can be used to pay not only for public transportation, but also to make payments at convenience stores and fast-food restaurants and for parking, and point-of-sale applications such as gas and vending machines. As of July 2008, there were over 17 million Octopus cards in circulation, used to conduct over 10 million transactions a day. The card can be recharged online, over the counter, or via special-purpose "add-value" machines. So far, smart cards have played a limited role in supporting electronic transactions on the fly, where the user is mobile (as in a subway train passenger) and wants to make small payments. However, in the future, smart card technology will be integrated with cell phones, and wireless payment to support mobile e-commerce will become more widespread.

DIGITAL ACCUMULATING BALANCE PAYMENT SYSTEMS

digital accumulating balance payment system

allows users to make micropayments and purchases on the Web, accumulating a debit balance for which they are billed at the end of the month

Digital accumulating balance payment systems allow users to make micropayments and purchases on the Web, accumulating a debit balance for which they are billed at the end of the month. Like a utility or phone bill, consumers are expected to pay the entire balance at the end of the month using a checking or credit card account. Digital accumulating balance systems are ideal for purchasing intellectual property on the Web such as single music tracks, chapters of books, or articles from a newspaper. such as ringtones and games. Balances accumulate and customers are billed monthly with their regular phone bill. A good example is Valista's PaymentsPlus, a system for accumulating balances for small transactions. PaymentsPlus is used by companies such as AOL, Vodafone, NTT DoCoMo, Tiscali, Wanadoo, and T-Online, among others.

Clickshare takes a different approach. Consumers have one account at a Web site of their choice, and then can use that account to purchase digital content from other Web sites without having to reenter credit card or other personal information. Clickshare has found its greatest acceptance with the online newspaper and publishing industry and has recently signed deals with papers as diverse as the *Chicago Sun-Times, Asian Banker, Lawton (Oklahoma) Constitution,* and *Daily Hampshire Gazette*, and publishers such as Crain Communications and the Globe Pequot Press. It also supplies subscription, authentication, and transaction billing for a variety of major newspapers' subscription Web sites aimed at NFL fans, such as Gannett's Packers Premium and the StarTribune's Purple Plus.

DIGITAL CHECKING PAYMENT SYSTEMS

digital checking payment system

seeks to extend the functionality of existing checking accounts for use as online shopping payment tool

In December 2004, the Federal Reserve announced that for the first time in history, the number of electronic payment transactions (credit, debit, and other forms of electronic payment) exceeded the number of paper checks. However, the venerable check is not yet moving into retirement. According to the 2007 Federal Reserve Payments Study, over 33 billion checks were written in the United States in 2006. **Digital checking payment systems** seek to extend the functionality of existing checking accounts for use as online shopping payment tools.

PayByCheck's system is based on the consumer's existing checking account. When a consumer wishes to pay by check at a merchant site that offers this service, an online authorization form appears that mimics the appearance of a paper check. The user is prompted to fill in checking account information, including a valid check number, bank routing number, and bank account number. To authorize payment, a user must type his or her full name, and in some instances, if required by the merchant, the last four digits of his or her social security number. The payment information is matched against PayByCheck's various databases containing information on known bad check writers, real-time information from the customer's bank about current bank account status, fraud databases, and an address verification system to verify the customer's name and address. Bio identification in the form of a fingerprint scanner attached to a PC can also be used. PayByCheck then produces a check or electronic debit for the amount of the purchase as indicated on the check, and delivers it to the merchant. The check is deposited by the merchant and routed to the consumer's bank for payment, just like a check written from a checkbook. eBillme is another option. eBillme links to a customer's online banking account. Digital checking has not been successful so far because of the difficulties of verifying the consumer online.

WIRELESS PAYMENT SYSTEMS

There are approximately 3 billion cell phones in use around the world, and in China, the number of cell phones exceeded 500 million in July 2008 more than the entire population of the United States. The United States' cell phone population is now estimated at 255 million. These numbers dwarf the global personal computer population of about 1 billion (TIA, 2007; PCWorld, July 2008). In Japan, more than 95% of households have cell phones.

Use of mobile handsets as payment devices is already well established in Europe, Japan, and South Korea. Japan is arguably the most advanced in terms of providing non-voice services to consumers, that is, real mobile commerce. Japanese cell phones can act as bar code readers, GPS locators, FM radios, voice recorders and analog TV tuners, and purchase things such as train tickets, newspapers, restaurant meals, groceries, books, and a host of common retail goods and services. Three kinds of mobile payments systems are used in Japan, and these provide a glimpse of the future of mobile payments in the United States Japanese cell phones support e-money (stored value systems charged by credit cards or bank accounts), mobile debit cards (tied to personal bank accounts), and mobile credit cards. Japanese cell phones act like mobile wallets, containing a variety of payment mechanisms. Consumers can pay merchants by simply waving the cell phone at a merchant payment device that can accept payments. How do the cell phones communicate with merchants when, say, buying a newspaper at a train station or restaurant meal? Japan's largest phone company, NTT DoCoMo, introduced wireless RFID cell phones and a related payment system (FeliCa) in 2004. Currently more than 10 million wallet phones are in use in Japan.

In the United States, the cell phone has not yet evolved into a fully capable mobile commerce and payment system. The vast majority of cell phone revenues

| 5.8 | **CASE STUDY** |

Paypal Has Company

PayPal—the online payment processor now owned by eBay—was the first truly successful Internet-based e-commerce payment system. Its origins were quite simple. On November 16, 1999, Peter Theil sat with friends at a restaurant. When the bill arrived, Theil used his Palm Pilot to "beam" his share to a friend sitting across the table. Theil and fellow co-founder Max Levchin had built a system that would allow them to send money to one another via a Palm Pilot's infrared links. From this idea sprang one of the first "peer-to-peer" payment systems: a system that allows individuals to send money to one another via e-mail.

PayPal emphasizes ease of use for both senders and receivers of cash. Here's a brief synopsis of how it works. First, you create a PayPal account at the PayPal Web site by filling out a one-page application form and providing credit or debit card or bank account information. Only PayPal is privy to this information, not the receiving party. Then, when you use PayPal to pay for a purchase, money is drawn from the credit card or bank account and transmitted to the Automated Clearing House (ACH) Network, a privately operated financial intermediary that tracks and transfers funds

between financial institutions. The party who is to receive the payment is notified via e-mail that money is waiting. If the receiving party has a PayPal account, the funds are automatically deposited into the account; if the person does not have a PayPal account, he or she must set one up, and then the money is credited to his or her account. Once the funds are in the PayPal account, the recipient can then transfer them electronically to a checking account, request a paper check, or use PayPal to send the funds to someone else.

Levchin and Theil originally conceived of PayPal as a method for "beaming" money to users of handheld PDAs. When this idea did not pan out, they changed their target to arranging payments between individuals who knew one another. However, they quickly realized that it would also work for a company such as eBay, providing purchasers and sellers with a way to short-cut the time-consuming and cumbersome process of mailing checks and money orders and waiting for checks to clear before shipping items. Moreover, for small merchants selling items on the Web, it is difficult and expensive to obtain the capability to accept credit cards. Credit companies extend these merchant services only to bona fide businesses, usually requiring a physical place of business as a requirement.

Today, PayPal is the largest and most popular online payment service, growing from a handful of users when it launched in late 1999 to over 165 million in 2007, of which about 57 million can be characterized as active users. In 2007, PayPal processed $45 billion in payments. About 70% of this gross volume ($30 billion) is tied to eBay users, and $15 billion comes from non-eBay transactions. One reason PayPal has grown so fast is because it experiences the benefits of network economics or the "viral effect": the more people who accept and use PayPal, the greater the benefit to the consumer. If I send you a PayPal payment via e-mail, then you are incentivised to open a PayPal account to receive the funds. If PayPal is to continue growing, it will have to break out of the eBay marketspace and find new payment opportunities.

PayPal earns money in many different ways. First, online sellers (who may be individuals or small businesses that do not want the difficulties associated with obtaining a merchant credit card account) pay a transaction fee for the service (30 cents plus 1.9%–2.9% of the proceeds of the transaction). This generally works out to 3.3% of the transaction on a $100 transaction. Credit card firms generally charge about the same or 0.3% more due to their higher customer acquisition costs. PayPal, in other words, can be slightly less costly than credit cards for merchants.

One advantage for merchants on eBay is that they are not required to have a merchant bank account, which is required by credit card issuers. Merchant banks clear credit card transactions and charge fees. Consumers are not charged directly for the use of their PayPal account although they do pay ultimately because retailers need to recover the costs of the transaction by raising the prices on goods sold using PayPal. Second, PayPal earns revenue by collecting the interest earned on consumer funds not yet transferred out of the PayPal system. PayPal has charges for transferring funds to foreign banks, converting currencies, and new financial products such as a PayPal credit card.

Part of the strength of PayPal lies in its simplicity: it piggybacks on existing credit card and checking payment systems. This is also one of its weaknesses, however. PayPal reportedly suffers relatively high levels of fraud related to the credit card system on which it relies. To protect against fraud, PayPal requires special authorization for payments over $200.

In 2002, PayPal went public and issued shares in an initial public offering. One of the main reasons PayPal grew so rapidly was because of its popularity on eBay. In an effort not to lose this lucrative transaction business to PayPal, eBay spent over $100 million promoting its own similar system called Billpoint—but to no avail. In October 2002, eBay purchased PayPal for $1.5 billion—about $20 a share. At the time, analysts felt the price was too high, but eBay has had the last laugh. Today, PayPal is valued at $7–$8 billion, and, according to the company, has a 10% share of the U.S. consumer e-commerce payments market and a 5% share of the global market. In 2007, PayPal generated $28 billion of the net total payment volume from eBay.com transactions, which represented approximately 58% of PayPal's total volume for the year .PayPal saw a 345 increase in revenue from 2006 to 2007, 25% of eBay's total net revenue, generated a TPV of $47.5 billion, a 33% increase from $35.8 billion in 2006. In 2007, PayPal had an average of 1.96 million transactions per day in 17 currencies.

For a brief period, PayPal enjoyed its position as the only widely adopted online platform (aside from the credit card companies). But this is changing rapidly. The largest direct competitor is Google's Checkout system, an online digital wallet. Google Checkout stores a user's financial information, including credit card information, and then presents this information to merchants when the user checks out. The customer does not have to fill out forms or reveal credit information to online merchants. Checkout does not support peer-to-peer payments, at least not yet. Google has been careful not to directly challenge PayPal in the P2P market, if only because eBay (the owner of PayPal) is the largest single advertiser on Google, and Google directs a significant traffic volume to eBay. They need one another. Google will also use Checkout to support its advertising network. Ads for online stores that accept Checkout are highlighted with an icon, increasing the chances that users will click on those sites. Once users click on an ad, they are more likely to purchase. Merchants who accept Checkout on their sites receive more traffic simply for offering the convenience of the service, and Google has frequent promotions where it eliminates all processing fees for periods of time, saving merchants the 2% plus 20 cents it charges for transactions.

An even more direct challenge is coming from unlikely sources: cell phone carriers such as ATT and Verizon, especially in P2P payments. PayPal and Google Checkout are both built upon the existing credit card system. What if you could eliminate the credit card intermediaries? In June 2007, Verizon announced a deal with mobile payment company Obopay, Inc. to allow subscribers to transfer money and make purchases through their cell phones. Users can send money to anyone with a cell phone on any wireless network. Now let's see: there's a billion PCs in the world, but around 4 billion cell phones. Around 255 million people in the U.S. have mobile phones. Currently, Verizon customers will have to load their Obopay accounts at the

Obopay Web site with a credit card. But in the future, Obopay hopes to integrate its service with Verizon's own monthly billing service, thereby eliminating credit card companies altogether from the payment loop, reducing transaction costs for merchants and customers, and making it easier to use the service (there's no sign up needed as long as you have a Verizon cell phone account).

PayPal also faces other challenges. PayPal's brand is closely associated with smaller merchants, P2P money transfer, and low-cost auctions. As a result, some larger firms might not want the PayPal brand image associated with their brands.

PayPal's business makes it a natural target for fraud, both by merchants that do not deliver goods or services paid for by its customers, and from outside forces who send fraudulent e-mails to its customers, attempting to steal the customers' password, credit card numbers, or other personal information. In 2007, PayPal's transaction loss was $139.3 million, .29% of the total payment volume. The loss rate in 2007 was lower than the 2006 loss rate, but the dollars lost increased. PayPal has been forced to institute a number of costly measures to combat fraud in the attempt to enhance its customers' confidence in its services. PayPal's protections for consumers are weaker than what credit card companies are required to offer. For instance, you can deny a credit card charge and have a $50 maximum liability if your credit card information is stolen and used in commerce. With PayPal, you may or may not receive your money back, depending on whether PayPal can receive its money back, and a host of other conditions. PayPal has developed a consumer protection program, but it also settled in 2006 with 28 state attorneys general involving concerns about certain business practices. Chief among these practices was encouraging users to allow PayPal to directly debit consumer bank accounts, because PayPal can avoid paying credit companies a 2% funds transfer fee, making the direct deduction option more profitable for PayPal. If you have given PayPal both your credit card information and bank account information, the default payment method used by PayPal is your bank account. Once funds are withdrawn from your bank account, they cannot be recovered, unlike credit card transactions. Hence, the risk to consumers is substantially greater. Credit card companies can retrieve funds from misbehaving merchants more quickly by simply reverse-crediting their merchant bank accounts, which generates a hefty penalty payment for them as well.

To cope with emerging new competitors, including the cell phone carriers with deep pockets, PayPal is pursuing a number of other growth initiatives. PayPal signed up both Napster and Apple's iTunes Music Store as merchants in its first foray into the micropayments market. The experience proved so successful that PayPal is now investigating similar deals for other micropayments markets, such as downloadable games, electronic greeting cards, and other online content. PayPal introduced a new micropayments pricing plan designed to increase and encourage the purchase of low-priced digital goods. PayPal is also pursuing an overseas expansion strategy. It has added localized Web sites in China, Australia, Italy, and Spain to a list that already included Canada, Austria, Belgium, France, Germany, the Netherlands, Switzerland, and the United Kingdom. In 2007, businesses or consumers with e-mail could use PayPal to send online payments in 190 countries, and receive payments in 65 of those countries. Payments can be made or accepted in any one of 17 different currencies.

SOURCES: "Profit Climbs for eBay, But Auction Growth Is Slowing," by Brad Stone, *New York Times*, July 17, 2008; "Google Checkout and PayPal spend big to lure buyers," by Saul Hansell, *New York Times*, November 26, 2007; "Verizon Announces Deal with Mobile Payment Firm Obopay," *Wall Street Journal*, June 20, 2007; eBay Inc. Form 10-K for the fiscal year December 31, 2006, filed with the Securities and Exchange Commission, February 28, 2007; "PayPal Plans Mobile Payment Service," by Vauhini Vara, *Wall Street Journal*, March 23, 2007; "Google Steps More Boldly Into PayPal's Territory," by Miguel Helft, *New York Times*, December 20, 2006; "How to Make PayPal Your Friend," by Ron Lieber, *Wall Street Journal*, October 7, 2006; ebay.com 2007 10K.

PayPal is attempting to expand beyond eBay sales by setting up preferred merchant relationships with other large Internet retailers such as Yahoo and Amazon, with mixed success. Amazon has its own credit card and preferred methods of payment, but Yahoo uses PayPal as a recommended payment method. In 2006, PayPal introduced its mobile text message payment system, which allows cell phone users to pay for goods and services by texting PayPal payments to merchants. Students in some schools can now buy school lunches using PayPal, and holiday promotions, which include $50 rebates have helped to increase usage and spending.

Despite the challenges, however, the future for PayPal appears bright. In fact, some analysts believe that PayPal may someday become an even bigger phenomenon than its acquirer, eBay.

Case Study Questions

1. What is the value proposition that PayPal offers consumers? How about merchants?

2. What are some of the risks of using PayPal when compared to credit cards and debit cards?

3. What strategies would you recommend that PayPal pursue in order to maintain its growth over the next five years?

4. Why are cell phone networks a threat to PayPal's future growth?

5.9 REVIEW

KEY CONCEPTS

■ **Understand the scope of e-commerce crime and security problems.**

While the overall size of cybercrime is unclear at this time, cybercrime against e-commerce sites is growing rapidly, the amount of losses is growing, and the management of e-commerce sites must prepare for a variety of criminal assaults.

■ **Describe the key dimensions of e-commerce security.**

There are six key dimensions to e-commerce security:
- *Integrity*—ensures that information displayed on a Web site or sent or received via the Internet has not been altered in any way by an unauthorized party.
- *Nonrepudiation*—ensures that e-commerce participants do not deny (repudiate) their online actions.
- *Authenticity*—verifies an individual's or business's identity.

- *Confidentiality*—determines whether information shared online, such as through e-mail communication or an order process, can be viewed by anyone other than the intended recipient.
- *Privacy*—deals with the use of information shared during an online transaction. Consumers want to limit the extent to which their personal information can be divulged to other organizations, while merchants want to protect such information from falling into the wrong hands.
- *Availability*—determines whether a Web site is accessible and operational at any given moment.

■ Understand the tension between security and other values.

Although computer security is considered necessary to protect e-commerce activities, it is not without a downside. Two major areas where there are tensions between security and Web site operations include:

- *Ease of use*: The more security measures that are added to an e-commerce site, the more difficult it is to use and the slower the site becomes, hampering ease of use. Security is purchased at the price of slowing down processors and adding significantly to data storage demands. Too much security can harm profitability, while not enough can potentially put a company out of business.
- *Public safety*: There is a tension between the claims of individuals to act anonymously and the needs of public officials to maintain public safety that can be threatened by criminals or terrorists.

■ Identify the key security threats in the e-commerce environment.

The nine most common and most damaging forms of security threats to e-commerce sites include:

- *Malicious code*—viruses, worms, Trojan horses, and bot networks are a threat to a system's integrity and continued operation, often changing how a system functions or altering documents created on the system.
- *Unwanted programs (adware, spyware, etc.)*—a kind of security threat that arises when programs are surreptitiously installed on your computer or computer network with
- *Phishing*—any deceptive, online attempt by a third party to obtain confidential information for financial gain.
- *Hacking and cybervandalism*—intentionally disrupting, defacing, or even destroying a site.
- *Credit card fraud/theft*—one of the most-feared occurrences and one of the main reasons more consumers do not participate in e-commerce. The most common cause of credit card fraud is a lost or stolen card that is used by someone else, followed by employee theft of customer numbers and stolen identities (criminals applying for credit cards using false identities).
- *Spoofing*—occurs when hackers attempt to hide their true identities or misrepresent themselves by using fake e-mail addresses or masquerading as someone else. Spoofing also can involve redirecting a Web link to an address different from the intended one, with the site masquerading as the intended destination.

- *Denial of Service attacks*—hackers flood a Web site with useless traffic to inundate and overwhelm the network, frequently causing it to shut down and damaging a site's reputation and customer relationships.
- *Sniffing*—a type of eavesdropping program that monitors information traveling over a network, enabling hackers to steal proprietary information from anywhere on a network, including e-mail messages, company files, and confidential reports. The threat of sniffing is that confidential or personal information will be made public.
- *Insider jobs*—although the bulk of Internet security efforts are focused on keeping outsiders out, the biggest threat is from employees who have access to sensitive information and procedures.
- *Poorly designed server and client software*—the increase in complexity and size of software programs has contributed to an increase in software flaws or vulnerabilities that hackers can exploit weaknesses.

■ **Describe how technology helps protect the security of messages sent over the Internet.**

Encryption is the process of transforming plain text or data into cipher text that cannot be read by anyone other than the sender and the receiver. Encryption can provide four of the six key dimensions of e-commerce security:

- *Message integrity*—provides assurance that the sent message has not been altered.
- *Nonrepudiation*—prevents the user from denying that he or she sent a message.
- *Authentication*—provides verification of the identity of the person (or computer) sending the message.
- *Confidentiality*—gives assurance that the message was not read by others.

There are a variety of different forms of encryption technology currently in use. They include:

- *Symmetric key encryption*—Both the sender and the receiver use the same key to encrypt and decrypt a message. AES (Advanced Encryption Standard) is the most widely used symmetric key encryption system on the Internet today.
- *Public key cryptography*—Two mathematically related digital keys are used: a public key and a private key. The private key is kept secret by the owner, and the public key is widely disseminated. Both keys can be used to encrypt and decrypt a message. Once the keys are used to encrypt a message, the same keys cannot be used to unencrypt the message.
- *Public key encryption using digital signatures and hash digests*—This method uses a mathematical algorithm called a hash function to produce a fixed-length number called a hash digest. The results of applying the hash function are sent by the sender to the recipient. Upon receipt, the recipient applies the hash function to the received message and checks to verify that the same result is produced. The sender then encrypts both the hash result and the original message using the recipient's public key, producing a single block of cipher text. To ensure both the authenticity of the message and nonrepudiation, the sender encrypts the entire block of cipher text one more time using the sender's private key. This produces a digital signature or "signed" cipher text that can be sent over the Internet to ensure the confidentiality of the message and authenticate the sender.
- *Digital envelope*—This method uses symmetric encryption to encrypt and decrypt the document, but public key encryption to encrypt and send the symmetric key.

- *Digital certificates and public key infrastructure*—This method relies on certification authorities who issue, verify, and guarantee digital certificates (a digital document that contains the name of the subject or company, the subject's public key, a digital certificate serial number, an expiration date, an issuance date, the digital signature of the certification authority, and other identifying information).

■ Identify the tools used to establish secure Internet communications channels and protect networks, servers, and clients.

In addition to encryption, there are several other tools that are used to secure Internet channels of communication, including:
- *Secure Sockets Layer (SSL)*—This is the most common form of securing channels. The SSL protocol provides data encryption, server authentication, client authentication, and message integrity for TCP/IP connections.
- *Secure Hypertext Transfer Protocol (S-HTTP)*—S-HTTP secures only Web protocols and cannot be used to secure non-HTTP messages.
- *Virtual private networks (VPNs)*—These allow remote users to securely access internal networks via the Internet, using the Point-to-Point Tunneling Protocol (PPTP), an encoding mechanism that allows one local network to connect to another using the Internet as the conduit.

After communications channels are secured, tools to protect networks, the servers, and clients should be implemented. These include:
- *Firewalls*—software applications that act as filters between a company's private network and the Internet itself, denying unauthorized remote client computers from attaching to your internal network.
- *Proxies*—software servers that act primarily to limit access of internal clients to external Internet servers and are frequently referred to as the gateway.
- *Operating system controls*—built-in username and password requirements that provide a level of authentication. Some operating systems also have an access control function that controls user access to various areas of a network.
- *Anti-virus software*—a cheap and easy way to identify and eradicate the most common types of viruses as they enter a computer, as well as to destroy those already lurking on a hard drive.

■ Appreciate the importance of policies, procedures, and laws in creating security.

In order to minimize security threats:
- E-commerce firms must develop a coherent corporate policy that takes into account the nature of the risks, the information assets that need protecting, and the procedures and technologies required to address the risk, as well as implementation and auditing mechanisms.
- Public laws and active enforcement of cybercrime statutes are also required to both raise the costs of illegal behavior on the Internet and guard against corporate abuse of information.

The key steps in developing a security plan are:
- *Perform a risk assessment*—an assessment of the risks and points of vulnerability.
- *Develop a security policy*—a set of statements prioritizing the information risks, identifying acceptable risk targets, and identifying the mechanisms for achieving these targets.

- *Create an implementation plan*—a plan that determines how you will translate the levels of acceptable risk into a set of tools, technologies, policies, and procedures.
- *Create a security team*—the individuals who will be responsible for ongoing maintenance, audits, and improvements.
- *Perform periodic security audits*—routine reviews of access logs and any unusual patterns of activity

■ **Describe the features of traditional payment systems.**

Traditional payment systems include:
- *Cash*, whose key feature is that it is instantly convertible into other forms of value without the intermediation of any other institution.
- *Checking transfers*, which are funds transferred directly through a signed draft or check from a consumer's checking account to a merchant or other individual; these are the second most common form of payment.
- *Credit card accounts*, which are accounts that extend credit to a consumer and allow consumers to make payments to multiple vendors at one time.
- *Stored value systems*, which are created by depositing funds into an account and from which funds are paid out or are withdrawn as needed. Stored value payments systems include debit cards, phone cards, and smart cards.
- *Accumulating balance systems*, which accumulate expenditures and to which consumers make periodic payments.

■ **Understand the major e-commerce payment mechanisms**

The major types of digital payment systems include:
- *Online credit card transactions,* which are the primary form of online payment system. There are five parties involved in an online credit card purchase: consumer, merchant, clearinghouse, merchant bank (sometimes called the "acquiring bank"), and the consumer's card issuing bank. However, the online credit card system has a number of limitations involving security, merchant risk, cost, and social equity.
- *Digital wallets*, which emulate the functionality of a traditional wallet containing personal identifying information and store value in some form.
- *Digital cash*, which are online numeric tokens based on bank deposits or credit card accounts.
- *Online stored value systems*, which permit consumers to make instant, online payments to merchants and other individuals based on value stored in an online account. Some stored value systems require the user to download a digital wallet, while others require users to simply sign up and transfer money from an existing account into an online stored value account.
- *Digital accumulating balance systems*, which allow users to make purchases on the Web, accumulating a debit balance for which they are billed at the end of the cycle (such as at the end of a day or month); consumers are then expected to pay the entire balance using a checking or credit card account. Accumulating balance systems are ideal for purchasing digital content such as music tracks, chapters of books, or articles from a newspaper.
- *Digital checking payment systems*, which are extensions to the existing checking and banking infrastructure.

- *Wireless payment systems*, which are cell phone-based payment systems that enable mobile payments.

■ Describe the features and functionality of electronic billing presentment and payment systems.

EBPP systems are a form of online payment systems for monthly bills. EBPP services allow consumers to view bills electronically and pay them through electronic funds transfers from bank or credit card accounts. Major players in the EBPP marketspace include:

- *Biller-direct systems*, which were originally created by large utilities to facilitate routine payment of utility bills, but which are increasingly being used by other billers.
- *Consolidators*, which attempt to aggregate all bills for consumers in one place and ideally permit one-stop bill payment.
- *Infrastructure providers* which support the biller-direct and consolidator business models.

QUESTIONS

1. Why is it less risky to steal online? Explain some of the ways criminals deceive consumers and merchants.
2. Explain why an e-commerce site might not want to report being the target of cybercriminals.
3. Give an example of security breaches as they relate to each of the six dimensions of e-commerce security. For instance, what would be a privacy incident?
4. How would you protect your firm against a Denial of Service attack?
5. Explain why the U.S. government wants to restrict the export of strong encryption systems. And why would other countries be against it?
6. Name the major points of vulnerability in a typical online transaction.
7. How does spoofing threaten a Web site's operations?
8. Why is adware or spyware considered to be a security threat?
9. What are some of the steps a company can take to curtail cybercriminal activity from within a business?
10. Explain some of the modern-day flaws associated with encryption. Why is encryption not as secure today as it was earlier in the century?
11. Briefly explain how public key cryptography works.
12. Compare and contrast firewalls and proxy servers and their security functions.
13. Is a computer with anti-virus software protected from viruses? Why or why not?
14. Identify and discuss the five steps in developing an e-commerce security plan.
15. How do biometric devices help improve security? What particular type of security breach do they particularly reduce?
16. What are tiger teams, who uses them, and what are some of the tactics they use in their work?
17. How do the interests of the four major payment systems stakeholders impact each other?
18. Compare and contrast stored value payment systems and checking transfers.

19. Why is a credit card not considered an accumulating balance payment system?
20. Name six advantages and six disadvantages of using cash as a form of payment.
21. Describe the relationship between credit card associations and issuing banks.
22. What is Regulation Z, and how does it protect the consumer?
23. Briefly discuss the disadvantages of credit cards as the standard for online payments. How does requiring a credit card for payment discriminate against some consumers?
24. Describe the major steps involved in an online credit card transaction.
25. Compare and contrast smart cards and traditional credit cards.
26. How is money transferred in transactions using wireless devices?
27. Discuss why EBPP systems are becoming increasingly popular.
28. How are the two main types of EBPP systems both alike and different from each other?

PROJECTS

1. Imagine you are the owner of an e-commerce Web site. What are some of the signs that your site has been hacked? Discuss the major types of attacks you could expect to experience and the resulting damage to your site. Prepare a brief summary presentation.

2. Given the shift toward mobile commerce, identify and discuss the new security threats to this type of technology. Prepare a presentation outlining your vision of the new opportunities for cybercrime.

3. Find three certification authorities and compare the features of each company's digital certificates. Provide a brief description of each company as well, including number of clients. Prepare a brief presentation of your findings.

4. Research the challenges associated with payments across international borders and prepare a brief presentation of your findings. Do most e-commerce companies conduct business internationally? How do they protect themselves from repudiation? How do exchange rates impact online purchases? What about shipping charges? Summarize by describing the differences between a U.S. customer and an international customer who each make a purchase from a U.S. e-commerce merchant.

WEB SITE RESOURCES www.prenhall.com/laudon

- Additional projects, exercises, and tutorials
- Careers: Explore career opportunities in e-commerce
- Raising capital and business plans

Business Concepts
and Social Issues

CHAPTER 6

E-commerce Marketing Concepts

After reading this chapter, you will be able to:

- Identify the key features of the Internet audience.
- Discuss the basic concepts of consumer behavior and purchasing decisions.
- Understand how consumers behave online.
- Describe the basic marketing concepts needed to understand Internet marketing.
- Identify and describe the main technologies that support online marketing.
- Identify and describe basic e-commerce marketing and branding strategies.

Netflix Develops and Defends its Brand

Netflix is the largest online entertainment subscription service in the United States, providing more than 8 million customers with access to over 100,000 DVD titles (and more than 55 million DVDs in stock). Netflix's basic business is renting DVD titles on a subscription basis, with different plans ranging from $4.99 a month to $47.99 a month. Since 1999, Netflix subscribers have grown at an annual rate of 79%, and its revenues have grown at 113%. Its 2007 revenues were $1.2 billion. Subscription and revenue growth have subsided during this period as new competitors entered the market. If you ever wondered how many of its 100,000 DVD titles are rented at least once on a typical day, the answer is an astounding 51,000. Most people guess about 1,000, and they seriously underestimate the breadth of American tastes in movies, and the overall demand for Hollywood fare.

But how did Netflix build up a nationally recognized successful brand in a marketplace filled with established brand names such as behemoth Blockbuster, which has over 25 million customers and 85,000 rental DVD titles distributed through over 8,000 local neighborhood stores?

Netflix started out in Los Gatos, California (in the heart of Silicon Valley and the San Francisco Bay Area) as a regionally based online movie store. It offered Bay Area customers a simple list of videos arranged by title and lead actor. Rentals were mailed out, and renters were charged the usual late fees for failure to return within a week. Despite the simplicity of its business model and regional character, Netflix had gross revenues of over $1 million in 1998, but lost over $11 million. It was hardly an auspicious beginning, even though these first years demonstrated a market for online video rentals.

In 2000, Netflix changed its business model to that of a nationally based subscription model, entered into a number of relationships with Hollywood producers to speed up access to recent titles, expanded the functionality of its Web site, and changed its strategic marketing objectives toward becoming a nationally recognized online brand name.

Unlike most neighborhood video rental stores at the time, Netflix changed from charging a fee for each video rental to assessing a monthly service charge for unlimited video rentals. Customers can rent as many videos as they want (with its most popular plan allowing a limit of three videos signed out at any given time) every month. For hard-core video fans, Netflix has developed a $47.99 a month plan that allows eight movies to be checked out at once. Moreover, Netflix eliminated late fees—the single largest complaint of video store customers around the country. To fulfill orders on a national basis, Netflix established video warehouse operations in various metropolitan areas around the United States (now totaling 44) and entered into a long-term relationship with the United States Postal Service to ensure delivery within one or two days for 95% of its subscribers in most parts of the country at very low cost for high-volume deliveries. Netflix provides a pre-stamped mailer for postal returns, absorbing the cost by using revenues from sales of DVDs to some renters.

To build national brand awareness, Netflix used every method in the e-commerce playbook. Netflix marketed its service by purchasing pay-for-performance banner advertising from Yahoo, MSN, and AOL. It used search engine marketing and pay-for-placement ads on major search engines and permission-based e-mail. It also developed an active affiliate marketing program where third parties can automatically download Netflix ads and logos, place them on their sites, and collect revenues for steering customers to Netflix. Netflix also entered into a relationship with Best Buy—an online and offline electronics store—to place Netflix flyers offering a free 14-day trial of Netflix service inside every DVD player Best Buy shipped, and place Netflix on its site as the sole provider of DVDs.

On its own Web site, Netflix offered free trial periods and experienced high conversion rates. Hollywood studios typically distribute their filmed entertainment to the home video market six months after the theater release, to the pay-per-view (PPV) market seven months after theater release, to premium satellite and cable systems one year after release, and to general broadcast television and basic cable about two to three years after release. Rather than invest heavily in the purchase of DVDs from Hollywood, Netflix entered into a revenue-sharing arrangement with several studios, which allowed Netflix to purchase the DVDs below cost but to share the revenues from rentals with the studios. In this way, Netflix was able to build a bigger inventory faster and with less investment.

But building a brand also involves building a trusted high-value relationship with the customer, a unique value proposition that the customer cannot obtain elsewhere and might even pay a premium to receive. To build this relationship, Netflix enlarged the titles library from a few thousand to over 100,000 titles, providing customers 10 times more titles than can be found in the typical large Blockbuster store (and adding customer value through the "library effect" described later in the chapter).

In an effort to provide personalized video rental advice, Netflix also added a recommender system to its Web site. Using its own customers as a knowledge base, it asked customers to submit online reviews, comments, and recommendations on videos they rented. So far, Netflix has gathered over 1 billion customer recommendations, which it then makes available to the entire online customer base—a valuable and inimitable resource. Using data mining techniques and a collaborative filtering tool similar to

Amazon's, Netflix is able to recommend to its customers new videos based on each customer's personal profile of previous rentals and the rentals of other similar customers. Netflix can tell customers who have selected one video, "Other customers who selected this video also chose the following videos." Using the results from its data mining efforts, Netflix sends e-mail to its customer base offering recently released videos that, given the customer's previous rental history, might be of special interest to that customer.

Providing a superior customer experience based on convenience, selection, personalization, and service, Netflix has been able to fend off its major competitors such as Blockbuster, at least for now. Wall Street analysts have been predicting a slide at Netflix for many years despite its growth because of the possibility of serious competition and bruising price wars for subscribers with Blockbuster. In the last year its stock was hammered from the $40 range down to $23 a share. Blockbuster developed its own subscription service in 2006 and has grown the initial 1 million subscribers to over 4 million in 2008. However, Blockbuster has had a difficult time moving from a physical rental store model to an online DVD rental model. In 2005, it began the transition with a Total Service Plan that allows customers to drop off rental DVDs at any of the 20,000 local stores, and even exchange them for other DVDs. It also offers digital downloads of selected videos to customer PCs, and in August 2007, acquired Movielink, a movie download service provider. Blockbuster forced Netflix to drop subscription prices as well. In the meantime, Amazon has entered the fray by offering a movie download service to Tivo subscribers for direct play on television. Hollywood's own efforts at digital distribution (at sites such as CinemaNow, HBO, and Showtime) currently still have very limited selections. To counter this competition, Netflix is building on its brand strength in customer service strength by offering real human telephone customer service (as opposed to online digital help), and a new service of streaming selected videos to subscriber PCs for free. Netflix has also sued Blockbuster, alleging patent infringement, and Blockbuster has countersued Netflix alleging anti-trust violations. As the competition heats up, Netflix's founder and CEO Reed Hastings says, "We have a lot of room to grow. Our relative execution will determine what the share split is between Netflix and Blockbuster." So far, neither Blockbuster or Amazon have succeeded in stealing Netflix customers. Netflix has started its own download service that offers 12,000 titles for play on a PC, and also offers an Internet-TV set top box that feeds movies directly to a TV. Blockbuster stock has fallen from $5.00 a share in 2007, to less than $2.00 a share in 2008.

SOURCES: "Blockbuster's Loss Widens As Same-Store Sales Climb," by Shara Tibken, *Wall Street Journal*, August 7, 2008; Netflix Announces Q2 2008 Financial Results," Netflix Press Release, Los Gatos, July 25, 2008 "Netflix to Sell a Device for Instantly Watching Movies on TV Sets," by Saul Hansell, *New York Times*, May 20, 2008; "Blockbuster Faces the Critics," by Conrad de Aenlle, *New York Times*, April 26, 2008; "Netflix Fact Sheet," Netflix.com, October 5, 2007; Netflix Inc Form 10-K for the fiscal year ended December 31, 2007, filed with the Securities and Exchange Commission on March 15, 2008; "At Netflix, Victory for Voices Over Keystrokers," by Katie Hafner, *New York Times*, August 16, 2007; "Blockbuster Marries Stores to Internet," by Justin Jones, *New York Times*, January 20, 2007; "Netflix to Deliver Movies to the PC," by Miguel Helft, *New York Times*, January 16, 2007.

N etflix provides an example of how the Internet has changed the nature of entire industries and how it enables new types of businesses to thrive even in highly competitive environments. But perhaps no area has been more affected than marketing and marketing communications. As a communications tool, the Internet affords marketers new ways of contacting millions of potential customers at costs far lower than traditional media. The Internet also provides new ways—often instantaneous and spontaneous—to gather information from customers, adjust product offerings, and increase customer value. In the case of Netflix, and in the other cases in this and the following chapter, the Internet has spawned entirely new ways to identify and communicate with customers, including search engine marketing, data mining, recommender systems, and targeted e-mail.

In the Web 2.0 environment of 2008 and 2009, advertisers are following huge shifts in audience away from traditional media and towards social networking, user-generated content, and online content destinations. For example, Intel has moved 50% of its marketing budget to the online channel, and Procter & Gamble, the world's largest advertiser, has moved over 35% of its marketing online. Nike has reduced its traditional media marketing budget to 35%, with the rest going to Internet and event marketing (Burns, 2007). In this chapter and Chapter 7, we discuss avenues for marketing and advertising on the Internet. This chapter focuses on the basic marketing concepts you need to understand to evaluate e-commerce marketing programs. Here, we examine consumer behavior on the Web, brands, the unique features of electronic markets, and special technologies that support new kinds of branding activities. For some of you, this will be a useful review of material you first learned in marketing classes, while for others this will be a first-time exposure to basic marketing concepts. Chapter 7 discusses e-commerce marketing communications, including advertising and other tools.

6.1 CONSUMERS ONLINE: THE INTERNET AUDIENCE AND CONSUMER BEHAVIOR

Before firms can begin to sell their products online, they must first understand what kinds of people they will find online and how those people behave in the online marketplace. In this section, we focus primarily on individual consumers in the B2C arena. However, many of the factors discussed apply to the B2B arena as well, insofar as purchasing decisions by firms are made by individuals.

THE INTERNET AUDIENCE

We will start with an analysis of some basic background demographics of Web consumers in the United States. The first principle of marketing and sales is "know thy customer." Who uses the Web, who shops on the Web and why, and what do they buy?

INTERNET TRAFFIC PATTERNS: THE ONLINE CONSUMER PROFILE

In 2009, over 84 million U.S. households (about 70% of all U.S. households) will have access to the Internet (eMarketer, Inc., 2008a). By comparison, 98% of all U.S. households currently have televisions and 94% have telephones.

Although the number of new online users increased at a rate of 30% a year or higher in the late 1990s, over the last several years, this growth rate has slowed to about 2%-3% a year. Because of the cost and complexity of computer use required for Internet access, it is unlikely that Internet use will equal that of television or radio use in the near future, although this may change as computers become less expensive and complex. E-commerce businesses can no longer count on an annual 30% growth rate in the online population to fuel their revenues. The days of extremely rapid growth in the U.S. Internet population are over.

Intensity and Scope of Usage

The slowing rate of growth in the U.S. Internet population is compensated for in part by an increasing intensity and scope of use. Several studies show that a greater amount of time is being spent online by Internet users. Overall, users are going online more frequently, with 72% of adult users in the United States (124 million people) logging on in a typical day (Pew Internet & American Life Project, 2008a). The more time users spend online, becoming more comfortable and familiar with Internet features and services, the more services they are likely to explore, according to the Pew Internet & American Life Project.

People who go online are engaging in a wider range of activities than in the past. While e-mail remains the most-used Internet service, other popular activities include using search engines, researching products and services, catching up on news, gathering hobby-related information, seeking health information, conducting work-related research, and reviewing financial information. **Table 6.1** identifies the range of online activities for the typical U.S. Internet user. Each percent translates into about 1.17 million people.

Demographics and Access

Some demographic groups have much higher percentages of online usage than other groups. **Table 6.2** on page 344 summarizes some of the major intergroup differences and their pace of change. All groups increased their use of the Internet over the period surveyed, but some groups increased their participation at a greater rate.

The demographic profile of the Internet—and e-commerce—has changed greatly since 1995. Up until 2000, single, white, young, college-educated males with high incomes dominated the Internet. This inequality in access and usage led to concerns about a possible "digital divide." However, in recent years, there has been a marked increase in Internet usage by females, minorities, and families with modest incomes, resulting in a notable decrease—but not elimination—in the earlier inequality of access and usage.

Gender Although men accounted for a small majority of Internet users in 2002, today a fairly equal percentage of both men (71%) and women (70%) use the Internet.

TABLE 6.1	A GROWING RANGE OF ONLINE ACTIVITIES: AN AVERAGE DAY IN THE LIFE OF AN INTERNET USER	
ACTIVITY		PERCENT OF INTERNET USERS WHO REPORTED ENGAGING IN ACTIVITY "YESTERDAY"
		2008
Use the Internet		72%
Send e-mail		60%
Use a search engine to find information		41%
Get news		37%
Look for information on a hobby or interest		29%
Surf the Web for fun		28%
Do any type of research for your job		23%
Check the weather		22%
Banking online		21%
Watch a video on a video-sharing site like YouTube or Google Video		15%
Check sports scores		15%
Visit a local, state, or federal government Web site		14%
Send or receive text messages using a cell phone		11%
Get financial information online		10%
Search for a map or driving directions		10%
Send instant messages		10%
Log onto the Internet using wireless device		10%
Watch a video clip or listen to an audio clip		10%
Use an online social networking site like MySpace, Facebook, or Friendster		9%
Play online games		9%
Look for information on Wikipedia		8%
Get travel info		8%
Download music files		7%
Tag online content like a photo, news story, or blog post		7%
Read someone else's blog		7%
Pay bills online		7%
Look up a phone number or address		7%
Pay to access or download digital content online		6%
Use online classified ads or sites like Craigslist		6%
Look for religious or spiritual information		6%
Buy a product		6%
Download other files such as games, videos, or pictures		6%
Download video files		6%

TABLE 6.1	A GROWING RANGE OF ONLINE ACTIVITIES: AN AVERAGE DAY IN THE LIFE OF AN INTERNET USER (CONTINUED)

ACTIVITY	PERCENT OF INTERNET USERS WHO REPORTED ENGAGING IN ACTIVITY "YESTERDAY"
	2008
Look online for information about a job	5%
Look for information about a place to live	5%
Upload photos to share with others	5%
Chat in a chat room or in an online discussion	5%
Search for information about someone you know or might meet	5%
Look for "how-to," "do-it-yourself," or repair information	5%
Look for health/medical info	5%
Share files from own computer with others	5%
Buy or make a reservation for travel	4%
Rate a product or service or person using an online rating system	4%
Take a virtual tour of a location online	4%
Get info online about a college or other school	4%
Listen to a live recorded radio broadcast online	4%
Create content for the Internet	4%
Post a comment or review online about a product or service you bought	3%
Take material you find online and remix it into your own artistic creation	3%
Participate in an online auction	3%
View live images online of a remote location or person, using a webcam	2%
Create a blog	2%
Go to a dating Web site or other sites where you can meet other people online	2%
Take a class online just for personal enjoyment or enrichment	2%
Make a phone call online	2%
Create an avatar or online representation of yourself	1%
Sell something online	1%
Research your family's history	1%
Download a podcast	1%
Take a class online for credit toward a degree	1%
Make a donation to a charity online	1%
Buy or sell stocks, bonds, or mutual funds	1%
Visit an adult Web site	1%
Download or share adult content online	1%

SOURCE: Pew Internet & American Life Project, 2008a.

TABLE 6.2	CHANGING DEMOGRAPHIC DIFFERENCES IN INTERNET ACCESS	
GROUP	THE PERCENT OF EACH GROUP ONLINE	
	2008	2002
Total Adults	73%	50%
Women	73%	56%
Men	73%	60%
AGE		
18–29	90%	74%
30–49	85%	67%
50–64	70%	52%
65+	35%	18%
RACE/ETHNICITY		
White, Non-Hispanic	73%	60%
Black, Non-Hispanic	59%	45%
Hispanic	80%	54%
COMMUNITY TYPE		
Urban	74%	67%
Suburban	77%	66%
Rural	63%	52%
HOUSEHOLD INCOME		
Less than $30,000/yr	53%	38%
$30,000–$50,000	76%	65%
$50,000–$75,000	85%	74%
More than $75,000	95%	86%
EDUCATIONAL ATTAINMENT		
Less than High School	44%	N/A
High School	63%	45%
Some College	84%	72%
College +	91%	82%

SOURCE: Based on data from Pew Internet & American Life Project, 2008b; 2005a; 2005b.

Women are also almost as likely to use the Internet on a daily basis as men, although somewhat less likely to purchase online.

Age Young adults (18–29) form the age group with the highest percentage of Internet access at 90%. Adults in the 30–49 group (85%) are also strongly represented and growing their Internet presence. The percentage of the very young (under 12) and teens (12-17) going online is also growing dramatically, in part due to increased access to computers and the Internet both at school and at home. Another fast growing group online is the 65 and over segment, 35% of whom now use the Internet, nearly double the level of 2002.

Ethnicity Variation across ethnic groups is not as wide as across age groups. In 2002, there were significant differences among ethnic groups, but this has receded. The percentage of Hispanics with Internet access now exceeds that of whites. African-Americans continue to lag somewhat behind, with only 59% but this number is increasing over time. The growth rates for both Hispanics and African-Americans over the six-year period from 2002 to 2008 is higher than those for whites, which has helped close the gap.

Community Type Historically, Internet access rates have been lower in rural areas than other kinds of communities. Internet penetration in rural areas has grown significantly since 2002, but continues to lag over 10 percentage points below that of urban and suburban areas.

Income Level As can be seen in Table 6.2, 95% of households with income levels above $75,000 have Internet access, compared to only 53% of households earning less than $30,000. However, those households with lower earnings are gaining Internet access at faster rates than households with incomes of $75,000 and above. Over time, income differences have declined, but they remain significant.

Education Amount of education also makes a significant difference when it comes to online access. Of those individuals with a high school education or less, 44% were online in 2008, compared to 91% of individuals with a college degree or more. Even some college education boosted Internet usage, with that segment reaching 84% accessing the Web. In general, educational disparities far exceed other disparities in Internet access and usage.

Overall, there remains a strong relationship between age, income, ethnicity, and education on one hand and Internet usage on the other. The so-called "digital divide" has indeed moderated, but it still persists along the income, education, age, and ethnic dimensions.

Type of Internet Connection: Broadband Impacts

In 2008, around 75 million households had broadband service in their homes—62% of all households (eMarketer, Inc., 2008b; Pew Internet & American Life Project, 2008c). Research suggests the broadband audience is different from the dial-up audience (see **Table 6.3**) and marketers need to take this into account when devising marketing plans. The broadband audience is more educated, wealthier, and more middle-aged. The broadband audience is much more intensely involved with the Internet and much more capable of using the Internet. For marketers, this audience offers unique opportunities for the use of multimedia advertising and marketing campaigns, and for the positioning of products especially suited for this audience.

Community Effects: Social Contagion

For a physical retail store, the most important factor in shaping sales is location, location, and location. If you are located where thousands of people pass by every day, you will tend to do well. But for Internet retailers, physical location has almost no consequence as long as customers can be served by shipping services such as UPS or the post office. What does make a difference for consumer purchases on the Internet is whether or not the consumer is located in "neighborhoods" where others purchase on the Internet. These so-called neighborhood effects, and the role of social emulation in consumption decisions, are well-known for other goods such as personal computers. Research on an Internet grocery found that being located nearby other users of the online grocery increased the likelihood of purchasing at the site by 50% (Bell and Song, 2004). Online marketers are beginning to realize the importance of online and offline social ties, and communities, for branding and sales. Social networking sites, blogs, and social tagging sites are increasingly influential in consumer behavior as you will see throughout this chapter.

TABLE 6.3	THE IMPACT OF BROADBAND ON INTERNET ACTIVITIES	
ACTIVITY	HOME DIAL-UP	HOME BROADBAND
Use an online search engine	80%	94%
Check weather reports	75%	84%
Get news	61%	80%
Visit a state or local government Web site	55%	72%
Look for information on the 2008 election	37%	62%
Watch a video on a video sharing site like YouTube or Google Video	29%	60%
Look online for information about a job	36%	50%
Send instant messages	38%	44%
Read someone else's blog	15%	40%
Use a social networking site	21%	33%
Make a donation to a charity online	9%	23%
Download a podcast	8%	22%
Download or share files	17%	17%
Create or work on your blog	8%	15%

SOURCE: Pew Internet & American Life Project, 2008c.

Lifestyle and Sociological Impacts

There are some worrisome potential impacts to intensive Internet use. Ask many parents of young teenagers, and they will often complain their children are spending too much time instant messaging and playing games online. Early research suggested that the Internet might be causing a decline in traditional social activities, such as talking face-to-face with neighbors and family members, encouraging users to spend less time with family and friends, and more time working, whether at home or at the office. According to an early study performed at Stanford University by a group of political scientists, Internet users lose touch with those around them; individuals spending just two to five hours a week online spend far less time talking with friends and family face-to-face and on the phone. Users who spend up to five hours a week online frequently experience an increase in time spent working while at home, while those who spend more than five hours a week online find themselves working more at work as well; the Internet is taking up a larger portion of what used to be free time for some workers. On the other hand, e-mail, instant messaging, and chat groups, all decidedly social activities, albeit not face-to-face ones, are among the most popular uses of the Internet.

More recent research has found that the use of the Internet strengthens and compliments traditional face-to-face relationships. While Internet use involves a single user sitting in front of a screen—much like television—it is very different from television because of the high levels of social interaction possible on the Internet. Insofar as Internet use deters children from face-to-face interaction or from undirected "play" out of doors, undesirable effects on child social development may result (Nie and Erbring, 2000). On the other hand, a recent study demonstrated that the Internet has strengthened ties among cousins (the "clicking cousins effect"), children, and parents through the use of e-mail to stay in touch on a daily basis. A meta-analysis of multiple studies on the impact of the Internet on social interaction from 1995–2003 found mixed results, with offline and online interaction stimulating one another, but online communication did not translate into more visiting face-to-face (Saunders and Chester, 2008; Shklovski, et al., 2004).

Media Choices and Multitasking: The Internet versus Other Media Channels

What may be of even more interest to marketers, however, is that the more time individuals spend using the Internet, "the more they turn their back on traditional media," according to the Stanford study. For every additional hour users spend online, they reduce their corresponding time spent with traditional media, such as television, newspapers, and radio. Traditional media are competing with the Internet for consumer attention, and so far, the Internet appears to be gaining on print media (newspapers and magazines) but not television. Media multitasking is rising: 100 million U.S. adult Internet users watch television while going online. Others listen to the radio, read magazines, or newspapers (eMarketer, Inc., 2007a). We discuss media consumption in greater depth in Chapter 10.

CONSUMER BEHAVIOR MODELS

Once firms have an understanding of who is online, they need to focus on how consumers behave online. The study of **consumer behavior** is a social science

consumer behavior
a social science discipline that attempts to model and understand the behavior of humans in a marketplace

discipline that attempts to model and understand the behavior of humans in a marketplace. Several social science disciplines play roles in this study, including sociology, psychology, and economics. Models of consumer behavior attempt to predict or "explain" what consumers purchase and where, when, how much, and why they buy. The expectation is that if the consumer decision-making process can be understood, firms will have a much better idea how to market and sell their products. **Figure 6.1** illustrates a general consumer behavior model that takes into account a wide range of factors that influence a consumer's marketplace decisions.

Consumer behavior models seek to predict the wide range of decisions that consumers make on the basis of background demographic factors, and on a set of intervening, more immediate variables that shape the consumer's ultimate decisions.

Background factors are cultural, social, and psychological in nature. Firms must recognize and understand the behavioral significance of these background factors and adjust their marketing efforts accordingly. **Culture** is the broadest factor in consumer behavior because it shapes basic human values, wants, perceptions, and behaviors. Culture creates basic expectations that consumers bring to the marketplace, such as what should be bought in different markets, how things should be bought, and how things should be paid for. Generally, culture affects an entire nation, and takes on major significance in international marketing. For instance, an American-style e-commerce site that sells cooking spices might have difficulty in an Asian culture such as China or Japan, where food and spice shopping takes place at local neighbor-

culture

shapes basic human values, wants, perceptions, and behaviors

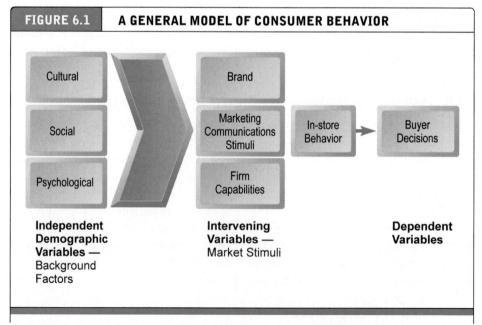

| FIGURE 6.1 | A GENERAL MODEL OF CONSUMER BEHAVIOR |

Independent Demographic Variables — Background Factors

Intervening Variables — Market Stimuli

Dependent Variables

Consumer behavior models try to predict the decisions that consumers make in the marketplace.
SOURCE: Adapted from Kotler and Armstrong, 2008.

hood markets, large food stores do not exist, and shoppers tend to pick out and smell each spice before purchasing it.

Within nations, subcultures are extremely important in consumer behavior. **Subcultures** are subsets of cultures that form around major social differences such as ethnicity, age, lifestyle, and geography. In the United States, ethnicity plays a very large role in consumer behavior. There are an estimated 40 million African-Americans with an annual purchasing power of over $845 billion, about 43 million Hispanics with a total annual purchasing power of $860 billion, and almost 15 million Asian-Americans with a total purchasing power of over $460 billion. (U.S. Census Bureau, 2007, Dodson, 2007). Each of these ethnic groups represents a significant market segment that firms can target. For instance, Toyota was one of the first automotive manufacturers to use the Internet to target Hispanic customers. Toyota places Web advertisements on Spanish-language portals such as MSNLatino, Yahoo en Espanol, AOL Latino, Univision, and Terra to direct Hispanic customers to its Toyota.com Spanish-language Web site. As a result, Toyota now ranks 1st in the new vehicle sales registered by Latinos. Among the important social factors that shape consumer behavior are the many reference groups to which all consumers "belong," either as direct participating members, or as indirect members by affiliation, association, or aspiration. **Direct reference groups** include one's family, profession or occupation, religion, neighborhood, and schools. **Indirect reference groups** include one's life-cycle stage, social class, and lifestyle group (discussed later). For instance, the concept of community-based Web sites is based on the notion that people choose to be members of groups and subgroups that express and reflect their interests, such as the home-schooling community, personal health-related-issues communities, and recreational activity communities.

Within each of these reference groups, there are **opinion leaders** (or **viral influencers**, as they are termed by online marketers), who because of their personality, skills, or other factors, influence the behavior of others. Marketers seek out opinion leaders in their communications and promotional efforts because of their influence over other people. For instance, many Web sites include testimonials submitted by successful adopters of a product or service. Generally, those giving the testimonials are portrayed as opinion leaders— "smart people in the know." At Procter & Gamble's Web site, for example, testimonials come from "P&G Advisors," who are consumers who take an active interest in Procter & Gamble products.

A unique kind of reference group is a **lifestyle group**, which can be defined as an integrated pattern of activities (hobbies, sports, shopping likes and dislikes, social events typically attended), interests (food, fashion, family, recreation), and opinions (social issues, business, government).

Lifestyle group classification systems—of which there are several—attempt to create a classification scheme that captures a person's whole pattern of living, consuming, and acting. The theory is that once you understand a consumer's lifestyle, or the lifestyles typical of a group of people—such as college students, for instance— then you can design products and marketing messages that appeal specifically to that

subculture
subset of cultures that form around major social differences

direct reference groups
one's family, profession or occupation, religion, neighborhood, and schools

indirect reference groups
one's life-cycle stage, social class, and lifestyle group

opinion leaders (viral influencers)
influence the behavior of others through their personality, skills, or other factors

lifestyle group
an integrated pattern of activities, interests, and opinions

lifestyle group. Lifestyle classification then becomes another method of segmenting the market.

psychological profile
set of needs, drives, motivations, perceptions, and learned behaviors

In addition to lifestyle classification, marketers are interested in a consumer's psychological profile. A **psychological profile** is a set of needs, drives, motivations, perceptions, and learned behaviors—including attitudes and beliefs. Marketers attempt to appeal to psychological profiles through product design, product positioning, and marketing communications. For instance, many health e-commerce sites emphasize that they help consumers achieve a sense of control over their health destiny by providing them with information about diseases and treatments. This message is a powerful appeal to the needs of a wealthy, educated, professional, and technically advanced set of Web users for self-control and mastery over what might be a complex, health-threatening situation.

Marketers cannot influence demographic background factors, but they can adjust their branding, communications, and firm capabilities to appeal to demographic realities. For instance, the National Basketball Association's Web site, NBA.com, appeals to a variety of basketball fan subgroups from avid fans interested in specific team statistics, to fashion-conscious fans who can purchase clothing for specific NBA teams, to fans who want to auction memorabilia.

PROFILES OF ONLINE CONSUMERS

Online consumer behavior parallels that of offline consumer behavior with some obvious differences. It is important to first understand why people choose the Internet channel to conduct transactions. **Table 6.4** illustrates the main reasons consumers choose the online channel.

While price appears on this list, overwhelmingly, consumers shop on the Web because of convenience, which in turn is produced largely by saving them time. Overall transaction cost reduction appears to be the major motivator for choosing the online channel, followed by other cost reductions in the product or service.

TABLE 6.4	WHY CONSUMERS CHOOSE THE ONLINE CHANNEL
REASON	PERCENTAGE OF RESPONDENTS
Can shop at any time of day	88%
Can research many products at the same time	66%
Can find products that are not available in stores	54%
Do not need to deal with salespeople	53%
Can get better information on products online	45%
Easier to find information on Web sites than it is to find in-store employees to help	44%
Prices are better online	40%
Products are usually in stock	40%

SOURCES: Based on data from eMarketer, Inc., 2007b; Sterling Commerce and Deloitte Consulting, 2007.

THE ONLINE PURCHASING DECISION

Once online, why do consumers actually purchase a product or service at a specific site? There are many models and several research studies that attempt to provide answers to this question. **Psychographic research** (research that combines both demographic and psychological data and divides a market into different groups based on social class, lifestyle, and/or personality characteristics) on the profile of active e-commerce shoppers attempts to understand the characteristics of users—in particular their various lifestyles—that lead to online buying behavior. For instance, in a study by the Wharton Forum on Electronic Commerce, a panel of 2,500 people was surveyed to understand the factors that predict e-commerce purchases. As shown in **Figure 6.2**, the survey found that the most important factors in predicting buying behavior were (1) looking for product information online, (2) leading a "wired lifestyle" (one where consumers spend a considerable amount of their working and home lives online), and (3) recently ordering from a catalog. Other studies identify the path to a purchase decision. Around 37% of respondents in this study used a search engine to find items online, and knew what they wanted before searching (eMarketer, 2007c).

But aside from individual characteristics, you need to consider how buyers make the actual decision to purchase and how the Internet environment affects consumers'

psychographic research

divides a market into different groups based on social class, lifestyle, and/or personality characteristics

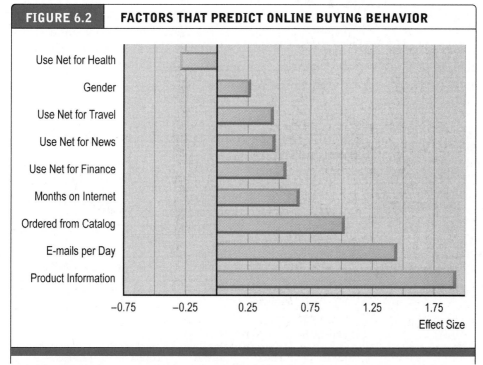

FIGURE 6.2 | **FACTORS THAT PREDICT ONLINE BUYING BEHAVIOR**

Actively looking for product information, the number of e-mails sent per day, and whether someone has recently ordered from a catalog are the most significant variables in predicting whether someone will purchase online (variables are listed from lowest to highest effect).

SOURCE: Lohse, Bellman, and Johnson, 2000.

decisions. There are five stages in the consumer decision process: awareness of need, search for more information, evaluation of alternatives, the actual purchase decision, and post-purchase contact with the firm (Kotler and Armstrong, 2008). **Figure 6.3** shows the consumer decision process and the types of offline and online marketing communications that support this process and seek to influence the consumer before, during, and after the purchase decision.

As shown in Figure 6.3, traditional mass media, along with catalogs and direct mail campaigns, are used to drive potential buyers to Web sites. What's new about online purchasing is the new media marketing communications capabilities afforded by the Web: community bulletin boards, chat rooms, listservs, banner ads, targeted permission e-mail, search engines, and online product reviews. Simply put, the Web offers marketers an extraordinary increase in marketing communications tools and power, and the ability to envelop the consumer in a very rich information and purchasing environment. In Chapter 7, we describe these new communications techniques and gauge their effectiveness in greater detail.

Both offline and online communications tools can be used to support the online consumer decision process at each of the five stages of the process.

A MODEL OF ONLINE CONSUMER BEHAVIOR

Is online consumer behavior fundamentally different from offline consumer behavior? Arguably not. Consumer behavior online and offline has both similarities and differences. The e-commerce world is not quite so revolutionary as some would have us believe. For instance, the stages of the consumer decision process are basically the same whether the consumer is online or offline. On the other hand, the general model of consumer behavior requires modification to take into account new factors. In **Figure 6.4**, we have modified the general model of consumer

FIGURE 6.3	THE CONSUMER DECISION PROCESS AND SUPPORTING COMMUNICATIONS

MARKET COMMUNICATIONS	Awareness— Need Recognition	Search	Evaluation of Alternatives	Purchase	Post-purchase Behavior— Loyalty
Offline Communications	Mass media TV Radio Print media	Catalogs Print ads Mass media Salespeople Product raters Store visits	Reference groups Opinion leaders Mass media Product raters Store visits	Promotions Direct mail Mass media Print media	Warranties Service calls Parts and Repair Consumer groups
Online Communications	Targeted banner ads Interstitials Targeted event promotions	Search engines Online catalogs Site visits Targeted e-mail	Search engines Online catalogs Site visits Product reviews User evaluations	Online promotions Lotteries Discounts Targeted e-mail	Communities of consumption Newsletters Customer e-mail Online updates

FIGURE 6.4	A MODEL OF ONLINE CONSUMER BEHAVIOR

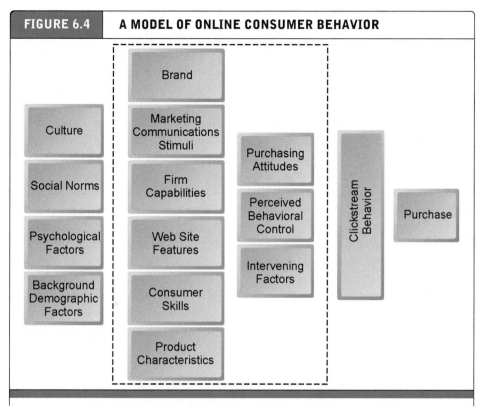

In this general model of online consumer behavior, the decision to purchase is shaped by background demographic factors, several intervening factors, and finally influenced greatly by clickstream behavior very near to the precise moment of purchase.

behavior to focus on user characteristics, product characteristics, and Web site features, along with traditional factors such as brand strength and specific market communications (advertising) (Li, et al., 1999; Lohse, et. al. 2000; Pavlou and Fygenson, 2005). Figure 6.4 attempts to summarize and simplify current research.

In the online model, Web site features, along with consumer skills, product characteristics, attitudes towards online purchasing, and perceptions about control over the Web environment come to the fore. Web site features include latency (delay in downloads), navigability, and confidence in a Web site's security. (We examine Web site design issues as they relate to marketing more fully in Chapter 7.) There are parallels in the analog world. For instance, it is well known that consumer behavior can be influenced by store design, and that understanding the precise movements of consumers through a physical store can enhance sales if goods and promotions are arranged along the most likely consumer tracks. For instance, because consumers almost invariably enter a store and move to the right, high-margin items—jewelry and cosmetics—tend to be located there. And because it is known that consumers purchase fresh dairy products frequently, they are put at the back of grocery stores. Wal-Mart uses consumer-tracking databases within its stores to optimize the convenience to consumers—putting clothing nearest the entry, and electronics and cameras toward the back. Proper store design and precision tracking of consumers is not new—but its technical implementation on the Web, its lowered cost, its ubiquity, and its comprehensiveness on the Web are new.

Consumer skills refers to the knowledge that consumers have about how to conduct online transactions (which increases with experience online). Product characteristics refers to the fact that some products can be easily described, packaged, and shipped over the Internet (such as books, software, and DVDs), whereas others cannot. Combined with traditional factors, such as brand, advertising, and firm capabilities, these factors lead to specific attitudes about purchasing at a Web site (trust in the Web site and favorable customer experience) and a sense that the consumer can control his or her environment on the Web site.

clickstream behavior

the transaction log that consumers establish as they move about the Web

Clickstream behavior refers to the transaction log that consumers establish as they move about the Web, from search engine, to a variety of sites, then to a single site, then to a single page, and then, finally, to a decision to purchase. These precious moments are similar to "point of purchase" moments in traditional retail.

A number of researchers have argued that understanding the background demographics of Internet users is no longer necessary, and not that predictive in any event. In most studies of consumer behavior, background demographics usually account for less than 5% of the observed behavior. Many believe instead that the most important predictors of online consumer behavior are the session characteristics and the clickstream behavior of people online very close to the moment of purchase. The theory is that this information will enable marketers to understand what the consumer was looking for at each moment, and how much they were willing to pay, thus allowing the marketers to precisely target their communications in an effort to sway the purchase decision in their favor.

For instance, a study by Booz Allen & Hamilton and NetRatings found that background demographics alone, and even background demographics with attitudinal and lifestyle factors, fail to take into account the different types of user sessions and different clickstream patterns. Analyzing the clickstream behavior of 2,466 individuals engaged in 186,797 user sessions, the study identified seven categories of user sessions: "Quickies," "Just the Facts," "Single Mission," "Do It Again," "Loitering," "Information Please," and "Surfing." Researchers called these segments "occasions," and suggested "occasion-based" marketing is more effective than static market segmentation based on demographics and/or consumer attitudes. Segmenting the market in this way, they found that in some types of sessions, users are more likely to buy, whereas in other sessions, they appear to be immune to online advertising. A study of over 10,000 visits to an online wine store found that detailed and general clickstream behavior were as important as customer demographics and prior purchase behavior in predicting a current purchase (Van den Poel and Buckinx, 2004). The most important clickstream factors were:

- Number of days since last visit
- Speed of clickstream behavior
- Number of products viewed during last visit
- Number of pages viewed
- Number of products viewed
- Supplying personal information (trust)

- Number of days since last purchase
- Number of past purchases

Clickstream marketing takes maximum advantage of the Internet environment. It presupposes no prior knowledge of the customer (and in that sense is "privacy-regarding"), and can be developed dynamically as customers use the Internet. For instance, the success of search engine marketing (the display of paid advertisements on Web search pages) is based in large part on what the consumer is looking for at the moment and how they go about looking (detailed clickstream data). After examining the detailed data, general clickstream data is used (days since last visit, past purchases). If available, demographic data is used (region, city, and gender).

SHOPPERS: BROWSERS AND BUYERS

The picture of Internet use sketched in the previous section emphasizes the complexity of behavior online. Although the Internet audience still tends to be concentrated among the well educated, affluent, and youthful, increasingly the audience is becoming more diverse. Clickstream analysis shows us that people go online for many different reasons. Online shopping is similarly complex. Beneath the surface of the $255 billion B2C e-commerce market in 2008 are substantial differences in how users shop online.

For instance, as shown in **Figure 6.5**, about 68% of online users are "buyers" who actually purchase something entirely online. Another 12% of online users research products on the Web ("browsers"), but purchase them offline. This combined group, referred to as "shoppers," constitutes approximately 80% of the online Internet audience. With the U.S. Internet audience (14 years or older) estimated at about 173–200 million in 2008, online shoppers (the combination of buyers and browsers) add up to a market size of around 140–160 million consumers. Most marketers find this number exciting.

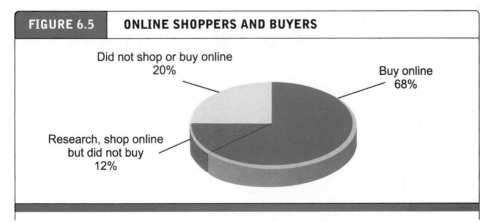

| FIGURE 6.5 | ONLINE SHOPPERS AND BUYERS |

About 80% of the online audience shops online, either by researching products or by purchasing products online. The percentage of the online audience actually purchasing has increased by 5% since 2005 to 68%, the number of their purchase transactions has increased, and the average annual amount spent has increased from $878 to $1,243 in 2008.

SOURCE: Based on data from eMarketer, Inc., 2008a; authors' estimates.

The significance of online browsing for offline purchasing should not be underestimated. Although it is difficult to precisely measure the amount of offline sales which occur because of online product research, several different studies have found that, in 2008, about one-third of all offline retail purchasing is influenced by online product research, blogs, banner ads, and other Internet exposure. The offline influence varies by product. This amounts to about $1 trillion in annual retail sales, a truly extraordinary number (eMarketer, Inc., 2008a).

E-commerce is a major conduit and generator of offline commerce. The reverse is also true: online traffic is driven by offline brands and shopping. While online research influences offline purchase, it is also the case that offline marketing media heavily influence online behavior including sales. Traditional print media (magazines and newspapers) and television are by far the most powerful media for reaching and engaging consumers with information about new products and directing them to the Web (see **Table 6.5**). Online communities and blogging are also very influential but not yet as powerful as traditional media.

TABLE 6.5	MEDIA THAT INFLUENCE CONSUMERS TO START SEARCH FOR MERCHANDISE ONLINE
MEDIA	PERCENTAGE OF RESPONDENTS
Magazines	47%
Reading an article	43%
Broadcast TV	43%
Newspapers	41%
Cable TV	36%
Coupons	36%
Face-to-face communication	34%
Radio	30%
Direct mail	30%
E-mail advertising	29%
In-store promotions	27%
Online advertising	26%
Outdoor billboards	12%
Online communities	10%
Instant messaging	9%
Mobile Phone	8%
Blogs	8%
Yellow pages	7%
Mobile pictures/video	5%
Text messaging	5%
Other	6%

SOURCES: Based on data from eMarketer, Inc., 2008f; BigResearch and the Retail Advertising and Marketing Association, 2008.

These considerations strongly suggest that e-commerce and traditional commerce are coupled and should be viewed by merchants (and researchers) as part of a continuum of consuming behavior and not as radical alternatives to one another. Commerce is commerce; the customers are often the same people. Customers use a wide variety of media, sometimes multiple media at once. The significance of these findings for marketers is very clear. Online merchants should build the information content of their sites to attract browsers looking for information, build content to rank high in search engines, put less attention on selling per se, and promote services and products (especially new products) in offline media settings in order to support their online stores.

WHAT CONSUMERS SHOP FOR AND BUY ONLINE

You can look at online sales as divided roughly into two groups: small ticket and big ticket items. Big ticket items include computer equipment and consumer electronics, where orders can easily be over $500. Small ticket items include apparel, books, health and beauty supplies, office supplies, music, software, videos, and toys, where the average purchase is typically less than $100. In the early days of e-commerce, sales of small ticket items vastly outnumbered those of large ticket items for a variety of reasons. First movers on the Web sold these products early on; the purchase price was low (reduced consumer risk); the items were physically small (shipping costs were low); margins were high (at least on CDs and software); and there was a broad selection of products (e-commerce vendors could compete on scope when compared to traditional offline stores). But the recent growth of big ticket items such as computer hardware, consumer electronics, furniture, and jewelry has changed the overall sales mix. Consumers are now much more confident spending online for big ticket items. Although furniture and large appliances were initially perceived as too bulky to sell online, these categories have rapidly expanded in the last few years. The types of purchases made also depend on levels of experience with the Web (U.S.C. Annenberg School Center for the Digital Future, 2004). New Web users tend primarily to buy small ticket items, while experienced Web users are more willing to buy large ticket items in addition to small ticket items. **Figure 6.6** illustrates how much consumers spent online for various categories of goods at the top 500 Internet retailers in 2007.

INTENTIONAL ACTS: HOW SHOPPERS FIND VENDORS ONLINE

Given the prevalence of "click here" banner ads, one might think customers are "driven" to online vendors by spur-of-the-moment decisions. In fact, only a tiny percentage of shoppers click on banners to find vendors. Once they are online, 37% of consumers use search engines as their preferred method of research or purchasing a product; 33% go directly to the company Web site. Comparison shopping sites (17%) and product rating sites (15%) also play a role. E-commerce shoppers are highly intentional. Typically, they are focused browsers looking for specific products, companies, and services. Merchants can convert these "goal-oriented," intentional shoppers into buyers if they can target their communications to them and design their sites in such a way as to provide easy-to-access and use product information, full selection, and customer service and do this at the

construction, and unique products. The Apple iPhone brand connotes to iPhone owners a cool, hip, technologically advanced style of life. Consumers are willing to pay a premium price for Apple iPhones not only because of the augmented product features, but also because of these brand expectations. **Figure 6.8** illustrates the process of brand creation or **branding**.

branding
process of brand creation

Marketers identify the differentiating features of the actual and augmented product. They engage in a variety of marketing communications activities to transmit the feature set to the consumer. Based on the consumers' experiences and the promises made by marketers in their communications, consumers develop expectations about a product. For instance, when a consumer purchases an Apple iPhone, he or she expects to receive a unique, high-quality, very easy-to-use cell phone. Consumers are willing to pay a premium price in order to obtain these qualities. If iPhones do not in fact perform according to these expectations, the brand will be weakened and consumers will be less willing to pay a premium price. In other words, a strong brand requires a strong product. But if iPhones do perform according to expectations, then customers will feel loyal to the product; they will purchase again or recommend it to others; and they will trust, feel affection for, and ascribe a good reputation to both the product and the company that makes it.

closed loop marketing
when marketers are able to directly influence the design of the core product based on market research and feedback from the market

Ideally, marketers directly influence the design of products to ensure the products have desirable features, high quality, correct pricing, product support, and reliability. When marketers are able to directly influence the design of a core product based on market research and feedback, this is called **closed loop marketing**. While ideal, it is more often the case that marketers are hired to "sell" a product that has already been

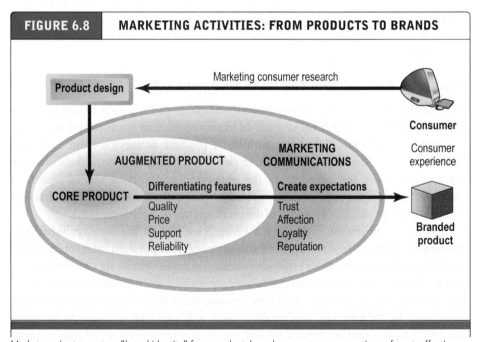

| FIGURE 6.8 | **MARKETING ACTIVITIES: FROM PRODUCTS TO BRANDS** |

Marketers aim to create a "brand identity" for a product, based on consumer perceptions of trust, affection, loyalty, and reputation.

designed. E-commerce—as we see next—offers some unique opportunities to achieve closed loop marketing.

Marketers devise and implement brand strategies. A **brand strategy** is a set of plans for differentiating a product from its competitor, and communicating these differences effectively to the marketplace. In developing new e-commerce brands, the ability to devise and develop a brand strategy has been crucial in the success and failure of many companies, as described throughout this book.

What kinds of products can be branded? According to many marketing specialists, there is no limit. Every product can potentially be branded. Sneakers that make you soar from Nike, cars from Volvo that make you feel safe on dark rainy nights, shirts from Polo that make you appear as if you were on the way to a country club—these are all examples of products with extraordinary brand names for which consumers pay premium prices.

How much is a brand worth? Brands differ in their power and value in the marketplace. A brand can represent corporate value as an asset, it can also represent customer loyalty or attachment, and it can be seen as a set of associations that consumers have about products. **Brand equity** is the estimated value of the premium customers are willing to pay for using a branded product when compared to unbranded competitors (Feldwick, 1996). According to Interbrand's 2008 World's Most Valuable Brands survey, the top five brands and their estimated equity value are Coca-Cola ($66.6 billion), IBM ($59 billion), Microsoft ($59 billion), General Electric ($53 billion), and Nokia ($35.9 billion) (Interbrand/BusinessWeek, 2008). Brand equity also affects stock prices insofar as brands strengthen future revenue streams, and insofar as brands are intangible assets that have a market value. There are several methodologies used to calculate brand value, but this discussion is beyond the scope of this book (Berg, et. al., 2007; Ailawadi, 2003).

SEGMENTING, TARGETING, AND POSITIONING

Markets are not unitary, but in fact are composed of many different kinds of customers with different needs. Firms seek to segment markets into distinct groups of customers who differ from one another in terms of product needs. Once the segments are established, each segment can be *targeted* with differentiated products. Within each segment, the product is *positioned* and branded as a unique, high-value product, especially suited to the needs of segment customers.

There are six major ways in which marketers segment and target markets (**Table 6.7**).

By segmenting markets, firms can differentiate their products to more closely fit the needs of customers in each segment. Rather than charge one price for the same product, firms can maximize revenues by creating several different variations on the same product and charging different prices in each market segment. While segmenting and targeting are not new, the Internet offers an unusual opportunity for very fine-grained segmenting down to the level of the individual. Potentially, with enough personal information, marketers on the Internet can personalize market messages to precisely fit an individual's needs and wants. In the physical world of marketing using

brand strategy
a set of plans for differentiating a product from its competitors, and communicating these differences effectively to the marketplace

brand equity
the estimated value of the premium customers are willing to pay for using a branded product when compared to unbranded competitors

TABLE 6.7	MAJOR TYPES OF ONLINE MARKET SEGMENTATION AND TARGETING
Behavioral	Segmenting on the basis of behavior in the marketplace. In traditional stores, this involves observing how customers walk through stores. On the Internet, Web site owners and members of advertising networks can dynamically assign users to groups, and merge their behavioral information with other data.
Demographic	Using age, ethnicity, religion, and other demographic factors to segment. On the Internet, using registration data or other self-revelations. Sites visited also serves as proxy measures of age, e.g., music sites are visited by young persons.
Psychographic	Using common interests, values, and opinions along with personality, attitude, and lifestyle preferences to segment consumers into groups. On the Internet, Web sites visited can substitute for direct measurement, e.g., the fashion Web sites visited by consumers reflect a self-chosen lifestyle and values.
Technical	Using information gathered by a shopping technology as a basis for segmentation. Nearly everyone who shops at malls owns a car. On the Internet, each consumer visit generates a record of the user's domain, IP address, browser, computer platform and connection type, as well as what URL the user linked to the site from and the date and time. People who connect using broadband media, for instance, are much more likely to download music from the Internet.
Contextual	Using the context of an event, or the content of an event, as a basis for segmentation. People who attend rock concerts tend to purchase music CDs as well. On the Internet, people who read the online *Wall Street Journal* are very good targets for financial service advertising,
Search	Using consumers' explicitly expressed interest at this moment to segment and target. Perhaps the simplest of all segmenting, search direct response follows the ageless maxim "sell them what they want."

other technologies like newspapers, radio and television, it is more difficult to personalize messages.

Once markets are segmented, the branding process proceeds within each segment by appealing to the segment members. For instance, automobile manufacturers segment their markets on many dimensions: demographics (age, sex, income, and occupation), geographic (region), benefits (special performance features), and psychographics (self-image and emotional needs). For each market segment, they offer a uniquely branded product.

ARE BRANDS RATIONAL?

Coca-Cola is one of the most enduring, powerful brands in U.S. commercial history. The core product is colored, flavored, carbonated sugar water. The augmented branded product is a delightful, refreshing, reputable, unique-tasting drink available worldwide, based on a secret formula that consumers willingly pay up to twice as much for when compared to unbranded store brands of cola. Coca-Cola is a marketing-created micro-monopoly. There is only one Coke and only one supplier.

Why would consumers pay twice as much for Coke compared to unbranded cola drinks? Is this rational?

The answer is a qualified yes. Brands introduce market efficiency by reducing the search costs and decision-making costs of consumers. Strong brands signal strong products that work. Brands carry information. Confronted with many different drinks, the choice of Coke can be made quickly, without much thought, and with the assurance that you will have the drinking experience you expect based on prior use of the product. Brands reduce consumer risk and uncertainty in a crowded marketplace. Brands are like an insurance policy against nasty surprises in the marketplace for which consumers willingly pay a premium—better safe than sorry.

The ability of brands to become a corporate asset (to attain brand equity) based on future anticipated premiums paid by consumers also provides an incentive for firms to build products that serve customer needs better than other products. Therefore, although brands create micro-monopolies, increase market costs, and lead to above-average returns on investment (monopoly rents), they also introduce market efficiencies for the consumer.

For business firms, brands are a major source of revenue and are obviously rational. Brands lower customer acquisition costs and increase customer retention. The stronger the brand reputation, the easier it is to attract new customers. **Customer acquisition costs** refer to the overall costs of converting a prospect into a consumer, and include all marketing and advertising costs. **Customer retention costs** are those costs incurred in convincing an existing customer to purchase again. In general, it is much more expensive to acquire a new customer than to retain an existing customer. For instance, Reichheld and Schefter calculated that e-commerce sites lose from $20 to $80 on each customer in the first year because of the high cost of acquiring a customer, but potentially can make up for this loss in later years by retaining loyal customers (Reichheld and Schefter, 2000). In some instances, however, e-commerce companies have gone out of business before they ever reached that point.

A successful brand can constitute a long-lasting, impregnable unfair competitive advantage. As we discussed in Chapter 2, a competitive advantage is considered "fair" when it is based on innovation, efficient production processes, or other factors that theoretically can be imitated and/or purchased in the marketplace by competitors. An "unfair competitive advantage" cannot be purchased in the factor markets and includes such things as patents, copyrights, secret processes, unusually skilled or dedicated employees and managers, and, of course, brand names. Brands cannot be purchased (unless one buys the entire company).

customer acquisition costs
the overall costs of converting a prospect into a consumer

customer retention costs
costs incurred in convincing an existing customer to purchase again

DO BRANDS LAST FOREVER?

Brands, however, do not necessarily last forever, and the micro-monopolies they create may not be stable over the long term. In a study of brand endurance, Golder found that between 1923 and 1997, only 23% of the firms that ranked first in market share in 1923 were still in the market-leading position in 1997, while 28% of the leaders failed altogether (Golder, 2000). Less than 10% of the Fortune 500 of 1917 still exists (Starbuck and Nystrom, 1997). Life at the top is sweet, but often short, and market efficiency is restored long-term as entrepreneurs exploit new technologies and new public tastes at a faster rate than the incumbent market leaders.

CAN BRANDS SURVIVE THE INTERNET? BRANDS AND PRICE DISPERSION ON THE INTERNET

As we noted in Chapter 1, during the early days of e-commerce, many academics and business consultants postulated that the Web would lead to a new world of information symmetry and "frictionless" commerce. In this world, newly empowered customers, using intelligent shopping agents and the nearly infinite product and price information available on the Internet, would shop around the world (and around the clock) with minimal effort, driving prices down to their marginal cost and driving intermediaries out of the market as customers began to deal directly with producers (Wigand and Benjamin, 1995; Rayport and Sviolka, 1995; Evans and Wurster, 1999; Sinha 2000).[1] The result was supposed to be an instance of the "**Law of One Price**": with complete price transparency in a perfect information marketplace, one world price for every product would emerge. "Frictionless commerce" would, of course, mean the end of marketing based on brands.

> **Law of One Price**
> with complete price transparency in a perfect information marketplace, there will be one world price for every product

But it didn't work out this way. Price has not proven to be the only determinant of consumer behavior. E-commerce firms continue to rely heavily on brands to attract customers and charge premium prices. Internet technologies can be used to infinitely differentiate products by using personalization, customization, and community marketing techniques (described in the next section), thereby overcoming the price-lowering effects of lower search costs and a large number of worldwide suppliers for goods. For instance, Bailey and Brynjolfsson (1997) found that prices for books, music CDs, and software were not substantially lower at e-commerce sites than in traditional stores or catalogs (see also Clay et al., 1999 for similar results). Later studies found that prices at e-commerce sites were 9%–16% lower than at conventional retail outlets for musical CDs (depending on whether taxes and shipping costs were included in the price), but also found substantial price dispersion—nearly as much as in traditional markets for the same goods (Brynjolfsson and Smith, 2000).

> **price dispersion**
> the difference between the highest and lowest prices in a market

Price dispersion refers to the difference between the highest and lowest prices in a market. In a perfect market, there is not supposed to be any price dispersion. Other evidence suggests that many suppliers and price comparisons can overwhelm consumers, and that consumers achieve efficiencies by quickly purchasing from a trusted, high-price provider. In general, the most frequently visited and used e-commerce sites are not the lowest-price sites (Smith et al., 1999).

Recent research on brands and price dispersion illustrates the complexities of Internet marketing as well as the continuing power of brands and customer loyalty. In general, online prices have been increasing relative to offline prices (Baye, et al., 2002a; Scholten and Smith, 2002). Moreover, the "relative dispersion" of prices for online goods has also increased, which means that some online merchants can charge

[1]The theory of frictionless commerce is not unique to the Internet. Computerized stock and options markets over the last 20 years have also attempted to achieve low-friction transactions.

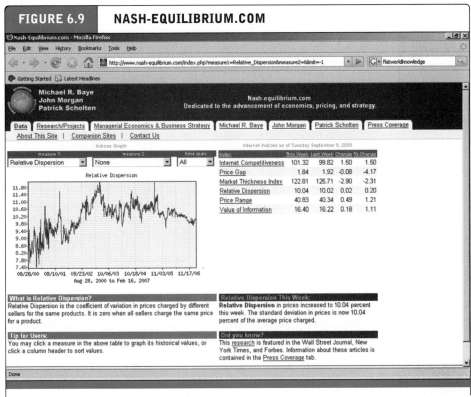

FIGURE 6.9 **NASH-EQUILIBRIUM.COM**

Nash-equilibrium.com is a Web site run by economists Michael Baye, John Morgan, and Patrick Scholten that provides a variety of economic indices related to the Internet, including Internet competitiveness, price gaps, price ranges, and relative dispersion statistics.

SOURCE: Nash-equilibrium.com, 2008.

more than others for certain items, according to Nash-equilibrium.com, a site run by economists that charts price movements on the Web (see **Figure 6.9**). Price dispersion, a measure of competitiveness, is less for commodities (memory chips) than for books or other differentiated products. Moreover, Internet-savvy users systematically seek out lowest prices. Sellers invest heavily in ways to differentiate their product or service—they create online brands that permit charging a premium for many products. The result is large differences in price sensitivity for the same products. For instance, researchers estimate that a 1% increase in prices at Amazon decreases sales by about 0.5%, while at Barnes & Noble, a 1% increase in prices results in a decrease in sales of about 4% (Baye, et al., 2002b).

One of the tactics used by online sellers is the "**library effect**" (or "catalog effect"). How much is it worth to you to shop at a store that has everything? Just one stop, and chances are that you can get what you want. Would you rather visit a library with 10 million volumes, or one with a few hundred thousand? The number of books on sale at Amazon is 23 times larger than the number of books found at a typical Barnes & Noble superstore, and 57 times larger than the number of books typically found at a large independent bookstore. One analysis put the gain in economic value (or "consumer welfare") produced by online bookstores at about $1 billion annually,

library effect
an attempt to appeal to consumers on the basis of the total number of products offered

five times larger than the gain in economic value produced by lower prices on the Internet (Brynjolfsson, Smith, and Hu, 2003). Stores such as Amazon make the size of their product offerings a part of their brand image and marketing communications in order to charge premium prices. Obviously, library effects apply only where there is a large number of SKUs or products available to sell—like music, DVDs, CDs, books, travel arrangements, airline tickets, and many of the products available on the Web— but not for unique collector items.

We can conclude from the research evidence that brands are alive and well on the Web, that consumers are willing to pay premium prices for products and services they perceive as differentiated, that consumers are willing to shop online as opposed to offline at stores where product variety is high, and that in many instances Web prices may be higher than those available in retail stores because of the premium consumers will pay for convenience. The evidence also suggests some solid reasons for the adage popular during the early days of e-commerce: "Get Big Fast." Selection, not price, may be your e-commerce site's biggest advantage and largest contributor to consumer welfare. Another strategic way to look at these data is to expect growing ownership concentration among Internet merchants as they pursue scale economies and library effects that derive from size.

Now that you have covered these basic concepts, the next section describes what makes Internet marketing different from ordinary marketing.

6.3   INTERNET MARKETING TECHNOLOGIES

Internet marketing has many similarities to and differences from ordinary marketing. The objective of Internet marketing—as in all marketing—is to build customer relationships so that the firm can achieve above-average returns (both by offering superior products or services and by communicating the feature set to the consumer). But Internet marketing is also very different from ordinary marketing because the nature of the medium and its capabilities are so different from anything that has come before. In order to understand just how different Internet marketing can be and in what ways, you first need to become familiar with some basic Internet marketing technologies.

In Chapter 7, we will describe marketing communications channels, and advertising, including search engine marketing, which tends to be used more for sales rather than marketing and branding.

THE REVOLUTION IN INTERNET MARKETING TECHNOLOGIES

In Chapter 1, we listed eight unique features of e-commerce technology. **Table 6.8** describes how marketing has changed as a result of these new technical capabilities.

On balance, the Internet has had three very broad impacts on marketing. First, the Internet, as a communications medium, has broadened the scope of marketing communications—in the sense of the number of people who can be easily reached. Second, the Internet has increased the richness of marketing communications by combining text, video, and audio content into rich messages. Arguably, the Web is richer as a medium than even television or video because of the complexity of

TABLE 6.8	IMPACT OF UNIQUE FEATURES OF E-COMMERCE TECHNOLOGY ON MARKETING
E-COMMERCE TECHNOLOGY DIMENSION	**SIGNIFICANCE FOR MARKETING**
Ubiquity	Marketing communications have been extended to the home, work, and mobile platforms; geographic limits on marketing have been reduced. The marketplace has been replaced by "marketspace" and is removed from a temporal and geographic location. Customer convenience has been enhanced, and shopping costs have been reduced.
Global reach	Worldwide customer service and marketing communications have been enabled. Potentially hundreds of millions of consumers can be reached with marketing messages.
Universal standards	The cost of delivering marketing messages and receiving feedback from users is reduced because of shared, global standards of the Internet.
Richness	Video, audio, and text marketing messages can be integrated into a single marketing message and consuming experience.
Interactivity	Consumers can be engaged in a dialog, dynamically adjusting the experience to the consumer, and making the consumer a co-producer of the goods and services being sold.
Information density	Fine-grained, highly detailed information on consumers' real-time behavior can be gathered and analyzed for the first time. "Data mining" Internet technology permits the analysis of terabytes of consumer data everyday for marketing purposes
Personalization/Customization	This feature potentially enables product and service differentiation down to the level of the individual, thus strengthening the ability of marketers to create brands.
Social technology	User-generated content and social networking sites, along with blogs, have created new, large, online audiences where the content is provided by users. These audiences have greatly expanded the opportunity for marketers to reach new potential customers in a nontraditional media format. Entirely new kinds of marketing techniques are evolving. These same technologies expose marketers to the risk of falling afoul of popular opinion by providing more market power to users who now can "talk back."

messages available, the enormous content accessible on a wide range of subjects, and the ability of users to interactively control the experience. Third, the Internet has greatly expanded the information intensity of the marketplace by providing marketers (and customers) with unparalleled fine-grained, detailed, real-time information about consumers as they transact in the marketplace.

WEB TRANSACTION LOGS

How can e-commerce sites know more than a department store does about consumer behavior? A primary source of consumer information on the Web is the transaction log maintained by all Web servers. A **transaction log** records user activity at a Web site. The transaction log is built into Web server software. **Figure 6.10** shows one second from the Web transaction log for Azimuth-interactive.com, a Web-based software training site. The log has been edited to eliminate the names of real persons and show only a few entries for each visitor. In fact, visitors usually create tens or hundreds of entries in the log, one entry for each page or object they request.

Table 6.9 on page 372 lists the data elements contained in a Web transaction log and shows how these elements can be used in marketing, using the first entry in the transaction log in Figure 6.10 as an example.

WebTrends, discussed in Chapter 4, is a leading log file analysis tool. Transaction log data becomes even more useful when combined with two other visitor-generated data trails: registration forms and the shopping cart database. Users are enticed through various means (such as free gifts or special services) to fill out registration forms. **Registration forms** gather personal data on name, address, phone, zip code, e-mail address (usually required), and other optional self-confessed information on interests and tastes. When users make a purchase, they also enter additional information into the shopping cart database. The **shopping cart database** captures all the item selection, purchase, and payment data. Other potential additional sources of information are information users submit on product forms, contribute to chat groups, or send via e-mail messages using the "Contact Us" option on most sites.

For a Web site that has a million visitors per month, and where, on average, a visitor makes 15 page requests per visit, there will be 15 million entries in the log each month. These transaction logs, coupled with data from the registration forms and shopping cart database, represent a treasure trove of marketing information for both individual sites and the online industry as a whole. Nearly all the new Internet marketing capabilities are based on these data-gathering tools. For instance, here are just a few of the interesting marketing questions that can be answered by examining a site's Web transaction logs, registration forms, and shopping cart database:

- What are the major patterns of interest and purchase for groups and individuals?
- After the home page, where do most users go first, and then second and third?
- What are the interests of specific individuals (those we can identify)?
- How can we make it easier for people to use our site so they can find what they want?
- How can we change the design of the site to encourage visitors to purchase our high-margin products?
- Where are visitors coming from (and how can we optimize our presence on these referral sites)?
- How can we personalize our messages, offerings, and products to individual users?

FIGURE 6.10 **ONE SECOND FROM THE WEB TRANSACTION LOG OF AZIMUTH-INTERACTIVE.COM**

dsl254-068-173.nyc1.dsl.speakeasy.net - - [22/Oct/2008:11:29:32 -0400] "GET /masthead.cgi?page=hompage&ad=1 HTTP/1.1" 200 3646 "http://www.azimuth-interactive.com/" "Mozilla/5.0 (Windows; U; Windows NT 5.0; en-US; rv:1.6) Gecko/20040113"

dsl254-068-173.nyc1.dsl.speakeasy.net - - [22/Oct/2008:11:29:32 -0400] "GET /images/newredspacer.gif HTTP/1.1" 200 35 "http://www.azimuth-interactive.com/homepage2.php" "Mozilla/5.0 (Windows; U; Windows NT 5.0; en-US; rv:1.6) Gecko/20040113"

dsl254-068-173.nyc1.dsl.speakeasy.net - - [22/Oct/2008:11:29:32 -0400] "GET /images/azimuthweblogo2.gif HTTP/1.1" 200 1494 "http://www.azimuth-interactive.com/masthead.cgi?page=hompage&ad=1" "Mozilla/5.0 (Windows; U; Windows NT 5.0; en-US; rv:1.6) Gecko/20040113"

dsl254-068-173.nyc1.dsl.speakeasy.net - - [22/Oct/2008:11:29:32 -0400] "GET /images/newmastheadart.gif HTTP/1.1" 200 26349 "http://www.azimuth-interactive.com/masthead.cgi?page=hompage&ad=1" "Mozilla/5.0 (Windows; U; Windows NT 5.0; en-US; rv:1.6) Gecko/20040113"

dsl254-068-173.nyc1.dsl.speakeasy.net - - [22/Oct/2008:11:29:32 -0400] "GET /images/whitespacer.gif HTTP/1.1" 200 45 "http://www.azimuth-interactive.com/masthead.cgi?page=hompage&ad=1" "Mozilla/5.0 (Windows; U; Windows NT 5.0; en-US; rv:1.6) Gecko/20040113"

dsl254-068-173.nyc1.dsl.speakeasy.net - - [22/Oct/2008:11:29:32 -0400] "GET /images/corpsolutionsnav.gif HTTP/1.1" 200 206 "http://www.azimuth-interactive.com/masthead.cgi?page=hompage&ad=1" "Mozilla/5.0 (Windows; U; Windows NT 5.0; en-US; rv:1.6) Gecko/20040113"

dsl254-068-173.nyc1.dsl.speakeasy.net - - [22/Oct/2008:11:29:32 -0400] "GET /images/softcoursesnav.gif HTTP/1.1" 200 239 "http://www.azimuth-interactive.com/masthead.cgi?page=hompage&ad=1" "Mozilla/5.0 (Windows; U; Windows NT 5.0; en-US; rv:1.6) Gecko/20040113"

dsl254-068-173.nyc1.dsl.speakeasy.net - - [22/Oct/2008:11:29:32 -0400] "GET /images/coursebooksnav.gif HTTP/1.1" 200 165 "http://www.azimuth-interactive.com/masthead.cgi?page=hompage&ad=1" "Mozilla/5.0 (Windows; U; Windows NT 5.0; en-US; rv:1.6) Gecko/20040113"

dsl254-068-173.nyc1.dsl.speakeasy.net - - [22/Oct/2008:11:29:32 -0400] "GET /images/onlinecoursesnav.gif HTTP/1.1" 200 174 "http://www.azimuth-interactive.com/masthead.cgi?page=hompage&ad=1" "Mozilla/5.0 (Windows; U; Windows NT 5.0; en-US; rv:1.6) Gecko/20040113"

dsl254-068-173.nyc1.dsl.speakeasy.net - - [22/Oct/2008:11:29:32 -0400] "GET /images/onlinetestingnav.gif HTTP/1.1" 200 175 "http://www.azimuth-interactive.com/masthead.cgi?page=hompage&ad=1" "Mozilla/5.0 (Windows; U; Windows NT 5.0; en-US; rv:1.6) Gecko/20040113"

TABLE 6.9	MARKETING USES OF DATA FROM WEB TRANSACTION LOGS
DATA ELEMENT	MARKETING USE
IP address of the visitor: dsl254-068-173.nyc1.dsl.speakeasy.net	Can be used to send return e-mails for marketing when the visitor is using a dedicated URL as opposed to a dial-in modem. Dial-in modems use temporary IPs and cannot be used for return mail.
Date and time stamp: [22/Oct/2008:11:29:32 -0400]	Used to understand patterns in the time of day and year of consumer activity.
Pages and objects requested and visited ("Get" statements): "GET /masthead.cgi?page=hompage& ad=1 HTTP/1.1"	Used to understand what this specific consumer ("Get" statements): was interested in finding (the clickstream). Can be used later to send "personalized" messages, "customized products," or simply return mail regarding related products.
Response of site server: 200	Used to monitor for broken links, pages not returned.
Size of pages sent (bytes of information): 3646	Used to understand capacity demands on servers and communications links.
Name of page or site from which the consumer came to this site: "http://www.azimuth-interactive.com/"	Used to understand how consumers come to a site, and once there, their patterns of behavior.
Name and version of the browser used: "Mozilla/5.0 (Windows; U; Windows NT 5.0; en-US; rv:1.6) Gecko/20040113"	Useful for understanding target browsers, ensuring your site is compatible with browsers being used.
Name and version of the operating system of the consumer's client computer: (Windows; U; Windows NT 5.0; en-US; rv:1.6)	Useful for understanding the capabilities of target client computers; more recent operating systems indicates new computer, or technically savvy user.
History of all the pages and objects visited during a session at the site.	Used to establish personal profiles of individuals, analyze site activity, and understand the most popular pages and resources.

Answering these questions requires some additional technologies. As noted by Jupiter Research, businesses can choke on the massive quantity of information found in a typical site's log file. We describe some technologies that help firms more effectively utilize this information below.

SUPPLEMENTING THE LOGS: COOKIES AND WEB BUGS

While transaction logs create the foundation of online data collection, they are supplemented by two other data collection techniques: cookies and Web bugs. As described in Chapter 3, a cookie is small text file that Web sites place on the hard disk of visitors' client computers every time they visit, and during the visit, as specific

FIGURE 6.11	**FIREFOX COOKIES DIALOG BOX**

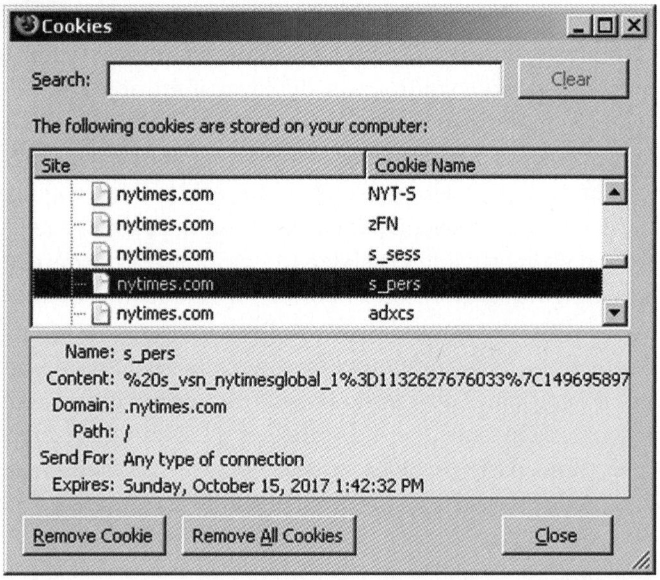

Firefox's Cookies dialog box identifies the various components of a typical cookie file on your computer.

pages are visited. Cookies allow a Web site to store data on a user's computer and then later retrieve it. The Firefox Cookies dialog box in **Figure 6.11** shows the components in a typical cookie file on a client computer (in this case, a cookie from the *New York Times* Web site). The cookie typically includes a name; a unique ID number for each visitor that is stored on the user's computer; the domain (which specifies the Web server/domain that can access the cookie); a path (if a cookie comes from a particular part of a Web site instead of the main page, a path will be given); a security setting that provides whether the cookie can only be transmitted by a secure server; and an expiration date (not required). First-party cookies come from the same domain name as the page the user is visiting, while third-party cookies come from another domain, such as ad serving or adware companies, affiliate marketers, or spyware servers.

A cookie provides Web marketers with a very quick means of identifying the customer and understanding his or her prior behavior at the site. Web sites use cookies to determine how many people are visiting the site, whether they are new or repeat visitors, and how often they have visited, although this data may be somewhat inaccurate because people share computers, they often use more than one computer, and cookies may have been inadvertently or intentionally erased. Cookies make shopping carts and "quick checkout" options possible by allowing a site to keep track of a user as he or she adds to the shopping cart. Each item added to the shopping cart is stored in the site's database along with the visitor's unique ID value.

The location of cookie files on a computer depends on the browser version being used. Cookie files can be accessed on a computer using Mozilla Firefox by opening the

Tools menu, clicking Options, selecting the Privacy tab, and clicking the Show Cookies button. Firefox neatly organizes all your cookies in an alphabetically arranged file based on the name of vendor placing the cookie. You can delete individual cookies or all cookies in Firefox. In Internet Explorer 7.0, and even more so with IE 8.0 released in 2008, users have a bit more control over the level of privacy. You can set the level of privacy you desire all the way from rejecting all cookies (Block All Cookies option) or accepting some cookies from third and first parties if they have a privacy policy in place (Medium) or accepting all cookies (Accept All Cookies option). In Internet Explorer 7.0, select Tools, Internet Options, and then the Privacy tab. You adjust the level of privacy you want by using the slider. In new browsers, users can opt for a privacy mode that extinguishes all records of browsing activity on the client computer.

Reports from a variety of Internet research firms indicate that most Americans do not delete cookies from their computers in large part because around 80% of U.S. computer users do not know how to do this. Of those that do know how to delete cookies, only about 30% in fact do so. Nevertheless, a large study of Yahoo (first party) and DoubleClick (third party) cookies in over 400,000 U.S. households found that about 58% of the cookies placed by these firms had been reset (deleted) (eMarketer Inc., 2007d). Over time, as users become more familiar with cookies, acceptance levels have gone up, and the number of users who report "never blocking cookies" has risen from 11% in 2004 to 24% in 2006. The more cookies are deleted, the less accurate are Web page and ad server metrics, and the less likely marketers will be able to understand who is visiting their sites or where they came from.

Although cookies are site-specific (a Web site can only receive the data it has stored on a client computer and cannot look at any other cookie), when combined with Web bugs, they can be used to create cross-site profiles. We discuss this practice further in the "Advertising Networks" section later in this chapter.

Web bugs are tiny (1 pixel) graphic files embedded in e-mail messages and on Web sites. Web bugs are used to automatically transmit information about the user and the page being viewed to a monitoring server. For instance, when a recipient opens an e-mail in HTML format or opens a Web page, a message is sent to a server calling for graphic information. This tells the marketer that the e-mail was opened, indicating at least that the recipient was interested in the subject header. Web bugs are often clear or colored white so they are not visible to the recipient. You may be able to determine if a Web page is using Web bugs by using the View Source option of your browser and examining the IMG (image) tags on the page. As noted above, Web bugs are typically 1 pixel in size and contain the URL of a server that differs from the one that served the page itself (see Web Bugs FAQ, Privacyfoundation.org). *Insight on Society: Marketing with Web Bugs* examines the use of Web bugs.

DATABASES, DATA WAREHOUSES, AND DATA MINING: DEVELOPING PROFILES

Databases, data warehouses, data mining, and the variety of marketing decision-making techniques loosely called *profiling* are at the heart of the revolution in Internet marketing. Together, these techniques attempt to identify precisely who the online customer is and what they want, and then, to fulfill the customer's criteria exactly.

INSIGHT ON SOCIETY

MARKETING WITH WEB BUGS

Images called "clear GIFs," "Web beacons," and "invisible GIFs" don't sound too threatening. But when they're referred to as "Web bugs," Internet users begin to get a better sense of their true purpose. Web bugs come in several different varieties, but the basic idea is that they are objects (in the form of an image or a tiny pixel) that are embedded invisibly on Web pages and in an e-mail that cause a part of the Web page (usually that image or pixel) to be retrieved by a completely different third-party Web site by sending a signal to that third-party site. As a result, the third-party Web site knows that you visited the original Web site, and they can know much more if they want to, such as where you've been and what you've bought.

Marketers using Web bugs claim their sole purpose is to aid in collecting statistics about Web usage, including how many visitors a particular site has had, which pages on a site are most popular, and which banner ads are providing the best results. Search engine marketing and portal companies such as Google, Microsoft, and AOL use them, as do advertising networks such as DoubleClick. Canadian Web security firm Security Space periodically samples over 15 million Web pages from 1.5 million Web domains to identify the top 100 bug-using sites. The leading Web bugger is Google Analytics followed by Google Syndication, Google, Yahoo, Amazon, and your favorite Web 2.0 sites, Youtube, Photobucket, Flickr, and Geocities. Anytime you use these sites, your every move is bugged. SecuritySpace also collects data on Web traffic that is bugged to identify who is bugging the most Web traffic. The leading traffic bugger is the advertising network DoubleClick, followed by

Akamai, other ad networks, ISPs such as Lycos, and of course, Google and Amazon.

Web bugs are used to track billions of monthly advertising promotions. Without such data, advertisers argue, they would be unable to determine which marketing techniques to use. All information collected is anonymous—so they say—and, on its own, cannot be linked back to any particular individual. For that reason, advertisers claim Web bugs are innocuous. Yet offline marketing information obtained from supermarkets and credit companies and collected by firms such as Acxiom is routinely sold to firms for targeted marketing. Therefore, there is no reason to believe firms abstain from mixing online behavioral data with offline personal information.

If Web bugs are so harmless, why go to the trouble of hiding them? Why not just let people know the site is bugged, perhaps using a yellow caution sign on each bug? That's what privacy advocates are asking. And what they've learned is that although Web bugs may have been designed to simply provide traffic counts, when combined with information from third-party sources, bugs can give marketers an all too complete picture of an individual consumer—right down to home address, online account balances, account numbers, and whatever else the user has entered into his or her computer.

When users visit a Web page with a Web bug on it, or read an e-mail with a bug inserted, unbeknownst to them, data about their online activities is forwarded to a third-party information collector, usually a marketing firm. Web bugs can report a user's IP address, referring URL, and cookie information from a visit to a site, and from an e-mail can link an e-mail address to

(continued)

previously set cookie data. The simplest and most common bug is the clear GIF image that works with cookies to transmit information to third parties about a user's online travels. The GIF can be a single white pixel on the screen you will never see. Truly insidious "executable bugs" can install a file onto someone's hard drive to collect information whenever the user goes online; such bugs can scan a computer and send information on all documents containing keywords, such as *medical* or *finance*. "Script-based executable bugs" can actually take documents from a computer without notice. So while the majority of bugs may be used simply to track a user's movements, there appears to be great potential for abuse.

Bugs enable marketers to know who's online, which Web sites they've visited, where they've spent money, what their address is, and more. When the technology is used by a network of sites linked to a third-party, such as DoubleClick, consumer profiling becomes even more detailed, leading to a potentially significant loss of privacy.

Use of Web bug technology is rising sharply as marketers seek to gain a foothold in Web 2.0 communities such as MySpace, YouTube, and Photobucket. Personal pages and user-generated content are favorite locations for buggers to place their works. Collecting information on consumers is nothing new, but the extent to which data can now be accumulated and combined to form very specific profiles of Internet users has led to calls for regulation.

The Privacy Foundation has issued guidelines for Web bug usage. The guidelines suggest that Web bugs should be visible as an icon on the screen, the icon should be labeled to indicate its function, and it should identify the name of the company that placed the Web bug on the page. In addition, if a user clicks on the Web bug, it should display a disclosure statement indicating what data is being collected, how the data is used after it is collected, what companies receive the data, what other data the Web bug is combined with, and whether or not a cookie is associated with the Web bug. Users should be able to opt-out of any data collection done by the Web bug, and the Web bug should not be used to collect information from Web pages of a sensitive nature, such as medical, financial, job-related, or sexual matters. The Privacy Foundation offers a bug alert program named Bugnosis 1.3 that notifies consumers when a Web bug is detected. If the program finds a possible Web bug, it alerts you with a sound or an image (our favorite is a little creeping bug) and gives the user some details about the Web bug in a window. It also makes visible the Web bugs hidden on the page.

In an effort to address privacy concerns and build consumer trust online, an industry advertising group, the Network Advertising Initiative (NAI), released self-regulatory guidelines for the industry. The NAI renamed Web bugs as "Web beacons" and requires online firms to notify customers of Web bug usage whether in e-mail or on Web sites, state the purpose of their use, and disclose any data that could be released to third parties. The NAI also called for users to be given a choice (whether opt-in or opt-out) of any release of personally identifiable information (PII) to third parties, and to provide an opt-in choice for any release of information related to PII. These restrictions do not apply to the Web site itself (agents). In addition, the NAI provides a capability open to all Web users to opt out of online advertising networks collecting non-personal information on them. However, for this to work, users need to have a cookie downloaded to their browser that will inform the networks not to collect information on this user.

There are also technology solutions that depend on the browser or e-mail provider. For

(continued)

instance, Microsoft retooled its Hotmail service by adding a feature that allows users to block Web bugs placed inside e-mail messages. A similar option is now a part of the Outlook Express and Outlook e-mail programs. Mozilla's Thunderbird e-mail program also allows users to prevent incoming e-mail from displaying any images, hence blocking reports back to third parties. However, this kind of protection would be impossible for ordinary Web pages, which depend on images. Indeed, images are at the heart of the Web.

Currently, Internet users are not protected by government regulation against Web bugs. Most users probably have no idea that Web bugs are in use, how to adjust their browsers to block Web bug images, or how Web bugs are used to track their movements on the Web. According to Rich Howe, Chief of Marketing and Strategy at the offline marketing giant Acxiom, "Most consumers don't know exactly who will be using the data. The majority of individuals don't know a lot about it." For instance, a firm called Omniture uses persistent cookies and Web bugs to track PayPal payments on many sites, including to whom the payment is being made. Most PayPal users do not have a clue about this activity.

SOURCES: "Paypal and Web Bugs," iDunno.org, September 3, 2008; "A Push to Limit the Tracking of Web Surfers' Clicks," By Louise Story, March 20, 2008.Firm Mines Offline Data to Target Online Ads," by Kevin Delaney and Emily Steel, *Wall Street Journal*, October 17, 2007; "Bugnosis FAQ," Bugnosis.org, October 17, 2007; "Web Bug Report," SecuritySpace, October 1, 2007; "Non-PII (Anonymous Information) Opt-Out," Network Advertising Initiative, Networkadvertising.org, October 17, 2007; "Online Retailers Are Watching You," by Jessica E. Vascellaro, *Wall Street Journal*, November 28, 2006.

These techniques are more powerful and far more precise and fine-grained than the gross levels of demographic and market segmentation techniques used in mass marketing media or by telemarketing.

In order to understand the data in transaction logs, registration forms, shopping carts, cookies, Web bugs, and other sources, Internet marketers need massively powerful and capacious databases, database management systems, and data modeling tools. Just examine the transaction log in Figure 6.10 again, and then imagine trying to find the patterns in millions of entries each day!

Databases

The first step in interpreting huge transaction streams is to store the information systematically. A **database** is a software application that stores records and attributes. A telephone book is a physical database that stores records of individuals and their attributes such as names, addresses, and phone numbers. A **database management system** (**DBMS**) is a software application used by organizations to create, maintain, and access databases. The most common DBMS are DB2 from IBM and a variety of SQL databases from Oracle, Sybase, and other providers. **SQL** (**structured query language**) is an industry-standard database query and manipulation language used in relational databases. **Relational databases** such as DB2 and SQL represent data as two-dimensional tables with records organized in rows, and attributes in columns, much like a spreadsheet. The tables—and all the data in them—can be flexibly related to one another as long as the tables share a common data element.

database
a software application that stores records and attributes

database management system (DBMS)
a software application used by organizations to create, maintain, and access databases

SQL (structured query language)
an industry-standard database query and manipulation language used in relational databases

relational databases
represent data as two-dimensional tables with records organized in rows and attributes in columns; data within different tables can be flexibly related as long as the tables share a common data element

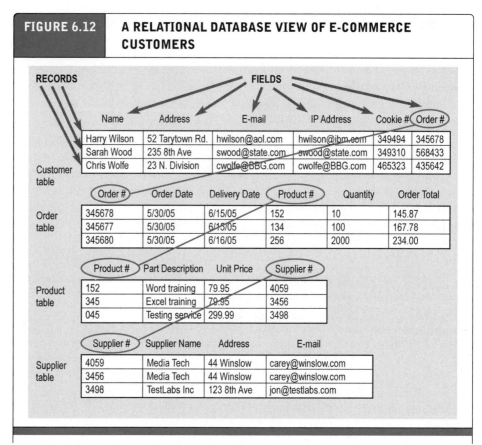

FIGURE 6.12   **A RELATIONAL DATABASE VIEW OF E-COMMERCE CUSTOMERS**

In a relational database, data gathered from an e-commerce site is stored on hard drives and presented to managers of sites in the form of interrelated tables.

Relational databases are extraordinarily flexible and allow marketers and other managers to view and analyze data from different perspectives very quickly. **Figure 6.12** illustrates a relational database view of customers. The data are organized into four tables: customer, order, product, and supplier. The tables all share at least one data element. Using this model, it would be possible to query the database for a list of all customers who bought a certain product, or to message a supplier when the inventory falls below a certain level (and message a customer automatically via e-mail that the product is temporarily out of stock).

Data Warehouses and Data Mining

data warehouse
a database that collects a firm's transactional and customer data in a single location for offline analysis

A **data warehouse** is a database that collects a firm's transactional and customer data in a single location for offline analysis by marketers and site managers. The data originate in many core operational areas of the firm, such as Web site transaction logs, shopping carts, point-of-sale terminals (product scanners) in stores, warehouse inventory levels, field sales reports, external scanner data supplied by third parties, and financial payment data. The purpose of a data warehouse is to gather all the firm's transaction and customer data into one logical repository where it can be analyzed and modeled by managers without disrupting or taxing the firm's primary transactional systems and databases. Data warehouses grow quickly into storage repositories containing terabytes of data (trillions of bytes) on consumer behavior at a firm's stores and Web sites. With a data warehouse, firms can answer such questions as: What products are the most profitable by region and city? What regional marketing campaigns are working? How effective is store promotion of the firm's Web site? Data warehouses can provide business managers with a more complete awareness of customers through data that can be accessed quickly.

Data mining is a set of different analytical techniques that look for patterns in the data of a database or data warehouse, or seek to model the behavior of customers. Web site data can be "mined" to develop profiles of visitors and customers (see **Figure 6.13**). A **customer profile** is simply a set of rules that describe the typical behavior of a customer or a group of customers at a Web site. Customer profiles help to identify the patterns in group and individual behavior that occur online as millions of visitors use a firm's Web site. For example, almost every financial transaction you engage in is processed by a data mining application to detect fraud. Phone companies closely monitor your cell phone use as well to detect stolen phones and unusual calling patterns. Financial institutions and cell phone firms use data mining to develop fraud profiles. When a user's behavior conforms to a fraud profile, the transaction is not allowed or terminated.

There are many different types of data mining. The simplest type is **query-driven data mining**, which is based on specific queries. For instance, based on hunches of marketers who suspect a relationship in the database or who

data mining
a set of analytical techniques that look for patterns in the data of a database or data warehouse, or seek to model the behavior of customers

customer profile
a description of the typical behavior of a customer or a group of customers at a Web site

query-driven data mining
data mining based on specific queries

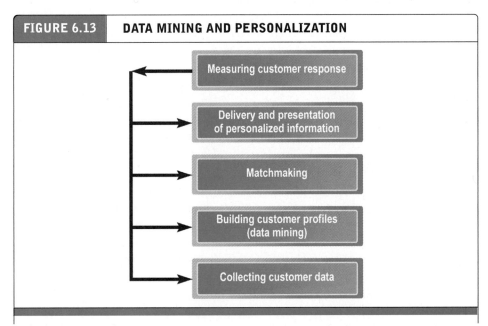

| FIGURE 6.13 | **DATA MINING AND PERSONALIZATION** |

Measuring customer response

Delivery and presentation of personalized information

Matchmaking

Building customer profiles (data mining)

Collecting customer data

Personalization of content and marketing is based on data mining techniques that can produce reliable profiles of individual consumer behavior.

SOURCE: Adomavicius and Tuzhilin, 2001b. ©2001 IEEE.

need to answer a specific question, such as "What is the relationship between time of day and purchases of various products at the Web site?", marketers can easily query the data warehouse and produce a database table that rank-orders the top 10 products sold at a Web site by each hour of the day. Marketers can then change the content of the Web site to stimulate more sales by highlighting different products over time or placing particular products on the home page at certain times of day or night.

model-driven data mining
involves the use of a model that analyzes the key variables of interest to decision makers

Another form of data mining is model-driven. **Model-driven data mining** involves the use of a model that analyzes the key variables of interest to decision makers. For example, marketers may want to reduce the inventory carried on the Web site by removing unprofitable items that do not sell well. A financial model can be built showing the profitability of each product on the site so that an informed decision can be made.

rule-based data mining
examines demographic and transactional data of groups and individuals at a Web site and attempts to derive general rules of behavior for visitors

A more interesting kind of data mining is rule-based. **Rule-based data mining** examines demographic and transactional data of groups and individuals at a Web site and attempts to derive general rules of behavior for visitors. There are factual and behavioral approaches as well as different levels of granularity, from market segments down to individuals. In the *factual approach*, factual demographic and transactional data (purchase price, products purchased) and material viewed at the site are analyzed and stored in a customer profile table in order to segment the marketplace into well-defined groups. For instance, female customers who purchased items worth more than $50 in an average visit and who viewed travel articles might be shown a vacation travel advertisement. The rules are specified by marketing managers as a set of *filters* based on their expert opinions, as well as trial and error, and are applied to aggregate groups of visitors or market segments. There can be thousands of different types of visitors, and hence thousands of marketing decisions or filters that marketers have to make.

collaborative filtering
site visitors classify themselves into affinity groups characterized by common interests; products are then recommended based on what other people in the group have recently purchased

A different *behavioral approach* to data mining is **collaborative filtering** (see *Insight on Technology: The Long Tail: Big Hits and Big Misses*). Behavioral approaches try to "let the data speak for itself" rather than impose rules set by expert marketers. Collaborative filtering was first developed at the MIT Media Lab and commercialized by an MIT Media Lab-backed startup company, Firefly. Rather than having expert marketers make decisions based on their own "rules of thumb," experience, and corporate needs (a need to move old inventory, for instance), site visitors collaboratively classify themselves based on common selections. The idea is that people classify themselves into "affinity groups" characterized by common interests. A query to the database can isolate the individuals who all purchased the same products. Later, based on purchases by other members of the affinity group, the system can recommend purchases based on what other people in the group have bought recently. For example, visitors who all purchased books on amateur flying could be pitched a video that illustrates small-plane flying techniques. And then later, if several members of this "amateur flying interest group" purchased books on parachuting, then all members of the group would be pitched a recommendation to buy parachuting books, based on what other people collaboratively "like themselves" were purchasing. This pitch would be made regardless of the demographic background of the individuals.

INSIGHT ON TECHNOLOGY

THE LONG TAIL: BIG HITS AND BIG MISSES

The "Long Tail" is a colloquial name given to various statistical distributions characterized by a small group of events of high amplitude and a very large group of events with low amplitude. Coined by *Wired Magazine* writer Chris Anderson in 2004, the Web's Long Tail has since gone on to perplex academics and challenge online marketers. The concept is straightforward. Think Hollywood movies: there are big hits that really hit big, and thousands of films that no one ever hears about. In economics, it's the Pareto principle: 20% of anything produces 80% of the effects. It's these non-hit misses that make up the Long Tail. Anderson claims to have discovered a new 98% rule: no matter how much content you put online, someone, somewhere will show up to buy it. eBay would seem to be a perfect example. The online tag sale contains millions of items drawn from every Aunt Tilly's closet in the world and still seems to find a buyer somewhere for just about anything.

On the Internet, where storage and distribution costs are near zero, Amazon is able to offer 3 million books for sale compared to a typical large bookstore with 40,000–100,000 titles. The same is true of CDs, DVDs, digital cameras, and portable MP3 players. Wherever you look on the Web, you find huge inventories, and a great many items that few people are interested in buying. But someone is almost always searching for something. With a billion people online, even a one-in-a-million product will find 1,000 buyers. According to Anderson, online music sites sell access to 98% of their titles once a quarter. According to Netflix, 60% of its 100,000 titles are rented at least once a day by someone. Unlike physical stores such as Wal-Mart and Sears, online merchants have much lower overhead costs because they do not have physical stores and have lower labor costs. Therefore they can load up on inventory including items that rarely sell.

There are several implications of the Long Tail phenomenon for Web marketing. Some writers like Anderson claim that the Internet revolutionizes digital content by making even niche products highly profitable, and that the revenues produced by small niche products will ultimately outweigh the revenues of hit movies, songs, and books. For Hollywood, and all content producers, this means less focus on the blockbusters that bust the budget, and more emphasis on the steady base-hit titles that have smaller audiences but make up for it in numbers of titles. The Long Tail is a democratizing phenomenon: even less well-known movies, songs, and books can now find a market on the Web. There's hope for your blog and garage band! For economists, the Long Tail represents a net gain for social welfare because now customers can find exactly the niche content they really want rather than accept the "big hits" on the shelf. The Web's Long Tail makes more customers happy, and the possibility of making money on niche products should encourage more production of "indy" music and film.

The problem with all these misses in the Long Tail is that few people can find them because they are—by definition—largely unknown. Hence, in their native state, the revenue value of low-demand products is locked up in collective ignorance. Here's where recommender systems come into play: they can guide consumers to obscure but wonderful works based on the recommendations of others.

Recommender systems use historical data on user preferences or behavior to predict how new

(continued)

users will behave. Memory-based systems use the entire database to make predictions, and model-based systems use past data to build a model of consumer behavior and then apply the model to new consumers. Using a similarity metric, which is a means of segmenting the user base, a subsegment of users are selected whose behavior or preferences are similar to the user seeking recommendations. An average purchase propensity for a specific product by members of that subsegment is calculated, with a recommendation made based on that average.

In many cases, recommendations are made based on past purchasing behavior of the user, which may or may not reflect the needs or preferences of the user today. The ability to narrow down the list of potential options, however, makes the information-gathering process more efficient and, for many users, very helpful.

But recent research casts some doubt on the revenue potential in the Long Tail. In an odd twist, the number of DVD titles online that never get played is increasing rapidly, while at the same time the big blockbuster "winner take all" titles are also declining. Solid "best sellers" have expanded and produce the vast

part of online DVD revenues. Over time, the number of titles in the Long Tail has exploded, and the "no play" rate has expanded at music sites from 2% to 12%. Rhapsody is reporting a no play rate of 22% in 2007. When Anderson wrote his paper in 2004, user-generated content sites were just beginning. Now 11 million people in the United States are posting to blogs. The average blog has no subscribers, and a readership of just above 1 (the person who wrote it and part of a friend). Likewise with YouTube, which stores around 80 million videos, adding about 2 million a month. YouTube has not announced its no play rate, but it is likely to be a growing phenomenon: millions of digital titles gathering digital dust. For marketers, then, the lesson is that the marketing opportunities in the Long Tail are much less than the popularity of social networking sites would lead you to believe. Placing ads at the foot of YouTube videos without regard to their play rate does not make good business sense, and the number of opportunities for reaching large numbers of online content consumers is perhaps much less than popularly believed.

SOURCES: "How Big Is the Free Economy?" by Kevin Kelly, longtail.com, July 30, 2008; "The Dynamics of Viral Marketing," by Jure Leskovec, Lada A. Adamic and Bernardo A. Huberman, ACM Transactions on the Web, Vol. 1, No. 1, Article 5, Publication date: May 2007. "Superstars and Underdogs: An Examination of the Long Tail Phenomenon in Video Sales," by Anita Elberse and Felix Oberholzer-Gee, Harvard Business School Working Paper Series, No. 07-015, December, 2006; "It May Be a Long Time Before the Long Tail Is Wagging the Web," by Lee Gomes, *Wall Street Journal*, July 26, 2006; "Will All of Us Get Our 15 Minutes On a YouTube Video," by Lee Gomes, *Wall Street Journal*, August 30, 2006; "From Niches to Riches: Anatomy of the Long Tail," by Eric Brynjolfsson, Yu Hu, and Michael Smith, *MIT Sloan Management Review*, Summer 2006; "Like This? You'll Hate That. (Not All Web Recommendations Are Welcome.)," by Laurie Flynn, *New York Times*, January 23, 2006; "Multi Agent Information Retrieval and Recommender Systems," International Joint Conference on Artificial Intelligence," University of Montreal, January 2005; "The Long Tail," by Chris Anderson, *Wired Magazine*, October 2004.

A more fine-grained behavioral approach that seeks to deal with individuals as opposed to market segments or affinity groups derives rules from individual consumer behavior (along with some demographic information) and seeks to deal specifically with individuals (Adomavicius and Tuzhilin, 2001a; Chan, 1999; Fawcett and Provost, 1996; 1997). Here, the pages actually visited by specific users are stored as a set of conjunctive rules. For example, if an individual visits a site and typically ("as a rule") moves from the home page to the financial news section to the Asian report section, and then often purchases articles from the "Recent Developments in Banking" section, then this person—based on purely past behavioral patterns—

might be shown an advertisement for a book on Asian money markets. These rules can be constructed to follow an individual across many different Web sites.

There are many drawbacks to all these techniques, not least of which is that there may be millions of rules, many of them nonsensical, and many others of short-term duration. Hence, the rules need extensive validation and culling (Adomavicius and Tuzhilin, 2001a). Also, there can be millions of affinity groups and other patterns in the data that are temporal or meaningless. The difficulty is isolating the valid, powerful (profitable) patterns in the data and then acting on the observed pattern fast enough to make a sale you would otherwise not have made. As we see later, there are practical difficulties and trade-offs involved in achieving these levels of granularity, precision, and speed.

CUSTOMER RELATIONSHIP MANAGEMENT (CRM) SYSTEMS

Customer relationship management systems are another important Internet marketing technology. A **customer relationship management (CRM) system** is a repository of customer information that records all of the contacts that a customer has with a firm (including Web sites) and generates a customer profile available to everyone in the firm with a need to "know the customer." CRM systems also supply the analytical software required to analyze and use customer information. Customers come to firms not just over the Web but also through telephone call centers, customer service representatives, sales representatives, automated voice response systems, ATMs and kiosks, in-store point-of-sale terminals, and mobile devices (m-commerce). In the past, firms generally did not maintain a single repository of customer information, but instead were organized along product lines, with each product line maintaining a customer list (and often not sharing it with others in the same firm).

customer relationship management (CRM) system
a repository of customer information that records all of the contacts that a customer has with a firm and generates a customer profile available to everyone in the firm with a need to "know the customer"

In general, firms did not know who their customers were, how profitable they were, or how they responded to marketing campaigns. For instance, a bank customer might see a television advertisement for a low-cost auto loan that included an 800-number to call. However, if the customer came to the bank's Web site instead, rather than calling the 800-number, marketers would have no idea how effective the television campaign was because this Web customer contact data was not related to the 800-number call center data. **Figure 6.14** illustrates how a CRM system integrates customer contact data into a single system.

CRMs are part of the evolution of firms toward a customer-centric and marketing-segment-based business, and away from a product-line-centered business. CRMs are essentially a database technology with extraordinary capabilities for addressing the needs of each customer and differentiating the product or service on the basis of treating each customer as a unique person. Customer profiles can contain the following information:

- A map of the customer's relationship with the institution
- Product and usage summary data
- Demographic and psychographic data
- Profitability measures

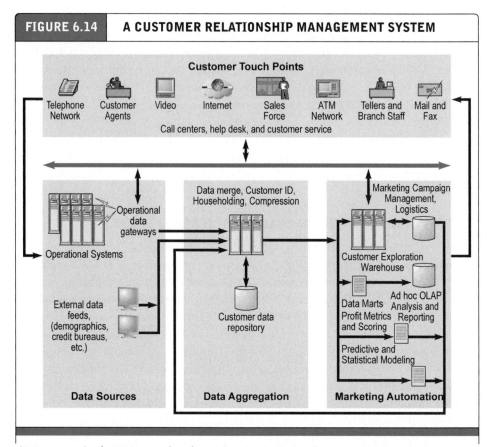

FIGURE 6.14   **A CUSTOMER RELATIONSHIP MANAGEMENT SYSTEM**

This is an example of a CRM system for a financial services institution. The system captures customer information from all customer "touch" points as well as other data sources, merges the data, and aggregates it into a single customer data repository or data warehouse where it can be used to provide better service, as well as to construct customer profiles for marketing purposes. Online Analytical Processing (OLAP) allows managers to dynamically analyze customer activities to spot trends or problems involving customers. Other analytical software programs analyze aggregate customer behavior to identify profitable and unprofitable customers as well as customer activities.
SOURCE: Compaq, 1998.

- Contact history summarizing the customer's contacts with the institution across most delivery channels
- Marketing and sales information containing programs received by the customer and the customer's responses
- E-mail campaign responses

    With these profiles, CRMs can be used to sell additional products and services, develop new products, increase product utilization, reduce marketing costs, identify and retain profitable customers, optimize service delivery costs, retain high lifetime value customers, enable personal communications, improve customer loyalty, and increase product profitability.

For instance, Home Depot saw increased competition from online hardware stores and decided to emphasize e-commerce as part of its business strategy. The company sought a comprehensive CRM solution that could organize and analyze information from both clicks and mortar. They used a CRM software package called Epiphany Insight to gain a better understanding of which Home Depot products were selling on the Web and enabled their customer service focus from their stores to exist on the Web as well. Epiphany has since been acquired by Infor. Other leading CRM vendors include SAP, SalesForce.com, Oracle, Kana, and eGain.

6.4 B2C AND B2B E-COMMERCE MARKETING AND BRANDING STRATEGIES

The new marketing technologies described previously have spawned a new generation of marketing techniques and added power to some traditional techniques (such as direct mail campaigns with Web site addresses displayed). In this section, we describe a variety of Internet marketing strategies for market entry, customer acquisition, customer retention, pricing, and dealing with channel conflict. It is important to note that although B2C and B2B e-commerce do have differentiating features (for instance, in B2C e-commerce, marketing is aimed at individual consumers, whereas in B2B e-commerce, typically more than just one individual is involved with the purchase decision), the strategies discussed in this section in most instances can be, and are, applied in both the B2C and B2B arenas.

MARKET ENTRY STRATEGIES

Both new firms and traditional existing firms have choices about how to enter the market, and ways to establish the objectives of their online presence. **Figure 6.15** illustrates four basic market entry strategies.

| FIGURE 6.15 | GENERIC MARKET ENTRY STRATEGIES |

Both new and traditional firms face a basic choice—"clicks" or "bricks and clicks"—when entering the e-commerce marketplace.

Let's examine the situation facing new firms—quadrants 1 and 2 in Figure 6.15. In the early days of e-commerce, the typical entry strategy was pure clicks/first-mover advantage, utilized by such companies as Amazon, eBay, and E*Trade (quadrant 1). Indeed, this strategy was at the heart of the so-called new economy movement, and provided the capital catch basin into which billions of investment dollars flowed. The ideas are beguiling and simplistic: enter the market first and experience "first-mover" advantages—heightened user awareness, followed rapidly by successful consumer transactions and experiences—and grow brand strength. According to leading consultants of this era, first movers would experience a short-lived mini-monopoly. They would be the only providers for a few months, and then other copycats would enter the market because entry costs were so low. To prevent new competitors from entering the market, growing audience size very rapidly became the most important corporate goal rather than profits and revenue.

Firms following this strategy typically spent the majority of their marketing budget (which, in and of itself, may have constituted a large part of their available capital) on building brand (site) awareness by purchasing high-visibility advertising in traditional mass media such as television (Super Bowl game ads), radio, newspapers, and magazines. If the first mover gathered most of the customers in a particular category (pets, wine, gardening supplies, and so forth), the belief was that new entrants would not be able to enter because customers would not be willing to pay the switching costs. Customers would be "locked in" to the first-mover's interface. Moreover, the strength of the brand would inhibit switching, even though competitors were just a click away.

In retrospect, it is now clear that pursuing first-mover advantage as a marketing strategy was not particularly successful for most firms. Although first movers may have interesting advantages, they also have significant liabilities. The history of first movers in most areas of business is that statistically, they are losers for the most part because they lack the complementary assets and resources required to compete over the long term. While innovative, first movers usually lack financial depth, marketing and sales resources, loyal customers, strong brands, and production or fulfillment facilities needed to meet customer demands once the product succeeds (Teece, 1986). Research on Internet advertising indicates that while expensive ad campaigns may have increased brand awareness, the other components of a brand such as trust, loyalty, and reputation did not automatically follow, and more important, site visits did not necessarily translate into purchases (Ellison, 2000).

Another possibility for new firms is to pursue a mixed bricks-and-clicks strategy, coupling an online presence with other sales channels (quadrant 2). However, few new firms can afford the "bricks" part of this strategy. Therefore, firms following this entrance strategy often ally themselves with established firms that have already developed brand names, production and distribution facilities, and the financial resources needed to launch a successful Internet business. For instance, BrainPlay, Inc., an e-tailer of children's goods, entered into an alliance with the established Consolidated Stores Corporation KB Toys unit to form a new online presence called KBkids.com. KBkids was later closed, but KBtoys.com survives today.

Now let's look at traditional firms. Traditional firms face some similar choices, with of course one difference: they have significant amounts of cash flow and capital to fund their e-commerce ventures over a long period of time. For example, Barnes & Noble, the world's largest book retailer, formed Barnesandnoble.com (quadrant 3), a follower site, when faced with the success of upstart Amazon.com (quadrant 1). The Web site was established as an independent firm, a Web pure-play, although obviously making use of the Barnes & Noble brand name. Likewise, Rite Aid followed the success of online pharmacies by establishing its own Web site (Riteaid.com) and then forming an alliance with Drugstore.com to fulfill and service prescriptions ordered online at Drugstore.com (and perform backend processing of insurance payments).

The most common strategy for existing firms is to extend their businesses and brands by using a mixed bricks-and-clicks strategy in which online marketing is closely integrated with offline physical stores (quadrant 4). These "brand-extension" strategies characterize REI, L.L.Bean, Wal-Mart, and many other established retail firms. Like fast followers, they have the advantage of existing brands and relationships. However, even more than fast followers, the brand extenders do not set up separate pure-play online stores, but instead typically integrate the online firm with the traditional firm from the very beginning. L.L.Bean and Wal-Mart both saw the Web as an extension of their existing order processing and fulfillment, marketing, and branding efforts.

Each of the market entry strategies discussed above has seen its share of successes and failures. While the ultimate choice of strategy depends on a firm's existing brands, management strengths, operational strengths, and capital resources (Gulati and Garino, 2000), today most firms are opting for a mixed bricks-and-clicks strategy in the hope that it will enable them to reach profitability more quickly.

ESTABLISHING THE CUSTOMER RELATIONSHIP

Once a firm chooses a market entry strategy, the next task is establishing a relationship with the customer. Traditional public relations and advertising media (newsprint, direct mail, magazines, television, and even radio) remain vital for establishing awareness of the firm. However, a number of unique Internet marketing techniques have emerged that have proven to be very powerful drivers of Web site traffic and purchases. Here we discuss several of these new techniques, including advertising networks, permission marketing, affiliate marketing, viral marketing, blog marketing, and social network marketing. The use of keyword purchases and pay-for-placement and rank on search engines (so-called "search engine marketing") is discussed in some detail in Chapter 8 as a special type of advertising or marketing communications.

Advertising Networks

In the early years of e-commerce, firms placed ads on the few popular Web sites in existence, but by early 2000, there were hundreds of thousands of sites where ads could be displayed. Most firms by themselves, even very large firms, did not have the capabilities to place banner ads and marketing messages on thousands of Web sites,

advertising networks
present users with banner advertisements based on a database of user behavioral data

and monitor the results. Specialized marketing firms called **advertising networks** appeared to help firms take advantage of the powerful tracking and marketing potential of the Internet.

Advertising networks represent the most sophisticated application of Internet database capabilities to date, and illustrate just how different Internet marketing is from traditional marketing. These networks sell advertising and marketing opportunities (slots) to companies who wish to buy exposure to an online audience. Advertising networks obtain their inventory of ad opportunities from a network of participating sites that want to display ads on their sites in return for receiving a payment from advertisers. These sites are usually referred to as Web publishers. The advertising network shares the revenue with the publisher. Advertising networks have developed software that tracks customer movements among the network members, say, from Amazon, to Travelocity, to Google, Yahoo, and eBay. At each visit the ad network software decides which banner ads, videos, and other ads to show the customer based in part on the customer's behavior at various sites on the network. For instance, at Travelocity, the customer may research a vacation to England. On Google, the customer may search for English cities. When the customer goes to Yahoo, he or she may be shown ads for raincoats. The advertiser works with the network to determine the rules for showing ads. If you wonder, for instance, why you see so many ads for home mortgages despite the fact you have never looked at an apartment or house for sale, it is because the advertising mortgage company and the ad network have determined your age demographic and geographic location, and on that basis, show mortgage ads to everyone meeting those criteria regardless of previous network behavior. Ad networks are not always very discriminating in their behavior.

Perhaps the best-known advertising network is DoubleClick, which released its first-generation tracking system, DART, in 1996. Google purchased DoubleClick for $3.1 billion in April 2007. Other advertising networks include 24/7 Real Media's Open AdStream (purchased by WPP, the world's largest advertising firm, for $649 million in June 2007), and aQuantive (purchased by Microsoft for $6.1 billion in May 2007).

Why are billions of dollars being invested in these companies? For technology firms such as Google and Microsoft, purchasing these companies allows them to buy large chunks of the online display advertising business, which amounts to about $3 billion a year in revenue. For marketing firms such as WPP, the purchase of 24/7 Real Media allows it to extend its traditional business of creating and placing ads, and develop a third line business in the Internet display ad market.

DoubleClick serves about 60 billion ads per month (in round numbers, about 24,000 ads per second) and maintains over 100 million user profiles on individual Web consumers. Specialized ad servers are used to store and send to users the appropriate banner ads. All these systems rely on cookies, Web bugs, and massive backend user profile databases to pitch banner ads to users and record the results, including sales. This process allows feedback from the market to be entered into the database. For instance, DoubleClick's Intelligent Targeting service allows advertisers to send ads to consumers who have indicated a specific interest area, either through recent or frequent visits to particular types of Web sites, while its Boomerang service allows a Web site to target visitors to that site by advertising to those anonymous visitors when they visit other DoubleClick client sites.

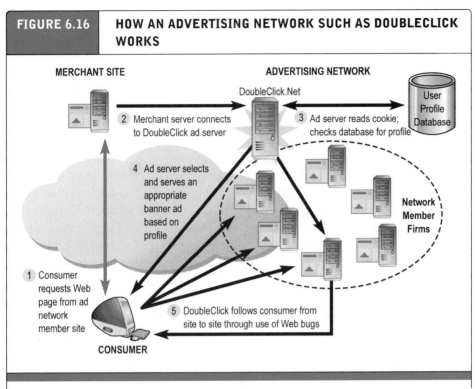

FIGURE 6.16 **HOW AN ADVERTISING NETWORK SUCH AS DOUBLECLICK WORKS**

Advertising networks have become controversial among privacy advocates because of their ability to track individual consumers across the Internet. We discuss privacy issues further in Chapter 8.

Figure 6.16 illustrates how these systems work. Advertising networks begin with a consumer requesting a page from a member of the advertising network (1). A connection is established with the third-party ad server (2). The ad server identifies the user by reading the cookie file on the user's hard drive and checks its user profile database for the user's profile (3). The ad server selects an appropriate banner ad based on the user's previous purchases, interests, demographics, or other data in the profile (4). Whenever the user later goes online and visits any of the network member sites, the ad server recognizes the user and serves up the same or different ads regardless of the site content. The advertising network follows users from site to site through the use of Web bugs (5).

Permission Marketing

The phrase "**permission marketing**" was coined by author and consultant Seth Godin to describe the strategy of obtaining permission from consumers before sending them information or promotional messages (Godin, 1999). Godin's premise was that by obtaining permission to send information to consumers up front, companies are much more likely to be able to develop a customer relationship. When consumers agree to receive promotional messages, they are *opting-in*; when they decide they do not want to receive such messages, they *opt-out*.

permission marketing
marketing strategy in which companies obtain permission from consumers before sending them information or promotional messages

Most consumers need an incentive to spend time reading promotional material, or to provide personal information companies can use to improve their own marketing. Godin's former company, Yoyodyne, pioneered the creation of online sweepstakes and games that gathered information from participants in return for the chance to win money and prizes. Another company, portal Iwon.com, gives users the chance to win money each week for visiting the site; each month, the company offers special bonus prizes to users who are willing to complete a more in-depth survey about their personal life. The site gains useful personal information, and the user earns the chance to win a free prize.

A key component of e-mail involves permission marketing. Typically, when placing an order online, consumers are given the option of receiving newsletters or announcements of products and sales via e-mail. In the United States, the default is usually "opt-in," and the consumer is required to check off an option to not receive e-mail. Federal law now requires merchants sending e-mail to consumers to provide an Unsubscribe link for all e-mail. We discuss e-mail as a marketing communication tool in greater detail in Chapter 7

Affiliate Marketing

affiliate marketing
one Web site agrees to pay another Web site a commission for new business opportunities it refers to the site

In the offline world, referrals are one of the best sources of qualified leads. **Affiliate marketing** is the online application of this marketing method, where one Web site agrees to pay another Web site or an individual writing a blog a commission for new business opportunities it refers to the site. The affiliate adds a link to the company's Web site on its own site and encourages its visitors to patronize its marketing partner. Some affiliates are paid a commission based on any sales that are generated, while others may be paid a fee based on number of click-throughs or new registrations, or a flat fee, or some combination of these.

For instance, Amazon has a strong affiliate program consisting of more than 1 million participant sites, called Associates, which receive up to 10% on sales their referrals generate. Members of eBay's Affiliates Program can earn between $20 and $35 for each active registered user sent to eBay. Amazon, eBay, and other large e-commerce companies with affiliate programs typically administer such programs themselves. Smaller e-commerce firms who wish to use affiliate marketing often decide to join an *affiliate network* (sometimes called an *affiliate broker*), which acts as an intermediary. The affiliate network brings would-be affiliates and merchants seeking affiliates together, helps affiliates set up the necessary links on their Web site, tracks all activity, and arranges all payments. Leading affiliate networks include Commission Junction, LinkShare, and eAdExchange.com. In return for their services, affiliate networks typically take about 20% of any fee that would be payable to the affiliate. The total size of the affiliate market is not known, but industry experts estimate that around 10% of all retail online sales are generated through affiliate programs (as compared, say, to search engine ads which account for over 30% of online sales).

A key benefit of affiliate marketing is the fact that it typically operates on a "pay-for-performance" basis. Affiliates provide qualified sales leads in return for pre-agreed upon compensation. Another advantage, however, is the existence of an established user base that a marketer can immediately tap into through an affiliate. For affiliates, the appeal is a steady income—potentially large—that can result from such relationships. In addition, the presence of another company's logo or brand name can provide a measure of prestige and credibility.

Affiliate marketing can have some drawbacks, however, if not managed carefully. Too many links that are not relevant to a firm's primary focus can lead to brand confusion, for instance. Affiliate marketing works best when affiliates choose products and services that match and supplement the content of their own Web site. Web sites with affiliate links also risk "losing" those customers who click on a link and then never return, unless the Web site takes action to prevent this, such as by having the link open a new window that when closed returns the customer to the original site.

Viral Marketing in the Web 2.0 Milieu

Just as affiliate marketing involves using a trusted Web site to encourage users to visit other sites, **viral marketing** is the process of getting customers to pass along a company's marketing message to friends, family, and colleagues. It's the online version of word-of-mouth advertising, which spreads even faster than in the real world. In the offline world, next to television, word of mouth is the second most important means by which consumers find out about new products (eMarketer, Inc., 2007e). It is believed that about 27 million online adults in the United States are "influencers" who share their opinions about products in a variety of online settings. In addition to increasing the size of a company's customer base, customer referrals also have other advantages: they are less expensive to acquire since existing customers do all the acquisition work, and they tend to use online support services less, preferring to turn back to the person who referred them for advice. Also, because they cost so little to acquire and keep, referred customers begin to generate profits for a company much earlier than customers acquired through other marketing methods. There are a number of online venues where viral marketing appears in the Web 2.0 era. E-mail used to be the primary online venue for e-mail marketing ("please forward this e-mail to your friends"), but Web 2.0 venues such as blogs and social networking sites are beginning to play a major role as described below.

Half.com's Take Five! program is an example of viral marketing, where registered users at the site selling used books, music, movies, and games are given an incentive (coupons) to tell their friends about the site. When a user submits a friend's name and e-mail address on Half.com's Take Five page, Half.com sends the friend a coupon valid for $5 off the friend's first order of $10 or more. Then, when the friend uses the Take Five coupon, Half.com gives the referring user a $5 coupon that also can be used off a $10 order. The process of viral marketing can also involve users who do not know each other. When a consumer decides to make a major purchase, such as a new mountain bike, getting advice and opinions from people who own such bikes is usually the first step. And with the Internet, it is fairly easy to find and read reviews of various bike models written by knowledgeable consumers. Sites such as Epinions and ConsumerReports.org provide objective product reviews by people who have bought and used a long list of products and services. Armed with feedback and input from online aficionados, consumers can

viral marketing
the process of getting customers to pass along a company's marketing message to friends, family, and colleagues

then click through to an e-commerce site and make a purchase. Epinions has links to a number of affiliate online retailers who pay a fee back to the site for each purchase that originates there.

Blog Marketing

Blogs have become a part of mainstream online culture (see Chapter 3 for a description of blogs and RSS). Over 67 million Americans (39% of adult users) visited a blog in 2008, and around 21 million (12% of Internet users) have created blogs (Pew Internet & American Life Project, 2008a). Blog traffic in 2008 grew 23% over 2007. Thousands of high-ranking corporate officials, politicians, journalists, academics, and government officials have created blogs, along, of course, with the rest of us. Blog creators tend to be young, broadband users, Internet veterans, wealthy, and educated. It did not take long for marketers to discover this large number of "eyeballs" and seek out ways to market and advertise to them. Because blogs are based on the personal opinions of the writers, they are ideal locations to start a viral marketing campaign.

Blogs, like ordinary Web sites, can be used to display both branding ads not geared towards sales, as well as advertising aimed at making sales. But because blogs are usually created by private individuals wishing to make a public statement, bloggers do not have the Web marketing and advertising resources of large corporations, and the number of eyeballs viewing any one site is miniscule compared to portal Web sites such as Yahoo. The problem is how to efficiently aggregate these tiny audiences into a significant block of eyeballs worthy of an advertiser's attention.

One solution is to build an advertising network of bloggers and allow bloggers to subscribe to this network, agreeing to display ads on their blogs, and then paying them a fee for each visitor who clicks on the ad. CrispAds.com is one such network. Users of this service can choose from categories of ads to display. CrispAds also allows users to place ads in their RSS feeds to other sites. Blogads.com provides a similar service.

Google's AdSense is also a major blog marketer. The AdSense service "reads" a blog and identifies the subject of the blog's postings. Then AdSense will place appropriate ads on the blog, adjusted to the blog's content. For instance, BoingBoing.net, a very popular technology blog known for its love of gadgets, displays ads from major advertisers like HP, Verizon, and RackSpace.

The metrics of blog marketing at this time are not well understood. No one knows the size of the blog marketing phenomenon or the revenues produced by blog marketing at this time. The authors estimate that less than 5% of online advertising and marketing expenditures occurs on blogs. Given the growth of this phenomenon—well over 50% a year in the past few years—and the novelty, blog marketing will likely show substantial gains over the next several years. There may be limits on this phenomenon just as with e-mail marketing. The *blogosphere* (the Internet's aggregate blogging community) is already buzzing about blogs set up merely for personal financial gain. The founder of one site on asbestos litigation, for instance, freely admits he set up the site in order to tap into the revenues flowing to individuals and law firms in connection with asbestos litigation (Rodgers, 2005). Firms are tempted to hire bloggers to report favorably on their products, leading to what one wag called "blogola." This behavior reduces the credibility and effectiveness of blog marketing, and makes larger advertisers fearful of advertising on blogs when they cannot control the content of the blog.

Social Network Marketing and Social Shopping

Social networks in the offline world are collections of people who voluntarily communicate with one another over an extended period of time. Online social networks, such as MySpace, Facebook, Xanga, Friendster, Buzznet, and Bibo, are Web sites that enable users to communicate with one another, form close group and individual relationships, and share interests, values, and ideas. Individuals establish online profiles including pictures and then invite their friends to create their own profiles and link to their profile. The network grows by word of mouth and through e-mail links. In 2008, over 76 million Internet users visited social networking sites (up over 300% since 2007), and related user-generated content sites such as Photobucket, YouTube, and Flickr. Marketers spent about $1.4 million on social network marketing in 2008, about 5% of all online marketing. MySpace, the most popular social network, generated $850 million in online ad revenues in 2008, and FaceBook 325 million (up over 300% above 2007). These two sites together account for about 75% of all online social networking ad revenues, and traffic grew by 33% in 2008 (up 60% over 2007). Neither site is profitable as of late 2008, but at these rates of growth, they are both expected to become profitable in 2009 (eMarketer Inc., 2008e).

Firms are beginning to harness the spectacular popularity and growth of social networking sites by marketing to participants. The idea is that consumers will tend to buy what their friends buy and recommend. At Yub.com, which has several patents on **social shopping**, users can view their friend's purchases and interests, click an image of the products, and link to a Web site where they can buy the products. Yub.com keeps the referral fees of 10%–15%. Friendster uses similar techniques to send customers to Amazon, keeping a referral fee. Other online retail sites are attempting to create their own user communities. At Overstock.com, users of that site's auction service are invited to create free online profiles, and share news of their recent purchases with friends at the site. The Insight on Business story, *Social Network Marketing: New Influencers Among the Chattering Masses*, further examines the emergence of social network marketing.

social shopping
sharing product choices with friends online

Leveraging Brands

Brand leveraging is one of the most successful online customer acquisition strategies (Carpenter, 2000). **Brand leveraging** refers to the process of using the power of an existing brand to acquire new customers for a new product or service. For instance, while Tab was the first to discover a huge market for diet cola drinks, Coca-Cola ultimately succeeded in dominating the market by leveraging the Coke brand to a new product called Diet Coke.

In the online world, some researchers predicted that offline brands would not be able to make the transition to the Web because customers would soon learn who was offering products at the cheapest prices and brand premiums would disappear

brand leveraging
using the power of an existing brand to acquire new customers for a new product or service

INSIGHT ON BUSINESS

SOCIAL NETWORK MARKETING: NEW INFLUENCERS AMONG THE CHATTERING MASSES

Social network marketing is arguably the single most exciting, and fastest growing online marketing development in the last 10 years. With over 100 million unique visitors a month, social networking sites such as MySpace, Facebook, and scores of niche sites are natural targets for marketers who want to be where their customers are. Alongside these sites are social news/social bookmarking sites such as Digg, Reddit, Del.icio.us, NewsVine, the new Netscape, and StumbleUpon, which attract additional millions of viewers. At social news/bookmarking sites, visitors submit links to stories or their favorite bookmarked sites, and depending on how popular their stories and bookmarks become, their recommendations rise or fall. Blogs are yet another online forum for writers to express themselves and readers to respond, creating a community of responses. The top 50 most popular blogs tracked by Technorati.com, an online buzz tracker, draw over 20 million visitors a day! There are an estimated 27 million "influential" people on social networking sites who express opinions on products and brands. Social networking sites are the equivalent of offline word-of-mouth networks, which are the most powerful influence on consumer behavior. It's word of mouth on digital steroids.

A whole new lexicon has emerged to describe the new social network marketing opportunities:

- Online word-of-mouth-marketing: giving people a reason to talk about your products online
- Buzz marketing: using high profile entertainment, games or news to get people talking about your products online

- Online viral marketing: creating messages designed to be passed along by e-mail, blogging, or networking with others
- Online community marketing: forming online niche communities to share interests about your brand
- Online grassroots marketing: organizing volunteers or paying people to reach out to their friends online
- Influencer marketing: finding people in online communities who are opinion leaders or key influencers
- Conversation marketing: interesting or fun online advertising to start word-of-mouth campaigns via e-mail, blogs, and networking profiles
- Brand blogging: creating blogs, or participating on blogs, or hiring bloggers to share and promote the value of your brands

Marketers are starting to follow the opportunity, though: social network marketing hit $2 billion in 2009, still less than one-tenth of all online marketing, but growing at 52% a year. This makes social marketing the fastest growing form of online marketing just at a time when search engine marketing growth is slowing.

There are risks, however. For instance, you cannot control what bloggers, chatters, and networkers say about your brand or products, and while they may provide valuable feedback that is useful for product design and improvement, unfair characterizations of your products, intentions, or policies can kill sales. How do you know what the chattering masses are saying about your brand, and what can you do about it? Social network marketing is very different from traditional media marketing where the firm can control the message and the medium. Social network marketing

(continued)

is a no-holds-barred dialogue between the customer and the company. A number of firms have sprung up to help solve this problem. For instance, Nielsen BuzzMetrics is a company formed by the media ratings firm A.C. Nielsen that uses search engines to sweep the Internet for phrases, opinions, opinions, keywords, sentences, and images that impact one of its customers' brands. It then analyzes the vocabulary, language patterns, and phrasing to determine if the comments are positive or negative, and the demographics of the people making the comments wherever possible. In a sense, it is using the Internet as an online focus group. Other firms performing similar services are Umbria, Cymfony, and Biz360. Coke has used BuzzMetrics to gauge responses to a video it posted on YouTube; ConAgra has used these techniques to anticipate lifestyle and food trends; Sony has used these firms to track interest in its computer games.

The online brand intelligence field is also moving towards real-time monitoring of the social network ecosystem. VML, based in Kansas City, a unit of WPP Group, tracks the blogosphere in real time with its SEER ™ brand management tool and produces visual maps of the blogosphere that pinpoint the originators of comments about a firm, the subscribers, and the links among them (see screenshot below). They can tell a customer such as Adidas that the blogosphere is complaining about fading colors on the Predator, a new soccer cleat. As a result, Adidas began to tell customers at the point of purchase to treat the leather before wearing the cleats and then changed the formulation of dyes used in the color process.

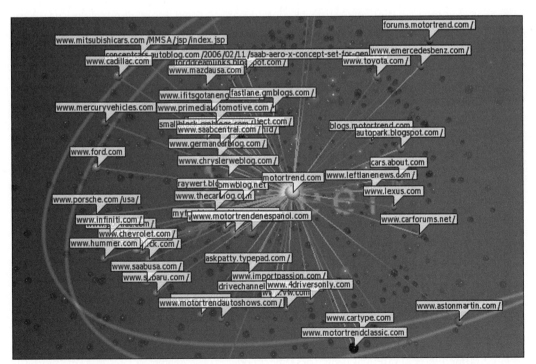

SOURCES: "Use Social Media to Bond With Consumers," by Kelly Spors, Wall Street Journal, September 3, 2008; "Make Social Networking Work for Your Business," by Kelly Spors, Wall Street Journal, July 8, 2008; "Social Network Marketing," eMarketer, May 2007; "Tapping Into Customers' Online Chatter," by Aaron Patrick, *Wall Street Journal*, May 18, 2007; "To Create Buzz, TV Networks Try a Little 'Blogola'," by Brooks Barnes, *Wall Street Journal*, May 15, 2007; "The Wizards of Buzz," by Jamie Warren and John Jurgenson, *Wall Street Journal*, February 10, 2007.

(price transparency). But this has not occurred. In retail, firms such as Wal-Mart and JCPenney have leaped into the top 10 online retail firms in a very short period in large part because of the strength of their offline brand, which gave them the ability to attract millions of their offline customers to their Web sites. In the financial service industry sector, firms such as Wells Fargo, Citibank, Fidelity, and Merrill Lynch have all succeeded in acquiring millions of online customers based on their large offline customer bases and brands. In the content provider industry, the *Wall Street Journal* and *Consumer Reports* have become among the most successful subscription-based content providers. In manufacturing and retail, Dell has been very successful in leveraging its brand of custom-built computers ordered by telephone into a made-to-order computer ordered over the Internet (Kraemer et al., 2000). A major advantage of brand leveraging—when compared to a startup venture with no brand recognition—is that it significantly reduces the costs of acquiring new customers (Kotler and Armstrong, 2008).

CUSTOMER RETENTION: STRENGTHENING THE CUSTOMER RELATIONSHIP

The Internet offers several extraordinary marketing techniques for building a strong relationship with customers and for differentiating products and services.

Personalization and One-to-One Marketing

one-to-one marketing
segmenting the market based on a precise and timely understanding of an individual's needs, targeting specific marketing messages to these individuals, and then positioning the product vis-à-vis competitors to be truly unique

No Internet-based marketing technique has received more popular and academic comment than "one-to-one" or "personalized marketing." **One-to-one marketing** segments the market on the basis of individuals (not groups), based on a precise and timely understanding of their needs, targeting specific marketing messages to these individuals, and then positioning the product vis-à-vis competitors to be truly unique (Peppers and Rogers, 1997). One-to-one marketing is the ultimate form of market segmentation, targeting, and positioning—where the segments are individuals.

The movement toward market segmentation has been ongoing since the development of systematic market research and mass media in the 1930s. However, e-commerce and the Internet are different in that they enable personalized one-to-one marketing to occur on a mass scale. **Figure 6.17** depicts the continuum of marketing: from mass marketing of undifferentiated products, where one size and one price fits all, to personalized one-to-one marketing.

Mass marketing, based on national media messages aimed at a single national audience and with a single national price, is appropriate for products that are relatively simple and attractive to all consumers in a single form. Think of Coke, Tide, and McDonalds. *Direct marketing*, which is based on direct mail or phone messages and aimed at segments of the market likely to purchase and which has little variation in price (but special offers to loyal customers), is most often used for products that can be stratified into different categories. *Micromarketing*, which is aimed at geographical units (neighborhoods, cities) or specialized market segments (technology buffs), is the first form of true database marketing. Frito-Lay, for instance, maintains a national sales database for each of 10,000 route sales personnel and over 50,000 store outlets. Frito-Lay marketers know precisely at the end of every day how many small bags of Salsa Chips sell in Los Angeles, and how many bags of Ranch

---

FIGURE 6.17 | **THE MASS MARKET-PERSONALIZATION CONTINUUM**

MARKETING ATTRIBUTES

MARKETING STRATEGIES	Product	Target	Pricing	Techniques
Mass Marketing	Simple	All consumers	One nation, one price	Mass media
Direct Marketing	Stratified	Segments	One price	Targeted communications, e.g., mail and phone
Micromarketing	Complex	Micro-segments	Variable pricing	Segment profiles
Personalized, One-to-One Marketing	Highly complex	Individual	Unique pricing	Individual profiles

Personalized one-to-one marketing is part of a continuum of marketing strategies. The choice of strategy depends on the nature of the product as well as the technologies that are available to enable various strategies.

Chips sell in Cambridge, Massachusetts, store by store. Although seemingly simple, the corn chip can take on fairly complex and nuanced taste experiences that attract different customers in different neighborhoods. Using its database, Frito-Lay dynamically adjusts prices to market conditions and competitor product and pricing, every day.

Personalized one-to-one marketing is suitable for products (1) that can be produced in very complex forms, depending on individual tastes, (2) whose price can be adjusted to the level of personalization, and (3) where the individual's tastes and preferences can be effectively gauged.

A good example of personalization at work is Amazon or Barnesandnoble.com. Both sites greet registered visitors (based on cookie files), recommend recent books based on user preferences (based on a user profile in their database), and expedite checkout procedures based on prior purchases.

Several U.S. firms such as the *New York Times* and Orbitz have adopted a form of permission-based, personalized "direct-messaging" banner advertising in which customers are shown ads addressed to them by name, mentioning some of their past purchases. Dotomi Direct Messages differ from banner ads and e-mail messages because consumers agree to receive messages from various companies, and the ads are personal in the sense of being based on the consumer's prior purchases and behavior. Invented by Yair Goldfinger, who created instant messaging while working for AOL, the system uses cookies to identify returning visitors to a network of sites. In a sense, the ads are specially built for each unique user. The response rate to traditional banner ads is currently about 0.5%, whereas the response rate to personalized banner ads is about 34% (Tedeschi, 2004). Unfortunately, consumers who sign up for this service do not receive fewer of the old-style, mass market, banner ads.

Is Web-based personalization as good as the personal attention you would receive from a local, independent bookstore owner? Probably not. Nevertheless, these Web-based techniques use more individual knowledge and personalization than traditional mass media, and more than a direct mail post card.

Personalization is not necessarily an unmitigated good, however. Research indicates that most consumers appreciate personalization when it increases their sense of control and freedom, such as through personalized order tracking, purchase histories, databases of personalized information to ensure quicker transactions during future sessions, and opt-in e-mail notification of new products and special deals. The online buyers participating in Wolfinbarger and Gilly's focus groups saw personalization as negative, however, when it resulted in unsolicited offers or reduced anonymity; such features are perceived to take away user control and freedom (Wolfinbarger and Gilly, 2001). Furthermore, although personalization technologies have made significant advances over the past several years, it is still difficult for a computer to accurately understand and anticipate the interests and needs of a customer. "Personalized" offers that miss the mark can lead to more customer disdain than satisfaction (Waltner, 2001). How often do you open up a Web site such as Yahoo and find ads that are totally irrelevant to your interests?

Customization and Customer Co-Production

customization

changing the product, not just the marketing message, according to user preferences

customer co-production

in the Web environment, takes customization one step further by allowing the customer to interactively create the product

Customization is an extension of personalization. **Customization** means changing the product—not just the marketing message—according to user preferences. **Customer co-production** means the users actually think up the innovation and help create the new product. For instance, studies of new and improved products find that many come directly from intensive users. The operating system Linux is entirely built by users and innovations in mountain bikes, sail boards, sailboats and gear, ski equipment, and thousands of other industrial products often came from "lead users" (von Hippel, 2005; 1994). Customer co-production in the Web environment takes customization one step further by allowing the customer to interactively create the product.

Many leading companies now offer "build-to-order" customized products on the Internet on a large scale, creating product differentiation and, hopefully, customer loyalty. Customers appear to be willing to pay a little more for a unique product. The key to making the process affordable is to build a standardized architecture that lets consumers combine a variety of options. For example, Nike has been offering customized sneakers through its Nike iD program on its Web site since 1999. Consumers can choose the type of shoe, colors, material, and even a logo of up to eight characters. Nike transmits the orders via computers to specially equipped plants in China and Korea. The sneakers cost only $10 extra and take about three weeks to reach the customer. At the Shop M&M's Web site, customers can get their own message printed on custom-made M&Ms; Timberland.com also offers online customization of its boots.

Information goods—goods whose value is based on information content—are also ideal for this level of differentiation. For instance, the *New York Times*—and many other content distributors—allows customers to select the news they want to see on a daily basis. Many Web sites, particularly portal sites such as Yahoo, MSN, Netscape, and AOL, allow customers to create their own customized version of the Web site. Such pages frequently require security measures such as usernames and passwords to ensure privacy and confidentiality.

Transactive Content

According to several studies, the most common reasons people go online are to communicate (e-mail) and to find information. As we noted in Section 6.1, shopping is not the primary Internet consumer activity.

Marketers have adjusted their Web marketing strategies accordingly. The result is "transactive content," a term originally coined by Forrester Research (Forrester Research, 1997; 1998). **Transactive content** results from the combination of traditional content, such as articles and product descriptions, with dynamic information—such as new product announcements—culled from product databases, tailored to each user's profile. Such applications dynamically respond to user needs and preferences, for instance, by featuring a product within a price range typically preferred by the customer on the order page. You might be reading an article on travel to Africa at Iexplore.com, a travel company with an extensive Web site for adventure-travel advice, products, and services. Based on data drawn from your user profile as well as real-time clickstream behavior (for instance, you had previously expressed an interest in water sports), you might be served a link to information on kayaking safaris in Africa. Transactions, content, and interactivity are combined into a seamless experience.

transactive content
results from the combination of traditional content, such as articles and product descriptions, with dynamic information culled from product databases, tailored to each user's profile

Customer Service

A Web site's approach to customer service can significantly help or hurt its marketing efforts. Online customer service is more than simply following through on order fulfillment; it has to do with users' ability to communicate with a company and obtain desired information in a timely manner. Customer service can help reduce consumer frustration, cut the number of abandoned shopping carts, and increase sales.

According to Wolfinbarger and Gilly, most consumers want to, and will, serve themselves as long as the information they need to do so is relatively easy to find. Online buyers largely do not expect or desire "high-touch" service unless they have questions or problems, in which case they want relatively speedy answers that are responsive to their individual issue. Wolfinbarger and Gilly noted that participants in their study said that the first opportunity to cement them to an online brand came when they had a problem with the order; customer loyalty increased substantially when online buyers learned that customer service representatives were available online or at an 800-number and were willing and able to resolve the situation quickly. Conversely, online buyers who did not receive satisfaction at these critical incidents terminated their relationship and became willing to do business with a site that might charge more, but offered better customer service (Wolfinbarger and Gilly, 2001).

There are a number of tools that companies can use to encourage interaction with prospects and customers and provide customer service, including the customer relationship management systems described in the preceding section—FAQs, customer service chat systems, intelligent agents, and automated response systems.

Frequently asked questions (**FAQs**), a text-based listing of common questions and answers, provide an inexpensive way to anticipate and address customer concerns. Adding an FAQ page on a Web site linked to a search engine helps users track down needed information more quickly, enabling them to help themselves resolve questions and concerns. By directing customers to the FAQs page first, Web sites can give customers answers to common questions. If a question and answer do not appear, it is important for sites to make contact with a live person simple and easy. Offering an e-mail link to customer service at the bottom of the FAQs page is one solution.

Real-time customer service chat systems (in which a company's customer service representatives interactively exchange text-based messages with one or more customers on a real-time basis) are an increasingly popular way for companies to assist online shoppers during a purchase. Chats with online customer service representatives can provide direction, answer questions, and troubleshoot technical glitches that can kill a sale. Leading vendors of customer service chat systems include LivePerson, Groopz, and SightMax. Vendors claim that chat is significantly less expensive than telephone-based customer service. However, critics point out this conclusion may be based on optimistic assumptions that chat representatives can assist three or four customers at once, and that chat sessions are shorter than phone sessions. Also, chat sessions are text sessions, and not as rich as talking with a human being over the phone. On the plus side, chat has been reported to raise per-order sales figures, providing sales assistance by allowing companies to "touch" customers during the decision-making process. According to Jupitermedia Metrix, anecdotal evidence suggests that chat can lower shopping cart abandonment rates, increase the number of items purchased per transaction, and increase the dollar value of transactions. In 2008, about 30% of U.S. online retailers offer live chat (Brohan, 2008).

Intelligent agent technology, described in Chapter 3, is another way customers are providing assistance to online shoppers. Intelligent agents are part of an effort to reduce costly contact with customer service representatives. **Automated response systems** send e-mail order confirmations and acknowledgments of e-mailed inquiries, in some cases letting the customer know that it may take a day or two to actually research an answer to their question. Automating shipping confirmations and order status reports are also common. Although the upfront expenditure to install and implement automated systems may be costly, the potential reduction in calls to live telephone operators and online help centers is an incentive for companies to increasingly automate as many aspects of the online shopping experience as possible. Firms must use and monitor automated response systems carefully, however, or they may backfire. Many customers still resent automated communications, even if they appear personal-

frequently asked questions (FAQs)
a text-based listing of common questions and answers

real-time customer service chat systems
a company's customer service representatives interactively exchange text-based messages with one or more customers on a real-time basis

automated response system
sends e-mail order confirmations and acknowledgments of e-mailed inquiries

ized. If automated replies are not useful, they may drive consumers to use live support even more.

NET PRICING STRATEGIES

In a competitive market, firms compete for customers through price as well as product features, scope of operations, and focus. **Pricing** (putting a value on goods and services) is an integral part of marketing strategy. Together, price and quality determine customer value. Pricing of e-commerce goods has proved very difficult for both entrepreneurs and investors to understand.

In traditional firms, the prices of traditional goods—such as books, drugs, and automobiles—are usually based on their fixed and variable costs as well as the market's **demand curve** (the quantity of goods that can be sold at various prices). Fixed costs are the costs of building the production facility. *Variable costs* are costs involved in running the production facility—mostly labor. In a competitive market, with undifferentiated goods, prices tend toward their *marginal costs* (the incremental cost of producing the next unit) once manufacturers have paid the fixed costs to enter the business.

Firms usually "discover" their demand curves by testing out various price and volume bundles, closely watching their cost structure. Normally, prices are set to maximize profits. A profit-maximizing company sets its prices so that the marginal revenue (the revenue a company receives from the next unit sold) from a product just equals its marginal costs. If a firm's marginal revenue is higher than its marginal costs, it would want to lower prices a bit and sell more product (why leave money on the table when you can sell a few more units?). If its *marginal revenue* for selling a product is lower than its marginal costs, then the company would want to reduce volume a bit and charge a higher price (why lose money on each additional sale?).

During the early days of e-commerce, something unusual happened. Sellers were pricing their products far below their marginal costs. Some sites were losing money on every sale. How could this be? New economics? New technology? The Internet Age? No. Internet merchants could sell below their marginal costs (even giving away products for free) simply because a large number of entrepreneurs and their venture capitalist backers thought this was a worthwhile activity, at least in the short term. The idea was to attract "eyeballs" with free goods and services, and then later, once the consumer was part of a large, committed audience, charge advertisers enough money to make a profit, and (maybe) charge customers subscription fees for value-added services (the so-called *"piggy-back" strategy* in which a small number of users can be convinced to pay for premium services that are piggy-backed upon a larger audience that receives standard or reduced value services). To a large extent, social networking sites and user-generated content sites have resurrected this revenue model with a focus on the growth in audience size and not short-term profits. To understand the behavior of entrepreneurial firms, it is helpful to examine a traditional demand curve (see **Figure 6.18**).

pricing
putting a value on goods and services

demand curve
the quantity of goods that can be sold at various prices

A small number of customers are willing to pay a great deal for the product—far above P_1. A larger number of customers would happily pay P_1, and an even larger number of customers would pay less than P_1. If the price were zero, the demand might approach infinity! Ideally, in order to maximize sales and profits, a firm would like to pick up all the money in the market by selling the product at the price each customer is willing to pay. This is called **price discrimination**—selling products to different people and groups based on their willingness to pay. If some people really want the product, sell it to them at a high price. But sell it to indifferent people at a much lower price; otherwise, they will not buy. This only works if the firm can (a) identify the price each individual would be willing to pay, and (b) segregate the customers from one another so they cannot find out what the others are paying. Therefore, most firms adopt a fixed price for their goods (P_1), or a small number of prices for different versions of their products.

During the early days of e-commerce, and even today in the case of Web 2.0 firms, e-commerce firms were willing to charge far below their costs, sometimes giving away valuable services, in order to attract huge audiences. Millions of visitors accepted free or nearly free services and products being sold below their cost.

What if the marginal cost of producing a good is zero? What should the price be for these goods? It would be impossible then to set prices based on equalizing marginal revenue and marginal cost—because marginal cost is zero. The Internet is primarily filled with information goods—from music to research reports, to stock

price discrimination
selling products to different people and groups based on their willingness to pay

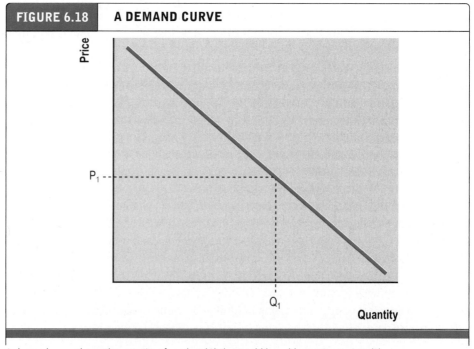

| FIGURE 6.18 | A DEMAND CURVE |

A demand curve shows the quantity of product (Q) that could be sold at various prices (P).

quotes, stories, weather reports, articles, pictures, and opinions—whose marginal cost of production is zero when distributed over the Internet. Thus, another reason certain goods, such as information goods, may be free on the Internet is that they are "selling" for what it costs to produce them—nothing. Content that is stolen from television, CDs, and Hollywood movies has zero production costs. Content that is contributed by users also has zero production costs for the Web sites themselves.

It's Free!

Let's examine free pricing of Internet services. Everyone likes a bargain, and the best bargain is something for free. Businesses give away free PCs, free data storage, free music, free Web sites, free photo storage, and free Internet connections. Google offers free office apps, free email, and free collaboration sitesThere can be a sensible economic logic to giving things away. Free content can help build market awareness (such as the free online *New York Times* that contains only the daily stories—not the archived stories) and can lead to sales of other follow-on products. In addition, widely dispensing one's software for free also builds network effects (millions use the free version of WinZip bundled with Windows to compress and share files). Finally, free products and services knock out potential and actual competitors (the free browser Internet Explorer from Microsoft spoiled the market for Netscape's browser) (Shapiro and Varian, 1999).

"Free" as a pricing strategy does have limits. Many e-commerce businesses were unable to convert the eyeballs into paying customers. Free sites attracted hundreds of thousands of price-sensitive "free loaders" who had no intention of ever paying for anything, and who switched from one free service to another at the very mention of charges. The piggyback strategy has not been a great success. The Web's largest subscription service is the *Wall Street Journal*, which charges 930,000 subscribers from $79 to $99 a year, but the largest free financial news sites have over 5 million daily visitors. Many companies started offering their services for free, but now charge an annual subscription fee.

In the case of Google in 2008, its "free" services are advertising supported, another Web page on which to display ads and generate revenue. Where this is not the case, Google nevertheless builds brand and builds the total Web audience for its services which can later be translated into ad exposures. There probably is no free lunch after all.

Versioning

One solution to the problem of free information goods is **versioning**—creating multiple versions of the goods and selling essentially the same product to different market segments at different prices. In this situation, the price depends on the value to the consumer. Consumers will segment themselves into groups that are willing to pay different amounts for various versions (Shapiro and Varian, 1998). Versioning fits well with a modified "free" strategy. A reduced value version can be offered for free, while premium versions can be offered at higher prices. What makes a "reduced-value version?" Low-priced—or in the case of information goods, even "free"— versions might be less convenient to use, less comprehensive, slower, less powerful,

versioning
creating multiple versions of information goods and selling essentially the same product to different market segments at different prices

and offer less support than the high-priced versions. Just as there are different General Motors car brands appealing to different market segments (Cadillac, Buick, Chevrolet, and Pontiac), and within these divisions, hundreds of models from the most basic to the more powerful and functional, so can information goods be "versioned" in order to segment and target the market and position the products. In the realm of information goods, online magazines, music companies, and book publishers offer sample content for free, but charge for more powerful content. The *New York Times*, for instance, offers free daily content for several days after publication, but then charges per article for access to the more powerful archive of past issues. Writers, editors, and analysts are more than willing to pay for access to archived, organized content. Some Web sites offer "free services" with annoying advertising, but turn off the ads for a monthly fee.

Bundling

"Ziggy" Ziegfeld, a vaudeville entrepreneur at the turn of the century in New York, noticed that nearly one-third of his theater seats were empty on some Friday nights, and during the week, matinee shows were often half empty. He came up with an idea for bundling tickets into "twofers": pay for one full-price ticket and get the next ticket free. Twofers are still a Broadway theater tradition in New York. They are based on the idea that (a) the marginal cost of seating another patron is zero, and (b) a great many people who would not otherwise buy a single ticket would buy a "bundle" of tickets for the same or even a slightly higher price.

bundling
offers consumers two or more goods for one price

Bundling of information goods online extends the concept of a twofer. **Bundling** offers consumers two or more goods for one price. The key idea behind the concept of bundling is that although consumers typically have very diverse ideas about the value of a single product, they tend to agree much more on the value of a bundle of products offered at a fixed price. In fact, the per-product price people are willing to pay for the bundle is often higher than when the products are sold separately. Bundling reduces the variance (dispersion) in market demand for goods. **Figure 6.19** illustrates how the demand curve changes when information goods are offered in a bundle.

Examples of bundling abound in the information goods marketplace. Microsoft bundles its separate Office tools (Word, Excel, PowerPoint, and Access) into a single Microsoft Office package. Even though many people want to use Word and Excel, far fewer want Access or PowerPoint. However, when all products are put into a single bundle, a very large number of people will agree that about $399 (or around $100 per tool) is a "fair" price for so many products. Likewise, the more software applications that Microsoft bundles with its basic operating system, the more the marketplace agrees that as a package of functionality, it is reasonably priced. On the Web, many content sites bundle as opposed to charge individual prices. Electronic libraries such as NetLibrary.com offer access to thousands of publications for a fixed annual fee. Theoretically, bundlers have distinct competitive advantages over those who do not or cannot bundle. Specifically, on the supply side, bundler firms can pay higher prices for content, and on the demand side, bundlers can charge higher prices for their bundles than can single-good firms (Bakos and Brynjolfsson, 2000).

FIGURE 6.19	THE DEMAND FOR BUNDLES OF 1–20 GOODS

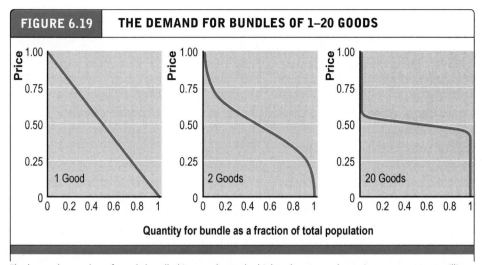

Quantity for bundle as a fraction of total population

The larger the number of goods bundled in a package, the higher the per-product price consumers are willing to pay.
SOURCE: Bakos and Brynjolfsson, 1999.

However, bundling of digital goods does not always work. It depends on the bundle and the price. For instance, Reed Elsevier, the world's largest publisher of scientific journals, created a bundle of 1,500 digital scientific journals for American universities, and priced the bundle at a substantial markup to what universities were paying for a much smaller number of journals. It then raised the price to universities that did not want the bundle. The result was a marketplace rebellion shaped in part by the fact that much of the research in these journals was paid for by taxpayers through government grants.

Dynamic Pricing

The pricing strategies we have discussed so far are all fixed-price strategies. Versions and bundles are sold for fixed prices based on the firm's best effort at maximizing its profits. But what if there is product still left on the shelf along with the knowledge that someone, somewhere, would be willing to pay something for it? It might be better to obtain at least some revenue from the product, rather than let it sit on the shelf, or even perish. Imagine also that there are some people in every market who would pay a hefty premium for a product if they could have it right away. In other situations, such as for an antique, the value of the product has to be discovered in the marketplace (usually because there is a belief that the marketplace would value the product at a much higher price than its owner paid as a cost). In other cases, the value of a good is equal to what the market is willing to pay (and has nothing to do with its cost). Here is where dynamic pricing mechanisms come to the fore, and where the strengths of the Internet can be seen.

Two prevalent kinds of *dynamic pricing mechanisms* are auctions and yield management. Auctions have been used for centuries to establish the instant market price for goods. Auctions are flexible and efficient market mechanisms for pricing unique or unusual goods, as well as commonplace goods such as computers, flower bundles, and cameras.

Yield management is quite different from auctions. In *auctions*, thousands of consumers establish a price by bidding against one another. In *yield management*, managers set prices in different markets, appealing to different segments, in order to sell excess capacity. Airlines exemplify yield management techniques. Every few minutes during the day, they adjust prices of empty airline seats to ensure at least some of the 50,000 empty airline seats are sold at some reasonable price—even below marginal cost of production. Frito-Lay, as mentioned earlier, also uses yield management techniques to ensure products move off the shelf in a timely fashion.

Yield management works under a limited set of conditions. Generally, the product is perishable (an empty airline seat perishes when the plane takes off without a full load); there are seasonal variations in demand; market segments are clearly defined; markets are competitive; and market conditions change rapidly (Cross, 1997). In general, only very large firms with extensive monitoring and database systems in place have been able to afford yield management techniques.

The Internet has truly revolutionized the possibilities to engage in dynamic, and even misleading pricing strategies. With millions of consumers using a site every hour, and access to powerful databases, merchants can raise prices one minute, and drop them another minute when a competitor threatens. Bait and switch tactics become more common: a really low-price on one product is used to attract people to a site where in fact the product is not available.

We discuss dynamic pricing, auctions, and yield management techniques in greater detail in Chapter 11.

CHANNEL STRATEGIES: MANAGING CHANNEL CONFLICT

channel
refers to different methods by which goods can be distributed and sold

channel conflict
occurs when a new venue for selling products or services threatens to destroy existing venues for selling goods

In the context of commerce, the term **channel** refers to different methods by which goods can be distributed and sold. Traditional channels include sales by manufacturers, both directly and through intermediaries such as manufacturer representatives, distributors, and retailers. The emergence of e-commerce on the Web has created a new channel and has led to channel conflict. **Channel conflict** occurs when a new venue for selling products or services threatens to destroy existing venues for selling goods. Channel conflict is not new, but the Web creates incentives for producers of goods and services to establish direct relationships with consumers and thereby eliminate "middle persons" such as distributors and retailers.

For instance, Levi Strauss & Co. decided to begin selling Levi's jeans and Dockers on its Levi.com and Dockers.com sites. Initially, it forbade retailers (such as Macy's—one of Levi's largest retailers) from selling Levi products on the Web. However, the storm of protest from retailers, falling sales, and drooping profits forced Levi to allow retailers to sell through their Web channels.

Rather than engage in direct confrontation with alternative channels, some manufacturers have turned toward a partnership model. For instance, Ethan Allen developed its own Web site for direct sales of its entire line of furniture. At the same time, Ethan Allen recognizes the importance of its independent retail stores for delivery, service, and support, and pays dealers in a local area 25% of the Internet sale for delivery and service, and 10% of the Internet sale even if the dealer does not participate in any way.

At the other end of the spectrum, some manufacturers use the Web solely as a marketing and branding mechanism in order to prevent channel conflict. For instance, Ford, General Motors, and most automobile manufacturers continue to rely on sales made by their dealerships rather than attempt to sell their cars directly online.

Liquidation.com:
B2B Marketing Success Story

What would you do if you wanted to sell 1,300 pounds of scrap titanium? A truckload of new kitchen cabinets or four pallets of used Dell computers? How about 100 designer blouses from a name-brand manufacturer? Or six German-made circular knitting machines worth about $42,000 each when new but no longer needed because of changes in the U.S. textile marketplace? You might want to unload that strip mall in San Francisco now that real estate prices have tanked. If you wanted to sell these industrial goods, large lot sizes, and real estate, you would look for an online B2B liquidator site such as Liquidation.com or Bid4assets.com. These and other smaller firms provide eBay-style auctions that create a market for production overruns, store returns, and goods of bankrupt firms. These firms live off the misfortunes of some, while creating fortunes for other entrepreneurs who can buy large lots of goods at pennies on the dollar and resell them for large profits. In the case of the used Dell computers, the seller at Liquidation.com squeezed out nearly $200 for each of the computers, which in the past might have been sold to a traditional liquidator for $50

a piece. On average, sellers who use online liquidation services receive 20%–200% more than if they had used traditional liquidators. But how do these liquidation firms compete against their much larger rival eBay, which also provides liquidation services? The answer is precision online marketing and branding.

Liquidity Services operates four online auction marketplaces: Liquidation.com, Govliquidation.com, Liquibiz.com, and a wholesale industry portal, GoWholesale.com, that connects advertisers with buyers seeking products for resale and related business services. Liquidity Services is in what is called the "reverse supply chain business." We normally think of the supply chain business as one where firms work through a variety of mechanisms to gather the resources needed to produce goods. In the reverse supply chain, firms start with finished products and try to dispose of them. While a well-established forward supply chain exists for the procurement of assets, most manufacturers, retailers, corporations, and government agencies have not made significant investments in the reverse supply chain process. The reverse supply chain addresses the redeployment and remarketing of wholesale, surplus, and salvage assets. These assets generally consist of retail customer returns, overstock products, and end-of-life goods from both the corporate and government sectors. According to D.F. Blumberg Associates, Inc., a research and consulting firm, the estimated reverse logistics market in North America will be $63.1 billion in 2008, up from $38 billion in 2004.

Liquidity Services, Inc. (the parent firm of Liquidation.com) utilizes online marketplaces, B2B product sales and marketing expertise, and value-added services to complete over 500,000 bulk sale transactions in 2007. Liquidity Services, which went public in February 2006, had $198 million in revenue in 2007 and has been profitable since 2002. It has over 550 employees worldwide and is headquartered in Washington, D.C. While the offline world of liquidation is populated with discount hunters, local wholesalers, scrap yards, and musty warehouses, and where returns for sellers are a few pennies on the dollar, at Liquidation.com, sellers are offered a global marketplace, complete support for presentation on the Web site (including graphics and text), and support for transactions (an auction and bidding engine). Liquidation.com offers sellers at least twice as much value as they would recover in the offline world. The firm is used by over 675,000 qualified professional buyers who purchase bulk products from Fortune 500 retailers, leading e-tailers, manufacturers and distributors. These buyers may be retailers, wholesalers, or eBay PowerSellers located in the United States and around the world in about 116 countries. The sellers tend to be manufacturers, distributors, and large retailers. At large retail stores like Wal-Mart and JCPenney, over 6% of in-store sales are returned. For e-commerce online transactions, the return rate is an astounding 12% of sales. Most of these items cannot be re-sold because the original packaging or the item itself is damaged in some way. Hence they must be sold off at the best available price.

The sellers on Liquidation.com are a mixed bag of national manufacturers, retailers, e-tailers, and government agencies. Recently, Liquidation.com won a federal contract as the exclusive liquidator for the U.S. Department of Defense, and was selected as one of eight firms liquidating materials from other federal agencies. The U.S. government alone disposes of 10,000 computers a month. How much money is invovled in "surplus?" In a recent deal, Liquidator Services Inc. signed an agreement with U.S.

Defense Department to pay 3.26% of the original value on usable surplus gear and gets to keep all the profits.

Auctions at Liquidation.com close every two to three days, and there is no sniping allowed. (*Sniping* is the practice of standing on the sidelines and not bidding, and then coming into the bidding in the last few seconds and winning the auction.) Bidding is extended every three minutes until there is just one bidder left. Extending the auction when there are multiple bidders allows time for bidders to raise their bids, and also creates a sense of fairness among bidders. One happy user of Liquidation auctions is Jose Guitan, who runs an eBay store called Bargainmaze.com. He uses it to acquire inventory of electronics, watches, and toys. "The time I used them," Jose notes, "I took a chance. But they delivered what they said they would. You have to rely heavily on the description online and hope it's accurate, but most of the time it is very precise." The one time Guitan did have a problem because the merchandise delivered did not match its description, Liquidation.com forced the seller to take the merchandise back and return the money. All Guitan lost was the shipping expense. Guitan quit his restaurant job recently and became a full-time eBay merchant, reselling products he sources from online liquidators.

But Liquidation.com faces some difficult issues of marketing and branding. First, it had to discover how to attract buyers to its Web site when the inventory itself changes daily, and the potential buyer never knows what will be for sale on any day. Second, it had to appeal to a very broad audience of potential purchasers who might be interested in anything at the right price. This was not targeted marketing so much as shotgun marketing to a world audience of businesses. Last, it had to build trust by ensuring that customers received exactly what they bid for even though Liquidation.com does not own the goods. Like eBay, Liquidation.com provides the transaction platform for buyers and sellers. However, it also provides a wide range of value added services for both buyers and sellers, taking, on average, a 20% profit-share cut or commission from sellers.

Some of the tactics Liquidation.com used to build a site that looks trustworthy are a home page with links on top, bottom, and side to customer service; logos of Dun & Bradstreet, VeriSign, PayPal, and TrustE on the bottom of many pages; and a news section for press releases and press mentions so that the site looks as if it is well known by trusted third parties (such as the *Wall Street Journal*, which occasionally mentions Liquidation. com).

The marketing team at Liquidation.com knew it needed to understand what was working at the Web site and how it worked, and then focus on driving customers to the Web site. Liquidation.com first invested in building a tracking program that focused on conversion metrics such as the average number of auctions viewed per name, average number of bids placed, average number of transactions, percentage of opt-in e-mail, and percentage of visitors who registered. The marketing team discovered that first-time visitors did not like to fill out the existing five-page registration form, so it was simplified to a half page. That increased registrations and opt-in to e-mail messages. They also discovered that first-time visitors rarely purchase anything, and the average length of time from first visit to first bid was 60 days. Therefore, the team reasoned it was important to keep in touch with first-time visitors and registrants through e-mail or other means. Looking at the sales metrics, the marketing and sales teams can use the information collected over the past eight years to lot and merchandise incoming inventory into batches that are attractive to its buyer base. In some instances, there is more demand and higher bids from smaller buyers who might be able to handle 100 briefcases as opposed to a lot of 1,000 briefcases. In other cases, larger buyers are increasingly attracted to truckload lots to help stock discount stores, flea market kiosks and other small businesses. As Liquidation.com increases the volume of goods on its site from large retailers and manufacturers, it has the flexibility to provide a broad range of product offerings to better suit customer demand and increase the total amount returned to sellers as well as the amount it keeps.

While these changes helped optimize results from customers who visit the site, the question of how to bring people to the site in the first place remained. The initial budget for marketing was very small, and the potential audience huge. Liquidation.com's first tactic was to start using search engine marketing offered by Google and Overture (now Yahoo). They purchased hundreds of words on Overture and Google that would point directly to Liquidation.com product pages. At the same time, they checked the "organic" listings on Google to see if the product pages were turning up on their own as a result of Google's Web-based search engine. If not, they would purchase keywords. To drive more traffic without much cost, the team engaged in guerilla marketing public relations campaigns, trying to get the company name into major media business coverage wherever possible. When a huge blizzard hit the East Coast, the PR team immediately called reporters at metropolitan newspapers to suggest stories about retailers using Liquidation.com to get rid of inventory. Liquidation.com has appeared in the *Wall Street Journal, Christian Science Monitor, USA Today*, and *Business Week*, among others.

Looking at how his competitors used print ads in trade magazines, the marketing staff laid copies of all the magazines side by side and discovered the competitors' ads were "pretty cheesy looking." They decided to place a small number of ads that emphasized a professional level of service, efficient business processes, and the trustworthiness of their company.

While Liquidation.com is primarily intended as a site that makes it easy for bulk sellers to find retail buyers, Liquidity Services realized there was also a market for a Web site that would cater to retailers seeking out suppliers. In June 2004, Liquidity Services launched GoWholesale.com for retailers seeking long-term wholesale suppliers. Taking a page from Google, GoWholesale lets wholesalers bid on keywords for sponsored listings on the site. Retailers will see sponsored listings first, and then unsponsored links.

Perhaps the most effective tactic for driving traffic is e-mail marketing. Liquidation.com rents a small number of opt-in e-mail lists that have proved effective. Two precautions they have taken are to assume people on these lists may already be customers, and not to rent too frequently and annoy customers. But the most effective use of e-mail turns out to be mailing to the over 675,000 registered buyers on a regular basis, offering new products each time. About one-quarter of the mailing list receives a targeted mailing for a specific item at auction. On the registration page, users are asked to describe their interests in broad terms, and these self-selections (like a collaborative filter) are used to target e-mail campaigns. The open, click, and

SOURCES: "Liquidity Services, Inc. Awarded New Surplus Contract with the U.S. Department of Defense," Liquidity Services, Inc., August 4, 2008; Liquidity Services Inc. Form 10-k, filed with the Securities and Exchange Commission, December 7, 2007; "Casting a Web From Business to Business," by Peter Morton, Canada.com, May 26, 2007; "Liquidity Services, Inc. Honored With Three International WebAwards for Outstanding Web Site Development," Liquiditiy Services, Inc., October 15, 2007; "Liquidity Services, Inc. Ranks #18 On BusinessWeek's Hot 100 Growth Companies," Liquidity Services, Inc., June 4, 2007; Liquidity Services Inc. Form 10-k, filed with the Securities and Exchange Commission, December 22, 2006; "Liquidity Services Says Its Ready to Handle the Government's Used Equipment," by Aliza Sternstein, *Federal Computer Week*, February 2, 2005.

conversion rates on these targeted mailings is 20% higher than the general campaigns.

As a result of its successful marketing and branding campaigns, Liquidation.com has turned a murky world of inefficient, local liquidation markets into a global, trusted, online niche in the expanding Web liquidation industry. In 2007, Liquidity Services won three international Web awards for outstanding Web site development. Among the features cited in the awards were a robust search engine, customized e-mail alerts to keep buyers informed, superior product information, shipping quotes to assure final prices for buyers, and real-time tracking of transactions.

Case Study Questions

1. Why is Liquidation.com able to compete against eBay?

2. How did Liquidation.com build trust in its site and services?

3. Why would retailers rather have a site dedicated to finding wholesalers rather than use the existing Liquidation.com site?

4. What are the key elements in Liquidation.com's core product and how does it create an augmented product?

5. Find a product on the Liquidation.com site that is also for sale on eBay. Compare the prices per unit. What accounts for the price differential?

6.6 REVIEW

KEY CONCEPTS

■ **Identify the key features of the Internet audience.**

Key features of the Internet audience include:
• *The number of users online in the United States.* In 2008, around 175 million. However, the rate of growth in the U.S. Internet population has begun to slow.
• *Intensity and scope of use.* Both are increasing, with around 72% of adult users in the United States logging on in a typical day and engaging in a wider set of activities, including sending and reading e-mail, gathering hobby-related information, catching up on news, browsing for fun, buying products, seeking health information, conducting work-related research, and reviewing financial information.

- *Demographics and access.* Although the Internet population is growing increasingly diverse, some demographic groups have much higher percentages of online usage than other groups, and different patterns of usage exist across various groups.
- *Gender.* Although men accounted for the majority of Internet users in 2000, today an equal percentage of both men and women (73%) use the Internet.
- *Ethnicity.* Variation across ethnic groups is not as wide as across age groups. In 2008, Hispanics had the highest Internet access rates, at 80%, with whites at 73% and African-Americans at 59%. Hispanics and African-Americans are both going online at higher rates than whites.
- *Education.* Amount of education seems to make a difference when it comes to online access. Of those individuals with less than a high school education, about 44% were online in 2008, while 91% of individuals with a college degree or more were online.
- *Lifestyle impacts.* Intensive Internet use may cause a decline in traditional social activities. The social development of children who use the Internet intensively instead of engaging in face-to-face interactions or undirected play out of doors may also be negatively impacted.
- *Media choices.* The more time individuals spend using the Internet, the less time they spend using traditional media.

■ Discuss the basic concepts of consumer behavior and purchasing decisions.

Models of consumer behavior attempt to predict or explain what consumers purchase, and where, when, how much, and why they buy. Factors that impact buying behavior include:
- Cultural factors
- Social factors
- Psychological factors

There are five stages in the consumer decision process:
- Awareness of need
- Search for more information
- Evaluation of alternatives
- The actual purchase decision
- Post-purchase contact with the firm

The online consumer decision process is basically the same, with the addition of two new factors:
- *Web site capabilities*—the content, design, and functionality of a site.
- *Consumer clickstream behavior*—the transaction log that consumers establish as they move about the Web and through specific sites. Analysts believe the most important predictors of online consumer behavior are the session characteristics and the clickstream behavior of people online, rather than demographic data.

■ Understand how consumers behave online.

Clickstream analysis shows us that people go online for many different reasons, at different times, and for numerous purposes.
- About 68% of online users are "buyers" who actually purchase something entirely online. Another 12% of online users research products on the Web, but

purchase them offline. This combined group, referred to as "shoppers," constitutes approximately 80% of the online Internet audience.

- Online sales are divided roughly into two groups: small ticket and big ticket items. In the early days of e-commerce, sales of small ticket items vastly out-numbered those of large ticket items. However, the recent growth of big ticket items such as computer hardware and consumer electronics has changed the overall sales mix.

- There are a number of actions that e-commerce vendors could take to increase the likelihood that shoppers and non-shoppers would purchase online more frequently. These include better security of credit card information and privacy of personal information, lower shipping costs, and easier returns.

■ **Describe the basic marketing concepts needed to understand Internet marketing.**

The key objective of Internet marketing is to use the Web—as well as traditional channels—to develop a positive, long-term relationship with customers (who may be online or offline) and thereby create a competitive advantage for the firm by allowing it to charge a higher price for products or services than its competitors can charge.

- Firms within an industry compete with one another on four dimensions: differentiation, cost, focus, and scope. "Competitive markets" are ones with lots of substitute products, easy entry, low differentiation among suppliers, and strong bargaining power of customers and suppliers.

- Marketing is an activity designed to avoid pure price competition, and to create imperfect markets where returns on investment are above average, competition is limited, and consumers are convinced to pay premium prices for products that have no substitute because they are unique. Marketing encourages customers to buy on the basis of perceived and actual nonmarket, that is, non-price, qualities of products.

- A product's brand is what makes products truly unique and differentiable in the minds of consumers. A brand is a set of expectations, such as quality, reliability, consistency, trust, affection, and loyalty, that consumers have when consuming, or thinking about consuming, a product or service from a specific company.

- Marketers devise and implement brand strategies—a set of plans for differentiating a product from its competitors and communicating these differences effectively to the marketplace. Segmenting the market, targeting different market segments with differentiated products, and positioning products to appeal to the needs of segment customers are key parts of brand strategy.

- Brand equity is the estimated value of the premium customers are willing to pay for using a branded product when compared to unbranded competitors. Consumers are willing to pay more for branded products in part because they reduce consumers' search and decision-making costs. The ability of brands to attain brand equity also provides incentive for firms to build products that serve customer needs better than other products. Brands also lower customer acquisition cost and increase customer retention.

- Although some predicted that the Web would lead to "frictionless commerce" and the end of marketing based on brands, recent research has shown that brands are alive and well on the Web and that consumers are still willing to pay price premiums for products and services they perceive and differentiate.

■ Identify and describe the main technologies that support online marketing.

- *Web transaction logs*—records that document user activity at a Web site.
- *Transaction logs*—coupled with data from the registration forms and shopping cart database, these represent a treasure trove of marketing information for both individual sites and the online industry as a whole.
- *Cookies*—small text files that Web sites place on visitors' client computers every time they visit, and during the visit, as specific pages are visited. Cookies provide Web marketers with a very quick means of identifying the customer and understanding his or her prior behavior at the site.
- *Web bugs*—tiny (1 pixel) graphic files hidden in marketing e-mail messages and on Web sites. Web bugs are used to automatically transmit information about the user and the page being viewed to a monitoring server.
- *Databases, data warehouses, data mining, and "profiling"*—technologies that allow marketers to identify exactly who the online customer is and what they want, and then to present the customer with exactly what they want, when they want it, for the right price.
- *CRM systems*—a repository of customer information that records all of the contacts that a customer has with a firm and generates a customer profile available to everyone in the firm who has a need to "know the customer."

■ Identify and describe basic e-commerce marketing and branding strategies.

The marketing technologies described above have spawned a new generation of marketing techniques and added power to some traditional techniques.

- Internet marketing strategies for market entry for new firms include pure clicks/first-mover and mixed bricks-and-clicks/alliances; and for existing firms include pure clicks/fast-follower and mixed bricks-and-clicks/brand extender.
- Online marketing techniques to online customers include the use of advertising networks, permission marketing, affiliate marketing, viral marketing, blog marketing, social network marketing, and brand leveraging.
- Online techniques for strengthening customer relationships include one-to-one marketing, customization and customer co-production, transactive content, and customer service (such as CRMs, FAQs, live chat, intelligent agents, and automated response systems).
- Online pricing strategies include offering products and services for free, versioning, bundling, and dynamic pricing.
- Companies operating in the e-commerce environment must also have marketing strategies in place to handle the possibility of channel conflict.

QUESTIONS

1. Is growth of the Internet, in terms of users, expected to continue indefinitely? What will cause it to slow, if anything?
2. Other than search engines, what are some of the most popular uses of the Internet?
3. Would you say that the Internet fosters or impedes social activity? Explain your position.

4. Why would the amount of experience someone has using the Internet likely increase future Internet usage?

5. Research has shown that many consumers use the Internet to investigate purchases before actually buying, which is often done in a physical storefront. What implication does this have for online merchants? What can they do to entice more online buying, rather than pure research?

6. Name four improvements Web merchants could make to encourage more browsers to become buyers.

7. Name the five stages in the buyer decision process and briefly describe the online and offline marketing activities used to influence each.

8. Why are "little monopolies" desirable from a marketer's point of view?

9. Describe a perfect market from the supplier's and customer's perspective.

10. Explain why an imperfect market is more advantageous for businesses.

11. What are the components of the core product, actual product, and augmented product in a feature set?

12. List some of the major advantages of having a strong brand. How does a strong brand positively influence consumer purchasing?

13. How are product positioning and branding related? How are they different?

14. List the differences among databases, data warehouses, and data mining.

15. Name some of the drawbacks to the four data mining techniques used in Internet marketing.

16. Why have advertising networks become controversial? What, if anything, can be done to overcome any resistance to this technique?

17. Which of the four market entry strategies is most lucrative?

18. Compare and contrast four marketing strategies used in mass marketing, direct marketing, micromarketing, and one-to-one marketing.

19. What pricing strategy turned out to be deadly for many e-commerce ventures during the early days of e-commerce? Why?

20. Is price discrimination different from versioning? If so, how?

21. What are some of the reasons that freebies, such as free Internet service and giveaways, don't work to generate sales at a Web site?

22. Explain how versioning works. How is this different from dynamic pricing?

23. Why do companies that bundle products and services have an advantage over those that don't or can't offer this option?

PROJECTS

1. Go to the SRI site (www.sric-bi.com/VALS/presurvey.shtml). Take the survey to determine which lifestyle category you fit into. Then write a brief two-page paper describing how your lifestyle and values impact your use of the Web for e-commerce. How is your online consumer behavior affected by your lifestyle?

2. Find an example of a Web site that you feel does a good job appealing to both goal-directed and experiential consumers. Explain your choice.

3. Choose a digital content product available on the Web and describe its feature set.

4. Visit Eluxury.com and create an Internet marketing plan for it that includes each of the following:

   - One-to-one marketing
   - Affiliate marketing
   - Viral marketing
   - Blog marketing
   - Social network marketing

   Describe how each plays a role, and create a PowerPoint or other form of presentation of your marketing plan.

WEB SITE RESOURCES www.prenhall.com/laudon

- Additional projects, exercises, and tutorials
- Careers: Explore career opportunities in e-commerce
- Raising capital and business plans

E-commerce Marketing Communications

After reading this chapter, you will be able to:

- Identify the major forms of online marketing communications.
- Understand the costs and benefits of online marketing communications.
- Discuss the ways in which a Web site can be used as a marketing communications tool.

Video Ads Cure Banner Blindness:
String Master

The age of video ads is upon us, just in case you haven't noticed. In fact, the country seems to have gone fairly crazy over videos: there are over 50 million YouTube viewers every month, several hundred thousand videos uploaded every day, and over 120 million Internet users who watch online videos. The online audience for videos is huge, larger than the combined visitors to AOL, Yahoo, and Google. This makes video an obvious advertising medium. And just in time: Internet users have learned how to avoid the traditional banner ad by instinctively moving their eyes to a different part of the screen. Click-throughs on banner ads are miniscule. Videos are another story. How to use them effectively in ad campaigns is still being worked out.

Take the experience of Evan Sofron, who markets String Master, a robotic guitar tuner that uses a computer-based listening device and a geared motor to tune a guitar to a perfect pitch. His small online company, Actiontuners in Deland, Florida, sells the String Master tuner through his Web site, Actiontuners.com. Evan used Google AdWords and text ads in both keyword and site-targeted campaigns. It worked. He saw a 15% increase in sales, but felt it was difficult to convey the features of his product, or what it looked like, with just text ads. Evan was also disappointed that the click-through rates for the ads were only 0.5%.

Around that time, Google began developing the capability to distribute video ads on its AdSense network. Evan had spent 20 years in the commercial video industry making television videos for a variety of firms and products. He created a 30-second video that demonstrated how String Master actually worked. Then, working with the Google Content Network, he chose various guitar, music, and musician sites on which the video ad would be displayed.

Rather than focus on a traditional metric such as click-through rates, Evan wanted to optimize the number of plays for his video and the time viewers spent watching his ads on the various sites. In a few weeks he could tell which sites were most productive, and focused his ads on these sites while removing them from the other sites. In a few months, Evan increased sales of his String Master by 40%. Click-through rates averaged 8.5% across all sites, and went as high as 30% on some sites.

Major Fortune 500 companies have learned a similar lesson: people are far more likely to watch a video, and pay attention to the content, than look at a banner ad or remember a text ad on Google. The large firms are also moving into the online video advertising marketplace with more sophisticated campaigns and big budgets. Dove soap (owned by Unilever) created one of the most successful commercial viral videos to date as a part of its Dove Self Esteem Fund, which seeks to "save the next generation from self-limiting beauty stereotypes" and promotes a wider definition of beauty. Its slogan is "Talk to your daughter before the beauty industry does," and its video is titled "Onslaught," which vividly illustrates the tsunami of beauty industry ads that young girls are exposed to and that offer impossible images for girls to emulate. Dove posted the video on YouTube, where it has received 800,000 views and has been "favorited" over 2,300 times. Dove also illustrates the perils of video advertising on YouTube: there are thousands of user-generated videos that disparage the Dove video and brand name.

Other companies are developing YouTube videos to advertise and brand their products. Microsoft launched its Halo 3 game with a TV ad that aired during Monday Night football, and then was quickly posted by viewers to YouTube, where it has received 3.7 million views to date. McDonalds created a spoof of its Chicken McNuggets product showing a couple of guys rapping about McNuggets. The original video surfaced on YouTube in 2006 and so far has over 700,000 views, was favorited 4,000 times, and produced 1,300 ratings and 1,400 comments.

In a twist, the H.J. Heinz company ("Doing common things uncommonly well") ran a user-generated ad contest asking viewers to submit video ads for Heinz Ketchup. The top 15 videos will be voted on by the public, and the winner will receive $57,000 (Heinz 57 Ketchup). So far, the original contest video has been viewed 1.1 million times, 2,200 people have submitted videos, and all of those ads were viewed over 500,000 times. Not bad for a media buy that cost only $33,000 to produce! That's about 2 cents per thousand impressions compared to $20 per thousand for a television ad.

People care and get excited about videos far more than banner ads and e-mail. This makes them an ideal advertising medium. The challenge is figuring out how to package advertising messages more directly with the videos, or how to piggyback advertising onto millions of user-generated video, and subsequently trying to measure the impact on sales. Google, Yahoo, AOL and literally hundreds of smaller firms, are hard at work trying to attach the right ads to the right videos, a tricky process since computers cannot "understand" the content of videos (they can "understand" the audio script—sort of). No one wants their product ads attached to stolen, pornographic, or inappropriate videos. Another challenge is to figure out how to show the ad while the video plays without destroying the viewing experience.

Advertising firms and Web sites are trying to move beyond the traditional "preroll" where the user clicks on a video, then is forced to watch an advertisement. Several new techniques are being explored: skins, which display alongside the video screen; bugs (overlays), which appear over the lower part of the video screen; and tickers, which scroll ads underneath the video.

The final challenge is to avoid turning the viewer off, and causing a kind of video blindness on a mass scale.

SOURCES: "Camera Ready: New Tools and Services for Small Companies to Create Video Ads," by Shelly Banjo, *Wall Street Journal*, August 28, 2008; "Lights! Camera! Sales!," by Raymund Flandez, *Wall Street Journal*, November 26, 2007; "Web Videos Stealing TV Viewers and Marketers," *New York Times*, November 16, 2007; "Are Skins, Bugs, or Tickers The Holy Grail of Web Advertising," by Kevin Delaney, *Wall Street Journal*, August 13, 2007; "Marketers See a Banner-Blindness Cure," by Emily Steel, *Wall Street Journal*, June 20, 2007; "Case Study: Using Video Advertising to Engage Your Customers," by Feng and Vivian, Inside AdWords, May 18, 2007; "Start-Ups Seek to Cash in on Web-Video Ads," *Wall Street Journal*, March 2, 2007; "Online Sellers Discover the Power of Video Clips," by Bob Tedeschi, *New York Times*, February 5, 2007.

The opening case provides an interesting glimpse into how the new broadband video capacity of homes and businesses, coupled with new Internet technologies, and widespread distribution of digital video cameras, is being used to influence consumer choice and build brand awareness. It also illustrates some of the challenges that marketers should be aware of when using these new forms of advertising.

In the last two years, Internet advertising has been on a tear. At the same time, the advertising industry as a whole—both offline and online—is going through a period of tumultuous change. The Internet and online advertising are disrupting the traditional advertising business which was dominated by television and print media. Advertising budgets are following customer eyeballs and moving onto the Web, while expenditures for print and television are static or declining. **Table 7.1** summarizes the significant changes in the advertising industry for 2008–2009.

TABLE 7.1	WHAT'S NEW IN INTERNET ADVERTISING 2008–2009
SEARCH ENGINE	**CRITERIA**
Growth of Internet advertising's share of total advertising budget at the expense of traditional media	In United States, growth is 25% a year and in Great Britain, 40% a year and 15% of the total market. Key difference: in Great Britain, advertisers control where their ads appear by dealing directly with publishers, unlike in the United States, where intermediaries such as DoubleClick control this function.
Industry giants embrace Internet advertising	Large packaged goods companies from Procter & Gamble to Budweiser are moving onto the Web with new branding ad formats such as video and BudTV.
Video, games, widgets and virtual lives: new ad formats	The banner display ad, in all its forms, gives way to an explosion in video ads, games and in-game ads, ads in widgets, and ads on social networks and virtual sites.
Behavioral targeting: customized ads and Web sites	New technologies come closer to the ideal of showing ads at the right time, to the right person, by analyzing online behavior
Metrics: challenges and solutions	Lack of industry standards, and new technologies such as AJAX, complicate the problem of measuring the impact of online ads, and understanding how much these ads are worth.
Google, AOL, Microsoft, and Yahoo enter the display ad industry.	Internet titans are seeking to leverage their online positions in search advertising into the display ad industry by purchasing online ad networks.
Social network marketing	Social networks gather the Web's largest audiences, and advertisers attempt to follow

After taking a steep plunge in 2001 following the dot-com bust, aggressive forms of "push" advertising such as animated banners, and even more aggressive pop-ups that greet you on entering and leaving Web sites have exploded, along with unsolicited e-mail or "spam," which now consumes about 70%–80% of all e-mail traffic on the Internet. Paid search advertising (also called "pull" advertising)—where consumers search for and find information and advertisers pay for text ads, such as that offered by Google, Yahoo, MSN and many others, has skyrocketed in popularity to become the single largest online ad form. Video advertising is still a small part of the overall Internet ad pie, but it is the fastest growing form of advertising. Internet advertising has become more costly as demand has exploded but still costs far less than traditional media advertising.

online marketing communications
methods used by online firms to communicate to the consumer and create strong brand expectations

In Chapter 6, we described brands as a set of expectations that consumers have about products offered for sale. We discussed some of the marketing activities that companies engage in to create those expectations. In this chapter, we focus on understanding **online marketing communications**—all the major methods that online firms use to communicate to the consumer, create strong brand expectations, and drive sales. What are the best methods for attracting people to a Web site and converting them into customers? We also examine the Web site as a marketing communications tool. How does the design of a Web site affect sales? How can you optimize a Web site for search engines?

7.1   MARKETING COMMUNICATIONS

Marketing communications have a dual purpose: branding and sales. One purpose of marketing communications is to develop and strengthen a firm's brands by informing consumers about the differentiating features of the firm's products and services. In addition, marketing communications are used to promote sales directly by encouraging the consumer to buy products (the sooner, the better). The distinction between the branding and sales purposes of marketing communications is subtle but important because branding communications differ from promotional communications.

promotional sales communications
suggest the consumer "buy now" and make offers to encourage immediate purchase

Promotional sales communications almost always suggest that the consumer "buy now," and they make offers to encourage immediate purchase. **Branding communications** rarely encourage consumers to buy now, but instead emphasize the differentiable benefits of consuming the product or service.

branding communications
focus on extolling the differentiable benefits of consuming the product or service

There are many different forms of online marketing communications, including online advertising, e-mail marketing, and public relations. Even the Web site itself can be viewed as a marketing communications tool.

ONLINE ADVERTISING

online advertising
a paid message on a Web site, online service, or other interactive medium

Advertising is the most common and familiar marketing communications tool. Companies will spend an estimated $299 billion on advertising in 2009, and an estimated $30 billion of that amount on **online advertising** (defined as a paid message on a Web site, paid search listing, video, widget, game, or other online medium, such as instant messaging) (see **Figure 7.1**) (eMarketer, Inc., 2008a).

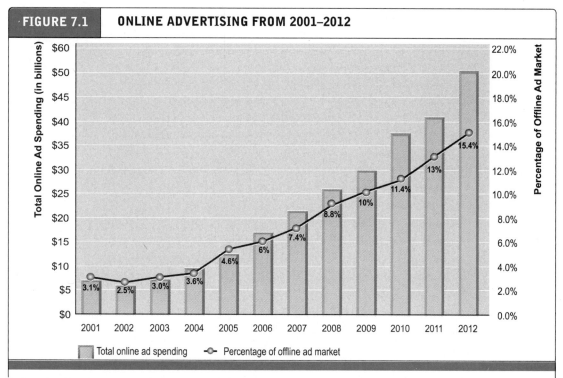

| FIGURE 7.1 | ONLINE ADVERTISING FROM 2001–2012 |

Online advertising is growing at about 20% a year, three times faster than the ad market as a whole. It will constitute nearly 10% of all advertising, and in 2012 will amount to 15% of all advertising.
SOURCES: Based on data from eMarketer, Inc., 2008a.

In the last five years, online advertising has grown over 200%, and advertisers are aggressively increasing online spending and cutting outlays on traditional channels such as radio, television, and newspapers. However, while online advertising is the fastest growing form of advertising, it will still remain a small part of total advertising for some time to come, reaching only 15% of all advertising by 2012.

Spending on online advertising among different industries is highly skewed. The top five industries—consumer (retail, automotive, travel, and packaged goods), financial services, computers, telecommunications, and media (television and radio broadcasting and print publishing)—account for more than 75% of all online advertising (Interactive Advertising Bureau/PricewaterhouseCoopers, 2008). Online advertising has both advantages and disadvantages when compared to advertising in traditional media, such as television, radio, and print (magazines and newspapers). One big advantage for online advertising is that the Internet is where the audience is moving, especially the very desirable 18–34 year olds, as well as the ballooning baby boomers who are post-65 years of age. A second large advantage for online advertising is the ability to target ads to narrow segments and track performance of advertisements in almost real time. **Ad targeting**, the sending of market messages to specific sub-groups in the population in an effort to increase the likelihood of a purchase, is as old as advertising itself. Ad targeting is also the foundation of price discrimination: the ability to charge different types of consumers different prices for the same product or service. The six

ad targeting
the sending of market messages to specific sub-groups in the population

major online segmentation and targeting methods (behavior, demographic, pyschographic, technical, contextual, and search) were described in Table 6.7 in Chapter 6. We further discuss ad targeting later in this section.

Theoretically, online advertising can personalize every ad message to precisely fit the needs, interests, and values of each consumer. In practice, as we all know from spam and constant exposure to pop-up ads that are of little interest, the reality is very different. Online advertisements also provide greater opportunities for interactivity—two-way communication between advertisers and potential customers. The primary disadvantages of online advertising are concerns about its cost versus its benefits, how to adequately measure its results, and the supply of good venues to display ads. For instance, the owners of Web sites who sell advertising space ("publishers") do not have agreed-upon standards or routine audits to verify their claimed numbers as do traditional media outlets. We examine the costs and benefits of online advertising as well as research on its effectiveness in Section 7.2.

There are a number of different forms of online advertisement:
- Display ads (banners and pop-ups)
- Rich media and video ads
- Search engine advertising
- In-game ads
- Social network, blog, and game advertising
- Sponsorships
- Referrals (affiliate relationship marketing)
- E-mail marketing
- Online catalogs

Table 7.2 provides some comparative data on the amount of spending for certain advertising formats. The online advertising format that currently produces the highest revenue is paid search, followed by display ads, but the fastest growing online ad format is rich media/video ads. We discuss the various online ad formats in more depth next.

Display Ads: Banners and Pop-Ups

banner ad

displays a promotional message in a rectangular box at the top or bottom of a computer screen

Display ads were the first Internet advertisements. A **banner ad** displays a promotional message in a rectangular box at the top or bottom of a computer screen. A banner ad is similar to a traditional ad in a printed publication but has some added advantages. If clicked on, it can bring a potential customer directly to the advertiser's Web site. It also is much more dynamic than a printed ad: it can present multiple images or otherwise change its appearance.

Banner ads sometimes feature Flash video and animations or animated GIFs, which display different images in relatively quick succession, creating an animated effect. The Interactive Advertising Bureau (IAB), an industry organization, has established voluntary industry guidelines for banner ads. A full banner, the most common, is 468 pixels wide by 60 pixels high with a resolution of 72 dpi (dots per inch) and a maximum file size of 13 KB.

TABLE 7.2	ONLINE ADVERTISING SPENDING FOR SELECTED FORMATS		
FORMAT	2008	2012	%CHANGE
Search	$10,360	$19,023	84%
Rich media/video	$2,654	$9,444	256%
Display ads	$5,465	$9,394	72%
Classified	$4,287	$7,575	77%
Lead generation	$2,124	$4,233	99%
E-mail	$492	$765	55%
Sponsorships	$518	$566	9%
Total	$25,900	$51,000	96%

SOURCES: Based on data from eMarketer, Inc., 2008a; Veronis Suhler Stevens, 2007; authors' estimates.

The IAB guidelines include specifications for virtually all types of ads and buttons, including skyscrapers (a tall, narrow banner ad almost three times the height of the traditional vertical banner ad), rectangles of various sizes, and a square pop-up (which opens in a separate window), to allow marketers to develop ads featuring enhanced interactivity as well as expanded creativity. The various types of ads (including the rich media/video ads discussed in the next section) are designed to help advertisers break through the "noise" and clutter created by the high number of display ad impressions that a typical user is exposed to within a given day. Advertising networks such as DoubleClick serve over 500 billion impressions of various types in a single year, and research firms estimate that Internet users are exposed to over 1,000 display ads per day. **Figure 7.2** shows examples of some of the different types of display ads, as specified by the IAB.

Pop-up ads are those banners and buttons that appear on the screen without the user calling for them. Generally, these ads conform to the size specifications of the IAB banner and button specifications. One type of pop-up ad is the **pop-under ad** that opens underneath a user's active browser window and does not appear until the user closes the active window. The ad remains visible until the user takes action to close it. Pop-ups can appear prior to display of the consumer's target page, during, or after the display on leaving.

Multiple surveys have found that pop-up ads that appear over a user's Web page cause negative consumer sentiment. Online consumers rate pop-ups right next to telemarketing as the most annoying form of marketing communication. A number of ISPs and search engine/portal sites, such as Yahoo, Google, AOL, and Earthlink now offer consumers pop-up blocking toolbars, as do Web browsers such as Mozilla Firefox and Internet Explorer 7 and 8. Unfortunately, studies have found that pop-up ads are twice as effective in terms of click-through rates than normal banner ads (although this may occur because people get confused about how to close the ads and end up unintentionally clicking to the advertised site). As a result, despite the backlash, although the number of pop-ups and pop-unders are likely to decline, they will not disappear entirely.

pop-up ad
banners and buttons that appear on the screen without the user calling for them

pop-under ad
opens underneath a user's active browser window and does not appear until the user closes the active window

FIGURE 7.2	TYPES OF DISPLAY ADS

Full Banner:
468 x 60 pixels

Skyscraper:
120 ´ 600 pixels

Half Banner:
234 x 60 pixels

Micro Bar:
88 x 31 pixels

Vertical Banner:
120 x 240 pixels

Button-1:
120 x 90 pixels

Button-2:
120 x 60 pixels

Square Button:
125 x 125 pixels

Rectangle:
180 x 150 pixels

In addition to the various display ads shown above, IAB also provides standards for a medium, large, and vertical rectangle, a square pop-up, a wide skyscraper, a half-page ad, and an ad it calls a "leaderboard" (728 x 90 pixels).

SOURCE: Interactive Advertising Bureau, 2008.

Rich Media/Video Ads

While traditional banner ads will undoubtedly remain a dominant form for some time to come, the use of video and **rich media/video ads** (ads employing Flash, dynamic HTML (DHTML), Java, and streaming audio and/or video) is the fastest growing form of online advertising although in total revenue, the amount spent still totals only one-fifth of the amount spent on search engine advertising. As with display ads, the IAB has published voluntary guidelines for rich media ads. **Table 7.3** illustrates some of the IAB standards for video ads. Rich media/video ads are also increasingly interactive, seeking to involve the user even more deeply by forcing him or her to interact with the ad in some fashion, such as by requiring the user to assemble on-screen objects or click on related objects. Rich media/video ads tend to be more about branding than driving sales per se.

Why are rich media/video ads so effective? One research report found that exposure to rich media/video ads boosted brand awareness by 10% over a control group. The same methodology applied to normal banner ads found that it took three exposures to a large rectangle ad to produce a similar increase, six exposures to a skyscraper unit to get an 8% increase, and ten exposures to a regular banner ad to get a 6% increase (Dynamic Logic, 2004). Industry reports indicate that rich media/video ad spending will grow about 212% from 2008 to 2012, faster than paid search engine advertising (which is estimated to grow about 92% during the same time period). (eMarketer, Inc. 2008a). And it isn't just that advertisers are using video to get their message across. They are also linking up their banner and video ads to user-generated videos—millions of them. **Table 7.4** illustrates the wide variety of Web sites that offer videos, and which represent excellent marketing opportunities for advertisers.

The explosion of online video content across major news and entertainment sites, Web portals, and humor and user-generated sites has created huge opportunities for brand marketers to better reach their target audiences. About 80% of the entire U.S. Internet audience (around 138 million viewers) now watch online videos. This audience will grow to 183 million by 2012. Online video has become the audience aggre-

rich media/video ad
ad employing Flash, DHTML, and Java, and streaming audio and/or video

TABLE 7.3	TYPES OF VIDEO ADS		
FORMAT	DESCRIPTION	WHEN USED	USED WITH
Linear video ad	Pre-roll; takeover; ad takes over video for a certain period of time	Before, between, after video	Text, banners, rich media video player skins
Non-linear video ad	Overlay; Web bugs; ad runs at same time as video content and does not take over full screen	During, over, or within video	
In-banner video ad	Rich media; ad is triggered within banner, may expand outside banner	Within Web page, generally surrounded by content	None
In-text video ad	Rich media; ad is delivered when user mouses over relevant text	Within Web page, identified as a highlighted word within relevant content	None

TABLE 7.4	TOP TEN U.S. ONLINE VIDEO SITES (JULY 2008) (in millions)	
SITE	VISITORS	AVG. VIDEOS PER VIEWER
1. Google sites (YouTube)	92.1	54.7
2. Fox Interactive Media (MySpace)	54.8	8.1
3. Yahoo! sites	37.6	7.2
4. Microsoft sites	32.6	8.7
5. AOL	23.0	4.1
6. Viacom Digital	21.1	11.7
7. Turner Network	18.7	9.2
8. Disney Online	15.9	11.7
9. Time Warner (excluding AOL)	15.3	3.2
10. Amazon sites	11.7	2.5

SOURCE: eMarketer, Inc., 2008b.

gator of the 21st century, displacing television broadcast networks and Hollywood film producers (eMarketer, Inc., 2008a).

Exactly how to take advantage of this opportunity is still a puzzle. A small group of users will pay for premium online content, but the vast majority of Internet users expect video to be free and advertising-supported. Internet users are willing to listen to advertising in order to see short video clips as long as the ads don't interfere, and the ads are not too long. There are many formats for displaying ads with videos. Currently, the most widely used format is the "pre-roll" (followed by the mid-roll and the post-roll) where users are forced to watch an ad, often another video, either before, in the middle, or at the end of the video they originally clicked on. While advertising firms have been successful in selling the video ad format to firms, the major video sites like YouTube and MySpace have had a difficult time selling their ad space and monetizing their huge audiences.

There are many specialized video advertising networks such as Videoegg, Advertsing.com, Broadband, Roo and others who run video advertising campaigns for national advertisers and place these videos on their respective network of Web sites. Firms can also establish their own video and television sites to promote their products. For instance in 2007, Budweiser created BudTV and Procter & Gamble created an online sitcom called *Crescent Heights*.

interstitial ad

a way of placing a full-page message between the current and destination pages of a user

Interstitial ads are typically considered a kind of "rich media" ad. **An interstitial ad** (interstitial means "in between") is a way of placing a full-page message between the current and destination pages of a user. Interstitials are usually inserted within a single Web site, and displayed as the user moves from one page to the next. The interstitial typically moves automatically to the page the user requested after allowing enough time for the ad to be read. Interstitials can also be deployed over an advertising network and appear as users move among Web sites.

Since the Web is such a busy place, people have to find ways to cope with overstimulation. One means of coping is known as sensory input filtering. This means that people learn to filter out the vast majority of the messages coming at them. Internet users quickly learn at some level to recognize banner ads or anything that looks like a banner ad and to filter out most of the ads that are not exceptionally relevant. Video ads and interstitial messages, like TV commercials, attempt to make viewers a captive of the message. Typical interstitials last ten seconds or less and force the user to look at the ad for that time period. IAB standards for pre-roll ads also limit their length. To avoid boring users, video ads typically use animated graphics and music to entertain and inform them. A good video ad or interstitial will also have a "skip through" or "stop" option for users who have no interest in the message.

A **superstitial** (now offered by a firm by the name of Viewpoint and sometimes referred to as a Unicast Transitional with Flash) is a rich media ad that can be any screen display size up to full screen 900 x 500 (the full-screen superstitial), and with a file size of up to 600 KB. Superstitials differ from interstitials in that they are pre-loaded into a browser's cache and do not play until fully loaded. When the file is finished downloading, like an interstitial, it waits until the user clicks to another page before popping up in a separate window. Video ads are displacing superstitials.

Regardless of the type of display advertising, most large advertisers work through intermediaries such as advertising networks (e.g. DoubleClick), or advertising agencies that have an ad placement and creative staff. Other options include swapping ad space with other sites, and dealing directly with the publisher (the Web site that will post the advertisement). **Banner swapping** arrangements among firms allow each firm to have its banners displayed on other affiliate sites for no cost. **Advertising exchanges** arrange for banner swapping among firms, usually small firms that cannot afford expensive ad networks such as DoubleClick. By displaying the banners of other firms, the firm can earn credits toward the display of its banner on other Web sites. Smaller firms have many more opportunities than in the past to place banner ads inexpensively using Yahoo Advertising, Google Ads, and Microsoft's Digital Advertising Solutions. Each of these firms provides targeting, segmentation, cross-selling techniques, and ad customization.

superstitial
a rich media ad that is pre-loaded into a browser's cache and does not play until fully loaded and the user clicks to another page

banner swapping
an arrangement among firms that allows each firm to have its banners displayed on other affiliate sites for no cost

advertising exchanges
arrange for banner swapping among firm

Search Engine Advertising: Paid Search Engine Inclusion and Placement

Arguably, the most significant change in online marketing in the past five years has been the explosive growth in search engine marketing. More than any other form of online advertising, search engine marketing has altered the entire marketing communications industry. This form of marketing communications has been one of the fastest-growing: revenues generated by search engine marketing have grown from 1% of total online advertising spending in 2000 to over 40% in 2008 (see **Figure 7.3**), although the rate of growth is slowing to around 20%-25% a year (eMarketer, Inc. 2008c). The search engine audience is huge—almost as big as the e-mail user population. On an average day in the United States, around 71 million Americans (over 40% of the online population) will use a search engine (Pew Internet & American Life Pro-

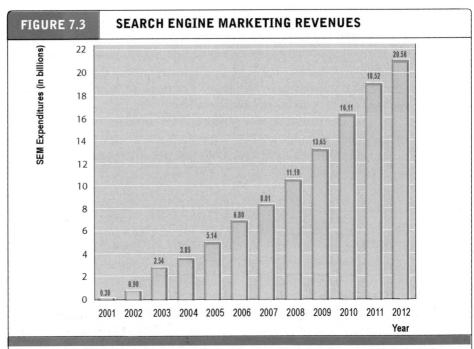

| FIGURE 7.3 | **SEARCH ENGINE MARKETING REVENUES** |

Search engine marketing has grown to about 40% of all online advertising. However, its growth rate has slowed considerably to the low double-digits.

SOURCES: Based on data from eMarketer, Inc., 2008c, 2007a, 2005b; 2005c; Interactive Advertising Bureau PricewaterhouseCoopers, 2008, 2007, 2005.

ject, 2008). Collectively, they generate around 10 billion searches a month. Briefly, this is where the eyeballs are (at least for a few moments) and this is where advertising can be very effective by responding with ads that match the interests and intentions of the user. The click-through rate for search marketing generally is 10%–12% and has been fairly steady over the years.

Today there are hundreds of search engines on the Internet, with about 20 "major" search sites that generate most of the search traffic. Search engine marketing is highly concentrated. The top three search engine providers (Google, Yahoo, and MSN) supply over 95% of all the searches to these top twenty sites (see Figure 3.20). Over time, the search engine market has gradually shifted towards Google at about 1% a year, with Yahoo and MSN slowly losing share. Ask.com remains a steady player with around 4% of the market.

Types of Search Engine Marketing There are at least three different types of search engine marketing: keyword paid inclusion or rank, advertising keywords, and search engine-based advertising networks. Search engine sites originally performed unbiased searches of the Web's huge collection of Web pages and derived most of their revenue from banner advertisements. This form of search engine results is often called **organic search** because the inclusion and ranking of Web sites depends on a more or less "unbiased" application of a set of rules (an algorithm) imposed by the search engine. Since 1998, search engine sites have slowly been transforming themselves into digital yellow pages, where firms pay for inclusion in the search engine index

organic search

inclusion and ranking of sites depends on a more or less unbiased application of a set of rules imposed by the search engine and/or pay for specific locational placement or rank in the results of searches—so-called paid placement or paid rank.

Most search engines offer **paid inclusion** programs which, for a fee, guarantee a Web site's inclusion in its list of search results, more frequent visits by its Web crawler, and suggestions for improving the results of organic searching. Search engines claim that these payments—costing some merchants hundreds of thousands a year do not influence the organic ranking of a Web site in search results, just inclusion in the results. However, it is the case that page inclusion ads get more hits, and the rank of the page appreciates, causing the organic search algorithm to rank it higher in the organic results.

Some search engines do not have a paid inclusion program, but do charge for placing small text ads in either sponsored link areas of the results pages or sometimes mixed with organic results (unbeknownst to the user). Google claims it does not permit firms to pay for their rank in the organic results, although it does allocate two to three sponsored links at the very top of their pages, albeit labeling them as "Sponsored Links." Some search engines make it very difficult for the user to know if the top-listed results of a search are paid inclusions or the result of objective search criteria. Merchants who refuse to pay for inclusion typically fall far down on the list and off the first page of results, which is akin to commercial death.

Research demonstrates the significance of rank in both organic and paid placements, and equally important, the greater power that users attach to organic search results (see **Figure 7.4**). Researchers used an eye-tracking tool to gauge Web

paid inclusion

for a fee, guarantees a Web site's inclusion in its list of sites, more frequent visits by its Web crawler, and suggestions for improving the results of organic searching

---

FIGURE 7.4	**THE IMPORTANCE OF RANK FOR CUSTOMER VIEWING BY TYPE OF SEARCH**

Nearly everyone reads the top three-ranked results in organic search results, but readership drops off rather dramatically for the 4th through 10th-ranked results. Sponsored links are heavily discounted by readers—only 50% read the top-ranked sponsored results listed, and readership drops off sharply after that.

SOURCE: Based on data from Hotchkiss, et al., 2007.

users' behavior at search engines. They discovered an "F" shaped pattern in which viewers scan search result pages from top to bottom, with greater attention to the left side of the page looking for clues. They spend less time on the right side of the page looking at paid text advertisements, and usually only at the top three advertisements. Users always viewed the first three organic listings, but were much less likely to view the sponsored listings. These results have been replicated several times using eye heat maps (Shrestha and Lenz, 2007; Nielsen, 2006).

The two other types of search engine marketing rely on selling keywords in online auctions.

keyword advertising

merchants purchase keywords through a bidding process at search sites, and whenever a consumer searches for that word, their advertisement shows up somewhere on the page

In **keyword advertising**, merchants purchase keywords through a bidding process at search sites, and whenever a consumer searches for that word, their advertisement shows up somewhere on the page, usually as a small text-based advertisement on the right, but also as a listing on the very top of the page. The more merchants pay, the higher the rank and greater the visibility of their ads on the page. Generally, the search engines do not exercise editorial judgment about quality or content of the ads although they do monitor the use of language. In addition, some search engines rank the ads in terms of their popularity rather than merely the money paid by the advertiser so that the rank of the ad depends both on the amount paid and the number of clicks per unit time. Google's keyword advertising program is called AdWords, Yahoo's is called PrecisionMatch, and Microsoft's is called adCenter.

network keyword advertising (context advertising)

network of publishers accepts ads placed by Google on their Web sites, and receive a fee for any click-throughs from those ads

Network keyword advertising (**context advertising**), introduced by Google in 2002, differs from ordinary keyword advertising described previously. Here's how these search engine networks operate. Publishers (Web site owners) join the network, and allow the search engine to place "relevant" ads on their sites. The ads are paid for by advertisers who want their messages to appear across the Web. Google-like text messages are the most common. The revenue from the resulting clicks is split between the search engine and the site publisher although in some cases the publisher gets much more than half. The publisher has no direct control over what ads are shown on his/her site. The advertiser has no control over where their ads appear either. But the search engines use a variety of tools (keyword analysis and propinquity of keywords) to ensure only "relevant" and "appropriate" ads appear. For this reason, network keyword advertising is often called "context marketing" because an effort is made to understand the context where the ad will be shown. Google calls this "AdSense," knowing where to place ads based on the surrounding context. Yahoo's program is called ContentMatch. Together, keyword and network keyword advertising account for most of the revenue growth in search engine marketing. About half of Google's revenue comes from AdWords and the rest comes from AdSense.

In this manner, the search engines have greatly extended their keyword advertising beyond their own sites (where users do not linger) to tens of thousands of other sites on the Web. Unfortunately, these programs have also led to the creation of "junk AdSense" sites composed of re-hashed links from the Web, and an entire industry of illegitimate poachers who nevertheless are paid when their Web site visitors click on an adSense link.

Keywords for both types of keyword advertising range in price from a few pennies per click, to $25 or above for high-priced popular items (see **Figure 7.5**). The highest

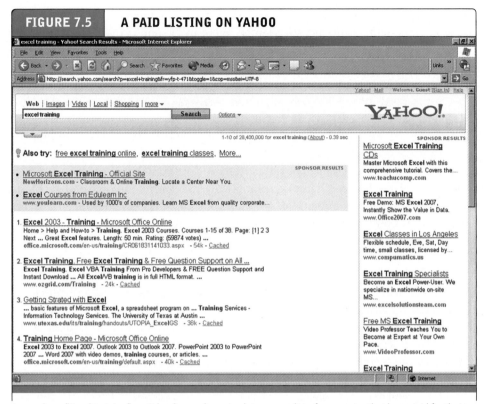

A search on "Excel training" on Yahoo's search engine brings up a list of companies that have paid for their inclusion and placement on the search results list.

SOURCE: Yahoo.com . Reproduced with permission of Yahoo! Inc. © 2008 Yahoo! Inc. YAHOO! and the YAHOO! logo are trademarks of Yahoo! Inc.

keyword prices are paid for potential litigation customers by law firms. The family of "mesothelioma" keywords sell for up to $800 a click. How much would you pay (or should you pay) to place your company's listing in front of the consumer just at the precise moment the consumer is looking for products provided by your company? This depends, of course, on how much customers are likely to spend at your site. And it depends on how much your competitors are willing to pay for the same keyword. In an auction environment, it is easy to overpay or under pay.

Search engine marketing is nearly an ideal targeted marketing technique: at precisely the moment that a consumer is looking for a product, an advertisement for that product is presented. While originally this was the idea behind advertising networks such as DoubleClick and Real Media 24/7, their database techniques cannot deliver the advertisement with as much accuracy or speed at the moment of interest. Unlike traditional online and offline targeted marketing approaches, which are based on searching large databases for customer profiles and information, search engine marketing is based on the much more efficient idea of responding to keyword searches at that moment (although prior searches from the IP address, or keywords gleaned from other sources such as Google's Gmail can also influence the results).

No databases on clickstream behavior or background demographics are generally used. The most important fact for search engine marketers is that the customer is looking for a product like the one sold by the merchant.

In some cases, search engines do not inform the user that the results of a query have been paid for by participating firms, or they make it difficult to tell what is paid and what is the result of unbiased search. Some analysts argue that users don't care if merchants pay for listings—just as they don't care when they use the yellow pages—as long as the searches produce relevant results. Some have even argued that informing the user about the commercial nature of placement and listings would harm e-commerce because users have been trained by the industry to "avoid anything that looks commercial." Users might actually not pursue appropriate and relevant links if they thought the listing was commercially influenced. A number of complaints have been filed with the Federal Trade Commission (FTC) that search engines that fail to clearly indicate they accept payments for higher search ranking are engaging in deceptive practices. In July 2002, the FTC recommended to the search engine industry that it should improve the disclosure of paid content within search results (Sullivan, 2003). A follow-up study by Consumer Reports WebWatch found that paid inclusion was not satisfactorily disclosed or explained by any of the search engines tested; meta-engines, which present results from several search engines simultaneously, repeatedly failed to adequately disclose the presence of paid placement and paid inclusion within search results; and disclosures when made are generally hard to find, making them easy for consumers to overlook. The report also found that information disclosed by Web sites about business practices with advertisers—and how these practices may affect search results—was often confusing and jargon-laden. Some search engines, such as Google (one of the few major search engines not named in the original FTC complaint) took pains to visually segregate paid results from non-paid results (Consumer Reports WebWatch, 2004; 2005). The search engine industry has the online population pretty confused about where the results come from. A Pew Internet & American Life Project study found that 62% of search engine users were not aware of the difference between paid and unpaid results, and 70% accepted the concept of sponsored results. Half said they would stop using a search engine if they felt it was not being honest about how the results are produced (Pew Internet & American Life Project, 2005).

Why does search engine marketing work so well and why is it so popular with both merchants and consumers? For merchants, search engine marketing is close to ideal for sales promotion. Paid search engine inclusion and placement is one of the most effective marketing communications tools on the Web, given that on any given day about 71 million Americans use a search engine to find products and information.

The major search engines have been very helpful to small businesses that cannot afford large marketing campaigns. Because shoppers are looking for a specific product or service when they use search engines, they are what marketers call "hot prospects"—people who are looking for information and often intending to buy. Moreover, search engines charge only for click-throughs to a site. Merchants do not have to pay for ads that don't work. Last, merchants do not have to be at the mercy of search engine ranking and listing rules that they—and most others—cannot understand. No one really knows, for instance, exactly how or why Google decides to organically rank one company over another, or to refuse a company a listing in the front pages. No one really knows how to improve their rankings (although there are hundreds of firms who claim otherwise). In fact, according to Google's own self-description of its search engine, listings are biased toward already popular Web sites to whom many consumers connect, and ignore new startup companies or put them on back pages. Google editors intervene in unknown ways to punish certain Web sites and reward others. Search engines such as Google maintain a stranglehold over small companies trying to get national market exposure. Paid listings change much of this. A company simply pays Google or other search engine and has the certain knowledge that its ad will appear on the page and with a rank that reflects its bid. For many merchants who can afford this, the reduction in uncertainty is worth the price.

What about consumers? Consumers benefit from search engine marketing because ads for merchants appear only when consumers are looking for a specific product. There are no pop-ups, Flash animations, videos, interstitials, e-mails, or other irrelevant communications to deal with. Thus, search engine marketing saves consumers cognitive energy. Search engine marketing works because it is primarily pull-oriented: consumers pull the information they are looking for.

Search Engine Click Fraud and Ad Nonsense The Achilles' heel of search engine marketing is "click fraud." Just as spam has greatly reduced the utility of e-mail marketing, so has click fraud raised the costs and reduced the attractiveness of search engine marketing to merchants. So much of the Internet depends on openness, trust, and ethical behavior by participants. Click fraud strikes at the heart of these assumptions.

Anyone, including competitors, can click on search engine ads, driving up a merchant's costs, without ever purchasing anything. If you are a Web site publisher, you can increase your revenue by having friends and relatives click on the ads Google or Microsoft place on your site. **Click fraud** occurs when (a) a competitors fraudulently click on competitor ads in order to drive up their marketing costs, or (b) a Web site publisher fraudulently clicks on ads posted on their sites in order to increase ad revenue. Some fraudsters have developed "click bots" that automatically click on ads from hundreds of different IP addresses, and utilize zombie computers (unprotected clients on the Web that have been captured by adware programs) to generate the clicks, which are untraceable. A related type of click fraud involves fraudsters who call up a search results page where their competitors' ads appear, and then fail to click on competitor ads. This results in a low ad popularity rank for these Google AdWords and AdSense ads, which in turn can result in their being pushed down the rank order of ads onto the lower part of the page.

Search engines attempt to monitor and prevent this behavior by observing traffic patterns, but find it difficult to trace fraudulent clicks because defrauders can hide their offshore IP addresses. Current research suggests the click fraud rate in the United States is around 16% of all clicks, and 20% on "high-priced keywords" (Click Forensics, 2008). The amount of publisher-originated click fraud is not known. SEMPO, the Search Engine Marketing Professional Organization (a trade association

click fraud
occurs when a competitor hires third parties (typically from low-wage countries) to fraudulently click on competitor ads

of marketers in part sponsored by search engine firms) reports that 40% of large advertisers felt click fraud was a problem, 19% of advertisers attempt to track click fraud, and about 50% of advertisers have reduced their keyword search budgets because of click fraud (Fair Isaac Corporation, 2007). Click fraud can be difficult but not impossible to detect. The typical click fraud pattern is one where clicks increase and sales remain the same or decline. Large departures from historical click rates (such as one standard deviation or more) are suspect. Search engine firms such as Google and Yahoo do refund charges in suspicious situations. A somewhat less severe issue is the appearance of "ad nonsense" which occurs because Google's AdSense program places ads on thousands of Web sites using a computer program that attempts to understand the content of the Web page, and place an appropriate ad. Sometimes, the computer program makes mistakes, such as when a search on the term "lost dogs" produces ads on Google offering "great deals" on lost dogs, and ads for "disease," "sewage" and "rot." Even more disturbing to advertisers, sometimes ads for products show up on Web sites totally unrelated to that product. For instance, Kraft Foods ads for cheese appeared on a Web site of a "White Nationalist" hate group that used the words "Thanksgiving" on its Web site. Advertisers lose control over where their ads appear when they use the Google AdSense program.

Sponsorships

sponsorship
a paid effort to tie an advertiser's name to information, an event, or a venue in a way that reinforces its brand in a positive yet not overtly commercial manner

A **sponsorship** is a paid effort to tie an advertiser's name to particular information, an event, or a venue in a way that reinforces its brand in a positive yet not overtly commercial manner. Sponsorships typically are more about branding than immediate sales. A common form of sponsorship is targeted content (or advertorials), in which editorial content is combined with an ad message to make the message more valuable and attractive to its intended audience. For instance, WebMD.com, the leading medical information Web site in the United States, offers "sponsorship sites" on the WebMD Web site to companies such as Phillips to describe their home defibrillators, and Lilly to describe their pharmaceutical solutions for attention deficit disorders among children. According to eMarketer, sponsorships accounted for around $535 million in online advertising revenues in 2007 (eMarketer, Inc., 2008a).

Referrals (Affiliate Relationship Marketing)

affiliate relationships
permit a firm to put its logo or banner ad on another firm's Web site from which users of that site can click through to the affiliate's site

An **affiliate relationship** permits a firm (the originating Web site) to place its logo, banner ad, or text link on another firm's Web site (called the affiliate) from which users of that site can click through to the originating site. Millions of personal Web sites have Amazon and other logos which when clicked will take the visitor to Amazon, and generate revenue for the Web site. Among large firms, affiliate relationships are sometimes called "tenancy deals" because they allow a firm to become a long-term "tenant" on another site. Amazon has tenancy relationships with a number of retailers. Referrals (affiliate marketing) generated about $2.1 million a year in 2008 (eMarketer, Inc., 2008a). In some cases, the firms share a single corporate parent or investor group that is seeking to optimize the performance of all its Web sites by creating links among its "children" sites. In other cases, two Web sites may sell complementary products and the firms may strike an affiliate relationship to make it easier for their customers to find the products they are looking for.

E-MAIL MARKETING AND THE SPAM EXPLOSION

In the early days of e-commerce, **direct e-mail marketing** (e-mail marketing messages sent directly to interested users) was one of the most effective forms of marketing communications. Direct e-mail marketing messages were sent to an "opt-in" audience of Internet users who, at one time or another, had expressed an interest in receiving messages from the advertiser. Unsolicited e-mail was not common. By sending e-mail to an opt-in audience, advertisers were targeting interested consumers. Response rates to legitimate, opt-in e-mail campaigns average just over 6%, depending on the targeting and freshness of the list. By far, in-house e-mail lists are more effective than purchased e-mail lists. Because of the comparatively high response rates and low cost, direct e-mail marketing remains a common form of online marketing communications. In 2008, according to a McKinsey & Company, over 80% of companies worldwide used e-mail campaigns to reach customers, and the total amount U.S. companies spend on e-mail marketing was about $430 million (McKinsey & Company, 2007). Click rates for legitimate e-mails depend on the promotion (the offer), the product, and the amount of targeting, but they average in the 5%–7% range, higher than postal mail response rates (less than 2%–4%). Despite the deluge of spam mail, e-mail remains a highly cost effective way of communicating with existing customers, and to a lesser extent finding new customers.

E-mail marketing and advertising is inexpensive and somewhat invariant to the number of mails sent. The cost of sending 1,000 mails is about the same as the cost to send 1 million. The primary cost of e-mail marketing is for the purchase of the list of names to which the e-mail will be sent. This generally costs anywhere from 5 to 20 cents a name, depending on how targeted the list is. Sending the e-mail is virtually cost-free. In contrast, a direct mail 5 x 7-inch post card mailing costs about 15 cents per name, but printing and mailing costs raise the overall cost to around 75 to 80 cents a name. While the cost of legitimate e-mail messages based on high-quality commercial opt-in e-mail lists is $5 to $10 per thousand, the direct mail cost is $500 to $700 per thousand when all costs are added up.

In 2008, however, e-mail no longer commands quite as much respect as it once did because of three factors: spam, software tools used to control spam that eliminate much e-mail from user in-boxes, and poorly targeted purchased e-mail lists. **Spam** is "junk e-mail" and spammers are people who send unsolicited e-mail to a mass audience of Internet users who have expressed no interest in the product. Worse, spammers tend to market pornography, fraudulent deals and services, outright scams, and other products not widely approved in most civilized societies. Legitimate direct opt-in e-mail marketing is not growing as fast as behaviorally targeted banners, pop-ups, and search engine marketing because of the explosion in spam. Consumer response to even legitimate e-mail campaigns has become more sophisticated. Almost three-quarters of Internet users say they see value in e-mail from companies they do business with, while only 17% saw value when the

direct e-mail marketing
e-mail marketing messages sent directly to interested users

spam
unsolicited commercial e-mail

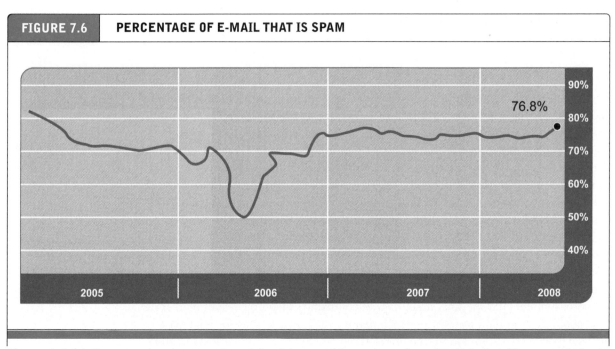

After a period of decline, spam volume has resumed growth largely because of the greater number and sophistication of "spam zombies" and "bot networks," which consist of thousands of captured PCs that can initiate and relay spam messages. Spam is seasonally cyclical, and varies monthly due to the impact of new technologies (both supportive and discouraging of spammers), new prosecutions, and seasonal demand for products and services. Spam seems to peak in June.

SOURCE: MessageLabs.com, 2008.

e-mail came from companies they do not do business with (Acxicom, 2006). As Internet users become more experienced with spam filters, more and more (currently around 70%) delete spam before opening based on the "From" line or the "Subject" line. Over 60% of users find e-mail commercial spam unpleasant and 20% report reduced overall use of e-mail because of spam (eMarketer, Inc., 2007c). In general, e-mail works well for maintaining the customer relationship, but poorly in acquiring new customers.

While click fraud may be the Achilles heel of search engine marketing, spam is the nemesis of effective e-mail marketing and advertising. The percentage of all e-mail that is spam is estimated at around 70%–80% in 2007 (Symantec, 2008; MessageLabs, 2008) (see **Figure 7.6**).

Figure 7.7 illustrates the average breakdown for the most common categories of spam, as recorded by Symantec and its subsidiary Brightmail, a San Francisco-based anti-spam software company, during the first half of 2008.

The cost of entry to the spam business or "mass bulk e-mailing business" is small. Hundreds of programs that can be purchased on the Web allow spammers to harvest e-mail addresses across the Web from message boards and chat rooms; downloads of millions of names are available. Spammers do not generally pay anything for the cost of distributing their spam because they send the messages using captured client and

---

FIGURE 7.7	SPAM CATEGORIES

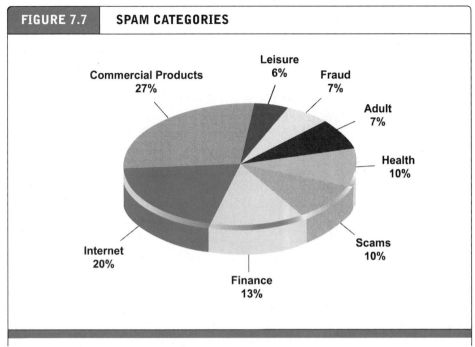

On average, the leading category of spam during the first half of 2007 involved commercial products, followed closely by finance and health (drug offers).
SOURCE: Symantec, 2008.

server computers. The explosion in spam has led to many unsuccessful efforts to control the deluge. There are four solutions to spam: technology, government legislation, voluntary self-regulation, and volunteer efforts to identify spammers and either shut them down or inform authorities. Obviously, none of these approaches has been successful to date, each approach has many advocates and entrepreneurs, and together all approaches just might make a difference

Filtering software on client computer browsers has helped companies and individual users cope with spam, but spammers purchase the same software to understand how to defeat them. Moreover, company mail servers still fill up with spam messages. Filters on corporate servers are more effective and reduce server loads by deleting spam or compressing it in smaller files. Large ISPs such as AOL and MSN are able to filter a lot of, but not all, spam, as spammers are able to capture thousands of unprotected client computers in homes and offices and to use them to originate spam mail without the owner's knowledge. ISPs set up "honey pots"— dummy e-mail accounts—that quickly receive spam mail to study the subject lines of spam and to develop filters on specific words and phrases. Spammers reply by creating new variations on words, often with dummy characters such as "V1agra" and "F*A*S*T M*O*N*E*Y".

More promising technology approaches may result from cooperation among the big technology players and ISPs. AOL, Yahoo, EarthLink, and Microsoft—the nation's largest ISPs—have agreed on technical standards called Sender ID which requires large-scale e-mailers to verify their identify with the ISPs as a condition of sending their e-mail. Currently, spammers can hide their identity in the e-mail protocol and there are no formal restrictions on e-mail being sent from computers with specific IP addresses. A more aggressive approach called FairUCE is being marketed by IBM, and a similar program is being marketed by Symantec to large corporations. IBM's service is based on a huge database that identifies actual computers with specific IP addresses that are sending spam, and adds them to a spam list. Once identified, e-mails coming from these computers are immediately returned to the actual spamming machine (not the e-mail address in the From: field), causing the spammer computer to overload, slowdown, and choke. It is not clear at this time how well IBM's technology solution will work on a large scale. Symantec has developed software for corporations that intentionally slow down their bit rate to that of a very slow modem, slowing down the spam sending process.

Legislative attempts to control spam have also largely not succeeded. Thirty-eight states in the United States have laws regulating or prohibiting spam (National Conference of State Legislatures, 2008). State legislation typically requires that unsolicited mail (spam) contain a label in the subject line ("ADV") indicating the message is an advertisement, require a clear opt-out choice for consumers, and prohibit e-mail that contains false routing and domain name information (nearly all spammers hide their own domain, ISP, and IP address). Some states, such as California and Delaware, are much stricter and prohibit all unsolicited e-mail to or from state citizens and require a specific "opt-in" choice before consumers can be sent e-mail. In Virginia, sending spam is a criminal felony offense.

Congress passed the first national anti-spam law ("Controlling the Assault of Non-Solicited Pornography and Marketing Act" or CAN-SPAM) in 2003, and it went into effect in January 2004. The act does not prohibit unsolicited e-mail (spam) but instead requires unsolicited commercial e-mail messages to be labeled (though not by a standard method) and to include opt-out instructions and the sender's physical address. It prohibits the use of deceptive subject lines and false headers in such messages. The FTC is authorized (but not required) to establish a "do-not-e-mail" registry. State laws that require labels on unsolicited commercial e-mail or prohibit such messages entirely are pre-empted, although provisions merely addressing falsity and deception may remain in place. The act imposes fines of $10 for each unsolicited pornographic e-mail and authorizes state attorneys general to bring lawsuits against spammers. The act obviously makes lawful legitimate bulk mailing of unsolicited e-mail messages (what most people call spam), yet seeks to prohibit certain deceptive practices and provide a small measure of consumer control by requiring opt-out notices. In this sense, critics point out, CAN-SPAM ironically legalizes spam as long as spammers follow the rules. For this reason, large spammers have been among the bill's biggest supporters, and consumer groups have been the Act's most vociferous critics. Major business interest groups also lobbied against the CAN-SPAM bill. Citicorp, Schwab, Procter & Gamble, the National Retail Foundation, the Securities Industry Association, and the American Insurance Association all argued that the act would harm legitimate e-mail marketing and put e-commerce at a disadvantage.

There have been a number of state and federal prosecutions of spammers, and private civil suits by large ISPs such as Microsoft. For instance, in May 2007, Robert Soloway, a 27-year-old Seattle man also known as the "Spam King," was arrested after being indicted by a federal grand jury on 16 counts of mail fraud, e-mail fraud, wire fraud, and aggravated identity theft. According to the indictment, Soloway operating under the name "Newport Internet Marketing," claimed to have a list of 158 million e-mail addresses, and charged $495 for a typical blast of 20 million e-mails sent over 15 days. Soloway obtained the e-mail addresses from "harvesting" programs and spyware programs which read lists from infected computers. He sold the lists to businesses claiming they contained only the addresses of "opt-in" prospects. Then, using remote botnets, he sent out blast e-mails of 20 to 100 million spam messages at a time. In 2007 prosecutors won a $7.8 million judgement against the King, and in March 2008 he pleaded guilty to federal criminal charges that he failed to pay income taxes on his spam income. Soloway faces twenty six years in prison. Currently the FBI and Justice Department have over 100 spam and phishing investigations under way.

Volunteer efforts by industry are another potential control point. Notably, the Direct Marketing Association (DMA), an industry trade group that represents companies that use the postal mail system as well as e-mail for solicitations, is now strongly supporting legislative controls over spam, in addition to its voluntary guidelines. The DMA would like to preserve the legitimate use of e-mail as a marketing technique. The DMA has formed a 15-person anti-spam group and spends $500,000 a year trying to identify spammers; the DMA also is a supporter of the National Cyber-Forensics & Training Alliance, a purportedly non-profit organization with "close ties" to the FBI, that operates a program called Operation Slam Spam that seeks to identify the IP addresses of the largest spammers and has a database of over 400 known spam addresses.

ONLINE CATALOGS

Online catalogs are the equivalent of a paper-based catalog. Online catalogs were popular in the early years of e-commerce but quickly went out of favor among advertisers because the pages took so long to load. But with about 89% of the online households using broadband high-speed connections in 2009, graphic-intense pages load quickly, and the possibilities for advertisers to re-use their paper catalog photos increase. Web publishers such as Google Catalogs and Catalog.com com have made it far easier for even small merchants to find an audience and re-purpose their expensive four-color offline catalogs. The result is a resurgence in online catalogs. The number of online catalogs in 2009 has more than doubled since 2005. E-catalog sales have risen to about 36% of U.S. multi-channel retailers (Direct Marketing Association, 2008; eMarketer, Inc., 2008f).

The basic function of a catalog is to display the merchant's wares (see **Figure 7.8**). The electronic version typically contains a color image of each available product and a description of the item, as well as size, color, material composition, and

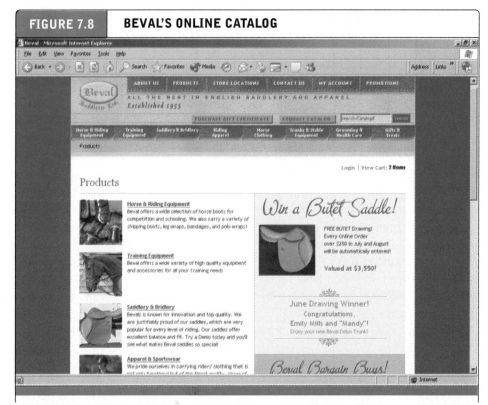

Beval Saddlery Ltd.'s Web site offers a variety of riding apparel and equipment. Customers can click on one of the product categories listed on the left side of the screen and are taken to a page listing products within that category. Clicking on a particular product takes the customer to a page with a description and photo of the product and an order button.
SOURCE: Beval.com, 2008.

pricing information. There are two different types of online catalogs: full-page spreads and grid displays. Most online retailers use a grid display in which multiple products are shown in very small postage-stamp photos. This is typical of Amazon, LLbean.com, and Gap.com. The other alternative is to use larger page spreads using large photos to display one or two products; HammacherSchlemmer.com, Landsend.com, and Restorationhardware.com use this approach, among others. The cost of building an online catalog ranges from $30,000–$50,000 for smaller Web sites, to several million for an online catalog with thousands of products and images.

How do companies integrate online catalogs with physical catalogs? Most direct mail catalog companies continue to use physical direct mail catalogs, and pure online companies have begun to supplement their online advertising with physical catalogs. Direct mail companies can increase their operational efficiency by sending electronic catalogs to customers before sending out the physical catalogs. This evens out the flow of orders. In general, merchants find that online and offline catalogs are complementary and do not cannibalize or substitute for one another. The flow of orders increases as the overall awareness of the company brand increases when both channels are used simultaneously. On the other hand, research suggests that the effects are subtle, and that much depends on the type of customer ("good" versus "best" customers) and their prior Internet experience (Anderson, et al., 2005).

SOCIAL MARKETING: BLOGS, SOCIAL NETWORKS, AND GAMES

The two key elements of Web 2.0 are the rapid growth of user-generated content and the use of the Internet for socializing and sharing. 40% of Internet users visit a social networking site at least once a month. With 72 million monthly MySpace users, 32 million Facebook users, 67 million blog readers, and 70 million YouTube visitors, it's little wonder that marketers and advertisers are joyous at the prospect of dominating this new audience. Microsoft's purchase of an interest in Facebook, and Google's purchase of YouTube, suggest the excitement in the marketing community for the advertising potential of social networking. Although in the past, major brands have been reluctant to risk advertising on sites whose content they cannot control, they are beginning to experiment with a number of new formats. In 2009, all forms of social marketing are expected to generate $2.8 billion in revenues, and it is expected these revenues will double to over $4 billion in 2012.

It is difficult to define 'social marketing' precisely, but a working definition might be that it is advertising which adopts a many-to-many model as opposed to a one-to-many model of traditional advertising, where a central broadcaster sends the same message to millions of people. For instance, over 400,000 viewers saw Microsoft's Halo 3 trailer on YouTube in a single month after being posted by a handful of posters. About 2,500 added the video to their favorites lists, which are broadcast to all their friends. So an existing social network composed of many people distributes the Microsoft message to a great many other people.

This kind of marketing is "social" because like traditional word-of-mouth and viral marketing, it relies on pre-existing social networks to spread the message. However, in this case, the social networks exist on the Internet, and they are digitally enabled networks whose members have extraordinary tools to spread the message far, wide, and very quickly. The vast majority of online social network members are also friends offline, or friends of friends offline (Ellison, et. al., 2006). Hence the offline world and the online world are intimately connected.

The three main areas of social marketing are blog, social network and game advertising.

Blog Advertising

Blogs are very high on the list of advertising tactics that marketing executives consider. In 2009, blog advertising revenue will be about $549 million (out of a total online ad spend of $30 billion) during that year. However, it is expected to grow to $746 million by 2012 (eMarketer, Inc., 2008e). Blogs have proved difficult to monetize because few blogs attract large audiences, and the subject matter of most blogs is highly personal and idiosyncratic. Search engines have a difficult time "reading" blogs, understanding their content, and making a judgment about the appropriateness of their ad inventory. Advertising dollars are therefore concentrated in the top 100 blogs, which have a coherent theme that consistently attracts larger audiences. Because blog readers and creators tend to be more educated, have higher incomes, and be opinion leaders, they are ideal recipients of ads for many products and services that cater to this kind of an audience. Advertising networks that specialize in blogs provide some efficiency in placing ads, as do blog networks, which are collections of a small number of popular blogs, coordinated by a central management team, and which can deliver a larger audience to advertisers.

Social Network Advertising

Although still in its infancy, social network advertising is the largest and fastest growing form of social marketing, generating $2 billion in revenue for 2009. There are a number of different types of social networks from general purpose (MySpace), to niche networks of professionals and hobbyists, to sponsored networks created by firms. However, most of the advertising action centers on the leading sites—MySpace ($850 million), Facebook ($305 million), and YouTube ($130 million). These three sites account for 94% of social network advertising (eMarketer, Inc. 2007d).

Social networks offer advertisers all the formats found on portal and search sites including banner ads (the most common), short pre-roll and post-roll ads before a video, and sponsorship of content. For instance, Adidas, Burger King, General Electric, Toyota Yaris, and Verizon have profile pages on MySpace, and other national brand names have posted videos on YouTube. Chevrolet, Geico, and Mars have encouraged users to create their own ads, and sponsored contests to choose the best ads.

There are several dangers to social network advertising. User-generated ads can obviously generate negative messages that are widely distributed. The content of many YouTube videos and MySpace profiles is repugnant to many American consumers and could taint brands associated with sites that permit this kind of content although entertainment firms may benefit from this milieu. While Google and YouTube have developed ways to display text and background ads alongside playing videos, many advertisers do not yet trust the software used to select the appropriate videos for an ad.

It is easy to overstate the growth in social marketing, and it is risky to ignore it. Currently, the three major search engines/portals have a much higher Internet audience share of the U.S. online population visiting their sites on a daily and weekly basis than even the largest social networking sites, or even all of the social sites combined. Google and Yahoo both have more than a 140 million unique visitors a month, Microsoft 120 million, and AOL 111 million. These audiences are twice the size of social sites. Still the social sites have substantial audiences. Therefore, marketers should continue investing in search engine and portal display advertising, while experimenting in social marketing. In the longer term of the next five years, with current trends, it is likely that social networking sites will equal the audience share of major portals and search engines, challenging these "older" venues for dominance in advertising platforms.

Game Advertising

More than 100 million people in the United States use video game consoles. From January to June 2008, 11 million Xbox 360s, 11 million Nintendo Wiis, and 5 million Sony

Playstation 3s were sold. About 60 million new units are sold each year in the U.S. alone. Worldwide sales are approximately 120 million. Today most games are played in social environments with multiple players in the same room, or over the Internet. We include them in a discussion of social marketing because of the mutually influential social environment in which most digital video games are played today. There are, of course, many kinds of games that are broadcast by a game sponsor—over 800 million sponsored games were downloaded in 2008 to millions of users. So-called "advergames" are sponsored games to promote brands. Coca-Cola, Burger King, and Taco Bell, along with many other national brands, have used advergames. These kinds of games could be considered a unique kind of display ad that is highly interactive, but not necessarily social.

U.S. video in-game advertising will generate about $510 million in 2009, but it is growing at a 15% compound rate, and will hit nearly a $650 million by 2012. While we tend to think of online gamers as mostly male, in fact 47% of online gamers are female. Over 40% of gamers are female, a percentage that increased significantly with the introduction of the Nintendo Wii. One quarter of gamers are over 50, and half of gamers are 18-49.

The limitations of game advertising are due in part to game content which tends to be attractive to young males and females, but not to a much larger audience. Many advertisers do not want their brands to be associated with violence, mayhem, and war-like scenarios, or sexual content that is often present in video games. *Insight on Society: Marketing to Children of the Web in the Age of Social Networks and Viral Marketing* considers some of the social issues that marketing to children on the Web present.

BEHAVIORAL TARGETING: GETTING PERSONAL

In Chapter 6, you learned about the six major ways that marketers target markets (refer to Table 6.7)—through behavioral, demographic, pysychographic, technical contextual and search data collected online. One of the original promises of the Web has been that it can deliver a marketing message tailored to each consumer based on this data, and then measure the results in terms of click-throughs and purchases. For a variety of technical and other reasons, this vision has, thus far, not been achieved. The quality of the data, largely owned by the online advertising networks, is quite good, but the ability to understand and respond—the business intelligence and analytics— are weak, preventing companies from being able to respond quickly in meaningful ways when the consumer is online. Non-targeted ads are doing about as well as targeted ads for many firms. And marketing companies are not yet prepared to understand or accept the idea that there needs to be several hundred or a thousand variations on the same display ad depending on the customer's profile. Such a move would raise costs.

Several consequences follow. First, just about everyone using the major Web portals is exposed to advertising that has nothing to do with their personal interests, or intentions. Second, search-engine marketing is the only technique that comes close to revealing consumers' intentions. In 2003, the author John Battelle coined the phrase and the notion that the Web is a database of intentions:

INSIGHT ON SOCIETY

MARKETING TO CHILDREN OF THE WEB IN THE AGE OF SOCIAL NETWORKS

About 70% of children ages 8-11 go online from home. That translates to millions of kids visiting Web sites such as Wrigley's Candystand.com ("the hottest online games"), Postopia.com ("a fun site for kids") and Millsberry.com, a General Mills-sponsored site with games encouraging kids to watch Lucky Charms webisodes and play games hunting for Reese's Puffs online. They spend more time on these sites than they do with TV commercials. Industry self-regulation requires firms not to advertise to kids younger than 12, but sites like Kraft's NabiscoWorld.com includes games that appeal to younger audiences, such as Oreos Race for the Stuf, whereby a player-controlled character can twist, lick, and dunk oversize Oreo cookies. NabiscoWorld.com, along with Wrigley's (WWY) Candystand, Pizza Hut, and Pepsi (PEP) Stuf were among the 10 most popular food sites on the Web in July, according to research firm Hitwise.

An FTC report in 2008 concluded that U.S. $1.6 billion firms were spending $1.6 billion on advertising to children, about half of that to children under 12. The Web provides marketers an entirely new arsenal to influence really young children. What's in the arsenal? Here are some of the most common child-advertiser tools: mobile phone marketing; behavioral profiling; digital "360 buzz" campaigns; commercialized online "communities," viral videos; gamevertising; and avatar advertising. No one knows how much money is spent on Web advertising by food firms and others. Critics argue, and the FTC expresses concern, that most of this advertising is for foods that make children obese and pose a health threat to children.

Children as young as three or four years old can often recognize brands and status items before they can even read, and 73% of four-year-olds generally ask their parents for specific brands. These findings are cause for celebration for some marketers. In the United States, 53 million school-age children spend approximately $100 billion annually of their own and their family's money on food, drinks, video and electronic products, toys, and clothing, and they influence family spending decisions valued at another $165 billion. In order to capture a portion of this spending and position themselves for future purchases as the child ages, marketers are becoming increasingly interested in advertising aimed at children.

In addition to investing in television advertising, which accounts for around 70% of the total amount spent on advertising to children in the United States, marketers focused on children are now migrating to the Web, where over 20% of all Internet users are children, totaling more than 35 million users between the ages of 3 and 17. Unbelievable as it may sound, 23% of nursery school children use the Internet. This rises to 68% of 12–17 year olds. The 3–17 age group makes up about 20% of the total Internet audience in the United States. Using online custom banner ads, product characters, games, and surveys, marketers are both influencing behaviors and gathering valuable data about purchasing preferences and family members. Coupled with in-bedroom televisions, video games, cell phones, and other digital paraphernalia, a children's "digital culture" has been created with built-in avenues to the psyche of very young minds—minds that are so young

(continued)

they are unlikely to know when they are being marketed to and when they are given misleading or even harmful information.

And then came social networking sites, virtual worlds aimed at kids, and social bookmarking sites. A recent study funded by Microsoft, News Corp. (MySpace), and Verizon, found that 70% of children visit social networking sites weekly and over 50% had participated in some kind of advertiser-branded activity such as visiting a company profile page in the past month. Marketers are moving aggressively to use online social networks and viral marketing to get kids hooked on brands early in life. For instance, Red Bull does little traditional TV advertising in the 100 countries where it sells energy drinks. Instead it has been using Web-based contests and games such as the Red Bull Art of the Can, where youngsters create sculptures out of Red Bull cans and submit photos of their handiwork. The prize: a trip for two to Switzerland.

You may not have heard of Axe (a product of Unilever), a deodorant for young men that apparently drives girls crazy for them. Axe Vice President Russell Taylor's goal is for the brand to become truly global. The sales pitch is simple: "Hey, dude, spray Axe deodorant all over your body, and you will become irresistible to beautiful young women." The branding message: a female wolf whistle and the phrase "Bom Chicka Wah Wah," expressed in a woman's sexy voice. Armed with this powerful message to the world's teenagers, Axe launched the product in the United States by posting three videos online that supposedly showed the "Axe effect" of women chasing men who used the spray (viewable at TheAxeEffect.com). The response was sensational: millions of people forwarded the videos to friends by e-mail in a massive viral outpouring. Marketers also created an online game wherein guys indicated the kind of young woman they were interested in and got recommendations on which Axe fragrance to buy.

With tactics like these, Axe has grown its U.S. business to more than $500 million last year.

You can bet that many of these postings and shared experiences were by children under the age of 13. Using social networks, blogs, and YouTube, in a way much more powerful than earlier Web marketing to children, marketers are able to circumvent what few restrictions on marketing to children exist.

While such moves may be savvy marketing, are they ethical? Some people say no. Research conducted in 1996 by the Center for Media Education (CME), showed that young children cannot understand the potential effects of revealing their personal information; neither can they distinguish between substantive material on Web sites and the advertisements surrounding it. While some parents tried to monitor their children's use of the Internet services, many of them failed due to lack of time, computer skills, or awareness of risk. Targeting of children by marketing techniques resulted in the release of a large amount of private information into the market and triggered the need for regulation.

Experts argue that since children don't understand persuasive intent until they are eight or nine years old, it is unethical to advertise to them before they can distinguish between advertising and the real world. Others believe that fair advertising is an important, and necessary, process of the maturation process for future adults in today's society. But does that argument hold when children are gaining increased access to information about unhealthy activities, such as beer drinking through Web sites geared to a younger audience? Although brewers admit they are targeting a younger market segment—twenty-somethings—they have set up warning screens and registration pages that require users to enter a birth date proving they are of legal drinking age. Of course, there is no process to verify such data, making it easy for underage consumers to gain access to, and be influenced by,

(continued)

entertaining content at drinking-oriented Web sites.

In 1998, Congress passed the Children's Online Privacy Protection Act (COPPA) after the FTC discovered that 80% of Web sites were collecting personal information from children, but only 1% required their parents' permission. Under COPPA, companies must post a privacy policy on their Web sites, detailing exactly how they collect information from consumers, how they'll use it, and the degrees to which they'll protect consumer privacy. Companies are not permitted to use personal information collected from children under 13 years of age without the prior, verifiable consent of parents. But the problem is that the FTC and others have been unable to specify exactly what "verifiable consent" means. Until technologies such as digital signatures are widely available, there appears to be no reliable way to provide verifiable consent online. The FTC recognized this fact by issuing a temporary ruling (now permanent) requiring a "sliding scale of verifiable parental consent." If firms want to use the personal information of children for internal uses only, the FTC requires an e-mail from the parent plus one other form of verification (such as a credit card or phone number). A stricter standard is required of firms who want to sell personal information about children: these Web sites are required to use one of the following means of verification in addition to an e-mail: a print-and send consent form, credit card transaction, a toll free number staffed by trained personnel, or an e-mail with a password or PIN.

Since the law took effect, the FTC has filed a complaint and obtained settlements in 14 cases and issued fines as high as $1 million. Xanga got clipped for $1 million in 2006 because it collected, used, and disclosed personal information from children under the age of 13 without first notifying parents and obtaining their consent. The complaint charged that the defendants had actual knowledge they were collecting and disclosing personal information from children. The Xanga site stated that children under 13 could not join, but then allowed visitors to create Xanga accounts even if they provided a birth date indicating they were under 13. Further, they failed to notify the children's parents of their information practices or provide the parents with access to and control over their children's information. The defendants created 1.7 million Xanga accounts over the past five years for users who submitted age information indicating they were under 13. Previous FTC COPPA cases included Mrs. Fields' Original Cookies, Hershey Foods, UMG recordings, and Bonzi Software. These cases involve no actual intent or knowledge, just lack of attention.

While in general, voluntary compliance with COPPA has been good, and most Web sites are careful to avoid gathering personal information on children as a part of their marketing effort, some Web sites are directly aimed at very young children. Sites such as ClubPenguin, Webkinz, and NeoPets provide online tools and play environments that enable young users to interact, adopt pets, play sponsored advergames, and reveal personal information. In the process of playing the games, children produce marketing information for product designers. While each of these Web sites' privacy policies claim strict adherence to the restrictions of COPPA, it is unclear how they ascertain who is over 13 and who is under 13, or if those under 13 have parental consent. Even less clear is how social networking sites where marketers are posting brand videos can protect the identities and privacy of children who expose their friends' e-mails every time they favorite a video.

▬▬ **SOURCES:** "Crying Foul Over Online Junk Food Marketing," by Catherine Holahan, *BusinessWeek*, August 12, 20008; "No Escape: Marketing to Kids in the Digital Age," by Jeff Chester and Kathryn Montgomery, Multinational Monitor, July/August 2008; "Marketing Food to Children and Adolescents. A Review of Industry Expenditures, Activities, and Self-Regulation," Federal Trade Commission, July 2008; "Children's Safety on the Internet: A Resource Guide for Parents," The Privacy Rights Clearinghouse, Privacyrights.org, October, 2007; "Kids, Teens and Virtual Worlds," eMarketer, Inc., September 25, 2007; "Children Of The Web" Businessweek.com, July 2, 2007; Federal Trade Commission, "Implementing the Children's Online Privacy Protection Act. A Report to Congress," February, 2007; "Social Networking and Advertising Study," Alloy Media, January 2, 2007.

"The Database of Intentions is simply this: The aggregate results of every search ever entered, every result list ever tendered, and every path taken as a result. It lives in many places, but three or four places in particular hold a massive amount of this data (i.e., MSN, Google, and Yahoo). This information represents, in aggregate form, a place holder for the intentions of humankind—a massive database of desires, needs, wants, and likes that can be discovered, subpoenaed, archived, tracked, and exploited to all sorts of ends. Such a beast has never before existed in the history of culture, but is almost guaranteed to grow exponentially from this day forward. This artifact can tell us extraordinary things about who we are and what we want as a culture. And it has the potential to be abused in equally extraordinary fashion." (Battelle, 2003.)

However, now that search engine marketing growth has slowed somewhat, attention has returned to the various ways that content can be customized, and sales optimized, by using the information that Web visitors reveal about themselves online, and if possible, combine this with offline identity and consumption information gathered by companies such as Acxiom. So-called "behavioral targeting" is based on real-time information about visitors use of Web sites, including pages visited, content viewed, search queries, ads clicked, videos watched, content they share, and products they purchase. Once this information is collected and analyzed, behavioral targeting programs attempt to develop profiles of individual users, and then showing advertisements most likely to be of interest to the user. In 2008, U.S. firms will spend $1 billion on behavioral targeting, and this will quadruple by 2012 to be the fastest growing form of online marketing techniques (eMarketer, Inc., 2008f). Interest in this area has been sparked by four recent acquisition announcements: Google-DoubleClick, Yahoo-Right Media, WPP Group-24/7 Media, and Microsoft-aQuantive. Many of these techniques are not new, just extensions of offline techniques. The difference is obtaining this information online, unobtrusively, without the user knowing, dynamically analyzing the information on the fly, and taking the appropriate action within a tolerable 1–2 seconds response time.

These capabilities are not fully developed yet, but firms are experimenting with more precise targeting methods. Snapple used behavioral targeting methods (with the help of an online ad firm Tacoda) to identify the types of people attracted to Snapple Green Tea. Answer: people who like the arts and literature, travel internationally, and visit health sites. Microsoft is offering MSN advertisers access to personal data derived from 263 million Hotmail users. Some advertisers have reported over 50% increases in click-through rates. General Motors is using Digitas (a Boston-based online ad firm) to create several hundred versions of a single ad for its new Acadia crossover vehicle. Viewers are initially shown ads that emphasize brand, features, and communities. On subsequent viewing, they are shown different ads based on demographics, lifestyle, and behavioral considerations. Men are shown versions of the ads emphasizing engines, specifications, performance, while women are shown versions that emphasize comfort, accessibility, and families (Story, 2007).

The growth in the power, reach and scope of behavioral targeting has drawn the attention of privacy groups and the Federal Trade Commission (FTC). In

November 2007, the FTC opened hearings to consider proposals from privacy advocates to develop a "do not track list," develop visual online cues for people to alert them to tracking, and allow people to opt-out. In June, 2008, the Senate held hearings on behavioral marketing and privacy. While Google, Microsoft and Yahoo pleaded for legislation to protect them from consumer lawsuits, the FTC refused to consider new legislation to protect the privacy of Internet users. Instead, the FTC proposed industry self-regulation. Perhaps the central question is understanding what rights individuals have in their own personally identifiable Internet profiles. Do they have viewing and editing rights? Further, who can possibly "own" the intentions of an entire culture? We consider these issues further in Chapter 8.

MIXING OFFLINE AND ONLINE MARKETING COMMUNICATIONS

Many early proponents of e-commerce believed that the traditional world of marketing based on mass media was no longer relevant to the exploding online commercial world and that in the "new Internet economy," nearly all marketing communications would be online. As it turned out, this did not happen. What did happen is that offline marketing powerhouses in consumer-oriented industries learned how to use the Web to extend their brand images and sales campaigns to an educated, wealthy, and computer literate, online audience. The large advertising agencies that specialized in mass media opened up Internet practices, and learned quickly how to integrate online and offline campaigns. Pure online companies learned how to use traditional print and television advertising as a means for driving sales to their Web sites.

The marketing communications campaigns most successful at driving traffic to a Web site have incorporated both online and offline tactics, rather than relying solely on one or the other. The objective is to draw the attention of people who are already online and persuade them to visit a new Web site, as well as attract the attention of people who will be going online in the near future in order to suggest that they, too, visit the Web site. Several research studies have shown that the most effective online advertisements are those that use consistent imagery with campaigns running in other media at the same time (Briggs, 1999). Offline mass media such as television and radio have nearly a 100% market penetration into the 120 million households in the United States. U.S. daily newspapers have a total circulation of around 55 million. It would be foolish for pure online companies not to use these popular media to drive traffic to the online world of commerce. In the early days of e-commerce, the Internet audience was quite different from the general population, and perhaps was best reached by using online marketing alone. This is no longer true as the Internet population becomes much more like the general population.

Many online ventures have used offline marketing techniques to drive traffic to their Web sites, increase awareness, and build brand equity. For instance, LendingTree.com has used television advertising to direct people to its Web site to look for mortgages. Barnes & Noble, as well as JCPenney and REI Inc., use print media to inform customers of their in-store Web kiosks. In 2007, Sears brought back its holiday Wish Catalog both in print and online to drive consumers to its Web sites.

Such "tie-ins" between a print product and a firm's Web site have proven to be very successful in driving Web traffic (Elliot, 2007).

Another example of the online/offline marketing connection is the use of print catalogs by heretofore entirely online ventures. Some online ventures have created paper catalogs and mailed them to their customers to improve their relationship with that group.

The development of multi-channel marketing and communications reflects the fact that the behavior of consumers is increasingly multi-channel (see Chapter 9). Almost 40% of all consumers purchased products offline that they researched online, and 75% of all online retail sales in the United States were made by multi-channel retailers—retailers who had physical stores and catalogs in addition to Web sites (eMarketer, Inc., 2007g).

Insight on Business: The Very Rich Are Different from You and Me: Neiman Marcus, Tiffany & Co., and Armani examines how luxury good providers use online marketing in conjunction with their offline marketing efforts.

7.2 UNDERSTANDING THE COST AND BENEFITS OF ONLINE MARKETING COMMUNICATIONS

As we saw in Section 7.1, online marketing communications still comprise only a very small part of the total marketing communications universe. While there are several reasons why this is the case, two of the main ones are concerns about whether online advertising really works and about how to adequately measure the costs and benefits of online advertising. We will address both of these topics in this section. But first, we will define some important terms used when examining the effectiveness of online marketing.

ONLINE MARKETING METRICS: LEXICON

In order to understand the process of attracting prospects to your firm's Web site via marketing communications and converting them into customers, you will need to be familiar with Web marketing terminology. **Table 7.5** on page 455 lists some terms commonly used to describe the impacts and results of online marketing.

The first nine metrics focus primarily on the success of a Web site in achieving audience or market share by "driving" shoppers to the site. In the early years of e-commerce, these measures often substituted for solid information on sales revenue as e-commerce entrepreneurs sought to have investors and the public focus on the success of the Web site in "attracting eyeballs" (viewers).

Impressions are the number of times an ad is served. **Click-through rate (CTR)** measures the percentage of people exposed to an online advertisement who actually click on the advertisement. Because not all ads lead to an immediate click, the industry has invented a new term for a "long term" hit called **view-through rate** (VTR), which measures the 30-day response rate to an ad. **Hits** are the number of http requests received by a firm's server. Hits can be misleading as a measure of Web site activity because a "hit" does not equal a page. A single page may account for several

impressions
number of times an ad is served

click-through rate (CTR)
the percentage of people exposed to an online advertisement who actually click on the banner

view-through rate (VTR)
measures the 30-day response rate to an ad

hits
number of http requests received by a firm's server

INSIGHT ON BUSINESS

THE VERY RICH ARE DIFFERENT FROM YOU AND ME: NEIMAN MARCUS, TIFFANY & CO, AND ARMANI

"The very rich are different from you and me," Nick Carroway observed, in a memorable line from *The Great Gatsby*, a novel by F. Scott Fitzgerald about life among the very wealthy in the 1920s. Palm Beach has its Worth Avenue, New York has its Fifth Avenue, Los Angeles has its Rodeo Drive, and Chicago has the Magnificent Mile. So where to go on the Web to get that $5,000 cocktail dress, or that $3,000 Italian suit?

The rich just can't seem to get enough of a good thing. Times are good for luxe on the Web: around 80% of U.S. consumers with a net worth greater than $5 million use the Web everyday, and shop on the Web for clothes, jewelry, as well as more common items such as music and videos. Around 60% of rich Internet users hobnob on social sites. US luxury e-commerce sales are expected to nearly triple in the next three years, to $7 billion in 2010 from $2.5 billion in 2007, according to Forrester Research. Sales at Coach.com, the luxury bag maker, were up 50% in 2007, but slowed a bit to just a 30% increase in 2008. And aside from political sites, the second fastest growing Web site category is jewelry/luxury goods/accessories. Yoox, Saks.com, Zagliani, and Marni all report their online sales are now approaching the sales of their flagship stores.

Yet luxury retailers such as Neiman Marcus, Tiffany, Armani, and Christian Dior have had a difficult time developing an online presence for their wealthy customers. Critics argue they have had a difficult time understanding their wealthy online customers. Luxury brands and retailers must try to please not only their wealthy older customers, but also their younger children who are used to shopping online.

For instance, when Neiman Marcus introduced its first Web site with two virtual boutiques, featuring tours of Kate Spade handbags and John Hardy silver cufflinks, Web designers were awed by the display of graphics and motion. But most customers were turned off because they could not find enough goods for sale, and could not easily navigate the site. Pretty snazzy stuff, but today it's all gone. Neimanmarcus.com now features no animations, no Flash graphics, but much more merchandise neatly arranged by category and designer: in short, an online catalog much like JCPenney's. The current Neiman Marcus Web site gets generally high marks for the simplicity of design and efficiency of navigation, although critics point out that it's still somewhat difficult to find the online version of Neiman Marcus' most popular off-line marketing tool: its Christmas catalog that features "beyond the pale" luxury items such as a "his and hers" double portrait in chocolate for $100,000 and an underwater personal submarine for $1.4 million. The best proof is in the sales results, however: Neiman Marcus recorded $500 million in sales at its three Web sites in 2008, an increase of over 29% from the previous year, and putting it in sixth place overall for the online apparel/accessories group. Neiman Marcus further reports that sales have been exploding in the last 18 months with basic garments selling slowly, but items such as $7,900 Valentino gowns, $5500 Carolina Herrera jackets and other items with more "camera" appeal selling quickly. Neiman believes that the increasing prevalence of high-speed Internet connections allowing customers to zoom and rotate garments, and look more closely at the fabrics is a primary reason.

(continued)

Luxe sales are not recession-proof, but they are recession-resistant. Sales at luxury sites have slowed from annual 30% increases a few years ago to a more sedate 25% growth in the last half of 2008.

Developing an online marketing approach that increases a company's access to consumers while retaining an image of exclusivity was the challenge faced by the world-renowned jeweler Tiffany & Co. when it redesigned its Web site in 1999. The company was in the enviable position of being perhaps the most famous jewelry company in the United States. Tiffany's offline marketing communications sought to engender feelings of beauty, quality, and timeless style—all hallmarks of the Tiffany brand. How could Tiffany maintain its approach on the Web, a medium that often emphasizes speed and flashy graphics over grace and elegance, and low cost bargains over high-priced exclusive fashion? The Web, at least in its early days, was all about price, bargains, and free—words that are anathema to the high fashion merchant.

Tiffany's first effort on the Web was designed by Oven Digital Inc., who built a Web site that used soft, neutral colors throughout, sparse wording, and pictures that faded slowly onto the screen. The shopping portion of the Web site showed just one large item, with some smaller photos that could be enlarged by clicking at the bottom of the screen. The Web site also included information on buying and caring for jewelry. Caroline Naggiar, Tiffany's senior vice president of marketing at the time, characterized the site "as an enormous exercise in reserve." But that same "reserved" quality made it difficult for consumers to find out what was for sale. Critics complained that the Tiffany Web site had too few products online, the Flash graphics were slow, there were too many animations, and the product line available was poorly organized. While Tiffany claimed there were 2,000 products online, finding them and buying them was an arduous process. Critics complained the Web site was dull with all the white space, surfing was tedious, and only those not in a hurry could navigate it. The site was re-designed by an in-house team with a view toward making it more focused. Today, Tiffany has shifted more of its direct marketing effort from the offline catalog to the online catalog. The results improved dramatically. In 2006, online sales soared to $120 million, expanding at a 10% rate—much better than earlier. It has opened new sites in Canada, the United Kingdom and Japan. Tiffany sites carry over 2,800 products in five categories of goods: diamonds, jewelry, watches, table settings, gifts, and accessories.

Other cutting edge fashion houses such as Christian Dior, Armani, and Bottega Veneta insisted in their first efforts on managing their own Web sites. The results were not impressive. The Web sites were typically a collection of photos with directions to the nearest store. Embracing the Internet ran counter to their strategies to keep tight control over their images and customers. Many luxe sites still are for display only, no purchases online please.

As a result of the difficulties they encountered, some luxury sites have begun reluctantly to outsource their Web sites. For instance, Louis Vuitton, DKNY and Armani have all outsourced their online boutiques to Web operations outfits such as Yoox, a fashion retailer with a long experience on the Web. In the case of Armani, Emporio Armani personally directed the online effort. To avoid the cheaper catalog look, he had his store design team hand over architectural plans to the flagship store in Milan so that Yoox could use it as a metaphor and model for the Web site. Now visitors can turn left or right as they would at the Milan store, and take a virtual tour of the goods on display. Armani wanted a three-dimensional look, and the ability to shine bright lights on the products being

(continued)

examined, a trick used in his stores to impart the sense of elegance. Robert Trefus, Armani's vice president in charge of the Web site, expects the Internet Boutique to become the line's biggest store in a few years. The cost of opening the site has been a fraction of the cost of launching a new store, and less risky. "At least we don't have to worry about the location, or opening a store on the wrong corner." A trip to the Armani Web site is a trip all unto itself: stunning video images of the latest Fall collections, Armani Jeans, and the Armani Exchange, where you can actually buy something from the Emporio Armani retail collection.

While many luxe retailers have had difficulty selling goods and still preserving their exclusive image online, one exception has been Nordstrom (the Washington-based high-end department store known for service and customer loyalty). Not surprisingly, the Nordstrom.com Web site is a marvel of simplicity. There are few gimmicks or gadgetry, and no Flash animations, streaming videos of happy customers, or travelogues. Instead, you find tons of products—5,000 in all—shown in big clear pictures and organized in a thoughtful manner.

■■■■ **SOURCES:** ""Getting Luxury Goods Online," by Thomas Grose, *Time Magazine*, June 23, 2008; "Luxury Brands Lag in Adopting e-Commerce," *Internet Retailer*, May 30, 2008; "Affluent Hobnob on Social Networks," eMarketer, March 19, 2008.$7,900 Valentino Gowns, a Click Away," by Bob Tedeschi, *New York Times*, November 5, 2007; "Fashion's Trend: Outsource the Web," by Christina Passariello, *Wall Street Journal*, September 12, 2007; "Affluent Like Shopping Online Too," eMarketer, Inc., October 9, 2007; "Rich, Online, and Nowhere To Buy: Online Retailers Are the Wave of the Future, So Why Are the World's Trendsetting Luxury Brands So Far Behind?," By Jessica Dickler, CNNMoney.com, July 1, 2007; "Top 100 Web Retailers: Tiffany & Company," Internet Retailer Top 500 Guide, 2008.

hits if the page contains multiple images or graphics. A single Web site visitor can generate hundreds of hits. For this reason, hits are not an accurate representation of Web traffic or visits, even though they are generally easy to measure; the sheer volume of hits can be huge—and sound impressive, but not be a true measure of activity. **Page views** are the number of pages requested by visitors. However, with increased usage of Web frames that divide pages into separate sections, a single page that has three frames will generate three page views. Hence, page views per se are also not a very useful metric.

page views
number of pages requested by visitors

Stickiness (sometimes called *duration*) is the average length of time visitors remain at a Web site. Stickiness is important to marketers because the longer the amount of time a visitor spends at a Web site, the greater the probability of a purchase. For instance, eBay, which is one of the stickiest and most profitable sites on the Web, is often held up as evidence that stickiness correlates with success. However, experience at other Web sites counters this argument, calling into question the relevance of stickiness as a measure. Search engine Google, for example, is a very popular destination and yet reports very low stickiness ratings (Weber, 2001). Its founders take this as a sign that they have achieved their objective—sending users to their desired destination quickly.

stickiness (duration)
average length of time visitors remain at a site

The number of unique visitors is perhaps the most widely used measure of a Web site's popularity. The measurement of **unique visitors** counts the number of distinct, unique visitors to a Web site, regardless of how many pages they view.

unique visitors
the number of distinct, unique visitors to a site

TABLE 7.5	MARKETING METRICS LEXICON
COMMON MARKETING E-METRICS	**DESCRIPTION**
Impressions	Number of times an ad is served
Click-through rate (CTR)	The percentage of times an ad is clicked
View-through rate (VTR)	The percentage of times an ad is not clicked immediately but the Web site is visited within 30 days.
Hits	Number of http requests
Page views	Number of pages viewed
Stickiness (duration)	Average length of stay at a Web site
Unique visitors	Number of unique visitors in a period
Loyalty	Measured variously as the number of page views, frequency of single user visits to the Web site, or percentage of customers who return to the site in a year to make additional purchases
Reach	Percentage of Web site visitors who are potential buyers; or the percentage of total market buyers who buy at a site
Recency	Time elapsed since the last action taken by a buyer, such as a Web site visit or purchase
Acquisition rate	Percentage of visitors who indicate an interest in the Web site's product by registering or visiting product's pages
Conversion rate	Percentage of visitors who become customers
Browse to buy ratio	Ratio of items purchased to product views
View to cart ratio	Ratio of "Add to cart" clicks to product views
Cart conversion rate	Ratio of actual orders to "Add to cart" clicks
Checkout conversion rate	Ratio of actual orders to checkouts started
Abandonment rate	Percentage of shoppers who begin a shopping cart purchase but then leave the Web site without completing a purchase (similar to above)
Retention rate	Percentage of existing customers who continue to buy on a regular basis (similar to loyalty)
Attrition rate	Percentage of customers who do not return during the next year after an initial purchase
E-MAIL METRICS	
Open rate	Percentage of e-mail recipients who open the e-mail and are exposed to the message
Delivery rate	Percentage of e-mail recipients who received the e-mail
Click-through rate (e-mail)	Percentage of recipients who clicked through to offers
Bounce-back rate	Percentage of e-mails that could not be delivered
Unsubscribe rate	Percentage of recipients who click unsubscribe
Conversion rate (e-mail)	Percentage of recipients who actually buy

loyalty

percentage of purchasers who return in a year

reach

percentage of the total number of consumers in a market who will visit a site

recency

average number of days elapsed between visits

acquisition rate

measures the percentage of visitors who register or visit product pages

conversion rate

percentage of visitors who purchase something

browse-to-buy ratio

ratio of items purchased to product views

view-to-cart ratio

ratio of "Add to cart" clicks to product view

cart conversion rate

average number of days elapsed between visits

checkout conversion ratio

ratio of actual orders to checkouts started

abandonment rate

percentage of shoppers who begin a shopping cart form, but then fail to complete the form

retention rate

percentage of existing customers who continue to buy on a regular basis

attrition rate

percentage of customers who purchase once, but do not return within a year

open rate

percentage of customers who open the e-mail and are exposed to the message

Loyalty measures the percentage of visitors who return in a year. This can be a good indicator of a site's Web following, and perhaps the trust shoppers place in a site. **Reach** is typically a percentage of the total number of consumers in a market who visit a Web site; for example, 10% of all book purchasers in a year will visit Amazon at least once to shop for a book. This provides an idea of the power of a Web site to attract market share. **Recency**—like loyalty—measures the power of a Web site to produce repeat visits and is generally measured as the average number of days elapsed between shopper or customer visits. For example, a recency value of 25 days means the average customer will return once every 25 days.

The metrics described so far do not say much about commercial activity or help understand the conversion from visitor to customer. Several other measures are more helpful in this regard. **Acquisition rate** measures of the percentage of visitors who register or visit product pages (indicating interest in the product). **Conversion rate** measures the percentage of visitors who actually purchase some-thing. Industry-wide conversion rates average between 3%–5% (Internet Retailer, 2008). The **browse-to-buy ratio** measures the ratio of items purchased to product views. The **view-to-cart ratio** calculates the ratio of "Add to cart" clicks to product views. **Cart conversion rate** measures the ratio of actual orders to "Add to cart" clicks. **Checkout conversion rate** calculates the ratio of actual orders to check-outs started. **Abandonment rate** measures the percentage of shoppers who begin a shopping cart form but then fail to complete the form and leave the Web site. Abandonment rates can signal a number of potential problems—poor form design, lack of consumer trust, or consumer purchase uncertainty caused by other factors. A MarketLive survey found that about 59% of consumers abandoned the items in their shopping cart prior to checkout, with the main reasons cited being additional costs for shipping and handling that only became clear during the checkout process (eMarketer, Inc., 2008g). Given that more than 80% of online shoppers generally have a purchase in mind when they visit a Web site, a high abandonment rate signals many lost sales. **Retention rate** indicates the percentage of existing customers who continue to buy on a regular basis. **Attrition rate** measures the percentage of customers who purchase once but never return within a year (the opposite of loyalty and retention rates).

E-mail campaigns have their own set of metrics. **Open rate** measures the percentage of customers who open the e-mail and are exposed to the message. Generally, open rates are quite high, in the area of 50% or greater. However, some browsers open mail as soon as the mouse cursor moves over the subject line, and therefore this measure can be difficult to interpret. **Delivery rate** measures the percentage of e-mail recipients who received the e-mail. **Click-through rate (e-mail)** measures the percentage of e-mail recipients who clicked through to the offer. Finally, **bounce-back rate** measures the percentage of e-mails that could not be delivered.

There is a lengthy path from simple online ad impressions, Web site visits, and page views to the purchase of a product and the company making a profit (see **Figure 7.9**). You first need to make customers aware of their needs for your product and somehow drive them to your Web site. Once there, you need to convince them you have the best value—quality and price—when compared to alternative providers. You then must persuade them to trust your firm to handle the transaction (by providing a secure environment and fast fulfillment). Based on your success, a percentage of customers will remain loyal and purchase again or recommend your Web site to others.

HOW WELL DOES ONLINE ADVERTISING WORK?

What is the most effective kind of online advertising? How does online advertising compare to offline advertising? The answers depend on the goals of the campaign, the nature of the product, and the quality of the Web site you direct customers toward. The answers also depend on what you measure. Click-through rates are interesting, but ultimately it's the return on the investment in the ad campaign that counts. A broader understanding of the matter requires that you consider the cost of purchasing the promotional materials and mailing lists, and the studio production costs for radio and TV ads. Also, each media has a different revenue per contact

delivery rate
percentage of e-mail recipients who received the e-mail

click-through rate (e-mail)
percentage of e-mail recipients who clicked through to the offer

bounce-back rate
percentage of e-mails that could not be delivered

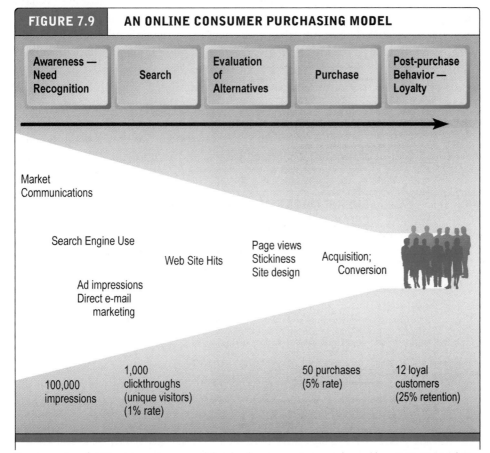

| FIGURE 7.9 | AN ONLINE CONSUMER PURCHASING MODEL |

The conversion of visitors into customers, and then loyal customers, is a complex and long-term process that may take several months.

potential because the products advertised differ. For instance, online purchases tend to be for smaller items when compared to newspaper, magazine, and television ads (although this too seems to be changing).

Table 7.6 lists the click-through rates for various types of online marketing communications tools. There is a great deal of variability within any of these types so the figures in Table 7.5 should be taken as "typical." Click-through rates on all these formats are a function of personalization, and other targeting techniques. Permission e-mail campaigns produce the highest response rate and the click-through rate has been fairly consistent over the last five years, in the 4%–5% range (for unsolicited e-mail and outright spam, response rates are much lower even though about 20% of U.S. e-mail users report clicking occasionally on an unsolicited e-mail). Putting the recipient's name in the subject line can double the click-through rate.

The click-through rates for video ads may seem low, but it is twice the rate for display ads. The "interaction rate" with videos is quite high, about 7%. "Interaction" means the user clicks on the video, plays it, stops it, or takes some other action (possibly skips the ad altogether).

As consumers become more accustomed to new online advertising formats, click-through rates tend to fall (see **Figure 7.10**). Response rates to banner ads have fallen about 40% over the last four years, and e-mail response has also fallen from its initial high rates. This is not true of video and rich media where response rates which have remained steady, perhaps due to the growing quality and novelty of online video.

How effective is online advertising when compared to offline advertising? **Figure 7.11** on page 460 provides some insight into this question. In general, the online channels (e-mail, banner ads, and video) compare favorably with traditional channels. Search engine marketing over the last two years has grown to be the most cost effective form of marketing communications and accounts for large part in the

TABLE 7.6	ONLINE MARKETING COMMUNICATIONS: TYPICAL CLICK-THROUGH RATES
MARKETING METHODS	**TYPICAL CLICK-THROUGH RATES**
Display ads	.1%–.2%
Interstitials	.2%–.3%
Superstitials	.2%–.3%
Search engine keyword purchase	3%–7%
Video and rich media	.4%–.6%
Sponsorships	1.5%–3%
Affiliate relationships	.2%–.4%
E-mail marketing in-house list	4%–5%
E-mail marketing purchased list	.01%–.02%
Online catalogs	3%–6%

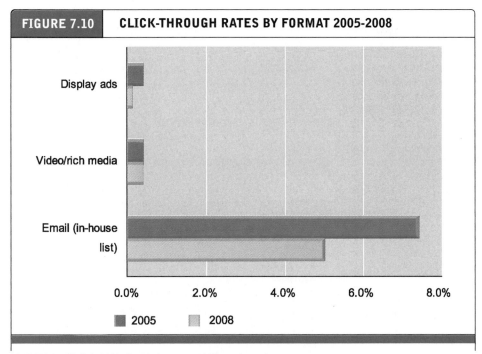

| FIGURE 7.10 | **CLICK-THROUGH RATES BY FORMAT 2005-2008** |

SOURCES: Doubleclick, 2007a, b; eMarketer, Inc., 2008h; author estimates.

growth of Google, as well as other search engines. The cost effectiveness of targeted, opt-in e-mail remains very strong.

There is growing evidence that the cost effectiveness of search engine marketing has peaked, and may actually be declining because the cost of keywords has grown significantly, and the number of keywords being purchased has also expanded as retailers branch out from their core keywords into more peripheral words. The result is a rising cost per click and a declining efficacy of keywords that are peripheral to the brand (DoubleClick, 2007b). Growth in search engine advertising revenues are likely to slow in the near future, and search engine firms are seeking other opportunities for growth by purchasing advertising networks, and moving into the ad brokerage business for traditional media like radio, newspapers, and television.

A study of the comparative impacts of offline and online marketing concluded that the most powerful marketing campaigns used multiple forms of marketing, including online, catalog, television, radio, newspapers, and retail store. Traditional media like television and print media remain the primary means for consumers to find out about new products even though advertisers have reduced their budgets for print media ads. The consensus conclusion is that consumers who shop multiple channels are spending more than consumers who shop only with a single channel, in part because they have more discretionary income but also because of the combined number of "touch points" which marketers are making with the consumers. The fastest growing channel in consumer marketing is the multi-channel shopper.

Banner ads can be made far more effective if they are targeted to specific occasions (occasion-based marketing), particular keyword search arguments, or users who have an identified user profile and can be pitched the ad at just the right moment.

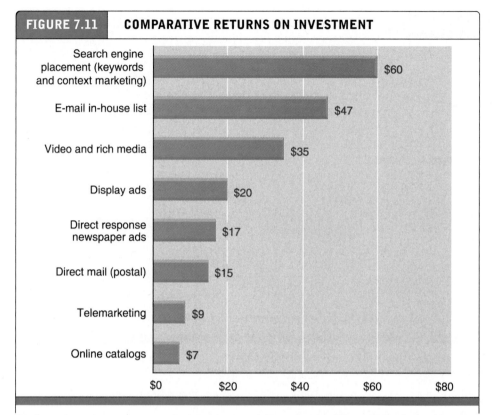

| FIGURE 7.11 | **COMPARATIVE RETURNS ON INVESTMENT** |

This figure shows the average returns in dollars for every dollar spent using different types of advertising techniques. Search engine placement has replaced e-mail as the most cost-effective form of online advertising.

SOURCES: Industry sources; author estimates.

Usually, this kind of precision ad pitching requires the services of an advertising network firm such as DoubleClick or 24/7 Real Media.

THE COSTS OF ONLINE ADVERTISING

cost per thousand (CPM)
advertiser pays for impressions in 1,000-unit lots

cost per click (CPC)
advertiser pays prenegotiated fee for each click an ad receives

cost per action (CPA)
advertiser pays only for those users who perform a specific action

Effectiveness cannot be considered without an analysis of costs. Initially, most online ads were sold on a barter or **cost per thousand (CPM)** (M is the symbol for thousand in Latin) basis, with advertisers purchasing impressions in 1,000-unit lots. Today, other pricing models have developed, including **cost per click (CPC)**, where the advertiser pays a prenegotiated fee for each click an ad receives, **cost per action (CPA)**, where the advertiser pays a prenegotiated amount only when a user performs a specific action, such as a registration or a purchase, and hybrid arrangements, combining two or more of these models (see **Table 7.7**).

While in the early days of e-commerce, a few online sites spent as much as $400 on marketing and advertising to acquire one customer, the average cost was never that high. **Table 7.8** shows the average cost per acquisition for various different types of media

TABLE 7.7	DIFFERENT PRICING MODELS FOR ONLINE ADVERTISEMENTS
PRICING MODEL	**DESCRIPTION**
Barter	Exchange of ad space for something of equal value
Cost per thousand (CPM)	Advertiser pays for impressions in 1,000 unit lots
Cost per click (CPC)	Advertiser pays pre-negotiated fee for each click ad receives
Cost per action (CPA)	Advertiser pays only for those users who perform a specific action, such as registering, purchasing, etc.
Hybrid	Two or more of the above models used together
Sponsorship	Term-based; advertiser pays fixed fee for a slot on a Web site

While the costs for offline customer acquisition are higher than online, typically the offline items are far more expensive. If you advertise in the *Wall Street Journal* you are tapping into a wealthy demographic interested in buying islands, jets, other corporations, and expensive homes in France. A full-page black and white ad in the *Wall Street Journal* National Edition costs about $170,000, whereas other papers are in the $100,000 range. For these kinds of prices you will need to either sell quite a few apples, or a small number of corporate jet lease agreements.

One of the advantages of online marketing is that online sales can generally be directly correlated with online marketing efforts. The online merchant can measure precisely just how much revenue is generated by specific banners or e-mail messages sent to prospective customers. One way to measure the effectiveness of online marketing is by looking at the ratio of additional revenue received divided by the cost of the campaign (Revenue/Cost). Any positive whole number means the campaign was worthwhile.

TABLE 7.8	AVERAGE COST PER CUSTOMER ACQUISITION FOR SELECT MEDIA IN THE UNITED STATES, 2008
Internet search	$8.50
Yellow pages	$20.00
Online display ads	$50.00
E-Mail	$60.00
Direct mail	$70.00
Newspaper	$25.00
Magazine	$19.00
Television	$17.00

SOURCES: Industry sources; authors' estimates.

A more complex situation arises when both online and offline sales revenues are affected by an online marketing effort. A large percentage of the online audience uses the Web to "shop," but not buy. These shoppers buy at physical stores. Merchants such as Sears and Wal-Mart will use e-mail to inform their registered customers of special offers available for purchase either online or at stores. Unfortunately, purchases at physical stores cannot be tied precisely with the online e-mail campaign. In these cases, merchants have to rely on less precise measures such as customer surveys at store locations to determine the effectiveness of online campaigns.

In either case, measuring the effectiveness of online marketing communications—and specifying precisely the objective (branding versus sales)—is critical to profitability. To measure marketing effectiveness, you need to understand the costs of various marketing media and the process of converting online prospects into online customers.

In general, online marketing communications are more costly on a CPM basis than traditional mass media marketing, but are more efficient in producing sales. **Table 7.9** shows costs for typical online and offline marketing communications. For instance, a local television spot (30 seconds) can cost $4,000–$40,000 to run the ad and an additional $40,000 to produce the ad, for a total cost of $44,000–$80,000. The ad may be seen by a population of, say, 2 million persons (impressions) in a local area for a CPM ranging from 2-4 cents, which makes television very inexpensive for reaching large audiences quickly. A Web site banner ad costs virtually nothing to produce and can be purchased at Web sites for a cost of from $2–$15 per thousand impressions. Direct postal mail can cost 80 cents to $1 per household drop for a post card, but e-mail can be sent for virtually nothing and costs only $5–$15 per thousand targeted names. Hence e-mail is far less expensive than postal mail on a CPM basis.

SOFTWARE FOR MEASURING ONLINE MARKETING RESULTS

A number of software programs are available to automatically calculate activities at a Web site. **Figure 7.12** illustrates the information that a Web site activity analysis might provide.

Other software programs and services assist marketing managers in identifying exactly which marketing initiatives are paying off and which are not. See *Insight on Technology: It's 10 P.M. Do You Know Who Is On Your Web Site?* on pages 465-466 for a description of one such program, offered by Visual Sciences.

7.3 THE WEB SITE AS A MARKETING COMMUNICATIONS TOOL

One of the strongest online marketing communications tools is a functional Web site that customers can find easily, and once there, locate what they are looking for quickly. In some ways, a Web site can be viewed as an extended online advertisement.

TABLE 7.9	TRADITIONAL AND ONLINE ADVERTISING COSTS COMPARED
TRADITIONAL ADVERTISING	
Local television	$4,000 for a 30-second commercial during a movie; $45,000 for a highly rated show
Network television	$80,000–$600,000 for a 30-second spot during prime time; the average is $120,000 to $140,000
Cable television	$5,000–$8,000 for a 30-second ad during prime time
Radio	$200–$1,000 for a 60-second spot, depending on the time of day and program ratings
Newspaper	$120 per 1,000 circulation for a full-page ad
Magazine	$50 per 1,000 circulation for an ad in a regional edition of a national magazine, versus $120 per 1,000 for a local magazine
Direct mail	$15–$20 per 1,000 delivered for coupon mailings; $25–$40 per 1,000 for simple newspaper inserts
Billboard	$5,000–$25,000 for a 1-3 month rental of a freeway sign
ONLINE ADVERTISING	
Banner ads	$2–$15 per 1,000 impressions on a Web site, depending on how targeted the ad is (the more targeted, the higher the price)
Video and rich media	$20–$25 per 1,000 ads, depending on the Web site's demographics
E-mail	$5–$15 per 1,000 targeted e-mail addresses
Sponsorships	$30–$75 per 1,000 viewers, depending on the exclusivity of the sponsorship (the more exclusive, the higher the price)

An appropriate domain name, search engine optimization, and proper Web site design are integral parts of a coordinated marketing communications strategy and ultimately, necessary conditions for e-commerce success.

DOMAIN NAMES

One of the first communications an e-commerce Web site has with a prospective customer is via its URL. Domain names play an important role in reinforcing an existing brand and/or developing a new brand. There are a number of considerations to take into account in choosing a domain name. Ideally, a domain name should be short, memorable, not easily confused with others, and difficult to misspell. The name of a Web site may or may not reflect the nature of the

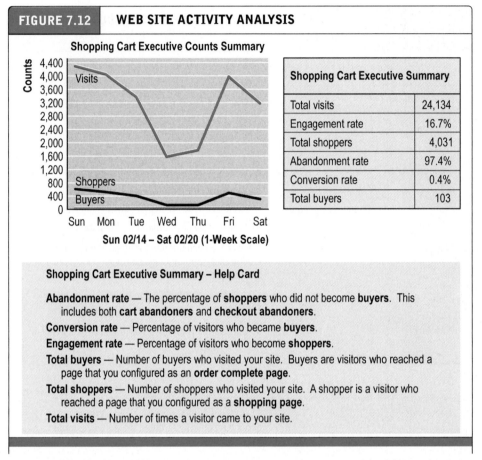

FIGURE 7.12 | **WEB SITE ACTIVITY ANALYSIS**

Shopping Cart Executive Counts Summary

Shopping Cart Executive Summary

Total visits	24,134
Engagement rate	16.7%
Total shoppers	4,031
Abandonment rate	97.4%
Conversion rate	0.4%
Total buyers	103

Shopping Cart Executive Summary – Help Card

Abandonment rate — The percentage of **shoppers** who did not become **buyers**. This includes both **cart abandoners** and **checkout abandoners**.

Conversion rate — Percentage of visitors who became **buyers**.

Engagement rate — Percentage of visitors who become **shoppers**.

Total buyers — Number of buyers who visited your site. Buyers are visitors who reached a page that you configured as an **order complete page**.

Total shoppers — Number of shoppers who visited your site. A shopper is a visitor who reached a page that you configured as a **shopping page**.

Total visits — Number of times a visitor came to your site.

company's business. The name of most major brands do not. Companies that choose a name unrelated to the nature of their business must be willing to spend extra time, effort, and money to establish the name as a brand. Dot-com domain names (as opposed to .net or .org) are still considered the most preferable, especially in the United States.

Today, however, it may be difficult to find a domain name that satisfies all of the above criteria. Many of the "good" .com domain names have already been taken. A number of companies exist that list domain names for sale (such as GreatDomains.com and BuyDomains.com). Most of the online domain registration sites such as Networksolutions.com, Godaddy.com, and Register.com have tools that can help you find appropriate names.

SEARCH ENGINE OPTIMIZATION

Given that nearly 71 million Americans use search engines daily, and given that about half of these users search for products and services using a search engine, it makes sense for a company to optimize its Web site for search engine recognition. Despite the fact that, with the exception of Google, most major search engines allow Web sites to pay for inclusion in their search results listing (but not the organic ranking), and most major search engines have also adopted a paid search engine advertising model,

INSIGHT ON TECHNOLOGY

IT'S 10 P.M. DO YOU KNOW WHO IS ON YOUR WEB SITE?

Chances are you don't, but if you used a Web site analytics company such as Omniture you might. And if you did pay attention to these matters, you most surely would be making more money from your Web site. Why? Because if you knew in real time what types of people were on your Web site hour by hour, minute by minute, you would be able to adjust your marketing and advertising messages, adjust your product mix, change product placement, and greatly improve the conversion process from mere visitors to actual purchasers.

In an industry where the players cannot seem to agree on standards for measuring Web site performance, and where webmasters are overwhelmed with literally millions of bits of information about the behavior of consumers on their Web sites, Omniture is working to help Web managers make sense out of their clickstream traffic. Omniture is an ASP (applications service provider) that sells Web site analytics and optimization services to other firms. In 2007, Omniture generated $143 million in revenue, up considerably from the post dot-com bust years. The company has approximately 4,400 customers in the United States and Europe, most of whom subscribe to their flagship product SiteCatalyst, a collection of tools which allow managers to see in real-time who is on their site, how customers flow through their site, and which are the most popular and profitable pages. The company was founded in 1996, and began selling on-demand Web site optimization and mangaement tools in 2002. Since then, the company has made several acquisitions to grow its business rapidly.

Other competitors in the same business include Coremetrics and Nedstat; network management software and business intelligence vendors such as NetIQ and SPSS that offer Web analytics as part of their larger product offerings; and digital marketing and e-commerce services providers such as aQuantive and Digital River that incorporate Web analytics in their services.

Omniture SiteCatalyst allows webmasters to monitor and analyze their Web traffic in real time, collect visitor intelligence, and enable faster adjustments to underperforming pages. It also provides most, if not all, of the answers to questions about performance and ROI that Web site marketing managers want.

SiteCatalyst collects, processes, stores, and reports on Internet user behavior based on browser activity. Reports allow customers to measure which marketing initiatives visitors responded to, what search engines they used, what keywords they entered, how much time they spent on pages, what they bought online, when they abandoned shopping carts, and where they live. The available reports and features include Web site navigation analysis, conversion rate analysis including calculating the long-term value of customers, marketing campaign measurement,and executive dashboards.

SiteCatalyst can evaluate a page-by-page navigation path a visitor has taken through a Web site. The service works by imbedding a small piece of code into each HTML page a client wants to track and analyze. One benefit to clients is that SiteCatalyst eliminates the need to capture, store, and process log files, which are expensive to run and maintain and consume a good bit of a company's time and resources.

SiteCatalyst does not need to be installed on a customer's own computers and infrastructure, but instead operates as Web service. There is no "installation" involved. Hence maintenance and operational costs are borne by Omniture.

(continued)

SiteCatalyst is able to segment customers live, in real-time, as they poke around a Web site. For instance, some visitors come for replacement parts, and can be cross-sold to other products from your firm in the process. Looking for a printer cartridge? Why not consider buying a whole new printer on sale today? Most visitors come to Web sites (especially brand name Web sites like Microsoft, HP, or Macy's) looking for specific products. But as long as they are on your site, why not entice them to consider related products or services? If an LL Bean customer comes to llbean.com looking for pajamas, Omniture is able to determine which ads and prompts lead to additional sales. In general, people looking for pajamas can be sold sleep and warmth-related products like underwear, blankets and pillows.

Not to be left behind by Web 2.0, Omniture also provides "Social Networking Optimization" tools. If you have social networking elements to your Web site like user comments, user generated content, video with sharing possibilities, or bookmarking, Omniture networking optimization can help you understand the consumption and creation habits of visitors, identify how much the social networking elements add to sales, engage users with content that is motivational, and help create emotional links to your products and brand.

HP, one of the world's largest PC and printer manufacturers, uses Omniture SiteCatalyst to manage its Web site, HP.com. An incredibly complex business, HP is segmented into largely independent product and service groups: printers, PCs, commercial servers, commercial printers, and software. It is also segmented into market segments: home/office, small business, enterprise business, government systems, and graphic arts. A visit to the Web site shows the complexity of having a single Web site to deliver service to customers coming from all of these segments. Behind the scenes, in the past HP had no systemic way of understanding how well users navigated the site, found what they want, and purchased a product. It did not have tracking data on customers visiting the site. Therefore, it did not know if printer customers were also PC or corporate customers. Also the independent business groups contributed their own ideas to how the user would be treated, creating many different and inconsistent marketing messages. HP did use surveys of visitors and specialized reports performed by various HP employees on an ad hoc basis. The absence of an overall coordinated Web site management tool meant that HP could not run its business as an integrated, cohesive firm.

In 2006 HP began using SiteCatalyst with the goal of complete customer tracking, a unified set of reports available on-demand and nearly instantly to more than 1,300 HP managers, and a full 360 degree view of their customer. HP tripled its conversion rates for its email campaigns, largely due to knowing who visited the site, capturing their email, and sending appropriate marketing emails for products and services. HP was also able to improve the navigation of its Web site by examining closely the click-path that users followed on the HP site. When people get lost on a Web site, it usually results in nearly randomized clicking in an effort by the user to find their way. Understanding these faulty navigation areas, HP revised its navigation to minimize "the lost user" phenomenon. For instance, the Customer Experience Group (a newly formed group responsible for the overall operation of HP.com) discovered that visitors seeking parts were much more likely to buy online from HP if they could arrive at the Parts store in one or two clicks (rather than a much more lengthy navigation path for the old site). HP estimates this change in navigation produced an annual increase of $775,000 in revenue from the Parts Store.

SOURCES: "Omniture, Inc. Form 10-K for the fiscal year ended December 31, 2007 filed with the Securities and Exchange Commission; "HP Uses Omniture to Get a 360 Degree View of Its Customers," Case Study, Omniture.com, September, 2008; "SiteCatalyst Business Optimizations: Social Networking Optimization," White Paper, Omniture.com, September, 2008;"Omniture's SiteCatalyst Turns 14," By Enid Burns, The ClickZ Network, Mar 5, 2008.

provide guidance on how to enhance the visibility of a Web site to crawler programs. Most of this advice is quite commonsensical and none of it is guaranteed to work despite the promises.

The first step in improving a firm's search engine ranking is to register with as many search engines as possible, so that a user looking for similar Web sites has a chance of coming across the firm's site. Nearly all search engines have registration pages, and some may charge an "inclusion fee" of around $50 per year.

The second step to improve a firm's ranking is to ensure that keywords used in the Web site description match keywords likely to be used as search terms by prospective customers. Using the keyword "lamps," for example, will not help your search engine ranking if most prospective customers are searching for "lights." Search engines differ, but most search engines read home page title tags, metatags, and other text on the home page in order to understand and index the content of the page.

Third, place keywords in a Web site's metatag and page title. A metatag is an HTML tag containing a list of words describing the Web site. Metatags are heavily used by search engines to determine the relevance of Web sites to search terms used frequently by users. The title tag provides a brief description of the Web site's content. The words in both the metatags and the title tags should match words on the home page. In addition, it is wise to include many references on the home page to the subject matter of likely consumer searches. Most crawlers will index the text content of the home page and may not go deeper into the Web site's secondary pages.

Fourth, link the Web site to as many other Web sites as possible, both in-coming links and out-going links. Search engines evaluate both kinds of links, and their quality to identify how popular a page is and how linked it is to other content on the Web. Search engines such as Google are guessing that when you enter a query for a product, chances are good that the product is located at one of the highly connected Web sites. The assumption is that the more links there are to a Web site, the more useful the Web site must be. How can a firm increase links to its Web site? Placing advertising is one way: banner ads, buttons, interstitials, and superstitials are all links to a firm's Web site. You can also create Web sites, even hundreds of Web sites, whose only function is to link to your main Web site although search engines can discover his and place you on the last page of search returns. Entering into affiliate relationships with other Web sites is another method. Search engines attempt to cancel out all efforts to mislead their search engines with varying and unknown success.

While the steps listed above are a beginning, increasing a firm's ranking is still a bit of an art form and usually requires a full-time professional effort to tweak metatags, keywords, and network links before solid results are obtained. The task often requires several months and is complicated by the fact that each search engine uses slightly different indexing methods, and changes their indexing methods in order to fool search engine optimizers.

WEB SITE FUNCTIONALITY

Attracting users to a company's Web site is the objective of marketing, but once a consumer is at a Web site, the sales process begins. This means that whatever brought the individuals to the Web site becomes much less relevant, and what they find at the Web site will ultimately determine whether they will make a purchase or return. Recall that a Web page and Web site are, first and foremost, a software interface. The question is: What makes for an effective software interface? In general, people use software inter-faces that they perceive to be useful and easy to use (a literature that is referred to as the "technology acceptance model"). Utility and ease of use are, therefore, the main factors to focus on when designing a site. Other factors involved in the credibility and trust that users place in a Web site—both very important for making decisions—are described in a growing literature on Web site design (Fogg, et al., 2003). In an exploratory study of Web site credibility based on 2,600 participants, the top three factors in Web site credibility were design look, information design/structure, and information focus (Fogg, et al., 2003) (see **Figure 7.13**.). Similar results were reported by Flanigan and Metzger in a 2007 study (Flanigan and Metzger, 2007). The message is: design counts.

The authors of this study were disappointed that users were most impressed by the design look of a Web site rather than its utility or ease of use.

Research on Web site utilization has found that the way information is organized on a Web site, while important for first-time users, declines in importance over time. Gradually, information content becomes the major factor attracting further visits (Davern, et al., 2001). In this research, frequency of Web site use is a function of four independent variables: content quality, Web site organization, perceived usefulness of the Web site, and perceived ease of use. Over time, people get used to the organization of a Web site and learn how to use it effectively to gather information. This suggests that improving content and usefulness ought to be the first priority of a firm, and that Web site redesign should be implemented carefully and incrementally. Radically redesigning a site runs the risk of losing the "lock in" effects that Web sites can induce (Davern, et al., 2001).

In Chapter 4 (Section 4.4), we identified eight basic design features that were necessary, from a business point of view, to attract and retain customers. The Web site must be functional, informative, employ simple navigation (ease of use), use redundant navigation, make it easy for customers to purchase, and feature multi-browser functionality, simple graphics, and legible text. Researchers have also found a number of other design factors that marketing managers should be aware of (see **Table 7.10** on page 470).

Sites that offer a "compelling experience" in the sense of providing entertainment with commerce or interactivity, or that are perceived as "fun" to use, are more successful in attracting and keeping visitors (Novak, et al., 2000). Web sites with editorial content that informs users also increases the time users spend on the Web site and increases the chance of them purchasing a product or service. While simplicity of design is hard to define, Lohse et al. (2000) found that the most important factor in predicting monthly sales was product list navigation and choice features that save consumers time. Thus, Amazon's "one-click" purchase capability is a powerful tool for increasing sales. eMarketer reports that between 50% and 60% of shopping carts are abandoned by confused and worried consumers, and that shopping carts are places where transactions go to die (eMarketer, Inc., 2008g). In

FIGURE 7.13	**FACTORS IN THE CREDIBILITY OF WEB SITES**

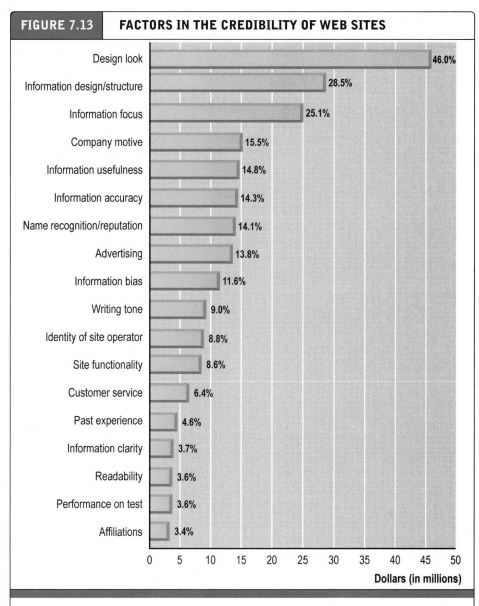

When evaluating the credibility of a Web site, survey participants commented on the design look of the Web site more than any other Web site feature.

SOURCE: Based on data from Fogg, et al., 2003.

difficult economic times, more customers "fantasy shop": enter the purchase process and pull out at the last possible moment before purchase.

More and more Web sites are using interactive consumer-decision aids to help the shopper make choices. Recommendation agents are programs that can suggest a product based on either consumer surveys or a review of a consumer's profile. Dell uses an online configurator to help consumers decide what computer to order.

TABLE 7.10	WEB SITE DESIGN FEATURES THAT IMPACT ONLINE PURCHASING
DESIGN FEATURE	**DESCRIPTION**
Compelling experience	Provide interactivity, entertainment, human interest; site is fun to use.
Editorial content	Provide helpful content, opinions, and features on subjects of interest to visitors in order to increase stickiness.
Fast download times	Quicker is better; if longer, provide amusement.
Easy product list navigation	Consumers can easily find the products they want.
Few clicks to purchase	The shorter the click list, the greater the chance of a sale.
Customer choice agents	Recommendation agents/configurators help the consumer make quick, correct choices.
Responsiveness	Personal e-mail response; 1–800 phone capability shown on Web site.

Responsiveness of Web sites is also important to credibility. Firms are improving but have a long way to go. A study of large firms found that while 90% of firms have a privacy policy, 75% don't tell users how to have their personal information destroyed so it can't be used by others, 12% of large companies did not respond to e-mail queries, and 21% responded only to half the queries sent to their Web sites. In general, large companies with Web sites receive favorable respect ratings for "simplicity of design and use" but weak ratings on responding to customers (Walker, 2004; Customer Respect Group, 2005). Other researchers have found that consumers purchase more at sites where there are strong privacy policies and these are known to visitors (Tsai, et. al., 2007).

No matter how successful the offline and online marketing campaign, a Web site that fails to deliver information, customer convenience, and responsiveness spells disaster. Attention to these Web site design features will help ensure success.

CASE STUDY

Adware, Spyware, Ad Bombs, Ambush Marketing, and Customer Hijacking:

Invasive Marketing Techniques Grow on the Web

Imagine you turn on your television and tune in *American Idol*, looking forward to another exciting evening. At 9:00 PM, the show comes on, but suddenly the opening credits are blocked by a pop-up ad that takes up half the screen and lasts for 30 seconds. You fiddle with the remote, but it doesn't stop. Other pop-ups continue to appear throughout the show, preventing you from really enjoying it. Finally, you turn it off. Of course, this doesn't happen on TV, or the radio, or with the telephone system. At least not yet. But on the Web, it happens all the time.

Spying, phishing, and spamming. Sometimes you have to wonder if the Web will just self-destruct and take most of e-commerce with it. The Holy Grail of advertising and marketing is to deliver the right message to the right person at the right time. If this were possible, no one would receive ads they did not want to see and then no advertising dollars would be wasted, reducing the costs to end users and increasing the efficiency of each ad dollar. One early vision of e-commerce was a trade-off between privacy and efficiency: let us know a little more about you and we will show you only the advertising and products you are interested in seeing, and even offer free content. E-commerce was supposed to end the mass advertising that exploded in the television era. But you quickly learn on the Web that your e-mail address can easily be discovered by marketing firms—who often share your address with one another—and thereafter you are treated to hundreds of e-mail messages a week offering "free" credit cards, cash prizes, coupons, no-money-down mortgages, lifetime income without work, and other get-rich quick schemes. Rather than achieve the holy grail of advertising, much of Web-based marketing is extraordinarily ignorant of who you are or what you are looking for.

Sometimes the technology can lead aggressive marketers in the opposite direction, increasing the chances that you will see the wrong ads at the wrong time without your consent. Adware and spyware are technologies that would seem to defeat the very purpose of the Internet, namely, a global interactive information environment under user control.

Adware is software that is typically installed without a user's knowledge, or without full disclosure that it will be used to gather personal information and/or show the user advertising. Adware logs information about the user, possibly including passwords, e-mail addresses, Web browsing history, online buying habits, the computer's hardware and software configuration, and the name, age, sex, and so on of the user. This information is periodically sent to an adware server, and then sold to legitimate advertisers and spammers. In addition, as the user visits certain sites, ads pop up often directing the user to a competitor's site, or a malicious site.

Spyware is software installed without the user's knowledge for the purpose of tracking a user's online behavior, such as e-mail, documents created, sites visited, and documents downloaded. This software includes key loggers, screen capture devices, and Trojan horses. In some cases, spyware may be a legitimate program used by parents or corporations to track use of the Internet by children or employees, or by law enforcement or intelligence agencies. However, typically, it is used for malicious purposes.

To get a better understanding of how adware works, let's follow an "ad bomb" as it moves through the system that is not protected by an adware blocker. Suppose a ten-year-old relative visits your house and wants to "play with the computer" as adults go about their business. You have DSL service. Surfing to a game site, she sees an offer for $100 in "free" prizes. She clicks and up pops the following proposition: "Click Here to Get Your Free Prizes." She clicks and up pops pictures of ten free prizes, ranging from free CDs to free clothing. But in the background a program is loaded onto your computer that automatically—without your intervention—requests that pop-up advertisements served by an advertising network be displayed every few minutes whenever you are using your computer. It is not even necessary to have launched your browser because the program automatically launches your browser whenever it wants to serve up an ad. Thankfully, however, most of the ads served up are appropriate for a ten-year-old (more offers of free prizes, CDs for children, and clothing), although there are some inappropriate advertisements, such as those for credit cards.

Following one of these ads back to its originator, you discover a direct marketing firm called Zango.com that specializes in putting together a network of millions of users offering free videos, games, screen savers, and music. There, in order to actually obtain your free content, you are required to register and give your name and e-mail address. Zango adds your name to millions of other consumers. Then, when you download your free content, Zango automatically installs a program that tracks your every online movement, and reports back to Zango servers. Zango then sells this information to marketers looking for specific market segments. For instance, as a marketer for a sportswear site, you might want to pop an ad for your monogrammed t-shirts every time a user enters a search term for t-shirts on Google, or enters the URL of L.L.Bean. In this case, both Google and L.L.Bean are denied revenue, and their customers are hijacked to another competing site. In an effort to rid your computer of the offending ad bomb, you contact the ad network. Technicians explain in an e-mail that they are just serving the ads and bear no responsibility for the downloaded program. They explain that "you may have unknowingly downloaded an application from one of these sites. An application downloaded from one of these sites may be requesting an advertisement from our ad server. Please note that we do not download any applications to your computer. We do not control these Web sites who did download the program to your computer." The ad network technicians fail to mention that they are paid by the advertisers involved to respond to the ads. The network does offer to help, however. Technical support advises you to close down ad windows as they appear, or press CTRL + N to display the URL of the advertisers and then send the URLs to the network, which will, in turn notify the advertisers to unsubscribe you from their lists. Finally, you open Windows' Add/Remove Programs utility in the hope of identifying the program and removing it. After scanning the list of programs, you discover an unfamiliar program. Guessing this oddly named program is the offender, you remove it, and finally the ad bomb event is over. Sometimes. In other cases, the adware is hidden from Windows altogether. Zango's position, and that of other adware distributors, is that consumers voluntarily consent to receive the ads when they install the file-swapping or other programs that typically have notices on install pages in very small print that say "You agree to receive occasional advertising messages from us directly or our affiliates." Consumer groups and the federal government think otherwise. They claim the programs are installed without consumer consent or knowledge.

Claria (formerly Gator.com) was one of the first to use an adware technique that could be called ambush advertising. Claria originally started business as a provider of a client-side digital wallet that stored personal information and automatically filled out Web forms. From there, Claria added a product called the OfferCompanion that could follow a consumer's movements on the Web, and when the user surfed to a site such as Staples.com, notify Claria's servers, which would search their ad database for an ad purchased by a Staples competitor such as OfficeMax, and then serve that as a "mini-billboard" that would appear directly over the Staples Web site. In 2001, the IAB—a trade group that represents Internet advertising agencies—announced its opposition to OfferCompanion, charging that it infringed on the trademark, copyright, and intellectual property rights of Web site publishers and other advertisers whose ads were being covered up by the mini-billboard. IAB demanded that Claria cease use of the program. Claria in turn sued the IAB in a California federal court for IAB's "malicious disparagement" of its products. The suit was settled out of court, but in June 2002, the *Washington Post*, *New York Times*, Dow Jones, and seven other publishers sued Claria on the grounds that its ads violated their copyrights and stole revenue. In February 2003, Claria settled this suit out of court as well, on confidential terms, and has subsequently settled a number of other suits that had been also been filed. Other companies offering similar services, such as WhenU and 180Solutions, have also been subjected to lawsuits.

P2P file-swapping music services also typically bundle small self-executing programs onto consumer computers that permit them or their affiliates to hijack customers. This is big business and very harmful to a typical small affiliate marketing site that may have clickable logos to Amazon, Barnes & Noble, JCPenney, Wal-Mart, or other large online retailers that have affiliate programs. According to Forrester Research analyst Carrie Johnson, affiliate marketing accounts for about 15% to 20% of B2C revenues. Here's how it works. When you download file-swapping software, you also download (and voluntarily consent to install) highjack adware. When you click on any of several hundred well-known Web destinations with affiliate programs, the adware intercepts the transaction and substitutes the affiliate ID of the music site for the affiliate number you launched from. The result: The 5% commission paid by the large retailers goes to the music site or its affiliate companies, and not to the affiliate site you were visiting. LimeWire, a Bit Torrent P2P site in the United Kingdom, distributed an adware program such as this in the past, but now claims to be adware free.

While many early purveyors of adware, under pressure from consumer groups, Internet security firms, and the Federal Trade Commission, have closed shop, others persist and new firms emerge. The most notorious recent offender is Zango.com (formerly ePIPO, and 180Solutions), mentioned previously. Identified by security firms such as McAfee and Symantec as "an adware downloader" and a "potentially unwanted program," Zango downloads programs to user computers that display popup ads without user consent. It automatically runs on startup, and the software cannot be shut down by the user or removed without requesting a separate uninstall program. Adware typically infects social networks and user-generated content sites. A security firm has discovered a number of user pages on MySpace that have videos that look like YouTube videos but when clicked, automatically install the Zango Case Toolbar. Users are sent to site called Youtube.info where prizes, games, music and sports entertainment are offered. It's all "free," but you pay the "price" by installing more adware.

In January 2006, the FTC charged Zango with deceptive failure to disclose adware, unfair installation of adware, and unfair uninstall practices in violation of the Federal Trade Commission Act. Zango settled in November 2006 in a consent decree in which it agreed to stop the identified practices and give up $3 million in ill-gotten gains. Its two top executives and owners, Keith Smith and Daniel Todd, are required to report their business activities to the FTC for 10 years given their history of illegal adware distribution. However, an independent security research in July 2007 found Zango was still engaging in practices designed to deceive, confuse and harm visitors contrary to its FTC settlement.

Despite this judgement and fine in which Zango agreed to cease non-consensual installation of software, Zango continues to innovate. In January, 2008, Zango was discovered on social networking sites like Facebook and MySpace hawking an application called "Crush Calculator." This application that tells Facebook members that one of their friends has a crush on them, and then leads users through several screens where they reveal their friends' email addresses and other personal information. On the last screen there is a disclosure notice that Zango software will be downloaded when the user clicks "submit." Click submit, and load Zango adware that follows you around the Internet. In another sign of Zango's irrepressible urge to innovate and survive, it has launched a number of Web sites that purport to offer you free movies and TV shows (Movietvonline.com and Bestcinemaonline.com). At these sites visitors are offered partial movie scenes, and encouraged to install Zango adware to see the entire movies. Of course the "movies" are in fact links to pirated copies served up by a variety of BitTorrent sites off shore.

How big a problem is adware and spyware? Well over 120 billion ad impressions a month are flashed in front of Internet users paid for by thousands of firms. No one has any idea how many of these billions of ads are served up by adware. The FTC believes that about 10% of all ad impressions are generated by spyware. An academic and industrial consortium, Stopbadware.org, a joint venture of the Harvard Berkman Center for Internet and Society and the Oxford Internet Institute, backed by Google, Lenovo, PayPal, Sun Microsystems, and VeriSign, began tracking Web sites where adware and malware is found. By November 2007, it had identified 257,618 Web sites that either intentionally or unintentionally are distributing adware. It also identified the top five ISPs that host these sites. The worst was iPowerWeb, which hosted over 10,000 offending Web sites. By 2008, malware had become a $2 billion industry, and an estimated 59 million Americans currently have spyware or other malicious badware installed on their computers.

Why do companies use adware? They do so primarily because research shows that adware can be twice as effective as other forms of online advertising. As Zango's Web site points out, "With Zango, you can truly target consumers when they are most interested in products or services. You'll achieve a higher ROI while exposing people to fewer ads than hit-or-miss pop-ups and banners." When a user searches for a product, or tries to go to a competitor's Web site (indicating interest and willingness to purchase), the user can be hit immediately with either an ad for that product, or diverted to a competitor's Web site. Zango claims to have been profitable for 24 consecutive quarters. The Zango Web site has three success story cases: FirstPremiere Bank (a purveyor of credit cards to the sub-prime market), Loanbright.com (a purveyor of software tools to small mortgage brokers), and an unnamed automobile company. Economic incentives drive the key participants in adware and make it a profitable enterprise. Internet ISPs benefit from new clients and network traffic, as do the large telecommunications companies that own the Internet backbone. Adware software makers obviously benefit by presenting their clients with a built-in, captive, targeted audience. PC software companies have in the past not felt it was in their interests to build-in protections to adware or malware. Obviously many firms are hurt and threatened by adware, and consumers suffer negative externalities. The corporate sponsors of Stopbadware.com are threatened by adware, and ISPs such as Verizon and others see that corruption of the marketing process is not in the long-term interests of e-commerce.

A number of bills have been introduced before Congress and various state legislatures to knock off adware. In May 2007, the House of Representatives passed the Internet Spyware Prevention Act of 2007. Like previous attempts in 2004 and 2005, the bill died in the Senate because of large-scale institutional forces that oppose any legislation that would criminalize phishing, spyware, adware, and other malware or put limits on what market forces are generating. Key players in the marketing industry oppose this legislation because it could outlaw the use of cookies, which are typically downloaded to a user's computer without the user's knowledge or consent. In the proposed legislation, cookies are expressly exempted from the provisions of the bill. In 2008, the Senate Committee on Commerce considered the Counter Spy Act, which prohibits the use of unfair or deceptive means to install software on computers, as well as the unauthorized acquisition, use, or commercialization of information from individuals. Software firms in the security business also want a Good Samaritan

SOURCES: "NebuAd Halts Plans for Web Tracking," by Ellen Nakashima, Washington Post.com, September 4, 2008; "Adware Vendor Zango Profits from Pirated Movies," by Gregg Keizer, *Computerworld*, August 18, 2008; "Experts: Spyware Legislation Needs More Work," by Grant Gross, *Computerworld*, June 12, 2008; "Red In the Face: Zango Adware Surfaces on Facebook," by Wendy Davis, MediaPost.com, January 4, 2008; "Badware Websites Report 2008," Stopbadware.org, September, 2008; "Trends in Badware 2008," Stopbadware.org, September, 2008; "Malware is Getting Sneakier," by Robert McMillan, IDG News Service, October 3, 2007; "The Economics of Malware," by Michel J. van Eeten, J. Bauer, J. Groenwegen, and W. Lemstra, University of Delft, 35th Telecommunications Policy Research Conference, September 28, 2007; "Internet Spyware (I-SPY) Prevention Act of 2007," (HR 1525) United States House of Representatives, May 2007; "Bad Practices Continue at Zango, Notwithstanding Proposed FTC Settlement," by Ben Edelman and Eric Howes, Benedelman.org/news, November 20, 2006.

provision in the legislation which would protect makers of anti-spyware programs who are being sued by adware firms because the anti-spyware programs prevent their adware from working. Now there's a twist.

While most firms are opposed to spyware, major institutions like hardware, software, financial service, search engine, and cell phone operators all want to be able to download programs to users that will scan computers for illicit copies of software, attempted attacks on Web sites, and other illicit activities. Start-up marketing firms (like NebuAd.com) looking for an edge want to install "deep packet inspection" software on ISP servers that handle your Web traffic. Deep packet inspection will allow the ISP and marketing firm to trace your every click on the Web. Deep packet inspection does not involve installing adware, but does accomplish the same purpose using the ISP servers, namely, tracing your online movements for the purpose of making a profit. Privacy groups are opposed to this level of surveillance. Once NebuAd plans became public, they came to the attention of Congress. In August, 2008 NebuAd fired its CEO, and withdrew its products from the market, as seven large ISPs dropped plans to use NebuAd software or engage in deep packet inspection (including CableOne).

Case Study Questions

1. Do you believe ISPs who host adware sites should be held legally responsible for these adware Web sites? Do you think the ad sponsors who pay firms like Zango should be held responsible? Why or why not?

2. Do these programs result in greater "targeting" of advertising, or are they just as mass market in nature as television ads?

3. What types of industry or government regulations might be needed to control these forms of advertising?

4. In what ways does adware contribute to a more efficient marketplace? Does it increase consumer choice, speed product search, or increase the efficiency of matching buyers and sellers?

7.5 REVIEW

KEY CONCEPTS

- Identify the major forms of online marketing communications.

Marketing communications include promotional sales communications that encourage immediate purchases and branding communications that focus on extolling the differentiable benefits of consuming a product or service. There are a number of different forms of marketing communications:

- *Banner and rich media/video ads* are promotional messages that users can respond to by clicking on the banner and following the link to a product description or offering. Variations include different size banners, buttons, skyscrapers, pop-ups, and pop-unders. Rich media ads use Flash, DHTML, Java, and streaming audio and/or video and typically seek to involve users more deeply than static banner ads.
- *Interstitial ads* are a way of placing full-page messages between the current and destination pages of a user. They are usually inserted within a single site, and are displayed as the user moves from one page to the next; they can also be made to appear as users move among sites.
- *Superstitials* are rich media ads developed by Unicast that pre-load into a browser's cache and do not play until fully loaded and the user clicks to another page.
- *Paid search engine inclusion and placement* is a relatively recent phenomenon. Firms now pay search engines for inclusion in the search engine index (formerly free and based on "objective" criteria), receiving a guarantee that their firm will appear in the results of relevant searches.
- *Sponsorships* are paid efforts to tie an advertiser's name to particular information, an event, or a venue in a way that reinforces its brand in a positive yet not overtly commercial manner. Advertorials are a common form of online sponsorship.
- *Affiliate relationships* permit a firm to put its logo or banner ad on another firm's Web site from which users of that site can click through to the affiliate's site.
- *Direct e-mail marketing sends* e-mail directly to interested users, and has proven to be one of the most effective forms of marketing communications. The key to effective direct e-mail marketing is "interested users"—Internet users who, at one time or another, have expressed an interest in receiving messages from the advertiser (people who have "opted in").
- *Online catalogs* are the online equivalent of paper-based catalogs. Their basic function is to display an e-commerce merchant's wares.
- Offline marketing combined with online marketing communications is typically the most effective. Although many e-commerce ventures want to rely heavily on online communications, marketing communications campaigns most successful at driving traffic to a Web site have incorporated both online and offline tactics.

■ Understand the costs and benefits of online marketing communications.

Key terms that one must know in order to understand evaluations of online marketing communications' effectiveness and its costs and benefits include:

- *Impressions*—the number of times an ad is served.
- *Click-through rate*—the number of times an ad is clicked.
- *Hits*—the number of http requests received by a firm's server.
- *Page views*—the number of pages viewed by visitors.
- *Stickiness (duration)*—the average length of time visitors remain at a site.
- *Unique visitors*—the number of distinct, unique visitors to a site.
- *Loyalty*—the percentage of purchasers who return in a year.
- *Reach*—the percentage of total consumers in a market who will visit a site.
- *Recency*—the average number of days elapsed between visits.

- *Acquisition rate*—the percentage of visitors who indicate an interest in the site's product by registering or visiting product's pages.
- *Conversion rate*—the percentage of visitors who purchase something.
- *Browse-to-buy ratio*—the ratio of items purchased to product views
- *View-to-cart ratio*—the ratio of "Add to cart" clicks to product views.
- *Cart conversion rate*—the ratio of actual orders to "Add to cart" clicks.
- *Checkout conversion rate*—the ratio of actual orders to checkouts started.
- *Abandonment rate*—the percentage of shoppers who begin a shopping cart form, but then fail to complete the form.
- *Retention rate*—the percentage of existing customers who continue to buy on a regular basis.
- *Attrition rate*—the percentage of customers who purchase once, but do not return within a year.
- *Open rate*—the percentage of customers who open the mail and are exposed to the message.
- *Delivery rate*—the percentage of e-mail recipients who received the e-mail.
- *Click-through rate (e-mail)*—the percentage of e-mail recipients who clicked through to the offer.
- *Bounce-back rate*—the percentage of e-mails that could not be delivered

Studies have shown that low click-through rates are not indicative of a lack of commercial impact of online advertising, and that advertising communication does occur even when users do not directly respond by clicking. Online advertising in its various forms has been shown to boost brand awareness and brand recall, create positive brand perceptions, and increase intent to purchase.

Effectiveness cannot be considered without analysis of cost. Typical pricing models for online marketing communications include:

- *Barter*—the exchange of ad space for something of equal value.
- *Cost per thousand (CPM)*—the advertiser pays for impressions in 1,000-unit lots.
- *Cost per click (CPC)*—the advertiser pays a prenegotiated fee for each click an ad receives.
- *Cost per action (CPA)*—the advertiser pays only for those users who perform a specific action.
- *Hybrid models*—combines two or more other models.
- *Sponsorships*—the advertiser pays a fixed fee for a particular term.

Online marketing communications are typically less costly than traditional mass media marketing. Also, online sales can generally be directly correlated with online marketing efforts, unlike with traditional marketing communications tactics.

The online merchant can measure precisely just how much revenue is generated by specific banners or specific e-mail messages sent to prospective customers.

■ **Discuss the ways in which a Web site can be used as a marketing communications tool.**

A functional Web site that customers can find is one of the strongest online communications tools. The following are all integral parts of a coordinated marketing communications strategy:

- *Appropriate domain name*—companies should choose a domain name that is short, memorable, hard to confuse or misspell, and indicative of a firm's business functions, and that preferably uses dot.com as its top-level domain.

- *Search engine optimization*—companies should register with all the major search engines so that a user looking for similar sites has a better chance of finding that particular site; ensure that keywords used in the Web site description match keywords likely to be used as search terms by prospective customers; and link the site to as many other sites as possible.
- *Web site functionality*—once at a Web site, visitors need to be enticed to stay and to buy. Web site design features that impact online purchasing include how compelling the experience of using the Web site is, download time, product list navigation, the number of clicks required to purchase, the existence of customer choice agents, and the Web site's responsiveness to customer needs.

QUESTIONS

1. Explain the difference between marketing and marketing communications.
2. Explain the difference between branding communications and sales/promotional communications.
3. What are some reasons why online advertising constitutes only about 9% of the total advertising market?
4. What kinds of products are most suited to being advertised online?
5. What is the difference between an interstitial ad and a superstitial ad?
6. What are some of the reasons for the decline in click-through rates on banner ads today? How can banner ads be made more effective?
7. Why are some affiliate relationships called "tenancy" deals? How do they differ from pure affiliate arrangements?
8. There is some controversy surrounding paid placements on search engines. What are the issues surrounding paid-placement search engines? Why might consumers object to this practice?
9. What are some of the advantages of direct e-mail marketing?
10. Why is offline advertising still important?
11. What is the difference between hits and page views? Why are these not the best measurements of Web traffic? Which is the preferred metric for traffic counts?
12. Define CTR, CPM, CPC, and CPA.
13. What are the key attributes of a good domain name?
14. What are some of the steps a firm can take to optimize its search engine rankings?
15. List and describe some Web site design features that impact online purchasing.

PROJECTS

1. Use the Online Consumer Purchasing Model (Figure 7.9) to assess the effectiveness of an e-mail campaign at a small Web site devoted to the sales of apparel to the ages 18–26 young adult market in the United States. Assume a marketing campaign of 100,000 e-mails (at 25 cents per e-mail address). The expected click-through rate is 15%, the conversion to customer rate is 10%, and the loyal customer retention rate is 25%. The average sale is $60, and the profit margin is 50% (the cost of the goods is $30). Does the campaign produce a profit? What would you advise doing to increase the number of purchases and loyal customers? What Web design factors? What communications messages?

2. Surf the Web for at least 15 minutes. Visit at least two different sites. Make a list describing in detail all the different marketing communication tools you see being used. Which do you believe is the most effective and why?

3. Do a search for a product of your choice on at least three search engines. Examine the results page carefully. Can you discern which results, if any, are a result of a paid placement? If so, how did you determine this? What other marketing communications related to your search appear on the page?

4. Examine the use of rich media and video in advertising. Find and describe at least two examples of advertising using streaming video, sound, or other rich media technologies. (Hint: Check the sites of Internet advertising agencies for case studies or examples of their work.) What are the advantages and/or disadvantages of this kind of advertising? Prepare a short 3- to 5-page report on your findings.

5. Visit Spywareinfo.com and Spywarewarrior.com. Develop a presentation describing the major objections that authors at these sites have towards spyware.

WEB SITE RESOURCES www.prenhall.com/laudon

- Additional projects, exercises, and tutorials
- Careers: Explore career opportunities in e-commerce
- Raising capital and business plans

CHAPTER 8

Ethical, Social, and Political Issues in E-commerce

After reading this chapter, you will be able to:

- Understand why e-commerce raises ethical, social, and political issues.
- Recognize the main ethical, social, and political issues raised by e-commerce.
- Identify a process for analyzing ethical dilemmas.
- Understand basic concepts related to privacy.
- Identify the practices of e-commerce companies that threaten privacy.
- Describe the different methods used to protect online privacy.
- Understand the various forms of intellectual property and the challenges involved in protecting it.
- Understand how governance of the Internet has evolved over time.
- Explain why taxation of e-commerce raises governance and jurisdiction issues.
- Identify major public safety and welfare issues raised by e-commerce.

Second Life Gets a Life:
Discovering Law and Ethics in Virtual Worlds

Second Life is a massively multiplayer online role playing game (MMORPG) experience where upwards of 1 million active users (and over 15 million unique subscribers) engage in online virtual activities that can range from innocent social chitchat to hustling, buying, selling, and even stealing. With liquidity provided by Linden dollars that can be purchased with real dollars ($1=250-270 Linden dollars), avatars that you create can buy and sell virtual assets—goods and services—from handbags and cars, to real estate, avatar design, clothing, and accessories service businesses. Some popular services include simulated prostitution, strip clubs, and, not surprisingly, gambling. Second Life commerce generates between $250,000 and $1 million in U.S. dollar revenues each day.

For the most part, players come not to compete with one another, but to entertain themselves, escape their real worlds, and have some fun. Others come in an attempt to make a profit, and a small number come to create mischief. Mischief, so much a part of the real world where law and custom aim to hold it in check, poses an interesting challenge for virtual worlds where there are no laws, and yet where actions taken online can injure people and corporations offline. It's like the Old West, where law and order were not quite established and people sought solutions, looking at times for a strong High Noon sheriff to bring order. Every now and then, the Sheriff sets down the law in Second Life, when its owners declare certain activities illegal and attempt to set up a system of self-regulation (if not quite law).

For instance, many of the assets, goods, and services sold on Second Life do not "belong" to the people who are selling them. You can buy virtual Gucci bags, Ferrari cars (L$ 1,995—what a deal!), Rolex watches, Rayban sunglasses, Prada and Oakley clothes for your avatars, Nike shoes, and Apple iPods. In a small study conducted by several lawyers, of 10 randomly selected virtual stores on Second Life, seven sold knock-off goods that exhibited obvious trademark infringements. Some stores sold nothing but brand-name goods. But because this is all virtual, none of the mentioned trademark owners have thus far brought a lawsuit against residents. As lawyers point out, unless companies actively enforce their trademarks in the face of infringement, they can lose the trademark altogether. From a practical point of view, at some point, nearly all firms will have a virtual presence, and when they seek to develop their trademarks on virtual sites, they will not want to compete with hundreds or thousands of residents selling knockoffs.

In a further sign of emerging legal and ethical issues, six major content creators on Second Life filed a real-world copyright and trademark infringement lawsuit against Thomas Simon, a Queens, New York, resident. Simon allegedly found a flaw in the Second Life program, and used a third-party copy program to make thousands of copies of the creators' products. Included in the alleged theft were avatar clothing, skins and shapes, scripted objects, furniture, and other objects. To complicate matters, the plaintiffs "broke into" Rase Kenzo's skybox to find the evidence of infringement. In the real world, the evidence obtained by unlawful means would be disallowed. In December 2007, the plaintiffs settled the lawsuit, with Simon agreeing to pay $525 in damages for profits made as a result of unauthorized copying of the plaintiff's intellectual property. Linden takes the position that it is an ISP under the Digital Millennium Copyright Act and thus is not itself responsible for any copyright infringement by its users.

Linden Lab is struggling with issues of governance and ethics on Second Life. It has banned six behaviors: intolerance (including slurs against groups), harassment, assault (including use of software tools to attack people's avatars), disclosure of information about other people's real-world lives, indecency (sexual behavior outside areas rated as mature), and disturbing the peace. Violations prompt warnings, suspension or banishment, enforced by Linden managers. There is no appeal process or due process.

The large-scale trademark and copyright infringements raise concerns about virtual life and real life law and statutes. Stealing in virtual life would seem to parallel stealing in real life. Gambling is another matter. Linden Lab's terms of service ban any illegal activity, but the company itself is not sure whether in-world gambling or prostitution crosses the line. The FBI and federal prosecutors were invited to visit Second Life gambling operations in April 2007, but issued no opinion on the legality of the operation. According to Ginsu Yoon, Vice President of Business Affairs, "It's not always clear to us whether a 3-D simulation of a casino is the same thing as a casino, legally speaking—and it's not clear to the law enforcement authorities we have asked." Even if the law were clear, he said the company would have no way to monitor or prevent in-world gambling, much as law enforcement cannot police every neighborhood poker game or office basketball pool. "There are millions of registered accounts and tens of millions of different objects in Second Life; there is simply no way for us to monitor content prospectively even if we wanted to," Yoon said. "That would be a harder task than pre-monitoring all e-mail sent through Yahoo Mail or Gmail, and no one expects those services to prevent all possible use of e-mail for illegal activity." This sounds like no one is in control, and real-world laws just don't apply, an argument that used to be made by peer-to-peer music sites. Ultimately, the Supreme Court in the real world shut down those music sites because they intentionally established a mechanism to violate copyright laws. In July 2007, Linden Lab decided to outlaw all forms of gambling.

Linden Lab and Second Life have a strong libertarian history. Its founders envisaged Second Life as a self-regulating community where good people could amuse themselves in a fantasy world. Dealing with "griefers," and their growing numbers as evidenced by rapidly expanding abuse complaints at Second Life, suggest that Linden's executives should start thinking about what they have created and how they will police it. If not, real world prosecutors and courts will do it for them. Second Life will have to grow up someday.

SOURCES: "Virtual Knockoffs," by Steven Seidenberg, *Inside Counsel*, March 2008; "Second Life Content Creators' Lawsuit Against Thomas Simon (aka Avatar 'Rase Kenzo') Settles; Signed Consent Judgment Filed," Virtuallyblind.com, January 2008; "Rapid Trademark Infringement in Second Life Costs Millions, Undermines Future Enforcement," by Benjamin Duranske, Virtuallyblind.com, October 30, 2007; "Second Life Players Bring Virtual Reality to Court," by Emil Steiner, Washingtonpost.com, October 29, 2007; "Second Life Virtual Gamblers Told to Fold," by Mike Musgrove, *Washington Post*, August 1, 2007; "Fantasy Life, Real Law," by Stephanie Ward, *ABA Journal*, March, 2007; "Virtual Vandalism," by Don Clark, *Wall Street Journal*, November 27, 2006.

Determining how to regulate virtual behavior that may have a real-world impact is just one of many ethical, social, and political issues raised by the rapid evolution of the Internet and e-commerce. These questions are not just ethical questions that we as individuals have to answer; they also involve social institutions such as family, schools, and business firms. And these questions have obvious political dimensions because they involve collective choices about how we should live and what laws we would like to live under.

In this chapter, we discuss the ethical, social, and political issues raised in e-commerce, provide a framework for organizing the issues, and make recommendations for managers who are given the responsibility of operating e-commerce companies within commonly accepted standards of appropriateness.

8.1 UNDERSTANDING ETHICAL, SOCIAL, AND POLITICAL ISSUES IN E-COMMERCE

The Internet and its use in e-commerce have raised pervasive ethical, social, and political issues on a scale unprecedented for computer technology. Entire sections of daily newspapers and weekly magazines are devoted to the social impact of the Internet. But why is this so? Why is the Internet at the root of so many contemporary controversies? Part of the answer lies in the underlying features of Internet technology itself, and the ways in which it has been exploited by business firms. Internet technology and its use in e-commerce disrupt existing social and business relationships and understandings.

Consider for instance Table 1.2 (in Chapter 1), which lists the unique features of Internet technology. Instead of considering the business consequences of each unique feature, **Table 8.1** examines the actual or potential ethical, social, and/or political consequences of the technology.

We live in an "information society," where power and wealth increasingly depend on information and knowledge as central assets. Controversies over information are often disagreements over power, wealth, influence, and other things thought to be valuable. Like other technologies, such as steam, electricity, telephones, and television, the Internet and e-commerce can be used to achieve social progress, and for the most part, this has occurred. However, the same technologies can be used to commit crimes, despoil the environment, and threaten cherished social values. Before automobiles, there was very little interstate crime and very little federal jurisdiction over crime. Likewise with the Internet: before the Internet, there was very little "cybercrime."

Many business firms and individuals are benefiting from the commercial development of the Internet, but this development also exacts a price from individuals, organizations, and societies. These costs and benefits must be carefully considered by those seeking to make ethical and socially responsible decisions in this new environment. The question is: How can you as a manager make reasoned judgments about what your firm should do in a number of e-commerce areas—from

TABLE 8.1	UNIQUE FEATURES OF E-COMMERCE TECHNOLOGY AND THEIR POTENTIAL ETHICAL, SOCIAL, AND/OR POLITICAL IMPLICATIONS
E-COMMERCE TECHNOLOGY DIMENSION	**POTENTIAL ETHICAL, SOCIAL, AND POLITICAL SIGNIFICANCE**
Ubiquity—Internet/Web technology is available everywhere: at work, at home, and elsewhere via mobile devices, anytime.	Work and shopping can invade family life; shopping can distract workers at work, lowering productivity; use of mobile devices can lead to automobile and industrial accidents. Presents confusing issues of "nexus" to taxation authorities.
Global reach—The technology reaches across national boundaries, around the Earth.	Reduces cultural diversity in products; weakens local small firms while strengthening large global firms; moves manufacturing production to low-wage areas of the world; weakens the ability of all nations—large and small—to control their information destiny.
Universal standards—There is one set of technology standards, namely Internet standards.	Increases vulnerability to viruses and hacking attacks worldwide affecting millions of people at once. Increases the likelihood of "information" crime, crimes against systems, and deception.
Richness—Video, audio, and text messages are possible.	A "screen technology" that reduces use of text and potentially the ability to read by focusing instead on video and audio messages. Potentially very persuasive messages possible that may reduce reliance on multiple independent sources of information.
Interactivity—The technology works through interaction with the user.	The nature of interactivity at commercial sites can be shallow and meaningless. Customer e-mails are frequently not read by human beings. Customers do not really "co-produce" the product as much as they "co-produce" the sale. The amount of "customization" of products that occurs is minimal, occurring within predefined platforms and plug-in options.
Information density—The technology reduces information costs, raises quality.	While the total amount of information available to all parties increases, so does the possibility of false and misleading information, unwanted information, and invasion of solitude. Trust, authenticity, accuracy, completeness, and other quality features of information can be degraded. The ability of individuals and organizations to make sense of out of this plethora of information is limited.
Personalization/Customization—The technology allows personalized messages to be delivered to individuals as well as groups.	Opens up the possibility of intensive invasion of privacy for commercial and governmental purposes that is unprecedented.
Social technology—The technology enables user content generation and social networking.	Creates opportunities for cyberbullying, abusive language, and predation; challenges concepts of privacy, fair use, and consent to use posted information; creates new opportunities for surveillance by authorities and corporations into private lives.

securing the privacy of your customer's clickstream to ensuring the integrity of your company's domain name?

A MODEL FOR ORGANIZING THE ISSUES

E-commerce—and the Internet—have raised so many ethical, social, and political issues that it is difficult to classify them all, and hence complicated to see their relationship to one another. Clearly, ethical, social, and political issues are interrelated. One way to organize the ethical, social, and political dimensions surrounding e-commerce is shown in **Figure 8.1**. At the individual level, what appears as an ethical issue—"What should I do?"—is reflected at the social and political levels—"What should we as a society and government do?" The ethical dilemmas you face as a manager of a business using the Web reverberate and are reflected in social and political debates. The major ethical, social, and political issues that have developed around e-commerce over the past nine to ten years can be loosely categorized into four major dimensions: information rights, property rights, governance, and public safety and welfare.

Some of the ethical, social, and political issues raised in each of these areas include the following:

- **Information rights:** What rights to their own personal information do individuals have in a public marketplace, or in their private homes, when Internet technologies make information collection so pervasive and efficient? What rights do individuals have to access information about business firms and other organizations?

- **Property rights:** How can traditional intellectual property rights be enforced in an Internet world where perfect copies of protected works can be made and easily distributed worldwide in seconds?

- **Governance:** Should the Internet and e-commerce be subject to public laws? And if so, what law-making bodies have jurisdiction—state, federal, and/or international?

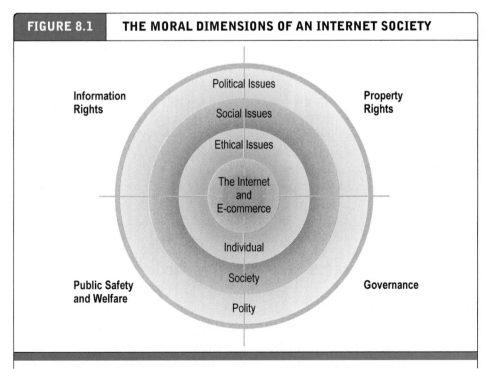

FIGURE 8.1	THE MORAL DIMENSIONS OF AN INTERNET SOCIETY

The introduction of the Internet and e-commerce impacts individuals, societies, and political institutions. These impacts can be classified into four moral dimensions: property rights, information rights, governance, and public safety and welfare.

- **Public safety and welfare:** What efforts should be undertaken to ensure equitable access to the Internet and e-commerce channels? Should governments be responsible for ensuring that schools and colleges have access to the Internet? Are certain online content and activities—such as pornography and gambling—a threat to public safety and welfare? Should mobile commerce be allowed from moving vehicles?

To illustrate, imagine that at any given moment, society and individuals are more or less in an ethical equilibrium brought about by a delicate balancing of individuals, social organizations, and political institutions. Individuals know what is expected of them, social organizations such as business firms know their limits, capabilities, and roles, and political institutions provide a supportive framework of market regulation, banking, and commercial law that provides sanctions against violators.

Now, imagine we drop into the middle of this calm setting a powerful new technology such as the Internet and e-commerce. Suddenly, individuals, business firms, and political institutions are confronted by new possibilities of behavior. For instance, individuals discover that they can download perfect digital copies of music tracks from Web sites without paying anyone, something that, under the old technology of CDs, would have been impossible. This can be done, despite the fact that these music tracks still "belong" as a legal matter to the owners of the copyright—musicians and record label companies. Then, business firms discover that they can make a business out of aggregating these digital musical tracks—or creating a mechanism for sharing musical tracks—even though they do not "own" them in the traditional sense. This, of course, is the story of Grokster, Kazaa, and Napster described in Chapter 1. The record companies, courts, and Congress were not prepared at first to cope with the onslaught of online digital copying. Courts and legislative bodies will have to make new laws and reach new judgments about who owns digital copies of copyrighted works and under what conditions such works can be "shared." It may take years to develop new understandings, laws, and acceptable behavior in just this one area of social impact. In the meantime, as an individual and a manager, you will have to decide what you and your firm should do in legal "gray" areas, where there is conflict between ethical principles but no clear-cut legal or cultural guidelines. How can you make good decisions in this type of situation?

Before examining the four moral dimensions of e-commerce in greater depth, we will briefly review some basic concepts of ethical reasoning that you can use as a guide to ethical decision making, and provide general reasoning principles about the social and political issues of the Internet that you will face in the future.

BASIC ETHICAL CONCEPTS: RESPONSIBILITY, ACCOUNTABILITY, AND LIABILITY

ethics
the study of principles that individuals and organizations can use to determine right and wrong courses of action

Ethics is at the heart of social and political debates about the Internet. **Ethics** is the study of principles that individuals and organizations can use to determine right and wrong courses of action. It is assumed in ethics that individuals are free moral agents who are in a position to make choices. When faced with alternative courses of action, what is the correct moral choice? Extending ethics from individuals to business firms and even entire societies can be difficult, but it is not impossible. As long as there is a decision-making body or individual (such as a Board of Directors or CEO in a business firm, or a governmental body in a society), their decisions can be judged against a variety of ethical principles.

If you understand some basic ethical principles, your ability to reason about larger social and political debates will be improved. In western culture, there are three basic principles that all ethical schools of thought share: responsibility, accountability, and liability. **Responsibility** means that as free moral agents, individuals, organizations, and societies are responsible for the actions they take. **Accountability** means that individuals, organizations, and societies should be held accountable to others for the consequences of their actions. The third principle—**liability**—extends the concepts of responsibility and accountability to the area of law. Liability is a feature of political systems in which a body of law is in place that permits individuals to recover the damages done to them by other actors, systems, or organizations. **Due process** is a feature of law-governed societies and refers to a process in which laws are known and understood and there is an ability to appeal to higher authorities to ensure that the laws have been applied correctly.

You can use these concepts immediately to understand some contemporary Internet debates. For instance, consider the *Metro-Goldwyn-Mayer v. Grokster* lawsuit discussed in the case study at the end of Chapter 1. MGM and other studios that joined it in the case argued that because the primary and intended use of Internet P2P file-sharing services such as Grokster, StreamCast, and Kazaa was the swapping of copyright-protected music and video files, the file-sharing services should be held accountable, and shut down. Although Grokster and the other networks acknowledged that the most common use of the software was for illegal digital music file-swapping, they argued that there were substantial, nontrivial uses of the same networks for legally sharing files. They also argued they should not be held accountable for what individuals do with their software, any more than Sony could be held accountable for how people use VCRs, or Xerox for how people use copying machines. Ultimately, the Supreme Court ruled that Grokster and other P2P networks could be held accountable for the illegal actions of their users if it could be shown that they intended their software to be used for illegal downloading and sharing, and had marketed the software for that purpose. The court relied on copyright laws to arrive at its decisions, but these laws reflect some basic underlying ethical principles of responsibility, accountability, and liability.

Underlying the *Grokster* Supreme Court decision is a fundamental rejection of the notion that the Internet is an ungoverned "Wild West" environment that cannot be controlled. Under certain defined circumstances, the courts will intervene into the uses of the Internet. No organized civilized society has ever accepted the proposition that technology can flaunt basic underlying social and cultural values. Through all of the industrial and technological developments that have taken place, societies have intervened by means of legal and political decisions to ensure that the technology serves socially acceptable ends without stifling the positive consequences of innovation and wealth creation. The Internet in this sense is no different, and we can expect societies around the world to exercise more regulatory control over the Internet and e-commerce in an effort to arrive at a new balance between innovation and wealth creation, on the one hand, and other socially desirable objectives on the

responsibility
as free moral agents, individuals, organizations, and societies are responsible for the actions they take

accountability
individuals, organizations, and societies should be held accountable to others for the consequences of their actions

liability
a feature of political systems in which a body of law is in place that permits individuals to recover the damages done to them by other actors, systems, or organizations

due process
a process in which laws are known and understood and there is an ability to appeal to higher authorities to ensure that the laws have been applied correctly

other. This is a difficult balancing act, and reasonable people will arrive at different conclusions.

ANALYZING ETHICAL DILEMMAS

dilemma

a situation in which there are at least two diametrically opposed actions, each of which supports a desirable outcome

Ethical, social, and political controversies usually present themselves as dilemmas. A **dilemma** is a situation in which there are at least two diametrically opposed actions, each of which supports a desirable outcome. When confronted with a situation that seems to present an ethical dilemma, how can you analyze and reason about the situation? The following is a five-step process that should help:

1. **Identify and clearly describe the facts.** Find out who did what to whom, and where, when, and how. In many instances, you will be surprised at the errors in the initially reported facts, and often you will find that simply getting the facts straight helps define the solution. It also helps to get the opposing parties involved in an ethical dilemma to agree on the facts.

2. **Define the conflict or dilemma and identify the higher-order values involved.** Ethical, social, and political issues always reference higher values. Otherwise, there would be no debate. The parties to a dispute all claim to be pursuing higher values (e.g., freedom, privacy, protection of property, and the free enterprise system). For example, supporters of the use of advertising networks such as DoubleClick argue that the tracking of consumer movements on the Web increases market efficiency and the wealth of the entire society. Opponents argue this claimed efficiency comes at the expense of individual privacy, and advertising networks should cease their activities or offer Web users the option of not participating in such tracking.

3. **Identify the stakeholders.** Every ethical, social, and political issue has stakeholders: players in the game who have an interest in the outcome, who have invested in the situation, and usually who have vocal opinions. Find out the identity of these groups and what they want. This will be useful later when designing a solution.

4. **Identify the options that you can reasonably take.** You may find that none of the options satisfies all the interests involved, but that some options do a better job than others. Sometimes, arriving at a "good" or ethical solution may not always be a balancing of consequences to stakeholders.

5. **Identify the potential consequences of your options.** Some options may be ethically correct, but disastrous from other points of view. Other options may work in this one instance, but not in other similar instances. Always ask yourself, "What if I choose this option consistently over time?"

Once your analysis is complete, you can refer to the following well-established ethical principles to help decide the matter.

CANDIDATE ETHICAL PRINCIPLES

Although you are the only one who can decide which ethical principles you will follow and how you will prioritize them, it is helpful to consider some ethical principles with deep roots in many cultures that have survived throughout recorded history:

- **The Golden Rule:** Do unto others as you would have them do unto you. Putting yourself into the place of others and thinking of yourself as the object of the decision can help you think about fairness in decision making.

- **Universalism:** If an action is not right for all situations, then it is not right for any specific situation (Immanuel Kant's categorical imperative). Ask yourself, "If we adopted this rule in every case, could the organization, or society, survive?"

- **Slippery Slope:** If an action cannot be taken repeatedly, then it is not right to take at all (Descartes' rule of change). An action may appear to work in one instance to solve a problem, but if repeated, would result in a negative outcome. In plain English, this rule might be stated as "once started down a slippery path, you may not be able to stop."

- **Collective Utilitarian Principle:** Take the action that achieves the greater value for all of society. This rule assumes you can prioritize values in a rank order and understand the consequences of various courses of action.

- **Risk Aversion:** Take the action that produces the least harm, or the least potential cost. Some actions have extremely high failure costs of very low probability (e.g., building a nuclear generating facility in an urban area) or extremely high failure costs of moderate probability (speeding and automobile accidents). Avoid the high-failure cost actions and choose those actions whose consequences would not be catastrophic, even if there were a failure.

- **No Free Lunch:** Assume that virtually all tangible and intangible objects are owned by someone else unless there is a specific declaration otherwise. (This is the ethical "no free lunch" rule.) If something someone else has created is useful to you, it has value and you should assume the creator wants compensation for this work.

- **The *New York Times* Test (Perfect Information Rule):** Assume that the results of your decision on a matter will be the subject of the lead article in the *New York Times* the next day. Will the reaction of readers be positive or negative? Would your parents, friends, and children be proud of your decision? Most criminals and unethical actors assume imperfect information, and therefore they assume their decisions and actions will never be revealed. When making decisions involving ethical dilemmas, it is wise to assume perfect information markets.

- **The Social Contract Rule:** Would you like to live in a society where the principle you are supporting would become an organizing principle of the entire society?

For instance, you might think it is wonderful to download illegal copies of music tracks, but you might not want to live in a society that did not respect property rights, such as your property rights to the car in your driveway, or your rights to a term paper or original art.

None of these rules is an absolute guide, and there are exceptions and logical difficulties with all of them. Nevertheless, actions that do not easily pass these guidelines deserve some very close attention and a great deal of caution because the appearance of unethical behavior may do as much harm to you and your company as the actual behavior.

Now that you have an understanding of some basic ethical reasoning concepts, let's take a closer look at each of the major types of ethical, social, and political debates that have arisen in e-commerce.

8.2   PRIVACY AND INFORMATION RIGHTS

privacy
the moral right of individuals to be left alone, free from surveillance or interference from other individuals or organizations, including the state

information privacy
includes both the claim that certain information should not be collected at all by governments or business firms, and the claim of individuals to control the use of whatever information that is collected about them

Privacy is the moral right of individuals to be left alone, free from surveillance or interference from other individuals or organizations, including the state. Privacy is a girder supporting freedom: Without the privacy required to think, write, plan, and associate independently and without fear, social and political freedom is weakened, and perhaps destroyed. **Information privacy** is a subset of privacy. The right to information privacy includes both the claim that certain information should not be collected at all by governments or business firms, and the claim of individuals to control the use of whatever information that is collected about them. Individual control over personal information is at the core of the privacy concept.

Due process also plays an important role in defining privacy. The best statement of due process in record keeping is given by the Fair Information Practices doctrine developed in the early 1970s and extended to the online privacy debate in the late 1990s (described later in this section).

There are two kinds of threats to individual privacy posed by the Internet. One threat originates in the private sector and concerns how much personal information is collected by commercial Web sites and how it will be used. A second threat originates in the public sector and concerns how much personal information federal, state, and local government authorities collect, and how they use it. While these threats are conceptually distinct, in practice they are related as the federal government increasingly relies on Internet companies to provide intelligence on specific individuals and groups, and as Internet records held by search engine companies and others (like Amazon) are sought by legal authorities and attorney's.

Privacy claims—and thinking about privacy—mushroomed in the United States at the end of the nineteenth century as the technology of photography and tabloid journalism enabled the invasion of the heretofore private lives of wealthy industrialists. For most of the twentieth century, however, privacy thinking and legislation focused on restraining the government from collecting and using personal information. With the explosion in the collection of private personal information by Web-based marketing firms since 1995, privacy concerns are increasingly directed toward restraining the activities of private firms in the collection and use of information on the Web. Claims to privacy are also involved at the workplace. Millions of employees are subject to various forms of electronic surveillance that in many cases is enhanced by firm intranets and Web technologies. For instance, the majority of U.S. companies monitor which Web sites their workers visit, as well as employee e-mail and instant messages. Employee posts on message boards and blogs are also coming under scrutiny (Vaughan, 2007).

In general, the Internet and the Web provide an ideal environment for both business and government to invade the personal privacy of millions of users on a scale unprecedented in history. Perhaps no other recent issue has raised as much widespread social and political concern as protecting the privacy of over 173 million Web users in the United States alone. The major ethical issues related to e-commerce and privacy include the following: Under what conditions should we invade the privacy of others? What legitimates intruding into others' lives through unobtrusive surveillance, market research, or other means? The major social issues related to e-commerce and privacy concern the development of "expectations of privacy" or privacy norms, as well as public attitudes. In what areas of life should we as a society encourage people to think they are in "private territory" as opposed to public view? The major political issues related to e-commerce and privacy concern the development of statutes that govern the relations between record keepers and individuals. How should both public and private organizations—which may be reluctant to remit the advantages that come from the unfettered flow of information on individuals—be restrained, if at all? In the following section, we look first at the various practices of e-commerce companies that pose a threat to privacy.

INFORMATION COLLECTED AT E-COMMERCE SITES

As you have learned in previous chapters, e-commerce sites routinely collect a variety of information from or about consumers who visit their site and/or make purchases. Some of this data constitutes **personally identifiable information (PII)**, which is defined as any data that can be used to identify, locate, or contact an individual (Federal Trade Commission, 2000a). Other data is **anonymous information**, composed of demographic and behavioral information, such as age, occupation, income, zip code, ethnicity, and other data that characterizes your life without identifying who you are. **Table 8.2** lists some of the personal identifiers routinely collected by online e-commerce sites. This is not an exhaustive list.

Advertising networks and search engines also track the behavior of consumers across thousands of popular sites, not just at one site, via cookies, spyware, and other techniques

Table 8.3 illustrates some of the major ways online firms gather information about consumers.

personally identifiable information (PII)
any data that can be used to identify, locate, or contact an individual

anonymous information
demographic and behavioral information that does not include any personal identifiers

TABLE 8.2	PERSONAL INFORMATION COLLECTED BY E-COMMERCE SITES	
Name	Bank accounts	Education
Address	Credit card accounts	Preference data
Phone number	Gender	Transaction data
E-mail address	Age	Clickstream data
Social Security number	Occupation	Browser type

TABLE 8.3	THE INTERNET'S MAJOR INFORMATION GATHERING TOOLS AND THEIR IMPACT ON PRIVACY
INTERNET CAPABILITY	**IMPACT ON PRIVACY**
Cookies	Used to track individuals at a single site.
Third-party cookies	Cookies placed by outside third-party advertising networks. Used to monitor and track online behavior, searches, and sites visited across thousands of sites that belong to the advertising network for the purpose of displaying "relevant" advertising.
Spyware	Can be used to record all the keyboard activity of a user, including Web sites visited and security codes used; also used to display advertisements to users based on their searches or other behavior.
Search engine behavioral targeting (Google, and other search engines)	Uses prior search history, demographic, expressed interests, geographic, or other user-entered data to target advertising.
Deep packet inspection	Uses software installed at the ISP level to track all user clickstream behavior, sells this information to advertisers, and then attempts to show users "relevant ads."
Shopping carts	Can be used to collect detailed payment and purchase information.
Forms	Online forms that users voluntarily fill out in return for a promised benefit or reward that are linked with clickstream or other behavioral data to create a personal profile.
Site transaction logs	Can be used to collect and analyze detailed information on page content viewed by users.
Search engines	Can be used to trace user statements and views on newsgroups, chat groups, and other public forums on the Web, and profile users' social and political views. Google returns name, address, and links to a map with directions to the address when a phone number is entered.
Digital wallets (single sign-on services)	Client-side wallets and software that reveal personal information to Web sites verifying the identity of the consumer.
Digital Rights Management (DRM)	Software (Windows Media Player) that requires users of online media to identify themselves before viewing copyrighted content.
Trusted Computing Environments	Hardware and software that controls the viewing of copyrighted content and requires users identification.

PROFILING AND BEHAVIORAL TARGETING

On an average day, around 125 million Americans go online (Pew Internet & American Life Project, 2008). Marketers would like to know who these people are, what they are interested in, and what they buy. The more precise the information, the more complete the information, the more valuable it is as a predictive and marketing tool. Armed with this information, marketers can make their ad campaigns more efficient by targeting specific ads at specific groups or individuals, and they can even adjust the ads for specific groups.

Many Web sites allow third parties—including online advertising networks such as aQuantive, DoubleClick, and others—to place "third-party" cookies on a visitor's hard drive in order to engage in profiling the user's behavior across thousands of Web sites. A third-party cookie is used to track users across hundreds or thousands of other Web sites who are members of the advertising network. **Profiling** is the creation of digital images that characterize online individual and group behavior. **Anonymous profiles** identify people as belonging to highly specific and targeted groups, for example, 20-to 30-year-old males, with college degrees and incomes greater than $30,000 a year, and interested in high-fashion clothing (based on recent search engine use). **Personal profiles** add a personal e-mail address, postal address, and/or phone number to behavioral data. Increasingly, online firms are attempting to link their online profiles to offline consumer data collected by established retail and catalog firms. In the past, individual stores collected data on customer movement through a single store in order to understand consumer behavior and alter the design of stores accordingly. Also, purchase and expenditure data was gathered on consumers purchasing from multiple stores—usually long after the purchases were made—and the data was used to target direct mail and in-store campaigns, in addition to mass-media advertising.

The online advertising networks such as DoubleClick and 24/7 Media have added several new dimensions to established offline marketing techniques. First, they have the ability to precisely track not just consumer purchases, but all browsing behavior on the Web at thousands of the most popular member sites, including browsing book lists, filling out preference forms, and viewing content pages. Second, they can dynamically adjust what the shopper sees on screen—including prices. Third, they can build and continually refresh high-resolution data images or behavioral profiles of consumers (Laudon, 1996). Other advertising firms have created spyware software that, when placed on a consumer's computer, can report back to the advertiser's server on all consumer Internet use, and is also used to display advertising on the consumer's computer.

A different kind of profiling and a more recent form of behavioral targeting is Google's results-based personalization of advertising. In October 2005, Google applied for a patent on a program that allows advertisers using Google's AdWord program to target ads to users based on their prior search histories and profiles which Google constructs based on user searches, along with any other information the user submits to Google or Google can obtain, such as age, demographics, region, and other Web activities (such as blogging). Google also applied for a second patent on a program that allows Google to help advertisers select keywords and design ads for various market segments based on search histories, such as helping a clothing Web site create and test ads targeted at teenage females. In August 2007, Google began to put some of those ideas into practice, using behavioral targeting to help it display more relevant ads based on keywords. According Google, the new feature is aimed at capturing a more robust understanding of user intent, and thereby delivering a better ad (Tehrani, 2007). Google's Gmail, a free e-mail service, offers a powerful interface, and as of September 2008, 7.1 gigabytes of free storage. In return, Google computers read all incoming and outgoing e-mail and place "relevant" advertising in the margins of the

profiling
the creation of digital images that characterize online individual and group behavior

anonymous profiles
identify people as belonging to highly specific and targeted groups

personal profiles
add a personal e-mail address, postal address, and/or phone number to behavioral data

mail. Profiles are developed on individual users based on the content in their e-mail (Story, 2007a).

The technology of tracking and profiling continues to evolve. In 2008 Google announced its Chrome Web browser. Chrome has a Suggest feature which automatically suggests related queries and Web sites a the user enters a search. Critics pointed out this was a "key logger" device that would record every keystroke of users forever. Google has since announced it would anonymize the data in twenty four hours.

deep packet inspection

a technology for recording every key stroke at the ISP level

Deep packet inspection is a recent technology for recording every key stroke at the ISP level of everyone (no matter where they ultimately go on the Web), and then use that information to make suggestions, and target ads. While advertising networks are limited, and even Google does not constitute the universe of search, deep packet inspection at the ISP level really does capture the universe of all Internet users. The leading firm in this technology is NebuAd. After testing the hardware and software with several ISPs in 2008, the outcry from privacy advocates and Congress caused these ISPs to withdraw from the experiment, and NebuAd withdrew the product from the market (Nakashima, 2008).

What is different about these efforts at online profiling and behavioral targeting (when compared to offline methods used in the past) is the scope and intensity of the data dragnet, and the ability to manipulate the shopping environment to the advantage of the merchant. Most of this activity occurs in the background without the knowledge of the shopper, and it takes place dynamically online in less than a second. Arguably, no other Web-based technique comes so close to being a real-world implementation of George Orwell's novel *1984* and its lead character, Big Brother. Here's an illustration of online profiling from "Online Profiling: A Report to Congress," an FTC report:

Online consumer Joe Smith goes to a Web site that sells sporting goods. He clicks on the pages for golf bags. While there, he sees a banner ad, which he ignores as it does not interest him. The ad was placed by USAad Network. He then goes to a travel site and enters a search on "Hawaii." The USAad Network also serves ads on this site, and Joe sees an ad for rental cars there. Joe then visits an online bookstore and browses through books about the world's best golf courses. USAad Network serves ads there as well. A week later, Joe visits his favorite online news site, and notices an ad for golf vacation packages in Hawaii. Delighted, he clicks on the ad, which was served by USAad Network. Later, Joe begins to wonder whether it was a coincidence that this particular ad appeared and, if not, how it happened (Federal Trade Commission, 2000b).

The sample online profile illustrates several features of such profiles. First, the profile created for Joe Smith was completely anonymous and did not require any personal information, such as a name, e-mail address, or Social Security number. Obviously, this profile would be more valuable if the system did have personal information because then Joe could be sent e-mail marketing. Second, ad networks do not know who is operating the browser. If other members of Joe's family used the same computer to shop the Web, they would be exposed to golf vacation ads, and Joe could be exposed to ads more appropriate to his wife or children. Third, profiles are usually very imprecise, the result of "best guesses" and just plain guesses. Profiles are built using a product/service scoring system that is not very detailed, and as a result, the profiles tend to be very crude.

In the preceding example, Joe is obviously interested in golf and travel because he intentionally expressed these interests. However, he may have wanted to scuba dive in Hawaii, or visit old friends, not play golf. The profiling system in the example took a leap of faith that a golf vacation in Hawaii is what Joe really wants. Sometimes these guesses work, but there is considerable evidence to suggest that simply knowing Joe made an inquiry about Hawaii would be sufficient to sell him a trip to Hawaii for any of several activities and the USAad Network provided little additional value.

Network advertising firms argue that Web profiling benefits both consumers and businesses. Profiling permits targeting of ads, ensuring that consumers see advertisements mostly for products and services in which they are actually interested. Businesses benefit by not paying for wasted advertising sent to consumers who have no interest in their product or service. The industry argues that by increasing the effectiveness of advertising, more advertising revenues go to the Internet, which in turn subsidizes free content on the Internet. Last, product designers and entrepreneurs benefit by sensing demand for new products and services by examining user searches and profiles.

Critics argue that profiling undermines the expectation of anonymity and privacy that most people have when using the Internet, and change what should be a private experience into one where an individual's every move is recorded. As people become aware that their every move is being watched, they will be far less likely to explore sensitive topics, browse pages, or read about controversial issues. In most cases, the profiling is invisible to users, and even hidden. Consumers are not notified that profiling is occurring. Profiling permits data aggregation on hundreds or even thousands of unrelated sites on the Web. The cookies placed by ad networks are persistent, and they can be set to last days, months, years, or even forever. Their tracking occurs over an extended period of time and resumes each time the individual logs on to the Internet. This clickstream data is used to create profiles that can include hundreds of distinct data fields for each consumer. Associating so-called anonymous profiles with personal information is fairly easy, and companies can change policies quickly without informing the consumer. Some critics believe profiling permits **weblining**—charging some customers more money for products and services based on their profiles. Although the information gathered by network advertisers is often anonymous (non-PII data), in many cases, the profiles derived from tracking consumers' activities on the Web are linked or merged with personally identifiable information. DoubleClick and other advertising network firms have attempted to purchase offline marketing firms that collect offline consumer data for the purpose of matching offline and online behavioral data at the individual level. However, public reaction was so negative that no network advertising firm publicly admits to matching offline PII with online profile data. Nevertheless, client Web sites encourage visitors to register for prizes, benefits, or content access in order to capture personal information such as e-mail addresses and physical addresses. Anonymous behavioral data is far more valuable if it can be linked with offline consumer behavior, e-mail addresses, and postal addresses.

This consumer data can also be combined with data on the consumers' offline purchases, or information collected directly from consumers through surveys and registration forms. As the technology of connection to the Internet for consumers moves away from telephone modems where IP addresses are assigned dynamically,

weblining
charging some customers more money for products and services based on their profiles

and toward static assigned IP addresses used by DSL and cable modems, then connecting anonymous profiles to personal names and e-mail addresses will become easier and more prevalent.

From a privacy protection perspective, the advertising network raises issues about who will see and use the information held by private companies, whether the user profiles will be linked to actual personally identifying information (such as name, Social Security number, and bank and credit accounts), the absence of consumer control over the use of the information, the lack of consumer choice, the absence of consumer notice, and the lack of review and amendment procedures.

The pervasive and largely unregulated collection of personal information online has raised significant fears and opposition among consumers. According to a 2008 survey of 1,105 respondents, 57% said they were uncomfortable with advertisers using browsing history to serve relevant ads,and 54% delete cookies every two to three months. 44% would click a button that said "Reduce unwanted ads" and 42% would sign up for a online registry to ensure advertisers are not able to track browsing behavior. Even worse for advertisers, 87% said that less than 25% of the ads they do see online are relevant. Another study found that over six in 10 U.S. Web searchers do not trust search engines with their information (eMarketer Inc. 2007a). One result of the lack of trust toward online firms and specific fears of privacy invasion is a reduction in online purchases. For instance, one survey found that over 70% of respondents had decided against registering or making a purchase online because those actions required them to provide information that they did not want to divulge. A Gartner survey found that nearly half of online U.S. adults said that concerns about theft of information, data breaches, or Internet-based attacks affected their purchasing, payment, online transaction or e-mail behavior (TRUSTe, 2006; eMarketer, Inc., 2007b). The actual amount of lost sales is unknown, but if 25% of consumers stopped purchasing online, that would add up to a hefty $56 billion in lost sales. If even just 10% of this number turned out to be accurate, that would still be a $22.5 billion loss in sales. A Harris survey in 2008 found that 59% of Internet users were not very comfortable with Web sites that target ads based on browser history or click streams (eMarketer Inc., 2008).

The Internet and e-commerce—as we have seen in previous chapters—strengthen the ability of private firms to collect, store, and analyze personal information at a level never envisioned by privacy thinkers and legislators. With Web technologies, the invasion of individual privacy is low-cost, profitable, and effective.

The Internet and Government Invasions of Privacy: E-commerce Surveillance

Today, the e-commerce behavior, profiles, and transactions of consumers are routinely available to a wide range of government agencies and law enforcement authorities, contributing to rising fears among online consumers, and in many cases, their withdrawal from the online marketplace. While the Internet used to be thought of as impossible for governments to control or monitor, nothing could be actually further from the truth. Law enforcement authorities have long claimed the right under numerous statutes to monitor any form of electronic communication pursuant to a court order and judicial review and based on the reasonable belief that a crime is being committed. This includes the surveillance of consumers engaged in e-commerce. In the case of the Internet, this is accomplished by placing sniffer software and servers at the ISP being used by the target suspect, in a manner similar to pen registers and trap-and-trace devices used for telephone surveillance. The Communications Assistance for Law Enforcement Act (CALEA), the USA PATRIOT Act, the Cyber Security Enhancement Act, and the Homeland Security Act all strengthen the ability of law enforcement agencies to monitor Internet users without their knowledge and, under certain circumstances when life is purportedly at stake, without judicial oversight. In addition, government agencies are among the largest users of private sector commercial data brokers, such as ChoicePoint, Acxiom, Experian, and TransUnion Corporation, that collect a vast amount of information about consumers from various offline and online public sources, such as public records and the telephone directory, and non-public sources, such as "credit header" information from credit bureaus (which typically contains name, aliases, birth date, Social Security number, current and prior addresses, and phone numbers). Information contained in individual reference services' databases ranges from purely identifying information (e.g., name and phone number) to much more extensive data (e.g., driving records, criminal and civil court records, property records, and licensing records). This information can be linked to online behavior information collected from other commercial sources to compile an extensive profile of individual's online and offline behavior (Frackman, Ray, and Martin, 2002; Federal Trade Commission, 1997).

In June 2006, the Justice Department appointed a task force to investigate a proposal that Internet companies retain records that would allow the government to identify which individuals visited certain Web sites and conducted searches using certain terms, and also records about whom users exchange e-mail with, for as long two years. The European Parliament passed similar legislation in December 2005. In 2007, the four major search engines (Google, Yahoo, MSN, and Ask.com) all announced new policies on how long they would retain search information, ranging from 18 months (Google and MSN) to 13 months (Yahoo), while Ask.com announced a new tool, Ask Eraser, that would allow users to block any retention of specific search terms and the user's IP address (Hansell and Lichtblau, 2006; Zeller, 2006; Leidtke, 2007). In September 2008, under pressure from European regulators, Google announced that it would reduce the amount of time it stores IP address on its server logs to 9 months.

Growing privacy concerns in the United states have changed Google's U.S. policy. In 2008 Google reduced its retention period to nine months after which it "anonymizes" data. Other search engines are following Google and reducing their retention. Unfortunately, no one knows what "anonymizing" means.

In April 2008 the European Parliament's Data Protection Working Party called for search engines to set their data retention at six months. Currently, the EU requires search engines to set their data retention limit at 18 months.

Congress, aware of the dangers of unregulated government intrusion into Internet communications, and its threat to e-commerce privacy, created a Privacy and Civil Liberties Oversight Board in the Office of the President in 2004 to ensure anti-terrorism laws do not decimate other privacy protection laws. The Board began meeting in 2006, and issued its first annual report to Congress in April 2007 (Privacy and Civilities Oversight Board, 2007).

LEGAL PROTECTIONS

In the United States, Canada, and Germany, rights to privacy are explicitly granted in, or can be derived from, founding documents such as constitutions, as well as in specific statutes. In England and the United States, there is also protection of privacy in the common law, a body of court decisions involving torts or personal injuries. For instance, in the United States, four privacy-related torts have been defined in court decisions involving claims of injury to individuals caused by other private parties: intrusion on solitude, public disclosure of private facts, publicity placing a person in a false light, and appropriation of a person's name or likeness (mostly concerning celebrities) for a commercial purpose (Laudon, 1996). In the United States, the claim to privacy against government intrusion is protected primarily by the First Amendment guarantees of freedom of speech and association, the Fourth Amendment protections against unreasonable search and seizure of one's personal documents or home, and the Fourteenth Amendment's guarantee of due process.

In addition to common law and the Constitution, there are both federal laws and state laws that protect individuals against government intrusion and in some cases define privacy rights vis-à-vis private organizations such as financial, educational, and media institutions (cable television and video rentals) (see **Table 8.4**).

Informed Consent

informed consent
consent given with knowledge of all material facts needed to make a rational decision

The concept of **informed consent** (defined as consent given with knowledge of all material facts needed to make a rational decision) also plays an important role in protecting privacy. In the United States, business firms (and government agencies) can gather transaction information generated in the marketplace and then use that information for other marketing purposes, without obtaining the informed consent of the individual. For instance, in the United States, if a Web shopper purchases books about baseball at a site that belongs to an advertising network such as DoubleClick, a cookie can be placed on the consumer's hard drive and used by other member sites to sell the shopper sports clothing without the explicit permission or even knowledge of the user. This online preference information may also be linked with personally identifying information. In Europe, this would be illegal. A business in Europe cannot use marketplace transaction information for any purpose other than supporting the current transaction, unless of course it obtains the individual's consent in writing or by filling out an on-screen form.

opt-in
requires an affirmative action by the consumer to allow collection and use of consumer information

There are traditionally two models for informed consent: opt-in and opt-out. The **opt-in** model requires an affirmative action by the consumer to allow collection and use of information. For instance, using opt-in, consumers would first be asked if they approved of the collection and use of information, and then directed to check a

TABLE 8.4	FEDERAL AND STATE PRIVACY LAWS

NAME	DESCRIPTION
GENERAL FEDERAL PRIVACY LAWS	
Freedom of Information Act of 1966	Gives people the right to inspect information about themselves held in government files; also allows other individuals and organizations the right to request disclosure of government records based on the public's right to know.
Privacy Act of 1974, as amended	Regulates the federal government's collection, use, and disclosure of data collected by federal agencies. Gives individuals a right to inspect and correct records.
Electronic Communications Privacy Act of 1986	Makes conduct that would infringe on the security of electronic communications illegal.
Computer Matching and Privacy Protection Act of 1988	Regulates computerized matching of files held by different government agencies.
Computer Security Act of 1987	Makes conduct that would infringe on the security of computer-based files illegal.
Driver's Privacy Protection Act of 1994	Limits access to personal information maintained by state motor vehicle departments to those with legitimate business purposes. Also gives drivers the option to prevent disclosure of driver's license information to marketers and the general public.
E-Government Act of 2002	Regulates the collection and use of personal information by federal agencies.
FEDERAL PRIVACY LAWS AFFECTING PRIVATE INSTITUTIONS	
Fair Credit Reporting Act of 1970	Regulates the credit investigating and reporting industry. Gives people the right to inspect credit records if they have been denied credit and provides procedures for correcting information.
Family Educational Rights and Privacy Act of 1974	Requires schools and colleges to give students and their parents access to student records and to allow them to challenge and correct information; limits disclosure of such records to third parties.
Right to Financial Privacy Act of 1978	Regulates the financial industry's use of personal financial records; establishes procedures that federal agencies must follow to gain access to such records.
Privacy Protection Act of 1980	Prohibits government agents from conducting unannounced searches of press offices and files if no one in the office is suspected of committing a crime.
Cable Communications Policy Act of 1984	Regulates the cable industry's collection and disclosure of information concerning subscribers
Video Privacy Protection Act of 1988	Prevents disclosure of a person's video rental records without court order or consent.
Child Online Privacy Protection Act (1998)	Prohibits deceptive practices in connection with collection, use and/or disclosure of personal information from and about children on the Internet.
Financial Modernization Act (Graham-Leach-Bliley Act) (1999)	Requires financial institutions to inform consumers of their privacy policies and permits consumers some control over their records.
Health Insurance Portability and Accountability Act of 1996 (HIPAA)	Requires health care providers and insurers and other third parties to promulgate privacy policies to consumers and establishes due process procedures.

TABLE 8.4	FEDERAL AND STATE PRIVACY LAWS (CONT'D)
NAME	DESCRIPTION
SELECTED STATE PRIVACY LAWS	
Online Privacy Policies	The California Online Privacy Protection Act of 2003 was the first state law in the United States requiring owners of commercial Web sites or online services to post a privacy policy. The policy must, among other things, identify the categories of PII collected about site visitors and categories of third parties with whom the information may be shared. Failure to comply can result in a civil suit for unfair business practices. Nebraska and Pennsylvania prohibit false and misleading statements in online privacy policies. At least 16 states require government Web sites to establish privacy policies or procedures or incorporate machine-readable privacy policies into their Web sites.
Spyware Legislation	A number of states, including California, Utah, Arizona, Arkansas, and Virginia, among others, have passed laws that make the installation of spyware on a user's computer without consent, illegal.
Disclosure of Security Breaches	In 2002, California enacted legislation that requires state agencies or businesses that own or license computer data with personal information to notify state residents if they experience a security breach involving that information; over 22 other states have enacted similar legislation
Privacy of Personal Information	Two states, Nevada and Minnesota, require ISPs to keep their customers' PII private unless the customer consents to disclose the information. Minnesota also requires ISPs to get permission from subscribers before disclosing information about subscribers' online surfing habits
Data Encryption	In October 2007, Nevada passed the first law that requires encryption for the transmission of customer personal information. The law takes effect October 1, 2008.

opt-out

the default is to collect information unless the consumer takes an affirmative action to prevent the collection of data

selection box if they agreed. Otherwise, the default is not to approve the collection of data. In the **opt-out** model, the default is to collect information unless the consumer takes an affirmative action to prevent the collection of data by checking a box, or by filling out a form.

Until recently, many U.S e-commerce companies rejected the concept of informed consent and instead simply published their information use policy on their site. U.S. businesses argue that informing consumers about how the information will be used is sufficient to obtain the users' informed consent. Most U.S. sites that offer informed consent make opting in the default option, and require users to go to special pages to request to opt-out of promotional campaigns. Some sites have an opt-out selection box at the very bottom of their information policy statements where the consumer is unlikely to see it. Privacy advocates argue that many information/privacy policy statements on U.S. Web sites are obscure, difficult to read, and legitimate just about any use of personal information. For instance, Yahoo's privacy policy begins with the statement that "Yahoo! takes your privacy seriously."

It then states that it "does not rent, sell, or share personal information about you with other people or non-affiliated companies." However, there are a number of exceptions that significantly weaken this statement. For instance, Yahoo may share the information with "trusted partners," which could be anyone that Yahoo does business with, although perhaps not a company that the user might choose to do business with.

The FTC's Fair Information Practices Principles

In the United States, the FTC has taken the lead in conducting research on online privacy and recommending legislation to Congress. The FTC is a cabinet-level agency charged with promoting the efficient functioning of the marketplace by protecting consumers from unfair or deceptive practices and increasing consumer choice by promoting competition. In addition to reports and recommendations, the FTC enforces existing legislation by suing corporations it believes are in violation of federal fair trade laws.

In 1995, the FTC began a series of investigations of online privacy based on its belief that online invasion of privacy potentially involved deceit and unfair behavior. In 1998, the FTC issued its Fair Information Practice (FIP) principles, on which it has based its assessments and recommendations for online privacy. **Table 8.5** describes these principles. Two of the five are designated as basic, "core" principles that must be present to protect privacy, whereas the other practices are less central. The FTC's FIP principles restate and strengthen in a form suitable to deal with online privacy the Fair Information Practices doctrine developed in 1973 by a government study group (U.S. Department of Health, Education and Welfare, 1973).

The FTC's FIP principles set the ground rules for what constitutes due process privacy protection procedures at e-commerce and all other Web sites—including government and nonprofit Web sites—in the United States.

At this point, the FTC's FIP principles are guidelines, not laws. They have stimulated private firms and industry associations to develop their own private guidelines (discussed next). However, the FTC's FIP guidelines are being used as the basis of new legislation. The most important online privacy legislation to date that was directly influenced by the FTC's FIP principles is the Children's Online Privacy Protection Act (COPPA) (1998), which requires Web sites to obtain parental permission before collecting information on children under 13 years of age.

In July 2000, the FTC recommended legislation to Congress to protect online consumer privacy from the threat posed by advertising networks. **Table 8.6** on page 505 summarizes the Commission's recommendations. The FTC profiling recommendations significantly strengthen the FIP principles of notification and choice, while also including restrictions on information that may be collected.[1] Although the FTC

---

[1] Much general privacy legislation affecting government, e.g., the Privacy Act of 1974, precludes the government from collecting information on political and social behavior of citizens. The FTC restrictions are significant because they are the FTC's first effort at limiting the collection of certain information.

TABLE 8.5	FEDERAL TRADE COMMISSION'S FAIR INFORMATION PRACTICE PRINCIPLES
Notice/Awareness (Core principle)	Sites must disclose their information practices before collecting data. Includes identification of collector, uses of data, other recipients of data, nature of collection (active/inactive), voluntary or required, consequences of refusal, and steps taken to protect confidentiality, integrity, and quality of the data
Choice/Consent (Core principle)	There must be a choice regime in place allowing consumers to choose how their information will be used for secondary purposes other than supporting the transaction, including internal use and transfer to third parties. Opt-in/Opt-out must be available.
Access/Participation	Consumers should be able to review and contest the accuracy and completeness of data collected about them in a timely, inexpensive process.
Security	Data collectors must take reasonable steps to assure that consumer information is accurate and secure from unauthorized use.
Enforcement	There must be in place a mechanism to enforce FIP principles. This can involve self-regulation, legislation giving consumers legal remedies for violations, or federal statutes and regulation.

SOURCE: Based on data from Federal Trade Commission, 1998; 2000a.

supports industry efforts at self-regulation, it nevertheless recommended legislation to ensure that all Web sites using network advertising and all network advertisers comply. To date, however, Congress has not passed such legislation.

In November 2007, the FTC held a two-day workshop on online advertising, behavioral targeting, and online privacy. Consumer privacy groups have asked for the institution of a "Do Not Track" list similar to the FTC's "Do Not Call" telemarketing list, that would permit people to more easily opt out of behavioral tracking programs, as well as disclosure notices that tracking is occurring, and the ability for consumers to view and edit any profiles about themselves that ad networks build. The online advertising industry, not surprisingly, believes that FTC regulation would stifle innovation in the industry. Although at least one FTC member suggested at the conference that rules about privacy policies might need to be established, and that the FTC needed to increase its scrutiny of the online targeting, whether any new FTC regulations will result from these efforts in the near future is unknown (Story, 2007b).

In 2008, the growing fear of widespread behavioral targeting, strengthened by the buyouts of the largest advertising networks by search engines (e.g. Google's purchase of DoubleClick), led to a Congressional hearings in June. Industry leaders like Google and Microsoft called for new privacy legislation which would legitimate their behavioral targeting programs. Neither Congress or the FTC is willing to pass new legislation at this time. In August, 2008, four legislators sent a letter to thirty-three Internet companies,

TABLE 8.6	FTC RECOMMENDATIONS REGARDING ONLINE PROFILING
PRINCIPLE	DESCRIPTION OF RECOMMENDATION
Notice	Complete transparency to user by providing disclosure and choice options on the host Web site. "Robust" notice for PII (time/place of collection; before collection begins). Clear and conspicuous notice for non-PII.
Choice	Opt-in for PII, opt-out for non-PII. No conversion of non-PII to PII without consent. Opt-out from any or all network advertisers from a single page provided by the host Web site.
Access	Reasonable provisions to allow inspection and correction.
Security	Reasonable efforts to secure information from loss, misuse, or improper access.
Enforcement	Done by independent third parties, such as seal programs and accounting firms.
Restricted collection	Advertising networks will not collect information about sensitive financial or medical topics, sexual behavior or sexual orientation, or use Social Security numbers for profiling.

including the top search engines, requesting detailed explanations of their privacy policies (Clifford, 2008).

The European Directive on Data Protection

In Europe, privacy protection is much stronger than it is in the United States. In the United States, private organizations and businesses are permitted to use PII gathered in commercial transactions for other business purposes without the prior consent of the consumer (so-called secondary uses of PII). In the United States, there is no federal agency charged with enforcing privacy law. Instead, privacy law is enforced largely through self-regulation by businesses, and by individuals who must sue agencies or companies in court to recover damages. This is expensive and rarely done. The European approach to privacy protection is more comprehensive and regulatory in nature. European countries do not allow business firms to use PII without the prior consent of consumers. They enforce their privacy laws by creating data protection agencies to pursue complaints brought by citizens and to actively enforce privacy laws.

On October 25, 1998, the European Commission's Directive on Data Protection went into effect, standardizing and broadening privacy protection in the European Union (EU) nations. The Directive is based on the Fair Information Practices doctrine, but extends the control individuals can exercise over their personal information. The Directive requires companies to inform people when they collect information about them and to disclose how it will be stored and used. Customers must provide their informed consent before any company can legally use data about them, and they have the right to access that information, correct it, and request that no further data be collected. Further, the Directive prohibits the transfer of PII to organizations or countries that do not have similarly strong privacy protection policies. This means that data collected in Europe by American business firms cannot be transferred or processed in the United States (which has weaker privacy protection laws). This would potentially interfere with a $350 billion annual trade flow between the United States and Europe.

safe harbor

a private self-regulating policy and enforcement mechanism that meets the objectives of government regulators and legislation but does not involve government regulation or enforcement

The Department of Commerce, working with the European Commission, developed a safe harbor framework for U.S. firms. A **safe harbor** is a private self-regulating policy and enforcement mechanism that meets the objectives of government regulators and legislation, but does not involve government regulation or enforcement. The government plays a role in certifying safe harbors, however. Organizations that decide to participate in the safe harbor program must develop policies that meet European standards, and they must publicly sign on to a Web-based register maintained by the Department of Commerce. Enforcement occurs in the United States and relies to a large extent on self-policing and regulation, backed up by government enforcement of fair trade statutes. For more information on the safe harbor procedures and the EU Data Directive, see www.export.gov/safeharbor.

PRIVATE INDUSTRY SELF-REGULATION

The online industry in the United States has historically opposed privacy legislation, arguing that industry can do a better job of protecting privacy than government. However, individual firms like AOL, Yahoo and Google have adopted policies on their own in an effort to address the concerns of the public about personal privacy on the Internet. The online industry formed the Online Privacy Alliance (OPA) in 1998 to encourage self-regulation in part as a reaction to growing public concerns and the threat of legislation being proposed by FTC and privacy advocacy groups.

Private industry in the United States has created the idea of safe harbors from government regulation. For instance, COPPA includes a provision enabling industry groups or others to submit for the FTC's approval self-regulatory guidelines that implement the protections of the FIP principles and FTC rules. In May 2001, the FTC approved the TRUSTe Internet privacy protection program under the terms of COPPA as a safe harbor.[2]

OPA has developed a set of privacy guidelines that members are required to implement. The primary focus of industry efforts has been the development of online "seals" that attest to the privacy policies on a site. The Better Business Bureau (BBB), TRUSTe, WebTrust, and major accounting firms—among them PricewaterhouseCoopers' BetterWeb—have established seals for Web sites. To display a seal, Web site operators must conform to certain privacy principles, a complaint resolution process, and monitoring by the seal originator. Around 2,250 sites now display the TRUSTe seal, and over 45,000 display the BBB's Reliability seal.

[2]Another longstanding industry group with a safe harbor program for children online is CARU (Children's Advertising Review Unit), founded in 1974 as the advertising industry's self-regulation program for the protection of children.

Nevertheless, online privacy seal programs have had a limited impact on Web privacy practices. Critics argue that the seal programs are not particularly effective in safeguarding privacy. For these reasons, the FTC has not deemed the seal programs as "safe harbors" yet (with the exception of TRUSTe's children's privacy seal under COPPA), and the agency continues to push for legislation to enforce privacy protection principles.

The advertising network industry has also formed an industry association, the Network Advertising Initiative (NAI), to develop privacy policies. NAI member companies include Advertising.com, Atlas (part of aQuantive), DoubleClick, Revenue Science, Tacoda, and 24/7 Real Media. The NAI has developed a set of privacy principles in conjunction with the FTC. The NAI policies have two objectives: to offer consumers a chance to opt-out of advertising network programs (including e-mail campaigns), and to provide consumers redress from abuses. In order to opt-out, the NAI has created a Web site—Networkadvertising.org—where consumers can use a global opt-out feature to prevent network advertising agencies from placing their cookies on a user's computer. If a consumer has a complaint, the NAI has a link to the Truste.org Web site where the complaints can be filed (Network Advertising Initiative, 2008). Consumers still receive Internet advertising just as before, but the ads will not be targetted to their browsing behavior.

Responding to public concerns about tracking people online, AOL established an opt-out policy which allows users of its site to not be tracked. Yahoo follows the NAI guidelines and also allows opt out for tracking and web beacons (Web bugs). Google has reduced retention time for tracking data.

In general, industry efforts at self-regulation in online privacy have not succeeded in reducing American fears of privacy invasion during online transactions, or in reducing the level of privacy invasion. At best, self-regulation has offered consumers notice about whether a privacy policy exists, but usually says little about the actual use of the information, does not offer consumers a chance to see and correct the information or control its use in any significant way, offers no promises for the security of that information, and offers no enforcement mechanism (Hoofnagle, 2005). At the same time, the FTC and Congress point to efforts at self-regulation as a reason for not legislating in this area. Read *Insight on Business: Chief Privacy Officers* to see a different approach to industry self-regulation.

PRIVACY ADVOCACY GROUPS

There are a number of privacy advocacy groups on the Web that monitor developments in privacy. Some of these sites are industry-supported, while others rely on private foundations and contributions. Some of the better-known sites are listed in **Table 8.7**.

TECHNOLOGICAL SOLUTIONS

There are a number of privacy-enhancing technologies for protecting user privacy during interactions with Web sites that have been developed (see **Table 8.8**). Most of these tools emphasize security—the ability of individuals to protect their communications and files

TABLE 8.7	PRIVACY ADVOCACY GROUPS
ADVOCACY GROUP	FOCUS
Epic.org (Electronic Privacy Information Center)	Washington-based watch-dog group
Privacyinternational.org	Tracks international privacy developments
Cdt.org (Center for Democracy and Technology)	Foundation- and business-supported group with a legislative focus
Privacy.org	Clearinghouse sponsored by EPIC and Privacy International
Privacyrights.org	Educational clearinghouse
Privacyalliance.org	Industry-supported clearinghouse

TABLE 8.8	TECHNOLOGICAL PROTECTIONS FOR ONLINE PRIVACY	
TECHNOLOGY	PRODUCTS	PROTECTION
Spyware blockers	Spyware Doctor, ZoneAlarm, Ad-Aware and Spybot—Search and Destroy (Spybot-S&D) (freeware)	Detects and removes spyware and adware, keyloggers and other malware
Pop-up blockers	Browsers: Firefox, Internet Explorer 6.0 SP2 and 7, Safari, Opera Toolbars: Google, Yahoo, MSN Add-on programs: STOPzilla, Adblock, NoAds	Prevents calls to ad servers that push pop-up, pop-under and leave behind ads; restricts downloading of images at user request
Secure e-mail	ZL Technologies; SafeMessage.com; Hushmail.com; Pretty Good Privacy (PGP)	E-mail and document encryption
Anonymous remailers	W3-Anonymous Remailer; Jack B Nymble; Java Anonymous Proxy	Send e-mail without trace
Anonymous surfing	Freedom Websecure; Anonymizer.com; Tor; GhostSurf	Surf without a trace
Cookie managers	CookieCrusher, and most browsers	Prevents client computer from accepting cookies
Disk/file erasing programs	Mutilate File Wiper; Eraser; DiskVac 2.0	Completely erases hard drive and floppy files
Policy generators	OECD Privacy Policy Generator	Automates the development of an OECD privacy compliance policy
Privacy Policy Reader	P3P	Software for automating the communication of privacy policies to users
Public Key Encryption	PGP Desktop 9.0	Program that encrypts your mail and documents

INSIGHT ON BUSINESS

CHIEF PRIVACY OFFICERS

How can you tell if your own corporate practices actually conform to the privacy policy stated on your Web site? How can your business keep track of all the new privacy legislation and changes in European policies? The answer for many corporations is to create an executive position—chief privacy officer (CPO). The position is a relatively new one that firms first started to create about 10 years ago, but today is one of fastest growing in corporate management. Many firms, such as IBM, AT&T, Eastman Kodak, DoubleClick, New York Life, ChoicePoint, Marriott International and many others, have added this position to senior management ranks, and it is becoming more and more common in the health care, financial services, technology, and consumer goods industries, in part due to growing regulatory requirements with respect to data privacy.

What does a CPO do? The job has several aspects. Often, a CPO's first job is to plan and then implement a privacy plan for the firm to follow. Once a plan is in place, it needs to be enforced, and monitored, and the company's business units and employees may need to be educated about the plan and the importance of privacy. For instance, at Marriott International, Chris Zoladz, vice president of information protection and privacy, notes that "Good privacy is good business." When Marriott marketing executives proposed personalizing the information that appears on the hotel chain's Web site so that it was customized based on personal information collected from guests as part of the reservation process, Zoladz got involved to make sure the information was used properly.

Another job is helping the company avoid privacy "landmines," which are mistakes in policy or technology that, had any one thought about it, would obviously be embarrassing to the company because of the potential for a storm of protest from privacy protection groups. For instance, IBM's CPO proactively led the fight within the company to ban the use of genetic data in the employment recruiting and promotion process. AOL proactively changed its privacy policy for the first time since 1998 by stopping the practice of selling mailing lists to retailers, and stopped using information from advertising networks and non-AOL sites to customize ads. In other cases, in the absence of a CPO, disaster is possible. U.S. Bancorp decided to sell personal financial data to a direct-marketing company in violation of its own stated policies. This cost Bancorp $3 million in a legal settlement in Minnesota. Real Networks had to apologize to users and change its data collection policies after a disclosure that the company's RealJukebox Internet music software captured data about users' preferences. A string of data losses, criminal intrusions, and accidents at data brokerage firms such as ChoicePoint and Reed Elsevier's LexisNexis unit resulted in the diversion and theft of hundreds of thousands of complete personal profiles. This in turn has led to Congressional investigations, fines, and the threat of restrictive legislation for the entire data brokerage industry.

The new corporate emphasis on privacy has also created a new business for the big accounting firm PricewaterhouseCoopers as one part of its Global Risk Management Solutions. PWC has

(continued)

conducted hundreds of privacy audits. Companies are taking this issue very seriously because data theft or loss and invasions of privacy directly threaten the brand names of firms. Privacy audits identify the risks that firms face and prescribe corrective actions with a view to avoiding class-action suits, Internet-based protests, and shareholder enmity. And what do the auditors find? About 80% of the companies audited by PWC do not follow their own stated privacy policies. Most of the time this is the result of poor training and human error.

After Expedia completed a privacy audit led by PWC, it changed its information collection policy from opt-out to opt-in. Now Expedia's customers have to actively click a button and ask to be informed of new offers from the travel site. The result is that far fewer customers ask to unsubscribe from mailing solicitations. Expedia executives believe trust and privacy are major concerns of their customers, and anything they can do to enhance trust is good for their business.

What do CPOs worry about? They often have a hard time with their own employees taking privacy seriously and changing policies to cope with the risks. In the case of ChoicePoint's loss of 145,000 personal dossiers to criminals posing as real companies, ChoicePoint has hired a CPO who reports directly to the Board of Directors and the CEO, and has changed its procedures for verifying the authenticity of people claiming to be legitimate businesses. Prior to this breach of its database, ChoicePoint did not verify the authenticity or legitimacy of people claiming a business need to access their databases.

Perhaps the biggest challenge facing CPOs is federal legislation that requires companies to inform consumers of their privacy policies, and the trend away from a pro-active, pro-consumer privacy officer and towards a narrow legalistic emphasis on compliance. The Graham-Leach-Bliley Act of 1999 requires all financial service firms to inform consumers of their privacy policies. This results in tens of millions of pamphlets being sent to consumers, often written in confusing legal jargon that few can understand. HIPAA, designed to make the transfer of records among health care agencies more efficient as well as to safeguard the privacy of those records, has also unleashed a flood of privacy pamphlets that few can understand. HIPAA requires that all health care providers and insurers have a privacy officer, even in small medical practices with seven doctors. Professional associations such as the International Association of Privacy Professionals openly worry that legalistic compliance with federal laws fails to take into account the real interests of consumers and the strategic implications for the firm.

SOURCES: "Q&A: Jules Polonetsky, Chief Privacy Officer, AOL" by Kenneth Corbin, Internetnews.com, May 12, 2008; "Gartner for IT Leaders Overview: The Chief Privacy Officer," by Arabella Hallawell and Paul E. Proctor, October 1, 2007; "Why Your Company Needs a Chief Privacy Officer," by Cara Garretson, *Network World*, May 22, 2007; "Shocking Number of Organizations without Chief Privacy Officer," Hr.com, January 26, 2007; "IBM Policy Bars Use of Gene Data in Employment," by Charles Forelle, *Wall Street Journal*, October 11, 2005; "AOL Recasts Privacy Policy," by Colin C. Haley, Internetnews.com, October 7, 2005; "Internal Privacy Audits Can Provide Companies With Excellent Value," by Jacqueline Kloske and John Kellenberger, *The Legal Intelligencer*, July 6, 2005; "What the Creation of a Chief Privacy Officer Means for CIOs," *IT BusinessEdge*, February 16, 2005.

from illegitimate snoopers. This is just one element of privacy. The other is the development of private and public policies that enable consumers to control the collection and use of information that is gathered in the course of market transactions.

The growth in consumer use of spyware blockers, cookie blockers, and pop-up controls on browsers threatens the online advertising industry that relies on cookies, placed mostly by advertising networks, although thus far, it has not appreciably reduced reliance on these techniques by advertisers.

Perhaps the most comprehensive technological privacy protection effort is **P3P**, the **Platform for Privacy Preferences** sponsored by W3C (the World Wide Web Consortium—an international, nonprofit, industry-supported Web standards group). P3P is a standard designed to communicate a Web site's privacy policy to Internet users, and to compare that policy to the user's own preferences, or to other standards such as the FTC's FIP principles or the EU Data Protection Directive. P3P does not establish privacy standards and relies on government and industry to develop them. The basic idea behind P3P and subsequent efforts like TAMI (MIT) and PRIME (Europe) is to allow individuals to express their privacy preferences in a machine readable form that all Web sites can universally understand.

P3P works through a user's Web browser. On the server side, P3P enables sites to translate their privacy policies into a standardized machine-readable XML format that can be read either by the browser or by installed software plug-ins. On the user client side, the browser automatically fetches a Web site's privacy policy and informs the user. **Figure 8.2(A)** illustrates how this could work.

P3P (Platform for Privacy Preferences)
a standard designed to communicate to Internet users a Web site's privacy policy, and to compare that policy to the user's own preferences, or to other standards such as the FTC's FIP guidelines or the EU Data Protection Directive

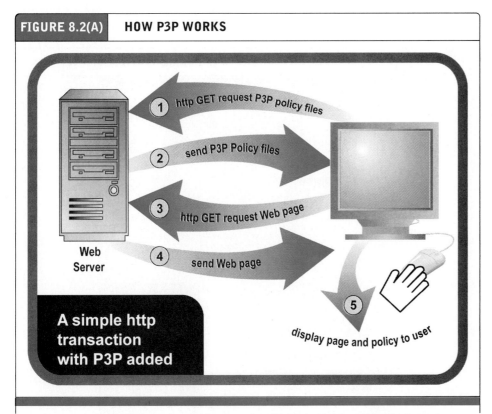

FIGURE 8.2(A)   HOW P3P WORKS

1 http GET request P3P policy files
2 send P3P Policy files
3 http GET request Web page
4 send Web page
5 display page and policy to user

Web Server

A simple http transaction with P3P added

The Platform for Privacy Preferences enables the automatic communication of privacy policies between e-commerce sites and consumers.

SOURCE: W3C Platform for Privacy Preferences Initiative, 2003.

P3P is now built into browsers such as Firefox and Internet Explorer 6.0/7.0. By using a slider, users can set the privacy policy they desire, and their browser will automatically read the privacy policy of sites they visit, and warn them when a site does not match their preferences (see **Figure 8.2 (B)**). According to a Carnegie Mellon study, about 10% of Web sites overall, and more than 20% of e-commerce sites, now feature P3P, as well as about one-third of the top 100 Web sites (eMarketer, Inc., 2007c).

While P3P is one step in the direction of increasing consumer awareness and understanding of Web site privacy, it fails to achieve other goals of fair information policies such as limits on what information is collected, the use of personal information, user control of over personal information, security, and enforcement of privacy rights. In this sense, it has failed to increase the consumer's sense of trust when shopping online. Most users simply leave the default settings for P3P at "medium," not knowing exactly what this means (Van Kirk, 2005).

Insight on Technology: The Privacy Tug of War: Advertisers vs. Consumers describes some other new technologies being used to both invade and protect privacy.

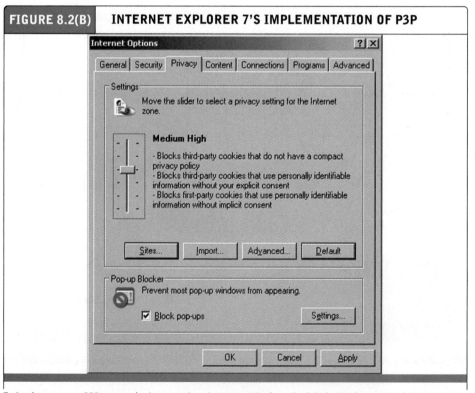

FIGURE 8.2(B)   INTERNET EXPLORER 7'S IMPLEMENTATION OF P3P

To implement your P3P personal privacy settings in Internet Explorer 7, click the Tools command, then Internet Options. Then click the Privacy tab in the Internet Options dialog box.

INSIGHT ON TECHNOLOGY

THE PRIVACY TUG OF WAR: ADVERTISERS VS. CONSUMERS

We are in a technological tug of war between technologies that make invading customer privacy very easy versus other technologies that make protecting privacy easier. On the privacy invasion side, Experian links Web sites to its database and provides the names and addresses of visitors to the sites in real time. Other companies such as Acxiom combine offline and online purchasing and behavioral data into one central database. In October 2007, Acxiom launched a new service, Relevance-X, that draws on that database to determine which online ads to show. MySpace has developed its HyperTargeting ad program, which scours user profiles for interests and then delivers related ads; In November, 2007, Facebook introduced Beacon, an advertising system that broadcast members' activities on other Web sites (what you purchased) to your friends on Facebook. Beacon was launched with the support of forty other Web sites fromm Cocal Cola to . Beacon created a fire storm of resistance from Facebook members, and privacy groups. By December, 2007, Facebook CEO, Mark Zuckerberg, apologized to Facebook members and changed the Beacon program so that users needed to explicitly approve of their activities being shared with others. In August, 2008, Facebook was sued in a class action suit for violating several federal and state laws which prohibit the unauthorized release of personal information. Currently, Beacon requires users to opt-in to the program.

Meanwhile, you have to be very careful not to open e-mail attachments or click on a promise of "instant rewards" on a Web site lest you accidentally download and install a spyware or adware program that will either be used to track your every keystroke or, more benignly, to swamp your screen with ads you never wanted to see in the first place.

How do the advertisers justify their intrusions into our private use of the Internet? The answer is profoundly interesting. Here's the idea, according to senior executives at advertising networks such as DoubleClick: the implicit bargain underlying the "free" Internet is that consumers get content because they are looking at ads. Never mind that you paid around $1,000 for your computer system, and $20–$50 monthly for Internet service. Take away the ads, and some other way will have to be found to pay for what you get on the Internet. The other main rationale behind all these intrusive behaviors is marketing efficiency and effectiveness: the more advertisers know about you, the more they can customize and personalize the advertising to exactly what you are looking for at right time, and, of course, the more they can charge their customers, the firms that pay for the advertising. Online advertisers believe consumers are saying, "Take my privacy, but please send the content."

The problem is that most consumers don't really accept this deal. It's possible that the advertisers don't know the consumer very well. An industry-backed survey of over 1,000 Web users found that only 14% said they liked giving information to Web sites in order to receive customized content, and 71% said they disliked it but did so only if necessary to obtain content or information. Another survey found that 41% said that, in the past six months, they had provided inaccurate information to Web sites that required personal information which respondents did not want to share. Consumers seem to be saying, "Send the content, but let me keep my privacy!" While some studies suggest that many teenagers

(continued)

and young adults do not care as much about privacy as older adults, privacy experts believe that this is because they do not understand how much information is being gathered about them.

On the privacy protection side, there are a great many more tools available to consumers than just a few years ago. Admittedly, P3P, an industry-sponsored effort to provide users some choice in privacy by making them aware of Web site privacy policies, has not been too successful. But ISPs and independent software companies now provide a host of tools that work wonders and are easy to use. AOL recently announced that it would offer a "Do Not Track" service that will link consumers directly to opt-out lists offered by the large advertising networks. The open source browser Firefox and Internet Explorer 6.0/7 have effective pop-up and image blockers. Google, Yahoo, MSN, and AOL also offer toolbars that provide similar help. Adoption rates of cookie blockers and anti-spyware software are increasing as software makers such as Symantec make them available as a part of their software suites that install automatically. For instance, a recent

survey found that anti-virus, anti-spyware, and firewall software are used by over 80% of U.S. adult Internet users, and that over two-thirds had configured their browser or operating system to block pop-ups, reject cookies or block specific Web sites. Even if these estimates are off by 50%, a significant number of ads are not actually being shown to consumers.

All these consumer self-help activities have traditional Web advertisers worried. What if consumers rejected the idea of pop-up ads, tracking their behavior, and storing all this information about them? What if consumers did not buy into the "free Internet with ads" deal? What if 50% of Internet users adopted ISP-provided privacy protection or bought their equivalents on the market? While Internet advertisers have pretty much blocked effective legislation in Washington that would preserve privacy, and while their industry associations have quite clearly failed to bring about meaningful self-regulation, the market has responded by providing consumers with some powerful tools for protecting their own privacy.

SOURCES: "Brave New World of Digital Intimacy," by Clive Thompson, The New York Times, September 5, 2008; "Facebook Retreats on Online Tracking," By Louise Story and Brad Stone, The New York Times, November 30, 2007; "Are Facebooks Social Ads Illegal?", by Saul Hansell, New York Times, November 8, 2007; "Tracking of Web Use by Marketers Gains Favor," by Louise Story, New York Times, November 5, 2007; "The Higher Value of Eyeballs," by Louise Story, New York Times, November 5, 2007; "AOL's 'Do Not Track' Effect," by Ben Macklin, eMarketer, Inc., November 3, 2007; "Privacy Groups Seek 'Do Not Track' Web List," Reuters, November 1, 2007; "F.T.C. to Review Online Ads and Privacy," by Louise Story, New York Times, November 1, 2007; "Online Privacy? For Young People, That's Old-School," by Janet Kornbum, USA Today, October 22, 2007; "Firm Mines Offline Data to Target Online Ads," by Kevin J. Delaney and Emily Steel, Wall Street Journal, October 17, 2007;

8.3 INTELLECTUAL PROPERTY RIGHTS

Congress shall have the power to "promote the progress of science and useful arts, by securing for limited times to authors and inventors the exclusive right to their respective writings and discoveries."
—Article I, Section 8, Constitution of the United States, 1788.

Next to privacy, the most controversial ethical, social, and political issue related to e-commerce is the fate of intellectual property rights. Intellectual property encompasses all the tangible and intangible products of the human mind. As a general rule, in the United States, the creator of intellectual property owns it. For instance, if you personally create an e-commerce site, it belongs entirely to you, and you have exclusive rights to use this "property" in any lawful way you see fit. But the Internet potentially changes things. Once intellectual works become digital, it becomes difficult to control access, use, distribution, and copying. These are precisely the areas that intellectual property seeks to control.

Digital media differ from books, periodicals, and other media in terms of ease of replication, transmission, and alteration; difficulty in classifying a software work as a program, book, or even music; compactness—making theft easy; and difficulty in establishing uniqueness. Before widespread use of the Internet, copies of software, books, magazine articles, or films had to be stored on physical media, such as paper, computer disks, or videotape, creating some hurdles to distribution.

The Internet technically permits millions of people to make perfect digital copies of various works—from music to plays, poems, and journal articles—and then to distribute them nearly cost-free to hundreds of millions of Web users. The proliferation of innovation has occurred so rapidly that few entrepreneurs have stopped to consider who owns the patent on a business technique or method their site is using. The spirit of the Web has been so free-wheeling that many entrepreneurs ignored trademark law and register domain names that can easily be confused with another company's registered trademarks. In short, the Internet has demonstrated the potential for destroying traditional conceptions and implementations of intellectual property law developed over the last two centuries.

The major ethical issue related to e-commerce and intellectual property concerns how we (both as individuals and as business professionals) should treat property that belongs to others. From a social point of view, the main questions are: Is there continued value in protecting intellectual property in the Internet age? In what ways is society better off, or worse off, for having the concept of property apply to intangible ideas? Should society make certain technology illegal just because it has an adverse impact on some intellectual property owners? From a political perspective, we need to ask how the Internet and e-commerce can be regulated or governed to protect the institution of intellectual property while at the same time encouraging the growth of e-commerce and the Internet.

TYPES OF INTELLECTUAL PROPERTY PROTECTION

There are three main types of intellectual property protection: copyright, patent, and trademark law. In the United States, the development of intellectual property law begins in the U.S. Constitution in 1788, which mandated Congress to devise a system of laws to promote "the progress of science and the useful arts." Congress passed the first copyright law in 1790 to protect original written works for a period of 14 years, with a 14-year renewal if the author was still alive. Since then, the idea of copyright has been extended to include music, films, translations, photographs, and most recently (1998), the designs of vessels under 200 feet (Fisher, 1999). The copyright law has been amended (mostly extended) 11 times in the last 40 years.

The goal of intellectual property law is to balance two competing interests—the public and the private. The public interest is served by the creation and distribution of inventions, works of art, music, literature, and other forms of intellectual expression. The private interest is served by rewarding people for creating these works through the creation of a time-limited monopoly granting exclusive use to the creator.

Maintaining this balance of interests is always challenged by the invention of new technologies. In general, the information technologies of the last century—from radio and television to CD-ROMs, DVDs, and the Internet—have at first tended to weaken the protections afforded by intellectual property law. Owners of intellectual property have often but not always been successful in pressuring Congress and the courts to strengthen the intellectual property laws to compensate for any technological threat, and even to extend protection for longer periods of time and to entirely new areas of expression. In the case of the Internet and e-commerce technologies, once again, intellectual property rights are severely challenged. In the next few sections, we discuss the significant developments in each area: copyright, patent, and trademark.

COPYRIGHT: THE PROBLEM OF PERFECT COPIES AND ENCRYPTION

copyright law
protects original forms of expression such as writings, art, drawings, photographs, music, motion pictures, performances, and computer programs from being copied by others for a minimum of 70 years

In the United States, **copyright law** protects original forms of expression such as writings (books, periodicals, lecture notes), art, drawings, photographs, music, motion pictures, performances, and computer programs from being copied by others for a period of time. Up until 1998, the copyright law protected works of individuals for their lifetime plus 50 years beyond their life, and for works created for hire and owned by corporations such as Mickey Mouse of the Disney Corporation, 75 years after initial creation. Copyright does not protect ideas—just their expression in a tangible medium such as paper, cassette tape, or handwritten notes.

In 1998, Congress extended the period of copyright protection for an additional 20 years, for a total of 95 years for corporate-owned works, and life plus 70 years of protection for works created by individuals (the Copyright Term Extension Act, also known as CETA). In *Eldred v. Ashcroft*, the Supreme Court ruled on January 16, 2003, that CETA was constitutional, over the objections of groups arguing that Congress had given copyright holders a permanent monopoly over the expression of ideas, which ultimately would work to inhibit the flow of ideas and creation of new works by making existing works too expensive (Greenhouse, 2003a). Librarians, academics, and others who depend on inexpensive access to copyrighted material opposed the legislation.

Since the first federal Copyright Act of 1790, the congressional intent behind copyright laws has been to encourage creativity and authorship by ensuring that creative people receive the financial and other benefits of their work. Most industrial nations have their own copyright laws, and there are several international conventions and bilateral agreements through which nations coordinate and enforce their laws.

In the mid-1960s, the Copyright Office began registering software programs, and in 1980, Congress passed the Computer Software Copyright Act, which clearly provides protection for source and object code and for copies of the original sold in commerce, and sets forth the rights of the purchaser to use the software while the creator retains legal title. For instance, the HTML code for a Web page—even though easily available to every browser—cannot be lawfully copied and used for a commercial purpose, say, to create a new Web site that looks identical.

Copyright protection is clear-cut: it protects against copying of entire programs or their parts. Damages and relief are readily obtained for infringement. The drawback to copyright protection is that the underlying ideas behind a work are not protected, only their expression in a work. A competitor can view the source code on your Web site to see how various effects were created and then reuse those techniques to create a different Web site without infringing on your copyright.

Look and Feel

"Look and feel" copyright infringement lawsuits are precisely about the distinction between an idea and its expression. For instance, in 1988, Apple Computer sued Microsoft Corporation and Hewlett-Packard Inc. for infringing Apple's copyright on the Macintosh interface. Among other claims, Apple claimed that the defendants copied the expression of overlapping windows. Apple failed to patent the idea of overlapping windows when it invented this method of presenting information on a computer screen in the late 1960s. The defendants counterclaimed that the idea of overlapping windows could only be expressed in a single way and, therefore, was not protectable under the "merger" doctrine of copyright law. When ideas and their expression merge (i.e., if there is only one way to express an idea), the expression cannot be copyrighted, although the method of producing the expression might be patentable (*Apple v. Microsoft*, 1989). In general, courts appear to be following the reasoning of a 1992 case—*Brown Bag Software vs. Symantec Corp.*—in which the court dissected the elements of software alleged to be infringing. There, the Federal Circuit Court of Appeals found that neither similar concept, function, general functional features (e.g., drop-down menus), nor colors were protectable by copyright law (*Brown Bag vs. Symantec Corp.*, 1992).

Fair Use Doctrine

Copyrights, like all rights, are not absolute. There are situations where strict copyright observance could be harmful to society, potentially inhibiting other rights such as the right to freedom of expression and thought. As a result, the doctrine of fair use has been created. The **doctrine of fair use** permits teachers and writers to use copyrighted materials without permission under certain circumstances. **Table 8.9** describes the five factors that courts consider when assessing what constitutes fair use.

doctrine of fair use
under certain circumstances, permits use of copyrighted material without permission

The fair use doctrine draws upon the First Amendment's protection of freedom of speech (and writing). Journalists, writers, and academics must be able to refer to, and cite from, copyrighted works in order to criticize or even discuss copyrighted works. Professors are allowed to clip a contemporary article just before class, copy it, and hand it out to students as an example of a topic under discussion. However, they are not permitted to add this article to the class syllabus for the next semester without compensating the copyright holder.

TABLE 8.9	FAIR USE CONSIDERATIONS TO COPYRIGHT PROTECTIONS
FAIR USE FACTOR	**INTERPRETATION**
Character of use	Nonprofit or educational use versus for-profit use.
Nature of the work	Creative works such as plays or novels receive greater protection than factual accounts, e.g., newspaper accounts.
Amount of work used	A stanza from a poem or a single page from a book would be allowed, but not the entire poem or a book chapter.
Market effect of use	Will the use harm the marketability of the original product? Has it already harmed the product in the marketplace?
Context of use	A last-minute, unplanned use in a classroom versus a planned infringement.

What constitutes fair use has been at issue in a number of recent cases, including the Google Book Search Project described in the case study at the end of the chapter, and in several recent lawsuits. In *Kelly v. ArribaSoft* (2003) and *Perfect 10, Inc. v. Amazon.com, Inc.* (2007), the federal Circuit Court of Appeals for the 10th circuit held that the display of thumbnail images in response to search requests constituted fair use. A similar result was reached by the district court for the District of Nevada with respect to Google's storage and display of Web sites from cache memory, in *Field v. Google, Inc.* (2006). In all of these cases, the courts accepted the argument that caching the material and displaying it in response to a search request was not only a public benefit, but also a form of marketing of the material on behalf of its copyright owner, thereby enhancing the material's commercial value. Fair use is also at issue in the lawsuit filed by Viacom against Google and YouTube in March 2007, described further in the next section.

The Digital Millennium Copyright Act of 1998

Digital Millennium Copyright Act (DMCA)
the first major effort to adjust the copyright laws to the Internet age

The Digital Millennium Copyright Act (DMCA) of 1998 is the first major effort to adjust the copyright laws to the Internet age. This legislation was the result of a confrontation between the major copyright holders in the United States (publishing, sheet music, record label, and commercial film industries), ISPs, and users of copyrighted materials such as libraries, universities, and consumers. While social and political institutions are sometimes thought of as "slow" and the Internet as "fast," in this instance, powerful groups of copyright owners anticipated Web music services such as Napster by several years. Napster was formed in 1999, but work by the World Intellectual Property Organization—a worldwide body formed by the major copyright—holding nations of North America, Europe, and Japan—began in 1995. **Table 8.10** summarizes the major provisions of the DMCA.

The penalties for willfully violating the DMCA include restitution to the injured parties of any losses due to infringement. Criminal remedies are available to federal prosecutors that include fines up to $500,000 or five years imprisonment for a first

TABLE 8.10	THE DIGITAL MILLENNIUM COPYRIGHT ACT
SECTION	IMPORTANCE
Title I, WIPO Copyright and Performances and Phonograms Treaties Implementation	Makes it illegal to circumvent technological measures to protect works for either access or copying or to circumvent any electronic rights management information.
Title II, Online Copyright Infringement Liability Limitation	Requires ISPs to "take down" sites they host if they are infringing copyrights, and requires search engines to block access to infringing sites. Limits liability of ISPs and search engines.
Title III, Computer Maintenance Competition Assurance	Permits users to make a copy of a computer program for maintenance or repair of the computer.
Title IV, Miscellaneous Provisions	Requires the copyright office to report to Congress on the use of copyright materials for distance education; allows libraries to make digital copies of works for internal use only; extends musical copyrights to include "webcasting."

SOURCE: Based on data from United States Copyright Office, 1998.

offense, and up to $1 million in fines and 10 years in prison for repeat offenders. These are serious remedies.

The DMCA attempts to answer two vexing questions in the Internet age. First, how can society protect copyrights online when any practical encryption scheme imaginable can be broken by hackers and the results distributed worldwide? Second, how can society control the behavior of thousands of ISPs, who often host infringing Web sites, or who provide Internet service to individuals who are routine infringers? ISPs claim to be like telephone utilities—just carrying messages—and they do not want to put their users under surveillance or invade the privacy of users. The DMCA recognizes that ISPs have some control over how their customers use their facilities.

The DMCA implements a World Intellectual Property Organization (WIPO) treaty of 1996, which declares it illegal to make, distribute, or use devices that circumvent technology-based protections of copyrighted materials, and attaches stiff fines and prison sentences for violations. WIPO is an organization within the United Nations. Recognizing that these provisions alone cannot stop hackers from devising circumventions, the DMCA makes it difficult for such inventors to reap the fruits of their labors by making the ISPs (including universities) responsible and accountable for hosting Web sites or providing services to infringers once the ISP has been notified. ISPs are not required to intrude on their users. However, when copyright holders inform the ISP that a hosted site or individual users are infringing, they must "take down" the site immediately to avoid liability and potential fines. ISPs must also inform their subscribers of their copyright management policies. Copyright owners can subpoena the personal identities of any infringers using an ISP. There are important limitations on these ISP prohibitions that are mostly concerned with the transitory caching of materials for short periods without the knowledge of the ISP. However, should the ISP be deriving revenues from the infringement, it is as liable as the infringer, and is subject to the same penalties.

Title I of the DMCA provides a partial answer to the dilemma of hacking. It is probably true that skilled hackers can easily break any usable encryption scheme, and the means to do so on a large scale through distribution of the decryption programs already exists. The WIPO provisions accept this possibility and simply make it illegal to do so, or to disseminate, or to enable such dissemination or even storage and transmission of decrypted products or tools. These provisions put large ISPs on legal notice.

There are a number of exceptions to the strong prohibitions against defeating a copyright protection scheme outlined above. There are exceptions for libraries to examine works for adoption, for reverse engineering to achieve interoperability with other software, for encryption research, for privacy protection purposes, and for security testing. Many companies, such as YouTube, Google, and MySpace have latched on the provision of the DMCA that relates to removing infringing material upon request of the copyright owner as a "safe harbor" that precludes them from being held responsible for copyright infringement. This position is currently being tested in a $1 billion lawsuit brought by Viacom against Google and YouTube for willful copyright infringement, and by Vivendi's Universal Music Group against the News Corp.'s MySpace. These lawsuits are interesting because, unlike efforts against individuals accused of file-sharing, or offshore renegade outfits such as Kazaa, they pit large established corporate institutions against one another.

In the Viacom case, Viacom alleges that YouTube and Google engaged in massive copyright infringement by deliberately building up a library of infringing works to draw traffic to the YouTube site and enhance its commercial value. In response, Google and YouTube claim that they are protected by the DMCA's safe harbor and fair use, and that it is often impossible to know whether a video is infringing or not. YouTube also does not display ads on pages where consumers can view videos unless it has an agreement with the content owner. In October 2007, Google announced a filtering system aimed at addressing the problem. It requires content owners to give Google a copy of their content so Google can load it into an auto-identification system. The copyright owner can specify whether it will allow others to post the material. Then after a video is uploaded to YouTube, the system attempts to match it with its database of copyrighted material, and removes any unauthorized material. Whether content owners will be satisfied with this system is unknown, particularly since guidelines issued by a coalition of major media and Internet companies with respect to the handling of copyrighted videos on user-generated Web sites calls for the use of filtering technology that can block infringing material before it is posted online (Helft and Fabrikant, 2007; Gentile, 2007; Swartz, 2007).

PATENTS: BUSINESS METHODS AND PROCESSES

"Whoever invents or discovers any new and useful process, machine, manufacture, or composition of matter, or any new and useful improvement thereof, may obtain a patent therefore, subject to the conditions and requirements of this title."

—Section 101, U.S. Patent Act

A **patent** grants the owner a 20-year exclusive monopoly on the ideas behind an invention. The congressional intent behind patent law was to ensure that inventors of new machines, devices, or industrial methods would receive the full financial and other rewards of their labor and yet still make widespread use of the invention possible by providing detailed diagrams for those wishing to use the idea under license from the patent's owner. Patents are obtained from the United States Patent and Trademark Office (USPTO), created in 1812. Obtaining a patent is much more difficult and time-consuming than obtaining copyright protection (which is automatic with the creation of the work). Patents must be formally applied for, and the granting of a patent is deter-mined by Patent Office examiners who follow a set of rigorous rules. Ultimately, federal courts decide when patents are valid and when infringement occurs.

patent
grants the owner an exclusive monopoly on the ideas behind an invention for 20 years

Patents are very different from copyrights because patents protect the ideas themselves and not merely the expression of ideas. There are four types of inventions for which patents are granted under patent law: machines, man-made products, compositions of matter, and processing methods. The Supreme Court has determined that patents extend to "anything under the sun that is made by man" (*Diamond v. Chakrabarty*, 1980) as long as the other requirements of the Patent Act are met. There are three things that cannot be patented: laws of nature, natural phenomena, and abstract ideas. For instance, a mathematical algorithm cannot be patented unless it is realized in a tangible machine or process that has a "useful" result (the mathematical algorithm exception).

In order to be granted a patent, the applicant must show that the invention is new, original, novel, nonobvious, and not evident in prior arts and practice. As with copyrights, the granting of patents has moved far beyond the original intent of Congress's first patent statute that sought to protect industrial designs and machines. Patent protection has been extended to articles of manufacture (1842), plants (1930), surgical and medical procedures (1950), and software (1981). The Patent Office did not accept applications for software patents until a 1981 Supreme Court decision that held that computer programs could be a part of a patentable process. Since that time, thousands of software patents have been granted. Virtually any software program can be patented as long as it is novel and not obvious.

Essentially, as technology and industrial arts progress, patents have been extended to both encourage entrepreneurs to invent useful devices and promote widespread dissemination of the new techniques through licensing and artful imitation of the published patents (the creation of devices that provide the same functionality as the invention but use different methods) (Winston, 1998). Patents encourage inventors to come up with unique ways of achieving the same functionality as existing patents. For instance, Amazon's patent on one-click purchasing caused Barnesandnoble.com to invent a simplified two-click method of purchasing.

The danger of patents is that they stifle competition by raising barriers to entry into an industry. Patents force new entrants to pay licensing fees to incumbents, and thus slow down the development of technical applications of new ideas by creating lengthy licensing applications and delays.

E-commerce Patents

Much of the Internet's infrastructure and software was developed under the auspices of publicly funded scientific and military programs in the United States and Europe. Unlike Samuel F. B. Morse, who patented the idea of Morse code and made the telegraph useful, most of the inventions that make the Internet and e-commerce possible were not patented by their inventors. The early Internet was characterized by a spirit of worldwide community development and sharing of ideas without consideration of personal wealth (Winston, 1998). This early Internet spirit changed in the mid-1990s with the commercial development of the World Wide Web.

In 1998, a landmark legal decision, *State Street Bank & Trust v. Signature Financial Group, Inc.*, paved the way for business firms to begin applying for "business methods" patents. In this case, a Federal Circuit Court of Appeals upheld the claims of Signature Financial to a valid patent for a business method that allows managers to monitor and record financial information flows generated by a partner fund. Previously, it was thought business methods could not be patented. However, the court ruled there was no reason to disallow business methods from patent protection, or any "step by step process, be it electronic or chemical or mechanical, [that] involves an algorithm in the broad sense of the term" (*State Street Bank & Trust Co. v. Signature Financial Group*, 1998). The State Street decision led to an explosion in applications for e-commerce "business methods" patents, with over 11,000 in 2007 (see **Figure 8.3**). Note that the overall number of patent applications filed has also increased dramatically, from about 237,000 in 1995 to almost 456,000 in 2007.

Table 8.11 on page 524 lists some of the better-known, controversial e-commerce patents. Reviewing these, you can understand the concerns of commentators and corporations. Some of the patent claims are very broad (for example, "name your price" sales methods), have historical precedents in the pre-Internet era (shopping carts), and seem "obvious" (one-click purchasing). Critics of online business methods patents argue that the Patent Office has been too lenient in granting such patents and that in most instances, the supposed inventions merely copy pre-Internet business methods and thus do not constitute "inventions" (Harmon, 2003; Thurm, 2000; Chiappetta, 2001). The Patent Office argues, on the contrary, that its Internet inventions staff is composed of engineers, lawyers, and specialists with many years of experience with Internet and network technologies, and that it consults with outside technology experts before granting patents. To complicate matters, the European Patent Convention and the patent laws of most European countries do not recognize business methods per se unless the method is implemented through some technology (Takenaka, 2001).

Patent Reform

Issues related to business method patents, patent "trolls" (companies such as Acacia Technologies that buy up broadly-worded patents on a speculative basis and then use

FIGURE 8.3	INTERNET AND E-COMMERCE BUSINESS METHODS PATENTS

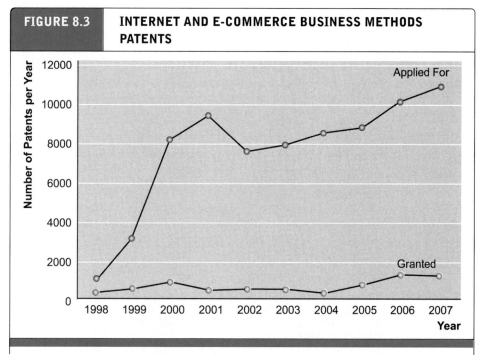

Bolstered by the 1998 *State Street Bank* decision, patents on computer-related business methods increased exponentially from 1998 when 1,337 applications were filed, to 2001, when 9,288 applications were submitted. During the period 2002–2005, applications dropped off somewhat and remained relatively steady at around 7,500–8,500 per year, but in 2006, they increased significantly again, to over 10,000 applications.
SOURCE: Based on data from U.S. Patent and Trademark Office, 2008.

them to threaten companies that are purportedly violating the patent) and confusing legal decisions have led to increasing calls for patent reform over the last few years, particularly by companies in the technology sector. One target of such legislation are firms that produce nothing but simply collect patents and then seek to enforce them. In 2000, Nathan Myhrvold formed a new kind of patent investment firm called Intellectual Ventures. A former Microsoft Chief Technology Officer, Myhrvold has amassed a collection of over 20,000 patents in the digital technology field, including e-commerce by purchasing them from small companies and entrepreneurs. He discovers large firms which are violating those patents and threatens to sue. Sony, Verizon, Google, Verizon and many other large firms pay up, and in addition, invest in the company so they can participate in future revenues (Sharma and Clark, 2008).

In September 2007, the House of Representatives passed its version of a patent reform bill that includes provisions that change the patent system from a "first to invent" system to a "first to file" system, change the way damages for patent infringement are calculated, provide a new way to challenge patents out of court, limit where patent suits can be filed (to prevent suits from being filed in districts that have a reputation for being more favorable), and impose heightened standards for a finding of willful infringement. This legislation will be considered in the Senate in 2009.

TABLE 8.11	SELECTED E-COMMERCE PATENTS	
COMPANY	SUBJECT	UPDATE
Leon Stambler	Secure communications	Private inventor with seven patents (1992–1998) covering creation of an authentication code to be used in electronic communications. In 2003, a Delaware jury found that RSA Security and VeriSign did not infringe on the patents. Stambler's appeal to the U.S. Court of Appeals for the Federal Circuit was rejected in February 2005.
Amazon	One-click purchasing	Amazon attempted to use patent originally granted to it in 1999 to force changes to Barnes & Noble's Web site, but a federal court overturned a previously issued injunction. Eventually settled out of court. In September 2007, a USPTO panel rejected most of the patent because of evidence another patent predated it, sending it back to the patent examiner for reconsideration.
Eolas Technologies	Embedding interactive content in a Web site	Eolas Technologies, a spin-off of the University of California, obtained patent in 1998. Eolas filed suit against Microsoft in 1999 for infringing the patent in Internet Explorer and was award a $520 million judgment in 2003. Decision was partially reversed in 2005, and sent back to district court for a new trial. The patent was reaffirmed in September 2005 by the USPTO. In August 2007, Eolas and Microsoft finally settled the suit on undisclosed terms.
Priceline	Buyer-driven "name your price" sales	Originally invented by Walker Digital, an intellectual property laboratory, and then assigned to Priceline. Granted by the USPTO in 1999. Shortly thereafter, Priceline sued Microsoft and Expedia for copying its patented business method. Expedia settled and agreed to pay a royalty in 2001.
Sightsound	Music downloads	Sightsound won a settlement in 2004 against Bertelsmann subsidiaries CDNow and N2K music sites for infringing its patent.
Akamai	Internet content delivery Global Hosting System	A broad patent granted in 2000 covering techniques for expediting the flow of information over the Internet. Akamai sued Digital Island (subsequently acquired Cable & Wireless) for violating the patent and, in 2001, a jury found in its favor. In 2004, Akamai accepted a damages payment to finally settle the suit.
DoubleClick	Dynamic delivery of online advertising	The patent underlying DoubleClick's business of online banner ad delivery, originally granted in 2000. DoubleClick sued competitors 24/7 Media and L90 for violating the patent and ultimately reached a settlement with them.
Overture	Pay for performance search	System and method for influencing position on search result list generated by computer search engine, granted in 2001. Competitor FindWhat.com sued Overture, charging that patent was obtained illegally; Overture countered by suing both FindWhat and Google for violating patent. Google agreed to pay a license fee to Overture in 2004 to settle the suit, and the lawsuit with FindWhat resulted in a hung jury in 2005, with both sides claiming victory.
Acacia Technologies	Streaming video media transmission	Patents for the receipt and transmission of streaming digital audio and or video content originally granted to founders of Greenwich Information Technologies in 1990s. Patents were purchased by Acacia, a firm founded solely to enforce the patents, in 2001. Acacia has subsequently secured dozens of licenses.
Soverain Software	Purchase technology	The so-called "shopping cart" patent for network-based systems, which involves any transaction over a network involving a seller, buyer, and payment system. In other words, e-commerce!. Originally owned by Open Markets, then Divine Inc., and now Soverain. Soverain filed suit against Amazon for patent infringement in 2004; Amazon settled for $40 million in August 2005.
MercExchange (Thomas Woolston)	Auction technology	Patents on person-to-person auctions and database search, originally granted in 1995. eBay ordered to pay $25 million in 2003 for infringing on patent. In July 2007, the U.S. district court denied a motion for permanent patent injunction against eBay using the "Buy It Now" feature, and moved to the final stages of allowing the damages award to be paid. Issues related to a second patent were deferred pending a USPTO office reexamination.
Google	Search technology	Google PageRank patent was filed in 1998 and granted in 2001.

TRADEMARKS: ONLINE INFRINGEMENT AND DILUTION

> Trademark is "any word, name, symbol, or device, or any combination thereof ... used in commerce ... to identify and distinguish ... goods . . . from those manufactured or sold by others and to indicate the source of the goods."
>
> —The Trademark Act, 1946

Trademark law is a form of intellectual property protection for **trademarks**—a mark used to identify and distinguish goods and indicate their source. Trademark protections exist at both the federal and state levels in the United States. The purpose of trademark law is twofold. First, the trademark law protects the public in the marketplace by ensuring that it gets what it pays for and wants to receive. Second, trademark law protects the owner—who has spent time, money, and energy bringing the product to the marketplace—against piracy and misappropriation. Trademarks have been extended from single words to pictures, shapes, packaging, and colors. Some things may not be trademarked: common words that are merely descriptive ("clock"), flags of states and nations, immoral or deceptive marks, or marks belonging to others. Federal trademarks are obtained, first, by use in interstate commerce, and second, by registration with the USPTO. Trademarks are granted for a period of ten years, and can be renewed indefinitely.

trademark
a mark used to identify and distinguish goods and indicate their source

Disputes over federal trademarks involve establishing infringement. The test for infringement is twofold: market confusion and bad faith. Use of a trademark that creates confusion with existing trademarks causes consumers to make market mistakes, or misrepresents the origins of goods is an infringement. In addition, the intentional misuse of words and symbols in the marketplace to extort revenue from legitimate trademark owners ("bad faith") is proscribed.

In 1995, Congress passed the Federal Trademark Dilution Act, which created a federal cause of action for dilution of famous marks. This legislation dispenses with the test of market confusion (although that is still required to claim infringement), and extends protection to owners of famous trademarks against **dilution**, which is defined as any behavior that would weaken the connection between the trademark and the product. Dilution occurs through blurring (weakening the connection between the trademark and the goods) and tarnishment (using the trademark in a way that makes the underlying products appear unsavory or unwholesome).

dilution
any behavior that would weaken the connection between the trademark and the product

Trademarks and the Internet

The rapid growth and commercialization of the Internet have provided unusual opportunities for existing firms with distinctive and famous trademarks to extend their brands to the Internet. These same developments have provided malicious individuals and firms the opportunity to squat on Internet domain names built upon famous marks, as well as attempt to confuse consumers and dilute famous or distinctive marks (including your personal name or a movie star's name). The conflict between legitimate trademark owners and malicious firms was allowed to fester and grow because Network Solutions Inc. (NSI), originally the Internet's sole agency for domain name registration for many years, had a policy of "first come, first served." This meant anyone could register any domain name that had not already been registered, regardless of the trademark status of the domain name. NSI was not authorized to decide trademark issues (Nash, 1997).

In response to a growing number of complaints from owners of famous trademarks who found their trademark names being appropriated by Web entrepreneurs, Congress passed the **Anticybersquatting Consumer Protection Act (ACPA)** in November 1999. The ACPA creates civil liabilities for anyone who attempts in bad faith to profit from an existing famous or distinctive trademark by registering an Internet domain name that is identical, confusingly similar, or "dilutive" of that trademark. The Act does not establish criminal sanctions. The Act proscribes using "bad faith" domain names to extort money from the owners of the existing trademark (**cybersquatting**), or using the bad faith domain to divert Web traffic to the bad faith domain that could harm the good will represented by the trademark, create market confusion, tarnish, or disparage the mark (**cyberpiracy**). The Act also proscribes the use of a domain name that consists of the name of a living person, or a name confusingly similar to an existing personal name, without that person's consent, if the registrant is registering the name with the intent to profit by selling the domain dame to that person.

Trademark abuse can take many forms on the Web. **Table 8.12** lists the major behaviors on the Internet that have run afoul of trademark law, and the some of the court cases that resulted.

Cybersquatting

In one of the first cases involving the ACPA, E. & J. Gallo Winery, owner of the registered mark "Ernest and Julio Gallo" for alcoholic beverages, sued Spider Webs Ltd. for using the domain name Ernestandjuliogallo.com. Spider Webs Ltd. was a domain name speculator that owned numerous domain names consisting of famous company names. The Ernestandjuliogallo.com Web site contained information on the risks of alcohol use, anti-corporate articles about E. & J. Gallo Winery, and was poorly constructed. The court concluded that Spider Webs Ltd. was in violation of the ACPA and that its actions constituted dilution by blurring because the Ernestandjuliogallo.com domain name appeared on every page printed off the Web site accessed by that name, and that Spider Webs Ltd. was not free to use this particular mark as a domain name (*E. & J. Gallo Winery v. Spider Webs Ltd.*, 2001).

Cyberpiracy

Cyberpiracy involves the same behavior as cybersquatting, but with the intent of diverting traffic from the legitimate site to an infringing site. In *Ford Motor Co. v. Lapertosa*, Lapertosa had registered and used a Web site called Fordrecalls.com as an adult entertainment Web site. The court ruled that Fordrecalls.com was in violation of the ACPA in that it was a bad faith attempt to divert traffic to the Lapertosa site and diluted Ford's wholesome trademark (*Ford Motor Co. v. Lapertosa*, 2001).

Anticybersquatting Consumer Protection Act (ACPA)

creates civil liabilities for anyone who attempts in bad faith to profit from an existing famous or distinctive trademark by registering an Internet domain name that is identical, or confusingly similar, or "dilutive" of that trademark

cybersquatting

involves the registration of an infringing domain name, or other Internet use of an existing trademark, for the purpose of extorting payments from the legitimate owners

cyberpiracy

involves the same behavior as cybersquatting, but with the intent of diverting traffic from the legitimate site to an infringing site

TABLE 8.12	**INTERNET AND TRADEMARK LAW EXAMPLES**	
ACTIVITY	DESCRIPTION	EXAMPLE CASE
Cybersquatting	Registering domain names similar or identical to trademarks of others to extort profits from legitimate holders.	*E. & J. Gallo Winery v. Spider Webs Ltd.*, 129 F. Supp. 2d 1033 (S.D. Tex., 2001) aff'd 286 F. 3d 270 (5th Cir.,2002)
Cyberpiracy	Registering domain names similar or identical to trademarks of others to divert Web traffic to their own sites.	*Ford Motor Co. v. Lapertosa*, 2001 U.S. Dist. LEXIS 253 (E.D. Mich., 2001); *PaineWebber Inc. v. Fortuny*, Civ. A. No. 99-0456-A (E.D. Va., 1999); *Playboy Enterprises, Inc. v. Global Site Designs, Inc.*, 1999 WL 311707 (S.D. Fla., 1999)
		Audi AG and Volkswagen of America Inc. v. Bob D'Amato (No. 05-2359; 6th Cir., November 27, 2006).
Metatagging	Using trademark words in a site's metatags.	*Bernina of America, Inc. v. Fashion Fabrics Int'l, Inc.*, 2001 U.S. Dist. LEXIS 1211 (N.D. Ill., 2001); *Nissan Motor Co., Ltd. v. Nissan Computer Corp.*, 289 F. Supp. 2d 1154 (C.D. Cal., 2000), aff'd, 246 F. 3rd 675 (9th Cir., 2000).
Keywords	Placing trademarked keywords on Web pages, either visible or invisible.	*Playboy Enterprises, Inc. v. Netscape Communications, Inc.*, 354 F. 3rd 1020 (9th Cir., 2004); *Nettis Environment Ltd. v. IWI, Inc.*, 46 F. Supp. 2d 722 (N.D. Ohio, 1999); *Government Employees Insurance Company v. Google, Inc.*, Civ. Action No. 1:04cv507 (E.D. VA, 2004); *Google, Inc. v. American Blind & Wallpaper Factory, Inc.*, Case No. 03-5340 JF (RS) (N.D. Cal., April 18, 2007)
Linking	Linking to content pages on other sites, bypassing the home page.	*Ticketmaster Corp. v. Tickets.com*, 2000 U.S. Dist. Lexis 4553 (C.D. Cal., 2000)
Framing	Placing the content of other sites in a frame on the infringer's site.	*The Washington Post, et al. v. TotalNews, Inc., et al.*, (S.D.N.Y., Civil Action Number 97-1190)

The Ford decision reflects two other famous cases of cyberpiracy. In the *Paine Webber Inc. v. Fortuny* case, the court enjoined Fortuny from using the domain name Wwwpainewebber.com—a site that specialized in pornographic materials—because it diluted and tarnished Paine Webber's trademark and diverted Web traffic from Paine Webber's legitimate site—Painewebber.com (*Paine Webber Inc. v. Fortuny*, 1999). In the *Playboy Enterprises, Inc. v. Global Site Designs, Inc.* case, the court enjoined the defendants from using the Playboy and Playmate marks in their domain names Playboyonline.net and Playmatesearch.net and from including the Playboy trademark in their metatags. In these cases, the defendants' intention was diversion for financial gain (*Playboy Enterprises, Inc. v. Global Site Designs, Inc.*, 1999).

In a more recent case, *Audi AG and Volkswagen of America Inc. v. Bob D'Amato*, the Federal Circuit Court of Appeals for the Sixth Circuit affirmed the District Court's ruling that the defendant Bob D'Amato infringed and diluted the plaintiffs' Audi, Quatro and Audi Four Rings logo marks, and violated the ACPA by operating the

Audisport.com Web site (*Audi AG and Volkswagen of America Inc. v. Bob D'Amato*, 2006).

Typosquatting is a form of cyberpiracy in which a domain name contains a common misspelling of another site's name. Often the user ends up at a site very different from one they intended to visit. For instance, John Zuccarini is an infamous typosquatter who was jailed in 2002 for setting up pornographic Web sites with URLs based on misspellings of popular children's brands, such as Bob the Builder and Teletubbies. The FTC fined him again in October 2007 for engaging in similar practices (McMillan, 2007).

Metatagging

The legal status of using famous or distinctive marks as metatags is more complex and subtle. The use of trademarks in metatags is permitted if the use does not mislead or confuse consumers. Usually this depends on the content of the site. A car dealer would be permitted to use a famous automobile trademark in its metatags if the dealer sold this brand of automobiles, but a pornography site could not use the same trademark, nor a dealer for a rival manufacturer. A Ford dealer would most likely be infringing if it used "Honda" in its metatags, but would not be infringing if it used "Ford" in its metatags. (Ford Motor Company would be unlikely to seek an injunction against one of its dealers.)

In the *Bernina of America, Inc. v. Fashion Fabrics Int'l, Inc.* case, the court enjoined Fashion Fabrics, an independent dealer of sewing machines, from using the trademarks "Bernina" and "Bernette," which belonged to the manufacturer Bernina, as metatags. The court found the defendant's site contained misleading claims about Fashion Fabrics' knowledge of Bernina products that were likely to confuse customers. The use of the Bernina trademarks as metatags per se was not a violation of ACPA, according to the court, but in combination with the misleading claims on the site would cause confusion and hence infringement (*Bernina of America, Inc. v. Fashion Fabrics Int'l, Inc.*, 2001).

In the *Nissan Motor Co. Ltd. v. Nissan Computer Corp.* case, Uzi Nissan had used his surname "Nissan" as a trade name for various businesses since 1980, including Nissan Computer Corp. He registered Nissan.com in 1994 and Nissan.net in 1996. Nissan.com had no relationship with Nissan Motor, but over the years began selling auto parts that competed with Nissan Motor. Nissan Motor Company objected to the use of the domain name Nissan.com and the use of "Nissan" in the metatags for both sites on grounds it would confuse customers and infringe on Nissan Motor's trademarks. Uzi Nissan offered to sell his sites to Nissan Motor for several million dollars. Nissan Motor refused. The court ruled that Nissan Computer's behavior did indeed infringe on Nissan Motor's trademarks, but it refused to shut the site down. Instead, the court ruled Nissan Computer could continue to use the Nissan name, and metatags, but must post notices on its site that it was not affiliated with Nissan Motor (*Nissan Motor Co. Ltd. v. Nissan Computer Corp.*, 2000). In November 2002, a U.S. District Court issued a permanent injunction, allowing Mr. Nissan to keep the domains, but restricting the commercial, advertising, and anti-Nissan Motor content that could be placed on the Web sites. Mr. Nissan appealed, and in August

2004, the Ninth Circuit Court of Appeals found that while Nissan Computer in fact capitalized on Nissan Motors' good-will in the Nissan trademark to the extent that use of the mark for automobiles captured the attention of customers interested in Nissan cars, Nissan Motor could not gain protection against any resultant dilution of the trademark because Nissan Computer had made its first commercial use of the mark over five years before Nissan Motor's mark became famous in the United States. In addition, requiring that the Web site not contain links to anti-Nissan Web sites was inconsistent with free speech rights. The Court of Appeals therefore reversed the previous ruling, ordering Mr. Nissan to refrain only from showing car-related ads, and remanded the case back to the District Court for consideration as to whether the injunction should be broadened to include the transfer of the domains. In April 2005, the Supreme Court turned down an appeal made by Nissan Motor.

Keywording

The permissibility of using trademarks as keywords on search engines is also subtle and depends on the extent to which such use is considered to be a "use in commerce", causes "initial customer confusion" and on the content of the search results.

In *Playboy Enterprises, Inc. v. Netscape Communications, Inc.*, Playboy objected to the practice of Netscape's and Excite's search engines displaying banner ads unrelated to Playboy Magazine when users entered search arguments such as "playboy," "playmate," and "playgirl." The Ninth Circuit Court of Appeals denied the defendant's motion for a summary judgment and held that when an advertiser's banner ad is not labeled so as to identify its source, the practice could result in trademark infringement due to consumer confusion (*Playboy Enterprises, Inc. v. Netscape Communications, Inc.*, 2004).

In the *Nettis Environment Ltd. v. IWI, Inc.* case, Nettis and IWI Inc. were competitors in the ventilation business. IWI had registered the trademarks "nettis" and "nettis environmental" on over 400 search engines, and in addition, used these marks as metatags on its site. The court required IWI to remove the metatags and de-register the keywords with all search engines because consumers would be con fused—searching for Nettis products would lead them to an IWI Web site (*Nettis Environment Ltd. v. IWI, Inc.*, 1999).

Google has also faced lawsuits alleging that its advertising network illegally exploits others' trademarks. For instance, insurance company GEICO challenged Google's practice of allowing competitors' ads to appear when a searcher types "Geico" as the search query. In December 2004, a U.S. District Court ruled that this practice did not violate federal trademark laws so long as the word "Geico" was not used in the ads' text (*Government Employees Insurance Company v. Google, Inc.*, 2004). Google quickly discontinued allowing the latter, and settled the case (Associated Press, 2005). Google settled another similar lawsuit, *Google Inc. v American Blind & Wallpaper Factory, Inc.*, in August 2007, following a court ruling in April that Google's display of competitor's ads as part of Google's AdWords program was a use of those marks in commerce, and allowing American Blind to proceed with trademark infringement claims arising from the use of those marks, finding that American Blind had presented sufficient evidence of consumer confusion to survive Google's motion for summary judgment on the matter. However, these settlements have not prevented other companies from also suing Google. For instance, in August 2007, American Airlines filed suit against Google over sponsored ads that appear when a user enters a keyword search using American Airlines trademarks. Thus far, although Google has lost some trademark cases in Europe, no definitive ruling against it has been issued in the United States.

The state of Utah has attempted to pre-empt the issue and passed a controversial Trademark Protection Act in March 2007 that bans advertisers from using the trademarked terms of their competitors to target ads to Utah users. The statute also establishes an "electronic registration mark" protecting trademark owners that file marks with a registry the state intends to create. Not surprisingly, the statute has been severely criticized by search providers such as Google, AOL, Yahoo and Microsoft, and will likely face constitutional challenges (Seidenberg, 2007).

Linking

linking
building hypertext links from one site to another site

Linking refers to building hypertext links from one site to another site. This is obviously a major design feature and benefit of the Web. **Deep linking** involves bypassing the target site's home page and going directly to a content page. In *Ticketmaster Corp. v. Tickets.com*, Tickets.com—owned by Microsoft—competed directly against Ticketmaster in the events ticket market. When Tickets.com did not have tickets for an event, it would direct users to Ticketmaster's internal pages, bypassing the Ticketmaster home page. Even though its logo was displayed on the internal pages, Ticketmaster objected on the grounds that such "deep linking" violated the terms and conditions of use for its site (stated on a separate page altogether and construed by Ticketmaster as equivalent to a shrink-wrap license), and constituted false advertising, as well as the violation of copyright. The court found, however, that deep linking per se is not illegal, no violation of copyright occurred because no copies were made, the terms and conditions of use were not obvious to users, and users were not required to read the page on which the terms and conditions of use appeared in any event. The court refused to rule in favor of Ticketmaster, but left open further argument on the licensing issue. In an out-of-court settlement, Tickets.com nevertheless agreed to stop the practice of deep linking (*Ticketmaster v. Tickets.com*, 2000).

deep linking
involves bypassing the target site's home page, and going directly to a content page

Framing

framing
involves displaying the content of another Web site inside your own Web site within a frame or window

Framing involves displaying the content of another Web site inside your own Web site within a frame or window. The user never leaves the framer's site and can be exposed to advertising while the target site's advertising is distorted or eliminated. Framers may or may not acknowledge the source of the content. In *The Washington Post, et al. v. TotalNews, Inc. case, The Washington Post*, CNN, Reuters, and several other news organizations filed suit against TotalNews Inc., claiming that TotalNews's use of frames on its Web site, TotalNews.com, infringed upon the respective plaintiffs' copyrights and trademarks, diluted the content of their individual Web sites, and the content of those Web sites. The plaintiffs claimed additionally that TotalNews's framing practice effectively deprived the plaintiffs' Web sites of advertising revenue.

TotalNews's Web site employed four frames. The TotalNews logo appeared in the lower left frame, the various links were located on a vertical frame on the left side of the screen, TotalNews's advertising was framed across the screen bottom, and the "news frame," the largest frame, appeared in the center and right. Clicking on a specific news organization's link allowed the reader to view the content of that particular organization's Web site, including any related advertising, within the context of the "news frame." In some instances, the framing distorted or modified the appearance of the linked Web site, including the advertisements, while the appearance of TotalNews's advertisements, in a separate frame, remained unchanged. In addition, the URL remained fixed on the TotalNews address, even though the content in the largest frame on the Web site was from the linked Web site. The "news frame" did not, however, eliminate the linked Web site's identifying features.

The case was settled out of court. The news organizations allowed TotalNews to link to their Web sites, but prohibited framing and any attempt to imply affiliation with the news organizations (*The Washington Post, et al. v. TotalNews, Inc.*, 1997).

CHALLENGE: BALANCING THE PROTECTION OF PROPERTY WITH OTHER VALUES

In the areas of copyright, patent law, and trademark law, societies have moved quickly to protect intellectual property from challenges posed by the Internet. In each of these areas, traditional concepts of intellectual property have not only been upheld, but often strengthened. The DMCA seems to restrict journalists and academics from even accessing copyrighted materials if they are encrypted, a protection not true of traditional documents (which are rarely encrypted anyway). Patents have been extended to Internet business methods, and trademarks are more strongly protected than ever because of fears of cybersquatting. In the early years of e-commerce, many commentators believed that Internet technology would sweep away the powers of corporations to protect their property (Dueker, 1996). The case of Napster and digital music files was a powerful example of how a new technology could disrupt an entrenched business model and an entire industry. In the case of Napster, though, the industry won in court suits and forced Napster's demise. Score one for the industry. Napster was quickly replaced by a newer technology (true peer-to-peer networks). Score one for file swappers. However, the U.S. Supreme Court and courts in Australia have found Grokster and other P2P networks liable for the infringement they enable. Australian courts ordered Sharman Network's P2P network software to track over 3,000 words (author and song names) and remove them from their network. In November 2005, Grokster shut down entirely as part of a legal settlement with the record industry, and paid $50 million in damages (McBride, 2005). Advantage: industry.

Despite these legal victories, the software for file-sharing itself is now widely distributed (bit torrent for instance is in the public domain and can be used by anyone with a computer). Because shared music files can be split up across thousands of user computers on these networks, there is no one in charge, no corporate entity to sue. Score one for file sharers. On the other hand, industry associations can identify, and sue the operators of really large computing systems on the networks who act as primary repositories and distributors of stolen music.

In 2008 the RIAA successfully pursued a number of civil suits against individuals storing even modest numbers of music tracks on their computers and making them available to others for downloading, as well as against universities who permit their servers to download stolen files. In September, 2008, the Federal Bureau of Investigation arrested a Los Angeles man on copyright-infringement charges for posting on his Web site nine songs from a yet-to-be-released album by the rock band Guns N' Roses. This is the only the second criminal prosecution for piracy in U.S. history, but it may signal a growing belief among copyright owners that only the reality of going to jail can stop illegal file sharing.

It is apparent that corporations have some very powerful legal tools for protecting their digital properties. By 2008, the record industry had filed over 30,000 lawsuits for sharing files (Kravets, 2008). In addition, there are five arbitration panels established to hear trademark disputes: WIPO, ICANN, the National Arbitration Forum (Minneapolis), eResolutions Consortium (Amherst, Massachusetts), and C.P.R. Institute for Dispute Resolutions in New York. The difficulty now may be in going too far to protect the property interests of the powerful and the rich, preventing parody sites or parody content from receiving wide distribution and recognition, and in this sense interfering with the exercise of First Amendment guarantees of freedom of expression.

8.4   GOVERNANCE

governance

has to do with social control: Who will control e-commerce, what elements will be controlled, and how the controls will be implemented

Governance has to do with social control: Who will control the Internet? Who will control the processes of e-commerce, the content, and the activities? What elements will be controlled, and how will the controls be implemented? A natural question arises and needs to be answered: "Why do we as a society need to 'control' e-commerce?" Because e-commerce and the Internet are so closely intertwined (though not identical), controlling e-commerce also involves regulating the Internet.

WHO GOVERNS E-COMMERCE AND THE INTERNET?

Governance of both the Internet and e-commerce has gone through four stages. **Table 8.13** summarizes these stages in the evolution of e-commerce governance.

Prior to 1995, the Internet was a government program. Beginning in 1995, private corporations were given control of the technical infrastructure as well as the process of granting IP addresses and domain names. However, the NSI monopoly created in this period did not represent international users of the Internet, and was unable to cope with emerging public policy issues such as trademark and intellectual property protection, fair policies for allocating domains, and growing concerns that a small group of firms were benefiting from growth in the Internet.

In 1995, President Clinton, using funds from the Department of Commerce, encouraged the establishment of an international body called the Internet Corporation for Assigned Names and Numbers (ICANN) that hopefully could better represent a wider range of countries and a broad range of interests, and begin to address emerging public policy issues. ICANN was intended to be an Internet/ e-commerce industry self-governing body, not another government agency.

TABLE 8.13	THE EVOLUTION OF GOVERNANCE OF E-COMMERCE
INTERNET GOVERNANCE PERIOD	**DESCRIPTION**
Government Control Period 1970–1994	DARPA and the National Science Foundation control the Internet as a fully government-funded program.
Privatization 1995–1998	Network Solutions Inc. is given a monopoly to assign and track high-level Internet domains. Backbone is sold to private telecommunications companies. Policy issues are not decided.
Self-Regulation 1995–present	President Clinton and the Department of Commerce encourage the creation of a semiprivate body, the Internet Corporation for Assigning Numbers and Names (ICANN), to deal with emerging conflicts and establish policies. ICANN currently holds a contract with the Department of Congress to govern some aspects of the Internet.
Governmental Regulation 1998–present	Executive, legislative, and judicial bodies worldwide begin to implement direct controls over the Internet and e-commerce.

The explosive growth of the Web and e-commerce created a number of issues over which ICANN had no authority. Content issues such as pornography, gambling, and offensive written expressions and graphics, along with commercial issue of intellectual property protection, ushered in the current era of growing governmental regulation of the Internet and e-commerce throughout the world. Currently, we are in a mixed-mode policy environment where self-regulation through a variety of Internet policy and technical bodies co-exists with limited government regulation.

Today, ICANN remains in charge of the domain name system that translates domain names (such as www.company.com) into IP addresses. It has subcontracted the work of maintaining the databases of the domain registries to several private corporations. The U.S. government controls the "A-root" server. However, these arrangements are increasingly challenged by other countries, including China, Russia, Saudi Arabia, and most of the European Union, all of whom want the United States to give up control over the Internet to an international body such as the International Telecommunication Union (ITU) (a UN agency). In November 2005, an Internet Summit sponsored by the ITU agreed to leave control over the Internet domain servers with the United States and instead called for an international forum to meet in future years to discuss Internet policy issues (Miller and Rhoads, 2005). For its part, the United States is currently loathe to give up control over the Internet as originally envisaged by earlier presidents.

Can the Internet Be Controlled?

Early Internet advocates argued that the Internet was different from all previous technologies. They contended that the Internet could not be controlled, given its inherent decentralized design, its ability to cross borders, and its underlying packet switching technology that made monitoring and controlling message content impossible. Many still believe this to be true today. The slogans are "Information wants to be free," and "the Net is everywhere" (but not in any central location). The implication of these slogans is that the content and behavior of e-commerce sites—indeed Internet sites of any kind—cannot be "controlled" in the same way as traditional media such as radio and television. However, attitudes have changed as many governments and corporations extend their control over the Internet and the World Wide Web (Markoff, 2005).

In fact, the Internet is technically very easily controlled, monitored, and regulated from central locations (such as network access points, as well as servers and routers throughout the network). For instance, in China, Saudi Arabia, North Korea, Thailand, Singapore, and many other countries, access to the Web is controlled from government-owned centralized routers that direct traffic across their borders and within the country, such as China's "Great Firewall of China," which permits the government to block access to certain U.S. or European Web sites, or via tightly regulated ISPs operating within the countries. In China, for instance, all ISPs need a license from the Ministry of Information Industry (MII), and are prohibited from disseminating any information that may harm the state or permit pornography, gambling, or the advocacy of cults. In addition, ISPs and search engines such as Google, Yahoo, and MSN typically self-censor their Asian content by using only government-approved news sources. MySpace also self-censors content it believes might upset the Chinese government. Despite this, in October 2007, it was reported that China was redirecting traffic from search engines operated by Google, Microsoft and Yahoo to Chinese-operated Baidu.com (Ho, 2007; Elgin and Einhorn, 2006). In the 2008 Olympics, China routinely censored access by Western media to common Internet sites, including BBC.com.

In some instances, the firms have also cooperated with the Chinese government's pursuit of bloggers and journalists as a condition of its continuing business in China. For instance, Yahoo has been roundly denounced for helping the Chinese government convict and sentence a man to ten years in jail for posting information to a U.S. Web site.

In the United States, as we have seen in our discussion of intellectual property, e-commerce sites can be put out of business for violating existing laws, and ISPs can be forced to "take down" offending content, or stolen content. Government security agencies such as the FBI can obtain court orders to monitor ISP traffic and engage in widespread monitoring of millions of e-mail messages. Under the USA PATRIOT Act, passed after the World Trade Center attack on September 11, 2001, American intelligence authorities are permitted to tap into whatever Internet traffic they believe is relevant to the campaign against terrorism, in some circumstances without judicial review. And many American corporations are developing restrictions on their employees' at-work use of the Web to prevent gambling, shopping, and other activities not related to a business purpose.

In the United States, efforts to control media content on the Web have run up against equally powerful social and political values that protect freedom of expression, including several rulings by the Supreme Court which have struck down laws attempting to limit Web content in the United States. The U.S. Constitution's First Amendment says "Congress shall make no law ... abridging the freedom of speech, or of the press." As it turns out, the 200-year-old Bill of Rights has been a powerful brake on efforts to control 21st-century e-commerce content.

PUBLIC GOVERNMENT AND LAW

The reason we have governments is ostensibly to regulate and control activities within the borders of the nation. What happens in other nations, for the most part, we generally ignore, although clearly environmental and international trade issues require multinational cooperation. E-commerce and the Internet pose some unique problems to public government that center on the ability of the nation-state to govern activities within its borders. Nations have considerable powers to shape the Internet.

TAXATION

Few questions illustrate the complexity of governance and jurisdiction more potently than taxation of e-commerce sales. In both Europe and the United States, governments rely on sales taxes based on the type and value of goods sold. In Europe, these taxes are collected along the entire value chain, including the final sale to the consumer, and are called "value-added taxes" (VAT), whereas in the United States, taxes are collected on final sales to consumers and are called consumption taxes. In the United States, there are 50 states, 3,000 counties, and 12,000 municipalities, each with unique tax rates and policies. Cheese may be taxable in one state as a "snack food" but not taxable in another state (such as Wisconsin), where it is considered a basic food. Consumption taxes are generally recognized to be regressive because they disproportionately tax poorer people, for whom consumption is a larger part of total income.

Sales taxes were first implemented in the United States in the late 1930s as a Depression era method of raising money for localities. Ostensibly, the money was to be used to build infrastructure such as roads, schools, and utilities to support business development, but over the years the funds have been used for general government purposes of the states and localities. In most states, there is a state-based sales tax, and a smaller local sales tax. The total sales tax ranges from zero in some states (North Dakota) to as much as 13% in New York City.

The development of "remote sales" such as mail order/telephone order (MOTO) retail in the United States in the 1970s broke the relationship between physical presence and commerce, complicating the plans of state and local tax authorities to tax all retail commerce. States sought to force MOTO retailers to collect sales taxes for them based on the address of the recipient, but Supreme Court decisions in 1967 and 1992 established that states had no authority to force MOTO retailers to collect state taxes unless the businesses had a "nexus" of operations (physical presence) in the state. Congress could, however, create legislation giving states this authority. But every congressional effort to tax catalog merchants has been beaten back by a torrent of opposition from catalog merchants and consumers, leaving intact an effective tax subsidy for MOTO merchants (Swisher, 2001).

The explosive growth of e-commerce, the latest type of "remote sales," has once again raised the issue of how—and if—to tax remote sales. Since its inception, e-commerce has benefited from a tax subsidy of up to 13% for goods shipped to high sales tax areas. Local retail merchants have complained bitterly about the e-commerce tax subsidy. E-commerce merchants have argued that this new form of commerce needs to be nurtured and encouraged in its early years, and that in any event, the crazy quilt of sales and use tax regimes would be difficult to administer for Internet merchants. State and local governments meanwhile see a potential source of new revenue slipping from their reach.

In 1998, Congress passed the Internet Tax Freedom Act, which placed a moratorium on "multiple or discriminatory taxes on electronic commerce" as well as on taxes on Internet access, for three years until October 2001, and in November 2001, extended the moratorium to November 2003. In November 2002, delegates from 32 states approved model legislation designed to create a system to tax Web sales. Spearheaded by the National Governor's Association (NGA), the Streamlined Sales Tax Project (SSTP) requires participating states to have only one tax rate for personal property or services effective by the end of 2005. By 2007, 15 states had agreed to support the SSTP. The governors are trying to get Congress to override judicial opinions and force online merchants to start collecting taxes. Nevertheless, in December 2004, Congress enacted the Internet Tax Nondiscrimination Act (Public Law 108–435), which extended the moratorium on states and local governments imposing taxes on Internet access and taxes on electronic commerce through November 1, 2007. In October 2007, Congress extended the moratorium once again, this time for an additional seven years. (Gross, 2007).

The merger of online e-commerce with offline commerce further complicates the taxation question. Currently, almost all of the top 100 online retailers collect taxes when orders ship to states where these firms have a physical presence. But others, like eBay, still refuse to collect and pay local taxes, arguing that the so-called tax simplification project ended up with taxes for each of 49,000 ZIP codes, hardly a simplification (Broache, 2005). The taxation situation is also very complex in services. For instance, none of the major online travel sites collect the full amount of state and local hotel occupancy taxes, or state and local airline taxes. Instead of remitting sales tax on the full amount of the consumer's purchase, these sites instead collect taxes on the basis of the wholesale price they pay for the hotel rooms or tickets (Hansell, 2002).

The taxation situation in Europe, and trade between Europe and the United States, is similarly complex. The Organization for Economic Cooperation and Development (OECD), the economic policy coordinating body of European, American, and Japanese governments, is currently investigating different schemes for applying consumption and business profit taxes for e-commerce digitally downloaded goods. The EU began collecting a VAT on digital goods such as music and software delivered to consumers by foreign companies in 2003. Previously,

European Union companies were required to collect the VAT on sales to EU customers, but U.S. companies were not. This gave American companies a huge tax edge.

Thus, there is no integrated rational approach to taxation of domestic or international e-commerce (Varian, 2001). In the United States, the national and international character of Internet sales is wreaking havoc on taxation schemes that were built in the 1930s and based on local commerce and local jurisdictions. Although there appears to be acquiescence among large Internet retailers such as Amazon to the idea of some kind of sales tax on e-commerce sales, their insistence on uniformity will probably delay taxation for many years, and any proposal to tax e-commerce will likely incur the wrath of almost 120 million U.S. e-commerce consumers. Congress is not likely to ignore their voices.

NET NEUTRALITY

"Net neutrality" is more a political slogan than a concept. It means different things to different people. Currently, all Internet traffic is treated equally (or "neutrally") by Internet backbone owners in the sense that all activities--- word processing, emailing, video downloading, etc.-- are charged the same flat rate regardless of how much bandwidth is used.. However, telephone and cable companies that provide the Internet backbone would like to be able to charge differentiated prices based on the amount of bandwidth consumed by content being delivered over the Internet. They would also like to ration bandwidth so that in times of excessive demand they would slow down some traffic ("bandwidth hogs") so that other traffic like email could proceed. There are two ways to achieve this rationing: pricing or speed (bandwidth controls). Heavy bandwidth users can be charged higher usage fees if they overstep a limit. This is referred to as "congestion pricing" or "web metering."

Heavy bandwidth users can also have their applications slowed down based on metering of their usage. In addition, high bandwidth vendors like YouTube could be charged additional fees.The content of companies that pay an additional fee would be given preferential treatment in terms of delivery speed. The content of companies that refused to pay would be delivered at a slower rate.

Likewise, individual home users who downloaded enormous movie files would be charged a higher monthly fee for Internet service compared to neighbors who use the Internet only for email and surfing. For instance, in 2008 the largest ISP in the U.S., Comcast, began to slow down traffic using the Bit Torrent protocol not because the content was pirated but because these video users were consuming huge chunks of the Comcast network capacity. During peak load times, Comcast claims its policy was a legitimate effort to manage capacity. The FCC disagree, and ruled in August, 2008, that Comcast illegally inhibited users of its high-speed network from using file-sharing software. Comcast has appealed. Currently Time Warner Cable is experimenting with Web metering in Beaumont, Texas, charging $1 for every gigabyte over a 5 gigabyte base service.

One minute of a high definition video is about 50 megabytes, 10,000 times larger than an 800 word email message. Those who oppose the idea of "net metering" and charging more for heavy users of bandwidth have been lobbying Congress to create a new layer of Internet regulation that would require network providers to manage their networks in a nondiscriminatory manner. So far, Congress has not yet passed any legislation, although the issue is likely to be revisited as certain types of content, such as online videos and other types of file-sharing, consume more and more bandwidth.

8.5   PUBLIC SAFETY AND WELFARE

Governments everywhere claim to pursue public safety, health, and welfare. This effort produces laws governing everything from weights and measures to national highways, to the content of radio and television programs. Electronic media of all kinds (telegraph, telephone, radio, and television) have historically been regulated by governments seeking to develop a rational commercial telecommunications environment and to control the content of the media—which may be critical of government or offensive to powerful groups in a society. Historically, in the United States, newspapers and print media have been beyond government controls because of constitutional guarantees of freedom of speech. Electronic media such as radio and television have, on the other hand, always been subject to content regulation because they use the publicly owned frequency spectrum. Telephones have also been regulated as public utilities and "common carriers," with special social burdens to provide service and access, but with no limitations on content.

In the United States, critical issues in e-commerce center around the protection of children, strong sentiments against pornography in any public media, efforts to control gambling, and the protection of public health through restricting sales of drugs and cigarettes.

PROTECTING CHILDREN

Pornography is an immensely successful Internet business. According to various statistics, online pornography in 2007 generated somewhere between $2–$3 billion in revenue. According to comScore Media Metrix, more than one-third of U.S. Internet users visit adult Web sites each month, and 4% of all Web traffic and 2% of all time spent Web surfing involved an adult site (eMarketer, Inc., 2007d; Moore, 2007).

To control the Web as a distribution medium for pornography, in 1996, Congress passed the Communications Decency Act (CDA). This act made it a felony criminal offense to use any telecommunications device to transmit "any comment, request, suggestion, proposal, image or other communications which is obscene, lewd, lascivious, filthy, or indecent" to anyone, and in particular, to persons under the age of 18 years of age (Section 502, Communications Decency Act of 1996). In 1997, the Supreme Court struck down the CDA as an unconstitutional abridgement of freedom of speech protected by the First Amendment. While the government argued the CDA was like a zoning ordinance designed to allow "adult" Web sites for people over 18 years of age, the Court found the CDA was a blanket proscription on content and rejected the "cyberzoning" argument as impossible to administer. Another 1996 law, the Child Pornography Prevention Act, which made it a crime to create, distribute, or posses "virtual" child pornography that uses computer-generated images or young adults rather than real children, was also struck down as overly broad by the Supreme Court in 2002, in the *Ashcroft v. Free Speech Coalition* case.

In 1998, Congress passed the Children's Online Protection Act (COPA). This act made it a felony criminal offense to communicate for "commercial purposes" "any material harmful to minors." Harmful material was defined as prurient, depicting sexual acts, and lacking value for minors. The act differed from the CDA by focusing on "commercial speech" and minors exclusively. In February 1999, however, a Federal District Court in Pennsylvania struck down COPA as an unconstitutional restriction on Web content that was protected under the First Amendment. The court nevertheless recognized the interest of Congress and society to protect children on the Internet and in e-commerce. In May 2002, the U.S. Supreme Court returned the case to the Court of Appeals for a decision, leaving in place an injunction barring enforcement of the law. In March 2003, the Third Circuit Court of Appeals ruled for the second time that COPA was unconstitutional, finding that the law violated the First Amendment because it improperly restricts access to a substantial amount of online speech that is lawful for adults. In 2004, the Supreme Court blocked enforcement of the law again, saying that it likely violated the First Amendment, but remanded it to the District Court for a further trial examining Internet filtering technologies that might be used to achieve the law's goals. In January 2006, it was revealed that in preparation for this trial, the Department of Justice had issued subpoenas to Google, AOL, Yahoo, and MSN seeking a week's worth of search queries and a random sampling of 1 million Web addresses in the effort to understand the prevalence of material that could be deemed harmful to minors and the effectiveness of filtering technology, raising a storm of additional controversy. AOL, MSN, and Yahoo all agreed to supply the requested data, but Google refused on a variety of grounds, including protection of its trade secrets, privacy, and public relations (Hafner and Richtel, 2006). In response, the court limited the subpoena to just a sample of URLs in Google's database. In March 2007, the district court struck down COPA, ruling once again that the law violated the 1st and 5th Amendments, and issued an order permanently enjoining the government from enforcing COPA. The government once again appealed, and in July 2008, the 3rd Circuit Court of Appeals upheld the district court opinion that COPA violated the 1st amendment. The government indicated that it once again was likely to appeal the decision to the Supreme Court (Singel, 2008).

The 2003 Protect Act is an omnibus bill intended to prevent child abuse that includes prohibitions against computer-generated child pornography." Part of that statute was previously held to be unconstitutional by the 11th Circuit Court of Appeals, but in May 2008, the Supreme Court reversed the 11th Circuit, and upheld the provision (Greenhouse, 2008).

Although Congress has had a difficult time framing constitutionally acceptable legislation to protect children and other consumers from pornography, in the Children's Online Privacy Protection Act (COPPA) (1998) (described in Section 8.2), it appears to have been successful in preventing e-commerce sites from collecting information on minors without parental consent. Pornographers who collect information on children without parental consent are potential felons. Because COPPA does not regulate e-commerce content per se, to date it has not been challenged in the courts.

In 2001, Congress passed the Children's Internet Protection Act (CIPA), which required schools and libraries in the United States to install "technology protection measures" (filtering software), in an effort to shield children from pornography. In June 2003, the Supreme Court upheld CIPA, overturning a Federal District Court that found the law interfered with the First Amendment guarantee of freedom of expression. The Supreme Court, in a 6-3 opinion, held that the law's limitations on access to the Internet posed no more a threat to freedom of expression than limitations on access to books that librarians choose for whatever reason not to acquire. The dissenting justices found this analogy inappropriate and instead argued the proper analogy was if librarians were to purchase encyclopedias and then rip out pages they thought were or might be offensive to patrons. All the justices agreed that existing blocking software was overly blunt, unable to distinguish child pornography from sexually explicit material (which is protected by the First Amendment), and generally unreliable (Greenhouse, 2003b). Other legislation such as the 2002 Domain Names Act seeks to prevent unscrupulous Web site operators from luring children to pornography using misleading domain names or characters known to children, while the 2002 Dot Kids Act authorizes the creation of a second-level domain on the Internet where all Web sites would have to declare they contain no material harmful to children. An alternative plan, to create an .xxx domain for adult Web site content, was rejected by ICANN for the third time in March 2007 (Moore, 2007).

In addition to government regulation, private pressure from organized groups has also been successful in forcing some Web sites to eliminate the display of pornographic materials. In June 2008, in response to pressure from Andrew Cuomo, New York's attorney general, Verizon, Time Warner Cable, and Sprint, agreed to limit access to some or all Usenet groups in an effort to block access to child pornography. A T&T AOL, and Comcast followed suit in July 2008.

CIGARETTES, GAMBLING, AND DRUGS: IS THE WEB REALLY BORDERLESS?

In the United States, both the states and the federal government have adopted legislation to control certain activities and products in order to protect public health and welfare. Cigarettes, gambling, medical drugs, and of course addictive recreational drugs, are either banned or tightly regulated by federal and state laws (see *Insight on Society: The Internet Drug Bazaar*). Yet these products and services are ideal for distribution over the Internet through e-commerce sites. Because the sites can be located offshore, they can operate beyond the jurisdiction of state and federal prosecutors. Or so it seemed until recently. In the case of cigarettes, state and federal authorities have been quite successful in shutting down tax-free cigarette Web sites within the United States and pressuring credit card firms to drop cigarette merchants from their systems. The major shipping companies—UPS, FedEx and DHL—have been pressured into refusing shipment of untaxed cigarettes, and in September 2008, the House passed a bill that would impose shipping and record-keeping requirements on those selling cigarettes and smokeless tobacco over the phone or through the mail or via the Internet, and makes failure to comply with state tax laws a felony. The bill also requires Internet and other remote sellers to verify the age and identity of purchasers, and prohibits use of the U.S. Postal Service for delivery. A similar bill is pending in the Senate (Abrams, 2008). Phillip Morris has also agreed not to ship cigarettes to any resellers that have been found to be engaging in illegal Internet and mail order sales. However, East European sites and Web sites located on American Indian reservations continue to operate using checks and money orders as payments and the postal system as logistics partner, but their level of business has plummeted as consumers fear state tax authorities will present them with huge tax bills if they are discovered using these sites. As a result of these pressures and the threat of ultimately collecting taxes from consumers who purchase at these sites, online tax-free cigarette sales have dropped precipitously.

Gambling also provides an interesting example of the clash between traditional jurisdictional boundaries and claims to a borderless, uncontrollable Web. The online gambling market, based almost entirely offshore—primarily in United Kingdom and various Caribbean Islands—grew by leaps and bounds between 2000 and 2006, generating as much as $50 billion to $60 billion a year, and with much of the action (some estimate up to 50%) coming from customers based in the United States. Although the federal government contended online gambling was illegal under U.S. federal law, they were initially unable to stop it, with various federal courts offering mixed opinions. However, in the summer of 2006, federal officials turned up the heat and arrested two executive officers of offshore gambling operations as they passed through the United States, leading their companies to cease U.S. operations. Then in October 2006, Congress passed the Unlawful Internet Gambling Enforcement Act, which makes it a crime to use credit cards or online payment systems for Internet betting. This effectively bars online gambling companies from operating legally in the United States, and shortly thereafter a number of the leading, publicly traded companies suspended their business in the United States. However, the bill has not eliminated all online gambling in the United States, with some smaller companies still offering offshore gambling. An association of online gambling groups is also challenging the law as unconstitutional, claiming that Internet gambling is protected by First Amendment privacy rights and that filtering technology exists to make sure that children and compulsive gamblers cannot access offshore betting sites. Several countries are also seeking compensation from the United States on the basis of a World Trade Organization ruling that American Internet gambling restrictions are illegal (Parry, 2007; Rivlan, 2007; Pfanner, 2006).

In September 2008, Representative Barney Frank, chairman of the House Financial Services Committee, introduced a bill that would require federal agencies to define the term "unlawful Internet gambling," on the grounds that existing legislation and regulation failed to define to do so, leaving financial institutions to figure out for themselves whether or not it was legal to process a given transaction.

INSIGHT ON SOCIETY

THE INTERNET DRUG BAZAAR

In August 2008, the president of Hi-Tech Pharmaceuticals and three other company officers pleaded guilty to conspiracy charges in connection with the importation and distribution of adulterated and unapproved drugs without valid prescriptions. The company used spam e-mail to market inexpensive, generic versions of Valium, Xanax, Ambien, Vioxx, Viagra and Cialis, among others, that were supposedly made in Canada, but were instead produced in an unsanitary 4-room house in Belize. The defendants face up to 5 years in prison, and fines of $250,000 each. The company also faces a fine of the greater of $500,000 or double the amount of fraud. The company sold millions of dollars worth of pharmaceuticals before being shut down in late 2006.

In another case, in July 2008, Alvin Woody, the owner of two North Carolina pharmacies, pleaded guilty to charges of conspiracy to distribute controlled substances and money laundering in connection with an unlawful prescription drug operation. According to the indictment, from August 2002 to May 2006, Kathleen Giacobbe, the owner and operator of Youronlinedoctor.com, as well as four other defendants, including a doctor and Woody conspired to distribute millions of dosage units of powerful and addictive painkillers and anxiety medications to thousands of customers nationwide based on unlawful and illegitimate prescriptions. The purported prescriptions were in fact merely drug "orders" taken by the Web site and then filled by the North Carolina pharmacies, which by pre-arrangement had agreed not to challenge the legitimacy of the orders. The Web site employed a doctor to give it the façade of legitimacy, and used a photocopy of his signature when it submitted the orders.

According to a study done by the Treatment Research Institute at the University of Pennsylvania, addictive and potentially lethal medications are available without prescription from more than 2 million Web sites around the world, with many sites based in countries that impose little if any regulation on pharmaceuticals. The National Center on Addiction and Substance Abuse (CASA) at Columbia University found in 2006 that a majority of Web sites selling controlled prescription drugs did not require a prescription. MarkMonitor, a company specializing in online brand protection, studied 2,968 online pharmacies in the summer of 2008. It found that questionable business practices were more the norm than the exception. A Google search on "drugs" "no prescription" returns over 2 million results.

The sale of drugs without a prescription is not the only danger posed by the Internet drug bazaar. Rogue online pharmacy sites may be selling counterfeit drugs, or unapproved drugs. For example, in February 2007, the FDA issued a warning that a number of consumers who had purchased Ambien, Xanax, and Lexapro online from several different Web sites had instead received a product containing haloperial, a powerful anti-psychotic drug. In May 2007, the FDA issued another warning that 24 apparently related Web sites were involved in the distribution of counterfeit versions of Xenical, a prescription weight loss drug.

But despite these dangers, online pharmacies remain alluring and are one of the fastest-growing business models, with, oddly, senior citizens—usually some of the most law-abiding citizens—leading the charge for cheaper drugs. The top 1,000 Internet pharmacies are estimated to generate about $4 billion in revenue. The main

(continued)

attraction of online drug sites is price. Typically, they are located in countries where prescription drugs are price-controlled, or where the price structure is much lower, such as in Mexico. U.S. citizens can often save 50%–75% by purchasing from online pharmacies located in other countries.

Currently a patchwork regulatory structure governs the sale of drugs online. At the federal level, the 1938 Food, Drug, and Cosmetic Act (FDCA) requires that certain drugs may only be purchased with a valid doctor's prescription and must be dispensed by a state-licensed pharmacy. To get around this requirement, some online pharmacies use questionnaires to diagnose disease and have these questionnaires reviewed by doctors that write the prescription. Whether this constitutes a "valid" prescription differs from state to state, which regulate both pharmacies and the practice of medicine within their borders. Congress has considered legislation to establish a federal definition of what constitutes a valid prescription, but to date such legislation has not passed. Complicating matters is the fact that many online pharmacies

operate offshore, making it difficult for federal and state authorities to exercise jurisdiction over them. In September 2008, Congress strengthened its regulation of online pharmacies considerably by passing the Ryan Haight Online Pharmacy Consumer Protection Act, which bans the sale of prescription drugs over the Internet without a prescription issued by a practitioner that has examined the patient at least once. The act will also require online pharmacies to comply with pharmacy licensing laws in every state where they do business.

In the meantime, the Food and Drug Administration recommends that consumers look for the National Association of Boards of Pharmacy (NABP) Verified Internet Pharmacy Practices Sites (VIPPS) Seal, which verifies that the site is legitimate. So far, 15 major Internet pharmacies have signed on, including Drugstore.com, Caremark.com, CVS.com, Walgreens.com, among others. However, that leaves thousands of sites that consumers should approach with a "buyer beware" attitude.

SOURCES: "MarkMonitor Reports Continuing Rise in Online Abuse of Top Drug Brands," Markmonitor.com, August 26, 2008; "From Diet Supplements to Illegal Net Pharmacy," by Mike Brunker, msnbc.com, August 19, 2008; "Mooresville Pharmacist Pleads Gulity to Conspiracy, Money Laundering Charges," Mooresville Tribune, July 30, 2008; "Online Pill Pushers Busted," by Roy Mark, Internetnews.com, August 3, 2007; "Five Defendants Indicted in Unlawful Prescription Drug Operation," Department of Justice, July 20, 2007; "Legal Issues Related to Prescription Drug Sales on the Internet," by Vanessa Burrows, CRS Report for Congress, July 12, 2007; "The Possible Dangers of Buying Medicine Online," U.S. Food and Drug Administration, July 2, 2007; "FDA Warns Consumers about Counterfeit Drugs from Multiple Internet Sellers," U.S. Food and Drug Administration, May 1, 2007; "Vantage Point: Internet Sales of Dangerous Drugs without a Prescription," by Keith Humphreys, *Stanford Report*, May 30, 2007; "FDA Alerts Consumers to Unsafe, Misrepresented Drugs Purchased Over the Internet," U.S. Food and Drug Administration, February 16, 2007; "Internet Prescriptions as Public Health Threat," by Edmund Scanlan, Chicago Accident Law Blog, February 13, 2007.

Print the Library [Online]:
Is Google Playing Fair, or Just Out to Make a Buck?

Google is on a tear to put everything digital on its servers and then, as the founders promise in ceaseless self-congratulatory announcements, provide access to "all the world's information" through its efforts. And make a buck, as it turns out, by selling ads aimed at you that are "relevant" to your searches. A problem arises, however, when what Google wants to put on their servers does not belong to them. We're all familiar with the copyrighted music and video situation, where firms often operating offshore, beyond the law (or so they think) enable, induce, and encourage Internet users to illegally download copyrighted material without paying a dime for it, while in the meantime raking in millions of advertising dollars from companies willing to advertise on their networks.

But Google is no criminal organization. For a firm who's motto is "Don't be evil," it seems out of character for it to initiate a program of scanning millions of copyrighted books it does not own and then, without permission, providing its search

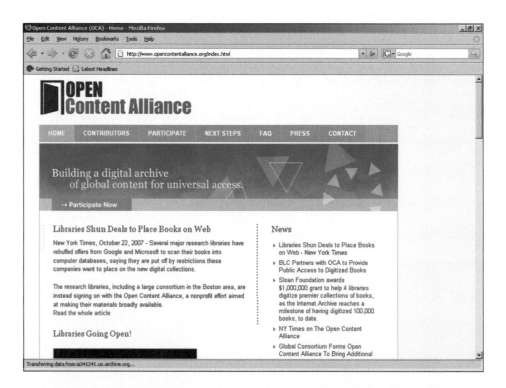

engine users with access to those books without charge, while selling ad space and pocketing millions for its own account without sharing that revenue with publishers or authors. One major difference between Google and most file-sharing firms is that Google has very deep pockets filled with cash, and they are based in the United States, making it an excellent legal target.

It's a complicated story with exaggerations on all sides. In 2004, Google announced a program it now calls the Google Book Search Project (previously called Google Print). There are two parts to the project. Under the Partner Program (previously called the Publisher Program), publishers give permission to Google to scan their books, or make scans available, and then make parts of the work, or simply bibliographic information (title, author, and publisher), available on Google's search engine. No problem there: publishers and authors get a chance to find a wider market, and Google sells more ads.

It's the second part of the project that is controversial. Under the Library Project (previously called Google Print Library), Google proposes to scan millions of books in university and public libraries and then allow users to search for key phrases, and display "relevant" portions of the text (what it calls "snippets"), all without contacting the publisher or seeking permission or paying a royalty fee. Google said it would "never show a full page without the right from the copyright holder," just the "relevant" portion. Google gave the publishing industry until November 2005 to opt-out by providing Google with a list of books they did not want to be included.

Google has the backing of a number of prestigious libraries, such as the University of Michigan, Harvard University, Stanford University, the New York Public Library, and Oxford University. But not all librarians agree. Some believe this is a marvelous extension of public access to library collections, while other librarians fear it is harmful to book authors and publishers. A number of well-known libraries, such as the Smithsonian Institution, and the Boston Public Library, as well as a consortium of 19 research and academic libraries in the Northeast, have refused to participate, in part because of restrictions that Google wants to place on the collection. Libraries that work with Google must agree to make the material unavailable to other commercial search services.

Google claims it is performing a public service by making an index of books, and relevant portions, available to millions on the Internet, and perhaps even helping publishers sell new copies of books that currently sit on dusty library shelves. The publishing industry disagrees with Google and two lawsuits were quickly filed in federal court in New York, one a class-action suit by the Authors Guild, and the second by five major publishing companies (McGraw Hill, Pearson Education, Penguin Group, Simon & Schuster, and John Wiley & Sons), claiming copyright infringement. The American Association of Publishers alleges that Google is claiming the right to "unilaterally change copyright law and copy anything unless somebody tells [them] "No" [making it] impossible for people in the intellectual property community to operate. They [Google] keep talking about doing this because it is good for the world. That has never been a principle in law. They 'do no evil' except they are stealing people's property." Or, as one wag put it, it's like having a thief break into your house and clean the kitchen—it's still breaking and entering.

Google, on the other hand, claims this use is "fair" under the "fair use" doctrine that has emerged from a number of court decisions issued over the years, and which is codified in the Copyright Act in 1976 (refer to Table 8.11). The copying and lending of books by libraries has been considered a fair use since the late 1930s under a "gentleman's agreement" between libraries and publishers, and a library exemption was codified as Section 108 of the Copyright Act of 1976. Libraries loan books to patrons for a limited period, and they must purchase at least one copy. Many people read books borrowed from libraries and recommend them to friends, who often buy the books rather than take the time and effort to go to a library. Libraries are also considered by many in the publishing industry as helping to market a book to a larger public, and libraries are believed to be performing a public service by increasing literacy and education.

There are two lines of cases that suggest potentially different outcomes for the Google litigation. In New York, in the *UMG Recording v. MP3* case, the federal district court for the Southern District of New York ruled that a defendant that copied copyrighted works onto a server and allowed access to third-party subscribers was not protected by fair use. But in California, two Ninth Circuit cases, *Kelly v. Arriba Soft*, and *Perfect 10, Inc. v. Amazon.com Inc.*, held that the storage and display of "thumbnail" images of copyrighted works in order to make them accessible via a search engine was fair use. Motions for summary judgment in both Google lawsuits were filed in July 2007, and in 2008 the cases are plodding along in federal court with no trial dates set. It will be many years before this litigation is completed.

In 2006 Microsoft launched a similar book search project called Microsoft Live Books Search that operated just like Google Search Books but it did not scan books without permission from publishers. In a see-saw battle through 2007 and 2008, Microsoft and Google issued press releases on the number of publishing firms that had signed up to support them. Finally in May, 2008, Microsoft closed the project down after scanning 750,000 books and 80 million academic articles. Microsoft said it did not see a viable business model in this space.

Meanwhile, the Open Content Alliance (OCA) has begun its own mammoth book-scanning project to produce an open database of book contents that will be accessible from any search engine, including Google's. For the most part, the OCA will focus on books in the public domain, often of historical interest. But for books still under copyright protection, they will obtain permission from the publishers before scanning. In contrast, Google wants to own and control its database of books. Proponents of the OCA approach worry that allowing one company, such as Google, to dominate the digital conversion of books is a dangerous proposition that gives too much control to a private entity that has profit as its primary goal. Major public and academic libraries (such as the Smithsonian Library and the Boston Public Libraries) have refused to join Google and instead want any scanned books to be available to all search engines and Internet devices without commercial restriction.

The book industry isn't the only industry likely to have to worry about Google. Just about any digital content is in the cross-hairs of Google's plans to dominate the Internet search industry. The more digital content Google can index, from maps, to music, TV programs, books, newspapers, and reports, the larger its audience, and the more money it can make from selling space to advertisers.

SOURCES: "Update on Authors Guild V. Google, Inc.," by Maya Reynolds, mayareynoldswriter.blogspot.com, July 21, 2008; "Three Years Later, Google Book Search, Mass Digitization, Continue to Spark Debate, by Cary Lening, Bureau of National Affairs, Patent, Trademark & Copyright Journal, Vol. 76, No. 1872, June 13, 2008; "Microsoft's Live Search scraps book digitization project," by Caroline McCarthy, CNETNews.com, May 23, 2008; "Envisioning the Next Chapter for Electronic Books," by Brad Stone, The New York Times, September 6, 2007; "Libraries Shun Deals to Place Books on Web," by Katie Hafner, *New York Times*, October 22, 2007; "The Google Book Search Project Litigation," by Lawrence Jordan, *Michigan Bar Journal*, September 2007; "Scan This Book!," by Andrew Richard Albanese, *Library Journal*, August 15, 2007; "Search Me?, " by Bob Thompson, *Washington Post*, August 13, 2006.

Case Study Questions

1. Who is harmed by Google's Library Project? Make a list of harmed groups, and for each group, try to devise a solution that would eliminate or lessen the harm.

2. If you were a librarian, would you support Google's Library Project? Why or why not?

3. Do you believe Google's claim that scanning entire books fits within the concept of "fair use"? Why or why not?

4. What are some of the important differences between Google's Library Project program and the Open Content Alliance program?

5. Why is Google pursuing the Library Project program? What is in it for Google? Make a list of benefits to Google.

8.7 REVIEW

KEY CONCEPTS

■ Understand why e-commerce raises ethical, social, and political issues.

Internet technology and its use in e-commerce disrupts existing social and business relationships and understandings. Suddenly, individuals, business firms, and political institutions are confronted by new possibilities of behavior for which understandings, laws, and rules of acceptable behavior have not yet been developed. Many business firms and individuals are benefiting from the commercial development of the Internet, but this development also has costs for individuals, organizations, and societies. These costs and benefits must be carefully considered by those seeking to make ethical and socially responsible decisions in this new environment, particularly where there are as yet no clear-cut legal or cultural guidelines.

■ Recognize the main ethical, social, and political issues raised by e-commerce.

The major issues raised by e-commerce can be loosely categorized into four major dimensions:
- *Information rights*—What rights do individuals have to control their own personal information when Internet technologies make information collection so pervasive and efficient?
- *Property rights*—How can traditional intellectual property rights be enforced when perfect copies of protected works can be made and easily distributed worldwide via the Internet?
- *Governance*—Should the Internet and e-commerce be subject to public laws? If so, what law-making bodies have jurisdiction-state, federal, and/or international?

- *Public safety and welfare*—What efforts should be undertaken to ensure equitable access to the Internet and e-commerce channels? Do certain online content and activities pose a threat to public safety and welfare?

■ **Identify a process for analyzing ethical dilemmas.**

Ethical, social, and political controversies usually present themselves as dilemmas. Ethical dilemmas can be analyzed via the following process:
- Identify and clearly describe the facts.
- Define the conflict or dilemma and identify the higher-order values involved.
- Identify the stakeholders.
- Identify the options that you can reasonably take.
- Identify the potential consequences of your options.
- Refer to well-established ethical principles, such as the Golden Rule, Universalism, Descartes' Rule of Change, the Collective Utilitarian Principle, Risk Aversion, the No Free Lunch Rule, the *New York Times* Test, and the Social Contract Rule to help you decide the matter.

■ **Understand basic concepts related to privacy.**

To understand the issues concerning online privacy, you must first understand some basic concepts:
- *Privacy* is the moral right of individuals to be left alone, free from surveillance or interference from others.
- *Information privacy* includes both the claim that certain information should not be collected at all by governments or business firms, and the claim of individuals to control the use of information about themselves.
- *Due process* as embodied by the Fair Information Practices doctrine, informed consent, and opt-in/opt-out policies also play an important role in privacy.

■ **Identify the practices of e-commerce companies that threaten privacy.**

Almost all e-commerce companies collect some personally identifiable information in addition to anonymous information and use cookies to track clickstream behavior of visitors. Advertising networks and search engines also track the behavior of consumers across thousands of popular sites, not just at one site, via cookies, spyware, search engine behavioral targeting, and other techniques

■ **Describe the different methods used to protect online privacy.**

There are a number of different methods used to protect online privacy. They include:
- Legal protections deriving from constitutions, common law, federal law, state laws, and government regulations. In the United States, rights to online privacy may be derived the U.S. Constitution, tort law, federal laws such as the Children's Online Privacy Protection Act (COPPA), the Federal Trade Commission's Fair Information Practice principles, and a variety of state laws. In Europe, the European Commission's Directive on Data Protection has standardized and broadened privacy protection in the European Union nations.
- Industry self-regulation via industry alliances, such as the Online Privacy Alliance and the Network Advertising Initiative, that seek to gain voluntary adherence to industry privacy guidelines and safe harbors. Some firms also hire chief privacy officers.

- Privacy-enhancing technological solutions include secure e-mail, anonymous remailers, anonymous surfing, cookie managers, disk file-erasing programs, policy generators, and privacy policy readers.

■ **Understand the various forms of intellectual property and the challenge of protecting it.**

There are three main types of intellectual property protection: copyright, patent, and trademark law.

- *Copyright law* protects original forms of expression such as writings, drawings, and computer programs from being copied by others for a minimum of 70 years. It does not protect ideas—just their expression in a tangible medium. "Look and feel" copyright infringement lawsuits are precisely about the distinction between an idea and its expression. If there is only one way to express an idea, then the expression cannot be copyrighted. Copyrights, like all rights, are not absolute. The doctrine of fair use permits certain parties under certain circumstances to use copyrighted material without permission. The Digital Millennium Copyright Act (DMCA) is the first major effort to adjust the copyright laws to the Internet Age. The DMCA implements a World Intellectual Property Organization treaty, which declares it illegal to make, distribute, or use devices that circumvent technology-based protections of copyrighted materials, and attaches stiff fines and prison sentences for violations.

- *Patent law* grants the owner of a patent an exclusive monopoly to the ideas behind an invention for 20 years. Patents are very different from copyrights in that they protect the ideas themselves and not merely the expression of ideas. There are four types of inventions for which patents are granted under patent law: machines, man-made products, compositions of matter, and processing methods. In order to be granted a patent, the applicant must show that the invention is new, original, novel, non-obvious, and not evident in prior arts and practice. Most of the inventions that make the Internet and e-commerce possible were not patented by their inventors. This changed in the mid-1990s with the commercial development of the World Wide Web. Business firms began applying for "business methods" and software patents.

- *Trademark protections* exist at both the federal and state levels in the United States. The purpose of trademark law is twofold. First, trademark law protects the public in the marketplace by ensuring that it gets what it pays for and wants to receive. Second, trademark law protects the owner who has spent time, money, and energy bringing the product to market against piracy and misappropriation. Federal trademarks are obtained, first, by use in interstate commerce, and second, by registration with the U.S. Patent and Trademark Office (USPTO). Trademarks are granted for a period of ten years and can be renewed indefinitely. Use of a trademark that creates confusion with existing trademarks, causes consumers to make market mistakes, or misrepresents the origins of goods is an infringement. In addition, the intentional misuse of words and symbols in the marketplace to extort revenue from legitimate trademark owners ("bad faith") is proscribed. The Anticybersquatting Consumer Protection Act (ACPA) creates civil liabilities for anyone who attempts in bad faith to profit from an existing famous or distinctive trademark by registering an Internet domain name that is identical, confusingly similar, or "dilutive" of that trademark. Trademark abuse can take many forms on the Web. The major behaviors on the Internet that have run afoul of trademark law include cybersquatting, cyberpiracy, metatagging, keywording, linking, and framing.

■ Understand how governance of the Internet has evolved over time.

Governance has to do with social control: who will control e-commerce, what elements will be controlled, and how the controls will be implemented. Governance of both the Internet and e-commerce has gone through four stages:

- *Government control (1970–1994)*. During this period, DARPA and the National Science Foundation controlled the Internet as a fully government funded program.
- *Privatization (1995–1998)*. Network Solutions was given a monopoly to assign and track high-level Internet domain names. The backbone was sold to private telecommunications companies and policy issues remained undecided.
- *Self-regulation (1995–present)*. President Clinton and the Department of Commerce encouraged creation of ICANN, a semi-private body, to deal with emerging conflicts and to establish policies.
- *Governmental regulation (1998–present)*. Executive, legislative, and judicial bodies worldwide began to implement direct controls over the Internet and e-commerce.

We are currently in a mixed-mode policy environment where self-regulation, through a variety of Internet policy and technical bodies, co-exists with limited government regulation.

■ Explain why taxation of e-commerce raises governance and jurisdiction issues.

E-commerce raises the issue of how—and if—to tax remote sales. The national and international character of Internet sales is wreaking havoc on taxation schemes in the United States that were built in the 1930s and based on local commerce and local jurisdictions. E-commerce has benefited from a tax subsidy since its inception. E-commerce merchants have argued that this new form of commerce needs to be nurtured and encouraged, and that in any event, the crazy quilt of sales and use tax regimes would be difficult to administer for Internet merchants. In 1998, Congress passed the Internet Tax Freedom Act, which placed a moratorium on multiple or discriminatory taxes on electronic commerce, and any taxation of Internet access, and since that time has extended the moratorium three times, most recently until November 2014. In November 2002, delegates from 32 states approved model legislation designed to create a system to tax Web sales, and by 2007, 15 states had agreed to support the program. Although there appears to be acquiescence among large Internet retailers to the idea of some kind of sales tax on e-commerce sales, insistence on uniformity will delay taxation for many years, and any proposal to
tax e-commerce will likely incur the wrath of U.S. e-commerce consumers.

■ Identify major public safety and welfare issues raised by e-commerce.

Critical public safety and welfare issues in e-commerce include:

- The protection of children and strong sentiments against pornography. The Children's Online Protection Act (COPA) of 1998 made it a felony criminal offense to communicate for commercial purposes any material harmful to minors. This law has thus far been struck down as an unconstitutional restriction on Web content that is protected under the First Amendment. The Children's Internet Protection Act (CIPA), which requires schools and libraries in the United States to install "technology protection measures" (filtering soft-ware) in an effort to shield children from pornography, has however, been upheld by the Supreme Court. In addition to government regulation, private pressure from organized groups has also been successful in forcing some Web sites to eliminate the display of pornographic materials.

- Efforts to control gambling and restrict sales of cigarettes and drugs. In the United States, cigarettes, gambling, medical drugs, and addictive recreational drugs are either banned or tightly regulated by federal and state laws. Yet these products and services are often distributed via offshore e-commerce sites operating beyond the jurisdiction of federal and state prosecutors. At this point, it is not clear that the Web will remain borderless or that e-commerce can continue to flaunt national, state, and local laws with impunity.

QUESTIONS

1. What basic assumption does the study of ethics make about individuals?
2. What are the three basic principles of ethics? How does due process factor in?
3. Explain Google's position that YouTube does not violate the intellectual property rights of copyright owners.
4. Define universalism, slippery slope, the *New York Times* test, and the social contract rule as they apply to ethics.
5. Explain why someone with a serious medical condition might be concerned about researching his or her condition online, through medical search engines or pharmaceutical sites, for example. What is one technology that could prevent one's identity from being revealed?
6. Name some of the personal information collected by Web sites about their visitors.
7. How does information collected through online forms differ from site transaction logs? Which potentially provides a more complete consumer profile?
8. How is the opt-in model of informed consent different from opt-out? In which type of model does the consumer retain more control?
9. What are the two core principles of the FTC's Fair Information Practice principles?
10. How do safe harbors work? What is the government's role in them?
11. Name three ways online advertising networks have improved on, or added to, traditional offline marketing techniques.
12. Explain how Web profiling is supposed to benefit both consumers and businesses.
13. What are some of the challenges that chief privacy officers (CPOs) face in their jobs?
14. How could the Internet potentially change protection given to intellectual property? What capabilities make it more difficult to enforce intellectual property law?
15. What does the Digital Millennium Copyright Act attempt to do? Why was it enacted? What types of violations does it try to prevent?
16. Define cybersquatting. How is it different from cyberpiracy? What type of intellectual property violation does cybersquatting entail?
17. What is deep linking and why is it a trademark issue? Compare it to framing—how is it similar and different?

18. What are some of the tactics illegal businesses, such as betting parlors and casinos, successfully use to operate outside the law on the Internet?

PROJECTS

1. Go to Google's Preferences page and examine its SafeSearch filtering options. Surf the Web in search of content that could be considered objectionable for children using each of the options. What are the pros and cons of such restrictions? Are there terms that could be considered inappropriate to the filtering software but be approved by parents? Name five questionable terms. Prepare a brief presentation to report on your experiences and to explain the positive and negative aspects of such filtering software.

2. Develop a list a privacy protection features that should be present if a Web site is serious about protecting privacy. Then, visit at least four well-known Web sites and examine their privacy policies. Write a report that rates each of the Web sites on the criteria you have developed.

3. Review the provisions of the Digital Millennium Copyright Act of 1998. Examine each of the major sections of the legislation and make a list of the protections afforded property owners and users of copyrighted materials. Do you believe this legislation balances the interests of owners and users appropriately? Do you have suggestions for strengthening "fair use" provisions in this legislation?

4. Visit at least four Web sites that take a position on e-commerce taxation, beginning with The National Conference of State Legislatures (Ncsl.org) and The National Governor's Association (Nga.org). You might also include national associations of local businesses or citizen groups opposed to e-commerce taxation. Develop a reasoned argument for, or against, taxation of e-commerce.

5. Consider the issue of the Department of Justice's subpoena of search query records discussed on page 539. Prepare a list of reasons why the firms subpoenaed should or should not comply with this request. What moral dilemmas present themselves? What higher-order values, and what kind of value conflicts, are revealed in this list. How do you propose that we as a society resolve these dilemmas. You might conclude by applying each of the Candidate Ethical Principles described in Section 8.1.

6. The opening case describes the virtual world created by Second Life. Find another virtual world on the Web and compare and contrast it to the features offered by Second Life. Prepare a brief presentation or report on your findings.

WEB SITE RESOURCES www.prenhall.com/laudon

- Additional projects, exercises, and tutorials
- Careers: Explore career opportunities in e-commerce
- Raising capital and business plans

E-commerce in Action

CHAPTER 9

Online Retail and Services

Blue Nile Sparkles
For Your Cleopatra

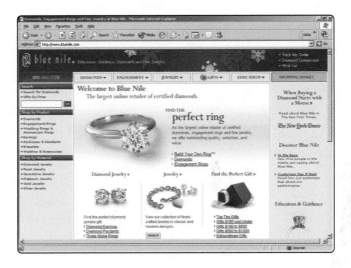

Men: looking for that special gift for your Cleopatra, but don't want to spend a lot of time shopping? Want to give the "Big Rock" certified by the independent Gemological Institute of America (GIA) or the American Gem Society Laboratories (AGSL) without spending a mountain of cash for the engagement experience? How about 35% less than retail prices? Not sure about the future value of diamonds? Then how about pearls, gold, or platinum?

Your answer has arrived: BlueNile.com offers you an online selection of over 60,000 diamonds for that special someone. You can buy them cut and polished, or put them into settings like rings, bracelets, earrings, necklaces, pendants, watches, and broaches that you can choose online. All the diamonds are graded by the 4Cs: carats (size), cut, color, and clarity, and a report for each diamond prepared by the GIA is available online. To make it easier, fellas, the carats are translated into milligrams, and one carat is exactly 200 milligrams of mass (if that helps). Just ask her what size she wants, and then look in your wallet. Although the majority of visitors to the site are women, about 85% of Blue Niles customers are men.

In June 2007, Blue Nile sold the biggest item in Internet history, a $1.5 million single diamond of around 10 carats, a size that would cover your finger with a penny-size rock. That's about 2,000 milligrams, the biggest mouse click ever. The mouse that roared?

BlueNile.com started out as RockShop.com in March 1999 in Seattle, Washington. In May 1999, the company purchased Williams and Son, a Seattle jeweler with a Web site, and changed its name to Internet Diamonds, Inc. In November 1999, the company launched the Blue Nile brand and changed its name to Blue Nile Inc., opening up its Web site, BlueNile.com, in December 1999. In May 2004, Blue Nile went public at $20, and jumped to $28 (a 38% pop) in the first day of trading. The received wisdom of Web gurus in 1999 was that the Internet would never be a place where fine jewelry could be sold. Why? CDs and books are what everyone thought the Web was good at back then.

Purchasing jewelry, especially high-cost diamonds, is what marketers call a "significant event." Typically, gifts of diamonds are associated with a significant emotional event, such as an engagement, marriage, or an anniversary. Generally, the event is shared with a significant other and often involves shopping together for the gem. Shopping on the Web (alone or together) hardly matches the emotional impact of walking into Tiffany's or another established retail store, with marvelous clear glass cases filled with brilliantly shining baubles, attended by a small army of unctuous perfumed sales clerks that make you feel so special. Diamonds represent a significant cost, and there is significant uncertainty about their value and pricing. Surveys show that most shoppers believe jewelry is highly overpriced, but they lack the knowledge and information to negotiate a better price or even judge the quality of what they are buying. Consumers generally have no rational way to compare diamonds, and face a limited selection at a single store, often in a high-pressured environment where sales employees are helping several customers at the same time. Most experts thought that, given the emotional significance and uncertainty of purchasing diamonds, few consumers would heighten the built-in anxiety by going to a strange Web site and plunking down $5,000 or more for a diamond they could not see or touch for several days.

But jewelry and high fashion retailers are leading the second act of online retailing, bursting on the scene in 2004 with high growth rates and spectacular average sales transaction levels. As it turns out, the retail jewelry industry is an ideal candidate for Web sales. Here's why.

The $51 billon traditional jewelry industry is a byzantine, fragmented collection of 126,000 physical stores in the United States, including 28,000 locations classified as specialty jewelry stores. About 95% of all retail jewelry firms operate only a single store. To supply this fragmented market, several layers of wholesalers and middlemen intervene, from rough diamond brokers, diamond cutters, diamond wholesalers, jewelry manufacturers, jewelry wholesalers, and finally, regional distributors. Oddly, the source of raw mined diamonds is monopolized by a single company, DeBeers, which controls over two-thirds of the world market. The fragmented supply and distribution chains add to huge markups based on monopoly-set prices for the raw diamonds. Currently, the typical retail store markup for diamonds is 48%, down from 51% a few years ago. Blue Nile's markup is 20%.

Beginning in 2003, online jewelry sites began selling about $4.8 billion a year, and Blue Nile accounts for 6% of that revenue. Blue Nile revenues hit $305 million in 2007, up 21% from the previous year. It had revenues of $144 million for the first six months of 2008, and a net profit of $5.8 million, and expected to achieve mid-single digit growth for the full year. Start-ups such as Blue Nile, Ice.com, Abazias, Diamond.com, and even Amazon are transforming the high-end jewelry business. Blue Nile, for instance, has simplified the supply-side of diamonds by only ordering and paying for a diamond after the customer has ordered it. Blue Nile has cut out several supply-side layers of middlemen and instead deals directly with wholesale diamond owners and jewelry manufacturers. Blue Nile minimizes its inventory costs and limits its risk of inventory markdowns. On the sell-side of distribution, Blue Nile has eliminated the expensive stores, sales clerks, and beautiful but expensive glass cases. Instead, Blue Nile offers a single Web site at which it can aggregate the demand of thousands of unique visitors for diamonds and present them with a more attractive shopping experience than a typical retail store. The result of rationalizing the supply and distribution chain is much lower markups. For example, Blue Nile will purchase a pair of oval emerald and diamond earrings from a supplier for $850 and charge the consumer $1,020. A traditional retailer would charge the consumer $1,258.

Blue Nile and other start-ups have improved the shopping experience primarily by creating a trust- and knowledge-based environment that reduces consumer anxiety about the value of diamonds. In essence, Blue Nile and the other online retailers give the consumer as much information as a professional gemologist would give them. The Web site contains educational guides to diamonds and diamond grading systems, and provides independent quality ratings for each diamond provided by non-profit industry associations, such as the GIA. There's a 30-day, money back, no-questions-asked guarantee.

Despite its lower gross margins due to its low prices, Blue Nile has higher net operating margins than its chief offline physical store competitor, Zales Inc., the country's largest jewelry chain. To get an idea of Blue Nile's efficiency, in order to sell $129 million in jewelry, a traditional physical store chain would need 116 stores and 900 workers. Blue Nile achieved $129 million in sales with one Web site, a 10,000-square-foot warehouse, and 115 workers.

After a strong 2007, Blue Nile stock ranged between $40 and $70 per share in 2008, and in September 2008 was selling at around $50 a share. The average ticket price for Blue Nile diamonds is $5,500, compared to $2,500 in typical retail stores.

So far the "Blue Nile" effect of lower margins and Internet efficiency has mainly impacted the small mom and pop jewelry stores. About 3,000 small retailers have disappeared in the last few years for a variety of reasons. The big retailers, such as Tiffany, Zales, and others sell more than Blue Nile, and continue to benefit from consumer interest in diamond engagement and wedding rings. Both Tiffany and Zales have online Web sites. Tiffany's site is a branding site, sending customers to their stores. The Zales site is a much more effective sales site than Tiffany's, with a marvelous build-a-ring capability, but still not quite up to the level of Blue Nile with respect to certification. Still, the success of Blue Nile, and the size of its competitors mean that Blue Nile will have to keep a keen watch on its competitors who are not far behind. But for now, the future of Blue Nile looks, well, sparkling.

SOURCES: "Blue Nile Announces 2008 Financial Results," Blue Nile Inc., August 5, 2008; "Blue Nile: A Guy's Best Friend," Jay Greene, *Business Week*, May 29, 2008; "Internet Jewelers: A Boy's Best Friend," *The Economist*, March 19, 2008; "The Digital Diamond District," by Victoria Barrett, *Forbes*, October 25, 2007; "Blue Nile.com: A Passion for Customer Service Makes Blue Nile the Top Niche Merchant in the *Internet Retailer* Top 500," by Mark Brohan, Internet Retailer, June, 2007; Blue Nile Inc. Report on Form 10-K for the fiscal year ended January 2, 2006, filed with the Securities and Exchange Commission on March 25, 2007; "When Buying a Diamond Starts With a Mouse," by Gary Rivlin, *New York Times*, January 7, 2007.

The Blue Nile case illustrates some of the advantages that a pure-play, start-up services company has over traditional offline retailers, and some of the disadvantages. A pure-play consumer service company can radically simplify the existing industry supply chain and develop an entirely new Web-based distribution system that is far more efficient than traditional retail outlets. At the same time, an online pure-play retailer can create a better value proposition for the customer, improving customer service and satisfaction in the process. On the other hand, pure-play start-up companies often have razor-thin profit margins, lack a physical store network to bolster sales to the non-Internet audience, and are often based on unproven business assumptions that, in the long term may not prove out. In contrast, large offline retailers, such as Wal-Mart, JCPenney, Sears, and Target, have established brand names, a huge real estate investment, a loyal customer base, and extraordinarily efficient inventory control and fulfillment systems. As we shall see in this chapter, traditional offline catalog merchants are even more advantaged. We will also see that, in order to leverage their assets and core competencies, established offline retailers need to cultivate new competencies and a carefully developed business plan to succeed on the Web.

As with retail goods, the promise of pure-online service providers is that they can deliver superior-quality service and greater convenience to millions of consumers at a lower cost than established bricks-and-mortar service providers, and still make a respectable return on invested capital. The service sector is one of the most natural avenues for e-commerce because so much of the value in services is based on collecting, storing, and exchanging information—something for which the Web is ideally suited. And, in fact, online services have been extraordinarily successful in attracting banking, brokerage, travel, and job-hunting customers. The quality and amount of information online to support consumer decisions in finance, travel, and career placement is extraordinary, especially when compared to what was available to consumers before e-commerce.

The online service sector—like online retail—has shown both explosive growth and some recent impressive failures. Despite the failures, online services have established a significant beachhead and are coming to play a large role in consumer time on the Internet. In areas such as brokerage, banking, and travel, online services are an extraordinary success story, and are transforming their industries. As with the retail sector, many of the early innovators—delivery services such as Kozmo and WebVan and consulting firms such as BizConsult.com—are gone. However, some early innovators, such as E*Trade, Schwab, Expedia, and Monster, have been successful, while many established service providers, such as Citigroup, JPMorgan Chase, Wells Fargo, Merrill Lynch, and the large airlines, have developed successful online e-commerce service delivery sites. In Sections 9.5–9.7 of this chapter, we take a close at three of these most successful online services: financial services (including insurance and real estate), travel services, and career services.

9.1 THE ONLINE RETAIL SECTOR

Table 9.1 summarizes some of these leading trends in online retailing for 2008–2009. Perhaps the most important theme in online retailing is the effort by retailers—both online and offline—to integrate their operations so they can serve customers in the various ways they want to be served.

TABLE 9.1	MAJOR TRENDS IN ONLINE RETAIL, 2008–2009

- The rapid growth in social networks and user-generated content sites enables "social shopping" where users pass on their opinions and recommendations to others in several online viral networks.

- Online retail achieves increasingly profitable operations through revenue growth, increasing size of purchase tickets, and a focus on improving efficiency of operations. Online retail remains the fastest-growing retail channel, and should surpass the mail order/telephone order (MOTO) catalog sales channel by 2010 at current growth rates.

- Buying online becomes a normal, mainstream, everyday experience. Around 80% of Internet users in the United States are now online shoppers.

- The selection of goods for purchase online increases to include luxury goods, such as jewelry, gourmet groceries, furniture, wine, as customer trust and experience increase. Informational shopping for big-ticket items such as cars and appliances continues to expand rapidly to include nearly all retail goods (both durables and non-durables).

- The average annual amount of online purchases continues to increase.

- Specialty retail sites show the most rapid growth in online retail as they develop customized retail goods and customer online configuration of goods.

- Online retailers place an increased emphasis on providing an improved "shopping experience," including ease of navigation and use, and online inventory updates.

- Online retailers increase the use of interactive multimedia marketing technologies and Web 2.0 techniques such as blogs, user-generated content, and video that exploit the dominance of broadband connections and offer features such as zoom, color switch, product configuration, and virtual simulations of households and businesses.

- Retail intermediaries strengthen in many areas, including groceries, automobiles, appliance and furniture dealers.

- Retailers become increasingly efficient in integrating multiple retailing channels, beyond "bricks-and-clicks" to "click and drive" and in-store Web kiosk ordering.

- Personalized goods, especially in apparel, become financially successful and begin to spread to many sites beyond specialty retailers.

- Online shopping becomes more multi-seasonal and less gift-oriented as consumers come to accept the Web as a routine shopping venue that is neither a novelty nor a special-occasion marketplace.

- More than half of online shopping and nearly a third of online purchases occur at work. However, growth of at-home broadband connections increases, making evening purchases from home the fastest-growing time segment for retail purchases online, relieving some pressure on workplace purchasing.

By any measure, the size of the U.S. retail market is huge. In a $13.2 trillion economy, personal consumption of retail goods and services accounts for over $9.3 trillion (about 70%) of the total gross domestic product (GDP)—or over two-thirds of all economic activity (U.S. Census Bureau, 2008).

If we examine the personal consumption sector more closely, we find that about 59% of personal consumption is for services, 11.5% is for durable goods, and 29% is for nondurable goods. Services include medical, educational, financial, and food services. **Durable goods** are those that are consumed over a longer period of time (generally more than a year), such as automobiles, appliances, and furniture. **Nondurable goods** are consumed quickly and have shorter life spans, and include general merchandise, clothing, music, drugs, and groceries.

The distinction between a "good" and a "service" is not always clear-cut, and is becoming more ambiguous over time. Increasingly, manufacturers and retailers of physical goods sell support services that add value to the physical product. It is difficult to think of a sophisticated physical good that does not include significant services in the purchase price. The movement toward "product-based services" can be seen in the packaged software market. Microsoft's Windows Vista and Office 2007 offer purchasers of the products additional value-added services from a variety of Microsoft Web sites. Charging for services, particularly on a monthly subscription basis, can be highly profitable. For instance, warranties, insurance policies, after-sale repairs, and purchase loans are increasingly a large source of revenue for manufacturers and retailers. Nevertheless, in this chapter, retail goods refer to physical products, and retailers refer to firms that sell physical goods to consumers, recognizing that retail goods include many services.

THE RETAIL INDUSTRY

The retail industry is composed of many different types of firms. **Figure 9.1** divides the retail industry into nine segments: clothing, durable goods, general merchandise, groceries, specialty stores, gasoline and fuel, eating and drinking, MOTO, and online retail firms.

Each of these segments offers opportunities for online retail, and yet in each segment, the uses of the Internet may differ. Some eating and drinking establishments use the Web to inform people of their physical locations and menus, while others offer delivery via Web orders (although this has not been a successful model). Retailers of durable goods typically use the Web as an informational tool rather than as a direct purchasing tool, although this is beginning to change as consumers have begun to purchase furniture and building supplies over the Internet. For instance, automobile manufacturers still do not sell cars over the Web, but they do provide information to assist customers in choosing among competing models. In fact, more than 70% of U.S. consumers research new car purchases on the Web before visiting a dealer to "kick the tires" and test-drive (J.D. Power and Associates, 2007).

The largest segment of the U.S. retail market is consumer durables, followed by general merchandise. These segments, particularly general merchandise, are highly concentrated, with large firms dominating sales. These very large firms have developed highly automated real-time inventory control systems (systems that collect

FIGURE 9.1	COMPOSITION OF THE U.S. RETAIL INDUSTRY

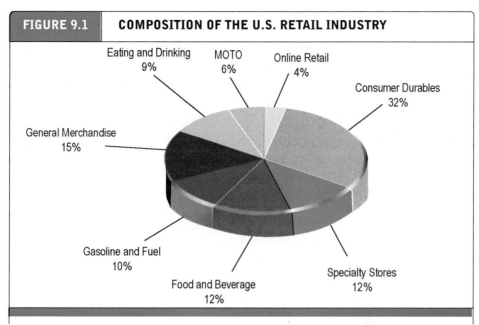

The retail industry can be grouped into eight major segments.
SOURCE: Based on data from U.S. Census Bureau, 2008.

point-of-sale data from cash registers, update inventory records, and inform vendors of stock levels), large national customer bases, and customer databases containing detailed purchasing information.

General merchandisers have always competed against a more traditional form of retail commerce called specialty retailers. In fact, modern retail trade began as a collection of small retail shops in a concentrated location that customers visited in serial order. Shopping used to mean a visit to a shoemaker, dressmaker, pharmacy, butcher, and dry goods store. While mass-market general department stores were the fastest-growing form of retail commerce for most of the twentieth century, in the 1960s, boutique and specialty stores catering to much smaller market segments with higher priced goods became the fastest-growing form of physical retail stores. Stores such as The Gap, Banana Republic, Athlete's Foot, Sports Authority, Victoria's Secret, Staples, Circuit City, and many others developed national and international chain store strategies based on up-scale youth market segments. The success of specialty retailing depends on building unique products for a market segment, offering strong customer service, and providing a persuasive shopping experience to support the brand image.

The MOTO sector is the most similar to the online retail sales sector. In the absence of physical stores, MOTO retailers distribute millions of physical catalogs (their largest expense) and operate large telephone call centers to accept orders. They have developed extraordinarily efficient order fulfillment centers that generally ship customer orders within 24 hours of receipt. MOTO was the fastest growing retail segment throughout the 1970s and 1980s. It grew as a direct result of improvements in the national toll-free call system, the implementation of digital switching in telephone systems, falling long distance telecommunications prices, and of course, the expansion of the credit card industry and associated technologies, without which neither MOTO nor e-commerce would be possible on a large national scale. MOTO was the last "technological" retailing revolution that preceded e-commerce. Because of their experience in fulfilling small orders rapidly, MOTO firms are advantaged when competing in e-commerce, and the transition to e-commerce has not been difficult for these firms.

Like general merchandisers, MOTO retailers have sophisticated inventory control systems, substantial customer databases, and large scale, giving them significant market power over vendors. In addition, MOTO retailers are advantaged in online retailing because they also have very effective order fulfillment systems and procedures—something with which general merchandisers have little experience. For these reasons, MOTO retailers are among the fastest growing online retail firms.

ONLINE RETAILING

Online retail is perhaps the most high-profile sector of e-commerce on the Web. Over the past decade, this sector has experienced both explosive growth and spectacular failures.

Many of the early pure-play online-only firms that pioneered the retail marketspace failed. Entrepreneurs and their investors seriously misjudged the factors needed to succeed in this market. But the survivors of this early period emerged much stronger, and along with traditional offline general and specialty merchants, as well as new start-ups, the e-retail space is growing very rapidly and is increasing its reach and size.

E-commerce Retail: The Vision

In the early years of e-commerce, literally thousands of entrepreneurial Web-based retailers were drawn to the marketplace for retail goods, simply because it was one of the largest market opportunities in the U.S. economy. Many entrepreneurs initially believed it was easy to enter the retail market. Early writers predicted that the retail industry would be revolutionized, literally "blown to bits"—as prophesized by two consultants in a famous Harvard Business School book (Evans and Wurster, 2000). The basis of this revolution would be fourfold. First, because the Internet greatly reduced both search costs and transaction costs, consumers would use the Web to find the lowest-cost products. Several results would follow. Consumers would increasingly drift to the Web for shopping and purchasing, and only low-cost, high-service, quality online retail merchants would survive. Economists assumed that the Web consumer was rational and cost-driven—not perceived-value or brand-driven, both of which are nonrational factors.

Second, it was assumed that the entry costs to the online retail market were much less than those needed to establish physical storefronts, and that online merchants were inherently more efficient at marketing and order fulfillment than offline stores.

The costs of establishing a powerful Web site were thought to be minuscule compared to the costs of warehouses, fulfillment centers, and physical stores. There would be no difficulty building sophisticated order entry, shopping cart, and fulfillment systems because this technology was well known, and the cost of technology was falling by 50% each year. Even the cost of acquiring consumers was thought to be much lower on the Web because of search engines that could almost instantly connect customers to online vendors.

Third, as prices fell, traditional offline physical store merchants would be forced out of business. New entrepreneurial companies—such as Amazon—would replace the traditional stores. It was thought that if online merchants grew very quickly, they would have first-mover advantages and lock out the older traditional firms that were too slow to enter the online market.

Fourth, in some industries—such as electronics, apparel, and digital content—the market would be disintermediated as manufacturers or their distributors entered to build a direct relationship with the consumer, destroying the retail intermediaries or middlemen. In this scenario, traditional retail channels—such as physical stores, sales clerks, and sales forces—would be replaced by a single dominant channel: the Web.

Many predicted, on the other hand, a kind of hypermediation based on the concept of a virtual firm in which online retailers would gain advantage over established offline merchants by building an online brand name that attracted millions of customers, and outsourcing the expensive warehousing and order fulfillment functions—the original concept of Amazon and Drugstore.com.

As it turned out, few of these assumptions and visions were correct, and the structure of the retail marketplace in the United States, with some notable exceptions, has not been blown to bits, disintermediated, or revolutionized in the traditional meaning of the word revolution. With several notable exceptions, online retail has often not been successful as an independent platform on which to build a successful "pure-play" Web-only business. As it turns out, the consumer is not primarily price-driven when shopping on the Internet but instead considers brand name, trust, reliability, and delivery time as at least as important as price (Brynjolfsson, Dick, and Smith, 2004).

However, the Internet has created an entirely new venue for multi-channel firms that have a strong offline brand, and in some cases, the Internet has supported the development of pure-play online-only merchants, both general merchandisers as well as specialty retailers. As predicted, online retail has indeed become the fastest-growing and most dynamic retail channel in the sense of channel innovation. The Web has created a new marketplace for millions of consumers to conveniently shop. The Internet and Web have continued to provide new opportunities for entirely new firms using new business models and new online products—such as BlueNile, as previously described. The new online channel can conflict with a merchant's other channels, such as direct sales forces, physical stores, and mail order, but this multi-channel conflict can be managed and turned into a strength.

The Online Retail Sector Today

Although online retailing is the smallest segment of the retail industry, constituting about 3% of the total retail market today, it is continuing to grow at a fast rate (around 14% a year), with new functionality and product lines being added every day (see **Figure 9.2**). When we refer to online retail we will not be including online services revenues such as travel, job-hunting, or music. Instead, for the purposes of this chapter, online retail refers solely to sales of physical goods over the Internet. The Internet provides a number of unique advantages and challenges to online retailers. **Table 9.2** summarizes these advantages and challenges.

Despite the high failure rate of online retailers in the early years, more consumers than ever are shopping online. For most consumers, the advantages of shopping on the Web overcome the disadvantages. In 2008, it is estimated that around 65%–70% of Internet users over the age of 14 (around 120 million people) bought at an online retail store, generating about $146 billion in online retail sales. While the number of new Internet users in the United States is not growing as rapidly at it was, with around 70% of the U.S. population over 14 years of age already on the Internet, this slowdown will not necessarily slow the growth in online retail e-commerce because the average shopper is spending more on the Internet each year, and finding many new categories of items to buy. For instance, in 2003, the average annual

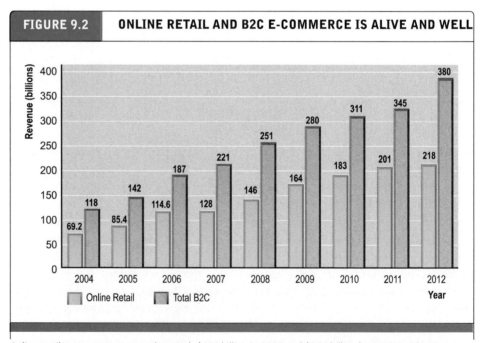

| FIGURE 9.2 | ONLINE RETAIL AND B2C E-COMMERCE IS ALIVE AND WELL |

Online retail revenues are expected to reach $146 billion in 2008 and $218 billion by 2012. Total B2C e-commerce revenues (including travel and other services) are projected to reach over $380 billion by 2012.

SOURCES: Based on data from eMarketer, Inc. 2008a; U.S. Department of Commerce, 2008; Forrester Research, 2008; authors' estimates.

TABLE 9.2	ADVANTAGES AND CHALLENGES TO ONLINE RETAIL
ADVANTAGES	**CHALLENGES**
Lower supply chain costs by aggregating demand at a single site and increasing purchasing power	Consumer concerns about the security of transactions
Lower cost of distribution using Web sites rather than physical stores	Consumer concerns about the privacy of personal information given to Web sites
Ability to reach and serve a much larger geographically distributed group of customers	Delays in delivery of goods when compared to store shopping
Ability to react quickly to customer tastes and demand	Inconvenience associated with return damaged or exchange goods
Ability to change prices nearly instantly	Overcoming lack of consumer trust in online brand names
Ability to rapidly change visual presentation of goods	
Avoidance of direct marketing costs of catalogs and physical mail	
Increased opportunities for personalization, customization	
Ability to greatly improve information and knowledge delivered to consumer	
Ability to lower consumers' overall market transaction costs	

amount spent online by users was $675, but by 2007, it had jumped to $1,153 (eMarketer, Inc., 2008a, 2005a). Also, as noted in Chapter 6, millions of additional consumers research products on the Web and are influenced in their purchase decisions at offline stores.

The primary beneficiaries of this growing consumer support are not only the first-mover dot-com companies, but also the established offline retailers who have the brand-name recognition, supportive infrastructure, and financial resources to enter the online marketplace successfully. Table 1.7 on page 42 lists the top online retail firms ranked by online sales. The list contains pure-play online retailers for whom the Internet is the only sales channel, such as Amazon (in first place) and Newegg (in 10th); multi-channel firms that have established brand names and for whom e-commerce plays a relatively small role when compared to their offline physical store channels, such as Staples (2nd), Office Depot (3rd), Office Max (6th), Sears (8th), Best Buy (13th), JCPenney (14th), and Wal-Mart (15th); and manufacturers of computer and electronic equipment, such as Dell (4th), HP (5th), Apple (7th), and Sony (12th). The top 15 retailers account for about one-third of all online retail. For pure-play firms heavily dependent on Web sales, the challenge is to turn visitors into customers, and to develop efficient operations that permit them to achieve long-term profitability. For traditional firms that are much less dependent on e-commerce sales, their challenge is to integrate the offline and online channels so customers can move seamlessly from one environment to another.

Multi-Channel Integration

Clearly one of the most important e-commerce retail themes of 2008–2009 and into the future, is the ability of offline traditional firms such as Wal-Mart, Target, JCPenney, Staples, and others to continue to integrate their Web operations with their physical store operations in order to provide an "integrated shopping customer experience," and leveraging the value of their physical stores. **Table 9.3** illustrates some of the various ways in which traditional retailers have integrated the Web and store operations to develop nearly seamless multi-channel shopping. This list is not exclusive, and retailers continue to develop new links between channels.

In the past, it has generally been traditional physical store retailers moving towards the development of powerful Web operations, but in the future, online, pure-play retailers such as Amazon and eBay may develop physical retail stores in order to process returns or even sell products. For instance, some local entrepreneurs

TABLE 9.3	RETAIL E-COMMERCE: MULTI-CHANNEL INTEGRATION METHODS
INTEGRATION TYPE	DESCRIPTION
Online order, in-store pickup	Probably one of the first types of integration.
Online order, store directory and inventory	When items are out of stock online, customer is directed to physical store network inventory and store location.
In-store kiosk Web order, home delivery	When retail store is out-of-stock, customer orders in store and receives at home. Presumes customer is Web familiar.
In-store retail clerk Web order, home delivery	Similar to above, but the retail clerk searches Web inventory if local store is out of stock as a normal part of the in-store check out process.
Web order, in-store returns and adjustments	Defective or rejected products ordered on the Web can be returned to any store location.
Online Web catalog	Online Web catalog supplements offline physical catalog and often the online catalog has substantially more product on display.
Manufacturers use online Web site promotions to drive customers to their distributors' retail stores	Consumer product manufacturers such as Colgate-Palmolive and Procter & Gamble use their Web channels to design new products and promote existing product retail sales.
Gift card, loyalty program points can be used in any channel	Recipient of gift card, loyalty program points can use it to purchase in-store, online or via catalog, if offered by merchant.

have opened up eBay "drop-off" stores. Like a traditional consignment shop, eBay drop-off stores take in merchandise from people who are too busy or not interested in running an eBay auction and then attempt to sell the merchandise on eBay, keeping as much as 50% of the proceeds for themselves.

Rather than demonstrate disintermediation, online retailing provides an example of the powerful role that intermediaries continue to play in retail trade. Established offline retailers have rapidly gained online market share. Increasingly, consumers are attracted to stable, well-known, trusted retail brands and retailers. The online audience is very sensitive to brand names (as described in Chapter 7) and is not primarily cost-driven. Other factors such as reliability, trust, fulfillment, and customer service are equally important.

9.2   ANALYZING THE VIABILITY OF ONLINE FIRMS

In this and the following chapters, we analyze the viability of a number of online companies that exemplify specific e-commerce models. We are primarily interested in understanding the near-to-medium term (1–3 years) economic viability of these firms and their business models. **Economic viability** refers to the ability of firms to survive as profitable business firms during the specified period. To answer the question of economic viability, we take two business analysis approaches: strategic analysis and financial analysis.

economic viability
refers to the ability of firms to survive as profitable business firms during a specified period

STRATEGIC ANALYSIS

Strategic approaches to economic viability focus on both the industry in which a firm operates and the firm itself (see Chapter 2, Section 2.4). The key industry strategic factors are:

- *Barriers to entry*: Can new entrants be barred from entering the industry through high capital costs or intellectual property barriers (such as patents and copyrights)?

- *Power of suppliers*: Can suppliers dictate high prices to the industry or can vendors choose from among many suppliers? Have firms achieved sufficient scale to bargain effectively for lower prices from suppliers?

- *Power of customers*: Can customers choose from many competing suppliers and hence challenge high prices and high margins?

- *Existence of substitute products*: Can the functionality of the product or service be obtained from alternative channels or competing products in different industries? Are substitute products and services likely to emerge in the near future?

- *Industry value chain*: Is the chain of production and distribution in the industry changing in ways that benefit or harm the firm?

- *Nature of intra-industry competition*: Is the basis of competition within the industry based on differentiated products and services, price, scope of offerings, or focus of offerings? How is the nature of competition changing? Will these changes benefit the firm?

The strategic factors that pertain specifically to the firm and its related businesses include:

- *Firm value chain*: Has the firm adopted business processes and methods of operation that allow it to achieve the most efficient operations in its industry? Will changes in technology force the firm to realign its business processes?

- *Core competencies*: Does the firm have unique competencies and skills that cannot be easily duplicated by other firms? Will changes in technology invalidate the firm's competencies or strengthen them?

- *Synergies*: Does the firm have access to the competencies and assets of related firms either owned outright or through strategic partnerships and alliances?

- *Technology*: Has the firm developed proprietary technologies that allow it to scale with demand? Has the firm developed the operational technologies (e.g., customer relationship management, fulfillment, supply chain management, inventory control, and human resource systems) to survive?

- *Social and legal challenges*: Has the firm put in place policies to address consumer trust issues (privacy and security of personal information)? Is the firm the subject of lawsuits challenging its business model, such as intellectual property ownership issues? Will the firm be affected by changes in Internet taxation laws or other foreseeable statutory developments?

FINANCIAL ANALYSIS

Strategic analysis helps us comprehend the competitive situation of the firm. Financial analysis helps us understand how in fact the firm is performing. There are two parts to a financial analysis: the statement of operations and the balance sheet. The statement of operations tells us how much money (or loss) the firm is achieving based on current sales and costs. The balance sheet tells us how many assets the firm has to support its current and future operations.

Here are some of the key factors to look for in a firm's Statement of Operations:

- *Revenues*: Are revenues growing and at what rate? Many e-commerce companies have experienced impressive, even explosive revenue growth, as an entirely new channel is created.

- *Cost of sales*: What is the cost of sales compared to revenues? Cost of sales typically includes the cost of the products sold and related costs. The lower the cost of sales compared to revenue, the higher the gross profit.

gross margin
gross profit divided by net sales

- *Gross margin*: What is the firm's gross margin, and is it increasing or decreasing? **Gross margin** is calculated by dividing gross profit by net sales revenues. Gross margin can tell you if the firm is gaining or losing market power vis á vis its key suppliers

- *Operating expenses*: What are the firm's operating expenses, and are they increasing or decreasing? Operating expenses typically include the cost of marketing, technology, and administrative overhead. They also include, in accordance with professional accounting standards (see below), stock-based compensation to employees and executives, amortization of goodwill and other intangibles, and impairment of investments. In e-commerce companies, these turn out to be very important expenses. Many e-commerce firms compensated their employees with stock shares (or options), and many e-commerce firms purchased other e-commerce firms as a part of their growth strategy. Many of the companies were purchased at extremely high values using company stock rather than cash; in numerous instances, the purchased companies fell dramatically in market value. All these items are counted as normal operating expenses.

- *Operating margin*: What did the firm earn from its current operations? **Operating margin** is calculated by dividing operating income or loss by net sales revenue. Operating margin is an indication of a company's ability to turn sales into pre-tax profit after operating expenses have been deducted. Operating margin tells us if the firm's current operations are covering its operating expenses, not including interest expenses and other non-operating expenses.

- *Net margin*: **Net margin** tells us the percentage of its gross sales revenue the firm was able to retain after all expenses are deducted. Net margin is calculated by dividing net income or loss by net sales revenue. Net margin sums up in one number how successful a company has been at the business of making a profit on each dollar of sales revenues. Net margin also tells us something about the efficiency of the firm by measuring the percentage of sales revenue it is able retain after all expenses are deducted from gross revenues, and within a single industry can be used to measure the relative efficiency of competing firms. Net margin takes into account many non-operating expenses such as interest and stock compensation plans.

When examining the financial announcements of e-commerce companies, it is important to realize that online firms often choose not to announce their net income according to generally accepted accounting principles (GAAP). These principles have been promulgated by the Financial Accounting Standards Board (FASB), a board of professional accountants that establishes accounting rules for the profession, and which has played a vital role since the 1934 Securities Act, which sought to improve financial accounting during the Great Depression. Many e-commerce firms in the early years instead reported an entirely new calculation called *pro forma earnings* (also called EBITDA—earnings before income taxes, depreciation, and amortization). Pro forma earnings generally do not deduct stock-based compensation, depreciation, or amortization. The result is that pro forma earnings are always better than GAAP earnings. The firms that report in this manner typically claim these expenses are non-recurring and special and "unusual." In 2002 and 2003, the SEC issued new guidelines (Regulation G) that prohibit firms from reporting pro forma earnings in official reports to the SEC, but still allow firms to announce pro forma earnings in public statements (Weil, 2003). Throughout this book, we consider a firm's income or loss based on GAAP accounting standards only.

A **balance sheet** provides a financial snapshot of a company's assets and liabilities (debts) on a given date. **Assets** refer to stored value. **Current assets** are those assets such as cash, securities, accounts receivable, inventory, or other

operating margin
calculated by dividing operating income or loss by net sales revenue

net margin
the percentage of its gross sales revenue the firm able to retain after all expenses are deducted; calculated by dividing net income or loss by net sales revenue

balance sheet
provides a financial snapshot of a company on a given date and shows its financial assets and liabilities

assets
refers to stored value

current assets
assets such as cash, securities, accounts receivable, inventory, or other investments that are likely to be able to be converted to cash within one year

liabilities
outstanding obligations of
the firm

current liabilities
debts of the firm that will
be due within one year

long-term debt
liabilities that are not due
until the passage of a year
or more

working capital
firm's current assets minus
current liabilities

investments that are likely to be able to be converted to cash within one year. **Liabilities** are outstanding obligations of the firm. **Current liabilities** are debts of the firm that will be due within one year. Liabilities that are not due until the passage of a year or more are characterized as **long-term debt**. For a quick check of a firm's short-term financial health, examine its **working capital** (the firm's current assets minus current liabilities). If working capital is only marginally positive, or negative, the firm will likely have trouble meeting its short-term obligations. Alternatively, if a firm has a large amount of current assets, it can sustain operational losses for a period of time.

9.3 E-COMMERCE IN ACTION: E-TAILING BUSINESS MODELS

So far, we have been discussing online retail as if it were a single entity. In fact, as we briefly discussed in Chapter 2, there are four main types of online retail business models: virtual merchants, multi-channel merchandisers (sometimes referred to as bricks-and-clicks or clicks-and-bricks), catalog merchants, and manufacturer-direct firms. In addition, there are small "mom and pop" retailers that use eBay, Amazon, and Yahoo Stores sales platforms, as well as affiliate merchants whose primary revenue derives from sending traffic to their "mother" sites. Each of these different types of online retailers faces a different strategic environment, as well as different industry and firm economics.

VIRTUAL MERCHANTS

virtual merchant
single-channel Web firms
that generate almost all of
their revenue from online
sales

Virtual merchants are single-channel Web firms that generate almost all their revenue from online sales. Virtual merchants face extraordinary strategic challenges. They must build a business and brand name from scratch, quickly, in an entirely new channel and confront many virtual merchant competitors (especially in smaller niche areas). Because these firms are totally online stores, they do not have to bear the costs associated with building and maintaining physical stores, but they face large costs in building and maintaining a Web site, building an order fulfillment infrastructure, and developing a brand name. Customer acquisition costs are high, and the learning curve is steep. Like all retail firms, their gross margins (the difference between the retail price of goods sold and the cost of goods to the retailer) are low. Therefore, virtual merchants must achieve highly efficient operations in order to preserve a profit, while building a brand name as quickly as possible in order to attract sufficient customers to cover their costs of operations. Most merchants in this category adopt low-cost and convenience strategies, coupled with extremely effective and efficient fulfillment processes to ensure customers receive what they ordered as fast as possible. In the following E-commerce in Action section, we take an in-depth look at the strategic and financial situation of Amazon, the leading online virtual merchant. In addition to Amazon, other successful virtual merchants include Newegg, Zappos, Drugstore.com, Buy.com, BlueNile (profiled in the opening case), Bluefly, and eBags.com.

E-COMMERCE IN ACTION

AMAZON.COM

Amazon, the Seattle-based pure-online merchant is one of the most best-known names on the Web. Never suffering from modesty, Amazon's founder, Jeff Bezos, has proclaimed in its annual report that the objective of Amazon is to "offer the Earth's Biggest Selection and to be Earth's most customer-centric company where customers can find and discover anything they may want to buy." Just exactly what these claims mean, and how it might be possible to achieve them, is still a matter of speculation for both customers and investors. Yet this has not stopped Bezos and his team from becoming the Web's most successful and innovative pure-play, online retailer.

Few business enterprises have experienced a similar roller-coaster ride from explosive early growth, to huge losses, and then on to profitability. No Internet business has been both so hotly reviled and so hotly praised. Its stock reflects these changing fortunes, hitting a high of $105 a share in the second quarter of 1999, and a low of $6 a share in 2001, climbing back up to $60 a share in 2003, bouncing between $30 to $50 during 2004–2005, dropping down to a low of $27 a share in 2006, then climbing back up to over $100 again in 2007, before dropping down again into the low $80s toward the end of the year, and remaining there in 2008. The story for now is that Amazon is an Internet survivor, one that is likely to succeed in the long term. It had its first profitable quarter in fall 2002, and its first profitable year in 2003. While controversial, Amazon has also been one of the most innovative online retailing stories in the history of e-commerce. From the earliest days of e-commerce, Amazon has continuously adapted its business model based both on its market experience and its insight into the online consumer.

The Vision

The original vision of founder Jeff Bezos and his friends was that the Internet was a revolutionary new form of commerce and that only companies that became really big early on (ignoring profitability) would survive. The path to success, according to founder Bezos, was to offer consumers three things: the lowest prices, the best selection, and convenience (which translates into feature-rich content, user-generated reviews of books and products, fast and reliable fulfillment, and ease of use). Currently Amazon offers consumers millions of unique new, used, and collectible items in 11 major categories: books; movies, music and games; digital downloads; computers and office; electronics; home and garden; grocery, health and beauty; toys, kids and baby; sports and outdoors; and tools, auto and industrial. And if Amazon does not carry it, they have created systems for helping you find it at online merchants who rent space from Amazon, or even at other places on the Web. In short, Amazon has come close to becoming the largest, single, one-stop merchant on the Web, a kind of combined "shopping portal" and "product search portal" that puts it in direct competition with other large online general merchants, eBay, and general portals such as Yahoo, MSN, and even Google. As Amazon has succeeded in becoming the world's largest online store, it expanded its original vision to become one of the Web's largest supplier of merchant and search services.

Business Model

Amazon's business is currently organized into two basic segments, Amazon Retail and Amazon Services. Amazon Retail sells goods that Amazon has purchased and then re-sells to consumers just like a traditional retailer. Amazon also operates Alexa.com and a9.com, which enable search and navigation, and Imdb.com, a comprehensive movie database. Amazon Services offers two basic types of services, merchant services and developer services.

The merchant services segment, Amazon Enterprise Solutions, enables third parties (individuals, small and large businesses) to integrate their products into Amazon's Web site, and use Amazon's customer technologies via the Amazon Marketplace and Merchants@ programs. Amazon Marketplace generally serves individuals and small businesses, while the Merchants@ program generally serves larger, branded businesses. Amazon is not the seller of record, does not own these products, and the shipping of products is handled by the third party. Amazon collects a fixed fee, sales commission (generally estimated to be between 10%–20% of the sale), per-unit activity fee, or some combination thereof from the third party. In this segment, Amazon acts as an online shopping mall, collecting "rents" from other merchants and providing "site" services such as order entry and payment. Amazon's third segment is the Amazon Services program. Under this program, Amazon provides e-commerce services to other businesses, operates their Web sites and sells their products, and in some instances, offers fulfillment services (for example, Target.com).

It is still too early to measure the impact and success of the Amazon Web Services segment. Through this segment, Amazon offers a variety of Web services that provide developers with direct access to Amazon's technology platform, and allow them to build their own applications based on that platform. The company launched the program in 2002, and five years later, Amazon had over 200,000 volunteers building applications and services, strengthening the business. Bezos, however, was not satisfied with only a slew of cool new applications for his company's Web site. In March 2006, Amazon introduced the first of several new services that Bezos hoped would transform the future of Amazon as a business. With Simple Storage Service (S3) and, later, Elastic Compute Cloud (EC2), Amazon entered the utility computing market. The company realized that the benefits of its $2 billion investment in technology could also be valuable to other companies. Amazon has tremendous computing capacity, but like most companies, only uses a small portion of it at any one time. Moreover, the Amazon infrastructure is considered by many to be among the most robust in the world. Amazon began to sell its computing power on a per-usage basis, just like a power company sells electricity. S3 is a data storage service that is designed to make Web-scale computing easier and more affordable for developers. Customers pay 15 cents per gigabyte of data stored per month on Amazon's network of disk drives. There is also a charge of 20 cents per gigabyte of data transferred. Customers pay for exactly what they use and no more. Working in conjunction with S3, EC2 enables businesses to utilize Amazon's servers for computing tasks, such as testing software. Using EC2 incurs charges of 10 cents per instance-hour consumed. An instance supplies the user with the equivalent of a 1.7 GHz x86 processor with 1.75 GB of RAM, a 160 GB hard drive, and 250 MB/s of bandwidth on the network. Other Web services offered by Amazon include Simple Queue Service (SQS), which offers a hosted queue for storing messages as they travel between computers, SimpleDB, a database Web service, Flexible Payments Service (FPS), which provides a payments service for developers, and Amazon Mechanical Turk, which provides a marketplace for work that requires human intelligence.

For now, Amazon generates revenue primarily by selling books, videos, electronics, and thousands of other products on domestic and international Web sites. 65% of its revenue still comes from media sales like books, CDs, and DVDs, and music from its streaming service. In addition to Amazon.com in the United States, Amazon also operates localized sites in Japan, Germany, United Kingdom, France, and Canada. The success of its international business is largely unrecognized. For instance, in 2007, Amazon derived over $6.7 billion, or 45%, of its $14.835 billion of gross revenues offshore, and international sales grew by 39% for the year. While Amazon started out as an online merchant of books, CDs, and DVDs, since 2002 it has diversified into becoming a general merchandiser of millions of other products. However, in its 2007 annual report, the company reported that 62% of its total sales revenue (about $9.2 billion) originated from the sale of media, and only 37% from electronics and other general merchandise. Heavily dependent on media sales, Amazon has not yet achieved the product diversification of offline mass-market merchants such as Wal-Mart, Costco, or Sears.

Amazon's business model has changed several times. It started originally as a no-inventory Web middleman between book distributors and the individual consumer. Amazon was a specialized online store in this phase, selling books and media. It claimed to be leveraging the unique features of the Web. When Amazon's ambitions grew beyond the book business and moved toward becoming a general merchandiser, executives realized Amazon would need to hold inventory, and soon began building huge warehouses and fulfillment centers located strategically around the country to fulfill orders for general merchandise. While Amazon has not abandoned its successful retail model, it has sought to increase growth by adopting a new business model where it simply provides a trading and commerce platform for other merchants and collects a fee, somewhat like the operator of a traditional shopping mall in the offline world. In 2001, it began a program called Z-Stores in which third-party merchants could set up their shops on the Amazon site. These shops were entirely separate from Amazon's own retail offerings and were difficult to find on the site. This program failed because of poor outreach to merchants, poor integration into Amazon's purchasing software, and lack of visibility for sites.

In 2003, Amazon began a larger program of allowing small and large retail merchants to establish storefronts within the larger Amazon site and to have their products integrated into Amazon's search engine. Large retailers such as Toys"R"Us Inc. and Target pioneered these sites within Amazon, which allowed these merchants to focus on sales while Amazon handled fulfillment of orders and maintained the

Web site. Thousands of smaller merchants have since joined the program, offering competing products that Amazon itself sells, and even competing against Toys"R"Us (with the result that Toys"R"Us sued Amazon in May 2004 for violating what it believed was its exclusive right to sell toys on Amazon). For instance, a single product on the Amazon Web site may be listed for sale simultaneously by Amazon, by a participant in the Amazon Merchants@ program, or by a business or individual selling a new, used, or collectible version of the product through Amazon Marketplace or Amazon Auctions.

In many respects, Amazon's Third Party Seller segment is an effort to compete directly with eBay, the Web's most successful third-party merchant sales platform, which offers, at any given time, has a registered trading community of active buyers and sellers of over 84 million people. In fact, eBay itself has moved closer to Amazon's business model by encouraging merchants to sell rather than auction goods on its sites ("Buy It Now", eBay stores, and other fixed-price trading features now accounts for around 40% of all products sold by eBay).

In 2007, Amazon expanded its Fulfillment by Amazon program to enable independent sellers, even those who do not sell through Amazon, to use the company's 20 distribution centers to fill their orders. Participants send their goods to be stored and shipped by Amazon. They pay Amazon a fee that varies according to the weight and shipping cost of the products.

Financial Analysis

Amazon's revenues have increased from about $600 million in 1998 to $14.835 billion in 2007. More recently, in the past three years, Amazon's revenues have grown an incredible 65% (see **Table 9.4**). This is very impressive, explosive revenue growth. In an effort to attract sales, Amazon has offered free shipping on orders over $25, and this has increased its operating costs and lowered net margins, a move that worries investors. This policy is one of a number of factors that contribute to Amazon's pattern of increasing revenues and decreasing profits.

However, Amazon has been able to compensate for the cost of its low price strategy and free shipping policies by reducing operating expenses and by eliminating marketing in offline magazines and television. costs have remained steady at a little over 2% of revenues despite huge increases in sales (72% in 2007). General and administrative costs as a percentage of sales have also remained nearly constant. This means that Amazon's huge increase in sales did not come about by huge increases in marketing, head count, or administrative overhead. Amazon instead relies heavily on affiliates and third-party merchants to drive sales. In addition, it has demonstrated an ability to scale its operations without rapidly increasing its administrative expenditures. As a result of its cost-saving measures, Amazon was able to grow its net income by a factor of more than 10 from 2003 ($35 million) to 2007 ($476). Net margin has fluctuated from a low of .7% in 2003, to a high of 8.5% in 2004, and was 3.2% in 2007. For every dollar in net sales in 2007, Amazon was earning a profit of about 3 cents—positive but not wonderful and not any better than a lot of bricks-and-mortar retailers. The reason for this fall off in net margin is clearly related to its free shipping policy and low cost policies.

TABLE 9.4	AMAZON'S CONSOLIDATED STATEMENTS OF OPERATIONS AND SUMMARY BALANCE SHEET DATA 2005–2007

CONSOLIDATED STATEMENTS OF OPERATIONS (in thousands)

For the fiscal year ended December 31, Revenue	2007	2006	2005
Net sales	$14,835,000	$10,711,000	$8,490,000
Cost of sales	$11,482,000	8,255,000	6,451,000
Gross profit	3,353,000	2,456,000	2,039,000
Gross margin	22.6	23%	24%
Operating expenses			
Marketing	344,000	263,000	198,000
Fulfillment	1,292,000	937,000	745,000
Technology and content	818,000	662,000	451,000
General and administrative	235,000	195,000	166,000
Other operating expense, net	9,000	10,000	47,000
Total operating expenses	2,698,000	2,067,000	1,607,000
Income from operations	655,000	389,000	432,000
Operating margin	4.4%	3.6%	5.1%
Total non-operating income (expense)	5,000	(12,000)	(4,000)
Income before income taxes	660,000	377,000	428,000
Provision for income taxes	184,000	187,000	95,000
Income before change in accounting principle	476,000	190,000	333,000
Cumulative effect of change in accounting principle	—	—	26,000
Net income (loss)	476,000	190,000	359,000
Net margin	3.2%	1.8%	4.2%

SUMMARY BALANCE SHEET DATA (in thousands)

At December 31, Assets	2007	2006	2005
Cash, cash equivalents and marketable securities	3,112,000	$2,019,000	$2,000,000
Total current assets	5,164,000	3,373,000	2,929,000
Total assets	6,485,000	4,363,000	3,696,000
Liabilities			
Total current liabilities	3,714,000	2,532,000	1,899,000
Long-term debt and other	1,574,000	1,400,000	1,521,000
Working capital	1,450,000	841,000	1,030,000
Stockholders' Equity (Deficit)	1,197,000	431,000	246,000

SOURCE: Amazon.com Inc., 2008.

Nevertheless, the prospect for Amazon based on this financial analysis looks much improved from earlier years when it was showing negative margins and losing money on every sale.

Amazon's balance sheet shows a company with a still heavy reliance on long-term debt. At the end of December 2007, it had about $3.1 billion in cash and marketable securities. The cash and securities were obtained from sales, sales of stock and notes to the public, venture capital investors, and institutional investors in return for equity (shares) in the company or debt securities. Total assets are listed at $6.4 billion. The company emphasizes the strength of its "free cash flow" as a sign of financial strength, suggesting it has more than enough cash available to cover short-term liabilities (such as financing holiday season purchasing). The balance sheet has improved over the last three years as asset to debt ratios are improving. Amazon's cash assets should certainly be enough to cover future short-term deficits should they occur. However, with $1.28 billion in long-term debt, and $77 million a year in interest expense, institutional investors are wary of investing more in Amazon. It is fair to conclude that Amazon's management is under a great deal of pressure to become a consistently profitable company and reduce its long term debt considerably. Amazon's stock has demonstrated investor uncertainty over its future. Rising to $100 in January 2000, the stock fell to $6 a share in December 2001, then began a slow climb back up, rising to $60 in December 2003. Since that time, the stock has been erratic, trading in the $35-$100 range (currently at $80+ per share in September 2008). Wall Street analysts are continually frustrated by Amazon's reporting of financial results, complaining the company refuses to explain its numbers or put them in proper context.

Strategic Analysis—Business Strategy

Amazon engages in a number of business strategies that seek to maximize growth in sales volume, while cutting prices to the bare bones. Its two main revenue growth strategies include moving towards a broader trading platform by expanding the third-party seller segment, and moving towards greater product focus by grouping its offerings into major categories called stores. In the last year or so, Amazon has created a number of new online stores that group together sellers and products: beauty, gourmet food, sporting goods, jewelry and watches, health and personal care, office supplies, a Software en Espanol store for Spanish-language and bilingual software products, and a motorcycle and ATV store. Early results suggest these stores are growing faster than Amazon as a whole, particularly jewelry and watches. Amazon is still following Wal-Mart's and eBay's examples by attempting to be a mass-market, low-price, high-volume online supermarket where you can get just about anything. To achieve profitability in this environment, Amazon has invested heavily in supply chain management and fulfillment strategies to reduce its costs to the bare minimum while still providing excellent customer service and even free shipping.

Specific programs to increase revenues are the continuation of free shipping from Amazon Retail (a strategy that has increased order sizes by 25%), greater product selection, and shorter order fulfillment times. Amazon's management is experimenting with "accelerated shipping" by offering customers next-day or even same-day shipping in selected areas such as Manhattan, while not charging additional fees. Internet customers have long been frustrated both by high shipping and handling charges as well as long delays in receiving goods. A ticking clock can be seen next to some Amazon sale items indicating the hours remaining for an order to make it to the customer by the next day.

Amazon began its Merchants@ and Amazon Marketplace programs in 2002 to allow other businesses and individuals to offer their new, used, and collectible products for sale on the Amazon Web site. These products are fully integrated onto the Amazon Web site and can be purchased by customers through a single checkout process. The program offers customers more than 500 brands, such as Target stores at Amazon. Amazon also operates other businesses' Web sites for them under its Amazon Services Merchant.com program. And under Amazon's Syndicated Stores Program, Amazon sells its own products through other businesses' Web sites, paying the other business a sales commission on any Amazon products sold.

Amazon has also made several strategic acquisitions in 2008, including Audible.com, a leading online provider of audio books and other digital spoken word audio content, Abebooks.com, an online marketplace primarily for used, rare and out-of-print books, and Fabric.com, an online fabric store that offers custom measured and cut fabrics, ad well as patterns, sewing tools, and accessories.

On the cost side, Amazon has taken significant steps to lower costs in the past two years. Important initiatives included the hiring of mathematicians and operations specialists to optimize the location of storing goods in Amazon's six warehouses, optimizing the size of shipments, and consolidating orders into larger batches prior to shipping. The company increasingly uses "postal injection" for shipping, in which Amazon trucks deliver pre-posted packages to U.S. Postal System centers.

Strategic Analysis—Competition

Amazon's competitors are general merchandisers who are both offline and online, and increasingly both. This includes the largest online competitor, eBay, and multi-channel retailers such as Wal-Mart, Sears, and JCPenney. Amazon also competes with catalog merchants such as L.L.Bean and Lands' End in a number of product areas. As the Web's largest bookseller, Amazon is in competition with specialty bookstores such as Barnesandnoble.com. Insofar as other portal sites such as MSN and Yahoo are involved in operating online stores or auctions, or selling their own products, Amazon also competes with these portals. In addition, Amazon competes with other firms who sell Web services such as hosting, shopping cart, and fulfillment services. Amazon has also engaged iTunes, Netflix, and Blockbuster in competition by offering video and audio downloads. In 2007, Amazon started selling MP3 music files without the Digital Rights Management (DRM) shackles that prevent iTunes users from playing their downloaded music on anything but an iPod, and by September 2008, was offering over 6 million DRM-free MP3 songs from all four major music labels and thousands of independent labels that can be played on virtually any hardware device and managed with any music software. In September 2008, Amazon also introduced its new Amazon Video On Demand Service, which offers thousands of movies and televisions that can be viewed instantly on a PC or Mac, as well as downloaded onto a computer or Tivo box.

Strategic Analysis—Technology

The person who said that "IT doesn't make a difference" clearly does not know much about Amazon. Amazon arguably has the largest and most sophisticated collection of online retailing technologies available at any single site on the Web. Amazon has implemented numerous Web site management, search, customer interaction, recommendation, transaction processing, and fulfillment services and systems using a combination of its own proprietary technologies and commercially available, licensed technologies. Amazon's transaction-processing systems handle millions of items, a number of different status inquiries, gift-wrapping requests, and multiple shipment methods. These systems allow the customers to choose whether to receive single or several shipments based on availability and to track the progress of each order. Amazon's technology extends to the employees as well. Every warehouse worker carries a shoehorn-size device that combines a bar code scanner, a display screen, and a two-way data transmitter. In 2007, Amazon spent $818 million (about 5.5% of its total revenues) on technology and new content, and in the first six months of 2008, spent $492 million, and said it was continuing to invest in several areas of technology and content including seller platforms, Web services, and digital initiatives, as well as expansion of new and existing product categories.

Strategic Analysis—Social and Legal Challenges

Amazon is currently facing a number of lawsuits concerning various aspects of its business. One series of lawsuits alleges that Amazon wrongfully failed to collect and remit sales and use taxes for sales of personal property and knowingly created records and statements falsely stating it was not required to collect or remit such taxes. Amazon historically has been faced with a number of patent infringement suits, which it typically settles out of court. Currently, there are several pending suits.

Perhaps the most troubling lawsuit against Amazon, however, is the suit filed by its own partner Toys"R"Us in 2004. Toys"R"Us sued Amazon over what it claimed was its exclusive right to sell toys on Amazon, and the fee which is reported to be $200 million for that right until 2010. This lawsuit aimed squarely at Amazon's Third Party Seller segment business. Toys"R"Us claimed the two companies agreed that Toys"R"Us would be the exclusive toy purveyor on the site. While in general this seems to be true because it is difficult to find toys on the Amazon site outside of the Toys"R"Us store, nevertheless Toys"R"Us is claiming some 4,000 items have slipped through the cracks. Amazon filed counter claims against Toys"R"Us. In March 2006, the Superior Court of New Jersey ruled in favor of Toys"R"Us, granting the toy company release from its contract with Amazon, but awarding no damages. Amazon is appealing the decision with the goal of reinstating the contract and compelling Toys"R"Us to pay the damages requested in the counterclaim. Because Amazon has come to rely heavily on the brand power of the largest third-party merchants, it would be particularly harmful to Amazon if it is deemed to have entered into "exclusivity" covenants with those retailers. For instance, eBay has no such exclusivity arrangement with any of its sellers.

In May 2008, Amazon filed a lawsuit against the State of New York, which in April 2008 amended its sales tax law to specifically cover sales by out-of-state online retailers who get customers through New York-based affiliate Web sites. Amazon has charged that the statute is unconstitutional and overly broad and vague. The suit remains pending as of the writing of this text.

Future Prospects

Amazon clearly has improved its financial performance through consistent gains in operational efficiency and extraordinary growth in sales. In 2007, net sales grew 36% to $14.8 billion, and net income rose to $476 million. Through the second quarter of 2008, Amazon showed significant gains over the previous year in net sales, operating income, and net income. For the first six months of the year, the company registered almost $8.2 billion in sales, as opposed to $5.9 billion for the same period in 2007. Operating income was $1.5 billion compared to $1.15 billion, and net income for the period was $425 million compared to $255 million. Projections for the full year indicated a growth in net sales of between 30% and 35% to between $19.35 -$20.1 billion. Although many worry about its ability to maintain high levels of customer service, Amazon routinely ranks among the top five online e-commerce sites for customer service, accuracy of delivery, and speed of fulfillment. While sales at traditional retailer stores are falling, in part due to high fuel costs, sales at online retail sites, including Amazon, are expanding. Amazon is well place to provide consumers with a viable alternative to visiting the suburban mall.

However, when compared to Wal-Mart, a very profitable retailing giant, Amazon comes up short because its net margins are paper-thin and could easily be reversed in an economic downturn. Although it seems to have turned the corner and achieved several years of consecutive profitability, when compared to Wal-Mart's return on invested capital and consistent growth rate in sales and profits, Amazon still has a long way to go. In the eyes of many critics, Amazon has shown it can be a very profitable bookseller, but it has yet to demonstrate it can be a profitable general merchandiser in the long term. Analysts express a mix of optimism and caution over Amazon's future in 2009 and beyond. Year-over-year sales growth percentages had risen for ten straight quarters starting with a 20% increase in the first quarter of 2006, and ending with a 41% increase in the second quarter of 2008. Despite the volatility of its stock price, Amazon is seen as a good investment due to its balance sheet showing a very positive ratio of cash on hand to long-term debt.

MULTI-CHANNEL MERCHANTS: BRICKS-AND-CLICKS

Also called multi-channel merchants, **bricks-and-clicks** companies have a network of physical stores as their primary retail channel, but also have introduced online offerings. These are multi-channel firms such as Wal-Mart, JCPenney, Sears, and other brand-name merchants. While bricks-and-clicks merchants face high costs of physical buildings and large sales staffs, they also have many advantages such as a brand name, a national customer base, warehouses, large scale (giving them leverage with suppliers), and a trained staff. Acquiring customers is less expensive because of their brand names, but these firms face challenges in coordinating prices across

bricks-and-clicks
companies that have a network of physical stores as their primary retail channel, but also have introduced online offerings

channels and handling returns of Web purchases at their retail outlets. However, these retail players are used to operating on very thin margins and have invested heavily in purchasing and inventory control systems to control costs, and in coordinating returns from multiple locations. Bricks-and-clicks companies face the challenge of leveraging their strengths and assets to the Web, building a credible Web site, hiring new skilled staff, and building rapid response order entry and fulfillment systems. According to Internet Retailer, in 2007, the 25 largest chain retailers accounted for over $33 billion (over 30%) of all online retail sales. However, there remains much room for growth. Many retail chains still have annual Web sales that represent less than 5% of their total sales (including Dillard's, Kohl's, CVS, Walgreen, and Lowes), while three companies (Rite Aid, TJX, and BJ's Wholesale) had no e-commerce business or only a limited or fledgling operation (Internet Retailer, 2008).

JCPenney.com (rebranded as JCP.com in 2007) is a prime example of a traditional merchant based on physical stores and an ailing catalog operation moving successfully to a multi-channel online store. Other examples include Sears.com, NeimanMarcus.com, Target.com and, of course, Walmart.com.

James Cash Penney founded JCPenney in 1902. Penney's original vision was to create a nationwide chain of stores based on the newly emerging business model called a "department store," which aggregated a wide variety of general merchandise at a central location, usually near local transportation hubs formed by streets, highways, and street car lines. In addition, Penney envisioned a national catalog mail-order business to rival the successful Sears model. Today, JCPenney is one of the largest national department store chains, with more than 1,000 department stores in the United States and Puerto Rico. In addition to its department stores, JCPenney operates one of the largest catalog operations in the United States, distributing over 400 million catalogs annually.

Like many traditional retailers, however, JCPenney has had to change its business model to accommodate the Internet and consumer demands for low cost and unparalleled product depth and selection, which could only be achieved by enhancing its Web operations. JCPenney opened its Web site for business in 1998 and placed its full catalog inventory online. Its department stores and Internet channels primarily serve the same target market: "modern spenders" and "starting-outers," or two-income families with median annual incomes of $50,000.

At JCPenney.com, customers can buy family clothing, jewelry, shoes, accessories, and home furnishings. And whether they buy merchandise in a bricks-and-mortar store, through the catalog, or on the Internet, customers can return items either at a store or through the mail. Indeed, the current essence of multi-channel retailing in 2007 is the nearly complete integration of offline and online sales and operations while presenting a single branded experience to the customer. A second feature of successful multi-channel retailing is understanding customer preferences so that each channel sells products appropriate to that channel. For instance, not only can customers pick up and return at a local store what they order from JCPenney.com, but they can also order from the store's counters items not in the store but available online. The in-store point-of-sale system is integrated with Penney's Web catalog, and they both share a common inventory system. Many items are too expensive to hold in physical store inventory, but they can be offered economically on the Web site. The company is also investing in state-of-the-art interactivity and imaging tools for the Web site, such as a tool that lets shoppers mix and match 142,000 combinations of window treatments, and fitting guides that enable shoppers to zoom in on products such as jeans and create more custom-fitted orders.

The company has achieved online success through some savvy decisions: putting approximately 250,000 products online, from lingerie to home furnishings, surpassing the competition in terms of selection, targeting women as the primary consumer, and making it easy to move from one category to the next on the site. JCPenney is able to directly compete against Amazon given its large selection, especially in apparel lines. In doing so, online sales are attracting new, younger JCPenney shoppers, 25% of whom have never bought anything in a JCPenney store. According to Internet Retailer, in 2008, 90% of JC Penney web customers also shop in their stores. Online sales are complementing, rather than cannibalizing, store and catalog sales. Shoppers who buy through all three channels spend four times more—$1,000—than the shopper who makes purchases only at the retail store.

As a result, JCPenney is experiencing a rejuvenation with the rapid growth of its online Web sales operation and appears to have successfully made the transition from department store/catalog merchant to store/Web merchant. Web sales in 2007 were $1.5 billion, an increase of 15.4% from 2006. Continued improvement in this segment, coupled with a strong focus on high-margin apparel products for families, an area where Amazon and eBay are weak, offers a chance for continuing improved long-term performance. JCPenney projects that it will generate $2 billion in Web sales within the next several years (JCPenney, 2008; Internet Retailer, 2008).

CATALOG MERCHANTS

Catalog merchants such as Lands' End, L.L.Bean, Eddie Bauer, Victoria's Secret, and Lillian Vernon are established companies that have a national offline catalog operation that is their largest retail channel, but who have also developed online capabilities. JCPenney could also be included here, given the large scale of its catalog operation. Catalog merchants face very high costs for printing and mailing millions of catalogs each year—many of which have a half-life of 30 seconds after the customer receives them. Nevertheless, catalog merchants have the highest margins in the retail sector because they have achieved very efficient operations. They generally have few, if any, physical stores. They also typically have developed centralized fulfillment and call centers, extraordinary service, and excellent fulfillment in partnership with package delivery firms such as FedEx and UPS. Catalog firms have suffered in recent years as catalog sales growth rates have fallen to levels that are still far above general retail but much slower than the early years of the 1980s, when annual revenues were growing at 30% a year. As a result, catalog merchants have had to diversify their channels either by building stores (L.L.Bean), being bought by store-based firms (Sears purchased Lands' End), or by building a strong Web presence.

Catalog merchants face many of the same challenges as bricks-and-mortar stores—they must leverage their existing assets and competencies to a new technology environment, build a credible Web presence, and hire new staff. Catalog firms are

catalog merchants
established companies that have a national offline catalog operation that is their largest retail channel, but who have recently developed online capabilities

uniquely advantaged, however, because they already possess very efficient, fast response order entry and fulfillment systems. In 2007, according to Internet Retailer, the 25 largest catalog merchants generated combined Web sales of $13 billion.

Arguably one of the most successful online catalog merchants is LandsEnd.com. Lands' End started out in 1963 in a basement of Chicago's tannery district selling sailboat equipment and clothing, handling 15 orders on a good day. Since then it expanded into a direct catalog merchant, distributing over 200 million catalogs annually and selling a much expanded line of "traditionally" styled sport clothing, soft luggage, and products for the home. Lands' End launched its Web site in 1995 with 100 products and travelogue essays. Located in Racine, Wisconsin, it has since grown into one of the Web's most successful apparel sites.

Land's End has always been on the leading edge of online retailing technologies, most of which emphasize personal marketing and customized products. Among these technologies are My Virtual Model, which allows customers to create a 3-D model of themselves to "try on" clothing; My Personal Shopper, where customers can create a personal wardrobe consultant to suggest items; Lands' End Live, which enables customers to chat online with customer service representatives; and Lands' End Custom, which allows customers to create custom-crafted clothing built for their personal measurements. While customized clothing built online was thought to be a gimmick in the early years of online retailing, today 40% of Lands' End clothing sold online is customized, and 25% of My Virtual Model customers are first-time customers. In 2003, Lands' End was purchased by Sears (which itself was purchased by Kmart in 2004) but retains an independent online presence and catalog operation. Sears has incorporated many of Lands' End's online techniques into its own Web site, Sears.com (Landsend.com, 2008).

MANUFACTURER-DIRECT

manufacturer-direct
single or multi-channel manufacturers who sell directly online to consumers without the intervention of retailers

Manufacturer-direct firms are either single or multi-channel manufacturers that sell directly online to consumers without the intervention of retailers. Manufacturer-direct firms were predicted to play a very large role in e-commerce, but this has generally not happened. The primary exception is computer hardware, where firms such as Dell, Hewlett-Packard, Sony, Apple, and Gateway, account for over 70% of computer retail sales online. Some of these firms had retail experience prior to the Web (Dell was built on the direct sales model), while others—such as Hewlett-Packard—had no prior direct sales experience.

supply-push model
products are made prior to orders received based on estimated demand

demand-pull model
products are not built until an order is received

As discussed in Chapter 6, manufacturer-direct firms face channel conflict challenges. Channel conflict occurs when physical retailers of products must compete on price and currency of inventory directly against the manufacturer, who does not face the cost of maintaining inventory, physical stores, or sales staffs. Firms with no prior direct marketing experience face the additional challenges of developing a fast-response online order and fulfillment system, acquiring customers, and coordinating their supply chains with market demand. Switching from a **supply-push model** (where products are made prior to orders received based on estimated demand and then stored in warehouses awaiting sale) to a **demand-pull model** (where products are not built until an order is received) has proved extremely difficult for traditional manufacturers. Yet for many products, manufacturer-direct firms have the advantage of an established national brand name, an existing large customer base, and a lower cost structure than even catalog merchants because they are the manufacturer of the goods and thus do not pay profits to anyone else. Therefore, manufacturer-direct firms should have higher margins.

The most frequently cited successful manufacturer-direct retailer is Dell Inc., the world's largest direct computer systems supplier, providing corporations, government agencies, small-to-medium businesses, and individuals with computer products and services ordered straight from the manufacturer's headquarters in Austin, Texas. Although sales representatives support corporate customers, individuals and smaller businesses buy direct from Dell by phone, fax, and via the Internet, with about $4 billion in sales generated online.

When Michael Dell started the company in 1984 in his college dorm room, his idea was to custom-build computers for customers, to eliminate the middleman and more effectively meet the technology needs of his customers. Today, the company sells much more than individual computer systems; it also offers enterprise systems, desktop, and laptop computers, as well as installation, financing, repair, and management services. By relying on a build-to-order manufacturing process, the company achieves faster inventory turnover (five days), and reduced component and finished goods inventory levels; this strategy virtually eliminates the chance of product obsolescence.

The direct model simplifies the company's operations, eliminating the need to support a wholesale and retail sales network, as well as cutting out the costly associated markup, and gives Dell complete control over its customer database. In addition, Dell can build and ship custom computers nearly as fast as a mail-order supplier can pull a computer out of inventory and ship it to the customer.

To extend the benefits of its direct sales model, Dell has aggressively moved sales, service, and support online. Each month, the company typically has 15–16 million unique visitors at Dell.com, where it maintains an estimated 80 country-specific Web sites. The Premier.Dell.com service enables companies to investigate product offerings, complete order forms and purchase orders, track orders in real time, and review order histories all online. For its small business customers, it has created an online virtual account executive, as well as a spare-parts ordering system and virtual help desk with direct access to technical support data. Dell has also continued to broaden its offerings beyond pure product sales, adding warranty services, product integration and installation services, Internet access, software, peripherals, and technology consulting, referring to them as "beyond the box" offerings. These include nearly 30,000 software and peripheral products from leading manufacturers that can be bundled with Dell products. Dell has also embraced Web 2.0, adding Web site features such as instruction on how to create and maintain a blog, edit and post online vidoes, and build and share online photo scrapbooks. Dell Lounge allows visitors to create video and audio mashups, while StudioDell shows how to work with digital photo and videos and allows visitors to upload videos they've created showing how they use Dell technology.

To improve customer service in 2007, Dell established a new call center operation in Canada, that features advanced online customer service applications, such as Dell-

Connect. DellConnect allows a customer service representative to remotely connect to a customer's computer via a broadband link to troubleshoot customer problems (Dell, Inc., 2008; Internet Retailer, 2008).

COMMON THEMES IN ONLINE RETAILING

We have looked at some very different companies in the preceding section, from entrepreneurial Web-only merchants to established offline giants. Online retail e-commerce is indeed alive and well for some retailers, particularly for established offline retailers with existing brands. Online retail is the fastest-growing channel in retail on a revenue basis, has the fastest-growing consumer base, and has growing penetration across many categories of nonessential goods. On the other hand, profits for new start-up ventures have been difficult to achieve, and it took even Amazon until 2003 to show its first profit.

The reasons for the difficulties experienced by online retailers in achieving profits are also now clear. The path to success in any form of retail involves having a central location in order to attract a larger number of shoppers, charging high enough prices to cover the costs of goods as well as marketing, and developing highly efficient inventory and fulfillment systems so that the company can offer goods at lower costs than competitors and still make a profit. In the early years, many online merchants failed to follow these fundamental ideas, and lowered prices below the total costs of goods and operations, failed to develop efficient business processes, or spent far too much on customer acquisition and marketing. Since 2002, however, online retail firms have begun to raise prices, often matching the prices in some categories of offline stores. Consumers have been willing to accept higher prices in return for the convenience of shopping online, and avoiding the costs of shopping at stores and malls.

For the most part, disintermediation did not occur and the retail middleman did not disappear. Indeed, virtual merchants, along with powerful offline merchants who moved online, maintained their powerful grip on the retail customer, with some notable exceptions in electronics and software. Manufacturers—with the exception of electronic goods—have used the Web primarily as an informational resource, driving consumers to the traditional retail channels for transactions.

The most significant online growth has been that of offline general merchandiser giants such as Wal-Mart and JCPenney and catalogers such as Lands' End and L.L. Bean. Many of the first-mover, Web pure-play merchants failed to achieve profitability and closed their doors en masse in 2000 and 2001 as their venture capital funds were depleted. Traditional retailers are the fast followers (although many of them cannot be characterized as particularly "fast") most likely to succeed on the Web by extending their traditional competencies and assets. In this sense, e-commerce technological innovation is following the historical pattern of other technology-driven commercial changes, from automobiles to radio and television.

To succeed online, established merchants need to create an integrated shopping environment that combines their catalog, store, and online experiences into one. Established retailers have significant fulfillment, inventory management, supply chain management, and other competencies that apply directly to the online channel. And although established merchants have moved online, their e-commerce operations are not always profitable. To succeed online, established retailers need to extend their brands, provide incentives to consumers to use the online channel, avoid channel conflict, and build partnerships with online portals such as AOL, MSN, and Yahoo.

A second area of very rapid online growth is a new crop of specialty merchants selling high-end, fashionable and luxury goods, such as BlueNile, the online diamond merchant, or selling discounted electronics, such as BestBuy.com (electronics), or apparel (Gap.com), or office products (OfficeDepot.com). For instance, at Gap, Inc., its Web sales provided the only bright spot in 2007 -- while store sales fell 4%, online sales grew by 23.7%. These firms are demonstrating the vitality and openness of the Internet for innovation and extending the range of products available on the Web. Many virtual merchants have developed large, online customer bases, as well as the online tools required to market to their customer base. These online brands can be strengthened further through alliances and partnerships that add the required competencies in inventory management and fulfillment services. Virtual merchants need to build operational strength and efficiency before they can become profitable.

Both Web-only and established offline retailers wishing to strengthen their e-commerce revenues will be favorably affected in the future by new retailing technologies—from extending high-speed Internet access to the majority of potential consumers, to mobile commerce using cell phones, to new services such as enhanced comparison shopping sites, as described in *Insight on Technology: Using the Web to Shop 'Till You Drop*.

9.4 THE SERVICE SECTOR: OFFLINE AND ONLINE

The service sector is typically the largest and most rapidly expanding part of the economies in advanced industrial nations such as the United States, and in European and some Asian countries. In the United States, services (broadly defined) employ about 108 million people (76% of the labor force) and account for about $7.7 trillion (about 58%) of the U.S's gross domestic product (GDP) (U.S. Census Bureau, 2008). Less than one-quarter of the U.S. workforce is involved in the production of physical goods.

On the other hand, productivity in the service sector has lagged far behind productivity in factories and on farms. Productivity in the service sector over the last decade has averaged about 1%, while farm and factory productivity has averaged about 5% (U.S. Census Bureau, 2008). While the explosion in information technology capital investment since 1995 has certainly added to overall productivity, "white collar" service sector employees did not benefit from this as much as factory employees. In part, this is because the very nature of services—performing activities for others in a highly personalized and customized manner—is somewhat immune to the beneficial aspects of computerization. The productivity of doctors, lawyers, accountants, and business consultants—all service occupations—has not been markedly affected in terms of unit output per unit time by the explosion in information technology, although the quality of their work has undoubtedly

INSIGHT ON TECHNOLOGY

USING THE WEB TO SHOP 'TILL YOU DROP

The original idea was simple and leveraged many of the unique features of e-commerce technology: Create a Web site listing thousands of products where consumers can compare prices, features, consumer reviews of the actual product performance, and reputations of merchants. Then, when visitors click on a product and price they like, they are taken to the merchant's Web site where they can make the purchase. The merchant pays the Web site a fee or commission for sending the customer. The idea: Shoppers would not have to shop till they drop, but instead could conveniently price compare at one site, and then buy from the lowest-price merchant on the Web. Merchants would support this service because they would obtain additional customers and sales. Merchants join the shopping services and provide a digital feed to the comparison sites providing information on both products and prices.

The idea first appeared in the mid-1990s in academic papers on potential uses of the Web and Internet, and was referred to as "shopping robots." Today, shopping bots have become big business. No one knows for sure, but observers believe there are about 60 of these sites on the Web in 2008. Now referred to much more descriptively as comparison shopping sites, with products tracked numbering in the millions, they are being snatched up by some of the biggest names in business. For instance, the leading stand-alone comparison shopping site, Shopping.com, with an estimated 18 million unique monthly visitors in 2008, was purchased in June 2005 by eBay for $634 million. (Shopping.com was formerly known as Dealtime.com, and also includes Epinions.com, an online consumer review and ratings platform). The second leading site, Shopzilla.com (which also operates a user

product review site called Bizrate.com), with an estimated 18 million monthly visitors, was also purchased in June 2005, by E.W. Scripps Co., for $525 million. Other competitors that have not yet been acquired include NexTag.com and PriceGrabber.com. General merchandisers such as Amazon, portals such as Yahoo and AOL, and search engines such as Google have also developed their own comparison shopping capabilities.

About 60% of consumers have used a comparison shopping Web site, according to Jupiter Research. The number of shoppers visiting such sites is growing at about 10% a year, after very rapid growth in the early years. Shopping comparison sites have become attractive acquisition candidates because they have done very well in attracting visitors, and are also profitable.

Comparison shopping sites focused originally on tracking online prices for electronic consumer goods and computers. Consumer electronics are fairly commoditized products by a few branded manufacturers, with standard features, making it fairly easy to compare one product to another. Type in digital camera, select the number of megapixels you want, enter the price and zoom range, press the Enter key on your keyboard, and you will receive a long list of cameras and dealers. You can refine your search as you move along the purchase process, and explore the reputations of dealers before you decide to purchase.

However, although Shopping.com tracks over 60 million products (Shopzilla, 30 million), very few of these items are so-called "soft goods" purchased by women, who have risen to equal the purchasing power of men on the Web. In 1998, 65% of Web purchases were made by men, while today, over 60% are made by women who are

(continued)

much more likely to be looking for soft goods, such as apparel, jewelry, accessories, luggage, and gifts. In fact, these are among the fastest-growing consumer product categories on the Web. For this reason, the shopping comparison sites are currently adding soft goods to their services.

But the process of comparison shopping for soft goods is not as simple as for hard goods such as digital TVs or digital cameras. The strength of a comparison shopping site is to present highly similar or identical items from different merchants at varying prices and reputation levels. Generally, these kinds of electronic goods have a limited number of suppliers (mostly solid brand names) and limited features. But in more complex product areas, such as apparel or jewelry, such standards do not exist. In fact, manufacturers of these products emphasize their uniqueness, not their similarity. One solution is to focus on the brands of soft goods and not the price: bags from Gucci, sweaters from Benneton, and mountain climbing gear from REI. Yahoo and search engines such as MSN and Google are moving closer to the brand model of comparison shopping as price becomes a less powerful factor in consumer purchases of soft goods.

As more and more attention focuses on comparison shopping sites, the sites themselves continue to innovate and add features, and they attempt to go beyond simply finding customers the lowest-price products. Shopping.com tracks its visitors to help consumers decide what to buy, and where to buy. It does this by showing visitors the most popular sites for each category of product selected. Shopzilla has developed a data categorization technology that it calls Robozilla, designed to help expedite the shopping process. PriceGrabber is focused on adding product tours and more content, such as user and third-party

reviews, and discussion boards. NexTag offers consumers e-mail price alerts and product price history charting, and for merchants, a new data feed auto-import option. Most of the larger sites are adding user-generated reviews and opinions of products.

New companies are also continuing to enter the market every day, such as HealthPricer, which lists over 360,000 health products, and StylePath, which finds consumers products based on their tastes and interests that they reveal to the shopping engine. This new site features 100,000 products from 1,500 online merchants.

One new site has upped the ante. Discount-More re-launched its search engine in 2007. The site enables consumers to get results from the top 26 shopping sites all on one page.

Despite these innovations, visitors to shopping comparison sites continue to be primarily price motivated: 85% of visitors press the "sort by price" button despite the search engines' efforts to provide more qualitative assessments of quality and reliability. The comparison sites are obviously in competition with search engines, such as Google (which has its own comparison service). As keyword prices have risen on search engines, shopping comparison sites become an excellent bargain. But in 2008, some merchants have begun to complain the comparison sites are getting greedy, and charging excessively high commissions. JellyFish, a new shopping site purchased by Microsoft, has a solution: it lets merchants pay per sale, not per click. And it shares half of its commission with customers by depositing their share in their accounts. Shopping.com has changed its pricing scheme so that merchants who receive few purchases do not pay as much per click.

SOURCES: "Online Shoppers Turn to Walmart.com as They Seek to Stretch Their Dollars," Internet Retailer, September 15, 2008; "Lots of Choices," by Mary Wagner, Internet Retailer, November, 2007; "New Shopping Site Finds Products Based on an Individuals Style Profile," October 19, 2007; "Staying on Top of Changes at Comparison Shopping Engines," Internet Retailer, October 10, 2007; "While Parents Procrastinate on Back-to-School Shopping, Shopzilla Discovers Hottest Items Are Not What You Think," Shopzilla.com, August 1, 2007; "Comparison Shopping Sites Expand and Narrow," Internet Retailer, July 2007; "Shopping.com Closes Holiday Season 2006 and Reports Record Traffic to Merchants," January 4, 2007.

improved. Unfortunately, increases in quality of service are not measured by productivity statistics. Being able to find the lowest price in the United States for a New York to Los Angeles flight in a matter of minutes (as opposed to many hours in the past) will never be measured in productivity statistics. What this means for e-commerce is that the service sector offers extraordinary opportunities insofar as e-commerce sites can deliver information, knowledge, and transaction efficiencies.

WHAT ARE SERVICES?

Just what are services? The U.S. Department of Labor defines **service occupations** as "concerned with performing tasks" in and around households, business firms, and institutions (U.S. Department of Labor, 1991). The U.S. Census Bureau defines **service industries** as those "domestic establishments providing services to consumers, businesses, governments and other organizations" (U.S. Census Bureau, 2001). The major service industry groups are finance, insurance, real estate, travel, professional services such as legal and accounting, business services, health services, and educational services. Business services include activities such as consulting, advertising and marketing, and information processing.

CATEGORIZING SERVICE INDUSTRIES

Within these service industry groups, companies can be further categorized into those that involve **transaction brokering** (acting as an intermediary to facilitate a transaction) and those that involve providing a "hands-on" service. For instance, one type of financial services involves stockbrokers who act as the middle person in a transaction between buyers and sellers. Online mortgage companies such as LendingTree refer customers to mortgage companies that actually issue the mortgage. Employment agencies put a seller of labor in contact with a buyer of labor. The service involved in all these examples is brokering a transaction.

In contrast, legal, medical, accounting, and other such industries perform specific hands-on activities for consumers. In order to provide their service, these professionals need to interact directly and personally with the "client." For these service industries, the opportunities for e-commerce are somewhat different. Currently, doctors and dentists cannot treat patients over the Internet. However, the Internet can assist their services by providing consumers with information, knowledge, and communication.

KNOWLEDGE AND INFORMATION INTENSITY

With some exceptions (for example, providers of physical services, such as cleaning, gardening, and so on), perhaps the most important feature of service industries (and occupations) is that they are knowledge and information intense. In order to provide value, service industries process a great deal of information and employ a highly skilled, educated work force. For instance, to provide legal services, you need lawyers with law degrees. Law firms are required to process enormous amounts of textual information. Likewise with medical services. Financial services are not so knowledge-intensive, but require much larger investments in information processing just to keep track of transactions and investments. In fact, the financial services

service occupations
occupations concerned with performing tasks in and around households, business firms, and institutions

service industries
establishments providing services to consumers, businesses, governments, and other organizations

transaction brokering
acting as an intermediary to facilitate a transaction

sector is the largest investor in information technology, with over 80% of invested capital going to information technology equipment and services (Laudon and Laudon, 2008).

For these reasons, many services are uniquely suited to e-commerce applications and the strengths of the Internet, which are to collect, store, and disseminate high-value information and to provide reliable, fast communication.

PERSONALIZATION AND CUSTOMIZATION

Services differ in the amount of personalization and customization required, although just about all services entail some personalization or customization. Some services, such as legal, medical, and accounting services, require extensive personalization—the adjustment of a service to the precise needs of a single individual or object. Others, such as financial services, benefit from customization by allowing individuals to choose from a restricted menu. The ability of Internet and e-commerce technology to personalize and customize service, or components of service, is a major factor undergirding the extremely rapid growth of e-commerce services. Future expansion of e-services will depend in part on the ability of e-commerce firms to transform their customized services—choosing from a list—into truly personalized services, such as providing unique advice and consultation based on a digital, yet intimate understanding of the client (at least as intimate as professional service providers).

9.5 ONLINE FINANCIAL SERVICES

Financial services (finance, insurance, and real estate) contribute over $2.7 trillion to the U.S. GDP. The online financial services sector is a shining example of an e-commerce success story, but the success is somewhat different than what had been predicted during the early days of e-commerce. While the innovative, pure-online firms have been instrumental in transforming the brokerage industry, the impacts of e-commerce have been less powerful in banking, insurance, and real estate, where consumers are more likely to use the Web for research but conduct transactions through traditional suppliers. As in the retail marketspace, it is the multi-channel, established financial services firms—the slow followers—who are showing the fastest growth and strongest prospects of long-term survival.

FINANCIAL SERVICES INDUSTRY TRENDS

The financial services industry provides four generic kinds of services: storage of and access to funds, protection of assets, means to grow assets, and movement of funds. Historically, in the United States and elsewhere, separate institutions provided these financial services (see **Table 9.5**).

However, two important global trends in the financial services industry that have direct consequences for online financial services firms are changing the institutional structure of financial services. The first trend is industry consolidation (see **Figure 9.3**).

TABLE 9.5	TRADITIONAL PROVIDERS OF FINANCIAL SERVICES
FINANCIAL SERVICE	**INSTITUTIONAL PROVIDER**
Storage of and access to funds	Banking, lending
Protection of assets	Insurance
Growth	Investment and brokerage firms
Movement of funds (payment)	Banks, credit card firms

In the United States, the banking, finance, brokerage, and insurance industries were legally separated by the Glass-Steagall Act of 1934, which prohibited banks, insurance firms, and brokerages from having significant financial interests in one another in order to prevent a repetition of the calamitous financial institution failures that followed the stock market crash of 1929 and the ensuing Depression. The Glass-Steagall Act also prevented large banks from owning banks in other states. This legal separation meant that financial institutions in the United States could not provide customers with integrated financial services, and could not operate nationwide. One result was the proliferation of small, inefficient, local banks in the United States, arguably the most "over-banked" country in the world. West European and Japanese financial institutions did not face similar restrictions, putting the American industry at a disadvantage. The Financial Reform Act of 1998 amended

FIGURE 9.3	INDUSTRY CONSOLIDATION AND INTEGRATED FINANCIAL SERVICES

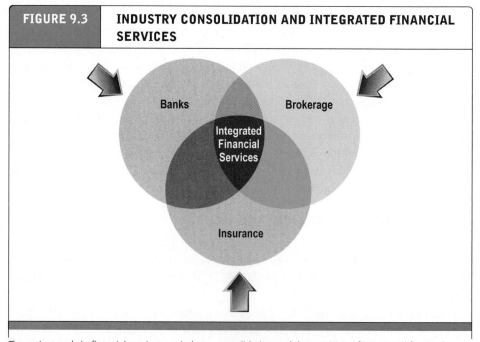

The major trends in financial services are industry consolidation and the provision of integrated financial services to consumers.

Glass-Steagall and permitted banks, brokerages, and insurance firms to merge and to develop nationwide banks. This new law touched off an avalanche of financial service sector consolidations.

A second related trend is the movement toward integrated financial services. Once banks, brokerages, and insurance companies are permitted to own one another, it becomes possible to provide consumers with what countless surveys have documented they really want: trust, service, and convenience. The movement toward financial service integration began in the 1980s when Merrill Lynch developed the first "cash management account" that integrated the brokerage and cash management services provided to Merrill Lynch's customers into a single account. Spare cash in each customer account was invested at the close of business each day into a money market fund. In the 1990s, Citibank and other large money center banks developed the concept of a financial supermarket, where consumers can find any financial product or service at a single physical center or branch bank. Nearly all large national banks now provide some form of financial planning and investment service.

The Internet has created the technical foundations for an online financial supermarket to operate, but, for the most part, it has still not arrived. It is not yet possible to arrange for a car loan, obtain a mortgage, receive investment planning advice, and establish a pension fund at any single financial institution with one account. Nevertheless, this is the direction in which large banking institutions are attempting to move.

The promise of the Internet in the long term is to take the financial supermarket model one step further by providing a truly personalized, customized, and integrated offering to consumers based on a complete understanding of the consumer and his or her financial behavior, life cycle status, and unique needs. It will take many years to develop the technical infrastructure, as well as change consumer behavior toward a much deeper relationship with online financial services institutions.

ONLINE FINANCIAL CONSUMER BEHAVIOR

Surveys show that consumers are attracted to financial sites because of their desire to save time and access information rather than save money, although saving money is an important goal among the most sophisticated online financial households. About 40% of U.S. Internet users go online to obtain financial information or use online banking or other financial services (Pew Internet & American Life Report, 2008; USC Annenberg School Center for the Digital Future, 2008). Most online consumers use financial services sites for mundane financial management, such as checking balances of existing accounts, most of which were established offline. Once accustomed to performing mundane financial management activities, consumers move on to more sophisticated capabilities such as using personal financial management tools, making loan payments, and considering offers from online institutions. **Table 9.6** shows the results of a survey of the online financial activities of U.S. adult Internet users during the previous 12 months.

Currently, the greatest deterrent to increased usage of online financial services is fears about security and confidentiality of sensitive financial information. In general, consumers are much more reluctant to conduct financial transactions

TABLE 9.6	ONLINE CONSUMERS' FINANCIAL ACTIVITIES
BANK	AMOUNT OF DEPOSITS
Checked bank accounts	65%
Moved/withdrew bank funds	43%
Applied for a credit card	25%
Traded stock	9%
Applied for a mortgage	6%

SOURCES: Based on data from eMarketer, Inc., 2007a; eBrain Market Research, 2006.

online than they are to shop online. For instance, surveys by both the Conference Board and TNS NFO have found that online households are much more concerned about the security of their financial transactions than about purchasing products online, communicating online, or using search engines. For instance, a Computer Associates July 2008 survey found that 58% of those surveyed felt that major financial institutions do not spend enough on online security (Computer Associates, 2008). Consumers are particularly concerned about the possibility of identity theft, fraud, and the risk of account intrusion.

ONLINE BANKING AND BROKERAGE

NetBank and Wingspan pioneered online banking in the United States in 1996 and 1997, respectively. Traditional banks had developed earlier versions of telephone banking, but did not use online services until 1998. Although late by a year or two, the established brand-name national banks have taken a substantial lead in market share as the percentage of their customers who bank online has grown rapidly. **Table 9.7** lists the amount of estimated online deposits held by various online banks, including online units of traditional banks. NetBank, one of the original pioneers, was forced to declare bankruptcy in October 2007, primarily as a result of the subprime mortgage loan crisis.

TABLE 9.7	LEADING ONLINE BANKS (NOVEMBER 2007) (IN BILLIONS)
BANK	AMOUNT OF DEPOSITS
ING Direct (online only)	$47.0 billion
Citibank Direct (online unit of traditional bank)	$9.0 billion
Emigrant Direct (online unit of traditional bank)	$6.0 billion
HSBC Direct (online unit of traditional bank)	$4.8 billion

According to eMarketer, nearly 91 million U.S. consumers are expected to conduct some online banking activity in 2008, an increase of about 14% over 2007, and this number is expected to grow to around 159 million by 2012 (eMarketer, Inc., 2007a) (see **Figure 9.4**).

The history of online brokerage has been similar to that of online banking. Early innovators such as E*Trade have been displaced from their leadership positions in terms of numbers of online accounts by discount broker pioneer Charles Schwab and financial industry giant Fidelity (which has more mutual fund customers and more funds under management than any other U.S. firm).

Today, according to Forrester Research estimates, about 6 million U.S. households trade online, a number Forrester expects to increase to approximately 12 million by 2011 (Forrester Research, 2007). According to a survey of online financial activities over the previous 12 months among U.S. adult Internet users, 9% traded stocks (eMarketer, Inc., 2007a). According to Nielsen, in terms of unique visitors, the top trading Web site among U.S. Internet users in July 2008 was Fidelity Investments, with over 5.2 million (see **Table 9.8**).

Multi-channel vs. Pure Online Financial Services Firms

Online consumers prefer to visit financial services sites that have physical outlets or branches. In general, multi-channel financial services firms that have both physical branches or offices and solid online offerings are growing faster than pure-online firms that have no physical presence, and they are assuming market

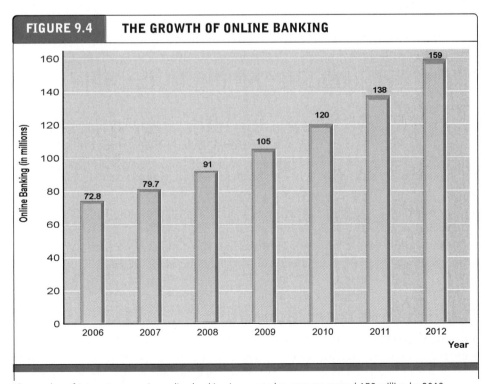

| FIGURE 9.4 | THE GROWTH OF ONLINE BANKING |

The number of Internet users using online banking is expected to grow to around 159 million by 2012.
SOURCE: Based on data from eMarketer, Inc., 2007a, authors' estimates.

TABLE 9.8	TOP ONLINE BROKERAGES JULY 2008
FIRM	NUMBER OF UNIQUE VISITORS (JULY 2008)
Fidelity Investments	5.20 million
Sharebuilder.com	2.54 million
Scottrade	2.43 million
TD Ameritrade	2.40 million
Vanguard	2.10 million
E*Trade	1.58 million
Charles Schwab	1.43 million
Merrill Lynch	1.14 million
Troweprice.com	0.95 million

SOURCES: Based on data from eMarketer, Inc., 2008b; MarketingCharts.com, 2008; Nielsen/NetRatings Netview, 2008.

leadership as well. Traditional banking firms have literally thousands of branches where customers can open accounts, deposit money, take out loans, find home mortgages, and rent a safety deposit box. Top online brokerage firms do not have the same physical footprint as the banks do, but each has a strong physical presence or telephone presence to strengthen its online presence. Fidelity has urban walk-in service center branches, but it primarily relies on the telephone for interacting with investors. Charles Schwab has decided to open investment centers around the country as an integral part of its online strategy. Pure-online banks and brokerages cannot provide customers with many services that still require a hands-on interaction.

Internet-only banks and brokerages lack physical client acquisition channels and therefore must rely on their Web sites and advertising to acquire customers, whereas established multi-channel institutions can convert existing branch customers into online customers at a far lower cost. In terms of loyalty and intensity, a different picture emerges. Users of pure-online institutions utilize these sites more intensively for a wide variety of services that used to be performed at branches, whereas the established multi-channel site users make fewer online transactions and visit the site less often. However, customers of pure-online institutions comparison shop more, are more price-driven, and are less loyal than customers of established multi-channel players.

Financial Portals and Account Aggregators

financial portals
sites that provide consumers with comparison shopping services, independent financial advice, and financial planning

Financial portals are sites that provide consumers with comparison shopping services, independent financial advice, and financial planning. Independent portals do not themselves offer financial services, but act as steering mechanisms to online providers. They generate revenue from advertising, referral fees, and subscription fees. For example, Yahoo's financial portal, Yahoo Finance, offers consumers credit card purchase tracking, market overviews, real-time stock quotes, news, financial advice, streaming-video interviews with financial leaders, and Yahoo Bill Pay, an EBPP system. Other independent financial portals include Intuit's Quicken.com, MSN's MSN Money, CNN Money, and America Online's Money and Finance channel.

In general, the financial portals do not offer financial services (they make their money from advertising); instead, they add to the online price competition in the industry and run counter to the strategy of large banking institutions to ensnare consumers into a single branded, financial institutional system, with a single account and high switching costs.

Account aggregation is the process of pulling together all of a customer's financial (and even nonfinancial) data at a single personalized Web site, including brokerage, banking, insurance, loans, frequent flyer miles, personalized news, and much more. For example, a consumer can see his or her Merrill Lynch brokerage account, Fidelity 401(k) account, Travelers Insurance annuity account, and American Airlines frequent flyer miles all displayed on a single site. The idea is to provide consumers with a holistic view of their entire portfolio of assets, no matter what financial institution actually holds those assets.

account aggregation
the process of pulling together all of a customer's financial (and even nonfinancial) data at a single personalized Web site

The leading provider of account aggregation technology is Yodlee. It uses screen-scraping and other techniques to pull information from over 8,000 different data sources. A smart-mapping technology is also used so that if the underlying Web sites change, the scraping software can adapt and still find the relevant information.

Financial portal sites were the first to adopt Yodlee's account aggregation technology. Established financial institutions initially opposed independent account aggregators as a threat to their customer base. But most such institutions have since signed deals with Yodlee to provide account aggregation at their sites as well. According to Yodlee, over 5 million consumers at more 100 financial institutions and portals such as Ameriprise Financial, AOL, Bank of America, Fidelity, JPMorgan Chase, Merrill Lynch, and MSN are now using Yodlee's Aggregation Platform (Yodlee, 2008).

Account aggregation raises a number of issues. In order to use account aggregation services, consumers must release all their login and password information to the aggregator. If one institution holds all account information, consumers face the risk of losing control over their information, which heretofore was spread across many largely inaccessible sites. Financial aggregators may be tempted to "cross sell" products to consumers at their sites, raising the possibility of fairly intense marketing campaigns, although aggregator sites claim they will not use their customers' information to promote products without explicit permission.

ONLINE MORTGAGE AND LENDING SERVICES

During the early days of e-commerce, hundreds of firms launched pure-play online mortgage sites to capture the U.S. home mortgage market. Early entrants hoped to radically simplify and transform the traditional mortgage value chain process, dramatically speed up the loan closing process, and share the economies with consumers by offering lower rates.

By 2003, over half of these early-entry, pure-online firms had failed. Early pure-play online mortgage institutions had difficulties developing a brand name at an affordable price and failed to simplify the mortgage generation process. They ended up suffering from high start-up and administrative costs, high customer acquisition costs, rising interest rates, and poor execution of their strategies.

Despite this rocky start, the online mortgage market is slowly growing; it is dominated by established online banks and other online financial services firms, traditional mortgage vendors, and a few successful online mortgage firms.

According to research firm TowerGroup, more than half of all mortgage shoppers research mortgages online, but few actually apply online (Whitehouse, 2004). According to another survey, 6% of those surveyed in 2006 had applied for a mortgage during the previous 12 months, compared to only 1% in 2000 (eMarketer, Inc., 2007b). Although online mortgage originations currently represent a small percentage of all mortgages, their number is expected to continue to grow slowly but surely over the next several years, although in 2008 the number of mortgages being originated in all forms has been negatively impacted by the subprime mortgage crisis.

There are three kinds of online mortgage vendors:

- Established banks, brokerages, and lending organizations such as Chase, Bank of America/Countrywide Credit Industries, Wells Fargo, Ameriquest Mortgage, and Citigroup (which operates Mortgage.com).

- Pure online mortgage bankers/brokers such as E-loan, QuickenLoans, and E*Trade Mortgage. These companies aim to expedite the mortgage shopping and initiation process, but still require extensive paperwork to complete a mortgage.

- Mortgage brokers such as Tree.com (formerly LendingTree), owned by IAC/InteractiveCorp, and comparison shopping site NexTag. These companies offer visitors access to hundreds of mortgage vendors who bid for their business.

Consumer benefits from online mortgages include reduced application times, market interest rate intelligence, and process simplification that occurs when participants in the mortgage process (title, insurance, and lending companies) share a common information base. Mortgage lenders benefit from the cost reduction involved in online processing of applications, while charging rates marginally lower than traditional bricks-and-mortar institutions.

Nevertheless, the online mortgage industry has not transformed the process of obtaining a mortgage. A significant brake on market expansion is the complexity of the mortgage process, which requires physical signatures and documents, multiple institutions, and complex financing details—such as closing costs and points—that are difficult for shoppers to compare across vendors (Perkins, 2004). Nevertheless, as in other areas, the ability of shoppers to find low mortgage rates on the Web has helped reduce the fees and interest rates charged by traditional mortgage lenders.

ONLINE INSURANCE SERVICES

In 1995, the price of a $500,000 20-year term life policy for a healthy 40-year-old male was $995 a year. In 2008, the same policy could be had for around $350—a decline of about 65%—while other prices have risen 15% in the same period (AccuQuote, 2008). In a study of the term life insurance business, Brown and Goolsbee discovered that Internet usage led to an 8%–15% decline in term life insurance prices industry-wide (both offline and online), and increased consumer surplus by about $115 million per year (and hence reduced industry profits by the same amount) (Brown and Goolsbee, 2000). Price dispersion for term life policies initially increased, but then fell as more and more people began using the Internet to obtain insurance quotes.

Unlike books and CDs, where online price dispersion is higher than offline, and in many cases online prices are higher than offline, term life insurance stands out as one product group supporting the conventional wisdom that the Internet will lower search costs, increase price comparison, and lower prices to consumers. Term life insurance is a commodity product, however, and in other insurance product lines, the Web offers insurance companies new opportunities for product and service differentiation and price discrimination.

The insurance industry forms a major part of the $2.7 trillion financial services sector. It has four major segments: automobile, life, health, and property and casualty. Insurance products can be very complex. For example, there are many different types of non-automotive property and casualty insurance: liability, fire, homeowners, commercial, workers' compensation, marine, accident, and other lines such as vacation insurance. Writing an insurance policy in any of these areas is very information-intense, often necessitating personal inspection of the properties, and it requires considerable actuarial experience and data. The life insurance industry has also developed life insurance policies that defy easy comparison and can only be explained and sold by an experienced sales agent. Historically, the insurance industry has relied on thousands of local insurance offices and agents to sell complex products uniquely suited to the circumstances of the insured person and the property. Complicating the insurance marketplace is the fact that the insurance industry is not federally regulated, but rather is regulated by 50 different state insurance commissions that are strongly influenced by local insurance agents. Before a Web site can offer quotations on insurance, it must obtain a license to enter the insurance business in all the states where it provides quotation services or sells insurance.

Like the online mortgage industry, the online insurance industry has been very successful in attracting visitors who are looking to obtain prices and terms of insurance policies. For instance, comScore reported that in 2007, during the period for 2004 to 2006, consumers requested more than 32 million auto insurance online price quotes up 35% from 2006. However, the industry has been less successful at getting customers to buy policies online, although this is changing, particularly in the areas of automobile insurance and term life insurance policies, which are less complex. For instance, a 2008 study by comScore showed that in 2007, auto insurance policies purchased online increased 37% from the previous year, and a record 2 million policies were purchased online. Almost two-thirds of those surveyed indicated that they would consider purchasing their next auto insurance policy online (insWeb, 2007; comScore, 2007).

While many national insurance underwriting companies initially did not offer competitive products directly on the Web because it might injure the business operations of their traditional local agents, the Web sites of almost all of the major firms now provide the ability to obtain an online quote. In 2007, the top five U.S. auto insurance companies in terms of number of online quotes requested were Progressive (33% market share), GEICO (31%), Esurance (15%), Allstate (8%), and State Farm (7%) (comScore, 2008). Even if consumers do not actually purchase insurance policies online, the Internet has proven to have a powerful influence on consumer insurance decisions by dramatically reducing search costs and changing the price discovery process.

See **Table 9.9** for a list and description of some of the leading online insurance services companies.

ONLINE REAL ESTATE SERVICES

Real estate is a $1.7 trillion industry. Commercial real estate involves around 4.9 million commercial buildings with around 72 billion square feet of floor space. During the second quarter of 2008, there were approximately 18.7 million vacant housing units for sale or rent. In 2007, total real estate transactions in the United States were over $270 billion. Real estate advertising expenditures account for about $11 billion a year. Finally, about $55 billion changed hands in real estate commissions for real estate transactions of all kinds. All together, these metrics make real estate a very attractive market (U.S. Census Bureau, 2008a, b; Gopal, 2007).

During the early days of e-commerce, real estate seemed ripe for an Internet revolution that would rationalize this historically local, complex, and local agent-driven industry that monopolized the flow of consumer information. Potentially, the Internet and e-commerce might have disintermediated this huge marketspace, allowing buyers and sellers, renters, and owners to transact directly; lower search costs to near zero; and dramatically reduce prices. However, this did not happen. What did happen is extremely beneficial to buyers and sellers, as well as to real estate agents. At one point, there was an estimated 100,000 real estate sites on the Internet worldwide. Many of these sites have disappeared. However, the remaining online sites have started to make headway toward transforming the industry. In addition, most local real estate brokers in the United States have their own agency Web sites to deal with clients, in addition to participating with thousands of other agencies in multiple listing services that list homes online. See **Table 9.10** for a list of some of the major online real estate sites.

Real estate differs from other types of online financial services because it is impossible to complete a property transaction online. Clearly, the major impact of Internet real estate sites is in influencing offline decisions. The Internet has become a compelling method for real estate professionals, homebuilders, property managers and owners, and ancillary service providers to communicate with and provide information to consumers. According to a survey conducted by the National Association of Realtors, the percentage of respondents receiving leads from the Internet grew

TABLE 9.9	LEADING MULTI-PRODUCT ONLINE INSURANCE SERVICES	
COMPANY	2007 REVENUES	DESCRIPTION
InsWeb	$33.2 million	Comparison shopping for consumers; insurance companies pay for client leads; also earns commissions from policies via two wholly owned insurance agencies. Auto, life, health, and homeowner's insurance quotes. Public company.
Insure.com (Quotesmith)	$18.02 million	Free quotes from 200 insurance companies on a full range of policies with no fee. Operates insurance agency and brokerage and earns revenue from insurance companies for client leads and commissions. Public company.
Insurance.com (operated by ComparisonMarket)	ND	Reportedly the nation's largest online auto insurance company. Consumers can compare quotes from 12 different carriers, and purchase policies online or from a licensed agent. Other products include life, health, and home insurance as well as travel, dental, and pet health insurance. Formerly owned by Fidelity, now privately held.
QuickQuote	ND	Free quotes on a range of policies. Revenue from advertising and client leads. Formerly owned by ING Group, now privately held.
Answerfinancial	ND	One-stop insurance shopping resource, featuring auto, home, life, health, dental, and long-term care insurance as well as annuity products, pet insurance, and more. Offers the products of more than 230 providers through intranets, the Internet, and by toll-free phone staffed by licensed agents.
NetQuote	ND	Provides quotes for auto, home, health, life, and business insurance. Has relationship with over 100 insurance companies, such as GEICO, Progressive, Allstate, and others. Claims to be the most visited insurance shopping site on the Web.

ND = Not Disclosed

from 30% in 2005 to 50% in 2007, and 93% of those who received Internet leads indicated that the leads ultimately resulted in a sale (Center for Realtor Technology, National Association of Realtors, 2007). Another survey, the California Association of Realtors "2008 Survey of California Home Buyers," found that over 78% of all first-time

TABLE 9.10	MAJOR ONLINE REAL ESTATE SITES
COMPANY	**DESCRIPTION**
Realtor.com	Official site of the National Association of Realtors. Operated by Move, Inc. Includes a searchable database of over 4 million existing homes for sale; listing content from over 1000 multiple listing services.
HomeGain	Online lead-generation and real estate marketing resource not affiliated with any traditional real estate agency. Acquired by Classified Ventures, a joint venture of six leading media companies, in July 2005.
RealEstate.com	Online lead generator for real estate brokers and agents. Owned by Tree.com, a spinoff of IAC/InterActive Corp.
ZipRealty	One of the first independent full-service residential real estate broker to leverage Internet to provide discount services. A public company with $103.8 million in net revenues for 2007. Currently operates in 18 states and District of Columbia. Shares a portion of its commission with buyer clients in the form of a cash rebate, and typically represents seller clients at fee levels below those offered by most traditional brokerage firms.
Move.com	Information on rental properties, builders, newly built homes, and housing plans. Owned by Move, Inc. (formerly Homestore).
Rent.com	Rental housing database with "millions" of apartments to rent. Owned by eBay.
Apartments.com	Rental housing listings. Exclusive provider of visual apartment listings for Web sites of over 140 newspapers. Owned by Classified Ventures.
Craigslist	Local community classifieds forum that includes advertisements for housing in over 450 communities around the world. Owned in part by eBay.
Loopnet	Leading online commercial real estate service with more than $525 billion of property listed for sale and 4.7 billion square feet of space for lease as of August 2008.
Zillow	Online real estate service that provides home sale data and estimates of home value.

homebuyers used the Internet for a significant part of the home-buying process, compared to only 28% in 2000. In general, Internet buyers were younger, wealthier, better educated, and more likely to be married than traditional buyers. According to the survey, more than nine out of 10 indicated that the Internet helped them better understand the process of buying a home. Most indicated that they preferred the dynamic online experience offered by the Internet compared to the static experience provided by newspaper advertisements. In particular, multiple pictures/slide shows, and maps showing the location of homes, were among the highest rated online features (California Association of Realtors, 2008).

The primary service offered by real estate sites is a listing of houses available. For example, Realtor.com, the official site of the National Association of Realtors, listed over 4 million homes, and had 6.3 million unique visitors in July 2008 (Move.com, 2008). The offerings have become sophisticated and integrated. Listings typically feature detailed property descriptions, multiple photographs, and virtual 360-degree tours. Consumers can link to mortgage lenders, credit reporting agencies, house inspectors, and surveyors. There are also online loan calculators, appraisal reports, sales price histories by neighborhood, school district data, crime reports, and social and historical information on neighborhoods. Some online real estate brokers now charge substantially less than traditional offline brokers who typically charge 6% of the sale price. They can do this because the buyers (and in some cases, the seller) do much of the work of traditional real estate agents, such as prospecting, choosing neighborhoods, and identifying houses of interest prior to contacting an online agent. For instance, Move.com also offers a "Find a Neighborhood" feature that allows users to choose the type of neighborhood they want to live in by weighing factors such as the quality (and tax costs) of schools, age of the population, number of families with children nearby, and available social and recreational services.

Despite the revolution in available information, there has not been a revolution in the industry value chain. The listings available on Web sites are provided by local multiple listing services supported by local real estate agents. Often, addresses of the houses are not available, and online users are directed to the local listing agent who is hired by the seller of house. Traditional hands-on real estate brokers will show the house and handle all transactions with the owner to preserve their fees, typically ranging from 5% to 6% of the transaction. See *Insight on Society: Turf Wars—Antitrust and the Online Real Estate Market* for a further examination of the real estate industry's reaction to the threats posed by the Internet to its traditional methods of doing business.

9.6 ONLINE TRAVEL SERVICES

Travel and tourism in the United States contribute over $1.1 trillion to the U.S. GDP, with online travel services becoming an ever larger part of the picture. Arguably, online travel is one of the most successful B2C e-commerce segments, accounting for more online revenues than any other online category. The Internet is becoming the most common channel used by consumers to research travel options, seek the best possible prices, and book reservations for airline tickets, hotel rooms, rental cars, cruises, and tours. According eMarketer, in 2007, about 42 million U.S. households booked travel online, and 2007 was the first year in which more travel (51%) was booked online than offline. By 2012, online travel booking revenues are expected to grow to about $162 billion from the 2008 level of $105 billion. (see **Figure 9.5** on page 607) (eMarketer, Inc., 2007c; 2008c; 2008d).

TURF WARS—ANTITRUST AND THE ONLINE REAL ESTATE MARKET

The promise of e-commerce is that it would create a fair, level playing field where thousands of suppliers and millions of consumers could negotiate prices and terms in a very efficient marketplace. These electronic markets would be more efficient in part because intermediaries—the distributors, wholesalers, and agents—would be eliminated by direct commerce between sellers and buyers.

Although these outcomes may have occurred in some e-commerce sectors, in many other sectors we see the emergence of oligopolies—near monopolies—characterized by three or four giant firms, or an even smaller number. Instead of disintermediation, e-commerce sometimes can cause a strengthening of existing intermediaries through exclusive market relationships. In certain markets, network effects occur which predispose that only a handful of competitors will exist, such as telephone markets and operating system markets. In other cases, the oligopoly is a function of market agreements among the top competitors. At times, the level of concentrated power and collusion online can become so strong that government agencies such as the U.S. Department of Justice and the Federal Trade Commission get involved.

Consider Move, Inc. (formerly Homestore, Inc.) which operates Realtor.com, the official site of the National Association of Realtors (NAR). Realtor.com lists more than 4 million homes based on exclusive agreements with over 900 local trade associations called multiple listing services (MLSs) that represent over 1.2 million real estate agents. In addition, Move Inc.'s recently consolidated Web site, Move.com, also handles 40,000 rental properties, representing approximately 5.5 million apartment units in more than 5,500 cities nationwide and its New Homes section offers information on more than 66,000 new and model homes for sale in over 6,500 new home communities and planned developments in the United States. Currently, its network of real estate industry Web sites (Realtor.com, Moving.com, and Seniorhousingnet.com) is the leading consumer destination for residential real estate, rental properties, and realtor listings. Move sites attract around 9 million unique monthly visitors. Move is also the exclusive provider of real estate listings to AOL, City Guide, CompuServe, Netscape, MSN, and Yahoo rentals. Move's aim is to provide consumers who are in the process of moving with all the services and information they need to make a successful move.

In April 2000, the Department of Justice opened an investigation into Homestore, Realtor.com, and the NAR. At issue were the exclusive agreements that Homestore had with the NAR and the potential it had to monopolize online MLS listings. In February 2001, Homestore eliminated its largest competitor by purchasing Move.com, which at that time was owned by Cendant. The Move.com acquisition gave Homestore access to more than 25% of the industry's brokers and transactions, and enabled Homestore to tap into more than 200,000 local real estate agents. Perhaps the biggest jewel in the Move.com purchase was a 40-year exclusive listing agreement with Century 21, Coldwell Banker, and ERA, three of Cendant's prized national franchises, as well as seven-year exclusive listing pacts with the nation's largest rental market brokers (NRT and Rent.net). This meant that Homestore.com acquired exclusive access to three of the largest bricks-and-mortar real estate firm listings in the United States. The Move.com deal also raised antitrust issues

(continued)

because it allegedly had the potential to give Homestore control of up to 90% of all online real estate listings. Homestore executives argued they had not violated antitrust laws or "restrained trade" in any way, but they had simply been successful in growing quite large. Industry experts argued that competitor sites could obtain local listings from sources other than local MLS agencies. For instance, competitors could obtain listings from local newspapers, although this clearly would not be as efficient as having access to local MLS listings. The Department of Justice apparently was swayed by these arguments because, in July 2001, it ended its inquiry into Homestore without comment. As noted previously, Homestore is now known as Move, Inc.

However, that did not end government interest in the issue of competition in the real estate market. In March 2005, the Department of Justice filed a complaint against the Kentucky Real Estate Commission, arguing that local rules prohibiting brokers from giving consumers rebates on real estate commissions (a key strategy for online real estate brokers such as Ziprealty and RealEstate.com) violated antitrust laws. The Department of Justice next focused on policies adopted by the NAR governing the Internet display of MLS listings. In September 2005, it filed an antitrust complaint alleging that the policies put Web-based brokerages at a competitive disadvantage vis-à-vis traditional brokers. The complaint claimed that provisions in the policy that enable brokers to unilaterally withhold their MLS listings from display on competitors' Web sites (known as a "blanket opt-out"), yet at the same time allow those listings to appear on Realtor.com, violated antitrust laws. In other words, the NAR, through its rules, was preventing the operators of online real estate Web sites (sometimes called virtual office Web sites—VOW) from getting access to local MLS listings. According to the Department of Justice, the policy allows traditional brokers to block

their competitors' customers from having full online access to all MLS listings, a critical component in the ability of a broker to effectively compete. In the government's view, the policy enables brokers to discriminate against other brokers based on their usage of new technologies and business models, denying them the benefits of MLS membership available to traditional brokers, discourages competition on price and quality, and deprives consumers of benefits that would flow from new ways of competing. The move by the Department of Justice was, not surprisingly, applauded by discount and non-traditional real estate firms. In response to the suit, the NAR announced that it strongly backed its policies and had no intention of settling. It asserted that the suit mischaracterized the purpose and effect of the "blanket opt-out," which it claimed was merely intended to protect brokers' ownership rights in their property listings. In 2006 the NAR moved to have the suit dismissed. The U.S. District Court in Chicago rejected this in November 2006.

In May 2008, the Justice Department announced that it had reached a proposed settlement with the NAR in which the NAR agreed to repeal its anticompetitive policies and require affiliated MLSs to repeal their rules based on those policies. The NAR also agreed to enact a new policy that Internet-based brokerage companies will not be treated differently from traditional brokers. Under the new policy, brokers participating in a NAR-affiliated MLS will not be permitted to withhold their listings from brokers who serve their customers through VOWs. In addition, brokers will be able to use VOWs to educate consumers, make referrals, and conduct brokerage services. The NAR agreed that such brokers would not be excluded from MLS membership based on their business model.

Every year, 1.5 million homes are sold, most of them through the MLS facilities located in the community. It's unclear how long the NAR and its local members can maintain their stranglehold

(continued)

on the local MLSs, and thereby maintain their 6% commissions. Undoubtedly, Craigslist (partially owned by eBay) and Google have their eyes on the $60 billion in annual commissions generated by traditional real estate agents. Alternatively, the future may be exemplified by firms such as Fsbo-Madison.com, one of the largest for-sale-by-owner sites in the country, and which currently has a 20% share of the Dane County, Wisconsin, market for real estate listings. The site charges just $150 to list a home, and provides a yard "For Sale" sign to boot. Lawyers are now offering advertisements to conduct a house closing for a fixed fee of $600. Consumers who in the past may have been frightened about the prospect of conducting a large transaction without a professional real estate agent holding their hand are now more confident they can do it themselves or with minimal help. Sellers, turned off by the huge 6% commissions of traditional agents, are also more confident they know how much to charge for their home. The technology for setting up a database with pictures and prices is now commonplace and inexpensive. Together, all of these factors may ultimately make it impossible for the NAR to continue to conduct business as usual.

SOURCES: "Justice Department Announces Settlement with the National Association of Realtors," Justice Department, May 27, 2008; "Court Allows Department of Justice Antitrust Lawsuit Against National Association of Realtors to Proceed," Department of Justice, December 2, 2006; "Five Multiple Listing Services Agree to Equal Treatment for Discount Brokers," by Vikas Bajaj, *New York Times*, October 16, 2006; "Court Greenlights DOJ Case Against Realtors," by Roy Mark, Internetnews.com, September 10, 2006; "Owners' Web Site Gives Realtors Run for Money," by Jeff Bailey, *New York Times*, January 3, 2006; "Discount Firms Blast Realtors," Bizreport.com, October 26, 2005; "Department of Justice Amends Antitrust Lawsuit Against National Association of Realtors," Department of Justice, October 4, 2005; "Real Estate's Turf War Heats Up," by Timothy J. Mullaney, *Business Week*, April 18, 2005; "Government Ends Homestore.com Inquiry," *New York Times*, July 17, 2001; "Homestore.com Faces Antitrust Probe," by Keith Regan, *E-Commerce Times*, April 26, 2000.

WHY ARE ONLINE TRAVEL SERVICES SO POPULAR?

Online travel sites offer consumers a one-stop, convenient, leisure and business travel experience where travelers can find content (descriptions of vacations and facilities), community (chat groups and bulletin boards), commerce (purchase of all travel elements), and customer service (usually through call centers). Online sites claim to offer much more information and many more travel options than traditional travel agents. For suppliers—the owners of hotels, rental cars, and airlines—the online sites aggregate millions of consumers into singular, focused customer pools that can be efficiently reached through onsite advertising and promotions. Online sites claim to create a much more efficient marketplace, bringing consumers and suppliers together in a low transaction cost environment.

Travel services appear to be an ideal service/product for the Internet, and therefore e-commerce business models should work well for this product. Travel is an information-intensive product requiring significant consumer research. It is an electronic product in the sense that travel requirements—planning, researching, comparison shopping, reserving, and payment—can be accomplished for the most part online in a digital environment. On the fulfillment side, travel does not require any "inventory": there are no physical assets. And the suppliers of the product—owners of hotels, airlines, rental cars, vacation rooms, and tour guides—are highly fragmented and often have excess capacity. Always looking for customers to fill vacant rooms and rent idle cars, suppliers will be anxious to lower prices and willing to advertise on Web sites that can attract millions of consumers. The online

FIGURE 9.5 **ONLINE TRAVEL SERVICES REVENUES**

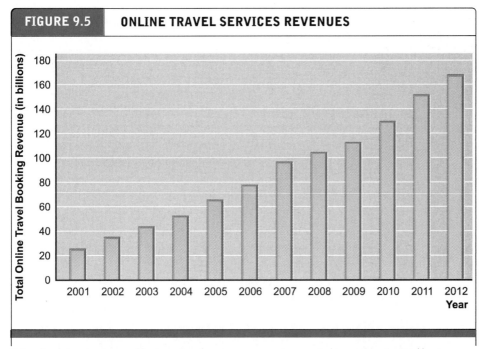

U.S. online leisure/unmanaged business travel service revenues are expected to continue to steadily grow through 2012.

SOURCES: Based on data from eMarketer, Inc., 2008c.

agencies—such as Travelocity, Expedia, and others—do not have to deploy thousands of travel agents in physical offices across the country but can instead concentrate on a single interface with a national consumer audience. Travel services may not require the kind of expensive multi-channel "physical presence" strategy required of financial services (although they generally operate centralized call centers to provide personal customer service). Therefore, travel services might "scale" better, permitting earnings to grow faster than costs.

THE ONLINE TRAVEL MARKET

There are four major sectors in the travel market: airline tickets, hotel reservations, car rentals, and cruises/tours. Airline tickets are the source of the greatest amount of revenue in online travel, accounting for an estimated $50 billion in 2008, and projected to grow at a rate of about 10% a year to $64 billion in 2012. Hotels and car rentals, although not as large from a dollar standpoint as airline reservations, are expected to grow at an even faster rate (see **Figure 9.6**).

The huge size and continued robust growth in online airline reservations reflects several factors. Airline reservations are largely a commodity. They can be easily described over the Web. The same is true with car rentals; most people can reliably rent a car over the phone or the Web and expect to obtain what they ordered (see the story *Insight on Business: Zipcars* on page 600 for a different kind of car rental business model). Although hotels are somewhat more difficult to describe, hotel branding,

FIGURE 9.6	PROJECTED GROWTH OF ONLINE TRAVEL MARKET SEGMENTS

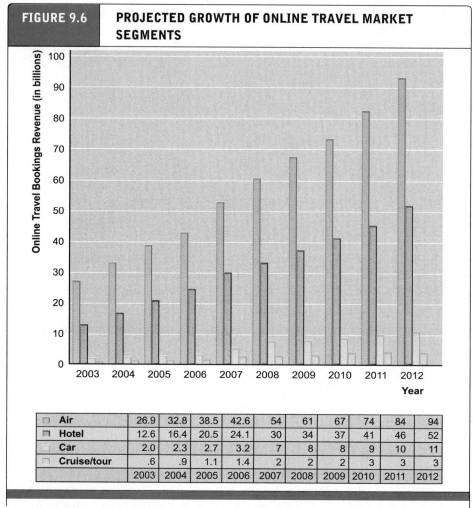

	2003	2004	2005	2006	2007	2008	2009	2010	2011	2012
Air	26.9	32.8	38.5	42.6	54	61	67	74	84	94
Hotel	12.6	16.4	20.5	24.1	30	34	37	41	46	52
Car	2.0	2.3	2.7	3.2	7	8	8	9	10	11
Cruise/tour	.6	.9	1.1	1.4	2	2	2	3	3	3
	2003	2004	2005	2006	2007	2008	2009	2010	2011	2012

Airline reservations will continue to dominate the online travel market, although hotel reservations and car reservations are growing at a faster rate.
SOURCES: Based on data from eMarketer, Inc. 2008c, 2007c, 2005b; authors' estimates.

supplemented by Web sites that include descriptions, photographs, and virtual tours, typically provide enough information to most consumers to allow them to feel as if they know what they are purchasing, making them more comfortable making hotel reservations online.

Analysts typically also divide the travel market into two major segments: leisure/unmanaged business travel and managed business travel. The online travel industry has concentrated mostly on the leisure/unmanaged business travel market, but this is expected to change in the future as the managed business travel segment offers greater growth opportunities compared to the more mature leisure/unmanaged business travel market. Managed travel business refers to mid-size and large corporations' efforts to control corporate travel costs by actively managing their employees' travel arrangements. In the past five years, corporate travel expenses have mushroomed, leading corporations to seek greater control over employee travel plans. Many corporations will not reimburse employee travel unless it is made through an approved in-house travel office or a contracted travel agency such as American Express, Rosenbluth International, or Carlson Travel, or increasingly, through Web-based solutions such as Sabre's GetThere.com.

Increasingly, corporations are outsourcing their travel offices entirely to vendors who can provide Web-based solutions, high-quality service, and lower costs. Online vendors to corporations provide **corporate online-booking solutions (COBS)** that provide integrated airline, hotel, conference center, and auto rental services at a single site.

corporate online-booking solutions (COBS)

provide integrated airline, hotel, conference center, and auto rental services at a single site

ONLINE TRAVEL INDUSTRY DYNAMICS

Because much of what travel agency sites offer is a commodity, and thus they face the same costs, competition among online providers is intense. Price competition is difficult because shoppers, as well as online site managers, can comparison shop easily. Therefore, competition among sites tends to focus on scope of offerings, ease of use, payment options, and personalization. Some well-known travel sites are listed in **Table 9.11**.

TABLE 9.11	**MAJOR ONLINE TRAVEL SITES**
NAME	DESCRIPTION
LEISURE/UNMANAGED BUSINESS TRAVEL	
Expedia	Largest online travel service; leisure focus.
Travelocity	Second-largest online travel service; leisure focus. Owned by Sabre Holdings.
Orbitz	Began as supplier-owned reservation system; now owned by Cendant.
Priceline	"Name your price" model; leisure focus.
CheapTickets	Discount airline tickets, hotel reservations, and auto rentals. Owned by Cendant.
Hotels.com	Largest hotel reservation network; leisure and corporate focus. Owned by Expedia.
Hotwire	Seeks out discount fares based on airline excess inventory. Owned by Expedia.
MANAGED BUSINESS TRAVEL	
GetThere.com	Corporate online booking solution (COBS). Owned by Sabre Holdings.
Egenica.com (an Expedia Company)	Online travel products and services for corporate customers in the United States and Europe. Special focus on small- and mid-sized businesses
Travelocity Business	Full-service corporate travel agency

INSIGHT ON BUSINESS

ZIPCARS

How would you like to have all the functionality of a car but not have to deal with any of the headaches typically associated with ownership of a car, such as maintenance and insurance, or even with the rental of a car from a traditional car rental agency that requires that you go to an office, stand in line, and fill out papers in order to rent, and that mandates a minimum rental period of at least one day?

This might sound like an impossible dream, but it's not. In the late 1990s, a new business model for renting cars was imported from Europe by a group of environmentally conscious entrepreneurs that leverages the power of the Web to make the dream a reality. Today, Zipcar, along with 30 other smaller companies, are using this model on their way towards sustained growth.

Zipcar began in 1999 with a few hundred members and 25 cars in Cambridge, Massachusetts. Members ("Zipsters") could pick up cars at any one of several parking spots around the city, use them for as long as they wanted, and then return them to the same parking spot. By 2005, Zipcar had grown to 700 cars, and 50,000 members paying $35 a year; expanded to include Boston, New York, Washington D.C., and San Francisco; and achieved revenue of around $15 million. In November 2007, Zipcar merged with its largest competitor, Flexcar. Today, the combinated company has 5,500 cars and 225,000 members, who pay $50 a year for membership, and around $10-11 an hour for using a car.

In order to make the business work, Zipcar uses a lot of technology and tries to reduce the human-customer contact as much as possible to keep expenses low. Here's how it works. Customers pay an annual subscription fee and are issued a Zipcar card. Customers go online or call an automated central number to reserve a car for around $10 an hour plus $56 a day. Once a car is rented, a central computer activates the car's key card entry system to permit a specific user to enter the car and start the engine. Customers return cars to the same locations and their credit cards are billed. Using wireless technology, the Internet, and automated voice recognition software at each city's central office, Zipcar is able to keep costs very low.

Zipcar is supported by universities as well as city governments looking for ways to discourage car ownership, and encourage car sharing, to reduce pollution and congestion. Zipcar has exclusive arrangements with Johns Hopkins, University of Michigan, University of North Carolina, Ohio State, Wellesley College, and many others. In these deals, the universities promise the car will make a certain revenue level per year (usually about $100,000) and make up the difference if they do not hit that revenue target.

Zipcar's customers are not Middle America, the people who own 200 million cars. Instead, most of Zipcar's customers are young urban professionals (lots of college and advanced degrees) or college students, a market shunned by traditional car rental companies who typically will not rent to drivers under 21. Zipcar started with a fleet of VW Beetles, but now offers Honda Civics, Toyota Prius Hybrids, Ford Escapes, and Mazda 3s. The attraction to college students is that they save money compared to owning cars that sit idle while they are in classes. In urban areas, Zipcar users report they are saving over $500 a month on car operational and parking costs alone. Consider that in Manhattan, where studio apartments rent for $2,500 a month, garage parking for your personal 4-wheeler will run another $300.

Car sharing is also green: national studies show that each shared car replaces up to 20 privately owned vehicles. Some corporations in major cities are thinking about eliminating their urban fleets and using car-sharing services.

However, whether or not hourly car rental services can expand beyond a few large cities and universities remains to be seen. The idea might not work as well in the suburbs, because customers would have to drive a car to pick up a Zipcar rental. On the other hand, Zipcar has expanded into New York, Boston, Washington D.C., Chicago, San Francisco, Vancouver, Toronto, and London. Zipcar executives see a fleet of about 1 million cars in the future just in urban areas. This fleet would replace 20 million privately owned vehicles, one-tenth of the U.S. private fleet. Who needs the burbs? Traditional car rental companies have begun to respond to Zipcar by opening small neighborhood rental shops that make it much more convenient to rent cars. But these firms are not Web-enabled like Zipcar, and lack the technology infrastructure to compete effectively. Zipcar, for instance, spent over $500,000 on a fleet reservation system that connects users, their Web site, and the cars themselves. Hertz, Avis, Budget, National? Call the 800-number.

SOURCES: "Top Car Sharing Services Join Forces," by Associated Press, *New York Times*, October 31, 2007; "Car-Sharing Firms to Merge," by Darren Everson, *Wall Street Journal*, November 1, 2007; "The Next Disruptors: 10 Game Changing Startups," by Eric Schonfeld and Chris Morrison, CNNMoney.com, August 22, 2007; "Zipcar Goes to College," by Darren Everson, *Wall Street Journal*, August 22, 2007; "By the Hour, Your Chariot Awaits," by Vikas Bajaj, *New York Times*, November 30, 2005.

The online travel services industry has gone through a period of consolidation as stronger offline, established firms such as Cendant (which purchased Orbitz in 2004 for $1.25 billion to add to previously purchased CheapTickets and Trip.com) and Sabre Holdings (which now owns Travelocity, Lastminute, and Site59, among others) purchasing weaker and relatively inexpensive online travel agencies in order to build stronger multi-channel travel sites. Expedia has also been involved in the industry consolidation. Originally begun by Microsoft, Expedia was purchased by Barry Diller's conglomerate IAC/InterActiveCorp (see the case study at the end of the chapter), but has now been spun off as an independent company once again, picking up IAC's Hotels.com, Hotwire, TripAdvisor, and Travelnow in the process.

In addition to industry consolidation, the online travel industry is also being roiled by new technologies in the form of meta-search engines which scour the Web for the best prices on travel and lodging, and then collect finder or affiliate fees for sending consumers to the lowest-price sites. For instance, Kayak.com has created a one-stop Web site where consumers can find the lowest price airfares and hotels by searching over 100 other Web travel sites and presenting the fares in rank order. Similar "travel aggregator" sites are SideStep, Yahoo's FareChase, and Mobissimo.

These sites, in the eyes of many industry leaders, commoditize the online travel industry even further, cause excessive price competition, and divert revenues from the leading, branded firms who have made extensive investments in inventory and systems. Kayak and other sites have been denied access to Expedia and Travelocity, and only search travel sites with permission, which explains why they have not been sued. Forced to work with smaller travel sites, the travel search engines have yet to show a profit but they are growing site traffic and revenues at a fast pace.

Opportunities for Disintermediation and Re-intermediation

The travel industry value chain is more complex than you may realize (see **Figure 9.7**). Suppliers such as large national airlines, international hotel chains, auto rental companies, and cruise/tour operators generally must deal through a group of intermediaries such as **global distribution systems** (**GDSs**) and travel agencies rather than directly with consumers. GDSs are merchants who buy reservations from suppliers and then resell the "inventory" to agencies, who then retail the inventory to consumers or create vacation packages that are then sold to retail agents. In the past, it was difficult if not impossible for suppliers to have a direct relationship with the consumer. Merchants and GDSs have far higher profit margins, with 50% markups not uncommon. Travel agencies, in contrast, receive fees and commissions that rarely rise above 10% to 15% of the amount of the travel booked.

GDSs and travel agencies are under pressure from both the supply side and the corporate demand side. Suppliers—such as airlines, hotels, and auto rental firms—would like to eliminate middlemen such as GDSs and travel agencies, and

global distribution systems (GDS)

merchants who buy reservations from suppliers, and then resell the "inventory" to agencies, which then retail the inventory to consumers or create vacation packages that are then sold to retail

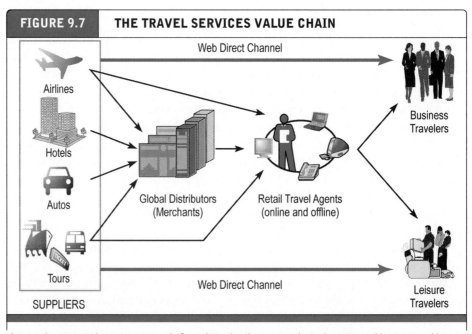

FIGURE 9.7 | **THE TRAVEL SERVICES VALUE CHAIN**

The travel services industry is composed of suppliers, distributors, retail travel agents, and business and leisure travelers. Internet travel sites are an example of how e-commerce can create new intermediaries while weakening existing intermediaries.

develop a direct relationship with consumers. Almost all airlines and hotel chains now offer online reservations directly to the public. The major auto rental firms have all also opened direct-to-customer Web sites (Alamo.com, Budget.com, and Hertz.com) in part to reduce agency fees and to combat Priceline's sale of unused rental capacity.

At the same time, successful online travel agencies are attempting to turn themselves into merchants by purchasing large blocks of travel inventory and then reselling it to the public, eliminating the global distributors and earning much higher returns (while assuming greater risk).

We examine the experience of Expedia in the online travel industry in more detail in the following E-commerce in Action section.

E-COMMERCE IN ACTION

EXPEDIA INC.

Expedia Inc. is a Bellevue, Washington-based online travel services company that provides access to information on scheduling, pricing, and availability of flights, hotel accommodations, and rental cars. Expedia began life as an operating unit of Microsoft and went public in 1999. In 2001, USA Networks (now IAC/InterActiveCorp) purchased a 70% interest in Expedia from Microsoft and acquired the remainder of the company in 2003. In August 2005, IAC spun Expedia off to its shareholders and it once again became an independent public company. Expedia is the largest player in online travel services, generating revenues of $2.7 billion in 2007 in an industry estimated to be $7 trillion worldwide, according to the World Travel and Tourism Council. There's still plenty of room for Expedia to grow.

The Vision

The vision behind Expedia was to create a global travel marketplace, enabling travel services suppliers to extend their marketing reach online, and giving consumers the ability to research, plan, and purchase travel services. Expedia's customer value proposition was to reduce customer transaction and search costs, and increase price transparency. By replacing many of the functions of local travel agents, Expedia potentially would change the industry structure.

To a large extent, Expedia has succeeded in achieving its vision. Through Expedia, consumers and business travelers (corporate travel business conducted through Egenica, an Expedia Company) can access real-time schedule and pricing information from more than 450 airlines, 35,000 lodging properties, and all major car rental agencies, 24 hours a day. Visitors can also consult extensive editorial content on hundreds of different destinations, review travel information and advice from industry experts, and learn from other travelers through chat groups and community bulletin boards. After gathering needed information, customers can also make reservations at the site.

Expedia also owns Hotels.com, which enables travelers to book lodging accommodations; Vacationspot, a vacation rental center; Hotwire, which offers discounted airline tickets, hotel rooms, rental cars, cruises, and vacation packages; TripAdvisor, a comprehensive online travel search engine and directory that aggregates unbiased articles, guidebook reviews, and user comments on cities, hotels, and activities; and eLong, a majority owned subsidiary based in Beijing, China.

Business Model

Expedia operates using two different business models: the agency model and the merchant model. Under the agency model, Expedia generates revenue in much the same way as a traditional travel agent—by earning a commission or flat fee on each transaction from the travel supplier. In the case of airline transactions, Expedia also receives fees from GDSs and service and delivery fees from its customers.

Under the merchant business model, Expedia purchases inventory from suppliers at discounted wholesale prices and then resells it to consumers at a retail price that it sets itself. This model enables Expedia to offer consumers more competitive prices and generates a higher gross profit per transaction than the commission-based agency model. The merchant model also provides travel suppliers with a cost-efficient way (as compared to traditional marketing initiatives) to increase the marketing and promotion of their brands.

In addition, Expedia earns revenue from paid advertising from suppliers such as airlines and hotels, and licenses core parts of its technology platform to Continental Airlines, Northwest Airlines, and American Express.

Financial Analysis

Expedia's gross revenues have grown by more than 25% during the three-year period from 2005 to 2007 to $2.7 billion, increasing from $2.1 billion in 2005 to almost $2.7 million in 2007..Its net income during the same period increased by almost 30%, from 229 million in 2005 to 296 million in 2007 (see **Table 9.12**).

According to Expedia, the increase in revenue for 2007 resulted primarily from increased worldwide merchant hotel revenue, and to a lesser extent, advertising and media revenue. International revenues increased by 34% compared to 13% growth for North American revenues, reflecting the maturity of the North American market and the opportunities for growth overseas.

Worldwide merchant hotel revenue increased 19%, driven in large part by a 12% increase in room nights stayed in conjunction with a 6% increase in revenue per room. Worldwide revenue from Expedia's airline ticket business decreased by 2% in 2007, due primarily to a decline of 12% in revenue per ticket, offset somewhat by an increase of 12% in air tickets sold.

On the cost side, operating expenses in 2007 were up slightly. Marketing expenses increased by nearly 20% in 2007 due to staffing costs. General and administrative costs increased by 14%. The primary component of this increase was driven by, according to Expedia, an increase in headcount and the related compensation expenditures. As a result of these changes, Expedia increased revenues, and its operating income

TABLE 9.12	EXPEDIA INC. CONSOLIDATED STATEMENTS OF OPERATIONS AND SUMMARY BALANCE SHEET DATA 2005–2007

CONSOLIDATED STATEMENTS OF OPERATIONS
(in thousands)

For the fiscal year ended December 31,	2007	2006	2005
Revenues			
Service Revenues	2,665,332	$2,237,586	$2,119,455
Cost of sales	562,401	502,638	470,716
Gross profit	**2,102,931**	**1,734,948**	**1,648,739**
Gross margin	**79%**	**77.5%**	**77.7%**
Operating expenses			
Selling and marketing expense	992,560	786,195	697,503
General and administrative expense	321,250	289,649	211,515
Technology and Content	182,483	140,371	130,507
Amortization of non-cash distribution and marketing expense	—	9,638	12,597
Amortization of intangibles	77,569	110,766	126,067
Impairment of intangible asset	—	47,000	—
Total operating expenses	1,573,862	1,383,619	1,098,127
Operating income	**529,069**	**351,329**	**397,052**
Operating margin	**20%**	**15.7%**	**18.7%**
Total other income (expense), net	(32,085)	33,569	16,819
Earnings before income taxes and minority interest	496,984	384,898	413,871
Income tax expense	(203,114)	(139,451)	(185,977)
Minority interest in loss (income) of consolidated subsidiaries	1,994	(513)	836
Net income	**295,864**	**244,934**	**228,730**
Net margin	**11.1%**	**10.9%**	**10.8%**

SUMMARY BALANCE SHEET DATA
(in thousands)

At December 31,	2007	2006	2005
Assets			
Cash, restricted cash, and cash equivalents	634,041	$864,367	$321,001
Accounts and notes receivable	268,007	211,430	174,019
Total current assets	1,045,655	1,182,685	590,244
Total assets	8,295,422	8,269,184	7,756,892
Liabilities			
Accounts payable, merchant and trade	852,277	720,737	642,821
Deferred merchant bookings	609,117	466,474	406,948
Total current liabilities	1,774,352	1,400,125	1,438,225
Total liabilities	3,477,341	2,364,894	2,023,099
Shareholders' equity	4,818,081	5,904,290	5,733,763

SOURCE: Expedia Inc., 2007.

grew 60%. As a further result, net income in 2007 increased by only 20% over the previous year.

The 2007 results represent a continued, albeit gradual, reversal in the company's financial performance. In earlier years, sales expanded very rapidly, but costs expanded even faster, resulting in net margins falling. Historically, the company was becoming less efficient as it grew, with expenses for people and marketing growing faster than sales. In 2007, the company continued to reverse that pattern through aggressive cost control, and its net profit margin stood at 11.1%.

Looking at the balance sheet, current assets are $1.04 billion and current liabilities are $1.77 billion. Expedia's current assets are catching up to their current liabilities, a reversal from 2005 when liabilities were nearly three times as large as assets. In previous years, Expedia's current assets typically exceeded its current liabilities.

Strategic Analysis—Business Strategy

Expedia's management is pursuing a number of strategies to grow the company: acquisition of complementary and competing travel companies, broadening the scope of offerings, and expanding into foreign markets, especially Asia.

Expedia has grown its business in part by acquiring a number of complementary travel services. Expedia acquired Travelscape and Vacationspot in 2000 and Classic Custom Vacations and Metropolitan Travel (corporate travel services) in 2002. IAC/InterActiveCorp, Expedia's former parent, acquired Hotels.com in 1999, Hotwire in 2003, TripAdvisor and Egencia (European corporate travel services) in 2004, and a majority stake in eLong (Chinese travel services) in 2005, and all of these acquisitions were included with Expedia when it was spun off from IAC in August 2005.

In 2008, Expedia made several acquisitions, including Holidaywatchdog, one of the most well-known user-generated travel sites in the United Kingdom, Airfaire-watchdog, a leading source of airfare sales, Carrentals.com, an online, direct-to-consumer car rental marketing and retail company, and Venere.com, which has relationships with approximately 29,000 hotels and bed and breakfast properties throughout Europe and the United States.

Expedia is also pursuing a multi-channel strategy by moving into customized vacation package planning. Expedia operates Classic Vacations, which offers customized luxury vacations in Hawaii, the Caribbean, Mexico, Costa Rica, Europe, Australia, New Zealand, and Tahiti, primarily through a national network of retail travel agents, and Expedia Corporate Travel, a full-service travel management company for corporate customers in the United States and Europe. Expedia also operates a network of in-destination travel desks located at hotels and resorts in Florida, Hawaii, and Mexico.

Recognizing the importance of expanding beyond U.S. borders, Expedia has developed localized versions of its core Web site in Canada, France, Germany, Italy, Netherlands, United Kingdom, India, New Zealand, and Spain. Hotels.com also has localized versions in the Americas, Europe, Asia Pacific, and South Africa. These local sites reflect language and cultural differences, as well as purchasing preferences; in the United Kingdom, for example, negotiated fares are the norm, rather than published fares. It also operates Anyway.com, a leading online travel company in France and in 2005, acquired a majority stake in eLong, an online travel service company based in China, that specializes in travel products and services in China, including corporate travel services.

Strategic Analysis—Competition

Expedia competes primarily with other online commercial travel Web sites, such as its main rivals Travelocity, Orbitz (as well as other travel sites owned by Cendant), and Priceline. It also faces growing competition from the direct suppliers of travel services, such as airlines, hotels, and car rental companies themselves, who increasingly are offering their products directly to the consumer online. Specialized travel search engines, such as Kayak, can also be considered competitors. Finally, traditional travel agencies that have established their own commercial Web sites are targeting the same customers. Perhaps the most worrisome competition is from the suppliers of inventory. Expedia is a middleman, dependent on the owners of inventory to sell their product to Expedia, such as empty hotel rooms and empty airline seats. Insofar as the suppliers go directly to the market by offering rooms and seats on their own Web sites, Expedia's supply of inventory is being squeezed. For instance, InterContinental Hotels Group (Holiday Inn and Crowne Plaza, among others) has stopped listing its 3,500 hotels on Expedia and Hotels.com, choosing instead to strike a deal with Sabre Holdings' Travelocity. In addition, many of the fastest-growing low-cost airlines like Southwest and JetBlue market directly to consumers over their own Web sites. In addition, in recent years, as the major airlines have struggled with high fuel prices and profitability, they have been less willing to sell their inventory to Expedia at discounted prices. As the technology for creating online travel services becomes less expensive and esoteric, there is every reason to believe that suppliers will come to the market directly. This will both squeeze the inventory of travel sites like Expedia, and raise marketing costs. Expedia's approach to competition involves differentiation through its quality and breadth of products.

Strategic Analysis—Technology

To ensure reliability, security, and scalability as the site grows, with the help and support of Microsoft, Expedia developed a multi-layered platform capable of handling large transaction volumes. It also created several powerful search tools to assist consumers in finding and acting on a wide range of travel information.

Best Fare Search, a Windows-based reservation and price comparison engine, allows Expedia to show customers many more priced itineraries than other travel Web sites. Expedia's Expert Searching and Pricing Platform (ESP Platform) uses two pieces to drive the company's global travel marketplace. One is a fare-searching engine that facilitates broad and deep searches for flight schedules airfares. The other is a common database platform that makes bundling different travel services into packages possible. Expedia began receiving the benefits of a new enterprise data warehouse in 2007, which provided a major upgrade to its data aggregation and data mining capabilities. Expedia and its competitors are facing a serious test as their number of customers begins to decline. Some analysts attribute the trend away from booking travel online to outdated technology that does not serve customers as well as it could. The reservation systems that feed travel sites date back to the 1960s and the online travel industry has not made the leaps forward in technology that, for example, online shopping has made.

Management increased technology spending by 7% in 2007. Technology expenditures are growing as the nature of its products becomes more complex, and as the company expands foreign operations. Expedia anticipates increases in spending in technology for 2008 both in terms of actual dollars and as a percentage of revenues.

Strategic Analysis—Social and Legal Challenges

The spin-off of Expedia from its former parent company IAC has been the catalyst for legal actions by shareholders against IAC and its former holdings. Expedia believes that the claims are without merit and will defend itself against them.

Expedia, along with other travel sites, also faces three other legal issues: taxation, international legal challenges, and emerging legislation on personal identifying information. For instance, unlike a local travel agent operating from a physical location, Expedia does not in all circumstances collect local room rental or car rental taxes, offering consumers a price advantage. Local and state taxing jurisdictions are protesting this, and as a result, Expedia and its competitors have been named in a number of statewide class action suits in several states. While international markets offer Expedia opportunities for growth, especially in China, the legal system in China is not yet stable enough to ensure Expedia's investments are safe. Finally, along with all other travel agencies, Expedia maintains an extensive database on its customers' travel interests and behavior. This personal information is likely to be the subject of consumer legislation in future years seeking to protect personal privacy, and this in turn will raise operating costs for Expedia.

Future Prospects

Expedia faces several challenges going forward: slowing growth in North American sales due to economic conditions, competition from suppliers, and cost control. Currently, U.S. consumer demand for travel has been affected by high fuel prices, the weaker dollar, and the threat of terrorism. To combat this, Expedia has focused on growing revenue by acquisition of other travel sites and expanding into foreign markets, a strategy that appears to be working. However, it is facing increasing competition from direct suppliers—airline, hotels, and car rental agencies. This is in turn is raising operating costs and marketing costs.

Now that Expedia is an independent company, it will have the stock currency to make additional acquisitions and pursue other strategies as well. For example, Expedia can expand by broadening its services towards more customized travel planning, and deepening its relationships with a wider variety of customers. In addition to offering the consumer lower costs, Expedia has an opportunity to offer the consumer customized travel planning which is more lucrative than mass-market cost-competitive airline seats.

9.7 ONLINE CAREER SERVICES

Next to travel services, one of the Internet's most successful online services has been job services (recruitment sites) that provide a free posting of individual resumes, plus many other related career services; for a fee, they also list job openings posted by companies. Career services sites collect revenue from other sources as well, by providing value-added services to users and collecting fees from related service providers.

The online job market is dominated by three large players: CareerBuilder, Monster, and Yahoo HotJobs. CareerBuilder also provides job listings for AOL and MSN. Other popular sites include Job.com, Indeed, SimplyHired, and USAjobs. These top sites generate more than $1 billion annually in revenue from employers' fees and consumer fees. Career sites rank 10th among the fastest growing Web site categories, based on number of unique visitors as complied by comScore Media Metrix (eMarketer, Inc., 2008d).

Traditionally, companies have relied on five employee recruitment tools: classified and print advertising, career expos (or trade shows), on-campus recruiting, private employment agencies (now called "staffing firms"), and internal referral programs. In comparison to online recruiting, these tools have severe limitations. Print advertising usually includes a per-word charge that limits the amount of detail employers provide about a job opening, as well as a limited time period within which the job is posted. Career expos do not allow for pre-screening of attendees and are limited by the amount of time a recruiter can spend with each candidate. Staffing firms charge high fees and have a limited, usually local, selection of job hunters. On-campus recruiting also restricts the number of candidates a recruiter can speak with during a normal visit and requires that employers visit numerous campuses. And internal referral programs may encourage employees to propose unqualified candidates for openings in order to qualify for rewards or incentives offered.

Online recruiting overcomes these limitations, providing a more efficient and cost-effective means of linking employers and potential employees, while reducing the total time-to-hire. Online recruiting enables job hunters to more easily build, update, and distribute their resumes while gathering information about prospective employers and conducting job searches.

IT'S JUST INFORMATION: THE IDEAL WEB BUSINESS?

Online recruitment is ideally suited for the Web. The hiring process is an information-intense business process that involves discovering the skills and salary requirements of individuals and matching them with available jobs. In order to accomplish this match up, there does not initially need to be face-to-face interaction, or a great deal of personalization. Prior to the Internet, this information sharing was accomplished locally by human networks of friends, acquaintances, former employers, and relatives, in addition to employment agencies that developed paper files on job hunters. The Internet can clearly automate this flow of information, reducing search time and costs for all parties.

Table 9.13 lists some of the most popular recruitment sites.

TABLE 9.13	POPULAR ONLINE RECRUITMENT SITES
RECRUITMENT SITE	**BRIEF DESCRIPTION**
General Recruitment Sites	
Careerbuilder	Owned by Gannett, Tribune, and McClatchy (all newspaper companies) and Microsoft. Provides job search centers for more than 1,000 partners, including AOL, MSN, and 150 newspapers.
Monster	One of the first commercial sites on the Web in 1994. Today, a public company offering general job searches in 23 countries, generating revenue of over $1 billion a year.
Yahoo HotJobs	General job searches. Partners with consortium of newspapers, including Hearst, Cox, MediaNews General, Scripps, and others for cross-listing of job postings.
Job.com	General job searches in 70 different disciplines. In August 2007, more than 7 million registered users, and 4th most visited site in category, according to comScore/Media Metrix.
Kenexa (formerly Brassring)	Management recruitment and job searches
Craigslist	Popular classified listing service focused on local recruiting
Indeed	Job site aggregator
SimplyHired	Job site aggregator
Executive Search Sites	
FutureStep	Korn/Ferry site. Low-end executive recruiting
Spencerstuart	Middle-level executive recruiting
Execunet	Executive search firm
Niche Job Sites	
USAJobs	Federal government jobs
HigherEdJobs	Education industry
EngineerJobs	Engineering jobs
Medzilla	Medical industry
ShowBizJobs	Entertainment industry
Salesjobs	Sales and marketing
Dice	Information technology jobs
MBAGlobalNet	MBA-oriented community site

Why are so many job hunters and employers using Internet job sites? Recruitment sites are popular largely because they save time and money for both job hunters and employers seeking recruits. For employers, the job boards expand the geographical reach of their searches, lower costs, and result in faster hiring decisions.

For job seekers, online sites are popular not only because their resumes can be made widely available to recruiters but also because of a variety of other related job-hunting services. The services delivered by online recruitment sites have greatly expanded since their emergence in 1996. Originally, online recruitment sites just provided a digital version of newspaper classified ads. Today's sites offer many other services, including skills assessment, personality assessment questionnaires, personalized account management for job hunters, organizational culture assessments, job search tools, employer blocking (prevents your employer from seeing your posting), employee blocking (prevents your employees from seeing your listings if you are their employer), and e-mail notification. Online sites also provide a number of educational services such as resume writing advice, software skills preparation, and interview tips.

For the most part, online recruitment sites work, in the sense of linking job hunters with jobs, but they are just one of many ways people actually find jobs. A survey by The Conference Board found that the majority (70%) of job seekers rely equally on both the Internet and newspapers to look for jobs, with about half relying on word-of-mouth leads, and about a quarter on employment agencies. However, most respondents felt that the Internet was the most productive in producing a job offer (eMarketer, Inc., 2006). Given that the cost of posting a resume online is zero, the marginal returns are very high.

The ease with which resumes can be posted online has also raised new issues for both job recruiters and job seekers. If you are an employer, how do you sort through and parse the thousands of resumes you may receive when posting an open job? If you are a job seeker, how do you stand out among the thousands or even millions of others? Perhaps one way is to post a video resume. In a survey by Vault, nearly nine in 10 employers said they would watch a video resume if it were submitted to them, in part because it would help them better assess a candidate's professional presentation and demeanor, and over half said they believed video would become a common addition to future job applications. CareerBuilder became the first major online job site to implement a video resume tool for job candidates, following a previous launch for an online video brand-building tool for employers (eMarketer, Inc., 2007d; CareerBuilder.com, 2007a).

In another sense, general online recruitment sites may be experiencing declining effectiveness. The advent of the Web and e-mail has increased the supply of resumes (the number of resumes landing on a recruiter's desktop) beyond the point where they can be rationally evaluated. On the other hand, most large companies rely heavily on their company's Web site as a source of employees. For instance, a Booz Allen Hamilton survey of recruiters from leading employers found that about 20% of new hires came directly from an organization's Web site (Booz Allen Hamilton, 2006). One way to avoid the clutter is to target and focus on specific companies, or, if you are a recruiter, to focus on niche sites that are likely to have people with the skills you are looking for. The use of corporate Web sites to find job candidates has also increased with the debut of the new .jobs top-level domain created to allow employers to create Web sites focused specifically at online recruiting.

Perhaps the most important function of online recruitment sites is not so much their capacity to actually match employees with job hunters but their ability to establish market prices and terms, as well as trends in the labor market. Online recruitment sites identify salary levels for both employers and job hunters, and categorize the skill sets required to achieve those salary levels. In this sense, online recruitment sites are online national marketplaces that establish the terms of trade in the labor markets. For instance, Monster.com offers its U.S. Monster Employment Index. This index monitors over 1,500 online job sites and calculates employment demand for the nation, regions, and specific occupations. The existence of these online national job sites should lead to a rationalization of wages, greater labor mobility, and higher efficiency in recruitment and operations because employers will be able to quickly find the people they need.

RECRUITMENT MARKET SEGMENTS

There are three segments in the recruitment business. General job recruitment is the largest segment and focuses on placing a wide range of individuals at all skill and salary levels. In the past, general job recruitment has been performed by government labor agencies and private placement firms, and through newspaper classified ads (a major source of revenue for newspapers). The executive search segment focuses on placing executives with annual salaries of $100,000 or more. Specialized executive placement firms conduct executive searches for employers, generally charging one-third of the first year's salary as a fee. A third segment is specialized job placement services, which are often run by professional societies such as the Society of Plastics Engineers site (4spe.org), and the police recruiting site, Policeemployment.com.

Online recruitment has focused primarily on the largest market for general job recruitment. However, many general sites—such as Monster—have begun listing lower- and middle-level management jobs. Indeed, the largest revenue potential for the general job online sites is in executive recruiting, where fees are currently very high. The traditional executive placement agencies such as Korn/Ferry and Spencer Stuart—realizing the threat from online sites—have also developed their own Web sites for lower- and middle-level managers seeking salaries above $100,000. Pitney Bowes and Accenture are just two firms hiring mid-level and even senior executives through the Internet. They are saving $50,000 per hire by avoiding expensive executive search firms.

ONLINE RECRUITMENT INDUSTRY TRENDS

Trends for 2008–2009 in the online recruitment services industry including the following:

- **Consolidation**: The three largest job services are CareerBuilder (owned by newspapers and Microsoft), Monster, and HotJobs (owned by Yahoo). In 2008–2009, these three sites dominate the market, and are expected to do so for some time to come.

- **Diversification**: While the national online market is becoming larger and consolidating into a few general sites, there is an explosion in specialty niche employment sites that focus on specific occupations. This is creating greater online job market diversity and choice.

- **Localization**: While local classified ads in newspapers remain a significant source of jobs, the large national online sites are also developing local boards in large metropolitan areas that compete more directly against local newspapers. The local newspapers themselves have responded by building local Web sites that focus on local job markets, especially hourly and contract jobs that often do not appear on the large national job boards. Craigslist is another source of local job listings. Hence there is a growing focus on local job markets by all participants in the marketplace because this is where so many new jobs first appear.

- **Job search engines/aggregators**: As with travel services, search engines that focus specifically on jobs are posing a new threat to established online career sites. For instance, Indeed, SimplyHired, and JobCentral "scrape" listings from thousands of online job sites such as Monster, CareerBuilder, specialty recruiting services, and the sites of individual employers, to provide a free, searchable index of thousands of job listings in one spot. Because these firms do not charge employers a listing fee, they are currently using a pay-per-click or other advertising revenue model

- **Social networking**: LinkedIn, probably the most well-known business-oriented social network, has grown significantly to over 25 million members representing over 150 different industries around the world as of September 2008. Members are using sites such as LinkedIn to establish business contacts and networks, while employers use them to conduct searches to find potential job candidates that may not be actively job hunting. In August 2007, CareerBuilder launched a job and internship matching application on Facebook that allows users to receive continuously updated listing based on the information found in their profiles. Social networking sites are also being used employers to "check up" on the background of job candidates. For instance, one survey found that 77% of recruiters surveyed used the Internet and social network sites to screen job candidates, and that over a third had eliminated a candidate based on information found there (eMarketer, Inc., 2007e; Careerbuilder.com, 2007b; LinkedIn.com, 2008).

IAC/InterActiveCorp
Online Services Spin-off

In August 2008, after almost a year of battling, Barry Diller, founder and CEO of the Internet giant conglomerate IAC/InteractiveCorp, was finally able to implement the "Big Breakup": splitting IAC into five separate businesses:

- IAC, a Web and advertising-focused business that includes Ask.com, Match.com, Evite, and CitySearch
- HSN, a retailing company that includes HSN home-shopping channel
- Ticketmaster, the concert ticket vendor
- Interval International, a resort-booking company
- LendingTree, an online lender.

Why would a "successful" Web conglomerate with the 10th-largest Internet audience in the world, with over 680,000 million unique visitors and generating over

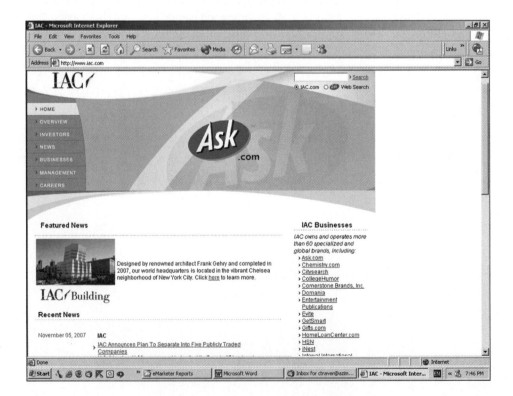

$6 billion in revenues, split up? Since 2002, when Diller put together a string of acquisitions to form IAC/InteractiveCorp, analysts wondered exactly what Diller had in mind. Each of its brands that it picked up were really in separate industries and had few if any apparent synergies. Diller himself defended the conglomerate as an interrelated set of brands with a powerful online future, but admitted in 2007 that, "I've always believed our complexity and many mouthfuls of sentences to explain who we are and what our strategy is have hampered clarity and understanding with all our constituencies, particularly investors. One of the reasons we've stayed with some of our more transactional businesses is that we needed their earnings to allow us to invest in emerging Internet businesses. Now that we have real scale in the pure Internet units, it makes nothing but sense to me to reorganize the whole."

Diller stands with Rupert Murdoch as quintessential traditional media people who have moved onto the Internet as the next big media opportunity. Murdoch moved from newspapers to satellite television, and then onto the Web with the purchase of MySpace in 2005 (way before social networking was so popular). Diller moved from Hollywood movie and television production, to cable system distribution, and then onto the Internet beginning in 2002. In fact, just when everyone was down on e-commerce in 2002, laughing about the failure of Pets.com as they felt the pain of losing their retirement plans in the stock market bubble they supported, Diller went on a multi-billion dollar buying spree of Web properties using a corporate vehicle that is now IAC/InterActiveCorp (formerly USA Interactive). How much money has IAC spent? In over 100 deals, about $20 billion. Where has IAC spent this money? Think Web services, mostly in travel, hotels, finance, event tickets and, most recently, search. IAC operates 60 different brands on the Web.

Diller is a legend in Hollywood. He worked his way up from the mailroom of William Morris, a talent agency in Hollywood. After William Morris, he joined ABC Entertainment and served as Vice President of Prime Time Television. Diller next moved to Paramount Pictures Corporation and for 10 years served as its Chairman and Chief Executive. In March 1983, in addition to Paramount, Diller became President of the conglomerate's newly formed Entertainment and Communications Group, which included Simon & Schuster, Inc., Madison Square Garden Corporation, and SEGA Enterprises, Inc. From October 1984 to April 1992, Diller served as Chairman and Chief Executive Officer of Fox, Inc. and was responsible for the creation of Fox Broadcasting Company, building it into a credible fourth television network, in addition to Fox's motion picture operations. Diller left Fox in 1992, went to the QVC home shopping network from 1992 to 1994, and then in 1995, was named Chairman and CEO of Silver King Communications. In 1996, Silver King, Home Shopping Network, and Savoy Pictures Entertainment merged, and took the name HSN, inc. In 1997, HSN inc. acquired 50% of Ticketmaster Group, and in 1998, cable channels USA Network and Sci Fi, and HSN was renamed USA Networks, Inc. (USAI). In 2001, USAI sold the most of the entertainment portion of the company to Vivendi SA of France for $11.7 billion in cash and stock. Besides Home Shopping Network, what was left included large holdings in Ticketmaster, Hotel Reservation Network (purchased in 1999), a local listing service called Citysearch.com (1998), and a dating service called Match.com (1999). In 2000, USAI purchased Precision Response

Corporation, which also conducts e-mail and database services for direct marketers. In 2002, USAI was renamed USA Interactive, and then in June 2003, changed its name once more, to IAC/InterActiveCorp (IAC).

Diller is not new to electronic commerce: In 1993, he was extolling the virtues of "buying underwear in your underwear." Barry Diller was among the very first to realize that millions of people wanted to shop without leaving the house. In 1998, IAC began its foray onto the Internet by attempting to purchase the search engine Lycos. This effort was terminated because the firms could not agree on the terms. IAC largely withdrew from the marketplace as it watched e-commerce properties plummet in value. Then, at or near their lows, IAC began buying in a march across the Web. In 2002 and 2003, it completed the purchase of LendingTree, Expedia, British firm uDate.com (an online personals site), TV Travel Group (a British vacation firm), Interval International (a time-share swapping service), the outstanding shares of Hotels.com, and the remaining shares of Ticketmaster. In 2004, it acquired TripAdvisor and ServiceMagic, an online marketplace that connects consumers with pre-screened, customer-rated home service professionals. In April 2005, IAC purchased Cornerstone Brands, a portfolio of leading print catalogs and online retailing sites that sell home products and leisure and casual apparel, for approximately $715 million, principally in cash. And in July 2005, it purchased search engine Ask Jeeves (now Ask.com) for $1.9 billion. In the two years since, it has added Shoebuy, a retail site; Connected Ventures, Inc., which operates CollegeHumor; InstantAction, a games site in a joint venture with Garage Games; and launched Pronto, a comparison shopping site.

Most of the company's businesses involved acting as an intermediary between supply and demand in interactive commerce, making it more like an eBay for services than an e-tailer such as Amazon. While some of the IAC's businesses did in fact hold inventory (such as HSN, Cornerstone, Home Shopping Europe, and Shoebuy.com), most of IAC's companies did not, and therefore have lower costs and potentially higher margins. "We want to be the largest and most profitable e-commerce company utilizing multiple brands," Diller said. IAC operated many distinct brands and business models. Some of its businesses are transactional where a fee is made on each transaction, some were subscription-based, and others are advertising-based. The Web is all about "searching and buying," he once said.

But the idea that 60 different Internet brands make a successful business did not convince Wall Street. By 2005, the prospects for Expedia and Hotels.com began to sour as travel became more competitive, and other Web sites vied for the airline and hotel reservation markets. Worse, hotel owners got the message and set up their own Web sites to sell excess inventory. As a result of these changes, in August 2005, Diller split IAC into two components, with all the travel businesses put under the Expedia brand in a single separately traded company called Expedia Inc. and all other brands, such as LendingTree, Ticketmaster, Match.com, and the recently acquired search engine Ask Jeeves, remaining under the IAC corporate umbrella and trading as a separate stock. Expedia is now a stand-alone company with revenues of around $2.7 billion for the 2007 fiscal year.

With the remaining brands, Diller hoped to create a "traffic ecosystem" in which users would be sent from one IAC site to another. Together, Ask.com and the other IAC sites had a combined audience that approaches MSN and Yahoo. Diller—ever the advertising man—along with others such as Rupert Murdoch and the News Corporation, was pursing eyeballs with a vengeance. Diller believed online search advertising would continue to grow rapidly over the next five years, and increasingly advertisers would switch to Web media to communicate with consumers.

IAC stock peaked at about $88 in July 2003, split in August 2005 in connection with its spin-off of Expedia, ramped back up to about $40 a share in February 2007, but has since traded in the $16–$33 range. Wall Street apparently did not accept the premise that all these businesses would add up to more than themselves standing alone.

As a result, by September 2007, Diller decided to abandon this plan also, coming to the realization that the stock market was not going to accept holding finance, ticketing, personal services, and search all in one company. The solution? Split IAC into five separate companies with each company focused on a specific industry. In August, 2008, the Diller empire was split into five companies trading on the NASDAQ: Tree.com (LendingTree.com and other financial services); HSN (the home television and /web shopping network); Ticketmaster (the world's largest event ticketing firm); Interval Group (online time-share properties), and the original IAC/InterActive Corporation (operating thirty five Web properties such as Ask.com, Match.com, and Evite.com). The stocks of the new companies got off to a good start: IAC jumped 8%, Ticketmaster, 7%, and HSN a whopping 21%. Even better: Diller was able to wring $1.3 billion in cash out of the stock offerings which Diller can use to develop new Web properties for IAC. These early gains have since subsided, and the value of the five separate companies is now just slightly higher than the old IAC company. So who has gained? Not, apparently, the shareholders who own a mixed bag of separate companies. Meanwhile, the remaining 35 Web properties in Diller's IAC/Interactive are arguable worth more if they just separated and went their separate ways. Consider that the value of Match.com, a leading match up site, could be worth $700 million on its own. Why stick Match.com into a company with Evite.com? What do they have in common?

In a harbinger of things to come, Diller immediately announced a spinoff of the two-year old virtual world Zwinky.com called "ZwinkyCuties." The new site is aimed at Disney's Penguin Club which is a bit hit with 6 to 12-year old girls. Zwinky.com is a social play site aimed at young girls with over 16 million registered users.

Meanwhile, Ask.com is doing very well. It struck a deal to continue its relationship with Google, which supplies ads to Ask.com's search engine. This will bring in about $3.5 billion over the next few years. Ask.com's market share expanded in 2007 to about 5% of the search market, up from less than 2% when IAC bought it. Ask.com owns the Teoma search engine, which it purchased in 2001. Teoma claims to be an improvement over Google. It ranks sites first based on related communities of sites that are "organically organized" and link to each other. After determining the relevant community of sites, it picks out the most popular based on incoming links

SOURCES: "IAC Story Not As Planned," by Martin Peers, Wall Street Journal, September 3, 2008; "Barry Diller's First Post-Split Launch at IAC: A Virtual World for Kids," IAC Press Release, August 8, 2008; "IAC: And The There Were Five," by Lisa LaMotta, Forbes, August 21, 2008; IAC/InterActiveCorp Form 10-K for the fiscal year ended December 31, 2007, filed with the Securities and Exchange Commission on March 16, 2008; "IAC Launches Comedy News Site," by Jessica Vascellaro, *Wall Street Journal*, November 9, 2007; "IAC Spinning Off HSN, Ticketmaster, Interval, and Lending Tree," *Internet Retailer*, November 5, 2007; "Barry Diller's Big Breakup," DealBook Blog, *New York Times*, November 5, 2007; "IAC/InteractiveCorp Takes Game Designer Stake," by Jessica Vascellaro, *Wall Street Journal*, September 18, 2007; "Back to His Roots: Diller's IAC Invests in Online Videos," by Jessica Vascellaro, *Wall Street Journal*, February 6, 2007.

(both numbers and quality of the linking sites, i.e., their popularity). Uses and search aficionados claim the Ask.com site produces more relevant, accurate results.

Whether or not Diller's "new, new" IAC will succeed this time is open to question. Most financial observers believe Diller has finally got it right, and that he should move into search and entertainment-based Internet advertising markets, which are growing very rapidly, and dump the older business models, which are not growing as fast. Diller readily admits that he makes up his Internet strategy as he moves along. "God knows we have plenty of money with which to screw up," he said, referring to IAC's $1.1 billion in available cash. If so, the stock is cheap, selling at 16 times earnings compared to Yahoo and Google's shares selling at 35–45 times earnings. Diller is preparing for a new string of acquisitions. IAC set up a venture capital investment arm in Silicon Valley called Primal Ventures (think primitive) to identify Internet opportunities. So far, Primal's head Jim Safka has identified opportunities in health, mental health, job recruitment, games, and entertainment for kids.

Case Study Questions

1. What are some of the ways in which Diller's e-commerce online service companies could cooperate to deliver superior value to the customer?

2. Would you recommend that IAC sites have a single Web site where users could find all the services of IAC, similar to a portal? Why or why not?

3. Based on reading of this chapter on services, what is the common thread that links together most of IAC/InterActiveCorp Web properties? How do these properties leverage the unique qualities of the Web?

4. Compare and contrast IAC/InterActiveCorp over the past three years with the merger of AOL and Time Warner. What mistakes did AOL/Time Warner make that IAC needs to avoid?

5. Suggest some likely ways in which the search engine Ask.com could help create a "traffic ecosystem" among IAC properties. Do you think users should be notified of this cross-marketing?

9.9 REVIEW

KEY CONCEPTS

■ **Understand the environment in which the online retail sector operates today.**

Personal consumption of retail goods and services comprise about 70% and account for over $8.7 trillion of total GDP. The retail sector can be broken down into three main categories:
- Services, which account for 58% of total retail sales
- Durable goods, which account for 13% of total retail sales
- Nondurable goods, which account for 29% of total retail sales

Although the distinction between a good and a service is not always clear-cut and "product-based services" are becoming the norm, we use the term retail goods to refer to physical products and retailers to refer to firms that sell physical goods to consumers. The retail industry can be further divided into nine major firm types:
- Clothing
- General merchandise
- Groceries
- Durable goods
- Specialty stores
- Eating and drinking
- Gasoline and fuel
- MOTO
- Online retail firms

Each type offers opportunities for online retail. The biggest opportunities for direct online sales are within those segments that sell small-ticket items (less than $100). This includes specialty stores, general merchandisers, mail-order catalogers, and grocery stores. The MOTO sector is the most similar to the online retail sales sector, and MOTO retailers are among the fastest-growing online retail firms.

During the early days of e-commerce, some predicted that the retail industry would be revolutionized, based on the following beliefs:
- Greatly reduced search costs on the Internet would encourage consumers to abandon traditional marketplaces in order to find the lowest prices for goods. First movers who provided low-cost goods and high-quality service would succeed.
- Market entry costs would be much lower than those for physical storefront merchants, and online merchants would be more efficient at marketing and order fulfillment than their offline competitors because they had command of the technology (technology prices were falling sharply).
- Online companies would replace traditional stores as physical store merchants were forced out of business. Older traditional firms that were too slow to enter the online market would be locked out of the marketplace.
- In certain industries, the "middleman" would be eliminated (disintermediation) as manufacturers or their distributors entered the market and built a direct relationship with the consumer. This cost savings would ensure the emergence of the Web as the dominant marketing channel.

- In other industries, online retailers would gain the advantage over traditional merchants by outsourcing functions such as warehousing and order fulfillment, resulting in a kind of hypermediation, in which the online retailer gained the upper hand by eliminating inventory purchasing and storage costs.

Today, it has become clear that few of the initial assumptions about the future of online retail were correct. Also, the structure of the retail marketplace in the United States has not been revolutionized. The reality is that:

- Online consumers are not primarily cost-driven—instead, they are as brand-driven and influenced by perceived value as their offline counterparts.
- Online market entry costs were underestimated, as was the cost of acquiring new customers.
- Older traditional firms, such as the general merchandising giants and the established catalog-based retailers, are taking over as the top online retail sites.
- Disintermediation did not occur. On the contrary, online retailing has become an example of the powerful role that intermediaries play in retail trade.

■ Explain how to analyze the economic viability of an online firm.

The economic viability, or ability of a firm to survive during a specified time period, can be analyzed by examining the key industry strategic factors, the strategic factors that pertain specifically to the firm, and the financial statements for the firm. The key industry strategic factors include:

- *Barriers to entry*, which are expenses that will make it difficult for new entrants to join the industry.
- *Power of suppliers*, which refers to the ability of firms in the industry to bargain effectively for lower prices from suppliers.
- *Power of customers*, which refers to the ability of the customers for a particular product to shop among the firm's competitors, thus keeping prices down.
- *Existence of substitute products*, which refers to the present or future availability of products with a similar function.
- *The industry value chain*, which must be evaluated to determine if the chain of production and distribution for the industry is changing in ways that will benefit or harm the firm.
- *The nature of intra-industry competition*, which must be evaluated to determine if the competition within the industry is based on differentiated products and services, price, the scope of the offerings, or the focus of the offerings and whether any imminent changes in the nature of the competition will benefit or harm the firm.

The key firm strategic factors include:

- The *firm value chain*, which must be evaluated to determine if the firm has adopted business systems that will enable it to operate at peak efficiency and whether there are any looming technological changes that might force the firm to change its processes or methods.
- *Core competencies*, which refer to unique skills that a firm has that cannot be easily duplicated. When analyzing the economic viability of a firm, it is important to consider whether technological changes might invalidate these competencies.
- *Synergies*, which refer to the availability to the firm of the competencies and assets of related firms that it owns or with which it has formed strategic partnerships.

- The firm's current *technology*, which must be evaluated to determine if it has proprietary technologies that will allow it to scale with demand and if it has developed the customer relationship, fulfillment, supply chain management, and human resources systems that it will need in order to be viable.
- The *social and legal challenges facing the firm*, which should be examined to determine if the firm has taken into account consumer trust issues such as the privacy and security of personal information and if the firm may be vulnerable to legal challenges.

The key financial factors include:

- *Revenues*, which must be examined to determine if they are growing and at what rate.
- *Cost of sales*, which is the cost of the products sold, including all related costs. The lower the cost of sales compared to revenue, the higher the gross profit.
- *Gross margin*, which is calculated by dividing gross profit by net sales revenue. If the gross margin is improving consistently, the economic outlook for the firm is enhanced.
- *Operating expenses*, which should be evaluated to determine if the firm's needs in the near interim will necessitate increased outlays. Large increases in operating expenses may result in net losses for the firm.
- *Operating margin*, which is calculated by dividing operating income or loss by net sales revenue, and is an indication of a company's ability to turn sales into pre-tax profit after operating expenses are deducted.
- *Net margin,* which is calculated by dividing net income or net loss by net sales revenue. It evaluates the net profit or loss for each dollar of net sales. For example, a net margin of -24 % indicates that a firm is losing 24 cents on each dollar of net sales revenue.
- The firm's *balance sheet,* which is a financial snapshot of a company on a given date that displays its financial assets and liabilities. If current assets are less than or not much more than current liabilities, the firm will likely have trouble meeting its short-term obligations

- ■ **Identify the challenges faced by the different types of online retailers.**

There are four major types of online retail business models, and each faces its own particular challenges:

- *Virtual merchants* are single-channel Web firms that generate all of their revenues from online sales. Their challenges include building a business and a brand name quickly, many competitors in the virtual marketplace, substantial costs to build and maintain a Web site, considerable marketing expenses, large customer acquisition costs, a steep learning curve, and the need to quickly achieve operating efficiencies in order to preserve a profit. Amazon is the most well-known example of a virtual merchant.
- *Multi-channel merchants* (bricks-and-clicks) have a network of physical stores as their primary retail channel, but have also begun online operations. Their challenges include high cost of physical buildings, high cost of large sales staffs, the need to coordinate prices across channels, the need to develop methods of handling cross-channel returns from multiple locations, building a credible Web site, hiring new skilled staff, and building rapid-response order

entry and fulfillment systems. JCP.com is an example of a bricks-and-clicks company.

- *Catalog merchants* are established companies that have a national offline catalog operation as their largest retail channel, but who have recently developed online capabilities. Their challenges include high costs for printing and mailing, the need to leverage their existing assets and competencies to the new technology environment, the need to develop methods of handling cross-channel returns, building a credible Web site, and hiring new skilled staff. Lands' End is an example of a catalog merchant.

- *Manufacturer-direct merchants* are either single or multi-channel manufacturers who sell to consumers directly online without the intervention of retailers. They were predicted to play a very large role in e-commerce, but this has not generally happened. Their challenges include channel conflict, which occurs when physical retailers of a manufacturer's products must compete on price and currency of inventory with the manufacturer who does not face the cost of maintaining inventory, physical stores, and a sales staff, quickly developing a fast-response online order and fulfillment system, switching from a supply-push (products are made prior to orders being received based on estimated demand) to a demand-pull model (products are not built until an order is received), and creating sales, service, and support operations online. Dell.com is an example of a manufacturer-direct merchant.

- **Describe the major features of the online service sector.**

The service sector is the largest and most rapidly expanding part of the economy of advanced industrial nations. Service industries are companies that provide services (i.e., perform tasks for) consumers, businesses, governments, and other organizations. The major service industry groups are financial services, insurance, real estate, business services, and health services. Within these service industry groups, companies can be further categorized into those that involve transaction brokering and those that involve providing a "hands-on" service. With some exceptions, the service sector is by and large a knowledge- and information-intense industry. For this reason, many services are uniquely suited to e-commerce and the strengths of the Internet.

The rapid expansion of e-commerce services in the areas of finance, including insurance and real estate, travel, and job placement, can be explained by the ability of these firms to:
- collect, store, and disseminate high value information
- provide reliable, fast communication
- personalize and customize service or components of service

E-commerce offers extraordinary opportunities to improve transaction efficiencies and thus productivity in a sector where productivity has so far not been markedly affected by the explosion in information technology.

- **Discuss the trends taking place in the online financial services industry.**

The online financial services sector is a good example of an e-commerce success story, but the success is somewhat different than what had been predicted in the early days of e-commerce. Today it is the multi-channel established financial firms that are growing the most rapidly and that have the best prospects for long-term viability. Other significant trends include the following:

- Management of financial assets online is growing rapidly.
- In the insurance and real estate industries, consumers still generally utilize the Internet just for research and use a conventional transaction broker to complete the purchase.
- Historically, separate institutions have provided the four generic types of services provided by financial institutions. Today, as a result of the Financial Reform Act of 1998, which permitted banks, brokerage firms, and insurance companies to merge, this is no longer true. This has resulted in two important and related global trends in the financial services industry that have direct consequences for online financial services firms: the move toward industry consolidation and the provision of integrated financial services.

Key features of the online banking and brokerage industries include the following:

- Multi-channel firms that have both physical branches and solid online offerings are growing faster and assuming market leadership over the pure-online firms that cannot provide customers with many services that still require hands-on interaction.
- Customer acquisition costs are significantly higher for Internet-only banks and brokerages that must invest heavily in marketing versus their established brand-name bricks-and-mortar competitors, which can simply convert existing branch customers to online customers at a much lower cost.
- Multi-channel institutions draw nearly four times the number of visitors, and significantly more of those visitors open a secure channel, indicating they are interested in transacting. However, visitors to pure-online firms use the sites more intensively and for a wider variety of services, while multi-channel site users visit less frequently and perform fewer transactions online. Unfortunately for the pure-online firms, their more active consumers are also more apt to comparison shop, are more cost-driven, and are therefore less loyal than established multi-channel users.
- The projected boom in online investment and banking has also attracted non-financial institutions. Financial portals provide comparison shopping services and steer consumers to online providers for independent financial advice and financial planning. They generate revenue from advertising, referral fees, and subscription fees. Financial portals add to the online price competition in the industry. They also thwart the ambitions of the large banking institutions that would like to ensnare consumers in a single branded financial supermarket in which the switching costs from a single, all-purpose account would be considerable.
- Account aggregation is another rapidly growing online financial service, which pulls together all of a customer's financial data on a single personalized Web site. Established financial institutions were originally opposed to these independent sites as a threat to their already established customer base, but consumer demand for this convenience has forced them to sign deals with the major account aggregation software providers in order to offer the service on their own sites. Privacy issues are raised by this new technology because in order to pull all of this data together in one place, consumers must release all of their login and password information to the account aggregator.

- During the early days of e-commerce, a radically altered online mortgage and lending services market was envisioned in which the mortgage value chain would be simplified and the loan closing process speeded up, with the resulting cost savings passed on to consumers. Affordably building a brand name, the resulting high customer acquisition costs, and instituting these value chain changes proved to be too difficult. Today it is the established banks and lenders who are reaping the benefits of a relatively small but rapidly growing market.
- There are four basic types of online mortgage lenders, including established banks, brokerages, and lending organizations; pure-online bankers/brokers; mortgage brokers; and mortgage service companies.

Key features of the online insurance industry include the following:

- Term life insurance stands out as one product group supporting the early visions of lower search costs, increased price transparency, and the resulting consumer savings. Policy prices for term life insurance have fallen as much as 54% in the last six years. However, in other insurance product lines, the Web offers insurance companies new opportunities for product and service differentiation and price discrimination.
- The insurance industry has several other distinguishing characteristics that make it difficult for it to be completely transferred to the new online channel, such as policies that defy easy comparison and that can only be explained by an experienced sales agent, a traditional reliance on local insurance offices and agents to sell complex products uniquely suited to the circumstances of the insured person and/or property, and a marketplace that is coordinated by state insurance commissions in each state with differing regulations. The result is that consumers for the most part will check the Web for prices and terms, but will not buy policies online. Although search costs have been dramatically reduced and price comparison shopping is done in an entirely new way, the industry value chain has so far not been significantly impacted.

Key features of the online real estate services industry include the following:

- The early vision that the historically local, complex, and agent-driven real estate industry would be transformed into a disintermediated marketplace where buyers and sellers could transact directly has not been realized. What has happened has been beneficial to buyers, sellers, and real estate agents alike.
- Since it is not possible to complete a property transaction online, the major impact of the online real estate industry is in influencing offline purchases.
- The primary service is a listing of available houses, with secondary links to mortgage lenders, credit reporting agencies, neighborhood information, loan calculators, appraisal reports, sales price histories by neighborhood, school district data, and crime reports.
- The industry value chain, however, has remained unchanged. Home addresses are not available online and users are directed back to the local listing agent for further information about the house.
- Buyers benefit because they can quickly and easily access a wealth of valuable information; sellers benefit because they receive free online advertising for their property; and real estate agents have reported that Internet-informed customers ask to see fewer properties.

- **Discuss the major trends in the online travel services industry today.**

Online travel services attract the largest single e-commerce audience and the largest slice of B2C revenues. The Internet is becoming the most common channel used by consumers to research travel options. It is also the most common way for people to search for the best possible prices and book reservations for airline tickets, rental cars, hotel rooms, cruises, and tours. Some of the reasons why online travel services have been so successful include the following:

- Online travel sites offer consumers a one-stop, convenient, leisure and business travel experience where travelers can find content, community, commerce, and customer service. Online sites offer more information and travel options than traditional travel agents, with such services as descriptions of vacations and facilities, chat groups and bulletin boards, and the convenience of purchasing all travel elements at one stop. They also bring consumers and suppliers together in a low transaction cost environment.

- Travel is an information-intensive product as well as an electronic product in the sense that travel requirements can be accomplished for the most part online. Since travel does not require any inventory, suppliers (which are highly fragmented) are always looking for customers to fill excess capacity. Also, travel services do not require an expensive multi-channel physical presence. For these reasons, travel services appear to be particularly well suited for the online marketplace.

- It is important to note that various segments of the travel industry fit this description better than others—for instance, airline reservations, auto rentals, and to a lesser extent, hotels. Cruises and tours are more differentiated with varying quality and a more complex level of information required for the decision-making process. Therefore, cruises, tours, and hotels to some extent will probably not grow as quickly in the online environment.

- In the past five years, corporate travel expenses have mushroomed, leading corporations to seek greater control over employee travel plans. Corporations are outsourcing their travel offices entirely to vendors who can provide Web-based solutions, high-quality service, and lower costs.

The major trends in online travel services include the following:

- The online travel services industry is going through a period of consolidation as stronger offline, established firms purchase weaker and relatively inexpensive online travel agencies in order to build stronger multi-channel travel sites that combine physical presence, television sales outlets, and online sites.

- Suppliers—such as airlines, hotels, and auto rental firms—are attempting to eliminate intermediaries such as GDSs and travel agencies, and develop a direct relationship with consumers. At the same time, successful online travel agencies are attempting to turn themselves into merchants by purchasing large blocks of travel inventory and then reselling it to the public, eliminating the global distributors and earning much higher returns.

■ **Identify current trends in the online career services industry.**

Next to travel services, job-hunting services have been one of the Internet's most successful online services because they save money for both job hunters and employers. In comparison to online recruiting, traditional recruitment tools have severe limitations:

- Online recruiting provides a more efficient and cost-effective means of linking employers and job hunters and reduces the total time-to-hire.
- Job hunters can easily build, update, and distribute their resumes, conduct job searches, and gather information on employers at their convenience and leisure.
- It is an information-intense business process that the Internet can automate, and thus reduce search time and costs for all parties.

Online recruiting can also serve to establish market prices and terms, thereby identifying both the salary levels for specific jobs and the skill sets required to achieve those salary levels. This should lead to a rationalization of wages, greater labor mobility, and higher efficiency in recruitment and operations as employers are able to more quickly fill positions.

The major trends in the online career services industry are:

- *Consolidation*: The online recruitment industry is going through a period of rapid consolidation led by Monster.
- *Diversification*: There is an explosion of specialty niche employment sites that focus on specific occupations.
- *Localization*: There is a growing focus on local job markets.
- *Job search engines*: New online job search engines that scrape listings from thousands of online job sites pose a threat to established career sites.
- *Social networking*: Many Internet users are beginning to use social networking sites to establish business contacts and find jobs; employers are also using them to identify and find out further information about job candidates.

QUESTIONS

1. Why were so many entrepreneurs drawn to start businesses in the online retail sector initially?
2. What frequently makes the difference between profitable and unprofitable online businesses today?
3. Which segment of the offline retail business is most like online retailing? Why?
4. Name the largest segment of U.S. retail sales. Explain why businesses in this segment have achieved and continue to dominate online retailing.
5. Describe the technological retail revolution that preceded the growth of e-commerce. What were some of the innovations that made later online retailing possible?
6. Name two assumptions e-commerce analysts made early on about consumers and their buying behavior that turned out to be false.
7. Why were customer acquisition costs assumed early on to be lower on the Web? What was supposed to reduce those costs?
8. Explain the distinction between disintermediation and hypermediation as it relates to online retailing.
9. How would you describe the top 10 online retailers as a group? Do they account for a small or a large percent of online business, for example?
10. Name two retail product categories that have been demonstrating greater than 50% annual growth.
11. Compare and contrast virtual merchants and bricks-and-clicks firms. What other type of online retailer is most like the virtual merchant?

11. Compare and contrast virtual merchants and bricks-and-clicks firms. What other type of online retailer is most like the virtual merchant?

12. What is the difference between a supply-push and a demand-pull sales model? Why do most manufacturer-direct firms have difficulty switching to one of these?

13. What are five strategic issues specifically related to a firm's capabilities? How are they different from industry-related strategic issues?

14. Which is a better measure of a firm's financial health: revenues, gross margin, or net margin? Why?

15. What are some of the difficulties in providing services in an online environment? What factors differentiate the services sector from the retail sector, for example?

16. Compare and contrast the two major types of online services industries. What two major features differentiate services from other industries?

17. Name and describe the three types of online mortgage vendors. What are the major advantages of using an online mortgage site? What factors are slowing the growth of such service businesses?

18. What is the biggest deterrent to growth of the online insurance industry nationally?

19. Define channel conflict and explain how it currently applies to the mortgage and insurance industries. Name two online insurance companies or brokers.

20. What is the most common use of real estate Web sites? What do most consumers do when they go there?

21. Name and describe the four types of services provided by financial services firms on the Web.

22. Who are the major players in the financial industry consolidation currently occurring worldwide?

23. Explain the two global trends impacting the structure of the financial services industry and their impact on online operations.

24. How have travel services suppliers benefited from consumer use of travel Web sites?

25. What are the two major segments of travel? Which one is growing the fastest and why?

26. Explain how global distribution systems (GDSs) function.

27. Name and describe the five traditional recruitment tools companies have used to identify and attract employees. What are the disadvantages of such tools in light of new online sites?

28. In addition to matching job applicants with available positions, what larger function do online job sites fill? Explain how such sites can affect salaries and going rates.

29. Given the popularity of online career sites, why are classified ads still the preferred information source for so many job seekers and employers?

PROJECTS

1. Find the Securities and Exchange Commission Web site at Sec.gov, and access the EDGAR archives, where you can review 10-K filings for all public companies. Search for the 10-K report for the most recent completed fiscal year for two online retail companies of your choice (preferably ones operating in the same area, such as Staples Inc. and Office Depot Inc.). Prepare a

presentation that compares the financial stability and prospects of the two businesses, focusing specifically on the performance of their respective Internet operations.

2. Examine the financial statements for Amazon and Best Buy Co. Inc. What observations can you make about the two businesses? Which one is stronger financially and why? Which one's business model appears to be weaker and why? If you could identify two major problem areas for each, what would they be? Prepare a presentation that makes your case.

3. Conduct a thorough analysis—strategic and financial—of one of the following companies or another of your own choosing: Bluefly Inc., Drugstore.com, Inc. or 1-800-Flowers.com, Inc. Prepare a presentation that summarizes your observations about the company's Internet operations and future prospects.

4. Find an example not mentioned in the text of each of the four types of online retailing business models. Prepare a short report describing each firm and why it is an example of the particular business model.

5. Drawing on material in the chapter and your own research, prepare a short paper describing your views on the major social and legal issues facing online retailers.

6. Conduct a thorough analysis—strategic and financial—of one of the following Web sites: Progressive.com, Insure.com, or Insweb.com. Prepare a presentation that summarizes your observations about the company's operations and future prospects.

7. Choose a services industry not discussed in the chapter (such as legal services, medical services, accounting services, or another of your choosing). Prepare a 3- to 5-page report discussing recent trends affecting online provision of these services.

8. Together with a teammate, investigate the use of wireless applications in the financial services industries. Prepare a short joint presentation on your findings.

9. Find at least two examples of companies not mentioned in the text that act as transaction brokers and at least two examples of companies that provide a hands-on service. Prepare a short memo describing the services each company offers and explaining why the company should be categorized as a transaction broker or a hands-on service provider.

WEB SITE RESOURCES www.prenhall.com/laudon

■ Additional projects, exercises, and tutorials
■ Careers: Explore career opportunities in e-commerce
■ Raising capital and business plans

CHAPTER 10

Online Content and Media

After reading this chapter, you will be able to:

- Identify the major trends in the consumption of media and online content.
- Discuss the concept of media convergence and the challenges it faces.
- Describe the five basic content revenue models.
- Discuss the key challenges facing content producers and owners.
- Understand the key factors affecting the online publishing industry.
- Understand the key factors affecting the online entertainment industry.

The Wall Street Journal Online Discovers Web 2.0

The *Wall Street Journal* was founded in 1889 by the Dow Jones News Service as a blend of general international and national news, along with in-depth financial reporting. It has a worldwide readership of 4 million. In April 1996, the Journal launched WSJ.com. In 2008, the Journal reached one million online subscribers, and attracted more than 4 million non-subscribing visitors , and it is the most successful online newspaper. The Journal is one of the very few online newspapers to successfully employ a subscription revenue model. Nearly all other news and magazine publishers have adopted an advertiser supported "free content" model. Currently, subscribers to the *Wall Street Journal* print edition pay $49 a year for access to the online edition; non-subscribers pay $99.

But the *Wall Street Journal* is different from most newspapers. Most of the 10,000 online newspapers in the world offer free content. The common view among newspaper publishers is that most online consumers expect information to be free. Switching to subscription fees has resulted in online magazines such as *Salon* losing 90% of their readers. Since then, *Salon*'s readership has stabilized and grown, and it has adopted a mixture of free content and premium paid subscriptions, but remains only barely profitable. As a result, online newspapers typically are supported by advertising and sales of classified ads—just as traditional print newspapers have been for centuries—rather than monthly subscription fees. While newspaper readership is down (especially in the important 18–49-year-old group), the demand for online advertising opportunities is up over 26% in 2007–2008. The demand for online general audiences is so hot that there is a shortage of Web pages. Newspapers—like the *Wall Street Journal* —are in a good position to provide Web pages. In 2004, Dow Jones bought a leading online business and investment site, MarketWatch.com, which has 7 million monthly unique visitors, in order to greatly increase its advertising pages.

Why has the *Wall Street Journal* succeeded with a subscription model where others have failed? Brand is certainly one reason. The *Wall Street Journal* has strong brand recognition among American investors. It is well known for its stock quotation services and in-depth reporting on business and general news issues. However, many newspapers such as the *New York Times*, *Los Angeles Times*, and *Washington Post* also have strong national brands, but do not charge subscription fees. The *New York Times* adopted a paid model called Times Select that charged for premium content, and access to the Times archives, but dropped that model in 2007 because users were gaining access to news from other sites such as Yahoo and Google.

Perhaps one key to the *Wall Street Journal's* success is that a subscription gives users access to premium content in the form of 25,000 in-depth background reports on companies, an archive of news articles going back to 1996, and access to the Dow Jones Publication Library, which features current and past articles from 7,000 newspapers, magazines, and business-news sources. If you are a stock analyst or an individual investor looking for information on a specific company, this archive of material may be well worth the relatively small annual subscription fee. Coupled with a fine-grained search engine, the *Wall Street Journal's* archives are unique and differentiated from most other online newspaper offerings. The *Journal* sells access to this premium archival content on a per article basis.

Readers of the *Journal* are also attracted to its timeliness and Web suitability. Using a structured markup technology provided by OmniMark's Content Engineering system, writers and editors are able to simultaneously author articles for both print and online editions, and then automatically generate Web pages that conform to the *Journal's* unique print style. This system also permits them to make dynamic changes in news story content, shortening or lengthening stories as needed, without costly page redesign. Writers and editors can post hundreds of up-to-date articles around the clock, and the key page elements—such as size of headlines, space between articles, positioning of navigation buttons, and placement of advertisements—are all generated by the OmniMark system. The same system creates a consistent content archive of news and opinion that can be searched by subscribers. In this sense, Internet distribution technology has led to a convergence in content creation and delivery: news is news, whether it is printed on paper or on a Web page. Like many online newspapers, the Journal now also makes extensive use of videos (listed on the home page), and has transformed many of its writers into online interviewers that provide a marvelous personal contact with newsmakers and current topics.

The new technology has transformed the online newspaper experience. Instead of having content trapped on static print pages that are updated daily, the online edition can offer timely breaking news much like a television or radio news show, and like television, provide video access to important news events and newsmakers. WSJ.com uses personalization features to make its content even more compelling. Subscribers can create a personalized WSJ.com home page with user-selected columnists, stock portfolio updates, and company news. In addition, along with other online publishers, users can have news stories on topics and subjects they choose pushed to them using a *Wall Street Journal* RSS feed. The *Journal* also has added major sections available only online: interactive features walk readers through complex stories, and in-depth reports explore topics such as retirement, mutual fund returns, and pension planning.

The *Journal* has multiple free Web sites from MarketWatch to the Real Estate and College journals. The *Journal* has been able to leverage this new functionality into higher subscription fees.

While many newspaper editors and reporters lament the decline in readership, and the movement of young adults to the Internet as a source of news and entertainment, clearly some newspapers are moving from an older, endearing technology called "print on paper," towards a new technology, "news on-screen." But even with these extensive changes in the *Wall Street Journal* product and delivery platform, its parent corporation, Dow Jones, has suffered lackluster earnings and poor stock price performance since 2005. In August 2007, the Bancroft family, the largest stockholder group and descendants of the founder Charles Dow who started the newspaper in 1899, accepted a $5 billion offer for Dow Jones from none other than Rupert Murdoch, the founder of News Corp, the largest newspaper print media company in the world, and the owner of MySpace, the most popular social networking site. One of Murdoch's anticipated first moves: make the online *Journal* free to greatly expand the audience, the size of the paper, and the advertising revenue. So far this has not happened, and the Journal remains subscription based but with more free teaser pages available to non-subscribers, and a small but growing number of display ads (despite its paid subscriber base).

In 2008 Murdoch redesigned the look and feel of the print Journal, still keeping its business focus, but adding more general news, a smaller page format, and started a week end magazine to compete more directly with the New York Times. In September, 2008 Murdoch redesigned the online edition as well.

The new online edition more clearly reflects the capabilities of the Internet and Web 2.0. There are reporter blogs, user comments on all articles, and videos, all updated in real time. The most radical departure is the addition of a social networking capability: the new online Journal will allow its one million subscribers to comment on any article, pose discussion questions, e-mail one another, and set up profiles that will allow other subscribers to see what they are doing on the site. The goal is to increase reader loyalty, expand the amount of time users spend on the site, and of course increase ad revenues. These changes point the way for newspapers and other traditional generators of content to remain viable and profitable long into the future.

SOURCES: "Social Networking coming to Wall Journal Website," by Anick Jesdahun, Time Magazine, September 15, 2008; "New Wall Street Journal Builds on Its Community of Subscribers," by Vindu Goel, The New York Times, September 15, 2008; "The Wall Street Journal Setting Online Content Free," by K.C. Jones, *Information Week*, November 14, 2007; "Murdoch: WSJ.com Expected to Be Free," *Associated Press*, November 13, 2007; "Murdoch's Next Focus: Business-News Battle," by Martin Peers, *Wall Street Journal*, August 2, 2007; "Murdoch Sees Journal as Hub for Empire," by Richard Siklos, *New York Herald Tribune*, June 10, 2007; Wall Street Journal Weighs Life Under Murdoch," by Richard Siklos, *New York Times*, May 2, 2007; WSJ.com, 2006; "The Newspaper of the Future," by Timothy O'Brien, *New York Times*, June 26, 2005.

The *Wall Street Journal Online* case illustrates how traditional media companies are adapting to the new opportunities of the Web by developing content experiences for online consumers that would be impossible offline, including video, blogs, interactive features like games and online crossword puzzles, and more recently, social networking opportunities. Today it is clear that the future of content—news, music, and video—is online. In the past, online companies had a difficult time becoming profitable. Today, the print industry, including newspapers and magazines, is having a difficult time coping with the movement of their readership to the Web. Broadcast and cable television, along with Hollywood and the music labels, are also wrestling with outdated business models based on physical media. Established media giants are continuing to make extraordinary investments in unique online content, new technology, new digital distribution channels, and entirely new business models. In this chapter, we focus primarily on the publishing and entertainment industries as they attempt to transform their traditional media into Web-deliverable forms and experiences for consumers.

10.1 ONLINE CONTENT

No other sector of the American economy has been so challenged by the Internet and the Web than the content industries. The content industries involve all those businesses that use print, television, and film to communicate, as well as the distribution businesses such as cable, broadcast television, satellite, printers, and retail content stores (like music and video rental stores). As a communications medium, the Web is, by definition, a source of online content. In this chapter, we will look closely at publishing (newspapers, books, and magazines) and entertainment (music, film, games, and television). These industries make up the largest share of the commercial content marketplace, both offline and online. In each of these industries, there are powerful offline brands, significant new pure-play online providers, consumer constraints and opportunities, a variety of legal issues, and technology constraints on rapid deployment of online content.

Table 10.1 describes the most recent trends in online content for 2007–2008.

CONTENT AUDIENCE AND MARKET: WHERE ARE THE EYEBALLS AND THE MONEY?

The average American adult spends over 3,800 hours each year consuming various media, nearly twice as much time spent at work (2,000 hours/year) (see **Figure 10.1**). By 2010, this amount is expected to grow to 4,000 hours or about 11 hours per day. While overall media time is growing at around 2.5% per year, Internet media time is growing at 5% per year. The Internet is the fastest-growing medium. Media revenues in 2008 were estimated to be $654 billion, and they are expected to grow at a compound rate of 9% (U.S. Census Bureau, 2008).

TABLE 10.1	**TRENDS IN ONLINE CONTENT, 2008–2009**

- **Media consumption**: Americans spend over 3,800 hours a year consuming various types of media, nearly twice as many hours as they work. Internet time exposure grows rapidly, surpassing newspapers, and music, but far behind traditional television and radio.

- **Revenue**: Revenues from Internet media are the fastest-growing media revenues.

- **Eyeballs**: Traditional content audience moves to the Internet, and the annual growth in the Internet audience outpaces all other media.

- **User-generated content**: The Internet inverts the traditional production and business model by having users create much content. Social network sites, video sites like YouTube, personal blogs, and photo sites, show extraordinary growth, threaten traditional entertainment firms, and challenge traditional media for user attention, total audience size, and even legitimacy. User-generated video and TV shows engage more and more users.

- **Technology**: Mobile smart phones and computers are brought to market, which make Web-based music, news, and entertainment available anytime and anywhere.

- **Advertising**: The growing Internet audience causes a rapid expansion in Internet advertising revenues as advertisers move to where the eyeballs are focused. The Internet adopts a traditional media business model: "free content" in exchange for viewing ads.

- **Business models:** A mixture of advertising support, subscription, and a la carte payment for unbundled products like individual songs, television shows, and movies proves to be the most successful business model.

- **Paid content and free content coexist**: The common notion of "Internet means free information" is being replaced by consumer acceptance of paying for premium content, which is growing far faster than other media or than the Internet itself in the United States. At the same time, music, television, and Hollywood studios are making some content free but supported by advertising revenues.

- **Convergence**: Traditional media—newspapers, magazines, and studios—are moving closer to a convergent model based on new technologies and new industry alignments among major media conglomerates. Hollywood and television studios begin video streaming of movies and shows. Internet television divisions of traditional TV studios are formed. Newspapers and magazines add video to their online sites. Internet media firms Yahoo, Google, AOL, MSN, and Apple move into traditional media spaces such as television, telephone, and movie distribution by offering a variety of new online services.

- **Print media**: Newspapers and magazines begin a painful transition to online models buoyed by the growth in online advertising, which is not sufficient to replace lost advertising revenues.

- **Entertainment content**: Led by music, an explosion in online video, and the growing interest in online television and feature length films, the Web emerges as an entertainment powerhouse rivaling broadcast networks, cable, and satellite distribution systems.

- **Consumer taste**: Consumers want to control their own programming. Consumers increasingly support time-shifting and space-shifting in media consumption by demanding to see or hear just about any media wherever and whenever they want using any of several devices like PCs, cell phones, PDAs, or conventional devices.

Media Utilization

The most popular medium is television, followed by radio and the Internet. Together, these three media account for over 80% of the hours spent consuming various media.

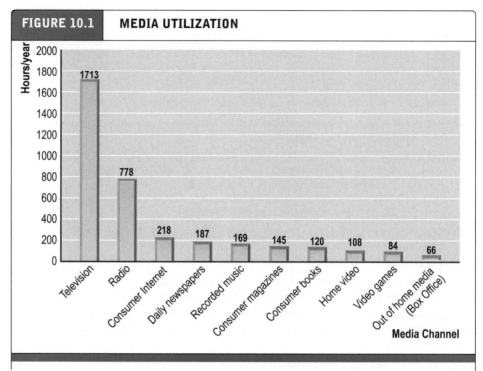

FIGURE 10.1 **MEDIA UTILIZATION**

Americans spend over 3,800 hours each, on average, annually, consuming various media, mostly television, radio, and recorded music. However, time spent on the Internet is growing rapidly. Internet time doubled since 2000, and it has overtaken newspapers, music, and magazine.

SOURCE: Based on data from U.S. Census Bureau, 2008.

While the Internet is currently a distant third, Internet utilization has been growing rapidly. If the time spent with text-based media (books, magazines, and newspapers) were combined, it would exceed that spent on recorded music. Surprisingly, non-television-based entertainment (home video, video games, and theater movies) consumes only 258 media hours per year (U.S Census Bureau, 2008).

Internet and Traditional Media: Cannibalization versus Complementarity

Most studies reveal that time spent on the Internet reduces consumer time available for other media (Pew Internet & American Life Project, 2006). There has been a massive shift of the general audience to the Web, and once there, an equally massive shift since 2003 towards viewing or listening to content. In 2008, consumers are spending 47% of their online time with content, up from 34% in 2003 (Online Publishers Association, 2007). A USC survey found that one-quarter of Web users report spending less time with offline print media, and 35% report less time with television (USC, 2007). In general, Internet users spend 15%–20% less time reading books, newspapers, magazines, and watching television, box office movies, and less time on the phone or listening to the radio. On the other hand, Internet users consume more media of all types than non-Internet users. This reflects the demographics of the Internet user as more literate, wealthier, more technically savvy, and more media aware. In addition, Internet users multitask when using the Internet, frequently listening to music, watching television, and using instant messaging while working on other tasks. Multimedia use reduces the cannibalization impact of the Internet for some visual and aural media, but obviously not for reading books or newspapers. And even for these print media, the Internet is simply an alternative source; Internet users are increasing the time they spend online reading newspapers, magazines, and even books.

Media Revenues

An examination of media revenues reveals somewhat different patterns (see **Figure 10.2**). Entertainment (box office events, home video, video games, and recorded music) garnered 27% of media revenues, even though this category consumes only 5% of consumer media hours.

Television—broadcast, cable, and satellite—remains a major producer of media revenues (42%), while newspapers generate 5% of revenues, down from 10% in previous years.

The Internet constitutes 12% of total media revenues, but this is substantially higher than the 5% of media channel revenues it produced in 2004. Once again, the Internet has grown in a few short years from a zero base to a substantial share of media revenues today. In the next section, we describe the current and emerging online content marketplace.

Figure 10.3 gives some idea of the relative size of the content market, based on per-person spending. Television and home video are more than three times the size of online content, but online content expenditures are rising at twice the rate of

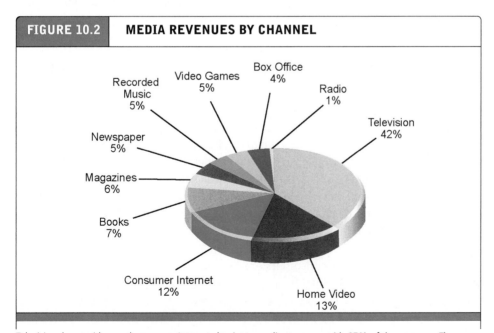

| FIGURE 10.2 | MEDIA REVENUES BY CHANNEL |

Television, home video, and consumer Internet dominate media revenues with 67% of the revenues. The revenue share for traditional media such as newspapers and magazines has shrunk, while book publishing revenues have remained fairly constant over many years.

SOURCE: Based on data from U.S. Census Bureau, 2008.

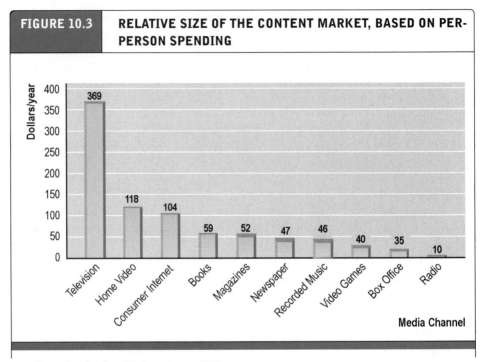

FIGURE 10.3   **RELATIVE SIZE OF THE CONTENT MARKET, BASED ON PER-PERSON SPENDING**

SOURCE: Based on data from U.S. Census Bureau, 2008.

home video or TV. At some point in the near future, online revenues will exceed those of home video, and then eventually, exceed those of broadcast and cable television.

Two Models For Digital Content Delivery: Paid and User-Generated Content

There are two commercial models for delivering content on the Internet: paid versus "free" with advertiser support. There is completely free user-generated content, which we will discuss later. Contrary to early analysts' projections that "free" would drive "paid" out of business ("information wants to be free"), it turns out that both models are viable now and in the near future. Consumers increasingly choose to pay for high-quality, convenient, and unique content, and they have gladly accepted "free" advertiser-supported content when that content is deemed not worth paying for but entertaining nevertheless. There's nothing contradictory about both models working in tandem, and cooperatively: free content can drive customers to paid content, as the recorded music firms have just discovered.

Now let's look at what consumers are buying on the Internet in terms of paid digital content. About 37% of Internet users (64 million users) have downloaded music, 17% have paid for downloading music, and less than 1% have paid for a video online (Pew Internet and American Life Report, 2008; eMarketer, Inc., 2008a). The online paid content audience, however, is growing at about 16% a year, faster than the Internet itself. Increasingly, the Internet is changing from primarily a communication medium to an entertainment medium. The growth in the audience size is largely attributable to the growth in the entertainment segment of music, and personals and dating content.

Figure 10.4 shows the estimated revenues from digital music, online TV, and digital movies.

Now let's look at the user-generated digital content audience. This audience is huge and growing very rapidly. User-generated content—music, videos, and text in the form of blogs—is free and typically advertiser supported. About 64 million users have created user-generated content, and 70 million have viewed it. Revenue is generated by advertisers who in 2008 will spend $1.5 billion, rising to $4 billion in 2012. Placing these numbers on user-generated content pages in the context of paid digital content, by 2011, user-generated content sites will be generating about as much money as paid music, and will be a substantial revenue stream. **Table 10.2** shows the top video and user-generated content sites. User-generated content falls into seven categories: video, audio, photos, information (news), personal data, reviews, and recommendations (favorites, social bookmarking). By far the largest and potentially most valuable to marketers is the online video audience. About 50% of all Internet video is now user generated, and this is expected to rise to 55% by 2012 (eMarketer, Inc., 2007b).

It will come as no surprise that YouTube is the leading advertiser-supported video site, and that the overall size of the online video audience (about 70 million monthly unique visitors) is much larger than traditional television audiences, which numbers in the 10 million range for exceptionally popular shows. A peak hourly load at

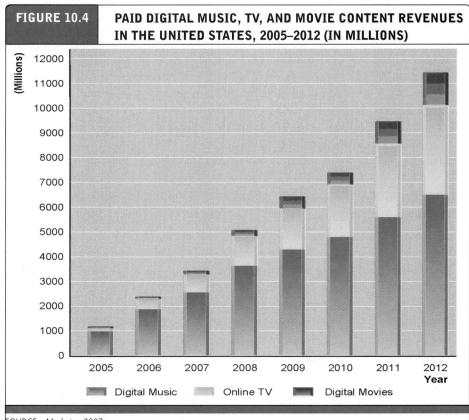

FIGURE 10.4 | **PAID DIGITAL MUSIC, TV, AND MOVIE CONTENT REVENUES IN THE UNITED STATES, 2005–2012 (IN MILLIONS)**

Legend: Digital Music, Online TV, Digital Movies

SOURCE: eMarketer, 2007a.

TABLE 10.2	TOP TEN U.S. ONLINE VIDEO SITES (JULY 2008) (in millions)	
SITE	VISITORS	AVG. VIDEOS PER VIEWER
1. Google sites (YouTube)	92.1	54.7
2. Fox Interactive Media (MySpace)	54.8	8.1
3. Yahoo! sites	37.6	7.2
4. Microsoft sites	32.6	8.7
5. AOL	23.0	4.1
6. Viacom Digital	21.1	11.7
7. Turner Network	18.7	9.2
8. Disney Online	15.9	11.7
9. Time Warner (excluding AOL)	15.3	3.2
10. Amazon sites	11.7	2.5

SOURCE: Based on data from comScore, 2008; eMarketer, Inc., 2008b.

YouTube can exceed 20 million unique visitors. The social networking sites are just now learning how to monetize this audience through advertising revenues, but so far they have had limited success.

The simultaneous growth of both paid and free advertiser-supported content on the Internet suggests that these phenomena are complimentary in some cases, and can grow together. This may not be true of newspapers and magazines where online content has lessened their readership, and substitution is taking place. But music offers an example of complementarity. Illegal P2P file sharing is just as prevalent as before, involving millions of songs. Yet the parallel growth of paid content sites such as iTunes suggest both models can exist and prosper.

One question remains: can the commercial content industries of movies, music, and text that depend on payments or subscriptions make enough money using the advertiser-supported model make up for losses caused to their traditional models?

Free or Fee: Attitudes About Paying For Content and the Tolerance of Advertising

Multiple surveys by many organizations have found that the Internet audience would prefer to pay nothing for content. However, it is willing to tolerate advertising support in order to obtain "free" video content and is willing to pay for selected, high-quality, convenient content such as iTunes and downloaded Hollywood movies. According to one survey, 63% of U.S. Internet users would agree to watch advertising before and after quality content, 28% would pay a few dollars per month for quality video, and only 6% would pay the equivalent of the price of a DVD as a monthly fee (eMarketer, Inc., 2007c). In contrast, most users expect news content to be advertiser supported. While the advertising support model is widely accepted, it also the case that paid digital content has shown extraordinary growth.

MEDIA INDUSTRY STRUCTURE

The media content industry prior to 1990 was composed of many smaller independent corporations specializing in content creation and distribution in the separate industries of film, television, book and magazine publishing, and newspaper publishing. During the 1990s and into this century, after an extensive period of consolidation, huge entertainment and publishing media conglomerates emerged (see **Table 10.3**).

The media industry is still organized largely into three separate vertical stovepipes, with each segment dominated by a few key players. We do not include the delivery platform firms here, such as AT&T, Verizon, Sprint, Dish Network, or Comcast, because in general they do not create content; they just move content across cable, satellite, and telephone lines. Generally, there is very little crossover from one segment to another. Newspapers do not also produce Hollywood films, and publishing firms do not own newspapers or film production studios. Even within media conglomerates that span several different media segments, separate divisions control each media segment. For instance, AOL/Time Warner is organized into six independent divisions (cable networks, publishing, music, film, cable programming, and digital media/Internet), each with its own separate management, production, marketing, distribution, and sales arrangements. The competition between corporate

TABLE 10.3	MEDIA TITAN REVENUES
MEDIA TITANS	2007 REVENUES (IN BILLIONS)
Entertainment	
AOL/Time Warner	$46.48
Walt Disney (ABC)	$35.51
News Corp (FOX)	$32.99
Vivendi	$31.09
Viacom (CBS)	$27.49
Bertelsmann	$27.04
Publishing	
Thomson Reuters	$12.44
Pearson PLC	$7.64
McGraw-Hill	$6.77
Newspapers	
Gannett (USA Today)	$7.44
Washington Post	$4.18
New York Times	$3.19
McClatchy Co.	$2.26
Dow Jones (WSJ)	$1.78

SOURCES: Based on data from Company SEC 10-K filings and author estimates.

divisions in mega-sized corporations is often more severe than with marketplace competitors. For instance, the AOL division may want to stream television shows over the Internet, but this desire could harm Time Warner's own cable network division. On the other hand, as the audience moves increasingly to the Internet, even large conglomerates will be forced to follow.

While the commercial media industry is highly concentrated, yet fragmented across media firms, the much larger media ecosystem includes literally millions of individuals and independent entrepreneurs creating content in the form of blogs, YouTube videos, and independent music bands on MySpace. At times, the viewership (or readership) of these much smaller but numerous players exceeds that of the media titans.

MEDIA CONVERGENCE: TECHNOLOGY, CONTENT, AND INDUSTRY STRUCTURE

Media convergence is a much used but poorly defined term. There are at least three dimensions of media where the term convergence has been applied: technology, content (artistic design, production, and distribution), and to the industry's structure as a whole. Ultimately for the consumer, convergence means being able to get any content you want, when you want it, on whatever platform you want it—from an iPod to a wireless PC to a handheld computer.

Technological Convergence

technological convergence

development of hybrid devices that can combine the functionality of two or more existing media platforms into a single device

Convergence from a technology perspective (**technological convergence**) has to do with the development of hybrid devices that can combine the functionality of two or more existing media platforms, such as books, newspapers, television, radio, and stereo equipment, into a single device. Examples of technological convergence include the iPhone, Blackberry, and Palm Treo ("smart phones,") that combine voice, Internet, Wi-Fi, and media services; iPod, which can combine in a handheld computing device music, video, photos, and text; digital interactive television sets that can surf the Web; video game machines that can also surf the Internet; and PCs that play and record music and videos.

Content Convergence

content convergence

convergence in the design, production, and distribution of content

A second dimension of convergence is **content convergence**. There are three aspects to content convergence: design, production, and distribution.

There is a historical pattern in which content created in an older media technology migrates to the new technology largely intact, with little artistic change. Slowly, the different media are integrated so that consumers can move seamlessly back and forth among them, and artists (and producers) learn more about how to deliver content in the new media. Later, the content itself is transformed by the new media as artists learn how to fully exploit the capabilities in the creation process. At this point, content convergence and transformation has occurred—the art is different because of the new capabilities inherent to new tools. For instance, European master painters of the fifteenth century in Italy, France, and the Netherlands (such as van Eyck, Caravaggio, Lotto, and Vermeer) quickly adopted new optical devices such as lenses, mirrors, and early projectors called *camera obscura* that could cast near-photographic quality images on canvases, and in the process they developed new theories of perspective and new techniques of painting landscapes and portraits. Suddenly, paintings took on the qualities of precision, detail, and realism found only in photographs (Boxer, 2001). A similar process is occurring today as artists and writers assimilate new digital and Internet tools into their toolkits. For instance, GarageBand from Apple enables low-budget independent bands (literally working in garages) to mix and control eight different digital music tracks to produce professional sounding recordings on a shoestring budget.

On the production side, new tools for digital editing and processing (for film and television) are driving content convergence. Given that the most significant cost of content is its creation, if there is a wide diversity of target delivery platforms, then it is wise to develop and produce only once using technology that can deliver to multiple platforms. Generally, this means creating content on digital devices (hardware and software) so that it can be delivered on multiple digital platforms. Once captured on digital devices, the same content can be archived, sliced into atomistic units, and re-purposed for a wide variety of other platforms and distribution channels.

On the distribution side, it is important that distributors and ultimate consumers have the devices needed to receive, store, and experience the product. While for the most part, technology companies have succeeded in giving consumers portable devices to receive online content, it has been more difficult for the content owners to come up with new, profitable distribution platforms. The music industry has seen its music store model collapse. The feature-length film industry struggles with online digital distribution. Hollywood studios currently deliver copies of new films to thousands of theaters across the country in trucks. A feature-length film can require six large, heavy canisters containing reels of 35mm film. To be able to digitally download the film via satellite, local theaters must be equipped with servers and large hard drives to receive the film, as well as new digital projection equipment. This will take many years to achieve, and it is unclear who will pay for it—the studios or the retail theaters.

Figure 10.5 depicts the process of media convergence and transformation using the example of books. For example, consider this book. The book was designed from the beginning as content to be delivered using both traditional text and the Internet. In that sense, this book is in the media transformation stage. In subsequent years, this same book will be available both as a purely digital work and as a mixed book + Web product. Eventually, it is likely that this book will be available mostly as a purely digital product with substantial visual and aural content that can be displayed on many different digital devices including e-book readers. By that time, the "learning experience" will be transformed. Traditional bound books will probably still be available (books have many advantages), but most likely, print editions will be printed on demand by customers using their own print facilities.

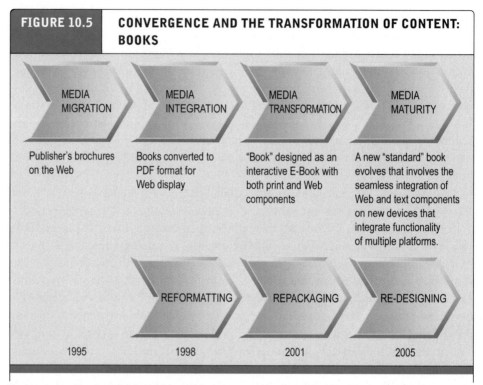

FIGURE 10.5 **CONVERGENCE AND THE TRANSFORMATION OF CONTENT: BOOKS**

MEDIA MIGRATION

MEDIA INTEGRATION

MEDIA TRANSFORMATION

MEDIA MATURITY

Publisher's brochures on the Web

Books converted to PDF format for Web display

"Book" designed as an interactive E-Book with both print and Web components

A new "standard" book evolves that involves the seamless integration of Web and text components on new devices that integrate functionality of multiple platforms.

REFORMATTING

REPACKAGING

RE-DESIGNING

1995   1998   2001   2005

The Internet is making it possible for publishers and writers to transform the standard "book" into a new form that integrates features of both text and the Internet, and also transforms the content of the book itself.

Industry Convergence

A third dimension of convergence is the structure of the various media industries. **Industry convergence** refers to the merger of media enterprises into powerful, synergistic combinations that can cross-market content on many different platforms and create new works that use multiple platforms. This can take place either through purchases or through strategic alliances. Traditionally, each type of media—film, text, music, television—had its own separate industry, typically composed of very large players. For instance, the entertainment film industry has been dominated by a few large Hollywood-based production studios; book publication is dominated by a few large book publishers; and music production is dominated by five global record label firms.

industry convergence
merger of media enterprises into synergistic combinations that create and cross-market content on different platforms

However, the Internet has created forces that make the merger of traditionally separate firms in separate media industries a plausible—perhaps necessary— business proposition. Media industry convergence may be necessary to finance the substantial changes in both the technology platform and the content. Traditional media firms by themselves generally do not possess the core competencies, financial heft, content ownership, or channel ownership to bring about Internet media convergence.

The best-known example of media industry convergence is the merger of AOL and Time Warner in January 2001. Time Warner was the largest multimedia conglomerate in the United States, but had no Web content per se, and had experienced an early failure in attempting to build a Web presence. AOL brought to the merger the largest online audience in the United States (nearly 40% of U.S. Internet users at that time), a substantial ISP operation with a monthly billing relationship with the consumer, and a successful track record in providing Internet and Web services and content. The merger plans called for the two companies to provide a single corporate platform for the creation and distribution of high-value content. AOL/Time Warner combines content with distribution. Senior executives at both AOL and Time Warner believed that new content would be created for distribution on both traditional and new media such as the Internet, and the process of transforming media and content to optimize the new Internet technology would begin in earnest with financing provided by successful traditional media such as cable subscriptions and feature film and television production revenue. However, the original vision has not materialized, and Time Warner has sold a stake in AOL to Google as a way to increase advertising revenue and audience reach.

Rupert Murdoch's News Corporation is another example. In 2005, the News Corporation (now a conglomerate with both newspaper and satellite distribution) purchased the Web's most dynamic and fast-growing social network, MySpace. This merger has been successful and MySpace is operating profitably. If traditional media companies have not done well in purchases of Internet platform companies, the technology owners like Apple, Microsoft, Google, and others have done better. Apple created its own online music store and now sells more labeled music than any other retailer; Microsoft created their xBox 360, and owns other content sources; Google has purchased a social network site, an online video repository, and has created software applications that include entertainment content.

In the end, consumers' demands for content anywhere, anytime, and with any device is pushing all the technology and content companies towards convergent experiences.

ONLINE CONTENT REVENUE MODELS AND BUSINESS PROCESSES

We have already discussed the "free" (with ad support) versus paid content models for delivering online content. But actually the situation is more complex: there are several different "free" revenue models. The basic content revenue models include: marketing, advertising, pay-per-view, subscription, value-added, and the mixed model, which combines several of the other types (see **Table 10.4**).

In the marketing revenue model, media companies give away content for free in the hope that visitors to the site will purchase the product offline or view a show offline. The Web site is intended to generate interest, develop word-of-mouth viral marketing, and deepen the emotional experience for offline product users. Consumer products companies like Procter & Gamble use this model. The revenues produced by this model are difficult to measure directly. Costs of operating the site can be hidden in larger marketing budgets and to some extent recovered through the sale of product-related paraphernalia, such as T-shirts, caps, and toys. This model appears to be effective in deepening the emotional involvement of consumers with the product,

Music Entertainment and Warner Music Group, which collectively control 50% of the market. In February, 2008, Amazon's music store passed Wal-Mart and became the number two paid download site behind Apple's iTunes. Why would any major record label sell music without DRM? One reason is that many believe current DRM practices severely limit the growth of paid digital downloading. EMI has much to gain by offering at least part of its catalog without DRM, and the other labels are following the Amazon effort closely to see if EMI's revenues expand, or contract, without DRM. EMI is hoping to expand the market for paid digital music that it owns.

Clearly consumers have accepted Apple's iPod and others' DRM compromise as basically fair—the restrictions constitute a reasonable speed bump in using copyrighted music for the price paid. Today, the number of people using legitimate music downloading sites such as

Apple's iTunes Music Store, Rhapsody, Yahoo, Amazon and Napster exceeded the number of users of P2P illegal services. Amazon's music store has attracted support from Pepsi and other marketers, shifting away from Apple's dominant control over online music. In 2008, about 10% of Amazon's customers are former Apple customers. While illegal sites still attract a majority of Internet consumers who are under the age of 25, by the time people are 30 and older, only 4% are still downloading music from illegal sites. Strengthened by the Supreme Court ruling against file-sharing sites, the last commercially viable U.S.-based file-sharing service, BearShare, collapsed under legal assault from the record label industry. BearShare settled allegations of copyright infringement for $30 million in 2006. However, pirate and offshore sites continue to fuel the P2P downloading phenomenon mostly among the under-twenty crowd.

■■■ **SOURCES:** "Amazon Gains Share of Shrinking Paid Music Market," by Saul Hansell, *New York Times*, April 17, 2008; "Music Industry, Souring on Apple, Embraces Amazon Service," by Jeff Leeds, *New York Times*, January 14, 2008; "Music Service From Amazon Takes on iTunes," by Ethan Smith and Vauhini Vara, *Wall Street Journal*, May 17, 2007; "Amazon to Sell Music Without Copy Protection," by Brad Stone and Jeff Leeds, *New York Times*, May 17, 2007; "Sharing Firm Settles Music Case," by Sarah McBride, *Wall Street Journal*, May 5, 2006; "CDs Recalled for Posing Risk to PCs," by Tom Zeller, *New York Times*, November 16, 2005.

overall footprint of the newspaper media. Offline print advertising at newspapers in 2008 is $42 billion, and declining at 10% a year. However, online newspaper ad revenues in 2008 are $3.2 billion and rising at 18% a year. In a nutshell this is the problem confronting newspapers: how to grow online revenues to offset the losses from print advertising. (Newspaper Association of America, 2008)

Audience Size and Growth

There are more than 10,000 online newspapers in the world. Online newspaper revenues are growing in the range of 18% per year According to Nielsen Online, the total Web audience for online newspapers in the United States during the first eight months of 2008 was typically between 65-70 million (Newspaper Association of America, 2008) (see **Figure 10.7** for a list of the top 10). The average online visitor stayed on the site for 20 minutes—about the same as visitors stay at Yahoo, the Web's most frequently visited content site. Online newspapers are the dominant local Web site: 62% of Internet users look for local news on a local newspaper Web site. Given this huge online newspaper audience, it is clear that the future of newspapers lies in the online market even as readership and subscriptions to the traditional print newspapers continues to decline at a steady pace.

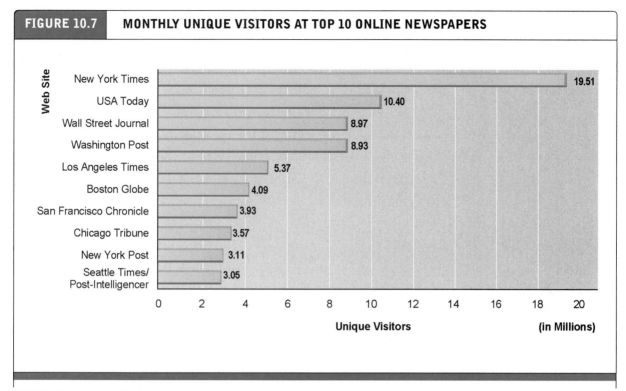

FIGURE 10.7 | **MONTHLY UNIQUE VISITORS AT TOP 10 ONLINE NEWSPAPERS**

SOURCES: Newspaper Association of America, 2008; authors' estimates.

Next to social networks, newspapers produce the largest online audiences of any media, and in that sense, contrary to popular opinion, are one of the most successful forms of online content to date. The Internet provides existing branded newspapers the opportunity to extend their brands to a new online audience, and also gives entrepreneurial firms the opportunity to offer services—such as classified job listings—on the Web that were previously delivered by newspapers. Online newspapers are the top choice for local news and information for Internet users in the United States.

While newspapers have done an excellent job at increasing their Web presence and audience, few have reached break-even operations, although some are close. Instead, online classified and advertising revenues have not kept pace with the fall in revenues from their traditional print editions. There are several reasons for this: increased competition from general portal sites moving into the content creation business, loss of classified ads to online portals, job sites, and free listing services such as Craigslist. Craigslist is reported to have wiped out $50 million in classified ads for San Francisco Chronicle.

The Web has provided an opportunity for newspapers to extend their offline brands, but at the same time it has given entrepreneurs the opportunity to take part of the newspapers' content—such as weather, classified ads, or current national and international news (but not local news).

Internet firms have emerged that threaten to take much of the classified ads business away from newspapers. Sites such as Monster, Craigslist, Autobytel, and CNET have moved aggressively to develop online classified ads for jobs, automobiles, and real estate, while others have developed deep and rich content in specialized areas such as automobiles, computers, cameras, and other hobbyist topics. Many of these firms have drained significant readership from newspapers for specialized, deep content; created nationwide marketplaces that did not exist before; and put a significant dent in local newspaper classified revenues. Classified revenues account for approximately 40% of newspaper revenue.

Online Newspaper Revenue Models and Results

The *New York Times*, the largest online general newspaper, has abandoned its Times Select subscription service that offered access to historical archives. The *Financial Times* is making more content available for free while retaining high-value content as a subscription service. And the *Wall Street Journal*, in competition with the *Financial Times*, is rumored to be considering planning the same strategy for the *Journal*.

Traditional newspapers make money by selling subscriptions for regular delivery and by selling advertising space, both fine-print classified ads as well as traditional ads placed on pages. Newspaper ads typically are paid for by local merchants selling goods and services in the area of a newspaper's circulation. Advertising accounts for 41% of newspaper revenues, up from 30% in 1980, and subscriptions account for 50% of revenue, with other miscellaneous income coming from printing legal notices. As a percentage of overall revenue, online revenues rarely exceed 10%, although online revenues are by far the faster growing. In general, newspapers are finding it difficult to replace offline readers with online readers simply because they cannot derive enough revenue from online readers. Advertisers are willing to pay much higher rates for print ads than online ads. The ratio of print revenue to online revenue per customer is roughly 3:1. For instance, a single offline subscriber, on average, generates $900 in revenue, while an online customer generates only $300 in revenue. Either the total number of online readers needs to increase dramatically relative to the offline audience, or newspapers need to figure out how to derive more revenue from each customer through increased advertising.

In response to declining or stagnant revenue growth, newspapers have sought alliances with one another and with online technology power houses such as Yahoo and Google in response to the challenge posed by pure-play online classified job sites, the newspaper industry has sought industry-wide alliances to develop competing sites and to move toward a value-added revenue model for this segment. To compete against Monster.com, the *New York Times*, Times-Mirror Company, the *Tribune*, and the *Washington Post* have created a territorial model called CareerBuilder.com, a job-listing site with 1.5 million jobs and 20 million monthly visitors. Gannett, McClatchy and Tribune Co., who collectively own hundreds of local newspapers, formed an alliance called Open Network to offer advertisers one-stop shopping for national (as opposed to local) newspaper advertising (Angwin, 2007). Yahoo and a consortium of seven newspaper chains representing 176 daily papers around the country have formed a partnership to share content, technology, and advertising.

The idea is to have newspapers place their ads on Yahoo's classified job site, and using HotJobs technology to run their own online career ads. Yahoo will in turn tag and index the newspapers' content so it can be found easily on the Web (Helft and Lohr, 2006). Google has created a system for auctioning ads for many of the largest newspaper companies, including Gannett, Tribune, the *New York Times*, Hearst, and others (Hansell, 2006).

Convergence

In terms of our schema of convergence—technology, content, and industry structure—the newspaper industry is rushing pell mell to a convergent model of news, content, and services. Soon newspapers will be offering social networking sites for local groups.

Technology The movement of published text to the Web was the first step toward technology platform convergence, but obviously this did not take advantage of the interactive features of the Web. The newspaper industry has been slow to invest in Internet technology, although this is changing as video, RSS feeds, blogs, and user feedback forums grow.

Content Online newspapers have transformed themselves into multimedia platforms with a variety of digital content. Four content changes are apparent: premium archived content, fine-grained search, videos reporting, and RSS feeds. **Figure 10.8** summarizes the transformation of online newspapers as digital outlets.

The online environment permits considerable extension to traditional newspaper content. For instance, newspapers can offer access to premium archive content by permitting users to search back issues. The inherent fine-grained search capability of the Internet platform increases ease of access to news and archival information for consumers. The most significant change in content is timeliness. The Internet frees newspapers from the time-bound character of paper and printing presses and allows for instant updates to breaking stories. In this sense, online newspapers can, for the first time, compete directly with television and radio for reporting breaking stories. Visit the online *New York Times* or *Wall Street Journal*, or a local online newspaper today, and you will see breaking news that is just a few minutes old. This is a sea change from traditional newspapers.

Industry Structure The newspaper industry is a mature industry that is ripe for further consolidation and expansion onto the Web. Historically, hundreds of local newspapers have been combined into larger national chains. Now the chains themselves need to be consolidated in order to create truly national advertising markets, and leverage their local readership (something Google, Microsoft, and Yahoo do not have). The problem has been finding deep-pocket media titans to purchase the papers and make hefty technology investments. Generally, the returns on newspaper investments do not meet the hurdle rates for most media titan firms. Instead, newspaper companies tend to buy one another, or are bought as play things for the idle and rich. The McClatchy Company purchased the second largest newspaper chain, Knight Ridder, in June 2006. In April 2007, Sam Zell, Chicago real estate magnate, purchased in the Tribune Company in an $8.2 billion deal, but only put up

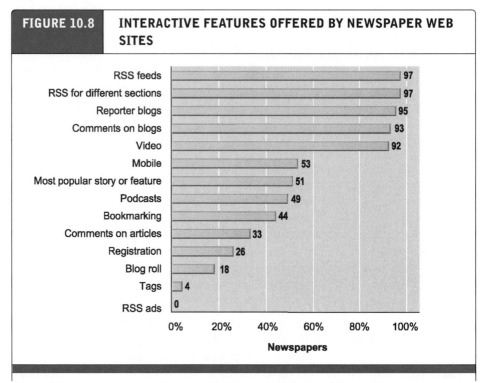

FIGURE 10.8

INTERACTIVE FEATURES OFFERED BY NEWSPAPER WEB SITES

This graph illustrates the adoption of interactive features on the Web sites of the top 100 newspapers as of August 2007.

SOURCES: Based on data from eMarketer, Inc. 2007d; The Bivings Group, 2007.

$315 million of his own money. The new company will take on $8 billion in debt, most of it owned by the employee pension plan. The only exception to this pattern has been the News Corporation (a multi-faceted media company which started out in the newspaper business but owns Fox television, and MySpace) purchase of Dow Jones, publisher of the *Wall Street Journal.*

Challenges: Disruptive Technologies

The online newspaper industry would appear at first glance to be a classic case of disruptive technology destroying a traditional business model based on physical products and physical distribution. This may turn out to be the case, but it cannot be the final assessment just yet. The industry is changing rapidly. There are significant assets that newspapers have—excellent content and writing, strong local readership, strong local advertising, and a fragmented but huge audience of nearly 100 million readers that rivals Yahoo, Google, and Microsoft's audience. Content is still king: the thousands of blogs in the blogospheres depend on traditional reporting media like television and newspapers to create the content which the blog writers can react to. Without the original content creators in the form of professional reporters and news organizations, the blogosphere would be a dull place. The people who read newspapers are very different from the people who visit YouTube: they are wealthier, more educated, and older. This is an ideal demographic for advertisers and a potential gold mine for newspapers. The online audience for newspapers will continue to grow in both sheer numbers and sophistication, demanding higher-quality online delivery and more services. The industry has made significant investments in technology for Web content creation and delivery. Many national newspapers have slowed down investment in online operations because they did not make a profit at first. The challenge is for newspaper owners and managers to invest heavily in the online editions even if they do not meet investment criteria at first. If the newspaper industry has a future, it will be online.

BOOKS: THE EVOLUTION OF E-BOOKS

In April 2000, Stephen King, one of America's most popular writers, published a novella called *Riding the Bullet*. This novella was only available as an e-book. King was the first major fiction writer to create an e-book-only volume of a new work. King's publisher, Simon & Schuster, arranged for sales online through online retailers such as Amazon. In the first day, there were 400,000 downloads, so many that Amazon's servers nearly crashed several times. More than 500,000 downloads occurred in the first week, for a price of $2.50 for a 66-page novella—about the same price per page as a standard King hardcover novel. While Amazon gave the book away for free in the first two weeks, when it began charging for the book, sales continued to be brisk. E-books have had a checkered history on the Internet, but they are still with us and growing rapidly. King's successful experiment with *Riding the Bullet* popularized the idea of e-books and introduced the prospect that e-books might be a commercially viable form of book publishing. The essential questions facing the book publishing industry are: If people are willing to buy physical books, would they also be willing to buy electronic versions of books? What kind of device would readers like to use when reading digital books? The next question is, "How much would they be willing to pay for an e-book?" And finally, "What changes to the concept of the book itself might be necessary to encourage people to buy e-books online?"

The Internet already has brought about significant changes in book sales and distribution, and is beginning to have an impact on the design, creation, and production of books. The book itself, and the reading experience, is starting to slowly morph into a truly different product. E-books, online print-on-demand books, and mixed media books are beginning to appear and are changing the concept of the traditional book from a passive form of entertainment to a more interactive form of engagement.

The modern book is not really very different from the first two-facing page, bound books that began to appear in seventeenth century Europe. The traditional book has a very simple, non-digital operating system: text appears left to right, pages are numbered, there is a hard front and back cover, and text pages are bound together by stitching or glue. In educational and reference books, there is an alphabetical index in the back of the book that permits direct access to the book's content. While these traditional books will be with us for many years given their portability, ease of use, and flexibility, a parallel new world of e-books is expected to emerge in the next five years.

E-books

E-books have had a glorious history of birth, death, re-birth, and death again. They're back, this time with powerful backers such as Amazon, Sony, Yahoo, Google, and Microsoft. In 2009, the idea is still receiving support from book readers, some publishers, and technology giants looking for the next "killer" gadget. The Google Book Search Project is scanning millions of books in large university libraries. When you click on a search result for a book from the Library Project, you will see basic bibliographic information about the book, and in many cases, a few sentences (called "snippets") showing your search term in context. If the book is out of copyright, you will be able to view and download the entire book. In all cases, you'll see links directing you to online bookstores where you can buy the book and libraries where you can borrow it. Google books will, of course, only be searchable with the Google search engine, and none of the scanned books will be compatible with similar efforts by Microsoft or members of the Open Content Alliance (see the case study at the end of Chapter 8).

Electronic books were around for many years before the Internet. In 1971, Michael Hart began Project Gutenberg at the Materials Research Lab at the University of Illinois. Hart began by typing in the Declaration of Independence, and proceeded to put more than 2,000 classic books online at the University's Computer Center. The books are all in ASCII plain text without traditional book fonts or formatting. While not a joy to read, they were free. In 1990, Voyager Company, a New York-based media company, began putting books such as *Jurassic Park* and *Alice in Wonderland* on CDs. However, with the exception of encyclopedias and large reference texts, popular books on CDs never were a commercial success. They were expensive to produce and distribute, and appeared in the marketplace before most PC users had CD-ROM drives.

The development of the Internet and the Web, along with small, powerful handheld devices has greatly changed the possibilities for e-books. The Web offered publishers much lower distribution costs (each "copy" on the Web can be downloaded for almost no cost), and unlike the early computer-based e-books, all the formatting, fonts, and colors used by publishers in high-quality books could be preserved when Adobe's Portable Document Format (PDF) is used to create the text.

There are many different types of commercial e-books (see **Table 10.6**). The two most common e-books are Web-accessed or Web-downloadable. **Web-accessed e-books** are stored on the publisher's servers and purchasers pay a fee for reading the book on-screen; in some cases these e-books can also be printed by the individual user. The most successful Web-accessed e-books are online encyclopedias such as the abridged edition of the *Encyclopedia Britannica*, and open source encyclopedias like Wikipedia.com. CourseSmart is a new e-textbook service formed by the six largest publishers of textbooks in the world. With CourseSmart, college students can subscribe to online textbooks for half the price of purchasing a physical textbook (including this book!). The book can be access from any Internet connected computer, anywhere, anytime. Students can also print chapters.

Web-downloadable e-books are a more user-friendly e-book that can be downloaded from the Web, stored as a file on the client PC, and in many cases

Web-accessed e-book
an e-book stored on a publisher's server that consumers access and read on the Web

Web-downloadable e-book
an e-book that can be downloaded from the Web, stored as a file on the client PC, and perhaps even printed

TABLE 10.6	TYPES OF E-BOOKS
E-BOOK TYPE	**DESCRIPTION**
Web-accessed e-books	E-book remains on publisher's Web site and is read only on the site. Purchasers pay a subscription fee for access.
Web-downloadable e-books	Contents of e-book can be downloaded to client PC for reading. Printing may or may not be possible. Purchaser pays for initial download and reading. Subsequent use may be metered or free.
Dedicated e-book reader	Contents of e-book can be downloaded only to dedicated hardware device either directly connected to the Web or through a PC connection.
General-purpose PDA reader	Contents of e-book can be downloaded from the Web to a general-purpose handheld personal digital assistant (PDA) such as an iPhone or Palm Pilot.
Print-on-demand books	Contents of a book are stored on a Web server; they can be downloaded on demand for local printing and even binding.

printed, although some e-books have security locks that prevent printing. The largest library of downloadable e-books is NetLibrary, claiming 150,000 e-books in 2008, followed by Questia's e-book collection of approximately 67,000 complete books. Access to these electronic libraries is only available through participating libraries and universities.

Dedicated e-book readers are a much less-common form of e-book even though they have received enormous publicity. **Dedicated e-book readers** are single-purpose devices that have proprietary operating systems that can download from the Web and read proprietary formatted files created for those devices. Each dedicated reader makes available to customers several thousand generally popular titles. Franklin Electronic Publisher's eBookMan was one of the first dedicated e-book readers. Prices ranged from a low of $129 to a high of $199 retail. The product was discontinued in 2001 after sales failed to reach expectations. Other players have since stepped up to the plate. Sony has brought back the concept of a mobile e-book reader in 2007 with its Sony Reader, a sleek, 9-ounce, half-inch thin reader about the size of a paperback book with an impressive six-inch display that uses an electronic ink that appears very much like ordinary ink on paper. The Sony Reader can hold 160 books. Amazon, the world's largest book retailer, has joined the fray with its Kindle, which includes a 10-ounce 6-inch screen. The Kindle uses electronic ink technology, and is connected to Sprint's EVDO wireless network, allowing users to purchase e-books directly from Amazon's Kindle Store, and download the books to the Kindle reader in real time. The Kindle Store The Kindle store has over 100,000 titles, and the Kindle reader can store about 200 titles. In 2008 the Kindle is the largest selling dedicated e-book reader.

dedicated e-book reader
a single-purpose device with a proprietary operating system that can download from the Web and read proprietary formatted files created for that device

An exciting new development in 2008 is the use of smartphones like iPhone and Blackberry as e-book devices. For instance, the New York Times has developed an iPhone App that displays the current New York Times newspaper on the iPhone. The print has been specially designed for the iPhone and is more readable than the Times regular online edition. Sales of dedicated e-book readers were only 200,000 in 2007, but are expanding to 1 million units in 2008, and are expected to hit 18 milion units in 2012 (a 160% CAGR).

print-on-demand book
custom-published book

Print-on-demand books are less well known, but arguably the largest form of electronic publishing. Sometimes called "custom publishing," print-on-demand books are usually professional or educational titles that are stored on mainframe storage devices ready for printing in small print runs on demand. For instance, most college publishers have a "custom book" program that allows professors to put together digitally stored chapters from many different books, along with articles from scholarly journals, and to publish a small print run of, say, 400 books for a single class. Generally, these books are no less costly to produce or purchase, but they have the advantage of flexible content that can be changed to meet the specific needs of users. "Print on demand" books is also a euphemism for vanity press books, or self-published books on the Internet. There is a lively market for self-published books on the Internet, although it is difficult to identify the precise size of this market, or who is paying the money for publishing—the writer or the reader.

Book Audience Size and Growth

In 2009, consumers will spend about $59 billion for the purchase of 3.2 billion books: $27 billion on consumer trade books, and $25 billion for professional, scholarly, and higher education textbooks (U.S. Census Bureau, 2008).

Publishing the same number of titles and raising prices, publishers have kept revenues about even with inflation. Unlike newspapers, the number of book readers has been constant and is anchored in the large, over-40-years-of-age demographic. Per capita spending for trade books was about $106 in 2008, higher than video games ($93), and in-theater movies and other box office events ($12). In other words, books are a substantial element in the consumer's time and revenue content budgets, and for professional and educational titles, book publishing is growing more than twice as fast as the general U.S. economy (U.S. Census Bureau, 2008).

Unlike reading newspapers, reading books on the Internet (or any electronic device) is not a popular activity. Only 3% of Internet users report reading books online (eMarketer, 2008). Online e-book sales—both reading online and downloading e-books for offline reading—generated over $500 million in 2008. This means that, currently, e-books of any kind are a tiny share of the $59 billion annual consumption of books—less than one percent! E-book sales are nevertheless the fastest-growing delivery platform for text content: 45% annual growth in revenues since 2004. Buying physical books online is one of the most popular activities of Internet users. The huge online audience for published books has had a significant impact on the book distribution and sales business, and represents an extraordinary opportunity to introduce new electronic editions of books in the future. It raises a few questions: Will people pay for e-books, and how much will e-book sales grow? Potentially, the market for online e-books could become large if consumers were willing to read electronic editions of books.

Figure 10.9 describes the estimated future growth of e-book sales on the Web. There is no single catalog of e-books, and therefore it is difficult to estimate the total number of new e-book titles each year. However, it is likely that between 2,000 and 3,000 new commercial e-book titles will be published in 2009, not counting several thousand self-published e-books.

Content: Advantages and Disadvantages of E-books

Stephen Riggio, CEO of Barnes & Noble, the world's largest bookseller, when asked about the future of e-books, said, "It's a very tiny, tiny market. The book is a perfect technology. If it were invented today, it would be revolutionary. It's user-friendly; it's portable. Books are relatively inexpensive. They have value as physical objects; they last a lifetime." (Jaworowski, 2006). Nevertheless, e-books offer many advantages compared to traditional published works. Among these are:

- Reduced transaction costs for the user via instant downloads

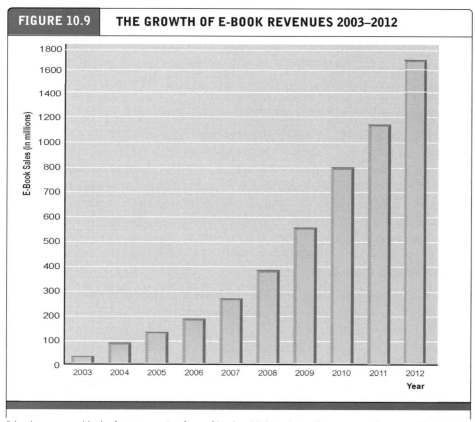

| FIGURE 10.9 | THE GROWTH OF E-BOOK REVENUES 2003–2012 |

E-books are arguably the fastest-growing form of book publishing, but still represent a tiny part of the book publishing industry.

SOURCE: Association of American Publishers, 2008; eMarketer, Inc., 2007f; authors' estimates.

- Increased accessibility to entire libraries from the home or office
- Searchable text
- Easy integration of e-book text with new text by cutting and pasting
- Modularization of the book's content down to the sentence and word level
- Ease in updating
- Lower production and distribution costs
- Longer lasting
- Increased opportunities for writers to publish
- Increased availability of out-of-print books and increased value of book archives
- Reduced cost of library functions, further democratizing access to books
- Reduced retail costs for the consumer
- Reduced weight for book bags

While this is a formidable list of advantages, e-books also have many disadvantages that have reduced their market acceptance. Among the most important disadvantages of e-books are:

- Require expensive and complex electronic devices to use
- Less portability than print books
- Reduced quality of on-screen print, making them more difficult to read
- Multiple competing standards and formats
- Uncertain business models
- Copyright management and royalty issues with authors

As one commentator noted, reading an e-book is just like reading a regular book except that it requires an expensive machine, it is not portable, and it is difficult to read. Worse, you need to replace batteries, and they are hard to read at the beach. However, the most recent devices from Sony and Amazon have enough battery power to read several books and are easily read at the beach (under an umbrella). Even better, the Kindle and the iPhone can download hundreds of books from the wireless Web even at the beach.

E-book Industry Revenue Models

The e-book industry is composed of intermediary retailers, traditional publishers, technology developers, and vanity presses. Some of the key players in the new e-book industry are listed in **Table 10.7**. Together, these players have pursued a wide variety of business models and developed many alliances in a collective effort to move text onto the computer screen.

In the traditional commercial book business model, publishers pay authors advances against earnings to write books. Publishers provide editorial, marketing, and sales expertise, and then sell these works to national distributors or directly to large retail book chains. In the case of noncommercial books, authors pay so-called vanity presses to publish and sell their books, receiving very little if any editorial or market-

TABLE 10.7	EXAMPLE E-BOOK INDUSTRY FIRMS
COMPANY	**E-BOOK ACTIVITIES**
Distributors	
Amazon	Largest online general retailer of books; creator of the Kindle e-book reader
Barnesandnoble.com	General audience online retailer of books and publisher of e-books.
NetLibrary	Second largest online e-library, now owned by Online Computer Library Center (50,000 volumes).
Questia	Largest online research library and e-book site by subscription (60,000 volumes).
Ebrary	Online research library by subscription using proprietary reader for PCs.
Fictionwise	Distributor of multi-platform e-books.
Adobe eBook Store	Online sales of e-books demonstrating the Acrobat platform.
Technology Developers	
Adobe Systems Inc.	Owners of Acrobat and PDF file format for e-book display on PC, CRT, and LCD screens
InterTrust Technologies	DRM software tools
Microsoft	Microsoft Reader software for e-book display on PDAs and PCs; supporter of Open eBook standard
Palm	PDA hardware and operating system; can be used for e-books
Sony	Manufacturer of e-book readers
MobiPocket	French company; creator of universal reader for PDAs and digital rights management software for publishers; secure and encrypted books based on serial number of handheld devices
Traditional Publishers	
Pearson PLC	Developing new models of online educational e-books
Thomson Learning	Educational publisher that plans to derive 50% of its revenue from e-materials by 2010
Random House	Largest trade book publisher; has developed a separate division to develop e-book titles
CourseSmart	Consortium of the six largest textbook publishers offering thousands of e-textbooks to college students at half price
Vanity e-Presses (on-demand publishers)	
Xlibris (Random House)	Self-publishing online
Ebooks-online	Online sales and publishing
Iuniverse	Self-publishing online
GreatUnpublished	Self-publishing online
Authorhouse	Self-publishing online

ing assistance. The development of e-books has brought about several changes in this traditional model.

The primary consumer e-book revenue model is pay-for-download, a model that involves traditional publishers and authors creating electronic editions of books, and publishers selling these works in their entirety through new online bookstore intermediaries such as Barnesandnoble.com and Amazon. E-books have not changed the traditional revenue model significantly. In general, publishers have not begun to sell e-books directly to the online audience simply because publishers have chosen not to develop these online capabilities, although in the future they could. Barnesandnoble.com is a special case. It occasionally acts as a publisher by commissioning new e-works; at the same time it is a retailer of those e-works.

A second e-book revenue model involves the licensing of entire e-libraries of content. This market involves major institutional customers like public and academic libraries, and corporate libraries. Licensing is similar to a subscription model; users pay either a monthly subscription fee or a flat fee for annual access to hundreds of titles. The licensing model is exemplified by NetLibrary. NetLibrary was the first large-scale experiment that involved the licensing of entire electronic libraries to universities and colleges. Many public libraries have begun to reach out to their Internet-enabled users, and greatly expand their local reach by offering e-books. For instance, New York City Public Library has over 3,000 electronic titles; the King County Library in Washington has over 8,500 online titles.

Convergence

The publishing industry is making very uneven progress toward media convergence in terms of technology platform, content, and industry structure. In the past, progress was slowed by poor business models and lack of financial resources. Today, it is slowed by greed and competition among technology firms, each of which is seeking to develop a proprietary solution to the problem of getting books online with a viable business model.

Technology One would think that it would be a simple matter to merge the world of text and books with that of the Internet and the Web, which originally were both text-based media. However, four technology-based difficulties have slowed this aspect of convergence: poor computer screen resolution, the lack of portable reader devices that can compete with the portability of the traditional book, the absence of a powerful DRM technology that can protect the copyrights of digital works, and the lack of standards to define cross-platform e-books.

One solution for the portability of e-books are smart phones like the iPhone and Blackberry. However, the screens on current smart phones and handheld computers are still too small for comfortable text reading. The printed page has a resolution of 1,200 dots per inch compared to computer displays with resolutions of about 72 to 96 dots per inch. Display of text on standard PC screens also produces eyestrain because of low resolution. Microsoft's ClearType and Adobe's CoolType represent two attempts to remedy this issue. Both are **sub-pixel display technologies** that enhance resolution by dividing the screen into sub-pixels and filling in sub-pixels with grey color to form a more uniform image of each letter. Horizontal resolution is increased by about 30% over traditional display software. ClearType and CoolType can be downloaded for free from Microsoft and Adobe Web sites. Other solutions involve doing away with the LCD screen and using elec-

sub-pixel display technologies

technologies that help enhance resolution of e-book reader display screens tronic paper displays (EPDs) and electronic ink technology developed at MIT in the late 1990s. An EPD looks like paper in appearance but is in fact an ultra-thin plastic film that encapsulates electronically charged particles that change from black to white in response to electronic signals. EPD gives the viewer the experience of reading from paper, while having the power of updatable information. EPDs have very low power consumption, are viewable in sunlight, and are very rugged (they don't break on dropping). The Sony Reader uses EPD technology.

As noted previously, several technology firms have developed **digital rights management (DRM)**, server software that helps prevent illegal distribution of paid content over the Web. Adobe's Acrobat comes with limited DRM software that can control printing and copying of downloaded matter. Intertrust is another industry leader in this field. Hackers can break most of these DRM technologies, however, and therefore, many publishing firms have been reluctant to publish works on the Web. MobiPocket has developed DRM software that encrypts content and provides a separate key for each work purchased that is based on the serial number of the PDA. This means the content can be played on only that device, it may not be copied for use on other devices, and it may be restricted in terms of the number of playbacks permitted (Mobipocket.com, 2007).

digital rights management (DRM) software
server software that helps prevent illegal distribution of paid content over the Web

Table 10.8 describes the current leading standards for e-books. The most widely adopted standard is the Adobe Acrobat PDF file format. Tens of millions of computer users have downloaded this file-formatting software. It preserves fonts, formatting, and graphics information and can be used on almost any computer including Macintosh, Unix-based, and PCs. Open eBook (OEB) is an emerging industry-formatting standard that is supported by publishers and software firms such as Microsoft. OEB provides a specification for representing the content of e-books, and is based on HTML and XML, making it universal across all platforms and types of screens. Currently, OEB supports only minimal formatting and is best for simple text, not complex graphics combined with text.

ONIX (Online Information Exchange) is an industry standard for transmitting information about books, or "meta data." For instance, a book jacket may contain review comments, a description of contents, a picture of the author, and an author biography. Currently, there is no way to communicate this information electronically from the publisher to the online bookstore that wants to display this meta data on a Web page. ONIX is an XML-based set of approximately 200 tags (e.g., < PublisherName > Scribner's < /PublisherName >) that can easily be read and communicated to book distributors and retailers (Editeur.org, 2007; Book Industry Study Group, 2007).

Content E-books today have made little progress toward content convergence. Most e-books contain only text and graphics, and often are simply PDF versions of files sent to the printers to run the physical presses. E-books can be placed along a continuum of transformation (and cost). E-books currently are in the media integration stage where text is being reformatted for electronic display. This is a low-cost beginning, allowing publishers to focus their attention and budgets on building their online distribution networks. However, some firms are beginning to experiment with more interactive experiences that will transform e-books into

TABLE 10.8	STANDARDS FOR E-BOOKS
E-BOOK STANDARD/SOFTWARE	**DESCRIPTION**
Screen Display	
Microsoft Reader "Clear Type"	Free software for improving LCD text display through sub-pixel rendering on Microsoft CE PDA devices.
Adobe CoolType	Free software for improving LCD text display through sub-pixel rendering on PDAs.
E-Ink	Electronic ink display for LCDs.
Formats	
Open eBook (OEB and OEB.LIT)	Microsoft-supported industry group to define e-book formatting. OEB.LIT adds DRM capabilities.
Adobe Portable Document Format (PDF)	Adobe's free viewer software for PC and PDA screen display of rich text, complex fonts, and formatting. Works best on PC screens. New versions contain DRM capabilities.
TK3 (NightKitchen)	CRT and LCD display of text, images, sounds, and video.
MobiPocket	Proprietary format that plays on all handheld devices.
Book Industry Product Description	
ONIX	Universal, international industry standard for describing book products and contents based on XML.

multimedia events containing lectures, speeches, interviews with the authors, online polls and quizzes, online updates of content, and videos to support the experience (see *Insight on Society: The Future of Books*).

Industry Structure Unlike the recorded music industry, the book industry has not been transformed by the Internet. However, it is being challenged by Google and Microsoft, who both want to index copyrighted books and make portions ("snippets" determined by Google) available online; by college students, their parents, and Congress, who want lower prices for textbooks; by very large distributors like Barnes & Noble, who want to move into actual publishing with very low-cost books; to a lesser extent by user-generated content in the form of blogs and self-published books; and by slow growth in physical book sales. The book publishing industry and the creation, production, and distribution of e-books is still dominated by a few titans, with the level of industry concentration increasing as large media companies such as Bertelsmann (Random House), and large text publishing companies, such as Pearson, Thomson, and McGraw Hill, absorb smaller presses. Nevertheless, the Internet has created many new opportu-

INSIGHT ON SOCIETY

THE FUTURE OF BOOKS

What do you think of when you think about what a "book" is, or looks like? Chances are you still think of the traditional "book," printed on paper, and bound with a hard or soft cover, with a finite beginning, middle and end. However, today the traditional notions about what constitutes a "book" are being exploded, as "books" take on varying degrees of forms and formats.

For instance, you've read in this chapter about different types of e-books. You can read a book on a Kindle, Sony Reader, on an iPhone, or an iPod. However, these are often traditional books just being delivered on a new format. Taking e-books one step further, say out to 2012, they most likely will evolve into much richer learning environments with substantial audio, video, and community participation than is true of today's text-only e-books. You can see the potential future of the e-book by visiting the Wall Street Journal Web site. There you will one of the world's most successful business publications integrate text with video, reporter blogs, user commentary, up-to-the-minute reporting, interviews, and podcasts. If newspapers can look like this, why can't online books?

But what about the form of the book itself? Why, for instance, should a book have just a single author or a few authors? Why should books be read alone? Sagas-the ancient lengthy stories of an entire people shared through an oral tradition-had multiple authors. It is possible on the Internet to have a community of readers contribute to both the authorship of the online e-book and the experience of reading the book. You can call it 'social publishing' or 'social writing.' Wikipedia, for instance, is a constantly updated online "e-book" encyclopedia written by thousands of contributors. Wikibooks,

its less well-known cousin, brings the wiki movement to the creation of textbooks. David Carr, a journalist for the New York Times, and Simon and Schuster, have collaborated to create TheNightoftheGun.com, a Web site that is part and parcel of Carr's memoir, The Night of the Gun. CAs Carr created his work, he developed a database of content, including hundreds of hours of recorded interviews, documents, reports, letters, legal communications, photos, and keepsakes. The Web site offers a fully immersive multimedia experience where the story is in the hands of the reader.

Unigo.com offers another take on the future of books. If you're like most college students, when you began to think about applying to college, probably one of the first places you turned to for information was a traditional college guide book, like those published by The Princeton Review, Peterson's Fiske, or U.S. News and World Report, or perhaps "The Insider's Guide to Colleges" by the staff of the Yale Daily News. But even books hundreds of pages long are limited in terms of the volume and type of information they can provide about the thousands of different colleges across the country. For Jordan Goldman, a 26-year-old recent Wesleyan graduate, this was a problem looking for a solution; and his solution is one that may threaten the publishing industry's stranglehold on the delivery of college information via traditionally published books.

What Goldman envisioned, and launched in September 2008, with the backing of Frank Sica, a former president of Soros Private Funds Management, is Unigo.com, a free, advertising-support site that offers a student-generated guide to North American colleges. The site features brief editorial overviews of each of the colleges featured, but the

(continued)

real meat is furnished by students in the form of responses to essay-based questionnaires, photos, videos, and uploaded writing samples. As of launch, over 30,000 individual bits of content had been submitted. At Davidson College, about 230 current students (1/8th of the student body) had submitted photos, reviews and video. As one person noted, its one thing to read in a guidebook that a school sits on a lake, and another to look at a video and see students hanging out in beautiful surroundings.

Every student who joins Unigo has a user profile, and users can search the site for material submitted by those who they believe might be similar to themselves. For instance, a user can search for reviews of Harvard by English majors, and contact students who submitted material with follow-up questions. Users can also search for schools by size, setting, region, selectivity and tuition. And branching into the social network space, the My Unigo section of the site allows users to organize all of the site's content according to their personal interests, and also add their own content.

As Goldman notes: "That the best resource for a four-year, $200,000 decision are these books - with no photos, no videos, no interactivity, only three-to-five pages per school on average, fully updated usually once every several years - just doesn't make the grade." He and Unigo's backers think their "grass-roots" movement to wrest control over the dissemination of information about colleges from traditional publishers will revolutionize the way students decide about which school to attend.

As we see throughout this chapter, the Internet is changing the consumer's sense of entertainment and even education. Heightened expectations for participation, involvement, engagement, and self-control are driving consumers toward Web sites and content providers that can provide these kinds of experiences, creating new opportunities for innovative publishers.

■■■ **SOURCES:** "The Unigo Blog", Unigoblog.wordpress.com, September 24, 2008; "About This Site," Nightofthegun.com, September 24, 2008; "The Tell-All Campus Tour," by Jonathan Dee, *New York Times*, September 21, 2008; "Envisioning the Next Chapter for Electronic Books," by Brad Stone, *New York Times*, September 7, 2007; "An Entire Bookshelf, in Your Hands," by Peter Wayner, *New York Times*, August 9, 2007.

nities for authors, publishers, distributors, and specialized book retailers. Entrepreneurial start-up firms such as NetLibrary demonstrated that a market existed for inexpensive digital libraries. Entrepreneurial online book distributors from Amazon and Barnesandnoble.com to much smaller, specialized topic, boutique online distributors have demonstrated a huge marketplace for online distribution of traditional books. Online book distributors such as Barnesandnoble.com have commissioned new e-book titles and moved into publishing. Authors have published works directly to the public without the intervention of publishers in the blogosphere, as well as through online vanity presses that charge authors for the privilege of publishing their works. The open source movement has created online encyclopedias like Wikipedia that offer incredible depth (but also occasional erroneous and misleading entries). Publishers such as Random House have simultaneously moved into direct distribution to the public of selected works (while continuing to utilize online distributors such as Amazon). Technology providers such as Adobe have begun limited distribution of e-books, and Palm has purchased the e-book assets of Peanutpress and begun selling e-books directly to the public. In this sense, the industry has become much more diverse than in the past, including hardware and software makers who have an interest in the success of e-books.

E-commerce in Action: CNET Networks, Inc. examines how one company, CNET Networks, Inc. has evolved from a television production company into a Web-based publishing firm, and the issues it has faced in the process.

E-COMMERCE IN ACTION

CNET NETWORKS, INC.

CNET Networks Inc. began as a television production company in 1992. In 1995, its first show, CNET Central, a half-hour weekly magazine-format program devoted to exploring the world of information technology and the Internet, debuted on USA Networks. CNET then repurposed this content and expanded its core skill set to the Web, and in 1995 launched CNET.com as the Web's largest resource on information technology products. The content was free for Web users, and the site generated revenues from advertising. The CNET.com site soon included reviews of products, pricing, vendors, and technology news. By 2001, after many acquisitions, CNET Networks had transformed itself into an Internet giant, one of the top 10 Web sites. In 2008, CNET Networks (a collection of several sites) is the world's ninth largest Internet network with over 200 million unique visitors worldwide each month (including 54 million unique visitors in the United States).

The Vision

CNET's mission is to be an interactive media company that builds brands for people and the things they are passionate about, such as gaming, music, entertainment, technology, business, food, and parenting. Founded in 1992, CNET Networks has a strong presence in the United States, Asia, and Europe. CNET started in a narrower niche of providing online information and forums for IT and technology professionals. It has since expanded into a much more general consumer base but still with a focus on content and niche brands.

CNET is a uniquely Internet content company because it combines elements of news, in-depth magazine style reporting, comparative shopping and reviews, video, and community services. In essence, CNET is a content company that rapidly exploited opportunities on the Internet for brand enhancement and extension. It is one of the first Internet content companies to have built a "successful" content business based on advertising revenues as opposed to subscriptions.

For the most part, content on CNET networks properties is advertiser supported and free to the user. CNET focuses on deep, rich content in a number of niche vertical markets. As we have seen throughout this chapter, the key to successful advertising and sales on Internet content sites is deep, rich, niche content targeted to narrow markets. CNET has been very successful in drawing a wealthy, educated, young, and technology-aware audience to its sites, making them ideal for advertisers in the tech marketplace. And who isn't in the tech marketplace for iPhones, Blackberrys, PCs, Macs, and cell phones?

CNET used to have a print publishing segment that published *Computer Shopper* magazine, a comparison shopping tabloid. However, it sold *Computer Shopper* in February 2006. CNET also sold a photo site called Webshots in 2006. This leaves an expanding stable of the following Internet brands:

- CNET focuses on technology and consumer electronics
- Gamespot provides gamers game information for consoles and PCs
- TV.com provides TV show summaries, guides, news, and biographies
- MP3.com is a music site that caters to independent musicians looking for an audience
- FilmSpot, launched in 2006, is an online movie resource featuring reviews, summaries, trailers, news, and photos
- TechRepublic provides information, articles, and reviews for IT professionals
- ZDNet focuses on business technologies and is aimed at technology and system managers
- BNET, launched in 2007, offers practical tools and reports for business managers
- CNETTV, launched in 2007, provides a collection of videos and blogs, with a focus on consumer electronics
- Urbanbaby is aimed at new and expectant mothers, providing child care and career information
- Chow.com is a food and drink Web site catering to young professionals

CNET has made an aggressive effort to move its brands to expanding overseas markets, especially in China. The company acquired OnlyLady, a fashion Web site in Shanghai, as well as extending its English-named brands throughout China, and operates in nine countries. In 2006, it purchased Xcar, a leading Chinese site aimed at car purchasers. In most of these efforts CNET has attempted to add Web 2.0 elements to all its branded sites by including more video, user-generated content, blogs, and podcasts.

Financial Analysis

Since 2000, CNET has operated with occasionally significant losses. In 2002, for instance, it sustained a $361 million loss on $183 million in revenue, but in 2004, it finally showed a positive net income of $1.8 million. Since then, it earned $19 million in 2005, then dropped down to around $7 million in 2006, and then rebounded strongly in 2007 with $176 million in net income due to an extraordinary tax benefit. (see **Table 10.9**). Revenues grew modestly by 10% in 2007, but so did costs. Sales and marketing shot up by 14% and general and administrative costs went up by the same amount, 10%. When a company is acquiring and disposing of divisions and entire firms, revenues can sink as divisions are sold off and new revenues are not yet being produced by new investments.

TABLE 10.9	**CNET NETWORK'S CONSOLIDATED STATEMENTS OF OPERATIONS AND SUMMARY BALANCE SHEET DATA, 2005–2007**

CONSOLIDATED STATEMENTS OF OPERATIONS (in thousands)

For the fiscal year ended December 31,	2007	2006	2005
Revenue	405,895	$369,259	$319,765
Cost of revenues	170,595	159,881	144,062
Gross profit	235,300	209,378	175,703
Gross Margin	58%	57%	55%
Operating expenses			
Sales and marketing	107,636	94,445	76,783
General and administrative	67,112	61,771	50,113
Stock option investigation	8,438	13,745	—
Depreciation	27,050	21,491	16,706
Amortization of intangible assets	9,177	7,622	6,001
Asset impairments	—	2,793	1,613
Total operating expenses	390,008	361,748	295,278
Operating income (loss)	15,887	7,511	24,487
Operating margin	4%	2%	8%
Other income (expenses)			
Realized gains on privately held investments	2,190	558	1,913
Impairments of privately held investments	—	—	(2,083)
Interest income	3,680	4,871	1,989
Interest expense	(5,702)	(5,023)	(3,086)
Other, net	1,470	(596)	19
Total non-operating income (expense)	1,638	(190)	(1,248)
Income before income taxes	17,525	7,321	23,239
Income tax expense (benefit)	(178,718)	1,334	(183)
Income from continuing operations	196,243	5,987	23,422
Loss from discontinued operations	(19,768)	(849)	(3,839)
Net income	176,475	6,836	19,583
Net margin	43%	2%	6%

SUMMARY BALANCE SHEET DATA
(in thousands)

At December 31,	2007	2006	2005
Assets			
Cash and cash equivalents	88,626	$31,327	$55,895
Investments in marketable debt securities	18,296	30,372	41,591
Accounts receivable	97,122	89,265	85,312
Deferred tax asset	23,745	141	—
Other current assets	12,758	10,371	14,337
Total current assets	240,547	161,476	197,135
Investments in marketable debt securities	510	13,915	12,432
Restricted cash	1,417	2,200	2,248
Property and equipment, net	72,547	72,625	72,000
Other assets	16,677	15,116	15,000
Deferred tax asset, long-term	193,549	438	—
Intangible assets, net	28,998	34,978	—
Goodwill	84,039	133,059	129,658
Total assets	638,284	433,807	455,566
Liabilities			
Current liabilities	79,729	164,240	63,122
Long term debt and other liabilities	55,108	4,498	139,908
Stockholders' equity	498,983	264,343	252,536

SOURCE: CNET Networks, Inc., 2007.

A brief look at CNET's balance sheet shows that at December 31, 2007, CNET had current assets of about $240 million and current liabilities of $80 million. This is a healthy balance sheet with a 3:1 ratio of assets to liabilities, suggesting the company was poised either to buy more web properties, or be acquired by another suitor who would find the assets attractive.

In May 2008, CBS bought CNET for $1.8 billion in cash (sic), paying $11 a share, about 45% higher than the stock market price. CBS has very little Internet audience share, largely restricted to its sports site CBSSports.com. Leslie Moonves, CEO of CBS, said "There are very few oppotunities to acquire a profitable, growing, well-managed Internet company like CNET Networks. Together CBS and CNET Networks will have additional significant exposure to the fastest growing advertising sector and can accelerate our growth through a number of new content, promotion, and advertising initiatives." Moonves hopes to add two percentage points to CNET's revenue and profit growth. Wall Street lowered its value of CBS stock on the announcement.

Strategic Analysis—Business Strategy

CNET and CBS management is pursuing a variety of strategies to improve its results going forward in 2009. Over the last five years, CNET has very deftly moved to build a huge international online audience, develop shopping services for this audience, build an advertising platform to this audience, and create deep, rich content. More importantly, it has tried to diversify out of the niche technology market and into areas of broader interest to consumers like games, TV, music, film, business and management, and cuisine (Chow.com).

CNET is also rapidly expanding its operations in foreign markets. Currently, it operates Web properties in nine countries and markets a multilingual database containing hundreds of thousands of products (CNET Data Services Division). CNET has focused its overseas growth efforts in China where it now operates 20 different Internet properties. CNET expanded into B2B commerce with its ChannelOnline Web site, which connects value added resellers (VARs) with potential commercial customers looking for providers (a Net marketplace e-procurement service). CNET has also expanded into radio programming with its launch of CNET Radio, an AM station devoted to technical topics, and CNET TV. In all these efforts, CNET has attempted to build in all the features found in the Web 2.0 experience, including user-generated content.

Strategic Analysis—Competition

CNET competes against a variety of content providers that focus on the information technology marketplace as well as other general content providers that also provide information technology news stories such as the *Wall Street Journal*, *PC World*, *Games Magazine*, and many others. CNET's main competitors are United Business Media, International Data Group, Internet.com, and Ziff-Davis Media. Each of these competitors has large magazine and newsletter publications (e.g., *Computerworld* and *Information Week*) that have large technology-oriented Internet audiences as well. Because content can be easily discovered and searched on the Internet through comprehensive search engines, CNET does not have a monopoly on information technology content, product data, or pricing information. CNET's position is weakened by the fact that it does not have a successful offline magazine or newsletter aimed at the professional information technology audience.

Strategic Analysis—Technology

Because CNET operates so many different Web sites, some acquired concurrently, it experienced large costs in simply updating and redesigning each Web site, and there was poor coordination among Web sites. In 2001, the company launched an effort to develop a global standardized Web site delivery platform, and by 2005 it had developed a scalable global content platform that allows it to feed content to all its different properties. By 2008, this platform has been able to achieve real economies of scale as it is used to support the nine major Web sites operated by CNET. This has eliminated many costs associated with site maintenance, permits the company to introduce new technologies worldwide at a single time, and increases the coordination of advertising data across many sites worldwide.

Strategic Analysis—Social and Legal Challenges

CNET faces no serious social and legal challenges. Changes in national policy on sales tax obviously will impair all e-commerce sites, including CNET. Following the acquisition of Ziff-Davis Inc., CNET inherited several shareholder and employee lawsuits that followed the decline in Ziff-Davis Inc. stock. These suits allege misrepresentation of financial condition and breach of fiduciary duty by Ziff-Davis Inc. management. If these suits are successful, they would have a small but material effect on CNET's financial condition. In 2004, CNET was sued by a group of social activists claiming that CNET, Google, MSN, and other search engines were violating California state law that prohibits Internet gambling by returning search results that identify gambling sites. CNET continues to be the subject of investor lawsuits related to its IPO in 2000.

Future Prospects

The question is: how does the merger of CNET and CBS add value to either company? Does CBS with very little Internet advertising experience really gain a significant advertising platform, or is it just purchasing eyeballs based on CNET content, and which it can sell to advertisers? Clearly, CBS itself is situated in the broadcast television industry which has been suffering flat revenue growth since 2006 due to the movement of ad dollars to the Internet. CNET gives CBS an opportunity to expand its Internet platform. But CNET itself has not shown strong growth in either revenue or profits compared to other Internet properties like Yahoo or Amazon, or YouTube, and MySpace. CBS has attached itself to a slow moving star. Yet there are potential synergies in this merger. CBS news stars like Katie Couric are starting to appear on CNET Web pages. CNET reporters are contributing content to CBS news technology coverage programs. CBS now uses its news and commentary shows like the CBS Early Show to drive visitors to CNET sites. While synergy does not have a good reputation in this business era, the CNET-CBS merger could be an exception to the rule.

How are sites based on lifestyle, technology, gaming, video, and music all related to one another? The answer is unclear. While it is laudable that CNET management has expanded beyond its narrow base, it has continued to pursue a niche strategy and become a kind of conglomerate of niches. Niches generally do not become big winners, by definition, and the upside growth is problematic. Because their content is so different, there are few synergies among these companies, and no reason for them to be lumped into a single company except for the fact they share a common infrastructure. Despite this diversity, the vast part of CNET's revenues continues to come from its premiere technology-oriented sites. On the bright side, the audience size of 200 million unique visitors is a tremendous asset. The only way to monetize this asset is to develop a powerful advertising platform and offer these pages to marketers.

10.3 THE ONLINE ENTERTAINMENT INDUSTRY

The entertainment industry is generally considered to be composed of four traditional, commercial players and one new arrival: television, radio broadcasting, Hollywood films, music, and video games (the new arrival). **Figure 10.10** illustrates the estimated relative sizes of these commercial entertainment markets as of 2008. By far, the largest entertainment producer is television (broadcast, satellite, and cable), followed by film, then radio, with music and video games tied for fourth. While PC and console games have grown to be larger than film box office revenues, total Hollywood film revenues dwarf the game industry when DVD sales and rentals, licensing, and ancillary products are added.

More than any of the content industries, the entertainment segment is undergoing a transformation brought about by the Internet. Several forces are at work. Accelerated platform development such as the iPod video and music platform, and digital cellular networks, have changed consumer preferences and increased demand for video, television, and game entertainment delivered over Internet devices whether in subscription or a la carte pay-per-view forms. Other social networking platforms are also spurring the delivery of entertainment content to desktop and laptop PCs, handhelds, and phones. iPod and other legitimate music subscription services like Rhapsody have also demonstrated a viable business model where millions of consumers are willing to pay reasonable prices for high-quality content, portability, and convenience. The growth in broadband has obviously made possible both wired and wireless delivery of all forms of entertainment over the Internet, potentially displacing cable and broadcast television networks. The development of several DRM schemes (including Apple's, RealNetworks', and Napster's) have demonstrated that copyrighted content can be delivered over the Internet in a reasonably secure fashion. All of these forces have combined in 2008 to bring about a transformation in the entertainment industries.

The ideal Internet content e-commerce world would allow consumers to watch any movie, listen to any music, watch any TV show, and play any game, when they wanted, where they wanted, and using whatever Internet device was convenient. Consumers would be billed monthly for these services by a single provider of Internet

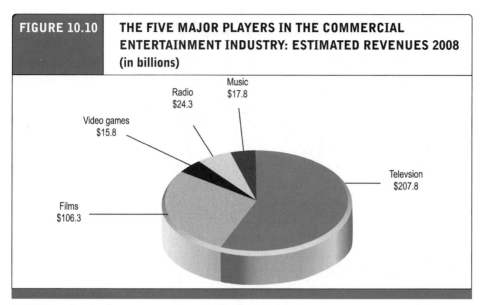

| FIGURE 10.10 | **THE FIVE MAJOR PLAYERS IN THE COMMERCIAL ENTERTAINMENT INDUSTRY: ESTIMATED REVENUES 2008 (in billions)** |

SOURCES: Based on data from U.S. Census Bureau, 2008; authors' estimates.

service. This idealized version of a convergent media world is many years away. But clearly this is the direction of the Internet-enabled entertainment industry in 2008.

When we think of the producers of entertainment in the offline world, we tend to think about television networks such as ABC, NBC, or CBS; Hollywood film studios such as MGM, Disney, Paramount, and Twentieth Century Fox; and music labels such as Sony BMG, Atlantic Records, Columbia Records, and Warner Records. Interestingly, none of these international brand names have a significant entertainment presence on the Internet. Although traditional forms of entertainment such as television shows and Hollywood movies are just now appearing on the Web, neither the television nor film industries have built an industry-wide delivery system. Instead, they are building alliances with portals like Yahoo, Google, AOL, and MSN, and a new player in media distribution, Apple Computer.

While industry titans waver, online consumers are redefining and considerably broadening the concept of entertainment. We refer to this development as "non-traditional" entertainment or what most refer to as user-generated content, which also have entertainment value including user videos uploaded to YouTube, photos uploaded to Photobucket and shared, as well as blogs. User-generated content reflects some of the same shifts in consumer preferences experienced by traditional media: people want to participate in the creation and distribution of content.

ONLINE ENTERTAINMENT AUDIENCE SIZE AND GROWTH

Measuring the size and growth of the Internet content audience is far less precise than measuring a television audience simply because there is no audience measurement service for the Internet. Estimates of audience size are typically based on responses to surveys rather than actual consumer behavior.

Online Traditional Entertainment

Recognizing the difficulties of measuring an Internet audience, let's first examine the use of "traditional" entertainment content, such as films, music, sports, and games; then we will look at non-traditional online entertainment. **Figure 10.11** shows the current and projected growth for commercial online entertainment revenues for the major players: music, Internet radio, online TV, online games, and online video. Music downloads lead the list of commercial entertainment revenues in 2008, followed by online games, TV, radio, and online video.

There are some surprising changes by 2012. Online games and Internet radio spurt ahead of online musical downloads. While online video lags behind, this could change if Hollywood studios decide upon a delivery system to homes. Online music-both downloads and Internet radio—together are the largest revenue-producing media in 2008 and 2012. Internet radio has a very low profile, but in 2008, 29 million people in the United States listen weekly to Internet radio, most often at work. This makes it an ideal advertising environment.

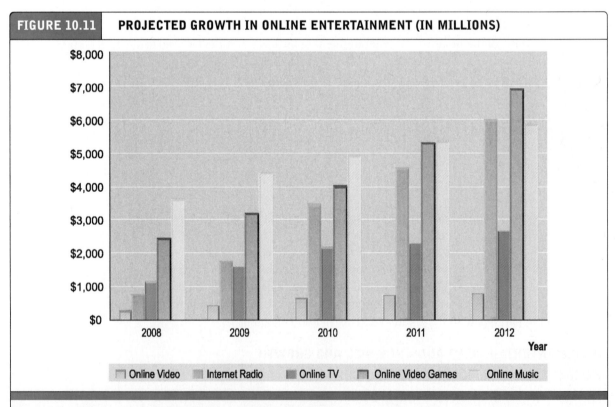

| FIGURE 10.11 | PROJECTED GROWTH IN ONLINE ENTERTAINMENT (IN MILLIONS) |

Among commercial forms of mass entertainment, online music downloads engages the largest number of people and revenues on the Web in 2008. However, online games and Internet radio revenues will overtake music by 2012.

SOURCES: Based on data from eMarketer, Inc., 2007a, 2007g, 2007h; authors' estimates.

User Generated Content: Where Does It Fit?

Whereas traditional commercial entertainment is produced by professional entertainers and producers, user-generated entertainment involves all those other activities that people voluntarily engage in to have fun, such as shooting videos, taking pictures, recording music and sharing it, and writing blogs. We have extensively documented the user-generated phenomenon in previous chapters. The question for this chapter is, "How does this content fit into the overall entertainment picture?"

The answer appears to be that user-generated content is both a substitute as well as a compliment to traditional commercial entertainment. As people spend more time consuming user-generated content, they may spend less time consuming commercial content. As advertising revenues grow on social networks and YouTube in order to capture an audience of nearly 90 million people, advertising revenues for commercial media may not grow as fast as they might have otherwise. On the other hand, box office and DVD video sales have not declined in the presence of alternative video formats. Instead people just watched more video of all kinds.

Figure 10.12 characterizes different types of Web entertainment experiences along two dimensions: user focus and user control. Sites that offer nontraditional user-generated forms of entertainment are unique not only because they afford access to large digital archives, promote fine-grained searching, and enable users to create their own archives, but also because they permit users high levels of control over both the program content and the program focus. For example, a social network site like MySpace offers user-generated content that is viewed by others as "entertaining." The hypothesis is that sites that offer both high user focus and high user control will have the fastest rates of growth. MySpace is illustrative of this hypothesis. MySpace started out as a independent, music-oriented social networking site where new bands not signed by major record labels could find new listeners, and where people could form networks of friends by creating their own home pages and displaying personal comments, text, photos, and music. By giving users control over their environment and focusing the site on users, the site routinely attracts over 35 million visitors a month in 2008.

CONTENT

The Internet has greatly changed the packaging, distribution, marketing, and sale of traditional entertainment content, with the largest impacts on music. Music may be a precursor to similar changes in the film and television segments. In the case of music, the package is being transformed from a traditional CD album containing 15 songs on average, to the download of single songs a la carte. In other words, the impact of the Internet has been to unbundle the traditional music package, permitting customers to buy what they want. The distribution is changing from retail stores selling physical product, to Internet delivery and playback on a wide variety of digital devices from iPods, to PCs, to PDAs. Finally, the marketing and sales have changed as well. New groups have their own Web sites, and can find their own niche audiences on MySpace and other sites, to some extent democratizing the process of establishing a music brand. Established groups can bypass traditional marketing and sales organizations by

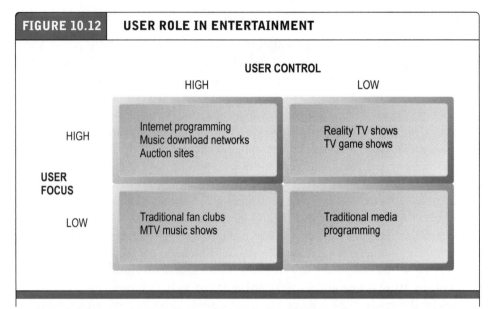

| FIGURE 10.12 | **USER ROLE IN ENTERTAINMENT** |

USER CONTROL

	HIGH	LOW
HIGH	Internet programming Music download networks Auction sites	Reality TV shows TV game shows
LOW	Traditional fan clubs MTV music shows	Traditional media programming

USER FOCUS

Popular Internet entertainment sites offer users high levels of control and user focus. Traditional media programming content is determined by programmers and has a celebrity focus. Traditional media has moved to become more participatory and more user-focused, but cannot match Internet levels of interactivity and user contribution to content.

creating their own Web distribution network. Not many established groups have gone this route entirely, but most such groups use the Web to market themselves.

ONLINE ENTERTAINMENT INDUSTRY REVENUE MODELS

Online entertainment sites have adopted many of the same revenue models as depicted previously in Table 10.4: marketing, advertising, pay-per-view, subscription, value-added, and mixed. Television networks, and Hollywood studios are beginning to sell episodes on a pay-per-view basis on iTunes, and entire series online on their own corporate sites.

CONVERGENCE

While there is clearly a movement toward convergence in technology platform, content, and industry structure, this movement has been slow because of both technological and market institutional forces.

Technology In musical entertainment, the technology platform has converged as PCs and handheld devices such as Apple's iPod and iPhone become music listening stations playing MP3 tracks, and general purpose computing and communication devices. The PC has also become a game station, capable of playing highly interactive rich media games with the same alacrity as dedicated game stations. In turn, many dedicated game stations such as Microsoft's Xbox 360 and Sony's PlayStation Portable (PSP) can be connected to the Web for interactive play and downloading new game software.

For movies and television, technology convergence has been hampered by the unwillingness of the movie industry to make its products available on a wide range of Internet-enabled devices, in large part because of concerns over piracy. Illegal downloading of movies has grown almost as fast as illegal music downloads, although because of the size of movie downloads, and the movie industry's efforts to close down illegal movie-sharing sites, illegal video downloads do not approach the volume of illegal musical downloads. The industry estimates it is losing $3 billion in sales a year from Internet piracy, and $4 billion a year from counterfeit DVDs (out a total industry revenue of $101 billion in 2008).

While Hollywood and New York television networks are obviously concerned about increasing piracy, and the lack of Internet security, they have made several important moves in 2007 and 2008 towards legitimate Internet distribution either through downloads from movie sites they control or through alliances with other platform owners like Apple Computer's iPod. There are several independent and industry-sponsored ventures: MovieFlix, Movies.com, Movielink, and iFilm. MovieFlix offers downloads of out-of-date and even out-of-copyright movies, some for free. It has alliances with Yahoo and other online portal movie distributors. Movies.com is sponsored by Disney and was intended to distribute films from Disney, Miramax, and Twentieth Century Fox using either high-speed Internet or digital cable systems. But these plans never materialized, and today Movies.com only offers trailers, theater reservation information, and general information service. iFilm is primarily a movie portal site with general information, that intended to provide legal movie downloads, but was purchased by Viacom and is now part of the MTV network where it only provides short film clips for advertisers. The only industry-supported sites currently offering Internet downloads of contemporary feature-length films are Movielink (a joint venture of Metro-Goldwyn-Mayer, Paramount Pictures, Sony Pictures, Universal, and Warner Bros.) and CinemaNow. Using a DRM envelope, users can download movies of about 500 megabytes in size for $1.99 to $4.99 per film. The consumer has 30 days to watch the movie, and once activated, 24 hours to view the movie on their PCs. After these time limits, the movie cannot be played. You can also rent movies for as low as 99 cents. CinemaNow holds the Internet distribution rights to the most extensive and comprehensive library of content available on-demand via the public Internet and private broadband networks. The CinemaNow library contains approximately 7,500 feature-length films, shorts, music concerts, and television programs from more than 250 film production studios. While these industry consortia may develop significant delivery capabilities, it is also the case that if millions of Americans decide to download movies over the Internet on a Saturday night, more than 50% of the Internet's capacity could be consumed, leading to significant brownouts and server outages in local areas. By 2008, the movie and television studios have began licensing some of their content to Amazon in a move to parry Apple's growing dominance in video and TV streaming and downloads. Amazon currently has several thousand movies and television episodes for sale.

The standards issue has largely been solved by movie sites letting the user decide which of three protocols will be used to download a movie: Microsoft's Windows Media Video, and RealNetworks Real System, or Apple's QuickTime.

Content In a convergent world, the creation, production, and distribution of entertainment content would be entirely digital, with few, if any, analog devices or physical products and their physical distribution channels. The Internet increasingly will come into direct competition with cable and satellite distribution channels. However, these physical and analog distribution channels are under increasing challenge from digital and Internet-based distribution. Hence, the content is moving off physical delivery platforms and toward Internet delivery platforms under user control.

In the areas of content creation and production, there has been significant progress for digital tools. Hollywood filmmakers are increasingly using digital cameras for selected movie scenes, and digital effects have come to play a larger role in many movies. Much of the editing of film is currently performed on digital editing computer workstations before the images are returned to analog 35mm film for distribution to theaters. Independent and low-budget film makers are creating feature-length films on digital cameras, editing in digital environments, and distributing directly on the Web to niche audiences at independent film sites. In television, digital cameras are now typical while editing and production is almost entirely digital. Likewise, in music, recording is performed on digital devices and mixed using digital mixers before production of digital CDs. Independent bands move their music directly from digital mixers to the Internet, skipping the CD production stage entirely. Composers, arrangers, and music educators have widely adopted two digital notation programs, Finale and Sibelius, to create music scores.

Industry Structure The existing industry value chain is highly inefficient and fractured. For the entertainment industry to move aggressively onto the Web there needs to be a reorganization of the value chain either through corporate mergers, or strategic alliances, or both. In the process of re-organization, traditional distributors (like cable TV and broadcast television) most likely will experience severe disruptions to their business models as the Internet replaces them as a distribution media.

Figure 10.13 illustrates the existing players and industry value chain and three alternative arrangements. The entertainment industry has never been a neat and tidy industry to describe. There are many players and forces—including government regulators and courts—that shape the industry. In the existing model, creators of entertainment such as music labels or television producers sell to distributors, who in turn sell to local retail stores or local television stations, who then sell or rent to consumers. In the film industry, court decisions in the 1930s and 1940s forced production studios to give up ownership of local theaters on antitrust grounds, fearing the large Hollywood production studios would monopolize the film industry. One possible alternative to this fractionated industry is the *content owner direct model*. The Internet offers entertainment content producers (the music labels, Hollywood studios, and television content producers) the opportunity to dominate the industry value chain by eliminating the distributors and retailers and selling directly to the consumer. This has not yet

FIGURE 10.13	ENTERTAINMENT INDUSTRY VALUE CHAINS

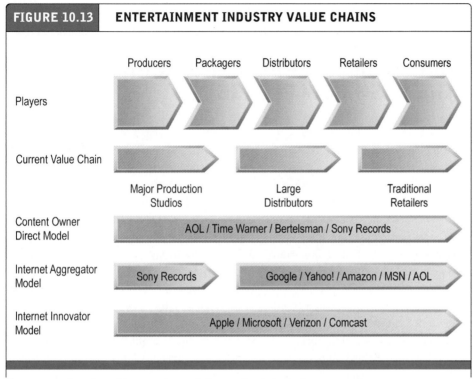

There are a variety of possible entertainment industry value chains in the near-term future.

been a successful model to date because the content producers know so little about the Internet and have not been successful on the Internet. A second possibility is the *aggregator model*. In this model, Web-based intermediaries such as Yahoo, Google, Amazon, and MSN who aggregate large audiences enter into strategic alliances with content owners to provide content to the aggregators. Yahoo fits into this model because it has begun hiring its own news reporters, and funding production of independent films that it can distribute on its portal.

A third possible model is the *Internet innovator model* in which successful Internet technology companies who develop the technology platforms such as Apple and Microsoft, as well as Internet communications platform providers like Verizon and Comcast Cable, move back into the value chain and begin creating their own content for exclusive distribution on their proprietary platform or channels. Good examples are Microsoft's Xbox video game platform, and Apple's iTunes Music Store, and Verizon's premium service package for DSL broadband (Grant, 2004).

Insight on Technology: Hollywood Needs a New Script: Pass the Cash Cow Please describes how Hollywood studios are struggling with the issues presented by the Internet.

INSIGHT ON TECHNOLOGY

HOLLYWOOD NEEDS A NEW SCRIPT: PASS THE CASH COW PLEASE

It's been a rebound year of sorts for the motion picture industry. Box office receipts in the United States of $9.6 billion in 2007 (and worldwide box office of $27 billion) brought the industry back to sales levels of 2002–2004. At the DVD rental store, however, DVD sales and rentals are flat—down 3% from the previous year. This is important because Hollywood makes a huge profit on DVD sales, about $17.62 per DVD, and its sells about 17 billion units a year, producing about $16 billion in revenues in the United States alone. Overall industry revenues have been flat, about $60 billion in the United States. This is in part due to slow or static growth in its products, with prices more or less stable, but the costs of producing the average Hollywood film have skyrocketed to about $100 million per title. The largest-grossing movie in 2007 was Spider-Man 3, which grossed $336 million in box office, and in 2008 another $100 million in DVD sales.

Hollywood has tried to grow by repackaging older movies into boxed sets, re-releasing so-called "producer" and "expanded" versions of older movies, and trying to extend the revenue life of its 68,000 DVD products. This can't go on forever. The problem is that Hollywood has come to count on the DVD platform for an increasing share of its revenue, using the box office release of films mostly as a marketing ploy to get word of mouth working for its films. The profit margins on DVDs are alleged to be over 45%, a real money-making machine. This machine is sputtering at a time when costs are spiraling, giving Hollywood investors and producers migraines. Industry experts believe that DVD sales will decline by 20% by 2010. The champagne has stopped flowing in Tinseltown, and industry leaders are pointing fingers at the Internet as one big cause of their problems.

There has been a dizzying array of new technologies and delivery vehicles that decidedly are a mixed blessing. DVD rentals are expanding nicely led by Netflix's Web/mail service, and competing Blockbuster mail and retail store channels. The problem with rentals, however, is that Hollywood only makes $2.25 per rental. The same with pay TV, and video on demand offered by cable TV companies: the studios make about the same $2.25 on these expanding sales. New technologies have introduced several low-profit channels and decreased consumer demand for the hi-profit DVD channel.

Now consider the impact of the Internet. In 2008, there were an estimated 62,000 digital videos on the Web available for illegal downloading, including all the top feature films of the last five years, and an estimated 1 million downloads per day worldwide. You can easily find these illegal copies by entering the title of any recent movie in Google to find a site to download it from without charge. It may take a couple of hours to download, and you end up with a movie that's usually of fair to poor quality (although sometimes of awful quality because it was shot with a camcorder in a theater). And then there are all the legal options for obtaining movies online. There are the streaming services now offered by Netflix, the Independent Movie Channel, RealTime, Joost, Limelight, Brightcove, and many others. With streaming technologies, the movie starts nearly instantly and is of acceptable quality but the viewer cannot store, or re-play the movie. Then there are the download sites, such as Wal-Mart (also the largest retailer of DVDs in the United States), Apple's iTunes Music Store, CinemaNow, and movie studio Web sites such as Movielink, owned and operated by Blockbuster, and supported by a joint effort of various Hollywood studios on a non-exclusive basis. The

(continued)

issue with downloads is that they take 2–3 hours, sometimes overnight for high-quality movies. Downloading a movie to your PC is straightforward, but getting it ported over to your TV can be problematic. You don't own these movies that you paid $12.95 to download, and they disappear in 30 days, and you have 24 hours to watch them once you start viewing. CinemaNow has introduced the possibility of burning DVDs from the downloads, but for a small number of titles.

With the proliferation of low-profit digital channels, the threat of piracy looms larger. The industry claims to be losing $5 billion a year on DVD sales and rentals because of Internet piracy. Technologies like a protocol called Bit-Torrent can increase the large file downloading capacity of a single server by several thousand times. The movie industry never counted on a young American programmer named Bram Cohen.

Cohen's BitTorrent protocol breaks large video files down into smaller fragments, called "seeds," typically a quarter of a megabyte (256 KB) in size. These fragments are distributed to all clients in the network depending on their bandwidth connections. Clients that want to download the entire file first obtain a list of all the clients who have fragments of the file, and then they query each client for the fragment, establishing a "bit storm" network for a few moments. After the fragments arrive, they are re-assembled into a single large file. Each client is both a downloader and uploader of the fragments it keeps, so that each client starts uploading its fragments before it has pulled down all the fragment files itself. In this way, the entire network is never over-taxed, and in fact as more and more clients come into the network to share "seeds" or fragments, the total throughput of the network increases. In a traditional server environment, where thousands of clients simultaneously request a file, the single server can easily be overloaded. In a traditional environment, the more people requesting large files, the slower the throughput and response time.

The movie industry was successful in converting the BitTorrent site into a legitimate site after the *Grokster v. MGM* decision in 2005. In 2005, Cohen made a deal with the Motion Picture Association of America (MPAA) to remove all links to illegal content on the official BitTorrent Web site. In 2006, Cohen's BitTorrent site entered into the legitimate movie downloading business in cooperation with the seven largest studios in America. The agreement means Bittorrent.com will comply with procedures outlined in the Digital Millennium Copyright Act (DMCA). But the code for the protocol is freely available to all, and most illegal movie download sites still use the BitTorrent protocol for distributing movies. In 2008 Bittorrent.com advertises itself as a legitimate content distributor with over 10,000 legal videos for download. With over 160 million clients downloaded, it sees itself as the consumer standard for software and content distribution on the Internet.

To add insult to injury, Hollywood also finds itself in the crosshairs of Google's YouTube site, Google's video search engine, and other social network sites that allow stolen, copyrighted materials to be posted. Google wants to organize the world's information, and that includes movies. So providing Web searchers access to snippets of digital movies is within Google's horizon, even if copyright holders don't agree. Google has its money invested in YouTube, and that's where it can make a killing by having users upload stolen Hollywood content and claim it is not responsible for what its users do. Rather than police its users, Google has demanded the movie studios identify any copyrighted content on the YouTube site, and send it a letter demanding it be taken down as required by the DMCA. Memories of the old Napster? Viacom has sued Google for $1 billion and the other studios are following closely. Google meanwhile is dragging its feet on the development of video fingerprinting software,

(continued)

which would allow it to prevent any watermarked video from being uploaded in the first place, although it has recently announced a filtering system that will help it identify copyrighted video material (see Chapter 8).

To show the industry there is hope in Hollywood-quality Internet video, Google has entered into an agreement with Dow Jones, Sony BMG, and other large content companies to syndicate their video content to other Web sites where the videos are shown within Google ad boxes. But this advertising revenue generated by playing Hollywood snippets will never replace the profits of DVDs.

Hollywood's response to the widespread looting of its treasure chest has been heated, but only barely more effective than the record industry response to Napster, Kazaa, and other file-sharing systems. Hollywood has created a sort of Entertainment Police force hired by the MPAA that trolls the Internet looking for free copies of the latest blockbusters. When found, they mail infringement notices to the owners of the IP address, warning them of potential liability. They also inform the Internet Service Provider. When they find an operation larger than a single P2P user, such as a constellation of IP addresses sharing video files, they get law enforcement agencies involved. The MPAA has sent thousands of letters to colleges, universities, and business networks urging them to prevent copyright infringement by students and employees. They have also sent letters to CEOs of all Fortune 1000 companies to ensure that high-speed corporate networks are not used to download or store infringing content.

The MPAA approach to new technologies has been to sue, threaten to sue, and establish research programs that build new technologies for destroying illegal copying and sharing.

MPAA and six major studios have established the Motion Pictures Laboratories Inc. to develop ways to jam camcorders used inside movie theaters; develop network management technology to detect and block illegal file transfers on campus and business networks; develop traffic analysis tools to detect illegal content sharing on P2P networks; and develop ways to allow legitimate customers to send wireless copies of movies around the house to various machines without interception by unauthorized users. One possibility for the Motion Pictures Lab is to exploit a recent patent issued to Professor John Hale at the University of Tulsa and a graduate student for a technique that distributes flawed decoy copies of copyrighted material over P2P networks. Called the "Gotcha" solution, these flawed files look and behave just like legitimate copies but when played have a buzzing sound, white noise, or announcements urging viewers of illegal films "Next time pay for what you take!" But the long-term hope of the industry is that new technologies will allow them to confidently release films in digital formats on customer accessible networks without losing control of the content and while still maintaining a healthy profit margin. To some extent, the only hope of the industry is to develop legal means for consumers to download or stream Hollywood movies in a legitimate, fee-based, secure environment. In 2008 Amazon launched a new service called Video on Demand that allows users for a fee to stream any of over 40,000 videos or movies, in real time, on their Windows or Macintosh computers. Without the fee or subscription-based profits, the money to make the Hollywood films will disappear, and all that will be left is 5-minute home videos on YouTube.

■ **SOURCES:** "The Ebb and Flow of Movies: Box Office Revenue 1986-2008," *New York Times*, February 22, 2008; "New Amazon Service Streams TV Shows and Films to PCs," by Walter Mossberg, *Wall Street Journal*, September 11, 2008; "DVD Feels First Sting of Slipping Sales," by Mike Snider, *USA Today*, January 7, 2008; "Theatrical Market Statistics," Motion Picture Industry Association, 2008. "Nothing to Watch on TV? Streaming Video Appeals to Niche Audiences," *New York Times*, August 7, 2007; "Policing Web Video With 'Fingerprints,'" by Kevin Delaney, Brooks Barnes and Matthew Karnitsching, *Wall Street Journal*, April 23, 2007; "Retailers Explore Movie Download Options," by Joshua Freed, Associated Press, April 9, 2007; "Push Comes to Shove for Control of Web Video," by Richard Siklos, *New York Times*, April 1, 2007; "Google in Content Deal With the Media Companies," by Louise Story, *New York Times*, February 26, 2007; "Media Consumption," by The Motion Picture Association, 2007.

Google and YouTube Together:
Can Google Monetize YouTube?

Ever since Google bought YouTube in November 2006, some have wondered just exactly how Google was going to make the $1.65 billion purchase price worthwhile. Wall Street, on the other hand, had no doubts that Google would make a killing, and Google's stock price quickly shot up from the unprecedented $500 level for most of 2007 to the super-unprecedented level of $700 in November 2007, before settling back down to around $630 in mid-November. This gives Google a price/earnings ratio of 49, just shy of the moon, and a market capitalization of $200 billion, which is over 10 times the market capitalization of General Motors, the largest car company on earth. In 2008, Google's stock dropped 40% to the 425 range, with a price/earnings ratio of 28 that is still in the upper atmosphere. Why did the market value the Google YouTube purchase so fondly at first, and then have second thoughts? What are the sceptics saying? Are are they just jealous of Google's evident success in purchasing the largest group of eyeballs on the Web, namely, YouTube's audience of 70 million unique visitors?

The answer from Google is that it plans to turn the Web's largest repository of video, and the largest video audience share, into the next big, killer app for advertising, namely, the largest advertising platform in history. Bigger than search, and bigger than television. Just how much video does YouTube have? To date, the estimate is that YouTube well over 20 million videos, stored on 600 terabytes of hard drives around the world, representing about 10 billion minutes of video. This is growing at the rate of about 1 million videos a year, and if the stars are right and millions of video cameras keep working, in five years, by 2012, YouTube will have about 40 million videos.

How many people are attracted to these videos and for how long? YouTube claims about 130 million unique visitors per month, but several independent Internet marketing firms put it closer to 70 million per month, with the average stay about five minutes, viewing on average two videos at a time. Analysts estimate YouTube streams over a billion video streams a month worldwide. Only 2% of these monthly visitors view daily, compared to Yahoo, for instance, where 40% of visitors visit every day. Yahoo really does have around 130 million unique visitors a month, who stay on average about one hour a visit to view content, generating a whopping 37 billion pages views a month! Each page view is an advertising opportunity. Google has about 112 million unique monthly visitors, who stay less than 24 minutes, generating 10 billion page views a month, on their way to their destination Web site. Over 30% of Google visitors visit daily. So while YouTube has grown explosively, it still has a way to go to catch Yahoo or Google and lacks the retention time (page views) and frequency of visits found at the major portals.

What YouTube needs is not just more content but quality content, content that is really interesting and that draws millions of viewers back every day. Chances are this

The primary e-book revenue model is pay-for-download, in which traditional publishers and authors create e-books and publishers sell these works in their entirety through online bookstore intermediaries. The traditional revenue model for the commercial book industry has not been changed much by the introduction of e-books, mainly because publishers most have chosen not to develop online capabilities. A second revenue model involves the licensing of entire e-libraries. This model is similar to the subscription model in that users pay either a monthly or an annual fee for access to hundreds of titles. Neither business model is yet profitable, but a five-year development period is expected.

- *Convergence.* The publishing industry is making steady progress toward media convergence. Technological convergence has been slowed by the poor resolution of computer screens, the lack of portable reader devices that can compete with the portability of a published book, the absence of DRM technology, and the lack of standards to define cross-platform e-books so that they can be viewed on many different devices. A likely solution to the portability problem is the use of PDAs, but the current PDAs are too small for comfortable reading. Several screen enhancement solutions have been developed using sub-pixel display technologies, and the development of electronic ink and electronic paper displays. Several technology firms have also developed DRM software to control printing and copying of downloaded materials; however, hackers have been able to break most DRM technologies, so the hesitancy of publishing firms to publish works on the Web has yet to be overcome. Some cross-platform standards are already available and new ones are beginning to emerge. Adobe Acrobat PDF files are the most commonly used standard to date; other standards include OEB and ONIX. Not much content design convergence has yet occurred. So far, text is simply being integrated into electronic display forms, and experimentations with more interactive formats are just beginning. Content production and distribution convergence have seen more progress. The development of XML and large-scale online text/graphic storage systems have transformed the book production process and made it more efficient. In distribution of book content, the Web has opened up an entirely new distribution channel. Industry structure has not changed much.

Huge publishing behemoths have long dominated the publishing industry, and the 1990s saw even further consolidation of power. Nevertheless, the Internet has created new opportunities for authors, publishers, and distributors. Authors have published works directly to the public; publishers have moved into direct distribution to the public of selected works; large online book distributors have commissioned new e-book titles and moved into publishing; technology providers have begun limited distribution of e-books; and NetLibrary has demonstrated that a market existed for inexpensive digital libraries that could be distributed to colleges, universities, and traditional libraries.

- **Understand the key factors affecting the online entertainment industry.**

There are five main players in the entertainment sector: television, film, music, video games, and radio broadcasting. The entertainment segment is currently undergoing great change, brought about the Internet. Consumers have begun to accept paying for content, and working with DRM restrictions.

Key factors include the following:

- *Audience size and growth.* Music downloads are the most popular form of entertainment, with online games second, followed by film, and sports. However, the amount of time users spend at music sites is not high because they typically download and store a track for future use. The sites with the highest usage levels are those that allow high levels of user control and participation. In the absence of film and TV on the Web, users are defining new forms of non-traditional entertainment that do not involve the traditional media titans including blogs, and user-generated content on social networking sites.

- *Content.* Packaging, distribution, marketing, and sales of music tracks have greatly changed in the Internet age. Huge online digital searchable music archives with millions of songs now exist from which users can mix and match to create their own personalized library. One main reason for the popularity of these services is that they enable users to become their own music packagers and distributors. This is the unique feature of online entertainment as compared to traditional entertainment. It offers users high levels of control over both program content and program focus.

- *Revenue models and results.* Television and movie sites typically use a marketing model, attempting to extend their brand influence and the audience for their offline product. Apple's a la carte model where users pay for a single music track download has been exceptionally successful. Many film sites use a pay-per-view rental model, or pay-for-download model. Many music entertainment sites are now successful with a monthly subscription model as well.

- *Convergence.* Convergence has been slow due to both technological and market forces. The technology platform for music has converged PCs and handheld devices such as Apple's iPod to become digital music listening systems. A new platform has arrived. The PC has also become a game station, with capabilities rivaling dedicated game stations. In turn, many dedicated game stations can now be connected to the Web for interactive play. Technology convergence for movies and television has been stalled by the lack of standards, the slow acceptance of high-bandwidth connections in the United States, and inadequate Internet backbone capacity. The film industry has moved very slowly in making content available on the Internet for fear of losing control over its content. There are only a few sites supporting legal Internet downloads of feature-length films. Technology standards are not a large issue as most consumers have become used to using one of three standards: Windows Media Player, Apple's QuickTime, or RealNetworks RealOne media player. Content creation and production convergence is occurring, with filmmakers and television studios increasingly using digital cameras and film editing done at digital computer workstations. Music is recorded on digital devices using digital mixers before it is digitally imprinted on CDs. Industry structure convergence in the entertainment industry, as in all content industries, is moving toward the merger of content and distribution. Content owners and producers are largely seeking to own their own distribution channels, cutting out the profits of distributors, resellers, and retailers. The belief appears to be widespread that successful media companies will need to own their entire value chain from content creation to consumer use.

QUESTIONS

1. What are the three dimensions in which the term convergence has been applied? What does each of these areas of convergence entail?
2. Why has media industry convergence not occurred as rapidly as predicted? What are the five basic revenue models for online content, and what is their major challenge? What will have to be done in order to overcome this obstacle to profitability?
3. What is the pay-per-view/pay-per-download revenue model, what type of content is it suitable for, and when is it expected to be successful?
4. What four things must content provider firms do in order to generate meaningful revenues?
5. What are the technological challenges facing content producers and owners?
6. Identify and explain the four other challenges facing content producers and owners.
7. How has the Internet impacted the content that newspapers can offer?
8. What changes have occurred for newspapers in the classified ads department?
9. What are the key challenges facing the online newspaper industry?
10. What are the advantages and disadvantages of e-book content?
11. How has the Internet changed the packaging, distribution, marketing, and sale of traditional music tracks?
12. What are the factors that make nontraditional, distinctly Web entertainment sites so popular with users?
13. What would complete content convergence in the entertainment industry look like? Has it occurred?

PROJECTS

1. Research the issue of media convergence in the newspaper industry. Do you believe that convergence will be good for the practice of journalism? Develop a reasoned argument on either side of the issue and write a 3- to 5-page report on the topic. Include in your discussion the barriers to convergence and whether these restrictions should be eased.

2. Go to Amazon and explore the different digital products that are available. Prepare a presentation to convey your findings to the class. For example, are there Web-accessed, Web-downloadable, dedicated e-books, or books for PDAs offered? Which are in greater abundance?

3. Go to TBO.com (Tampa Bay Online). Surf the site and sample the offerings. Prepare a presentation to describe and display the efforts you see at technology, content, and industry structure convergence as well as the revenue model being used. Who owns this site?

4. Examine and report on the progress, if any, made with respect to the delivery of movies on demand over the Internet.

5. Has technology platform, content design, or industry structure convergence occurred in the online magazine industry? Prepare a short report discussing this issue.

WEB SITE RESOURCES www.prenhall.com/laudon

- Additional projects, exercises, and tutorials
- Careers: Explore career opportunities in e-commerce
- Raising capital and business plans

CHAPTER 11

Social Networks, Auctions, and Portals

LEARNING OBJECTIVES

After reading this chapter, you will be able to:

- Explain the difference between a traditional social network and an online social network.
- Understand how a social network differs from a portal.
- Describe the different types of social networks and online communities and their business models.
- Describe the major types of auctions, their benefits and costs, and how they operate.
- Understand when to use auctions in a business.
- Recognize the potential for auction abuse and fraud.
- Describe the major types of Internet portals.
- Understand the business models of portals.

Social Network Fever Spreads to the Professions

When social networks first appeared a few years ago, it was widely believed this phenomenon would be limited to crazed teenagers already incapacitated by excessive time spent on video game machines. Most serious technoratis in Silicon Valley, and Wall Street, felt this was a blip on the horizon, and their full attention was occupied primarily by search engines, search engine marketing, and ad placement. But when the population of social network participants pushed past 50 million, then 75 million, even the technical elite woke up to the fact that these huge audiences were not just a bunch of teenagers, but that instead a wide slice of American society was also participating. Steve Ballmer, CEO of Microsoft, said in September 2007 that "I think these things [social networks] are going to have some legs, and yet there's a faddishness, a faddish nature about anything that basically appeals to younger people." This was a month before Microsoft paid $250 million for a small stake in Facebook, which valued the company at $15 billion. MySpace in the meantime had passed Yahoo as the most frequently visited site on the Web. Trying to sound convincing, Eric Schmidt, CEO of Google, declared that "I know a lot of people think this [social networking] is a blip, but it's real, it's serious." He said this just before spending $1.65 billion for YouTube.

The social networking craze obviously has awakened the technology giants, but they focus mostly on the really huge audiences attracted to the general networking sites such as MySpace, Facebook, YouTube, and Orkut (Google's social networking site that is the leader in Brazil but has flopped in the United States). However, in the background there are a fast-growing collection of social networks that are aimed at communities of practitioners or specific interest groups.

Take LinkedIn, for example, probably the best-known business networking site. LinkedIn is an online network with more than 24 million worldwide members, representing 150 different industries. Every 25 days or so, another million people joing LinkedIn. LinkedIn allows a member to create a profile, including a photo, that summarizes his or her professional accomplishments. Members' networks include their connections, their connections' connections, as well as people they know, potentially linking you to thousands of others.

Those with a particular interest in the stock market have a whole crop of Web sites that have sprouted that are aimed at stock investors who want to share their ideas with other investors. These social networks are not just bulletin boards with anonymous comments, but active communities where users are identified and their performance ranked according to the performance of their stock picks. One networker is Joey Fundora, a 32-year-old computer network architect from Miami. He logs on every day to StockTickr, which has about 2,500 members. The first page on the screen is a list of stocks that his friends are investing in, along with their stock picking scores. Fundora says that "If you know there's a user who is quite similar to your own investing strategy, they will often bring up stocks that aren't on your radar."

Like the larger social network sites, the financial sites allow users to connect with other investors, discuss issues focused on the stock market, and sometimes just show off users' investing prowess. Some of the new sites include BullPoo (does this sound like a reliable source?) where users are rated against other members on the performance of their "virtual" portfolios; Caps.fool.com, where users make predictions on whether a stock will beat the S&P 500 and are rated on their performance; and TradeKing, where users can search for others with similar styles and view recent trades. For day traders, work can be a lonely pursuit with little chance for interaction. The networking sites give day traders a chance to socialize and talk shop. While most of these sites have fewer than 5,000 members, they are relatively new. MotleyFool, one of the best known online stock investment services, just started its CAPS stock-rating social network and already has attracted 44,000 members.

You can find similar social networking sites springing up in a variety of specific professional groups such as health care (DailyStrength.org), law (LawLink), physicians (Sermo), Reuters customers (NewReuters), wireless industry executives (INmobile.org), and advertising professionals (AdGrabber.com). These social networks encourage members to intensely discuss the realities of their professions and practices, sharing successes and failures. There are also general business social networks designed more to develop a network for career advancement, such as LinkedIn, Ecademy, and Ryze.

The rapid growth of professional social networks linked to industry and careers shows how widespread and nearly universal the appeal of social networks are. While e-mail remains the Web's most popular activity, it is about to be eclipsed by social networking. What explains the very broad attraction to social networking? E-mail is excellent for communicating with other individuals, or even a small group. But e-mail is not very good at getting a sense of what others in the group are thinking, especially if the group numbers more than a dozen people. The strength of social networking lies in its ability to reveal group attitudes and opinions, values, and practices.

SOURCES: "About LinkedIn," Linkedin.com, September 2008; "Social Networking Goes Professional," by Jessica Vascellaro, *Wall Street Journal*, August 20, 2007; "A New Way to Rate Stock Tips," by Jane Kim, *Wall Street Journal*, January 3, 2007; "Social Networking Comes to Healthcare," by Laura Landro, *Wall Street Journal*, December 29, 2006; "When Outside the Loop, A Quicker Way to Get In," by Bob Tedeschi, *New York Times*, October 30, 2006.

I n this chapter, we discuss social networks, auctions, and portals. One might ask, "What do social networks, auctions, and portals have in common?" They are all based on feelings of shared interest and self-identification—in short, a sense of community. Social networks and online communities explicitly attract people with shared affinities, such as ethnicity, gender, religion, and political views, or shared interests, such as hobbies, sports, and vacations. The auction site eBay started as a community of people interested in trading unwanted but functional items for which there was no ready commercial market. That community turned out to be huge—much larger than anyone expected. Portals also contain strong elements of community by providing access to community-fostering technologies such as e-mail, chat groups, bulletin boards, and discussion forums.

11.1 SOCIAL NETWORKS AND ONLINE COMMUNITIES

The Internet was designed originally as a communications medium to connect scientists in computer science departments around the continental United States. From the beginning, the Internet was intended, in part, as a community building technology that would allow scientists to share data, knowledge, and opinions in a real-time online environment (see Chapter 3) (Hiltzik, 1999). The result of this early Internet was the first "virtual communities" (Rheingold, 1993). As the Internet grew in the late 1980s to include scientists from many disciplines and thousands of university campuses, thousands of virtual communities sprang up among small groups of scientists in very different disciplines that communicated regularly using Internet e-mail, listservs, and bulletin boards. The first articles and books on the new electronic communities began appearing in the mid to late 1980s (Kiesler et al. 1984; Kiesler, 1986). One of the earliest online communities, The Well, was formed in San Francisco in 1985 by a small group of people who once shared an 1800-acre commune in Tennessee. The Well is a online community that now has thousands of members devoted to discussion, debate, advice, and help (Hafner, 1997; Rheingold, 1998). With the development of the Web in the early 1990s, millions of people began obtaining Internet accounts and Web e-mail, and the community-building impact of the Internet strengthened. By the late 1990s, the commercial value of online communities was recognized as a potential new business model (Hagel and Armstrong, 1997).

The early online communities involved a relatively small number of Web aficionados, and users with intense interests in technology, politics, literature, and ideas. The technology was largely limited to posting text messages on bulletin boards sponsored by the community, and one-to-one, or one-to-many e-mails. In addition to The Well, early networks included GeoCities, a Web site hosting service based on neighborhoods. By 2002, however, the nature of online communities had begun to change. Cell phones and mobile Internet devices provided widespread access, making it possible to communicate nearly instantly with friends and relatives, and keep track of one another in a way not possible before. User-created Web sites called blogs became inexpensive and easy to set up without any technical expertise. These technologies also enabled sharing of rich media such as photos and videos made possible by the spreading use of digital cameras, digital video cameras, cell phones with cameras, and portable digital music players. Suddenly there was a much wider audience for sharing interests and activities, and much more to share.

A new culture emerged as well. The broad democratization of the technology and its spread to the larger population meant that online social networking was no longer limited to a small group but instead broadened to include a much wider set of people and tastes, especially pre-teens, teens, and college students who were the fastest to adopt many of these new technologies. The new social networking culture is very personal and "me" centered, displaying photos and broadcasting personal activities, interests, hobbies, and relationships on social network profiles. Today's social networks are as much a sociological phenomenon as they are a technology phenomenon.

Currently, social network participation is one of the most common usages of the Internet. About 44% of all Internet users in the United States—about 76 million Americans—have at one time or another gone online to a social network site (Pew Internet and American Life, 2008). MySpace reports storing over 100 million profiles, with Facebook, which has shown enormous growth over the past year, reporting 90 million.

WHAT IS AN ONLINE SOCIAL NETWORK?

social network
involves a group of people, shared social interaction, common ties among members, and people who share an area for some period of time

online social network
an area online, where people who share common ties can interact with one another

So exactly how do we define an online social network, and how is it any different from, say, an offline social network? Sociologists, who frequently criticize modern society for having destroyed traditional communities, unfortunately have not given us very good definitions of social networks and community. One study examined 94 different sociological definitions of community and found four areas of agreement. **Social networks** involve (a) a group of people, (b) shared social interaction, (c) common ties among members, and (d) people who share an area for some period of time (Hillery, 1955; Poplin, 1979). This will be our working definition of a social network. Social networks do not necessarily have shared goals, purposes, or intentions. Indeed, social networks can be places where people just "hang out," share space, and communicate.

Now it's a short step to defining an **online social network** as an area online where people who share common ties can interact with one another. This definition is very close to that of Howard Rheingold's—one of The Well's early participants—who coined the term *virtual communities* as "cultural aggregations that emerge when enough people bump into each other often enough in cyberspace. It is a group of people who may or may not meet one another face to face, and who exchange words and ideas through the mediation of an online social meeting space. The Internet removes the geographic and time limitations of offline social networks. To be in an online network, you don't need to meet face to face, in a common room, at a common time.

THE DIFFERENCE BETWEEN SOCIAL NETWORKS AND PORTALS

We describe portals in the last section of this chapter. Portals began as search engines and then added content, Internet, and e-commerce services. In order to survive, portals have added many community-building and social networking features including chat groups, bulletin boards, free Web site design and hosting, and other features that encourage visitors to stay on the site and interact with others who share their interests. Yahoo, for instance, uses deep vertical content features to retain its audience on site and maximize revenue opportunities. Portals have begun to measure their success in terms of their social networking features. For instance, Yahoo has purchased several Web properties, such as Flickr (a photo-sharing site) and HotJobs, which have social network features. Portals have moved toward becoming general community meeting places in an effort to enlarge and retain audience share and increase revenues. User-generated content on portals is one way to entice visitors to stay online at the site (and of course view more commercials).

Similarly, sites that began as narrowly focused content or affinity group community sites, such as iVillage, a site devoted to women's issues, have added more general portal-like services including general Web searching, general news, weather, travel information, and a wide variety of e-commerce services, often provided by portals seeking alliances. Browsers such as Mozilla's Firefox and Microsoft's Internet Explorer 7 are adding social networking features as well. There is no reason why social networking has to be limited to self-proclaimed social network sites such as MySpace. Social networking is a functionality, not a Web site. As a result, social networks and portals have moved closer together and at times are indistinguishable from one another.

THE GROWTH OF SOCIAL NETWORKS AND ONLINE COMMUNITIES

MySpace, Friendster, Tribe Networks, Flickr, and Facebook are all popular examples of online communities. **Figure 11.1** shows the top 10 social network sites, which together account for well over 90% of the Internet's social networking activity.

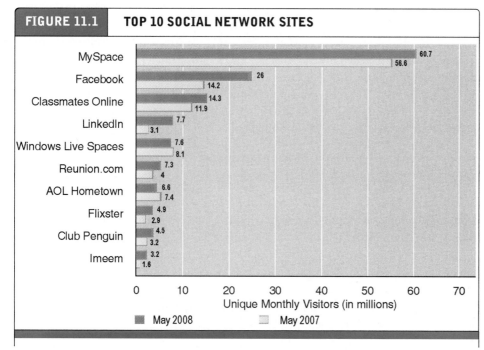

FIGURE 11.1 | **TOP 10 SOCIAL NETWORK SITES**

SOURCE: Based on data from Marketcharts.com, 2008; Hitwise, 2008.

Clearly, MySpace, with 60 million visitors a month, is the largest social network in terms of unique visitors, although it's growth has slowed from 25% a year to 7%. MySpace alone currently accounts for 50% of all social network traffic. In the past year, Facebook has grown 83%. While social networks originally attracted mostly Internet users under 35, today more than half of MySpace and Facebook users are over 35, wealthy (with average incomes of more than $75,000), and most have college degrees (eMarketer, Inc., 2008). Social networking is not just about teens and college students, but is a much larger social phenomenon.

It is easy to both overestimate and underestimate the significance of social networks. Unique visitors is just one way to measure the influence of a group of sites. Page views generated, time on site, attention (the percentage of time on a site divided by the percentage of time online for the average user), and frequency of visits provide a more detailed understanding of how social networks fit in the larger Internet scheme. While MySpace has 60 million unique visitors a month, Yahoo has 133 million. While the top 10 social networking sites together have about 143 million unique visitors, the top 10 portals, from Yahoo to Google to Ask, have over 800 million unique users. (Obviously, with 175–200 million people on the Internet, users are unique to more than one site.) In terms of page views, MySpace is generating about 67 billion page views per month, Yahoo about 50 billion. In terms of frequency of visits, only 2% of MySpace and Facebook users visit every day, while at Yahoo, 31% visit every day. In terms of attention (percentage of Internet time spent at the site), Yahoo leads the way with users reporting they spend 8% of their time on the site. MySpace users follow at 4%.

Perhaps the amount of advertising revenue generated by sites is the ultimate metric. The top four portals (Yahoo, Google, AOL, and MSN) generate about $12 billion annually in revenue. Social networking sites in the United States in 2008 are expected to generate a total of about $1.4 billion in advertising revenue, up from about $920 million in 2007 (eMarketer, Inc., 2008b). Social networking sites are the fastest-growing form of Internet usage, but they are not yet as powerful as traditional search engines/portals in terms of intensity of use and ad dollars generated, or unique visitors. But this is changing rapidly, and at current growth rates, social networks will exceed the reach, intensity, and scope of these "traditional" portals (eMarketer, Inc., 2006; Compete.com, 2008).

TURNING SOCIAL NETWORKS INTO BUSINESSES

While the early social networks had a difficult time raising capital and revenues, today's top networking sites are now learning how to monetize their huge audiences. Early networking sites relied on subscriptions, but today, social networks rely on advertising. Users of portals and search engines have come to accept advertising as the preferred means of supporting Web experiences rather than paying for it. **Figure 11.2** shows the amount of ad spending on social networks.

The techniques for marketing on social networks are still being worked out. Unlike portals where banner ads are an accepted phenomenon, this is not true on some social network sites such as Facebook, or LinkedIn.

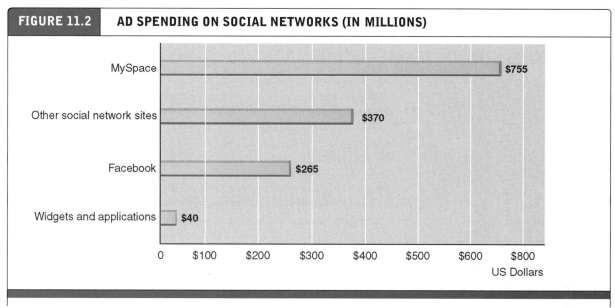

FIGURE 11.2 **AD SPENDING ON SOCIAL NETWORKS (IN MILLIONS)**

SOURCE: Based on data from eMarketer, Inc., 2008b.

TYPES OF SOCIAL NETWORKS AND THEIR BUSINESS MODELS

There are many types and many ways of classifying social networks and online communities. While the most popular general social networks have adopted an advertising model, other kinds of networks have different revenue sources. Social networks have different types of sponsors, and different kinds of members. For instance, some are created by firms such as IBM for the exclusive use of their sales force or other employees (intra-firm communities or B2E-business-to-employee communities); others are built for suppliers and resellers (inter-organizational or B2B communities); and others are built by dedicated individuals for other similar persons with shared interests (P2P-people-to-people communities). In this chapter, we will discuss B2C communities for the most part, although we also discuss briefly P2P communities of practice.

Table 11.1 describes in greater detail the five generic types of social networks and online communities: general, practice, interest, affinity, and sponsored. Each type of community can have a commercial intent or commercial consequence. We use this schema to explore the business models of commercial communities.

General communities offer members opportunities to interact with a general audience organized into general topics. Within the topics, members can find hundreds of specific discussion groups attended by thousands of like-minded members who share an interest in that topic. The purpose of the general community is to attract enough members to populate a wide range of topics and discussion groups. The business model of general communities is typically advertising supported by selling ad space on pages and videos.

general communities
offer members opportunities to interact with a general audience organized into general topics

TABLE 11.1	TYPES OF SOCIAL NETWORKS AND ONLINE COMMUNITIES
TYPE OF SOCIAL NETWORK /ONLINE COMMUNITY	**DESCRIPTION**
General	Online social gathering place to meet and socialize with friends, share content, schedules, and interests. Examples: MySpace and Facebook
Practice	Social network of professionals and practitioners, creators of artifacts such as computer code or music. Examples: JustPlainFolks (musicians community) and LinkedIn (business)
Interest	Community built around a common interest, such as games, sports, music, stock markets, politics, health, finance, foreign affairs, or lifestyle. Examples: E-democracy.org (political discussion group) and SocialPicks (stock market site)
Affinity	Community of members who self-identify with a demographic or geographic category, such as women, African Americans, or Arab Americans. Examples: BlackPlanet (African American community and networking site) and iVillage (focusing on women)
Sponsored	Network created by commercial, government, and nonprofit organizations for a variety of purposes. Examples: Nike, IBM, Cisco, and political candidates

practice networks
offer members focused discussion groups, help, information, and knowledge relating to an area of shared practice

interest-based social networks
offer members focused discussion groups based on a shared interest in some specific topic

affinity communities
offer members focused discussions and interaction with other people who share the same affinity

Practice networks offer members focused discussion groups, help, information, and knowledge relating to an area of shared practice. For instance, Linux.org is a non-profit community for the open source movement, a worldwide global effort involving thousands of programmers who develop computer code for the Linux operating system and share the results freely with all. Other online communities involve artists, educators, art dealers, photographers, and nurses. Practice networks can be either profit-based or nonprofit, and support themselves by advertising or user donations.

Interest-based social networks offer members focused discussion groups based on a shared interest in some specific subject, such as business careers, boats, horses, health, skiing, and thousands of other topics. Because the audience for interest communities is necessarily much smaller and more targeted, these communities have usually relied on advertising and tenancy/sponsorship deals. Sites such as Spoke, Jigsaw, Fool.com, Military.com, and Sailinganarchy all are examples of Web sites that attract people who share a common pursuit. These sites are usually advertising supported.

Affinity communities offer members focused discussions and interaction with other people who share the same affinity. Affinity refers to self- and group identification. For instance, people can self-identify themselves on the basis of religion, ethnicity, gender, sexual orientation, political beliefs, geographical location, and hundreds of other categories. For instance, iVillage, Oxygen, and Condenet, and NaturallyCurly, are affinity sites designed to attract women. These sites offer women discussion and services that focus on topics such as babies, beauty, books, diet and fitness, entertainment, health, and home and garden. These sites are supported by advertising along with revenues from sales of products.

Sponsored communities are online communities created by government, nonprofit, or for-profit organizations for the purpose of pursuing organizational goals. These goals can be diverse, from increasing the information available to citizens; for instance, a local county government site such as Westchestergov.com, the Web site for Westchester County (New York) government; to an online auction site such as eBay; to a product site such as Tide.com, which is sponsored by an offline branded product company (Procter & Gamble). Cisco, IBM, HP, and hundreds of other companies have developed their internal corporate social networks as a way of sharing knowledge.

sponsored communities
online communities created for the purpose of pursuing organizational (and often commercial) goals

SOCIAL NETWORK FEATURES AND TECHNOLOGIES

Social networks have developed software applications that allow users to engage in a number of activities. Not all sites have the same features, but there is an emerging feature set among the larger communities. Some of these software tools are built into the site, while others can be added by users to their profile pages as widgets (described in earlier chapters). **Table 11.2** describes some of social network functionalities.

THE FUTURE OF SOCIAL NETWORKS

While today's social networking scene is highly concentrated among the top 10 general networking sites, this is unlikely to remain the case. Networks are springing up all over the Internet based on intensely felt interests of smaller groups of people,

TABLE 11.2	SOCIAL NETWORK FEATURES AND TECHNOLOGIES
FEATURE	DESCRIPTION
Profiles	Users can create Web pages that describe themselves on a variety of dimensions.
Friends network	Ability to create a linked group of friends.
Network discovery	Ability to find other networks and find new groups and friends
Favorites	Ability to communicate favorite sites, bookmarks, content, and destinations.
E-mail	Send e-mail within the social network sites to friends.
Storage	Storage space for network members, content.
Instant messaging	Immediate one-to-one contact with friends through the community facility.
Message boards	Posting of messages to groups of friends, and other groups' members.
Online polling	Polling of member opinion.
Chat	Online immediate group discussion; Internet relay chat (IRC)
Discussion groups	Discussion groups and forums organized by topic.
Experts online	Certified experts in selected areas respond to queries.
Membership management tools	Ability of site managers to edit content, and dialog; remove objectionable material; protect security and privacy.

draining potential members from the general sites. General networking sites are poor places to meet new people, and most online social networks reflect offline friendships and associations.

Today's networks are places you go online, but in the future, browsers, portals like Yahoo and Google, and general Web sites will have social networking functionality built in, making it less necessary that you go to a social network site, and more likely that social networking will come to you (see *Insight on Technology: Social Operating Systems: Facebook vs. Google*). The biggest Web e-mail services (who also happen to be the big portals) are adding features that allow users to perform sociable functions like tracking friends, creating profiles, and joining other groups. Yahoo's 250 million e-mail users globally together are arguably the world's largest inactive and undiscovered network. Network aggregators are also emerging: SocialURL, ProfileFly, and ProfileLinker allow people to aggregate feeds from their different social network profiles, making it less necessary to visit the destination site itself.

11.2 ONLINE AUCTIONS

Online auction sites are among the most popular consumer-to-consumer (C2C) e-commerce sites on the Internet. The market leader in C2C auctions is eBay, which has 241 million registered users (one of the largest registered customer bases on the Internet) from all over the world, 85 million active users in the United States, over 12 million items listed each day within 18,000 categories, and in 2007, $7.6 billion in net revenues, a 29% growth over the previous year (eBay Inc., 2008). In the United States alone, there are several hundred auction sites, some specializing in unique collectible products such as stamps and coins, others adopting a more generalist approach in which just about any good can be found for sale. Increasingly, established portals and online retail sites—from Yahoo and MSN to JCPenney and Sam's Club—are adding auctions to their sites. And, as noted in Chapter 12, auctions constituted a significant part of all B2B e-commerce in 2008, and over a third of procurement officers use auctions to procure goods. What explains the extraordinary popularity of auctions? Do consumers always get lower prices at auctions? Why do merchants auction their products if the prices they receive are so low?

DEFINING AND MEASURING THE GROWTH OF AUCTIONS AND DYNAMIC PRICING

auctions
markets in which prices are variable and based on the competition among participants who are buying or selling products and services

dynamic pricing
the price of the product varies, depending directly on the demand characteristics of the customer and the supply situation of the seller

Auctions are markets in which prices are variable and based on the competition among participants who are buying or selling products and services. Auctions are one type of **dynamic pricing**, in which the price of the product varies, depending directly on the demand characteristics of the customer and the supply situation of the seller. There is a wide variety of dynamically priced markets, from simple haggling, bartering, and negotiating between one buyer and one seller, to much more sophisticated public auctions in which there may be thousands of sellers and thousands of buyers, as in a single stock market for a bundle of shares.

INSIGHT ON TECHNOLOGY

SOCIAL OPERATING SYSTEMS: FACEBOOK VS. GOOGLE

In the ongoing battles between hype and substance, fantasy and reality, hubris and humility, Silicon Valley takes no prisoners and has no equals. Google wants to organize the world's information, Amazon wants to be the world's store, and now Facebook wants to be the "social operating system" for the Internet, according to founder and CEO Mark Zuckerberg. Facebook wants to connect the world in one big social network (that it owns). Microsoft, owner of the world's desktops with a 95% market share, will just have to move on over while Facebook engineers this feat.

What can a social operating system possibly be? When we think of an operating system like Windows or Mac OS or Linux, we think of a software tool that controls the resources of the computer and provides the platform on which applications are built, launched, and operate. How can Facebook replace this? The answer is, it can't. But what Facebook can do is build, or encourage others to build, thousands of software applications, from tools such as iLike that let you find friends who share your musical tastes, to PopFly, a tool that lets you create links to Windows applications and Facebook, to the *Washington Post's* "political compass" application that allows you to calculate your place on a political spectrum of your friends, to games like Red Bull Roshambull, and a new program to "poke" people (mostly people of the opposite sex that you would like to know). iLike is now making more money on Facebook selling ads, and getting commissions from selling songs, and concert tickets, than it does from its own Web site, iLike.com.

In May 2007, Zuckerberg announced Facebook's new strategy of opening up its technology platform to outside developers or anyone who want to write an application and make it available to Facebook users. In short, Facebook is taking its two major assets—the 25-30 million unique users who visit each month, and its technology—and making them available to everyone. This allows developers to develop widgets and other Java applications to perform thousands of different tasks, and even allows developers to use their widgets to display ads and keep all the revenues. Facebook then becomes a kind of Web inside the Web—a platform or area where Web pages created by users (called "profiles") are linked together by the users themselves into networks, and where the applications are supplied by outside developers.

At some point in the future, these applications could include typical Office functionality like word processing and spreadsheets. But probably not, because these applications are already well performed by Microsoft Office and others. Instead businesses will be turning to Facebook to enhance the productivity of their employees by developing collaboration and meeting tools. Is Microsoft worried? Probably not, because people will still need a Windows or other operating system such as Mac OS to gain access to Facebook. So the social network operating system is not a substitute for a computer operating system. Not yet. Does Microsoft want to play in this new arena? Yes. It invested $250 million in Facebook in October 2007 for a 1.6% stake. This valued Facebook at $15 billion, and is a sign of how desperate Microsoft is to play in this new field. In 2007, Facebook had revenue of only $200 million a year, and for 2008, its revenues are estimated to be between $300-$350 million.. It's quite a distance to $15 billion.

(continued)

Not to be outdone by a mere start-up, Google refuses to give up the top spot in Silicon Valley's pantheon of creative genius. If Facebook promises to connect the world, Google wants to make sure it can play there too. Actually, Google wants to create a social networking world that runs on its standards and that would be universal to all social networks now and in the future. The problem with Facebook's opening to the world is that it's a closed world and creates applications that run only on Facebook. There are thousands of social networks that are more specialized, and are growing at faster rates than the big general social networks like Facebook and MySpace. Instead, Google has created a set of standard programs that enable three generic social network core functions and would be usable on all social networks. You can see these programs at Opensocial.com. These core functions are profile information (user data), friends information (social graph), and activities (events like news, schedules, reports of friends movements).

OpenSocial already has many friends who will host these applications: Engage, Friendster, hi5, Hyves, imeem, LinkedIn, MySpace, Ning, Oracle, Orkut, Plaxo, Salesforce.com, Six Apart, Tianji, Viadeo, and XING. Developers include Flixster, iLike, Friendster, Viadeo and Oracle,

along with thousands of individual small developers. All told, according if you add up all the social networks that host OpenSocial applications, as of October 2008, it will reach 500 million users. There seems to be a business network of social networking companies. The advantage for developers is that they can develop one application and have it run on all social networks. Another advantage is that this functionality can be added to any program, browser, or Microsoft Office application. For instance, you might be working on a particularly annoying spreadsheet and get help instantly from one of your business pals who's a wiz at spreadsheets. Or be in a Word document and suffer a loss of words. What better time to call in help from your friends? One consequence is that social networking functionality can be added to any program, and you will no longer have to go a social network site like Facebook in order to network. Social networking is a functionality, not a URL.

The company that seems to be in the crosshairs of all this activity is MySpace, the leading social network site by orders of magnitude. They have built a closed platform and do not allow outside developers to create applications, and certainly not to collect advertising revenues. It remains to be seen how long MySpace can maintain this isolation.

■■ **SOURCES:** "Report: Facebook Making $34.5M in Virtual Sales," by Mark Hefflinger, DMW Daily, September 2, 2008; "OpenSocial Now Reaches 350 Million Users, and Growing," by Erick Schonfeld, August 30, 2008; "Why So Many Want to Create Facebook Applications," by Riva Richmond, *Wall Street Journal*, September 4, 2007; "Facebook Gets Help From Its Friends," *Wall Street Journal*, June 22, 2007; "Exclusive: Facebook's New Face," by David Kirkpatrick, *Fortune*, May 25, 2007; "Facebook Opens Its Pages As a Way to Fuel Growth," *Wall Street Journal*, May 21, 2007.

In dynamic pricing, merchants change their prices based on both their understanding of how much value the customer attaches to the product and their own desire to make a sale. Likewise, customers change their offers to buy based on both their perceptions of the seller's desire to sell and their own need for the product. If you as a customer really want the product right now, you will be charged a higher price in a dynamic pricing regime, and you will willingly pay a higher price than if you placed less value on the product and were willing to wait several days to buy it. For instance, if you want to travel from New York to San Francisco to attend a last-minute business conference, and then return as soon as possible, you will be charged twice as much as a tourist who agrees to stay over the weekend.

In contrast, traditional mass-market merchants generally use **fixed pricing—** one national price, everywhere, for everyone. Fixed pricing first appeared in the nineteenth century with the development of mass national markets and retail stores that could sell to a national audience. Prior to this period, all pricing was dynamic and local, with prices derived through a process of negotiation between the customer and the merchant. Computers and the development of the Internet have contributed to a return of dynamic pricing. The difference is that with the Internet, dynamic pricing can be conducted globally, continuously, and at a very low cost.

There are many other types of dynamic pricing that preceded the Internet. Airlines have used dynamic pricing since the early 1980s to change the price of airline tickets depending on available unused capacity and the willingness of business travelers to pay a premium for immediate bookings. Airline yield management software programs seek to ensure that a perishable item (an empty airline seat is useless once the plane takes off) is sold before flight time at some price above zero.

The use of coupons sent to selected customers, and even college scholarships given to selected students to encourage their enrollment, are a form of both price discrimination and dynamic pricing. In these examples, the price of the item is adjusted to demand and available supply, and certain consumers are discriminated against by charging them higher prices while others are advantaged by receiving lower prices for the same products, namely, a reduced price for an item or a college education.

Newer forms of dynamic pricing on the Internet include bundling, trigger pricing, utilization pricing, and personalization pricing. As discussed in Chapter 7, bundling of digital goods is the practice of including low-demand products in a bundle "for free" in order to increase total revenues. **Trigger pricing**, used in m-commerce applications, adjusts prices based on the location of the consumer—for example, walking within 400 yards of a restaurant may trigger an immediate 10% dinner coupon on a portable Web device. **Utilization pricing** adjusts prices based on utilization of the product; for example, Progressive Insurance Company adjusts the annual cost of automobile insurance based on mileage driven. **Personalization pricing** adjusts prices based on the merchant's estimate of how much the customer truly values the product; for instance, Web merchants may charge committed fans of a musician higher prices for the privilege of receiving a new DVD before its official release to retail stores. Higher-cost hardbound books sell primarily to committed fans of writers, while less-committed fans wait for cheaper paperback versions to appear. For a look at some of the controversial issues of dynamic pricing, read *Insight on Society: Dynamic Pricing: Is This Price Right?*

Auctions—one form of dynamic pricing mechanism—are used throughout the e-commerce landscape. The most widely known auctions are **consumer-to-consumer (C2C) auctions**, in which the auction house is simply an intermediary market maker, providing a forum where consumers—buyers and sellers—can

fixed pricing
one national price, everywhere, for everyone

trigger pricing
adjusts prices based on the location of the consumer

utilization pricing
adjusts prices based on utilization of the product

personalization pricing
adjusts prices based on the merchant's estimate of how much the customer truly values the product

consumer-to-consumer (C2C) auctions
auction house acts as an intermediary market maker, providing a forum where consumers can discover prices and trade

business-to-consumer (B2C) auctions
auction house sells goods it owns, or controls, using various dynamic pricing models

INSIGHT ON SOCIETY

DYNAMIC PRICING: IS THIS PRICE RIGHT?

How do you set the price for goods on the Internet? Following an ancient Phoenician formula, most retailers calculate costs and multiply by two to come up with a price. But, this was just the beginning of the pricing process. Ancient merchants then went to market where they had to haggle before getting the sale. For a wealthy looking prospect, the price might start out very high, and for a commoner, at a much lower price. This kind of dynamic pricing can be found in the earliest of marketplaces: adjusting the price to a variety of market factors, including general demand, product-specific demand, supply, and specific attributes of the customer.

Now there are a host of online and offline dynamic pricing tools that can calculate what prices the market will bear at any given moment, for any given personal situation of the consumer. With new Web-based tools, there's a perfect price for every time of day, every hour, and for every customer. Hold on to your wallets!

There are many different kinds of dynamic pricing. Time-based dynamic pricing adjusts the price to different points in the product life cycle, charging more in the beginning with a new product because many customers want the latest fashions, music, literature, computers, and other innovations. Peak-load dynamic pricing adjusts prices to times of the day when the supply is relatively fixed. Clearance dynamic pricing is used when products lose value over time. All types of dynamic pricing segment the market according to the willingness of customers to pay through different channels, at different times, and with different amounts of effort. Just about all economic models of dynamic pricing assume a nearly perfect rational consumer who will always and instantly react to price changes (so-called "unbounded rationality"). We all have friends who seem like this sometimes and are willing to chase a deal for even marginal gains.

Web-based dynamic systems developed by SAP, DemandTec Inc., Hewlett-Packard, and General Electric sift through massive databases crammed with up-to-date information on orders, promotions, product revenues, and stock levels in warehouses. Based on this information, a pricing plan is developed for nearly all products. On the Web, menu costs—the cost of adjusting prices—are very low, and pricing plans can be implemented across the country nearly instantaneously. In the future, for offline physical stores, the dynamic pricing industry has solutions also: radio frequency tagging of price stickers in stores and electronic shopping cart screens attached to every physical shopping cart. Gartner estimates that 50% of the Global 2000 retailers have adopted dynamic pricing as their dominant pricing model.

DHL Worldwide Express used to establish its prices the old-fashioned way—one product, one price, across the nation and the world. Unfortunately, DHL's prices were often higher than those of rivals FedEx and UPS. "We knew we had to bring prices down, but didn't know by how much," says Aman Adinew, DHL's director of pricing and revenue management. To find out how to price products, DHL purchased dynamic pricing software from Zilliant Inc. in Austin, Texas. The system loaded in various test prices for services, including the prices of competitors. Then the system offered Web and telephone customers seeking rate information a number of different prices. DH L learned how low it needed to go in prices but still make a profit. Now DHL turns 25% of callers and Web queries into customers, up from 17% before, revenue is up 13%, and gross margins have jumped 5.4%.

In a recent survey, Consumer Reports Webwatch surveyed dynamic pricing at popular Web destinations. At BarnesandNoble, a hardcover book priced at $20.80 on Wednesday suddenly popped to $26.00 on Friday. The price for a pair of shoes at the fashion site Zappos increased $3.95 in four days. And after making multiple different reservations on Expedia and

(continued)

Travelocity, the researchers found real-time quotes on the precise same vacations based on the Web browser used, and whether the browser had cookies based on previous use of these sites.

Dynamic pricing has its opponents, such as consumer groups and individual consumers who oppose the idea of being exploited based on their personal situations. A June 2005 study by the Annenberg Center at the University of Pennsylvania found that nearly two-thirds of those surveyed believed incorrectly that it was illegal for online retailers to charge different people different prices. Almost 90% strongly objected to the idea of online stores charging people different prices for the same products based on information collected about their shopping habits. While the consuming public takes a dim view of paying, say, $500 more for an airline seat than the person next to them, marketing professors think dynamic pricing is a natural part of healthy markets where price is used to adjust supply and demand, as long as price discrimination does not take place along ethnic or religious lines. But when used badly, especially when the consumer becomes aware of paying a discriminate price that is higher (rather than lower—everyone loves a deal), then the merchant can pay a hefty price.

For instance, in September 2000, Amazon found itself in the midst of a public relations nightmare when customers in online chat rooms discovered that they had been charged different prices for the same DVDs. Amazon founder Jeff Bezos denied that the incongruent prices resulted from gathering customer purchasing and behavioral data, and claimed instead that they were simply the result of random price testing to determine the correct price point for the products. Amazon was forced to apologize and issue refunds to approximately 7,000 customers. Today, Amazon claims that it absolutely does not use dynamic pricing despite rumors that Amazon will adjust the prices for goods based on what the consumer has already put in their shopping carts. Carts with "high value" items suggest a wealthy customer who would pay higher prices.

Although some consumers become irate when they are charged more for a product than others, other reports on dynamic pricing have concluded that customers are also willing to pay more for quality and superior service, whether perceived or real. For instance, most customers are willing to pay for overnight shipping at a high price. It appears that some forms of dynamic pricing are acceptable and others not. Research on dynamic pricing has found that consumers find discrimination is considered fair as long as all buyers have the possibility to achieve all price levels. For instance, consumers think it's fair that someone pays less for a bottle of soda when they walk to a vendor's stand to get the drink, and more to have the soda delivered to them by a vendor. Consumers also consider it fair to pay a little less for a book online (and wait a week to get it), and pay a little more at a bookstore to get it immediately. Consumers find dynamic pricing unfair when they believe they never stand a chance to get the low price, never knew about it, could not reasonably find out about it, and, as a result, feel duped or taken advantage of.

Unfortunately, dynamic pricing on the Web seems to work most commonly when the consumer does not have a clue it is occurring. When price transparency is reduced, price discrimination flourishes. Most people on the Web (if not everywhere) are not unboundedly rational. Instead they are boundedly rational because they do not have perfect information, often cannot respond to random or instant changes in price even on the Internet, and would have to expend something to get more information. While the Internet probably increases price transparency when compared to physical markets, there are still plenty of opportunities to exploit consumers' bounded rationality.

SOURCES: "Pay Your Money, Or You're Taking a Chance," Consumer Reports, consumerwebwatch.org, July 6, 2007; "Dynamic Pricing of Network Goods With Boundedly Rational Consumers," by Roy Radner and Arun Sundararajan, Working Paper CeDEER, June, 2006; "Dynamic Pricing in Name-Your-Own-Price Channels: Bidding Behavior, Seller Profit, and Price Acceptance," by Ill-Horn Hann, Oliver Hinz and Martin Spann, WISE (Workshop on Information Systems and Economics), 2006; "What Consumers and Retailer Should Know About Dynamic Pricing," Knowledge@Wharton, July 27, 2005, "Web Sites Change Prices Based on Customers' Habits, by Anita Ramasastry, CNN.com, June 24, 2005; "Dynamic Pricing in Retail Will Only Work if Customers Approve," by Gartner (Hung LeHong) June 7, 2005; "Can differential prices be fair?," by J. Cox, J. *Journal of Product and Brand Management*, 10 (5), Cox, J. (2001); "The use and perceived fairness of price-setting rules in the bulk electricity market," by P. Dickson; and R. Kalapurakal, *Journal of Economic Psychology*, 15 (3), (1994).

discover prices and trade. Less well known are **business-to-consumer (B2C) auctions** where a business owns or controls assets and uses dynamic pricing to establish the price. Established merchants on occasion use B2C auctions to sell excess goods. This form of auction or dynamic pricing will grow along with C2C auctions. Online auctions are expected to grow in the range of 12%–18% annually between 2008 and 2012, with some firms such as eBay growing at faster rates because of international expansion to new markets. In 2008, C2C auction sites in the United States generated about $25 billion in gross revenue, and B2C auction sites generated about $19 billion (see **Figure 11.3**).

Some leading online auction sites are listed in **Table 11.3**. Auctions are not limited to goods and services. They can also be used to allocate resources, and bundles of resources, among any group of bidders. For instance, if you wanted to establish an optimal schedule for assigned tasks in an office among a group of clerical workers, an auction in which workers bid for assignments would come close to producing a nearly optimal solution in a short amount of time (Parkes and Ungar, 2000). In short, auctions—like all markets—are ways of allocating resources among independent agents (bidders).

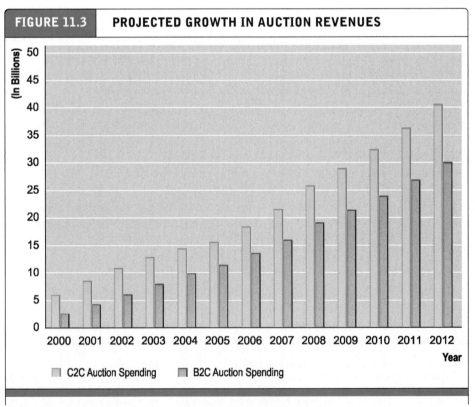

| FIGURE 11.3 | PROJECTED GROWTH IN AUCTION REVENUES |

C2C and B2C auctions are expected to continue growing in the U.S. at double-digit rates through 2012.
SOURCES: Based on data from eMarketer, 2005; Jupiter Research, 2001; authors' estimates.

TABLE 11.3	LEADING ONLINE AUCTION SITES
GENERAL	
eBay	The world market leader in auctions: 68 million visitors a month and hundreds of thousands of products.
uBid	uBid has registered over 5 million customers and sold over $2 billion dollars in merchandise since it started in 1997. The company currently attracts over 2 million unique visitors a month.
BidZ	General merchandise. Over 4 million monthly visitors.
Auctions.amazon	General consumer and business close-out auctions. Over 1 million monthly visitors.
Bid4Assets	Liquidation of distressed assets from government and the public sector, corporations, restructurings, and bankruptcies. Over 200,000 visitors monthly.
Auctions.samsclub	Sam's Club brand merchandise in a variety of categories. Over 400,000 monthly visitors.
SPECIALIZED	
Racersauction	Specialized site for automobile racing parts.
Philatelicphantasies	Stamp site for professionals, monthly online stamp auction.
Teletrade	America's largest fully automated auction company of certified coins including ancient gold, silver, and copper coins. Also offers sports cards.
Baseball-cards.com	The Internet's first baseball card store. Offers weekly 5,000 plus lot auctions of baseball, football, basketball, hockey, wire photos, and more.
Oldandsold	Online auction service specializing in quality antiques. Dealers pay a 3% commission on merchandise sold.

WHY ARE AUCTIONS SO POPULAR? BENEFITS AND COSTS OF AUCTIONS

The Internet is primarily responsible for the resurgence in auctions. Although electronic network-based auctions such as AUCNET in Japan (an electronic automobile auction for used cars) were developed in the late 1980s, these pre-Internet auctions required an expensive telecommunications network to implement. The Internet provides a global environment and very low fixed and operational costs for the aggregation of huge buyer audiences composed of millions of consumers worldwide who can use a universally available technology (Internet browsers) to shop for goods (Bapna, et al., 2001).

Benefits of Auctions

Aside from the sheer game-like fun of participating in auctions, consumers, merchants, and society as a whole derive a number of economic benefits from participating in Internet auctions. These benefits include:

- **Liquidity:** Sellers can find willing buyers, and buyers can find sellers. The Internet enormously increased the liquidity of traditional auctions that usually required all participants to be present in a single room. Now, sellers and buyers can be located anywhere around the globe. Just as important, buyers and sellers can find a global market for rare items that would not have existed before the Internet.

- **Price discovery:** Buyers and sellers can quickly and efficiently develop prices for items that are difficult to assess, where the price depends on demand and supply, and where the product is rare. For instance, how could a merchant (or buyer) price a Greek oil lamp made in 550 B.C. (to use just one example of the rare items that can be found on eBay)? How could a consumer even find a Greek oil lamp without the Internet? It would be difficult and costly for all parties.

- **Price transparency:** Public Internet auctions allow everyone in the world to see the asking and bidding prices for items. It is difficult for merchants to engage in price discrimination (charging some customers more) when the items are available on auctions. However, because even huge auction sites such as eBay do not include all the world's online auction items (there are other auction sites in the world), there still may be more than one world price for a given item (there are inter-market price differences).

- **Market efficiency:** Auctions can, and often do, lead to reduced prices, and hence reduced profits for merchants, leading to an increase in consumer welfare—one measure of market efficiency. Online auctions provide consumers the chance to find real bargains at potentially give-away prices; they also provide access to a very wide selection of goods that would be impossible for consumers to physically access by visiting stores.

- **Lower transaction costs:** Online auctions can lower the cost of selling and purchasing products, benefiting both merchants and consumers. Like other Internet markets, such as retail markets, Internet auctions have very low (but not zero) transaction costs. A sale at an auction can be consummated quickly and with very low transaction costs when compared to the physical world of markets.

- **Consumer aggregation:** Sellers benefit from large auction sites' ability to aggregate a large number of consumers who are motivated to purchase something in one marketspace. Auction-site search engines that lead consumers directly to the products they are seeking make it very likely that consumers who visit a specific auction really are interested and ready to buy at some price.

- **Network effects:** The larger an auction site becomes in terms of visitors and products for sale, the more valuable it becomes as a marketplace for everyone by providing liquidity and several other benefits listed previously, such as lower transaction costs, higher efficiency, and better price transparency. For instance, because eBay is so large—garnering close to 90% of all C2C auction commerce in the United States—it is quite likely you will find what you want to buy at a good price, and highly probable you will find a buyer for just about anything.

Risks and Costs of Auctions for Consumers and Businesses

There are a number of risks and costs involved in participating in auctions. In some cases, auction markets can fail—like all markets at times (we describe auction market failure in more detail later). Some of the more important risks and costs to keep in mind are:

- **Delayed consumption costs:** Internet auctions can go on for days, and shipping will take additional time. If you ordered from a mail-order catalog, you would likely receive the product much faster, or if you went to a physical store, you would be able to obtain the product immediately.

- **Monitoring costs:** Participation in auctions requires your time to monitor bidding.

- **Equipment costs:** Internet auctions require you to purchase a computer system, pay for Internet access, and learn a complex operating system.

- **Trust risks:** Online auctions are the single largest source of Internet fraud. Using auctions increases the risk of experiencing a loss.

- **Fulfillment costs:** Typically, the buyer pays fulfillment costs of packing, shipping, and insurance, whereas at a physical store these costs are included in the retail price.

Auction sites such as eBay have taken a number of steps to reduce consumer participation costs and trust risk. For instance, auction sites attempt to solve the trust problem by providing a rating system in which previous customers rate sellers based on their overall experience with the merchant. Although helpful, this solution does not always work. Auction fraud is the leading source of e-commerce complaints to federal law enforcement officials. One partial solution to high monitoring costs is, ironically, fixed pricing. At eBay, consumers can reduce the cost of monitoring and waiting for auctions to end by simply clicking on the "Buy It Now!" button and paying a premium price. The difference between the "Buy It Now" price and the auction price is the cost of monitoring. Also, most online auctions reduce monitoring costs by providing both a watch list and proxy bidding. **Watch lists** permit the consumer to monitor specific auctions of interest, requiring the consumer to pay close attention only in the last few minutes of bidding. **Proxy bidding** allows the consumer to enter a maximum price, and the auction software automatically bids for the goods up to that maximum price in small increments.

Nevertheless, given the costs of participating in online auctions, the generally lower cost of goods on Internet auctions is in part a compensation for the other additional costs consumers experience. On the other hand, consumers experience lower search costs and transaction costs because there usually are no intermediaries (unless, of course, the seller is an online business operating on an auction site, in which case there is a middleman cost), and usually there are no local or state taxes.

Merchants face considerable risks and costs as well. At auctions, merchants may end up selling goods for prices far below what they might have achieved in conventional markets. Merchants also face risks of nonpayment, false bidding, bid rigging, monitoring, transaction fees charged by the auction site, credit card transaction processing fees, and the administration costs of entering price and product information. We explore the benefits and risks for merchants later in this chapter.

watch lists
permit the consumer to monitor specific auctions of interest

proxy bidding
allows the consumer to enter a maximum price, and the auction software automatically bids for the goods up to that maximum price in small increments

Market-Maker Benefits: Auctions as an E-commerce Business Model

Online auctions have been among the most successful business models in retail and B2B commerce. eBay, the Internet's most lucrative auction site, has been profitable nearly since its inception. eBay has expanded into three lines of business that it believes are related: marketplaces (the original business), payments (PayPal), and communications (Skype). The strategy for eBay has been to make money off every stage in the auction cycle. eBay earns revenue in several ways: transaction fees based on the amount of the sale, listing fees for display of goods, financial service fees from payment systems such as PayPal, and advertising or placement fees where sellers pay extra for special services such as particular display or listing services. In addition, eBay purchased Skype, the Internet telephone company, so that buyers and sellers could communicate online with one another during the auction process. eBay has taken a significant write down in the value of Skype, but it remains the largest free Internet phone service.

However, it is on the cost side that online auctions have extraordinary advantages over ordinary retail or catalog sites. Auction sites carry no inventory and do not perform any fulfillment activities—they need no warehouses, shipping, or logistical facilities. Sellers and consumers provide these services and bear these costs. In this sense, online auctions are an ideal digital business because they involve simply the transfer of information.

Even though eBay has been extraordinarily successful, the success of online auctions is qualified by the fact that the marketplace for online auctions is highly concentrated. eBay dominates the online auction market, followed by BidZ and then Amazon Auctions; many of the smaller auction sites are not profitable because they lack sufficient sellers and buyers to achieve liquidity. In auctions, network effects are highly influential, and the tendency is for one or two very large auction sites to dominate, with hundreds of smaller specialty auction sites (sites that sell specialized goods such as stamps) being barely profitable.

TYPES AND EXAMPLES OF AUCTIONS

Auction theory is a well-established area of research, largely in economics (McAfee and McMillan, 1987; Milogram, 1989; Vickrey, 1961). Much of this research is theoretical, and prior to the emergence of public Internet auctions, there was not a great deal of empirical data on auctions or consumer behavior in auctions. Previous literature has identified a wide range of auction types, some of which are seller-biased, and others of which are more buyer-biased. Internet auctions are very different from traditional auctions (Morgan Stanley Dean Witter, 2000). Traditional auctions are relatively short-lived (such as a Sotheby's art auction), and have a fixed number of bidders, usually present in the same room. Online Internet auctions, in contrast, can go on much longer (a week), and have a variable number of bidders who come and go from the auction arena.

Internet Auction Basics

Before a business turns to auctions as a marketing channel, its managers need to understand some basic facts about online auctions.

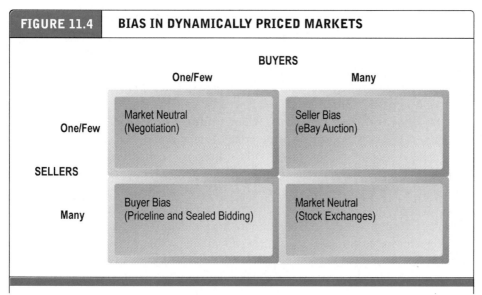

| FIGURE 11.4 | **BIAS IN DYNAMICALLY PRICED MARKETS** |

BUYERS

	One/Few	Many
One/Few	Market Neutral (Negotiation)	Seller Bias (eBay Auction)
Many	Buyer Bias (Priceline and Sealed Bidding)	Market Neutral (Stock Exchanges)

SELLERS

Dynamically priced markets can be either neutral or biased in favor of buyers or sellers.

Market Power and Bias in Dynamically Priced Markets Dynamically priced markets are not always "fair" in the sense of distributing market power to influence prices. **Figure 11.4** illustrates four different market bias situations that occur in dynamic markets.

In situations in which the number of buyers and sellers is few or equal in size, markets tend to be neutral, favoring neither the buyer nor the seller. One-on-one negotiations, barter markets, and stock exchanges all have this quality of neutrality, although specialists and market makers exact a commission for matching buy and sell orders. In stock markets, which are sometimes called a "double auction" because bids and offers are made continuously, many sellers and buyers call out prices for bundles of stock (of which there is a very large supply) until a deal is struck. In contrast, auctions such as those run by eBay and reverse auctions offered by companies such as Priceline have built-in biases. Usually on eBay, there is just one seller or a small number of sellers marketing goods that are in limited supply (or even rare goods) to millions of buyers who are competing on price. Priceline offers just the opposite bias and shares many features with a sealed-bid RFQ (request for quote) market. In Priceline's reverse auctions (described in greater detail later in this chapter), buyers post their unique needs for goods and services and a price they are willing to pay, while many sellers compete against one another for the available business. Of course, inherent bias in a marketplace does not mean consumers and merchants cannot find "good deals" and thousands of motivated customers willing to purchase goods at profitable prices.

However, the inherent biases should provide cautions to both merchants and consumers; namely, goods in auctions sometimes sell for far above their fair market value as they get bid too high, and sometimes for far less than their fair market value

fair market value
the average of prices for a product or service in a variety of dynamic and fixed-price markets around the world

uniform pricing rule
there are multiple winners and they all pay the same price

discriminatory pricing
winners pay different amounts depending on what they bid

bid rigging
bidders communicate prior to submitting their bids, and rig their bids to ensure that the lowest price is higher than it might otherwise be

price matching
sellers agree informally or formally to set floor prices on auction items below which they will not sell

as merchants become too desperate for business. **Fair market value** could be defined here as the average of prices for that product or service in a variety of dynamic and fixed-price markets around the world. We explore other auction market failures in a later section.

Price Allocation Rules: Uniform vs. Discriminatory Pricing There are different rules for establishing the winning bids and prices in auctions where there are multiple units for sale, say, 10 IBM laptop PCs. With a **uniform pricing rule**, there are multiple winners and they all pay the same price (usually the lowest winning bid—sometimes called a market clearing price). Other auctions use **discriminatory pricing** in which winners pay different amounts depending on what they bid. See, for instance, Ubid.com, which typically auctions multiple units from manufacturers. Like so many other auction rules, price allocation can change bidding strategy in auctions. For instance, in a uniform pricing auction for 10 IBM laptops, you may bid a very high price for a few units, knowing that others will not follow, but you will only pay a price equal to the lowest winning bid needed to clear out the units from the market. The person who bid for the tenth unit may have only bid 75% as high as your offer. Nevertheless, that is the price you will actually pay—the price needed to "clear the market" of all units. However, under a discriminatory pricing rule, you would be forced to pay your high bid. Obviously, from a buyer's point of view, uniform pricing is better, but from a merchant's point of view, discriminatory pricing is much better.

Public vs. Private Information in Dynamically Priced Markets In some dynamic markets, the prices being bid are secret, and are known only to one party. For instance, a firm may issue a request for bid to electrical contractors for provision of electrical service on a new building. Bidders are requested to submit sealed bids, and the lowest bidder (subject to qualifications) will be the winner. In this instance, the bidders do not know what others are bidding, and must bid their "best" price. The danger here is **bid rigging**, in which bidders communicate prior to submitting their bids, and rig their bids to ensure that the lowest price is higher than it might otherwise be (which benefits the bidder, who in this instance is receiving the bid price as payment for services to be rendered). This is a common problem in sealed bid markets. However, in auction markets, bid prices are usually public information, available to all. Here the risks are that bidders agree offline to limit their bids, that sellers use shills to submit false bids, or that sellers use the market itself as a signaling device, driving prices up. Open markets permit large players to signal prices or engage in **price matching**, where sellers agree informally or formally to set floor prices on auction items below which they will not sell. Generally such collusion exists on the sell side, where there are just a few sellers or auction houses in a position to fix prices.

Types of Auctions

Now that you have learned some basic auction market rules and practices, it's time to consider some of the major forms of dynamically priced markets and auctions, both online and offline. **Table 11.4** describes the major types of auctions, how they work, and their biases. As you can see in Table 11.4, aside from the different formats and rules, there are many other differences among auctions. As noted above, there are both discriminatory and uniform pricing rules, although the latter seem to be most

TABLE 11.4	TYPES OF AUCTIONS AND DYNAMIC PRICING MECHANISMS	
AUCTION TYPE	**MECHANISM**	**BIAS**
Sealed bid market (B2B e-procurement—Ariba Sourcing; eBay's Elance)	Sealed-bid auction, RFQs. Winner is chosen from lowest bidders at acceptable quality levels.	Buyer bias: Multiple vendors competing against one another.
Vickrey auction (private auction)	Sealed-bid auction, single unit; highest bidder wins at the second-highest bid price.	Seller bias: Single seller and multiple buyers competing against one another.
English auction (eBay)	Public ascending price, single unit; highest bidder wins at a price just above the second highest bid. Buyers can skip bidding at each price, but return at higher prices.	Seller bias: Single seller and multiple buyers competing against one another.
Dutch-traditional (Dutch flower market)	Public descending-price auction, single unit; seller lowers price until a buyer takes the product.	Seller bias: Single seller, and multiple buyers competing against one another.
Dutch-Internet (eBay Dutch Auction)	Public ascending price, multiple unit. Buyers bid on quantity and price. Final per-unit price is lowest successful bid, which sets a uniform price for all higher bidders as well (uniform price rule).	Seller bias: Small number of sellers and many buyers.
Japanese auction (private auction)	Public ascending price, single unit; highest bidder wins at a price just above second-highest bid (reservation price) and buyers must bid at each price to stay in auction.	Seller bias: Single seller and many buyers.
Yankee auction-Internet (variation on Dutch auction)	Public ascending price, multiple unit. Buyers bid on quantity and price per unit. Bidders ranked on price per unit, units, and time. Winners pay their actual bid prices (discriminatory rule).	Seller bias: Single seller and multiple buyers competing against one another.
Reverse auction	Public reverse English auction, descending prices, single unit. Sellers bid on price to provide products or services; winning bid is the lowest-price provider. Similar to sealed bid markets.	Buyer bias: Multiple sellers competing against one another.
Group buying (eSwarm)	Public reverse auction, descending prices, multiple units. Buyers bid on price per unit and units. Groups of sellers bid on price; winning bid is lowest-price provider.	Buyer bias: Multiple sellers competing against one another.
Name Your Own Price (Priceline)	Similar to a reverse auction except the price the consumer is willing to pay is fixed and the price offered is nonpublic. Requires a commitment to purchase at the first offered price.	Buyer bias: Multiple sellers competing against one another for an individual's business.
Double auction (NASDAQ and stock markets)	Public bid-ask negotiation; sellers ask, buyers bid. Sale consummated when participants agree on price and quantity.	Neutral: Multiple buyers and sellers competing against one another. Market bias: trading specialists (matchmakers)

NOTE: "Public" means all participants can observe prices offered.

common. Also, in some auctions, there are multiple units for sale, whereas in others, there is only a single unit for sale. The major types of Internet auctions are English, Dutch-Internet, Name Your Own Price, and Group Buying.

English auction

most common form of auction; the highest bidder wins

English Auctions The **English auction** is the easiest to understand and the most common form of auction on eBay. Typically, there is a single item up for sale from a single seller. There is a time limit when the auction ends, a reserve price below which the seller will not sell (usually secret), and a minimum incremental bid set. Multiple buyers bid against one another until the auction time limit is reached. The highest bidder wins the item (if the reserve price of the seller has been met or exceeded). English auctions are considered to be seller-biased because multiple buyers compete against one another—usually anonymously.

Traditional Dutch Auctions In the traditional Dutch auction in Aalsmeer, Holland, 5,000 flower growers—who own the auction facility—sell bundles of graded flowers to 2,000 buyers. The Dutch auction uses a clock visible to all that displays the starting price growers want for their flowers. Every few seconds, the clock ticks to a lower price. When buyers want to buy at the displayed price, they push a button to accept the lot of flowers at that price. If buyers fail to bid in a timely fashion, their competitors will win the flowers. The auction is very efficient: on average, Aalsmeer conducts 50,000 transactions daily for 15 million flowers. Dutch flower auctions are now conducted over the Internet. Buyers no longer have to be present at the market to bid, and sellers no longer have to have their flowers present in adjacent warehouses, but can ship directly from their farms (Kambil and vanHeck, 1996).

Dutch Internet auction

public ascending price, multiple unit auction. Final price is lowest successful bid, which sets price for all higher bidders

Dutch Internet Auctions In **Dutch Internet auctions**, such as those on eBay, OnSale, and others, the rules and action are different from the classical Dutch auction. The Dutch Internet auction format is perfect for sellers that have many identical items to sell. Sellers start by listing a minimum price, or a starting bid for one item, and the number of items for sale. Bidders specify both a bid price and the quantity they want to buy. The uniform price reigns. Winning bidders pay the same price per item, which is the lowest successful bid. This market clearing price can be less than some bids. If there are more buyers than items, the earliest successful bids get the goods. In general, high bidders get the quantity they want at the lowest successful price, whereas low successful bidders might not get the quantity they want (but they will get something). The action is usually quite rapid, and proxy bidding is not used. **Table 11.5** shows closing data from a sample Dutch Internet auction for a bundle of laptop computers.

In Table 11.5, the bids are arranged by price and then quantity. Under a uniform pricing rule, the lowest winning bid that clears the market of all 10 laptops is $568 and all winners pay this amount. However, the lowest winning bidder, JB505, will only receive three laptops, not four, because higher bidders are given their full allotments.

Name Your Own Price Auctions Auctions pioneered by Priceline are the second most-popular auction format on the Web. Although Priceline also acts as an intermediary, buying blocks of airline tickets and vacation packages at a discount and selling them at a reduced retail price or matching its inventory to bidders, it is best known for its Name Your Own Price auctions, where users specify what they are willing to pay for goods or services, and multiple providers bid for their business. Prices do not

TABLE 11.5	A MULTI-UNIT DUTCH INTERNET AUCTION

CLOSING AUCTION DATA

Lot number	8740240
Total Number of Units	10
Description	HP Pavilion dv6500t Laptop; Win Vista; Intel Celeron 1.73 GHz, 1 MB L2 cache; 15″ widescreen; 1 MB memory; Intel graphics accelerator
Reserve Price	None

BIDDER	DATE	TIME	BID	QUANTITY
JDMTKIS	10/25/08	18:35	$575	4
KTTX	10/25/08	18:55	$570	3
JB505	10/25/08	19:05	$568	4
VAMP	10/25/08	19:10	$565	2
DPVS	10/25/08	19:20	$565	1
RSF34	10/25/08	19:24	$560	1
CMCAL	10/25/08	19:25	$560	2

descend and are fixed: the initial consumer offer is a commitment to purchase at that price. In 2007, Priceline had over 16 million registered users, 5.1 million visitors a month, and over $1 billion in revenues. It is the eighth-ranked travel site in the United States. Today, it also arranges for the sale of new cars, hotel accommodations, car rentals, long distance telephone service, and home finance.

Table 11.6 describes the products and services available in Priceline's Name Your Own Price auctions. Clearly, a major attraction of Priceline is that it offers consumers a market biased in their favor and very low prices, up to 40% off. Brand-name suppliers compete with one another to supply services to consumers. However, it is unclear at this time if the Priceline business model can extend to other categories of products. Experiments to sell gasoline and groceries through Priceline failed.

But how can Priceline offer discounts up to 40% off prices for services provided by major name brand providers? There are several answers. First, Priceline "shields the brand" by not publicizing the prices at which major brands sell. This reduces conflict with traditional channels, including direct sales. Second, the services being sold are perishable: if a Priceline consumer did not pay something for the empty airline seat, rental car, or hotel room, sellers would not receive any revenue. Hence, sellers are highly motivated to at least cover the costs of their services by selling in a spot market at very low prices.

The strategy for sellers is to sell as much as possible through more profitable channels and then unload excess capacity on spot markets such as Priceline.

TABLE 11.6	PRICELINE NAME YOUR OWN PRICE OFFERINGS
SERVICE/PRODUCT	**DESCRIPTION**
Airline seats	Brand-name carriers bid for individual consumer business—perishable items that airlines are motivated to sell at the last minute.
Hotel rooms	Brand-name hotels bid for consumer business—perishable services that hotels are motivated to sell on a last-minute basis.
Rental cars	Brand-name rental companies bid for consumer business—perishable services that rental companies are motivated to sell on a last-minute basis.
Vacation packages	Brand-name hotels and air carriers bid for consumer business—perishable services that providers are motivated to sell on a last-minute basis.
Cruises	Cruise ship companies bid for consumer business, especially active in off-season periods.

demand aggregators

suppliers or market makers who group unrelated buyers into a single purchase in return for offering a lower purchase price. Prices on multiple units fall as the number of buyers increase

This works to the advantage of consumers, sellers, and Priceline, which charges a transaction fee to sellers.

Group Buying Auctions: Demand Aggregators A **demand aggregator** facilitates group buying of products at dynamically adjusted discount prices based on high-volume purchases. The originator of demand aggregation was Mercata, formed in 1998, and the Web's largest retail demand aggregator until it ceased operations in January 2001, when needed venture capital financing did not materialize. Mercata holds several patents covering online demand aggregation. The largest supplier today of demand aggregation software is Ewinwin, a B2B demand aggregator. In general, demand aggregation did not work well for retail sales, but it has found a home in B2B commerce as a way of organizing group buying. Trade associations and industry-buying groups have traditionally pursued group buying plans in order to reduce costs from large suppliers.

Online demand aggregation is built on two principles. First, sellers are more likely to offer discounts to buyers purchasing in volume, and, second, buyers increase their purchases as prices fall. Prices are expected to dynamically adjust to the volume of the order and the motivations of the vendors.

Although online sites dedicated to retail group buying were not a commercial success, their software and business practices have been integrated into B2B and Business-to-Government (B2G) sites as one of many dynamic-pricing mechanisms. For instance, the federal government's Department of Homeland Security is building a centralized purchasing portal that will aggregate the demand for IT commodities (such as PCs, routers, and other equipment) from many different constituent agencies in order to reduce costs. In general, demand aggregation is suitable for MRO products (commodity-like products) that are frequently purchased by a large number of organizations in high volume.

Professional Service Auctions Perhaps one of the more interesting uses for auctions on the Web is eBay's marketplace for professional services, Elance. This auction is a sealed-bid, dynamic-priced market for freelance professional services from legal and marketing services to graphics design and programming. Firms looking for professional services post a project description and request for bid on Elance. Providers of services bid for the work. The buyer can choose from among bidders on the basis of both cost and perceived quality of the providers that can be gauged from the feedback of clients posted on the site. This type of auction is a reverse Vickrey-like auction where sealed bids are submitted and the winner is usually the low-cost provider of services. Another similar site is SoloGig.

Auction Aggregators (Mega Auctions) With thousands of auctions available on the Web, how can you, your customers, or your business find the right auction for products of interest that you want to either buy or sell? **Auction aggregators** (sometimes called mega auctions) offer one solution to this problem of multiple Internet markets and inter-market price differences. Auction aggregators use computer programs to search thousands of Web auction sites, accumulating information on products, bids, auction duration, and bid increments. Consumers search auction aggregator sites for products of interest, and the site returns a list of both fixed-price sales locations and auction locations where the product is for sale. Auction aggregators work by sending Web crawlers to thousands of auction sites every night (and on some sites during the day as well), gathering all information on product listings—just like an ordinary single consumer would. However, the major sites have effectively prevented auction aggregators from searching their sites without a license.

auction aggregators
use computer programs to search thousands of Web auction sites, and aggregate information on products, bids, auction duration, and bid increments

WHEN TO USE AUCTIONS (AND FOR WHAT) IN BUSINESS

There are many different situations in which auctions are an appropriate channel for businesses to consider. For much of this chapter, we have looked at auctions from a consumer point of view. The objective of consumers is to receive the greatest value for the lowest cost. Switch perspectives now to that of a business. Remember the objective for businesses using auctions is to maximize their revenue (their share of consumer surplus) by finding the true market value of products and services, a market value that hopefully is higher in the auction channel than in fixed-price channels. **Table 11.7** provides an overview of factors to consider.

The factors to consider include:

- **Type of product:** Online auctions are most commonly used for rare and unique products for which prices are difficult to discover, and there may have been no market for the goods. However, Priceline has succeeded in developing auctions for perishable commodities (such as airline seats) for which retail prices have already been established, and some B2B auctions involve commodities such as steel (often sold at distress prices). New clothing items, new digital cameras, and new computers are generally not sold at auction because their prices are easy to discover; catalog prices are high, sustainable, and profitable; they are not

TABLE 11.7	FACTORS TO CONSIDER WHEN CHOOSING AUCTIONS
CONSIDERATIONS	DESCRIPTION
Type of product	Rare, unique, commodity, perishable
Stage of product life cycle	Early, mature, late
Channel-management issues	Conflict with retail distributors; differentiation
Type of auction	Seller vs. buyer bias
Initial pricing	Low vs. high
Bid increment amounts	Low vs. high
Auction length	Short vs. long
Number of items	Single vs. multiple
Price-allocation rule	Uniform vs. discriminatory
Information sharing	Closed vs. open bidding

perishable; and there exists an efficient market channel in the form of retail stores (online and offline).

- **Product life cycle:** For the most part, businesses have traditionally used auctions for goods at the end of their product life cycle and for products where auctions yield a higher price than fixed-price liquidation sales. However, products at the beginning of their life cycle are increasingly being sold at auction. Early releases of music, books, videos, games, and digital appliances can be sold to highly motivated early adopters who want to be the first in their neighborhood with new products. Online sales of event tickets from music concerts to sports events now account for upwards of 25% of all event ticket sales in the United States.

- **Channel management:** Established retailers such as JCPenney and Wal-Mart, and manufacturers in general, must be careful not to allow their auction activity to interfere with their existing profitable channels. For this reason, items found on established retail-site auctions tend to be late in their product life cycle, or have quantity purchase requirements.

- **Type of auction:** Sellers obviously should choose auctions where there are many buyers and only a few, or even one, seller. English ascending-price auctions such as those at eBay are best for sellers because as the number of bidders increases the higher the price tends to move.

- **Initial pricing:** Research suggests that auction items should start out with low initial bid prices in order to encourage more bidders to bid (see Bid Increments below). The lower the price, the larger the number of bidders will appear. The larger the number of bidders, the higher the prices move.

- **Bid increments:** It its generally safest to keep bid increments low so as to increase the number of bidders and the frequency of their bids. If bidders can be convinced that, for just a few more dollars, they can win the auction, then they will tend to make the higher bid and forget about the total amount they are bidding.

- **Auction length:** In general, the longer auctions are scheduled, the larger the number of bidders and the higher the prices can be go. However, once the new bid arrival rate drops off and approaches zero, bid prices stabilize. Most eBay auctions are scheduled for three days.

- **Number of items:** When a business has a number of items to sell, buyers usually expect a "volume discount," and this expectation can cause lower bids in return. Therefore, sellers should consider breaking up very large bundles into smaller bundles auctioned at different times.

- **Price allocation rule:** Most buyers believe it is "fair" that everyone pay the same price in a multi-unit auction, and a uniform pricing rule is recommended. eBay Dutch Internet auctions encourage this expectation. The idea that some buyers should pay more based on their differential need for the product is not widely supported. Therefore, sellers who want to price discriminate should do so by holding auctions for the same goods on different auction markets, or at different times, to prevent direct price comparison.

- **Closed vs. open bidding:** Closed bidding has many advantages for the seller, and sellers should use this approach whenever possible because it permits price discrimination without offending buyers. However, open bidding carries the advantage of "herd effects" and "winning effects" (described later in the chapter) in which consumers' competitive instincts to "win" drive prices higher than even secret bidding would achieve.

SELLER AND CONSUMER BEHAVIOR AT AUCTIONS

In addition to these structural considerations, you should also consider the behavior of consumers at auction sites. Research on consumer behavior at online auction sites is growing, but is still in its infancy. However, early research has produced some interesting findings.

Seller Profits: Arrival Rate, Auction Length, and Number of Units

The profit to the seller is a function of the arrival rate, auction length, and the number of units for auction. However, each of these relationships suffers a declining return to scale and rapidly falls off after an optimal point is reached (Vakrat and Seidman, 1998; 1999) (see **Figure 11.5**). For this reason, in real-world auctions on eBay, sellers with a large number of units to sell, say, hundreds of PC laptops, usually have multiple concurrent auctions with about 10 units for sale in each auction, with a duration of three days. The auction is just long enough to attract most of the likely bidders, but not so long as to run up the cost of posting the auction beyond a profitable level. The more popular an auction (the more bidders who arrive), the longer an auction should be, up to the point where the costs of maintaining the auction listing outweigh the additional profit brought by the last bidder. These dynamics suggest a kind of bidding frenzy for popular items,

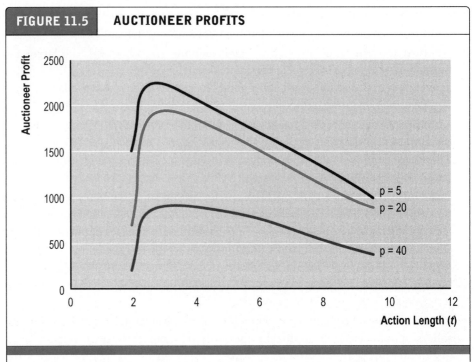

FIGURE 11.5   **AUCTIONEER PROFITS**

The auctioneer's profit is determined by the arrival rate at the auction (p), and the length of the auction (t). Profitability rises rapidly at first, but then falls off rapidly as costs rise. Profits also rise with the number of units auctioned up to a maximum point, and then fall off rapidly.

SOURCE: Based on data from Vakrat and Seidmann, 1998.

in which the prices bid depend on the number of bidders, length of time, and units offered.

Auction Prices: Are They the Lowest?

It is widely assumed that auction prices are lower than prices in other fixed-price markets. Empirical evidence is mixed on this assumption. Vakrat and Seidmann (1999) found auction prices were 25% lower on average than prices for the identical goods found in catalogs produced by the same retailers. Brynjolfsson and Smith (2001) also found that auction prices for CDs were lower than online store prices. Lee found, however, that auction prices for used cars in Japan on the AUCNET auction site were actually higher than fixed-price markets, in part because the quality of cars on the auction site was higher than cars found in car lots (Lee et al., 1999–2000).

There are many reasons why auction prices might be higher than those in fixed-price markets for items of identical quality, and why auction prices in one auction market may be higher than those in other auction markets. A considerable body of previous research has shown that consumers are not driven solely by value maximization, but instead are influenced by many situational factors, irrelevant and wrong information, and misperceptions when they make market decisions (Simonson and Tversky, 1992). Auctions are social events—shared social environments, where bidders adjust to one another (Hanson and Putler, 1996). Briefly, bidders base their bids on what others previously bid, and this can lead to an upward cascading effect (Arkes and Hutzel, 2000). In a study of hundreds of eBay auctions for Sony PlayStations, CD players, Mexican pottery, and Italian silk ties, Dholakia and Soltysinski (2001) found that bidders exhibited **herd behavior** (the tendency to gravitate toward, and bid for, auction listings with one or more existing bids) by making multiple bids on some auctions (coveted comparables), and making no bids at auctions for comparable items (overlooked comparables). Herd behavior was lower for products where there was more agreement and more objective clues on the value of the products—Sony PlayStations, for instance, compared to Italian silk ties. Herd behavior resulted in consumers paying higher prices than necessary for reasons having no foundation in economic reality.

> **herd behavior**
> the tendency to gravitate toward, and bid for, auction listings with one or more existing bids

The behavioral reality of participating in auctions can produce many unintended results. Winners can suffer **winner's regret**, the feeling after winning an auction that they paid too much for an item, which indicates that their winning bid does not reflect what they thought the item was worth but rather what the second bidder thought the item was worth. Sellers can experience **seller's lament**, reflecting the fact that they sold an item at a price just above the second place bidder, never knowing how much the ultimate winner might have paid or the true value to the final winner. Auction losers can experience **loser's lament**, the feeling of having been too cheap in bidding and failing to win. In summary, auctions can lead to both winners paying too much and sellers receiving too little. Both of these outcomes can be minimized when sellers and buyers have a very clear understanding of the prices for items in a variety of different online and offline markets.

> **winner's regret**
> the winner's feeling after an auction that he or she paid too much for an item
>
> **seller's lament**
> concern that one will never know how much the ultimate winner might have paid, or the true value to the final winner
>
> **loser's lament**
> the feeling of having been too cheap in bidding and failing to win

Consumer Trust in Auctions

Auction sites have the same difficulties creating a sense of consumer trust as all other e-commerce Web sites, although in the case of auction sites, the operators of the marketplace do not directly control the quality of goods being offered and cannot directly vouch for the integrity of customers. This opens the possibility for criminal actors to appear as either sellers or buyers. eBay is the single largest source of consumer fraud on the Internet. Several studies have found that trust and credibility increase as users gain more experience, if trusted third-party seals are present, and if the site has a wide variety of consumer services for tracking purchases (or fraud), thus giving the user a sense of control (Krishnamurthy, 2001; Stanford-Makovsky, 2002; Nikander and Karnonen, 2002; Bailey, et al., 2002; Kollock, 1999). Because of the powerful role that trust plays in online consumer behavior, eBay and most auction sites make considerable efforts to develop automated trust-enhancing mechanisms such as seller and buyer ratings, escrow services, and authenticity guarantees (see the next section).

WHEN AUCTION MARKETS FAIL: FRAUD AND ABUSE IN AUCTIONS

Markets fail to produce socially desirable outcomes (maximizing consumer welfare) in four situations: information asymmetry, monopoly power, public goods, and externalities.

Online and offline auction markets are particularly prone to fraud, which produces information asymmetries between sellers and buyers and among buyers, which in turn causes auction markets to fail. According to the Internet Crime Complaint Center (IC3), 35.7% of the fraud complaints reported to the Center related to online auctions, the most common frauds being merchants' failure to deliver after payment and consumers failing to pay after shipment (National White Collar Crime Center/FBI, 2008). The median loss was $484 and the most common fraudulent payment mechanisms were money orders and credit cards. The Federal Trade Commission (FTC), in 2008, had some good news: Internet auction fraud complaints dropped to seventh place in the Internet complaint category—only 24,000 complaints of fraud were reported to the FTC. The leading complaint was identity theft (258,000 complaints) (Federal Trade Commission, 2008). However, this data fails to measure the overall extent of auction fraud because many consumers do not report being defrauded to the FTC. **Table 11.8** lists the most common and important frauds.

eBay and many other auction sites have investigation units that receive complaints from consumers and investigate reported abuses. Nevertheless, with millions of visitors per week and hundreds of thousands of auctions to monitor, eBay is highly dependent on the good faith of sellers and consumers to follow the rules.

11.3 E-COMMERCE PORTALS

Port: From the Latin porta, an entrance or gateway to a locality.

Portals are the most frequently visited sites on the Web if only because they typically are the first page to which many users point their browser on startup. The top portals such as Yahoo, AOL, and MSN have hundreds of millions of unique visitors worldwide each month. Web portal sites are gateways to the more than 50 billion Web pages available on the Internet. Perhaps the most important service provided by portals is that of helping people find the information they are looking for on the Web. The original portals in the early days of e-commerce portals were search engines. Consumers would pass through search engine portals on their way to rich, detailed, in-depth content on the Web. But portals have evolved into much more complex Web sites that provide news, entertainment, maps, images, social networks, in-depth information, and education on a growing variety of topics all contained at the portal site. Portals today seek to be a sticky destination site, not merely a gateway through which visitors pass. In this respect, Web portals are very much like television networks: destination sites for content supported by advertising revenues. Portals today want visitors to stay a long time—the longer the better. For the most part they succeed: portals are places where people linger for a long time.

TABLE 11.8	TYPES OF AUCTION FRAUDS
TYPE OF FRAUD	**DESCRIPTION**
Feedback Offenses	
Shill feedback	Using secondary IDs or other auction site members to inflate seller ratings.
Feedback abuse	Any abuse of the feedback forum.
Feedback extortion	Threatening negative feedback in return for a benefit
Feedback solicitation	Offering to sell, trade, or buy feedback.
Buying Offenses	
Transaction interference	E-mailing buyers to warn them away from a seller.
Invalid bid retraction	Using the retraction option to make high bids, discovering the maximum bid of current high bidder, then retracting bid.
Persistent bidding	Persisting in making bids despite a warning that bids are not welcome.
Unwelcome buyer	Buying in violation of seller's terms.
Bid shielding	Using secondary user IDs or other members to artificially raise the bidding price of an item.
Nonpayment after buying	Blocking legitimate buyers by bidding high, then not paying.
Selling Offenses	
Shill bidding	Using secondary user IDs or bidders who have no actual intention to buy to artificially raise the price of an item.
Seller nonperformance	Accepting payment and failing to deliver the promised goods, either at all, or delivering goods not as described in auction (counterfeit or poor quality).
Nonselling seller	Refusing payment, failure to deliver after a successful auction.
Fee avoidance	Any of a variety of mechanisms for avoiding paying listing fees.
Transaction interception	Pretending you are a seller and accepting payment.
Contact Information/Identity Offenses	
Misrepresentation of identity	Claiming to be an employee of the auction site; representing oneself as another auction site member.
False or missing contact information	Providing false information or leaving information out
Dead/invalid e-mail addresses	Providing false contact information
Underage user	User under 18.
Miscellaneous Offenses	
Interference with site	Using any software program that would interfere with auction site operations.
Bid siphoning	E-mailing another seller's bidders and offering the same product for less.
Sending spam	Sending unsolicited offers to bidders.

enterprise portals

help employees navigate to the enterprise's human resource and corporate content

Portals also serve important functions within a business or organization. Most corporations, universities, churches, and other formal organizations have **enterprise portals** that help employees navigate to the enterprise's human resource and corporate content such as corporate news and announcements. For instance, your university has a portal through which you can register for courses, find out classroom assignments, and perform a host of other important student activities. Increasingly, these enterprise portals also provide general-purpose news and financial real-time feeds provided by content providers outside the organization, such as MSNBC News and generalized Web search capabilities. Corporate portals and intranets are the subject of other textbooks focused on the corporate uses of Web technology and are beyond the scope of this book (see Laudon and Laudon). Our focus here will be on e-commerce portals.

THE GROWTH AND EVOLUTION OF PORTALS

Web portals have changed a great deal from their initial function and role. As noted above, most of today's well-known portals began as search engines. The initial function provided by portals such as Yahoo, Lycos, Excite, AltaVista, Ask Jeeves, and later Google was to index Web page content and make this content available to users in a convenient form. Early portals expected visitors to stay only a few minutes at the site. As millions of people signed on to the Internet in the late 1990s, the number of visitors to basic search engine sites exploded commensurately. At first few people understood how a Web search site could make money by passing customers on to other destinations. But search sites attracted huge audiences, and therein lay the foundation for their success as vehicles for marketing and advertising. Search sites, recognizing the potential for commerce, expanded their offerings from simple navigation to include commerce (the sale of items directly from the Web site as well as advertising for other retail sites), content (in the form of news at first, and later in the form of weather, investments, games, health, and other subject matter), and distribution of others' content. These three characteristics have become the basic definition of portal sites since 2006, namely, sites that provide three functions: navigation of the Web, commerce, and content.

Because the value of portals to advertisers and content owners is largely a function of the size of the audience each portal reaches, portals compete with one another on reach and unique visitors. Reach is defined as the percentage of the Web audience that visits the site in a month (or some other time period), and unique visitors is defined as the number of uniquely identified individuals who visit in a month. Portals are inevitably subject to network effects: The value of the portal to advertisers and consumers increases geometrically as reach increases, which, in turn, attracts still more customers. These effects have resulted in the differentiation of the portal marketspace into three tiers: a few general-purpose mega portal sites that garner 60%–80% of the Web audience, second-tier general-purpose sites that hover around 20%–30% reach, and third-tier specialized vertical market portals that attract 2%–10% of the audience. As described in Chapter 3, the top five search engines (Google, Yahoo, MSN, AOL, and Ask.com)

FIGURE 11.6	**THE TOP 5 PORTAL/SEARCH ENGINE SITES IN THE UNITED STATES**

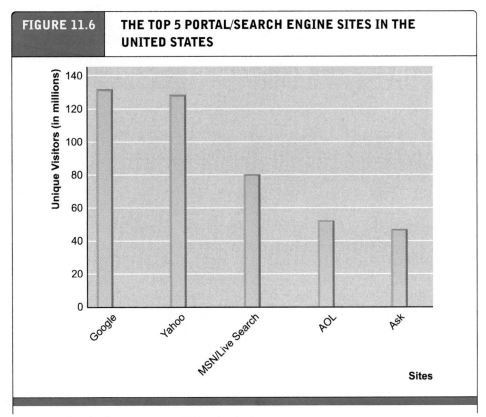

SOURCE: Based on data from Compete.com, 2008, authors' estimates.

account for over 90% of online searches. A similar pattern of concentration is observed when considering the audience share of portals/search engines as illustrated in **Figure 11.6**. However this picture is changing rapidly as large audiences move to social networking sites, and millions of users make these sites their opening or home pages.

For more insight into the nature of the competition and change among the top portals, read *Insight on Business: Battle of the Portals.*

TYPES OF PORTALS: GENERAL PURPOSE AND VERTICAL MARKET

There are two primary types of portals: general purpose portals and vertical market portals. **General purpose portals** attempt to attract a very large general audience and then retain the audience on-site by providing in-depth vertical content channels. Some general purpose portals—such as MSN and AOL—also offer limited ISP services usually in conjunction with a major telecommunications providers, plus Web search engines, free e-mail, personal home pages, chat rooms, community building software, and bulletin boards. Vertical content channels on general purpose portal sites offer content such as sports scores, stock tickers, health tips, instant messaging, automobile information, and auctions.

general purpose portals

attempt to attract a very large general audience and then retain the audience on-site by providing in-depth vertical content

INSIGHT ON BUSINESS

BATTLE OF THE PORTALS

What's the difference between NBC, ABC, and CBS—the three largest broadcasting networks in the United States? If you think there's not much difference, then you are in agreement with the vast majority of Americans who can't tell the difference either. Now, what's the difference between AOL, MSN, Yahoo, and Google? On the one hand that's easy: Google does not have its own content, and all the others do. Although this is not strictly true (Google has Google Earth, Google Maps, images, and video, for instance) for the most part, Google is a place you visit on your way somewhere else, whereas the other portals are places you go to and hang around for a while. Google is not a content company but an indexer of other people's content. But differences are what make life interesting, and in portals, the differences lead to different strategies. They all have decided to become the primary gateway to the Internet for the entire world. Why? Not because they want a "better world for all" but because that's what advertisers are willing to pay for: lots of eyeballs. The bigger your eyeball count, or in Web argot, "unique visitors" and "time on site," the more money you make.

The battle lines and players are clear. The top contenders, are Google, Yahoo, MSN, and AOL. Right now, each portal has different strengths. Each player is attempting to build on their core strengths, build new products and services before competitors, attack competitors' advantages by developing in their core areas of competence, and to build alliances or purchase other players to aid in the competition. Let's take a look at each major player and then think about what the landscape will look like in five years, say 2013.

Google and Microsoft are the most successful and aggressive competitors. Google's core strength is dominance in search, the ability to respond a query and search 50 billion Web pages in one second. Seventy one million Americans use a search engine each month, generating about 10 billion queries. In 2008, Google owns 58% of this huge audience, leaving Yahoo (22%), Microsoft MSN.com (10%), AOL (5%) and Ask (4%) with the rest of the market. Google's share has been growing slowly while Yahoo and MSN have lost share. Google has 119 million unique visitors each month (not counting the video site YouTube which it owns), and they spend on average 1 hour and 15 minutes on the site each month. Google has been able to monetize this audience advantage by displaying text ads to visitors on search return pages, charging advertisers for the privilege. Google has attempted to build on its search advertising business and expand into online banner advertising by purchasing the advertising network DoubleClick. Google's weakness is that it does not have much content to attract and keep users on its site for longer periods of time. Google is a place to go to search, and then leave once you find the content you are seeking. Google has developed many niche products from Gmail, to Google Apps, to photo sites and Google Maps to keep people on site for longer periods of time, and expose them to more ads. In addition to being an advertising agency selling space on its site, Google is also a cloud computing-platform company developing computer applications like word processing, spreadsheets, calendar and other functionality that operate as Web services, thereby going around Microsoft's monopoly of the PC desktop. This strikes at the

(continued)

heart of Microsoft's core competence (and revenue): PC operating systems and applications.

From a financial perspective Google is one of the most successful Web-based companies in history. Starting out as a fledgling dot.com start up in 1998, it went public in 2003 for an initial price of $85, and in 2008 is selling in the range of $400-$700, with a market capitalization at the low price of $138 billion. Google is sitting on $25 billion in cash and near cash equivalents.

Microsoft is one of the world's largest software companies and has built a monopoly based on its Windows operating system and Office applications package. Around 95% of the world's PCs use Windows and Office. Microsoft has sought to expand on this desktop presence by developing its Web portal and search site (MSN.com), Web-based services available at its WindowsLive.com site, and of course its video games (both software and hardware). Microsoft has been notably unsuccessful in its efforts to develop a competitive Web presence when compared to other players. Microsoft's search engine (now called LiveSearch) is used for only 10% of online searches, a share that has been slowly shrinking. MSN.com, Microsoft's general portal site, has about 100 million visitors a month, but they stay on average only 44 minutes a month, far less than competitors. Microsoft has been unable to monetize its search business or its Web portal. MSN's ad revenue in 2008 is only $3 billion, and its online services business is losing $1 billion annually. It has few search query pages to sell, and the banner ads on its portal site are not seen by many. In order to compete with Google, it has developed its own Web services business (WindowsLive), but here too it has failed to capture visitors. In order to compete with both Yahoo and Google in the display banner and advertising network market, Microsoft purchased the aQuantive advertising network company for $6 billion. Despite its poor performance in search and as a general Web portal, Microsoft is a formidable competitor with a cash hoard of $65 billion, and a market capitalization of $238 billion (twice the value of Google). Its stock hit a high of $50 in 2000, and in 2008, it is considered a slow growing, mature company unlikely to out-perform the market with a price of $25.

Yahoo is arguably the world's leading destination portal site with over 130 million visitors a month, who stay on average a whopping three hours a month, three times the Google exposure. Yahoo also leads in e-mail services. Yahoo's Web e-mail service has 10 times as many users as Google's Gmail. Yahoo has plenty of content on its pages, and began its life as a content-oriented portal providing general news, weather, commentary, plus in-depth information on targeted topics, and a host of Web-based services from mail, to calendars, to instant messaging. Yahoo's ad revenues are about $7 billion annually. While it has doubled revenues from 2004 to 2008, Yahoo's growth in the last few years has slowed dramatically. Its search engine accounts for 23% of searches, about 60 million a month, which is far better than Microsoft or AOL, but only half the size of Google.

Yahoo's weak financial performance in 2007 resulted in a flurry of takeover bids, led by Microsoft's $45 billion bid in 2008. Yahoo successfully fought off this offer and, seeking to maintain its independence, struck a deal with Google to display Google ads on the Yahoo search engine pages. In return, Yahoo would receive somewhere between $400- $800 million annually in new revenue. This arrangement is being examined by the Justice Department for its anti-competitive potential, and it is being opposed by large advertising agencies as well.

AOL was one of the first, successful general portals offering real content such as news, weather, sports, and email. AOL's network of Web

(continued)

properties is one of the top three in the United States, attracting an average of 110 million unique visitors each month. AOL's instant messaging service (AIM) is the leader in the U.S., and along with other services like MapQuest Maps, and AOL mail, it is a leading provider of Web services, entertainment, news and in-depth content to the general population.

Originally AOL was a paid subscription service tied to Internet dial-up access. This changed to an advertiser supported portal much like Yahoo. AOL's visitors stay on site an average of 4 hours a month (higher than any other portal). This gives AOL plenty of time to display ads, and it generated about $2.2 billion in ad revenues in 2007, still far below the leaders and not growing very rapidly. The ad revenues are not enough to make up for the loss in paid subscribers. AOL's overall revenue picture is still bleak. In 2005 AOL's parent company, TimeWarner, sold a 5% stake in AOL to Google. Google and AOL have had a partnership for several years in which Google displays its ads on AOL content pages, and pays AOL about $450 million a year.

The dynamics among these four leading portal sites has created some interesting strategic business situations. Clearly, AOL and Yahoo are too weak to pose a threat to the two strong players. Google and Microsoft not only compete head-to-head in search and Web services, but also by cutting deals with the two weak players, AOL and Yahoo. So far, Google is winning, and Microsoft is losing.

AOL's partnership with Google means that AOL now has both content and search, making it far more competitive with Yahoo, which has plenty of content and a new search engine that has not yet taken off in the marketplace. Meanwhile, Yahoo's stock price lingered all year long in 2007 around $25, until the board fired the CEO Terry Semel in June and convinced Yahoo's founder Jerry Yang to take the helm again. In an effort to speed up its slow growth, Yahoo tried to purchase MySpace earlier in 2005, but lost to the News Corp. In 2006 it tried to purchase YouTube, but lost to Google. Oddly, Yahoo has the largest user base in the world, a built-in social network, that it has failed to develop. Google has come to the rescue again (as it did for AOL earlier) and provided Yahoo a life line. In the process, Google has successfully prevented Microsoft from gaining access to additional content, eyeballs, and ad dollars by making both Yahoo and AOL off limits for Microsoft. Ultimately, this comes down to a battle between the two giants: Google and Microsoft.

In the end, the "traditional" portals face much more competition from the new upstart social networking sites. The traditional portals still do not have a strategy for dealing with the fact that millions of their customers are using the social network sites as their home page, and as the primary provider of content, from news, to videos and music. Isn't that what portals were supposed to do? The portal battle may be over, but the war for audience attention and ad dollars has moved to a different level.

■■■ **SOURCES:** "Google Tackles Microsoft in Launch of Browser," by Jessica Vascellaro, *Wall Street Journal*, September 2, 2008; "Yahoo Seeks Fresh Jolt With Ad Service," by Jessica Vascellaro, Shira Ovide and Emily Steel, *Wall Street Journal*, September 25, 2008 "Chief of AOL's Parent Is Open to Deal ," by Saul Hansell and Louise Story, *The New York Times*, March 12, 2008; "Google Gets Ready to Rumble With Microsoft," by Steve Lohr and Miguel Helft, The *New York Times*, December 16, 2007; "Portals vs. Social Networks: Which Will Prevail," by Tim Lebrecht, CNET News, October 6, 2007; "Semel out as Yahoo! CEO," by Paul R. La Monica, CNNMoney.com, June 18, 2007;

Vertical market portals (sometimes also referred to as destination sites or vortals) attempt to attract highly focused, loyal audiences with a deep interest either in community or specialized content—from sports to the weather. In addition to their focused content, vertical market portals have recently begun adding many of the features found in general purpose portals.

The concentration of audience share in the portal market reflects (in addition to network effects) the limited time budget of consumers. This limited time budget works to the advantage of general purpose portals. Consumers have a finite amount of time to spend on the Web, and as a result, most consumers visit fewer than 30 unique domains each month. Facing limited time, consumers concentrate their visits at sites that can satisfy a broad range of interests, from weather and travel information, to stocks, sports, and entertainment content.

General purpose sites such as Yahoo try to be all things to all people, and attract a broad audience with both generalized navigation services and also in-depth content and community efforts. For instance, Yahoo has become the Web's largest source of news: more people visit Yahoo news than any other news site including online newspapers. Yet recent changes in consumer behavior on the Web show that consumers are spending less time "surfing the Web" and on general browsing, and more time doing focused searches, research, and participating in social networks. These trends will advantage special purpose, vertical market sites that can provide focused, in-depth community and content.

As a general matter, the general purpose portals are very well-known brands, while the vertical content and affinity group portals tend to have less well-known brands. **Figure 11.7** lists examples of general purpose portals and the two main types of vertical market portals.

> **vertical market portals**
> attempt to attract highly focused, loyal audiences with a deep interest in either community or specialized content

FIGURE 11.7 — TWO GENERAL TYPES OF PORTALS: GENERAL PURPOSE AND VERTICAL MARKET PORTALS

GENERAL PURPOSE PORTALS	VERTICAL MARKET PORTALS — Affinity Group	VERTICAL MARKET PORTALS — Focused Content
Yahoo!	iVillage.com	ESPN.com
MSN	Newblackvoices.com	Bloomberg.com
AOL	T-online.com	NFL.com
Ask.com	Aflcio.org	WebMD.com
	Law.com	Greenpages.org
	Ceoexpress.com	Gamers.com
		Away.com
		Econline.com
		Sailnet.com

There are two general types of portals: general purpose and vertical market. Vertical market portals may be based on affinity groups or on focused content.

PORTAL BUSINESS MODELS

Portals receive income from a number of different sources. The revenue base of portals is changing and dynamic, with some of the largest sources of revenue declining. **Table 11.9** summarizes the major portal revenue sources.

ISP services revenue represents a declining part of the revenue base for portal sites. More and more Americans have switched to broadband connections provided by giant telephone and cable companies. The business strategies of both general and vertical portals have changed greatly because of the rapid growth in search engine advertising and intelligent ad placement networks such as Google's AdSense, which can place ads on thousands of Web sites based on the content of the Web site. General portal sites such as AOL, MSN, and Yahoo did not have well-developed search engines, and hence have not grown as fast as Google, which has a powerful search engine. Portal sites have invested billions of dollars to catch up with Google. On the other hand, general portals have content, which Google does not (with the exception of maps, images, and some software applications). Yahoo and MSN visitors stay on-site a long time reading news, content, and sending e-mail. General portals are attempting to provide more premium content focused on sub-communities of their portal audience. Advertisers on portals are especially interested in focused, revenue producing premium content available on Web portals because it attracts a more committed audience.

For instance, financial service firms pay premium advertising rates to advertise on portal finance service areas such as Yahoo's Finance pages. As noted in Chapters 6 and 7, there is a direct relationship between the revenue derived from a customer and the focus of the customer segment (see **Figure 11.8**).

The survival strategy for general purpose portals in the future is therefore to develop deep, rich, vertical content in order to reach customers at the site. The strategy for much smaller vertical market portals is to put together a collection of vertical portals to form a vertical portal network, a collection of deep, rich content

TABLE 11.9	TYPICAL PORTAL REVENUE SOURCES
PORTAL REVENUE SOURCE	DESCRIPTION
ISP services	Providing Web access and e-mail services for a monthly fee
General advertising	Charging for impressions delivered
Tenancy deals	Fixed charge for guaranteed number of impressions, exclusive partnerships, "sole providers"
Commissions on sales	Revenue based on sales at the site by independent providers
Subscription fees	Charging for premium content

| FIGURE 11.8 | **REVENUE PER CUSTOMER AND MARKET FOCUS** |

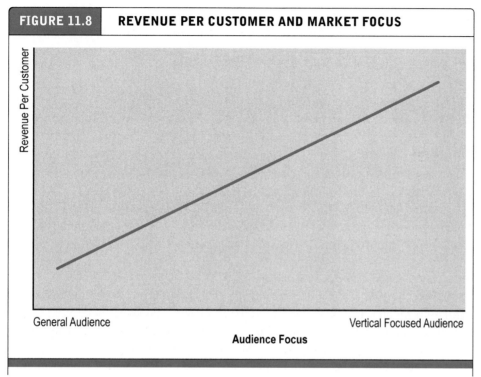

The more focused and targeted the audience, the more revenue that can be derived per customer for an appropriately targeted product or service.

sites. The strategy for search engine sites like Google is to obtain more content to attract users for a long time and expose them to more ad pages (or screens).

The following E-commerce in Action case illustrates how Yahoo is adapting to changing consumer and advertiser behavior.

E-COMMERCE IN ACTION

YAHOO! INC.

From its founding as a search engine in 1994 by two Stanford students, David Filo and Jerry Yang, Yahoo has grown into a $7 billion online brand-name juggernaut. Yahoo has had unprofitable periods in the past (in 2001, the company lost money as advertising revenues all but disappeared), but between 2002 and 2005, net income grew in leaps and bounds, from $42 million in 2002 to an astounding $1.89 billion in 2005, driven by the resurgence in Internet advertising, the spread of broadband connections, and changing tastes among the American public for Internet news, entertainment, and information. However, in 2006, earnings dropped for the first time in four years, to $750 million, due primarily to changes in financial accounting standards related to stock-based compensation, and in 2007 net income tanked down to $660 million. In 2008 Yahoo is on the brink of losing its independence, considering a major management shake up including ousting the founder, and fighting off shareholder revolts. The heavy hand of Microsoft was barely escaped in 2008, and only Google has extended a lifeline.

Yahoo today is at the very epicenter of the Web's action. In the difficult early years, it was unclear if Yahoo could remain independent and make the transition from an online portal to a general media and content company, something along the lines of America Online/Time Warner. By 2007, this was no longer a question.

The Vision

Yahoo was founded in 1994 to provide a comprehensive, intuitive, and user-friendly online guide to the Web. Since its inception, however, Yahoo has grown to be much more than a simple guide. In 2007, the company described itself in its investor relations documents and securities filings as "a leading global Internet brand and one of the most trafficked Internet destinations worldwide." Yahoo "seeks to provide Internet services that are essential and relevant to users and businesses through its global audience of users and advertisers."

Yahoo's general search offerings include Yahoo Search, Yahoo Toolbar, and Yahoo Search on Mobile. Its social search offerings include the social bookmarking site del.icio.us, Yahoo Answers, photo searches on Flickr, and Yahoo Video, which hosts Yahoo's video search products. It also offers local search products, such as Yahoo Local, Yahoo Yellow Pages, and Yahoo Maps. In addition to search, Yahoo offers a number of "marketplace" products, including Yahoo Shopping (which includes search functionality and comparison-shopping tools, a Shopping Bargains Center that provides users with coupons, rebates, etc., and Yahoo Auctions); Yahoo Real Estate, which provides information and services for users who are looking to buy, sell, or rent a home; Yahoo Travel, which provides a comprehensive online travel research and booking site; Yahoo Autos, which enables users to research, price, and compare cars online; and Yahoo Personals, an online dating service. Information and entertainment offering include Yahoo News, which aggregates news stories from news providers such as the Associated Press, Reuters, ABC News, CBS News, National Public Radio, and others; Yahoo Finance, which provides financial resources and personal financial management tools, Yahoo Food; Yahoo Tech; Yahoo Health; Yahoo Sports; Yahoo Music; Yahoo Movies; Yahoo TV; Yahoo Games; and Yahoo Kids.

Yahoo's communications and community offerings include Yahoo Mail, Yahoo Messenger with Voice; Yahoo Communities, such as Yahoo Groups; and Yahoo Photos. Its "connected life" products include Yahoo Mobile, Yahoo Broadband, and Yahoo Digital Home, which focus on delivering Yahoo content through user interfaces designed for viewing on the television or other devices.

For businesses, in addition to providing a general advertising platform, Yahoo also offers services such as Yahoo HotJobs (discussed in Chapter 9) and Yahoo Small Business, which provides fee-based online services such as Yahoo Domains, Yahoo Web Hosting, Yahoo Merchant Solutions, and Yahoo Business Mail.

Business Model

Yahoo gives away some user services for free (such as search, basic photo and video sharing, maps, personals, local weather, etc.), and earns money from marketing services (mostly advertising) and subscription fees for premium content. Approximately 88% of Yahoo's revenue in 2007 was derived from the sale of advertising, in many different forms, and the remaining 12% from all other fees. Yahoo's marketing services include online display advertising, including banner ads, rich media, video and targeting, placement fees, sponsorships, and direct marketing, and transaction fees from merchandise sales. Yahoo also generates revenue by allowing corporate partners access to its user base in return for a fee and a percentage of any revenue generated.

Financial Analysis

In 2007, net revenues continued to grow at Yahoo, reaching $6.9 billion, up 9% from 2006 (see **Table 11.10**). Overall, from 2004 to 2007, revenues have doubled. Yahoo has been aided considerably by the general acceptance of the Internet in the broader population, producing king-size audiences, and reaction of the advertising community, which has greatly expanded Internet advertising, Yahoo's main source of revenue. But can Yahoo possibly maintain this level of growth?

Yahoo's cost of revenue consists mainly of "traffic acquisition costs," which involves payments made to affiliates who have integrated its search and/or display advertising into their Web sites, and payments made to companies that direct traffic to Yahoo Web sites, fees paid to third-party content providers, Internet connection charges, and expenses for Web site production and delivery costs. Yahoo's cost of revenues has slowly increased, and its gross margin stayed basically the same from 2006 to 2007.

Yahoo's operating margins are positive but falling. In 2005 their net margin was 36%, but by 2007 it had fallen to 9.5%. How could this happen? Revenue growth in this 2005-2007 period was an acceptable 36% (but not spectacular when compared to Google), and the cost of producing its services proportionally not changing. You can see the sources of the earning decline by looking at operational expenses. Sales and marketing, for instance, went up 56%. Yahoo doubled its R&D budget in an effort to build a more powerful search engine called Panama to compete with Google, and a new display advertising system called APT. Finally, Yahoo got sloppy and let its corporate bureaucracy (general and administrative) costs balloon by 85% in the period. Yahoo's free cash flow remained about the same, growing from $1.7 billion in 2005 to $1.9 billion in 2007. Yahoo ended 2007 with $12.2 billion in total assets, of which $2 billion was cash and short-term investments. With only $2.4 billion in current liabilities, Yahoo's balance sheet is also strong and could support aggressive expansion plans. This makes Yahoo an attractive take over target—there's lots of cash in the bank.

Strategic Analysis—Business Strategies

In its quest to become the Internet's most widely visited online portal and search engine, Yahoo has grown through a combination of internal organic growth and acquisition, with the emphasis in recent years on acquisitions. Yahoo has grown

TABLE 11.10	YAHOO RESULTS OF OPERATIONS AND SUMMARY BALANCE SHEET DATA

YAHOO! INC. CONSOLIDATED STATEMENTS OF OPERATIONS (in thousands)

Revenue	2007	2006	2005
Net revenues	6,969,274	$6,425,679	$5,257,668
Cost of revenues	2,838,758	2,675,723	2,096,201
Gross profit	**4,130,516**	**3,749,956**	**3,161, 467**
Gross margin	**59%**	**58%**	**60%**
Operating expenses			
Sales and marketing	1,610,357	1,322,259	1,033,947
Product development	1,084,238	833,147	569,527
General and administrative	633,431	528,798	341,073
Amortization of intangibles	107,077	124,786	109,195
Total operating expenses	3,435,103	2,808,990	2,053,742
Income from operations	**695,413**	**940,966**	**1,107,725**
Operating margin	**10%**	**15%**	**21%**
Other income, net	154,011	157,034	1,435,857
Income before taxes and cumulative effect of accounting change	849,424	1,098,00	2,543,582
Provision for income taxes	(337,263)	(458,011)	(767,816)
Earnings in equity interests	150,689	112,114	128,244
Minority interests in operations of consolidated subsidiaries	(2,850)	(712)	(7,780)
Net income	**660,000**	**751,391**	**1,896,230**
Net margin	**9.5%**	**12%**	**36%**

CONSOLIDATED BALANCE SHEET DATA (in thousands)

At December 31	2007	2006	2005
Assets			
Cash, cash equivalents	1,513,930	$1,569,871	$1,429,693
Short-term investments	487,544	1,031,528	1,131,141
Accounts receivable	1,055,532	930,964	721,723
Prepaid expenses and other current assets	180,716	217,779	166,976
Working capital	937,274	2,276,148	2,245,481
Total assets	12,229,741	11,513,608	10,831,834
Liabilities			
Current liabilities	2,300,448	1,473,994	1,204,052
Long-term liabilities	384,208	870,948	1,061,367
Total stockholders' equity	9,532,831	9,160,610	8,566,415

SOURCE: Yahoo!, Inc., 2007.

organically by expanding its geographical coverage to foreign markets which now account for about 32% of revenues and growing at a faster pace than in the United States, and by extending its brand in the United States by adding new content and capabilities to its U.S. site. Geographical expansion increases the potential user base the company can acquire and is the impetus behind creating Yahoo properties in 20 countries, in 20 languages.

But Yahoo has primarily grown through acquisition and become a massive acquirer of Internet properties and capabilities, turning into one of the Internet's largest online media conglomerates. In the early years Yahoo purchased such companies as Four11, GeoCities, and Broadcast.com. In 2000–2002 it purchased Launch Media and HotJobs, the online job recruitment site, in a further effort to expand its revenue base. With the rise of Google's search engine, and growth of the Google audience, Yahoo purchased Inktomi in March 2003. Inktomi had developed a sophisticated Web search engine that provided improved relevance, paid inclusion, use of an XML interface, a larger index, and other features designed to gain better insight into a user's intent during his or her interaction on the Web. In October 2003, Yahoo purchased Overture, the originator of search engine paid advertising on the Internet. This purchase allowed Yahoo to compete with Google for paid search engine advertising. In 2004, Yahoo purchased Kelkoo, a European online comparison shopping site, for $571 million and MusicMatch, an online music site that uses the subscription model and competes against other online music sites such as iTunes, Rhapsody, and Napster, for $158 million. In October 2005, Yahoo acquired a 46% interest in Alibaba.com, a Chinese mainland shopping site that had successfully competed against Yahoo China and prevented Yahoo China from achieving a powerful market share, for $1 billion in cash and the contribution of Yahoo China. In November 2005, it purchased the remaining outstanding shares of Yahoo Europe and Yahoo Korea, which is had originally established in partnership with Softbank, for $501 million. It also acquired the social bookmarking site, del.icio.us, in 2005. Acquisitions in 2006 included a purchase of a 20% interest in RightMedia, an online advertising company, followed in 2007 by an acquisition of the remaining 80% for $680 million. Other acquisitions in 2007 included BlueLithium, an online global advertising network, for $300 million; and an additional 1% of Alibaba for $100 million.

Yahoo also acquired

• Zimbra, a provider of e-mail and collaboration software, expanding Yahoo!'s mail offerings and presence in universities, small and medium-sized businesses, and service provider partners, for $350 million;

• Rivals.com, an online destination for college and high school sports and recruiting information, expanding community offerings and open publishing capabilities on Yahoo! Sports.

• Right Media, an online advertising exchange that is an integral piece of Yahoo's strategy to build the industry's leading advertising and publishing network. Yahoo views its acquisition as a key step in its efforts to change how publishers connect to their audiences in one open advertising community.

Yahoo continued its expensive efforts to develop a search engine called Panama which would be able to rank Web pages according to their popularity and appropriateness just like Google. From the acquisitions list above, it is clear that Yahoo was making a major effort to build on its global advertising platform by providing advertisers more targeted online display ads. In 2008 Yahoo introduced its APT advertising service which allows newspapers, and other advertisers, to target ads on their own sites, as well as others. In this system, advertisers buy target audiences, like females between 21-35, and the system will find newspaper or Web properties where that demographic can be found. In short, management's strategy has been to respond to threats and opportunities by strategic acquisitions that solidify its grasp on users and secure its number one position on the Internet.

Yahoo has also sought to reduce its expenditures on content by forming strategic alliances and partnerships with leading content providers, including ABC News, AccuWeather, Reuters, and SportsTicker, to name a few. Yahoo also has a strategic alliance with Verizon to offer co-branded Internet access on a subscription basis to its DSL/broadband customers and to dial-up subscribers nationwide. The service includes a suite of Yahoo and Verizon customized products and services. In 2007, Yahoo combined its U.S. Hispanic business with Telemundo, the U.S. Spanish-language television network. On the advertising front, Yahoo has partnered with eBay to make Yahoo the exclusive provider of graphical advertising and search advertising on eBay's U.S. Web site. It also entered into a partnership with a consortium of more than 150 daily U.S. newspapers to deliver local search, display, and classified advertising. To expand its mobile offerings, it has partnered with Research in Motion and Motorola to distribute Yahoo Search and Yahoo Go for Mobile services on RIM's Blackberry devices and certain Motorola cell phones.

In addition to strategic acquisitions and alliances, Yahoo has also invested in new offerings to enhance its business. It redesigned the Yahoo home page, and launched Yahoo Answers, a free platform that allows users to ask and answer questions; a new version of Yahoo Messenger that now provides for high-quality PC-to-phone and phone-to-PC calling in the United States; a Windows version of Yahoo Go for Mobile; an enhanced Maps product; and a new version of Yahoo Video, with search and additional social networking features. It also enhanced its social media offerings with Flickr, its photo-sharing site.

Strategic Analysis—Competition

Yahoo's primary competition is Google, Microsoft, and, to a lesser extent, Time Warner (AOL). Until 2005, Yahoo considered the combined AOL/Time Warner operations and Microsoft MSN to be its biggest competition, mainly because of these companies' access to content, broad potential user base (as in the case of AOL/Time Warner), and direct billing relationship with the user, which Yahoo generally lacks. Both MSN and AOL have branded themselves as general purpose portals with deep, rich content and services, and secondarily, as search engines. In this sense, they are much like Yahoo. As Google has grown in audience, Yahoo, AOL, and MSN have made significant efforts to improve their search capabilities, while not stinting on their distinctive content. But as Google has added more content and services, from Google Earth to Google Scholar, television and video searching, mail, instant messaging, and many other services, so has Yahoo (and its competitors) come to see Google as the fastest-growing competitor and potentially, given its huge share of online search, the most dangerous competitor. Google's acquisition of YouTube makes it an even more dangerous competitor. The social networking sites MySpace and Facebook can also be considered competitors, although at this point in time, they do not offer the breadth of functionality that Yahoo does.

Yahoo considers the primary competitive factors to be the quality and relevance of its search results, and the usefulness, accessibility, integration, and personalization of the online services that it offers, as well as the overall user experience. In terms of attracting advertisers, it identifies the principal competitive factors as being the reach, effectiveness, and efficiency of its marketing services, as well as the creativity of the marketing solutions that it offers.

Strategic Analysis—Technology

Yahoo relies on several third-party technology providers for services related to the management and ongoing performance of Yahoo Web infrastructure, such as Internet connections, network access, hosting and co-location of Web servers, e-mail, and other service connections. Yahoo also licenses technology and related databases from a variety of third-party providers for various functionality, such as the technology underlying the delivery of news, stock quotes and other financial information, chat services, street mapping, telephone listings, streaming capabilities, and other services. While outsourcing the bulk of its technical operations lessens the risk of a major malfunction, it also places Yahoo at greater risk of having providers encounter problems that would disrupt access to the Yahoo site. Yahoo's success is also dependent in part on the continued growth and maintenance of the Internet infrastructure. Online security issues, such as spyware, viruses and worms, and denial of service attacks, could negatively impact Yahoo. Technologies that block the display of online advertising, such as pop-up blockers, may also harm Yahoo's operating results.

Strategic Analysis—Social and Legal Challenges

Yahoo does not at this time face significant legal challenges. As a portal, the main legal challenge faced by Yahoo is the nature of the content it makes available and the ownership of content posted by others on its servers. The Digital Millennium Copyright Act is intended to reduce the liability of online service providers for listing or linking to third-party Web sites that include materials that infringe copyrights or other rights of others. Yahoo nonetheless may be held liable or have its business impacted as a result of the online activities of individuals utilizing its services. Changes in regulations or user concerns regarding privacy and protection of user data could also adversely affect Yahoo's business, particularly its targeted marketing efforts. As noted above, cybercrime, as well as click fraud, may also create problems for Yahoo.

Future Prospects

In 2008, the prospects for Yahoo look dim. In February 2008, Microsoft offered to buy Yahoo for $44 billion. It was turned down by Yahoo's Board of Directors in May. In June, 2008, under pressure from shareholders and Wall Street, Yahoo fired its long-time CEO Terry Semel and brought back its founder, Jerry Yang. Yahoo turned to Google for a lifeline and reached an agreement with Google that will pour $500 million a year into Yahoo in return for allowing Google to place text ads on Yahoo's search pages. The system is opposed by the largest advertising firms in the United States, and is under investigation by the Justice Department for its potential to diminish competition in online advertising. When he was hired back, Yang promised to turn Yahoo around in 100 days, but in September 2008, Yahoo stock hit its all time low as investors believe the company has run out of strategies for competing against Microsoft, Google and AOL. Its expensive search engine effort has not worked, and its other investments have failed to produce the revenue in the short time frame that Wall Street expects.

While Yahoo is still the world's leader in online content and online audience, it has fallen behind Google in search advertising, and is challenged by a number of big players including Microsoft, Google, and AOL, all of whom have built up their display advertising networks. Its two great strengths are content and audience size. With its $1 billion-plus investment in China, it has assumed a leadership role in Asia as well, and done far better there than Google, eBay, or MSN. At the same time, like all portals, Yahoo faces the social networking sites such as Facebook and MySpace who are taking audience share from the portals as people increasingly linger on social networking sites. Therefore, Yahoo's future depends on developing an alliance with Google on search (and search engine marketing), and extending its lead in content, while at the same time leveraging its huge U.S. and international audience to become the world's largest social network. So far, Yahoo has faltered in addressing both these challenges.

iVillage Discovers the Path to Success: But Has It Since Lost Its Way?

iVillage was founded by Candice Carpenter, an Internet veteran of the 1990s, as a site devoted to women. It was one of the first "community" sites of the 1990s, a vertical market portal that focused on all issues dealing with women. iVillage was clearly among the most "successful" early Web sites to mix community, commerce, and content. A first mover in the rush to reach out to women and develop a women's community online, it is now owned by NBC and still ranks among the most popular online destinations for women, although it has recently been overtaken at the top by Glam Media's Glam.com.

iVillage has followed a winding path toward profitability. It grew its revenues from $12 million in 1998 to $100 million in 2006. But its losses grew as well, from $41 million in 1998, to a huge $179 million loss in 2000, and a further loss of $27 million in 2003. Finally, in 2004, it showed its first profit ever of $2.7 million and followed that with a $9.5 million profit in 2005. In 2006, NBC Universal purchased iVillage for $600 million. At the time, NBC said iVillage was profitable. Investors approved of NBC's purchase, and GE (the parent company of NBC) and iVillage shares both rose on the announcement.

Over the years, iVillage had not only become the leading source of news and information for and about women, it had also aggregated a collection of Web sites more or less related to the topic of women, including Women.com, gURL.com, Astrology.com, Substance.com, Promotions.com, Healthology.com, and Garden-web.com. None these sites was a killer application, but together the entire collection produced $100 million in revenue in 2006. NBC's purchase was seen both as an acceptance of the fact that the Internet had major potential as an advertising media, and recognition of the growing convergence among entertainment companies and Web properties. NBC had hardly any Web revenue properties or income in 2006, and iVillage would jump-start its entry to the Web.

NBC felt it could leverage its iVillage investment by using its NBC network to promote the Web property. Or was it the reverse: use the NBC network to promote iVillage? The idea was to re-use news and entertainment programming from shows such as the *Today Show* and *Access Hollywood*. Senior managers of content firms always love the idea of re-using content because it is so expensive to create in the first place, paying writers, sound technicians, camera operators, editors, and others. NBC was also talking about producing original Web content for iVillage, although exactly what that meant no one really knew.

By 2007, the success of the acquisition was less certain. NBC tried to promote iVil-lage on the *Today Show* as planned, but it had little effect on iVillage traffic. The women who watch the *Today Show* apparently do not visit iVillage. The move of cor-porate headquarters in New Jersey caused many iVillage veterans to leave. A major effort to increase traffic, a syndicated television program called iVillage Live, was cancelled in 200 due to low ratings, and then relaunched as "In the Loop with iVillage." The second effort did not prove to be any more successful tan the first, and ultimately In the Loop was also cancelled in February 2008, for the same reason -- low ratings.

The iVillage and NBC merger points to some of the pitfalls of merging a Web company with a media conglomerate that is based in television. Generally, the same strategies that work on TV will not work on the Web. At the time of the purchase, the technology of iVillage was out of date, and its editorial products were not necessarily leading edge. The focus has been on female beauty products, and not financial planning for women, or investing advice, or advancing in a profession. The new iVillage operated pretty much like the old iVillage: content was developed by experts and delivered to an audience. The opportunities for user-generated content were limited to posting on bulletin boards, or writing the editor.

In September 2007, a "new" iVillage Web site was launched. Videos are more apparent, opportunities to contribute are more visible, but the philosophy is unchanged: it's still reporting to women, and not letting women generate the news. As one pundit said, they should have turned iVillage into MyVillage, and gone into direct competition with MySpace. Meanwhile, iVillage has some big-name competitors for the female audience. Glam.com has cornered the style marketand in June 2007 overtook iVillage as the leading women's Web site. While iVillage and NBC dallied with TV, Glam Media used the opportunity to build what has become one of the fastest growing of the top 100 Web sites. From a start in 2003, Glam has built a network of 350 magazines, Web sites, and blogs, covering everything from health and beauty to shopping. Glam has negotiated long-term contracts with most of the independently owned sites, and in return offers those sites highly paid advertising. Glam is also continuing to build its own fully-owned sites as well. In an effort to combat the advance of Glam, iVillage entered into a three-year deal with BlogHer, a women's blog network. The deal is part of a new initiative at NBC Universal, called Women@NBCU, a female-targeted digital ad sales network designed to sell ads for iVillage, Oxygen.com, and other female-oriented sites. Whether this effort is too little, too late for iVillage remains to be seen.

SOURCES: "BlogHer Nabs iVillage Deal, NBC Investment," by Stephanie Olsen, CNET News, July 16, 2008; "iVillage's TV Show on NBC Shuts Down, Again," by Rafat Ali, PaidContent.org, February 18, 2008; "NBC Making a Clean Start in a House of Mixed Media," by Brooks Barnes, *New York Times*, August 13, 2007; "iVillage-NBC Dreams As Yet Unfulfilled," by Henry Blodget , *Silicon Valley Insider*, August 13, 2007; "Glam Surges to No.1 Women's Property, Overtakes iVillage," by Matt Marshall, VentureBeat, June 17, 2007. "NBC Universal Hopes To Cash In With iVillage," by Joe Flint, *Wall Street Journal*, March 9, 2006; "NBC Universal Takes an iVillage," by Steve Rosenbush, *BusinessWeek*, March 7, 2006; "iVillage Net Income More Than Triples for Fiscal 2005 Compared to Prior Years," iVillage.com, February 13, 2005.

Case Study Questions

1. Is iVillage a general purpose portal for all women, or a vertical portal? Visit the new iVillage site and make a list of both its general and vertical features to support your argument. How do you think visitors to the site will appreciate more general features? More focused features?

2. What recommendations do you have for iVillage management for new kinds of services and content that would generate revenue? What would attract more women to visit the site more often?

3. What were the assumptions that led NBC to purchase iVillage, and were those assumptions correct? Do you think $600 million was a reasonable price to pay? Why or why not?

4. What important concepts in e-commerce are demonstrated in the iVillage case?

5. How might iVillage have developed into MyVillage, and adopted a business model more like MySpace?

11.5 REVIEW

KEY CONCEPTS

- Explain the difference between a traditional social network and an online social network, and understand how an online community differs from a portal.

Social networks involve:
- A group of people
- Shared social interaction
- Common ties among members
- A shared area for some period of time

By extension, an online social network is an area online where people who share common ties can interact with one another.

- Understand how a social network differs from a portal

The difference between social networks and portals has become blurred. Originally, portals began as search engines. Then they added content and eventually many community building features such as chat rooms, bulletin boards, and free Web site design and hosting. Social network sites began as content-specific locations and added more general portal services such as Web searching, general news, weather, and travel information, as well as a wide variety of e-commerce services.

- Describe the different types of social networks and online communities and their business models.

- *General communities:* Members can interact with a general audience segmented into numerous different groups. The purpose is to attract enough members to populate a wide range of topical discussion groups. Most general communities began as non-commercial subscription-based endeavors, but many have been purchased by larger community portal sites.
- *Practice networks:* Members can participate in discussion groups and get help or simply information relating to an area of shared practice, such as art, education, or medicine. These generally have a nonprofit business model in which they simply attempt to collect enough in subscription fees, sales commissions, and limited advertising to cover the cost of operations.

- *Interest-based communities:* Members can participate in focused discussion groups on a shared interest such as boats, horses, skiing, travel, or health. The advertising business model has worked because the targeted audience is attractive to marketers. Tenancy and sponsorship deals provide another similar revenue stream.
- *Affinity communities:* Members can participate in focused discussions with others who share the same affinity or group identification, such as religion, ethnicity, gender, sexual orientation, or political beliefs. The business model is a mixture of subscription revenue from premium content and services, advertising, tenancy/sponsorships, and distribution agreements.
- *Sponsored communities:* Members can participate in online communities created by government, nonprofit, or for-profit organizations for the purpose of pursuing organizational goals. These types of sites vary widely from local government sites to branded product sites. They use community technologies and techniques to distribute information or extend brand influence. The goal of a branded product site is to increase offline product sales. These sites do not seek to make a profit and in fact are often cost centers.

- ■ **Describe the major types of auctions, their benefits and costs, and how they operate.**

Auctions are markets where prices vary (dynamic pricing) depending on the competition among the participants who are buying or selling products or services. They can be classified broadly as C2C or B2C, although generally the term C2C auction refers to the venue in which the sale takes place, for example, a consumer-oriented Web site such as eBay, which also auctions items from established merchants. A B2C *auction* refers to an established online merchant that offers its own auctions. There are also numerous B2B online auctions for buyers of industrial parts, raw materials, commodities, and services. Within these three broad categories of auctions are several major auction types classified based upon how the bidding mechanisms work in each system:

- *English auctions:* A single item is up for sale from a single seller. Multiple buyers bid against one another within a specific time frame, with the highest bidder winning the object, as long as the high bid has exceeded the reserve bid set by the seller, below which he or she refuses to sell.
- *Traditional Dutch auctions:* Sellers with many identical items sold in lots list a starting price and time for the opening of bids. As the clock advances, the price for each lot falls until a buyer offers to buy at that price.
- *Internet Dutch auctions:* Sellers with many identical items for sale list a minimum price or starting bid, and buyers indicate both a bid price and a quantity desired. The lowest winning bid that clears the available quantity is paid by all winning bidders. Those with the highest bid are assured of receiving the quantity they desire, but only pay the amount of the lowest successful bid (uniform pricing rule).
- *Name Your Own Price or reverse auctions:* Buyers specify the price they are willing to pay for an item, and multiple sellers bid for their business. This is one example of discriminatory pricing in which winners may pay different amounts for the same product or service depending on how much they have bid.
- *Group buying or demand aggregation auctions:* In the group-buying format, the more users who sign on to buy an item, the lower the price for the item falls.

These are generally B2B or B2G sites where small businesses can collectively receive discount prices for items that are purchased in high volumes.

Benefits of auctions include:

- *Liquidity:* Sellers and buyers are connected in a global marketplace.
- *Price discovery:* Even difficult-to price-items can be competitively priced based on supply and demand.
- *Price transparency:* Everyone in the world can see the asking and bidding prices for items, although prices can vary from auction site to auction site.
- *Market efficiency:* Consumers are offered access to a selection of goods that would be impossible to access physically, and consumer welfare is often increased due to reduced prices.
- *Lower transaction costs:* Merchants and consumers alike are benefited by the reduced costs of selling and purchasing goods compared to the physical marketplace.
- *Consumer aggregation:* A large number of consumers who are motivated to buy are amassed in one marketplace—a great convenience to the seller.
- *Network effects:* The larger an auction site becomes in the numbers of both users and products, the greater the benefits become and therefore the more valuable a marketplace it becomes.
- *Market-maker benefits:* Auction sites have no inventory carrying costs or shipping costs, making them perhaps the ideal online business in that their main function is the transfer of information.

Costs of auctions include:

- *Delayed consumption:* Auctions can go on for days, and the product must then be shipped to the buyer. Buyers will typically want to pay less for an item they cannot immediately obtain.
- *Monitoring costs:* Buyers must spend time monitoring the bidding.
- *Equipment costs:* Buyers must purchase, or have already purchased, computer systems and Internet service, and learned how to operate these systems.
- *Trust risks:* Consumers face an increased risk of experiencing a loss as online auctions are the largest source of Internet fraud.
- *Fulfillment costs:* Buyers must pay for packing, shipping, and insurance, and will factor this cost into their bid price.

Auction sites have sought to reduce these risks through various methods including:

- *Rating systems:* Previous customers rate sellers based on their experience with them and post them on the site for other buyers to see.
- *Watch lists:* These allow buyers to monitor specific auctions as they proceed over a number of days and only pay close attention in the last few minutes of bidding.
- *Proxy bidding:* Buyers can enter a maximum price they are willing to pay, and the auction software will automatically place incremental bids as their original bid is surpassed.

■ **Understand when to use auctions in a business.**

Auctions can be an appropriate channel for businesses to sell items in a variety of situations. The factors for businesses to consider include:

- *The type of product:* Rare and unique products are well suited to the auction marketplace as are perishable items such as airline tickets, hotel rooms, car rentals, and tickets to plays, concerts, and sporting events.
- *The product life cycle:* Traditionally, auctions have been used by businesses to generate a higher profit on items at the end of their life cycle than they would receive from product liquidation sales. However, they are now more frequently being used at the beginning of a product's life cycle to generate premium prices from highly motivated early adopters.
- *Channel management:* Businesses must be careful when deciding whether to pursue an auction strategy to ensure that products at auction do not compete with products in their existing profitable channels. This is why most established retail firms tend to use auctions for products at the end of their life cycles or to have quantity purchasing requirements.
- *The type of auction:* Businesses should choose seller-biased auctions where there are many buyers and only one or a few sellers, preferably using the English ascending price system to drive the price up as high as possible.
- *Initial pricing:* Auction items should start with a low initial bid in order to attract more bidders, because the more bidders an item has, the higher the final price will be driven.
- *Bid increments:* When increments are kept low, more bidders are attracted and the frequency of their bidding is increased. This can translate into a higher final price as bidders are prodded onward in small steps.
- *Auction length:* In general, the longer an auction runs, the more bidders will enter the auction, and the higher the final price will be. However, if an auction continues for too long, the bid prices will stabilize and the cost of posting the auction may outweigh the profit from any further price increases.
- *Number of items:* If a business has a large quantity of items to sell, it should break the lot up into smaller bundles and auction them at different times so that buyers do not expect a volume discount.
- *Price allocation rule:* Since most buyers are biased toward the uniform pricing rule, sellers should use different auction markets, or auction the same goods at different times in order to price discriminate.
- *Closed vs. open bidding:* Closed bidding should be used whenever possible because it benefits a seller by allowing price discrimination. However, open bidding can sometimes be beneficial when herd behavior kicks in, causing multiple bids on highly visited auctions, while overlooked and lightly trafficked auctions for the same or comparable items languish. This generally occurs when there are few objective measures of a product's true value in the marketplace.

■ **Recognize the potential for auction abuse and fraud.**

Auctions are particularly prone to fraud, which produces information asymmetries between buyers and sellers. Some of the possible abuses and frauds include:

- *Bid rigging:* Agreeing offline to limit bids or using shills to submit false bids that drive prices up.
- *Price matching:* Agreeing informally or formally to set floor prices on auction items below which sellers will not sell in open markets.

- *Shill feedback, defensive:* Using secondary IDs or other auction members to inflate seller ratings.
- *Shill feedback, offensive:* Using secondary IDs or other auction members to deflate ratings for another user (feedback bombs).
- *Feedback extortion:* Threatening negative feedback in return for a benefit.
- *Transaction interference:* E-mailing buyers to warn them away from a seller.
- *Bid manipulation:* Using the retraction option to make high bids, discovering the maximum bid of the current high bidder, and then retracting the bid.
- *Non-payment after winning.*
- *Blocking legitimate buyers by bidding high, then not paying.*
- *Shill bidding:* Using secondary user IDs or other auction members to artificially raise the price of an item.
- *Transaction non-performance:* Accepting payment and failing to deliver.
- *Non-selling seller:* Refusing payment or failing to deliver after a successful auction.
- *Bid siphoning:* E-mailing another seller's bidders and offering the same product for less.

■ **Describe the major types of Internet portals.**

Web portals are gateways to the more than 50 billion Web pages available on the Internet. Originally, their primary purpose was to help users find information on the Web, but they evolved into destination sites that provided a myriad of content from news to entertainment. Today, portals serve three main purposes: navigation of the Web, content, and commerce. Among the major portal types are:

- *Enterprise portals:* Corporations, universities, churches, and other organizations create these sites to help employees or members navigate to important content such as corporate news or organizational announcements.
- *General purpose portals:* Examples are AOL, Yahoo, and MSN, which try to attract a very large general audience by providing many in-depth vertical content channels. They also offer ISP services on a subscription basis, search engines, e-mail, chat, bulletin boards, and personal home pages.
- *Vertical market portals:* Also called destination sites, they attempt to attract a highly focused, loyal audience with an intense interest in either a community they belong to or an interest they hold. Recent studies have found that users with limited time resources are interested in concentrating their Web site visiting on focused searches in areas that appeal to them. Vertical market portals can be divided into two main classifications, although hybrids that overlap the two classifications also exist.
- *Affinity groups:* Statistical aggregates of people who identify themselves by their attitudes, values, beliefs, and behavior. Affinity portals exist to serve such broad constituencies as women, African Americans, and gays as well as much more focused constituencies such as union members, religious groups, and even home schooling families.
- *Focused content portals:* These sites contain in-depth information on a particular topic that all members are interested in. They can provide content on such broad topics as sports, news, weather, entertainment, finance or business, or

they can appeal to a much more focused interest group such as boat, horse, or video game enthusiasts.

- ■   Understand the business models of portals.

Portals receive revenue from a number of different sources. The business model is presently changing and adapting to declines in certain revenue streams, particularly advertising revenues. Revenue sources can include:

- *ISP services:* Providing Web access and e-mail services for a monthly fee.
- *General advertising:* Charging for impressions delivered.
- *Tenancy deals:* Locking in long-term, multiple-year deals so a company is guaranteed a number of impressions with premium placement on home pages and through exclusive marketing deals.
- *Subscription fees:* Charging for premium content.
- *Commissions on sales:* Earning revenue based on sales at the site by independent merchants.

The survival strategy for general purpose portals is to develop deep, rich, vertical content in order to attract advertisers to various niche groups that they can target with focused ads. The strategy for the small vertical market portals is to build a collection of vertical portals, thereby creating a network of deep, rich content sites for the same reason.

QUESTIONS

1. Why did most communities in the early days of e-commerce fail? What factors enable online social networks to prosper today?
2. How does a social network differ from a portal? How are the two similar?
3. What is an affinity community, and what is its business model?
4. What is personalization or personal value pricing, and how can it be used at the beginning of a product's life cycle to increase revenues?
5. List and briefly explain three of the benefits of auction markets.
6. What are the four major costs to consumers of participating in an auction?
7. Under what conditions does a seller bias exist in an auction market? When does a buyer bias exist?
8. What are the two price allocation rules in auction markets? Explain the difference between them.
9. What is an auction aggregator and how does it work?
10. What types of products are well suited for an auction market? At what points in the product life cycle can auction markets prove beneficial for marketers?
11. What three characteristics define a portal site today?
12. What is a vertical market portal, and how might recent trends in consumer behavior prove advantageous to this business model?
13. What are the two main types of vertical market portals, and how are they distinguished from one and other?
14. List and briefly explain the main revenue sources for the portal business model.

PROJECTS

1. Find two examples of an affinity portal and two examples of a focused content portal. Prepare a presentation explaining why each of your examples should be categorized as an affinity portal or a focused content portal. For each example, surf the site and describe the services each site provides. Try to determine what revenue model each of your examples is using and, if possible, how many members or registered visitors the site has attracted.

2. Examine the use of auctions by businesses. Go to any auction site of your choosing and look for outlet auctions or auctions directly from merchants. Research at least three products up for sale. What stage in the product life cycle do these products fall into? Are there quantity purchasing requirements? What was the opening bid price? What are the bid increments? What is the auction duration? Analyze why these firms have used the auction channel to sell these goods and prepare a short report on your findings.

3. Visit one for-profit and one nonprofit sponsored social network. Create a presentation to describe and demonstrate the offering at each site. What organizational objectives is each pursuing? How is the for-profit company using community building technologies as a customer relations management tool?

WEB SITE RESOURCES www.prenhall.com/laudon

- Additional projects, exercises, and tutorials
- Careers: Explore career opportunities in e-commerce
- Raising capital and business plans

CHAPTER 12

B2B E-commerce: Supply Chain Management and Collaborative Commerce

LEARNING OBJECTIVES

After reading this chapter, you will be able to:

- Define B2B commerce and understand its scope and history.
- Understand the procurement process, the supply chain, and collaborative commerce.
- Identify the main types of B2B e-commerce: Net marketplaces and private industrial networks.
- Understand the four types of Net marketplaces.
- Identify the major trends in the development of Net marketplaces.
- Identify the role of private industrial networks in transforming the supply chain.
- Understand the role of private industrial networks in supporting collaborative commerce.

Volkswagen
Builds Its B2B Net Marketplace

Volkswagen AG is Europe's largest car manufacturer, producing 6.1 million cars, trucks, and vans each year. In addition to the Volkswagen brand, the Volkswagen Group also owns luxury car makers such as Audi, Bentley, Bugatti, and Lamborghini, and family car makers SEAT in Spain and Skoda in the Czech Republic. The company has 325,000 employees and operates plants in Europe, Africa, the Asian/Pacific rim, and the Americas.

The various companies in the Volkswagen Group annually purchase components, automotive parts, and indirect materials worth about 62 billion euros, or about $88 billion (which constitutes about 84% of Volkswagen's annual revenue). Obviously, the procurement process and relationships with suppliers are absolutely critical for Volkswagen's success.

Today, the Volkswagen Group manages almost all of its procurement needs via the Internet. It began building its Internet platform, VWGroupSupply.com, in 2000. The Volkswagen Group was looking for ways to create more efficient relationships with its suppliers and reduce the cost of paper-based procurement processes. However, the company did not want to automate procurement using a public independent exchange or an industry consortium because it would have had fto adapt its own business processes to a common framework that could be used by many different organizations. Volkswagen hoped that by building its own B2B network, it could compete more effectively against other automakers. Volkswagen decided, for instance, not to participate in Covisint, the giant automotive industry consortium backed by major car manufacturers such as Ford, General Motors, and DaimlerChrysler, which provided procurement and other supply chain services for these companies, other automotive manufacturers, and their suppliers.

Instead, Volkswagen opted for a private platform which would allow it to integrate its suppliers more tightly with its own business processes, and where it could control more precisely who was invited to participate. VWGroupSupply now handles over 90% of all global purchasing for the Volkswagen Group, including all automotive and parts components. It is one of the most comprehensive Net marketplaces in the global automotive industry. From an initial seven applications, the platform now offers over 30 different online applications, such as requests for quotations (RFQs), contract negotiations, catalog purchases, purchase order management, engineering change management, vehicle program management, and payments, among others. The Volkswagen Group developed the platform using technology from a number of vendors, including Ariba, IBM, and i2 Technologies.

Suppliers of all sizes can access VWGroupSupply with standard Web browser software. The Web site is limited to suppliers who have done business with one or more companies in the Volkswagen Group and potential new suppliers who go through an authorization process. The system maintains a common data repository with details on each supplier concerning procurement, logistics, production, quality, technical design, and finance.

As of October 2007, its online catalog contained about 2.1 million items from 530 global suppliers. There were 14,200 internal users of the online catalog who had conducted over 1.2 million transactions with a value totaling 320 million euros ($486 million). The catalog uses the eCl@ss standard for classifying its contents. All suppliers who participate in the catalog ordering process classify their products using this standard.

Online negotiations involve multiple bids by suppliers for various purchasing contracts. VWGroupSupply ensures that all participants meet its technical and commercial qualifications. Before an online solicitation begins, the system informs vendors about the data and precise rules governing the negotiations. During 2007, more almost 3,300 online contract negotiations involving 6,850 companies were conducted online, with a value of 11.9 billion euros ($17.4 billion).

Shifts in market demand have a drastic impact on Volkswagen's production activities and affect the ability of suppliers to deliver. Production bottlenecks can result if suppliers are unprepared for a sudden upsurge in demand. If suppliers stock too much inventory, they may incur excess costs from running at overcapacity. VWGroupSupply has an application called electronic Capacity Management (eCAP) to alert both Volkswagen and its suppliers to changes in trends in advance.

eCAP enables suppliers to track Volkswagen's continually updated production plans and materials requirements in real time online. This capability captures information about participating suppliers' planned maximum and minimum capacities. If Volkswagen production requirements go beyond these limits, the system sets off an alarm so both parties can react quickly. As of June 2008, eCAP maintains information on over 400 suppliers and 4,000 critical parts.

During its first three years of operation, the material cost reductions and productivity gains from VWGroupSupply produced more than 100 million euros ($122 million) in cost reductions.

SOURCES: VWGroupSupply.com, September 2008; "Best Practices: VW Revs Up its B2B Engine," by Martin Hoffman, *Optimize*, March 2004.

The VWGroupSupply case illustrates the exciting potential for B2B e-commerce to lower production costs, speed up new product delivery, and ultimately revolutionize both the manufacturing process inherited from the early 20th century and the way we purchase industrial products. VWGroupSupply is an example of just one type of B2B e-commerce, but there are many other equally promising efforts to using the Internet to change the relationships among manufacturers and their suppliers. The success of VWGroupSupply and similar networks operated by the major automobile firms in the world stands in contrast to an earlier industry-sponsored Net marketplace called Covisint. Founded in 1999 by five of the world's largest automakers (General Motors, Ford, Chrysler, Nissan, and Peugeot), Covisint hoped to provide an electronic market connecting thousands of suppliers to a few huge buyers using auctions and procurement services. While initially successful, Covisint was dismantled and sold off in June 2004. Its auction business was sold to FreeMarkets, an early B2B auction company which itself was sold to Ariba later in 2004. The rest of Covisint's procurement software and operations were sold to CompuWare, a software services company, which maintains the Covisint brand name and provides software services to the automotive industry using Covisint.

The failure of Covisint and the simultaneous growth in B2B e-commerce efforts such as VWGroupSupply illustrates the difficulties of achieving the broad visions established during the early days of e-commerce. From a high point of 1,500 online B2B exchanges in 2000, the number has dwindled to less than 200 survivors today. Like B2C commerce, the B2B marketplace has consolidated, evolved, and moved on to more attainable visions. In the process, many B2B efforts have experienced extraordinary success. There are many failed efforts to consider as well; these provide important lessons to all managers.

In this chapter, we examine the many different types of Internet-based B2B commerce in detail. In Section 12.1, we define B2B commerce and place it in the con-text of trends in supply chain management, which, ultimately, is the objective of B2B commerce—to help businesses manage the flow of supplies needed for production. The next two sections describe the two fundamental types of B2B e-commerce: Net marketplaces and private industrial networks. We describe four major types of Net marketplaces, their biases (seller, buyer, and neutral), accessibility (private versus public), and value creation dynamics, and then the emergence of private Internet-based industrial networks that tie a smaller number of organizations into a collaborative commercial system.

Table 12.1 summarizes the leading trends in B2B e-commerce in the 2008-9 period. Perhaps the most important theme is the growing comfort level that business firms have with the Internet as a viable method of purchase, payment, and collaboration among partners in the supply chain.

TABLE 12.1	MAJOR TRENDS IN B2B E-COMMERCE, 2008–2009

- B2B e-commerce continues to grow at a double-digit 12-14% annual pace as business firms gain experience and knowledge in exploiting the Internet.
- Business firms increase their comfort level with Internet security and payments, helping to expand their use of B2B channels.
- Growing realization that the most important benefits to B2B commerce are not lower costs of raw materials (although these costs do decline), but rather gains in supply chain efficiency, better spend management, and improved business processes.
- Decline in growth of independent Net marketplace exchanges, but rapid growth in e-procurement firms and private industrial networks.
- Rapid growth in collaborative commerce B2B applications based on private networks.
- Continued consolidation in the B2B Net marketplace and software vendor markets as fewer but stronger firms purchase weaker firms born in early years of B2B e-commerce.

12.1   B2B E-COMMERCE AND SUPPLY CHAIN MANAGEMENT

The trade between business firms represents a huge marketplace. The total amount of B2B trade in the United States in 2008 was about $12 trillion, with B2B e-commerce (online B2B) contributing about $3.8 trillion of that amount (U.S. Census Bureau, 2008a, b). By 2012, B2B e-commerce should grow to about $6.3 trillion in the United States, assuming about a 12%–14% year-to-year growth rate.

The process of conducting trade among business firms is complex and requires significant human intervention, and therefore, it consumes significant resources. Some firms estimate that the average cost of each corporate purchase order for support products costs them at least $100 in administrative overhead. Administrative overhead includes processing paper, approving purchase decisions, spending time using the telephone and fax machines to search for products and arrange for purchases, arranging for shipping, and receiving the goods . Across the economy, this adds up to trillions of dollars annually being spent for procurement processes that could potentially be automated. If even just a portion of inter-firm trade were automated, and parts of the entire procurement process assisted by the Internet, then literally trillions of dollars might be released for more productive uses, consumer prices potentially would fall, productivity would increase, and the economic wealth of the nation would expand. This is the promise of B2B e-commerce. The challenge of B2B e-commerce is changing existing patterns and systems of procurement, and designing and implementing new Internet-based B2B solutions.

DEFINING AND MEASURING THE GROWTH OF B2B COMMERCE

total inter-firm trade
the total flow of value among firms

B2B commerce
all types of computer-enabled inter-firm trade

Before the Internet, business-to-business transactions were referred to simply as *trade* or the *procurement process*. The term **total inter-firm trade** refers to the total flow of value among firms. Today, we use the term **B2B commerce** to describe all types of computer-enabled inter-firm trade, such as the use of the Internet and other networking technologies to exchange value across organizational boundaries. This definition of B2B commerce does not include digital transactions that occur within the boundaries of a single firm—for instance, the transfer of goods and value from one subsidiary to another, or the use of corporate intranets to manage the firm. We use the term **Internet-based B2B commerce** (or **B2B e-commerce**) to describe specifically that portion of B2B commerce that is enabled by the Internet.

THE EVOLUTION OF B2B COMMERCE

B2B commerce has evolved over a 35-year period through several technology-driven stages (see **Figure 12.1**). The first step in the development of B2B commerce in the mid-1970s was **automated order entry systems** that involved the use of telephone modems to send digital orders to health care products companies such as Baxter Health Care. Baxter, a diversified supplier of hospital supplies, placed telephone modems in its customers' procurement offices to automate re-ordering from Baxter's computerized inventory database (and to discourage re-ordering from competitors). This early technology was replaced by personal computers using private networks in the late 1980s, and by Internet workstations accessing electronic online catalogs in the late 1990s. Automated order entry systems are **seller-side solutions**. They are owned by the suppliers and are seller-biased markets—they show only goods from a single seller. Customers benefited from these systems because they reduced the costs of inventory replenishment and were paid for largely by the suppliers. Automated order entry systems continue to play an important role in B2B commerce.

Internet-based B2B commerce (B2B e-commerce) that portion of B2B commerce that is enabled by the Internet

automated order entry systems involve the use of telephone modems to send digital orders

seller-side solutions seller-biased markets that are owned by, and show only goods from, a single seller

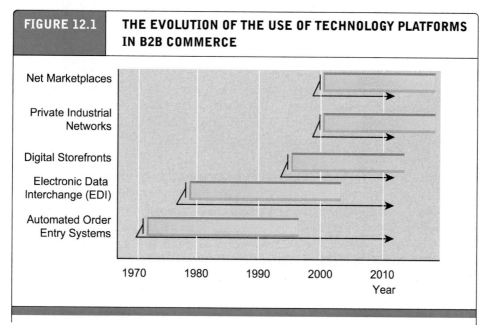

FIGURE 12.1 | **THE EVOLUTION OF THE USE OF TECHNOLOGY PLATFORMS IN B2B COMMERCE**

B2B commerce has gone through many stages of development since the 1970s. Each stage reflects a major change in technology platforms from mainframes to private dedicated networks, and finally to the Internet.

electronic data interchange (EDI)

a communications standard for sharing business documents and settlement information among a small number of firms

buyer-side solutions

buyer-biased markets that are owned by buyers and that aim to reduce the procurement costs of supplies for buyers

hub-and-spoke system

suppliers connected to a central hub of buyers via private dedicated networks

vertical market

one that provides expertise and products for a specific industry

horizontal markets

markets that serve many different industries

B2B electronic storefronts

online catalogs of products made available to the public marketplace by a single supplier

Net marketplace

brings hundreds to thousands of suppliers and buyers into a single Internet-based environment to conduct trade

By the late 1970s, a new form of computer-to-computer communication called **electronic data interchange** (**EDI**) emerged. We describe EDI in greater detail later in this chapter, but at this point, it is necessary only to know that EDI is a communications standard for sharing business documents such as invoices, purchase orders, shipping bills, product stocking numbers (SKUs), and settlement information among a small number of firms. Virtually all large firms have EDI systems, and most industry groups have industry standards for defining documents in that industry. EDI systems are owned by the buyers, and hence they are **buyer-side solutions** and buyer-biased because they aim to reduce the procurement costs of supplies for the buyer. Of course, by automating the transaction, EDI systems also benefit the sellers by reducing costs of serving their customers. The topology of EDI systems is often referred to as a **hub-and-spoke** system, with the buyers in the center and the suppliers connected to the central hub via private dedicated networks.

EDI systems generally serve vertical markets. A **vertical market** is one that provides expertise and products for a specific industry, such as automobiles. In contrast, **horizontal markets** serve many different industries.

Electronic storefronts emerged in the mid-1990s along with the commercialization of the Internet. **B2B electronic storefronts** are perhaps the simplest and easiest to understand form of B2B e-commerce, because they are just online catalogs of products made available to the public marketplace by a single supplier—similar to Amazon for the B2C retail market. Owned by the suppliers, they are seller-side solutions and seller-biased because they show only the products offered by a single supplier.

Electronic storefronts are a natural descendant of automated order entry systems, but there are two important differences: (1) the far less expensive and more universal Internet becomes the communication media and displaces private networks, and (2) electronic storefronts tend to serve horizontal markets—they carry products that serve a wide variety of industries. Although electronic storefronts emerged prior to Net marketplaces (described next), they are usually considered a type of Net marketplace.

Net marketplaces emerged in the late 1990s as a natural extension and scaling-up of the electronic storefronts. There are many different kinds of Net marketplaces that we describe in detail in Section 12.2, but the essential characteristic of a Net marketplace is that they bring hundreds to thousands of suppliers—each with electronic catalogs and potentially thousands of purchasing firms—into a single Internet-based environment to conduct trade.

Net marketplaces can be organized under a variety of ownership models. Some are owned by independent third parties backed by venture capital, some are owned by established firms who are the main or only market players, and some are a mix of both. Net marketplaces establish the prices of the goods they offer in four primary ways—fixed catalog prices, or more dynamic pricing, such as negotiation, auction, and bid/ask ("exchange" model). Net marketplaces earn revenue in a number of ways, including transaction fees, subscription fees, service fees, software licensing fees, advertising and marketing, and sales of data and information.

Although the primary benefits and biases of Net marketplaces have to be determined on a case-by-case basis depending on ownership and pricing mechanisms, it is often the case that Net marketplaces are biased against suppliers because they can force suppliers to reveal their prices and terms to other suppliers in the marketplace. Net marketplaces can also significantly extend the benefits of simple electronic storefronts by seeking to automate the procurement value chain of both selling and buying firms.

Private industrial networks also emerged in the late 1990s as natural extensions of EDI systems and the existing close relationships that developed between large industrial firms and their suppliers. Described in more detail in Section 12.3, **private industrial networks** (sometimes also referred to as a *private trading exchange*, or *PTX*) are Internet-based communication environments that extend far beyond procurement to encompass truly collaborative commerce. Private industrial networks permit buyer firms and their principal suppliers to share product design and development, marketing, inventory, production scheduling, and unstructured communications. Like EDI, private industrial networks are owned by the buyers and are buyer-side solutions with buyer biases. These systems are directly intended to improve the cost position and flexibility of large industrial firms (Kumaran, 2002).

Naturally, private industrial networks have significant benefits for suppliers as well. Inclusion in the direct supply chain for a major industrial purchasing company can allow a supplier to increase both revenue and margins because the environment is not competitive—only a few suppliers are included in the private industrial network. These networks are the most prevalent form of Internet-based B2B commerce, and this will continue into the foreseeable future.

private industrial networks (private trading exchange, PTX)
Internet-based communication environments that extend far beyond procurement to encompass truly collaborative commerce

THE GROWTH OF B2B E-COMMERCE 2001-2012

In the period 2008–2012, B2B e-commerce (including EDI) is projected to grow from about 32% to 40% of total inter-firm trade in the United States, or from $3.8 trillion in 2008 to $6.3 trillion in 2012 (see **Figure 12.2**).

Several observations are important to note with respect to Figure 12.2. First, it shows that the initial belief that electronic marketplaces would become the dominant form of B2B e-commerce is not supported. Second, private industrial networks play a dominant role in B2B e-commerce, both now and in the future. Third, non-EDI B2B e-commerce is the most rapidly growing type of B2B e-commerce, and EDI is still quite large but will decline over time. Well over 80% of U.S. firms buy indirect goods (maintenance and operations goods) on the Internet, which accounts for 11% of their overall indirect purchases. For goods used directly in production, likewise, about 70% of U.S. firms purchase over the Internet, which accounts for about 10% of their overall direct goods purchasing (eMarketer, Inc., 2004).

Industry Forecasts

Not all industries will be similarly affected by B2B e-commerce, and not all industries can similarly benefit from B2B. Several factors influence the speed with which industries migrate to B2B e-commerce and the volume of transactions. Those industries in which there is already significant utilization of EDI (indicating concentration of buyers and suppliers) and large investments in information

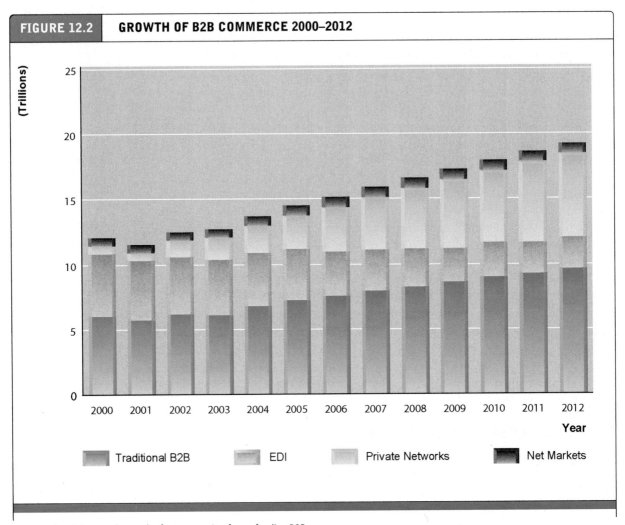

FIGURE 12.2 | **GROWTH OF B2B COMMERCE 2000–2012**

Private industrial networks are the fastest-growing form of online B2B e-commerce.
SOURCES: Based on data from U.S. Census Bureau, 2008a, b; authors' estimates.

technology and Internet infrastructure can be expected to move first and fastest to B2B e-commerce utilization. The aerospace and defense, computer, and industrial equipment industries meet these criteria. Where the marketplace is highly concentrated on either the purchasing or selling side, or both, conditions are also ripe for rapid B2B e-commerce growth, as in energy and chemical industries. In the case of health care, the federal government, health care providers (doctors and hospitals), and major insurance companies are moving rapidly towards a national medical record system and the use of Internet for managing medical payments.

POTENTIAL BENEFITS OF B2B E-COMMERCE

Regardless of the specific type of B2B e-commerce, as a whole, Internet-based B2B commerce promises many strategic benefits to participating firms—both buyers and sellers—and impressive gains for the economy as a whole. B2B e-commerce can:

- Lower administrative costs
- Lower search costs for buyers
- Reduce inventory costs by increasing competition among suppliers (increasing price transparency) and reducing inventory to the bare minimum
- Lower transaction costs by eliminating paperwork and automating parts of the procurement process
- Increase production flexibility by ensuring delivery of parts "just in time"
- Improve quality of products by increasing cooperation among buyers and sellers and reducing quality issues
- Decrease product cycle time by sharing designs and production schedules with suppliers
- Increase opportunities for collaborating with suppliers and distributors
- Create greater price transparency—the ability to see the actual buy and sell prices in a market

B2B e-commerce offers potential first-mover strategic benefits for individual firms as well. Firms who move their procurement processes online first will experience impressive gains in productivity, cost reduction, and potentially much faster introduction of new, higher-quality products. While these gains may be imitated by other competing firms, it is also clear from the brief history of B2B e-commerce that firms making sustained investments in information technology and Internet-based B2B commerce can adapt much faster to new technologies as they emerge, creating a string of first-mover advantages.

THE PROCUREMENT PROCESS AND THE SUPPLY CHAIN

The subject of B2B e-commerce can be complex because there are so many ways the Internet can be used to support the exchange of goods and payments among organizations. Ultimately, B2B e-commerce is about changing the **procurement process** (the way business firms purchase the goods they need to produce the goods they will ultimately sell to consumers) of thousands of firms across the United States and the world.

One way to enter this area of Internet-based B2B commerce is to examine the existing procurement process (see **Figure 12.3**). Firms purchase goods from a set of suppliers, and they in turn purchase their inputs from a set of suppliers. This set of firms is linked through a series of transactions referred to as the **supply chain**. The supply chain includes not just the firms themselves, but also the relationships among them and the processes that connect them.

There are seven separate steps in the procurement process. The first three steps involve the decision of who to buy from and what to pay: searching for suppliers of specific products; qualifying both the seller and the products they sell; and

procurement process
tthe way firms purchase the goods they need to produce goods for consumers

supply chain
firms that purchase goods, their suppliers, and their suppliers' suppliers. Includes not only the firms themselves, but also the relationships among them, and the processes that connect them

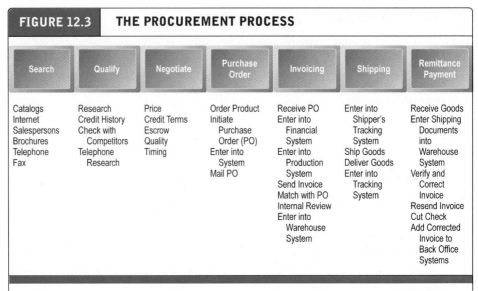

FIGURE 12.3 | **THE PROCUREMENT PROCESS**

Search	Qualify	Negotiate	Purchase Order	Invoicing	Shipping	Remittance Payment
Catalogs	Research	Price	Order Product	Receive PO	Enter into	Receive Goods
Internet	Credit History	Credit Terms	Initiate	Enter into	Shipper's	Enter Shipping
Salespersons	Check with	Escrow	Purchase	Financial	Tracking	Documents
Brochures	Competitors	Quality	Order (PO)	System	System	into
Telephone	Telephone	Timing	Enter into	Enter into	Ship Goods	Warehouse
Fax	Research		System	Production	Deliver Goods	System
			Mail PO	System	Enter into	Verify and
				Send Invoice	Tracking	Correct
				Match with PO	System	Invoice
				Internal Review		Resend Invoice
				Enter into		Cut Check
				Warehouse		Add Corrected
				System		Invoice to
						Back Office
						Systems

The procurement process is a lengthy and complicated series of steps that involves the seller, buyer, and shipping companies in a series of connected transactions.

negotiating prices, credit terms, escrow requirements, quality, and scheduling of delivery. Once a supplier is identified, purchase orders are issued, the buyer is sent an invoice, the goods are shipped, and the buyer sends a payment. Each of these steps in the procurement process is composed of many separate sub-activities. Each of these activities must be recorded in the information systems of the seller, buyer, and shipper. Often, this data entry is not automatic and involves some manual labor.

Types of Procurement

Two distinctions are important for understanding how B2B e-commerce can improve the procurement process. First, firms make purchases of two kinds of goods from suppliers: direct goods and indirect goods. **Direct goods** are goods integrally involved in the production process; for instance, when an automobile manufacturer purchases sheet steel for auto body production. **Indirect goods** are all other goods not directly involved in the production process, such as office supplies and maintenance products. Often these goods are called **MRO goods**—products for maintenance, repair, and operations.

Second, firms use two different methods for purchasing goods: contract purchasing and spot purchasing. **Contract purchasing** involves long-term written agreements to purchase specified products, with agreed-upon terms and quality, for an extended period of time. Generally, firms purchase direct goods using long-term contracts. **Spot purchasing** involves the purchase of goods based on immediate needs in larger marketplaces that involve many suppliers. Generally, firms use spot purchasing for indirect goods, although in some cases, firms also use spot purchasing for direct goods.

direct goods
goods directly involved in the production process

indirect goods
all other goods not directly involved in the production process

MRO goods
products for maintenance, repair, and operations

contract purchasing
involves long-term written agreements to purchase specified products, under agreed-upon terms and quality, for an extended period of time

spot purchasing
involves the purchase of goods based on immediate needs in larger marketplaces that involve many suppliers

According to several estimates, about 80% of inter-firm trade involves contract purchasing of direct goods, and 20% involves spot purchasing of indirect goods (Sodhi, 2001; Kaplan and Sawhney, 2000). This finding is significant for understanding B2B e-commerce, as we see below.

Although the procurement process involves the purchasing of goods, it is extraordinarily information-intense, involving the movement of information among many existing corporate systems. The procurement process today is also very labor-intensive, directly involving over 3.5 million employees in the United States, not including those engaged in transportation, finance, insurance, or general office administration related to the process (U.S. Census Bureau, 2008a).

In the long term, the success or failure of B2B e-commerce depends on changing the day-to-day behavior of these 3.5 million people. The key players in the procurement process are the purchasing managers. They ultimately decide who to buy from, what to buy, and on what terms. Purchasing managers ("procurement managers" in the business press) are also the key decision makers for the adoption of B2B e-commerce solutions.

The Internet could make an important contribution in simplifying the procurement process by bringing buyers and sellers together in a single marketplace and reducing search, research, and negotiating costs. This would appear to be very helpful for spot purchases of indirect goods. Later in the procurement process, the Internet could make an important contribution simply as a powerful communications medium, transferring information among the sellers, buyers, and shippers, and helping managers coordinate the procurement process. This would appear to be very helpful for contract purchases of direct goods. To a large extent, this is the promise of B2B e-commerce. But it is not the whole story.

Although Figure 12.3 captures some of the complexity of the procurement process, it is important to realize that firms purchase thousands of goods from thousands of suppliers. The suppliers, in turn, must purchase their inputs from their suppliers. Large manufacturers such as DaimlerChrysler Corporation have over 20,000 suppliers of parts, packaging, and technology. The number of secondary and tertiary suppliers is at least as large. Together, this extended **multi-tier supply chain** (the chain of primary, secondary, and tertiary suppliers) constitutes a crucial aspect of the industrial infrastructure of the economy. **Figure 12.4** depicts a firm's multi-tier supply chain.

The supply chain depicted in Figure 12.4 is a three-tier chain simplified for the sake of illustration. In fact, large Fortune 1000 firms have thousands of suppliers, who in turn have thousands of smaller suppliers. The complexity of the supply chain suggests a combinatorial explosion. Assuming a manufacturer has four primary suppliers and each one has three primary suppliers, and each of these has three primary suppliers, then the total number of suppliers in the chain (including the buying firm) rises to 53. This figure does not include the shippers, insurers, and financiers involved in the transactions.

Immediately, you can see from Figure 12.4 that the procurement process involves a very large number of suppliers, each of whom must be coordinated with the production needs of the ultimate purchaser—the buying firm.

multi-tier supply chain

the chain of primary, secondary, and tertiary suppliers

FIGURE 12.4	THE MULTI-TIER SUPPLY CHAIN

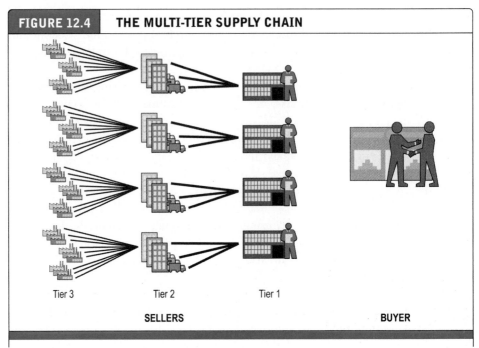

Tier 3   Tier 2   Tier 1

SELLERS   **BUYER**

The supply chain for every firm is composed of multiple tiers of suppliers.

legacy computer systems
generally are older mainframe and minicomputer systems used to manage key business processes within a firm in a variety of functional areas

materials requirements planning (MRP) system
legacy system that enables companies to predict, track, and manage all the constituent parts of complex manufactured goods

enterprise resource planning (ERP) system
a more sophisticated MRP system that includes human resource and financial components

The Role of Existing Legacy Computer Systems

Complicating any efforts to coordinate the many firms in a supply chain is the fact that each firm generally has its own set of legacy computer systems, often home-grown, that cannot easily pass information to other systems. **Legacy computer systems** generally are older mainframe and minicomputer systems used to manage key business processes within a firm in a variety of functional areas from manufacturing, logistics, financial, and human resources. Converting these older systems to new Internet and client/server-based systems is very expensive and takes many years.

One typical legacy system is a **materials requirements planning** (**MRP**) **system** that enables companies to predict, track, and manage all the constituent parts of complex manufactured goods such as automobiles, machine tools, and industrial equipment. An MRP system stores and generates a bill of material (BOM) that lists all the parts needed to manufacture a product. The MRP system also generates a production schedule that describes the order in which parts are used and the production time for each step in production. The BOM and production schedule are then used to generate purchase orders to suppliers. The MRP system can be run as often as needed, generating a dynamic production environment.

Many larger firms have installed **enterprise resource planning** (**ERP**) **systems**, which are more sophisticated MRP systems that include human resource and financial components. With an ERP system in place, orders from customers are translated into BOMs, production schedules, and human resource and financial requirements, including notifying the finance department to issue invoices to customers and pay suppliers. However, ERP systems were not originally designed to coordinate the flow of information among a large set of supplier firms, and they require expensive modification before they can become part of an enterprise-wide B2B system.

TRENDS IN SUPPLY CHAIN MANAGEMENT AND COLLABORATIVE COMMERCE

It is impossible to comprehend the actual and potential contribution of Internet-based B2B commerce, or the successes and failures of B2B e-commerce vendors and markets, without understanding ongoing efforts to improve the procurement process through a variety of supply chain management programs that long preceded the development of e-commerce.

Supply chain management (**SCM**) refers to a wide variety of activities that firms and industries use to coordinate the key players in their procurement process. For the most part, today's procurement managers work with telephones, fax machines, face-to-face conversations, and instinct, relying on trusted long-term suppliers for their strategic purchases of goods directly involved in the production process.

There have been four major developments in supply chain management over the two decades that preceded the development of the Internet and set the ground rules for understanding how B2B e-commerce works (or fails to work). These developments are supply chain simplification, electronic data interchange (EDI), supply chain management systems, and collaborative commerce.

supply chain management (SCM)
refers to a wide variety of activities that firms and industries use to coordinate the key players in their procurement process

Supply Chain Simplification

Many manufacturing firms have spent the past two decades reducing the size of their supply chains and working more closely with a smaller group of "strategic" supplier firms to reduce both product costs and administrative costs, while improving quality. Following the lead of Japanese industry, for instance, the automobile industry has systematically reduced the number of its suppliers by over 50%. Instead of open bidding for orders, large manufacturers have chosen to work with strategic partner supply firms under long-term contracts that guarantee the supplier business, but also establish quality, cost, and timing goals. These strategic partnership programs are essential for just-in-time production models, and often involve joint product development and design, integration of computer systems, and tight coupling of the production processes of two or more companies. **Tight coupling** is a method for ensuring that suppliers precisely deliver the ordered parts at a specific time and to a particular location, to ensure the production process is not interrupted for lack of parts.

tight coupling
a method for ensuring that suppliers precisely deliver the ordered parts, at a specific time and particular location, to ensure the production process is not interrupted for lack of parts

Electronic Data Interchange (EDI)

As noted in the previous section, B2B e-commerce did not originate with the Internet, but in fact has its roots in technologies such as EDI that were first developed in the mid-1970s and 1980s. EDI is a broadly defined communications protocol for exchanging documents among computers using technical standards developed by the American National Standards Institute (ANSI X12 standards) and international bodies such as the United Nations (EDIFACT standards).

EDI was developed to reduce the cost, delays, and errors inherent in the manual exchanges of documents such as purchase orders, shipping documents, price lists, payments, and customer data. EDI differs from an unstructured message because its messages are organized with distinct fields for each of the important pieces of information in a commercial transaction such as transaction date, product purchased, amount, sender's name, address, and recipient's name.

Each major industry in the United States and throughout much of the industrial world has EDI industry committees that define the structure and information fields of electronic documents for that industry. EDI communications at first relied on private point-to-point circuit-switched communication networks and private value-added networks that connected key participants in the supply chain (Laudon and Laudon, 2009). Estimates indicate that EDI transactions will total about $2.8 trillion in 2008. That is about 25% of the $12 trillion trade among firms (U.S. Census Bureau, 2008a, b). In this sense, EDI is particularly important in the development of B2B e-commerce.

EDI has evolved significantly since the 1980s (see **Figure 12.5**). Initially, EDI focused on document automation (Stage 1). Procurement agents created purchase orders electronically and sent them to trading partners, who in turn shipped order fulfillment and shipping notices electronically back to the purchaser. Invoices, payments, and other documents followed. These early implementations replaced the postal system for document transmission, and resulted in same-day shipping of orders (rather than a week's delay caused by the postal system), reduced errors, and lower costs.

The second stage of EDI development began in the early 1990s, driven largely by the automation of internal industrial processes and movement toward just-in-time production and continuous production. The new methods of production called for greater flexibility in scheduling, shipping, and financing of supplies. EDI evolved to become a system for document elimination. To support the new automated production processes used by manufacturers, EDI was used to eliminate purchase orders and other documents entirely, replacing them with production schedules and inventory balances. Supplier firms were sent monthly statements of production requirements and precise scheduled delivery times, and the orders would be fulfilled continuously, with inventory and payments being adjusted at the end of each month.

In the third stage of EDI, beginning in the mid-1990s, suppliers were given online access to selected parts of the purchasing firm's production and delivery schedules, and, under long-term contracts, were required to meet those schedules on their own without intervention by firm purchasing agents. Movement toward this continuous access model of EDI was spurred in the 1990s by large manufacturing and process firms (such as oil and chemical companies) that were implementing ERP systems. These systems required standardization of business processes and resulted in the automation of production, logistics, and many financial processes. These new processes required much closer relationships with suppliers, who were required to be more precise in delivery scheduling and more flexible in inventory management. This level of supplier precision could never be achieved economically by human purchasing agents. This third stage of EDI introduced the era of continuous replenishment. For instance,

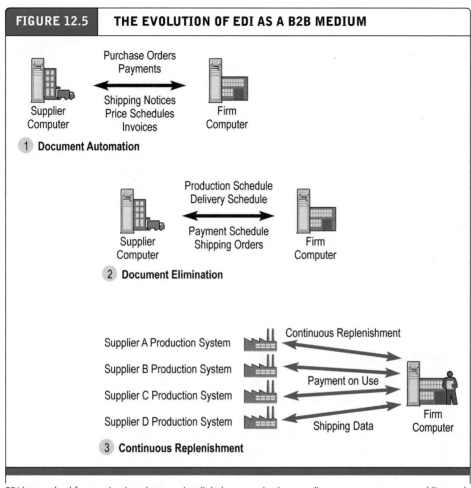

FIGURE 12.5   **THE EVOLUTION OF EDI AS A B2B MEDIUM**

EDI has evolved from a simple point-to-point digital communications medium to a many-to-one enabling tool for continuous inventory replenishment.

Wal-Mart and Toys"R"Us provide their suppliers with access to their store inventories, and the suppliers are expected to keep the stock of items on the shelf within pre-specified targets. Similar developments occurred in the grocery industry.

Today, EDI must be viewed as a general enabling technology that provides for the exchange of critical business information between computer applications supporting a wide variety of business processes. EDI is an important industrial network technology, suited to support communications among a small set of strategic partners in direct, long-term trading relationships. The technical platform of EDI has changed from mainframes to personal computers, and the telecommunications environment is changing from private, dedicated networks to the Internet (referred to as Internet-based EDI, or just Internet EDI). Most industry groups are moving toward XML as the language for expressing EDI commercial documents and communications.

The strength of EDI is its ability to support direct commercial transactions among strategically related firms in an industrial network, but this is its weakness as well. EDI is not well suited for the development of electronic marketplaces, where thousands of suppliers and purchasers meet in a digital arena to negotiate prices. EDI supports direct bilateral communications among a small set of firms and does not permit the multilateral, dynamic relationships of a true marketplace. EDI does not provide for price transparency among a large number of suppliers, does not scale easily to include new participants, and is not a real-time communications environment. It is instead a "batch processing" environment in which messages are exchanged in batches (although even this feature is changing as EDI moves toward XML and the Internet). EDI does not have a rich communications environment that can simultaneously support e-mail messaging, sharing of graphic documents, network meetings, or user-friendly flexible database creation and management. For these features, Internet-based software has emerged that is described below. EDI is also an expensive proposition, and a staff of dedicated programmers is required to implement it in large firms; in some cases, a considerable amount of time is also needed to reprogram existing enterprise systems to work with EDI protocols. Small firms are typically required to adopt EDI in order to supply large firms, and there are less-expensive, small-firm solutions for implementing EDI.

Supply Chain Management Systems

Supply chain simplification, focusing on strategic partners in the production process, ERP systems, and continuous inventory replenishment are the foundation for contemporary **supply chain management (SCM) systems**. Supply chain management systems continuously link the activities of buying, making, and moving products from suppliers to purchasing firms, as well as integrating the demand side of the business equation by including the order entry system in the process. With an SCM system and continuous replenishment, inventory is eliminated and production begins only when an order is received (see **Figure 12.6**). This is especially important in industries in which the product is perishable or experiences declining market value rapidly after production. Personal computers fit this description.

Hewlett-Packard (HP) has a Web-based order-driven supply chain management system that begins with either a customer placing an order online or the receipt of an order from a dealer. The order is forwarded from the order entry system to HP's production and delivery system. From there, the order is routed to one of several HP contractor supplier firms. One such firm is Synnex in Fremont, California. At Synnex, computers verify the order with HP and validate the ordered configuration to ensure the PC can be manufactured (e.g., will not have missing parts or fail a design specification set by HP). The order is then forwarded to a computer-based production control system that issues a bar-coded production ticket to factory assemblers. Simultaneously, a parts order is forwarded to Synnex's warehouse and inventory management system. A worker assembles the computer, and then the computer is boxed, tagged, and shipped to the customer. The delivery is monitored and tracked by HP's supply chain management system, which links directly to one of several overnight delivery systems operated by Airborne Express,

supply chain management (SCM) systems

continuously link the activities of buying, making, and moving products from suppliers to purchasing firms, as well as integrating the demand side of the business equation by including the order entry system in the process

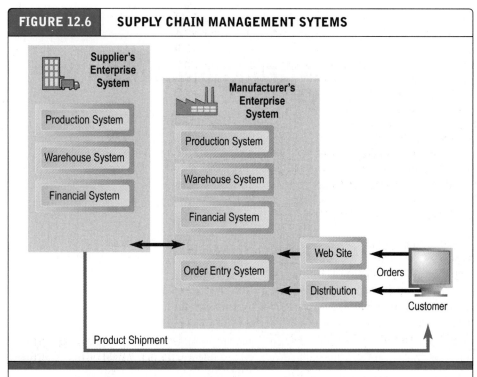

FIGURE 12.6	SUPPLY CHAIN MANAGEMENT SYTEMS

SCM systems coordinate the activities of suppliers, shippers, and order entry systems to automate order entry through production, payment, and shipping business processes.

Federal Express, and UPS. The elapsed time from order entry to shipping is 48 hours. With this system, Synnex and HP have eliminated the need to hold PCs in inventory, reduced cycle time from one week to 48 hours, and reduced errors. HP has extended this system to become a global B2B order tracking, reporting, and support system for large HP customers. The site now operates in 10 languages and more than 200 countries (Synnex Corporation, 2008; Hewlett-Packard, 2008).

Implementing an order-driven, Web-based supply chain management system is not always easy, however, as *Insight on Technology: RFID AutoIdentification: Making Your Supply Chain Visible* illustrates.

Collaborative Commerce

Collaborative commerce is a direct extension of supply chain management systems, as well as supply chain simplification. **Collaborative commerce** is defined as the use of digital technologies to permit organizations to collaboratively design, develop, build, and manage products through their life cycles. This is a much broader mission than EDI or simply managing the flow of information among organizations. Collaborative commerce involves a definitive move from a transaction focus to a relationship focus among the supply chain participants. Rather than having an arm's-length adversarial relationship with suppliers, collaborative

collaborative commerce
the use of digital technologies to permit organizations to collaboratively design, develop, build, and manage products through their life cycles

INSIGHT ON TECHNOLOGY

RFID AUTOIDENTIFICATION: MAKING YOUR SUPPLY CHAIN VISIBLE

It's 10 PM. Do you know where your containers are? If you're in business anywhere in the world today, and that business involves physical goods, then chances are quite good that your business depends on the movement of goods in containers. In fact, there are 200 million sea cargo containers moving every year among the world's seaports, and nearly 50% of the value of all U.S. imports arrive via sea cargo containers each year. The containers are loaded onto ships, and stacked high on the deck. The containers also fit on the back of trucks and on railway carriages. So when the containers are unloaded from the ship, they continue their journey from the port on the back of trucks or trains. It is a fast and efficient way of moving cargo. A standard container is 20 feet long, 8 feet wide, and 8 feet 6 inches high—big enough to hold a car.

Prior to the development of containers, all ocean-going cargo was loaded and unloaded onto ships in huge nets by dock workers, one package at a time. While the container revolutionized ocean shipping, vastly increasing productivity and reducing breakage, keeping track of 200 million cargo containers is difficult. While each container has its own permanent ID number painted on the side, as well as a bar code identification tag, this number must be entered manually by dock workers, or scanned up close. Identification of containers is prone to errors and slow. If you had to find one container on a dock containing over 1,000 containers, you would have to read each ID number until you found the one you wanted.

Tracking containers is just one part of the larger B2B product identification problem. Retailers such as Wal-Mart, Target, and Amazon find it difficult and expensive to track millions of

annual shipments into and out of their warehouses and sales floors; the automotive industry finds it costly and difficult to synchronize the flow of parts into its factories; the U.S. Department of Defense logistics system finds it difficult to keep track of the movement of troop supplies; and the airline industry often loses bags in transit.

Thirty years ago, the development of the Uniform Product Code (UPC) and the ubiquitous bar code label was an initial first step towards automating the identification of goods. But the bar code technology of the 1970s still required humans or sometimes machines to scan products. The problem with bar codes is that they don't talk—they are passive labels that must be read or scanned.

A new technology to replace bar codes is being deployed among the largest manufacturing and retailing firms. Radio frequency identification (RFID) involves the use of tags attached to products or product containers that transmit a radio signal in the 850 megahertz to 2.5 gigahertz range that continuously identifies themselves to radio receivers in warehouses, factories, retail floors, or on board ships. RFID labels are really tiny computer chips and a battery that are used to transmit each product's electronic product code to receivers nearby.

RFID has several key advantages over the old bar code scanner technology. RFID eliminates the line-of-sight reading requirement of bar codes and greatly increases the distance from which scanning can be done from a few inches up to 90 feet. RFID systems can be used just about anywhere—from clothing tags to missiles to pet tags to food—anywhere that a unique identification system is needed. The tag can carry information as simple as a pet owner's name and address or the cleaning

(continued)

instruction on a sweater to as complex as instructions on how to assemble a car. Best of all, instead of looking at a warehouse filled with thousands of packages that can't talk, you could be listening to these same thousands of packages each chirping a unique code, identifying themselves to you. Finding the single package you are looking for is much simplified. RFID tags produce a steady stream of data that can be entered into Internet—and intranet-based corporate applications such as SCM and ERP systems.

In mid-2007, there were about 375 million tags in use in the retail sector. Major computer firms such as Microsoft, IBM, and Hewlett-Packard are investing over several hundred million dollars each over the next five years to develop RFID software that will link RFID data to firms' SCM systems. Wal-Mart, the world's largest retailer, has made RFID an important part of its supply chain strategy. It began by mandating that its top 100 suppliers place RFID tags on all cases and pallets headed for the

firm's Dallas distribution centers by January 2005. Currently, about 600 of Wal-Mart's U.S. suppliers are tagging cases and pallets of some of the products they ship. About 1,000 Wal-Mart stores are RFID-enabled, with another 400 planned to be added by the end of 2007, as well as six of its distribution centers. As of January 2008, the RFID program at Sam's Club became mandatory, with suppliers charged $2 per pallet for deliveries without RFID tags.. Although Wal-Mart remains committed to the technology and estimates that it could increase sales by $287 million by using RFID technology, its implementation to date has had mixed results.

As adoption of the technology increases, RFID will have a profound impact on Internet-based B2B commerce by greatly reducing the cost of tracking goods through industry supply chains, reducing errors, and increasing the chances that the right product will be sent to the right customer.

SOURCES: "Wal-Mart RFID Plan Has Mixed Results," RFID News, April 28, 2008; "Wal-Mart Gets Tough on RFID," by Mary Hayes Weier, *Informa-tionWeek*, January 19, 2008; "Wal-Mart Eyes $287 Million Benefit from RFID," by Dan Nystedt, *Network World*, October 12, 2007; "Wal-Mart, Sam's Club Push RFID Further Along, *RFID Journal*, October 5, 2007; "How Wal-Mart Lost Its Technology Edge," by Thomas Wailgum, *Network World*, October 5, 2007; "RFID Progress in Retail to Mid 2007," Idtechex.com, May 29, 2007; "Who Gains, Who Loses, from RFID's Growing Presence in the Marketplace?," Knowl-edge@Wharton, March 23, 2005; "Technology for Tracking Goods Gets Boost from Microsoft, IBM," by Kevin Delaney, *Wal Street Journal*, January 26, 2004.

commerce fosters sharing of sensitive internal information with suppliers and purchasers. Managing collaborative commerce requires knowing exactly what information to share with whom. Collaborative commerce extends beyond supply chain management activities to include the collaborative development of new products and services by multiple cooperating firms.

A good example of a collaborative commerce system is provided by Group Dekko, a collection of 10 independently operated manufacturing companies headquartered in Kendallville, Indiana. Group Dekko produces a variety of components including wire harnesses, molded plastic parts, and metal stamping for automobiles, appliances, and office furniture. The group generates around $300 million in annual revenues. In order to work with its large customers—automobile and appliance manufacturers—Group Dekko had to implement quality control procedures conforming with international standard ISO 9000. The Group Dekko Services Department implemented a common, shared database of ISO documents using a software package called Lotus Domino to coordinate the efforts of the partner firms in Group Dekko. Lotus Domino is the Internet-based version of Lotus Notes, a collaborative document management and communications package. In this way, the separate Dekko companies could share standards, documents, graphics, and experiences in implementing the quality standards. This environment is being extended to share engineering drawings, bills of material, pricing, and routing information for new products. The goal is to involve Group Dekko companies, as well as their suppliers and customers, in the complete flow of design and product information (Group Dekko, 2008; IBM, 2005; 2003).

Although collaborative commerce can involve customers as well as suppliers in the development of products, for the most part, collaborative commerce is concerned with the development of a rich communications environment to enable inter-firm sharing of designs, production plans, inventory levels, delivery schedules, and even the development of shared products (see **Figure 12.7**).

Efforts to develop closer collaboration among suppliers and purchasers originated in the late 1970s at Xerox Parc, Xerox Corporation's research center in Palo Alto. Development of the appropriate software to enable rich communications was furthered by research conducted by Lotus Development Corporation in the early 1990s. The development of the Internet as a rich communications medium has displaced proprietary software tools, and today, collaborative commerce almost always involves the use of Internet technologies to support sharing of graphic designs, documents, messages, and network meetings.

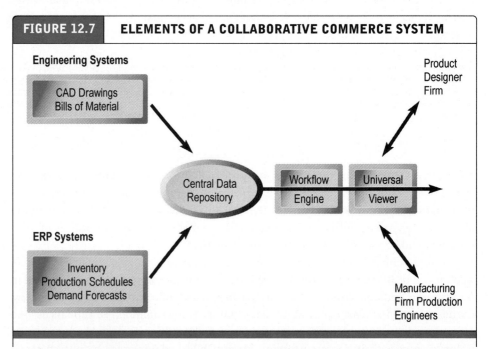

| FIGURE 12.7 | ELEMENTS OF A COLLABORATIVE COMMERCE SYSTEM |

A collaborative commerce application includes a central data repository where employees at several different firms can store engineering drawings and other documents. A workflow engine determines who can see this data and what rules will apply for displaying the data on individual workstations. A viewer can be a browser operating on a workstation.

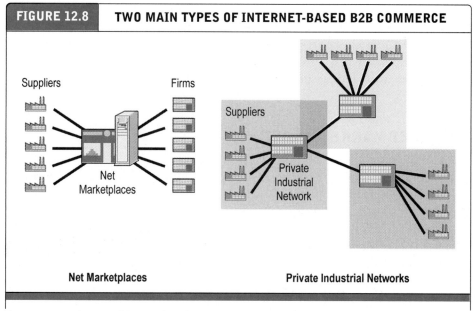

| FIGURE 12.8 | TWO MAIN TYPES OF INTERNET-BASED B2B COMMERCE |

There are two main types of Internet-based B2B commerce: Net marketplaces and private industrial networks.

Collaborative commerce is very different from EDI, which is a technology for structured communications among firms. Collaborative commerce is more like an interactive teleconference among members of the supply chain. EDI and collaborative commerce share one characteristic: they are not open, competitive marketplaces, but instead are, technically, private industrial networks that connect strategic partners in a supply chain.

In Section 12.3, we discuss collaborative commerce in greater depth as a private industrial network enabling technology.

MAIN TYPES OF INTERNET-BASED B2B COMMERCE

There are two generic types of Internet-based B2B commerce systems: Net marketplaces and private industrial networks (see **Figure 12.8**). Within each of these general categories there are many different subtypes that we discuss in the following sections.

Net marketplaces (also referred to as exchanges) bring together potentially thousands of sellers and buyers into a single digital marketplace operated over the Internet. Net marketplaces are transaction-based, support many-to-many as well as one-to-many relationships, and bear some resemblance to financial markets such as the New York Stock Exchange. There are many different types of Net marketplaces, with different pricing mechanisms, biases, and value propositions that will be explored in Section 12.2 (Kerrigan, et al., 2001). Private industrial networks bring together a small number of strategic business partner firms that collaborate to develop highly efficient supply chains and satisfy customer demand for products.

Private industrial networks are relationship-based, support many-to-one or many-to-few relationships, and bear some resemblance to internal collaborative work environments. There are many different types of private industrial networks, as discussed in Section 12.3. Private industrial networks are by far the largest form of B2B e-commerce, and account for over 10 times as much revenue as Net marketplaces.

12.2 NET MARKETPLACES

One of the most compelling visions of B2B e-commerce is that of an electronic marketplace on the Internet that would bring thousands of fragmented suppliers into contact with hundreds of major purchasers of industrial goods for the purpose of conducting "frictionless" commerce. The hope was that these suppliers would compete with one another on price, transactions would be automated and low cost, and as a result, the price of industrial supplies would fall. By extracting fees from buyers and sellers on each transaction, third-party intermediary market makers could earn significant revenues. These Net marketplaces could scale easily as volume increased by simply adding more computers and communications equipment.

In pursuit of this vision, well over 1,500 Net marketplaces sprang up in the early days of e-commerce. Unfortunately, many of them have since disappeared and the population is expected to stabilize at about 200. Still, many survive, and they are joined by other types of Net marketplaces—some private and some public—based on different assumptions that are quite successful

THE VARIETY AND CHARACTERISTICS OF NET MARKETPLACES

There is a confusing variety of Net marketplaces today, and several different ways to classify them. For instance, some writers classify Net marketplaces on the basis of their pricing mechanisms—auction, bid/ask, negotiated price, and fixed prices—while others classify markets based on characteristics of the markets they serve (vertical versus horizontal, or sell-side versus buy-side), or ownership (industry-owned consortia versus independent third-party intermediaries). **Table 12.2** describes some of the important characteristics of Net marketplaces.

TYPES OF NET MARKETPLACES

Although each of these distinctions helps describe the phenomenon of Net marketplaces, they do not focus on the central business functionality provided, and they are not capable by themselves of describing the variety of Net marketplaces.

In **Figure 12.9**, we present a classification of Net marketplaces that focuses on their business functionality; that is, what these Net marketplaces provide for businesses seeking solutions. We use two dimensions of Net marketplaces to create a four-cell classification table. We differentiate Net marketplaces as providing either indirect goods (goods used to support production) or direct goods (goods used in production), and we distinguish markets as providing either contractual purchasing (where purchases take place over many years according to a contract between the firm and its vendor) or spot purchasing (where purchases are episodic and

TABLE 12.2	OTHER CHARACTERISTICS OF NET MARKETPLACES: A B2B VOCABULARY
CHARACTERISTIC	**MEANING**
Bias	Sell-side vs. buy-side vs. neutral. Whose interests are advantaged: buyers, sellers, or no bias?
Ownership	Industry vs. third party. Who owns the marketplace?
Pricing mechanism	Fixed-price catalogs, auctions, bid/ask, and RFPs/RFQs.
Scope/Focus	Horizontal vs. vertical markets.
Value creation	What benefits do they offer the customer?
Access to market	In public markets, any firm can enter, but in private markets, entry is by invitation only.

FIGURE 12.9	PURE TYPES OF NET MARKETPLACES

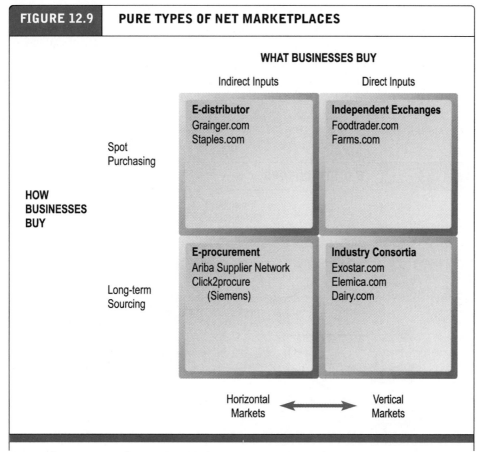

There are four main types of Net marketplaces based on the intersection of two dimensions: how businesses buy and what they buy. A third dimension—horizontal versus vertical markets—also distinguishes the different types of Net marketplaces.

anonymous—vendors and buyers do not have an ongoing relationship and may not know one another). The intersection of these dimensions produces four main types of Net marketplaces that are relatively straightforward: e-distributors, e-procurement networks, exchanges, and industry consortia. Note, however, that in the real world, some Net marketplaces can be found in multiple parts of this figure as business models change and opportunities appear and disappear. Nevertheless, the discussion of "pure types" of Net marketplaces is a useful starting point.

Each of these Net marketplaces seeks to provide value to customers in different ways. We discuss each type of Net marketplace in more detail in the following sections.

E-distributors

e-distributor

provides electronic catalog that represents the products of thousands of direct manufacturers

E-distributors are the most common and most easily understood type of Net marketplace. An **e-distributor** provides an electronic catalog that represents the products of thousands of direct manufacturers (see **Figure 12.10**). An e-distributor is the equivalent of Amazon.com for industry. E-distributors are independently owned intermediaries that offer industrial customers a single source from which to order indirect goods (often referred to as MRO) on a spot, as-needed basis. Reportedly, about 40% of corporate purchases cannot be satisfied under a company's existing contracts, and must be purchased on a spot basis (Jupiter Media Metrix, 2001a; Devine, et al., 2001). E-distributors make money by charging a markup on products they distribute.

Organizations and firms in all industries require MRO supplies. The MRO function maintains, repairs, and operates commercial buildings and maintains all the

FIGURE 12.10 E-DISTRIBUTORS

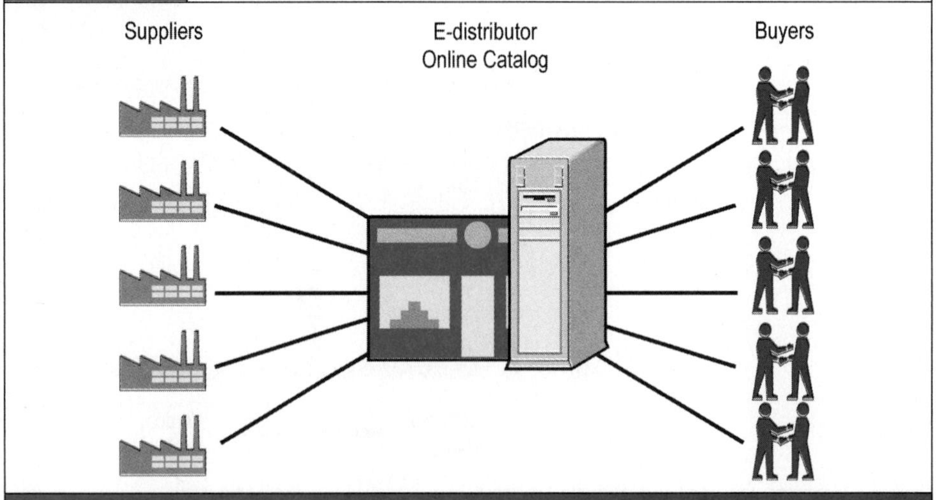

E-distributors are singular firms that bring the products of thousands of suppliers into a single online electronic catalog for sale to thousands of buyer firms. E-distributors are sometimes referred to as one-to-many markets, one seller serving many firms.

machinery of these buildings from heating, ventilating, and air conditioning systems to lighting fixtures.

E-distributors operate in horizontal markets because they serve many different industries with products from many different suppliers. E-distributors usually operate "public" markets in the sense that any firm can order from the catalog, as opposed to "private" markets, where membership is restricted to selected firms.

E-distributor prices are usually fixed, but large customers receive discounts and other incentives to purchase, such as credit, reporting on account activity, and limited forms of business purchasing rules (for instance, no purchases greater than $500 for a single item without a purchase order). The primary benefits offered to industrial customers are lower search costs, lower transaction costs, wide selection, rapid delivery, and low prices.

The most frequently cited example of a public e-distribution market is W.W. Grainger. Grainger is involved in both long-term systematic sourcing as well as spot sourcing, but its emphasis is on spot sourcing. Grainger's business model is to become the world's leading source of MRO suppliers, and its revenue model is that of a typical retailer: it owns the products, and takes a markup on the products it sells to customers. At Grainger.com, users get an electronic online version of Grainger's famous seven-pound catalog, plus other parts not available in the catalog (adding up to over 1 million parts), and complete electronic ordering and payment (W.W. Grainger Inc., 2008).

E-procurement

An **e-procurement Net marketplace** is an independently owned intermediary that connects hundreds of online suppliers offering millions of maintenance and repair parts to business firms who pay fees to join the market (see **Figure 12.11**). E-procurement Net marketplaces are typically used for long-term contractual purchasing of indirect goods (MRO); they create online horizontal markets, but they also provide for members' spot sourcing of MRO supplies. E-procurement companies make money by charging a percentage of each transaction, licensing consulting services and software, and assessing network use fees.

E-procurement companies expand on the business model of simpler e-distributors by including the online catalogs of hundreds of suppliers and offering value chain management services to both buyers and sellers. **Value chain management (VCM) services** provided by e-procurement companies include automation of a firm's entire procurement process on the buyer side and automation of the selling business processes on the seller side. For purchasers, e-procurement companies automate purchase orders, requisitions, sourcing, business rules enforcement, invoicing, and payment. For suppliers, e-procurement companies provide catalog creation and content management, order management, fulfillment, invoicing, shipment, and settlement.

E-procurement Net marketplaces are sometimes referred to as many-to-many markets. They are mediated by an independent third party that purports to represent both buyers and sellers, and hence claim to be neutral. On the other hand, because they may include the catalogs of both competing suppliers and competing e-distributors,

e-procurement Net marketplace
independently owned intermediary that connects hundreds of online suppliers offering millions of maintenance and repair parts to business firms who pay fees to join the market

value chain management (VCM) services
include automation of a firm's entire procurement process on the buyer side and automation of the selling business processes on the seller side

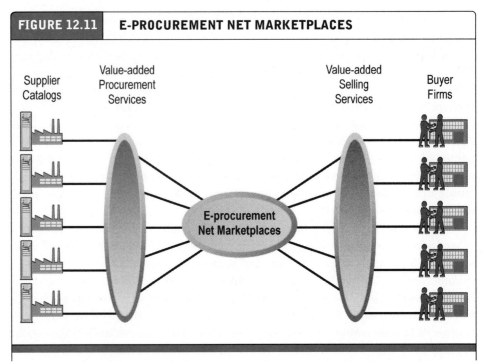

E-procurement Net marketplaces aggregate hundreds of catalogs in a single marketplace and make them available to firms, often on a custom basis that reflects only the suppliers desired by the participating firms.

they have a likely bias in favor of the buyers. Nevertheless, by aggregating huge buyer firms into their networks, they provide distinct marketing benefits for suppliers and reduce customer acquisition costs.

Players in this market segment include Ariba (which purchased its primary competitor, FreeMarkets, in 2004), Perfect Commerce, Verticalnet, A.T. Kearney Procurement Solutions, and Emptoris. The very large enterprise software firms—Oracle, SAP, i2, and JDA Software Group (which acquired Manugistics in 2006)—now also offer procurement solutions to their customers and compete directly against the early entrants in this market.

General Dynamics, for instance, one of the largest defense contractors, uses Ariba e-sourcing software to spend about $8.3 billion annually. General Dynamics uses Ariba's online e-auctions and automated RFQ software to reduce the cost of direct and indirect goods, and to reduce overall transaction costs with vendors. General Dynamics claims an overall reduction of 10%-15% in the cost of goods purchased through its new systems (Ariba, 2007; Hannon, 2003). We discuss Ariba's Net marketplace in depth in the following *E-commerce in Action* section.

E-COMMERCE IN ACTION

ARIBA

Ariba provides an excellent example of an e-procurement Net marketplace. Ariba provides what it calls Spend Management solutions to manage all of a company's non-payroll expenses. Spend Management solutions are a suite of products and services that help to identify and realize cost savings in corporate spending through analysis, sourcing, procurement, and supplier management. These solutions include software applications, services, and network access designed to streamline and automate the business processes related to all aspects of the purchasing process. Established in 1996, the Menlo Park, California, company sells its software and services in 25 countries and focuses primarily on large Fortune 1000 global firms.

Ariba's first application, introduced in June 1997, was Ariba Buyer, which it built to automate the procurement business process within single firms. Since then, the Ariba platform has grown beyond transactional buying and marketplace platforms to include multiple applications that permit users to establish B2B marketplaces internally on their corporate intranets, or externally on the public Internet covering the entire "spend" life cycle, from planning to invoicing. Built to leverage the Internet and provide real-time access to data and suppliers, these applications integrate with the Ariba Supplier Network, an Internet-based network that Ariba introduced in 1999 that connects suppliers to their customers and partners. Businesses can use the Ariba Supplier Network to search an open directory of trading partners, including over 174,000 suppliers worldwide; subscribe to and manage catalog content; and conduct transactions, including order management and fulfillment, invoicing, and settlement. By using the Ariba Supplier Network, businesses can realize cost savings through greater process efficiencies, better employee and contract compliance, reduced inventories, and fair pricing opportunities.

Ariba applications are designed to run on top of the major legacy and backend systems for business processes in the market today, eliminating the need for the manual transfer of data from Ariba to ERP systems such as SAP and Oracle. In 2006, Ariba began introducing Web-based "on-demand' versions of many of its applications.

Ariba's Spend Management solutions are organized around six key functions: (1) "spend visibility," (2) sourcing, (3) contract management, (4) procurement and expense, (5) invoice and payment, and (6) supplier management:

- *Visibility Solutions*: Ariba Analysis, Ariba Data Enrichment, and Ariba Spend Visibility On-Demand, a Web-based service, enable management to analyze spending, processes, and performance in order to identify and prioritize savings opportunities and enable more effective decision-making.

- *Sourcing Solutions*: Ariba Sourcing, Ariba Supplier Performance Management, Ariba Category Management, and Ariba Sourcing On-Demand, a Web-based service, allow companies to identify suppliers across a broad range of categories to negotiate procurement terms, leverage and aggregate spending, implement best practices, and manage procurement contracts.

- *Procurement and Expense Solutions*: The flagship Ariba Buyer application, Ariba Category Procurement, Ariba Travel and Expense, and Ariba Procure-to-Pay On-Demand, a Web-based service, are applications and services for requisitioning and procurement across all types of spending.

- *Contract Management Solutions*: Ariba Contract Workbench, Ariba Contract Compliance, and Ariba Contract Management On-Demand, a Web-based service, enable companies to streamline and automate the contract process from contract creation to compliance management.

- *Invoice and Payment Solutions*: Ariba Invoice and Settlement, and Ariba Electronic Invoice Presentment and Payment On-Demand, a Web-based service, enable companies to streamline and automate invoicing and payment processes to improve speed and accuracy.

- *Supplier Management Solutions*: Ariba Supplier Connectivity, which provides access to the Ariba Supplier Network, helps optimize buyer-supplier interactions throughout the spend management life cycle.

Customers can purchase Ariba Spend Management solution software application modules on a perpetual or term license, subscribe to Web-based on-demand solutions for a specified term, or pay for services on a time-and-materials or fixed-fee basis, depending upon their business requirements. Ariba offers three types of packages for on-demand solutions (Basic, Professional, Enterprise) with at different prices and varying levels of functionality.

Today, Ariba customers source more than $450 million every day in over 5,000 unique categories, Ariba manages more than $170 billion in procurement spending each year, and its procurement software can be found on over 4 million corporate desktops.

The Vision

Ariba's vision is to become the leading provider of spend management solutions, which are software and services to help firms manage what they buy.

During the early days of e-commerce (1996–1997), Ariba joined many other early B2B innovators such as Commerce One and Verticalnet in an effort to revolutionize the procurement and supply process in large corporations. Ariba wanted to replace the aging EDI platform used by large corporations to coordinate trade among a few firms at fixed prices and replace it with an Internet-based electronic marketplace where thousands of suppliers could be aggregated; open market prices could be seen by all; prices would be set dynamically, based on supply and demand; and the resulting price transparency would ensure buyers the lowest cost for their goods. In 1997, 95% of all corporate purchasing in the world was performed by hundreds of thousands of purchasing agents using paper and pencil documents, fax machines, and telephones. EDI was limited generally to contractual purchase of direct goods, which amounted to only 5% of all inter-firm trade, and ignored the MRO segment entirely, which accounts for 33% of all corporate purchasing. The average cost of these paper-based transactions was $75–$175. The traditional procurement process was slow to pay suppliers, and took several weeks to sometimes months to deliver supplies to corporate users. So-called "maverick purchasing" (off-contract purchasing by local units), the bane of all procurement officers, had grown to over 30% of the inter-firm procurement process in the United States, and resulted in premiums of 15% to 27%, according to AMR research. Ariba promised to use the Internet to radically change the procurement process, and to a large extent, has developed the tools needed to bring about the revolution in procurement that it originally envisioned. However, Ariba did not count on the fact that implementation of its software by large companies is complex, time-consuming, and expensive. It did not understand the power of existing EDI systems, or the ability of EDI to migrate to the Web. In most cases, customers must make significant changes in their business processes and expensive changes in existing systems if they want to use Ariba solutions.

Because many customers still have little experience with B2B e-commerce, Ariba must engage in a lengthy and expensive education program with customers. Inevitably, these considerations delay the sales cycle, which runs 6 to 9 months, and slow down implementation and payments. Ariba also did not count on the competitive response by Oracle, IBM, SAP, and other major technology players, each of which offers competing products (but who, in many cases, also partner with Ariba for specific customers). Finally, Ariba did not count on the difficulties it faced in getting suppliers to join its Ariba Supplier Network. Suppliers balked at the notion of joining buyer-dominated networks, where their products and services would be put into direct competition with others. This reduces the liquidity of the Net marketplace and makes it less valuable for buyers, and also reduces the transaction fees paid to Ariba.

Business Model

Ariba's original business model was to charge licensing and maintenance fees for use of its software. For corporate buyers, Ariba offers the prospect of a significant reduction in procurement costs and the cost of supplies, faster acquisition cycles, and reduced errors. Ariba offers suppliers similar reductions in selling costs, faster payment, and access to the aggregated purchasing power of hundreds of firms. Ariba developed a related business model in 1999 by creating its own Net marketplace (Ariba Supplier Network) that charged fees based on transaction value among trading partners. By providing firms quick and easy access to its own network, Ariba believed it could attract purchasing agents and firms to a turnkey solution that did not require adopting firms to radically change their behavior, install software, or implement costly organizational change programs. In 2006, Ariba began shifting the focus of its business model from the license/sale of its applications to a subscription- and maintenance-based revenue stream generated by its Web-based on-demand software solutions. Ariba expects that this shift in its software business from a perpetual model to a subscription-based on-demand delivery model will continue.

Financial Analysis

Ariba's early years (1997–2001) were marked by extraordinary growth in revenues, growing from $760,000 in 1997 to $399 million in 2001. The increases in revenues in these early years resulted from a number of factors, including acquisitions, growth in new customers, and growth in strategic relationships with computer services giants such as IBM and Oracle, who offered Ariba-based solutions to their customers. In the growth years, operating expenses mushroomed with gross revenues, primarily through large increases in the costs for marketing and sales that resulted from sales force compensation, advertising, and customer education programs. Both R&D (technology) costs and administrative costs grew rapidly as Ariba assimilated its acquisitions, assumed ongoing research projects of those businesses, and launched expensive human resource and financial management programs to control its own growth. But with the slowdown in the economy and decline in corporate spending on information technology beginning in 2001, revenue plunged in 2002 to $229 million. Over the period 2000–2004, the company paid $2.2 billion more for acquired companies than they were worth in book values! Fortunately (for Ariba), it paid for these acquisitions mostly with stock and little of its own cash. Unfortunately for those who received the stock, Ariba's stock values have plunged from their high of $183 to as low as $8. Its current price is around $16 per share.

Today, Ariba has begun to claw its way back, although amazingly, it has yet to show a profit. **Table 12.3** presents Ariba's operating results and summary balance sheet data for 2005-2007.

The results for 2007 show that Ariba's revenues increased slightly from $296 million in 2006 to $301 million in 2007, and its costs of revenues decreased from $174 million to $161 million. Operating expenses continued their three-year decline, going from $179 million to $166 million. Ariba's trend of decreasing net losses also continued. In 2005, its net loss was $350 million, as Ariba struggled to cope with expenses and write-offs associated in part with its acquisition of several companies in 2004. By 2007, the net loss was down to $15 million.

On the revenue side, license revenue continued to decline due primarily to a shift from perpetual software licenses to more subscription and hosted-term licenses, and what Ariba termed "a difficult selling environment," particularly for large enterprise software deals. Subscription and maintenance revenue increased 11%, while services and other revenues showed a small decline of 2%. As a result of these trends, Ariba experienced a shift in its revenue mix, with license revenues contributing only 6% of total revenues for 2007, down slightly from 8% in 2006, subscription and maintenance revenues contributing 46% of total revenues for 2007 compared to 43% for 2006, and services and other revenues contributing 48% of total revenues for 2007 compared to 49% for 2006. Reversing a trend that began in 2004, Ariba's gross margin increased from 2006 to 2007, but is still not as high as it was in 2005.

A look at the balance sheet shows that the company had about $43.5 million in working capital as of September 30, 2007. On the positive side, the company has only a small amount of long-term debt ($75 million). Ariba still has a little bit of breathing room to become a profitable company—if it makes the correct decisions in the near-term future.

However, Ariba appears to have taken a small step backward so far during 2008. For the nine months ended June 30, 2008, it had revenues of $243 million, com-

TABLE 12.3	**ARIBA, INC. CONSOLIDATED STATEMENTS OF OPERATIONS AND SUMMARY BALANCE SHEET DATA 2005–2007**

CONSOLIDATED STATEMENTS OF OPERATIONS
(in thousands)

For the fiscal year ended September 30,	2007	2006	2005
Revenues			
License	18,215	$23,914	$47,817
Subscription and maintenance	140,606	126,626	123,430
Services and other	142,846	145,476	151,796
Total revenues	301,667	296,016	323,043
Cost of revenues			
License	1,697	1,989	3,576
Subscription and maintenance	32,709	31,424	29,665
Services and other	112,918	129,562	125,222
Amortization of acquired technology and customer intangible assets	14,074	15,702	19,501
Total cost of revenues	161,398	178,677	177,964
Gross profit	**140,269**	**117,339**	**145,079**
Gross margin	**46.5**	**39.6%**	**44.9%**
Operating expenses			
Sales and marketing	93,904	78,071	92,262
Research and development	51,159	50,085	49,610
General and administrative	39,780	32,850	34,725
Other income-Softbank	(13,564)	(13,585)	(9,490)
Amortization of other intangible assets	525	800	798
Restructuring and integration costs	(4,194)	26,321	41,248
Goodwill impairment		–	247,830
Litigation provision		–	37,000
Total operating expenses	167,610	174,542	493,983
Loss from operations	**(27,341)**	**(57,203)**	**(348,904)**
Operating margin	**-9.1%**	**−19.3%**	**−108%**
Interest and other income, net	14,301	10.935	5,863
Net loss before income taxes and minority interests	(13,040)	(46,268)	(343,041)
Provision (benefit) for income taxes	1,937	1,533	6,570
Minority interests in net income (loss) of consolidated subsidiaries	–	17	
Net loss	**(14,997)**	**($47,801)**	**($349,628)**
Net margin	**-4.96%**	**−16.1%**	**−108%**

SUMMARY BALANCE SHEET DATA
(in thousands)

At September 30,	2007	2006	2005
Cash, cash equivalents, and short-term investments	183,046	$170,616	$147,435
Total current assets	185,670	183,137	164,780
Total current liabilities	149,790	124,641	132,476
Working capital (current assets less current liabilities)	35,880	58,496	32,304
Total assets	583,586	586,944	594,239
Restructuring and other long-term obligations, less current portion	74,734	103,074	90,540
Total stockholders' equity	351,144	333,023	336,242

SOURCE: Ariba, Inc., 2007.

pared to $226 million for the comparable period in 2007. Its cost of revenues during that period decreased from $123 million to $115 million in 2008. However, its operating expenses increased from $123 million to $170 million, and as a result, its net loss for the period increased, from $11 million in 2007 to $35 million for 2008. Its balance sheet at June 30, 2008, showed about $78.5 million of working capital.

Strategic Analysis—Business Strategies

In 2007, Ariba made a big bet on the future of subscription-based on-demand online software services. In September 2007, it announced that it had agreed to acquire Procuri, one of its competitors that also offers Web-based spend management solutions, for $93 million. Most of Procuri's customer base is in "middle market," which broaden's Ariba's reach from its traditional emphasis on the Fortune 1000. The Procuri acquisition follows three major purchases that Ariba made in 2004, when it acquired Alliente, a provider of business process outsourcing; FreeMarkets, one of the largest and most successful operators of independent Net marketplaces or exchanges; and Softface, a firm with expertise in spending analysis, catalogs, and contract management.

Strategic Analysis—Competition

While Ariba pioneered the market for Internet-based B2B e-commerce software, it was quickly joined by powerful competitors such as IBM, Oracle, and GE Information Services, as well as entrepreneurial start-up companies such as Commerce One and FreeMarkets. Since that time, Commerce One filed for bankruptcy and FreeMarkets has been eliminated though acquisition. Ariba remains one of the few strong survivors in the B2B Net marketplace arena. The company faces significant competition from major enterprise software firms such as SAP and Oracle, which have developed their own Internet-based procurement systems, and other small niche vendors such as Emptoris, Ketera Technologies, Verticalnet, Frictionless Commerce, and a reborn Commerce One (which was acquired by Perfect Commerce in February 2006). The entry barriers to the market for B2B e-commerce software are low, and there are few technology-based differentiating features among the offerings. Increasingly, trust, longevity, and stability are becoming important factors for customers to be concerned about as they review competing products and firms.

Ariba has entered into strategic partnerships with some of its competitors, such as IBM and i2Technologies, to develop targeted solutions for specific customers.

Strategic Analysis—Technology

Ariba is a B2B software applications company. All of Ariba's software is built for the Internet using standard software tools such as HTML, Java, and XML. Perhaps its most differentiated software technology is found in its Ariba Supplier Network. This network is an open-standards, multi-protocol transaction network that routes and translates transactions between buyers and suppliers using most major electronic commerce standards such as XML, CXML (an Internet version of XML for commercial transactions), Internet EDI, VAN EDI, OBI (Open Buying Internet), HTML, e-mail, and fax. This enables buyers and sellers to conduct business with one another regardless of what protocol they are using.

Strategic Analysis—Social and Legal Challenges

Ariba, like many other e-commerce companies that went public during the dot.com boom, and then suffered a revenue and share price crash, is the defendant in a number of lawsuits alleging improper activities at the time of its IPO and subsequent activities involving information about the financial health of the company. The company has also been sued by shareholders in connection with its acquisition of FreeMarkets. It also faced a patent infringement lawsuit filed by a firm named ePlus inc., alleging that three of its products—Ariba Buyer, Ariba Marketplace, and Ariba Category Procurement—infringed three U.S. patents owned by ePlus. In 2005, it settled this case and took a $37 million charge. Another patent infringement suit was filed against it by a firm called Sky in September 2007 that Ariba settled for $5.9 million in January 2008. In April 2007, Ariba sued Emptoris for patent infringement, and in November 2007, Emptoris cross-sued. Trials for both of these litigations are scheduled for the future.

A firm such as Ariba also could face significant liabilities should its software fail to perform or its Ariba Supplier Network be unavailable for a period of time. As firms become more dependent on Ariba for procurement, any glitch in operation could be very expensive.

Future Prospects

Ariba faced a number of daunting challenges after the Internet bubble burst, and it has successfully weathered that stormy period to emerge as a company about one-half it former size, but somewhat stronger financially. In the e-procurement Net marketplace business, it has greatly deepened its offerings through acquisitions, and while it faces significant competition from software firms such as SAP and Oracle, it remains the "best of breed" procurement software on the market.

Ariba anticipates that the shift in its software business from license sales to subscription sales will continue during 2009 and thereafter. It also believes its services revenue will continue to grow, led by continued expansion of its consulting services and growth in its procurement outsourcing business. However, when offset against an expected continued decline in software license revenues, it expects total revenue to remain relatively flat for the year. From an expense standpoint, its restructuring activities are largely complete, and costs and expenses in 2009 are expected to remain relatively consistent with its costs and expenses in 2008.

It is apparent that while Ariba's various strategies have worked to avoid a complete collapse of the company, and while the company appears stronger and more stable, investors believe the company is not yet out of the woods. In 2008, its stock price ranged from around $8 - $17 a share. With such a low stock price, Ariba may become an acquisition target for an established B2B software firm seeking to strengthen its offerings, or even for one of its large customers attempting to create its own Net marketplace from the vantage point of a firm that has an established reputation (see the Siemens case study at the end of the chapter).

Exchanges

exchange

independently owned online marketplace that connects hundreds to potentially thousands of suppliers and buyers in a dynamic, real-time environment

An **exchange** is an independently owned online marketplace that connects hundreds to potentially thousands of suppliers and buyers in a dynamic, real-time environment (see **Figure 12.12**). Exchanges generally create vertical markets that focus on the spot-purchasing requirements of large firms in a single industry, such as computers and telecommunications, electronics, food, and industrial equipment, although there are exceptions to this generalization as described in this section. Exchanges were the prototype Internet-based marketplace in the early days of e-commerce; as noted above, over 1,000 were created in this period, but most have failed.

Exchanges make money by charging a commission on the transaction. The pricing model can be through an online negotiation, auction, RFQ, or fixed buy-and-sell prices. The benefits offered to customers of exchanges include reduced search cost for parts and spare capacity. Other benefits include lower prices created by a global marketplace driven by competition among suppliers who would, presumably, sell goods at very low profit margins at one world-market price. The benefits offered suppliers are access to a global purchasing environment and the opportunity to unload production overruns (although at very competitive prices and low profit margins). Even though they are private intermediaries, exchanges are public in the sense of permitting any bona fide buyer or seller to participate.

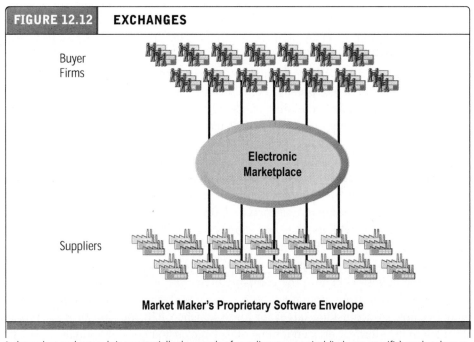

FIGURE 12.12 **EXCHANGES**

Buyer Firms

Electronic Marketplace

Suppliers

Market Maker's Proprietary Software Envelope

Independent exchanges bring potentially thousands of suppliers to a vertical (industry-specific) marketplace to sell their goods to potentially thousands of buyer firms. Exchanges are sometimes referred to as many-to-many markets because they have many suppliers serving many buyer firms.

Exchanges tend to be biased toward the buyer even though they are independently owned and presumably neutral. Suppliers are disadvantaged by the fact that exchanges put them in direct price competition with other similar suppliers around the globe, driving profit margins down. Exchanges have failed primarily because suppliers have refused to join them, and hence, the existing markets have very low liquidity, defeating the very purpose and benefits of an exchange. **Liquidity** is typically measured by the number of buyers and sellers in a market, the volume of transactions, and the size of transactions. You know a market is liquid when you can buy or sell just about any size order at just about any time you want. On all of these measures, many exchanges failed, resulting in a very small number of participants, few trades, and small trade value per transaction. The most common reason for not using exchanges is the absence of traditional, trusted suppliers.

While most exchanges tend to be vertical marketplaces offering direct supplies, some exchanges offer indirect inputs as well, such as electricity and power, transportation services (usually to the transportation industry), and professional services. **Table 12.4** lists a few examples of some current independent exchanges.

The following capsule description of several exchanges provides insight into their origins and current functions.

Global Wine & Spirits (GWS) is somewhat unique among independent exchanges, not only as a start-up that has managed to survive, but also as a latecomer to the B2B e-commerce community. GWS opened in 1999, but did not begin to trade products online until May 2001. Based in Montreal, Quebec, and operated by Mediagrif Interactive Technologies Inc., a Canadian company that operates a number of independent exchanges in a variety of industries, GWS divides its operations into two segments: a public eMarketplace and a division called GWSBusiness Solutions. More than 5,000 wine and spirits companies (2,900 wine and spirits producers and 2,100 wine and spirits wholesalers, importers, and retailers) in 100 countries are connected to private or public wine and spirits portals powered by GWS technology. (Global Wine & Spirits, 2008)

liquidity
typically measured by the number of buyers and sellers in a market, the volume of transactions, and the size of transactions

TABLE 12.4	EXAMPLES OF INDEPENDENT EXCHANGES
EXCHANGE	**FOCUS**
PowerSource Online	Computer parts exchange
Converge	Semiconductors and computer peripherals
Smarterwork	Spare professional services from Web design to legal advice
Active International	Trading in underutilized manufacturing capacity
Foodtrader	One of the largest B2B spot trading sites for the food products industry
IntercontinentalExchange	International online marketplace for over 600 commodities

Farms.com is yet another exchange that has managed to survive while several of its competitors have fallen by the wayside. Indeed, Farms.com has not only managed to survive, but it is also profitable. Farms.com's family of products and services now includes its Farms.com information portal; a trading/online marketplace (Mandf-trading) for the swine trade; PigCHAMP, which provides knowledge management and custom software for the swine industry; AgFreight, an online freight matching service for bulk agriculture commodities; AgSoftware, which provides a wide range of technology products and services such as IT consulting, programming, web hosting, and software products for the grain, seed, and livestock sectors; AgCareers, which operates an online job board; and AgPromote, which offers a variety of newsletters aimed at various sectors in the agriculture industry, as well as a number of other offerings (Farms.com, 2008).

Inventory Locator Service (ILS) has its roots as an offline intermediary, serving as a listing service for aftermarket parts in the aerospace industry. Upon opening in 1979, ILS initially provided a telephone and fax-based directory of aftermarket parts to airplane owners and mechanics, along with government procurement professionals. As early as 1984, ILS incorporated e-mail capabilities as part of its RFQ services, and by 1998, it had begun to conduct online auctions for hard-to-find parts. Today, ILS maintains an Internet-accessible database of over 5 billion aerospace and marine industry parts, and has also developed an eRFQ feature that helps users streamline their sourcing processes. The network's 20,000 subscribers in 93 different countries access the site over 50,000 times a day. (Inventory Locator Service, 2008).

Industry Consortia

industry consortium
industry-owned vertical market that enables buyers to purchase direct inputs (both goods and services) from a limited set of invited participants

An **industry consortium** is an industry-owned vertical market that enables buyers to purchase direct inputs (both goods and services) from a limited set of invited participants (see **Figure 12.13**). Industry consortia emphasize long-term contractual purchasing, the development of stable relationships (as opposed to merely an anonymous transaction emphasis), and the creation of industry-wide data standards and synchronization efforts. Industry consortia are more focused on optimizing long-term supply relationships than independent exchanges, which tend to focus more on short-term transactions. The ultimate objective of industry consortia is the unification of supply chains within entire industries, across many tiers, through common data definitions, network standards, and computing platforms. In addition, industry consortia, unlike independent exchanges described previously, take their marching orders from the industry and not from venture capitalists or investment bankers. This means any profits from operating industry consortia are returned to industry business firms.

Industry consortia sprang up in 1999 and 2000 in part as a reaction to the earlier development of independently owned exchanges, which were viewed by large industries (such as the automotive and chemical industries) as market interlopers that would not directly serve the interests of large buyers, but would instead line their own pockets and those of their venture capital investors. Rather than "pay-to-play," large firms decided to "pay-to-own" their markets. Another concern of large firms was that Net marketplaces would work only if large suppliers and buyers participated, and only if there was liquidity. Independent exchanges were not attracting enough players

---

| FIGURE 12.13 | **INDUSTRY CONSORTIA** |

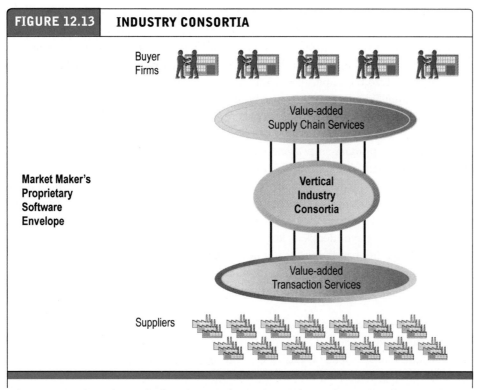

Buyer Firms

Market Maker's Proprietary Software Envelope

Value-added Supply Chain Services

Vertical Industry Consortia

Value-added Transaction Services

Suppliers

Industry consortia bring thousands of suppliers into direct contact with a smaller number of very large buyers. The market makers provide value-added software services for procurement, transaction management, shipping, and payment for both buyers and suppliers. Industry consortia are sometimes referred to as many-to-few markets, where many suppliers (albeit selected by the buyers) serve a few very large buyers, mediated by a variety of value-added services.

to achieve liquidity. In addition, exchanges often failed to provide additional value-added services that would transform the value chain for the entire industry, including linking the new marketplaces to firms' ERP systems. More than 60 industry consortia now exist, with many industries having more than one (see **Table 12.5**).

The industries with the most consortia are food, metals, and chemicals, although these are not necessarily the largest consortia in terms of revenue. Many very large Fortune 500 and private firms are investors in several industry consortia. For instance, Cargill—the world's largest private corporation—invested in six consortia that exist at various points in Cargill's and the food industry's tangled value chain.

Industry consortia make money in a number of ways. Industry members usually pay for the creation of the consortia's capabilities and contribute initial operating capital. Then industry consortia charge buyer and seller firms transaction and subscription fees. Industry members—both buyers and sellers—are expected to reap benefits far greater than their contributions through the rationalization of the procurement process, competition among vendors, and closer relationships with vendors.

Industry consortia offer many different pricing mechanisms, ranging from auctions to fixed prices to RFQs, depending on the products and the situation. Prices can also be negotiated, and the environment, while competitive, is nevertheless restricted to a smaller number of buyers—selected, reliable, and long-term suppliers who are often viewed as "strategic industry" partners. The bias of industry consortia is clearly toward the large buyers who control access to this lucrative market channel and can benefit from competitive pricing offered by alternative suppliers. Benefits to suppliers come from access to large buyer firm procurement systems, long-term stable relationships, and large order sizes.

Industry consortia can and often do force suppliers to use the consortia's networks and proprietary software as a condition of selling to the industry's members. Although exchanges failed for a lack of suppliers and liquidity, the market power of consortia members ensures suppliers will participate, so consortia may be able to avoid the fate of voluntary exchanges. Clearly, industry consortia are at an advantage when compared to independent exchanges because, unlike the venture-capital-backed exchanges, they have deep-pocket financial backing from the very start and guaranteed liquidity based on a steady flow of large firm orders. Yet industry consortia are a relatively new phenomenon, and the long-term profitability of these consortia, especially when several consortia exist for a single industry, has yet to be demonstrated.

The following capsule descriptions of two industry consortia illustrate their vitality and growth potential.

Exostar is an aerospace industry consortium. Its founding partners include BAE Systems, Boeing, Lockheed Martin, Raytheon, and Rolls-Royce. Exostar has taken a slow but steady approach to building its technology platform. It has kept its focus on the direct procurement and supply chain needs of its largest members, and taken its time developing a portfolio of technology solutions that meet its needs. Its current

TABLE 12.5	INDUSTRY CONSORTIA BY INDUSTRY (SEPTEMBER 2008)
INDUSTRY	**NAME OF INDUSTRY CONSORTIA**
Aerospace	Exostar
Automotive	SupplyOn
Chemical	Elemica, RubberNetwork
Financial	MuniCenter
Food	Dairy.com, eFSNetwork (iTrade Network)
Hospitality	Avendra
Medical Services, Supplies	GHX (Global Healthcare Exchange)
Metals and Mining	Quadrem
Paper and Forest Products	Liason
Shipping	OceanConnect
Textiles	TheSeam (Cotton Consortium)
Transportation	Transplace

products include Supply Pass, an integrated suite of tools that enables suppliers to handle buyer transactions via the Internet, SourcePass, which provides a dynamic bidding environment for buyers and sellers, and ProcurePass, which enables buyers to handle supplier transactions online, among others. As of September 2008, Exostar served a community of more than 40,000 trading partners, and in 2007, executed over 10 million transactions worth $38.5 billion (Exostar, 2008).

Serving the mining, minerals, and metals industries, Quadrem initially opened in May 2000 with 14 founding members. Its current shareholders include some of the world's largest natural resource companies, such as Alcoa, DeBeers, and Phelps Dodge, and together represent about $90 billion in annual spending. As of 2008, Quadrem's network includes more than 55,000 suppliers and 1,100 buyers, handles more than $17 billion in annual orders, and the number of transactions has been growing at a cumulative rate of 21% per month (Quadrem International Ltd., 2008).

THE LONG-TERM DYNAMICS OF NET MARKETPLACES

Net marketplaces are changing rapidly because of the widespread failures of early exchanges and a growing realization by key participants that real value will derive from B2B e-commerce only when it can change the entire procurement system, the supply chain, and the process of collaboration among firms. Several industry consortia have transformed themselves into industry data standards and synchronization forums. The consolidation of Net marketplaces in 2003 and 2004 has resulted in remaining firms that are much stronger and that are beginning to grow rapidly once again. In fact, B2B online transaction volumes are growing worldwide and within the United States at 20%–30% per year.

Figure 12.14 depicts some of these changes. Pure Net marketplace exchanges are moving away from the simple "electronic marketplace" vision, and toward playing a more central role in changing the procurement process. Independent exchanges are ideal buy-out candidates for industry consortia because they have often developed the technology infrastructure. In any event, consortia and exchanges are beginning to work together in selected markets. Likewise, e-distributors are securing admission to large e-procurement systems and also seeking admission to industry consortia as suppliers of indirect goods.

Other notable trends include the movement from simple transactions involving spot purchasing to longer-term contractual relationships involving both indirect and direct goods (Wise and Morrison, 2000). The complexity and duration of transactions is increasing, and both buyers and suppliers are becoming accustomed to working in a digital environment, and making less use of the fax machine and telephone. To date, Net marketplaces, as well as private industrial networks, have emerged in a political climate friendly to large-scale cooperation among very large firms. However, the possibility exists that Net marketplaces may provide some firms with an ideal platform to collude on pricing, market sharing, and market access, all of which would be anti-competitive and reduce the efficiency of the marketplace. *Insight on Society: Are Net Marketplaces Anti-Competitive Cartels?* considers the anti-competitive possibilities inherent in Net marketplaces.

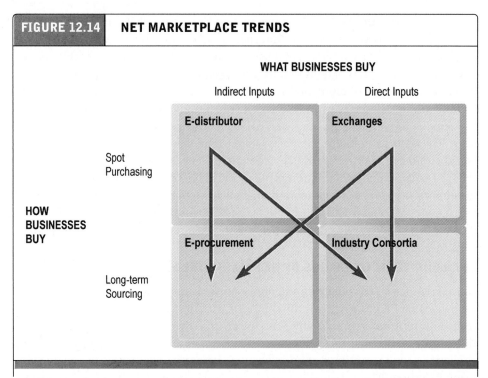

FIGURE 12.14   **NET MARKETPLACE TRENDS**

E-distributors and exchanges are migrating their business models toward more sustained, higher value-added relationships with buyer firms by providing e-procurement services and participating in industry consortia.

12.3 PRIVATE INDUSTRIAL NETWORKS

Private industrial networks today form the largest part of B2B e-commerce, both on and off the Internet. Industry analysts estimate that in 2009, about 50% of B2B expenditures by large firms will be for the development of private industrial networks. Private industrial networks can be considered the foundation of the "extended enterprise," and the notion that firms can extend their boundaries and their business processes to include supply chain and logistics partners.

WHAT ARE PRIVATE INDUSTRIAL NETWORKS?

As noted at the beginning of this chapter, private industrial networks are direct descendants of existing EDI networks, and they are closely tied to existing ERP systems used by large firms. A private industrial network (sometimes referred to as a private trading exchange, or PTX) is a Web-enabled network for the coordination of trans-organizational business processes (sometimes also called collaborative commerce). A **trans-organizational business process** requires at least two independent firms to perform (Laudon and Laudon, 2009). For the most part, these networks originate in and closely involve the manufacturing and related support industries, and therefore we refer to them as "industrial" networks, although in the future they could just as easily apply to some services. These networks can be

trans-organizational business process

process that requires at least two independent firms to perform

INSIGHT ON SOCIETY

ARE NET MARKETPLACES ANTI-COMPETITIVE CARTELS?

Although Net marketplaces and private industrial networks often lead to extraordinary gains in efficiency for both firms and industries as a whole, ironically, they also provide some equally powerful tools for reducing competition in the marketplace and driving up prices to consumers, and even reducing variety in the marketplace as well. There are two types of antitrust concerns: the market for goods and the market for B2B marketplaces themselves.

In the market for goods, the primary antitrust concerns are information sharing that permits or encourages price fixing, monopsony (when a cartel or monopoly drives down input prices below the value of goods), and exclusion (preventing new companies from entering a marketplace).

For instance, in a Net marketplace owned by large industry players (such as the chemical exchange Elemica), owner-members could collude with one another on the prices they are willing to pay for inputs. Price collusion does not necessarily involve a formal agreement among colluders, but can take place in highly efficient markets through "parallel pricing," or informal arrangements among suppliers to a market to "agree" on prices through market communication.

Information sharing may also lead to market-sharing agreements in which manufacturers divide the market into segments and agree to produce only enough for their allocated segment. In a monopsony, large buyers have so much power that they can control input prices by buying less of an input. Net marketplaces could be used to exclude rival competitive firms, forcing their rivals to pay higher prices for inputs. For instance, chemical firms that do not pay to support Elemica might be precluded from obtaining the best prices possible on the market.

The recent brief history of Net marketplaces suggests that they inherently consolidate into one or two Net marketplaces in each industry and therefore become the dominant players; they experience network effects in the sense that the larger Net marketplaces become, the more attractive they are to join; and they experience economies of scale insofar as the larger they become, the more efficient and liquid they become. Together, these factors lead to the surviving Net marketplaces having extraordinary market power. These concerns primarily apply to industry consortia, although they also arise in independent exchanges as well.

In the market for Net marketplaces, a very large Net marketplace formed by buyers or sellers could prevent other entrepreneurial market makers from starting up because of the high switching costs involved and the network effects of large markets. Such Net marketplaces may devise rules that specifically proscribe the members from purchasing in any other markets. Moreover, once a Net marketplace attracts, say, 90% of the buyers and sellers in a marketspace, it experiences powerful network effects and resulting high levels of liquidity; it becomes, in essence, the only marketplace with a sufficient number of buyers and sellers to support trading systematically.

Even though B2B Net marketplaces are new, the antitrust issues and concepts are not. Information sharing among competitors, monopsony, and exclusion from necessary facilities are issues that have arisen in the context of airline reservation systems, railroad terminal facilities, and film distribution by the motion picture industry. There are Justice

(continued)

Department rules (Competitor Collaboration Guidelines) that describe permissible information sharing and collaboration among competitors, and a large body of case law and scholarship that has developed principles for determining when collaboration among competing firms becomes illegal. In general, courts and scholars have sought to proscribe any behavior that would harm competition in the marketplace and harm customers by raising prices and/or reducing selection. A wide variety of behaviors are tolerated by courts up until the point where the consequences are harmful to competition, and ultimately to the consumer or buyers who are forced to pay higher prices.

In a report on competition in B2B markets, the Federal Trade Commission (FTC) concluded that no action was needed now to ensure B2B markets remained competitive. The FTC, however, continues to monitor the behavior of large Net marketplaces, as well as the trading that occurs within them, for signs of collusion, monopsony power, and exclusionary behavior that might harm competition.

SOURCES: "Competition Policy Implications of Electronic Business-to-Business Marketplaces: Issues for Marketers," by Andrew Pressey and John Ashton, Centre for Competition Policy Working Paper 07-15, June 2007; "The New Economy and Beyond: Past, Present, and Future," edited by Dennis W. Jansen, Edward Elgar Publishing, 2006; "B2B Companies Face Antitrust Questions," by Quentin Riegel, National Association of Manufacturers, 2005; "Diagnosing Physician-Hospital Organizations", by Susan A. Creighton, Federal Trade Commission, 2004; "FTC Finds Vivendi Subsidiaries Violated Antitrust Laws In Distribution of Three Tenors CDS," Federal Trade Commission, July 28, 2003; "Would B2B Exchanges Have Antitrust Issues?" by Tair-Rong Sheu, 30th Research Conference on Communication, Information and Internet Policy, September 29, 2002; "An Overview of Federal Trade Commission Antitrust Activities," Prepared statement of the Federal Trade Commission, Committee on the Judiciary, United States Senate, September 19, 2002; "Beyond Covisint: Antitrust Scrutiny of B2B Exchanges," by F. Martin Dajani, *Journal of the Missouri Bar*, July/August 2001; "Case Studies for Federal Trade Commission Public Workshop on Emerging Issues for Competition Policy in the World of E-Commerce," Federal Trade Commission, May 7, 2001; "Evaluating the Antitrust Risks of the Internet Entwined Business," by Shawn Potter, *West Virginia Journal of Law and Technology*, May 4, 2001; "Entering the 21st Century: Competition Policy in the World of B2B Marketplaces," Federal Trade Commission, October 2000.

industry-wide, but often begin and sometimes focus on the voluntary coordination of a group of supplying firms centered about a single, very large manufacturing firm. Private industrial networks can be viewed as "extended enterprises" in the sense that they often begin as ERP systems in a single firm, and are then expanded to include (often using an extranet) the firm's major suppliers. **Figure 12.15** illustrates a private industrial network originally built by Procter & Gamble (P&G) in the United States to coordinate supply chains among its suppliers, distributors, truckers, and retailers.

In P&G's private industrial network shown in Figure 12.15, customer sales are captured at the cash register, which then initiates a flow of information back to distributors, P&G, and its suppliers. This tells P&G and its suppliers the exact level of demand for thousands of products. This information is then used to initiate production, supply, and transportation to replenish products at the distributors and retailers. This process is called an efficient customer response system (a demand-pull production model), and it relies on an equally efficient supply chain management system to coordinate the supply side.

Not surprisingly, there is not a great deal of detailed information about private industrial networks. Most companies that originate and participate in these networks view them as a competitive advantage, and therefore they are reluctant to release information about how much they cost and how they operate.

GE, Dell Computer, Cisco Systems, Microsoft, IBM, Nike, Coca-Cola, Wal-Mart, Nokia, and Hewlett-Packard are among the firms operating successful private industrial networks.

CHARACTERISTICS OF PRIVATE INDUSTRIAL NETWORKS

The central focus of private industrial networks is to provide an industry-wide global solution to achieve the highest levels of efficiency. The specific objectives of a private industrial network include:

- Developing efficient purchasing and selling business processes industry-wide
- Developing industry-wide resource planning to supplement enterprise-wide resource planning
- Creating increasing supply chain visibility—knowing the inventory levels of buyers and suppliers
- Achieving closer buyer-supplier relationships, including demand forecasting, communications, and conflict resolution
- Operating on a global scale—globalization
- Reducing industry risk by preventing imbalances of supply and demand, including developing financial derivatives, insurance, and futures markets

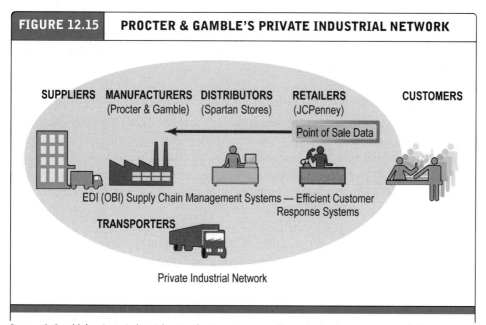

FIGURE 12.15 PROCTER & GAMBLE'S PRIVATE INDUSTRIAL NETWORK

Procter & Gamble's private industrial network attempts to coordinate the business processes of the many firms it deals with in the consumer products industry.

Private industrial networks serve different goals from Net marketplaces. Net marketplaces are primarily transaction-oriented, whereas private industrial networks focus on continuous business process coordination between companies. This can include much more than just supply chain management, such as product design, sourcing, demand forecasting, asset management, sales, and marketing. Private industrial networks do support transactions, but that is not their primary focus.

Private industrial networks usually focus on a single sponsoring company that "owns" the network, sets the rules, establishes governance (a structure of authority, rule enforcement, and control), and invites firms to participate at its sole discretion. Therefore, these networks are "private." This sets them apart from industry consortia, which are usually owned by major firms collectively through equity participation. Whereas Net marketplaces have a strong focus on indirect goods and services, private industrial networks focus on strategic, direct goods and services.

For instance, Ace Hardware, a cooperative of 5,100 retail hardware stores, uses a private industrial network to manage inventory levels and collaborate with suppliers by linking 14 Ace distribution centers and nine key suppliers. In the past, a team of 30 Ace procurement managers used faxes, phones, and an older EDI system to buy products for retail members. It took seven to ten days to process an order. Suppliers had no access to inventory levels in retail stores or Ace distribution centers, forcing them to guess their likely production requirements. Manco, one large supplier of Ace, now uses the Internet-based private industrial network to accurately gauge demand for more than 200 products, from duct tape to shelf liners, that it supplies Ace. The more streamlined ordering process has allowed Manco to reduce distribution costs by 28% and freight costs by 18% (VICS, 2004; ADX Corporation, 2004; Gleason, 2003).

Perhaps no single firm better illustrates the benefits of developing private industrial networks than Wal-Mart, described in *Insight on Business: Wal-Mart Develops a Private Industrial Network*.

PRIVATE INDUSTRIAL NETWORKS AND COLLABORATIVE COMMERCE

collaborative resource planning, forecasting, and replenishment (CPFR)

iinvolves working with network members to forecast demand, develop production plans, and coordinate shipping, warehousing, and stocking activities to ensure that retail and wholesale shelf space is replenished with just the right amount of goods

Private industrial networks can do much more than just serve a supply chain and efficient customer response system. They can also include other activities of a single large manufacturing firm, including design of products and engineering diagrams, as well as marketing plans and demand forecasting. Collaboration among businesses can take many forms and involve a wide range of activities—from simple supply chain management to coordinating market feedback to designers at supply firms (see **Figure 12.16**).

One form of collaboration—and perhaps the most profound—is industry-wide **collaborative resource planning, forecasting, and replenishment** (**CPFR**), which involves working with network members to forecast demand, develop production plans, and coordinate shipping, warehousing, and stocking activities to ensure retail and wholesale shelf space is replenished with just the right amount of goods. If this goal is achieved, hundreds of millions of dollars of excess inventory and capacity could be wrung out of an industry. This activity alone is likely to produce the largest benefits and justify the cost of developing private industrial networks.

A second area of collaboration is *demand chain visibility*. In the past, it was impossible to know where excess capacity or supplies existed in the supply and distribution chains. For instance, retailers might have significantly overstocked shelves, but suppliers and manufacturers—not knowing this—might be building excess capacity or supplies for even more production. These excess inventories would raise costs for the entire industry and create extraordinary pressures to discount merchandise, reducing profits for everyone.

A third area of collaboration is *marketing coordination and product design*. Manufacturers that use or produce highly engineered parts use private industrial networks to coordinate both their internal design and marketing activities, as well as related activities of their supply and distribution chain partners. By involving their suppliers in product design and marketing initiatives, manufacturing firms can ensure that the parts produced actually fulfill the claims of marketers. On the reverse flow, feedback from customers can be used by marketers to speak directly to product designers at the firm and its suppliers. For the first time, "closed-loop marketing"—customer feedback directly impacting design and production—described in Chapter 6—can become a reality.

FIGURE 12.16	PIECES OF THE COLLABORATIVE COMMERCE PUZZLE

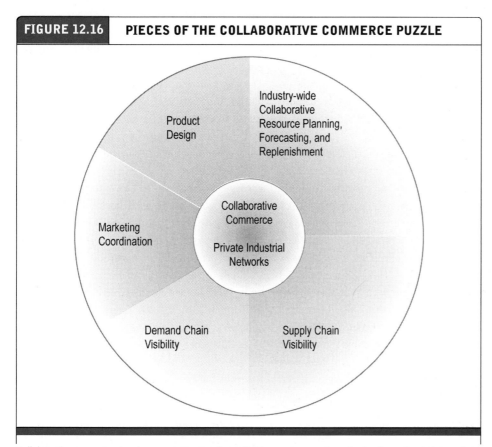

Collaborative commerce involves many cooperative activities among supply and sales firms closely interacting with a single large firm through a private industrial network.

WAL-MART DEVELOPS A PRIVATE INDUSTRIAL NETWORK

Wal-Mart is a well-known leader in the application of network technology to the coordination of its supply chain. With sales of more than $374 billion for the fiscal year ending January 31, 2008, Wal-Mart has been able to use information technology to achieve a decisive cost advantage over competitors. As you might imagine, the world's largest retailer also has the world's largest supply chain, with more than 60,000 suppliers worldwide. In the next five years, the company plans to expand from around 4,000 stores in the United States to over 5,000, and increase its selection of goods to include automobiles, pianos, groceries, high-fashion clothing, and personal computers. In other words, Wal-Mart's strategic plan is to be where they are not now. All of this will require an even more capable private industrial network than what is now in place.

In the late 1980s, Wal-Mart developed the beginnings of collaborative commerce using an EDI-based SCM system that required its large suppliers to use Wal-Mart's proprietary EDI network to respond to orders from Wal-Mart purchasing managers. In 1991, Wal-Mart expanded the capabilities of its EDI-based network by introducing Retail Link. This system connected Wal-Mart's largest suppliers to Wal-Mart's own inventory management system, and it required large suppliers to track actual sales by stores and to replenish supplies as dictated by demand and following rules imposed by Wal-Mart. Wal-Mart also introduced financial payment systems that ensure that Wal-Mart does not own the goods until they arrive and are shelved.

In 1997, Wal-Mart moved Retail Link to an extranet that allowed suppliers to directly link over the Internet into Wal-Mart's inventory management system. In 2000, Wal-Mart hired an outside firm to upgrade Retail Link from being a supply chain management tool toward a more collaborative forecasting, planning, and replenishment system. Using demand aggregation software provided by Atlas Metaprise Software, Wal-Mart purchasing agents can now aggregate demand from Wal-Mart's 4,000 separate stores in the United States into a single RFQ from suppliers. This gives Wal-Mart tremendous clout with even the largest suppliers. Wal-Mart and Atlas plan to first build a global sourcing network. Previously, Wal-Mart's foreign location buyers relied on a mix of telephones, fax, and e-mail to communicate their spending forecasts. The new system allowed them to submit forecasts via the Internet. Wal-Mart headquarters in turn issued worldwide RFQs for all stores. The Atlas software helps Wal-Mart purchasing agents select a winning bid and negotiate final contracts.

In addition, suppliers can now immediately access information on inventories, purchase orders, invoice status, and sales forecasts, based on 104 weeks of online, real-time, item-level data. The system now does not require smaller supplier firms to adopt expensive EDI software solutions. Instead, they can use standard browsers and PCs loaded with free software from Wal-Mart. There are now over 20,000 suppliers—small and large—participating in Wal-Mart's network.

In 2002, Wal-Mart switched to an entirely Internet-based private network. Wal-Mart adopted AS2, a software package from iSoft Corporation, a Dallas-based software company. AS2 implements EDI-INT (an Internet-based standard version of EDI), and the result is a

(continued)

radical reduction in communications costs. Wal-Mart uses Sterling Commerce (the largest single provider of EDI communication systems to industry) and IBM to support this EDI initiative. The AS2 initiative lets suppliers connect, deliver, validate, and reply to data securely over the Internet. IBM uses its expertise to assist Wal-Mart suppliers in selecting and implementing the appropriate AS2-certified solutions that best meet their needs. Sterling Commerce provides interoperability services for EDI-INT AS2 connectivity between Wal-Mart and its suppliers.

Wal-Mart's success spurred its competitors in the retail industry to develop industry-wide private industrial networks such as Global NetXchange (now Agentrics) in an effort to duplicate the success of Wal-Mart. Wal-Mart executives have said Wal-Mart would not join these networks, or any industry-sponsored consortium or independent exchange, because doing so would only help its competitors achieve what Wal-Mart has already accomplished with Retail Link. To compete with the efficiencies attained by Wal-Mart, other retailers, such as JCPenney, have implemented their own extensive private industrial networks to link suppliers to their stores' inventories directly over the Internet. JCPenney has even given over its inventory control and product selection to its largest apparel provider, TAL Apparel Ltd. of Hong Kong.

SOURCES: "Wal-Mart Stores Inc.-Requirements," Walmart.com, September 25, 2008; "How Wal-Mart Lost Its Technology Edge," by Thomas Wailgum, Network World, October 5, 2007; "Who Gains, Who Loses, from RFID's Growing Presence in the Marketplace?," Knowledge@Wharton, March 23, 2005; "Fruit Vendor Updates Systems to Satisfy Wal-Mart" by Stacy Cowley, *CIO*, August 1, 2004; "Suppliers May Miss Tracking Mandate Set by Wal-Mart," by Ann Zimmerman, *Wall Street Journal*, March 31, 2004.

DaimlerChrysler, for instance, developed a collaborative commerce application called the Supply Partner Information Network (SPIN) for its 20,000 suppliers. SPIN is an extranet-based supply chain management and support system that permits 12,000 supplier employees at 3,500 locations around the world to access DaimlerChrysler's real-time procurement, inventory, and demand forecasting systems, as well as longer-term strategy applications. DaimlerChrysler's Part Quality Supply System operating within SPIN tracks all production parts from supplier to shipper, factory installation, and after-market replacement. Chrysler estimates it has increased productivity of its entire "extended enterprise" family of suppliers by 20% (IBM, undated).

IMPLEMENTATION BARRIERS

Although private industrial networks represent a large part of the future of B2B, there are many barriers to its complete implementation (Watson and Fenner, 2000). Participating firms are required to share sensitive data with their business partners, up and down the supply chain. What in the past was considered proprietary and secret must now be shared. In a digital environment, it can be difficult to control the limits of information sharing. Information a firm gives gladly to its largest customer may end up being shared with its closest competitor.

Integrating private industrial networks into existing ERP systems and EDI networks poses a significant investment of time and money. Most ERP systems were not designed initially to work as extranets, or even to be very Internet-friendly. Most ERP systems are based on models of business processes that are entirely internal to the firm.

Adopting private industrial networks also requires a change in mindset and behavior for employees. Essentially, employees must shift their loyalties from the firm to the wider trans-organizational enterprise and recognize that their fate is intertwined with the fate of their suppliers and distributors. Suppliers in turn are required to change the way they manage and allocate their resources because their own production is tightly coupled with the demands of their private industrial network partners. All participants in the supply and distribution chains, with the exception of the large network owner, lose some of their independence, and must initiate large behavioral change programs in order to participate (Laudon, 2000).

INDUSTRY-WIDE PRIVATE INDUSTRIAL NETWORKS

Single-firm networks can be so successful that they become adopted by the entire industry, and they can be used also to coordinate activities among firms in different industries altogether. For instance, the P&G system described previously was so successful that P&G sold the software to IBM, which then re-sold the system to the entire consumer products industry in the United States. P&G believed that only by changing the entire industry of supply, procurement, and distribution could it achieve its goals of efficiency and effectiveness. Other examples of industry-wide private industrial networks include 1 SYNC and Agentrics. 1SYNC was formed by the merger of UCCnet and Transora in August 2005. 1SYNC offers a collaborative community of trading partners that includes 4,000 leading manufacturers in the alcohol and beverage, automotive, entertainment, grocery, healthcare, and office supplies industry. 1SYNC offers a range of data synchronization services that enable the elimination of costly data errors, increased supply chain efficiencies, and the advancement of next-generation technologies such as its Electronic Product Code (1SYNC, 2008).

Agentrics was established in 2000 under the name GlobalNetXchange (GNX) by eight of the world's largest retailers: Sears, Carrefour, Coles Myer, KarstadtQuelle, Kroger, MetroAG, Pinault-Printemps-Redoute, and Sainsbury. In 2005, GNX merged with WorldWide Retail Exchange, a retail industry consortium, and changed its name to Agentrics. Agentrics focuses on auctions and other services and standards for the retail industry. The combined entity is backed by 45 of the world's largest retailers and suppliers, who represent more than $1 trillion in sales (Agentrics, 2008).

Figure 12.17 illustrates an industry-wide private industrial network.

In the future, barring intervention by antitrust enforcers, we can expect many private industrial networks to expand into much larger industry-wide networks seeking to coordinate all the thousands of key players in vertical industries.

THE LONG-TERM DYNAMICS OF PRIVATE INDUSTRIAL NETWORKS

It is apparent that as large firms become more accustomed to working closely with both their supply chain partners and their distributors on the demand side, they will seek to push the boundaries of their networks to extend across the industry as a whole, to other industries, and to elaborate new roles for themselves and others. For instance, the computer manufacturer Hewlett-Packard discovered through its private

---

FIGURE 12.17   **AN INDUSTRY-WIDE PRIVATE INDUSTRIAL NETWORK**

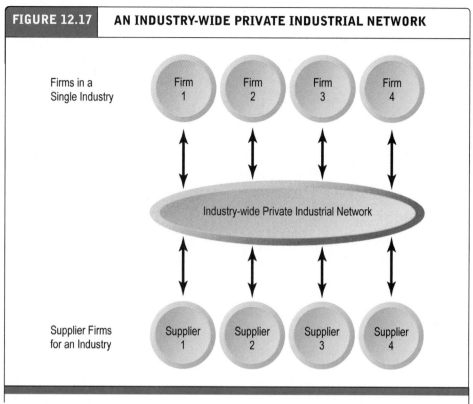

Some private industrial networks expand to encompass an entire industry, coordinating the business processes for suppliers, transporters, production firms, and ultimately distributors and retailers.

---

industrial network that resin manufacturers were charging higher prices for resins they shipped to the molding manufacturers who make the plastic cases for HP computers. The molding manufacturers historically are very slow in paying their bills, and as a result, their resin suppliers raised their prices. HP moved in as a market maker and purchased resins from the suppliers at a market price, then re-sold them at the same price to the molders. HP has more clout to collect from the molders than resin manufacturers (Turek and Gilbert, 2001). In the next five years, we may see that individual large firms will be able to intervene in global supply relationships in order to overcome bottlenecks that otherwise would be hidden from manufacturers.

In some instances, failed efforts to develop Net marketplaces lead to the development of collaborative networks. For instance, in the construction industry, there was an explosion of online exchanges for the purpose of bringing buyers and sellers together in a single digital marketplace. However, the construction companies and suppliers already knew one another and had long-established relationships. Construction companies were more interested in collaborating more closely with their suppliers and their customers for the purpose of exchanging and storing plans and documents, managing project costs and schedules, and developing new business leads (Fuscaldo, 2002).

12.4   CASE STUDY

Siemens
Clicks with Click2procure

Since 1999, Siemens has spent over $870 million building its e-procurement system called Click2procure, using technology provided by Commerce One and SAP, the Austrian manufacturer of a widely adopted ERP system. Click2procure is one of the world's largest private buy-side Net marketplaces. Siemens is a German electrical engineering and electronics giant with approximately 471,000 employees in 190 countries and revenue of over 73 billion (euro) in fiscal 2007. This multinational conglomerate is a leading manufacturer of automation and control systems, communications, lighting, medical, semi-conductors, power, and transportation products and services.

Click2procure is used today by 35,000 Siemens employees, of which 6,000 are involved with strategic purchasing. Siemens purchases over 45 billion (euro) a year in direct and indirect goods. Currently, Click2procure has about 9,000 registered suppliers. Suppliers can either register free of charge for a "Basic Registration" or pay a subscription fee of 3,000 (euro) a year for "Advanced Business Service," which entitles the supplier to additional marketing support, such as the contact information

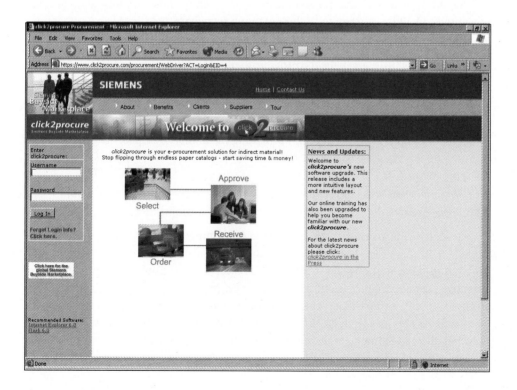

for relevant Siemens customers and an analysis of the supplier's individual competitive position. Click2procure has handled over 4 billion (euro) in purchasing volume for Siemens and conducted over 1,400 e-auctions within Siemens. According to Siemens, average savings achieved with e-auctions is around 18%. Suppliers have created almost 170 electronic catalogs within the system, with over 1.8 million direct and indirect goods available in about 40 different categories, such as copper and copper alloys, precious metals, plastic components and mold parts, microcontrollers, office materials, and so on. About 80,000 transactions are processed per month, and average savings in process costs range from 30%-60%, according to Siemens.

Click2procure provides a private, Web-based platform for standardizing and automating purchasing activities. The system also provides sourcing, procurement, and supply chain management services to outside firms. Siemens initially established a separate business called Siemens Procurement and Logistics Services (SPLS) as a separate business unit set up for the purpose of developing Click2procure as a profit center. SPLS was integrated into Siemens' Global Procurement and Logistics (GPL) in October 2004.

Prior to Click2procure, each of Siemens' business units around the globe did its own purchasing and followed its own rules. This bloated the supply base to 5,000 separate suppliers for MRO goods alone—about $10 billion worth of products. The decentralized purchasing system meant that Siemens could not aggregate orders across all business units to obtain better prices, and a significant amount of maverick purchasing occurred. Generally, maverick purchasing results in higher costs. Under the old system, 50,000 indirect purchases per month cost about $100 each to process, and there was no central review of the prices paid for products.

Siemens wanted to centralize control over global purchasing into a single unit. It wanted to build a solution with the following five characteristics:

- *Global reach*—supporting procurement in over 90 countries
- *Effective catalog management*—providing the ability to aggregate and manage catalogs from hundreds of suppliers
- *Web-based search engine*—providing the ability to compare prices from multiple suppliers
- *Rules-based and approval tracking*—providing the ability to impose its own business rules on purchasing based on the type of product and the ability to track the approval process
- *Integration with legacy systems*—pproviding a software solution that would easily integrate with a diverse range of legacy and ERP systems already in place

Guided by these criteria, Siemens opted for Commerce One's package Net Market Maker Solution. Net Market Maker Solution leveraged CommerceOne.net, a Web-based Net marketplace operated by Commerce One. CommerceOne.net provided catalog management and transaction processing capabilities. In addition, CommerceOne.net provided access to catalog management, transaction processing, and business services such as auctions and eRFQs. Using CommerceOne's packaged solution allowed Siemens to develop its own "private" Click2procure version in only four months. A system of this magnitude would have required three to five years if Siemens had chosen to build the system itself.

GPL is now the general contractor of the Click2procure service. GPL aggregates purchases from all Siemens buyers to negotiate better prices from suppliers. GPL also works with buyer firms—both Siemens business units and other firms who use Siemens's system—to integrate Click2procure with back-office legacy systems. This increases the switching costs for users who might want to use a different exchange. GPL issues a single monthly invoice to business units, reflecting items purchased, tax, and freight charges. GPL charges buyers either a flat fee per transaction, or takes a percentage of the discount it negotiates with suppliers.

For suppliers, Click2procure automates the invoicing and payment process, ensuring that suppliers get paid rapidly. In the past, receiving payment for supplies could take months as invoices wended their way through a number of differing accounts payable systems at local and global levels. GPL issues a single check to suppliers monthly for all orders processed through Click2procure. In addition, suppliers gain access to Click2procure's rapidly expanding network of buyers and potentially huge aggregated orders. For instance, whereas in the past, Siemens business units would buy PC computers from many different sources, by aggregating orders from all its business units, Siemens was able to purchase $30 million worth of PCs from a single vendor, Dell, up from $2 million in previous years.

Siemens reports a number of significant benefits from Click2procure:

- 10% reduction in prices paid for goods
- 75% reduction in administrative costs, bringing purchase order cost down to $25
- 60% reduction in ordering life cycles, from over eight days down to 48 hours
- Significant reduction in accounts payable staff now that bills are paid on time
- Enhanced inventory and asset utilization.
- Improved demand planning and forecasting

Despite these benefits, many business units at Siemens initially resisted joining. In some cases, favorite local suppliers were not included in the marketplace. Joining Click2procure meant that local units would have to give up their own purchasing process and forms, and completely change their procurement business procedures. Local units would also lose the ability to negotiate most favored terms, passing this activity on to central buyers who might not understand local requirements. To rectify this problem, Siemens elevated Click2procure to the status of a corporate standard, which meant that all Siemens operating groups were required to use its services and applications. This philosophy, known within Siemens as the "Shared Service Concept," makes all 14 Siemens operating groups "partners" in Click2procure. Click2procure's portfolio, strategy, and budget are jointly planned by a steering committee consisting of purchasing managers from the business groups. This organizational structure has been a significant factor in ensuring Click2procure's success.

SOURCES: Click2procure.com, October 2008; "BSM Internet—Facts and Figures," Siemens.com, October 2008; "About Us," Siemens.com, 2008; "Serving Internal Customers, by Demir Barlas, Line56.com, February 12, 2004; "Analyzing the Business Model of a Corporate Procurement Platform: The Case of Siemens click2procure," by Claas Muller-Lankenau and Stefan Klein, in: Lechner, Ulrike (Hrsg.), *Proceedings of the Tenth Research Symposium on Emerging Electronic Markets 2003, S. 159-167*, Bremen: University of Bremen, Germany, 2003; "Siemens Uses Catalog Software from jCatalog for Marketplace," Jcatalog.com, June 2003; "The New New Moneymakers," by Andrew Reese, Isourceonline.com, November 2002; "Companies Slash Order Times and Costs with Online Initiatives," by Steve Konicki, *Information Week*, August 5, 2002; "Siemens: Masters of Innovation," The Aberdeen Group, July 2002.

Case Study Questions

1. If you were the manager of a Siemens local business unit, what might be some of the disadvantages of using the Click2procure system for your unit?

2. If you were a manager of a manufacturing firm considering joining Click2procure, what are some of the concerns you might have about tightly integrating Click2procure with your backend legacy ERP systems? What recommendations would you make to your senior management on how to address your concerns?

3. In what ways does Siemens's Click2procure system impose switching costs on users? How might you minimize these if you were a user?

12.5 REVIEW

KEY CONCEPTS

■ **Define B2B commerce and understand its scope and history.**

Before the Internet, business-to-business transactions were referred to simply as *trade* or the *procurement process*. Today, we use the term *B2B commerce* to describe all types of computer-assisted inter-firm trade, and the term *Internet-based B2B commerce* or *B2B e-commerce* to describe specifically that portion of B2B commerce that uses the Internet to assist firms in buying and selling a variety of goods to each other. The process of conducting trade among businesses consumes many business resources, including the time spent by employees processing orders, making and approving purchasing decisions, searching for products, and arranging for their purchase, shipment, receipt, and payment. Across the economy, this amounts to trillions of dollars spent annually on procurement processes. If a significant portion of this inter-firm trade could be automated and parts of the procurement process assisted by the Internet, millions or even trillions of dollars could be freed up for other uses, resulting in increased productivity and increased national economic wealth.

In order to understand the history of B2B commerce, you must understand several key stages including:

- *Automated order entry systems*, developed in the 1970s, used the telephone to send digital orders to companies. Telephone modems were placed in the offices of the customers for a particular business. This enabled procurement managers to directly access the firm's inventory database to automatically reorder products.
- *EDI* or *electronic data interchange*, developed in the late 1970s, is a communications standard for sharing various procurement documents including invoices, purchase orders, shipping bills, product stocking numbers (SKUs), and settlement information for an industry. It was developed to reduce the costs, delays, and errors inherent in the manual exchange of documents.
- *Electronic storefronts* emerged in the 1990s along with the commercialization of the Internet. They are online catalogs containing the products that are made available to the general public by a single vendor.

- *Net marketplaces* emerged in the late 1990s as a natural extension and scaling-up of the electronic storefront. The essential characteristic of all Net marketplaces is that they bring hundreds of suppliers, each with its own electronic catalog, together with potentially thousands of purchasing firms to form a single Internet-based marketplace.
- *Private industrial networks* also emerged in the late 1 990s with the commercialization of the Internet as natural extensions of EDI systems and the existing close relationships that developed between large industrial firms and their suppliers.

Before you can understand each of the different types of Net marketplaces, you must be familiar with several other key concepts:

- *Seller-side solutions* are owned by the suppliers of goods and are seller-biased markets that only display goods from a single seller. Customers benefit because these systems reduce the costs of inventory replenishment and are paid for by and large by the suppliers. Automated order entry systems are seller-side solutions.
- *Buyer-side solutions* are owned by the buyers of goods and are buyer-biased markets because they reduce procurement costs for the buyer. Sellers also benefit because the cost of serving a company's customers is reduced. EDI systems are buyer-side solutions.
- *Vertical markets* provide expertise and products targeted to a specific industry. EDI systems usually serve vertical markets.
- *Horizontal markets* serve a myriad of different industries. Electronic storefronts are an example of a horizontal market in that they tend to carry a wide variety of products that are useful to any number of different industries.

■ Understand the procurement process, the supply chain, and collaborative commerce.

- The *procurement process* refers to the way business firms purchase the goods they need in order to produce the goods they will ultimately sell to consumers. Firms purchase goods from a set of suppliers who in turn purchase their inputs from a set of suppliers. These firms are linked in a series of connected transactions.
- The *supply chain* is the series of transactions that links sets of firms that do business with each other. It includes not only the firms themselves but also the relationships between them and the processes that connect them.

There are seven steps in the procurement process:

- Searching for suppliers for specific products
- Qualifying the sellers and the products they sell
- Negotiating prices, credit terms, escrow requirements, and quality requirements
- Scheduling delivery
- Issuing purchase orders
- Sending invoices
- Shipping the product

Each step is composed of separate sub-steps that must be recorded in the information systems of the buyer, seller, and shipper. There are two different types of procurements and two different methods of purchasing goods:

- *Purchases of direct goods*—goods that are directly involved in the production process.

- *Purchases of indirect goods*—goods needed to carry out the production process but that are not directly involved in creating the end product.
- *Contract purchases*—long-term agreements to buy a specified amount of a product. There are pre-specified quality requirements and pre-specified terms.
- *Spot purchases*—for goods that meet the immediate needs of a firm. Indirect purchases are most often made on a spot-purchase basis in a large marketplace that includes many suppliers.

The term *multi-tier supply chain* is used to describe the complex series of transactions that exists between a single firm with multiple primary suppliers, the secondary suppliers who do business with those primary suppliers, and the tertiary suppliers who do business with the secondary suppliers.

Trends in supply chain management (the activities that firms and industries use to coordinate the key players in their procurement process) include:

- *Supply chain simplification,* which refers to the reduction of the size of a firm's supply chain. Firms today generally prefer to work closely with a strategic group of suppliers in order to reduce both product costs and administrative costs. Long-term contract purchases containing pre-specified product quality requirements and pre-specified timing goals have been shown to improve end-product quality and ensure uninterrupted production.
- *Supply chain management systems,* which coordinate and link the activities of suppliers, shippers, and order entry systems to automate the order entry process from start to finish, including the purchase, production, and moving of a product from a supplier to a purchasing firm.
- *Collaborative commerce,* which is a direct extension of supply chain management systems as well as supply chain simplification. It is the use of digital technologies to permit the supplier and the purchaser to share sensitive company information in order to collaboratively design, develop, build, and manage products throughout their life cycles.

■ Identify the main types of B2B commerce: Net marketplaces and private industrial networks.

There are two generic types of B2B commerce and many different subtypes within those two main categories of Internet commerce:

- *Net marketplaces,* which are also referred to as exchanges or hubs, assemble hundreds to thousands of sellers and buyers in a single digital marketplace on the Internet. They can be owned by either the buyer or the seller, or they can operate as independent intermediaries between the buyer and seller.
- *Private industrial networks* bring together a small number of strategic business partners who collaborate with one another to develop highly efficient supply chains and to satisfy customer demand for product. They are by far the largest form of B2B commerce.

■ Understand the four types of Net marketplaces.

There are four main types of "pure" Net marketplaces:

- *E-distributors* are independently owned intermediaries that offer industrial customers a single source from which to make spot purchases of indirect or MRO goods. E-distributors operate in a horizontal market that serves many different industries with products from many different suppliers.

- *E-procurement Net marketplaces* are independently owned intermediaries connecting hundreds of online suppliers offering millions of MRO goods to business firms who pay a fee to join the market. E-procurement Net marketplaces operate in a horizontal market in which long-term contractual purchasing agreements are used to buy indirect goods.
- *Exchanges* are independently owned online marketplaces that connect hundreds to thousands of suppliers and buyers in a dynamic real-time environment. They are typically vertical markets in which spot purchases can be made for direct inputs (both goods and services). Exchanges make money by charging a commission on each transaction.
- *Industry consortia* are industry-owned vertical markets where long-term contractual purchases of direct inputs can be made from a limited set of invited participants. Consortia serve to reduce supply chain inefficiencies by unifying the supply chain for an industry through a common network and computing platform.

■ **Identify the major trends in the development of Net marketplaces.**

- In the early days of e-commerce, independent exchanges were the prototype Internet-based marketplace and over a thousand of them were created; however, most of them did not succeed. The main reason independent exchanges failed is that they did not attract enough players to achieve liquidity (measured by the number of buyers and sellers in the market, the transaction volume, and the size of the transactions).
- Industry consortia sprang up partly in reaction to the earlier development of independently owned exchanges that were viewed by large industries as interlopers who would not directly serve their needs. Industry consortia are profitable because they charge the large buyer firms transaction and subscription fees, but the rationalization of the procurement process, the competition among the vendors, and the closer relationship with the vendors are benefits that more than offset the costs of membership to the firms. However, the long-term profitability of consortia has yet to be proven.
- The failure of the early exchanges is one reason Net marketplaces are changing so rapidly. Participants have come to realize that the real value of B2B commerce will only be realized when it succeeds in changing the entire procurement system, the supply chain, and the process of collaboration among firms.

■ **Identify the role of private industrial networks in transforming the supply chain.**

- Private industrial networks, which presently dominate B2B commerce, are Web-enabled networks for coordinating trans-organizational business processes (collaborative commerce). These networks range in scope from a single firm to an entire industry.
- Although the central purpose of a private industrial network is to provide industry-wide global solutions to achieve the highest levels of efficiency, they generally start with a single sponsoring company that "owns" the network. This differentiates private industrial networks from industry consortia that are usually owned collectively by major firms through equity participation.
- Private industrial networks are transforming the supply chain by focusing on continuous business process coordination between companies. This coordination includes much more than just transaction support and supply chain management. Product design, demand forecasting, asset management, and sales and marketing plans can all be coordinated among network members.

■ Understand the role of private industrial networks in supporting collaborative commerce.

Collaboration among businesses can take many forms and involve a wide range of activities. Some of the forms of collaboration used by private industrial networks include the following:

- *CPFR* or *industry-wide collaborative resource planning, forecasting, and replenishment* involves working with network members to forecast demand, develop production plans, and coordinate shipping, warehousing, and stocking activities. The goal is to ensure that retail and wholesale shelf space is precisely maintained.

- *Supply-chain and distribution chain visibility* refers to the fact that, in the past, it was impossible to know where excess capacity existed in a supply or distribution chain. Eliminating excess inventories by halting the production of overstocked goods can raise the profit margins for all network members because products will no longer need to be discounted in order to move them off the shelves.

- *Marketing and product design collaboration* can be used to involve a firm's suppliers in product design and marketing activities as well as in the related activities of their supply and distribution chain partners. This can ensure that the parts used to build a product live up to the claims of the marketers. Collaborative commerce applications used in a private industrial network can also make possible closed-loop marketing in which customer feedback will directly impact product design.

QUESTIONS

1. Explain the differences among total inter-firm trade, B2B commerce, and B2B e-commerce.
2. What are the key attributes of an electronic storefront? What early technology are they descended from?
3. List at least five potential benefits of B2B e-commerce.
4. Name and define the two distinct types of procurements firms make. Explain the difference between the two.
5. Name and define the two methods of purchasing goods.
6. Define the term supply chain and explain what SCM systems attempt to do. What does supply chain simplification entail?
7. Explain the difference between a horizontal market and a vertical market.
8. How do the value chain management services provided by e-procurement companies benefit buyers? What services do they provide to suppliers?
9. What are the three dimensions that characterize an e-procurement market based on its business functionality? Name two other market characteristics of an e-procurement Net marketplace.
10. Identify and briefly explain the anti-competitive possibilities inherent in Net marketplaces.
11. List three of the objectives of a private industrial network.
12. What is the main reason why many of the independent exchanges developed in the early days of e-commerce failed?
13. Explain the difference between an industry consortium and a private industrial network.
14. What is CPFR, and what benefits could it achieve for the members of a private industrial network?

15. What are the barriers to the complete implementation of private industrial networks?

PROJECTS

1. Choose an industry and a B2B vertical market maker that interests you. Investigate the site and prepare a report that describes the size of the industry served, the type of Net marketplace provided, the benefits promised by the site for both suppliers and purchasers, and the history of the company. You might also investigate the bias (buyer versus seller), ownership (suppliers, buyers, independents), pricing mechanism(s), scope and focus, and access (public versus private) of the Net marketplace.

2. Examine the Web site of one of the e-distributors listed in Figure 12.9, and compare and contrast it to one of the Web sites listed for e-procurement Net marketplaces. If you were a business manager of a medium-sized firm, how would you decide where to purchase your indirect inputs—from an e-distributor or an e-procurement Net marketplace? Write a short report detailing your analysis.

3. Assume you are a procurement officer for an office furniture manufacturer of steel office equipment. You have a single factory located in the Midwest with 2,000 employees. You sell about 40% of your office furniture to retail-oriented catalog outlets such as Quill in response to specific customer orders, and the remainder of your output is sold to resellers under long-term contracts. You have a choice of purchasing raw steel inputs—mostly cold-rolled sheet steel—from an exchange and/or from an industry consortium. Which alternative would you choose and why? Prepare a presentation for management supporting your position.

4. Find a Net marketplace that has failed (possible candidates include Aerospan.com, Chemdex.com, Petrocosm.com, E-steel.com, or another of your choosing). Investigate the reasons behind its failure. Prepare a short report on your findings and your analysis of the lessons that can be learned from its demise.

WEB SITE RESOURCES www.prenhall.com/laudon

- Additional projects, exercises and tutorials
- Careers: Explore career opportunities in e-commerce
- Raising capital and business plans

References

CHAPTER 1

Bailey, Joseph P. *Intermediation and Electronic Markets: Aggregation and Pricing in Internet Commerce.* Ph. D., Technology, Management and Policy, Massachusetts Institute of Technology (1998a).

Bakos, Yannis. "Reducing Buyer Search Costs: Implications for Electronic Marketplaces." *Management Science* (December 1997).

Banerjee, Suman and Chakravarty, Amiya. "Price Setting and Price Discovery Strategies with a Mix of Frequent and Infrequent Internet Users." (April 15, 2005). SSRN: http://ssrn.com/abstract=650706.

Baye, Michael R. "Price Dispersion in the Lab and on the Internet: Theory and Evidence." *Rand Journal of Economics* (2004).

Baye, Michael R., John Morgan, and Patrick Scholten. "Temporal Price Dispersion: Evidence from an Online Consumer Electronics Market." *Journal of Interactive Marketing* (January 2004).

Bialik, Carl. "Lawyers Bid Up Value of Web-Search Ads." DowJonesNewswire (April 8, 2004).

Brynjolfsson, Erik, and Michael Smith. "Frictionless Commerce? A Comparison of Internet and Conventional Retailers." *Management Science* (April 2000).

eBay, Inc. Report on Form 10-K for the fiscal year ending December 31, 2007 filed with the Securities and Exchange Commission (February 28, 2008).

eMarketer, Inc. (Debra Aho Williamson). "Monetizing MySpace Traffic." (August 2008a).

eMarketer, Inc. (Jeffrey Grau). "U.S. Retail E-commerce: Slower But Still Steady Growth." (May 2008b or 2008d).

eMarketer, Inc. (Lisa Phillips). "U.S. Online Population," (February 2008c).

eMarketer, Inc. "Online Sales Revenues of Top 500 US Retail Websites by Company Type, 2007." (June 1, 2008e)

eMarketer, Inc. "Online Sales by Top 500 Retail Web Sites, by Product Category, 2007." (June 1, 2008f).

Evans, Philip, and Thomas S. Wurster. *Blown to Bits: How the New Economics of Information Transforms Strategy.* Cambridge, MA: Harvard Business School Press (2000).

Evans, Philip, and Thomas S. Wurster. "Getting Real About Virtual Commerce." *Harvard Business Review* (November-December 1999).

Evans, Philip, and Thomas S. Wurster. "Strategy and the New Economics of Information." *Harvard Business Review* (September-October 1997).

Facebook. Facebook.com. (September, 2008).

Fink, Eugene, Josh Johnson, and Jerry Hu. "Exchange Market for Complex Goods: Theory and Experiments." *Communications of the ACM.* (April, 2004).

Forrester Research, Inc. (Tamara Mendelsohn) "The Web's Impact on In-Store Sales: US Cross-Channel Sales Forecast, 2006 to 2012." (May 7, 2007).

Google, Inc. Report on Form 10-K for the Fiscal Year Ended December 31, 2007, filed with the Securities and Exchange Commission. (March 31, 2008).

Internet Systems Consortium, Inc. "ISC Internet Domain Survey." (January 2008).

Internet World Stats. Internetworldstats.com/stats.htm (June 2008).

Joost.com. "About Joost." (September 30, 2008).

Kalakota, Ravi, and Marcia Robinson. *e-Business 2.0: Roadmap for Success, 2nd edition.* Reading, MA: Addison Wesley (2003).

Kambil, Ajit. "Doing Business in the Wired World." *IEEE Computer* (May 1997).

Mesenbourg, Thomas L. "Measuring Electronic Business: Definitions, Underlying Concepts, and Measurement Plans." U. S. Department of Commerce Bureau of the Census (August 2001).

Nash-equilibrium.com. "Relative Dispersion." (September 5, 2008).

News Corporation. "MySpace Outperforms All Other Social Networking Sites." (July 12, 2007).

Nielsen Online. "Video Census." Center for Media Research. (April, 2008).

Pew Internet & American Life Project. "Daily Internet Activities." (July, 2008).

Photobucket.com. "About Photobucket." (September 2008.

PricewaterhouseCoopers/National Venture Capital Association. MoneyTree Report, Data: Thomson Financial (2008).

Rayport, Jeffrey F., and Bernard J. Jaworski. *Introduction to E-commerce, 2nd edition.* New York: McGraw-Hill (2003).

Richtel, Matt and Bob Tedeschi. "Online Sales Lose Steam." *New York Times* (June 17, 2007).

Secondlife.com. ""Economic Statistics." (September 2008).

Shapiro, Carl, and Hal R. Varian. *Information Rules. A*

Strategic Guide to the Network Economy. Cambridge, MA: Harvard Business School Press (1999).

Sinha, Indajit. "Cost Transparency: The Net's Threat to Prices and Brands." *Harvard Business Review* (March-April 2000).

Slatalla, Michelle. "Online Shopper: Price Comparison Sites Do the Legwork." *New York Times* (February 3, 2005).

Smith, Michael; Joseph Bailey; and Erik Brynjolfsson. "Understanding Digital Markets: Review and Assessment." In Erik Brynjolfsson and Brian Kahin (eds.) *Understanding the Digital Economy.* Cambridge MA: MIT Press (2000).

Tedeschi, Bob. "Web Videos Let Car Buyers Survey Their Many Choices." *New York Times* (May 14, 2007).

Telecommunications Industry Association. "TIA's 2007 Telecommunications Market Review and Forecast." (2008).

Tversky, A., and D. Kahneman. "The Framing of Decisions and the Psychology of Choice." *Science* (January 1981).

U.S. Census Bureau. "E-Stats Report 2006 E-commerce Multi-Sector Report." (May 2008).

Varian, Hal R. "5 Habits of Highly Effective Revolution." *Forbes ASAP* (February 21, 2000a).

Varian, Hal R. "When Commerce Moves On, Competition Can Work in Strange Ways." *New York Times* (August 24, 2000b).

Wikipedia.org. "Wikipedia: About." (September 29, 2008).

CHAPTER 2

Agentrics LLC. "Welcome to Agentrics." Agentrics.com (August 23, 2008).

Arthur, W. Brian. "Increasing Returns and the New World of Business." *Harvard Business Review* (July-August 1996).

Bakos, Yannis. "The Emerging Role of Electronic Marketplaces on the Internet." *Communications of the ACM* (August 1998).

Bakos, Yannis; Henry Lucas; Wonseok Oh; Sivakuman Viswanathan; Gary Simon; and Bruce Weber. "The Impact of Electronic Commerce in the Retail Brokerage Industry: Trading Costs of Internet Versus Full Service Firms." Center for Research on Information Systems, Stern School of Business, New York University (July 2000).

Barney, J. B. "Firm Resources and Sustained Competitive Advantage." *Journal of Management* Vol. 17, No. 1 (1991).

Bellman, Steven; Gerland L. Lohse; and Eric J. Johnson. "Predictors of Online Buying Behavior." *Communications of the ACM* (December 1999).

Brohan, Mark. "Great Expectations." *Internet Retailer* (September 2000).

Day, George S.; Adam J. Fein; and Gregg Ruppersberger. "Shakeouts in Digital Markets." *California Management Review* Vol. 45, No. 3 (Winter 2003).

eBay, Inc. Form 10-K for the fiscal year ended December 31, 2007, filed with the Securities and Exchange Commission (February 28, 2008).

eMarketer, Inc. (Noah Elkin). "Automotive Industry Online." (May 1, 2004).

eMarketer, Inc. (Lisa Phillips). "U.S. Online Population," (February, 2008a).

eMarketer, Inc. (Jeffrey Grau). "U.S. Retail E-commerce: Slower But Still Steady Growth." (May, 2008b).

eMarketer, Inc. (Ben Macklin). "Digital Downloading: Music, Movies, and TV." (January, 2007a).

eMarketer, Inc. (Paul Verna). "Recorded Music: Digital Falls Short." (November 2007b).

Nielsen Online. "Nielsen Online Releases April 2008 U.S. Search Rankings." (May 20, 2008).

Fisher, William W. III. "The Growth of Intellectual Property: A History of the Ownership of Ideas in the United States." Cyber.law.harvard.edu/people/tfisher/iphistory.pdf (1999).

Gebauer, Judith, and Michael Zagler. "Assessing the Status Quo and Future of B2B E-Commerce. *International Federation of Purchasing and Materials Management* (December 2000).

Gerace, Thomas. "Encyclopedia Britannica." Harvard Business School Case Study 396-051 (1999).

Ghosh, Shikhar. "Making Business Sense of the Internet." *Harvard Business Review* (March-April 1998).

Gulati, Ranjay, and Jason Garino. "Getting the Right Mix of Bricks and Clicks." *Harvard Business Review* (May-June 2000).

JiWire.com. "Wi-Fi Finder." (August 29, 2008).

Kambil, Ajit. "Doing Business in the Wired World." *IEEE Computer* (May 1997).

Kambil, Ajit; Ari Ginsberg; and Michael Bloch. "Reinventing Value Propositions." Working Paper, NYU Center for Research on Information Systems (1998).

Kanter, Elizabeth Ross. "The Ten Deadly Mistakes of Wanna-Dots." *Harvard Business Review* (January 2001).

Kaplan, Steven, and Mohanbir Sawhney. "E-Hubs: The New B2B Marketplaces." *Harvard Business*

Review (May-June 2000).

Kim, W. Chan, and Renee Mauborgne. "Knowing a Winning Business Idea When You See One." *Harvard Business Review* (September-October 2000).

Madnick, Stuart and Michael Siegel. "Seizing the Opportunity: Exploiting Web Aggregation." MIT Sloan School of Management, Working Paper 144 (December 2001).

Magretta, Joan. "Why Business Models Matter." *Harvard Business Review* (May 2002).

Nielsen Online. "Nielsen Online Releases April 2008 U.S. Search Rankings." (May 20, 2008).

Online Publishers Association. Paid Online Content U.S. Market Spending Report Fiscal Year 2005 (March 14, 2006).

Porter, Michael E. "Strategy and the Internet." *Harvard Business Review* (March 2001).

Porter, Michael E. *Competitive Advantage: Creating and Sustaining Superior Performance.* New York: Free Press (1985).

Porter, Michael E., and V. E. Millar. "How Information Gives You Competitive Advantage." *Harvard Business Review* (July-August 1985).

Rigdon, Joan I. "The Second-Mover Advantage." *Red Herring* (September 1, 2000).

Siwicki, Bill. It's a Small World. *Internet Retailer* (May 2007).

Teece, David J. "Profiting from Technological Innovation: Implications for Integration, Collaboration, Licensing and Public Policy." *Research Policy* 15 (1986).

Telecommunications Industry Association. "TIA's 2008 Telecommunications Market Review and Forecast." (2008).

Timmers, Paul. "Business Models for Electronic Markets" *Electronic Markets* Vol. 8, No. 2 (1998).

Ulfelder, Steve. "B2B Exchange Survivors." *Computerworld* (February 2, 2004).

U.S. Census Bureau, Economic and Statistics Administration. "Quarterly Retail E-commerce Sales 2nd Quarter 2008." (August 2008).

U.S. Census Bureau. "E-Stats Report 2006 E-commerce Multi-Sector Report." (May, 2008).

CHAPTER 3

Apple, Inc. "App Store Downloads Top 100 Million Worldwide." (Apple, September 9, 2008).

Berners-Lee, Tim; Robert Cailliau; Ari Luotonen; Henrik Frystyk Nielsen; and Arthur Secret. "The World Wide Web." *Communications of the ACM* (August 1994).

Bluetooth SIG. "Bluetooth: The Official Bluetooth Website." Bluetooth.com (2005).

Boingo Wireless. "Home Page." (September 20, 2007).

Brandt, Richard. "Net Assets: How Stanford's Computer Science Department Changed the Way We Get Information." *Stanford Magazine* (November/December 2004).

Bush, Vannevar. "As We May Think." *Atlantic Monthly* (July 1945).

Cerf, V., and R. Kahn, "A Protocol for Packet Network Intercommunication." *IEEE Transactions on Communications,* Vol. COM-22, No. 5, pp 637-648 (May 1974).

Cisco Systems, Inc. "IP Multicast Technical Overview." (August 2007).

Computer Science and Telecommunications Board. National Research Council (NRC). Networking Health: Prescriptions for the Internet." Washington DC: National Academy Press (2000).

comScore, Inc. "ComScore Media Metrix Ranks Top 50 Web Properties for July 2008." (August 15, 2008).

Cuil, Inc. (2008).

EmailStatcenter.com, Email Usage Patterns Report. (June 2008).

EmailStatcenter.com. (September 2008).

eMarketer, Inc. (Ben Macklin). "Broadband Services: VOIP and IPTV Trends," (April, 2008a).

eMarketer, Inc. "Mobile Phone Sales Worldwide, 2007 & 2008." (August 5, 2008b).

eMarketer, Inc. "Web Widgets and Applications: Destination Unknown." (Debra Aho Williamson). (February, 2008c).

eMarketer, Inc. "Widgets vs. Budget." (July 15, 2008d).

eMarketer, Inc. "Search Engine Marketing: User and Spending Trends." (January 2008e).

eMarketer, Inc. "Digital Downloading." (January 2007a).

eMarketer, Inc. "Recorded Music: Digital Falls Short." (November 2007b).

Federal Networking Council. "FNC Resolution: Definition of 'Internet.'" (October 24, 1995).

Gartner, Inc.. "Gartner Says More Than 1 Billion PCs in Use Worldwide and Headed to 2 Billion Units by 2014." (June 23, 2008a).

Gartner, Inc. "Cloud Computing Will Be As Influential as E-Business." (June 26, 2008b).

Geni.net. "Global Environment for Network Innovations." (September 2008).

Gross, Grant. "NSF Seeks Ambitious Next-Generation Internet Project." *Computerworld* (August 29, 2005).

Hamm, Steve. "Cloud Computing,: Eyes on the Skies." *BusinessWeek* (April 24, 2008).

IDC, Inc. "Worldwide Quarterly PC Tracker." Press release (September 2008).

Internet Corporation for Assigned Names and Numbers (ICANN). "Top-Level Domains (gTLDs)." Icann.org (2008).

InterNIC. "InterNIC FAQs on New Top-Level Domains." Internic.net (September 25, 2008).

Internet Retailer. Top 500 Guide. (2008).

Internet Society. "Internet Standards." Internet Society. (September 2008).

Internet Society. "RFC 2616: Hypertext Transfer Protocol—HTTP/1.1." (June 1999).

Internet Society. "RFC 2821: Simple Mail Transfer Protocol" (April 2001).

Internet Society. "RFC 1939: Post Office Protocol—Version 3." (May 1996).

Internet Society. "RFC 3501: Internet Message Access Protocol—Version 4rev1" (March 2003).

Internet Society. "RFC 0959: File Transfer Protocol." (October, 1985).

Internet Society. "RFC 854: Telnet Protocol Specification." (May 1983).

Internetworldstats.com. "World Internet Usage Statistics News and Population Stats." (September 20, 2008).

King, Rachael. "How Cloud Computing is Changing the World." *BusinessWeek* (August 4, 2008).

Kleinrock, Leonard. *1964 Communication Nets: Stochastic Message Flow and Delay.* New York: McGraw-Hill (1964).

Leiner, Barry M.; Vinton G. Cerf; David D. Clark; Robert E. Kahn; Leonard Kleinrock; Daniel C. Lynch; Jon Postel; Larry G. Roberts; and Stephen Wolff. "All About the Internet: A Brief History of the Internet." Internet Society (ISOC) (August 2000).

Mehta, Stephanie. "Verizon's Big Bet on Fiber Optics." money.cnn.com (February 22, 2007).

Merrill Lynch. "The Cloud Wars: $100+ Billion at Stake." Research Report (May 7, 2008).

National Research Council. "The Internet's Coming of Age." Washington DC: National Academy Press (2000).

Net Applications. "Browser Market Share Report." (June 2008).

Net Applications. "Website Statistics and Web Analytics." Hitlinks.com. (September 2008).

Netcraft. "September 2008 Web Server Survey." (September 2008).

Nielsen/NetRatings. "Nielsen/NetRatings Reports Topline U.S. Data for July 2007." (August 13, 2007a).

Nielsen/NetRatings. "Nielsen/NetRatings Announces July U.S. Search Share Rankings." (June 18, 2008).

Nielsen Online. "Megaview Search." (November 2007).

NLR.net. "National Lambda Rail." NLR.net. (September 2008).

Odlyzko, Andrew. "Data Networks are Lightly Utilized, and Will Stay That Way." *Review of Network Economics* Vol.2, Issue 3 (September 2003).

Perez, Juan Carlos. "Gadget Puts Google Talk on Web Pages." *Infoworld* (March 15, 2007).

Pew Internet & American Life Project. "Daily Internet Activities." (July 2008).

Pew Internet & American Life Project. "Podcast Downloading." (August 2008).

Technorati, Inc. "Welcome to Technorati." (September 2008).

Telecommunications Industry Association. "Telecom market heading for healthy growth 2008, TIA projects." (Kate Gerwig). SearchTelecom.com. (February 26, 2008).

Telecommunications Industry Association. "TIA's 2007 Telecommunications Market Review and Forecast." (January 2007).

Visualware, Inc., "VisualRoute Traceroute Server." Visualroute.visualware.com (September 2007).

Wayport, Inc. "Company Overview." (September 20, 2008).

Zakon, Robert H. "Hobbes' Internet Timeline v8.1." Zakon.org (2005).

Ziff-Davis Publishing. "Ted Nelson: Hypertext Pioneer." Techtv.com (1998).

ZigBee Alliance. "ZigBee Smart Energy: The Standard for Energy Efficiency." ZigBee.org. (June 23, 2008)

Zillman, Marcus. "Deep Web Research." LLRX.com (2005).

CHAPTER 4

Banker, Rajiv D., and Chris F. Kemerer. "Scale Economies in New Software Development." *IEEE Transactions on Software Engineering,* Vol. 15, No. 10 (1989).

Bluefly, Inc. Report Form 10-Q for the Quarterly Period Ended June 30, 2008 filed with the Securities & Exchange Commission (August 13, 2008).

CMSWatch.com (2008).

Doyle, Barry and Cristina Videria Lopes. "Survey of Technologies for Web Application Development."

ACM, Vol.2., No. 3. (June 2005).

eMarketer, Inc. (Lisa E. Phillips). "US Online Population" (February 2008).

Hostway. "Hostway Pet Peeves Survey: Top Line Results." Hostway.com, (2007).

IBM (High Volume Web Sites Team). "Best Practices for High-Volume Web Sites." *IBM Redbooks* (December 2002).

IBM (Nigel Trickett, Tatsuhiko Nakagawa, Ravi Mani, Diana Gfroerer). "Understanding IBM eServer pSeries Performance and Sizing." IBM Redbooks (January 24, 2003).

Laudon, Kenneth C. and Jane P. Laudon. *Management Information Systems: Managing the Digital Firm. 11th edition.* Upper Saddle River, NJ: Prentice Hall (2009).

Lientz, Bennet P., and E. Burton Swanson. *Software Maintenance Management.* Reading MA: Addison-Wesley (1980).

Story, Louise. "It's an Ad, Ad, Ad, Ad World." *New York Times* (August 6, 2007).

Telecommunications Industry Association, "TIA's 2008 Telecommunications Market Review and Forecast." (2008).

WebTrends, Inc. "WebTrends MarketingLab 2.0." (2007).

CHAPTER 5

Associated Press. "FBI Ditches Carnivore Surveillance System." Foxnews.com (January 18, 2005).

Boncella, Robert J. "Web Security for E-Commerce." *Communications of the Association for Information Systems,* Vol. 4. (November 2000).

Borden, Anne. "Credit Card Theft: An 'Inside Job'." Lawyersandsettlements.com (May 14, 2007).

Buckman, Rebecca. "Signing Up for E-Signatures." *Wall Street Journal* (July 3, 2007).

BusinessWire. "At a Project 150 Billion in 2007, the Mobile Phone Service Industry is one of the Largest Sectors in the US Economy." (February 11, 2008).

Butterfield, Ethan. "Agencies Making Little Progress Against Cybervandalism." *Government Computer News* (September 1, 2005).

CheckFree Corporation. "2007 Consumer Bill Payment Trends Survey." (January 2007).

CheckFree Corporation (Fiserv). "2008 Consumer Banking and Bill Payment Survey." (August 28, 2008).

CheckFree, Inc. "2007 Consumer Bills Payment Trends Survey: Volume of Electronic Payments." Checkfree.com (2007).

Computer Security Institute. "CSI Survey 2007." (September 2007).

Cybersource. "Cybersource 8th Annual Online Fraud Report." (2007).

Cybersource, Inc. "Online Fraud Report—2008 Edition." (2008).

Dash, Eric. "Data Breach Could Affect Millions of TJX Shoppers." *New York Times* (January 19, 2007).

Denning, Dorothy E., and William E. Baugh. "Hiding Crimes in Cyberspace." *Information, Communication, and Society* Vol. 2, No. 3 (Autumn 1999).

Electronic Privacy Information Center (EPIC). "Cryptography and Liberty 2000. An International Survey of Encryption Policy." Washington D. C. (2000).

Ellison, Carl, and Bruce Schneier. "Ten Risks of PKI: What You're Not Being Told About Public Key Infrastructure." *Computer Security Journal,* Vol. XVI, No. 1 (Winter 2000).

eMarketer, Inc. "Identity Theft Up 50% Since 2003." (March 9, 2007).

eMarketer, Inc. (Lisa Phillips). "Banking and Bill Paying Online: Chasing Those Digital Dollars." (May, 2007).

eMarketer, Inc. "Plastic Not Fantastic For Online Buyers?" (March 13, 2008).

eMarketer, Inc. "Most identity theft occurs offline." (February 14, 2008b).

eMarketer, Inc. "Are Online Security Worries Overblown?" (August 6, 2008c).

Federal Bureau Investigation. "Over 1 Million Potential Victims of Botnet CyberCrime." (June 13, 2007).

Forrester Research, Inc. (Catherine Graeber). "EBPP Forecast: 2006 to 2011." (January 25, 2007).

Gaudin, Sharon. "Ex-UBS Systems Admin Sentenced to 97 Months In Jail." *Informationweek* (December 13, 2006).

Gaudin, Sharon. "Storm Worm Botnet Attacks Anti-Spam Firms." *InformationWeek* (September 18, 2007).

Javelin Strategy & Research. "Online Payments Forecast: Alternative Payments to Go Mainstream as Consumers Seek Security and Convenience." (September 26, 2007).

Keizer, Gregg. "Mac, Windows Clipboards Poisoned by URL Attacks." Computerworld.com (August 19, 2008).

Keizer, Gregg. "Number of Malicious E-mails Bearing Bad Links Balloons Tenfold." *Computerworld* (September 27, 2007).

Koblentz, Evan. "Gunning for the Hockey Stick." Wirelessweek.com (September 1, 2008).

Markoff, John. "VeriSign Moves to Address an Internet Security Problem." *New York Times* (February 8, 2007).

Microsoft, Inc. "2H07 Microsoft Security Intelligence Report July through December 2007." (April 2008).

National White Collar Crime Center and the Federal Bureau of Investigation. "Internet Crime Complaint Center 2007 Internet Crime Report." (2008).

OpenDNS. "Phishtank Annual Report." (October 9, 2007).

Peretti, Kimberly. "Data Breaches: What the Underground World of 'Carding' Reveals," *Santa Clara Computer and High Technology Journal*, Vol. 25 (2008).

Regan, Keith. "Bill Me Later: The 'Frictionless' Online Payment Alternative." E-commerce-times.com (April 29, 2008).

Schwartz, John. "Fighting Crime Online: Who is in Harm's Way?" *New York Times* (February 8, 2001).

Steel, Emily. "Hackers Can Now Deliver Viruses via Web Ads," *Wall Street Journal* (July 19, 2007).

Stein, Lincoln D. *Web Security: A Step-by-Step Reference Guide.* Reading, MA: Addison-Wesley (1998).

Symantec, Inc. "Internet Security Threat Report Volume XII: April 2008." (April 2008).

Symantec, Inc. "Symantec Internet Security Threat Report. Trends for January 2007-June 2007." Volume XII (September 2007a).

Symantec, Inc. "Symantec Internet Security Threat Report. Trends for July 2006-December 2006." Volume XI (March 2007b).

Telecommunications Industry Association. "TIA's 2007 Telecommunications Market Review and Forecast." (2007).

United States Government Accountability Office. "Critical Infrastructure Protection: Department of Homeland Security Faces Challenges in Fulfilling Cybersecurity Responsibilities." (May 2005).

U.S. Census Bureau. *Statistical Abstract of the United States: 2006-2007,* Table 648. (2008).

US-CERT. "Cyber Security Bulletin SB08-252." (September 8, 2008).

US-CERT. "Vulnerability Summary for the Week of August 13, 2007," Cyber Security Bulletin SB07-232, Department of Homeland Security (August, 2007).

Vass, Lisa. "Citigroup Customer Data Leaked on LimeWire." Eweek.com (September 21, 2007).

Vijayan, Jaikumar. "Canadian Probe Finds TJX Breach Followed Wireless Hack." *Computerworld* (September 25, 2007).

Wang, Yi-Min, Ming Ma, Yuan Niu, and Hao Chen. "Spam Double-Funnel: Connecting Web Spammers with Advertisers," Microsoft Research University of California, Davis (2007).

CHAPTER 6

Adomavicius, Gediminas, and Alexander Tuzhilin. "Expert-Driven Validation of Rule-Based User Models in Personalization Applications." *Data Mining and Knowledge Discovery* (January 2001a).

Adomavicius, Gediminas, and Alexander Tuzhilin. "Using Data Mining Methods to Build Customer Profiles." *IEEE Computer* (February 2001b).

Ailawadi, K.L.; D.R. Lehmann; and S.A. Neslin. "Revenue Premium as an Outcome Measure of Brand Equity." *Journal of Marketing* (October 2003).

Akerlof, G. "The Market for 'Lemons' Quality Under Uncertainty and the Market Mechanism." *Quarterly Journal of Economics* (August 1970).

Ba, Sulin, and Paul Pavlou. "Evidence on the Effect of Trust Building Technology in Electronic Markets: Price Premiums and Buyer Behavior." *MIS Quarterly* (September 2002).

Bailey, J., and Erik Brynjolfsson. "An Exploratory Study of the Emerging Role of Electronic Intermediaries." *International Journal of Electronic Commerce* (Spring, 1997).

Bakos, J. Y., and Erik Brynjolfsson. "Bundling and Competition on the Internet: Aggregation Strategies for Information Goods." *Marketing Science* (January 2000).

Baye, Michael R.; John Morgan; and Patrick Scholten. "Price Dispersion in the Small and in the Large: Evidence from an Internet Price Comparison Site." Nash-equilibrium. com, (August 2002a).

Baye, Michael R.; John Morgan; and Patrick Scholten. "The Value of Information in an Online Consumer Market." *Journal of Public Policy and Marketing* (August 2002b).

Bell, David R. and Sangyoung Song. "Social Contagion and Trial on the Internet: Evidence from Online Grocery Retailing." Unpublished paper. The Wharton School, University of

Pennsylvania (May 12, 2004).

Berg, Julie, John Matthews, and Constance O'Hare, "Measuring Brand Health to Improve Top Line Performance." *MIT Sloan Management Review* (Fall 2007).

BIGresearch and Retail Advertising and Marketing Association. "Simultaneous Media Usage Study." (March 14, 2008).

Brohan, Mark. "Customer Driven." *Internet Retailer* (August 2008).

Brynjolfsson, Erik, and M. D. Smith. "Frictionless Commerce? A Comparison of Internet and Conventional Retailer." *Management Science* (April 2000).

Brynjolfsson, Erik; Michael D. Smith; and Yu Hu. "Consumer Surplus in the Digital Economy: Estimating the Value of Increased Product Variety at Online Booksellers." Working Paper, *Information, Operations, and Management Sciences Research Seminar Series,* Stern School of Business (April 17, 2003).

Burns, Enid. "Intel's Web Spend Mandate Could Mean Big Bucks for Online." ClickZ Network (October 18, 2007).

Business Week. "Global Brand Scorecard: The 100 Top Brands." (2007).

Carpenter, Phil. *eBrands: Building an Internet Business at Breakneck Speed.* Cambridge MA: Harvard Business School Press (2000).

Chan, P. K. "A Non-Invasive Learning Approach to Building Web User Profiles." In *Proceedings of ACM SIGKDD International Conference* (1999).

Clay, K.; K. Ramayya; and E. Wolff. "Retail Strategies on the Web: Price and Non-Price Competition in the On Line Book Industry." Working Paper, *MIT E-commerce Forum* (1999).

Compaq, Inc. "Compaq White Paper." Compaq.com (November 1998).

Corritore, C.L., B. Kracher, S. Wiedenbeck, "On-line trust: concepts, evolving themes, a model," *International Journal of Human-Computer Studies* (2006).

Cross, Robert. "Launching the Revenue Rocket: How Revenue Management Can Work For Your Business." *Cornell Hotel and Restaurant Administration Quarterly* (April, 1997).

Dodson, David. "Minority Groups' Share of $10 Trillion U.S. Consumer Market Is Growing Steadily." Terry College of Business, University of Georgia (July 31, 2007).

Ellison, Sarah. "Web-Brand Study Says Awareness Isn't Trust." *Wall Street Journal* (June 7, 2000).

eMarketer, Inc. (Jeffrey Grau). "US Retail E-Commerce." (May 2008a).

eMarketer, Inc. (Lisa Phillips). "US Online Population." (February 2008b).

eMarketer, Inc. "Online Sales by Top 500 US Retail Web Sites, by Product Category, 2007." (2008c).

eMarketer, Inc. "US Internet Users Who Know How to Delete Cookies Effectively, 2005-2008." (August 7, 2008d).

eMarketer, Inc. (Debra Williamson). "B2B Marketing in Social Networks." (August 2008e).

eMarketer, Inc. "Media that Influence Online Searchers by US Adult Internet Users, by Age, December 2007." (May 14, 2008f).

eMarketer, Inc. "Multitasking Consumers." (February 2007a).

eMarketer, Inc. "US Country Overview." (October 2007b).

eMarketer, Inc. (Jeffrey Grau). "US Retail E-Commerce: Entering the MultiChannel Era." (May 2007c).

eMarketer, Inc., "Average Number of First-Party and Third-Party Cookies Preserved vs. Reset on US Household Internet Computers." (June 2007d).

eMarketer, Inc. (Debra Williamson). "Word of Mouth Marketing." (June 2007e).

Evans, P., and T. S. Wurster. "Getting Real About Virtual Commerce." *Harvard Business Review* (November-December 1999).

Fawcett, Tom, and Foster Provost. "Adaptive Fraud Detection." *Data Mining and Knowledge Discovery* (1997).

Fawcett, Tom, and Foster Provost. "Combining Data Mining and Machine Learning for Effective User Profiling." In *Proceedings of the Second International Conference on Knowledge Discovery and Data Mining* (1996).

Feldwick, Paul. "What Is Brand Equity Anyway, and How Do You Measure It?" *Journal of the Market Research Society* (April 1996).

Forrester Research, Inc. "Designing Transactive Content." (February 1998).

Forrester Research, Inc. "Transactive Content." (October 1997).

Godin, Seth. *Permission Marketing.* New York: Simon & Schuster (1999).

Golder, Peter. "What History Teaches Us About the Endurance of Brands." *Stern Business* (Fall 2000).

Gulati, Ranjay, and Jason Garino. "Getting the Right Mix of Bricks and Clicks." *Harvard Business Review* (May-June 2000).

Internet Retailer. "E-retailers Face Tough Challenges

in Wooing Store Shoppers, New Study Says." (July 13, 2006).

Internet Retailer. "Top 500 Guide 2008 Edition." (2008).

Kim, D. and I. Benbasat. "The Effects of Trust-Assuring Arguments on Consumer Trust in Internet Stores," *Information Systems Research* (2006).

Kim, D. and I. Benbasat. "Designs for Effective Implementation of Trust Assurances in Internet Stores," *Communications of the ACM* (July 2007).

Kotler, Philip, and Gary Armstrong. *Principles of Marketing,* 12th Edition. Upper Saddle River, NJ: Prentice Hall (2008).

Kraemer, Kenneth L.; Jason Dedrick; and Sandra Yamashiro. "Refining and Extending the Business Model With Information Technology: Dell Computer Corporation." *The Information Society* (January-March 2000).

Lohse, L. G., G. Bellman, and E. J. Johnson. "Consumer Buying Behavior on the Internet: Findings from Panel Data." *Journal of Interactive Marketing* (Winter 2000).

Mishra, D. P., J. B. Heide, and S. G. Cort. "Information Asymmetry and Levels of Agency Relationships." *Journal of Marketing Research.* (1998).

Nie, Norman, and Lutz Erbring. "Internet and Society: A Preliminary Report." *Stanford Institute for the Quantitative Study of Society* (February 17, 2000).

Pavlou, Paul. "Institution-Based Trust in Interorganizational Exchange Relationships: The Role of Online B2B Marketplaces on Trust Formation." *Journal of Strategic Information Systems* (2002).

Pew Internet & American Life Project. "May-June 2005 Tracking Survey." (August 9, 2005a).

Pew Internet & American Life Project (Amanda Lenhart, Mary Madden and Paul Hitlin). "Teens and Technology." (July 27, 2005b).

Pew Internet & American Life Project (John B. Horrigan). "Home Broadband Adoption 2008." (July 2, 2008).

Pew Internet & American Life Project. "Daily Internet Activities." (February 15, 2008a).

Pew Internet & American Life Project. "Demographics of Internet Users." (July 22, 2008b).

Rayport, J. F., and J. J. Sviokla. "Exploiting the Virtual Value Chain." *Harvard Business Review* (November-December 1995).

Reichheld, Frederick F., and Phil Schefter. "ELoyalty: Your Secret Weapon on the Web." *Harvard Business Review* (July-August 2000).

Rodgers, Zachary. "Measuring Blog Marketing." Clickz.com (January 12, 2005).

Saunders, Peter Lee, and Andrea Chester. "Shyness and the Internet: Social Problem or Panacea?" Division of Psychology, School of Health Sciences, RMIT University, City Campus, Melbourne, Victoria, Australia (2008).

Scholten, Patrick, and S. Adam Smith. "Price Dispersion Then and Now: Evidence from Retail and E-tail Markets." Nash-equilibrium.com. (July 2002).

Shapiro, Carl, and Hal Varian. *Information Rules: A Strategic Guide to the Network Economy.* Cambridge, MA: Harvard Business School Press (1999).

Shapiro, Carl, and Hal Varian. "Versioning: The Smart Way to Sell Information." *Harvard Business Review* (November-December 1998).

Shklovski, Irina; Sara Kiesler, and Robert Kraut. "The Internet and Social Interaction: A Meta-analysis and Critique of Studies, 1995-2003." Carnegie Mellon University (2004).

Sinha, Indrajit. "Cost Transparency: The Net's Real Threat to Prices and Brands." *Harvard Business Review* (March-April 2000).

Smith, M. D.; J. Bailey; and E. Brynjolfsson. "Understanding Digital Markets: Review and Assessment," in E. Brynjolfsson and B. Kahin (eds.), *Understanding the Digital Economy.* Cambridge, MA: MIT Press (1999).

Starbuck, William, and Paul C. Nystrom. "Why Many Firms Run Into Crises, and Why Some Survive." Working Paper. Stern School of Business, Management and Organizational Behavior (1997).

Sterling Commerce and Deloitte Consulting. "What Consumers Want in Their Shopping Experience." (August 2007).

Tedeschi, Bob. "Web Marketers Get Personal." *New York Times* (June 28, 2004).

Teece, David J. "Profiting from Technological Innovation: Implications for Integration, Collaboration, Licensing and Public Policy." Research Policy, 15 (1986).

U.S. Census Bureau. "Minority Population Tops 100 Million." (May 17, 2007).

U.S.C Annenberg School Center for the Digital Future, "The Digital Future Report, Surveying the Digital Future, Year Four, Ten Years, Ten

Trends." (September, 2004).

Van den Poel, Dirk and Wouter Buckinx. "Predicting Online Purchasing Behavior." *European Journal of Operations Research*, Vol. 166, Issue 2 (2005).

von Hippel, Eric. *The Sources of Innovation.* Oxford University Press, New York (1994).

von Hippel, Eric. *Democratizing Innovation.* MIT Press, Cambridge (2005).

Wigand, R. T., and R. I. Benjamin. "Electronic Commerce: Effects on Electronic Markets." *Journal of Computer Mediated Communication* (December 1995).

Williamson, O. E. *The Economic Institutions of Capitalism.* New York: Free Press (1985).

Wolfinbarger, Mary, and Mary Gilly. "Shopping Online for Freedom, Control and Fun." *California Management Review* (Winter 2001).

CHAPTER 7

Anderson, Eric; Erik Brynjolfsson, Yu Hu, and Duncan Simester, "Understanding the Impact of Marketing Actions in Traditional Channels on the Internet: Evidence From a Large Field Experiment." (January 2005).

Battelle, John. "Search Blog." Battellemedia.com/archives/000063.php (November 13, 2003).

Beval Saddlery Ltd. "Products." Beval.com (February 2006).

Briggs, Rex. "How Internet Advertising Works." ESO-MAR "Net Effects" Conference, London. (February 22, 1999).

Click Forensics. "Industry Click Fraud Rate Holds at 16.2 Percent in Second Quarter 2008." (July 22, 2008).

comScore, Inc. "YouTube Draws 5 Billion U.S. Online Video Views in July 2008." (September 10, 2008).

Consumer Reports WebWatch. "Searching for Disclosure: How Search Engines Alert Consumers to the Presence of Advertising in Search Results." Consumerwebwatch.org (November 2004).

Consumer Reports Web Watch. "Still in Search of Disclosure: Re-evaluating How Search Engines Explain the Presence of Advertising in Search Results." (June 9, 2005).

Davern, Michael J.; Dov Te'eni; and Jae Yun Moon. "Information Environments and Human Behavior Over Time: From Initial Preferences to Mature Usage." Department of Information Systems, Stern School of Business, New York University (2001).

Direct Marketing Association (DMA). "State of the Catalog Industry, 2008 Edition." (August 27, 2008).

Doubleclick. "Video Ad Benchmarks: Average Campaign Performance." (February 2007a).

Doubleclick. "DoubleClick Performics Q1 Search Trend Report." (2007b).

Dynamic Logic. "Video Ads Achieve Greater Branding Impact With Fewer Impressions." *Beyond the Click: Insights from Marketing Effectiveness Research* (December 2004).

Elliot, Stuart. "Movies, TV and Magazines Work Together." *New York Times,* (November 5, 2007).

Ellison, Nicole, Charles Steinfeld, and Cliff Lampe. "Spatially Bounded Online Social Networks and Social Capital: The Role of Facebook." Department of Telecommunications, Information Studies, and Media, Michigan State University. Paper presented at the Annual Conference of the International Communication Association, Dresden, Germany (June 2006).

eMarketer, Inc. "eMarketer Sees Even Faster Online Ad Growth in 2005." (May 2, 2005a).

eMarketer, Inc. (David Hallerman). "Ad Spending Trends: The Internet and Other Media." (October 2005b).

eMarketer, Inc. "Catalogs Continue to Shift Online." (April 24, 2006).

eMarketer, Inc. (David Hallerman). "US Advertising Spending." (November 2007a).

eMarketer, Inc. (David Hallerman). "E-Mail Marketing." (September 2007b).

eMarketer, Inc. (Jeffrey Grau). "US Retail E-commerce: Entering the Multi-Channel Era." (May, 2007c).

eMarketer, Inc. (Debra A. Williamson) "Social Network Marketing: Ad Spending and Usage." (December 2007d).

eMarketer, Inc. (David Hallerman) "U.S. Online Advertising: Resilient in a Rough Economy." (March 2008a.)

eMarketer, Inc. "Top 10 Online Video Sites Properties Among U.S Internet Users. Ranked by Unique Viewers, July 2008." (September 2008b).

eMarketer, Inc. (David Hallerman) "Search Engine Marketing: User and Spending Trends." (January 2008c).

eMarketer, Inc. "US Multichannel Retailer Sales, by Channel, 2007 & 2008 (% of total sales)." (August 2008d).

eMarketer, Inc. (Paul Verna) "The Blogosphere: Mass Movement From the Grass Roots." (May 2008e).

eMarketer, Inc. (David Hallerman) "Behavioral Targeting: Marketing Trends." (June 2008f).

eMarketer, Inc. "Shopping Cart Abandonment Rises." (May 29, 2008g).

eMarketer, Inc. "US E-mail Marketing Click Rates, 2008." (April, 2008h).

Fair Isaac Corporation. "New Fair Isaac Research Indicates Click Fraud is Potentially Large Problem in Parts of Search Engine Advertising." (May 18, 2007).

Flanigan, Andrew, and Miriam J. Metzger. "The role of site features, user attributes, and information verification behaviors on the perceived credibility of web-based information." *New Media & Society*, Vol. 9, No. 2 (2007)

Fogg, B.J., Cathey Soohoo, David Danielson, Leslie Marable, Julliane Stanford, and Ellen Tauber. "How Do Users Evaluate the Credibility of Web Sites? A Study with Over 2,500 Participants." Proceedings of DUX2003, Designing for User Experiences. (2003).

Hotchkiss, Gord , Tracy Sherman, Rick Tobin, Cory Bates and Krista Brown. "Search Engine Results 2010." Enquiroresearch.com (September, 2007).

Interactive Advertising Bureau. "IAB Standards and Guidelines." Iab.net (September 2008).

Interactive Advertising Bureau (IAB)/ PricewaterhouseCoopers. "IAB Internet Advertising Revenue Report 2007 Full Year Results." (May 23, 2008).

Internet Retailer. "Top 500 Guide 2008 Edition." (2008).

Lohse, L. G.; G. Bellman; and E. J. Johnson. "Consumer Buying Behavior on the Internet: Findings from Panel Data." *Journal of Interactive Marketing* (Winter 2000).

McKinsey & Company. "How Companies Are Marketing Online: A McKinsey Global Survey." McKinsey Quarterly." (September 2007).

MessageLabs. "MessageLabs Intelligence Report: May 2008." (May 2008).

National Conference of State Legislatures. "State Laws Relating to Unsolicited Commercial of Bulk E-mail (SPAM)." (September 14, 2008).

Nielsen, Jakob. "F-Shaped Pattern For Reading Web Content, Nielsen's Alertbox." (April 17, 2006).

Novak, T. P.; D. L. Hoffman; and Y. F. Yung. "Measuring the Customer Experience in Online Environments: A Structural Modeling Approach." *Marketing Science* (Winter, 2000).

Pew Internet & American Life Project. "Daily Internet Activities." (February 15, 2008).

Pew Internet & American Life Project (Lee Rainie). "Search Engine Use November 2005." (November 2005).

Shrestha, Sav and Kelsi LenzEye. "Gaze Patterns while Searching vs. Browsing a Website." Software Usability Research Laboratory, Department of Psychology, Wichita State University, Wichita, KS 67260-0034 (September, 2007).

Story, Louise. "It's an Ad, Ad, Ad World." *New York Times* (August 6, 2007).

Sullivan, Danny. "FTC Recommends Disclosure to Search Engines." Searchenginewatch.com (February 13, 2003).

Symantec. "Symantec Global Internet Security Threat Report. Trends for July — December 2007." Volume XIII (April 2008).

Veronis Suhler Stevenson. "Communications Industry Forecast 2007-2011." (August 2007).

Walker, Marlon A. "Online Service Lags at Big Firms." *Wall Street Journal* (July 1, 2004).

Weber, Thomas. "A 'Sticky' Situation: How a Web Buzzword Spun Out of Control." *Wall Street Journal* (March 5, 2001).

CHAPTER 8

Abrams, Jim. "House Act to Block Cigarette Smugglers, Stop Internet Sales to Children." *Newsday*, (September 10, 2008).

Apple Computer, Inc. v. Microsoft Corp. 709 F. Supp. 925, 926 (N. D. Cal. 1989); 799 F. Supp. 1006, 1017 (N. D. Cal., 1992); 35 F. 3d 1435 (9th Cir.); cert. denied, 63 U. S. L. W. 3518 (U.S., Feb. 21, 1995) (No. 94-1121).

Associated Press. "Google Settles Final Piece of Geico Case." BizReport.com (September 8, 2005).

Audi AG and Volkswagen of America, Inc. v. Bob D'Amato No. 05-2359, 6th Circuit (November 27, 2006).

Bernina of America, Inc. v. Fashion Fabrics Int'l., Inc. 2001 U. S. Dist. LEXIS 1211 (N. D. Ill., Feb. 8, 2001).

Broache, Anne. "Renewing the Push to Collect Net Taxes." CNETnews.com (September 9, 2005).

Brown Bag vs. Symantec Corp., 960 F. 2d 1465 (9th Cir. 1992).

Chiappetta, Vincent. "Defining the Proper Scope of Internet Patents: If We Don't Know Where We Want to Go, We're Unlikely to Get There." Michigan Telecommunications Technology Law Review (May 2001).

Clifford, Stephanie. "Web Privacy on the Radar in Congress." *New York Times* (August 10, 2008).

Diamond v. Chakrabarty, 447 US 303 (1980).

Dueker, Kenneth Sutherlin. "Trademark Law Lost in Cyberspace: Trademark Protection for Internet Addresses." *Harvard Journal of Law and Technology* (Summer 1996).

E. & J. Gallo Winery v. Spider Webs Ltd. 129 F. Supp. 2d 1033 (S.D. Tex., 2001) aff'd 286 F. 3d 270 (5th Cir., 2002).

Elgin, Ben and Bruce Einhorn. "The Great Firewall of China." *BusinessWeek* (January 12, 2006).

eMarketer, Inc. (David Hallerman) "Behavioral Targeting Attitudes: The Privacy Issues." (June 2008).

eMarketer, Inc. "Some Users Distrust Search Engines." (July 23, 2007a)

eMarketer, Inc. "When Bad Ads Harm Good E-commerce." (July 3, 2007b)

eMarketer, Inc. "Online Buyers Will Pay Extra for Privacy." (June 14, 2007c)

eMarketer, Inc. "Adult Content Revenues in the US, by Segment, 2006 & 2006." (January 4, 2007d).

Federal Trade Commission. "FTC Staff Proposes Online Behavioral Advertising Privacy Principles." (December 20, 2007).

Federal Trade Commission. "Individual Reference Services: A Report to Congress." (December 1997).

Federal Trade Commission. "Privacy Online: Fair Information Practices in the Electronic Marketplace." (May 2000a).

Federal Trade Commission. "Online Profiling: A Report to Congress." (June 2000b).

Federal Trade Commission. "Privacy Online: A Report to Congress." (June 1998).

Field v. Google, Inc. 412 F.Supp. 2nd 1106 (D. Nev., 2006).

Fisher, William W. III. "The Growth of Intellectual Property: A History of the Ownership of Ideas in the United States." Law.harvard.edu/Academic_Affairs/coursepages/tfisher/iphistory.html (1999).

Ford Motor Co. v. Lapertosa 2001 U. S. Dist. LEXIS 253 (E. D. Mich. Jan. 3, 2001).

Frackman, Andrews; Claudia Ray, and Rebecca C. Martin. Internet and Online Privacy: A Legal and Business Guide ALM Publishing (2002).

Gentile, Gary. "Companies Set Guidelines on Copyrighted Video." *USA Today* (October 18, 2007).

Google, Inc. v. American Blind & Wallpaper Factory, Inc. Case No. 03-5340 JF (RS) (N.D. Cal., April 18, 2007).

Government Employees Insurance Company v. Google, Inc. Civ. Action No. 1:04cv507 (E.D. VA, December 15, 2004).

Greenhouse, Linda. "20 Year Extension of Existing Copyrights Is Upheld." *New York Times* (January 16, 2003a).

Greenhouse, Linda. "Justices Back Law to Make Libraries Use Internet Filters." *New York Times* (June 24, 2003b).

Greenhouse, Linda. "Supreme Court Upholds Child Pornography Law." *New York Times* (May 20, 2008).

Gross, Grant. "House Panel Votes to Extend Net Tax Ban." *InfoWorld* (October 11, 2007).

Hafner, Katie and Matt Richtel. "Google Resists U.S. Subpoena of Search Data." *New York Times* (January 20, 2006).

Hansell, Saul. "Experts Contend Travel Sites May Skimp on Hotel Taxes." *New York Times* (December 23, 2002).

Hansell, Saul and Eric Lichtblau. "U.S. Wants Internet Companies to Keep Web-Surfing Records." *New York Times* (June 2006).

Harmon, Amy. "Pondering Value of Copyright vs. Innovation." *New York Times* (March 3, 2003).

Helft, Miguel and Geraldine Fabrikant. "Viacom Sues Google Over Video Clips on Its Sharing Web Site." *New York Times* (March 14, 2007).

Ho, Victoria. "China Accused of Rerouting Search Traffic to Baidu." CNETNews.com (October 22, 2007).

Hoofnagle, Chris Jay. "Privacy Self-Regulation: A Decade of Disappointment." Electronic Privacy Information Center (Epic.org) (March 4, 2005).

Kelly v. ArribaSoft. 336 F3rd 811 (CA 9th, 2003).

Kravets, David. "File Sharing Lawsuits at a Crossroads, After 5 Years of RIAA Litigation." *Wired Magazine* (September 04, 2008).

Laudon, Kenneth. "Markets and Privacy." *Communications of the ACM* (September 1996).

Liedtke, Michael. "Microsoft, Yahoo Tweak Privacy Policies." *USA Today* (July 23, 2007).

Markoff, John. "Control the Internet? A Futile Pursuit, Some Say." *New York Times* (Nvember 14, 2005).

McBride, Sarah. "For Grokster, It's the Day the Music Died." *Wall Street Journal* (November 8, 2005).

McMillan, Robert. "Porn Typosquatter Fined Again by FTC." *InfoWorld* (October 16, 2007).

Miller, John W. and Christopher Rhoads, "U.S. Fights to Keep Control Of Global Internet Oversight." *Wall Street Journal* (November 16, 2005).

Moore, Matt. "ICANN Rejects Creation of ".XXX" Domain." *USA Today* (March 30, 2007).

Nakashima, Ellen. "NebuAd Halts Plans for Web Tracking." *Washington Post* (September 4, 2008).

Nash, David B. "Orderly Expansion of the International Top-Level Domains: Concurrent Trademark Users Need a Way Out of the Internet Trademark Quagmire." *The John Marshall Journal of Computer and Information Law* Vol. 15, No. 3 (1997).

Nettis Environment Ltd. v. IWI, Inc. 46 F. Supp. 2d 722 (N. D. Ohio 1999).

Network Advertising Initiative. "Participating Networks." (September 2008).

Nissan Motor Co., Ltd. v. Nissan Computer Corp. 289 F. Supp. 2d 1154 (C. D. Cal.), aff'd, 2000 U. S. App. LEXIS 33937 (9th Cir. Dec. 26, 2000).

PaineWebber Inc. v. Fortuny, Civ. A. No. 99-0456-A (E. D. Va. Apr. 9, 1999).

Parry, Wayne. "N.J. Judge Hears Challenge to Online Gambling Restrictions." *Associated Press* (September 26, 2007).

Perfect 10, Inc. v. Amazon.com, Inc. 487 F3rd 701 (CA 9th, 2007).

Pew Internet & American Life Project. "Daily Internet Activities." (February 15, 2008).

Pfanner, Eric. "Online Gambling Shares Plunge on Passage of U.S. Crackdown Law." *New York Times* (October 3, 2006).

Playboy Enterprises, Inc. v. Global Site Designs, Inc. 1999 WL 311707 (S. D. Fla. May 15, 1999).

Playboy Enterprises, Inc. v. Netscape Communications, Inc. 354 F. 3rd 1020 (9th Cir., 2004).

Seidenberg, Steve. "Keyword Protection." *Insidecounsel* (August 2007)

Sharma, Amol, and Don Clark. "Tech Guru Riles the Industry By Seeking Huge Patent Fees." *Wall Street Journal* (September 17, 2008).

Singel, Ryan. "Net Censorship Law Struck Down Again." Wired.com (July 22, 2008).

State Street Bank & Trust Co. v. Signature Financial Group, 149 F. 3d 1368 (1998).

Story, Louise. "F.T.C. to Review Online Ads and Privacy." *New York Times* (November 1, 2007a).

Story, Louise. "F.T.C. Member Vows Tighter Controls of Online Ads." *New York Times* (November 2, 2007b).

Swartz, Jon. "YouTube Gets Media Providers' Help Foiling Piracy." *USA Today* (October 15, 2007).

Swisher, Kara. "E-tailers Faced Death; Now Can They Handle Taxes?" *New York Times* (April 9, 2001).

Takenaka, Toshiko. "International and Comparative Law Perspective on Internet Patents." *Michigan Telecommunications Technology Law Review* (May 15, 2001).

Tehrani, Rich. "Behavioral Targeting at Google." VoIP Blog-Tehrani.com (August 1, 2007).

Thurm, Scott. "The Ultimate Weapon: It's the Patent." *Wall Street Journal* (April 17, 2000a).

Ticketmaster v. Tickets.com. 2000 U.S. Dist. Lexis 4553 (C.D. Cal., August 2000).

TRUSTe. "Consumers Have False Sense of Security About Online Privacy—Actions Inconsistent With Attitudes." Truste.org (December 6, 2006).

United States Copyright Office. "Digital Millennium Copyright Act of 1998: U.S. Copyright Office Summary." (December 1998).

United States Department of Health, Education and Welfare (US-DHEW). Records, Computers and Rights of Citizens. Cambridge, MA: MIT Press (1973).

United States Patent and Trademark Office. "Class 705 Application Filing and Patents Issued Data." (November 2007).

Van Kirk, Andrew. "Platform for Privacy Preferences (P3P): Privacy Without Teeth." (March 10, 2005).

Varian, Hal, "Forget Taxing Internet Sales. In Fact, Just Forget Sales Taxes Altogether." *New York Times* (March 8, 2001).

Vaughan, Sandra. "Evolution of Employee Monitoring Stretches Far Beyond Email." Scmagazineus.com (February 21, 2007).

The Washington Post, et al. v. TotalNews, Inc., et al. S.D.N.Y, Civil Action Number 97-1190. (February 1997).

Winston, Brian. *Media Technology and Society: A History From the Telegraph to the Internet.* Routledge (1998).

W3C Platform for Privacy Preferences Initiative." P3P 1. 0: A New Standard in Online Privacy." Platform for Privacy Preferences Initiative. (June 16, 2003).

Zeller, Tom, Jr. "Your Life As An Open Book." *New York Times* (August 12, 2006).

CHAPTER 9

AccuQuote. "AccuQuote.com, a Leading Provider of Affordable Term Life Insurance Quotes, Offers Advice on Using Life Insurance as an Investment." (May 19, 2008).

Amazon.com, Inc. Amazon.com Inc. Form 10-K for the fiscal year ended December 31, 2007, filed with the Securities and Exchange Commission (February 11, 2008).

Booz Allen Hamilton. "Internet is the Primary Hiring Source for Employers." (March 6, 2006).

Brohan, Mark. "Follow the Leader." *Internet Retailer* (September 2007).

Brown, Jeffrey, and Austan Goolsbee. "Does the Internet Make Markets More Competitive? Evidence from the Life Insurance Industry." John F. Kennedy School of Government, Harvard University. Research Working Paper RWP00-007 (2000).

Brynjolfsson, Erik; Astrid Andrea Dick and Michael D. Smith. "Search and Product Differentiation at an Internet Shopbot," Center for eBusiness@MIT (December, 2004).

California Association of Realtors. "2008 Survey of California Home Buyers." (September 11, 2008).

Careerbuilder.com. "CareerBuilder Launching Video Resumes for Job Seekers and Branding Videos for Employers." (April 18, 2007a).

Careerbuilder.com. "Careerbuilder.com Builds Job Matching Applications on Facebook Platform." (August 28, 2007b).

Center for Realtor Technology, National Association of Realtors. "2007 Technology Survey." (2007).

Computer Associates. "2008 Security and Privacy Survey." (July 2008).

comScore, Inc. "2007 Online Automobile Insurance Report." (April 12, 2007).

comScore, Inc. "comScore Reports the Number of Auto Insurance Policies Purchased Online Exceeded 2 Million In 2007." (March 12, 2008).

Dell Inc. Form 10-K for the fiscal year ended February 1, 2008, filed with the Securities and Exchange Commission (March 31, 2008).

eMarketer, Inc. (Jeffrey Grau). "E-commerce in the US: Retail Trends." (May 2005a).

eMarketer, Inc. (Jeffrey Grau). "Online Travel Worldwide." (December 2005b).

eMarketer, Inc. (Jeffrey Grau). "Career Planning and Job Hunting Online." (December 2006).

eMarketer, Inc. "Banking and Bill Paying Online: Chasing Those Digital Dollars." (May 2007a).

eMarketer, Inc. "Online Ads Build Mortgage Awareness." (July 19, 2007b).

eMarketer, Inc. (Jeffrey Grau). "U.S. Online Travel: The Threat of Commoditization." (April 2007c).

eMarketer, Inc. "Video Resumes Get Attention." (April 3, 2007d).

eMarketer, Inc. "Social Networking for Jobs." (April 25, 2007e).

eMarketer, Inc. (Jeffrey Grau). "US Retail E-commerce: Slower But Still Steady Growth." (May 27, 2008a).

eMarketer, Inc. "Top 10 Online Trading Sites in the US, Ranked by Unique Visitors, July 2008." (July 2008b).

eMarketer, Inc. (Jeffrey Grau). "US Online Travel: Planning and Booking." (August 2008c).

eMarketer, Inc. "Majority of 2007 Travel Booked Online." (January 15, 2008d).

eMarketer, Inc. "Top 10 Website Categories among US Internet Users Ranked by Growth in Unique Visitors, June & July 2008." (August 15, 2008e).

Evans, Philip, and Thomas S. Wurster. *Blown to Bits: How the New Economics of Information Transforms Strategy.* Cambridge, MA: Harvard Business School Press (2000).

Expedia, Inc. "Report on Form 10-K for the fiscal year ended December 31, 2007, filed with the Securities and Exchange Commission." (February 21, 2008).

Forrester Research, Inc. "The State of Retailing Online 2008" (April 2008).

Forrester Research, Inc. (Bill Doyle). "US Online Trading Forecast: 2006-2011." (February 1, 2007).

Gopal, Prashant. "Real Estate Agents Expected to Collect $55 Billion in Commissions This Year." *Business Week.* (December 14, 2007).

Insweb.com. "Q3 2007 InsWeb Earnings Conference Call—Final." (October 18, 2007).

Internet Retailer. "Top 500 Guide 2008 Edition." (2008).

JC Penney Company, Inc. Report on Form 10-K for the fiscal year ended February 2, 2008 filed with the Securities and Exchange Commission (March 2008).

J.D. Power and Associates. "2007 New Autoshopper.com Study." (October 10, 2007)

Lands' End, Inc. "About Lands' End." Landsend.com (2008).

Laudon, Kenneth C., and Jane P. Laudon. *Management Information Systems: Managing the Digital Firm,* 11th edition. Upper Saddle River, NJ: Prentice Hall (2009).

MarketingCharts.com. "Top 10 Online Trading Destinations — July 2008." (July 2008).

Move.com. "About Move." (September 2008).

Nielsen/NetRatings NetView. "Top 10 Online Trading Destinations — July 2008." (July 2008)

Perkins, Broderick. "Online Mortage Shopping Today." *Realty Times* (January 23, 2004).

Pew Internet & American Life Project. "Internet Activities." (February 15, 2008)

U.S. Census Bureau. "Census Bureau Reports on Residential Vacancies and Home Ownership." (July 24, 2008b)

U. S. Census Bureau. "Census of Service Industries." (2001).

U.S. Census Bureau. *Statistical Abstract of the United States 2007-2008* (2008a).

U.S. Department of Commerce. "E-Stats, 2006 E-commerce Multi-sector Report." (May 16, 2008).

U.S. Department of Labor. Dictionary of Occupational Titles, 4th edition. (1991).

University of Southern California Annenberg School Center for the Digital Future "2008 Digital Future Report." (January 17, 2008).

Weil, Jonathon. "Securities Rules Help to Close the Earning Reports GAAP." *Wall Street Journal* (April 24, 2003).

Whitehouse, Kaja. "Just Looking, Thanks." *Wall Street Journal* (June 14, 2004).

Yodlee, Inc. "Yodlee Announces $34 Million Financing." (June 4, 2008).

CHAPTER 10

Angwin, Julia. "Newspapers Set to Jointly Sell Ads on Web Sites." *New York Times* (January 10, 2007).

Association of American Publishers. "AAP Reports Book Sales Rose to $25 Billion in 2007." (March 31, 2008).

Bivings Group, The. "American Newspapers and the Internet: Threat or Opportunity?' (July 19, 2007).

Book Industry Study Group. "ONIX Downloads & Lists." Bisg.org (January 2006).

Boxer, Sarah. "Paintings Too Perfect? The Great Optics Debate." *New York Times* (December 4, 2001).

CNET Networks, Inc. Form 10-K for the fiscal year ended December 31, 2007, filed with the Securities and Exchange Commission (February 27, 2008).

comScore, Inc. "YouTube Draws 5 Billion U.S. Online Video Views in July 2008." (September 10, 2008).

Editeur.org. "ONIX for Books."(January 2006).

eMarketer, Inc. (Ben Macklin). "Digital Downloading." (January 2007a).

eMarketer, Inc. (Paul Verna). "Online Video: Making Content Pay." (August 2007b).

eMarketer, Inc. (Paul Verna). "User Generated Content: Will Web 2.0 Pay Its Way?" (June 2007c).

eMarketer, Inc. (Lisa Phillips). "Newspapers and Magazines." (October 2007d).

eMarketer, Inc. "Select Types of Online Content Services Used by US Adult Internet Users. (August 2007e).

eMarketer, Inc. "Books Sales by Type." (2007f).

eMarketer, Inc. "Video Game Advertising." (April 2007g).

eMarketer, Inc. "Radio Trends." (August 2007h).

eMarketer, Inc. (David Hallerman) "Online Video Content." (February 2008a.)

eMarketer, Inc. "Top 10 Online Video Sites Properties Among U.S Internet Users. Ranked by Unique Viewers, July 2008." (September 2008b).

eMarketer, Inc. "US E-Book Sales." (April 2008c).

Goel, Vindu. "New Wall Street Journal Builds on Its Community of Subscribers." *New York Times* (September 15, 2008).

Grant, Peter. "What's On." *Wall Street Journal* (March 22, 2004)

Hansell, Saul. "Newspapers to Test Plan to Sell Ads on Google," New York Times, November 6, 2006.

Helft, Miguel, and Steve Lohr. "Technology; 176 Newspapers to form a Partnership With Yahoo." *New York Times* (November 20, 2006).

Jaworowski, Ken. "Words Printed on Pages Still Sell Well." *New York Times* (April 15, 2006).

Jesdahun, Anick. "Social Networking coming to Wall Journal Website." *Time Magazine* (September 15, 2008).

Mobipocket.com. "Mobipocket Creator." (January 2008).

Newspaper Association of America. "Trends and Numbers." (September 2008).

Online Publishers Association. "Web Users Now Spend Half Their Time Visiting Content, Far Outpacing Time Spent With Search." (August 13, 2007).

Pew Internet & American Life Project. "Daily Internet Activities." (February 15, 2008)

Pew Internet & American Life Project (John B. Horrigan). "The Internet as a Resource for News and Information About Science." (November 20, 2006).

U.S. Census Bureau. *Statistical Abstract of the United States 2007-2008* (2008).

CHAPTER 11

Arkes, H. R., and L. Hutzel. "The Role of Probability of Success Estimates in the Sunk Cost Effect." *Journal of Behavioral Decisionmaking* (2000).

Bailey, Brian P.; Laura J. Gurak; and Joseph Konstan, "Do You Trust Me? An Examination of Trust in Computer-Mediated Exchange," In *Human Factors and Web Development,* 2nd Edition. Mahwah, NJ: Lawrence Erlbaum (2002).

Bapna, Ravi; Paulo Goes; and Alok Gupta. "Insights and Analyses of Online Auctions." *Communications of the ACM* (November 2001).

Brynjolfsson, Erik, and Michael Smith. "Frictionless Commerce? A Comparison of Internet and Conventional Retailers." *Management Science* (April 2000).

Compete.com. "Compete's Top 10 Sites Ranked by Unique Visitors August 2008." (September 2008).

Dholakia, Utpal, and Kerry Soltysinski. "Coveted or

Overlooked? The Psychology of Bidding for Comparable Listings in Digital Auctions." *Marketing Letters* (2001).

eBay, Inc. Report on Form 10-K for the fiscal year ended December 31, 2007, filed with the Securities and Exchange Commission (February 29, 2008).

eMarketer, Inc. "US Online Auction Spending 2005-2010 (in billions)." (October 6, 2005).

eMarketer, Inc. (Debra Williamson). "Social Network Ad Spending Keeps Rising." (August 13, 2007).

eMarketer, Inc. (Debra Williamson). "Social Network Marketing." (December 2007).

eMarketer, Inc. "US B2B and Total Online Social Network Advertising Spending, 2007-2012." (August 8, 2008a).

eMarketer, Inc. "US Online Social Network Advertising Spending, by Venue, 2007 & 2008." (May 9, 2008b).

Federal Trade Commission. "FTC Releases List of Top Consumer Fraud Complaints in 2007." (February 13, 2008).

Hafner, Katie. "The Epic Saga of The Well: The World's Most Influential Online Community (and It's Not AOL)." *Wired* (May 1997).

Hagel, John III, and Arthur G. Armstrong. *Net Gain: Expanding Markets Through Virtual Communities.* Cambridge, MA: Harvard Business School Press (1997).

Hanson, Ward, and D. S. Putler. "Hits and Misses: Herd Behavior and Online Product Popularity." *Marketing Letters* (1996).

Hillery, George A. "Definitions of Community: Areas of Agreement." *Rural Sociology* (1955).

Hiltzik, Michael. *Dealers of Lightning: Xerox PARC and the Dawn of the Computer Age.* New York: Harper Collins (1999).

Hitwise.com. "Facebook Visits Up 50 Percent Year over Year." (September 25, 2008).

Jupiter Research. (Jared Blank, Lead Analyst). "Personal Value Pricing." (June 6, 2001).

Kambil, Ajit, and Eric van Heck. "Competition in the Dutch Flower Market." New York University, Stern School of Business, Center for Information Systems Research (1996).

Kiesler, Sara. "The Hidden Messages in Computer Networks." *Harvard Business Review* (January-February 1986).

Kiesler, Sara; Jane Siegel; and Timothy W. McGuire. "Social Psychological Aspects of Computer-Mediated Communication." *American Psychologist* (October 1984).

Kollock, Peter. "The Production of Trust in Online Markets" In *Advances in Group Processes* (Vol 16) edited by E. J. Lawler, M. Macy, S. Thyne and H. A. Walker. Greenwich, CT: JAI Press (1999).

Krishnamurthy, Sandeep. "An Empirical Study of the Causal Antecedents of Customer Confidence in ETailers." *First Monday* (January 2001).

Laudon, Kenneth C. and Jane P. Laudon. *Management Information Systems: Managing the Digital Firm.* 11th edition. Upper Saddle River, NJ, Prentice Hall (2009).

Lee, H. G.; J. C. Westland; and S. Hong. "The Impact of Electronic Marketplaces on Product Prices: An Empirical Study of Aucnet." *International Journal of Electronic Commerce* (Winter 1999-2000).

Marketingcharts.com "Top 10 Social Networking Websites & Forums." (August 2008).

McAfee R., and John McMillan. "Auctions and Bidding." *Journal of Economic Literature* (June 1987).

Milogram, Paul R. "Auctions and Bidding: A Primer." *Journal of Economic Perspectives* (Summer 1989).

Morgan Stanley Dean Witter. "The B2B Internet Report: Collaborative Commerce." (April 2000).

National White Collar Crime Center/Federal Bureau of Investigation. "Internet Crime Report 2007." National White Collar Crime Center (2008).

Nikander, Pekka, and Kristina Karvonen. "Users and Trust in Cyberspace." In the *Proceedings of Cambridge Security Protocols Workshop 2000, April 3-5, 2000,* Cambridge University (2002).

Parkes, David C., and Lyle Ungar. "Iterative Combinatorial Auctions: Theory and Practice." Proceedings of the 17th National Conference on Artificial Intelligence (AAAI-00) (2000).

Pew Internet & American Life Report. "Daily Internet Activities, 2008." (February 15, 2008).

Rheingold, Howard. *Hosting Web Communities.* New York: John Wiley and Sons (1998). Also see Rheingold.com for more recent articles by Rheingold.

Rheingold, Howard. *The Virtual Community.* Cambridge MA: MIT Press (1993).

Stanford Persuasive Technology Lab and Makovsky & Company. "Stanford-Makovsky Web Credibility Study 2002." Stanford Persuasive Technology Lab. (Spring 2002).

Vakrat, Yaniv, and Abraham Seidmann. "Can Online Auctions Beat Online Catalogs?" Proceedings of the 20th Conference on Information Systems (December 1999).

Vakrat, Yaniv, and Abraham Seidmann. "Analysis and Design Models for Online Auctions." Proceedings of the 4th Informs Conference on Information Systems and Technology. (May

1998).

Vickrey, William. "Counterspeculation, Auctions and Competitive Sealed Tenders." *Journal of Finance* (March 1961).

Yahoo! Inc. Form 10-K for the fiscal year ended December 31, 2007, filed with the Securities and Exchange Commission (February 27, 2008).

CHAPTER 12

ADX Corporation. "Ace Hardware Expands Relationship with ADX for Improved Supply Chain Integration." (January 12, 2004).

Agentrics. "About Agentrics." (September 2008).

Ariba Inc. "Customers Overview: General Dynamics." Ariba.com (2007a).

Ariba, Inc. Form 10-K for the fiscal year ended September 30, 2007, filed with the Securities and Exchange Commission (November 15, 2007b).

Devine, Dennis A.; Christopher B. Dugan; Mikolaus D. Semaca; and Kevin J. Speicher. "Building Enduring Consortia." *McKinsey Quarterly* (2001).

eMarketer, Inc. (Steve Butler). "E-commerce Trade and B2B Exchanges." (July 2004).

Exostar LLC. "Exostar at a Glance." (September 2008).

Farms.com. "About Us." (September 2008).

Fuscaldo, Donna. "Building a Market. The Construction Industry Had Little Interest in Online Exchanges. Collaboration Services May Get Better Results." *Wall Street Journal* (April 15, 2002).

Gleason, Karen. "CPFR At Ace Hardware." (2003).

Global Wine & Spirits. "About Us." Globalwinespirits.com (September 2008).

Group Dekko. "About Us." (September 2008).

Hannon, David. "Bring E-Sourcing to a Decentralized Spend." *Purchasing* (May 15, 2003).

Hewlett-Packard. "HP.com Business to Business." Hp.com (September 2008).

IBM. "Chrysler Manages a Nationwide Supply Chain of Vendors." Ibm.com (undated).

IBM. "Group Dekko Harnesses Greater Efficiency Through Server Consolidation." IBM Case Study. Ibm.com (March 25, 2005).

IBM. "Group Dekko Collaborating With Customers on Product Development." IBM Case Study. Ibm.com (June 2003).

Inventory Locator Service LLC. ILSmart.com Home Page (September 2008).

Jupiter Media Metrix. (Jon Gibs, Lead Analyst). "B-to-B Supplier Strategies." (May 22, 2001).

Kaplan, Steven, and Mohanbir Sawhney. "E-Hubs: The New B2B Marketplaces." *Harvard Business Review* (May-June 2000).

Kerrigan, Ryan; Eric Roegner; Dennis Swinford; and Craig Zawada. "B2B Basics." *McKinsey Quarterly* (2001).

Kumaran, S. "A Framework-Based Approach to Building Private Trading Exchanges." *IBM Systems Journal* (July 2002).

Laudon, Kenneth C. and Jane P. Laudon. *Management Information Systems: Managing the Digital Firm.* 11th edition. Upper Saddle River, NJ: Prentice Hall (2009).

Laudon, Kenneth C. "The Promise and Potential of Enterprise Systems and Industrial Networks." The Concours Group (2000).

Quadrem. "About Quadrem" (September 2008).

Sodhi, Manmohan S. "2001: A Cyberspace Odyssey." *OR.MS Today* (February 2001).

Synnex Corporation. Form 10-K for the fiscal year ended November 30, 2007, filed with the Securities and Exchange Commission (February 13, 2008).

Turek, Norbert, and Gilbert, Alorie. "Atlas Shoulders The Private Exchange Load." *InfoWeek* (March 26, 2001).

U.S. Census Bureau. *"Statistical Abstract of the United States: 2007-2008."* (2008a).

U.S. Census Bureau. "eStats Report 2006 E-commerce Multi-sector Report." Table 7 (May 25, 2008b).

U.S. Census Bureau. "2006 Annual Survey of Manufactures." (2007).

VICS. (Voluntary Interindustry Commerce Standards). "Collaborative Planning, Forecasting, and Replenishment (CPFR)." (May 2004).

Watson, James K., and Joe Fenner. "So Many Choices, So Little Integration." Informationweek.com (October 16, 2000).

Wise, Richard, and Dave Morrison. "Beyond the Exchange: The Future of B2B." *Harvard Business Review* (November-December 2000).

W.W. Grainger. Inc. Form 10-K for the fiscal year ended December 31, 2007, filed with the Securities and Exchange Commission (February 27, 2008).

1Sync. "About Us" 1Sync.org (September 2008).

Index

A

abandonment rate, **455**, 456
About.com, 36, 76, 85
acceptance testing, **212**
access controls, **301**
accessibility rules, **243–245**
account aggregators, **596–597**
accountability, **488–490**
accumulating balance payment systems, **308–310**
Ace Hardware, 810
Ackerman, Jason, 64, 65
ACPA (Anticybersquatting Consumer Protection Act), **526**
acquisition rate, **455**, 456
Actiontuners.com, 419–422
active content, 237–242. *See also* content
ActiveX (Microsoft), **241–242**
actual products, **360**
Acxiom, 377, 449, 499
ad bombs, **471–476**
ad servers, **171**, 222, 472
ADA (American with Disabilities Act), 243
Adidas, 179, 395, 444
Adinew, Aman, 722
advertising, 4–5, 12, 25, 126, 237, 498. *See also* banner ads; marketing
  budgets, 421, 463
  business models and, 68–70, 76, 78–79, 110
  career services and, 619–623
  classified, 665–669
  contextual, 121
  effectiveness of, 457–356
  exchanges, **429**
  Google and, 40, 121, 175–176, 392, 436, 475, 697–700
  Internet II and, 121
  networks, **387–389**
  online, **422–424**
  portals and, 748, 753–756
  pricing models for, 461
  print, 423
  privacy issues and, 47
  push, 422
  revenue model, **68–70**, 654–658
  search engines and, 175–176
  social networks and, 714–715
  targeting, **423–424**
  traditional versus online, 463
  video, 421–422
adware, 47–48, 274, 298–299, 471–476
AES (Advanced Encryption Standard), **286**

affiliate(s)
  networks, **390**
  programs, 473–474
  relationship marketing, 424, **436–437**
  revenue model, **69–70**
affinity communities, **716**
Africa, 92
African-Americans, 349. *See also* racial differences
age, of Internet users, 344, 345
Agentrics, 87, 91–92, 814
aggregation, 726, 734–735. *See also* aggregators
aggregator(s), 623, 692. *See also* aggregation
  account, **596–597**
  auction, **735**
  demand, **734–735**
Agriculture Department (United States), 64
Ajax (Asynchronous JavaScript and XML), 240–241, 421
Akamai Technologies, 188–191, 214
Al Qaeda, 270. *See also* terrorism
algorithms, 286–289, 302
AltaVista, 26, 79, 173, 175
Amazon.com, 4, 120, 136, 492
  business models and, 65, 67–70, 72, 76–77, 83–85, 104, 573–582
  comparison shopping and, 588
  DRM and, 663–664
  dynamic pricing and, 723
  e-books and, 669, 670, 675, 678
  entertainment industry and, 692
  founding of, 126
  intellectual property issues and, 546
  intermediary role of, 39
  jewelry business and, 558
  marketing and, 339, 375, 386–387, 390, 397, 419, 436, 442, 473
  multi-channel integration and, 568–569
  overview, 573–582
  payment systems and, 328, 468
  privacy issues and, 47
  replacement of traditional stores by, 565
  retail sales model, 6
  RFID autoidentification and, 784
  sales statistics, 42
  security and, 277, 290
  service sector and, 626
  value proposition and, 67–68
  Web site construction and, 200, 205–206, 227, 243
  widgets and, 186
analytics, open source software for, 226
Anderson, Chris, 381
Anderson, Lloyd, 246

W

Credits

CHAPTER 1

p. 3, screenshot of facebook.com © facebook.com, 2008; Figure 1.2, reprinted by permission of Harvard Business School Press. From *Blown to Bits: How the New Economics of Information Transforms Strategy*, by Evans, Philip, and Thomas S. Wurster. Cambridge, MA, 2000. Copyright © 2000 by the Harvard Business School Publishing Corporation; all rights reserved; Figure 1.3, from Internet Systems Consortium, 2008; Figure 1.8, data provided by PricewaterhouseCoopers/National Venture Capital Association MoneyTree Report, Data: Thomson Financial; Figure 1.9, © 2008 eMarketer, Inc. Used with permission. Table 1.6 © 2008 eMarketer, Inc. Used with permission.

CHAPTER 2

p. 63, screenshot of freshdirect.com © Fresh Direct, LLC, 2007; Figure 2.1, screenshot of Ancestry.com subscription page, © Ancestry.com, 2008; p. 79, screenshot from Google.com; © 2008 Google; p. 89, screenshot from Onvia.com © Onvia, Inc. 2007. Used with permission; Figure 2.3, courtesy of Apple; Figure 2.4, reprinted by permission of Harvard Business Review. From "Strategy and the Internet" by Michael E. Porter, March 2001. Copyright © 2001 by the Harvard Business School of Publishing Corporation; all rights reserved; Figure 2.6, adapted from Laudon and Laudon, *Management Information Systems: Managing the Digital Firm*, 11th Edition, 2009. Reprinted with permission of Pearson Education, Inc., Upper Saddle River, NJ.; p. 108, screenshot of Priceline.com home page © 2007 Priceline.com Inc.

CHAPTER 3

p. 119, screenshot of GasBuddy.com © GasBuddy Organization, Inc., 2007; Figure 3.10, © Visualware, Inc., 2007. Used with permission; Figure 3.11, from National Academy Press, © 2000; Figure 3.14, from Internet2.edu, © 2007; Figure 3.17, adapted from Cisco Systems, 2007, Internet2.edu, 2000; p. 188 screenshot of Akamai.com © 2007 Akamai Technologies, Inc.

CHAPTER 4

p.199, simulator shot reprinted with permission from International Business Machines Corporation, © 2003; Figure 4.10, data © E-Soft Inc. Used with permission;

Figure 4.11, screenshots of WebTrends MarketingLab2, © WebTrends, Inc., 2007. Used with permission; Figure 4.17, based on data from Hostway Corporation's survey, Consumers' Pet Peeves about Commercial Web Sites; p. 210, screenshot of NaturallyCurly.com home page © NaturallyCurly.com, Inc. 2007. Used with permission.

CHAPTER 5

p. 259, screenshot of VisualDDoS, Sandia National Laboratories: Center for Cyber Defenders Program, 2007; Table 5.1, based on data from the 2008 Symantec Internet Security Threat Report, © Symantec Corporation, 2008; Figures 5.5 and 5.6, from Communications of the Association for Information Systems, Vol. 4, Article 11, November 2000; Table 5.6, from MacKie-Mason; K. Jeffrey; and Kimberly White: "Evaluating and Selecting Digital Payment Mechanisms," Selected Papers From the 1996 Telecommunications Policy Research Conference, published by Lawrence Erlbaum Associates, Inc.; p. 324, screenshot of PayPal.com home page: These materials have been reproduced with the permission of PayPal, Inc. Copyright © 2008 PayPal, Inc. All rights reserved.

CHAPTER 6

p. 337, screenshot of Netflix.com home page, reproduced by permission of Netflix, Inc., © 2007 Netflix, Inc. All rights reserved.; Figures 6.1 and 6.7 adapted from Kotler and Armstrong, *Principles of Marketing*, 12e, 2008. Reprinted by permission of Pearson Education, Inc., Upper Saddle River, NJ; Figure 6.2, from Lohse, Bellman, Johnson, "Consumer Buying on the Internet: Findings from Panel Data," Journal of Interactive Marketing, Winter 2000, © John Wiley & Sons, Inc. Reprinted by permission of John Wiley & Sons, Inc.; Figure 6.6, © 2008 eMarketer, Inc. Used with permission; Figure 6.9, from nash-equilibrium.com; Copyright 2008 by Michael R. Baye, John Morgan and Patrick Sholten. All rights reserved; Figure 6.10, from Azimuth Interactive, Inc., © 2008; Figure 6.13, from Adomavicius, Gediminas, and Alexander Tuzhilin, "Using Data Mining Methods to Build Customer Profiles," IEEE Computer (February 2001b) © IEEE 2001. Used with permission; Figure 6.19, reprinted by permission, Bakos and Brynjolfsson, "Bundling

Information Goods: Pricing, Profits, and Efficiency," Management Science, December, 1999. Copyright 1999, the Institute for Operations Research and the Management Sciences (INFORMS), 7240 Parkway Drive, Suite 310, Hanover, MD 21076 USA; p. 395, screenshot from VML SEER ™, © VML, 2007. Used with permission; p. 408, screenshot of Liquidation.com home page, © 2007 Liquidity Services, Inc; Table 6.1, from Pew Internet & American Life Project. "Daily Internet Activities," (last updated February 15, 2008) http://www.pewinternet.org/trends/Daily_Internet_Activities_2.15.08.htm, accessed October 2, 2008; Table 6.2, from Pew Internet & American Life Project, "Demographics of Internet Users," (last updated July 22, 2008), http://www.pewinternet.org/trends/User_Demo_7.22.08.htm, accessed October 2, 2008; Table 6.3, from Horrigan, John A. Home Broadband Adoption Report 2008, Pew Internet & American Life Project, July 2, 2008; http://www.pewinternet.org/ pdfs/ PIP_Broadband_2008.pdf, accessed October 2, 2008; p. 26.; Table 6.4 © 2007 eMarketer, Inc. Used with permission; Table 6.5 © 2008 eMarketer, Inc. Used with permission.

CHAPTER 7

p. 419, screenshot of Actiontuners.com home page © Action Marketing, 2008. Used with permission; Figure 7.2, from Interactive Advertising Bureau, 2007; Figure 7.5, screenshot of Yahoo! search results reproduced with permission of Yahoo! Inc. ® 2007 Yahoo! Inc. YAHOO! and the YAHOO! logo are trademarks of Yahoo! Inc; Figure 7.6, data from MessageLabs Intelligence Report, May 2008; Figure 7.7, based on data from the 2008 Symantec Internet Security Threat Report, © Symantec Corporation, 2008; Figure 7.8, screenshot from Beval.com © 2006 Beval Saddlery, Ltd.; Table 7.4, © 2008 eMarketer, Inc. Used with permission, Figure 7.13, from Fogg, B.J., Cathy Soohoo, David Danielson, Leslie Marable, Julianne Stanford, and Ellen Tauber. "How Do Users Evaluate the Creditability of Web Sites? A Study with Over 2,500 Participants." Consumer Reports WebWatch (www.consumerwebwatch.org) and Stanford University Persuasive Technology Lab. Proceedings of DUX2003, Designing for User Experiences (2003).

CHAPTER 8

p. 483, screenshot of Secondlife.com home page, © Linden Lab, 2007; Figure 8.2(A) from www.w3.org/P3P/brochure.html. © 3/16/2003 World Wide Web Consortium (Massachusetts Institute of Technology, European Research Consortium for Informatics and Mathematics, Keio University). All Rights Reserved; p. 544, screenshot of Opencontentalliance.org home page © 2007 Open Content Alliance. Used with permission.

CHAPTER 9

p. 557, screenshot of Bluenile.com home page © Blue Nile, Inc., 2007. Used with permission; Figure 9.4 © 2007 eMarketer, Inc. Used with permission; Figures 9.5, 9.6 © 2008 eMarketer, Inc. Used with permission; p. 624 screenshot of IAC.com home page © 2007 IAC/InterActiveCorp.

CHAPTER 10

p. 641, screenshot of WSJ.com reprinted with permission of Wall Street Journal Online, Copyright © 2008 Dow Jones & Company, Inc. All Rights Reserved Worldwide; Figure 10.4 © 2007 eMarketer, Inc. Used with permission; Table 10.2, © 2008 eMarketer, Inc. Used with permission.

CHAPTER 11

p. 709, screenshot of LinkedIn.com © LinkedIn Corporation, 2007. Used with permission; Figure 11.2, © 2008 eMarketer, Inc. Used with permission; Figure 11.5, reprinted by permission, Vakrat, Yaniv, and Abraham Siedmann, "Analysis and Design Models for Online Auctions." *Proceeds of the 4th Informs Conference on Information Systems and Technology, May 1998*. Copyright 1998, the Institute for Operations Research and the Management Sciences (INFORMS), 7240 Parkway Drive, Suite 310, Hanover, MD 21076 USA.

CHAPTER 12

p. 767, screenshot of VWGroupSupply.com home page, © Volkswagen AG; p. 817, screenshot of Click2procure.com home page © Siemens Corporation 2002-2006.